THE ARTHU

OF THE FRENCH

ARTHURIAN LITERATURE IN THE MIDDLE AGES

IV

THE
ARTHUR
OF THE
FRENCH

THE ARTHURIAN LEGEND IN MEDIEVAL FRENCH AND OCCITAN LITERATURE

edited by

Glyn S. Burgess and Karen Pratt

CARDIFF
UNIVERSITY OF WALES PRESS
2006

© The Vinaver Trust, 2006

First published in hardback in 2006 by the University of Wales Press.

First published in paperback in 2009 by the University of Wales Press.

www.uwp.co.uk

British Library Cataloguing-in-Publication Data
A catalogue record for this book is available from the British Library.

ISBN 978-0-7083-2196-6

Printed in the United Kingdom by CPI Antony Rowe, Chippenham, Wiltshire

ARTHURIAN LITERATURE IN THE MIDDLE AGES

Series Editor

Ad Putter

Further volumes in preparation

The ALMA series is a cooperation between
the University of Wales Press and the Vinaver Trust

CONTENTS

PREFACE

Ad Putter

This book is the fourth volume in the series Arthurian Literature in the Middle Ages. The purpose of the series is to provide a comprehensive and reliable survey of Arthurian writings in all their cultural and generic variety. For some time, the single-volume *Arthurian Literature in the Middle Ages: A Collaborative History* edited by R. S. Loomis (Oxford, 1959) served the needs of students and scholars of Arthurian literature admirably, but it has now been overtaken by advances in scholarship and by changes in critical perspectives and methodologies. The Vinaver Trust recognized the need for a fresh and up-to-date survey, and that several volumes were required to do justice to the distinctive contributions made to Arthurian literature by the various cultures of medieval Europe. The basis for this volume and its predecessors in the series is cultural rather than national. *The Arthur of the French* is primarily devoted to medieval Arthurian texts in French and Occitan, composed across a wide geographical area, though it also takes account of their historical, cultural and manuscript contexts, their afterlife in later periods, and of the formative influences by and on texts from extraneous cultures.

The series is mainly aimed at undergraduate and postgraduate students and at scholars working in the fields covered by each of the volumes. They have, however, also been written to be accessible to students and scholars from different fields, who want or need to learn what forms Arthurian narratives took in languages and literatures that they may not know, and how those narratives influenced the cultures they do know. Within these parameters the editors have had control over the shape and content of their individual volumes.

The mastermind behind this series was Ray Barron, who died without being able to see this latest instalment, *The Arthur of the French*, in its final form. This book is dedicated to his memory.

THE CONTRIBUTORS

PFA   Peter F. Ainsworth (University of Sheffield)

†EB   Emmanuèle Baumgartner (formerly Université de Paris III – Sorbonne nouvelle)

FB   Fanni Bogdanow (formerly University of Manchester)

GB   Geoffrey Bromiley (University of Durham)

GSB   Glyn S. Burgess (University of Liverpool)

KB   Keith Busby (University of Wisconsin)

LCB   Leslie C. Brook (University of Birmingham)

MTB   Matilda Tomaryn Bruckner (Boston College, Chestnut Hill, MA)

AC   Annie Combes (Université de Nantes)

FC   Fabrizio Cigni (Università di Pisa)

PDG   Peter Damian-Grint (University of Oxford)

PE   Penny Eley (University of Sheffield)

JTG   Joan Tasker Grimbert (Catholic University of America)

SG   Simon Gaunt (King's College London)

RH   Ruth Harvey (Royal Holloway, University of London)

TH   Tony Hunt (University of Oxford)

DK   Douglas Kelly (formerly University of Wisconsin)

EDK   Edward Donald Kennedy (University of North Carolina at Chapel Hill)

†EK   Elspeth Kennedy (formerly University of Oxford)

WWK   William W. Kibler (University of Texas)

NJL   Norris J. Lacy (Pennsylvania State University)

FLS   Françoise Le Saux (University of Reading)

RM   Roger Middleton (University of Nottingham)

†DDRO   D. D. R. Owen (formerly University of St Andrews)

KP   Karen Pratt (King's College London)

RTP   Rupert T. Pickens (University of Kentucky)

PVR   Paul V. Rockwell (Amherst College, MA)

MS   Michelle Szkilnik (Université de Paris III – Sorbonne nouvelle)

PS   Penny Simons (University of Sheffield)

JHMT   Jane H.M. Taylor (University of Durham)

RT   Richard Trachsler (Université de Paris IV – Sorbonne)

CVCS   Colette Van Coolput-Storms (Université Catholique de Louvain–la–Neuve)

AMLW   Andrea M. L. Williams (University of Sydney)

LJW   Lori J. Walters (Florida State University, Tallahassee)

ABBREVIATIONS

AfdA	*Anzeiger für deutsches Altertum*	*MF*	*Moyen Français*
AL	*Arthurian Literature*	*MLQ*	*Modern Language Quarterly*
AnFil	*Anuari de Filología*	*MLR*	*Modern Language Review*
Annales	*Annales. Économies, Sociétés,*	*MP*	*Modern Philology*
	Civilisations	*MR*	*Medioevo Romanzo*
Ann. Bret	*Annales de Bretagne*	*MRom*	*Marche Romane*
ANS	*Anglo-Norman Studies*	*MS*	*Medieval Studies*
ANTS	*Anglo-Norman Text Society*	*Neophil*	*Neophilologus*
AUMLA	*Journal of the Australasian*	*NFS*	*Nottingham French Studies*
	Universities Language and Literature	*NM*	*Neuphilologische Mitteilungen*
	Association	*NMS*	*Nottingham Medieval Studies*
AY	*Arthurian Yearbook*	*NZJFS*	*New Zealand Journal of French*
BBIAS	*Bibliographical Bulletin of the*		*Studies*
	International Arthurian Society	OPS	Occasional Publications Series
BEC	*Bibliothèque de l'École des Chartes*	*PAPS*	*Proceedings of the American*
BJRL	*Bulletin of the John Rylands Library*		*Philosophical Society*
BL	British Library	*PMLA*	*Publications of the Modern Language*
BNF	Bibliothèque Nationale de France		*Association of America*
BSCC	*Boletín de la Sociedad de*	*PQ*	*Philological Quarterly*
	Castellonense de Cultura	PRF	Publications Romanes et Françaises
CCM	*Cahiers de Civilisation Médiévale*	PTS	Plain Texts Series
CFMA	Classiques Français du Moyen Âge	*RBPH*	*Revue Belge de Philologie et d'Histoire*
CN	*Cultura Neolatina*	*RF*	*Romanische Forschungen*
DUJ	*Durham University Journal*	*RHLF*	*Revue d'Histoire Littéraire de la*
DVj	*Deutsche Vierteljahrsschrift für*		*France*
	Literaturwissenschaft und	*RHT*	*Revue d'Histoire des Textes*
	Geistesgeschichte	*RJ*	*Romanistisches Jahrbuch*
EETS	Early English Text Society	*RLR*	*Revue des Langues Romanes*
Esp	*L'Esprit Créateur*	*RMS*	*Reading Medieval Studies*
Ét. Celt	*Études Celtiques*	*Rom*	*Romania*
FCS	*Fifteenth-Century Studies*	*RomN*	*Romance Notes*
FF	*French Forum*	*RomQ*	*Romance Quarterly*
FMLS	*Forum for Modern Language Studies*	*RPh*	*Romance Philology*
FR	*French Review*	*RR*	*Romanic Review*
FS	*French Studies*	*SAR*	*South Atlantic Review*
FSB	*French Studies Bulletin*	SATF	Société des Anciens Textes Français
GRLMA	*Grundriß der romanischen Literaturen*	*SM*	*Studi Medievali*
	des Mittelalters	*SMC*	*Studies in Medieval Culture*
GRM	*Germanisch-romanische Monatsschrift*	*SMV*	*Studi Mediolatini e Volgari*
KRQ	*Kentucky Romance Quarterly*	*SN*	*Studia Neophilologica*
LR	*Lettres Romanes*	*SP*	*Studies in Philology*
MA	*Le Moyen Age*	*Spec*	*Speculum*
Man	*Manuscripta*	*StMed*	*Studies in Medievalism*
M&H	*Medievalia et Humanistica*	*Symp*	*Symposium*
Med	*Medievalia*	*TL*	*Travaux de Littérature*
Med. Aev	*Medium Aevum*	TLF	Textes Littéraires Français

TLL	*Travaux de Linguistique et de Littérature*	YFS	*Yale French Studies*
Tris	*Tristania*	ZfdA	*Zeitschrift für deutsches Altertum*
TrL	*Travaux de Littérature*	ZfSL	*Zeitschrift für französische Sprache*
UTSE	*University of Texas Studies in English*		*und Literatur*
VR	*Vox Romanica*	ZrP	*Zeitschrift für romanische Philologie*

INTRODUCTION

Karen Pratt

Li conte de Bretaigne sont si vain et plaisant,
Cil de Rome sont sage et de sens aprendant.
Cil de France sont voir chacun jour aparant.
            (Jean Bodel, *Chanson des Saisnes*, 9–11)

(*The tales of Britain are so frivolous and amusing; those
of Rome are wise and teach us good sense; those of
France are shown to be true every day.*)

The great paradox of King Arthur and his legend is that, although he is closely
identified with British (even English) history and culture, it was texts in the
French language that confirmed his status as a pan-European literary hero. There
is no doubt that the *matière de Bretagne* (matter of Britain), to which Bodel refers
above, was first made popular in written form by Geoffrey of Monmouth in his
Historia Regum Britanniae, which was in circulation by 1138. However,
Geoffrey's wonderfully imaginative, pseudo-historical account of Arthur's life
was made available to a much wider, non-literate audience in 1155, when the
Norman cleric Wace translated the *Historia* into French (chapter II).[1]
Significantly, it is Wace's French adaptation, rather than Geoffrey's Latin text,
that served as a source for Layamon's thirteenth-century dynastic chronicle, the
earliest work on Arthur to survive in the English language.[2] Wace's *Roman de
Brut* also has the distinction of being the earliest surviving text to mention the
Round Table, and was a key source of material for the father of Arthurian
romance, Chrétien de Troyes.

    Chrétien's legacy to Arthurian tradition was enormous, not least because it is
to him that we owe the first written accounts of the quest for the grail and of the
adultery of Lancelot and Guinevere.[3] Of his five romances, composed in the
second half of the twelfth century (chapter IV), most were subsequently adapted
into one or more of the following European languages: English, German, Norse,
Swedish and Welsh, if one accepts that *Erec*, *Yvain* and *Perceval* served as sources
for the Welsh romances *Geraint ab Erbin*, *Owein* and *Peredur*.[4] Chrétien's works
did not merely provide later writers, both French and non-French, with a rich
stock of Arthurian characters, themes and motifs; they also served as models of
romance composition in verse, to be emulated, adapted or reacted against by his
successors and continuators (chapters VI and X).

Almost contemporary with Chrétien's *œuvre* were the French Tristan romances of Beroul and Thomas, but it was Thomas of England's courtly treatment of this Celtic legend that soon gave rise to translations in German, English and Norse (chapter III). Equally influential, yet even more popular than the verse narratives, were the great thirteenth-century prose romance cycles. In the Vulgate Cycle (chapter VII) French writers presented the rise and fall of the Arthurian kingdom and the history of the Holy Grail, culminating in its Quest by Galahad and other, less perfect Knights of the Round Table. Later in the same century the matter of Arthur was combined with that of Tristan, producing in the prose *Tristan* (chapter VIII) and also in the Post-Vulgate *Roman du Graal* and related texts (chapter IX) veritable cornucopiae of Arthurian adventures. Once again, European literature gained in richness as foreign adapters translated French prose-romance material into English (most notably Sir Thomas Malory), Dutch, German, Spanish, Portuguese, Italian and Greek. As other volumes in the present series demonstrate, once Arthurian matter had been transplanted in foreign soil it flourished and diversified, fusing with native literary traditions. Yet all the major European literatures originally received their Arthurian rootstock from the Francophone world.

In post-conquest England the nobles who were the patrons of most literary production spoke the dialect of Old French known as Anglo-Norman, a fact that in the twelfth century facilitated cultural exchange between the France of the Capetians and the Anglo-Norman realm of the Plantagenets. Whatever Geoffrey of Monmouth's political motives may have been for composing his *Historia* (chapter II), his Arthur became for the Anglo-Normans a symbol of a strong monarchy with imperial ambitions, one which their rulers hoped could unite warring factions and provide the peoples of Britain with a unified national identity. If Wace did indeed dedicate his *Brut* to Eleanor of Aquitaine, as Layamon states, he could have been implying that her husband Henry II's recent ascent to the throne of England was continuing a tradition which had originated with the foundation of Britain by the Trojan Brutus, and which had reached its apogee in the illustrious reign of King Arthur.

However, although later English writers and their patrons fully exploited Arthur's potential in their constructions of an Anglo-British national identity, French authors operating beyond the Anglo-Norman kingdom had a more ambivalent attitude towards the legendary king. Whilst Chrétien's *Erec* presents a relatively positive view of the royal figure, leading some critics to speculate that the work was composed for Henry II,[6] his later romances present a deterioration in Arthur's status,[7] thereby problematizing his role as exemplary monarch. Chrétien's desire to please his noble patrons, Marie de Champagne and Philippe d'Alsace, Count of Flanders, who at times in the twelfth century found themselves in conflict with the King of France, may account for his less idealized portrayal of kingship in his later works. Moreover, Chrétien, hailing from Troyes, is more likely to have derived his sense of 'national' identity from the *matière de France* than from that of Britain, and his 'national' hero would therefore have been Charlemagne rather than Arthur. Perhaps this explains why he focused in his romances on young aristocratic heroes of unproven historicity: Erec, Cligés, Lancelot, Yvain and Perceval, rather than on the king at the centre of British history. Far less active than in the pseudo-chronicle accounts of his deeds, the Arthur of Chrétien's romances contents himself with attracting valiant knights and marvellous adventures to his court.

By the thirteenth century, Francophone Arthurian literature seems on the whole to have become the preserve of continental French authors, although many texts are either anonymous or have authors about whom we know little. Interesting exceptions to this rule are two Italians writing in French: the Venetian 'Maistre Richart d'Irlande', author of the *Prophecies de Merlin*, and Rustichello of Pisa (Rusticien de Pise), author of a prose Compilation of Arthurian, Grail and Tristan material (chapter IX). These 'non-British' writers are mostly uninterested in Arthur as a (pseudo-) historical figure capable of encouraging a sense of national identity. Instead, they use him as a cipher through which they can explore different moral and socio-political issues according to their tastes: some highlight political tensions between the monarchy and the aristocracy; others re-examine critically the universal values of honour, loyalty, love and friendship or specifically medieval concepts such as courtesy and chivalry; still others portray Arthur as an archetype of the tragic prince brought down by treachery or pride, or of the husband betrayed by his wife and best friend. He is, of course, surrounded by other colourful figures who lend themselves to constant rewriting: outspoken, sometimes spiteful Kay; beautiful, loving but unfaithful Guinevere; loyal, yet treacherous Lancelot; brave, womanizing, sometimes hot-headed Gauvain; deceitful, yet gifted Morgan; treacherous Mordred; ingenious Merlin. In addition, the Grail, transformed by Robert de Boron into a holy relic with eucharistic overtones (chapter VI), provides further scope for the exploration of Christian values, individual spirituality and Salvation History.

Whilst we find Arthur in the fourteenth century joining the ranks of the Nine Worthies, and, along with the myth of Jason and the Golden Fleece, being celebrated at the courts of the dukes of Burgundy as a model of courtesy and chivalry, the political, nation-building role of Arthurian literature has been largely eclipsed by concentration on notions of lineage and historical cyclicity (chapter XII). Thus, throughout its evolution, French Arthurian literature explores in varying degrees the ethical and socio-political concerns of each successive generation. However, perhaps more importantly, it is also characterized throughout by its sheer entertainment value, the ability of the matter of Britain to generate ever more complex and gripping narratives. Verse romance after Chrétien de Troyes (chapter X) exhibits a greater interest in intertextual, literary games than in the socio-political issues of the real world, although there is evidence that manuscript compilations may have been produced with ethical agendas in mind (chapter XI). Yet prose romance in particular demonstrates a desire for never-ending textuality. Indeed, French Arthurian literature's greatest strength seems to have been its ability constantly to generate new and exciting stories through the techniques of continuation, compilation, adaptation, interpolation and the complex interlacing of mysterious adventures.

The Arthur of the French is the fourth book to appear in this series commissioned by the Vinaver Trust to update R. S. Loomis's influential reference volume entitled *Arthurian Literature in the Middle Ages: A Collaborative History*, which was published in 1959. As should be clear from the above remarks, the word 'French' in our title refers to texts written in the French language rather than to a nation enclosed by strict geographical boundaries. Hence the inclusion of literature composed in England as well as in France. Moreover, although medieval Occitan (formerly often known as Old Provençal) was a separate language, distinct from Old French, the similarity of these languages and the geographical proximity of their speakers meant that in the Middle Ages there were close cultural and political links between Occitania and France. This volume therefore contains a chapter on Arthurian material in the Occitan lyric and romance (XIII), which argues that, from a southern perspective, Arthur was a foreign, northern French phenomenon.

Whilst the term 'French' of our title is relatively unproblematic, the definition of what constitutes Arthurian literature has created more editorial problems. In the volume as a whole a fairly broad definition has been adopted, especially in chapter X, although the statistical survey of Arthurian manuscripts in chapter I takes a slightly narrower view, and the section on narrative lays in chapter V, whilst referring to non-Arthurian examples, concentrates on those that feature Arthur or related characters. Our inclusion of the Tristan material, already present in Loomis's collective study, hardly requires justification; Arthur is mentioned by both Beroul and Thomas, and he plays a significant role in the prose *Tristan*, where Tristan becomes inextricably linked with the Knights of the Round Table.

The place of the British king in the historiographical tradition is treated in several contributions throughout this volume, especially in chapters II and XII, the latter including Jehan de Waurin's chronicle of the history of Britain and England and the pseudo-historical romance *Perceforest*. Yet other pseudo-historical texts in which Arthur plays a minor role have been excluded, and only a representative sample of works in genres other than romance has been treated in order to demonstrate how the matter of Britain was capable of crossing generic boundaries (see William Kibler, chapter XII).

In updating Loomis's volume to reflect modern scholarly interests, three chapters have been added, dealing with manuscripts (I), compilations (XI) and the post-medieval reception of the Arthurian legend in literature and film (XIV). By placing the chapter on manuscripts first, we are not only emphasizing the primary importance of the material nature of medieval textuality and its implications for the reception and interpretation of Arthurian literature, but also providing a broad overview of our subject, introducing the reader to the corpus of texts and contextualizing their production and transmission. It is noteworthy here that Arthurian literature in French was produced and copied during the Middle Ages not only in France, but also in England and Italy. The manuscript compiler's role as active editor, creating new reading experiences, is considered in chapter XI, and the enduring fascination of Arthurian material, both in scholarly and more popular contexts, is discussed in the last chapter.

The Arthur of the French is intended to meet the needs of undergraduate and postgraduate students of medieval French and Occitan literature, established scholars in these fields who are seeking information about the current state of research and students and scholars in other fields who require an introduction to Arthurian material within the French-speaking world. The volume attempts to guide Anglophone readers, some of whom may lack specialist knowledge, by expressing a consensus of academic opinion where this exists, pointing where necessary to significant differences of opinion and indicating fields in which further research would be fruitful. As far as possible, we have aimed at consistency and standardization, but in some cases this has been either impossible or undesirable. We have standardized the spelling in titles of medieval texts (though not in reference lists, where the form which appears in the title of a study is retained). Since the titles of many medieval works are modern inventions, and not universally accepted, our choice of title for individual texts may meet with some disapproval. We have, however, been consistent, as we have with proper names, where one form has been adopted per character throughout the volume, irrespective of the form employed by individual medieval authors. On the other hand, we have not attempted to eradicate conflicting scholarly views, in order to foster stimulating academic controversy. An example of this is to be found in chapters VIII and IX, where readers will find differing opinions expressed on the genesis of the prose *Tristan*.

In each chapter our aim has been to provide the following information concerning individual texts: their author, patron, possible audience, date, sources, social and literary context, manuscript transmission and reception, a plot summary, issues of interpretation and possibilities for further research. Some of this information, though, is simply unavailable, especially when authors are anonymous and no patrons are mentioned. The general assumption is that audiences were in the main aristocratic, including noblemen, ladies and clerics, and that works were read aloud (often in instalments) at large court gatherings or in small groups. However, private reading is not to be ruled out, and the larger, more ornate manuscripts containing the lengthy prose romances were clearly designed for visual as well as aural reception. The dates we offer for texts are often very approximate, and some works are at present undergoing redating, which may in turn affect the relative dating of other works. The multiple authorship of this volume has also led to some variation in the amount of space devoted to these different aspects, and here again consistency has not necessarily been viewed as a virtue. Indeed, more detailed synopses and longer literary analyses have been provided for lesser-known texts, especially if there is a dearth of secondary literature on them. More famous works may be treated fairly summarily, but ample supplementary reading material is cited. The reference lists contain all editions and studies mentioned in the accompanying chapter, plus additional helpful items. The first edition listed is that from which all unattributed citations in the text of the relevant chapter are taken and to which all line or page numbers relate. The Harvard system of reference (author, date, page number) is employed throughout for brevity, editions and translations of texts being distinguished from studies by the use of the editor's name, followed by the abbreviation 'edn' or transl., then by a line or page reference. Within the text the date of publication of an edition is included only where the same scholar has edited more than one work. Items accompanied by an asterisk are not found in the reference list to each chapter, but in the General Bibliography, which is designed to provide a list of the most important, and especially the most recent studies on French Arthurian romance, including reference works and bibliographies. Short titles which have been used for texts within a given chapter appear in square brackets either before or after the edition in the corresponding reference list.

Acknowledgements

The editors of this book owe many debts of gratitude – to its contributors (and especially those who submitted on time) for their forbearance; to Douglas Kelly, Elspeth Kennedy and Jane Taylor for organizing the material of multi-authored chapters into *molt beles conjointures*; to Simon Gaunt, Roger Middleton and above all to Elaine Polley for their advice, reference-checking and careful proof-reading; to Linda Gowans for her expert indexing; to the University of Wales Press for its continued interest in our project; to the Vinaver Trust for much-needed financial and moral support; and to the late Ray Barron, general editor of the series, who sadly did not live to see this volume brought to fruition. Finally, we should like to express our sorrow that three of our distinguished contributors,

Emmanuèle Baumgartner, Elspeth Kennedy and Roy Owen, died during the lengthy publication process. Arthurian Studies are much diminished by their loss.

Notes

[1] Thoughout this book chapter references in roman numerals relate to the present volume.

[2] See Barron ed. 1999*, 22–32. Items accompanied by an asterisk are to be found in the General Bibliography.

[3] See Lacy, Kelly and Busby eds 1987–8*, but also the review by R. Middleton (*MLR*, 85 (1990), 438–9).

[4] See Bromwich, Jarman and Roberts eds 1991*, chapters 6–8 and Lacy, Kelly and Busby eds 1987–8*, I, 337–42.

[5] Greek and Serbo-Russian versions of the Arthurian Compilation by Rustichello of Pisa (Rusticien de Pise) have survived (see chapter IX).

[6] See B. Schmolke-Hasselmann, 'Henri II Plantagenêt, roi d'Angleterre, et la genèse d'*Erec et Enide*', *CCM*, 24 (1981), 241–6.

[7] See B. N. Sargent-Baur, '*Dux bellorum/rex militum*/roi fainéant: la transformation d'Arthur au XIIᵉ siècle', *MA*, 90 (1984), 357–73.

I

THE MANUSCRIPTS

Roger Middleton

The texts of medieval French Arthurian literature in verse and prose are preserved in over 500 manuscripts and fragments, written over a period of rather more than three centuries, and produced over a wide area of French-speaking territory that included England and Italy. The earliest survivors are the remains of two copies of verse romances that have claims to be from the last years of the twelfth century. These are the Sneyd fragments of Thomas's *Tristan* (Oxford, Bodleian Library, MS French d. 16), and the defective copy of *Cligés* at Tours (Bibliothèque Municipale, MS 942). The earliest surviving manuscript of a prose romance is not very much later, there being at least four candidates for the period 1215–25. The most important of these is Rennes, Bibliothèque Municipale, MS 255, containing the beginning of the *Lancelot–Grail* Cycle (the *Estoire*, *Merlin* and an incomplete *Lancelot*). The possibility of a date in the region of 1220 for this manuscript poses a serious challenge to the view that the *Estoire* was not composed until 1225–30 or even later, and this has important consequences, not only for the dating of the individual texts, but also for our understanding of how the *Lancelot–Grail* Cycle came into existence.

The copying of Arthurian texts in verse continued throughout the thirteenth century, but apart from the necessary exception of the two copies of Froissart's *Meliador* (which was not composed until 1388) very few surviving manuscripts are later than 1350, and even the most recent (Turin, Biblioteca Nazionale, MS L. IV. 33) is no later than the early fifteenth century. Manuscripts of Arthurian prose romances were produced in significant numbers alongside the verse during the thirteenth century, and continued to be copied until the first quarter of the sixteenth century. The copy of *Lancelot* in BNF, fr. 1427 is dated 1504, and Gotha, Herzogliche Bibliothek, MS 688 (containing *Ysaÿe le Triste*) is probably from the period 1517–25, assuming that the arms of Louis de la Trémoïlle and his wife Louise Borgia are contemporary with the rest of the book. By this date manuscripts had been almost entirely superseded by the printed editions in which Arthurian prose texts were soon made available. The first of these was the two-volume *Lancelot* of 1488, of which the first volume was printed in Rouen by Jehan Le Bourgoys and the second in Paris by Jehan du Pré. This was quickly followed by the *Tristan* of 1489, printed by Le Bourgoys in collaboration with Antoine Vérard. After that, the succession of other texts and new editions continued steadily until the end of the sixteenth century, and even beyond.

The surviving manuscripts represent only some fraction of the number originally produced, certainly less than half, since every survivor must have been copied from an exemplar, and the very few cases where both exemplar and copy have survived, or where we have two copies from the same exemplar, are swamped by textual traditions that imply far more intermediaries. There are, however, important differences between the manuscript traditions of verse and prose, particularly in the ratio of surviving texts to surviving manuscripts. The vast majority of extant manuscripts are of prose romances, whereas the majority of Arthurian texts are in verse (though the figures are partly dependent upon our definition of what constitutes a text). In the extreme case, it could be said that something like 70 per cent of the manuscripts are of only two texts: the *Lancelot–Grail* and the prose *Tristan*. In another sense, however, these two works are so variable in their transmission that almost every manuscript could be treated as a separate text.

Manuscripts of Arthurian Verse

Texts and Manuscripts
In the case of productions that are in verse it is not usually very difficult to know what to count as a text, but there may be some doubt over what is Arthurian. The various copies of a particular verse text are not verbally identical, but the many differences are relatively trivial, the verse form making it much harder to introduce major new episodes. The episode of the King of the Red City in one manuscript of *L'Atre périlleux* (BNF, fr. 1433) presents some difficulty, but the only significant problems are those associated with the successive Continuations of *Perceval* and its two added prologues. Not only are there different Continuations (treated as separate texts for some purposes, but not for others), there is also the more delicate question of the short, long and mixed versions of the First Continuation, which requires the complex form of publication adopted by Roach (1949–83) in his edition.[1]

What counts as Arthurian can also vary according to context. For practical rather than theoretical reasons, the present chapter takes a very broad view so as to include those Breton romances discussed elsewhere in the volume, even though Arthur and his knights do not always appear. This results in counting the various Tristan poems, lays by Marie de France and other writers, *Ille et Galeron,* the *Roman de Silence* and *Galeran de Bretagne.* The inclusion of the Tristan poems is easy enough to justify because their material becomes Arthurian in the course of time (in the poem attributed to Beroul, in the Tristan episode of the Gerbert

Continuation, and definitively in the prose romance). Similarly, in the case of Marie de France, it would be invidious to distinguish too finely between *Lanval* (which is explicitly Arthurian), *Chevrefoil* (which is part of the Tristan corpus) and those other lays that draw upon the same Celtic motifs as Arthurian romance. The inclusion of the other lays and of *Ille et Galeron*, *Silence* and *Galeran de Bretagne* is for the sake of consistency and completeness (see chapter X). Excluded from this survey of the manuscripts are *Sone de Nansay* (which has too little Arthurian material), the *Roman du Hem* and *Le Tournoiement Antechrist* (which both have significant Arthurian content, but belong to genres that are quite different from Arthurian romance), all lyrics (even those with Arthurian content of one sort or another) and most historical texts (except for occasional mention of Wace). The lyrics are left out because the manuscripts that preserve them are almost invariably collections of songs (often with their music) chosen for their literary form, not for their content. Similarly in the case of the histories, the Arthurian material is coincidental to their purpose and to the manuscripts in which they are preserved. The partial exception for Wace is because the *Roman de Brut* paves the way for the later romances, and several manuscript collections seem to recognize this association (most notably BNF, fr. 1450).

On this basis (and not counting Wace in this context) the number of surviving texts in Old French verse that enter into consideration is sixty-nine. This number includes Froissart's *Meliador* (technically in Middle French) and *Jaufre* (in Occitan), but not the modernization of Chrétien's *Yvain* undertaken by Pierre Sala in the early sixteenth century (preserved in BNF, fr. 1638). Of those included, thirty-seven are (or were) full-length romances, whilst thirty-two are lays or other shorter texts. The figure for the romances is more reliable than that for the shorter texts, and can easily be adjusted to eliminate any or all of the texts that may be considered marginal for one reason or another. The figure for the shorter texts is less easy to adjust in this way, because it is much harder to draw the line between what is or is not Arthurian amongst the *Lais* of Marie de France and amongst other texts that are sometimes described as Breton lays and some-times not. The other variable is the ambiguous standing of those texts that survive only as fragments. The surviving portions of Beroul's *Tristran* and of *Hunbaut* are long enough in themselves to qualify as romances, and a similar status can easily be accorded to the *Tristan* of Thomas, when consideration is given to the range of the various fragments and to the foreign adaptations. The problems arise with the much smaller fragments of *Les Enfances Gauvain*, *Gogulor*, *Ilas et Solvas* and *Le Vallet a la cote mal tailliee* (counted here as romances), where the length and form of the original texts is pure speculation. The two prologues added to *Perceval* are both short, and so are counted here as shorter texts, but as they have no independent existence there are other contexts in which they are grouped with the Continuations. That said, however, the conclusions drawn from the statistics given below are not materially affected by any narrowing of the field. The numbers change, but the proportions do not alter by very much.

The 69 verse texts to be considered are known from a total of 217 copies, of which 163 are either complete or only partially defective, whilst the other 54 have been reduced to fragments. The more or less complete copies are to be found in 58 different manuscripts, with the fragments representing the remains of 46 others.

The relationships between the number of texts, copies and manuscripts are complex. The most notable anomaly is that the five romances by Chrétien de Troyes survive in a total of 67 copies, of which 46 (found in 30 manuscripts) are more or less complete, whilst 21 (from 17 different manuscripts) are in fragments. The four Continuations of *Perceval*, together with the *Elucidation* and *Bliocadran*, representing six texts, are known from a total of 41 copies, of which 34 (found in 12 manuscripts) are more or less complete, whilst 7 (representing 4 different manuscripts) are sets of fragments. Only one manuscript (Bern, Burgerbibliothek, MS 113) has any of these additions without also containing a copy of Chrétien's text.

The remaining 28 Arthurian verse romances are known from 55 copies, of which 30 (found in 21 manuscripts) are more or less complete, whilst 24 (representing 24 different manuscripts) are in fragments. Also worth noting is that 6 of the 21 manuscripts with more or less complete copies are compilations that include at least one romance by Chrétien or a *Perceval* Continuation. The 30 shorter verse texts (not including the *Perceval* prologues) are known from 54 copies, found in one fragment and only 14 other manuscripts, of which two also contain full-length romances. Taking all Arthurian verse texts together, the number of surviving copies (complete, partially defective or fragmentary) relative to the number of texts is 217 to 69 (a ratio of just over 3 to 1). However, this overall figure conceals a significant anomaly, for 67 of these copies are of Chrétien's five romances (a ratio of rather more than 13 to 1), and the figure remains almost as high even when the *Perceval* Continuations and prologues are added in (108 copies of just 11 texts giving a ratio of nearly 10 to 1). In contrast to this, for all other Arthurian verse romances there are 55 copies of 28 texts (a ratio of just under 2 to 1), and for the shorter Arthurian texts there are 54 copies of 30 texts (a very similar ratio of slightly less than 2 to 1). Another way of looking at this is to realize that over half the surviving copies of Arthurian texts in Old French verse are of Chrétien's five romances and the *Perceval* additions (108 out of the total 217). A further imbalance is that even amongst the five romances, *Perceval* is uniquely favoured, being represented by a total of 21 copies (of which 15 are more or less complete, and 6 reduced to fragments). The figures for the others are: *Erec* 12 (7 more or less complete + 5 fragments); *Cligés* 12 (8 + 4); the *Charrette* 8 (7 + 1); *Yvain* 14 (9 + 5). This distinction between Chrétien's romances and the others reappears in almost every aspect of manuscript production and survival that we shall examine, and it is unlikely to be coincidental. It is true that we are at the mercy of chance survivals, but there are two factors that distinguish Chrétien from the rest. In the first place, the numerical differences are sufficiently large to be meaningful in themselves, for whereas it may be no more than luck whether one, two or three copies of a particular text happen to survive, the existence of seven or more suggests a qualitative difference. Secondly, there is the fact that the difference is consistent for all five romances.[2]

One consequence of this imbalance between copies of Chrétien's romances and those of other texts is that we are presented with quite different types of textual tradition. What we cannot know is whether the textual traditions were in reality that different (though one suspects that they were) or whether the difference is in the way that they present themselves to modern eyes. For the majority of non-Chrétien verse texts, surviving in only one copy (plus the occasional fragment), the question of textual variants does not arise. The copy and the text are indistinguishable (apart from the 'correction of obvious scribal errors' practised by most editors). But not so for Chrétien, where each text survives in at least seven copies, and where the number of variants runs into many thousands. It is true that most of these variants are entirely trivial, but not all of them, and even some of those that might be considered trivial in purely scribal terms can have important consequences for literary interpretations. Thus, the loss or addition of a couplet here or there is so commonplace in any process of copying verse texts that we should hardly pay it much attention – unless it happened to be the couplet in which Lancelot hesitates for two steps before getting into the cart (Hult 1989). Nor is this particularly well-known example an isolated case. Even the alteration of a few letters can give rise to a range of conclusions, some more reliable than others, such that *(d)estregales/(d)outregales* as the name of Erec's homeland was the subject of an extended debate between Zimmer, Loth, Lot and G. Paris that was continued by Brugger (1904) and later by Loomis (1949, 70–1) and Ritchie (1952, 10–11). The point, however, is that discussions of this kind are necessarily confined to the works of Chrétien de Troyes and very few other texts. The survival of additional manuscripts places the scholar in an entirely different relationship to these particular texts, though this is often obscured by modern editions and the unwarranted reliance placed upon them.

Apart from Chrétien and the *Perceval* additions, and leaving aside the special case of *Jaufre* (the one Arthurian verse romance in Occitan), only two romances (*L'Atre périlleux* and *Meraugis*) survive in as many as three copies, and only three others (*Fergus*, *La Vengeance Raguidel* and *Ille et Galeron*) survive in as many as two. No fewer than twenty are known from single copies only, of which nearly half are to some extent defective. In addition, the copies of three of them (*Le Bel Inconnu*, *Hunbaut* and *Rigomer*) are to be found in the same collective manuscript (Chantilly, Musée Condé, MS 472).

Verse romances that exist in only one copy are: *Beaudous* (BNF, fr. 24301); *Le Bel Inconnu* (Chantilly, Musée Condé, MS 472); *Le Chevalier aux deux épées* (BNF, fr. 12603); *Claris et Laris* (BNF, fr. 1447); *Escanor* (BNF, fr. 24374, with two published fragments being now lost); *Floriant et Florete* (New York Public Library, MS 122); *Galeran de Bretagne* (BNF, fr. 24042); *Gliglois* (Turin, Biblioteca Nazionale, MS L. IV. 33); Robert de Boron's verse *Estoire dou Graal* and the fragment of his verse *Merlin* (BNF, fr. 20047); *Hunbaut* (Chantilly 472); *Silence* (Nottingham, on deposit in the University Library, MS Middleton L. M. 6); Beroul's *Tristran* (BNF, fr. 2171); and *Yder* (Cambridge University Library, MS Ee. 4. 26). To these may be added texts that survive in a single copy plus fragments: *Durmart le Galois* (Bern, Burgerbibliothek, MS 113; fragment in Carlisle Cathedral Library); *Meliador* (BNF, fr. 12557; fragment in BNF, nouv. acq. lat. 2374); and *Rigomer* (Chantilly 472; fragment in Turin, MS L. IV. 33). Also to be included here are the texts that each survive only in a single fragment: *Les Enfances Gauvain* (Paris, Bibliothèque de Sainte-Geneviève: Meyer 1910); *Gogulor* (owned by Charles H. Livingston: Livingston 1940–1); *Ilas et Solvas* (Lille, Bibliothèque Municipale: Langlois 1913); and *Le Vallet a la cote mal taillee* (BNF, nouv. acq. fr. 934: Meyer and Paris 1897).

The texts preserved by more than one extant copy are: *L'Atre périlleux* (BNF, fr. 1433; BNF, fr. 2168; Chantilly 472); *Fergus* (BNF, fr. 1553; Chantilly 472); *Ille et Galeron* (BNF, fr. 375; Nottingham, L. M. 6); *Meraugis de Portlesguez* (Vatican City, Biblioteca Apostolica Vaticana, MS Reg. lat. 1725; Vienna, Österreichische Nationalbibliothek, MS 2599; Turin, MS L. IV. 33; fragments in Berlin, Deutsche Staatsbibliothek, MS gall. qu. 48 and Draguignan, Archives Départementales de Var); *La Vengeance Raguidel* (Chantilly 472; Nottingham, L. M. 6; fragment in BNF, nouv. acq. fr. 1263; the first twenty-nine lines in BNF, fr. 2187, fol. 155v, and the scattered lines transcribed by Pierre Borel from an unknown manuscript of what he calls the 'Roman de Gauvain'); and the Occitan *Jaufre* (BNF, fr. 2164; BNF, fr. 12571; two different fragments in Nîmes, Archives Départementales du Gard, and excerpts in two *chansonniers*: Vatican City, Biblioteca Apostolica Vaticana, MS lat. 3206 and New York, Pierpont Morgan Library, MS M. 819).

Most shorter texts fall into the same categories. Those surviving in a single copy are: *Le Lai du Cor* (Oxford, Bodleian Library, MS Digby 86); *Le Chevalier à l'épée*, *La Mule sans frein* and the *Folie Tristan de Berne* (all in Bern, Burgerbibliothek, MS 354; with a fragment of the *Folie* in Cambridge, Fitzwilliam Museum, MS 302, fol. 100); *Le Donnei des amants* and *Nabaret* (in Cologny-Genève, cod. Bodmer 82); the *Folie Tristan d'Oxford* (Oxford, Bodleian Library, MS Douce d. 6); *Doon*, *Guingamor*, *Lecheor*, *Tydorel* and *Tyolet* (BNF, nouv. acq. fr. 1104); and *Trot*

(Paris, Bibliothèque de l'Arsenal, MS 3516). The twelve *Lais* of Marie de France are to be found (with a prologue) in British Library, MS Harley 978, and this is the collection that determines the canon. However, the prologue and three of the lays (*Eliduc*, *Chaitivel* and *Laustic*) are unique to this manuscript. The nine others also appear in BNF, nouv. acq. fr. 1104, with third copies of *Lanval*, *Guigemar* and *Yonec* in BNF, fr. 2168, a fourth of *Lanval* in British Library, MS Cotton, Vespasian B. xiv, and a fourth of *Yonec* in BNF, fr. 24432. All but *Eliduc* are also represented in the Old Norse *Strengleikar* (as are six of the anonymous lays as well as three others for which no French text has survived). Amongst the anonymous lays there are three that survive in two copies: *Desiré* (BNF, nouv. acq. fr. 1104; Bodmer 82); *Graelent* (BNF, nouv. acq. fr. 1104; BNF, fr. 2168); and *Melion* (Arsenal, MS 3516; Turin, MS L. IV. 33). Best represented of all is *Le Lai du Mantel*, which survives in five copies (BNF, fr. 353; BNF, fr. 837; BNF, fr. 1593; BNF, nouv. acq. fr. 1104; Bern 354).

The copies of *Le Lai du Mantel* are in manuscripts that are mainly collections of *fabliaux* (except for BNF, nouv. acq. fr. 1104), suggesting that the text was perceived as such. Similarly, the *Lais* of Marie de France occur mainly in collections of similar texts (particularly Harley 978, which also contains Marie's *Fables*, and BNF, nouv. acq. fr. 1104), and so do the anonymous lays (also in BNF, nouv. acq. fr. 1104 and, to a lesser extent, in Bodmer 82). Thus it looks as though their preservation is often a consequence of their respective genres (and supposed authorship) rather than any Arthurian content.

The most important text not included in the above lists is the *Tristan* of Thomas d'Angleterre. In one sense this is represented by several copies, but all are fragmentary. The most substantial single fragment is Oxford, Bodleian Library, MS Douce d. 6 (which also contains the closely related *Folie Tristan d'Oxford*), but almost as much text is contained in the two fragments from the collection of the Revd Walter Sneyd (now Bodleian Library, MS French d. 16). The four leaves that were once in the library of the Protestant Seminary at Strasbourg were destroyed by fire in 1870, but their text survives in the publication by Michel (1835–9, III, 83–94). There are other smaller fragments in Turin (once in a private collection, then lost, now rediscovered in the Accademia delle Scienze di Torino: Fontanella Vitale-Brovarone 1988, 299–314), in Cambridge University Library, MS Dd. 15. 12 and in Carlisle Cathedral Library (on deposit in the Cumbria Record Office: Benskin, Hunt and Short 1992–5). This provides material evidence of six manuscripts, and the translations into German, Norse and English imply the existence of three others. This number of manuscripts, and the fact that copying continued over an extended period until the end of the thirteenth century, suggest a manuscript tradition similar in principle to that of Chrétien's romances, but with a dramatic difference in the rate of survival. Various factors may have contributed to the losses, but the most obvious explanation is that the manuscripts reduced to fragments were not of the highest quality. It is true that the Sneyd fragment was illustrated to a certain extent (one small miniature survives), and true also that the Strasbourg fragments were illustrated by five miniatures in the space of four leaves, but it seems that they were of poor quality (according to Michel 1835–9, III, xxix). The Douce fragments have no miniatures and little decoration, and the recently discovered Carlisle fragment has a gap where a coloured initial has not been executed, implying that it was left undecorated, whatever the original intention may have been. We can, of course, have no knowledge of any illustrated manuscripts that have disappeared without leaving fragments or some other record, but there is no convincing example in the major inventories. Another factor may have been the length of the text (variously estimated at anything from 15,000 lines to not far short of 30,000), not merely a deterrent in itself when Old French verse is no longer either the form or the language of the day, but also a feature that would have reduced its chances of being incorporated into a collection of verse romances whose variety might have aided survival. The fact that as time went on there would have been more or less direct competition from the prose *Tristan*, whose more accessible text and illustrated manuscripts would have had more appeal, will also have had an effect. It is difficult to know whether the text's being Anglo-Norman had a direct influence upon its survival, but it may have affected the kind of manuscripts that were produced. Manuscripts of French literature made in England were often of the cheaper sort (Middleton 2003, 234).

The other most obvious point to emerge from this analysis is that certain manuscripts appear more than once. Chantilly 472 is particularly important, having *L'Atre périlleux*, *Le Bel Inconnu*, *Fergus*, *Hunbaut*, *Rigomer* and *La Vengeance Raguidel* (with three of them being unique); Bern 354 has *Le Chevalier à l'épée*, *La Mule sans frein*, *Le Lai du Mantel* and the *Folie Tristan de Berne*; Turin, MS L. IV. 33 has *Gliglois*, *Meraugis*, *Melion* and a fragment of *Rigomer*; BNF, fr. 2168 has *L'Atre périlleux*, *Lanval*, *Guigemar*, *Yonec* and *Graelent*; BNF, nouv. acq. fr. 1104 is a collection of lays, in which nine by Marie de France are accompanied by *Le Lai du Mantel*, *Desiré*, *Doon*, *Espine*, *Graelent*, *Guingamor*, *Lecheor*, *Tydorel* and *Tyolet*; Nottingham, L. M. 6 has *La Vengeance Raguidel*, *Ille et Galeron* and *Silence* (though the last two of these are stretching the boundary of what is Arthurian). The first two of these collective manuscripts also contain works by Chrétien de Troyes (Chantilly 472 has *Erec*, *Yvain* and the *Charrette*; Bern 354 has *Perceval*). Three other manuscripts noted above as containing only one non-Chrétien Arthurian romance also contain works by Chrétien (BNF, fr. 1433 has *Yvain* as well as *L'Atre périlleux*; BNF, fr. 12603 has *Yvain* as well as *Le Chevalier aux deux épées*; Vatican, Reg. lat. 1725 has the *Charrette* and *Yvain* as well as *Meraugis*). Similarly, Bern 113 contains the Second Continuation (without *Perceval* itself) as well as *Durmart*.

It is in fact characteristic for manuscripts of verse romances to contain several different texts, not necessarily all Arthurian but usually all in verse. Manuscripts that contain prose texts amongst the verse are: BNF, fr. 375; BNF, fr. 1553; Bern 113; and Chantilly 472. However, in all these cases, the prose constitutes only a small percentage of the whole. In Chantilly 472 the contents are almost exclusively Arthurian verse romances, the exceptions being a partial copy of *Perlesvaus* (Arthurian, but not in verse) and some branches of the *Roman de Renart* (in verse, but not Arthurian). Whether its present contents are those that were originally intended is difficult to say, because the manuscript is the work of several different scribes (though not all the numerous changes in the appearance of the script necessarily indicate a change of personnel), and there are parts where the physical structure is extremely complex.

In some cases the verse texts are all in octosyllabic rhyming couplets to the exclusion of texts in *laisses*. Whether this implies an awareness of a difference of genre (romance versus *chanson de geste*) or whether the distinction is purely formal is a more difficult question. Some notable exceptions are BNF, fr. 12603 and BNF, fr. 24403 (with its companion volume in Berkeley, California, Bancroft Library, MS UCB 140). In these cases it is the octosyllabic texts that are in the minority.

Some of the compilations show signs of deliberate planning, the most obvious example being BNF, fr. 1450. This begins with the 'historical' sequence of *Troie*, *Eneas* and the first part of the *Brut*, but then interrupts Wace's account of Arthur's reign to insert the five romances by Chrétien de Troyes (though two are now defective through loss of gatherings). It then continues with the rest of the *Brut*. All this is clearly deliberate, and it is probably not coincidental that the versions of Chrétien's romances in this manuscript are amongst the shortest preserved. On the other hand, the book ends with *Dolopathos*, which has no very obvious connection with the rest of the collection. Another, larger, compilation with several of the same texts is BNF, fr. 375, but the rationale behind its organization is less clear. The gatherings now bound at the beginning are not part of the original collection, but the rest was clearly a deliberate compilation, despite the somewhat disparate nature of its contents. It includes works by Chrétien (*Cligés* and *Erec* occur consecutively, and there is also a copy of the doubtfully attributed *Guillaume d'Angleterre*), and there are various other chivalric romances, but none that is Arthurian unless we count *Ille et Galeron*. In between, there are historical texts, *fabliaux*, religious works and lyrics. However, the defining feature of the collection is that it is introduced by a versified description that deals with each text in numerical order. This catalogue by Perrot de Nesle is now defective at the beginning through the loss of its opening leaf, but in its original form it must have been a substantial text in its own right (more than a thousand lines long). The first nine summaries are now missing and so is part of the tenth (*Floire et*

Blancheflor); the others, from the eleventh to the twenty-second, are intact. After the manuscript had been completed, someone other than the original scribes added the appropriate number to the *explicit* of each text. So, at this practical level, this collection is highly organized, but whether there is any underlying principle governing the choice of material is much more open to question. In its present state, the collection begins, like BNF, fr. 1450, with *romans d'antiquité*. The *Roman de Thèbes* is followed by *Troie* and *Athis et Prophilias*, but the sequence is then interrupted by the insertion of the *Congés* of Jean Bodel before the *Roman d'Alexandre*. However, the numbering system allows us to know that these were originally preceded by two other texts, because *Thèbes* is described in its *explicit* as 'the third branch' (*la tierce branke*). Since the opening leaf of the summaries by Perrot de Nesle has also been lost we cannot know how the collection began when it was complete, and whilst *Eneas* might be a reasonable guess for one of the two there is no obvious candidate for the other.

Several manuscripts other than BNF, fr. 1450 present what appear to be collected editions of Chrétien's works. Most notable are BNF, fr. 794 (the 'copie de Guiot') and the lost manuscript represented by the Annonay fragments. On the other hand, it should be remembered that, although the Guiot manuscript begins with four Chrétien romances (signed at the end by the scribe), there is a considerable amount of intervening material before *Perceval* and the First and Second Continuations with which the manuscript ends. There is, however, evidence to suggest that the book was made in three separate fascicles (Roques 1952, 182–3). What is now the middle section may have been the first to be written, followed by what is now last (containing *Perceval* and its Continuations) and finally the present opening section (Chrétien's four romances with Guiot's colophon). In this order the five Chrétien texts would be consecutive, and the book would end with Guiot's colophon. Yet the fact remains that when the volume was assembled (or soon afterwards) there was no requirement to keep the five romances together, the present order being guaranteed by the table of contents added later in the thirteenth century (Roques 1952, 184). Even with the Continuations, Chrétien's romances represent less than half the total (178 leaves out of 433). What form the Annonay manuscript took is pure speculation, though it is probably not coincidental that the surviving fragments were all written by the same scribe, and that they are exclusively from four of Chrétien's romances (*Erec*, *Cligés*, *Yvain* and *Perceval*), with nothing from any other text.

Amongst collections of non-Arthurian texts there are several that bring together the works of authors associated with a particular place or a particular region (be it through deliberate selection or through the simple availability of exemplars). As far as we know (given that so many texts are anonymous) there are no examples amongst the compilations of Arthurian verse that are made up of works by 'local authors'. It is true that the 'copie de Guiot' (BNF, fr. 794) has close connections with Champagne, having been copied as it seems in Provins (Roques 1952, 189). It does contain all five romances by Champagne's most famous poet as well as the unique surviving copy of the *Empereurs de Rome* by Calendre, who also seems to have been from the county. However, this accounts for less than half its contents, and the other texts are such as might be found anywhere.

Format and Appearance
Some compilations are large, both in physical dimensions and in the number of texts they contain. Amongst manuscripts containing works by Chrétien, the largest in format is BNF, fr. 375, which measures 395 x 305mm, has 313 leaves and contains 23 texts (not counting the extra gatherings at the beginning that are from a different book); but this is exceptional, most Chrétien manuscripts being between 260 and 300mm tall. Amongst the manuscripts without works by Chrétien, the largest is Bern 113, measuring 350 x 245mm with 291 leaves.

At the other end of the scale, nearly all the examples of manuscripts with just one Arthurian verse text are copies of *Perceval* and its Continuations, the few exceptions being the very early copy of *Cligés* in Tours 942, the unique copies of *Escanor*, *Floriant et Florete* and *Yder*, and the copy of *Meraugis* in Vienna. The main factor in producing volumes with a single text is presumably length. Once the Continuations are added to *Perceval* there are at least 30,000 lines, and usually over 40,000, enough to fill a book of standard size (and the same is true of *Escanor*). Oddly enough, however, the longest version of *Perceval* (incorporating the Gerbert Continuation) is followed in BNF, fr. 12576 by the works of the Renclus de Moliens, though this may not have been the original intention since the Grail section at one time ended with several blank leaves (some now missing, others now filled with later additions). By contrast, any romance of more typical length (about 6,000 lines for Chrétien and Raoul de Houdenc) would make only a very slim volume. It is not possible to say whether such small volumes were very rarely produced, or whether they have just failed to survive (with the exception of the *Cligés* in Tours and the very different case of the *Meraugis* in Vienna, which is slim but not small). Larger books, particularly if illustrated, are more likely to be preserved even when their text is no longer read. An imposing volume carries a certain prestige, and an illustrated one may be kept for the sake of its paintings. On the other hand, the small, single-text manuscript was a common enough format for copies of *chansons de geste*, provoking the rather improbable notion that they were used by *jongleurs* to refresh their memories before undertaking an oral performance. For a critique of the term 'manuscrit de jongleur', a discussion of suitable criteria (200mm or less, single column, minimal decoration, single text, or closely connected texts) and a list of survivors (some as late as the fourteenth century), see Duggan (1982). Amongst

Arthurian manuscripts only Tours 942 would meet all these criteria, and this may be an indication that there was at least some difference of practice between the two genres.

Some Arthurian manuscripts meet some of Duggan's criteria but not others. In single columns, with very limited decoration, each containing only *Perceval* and only slightly too large are Florence, Biblioteca Riccardiana, MS 2943 (126 leaves measuring 208/210 x 103/106mm) and Clermont-Ferrand, Bibliothèque Municipale et Interuniversitaire, MS 248 (152 leaves measuring 215 x 125mm). Not much larger (but with twice as many leaves) is Bern 354 (283 leaves measuring 240 x 165mm), which also has two small historiated initials. As now bound this consists of a collection of *fabliaux*, the *Sept Sages de Rome* in prose, and *Perceval*, but there are blank leaves with an owner's signature after the *Sept Sages* before *Perceval* begins a new gathering. As a separate volume the *Perceval* would be much closer to the relevant criteria, though still somewhat too large and in two columns. Amongst the single-text manuscripts without works by Chrétien, the two smallest are both in two columns: the unique copy of *Floriant et Florete* in New York Public Library, MS 122 (69 leaves measuring 228 x 168mm) and that of *Yder* in Cambridge University Library, MS Ee. 4. 26 (54 leaves, plus a gathering that is now missing from the beginning, measuring 255 x 185mm). Although it is the smaller of the two, the copy of *Floriant et Florete* has slightly more elaborate decoration, including some decorated initials and a few marginal illustrations. Also small and with little decoration is the collection of lays in Cologny-Genève, cod. Bodmer 82. This has only 24 leaves, and apparently measures somewhere near to 230 x 170mm. The Bodmer catalogue (Vielliard 1975, 103) gives the dimensions as '218 x 260mm. Justification env. 280 x 140mm' (which involves several obvious contradictions); G. Paris (1896, 497) described the leaves as 'mesurant 236 mill. en hauteur sur 160 en largeur'; most plausible is Tobin (1976, 15) with '23 par 17cm', and these dimensions are in the correct ratio for those of the leaf that is reproduced at a reduced scale as her frontispiece. Whatever the exact measurements may be (and it is clear from the photograph that not all leaves are the same) the fact remains that, despite its small size, the manuscript is in two columns and contains more than one text.

Significantly smaller than all those mentioned so far is Tours, Bibliothèque Municipale, MS 942, measuring 165 x 108mm, and containing only *Cligés*. In its present state it consists of just 59 leaves, but there are leaves missing from the beginning (probably 10) and from the end (probably 26) as well as a bifolium from quire 4 and a single leaf from quire 8. Assuming that *Cligés* really was the only text, this would suggest a manuscript with close to 98 leaves. It is tempting to extrapolate from this example and speculate that the early manuscripts now lost were often of this small size, containing a single text, and with little decoration. There is some support for this from the Sneyd fragments of Thomas (also early

and small, but with small miniatures) and from copies of other types of vernacular literature (Nixon 1993a, 18). The early copies of *Perceval* are also fairly small,
but not excessively so, and the Annonay fragments of four of Chrétien's
romances are from a manuscript that must have measured 280 x 210mm. This is
very much within the range that is normal for the collective manuscripts of fifty
years later. It used to be thought that the small-format manuscripts of *chansons
de geste* were all early, but this is not so (Duggan 1982, 38–9). The truth of the
matter is that we have no way of knowing whether the small, single-text *Cligés* is
typical of its time, one of several available formats that are all equally common,
or a unique exception.

Apart from Turin, Biblioteca Nazionale, MS L. IV. 33, all manuscripts of
Arthurian verse texts are on parchment. This is almost certainly no more than a
reflection of their dates, paper being rare during the period when most of the
manuscripts were copied, but common by the time the much later Turin book was
being made. Decoration is usually limited to coloured initials that alternate
between red and blue, with pen-flourishing in the opposite colour. Sometimes
there is a limited use of gold. These initials are mostly two lines high, with larger
examples at the beginning of a text and only occasionally elsewhere. On the other
hand, manuscripts without any decoration at all are very rare indeed, though this
may be a reflection of rates of survival rather than original production, and there
is an obvious connection here with their size. Large manuscripts of any text are
nearly always decorated; manuscripts without decoration are much more likely to
be small. This is simple economics. It makes no sense for a manuscript that is
already more costly because of its size to be made to look cheap by omitting all
decoration, whereas a manuscript that is being made as cheaply as possible needs
to be both small and plain.

The earliest surviving illustration in the verse manuscripts that we are considering is the one small miniature (the width of a narrow column) in the Sneyd
fragment of *Tristan*, which dates from the end of the twelfth century. There is
then a gap of more than thirty years before the small historiated initial (just over
half the width of the column) at the beginning of the *Charrette* in BNF, fr. 794,
but this is the only example in the manuscript, and it is very much smaller than
the miniatures in prose manuscripts of the same date (*c*.1230). It shows no more
than a seated female figure, depicted in an entirely conventional manner, probably representing the Countess of Champagne explaining the story, either to an
unseen author or perhaps directly to the reader. Not much later is the equally
small historiated initial at the beginning of *Perceval* in Bern 354 (showing
Perceval on horseback). More extensive illustration is to be found in the 82
miniatures found throughout Nottingham, MS Middleton, L. M. 6 (whose
Arthurian material comprises *Vengeance Raguidel*, *Ille et Galeron* and the *Roman
de Silence*), but these are still small (half the width of a column).

It is not until about 1270–80 that we have any example of a miniature to rival those of the prose romances. The earliest larger illustration of a scene from an Arthurian verse romance is probably in the manuscript of the non-Arthurian *Roman de la poire* (BNF, fr. 2186). Amongst several illustrations depicting famous pairs of lovers one is devoted to Cligés and Fénice, and another to Tristan and Yseut (Loomis 1938, 89–90, figs 202 and 203). From much the same time are the copies of *Perceval* and its Continuations in BNF, fr. 12576 and Montpellier, Bibliothèque Interuniversitaire, Section Médecine, MS H 249 (Stones 1993).

From then on, manuscripts of Chrétien's *Perceval* and its Continuations are nearly always illustrated with a significant number of miniatures. Such are: Mons, Bibliothèque de l'Université de Mons-Hainaut, MS 331/206; BNF, fr. 12577; and BNF, fr. 1453. There is, however, the exception of BNF, fr. 1429, which has no more than large decorated initials. Apart from the *Perceval* manuscripts the most elaborate illustration is in BNF, fr. 1433 (containing *Yvain* and *L'Atre périlleux*), and in Princeton, University Library, MS Garrett 125 (containing the *Charrette* and *Yvain*). Much less impressive are three miniatures in the *Erec* of BNF, fr. 24403, though other parts of the manuscript are well illustrated. Various manuscripts have no more than one illustration at the beginning of each text: a historiated initial for *Fergus* in BNF, fr. 1553; a miniature for *Claris et Laris* in BNF, fr. 1447; a historiated initial for *Le Chevalier aux deux épées* in BNF, fr. 12603; and a historiated initial for the beginning of *Erec* in BNF, fr. 1376. It has been speculated that the manuscript of *Escanor* (BNF, fr. 24374) once had a full-page miniature at the beginning, but the leaf is now missing. It is true that one of the manuscripts of *Jaufre* (BNF, fr. 2164) has so many small miniatures that they average more than one per page, but this stands apart from the rest of the tradition in several other ways: the text itself is in Occitan rather than French; the manuscript is from the south; and the paintings show considerable influence from Spain or Catalonia. The one real anomaly amongst the French manuscripts is the *Meraugis* in Vienna, Österreichische Nationalbibliothek, MS 2599. This is a manuscript of only 38 leaves, containing only one text, but of standard format (290 x 200mm) and with no fewer than seventeen miniatures and one historiated initial. That apart, only the Grail texts have anything approaching a complete programme of illustration, and to judge from the survivors the practice of illustrating Arthurian verse romances on any significant scale is at least half a century later than the equivalent illustration of the prose romances.

Dates and Places of Production

The earliest manuscripts of Arthurian verse romances must have been made when the texts themselves were first composed, probably in the 1170s. As far as we know, the first truly Arthurian romance was Chrétien's *Erec*, but this was surely preceded by some version of the Tristan story, possibly that by Thomas d'Angleterre, and perhaps also by the *Lais* of Marie de France.[3] The earliest surviving manuscripts are those that some have assigned to the later years of the twelfth century. This is almost certainly a valid claim in the case of the Sneyd fragments of *Tristan* (Oxford, Bodleian Library, MS French d. 16), and possibly also for the defective copy of *Cligés* at Tours (Bibliothèque Municipale, MS 942), now dated *c.*1200. The Annonay fragments of four Chrétien romances were at one time thought to be twelfth century or just after, but the current opinion is that they are more likely to be somewhat later, perhaps no earlier than 1220.

That manuscripts of Chrétien's romances enjoyed a reasonably wide circulation as early as the 1190s is demonstrated by the fact that copies were available to Hartmann von Aue for him to make his adaptations into German. Somewhat less reliable evidence for the movement of French Arthurian manuscripts is provided by Ulrich von Zatzikhoven, who claims to have derived his *Lanzelet* from a French book (presumably a manuscript of verse romances) brought to Germany by Hugh de Morville when he was one of the hostages for Richard the Lionheart. If true, this would have been in 1194, but none of it can be confirmed from other documents. Even if it is not entirely true, it is likely that by the time of writing both poet and audience took it to be plausible, but this may have been ten or more years later. In any event, by the first decade of the thirteenth century we have the evidence of Wolfram von Eschenbach's *Parzival* and the version of Thomas's *Tristan* produced by Gottfried von Straßburg.

On the other hand, despite this evidence for the availability of French manuscripts at an early date, we must not forget that most surviving copies are significantly later, and that there is no surviving complete copy before about 1220–30. There are three copies of *Perceval* that have claims to be this early, some thirty to forty years after the date of composition, but the dates suggested by different scholars are so varied that it is extremely difficult to be more precise. In Nixon (1993b) the suggested order of date (omitting smaller fragments) is: Tours, Bibliothèque Municipale, MS 942 (*Cligés*), with a suggested date of *c.*1200; Clermont-Ferrand, Bibliothèque Municipale et Interuniversitaire, MS 248 (*Perceval*); Annonay fragments (*Erec*, *Cligés*, *Yvain* and *Perceval*); London, British Library, Additional MS 36614 (*Perceval* plus *Bliocadran* and two Continuations); Florence, Biblioteca Riccardiana, MS 2943 (*Perceval*); and BNF, fr. 794 (all five Chrétien romances), with a suggested date of *c.*1230–40.

Perhaps even more revealing is the fact that Chrétien's *Perceval* is not only amongst the earliest of the survivors, but also amongst the latest. The survival of London, College of Arms, MS Arundel 14 (from the late fourteenth century) shows that this text continued to be copied for another 150 years (a total of some 200 years from the time of its composition). The latest manuscript to contain Arthurian verse texts is probably Turin, MS L. IV. 33, which includes *Meraugis*,

Gliglois, *Melion* and a fragment of *Rigomer*. This manuscript (the only one on paper) is apparently from the late fourteenth or early fifteenth century. Since it was badly damaged by the fire of 1904 any new assessment of its date is impracticable, and we are forced to rely upon the range of opinions given in nineteenth-century descriptions. It may in fact be more or less contemporary with Arundel 14 and with the manuscripts of Froissart's *Meliador* (which was not composed until 1388). Thus, the surviving copies of Arthurian verse in French span a period of just over 200 years (shortly before 1200 to not long after 1400). However, nearly all of them fall within a period of only half that (roughly speaking from 1220 to 1320), with a significant proportion being from the four decades 1280 to 1320 (precisely when literature of this type was no longer being produced).

There are no fixed relationships between the dates of the manuscripts and their contents, but there are certain features that are worth noticing. Obviously the later texts cannot occur in the earliest manuscripts, but the more interesting point is that they do not occur in the latest either. Manuscripts that are unequivocally from the fourteenth century are most likely to contain the earliest texts, the romances of Chrétien de Troyes, and especially *Perceval* and its Continuations.

It is also the case that the later romances exist in the fewest manuscripts. The latest of all, Froissart's *Meliador*, survives in one manuscript with fragments in one other, but since this text is so much later than all the others we might be wary of citing it as an example. On the other hand, it may be worth noting that Froissart's fame as a writer in another genre and his established contacts with possible patrons do not seem to have resulted in a great many copies of his romance. As far as we can tell, the latest Arthurian verse romance before *Meliador* was *Escanor*, composed by Girart d'Amiens about 1280. This too survives in only one copy, though there were at one time two other fragments, both apparently now lost. At over 30,000 lines *Escanor* is long enough to survive in isolation, and it is assumed that BNF, fr. 24374 never contained any other text, though since the manuscript is damaged at the beginning we could not be entirely sure of this.

Slightly earlier is *Claris et Laris*, thought to have been begun in 1268, and this too survives in only one copy (BNF, fr. 1447). Despite being much the same length as *Escanor*, this is accompanied by the early version of *Floire et Blancheflor* (an octosyllabic romance composed in the twelfth century) and by *Berte aus granz piés* by Adenet le roi (a *chanson de geste* in *laisses* composed at much the same time as *Claris et Laris*). This manuscript was made in Paris in the late thirteenth century by a team of craftsmen that was probably directed by the *libraire* Robert de l'Isle Adam. The same scribes and artists were responsible for a number of manuscripts that all contain either works by Adenet le roi or the *Meliacin* of Girart d'Amiens, which shares an origin with Adenet's *Cleomades*

(Rouse and Rouse 2000, I, 111). This tells us much about the commercial context in which this copy of *Claris et Laris* was produced, but what we do not know is who might have commissioned it or who might have been its medieval owners. It does have a later ex-libris indicating that its then owner lived in Rouen, but the name has been erased. It came to the Bibliothèque du Roi in 1732 with the collection of Jean-Baptiste Colbert, but it had not entered his collection until after his death in 1683 (item 62 in the list in BNF, MS Baluze 100, fol. 226v). Consequently, unlike many of the manuscripts acquired during Colbert's lifetime, it entered the collection in circumstances that are not documented.

Apart from the fact that each survives in only one copy (plus fragments), what these three late romances have in common is that their manuscripts were made within relatively few years of the time of their composition. So what we have is a small number of copies, all made within the space of a few years. The consequence of this, if matters really were as the surviving evidence seems to suggest, is that the textual tradition will have had little opportunity to become diffuse. Thus, in stemmatic terms, extant copies are likely to be close to the archetype. Unfortunately, this does not necessarily mean that their text is close to the original, for there is always the possibility of deliberate intervention. Indeed, the fragments of *Meliador* do seem to be from a recension of the text that is different from that in BNF, fr. 12557. This, however, is no particular surprise, because Froissart is notorious for his successive revisions of his *Chroniques*, and he may well have done the same with his romance.

Other relatively late romances that are poorly represented are *Rigomer* and *Hunbaut*, but here the gap between composition and surviving copies is more problematic. For one thing, the date of the texts is less easy to determine. Though *Hunbaut* in particular is sometimes said to be as late as 1250, this is no more than an estimate. The other part of the problem is that opinions differ on the date of the manuscript. The older view of Chantilly 472 would place it as late as the early fourteenth century, whereas Nixon (1993b, 40–1) has proposed that it is from nearer to the middle of the thirteenth century, and its date is now usually given as 1250–75. This would present us with a manuscript made within a very few years of some of the texts that it contains, but the copies of *Rigomer* and *Hunbaut* are both defective, implying at least one previous copy of each, and probably more (unless they were never finished).

A more important point about Chantilly 472 is that it contains Arthurian verse texts of different dates, so even if *Rigomer* and *Hunbaut* are relatively recent texts, Chrétien's romances are certainly not, and there are others between the two extremes. Of these *Le Bel Inconnu* is unique to this manuscript, but *Fergus* and *L'Atre périlleux* are the two non-Chrétien romances that occur in the largest number of copies. The most surprising case here is *Le Bel Inconnu*. Since this is a relatively early text that was still being copied as late as 1250, or even several decades after, one might have expected to find copies elsewhere, but none exists. However, there is evidence of various kinds that it was at one time a more popular text than its single copy would suggest. Certainly, the theme of the Fair Unknown is widely attested, for there are several versions in various different languages: *Lybeaus Desconus* in English, *Wigalois* in German and *Carduino* in Italian, as well as later reworkings in French such as the *Chevalier du Papegau*. These may have been made using written copies of the surviving French romance, but the differences between these versions allow for the possibility that the tale was transmitted orally. Better evidence for the existence of a lost French manuscript is provided by the adaptation into French prose that survives in the *Hystoire de Giglan* by Claude Platin (first printed in 1520), even though the story is there interwoven with that of *Jaufre*.

The copying of twelfth-century texts in the early fourteenth century implies a continuing tradition throughout the previous hundred years. In theory, the late copies could have been made directly from twelfth-century originals, but the textual evidence provided by Chrétien's romances suggests that the transmission was by means of a developing tradition that involved a significant number of stages. Consequently, it is probably fair to assume that the copying process was more or less continuous from the time of composition to the date of the latest surviving manuscript. This in turn implies the gradual disappearance of earlier copies (no doubt partly through continuing use rather than neglect), as well as sufficient continuing interest to justify the new ones. By the same token, the extreme scarcity of copies from the later fourteenth century onwards implies that interest had waned. The occasional exceptions (such as London, College of Arms, MS Arundel 14; Turin, Biblioteca Nazionale, MS L. IV. 33; and the copies of Froissart's *Meliador*) prove that some interest continued into the late fourteenth and early fifteenth century, and the presence of fifteenth-century marginalia in various manuscripts indicates that some people were still reading older copies, but it looks as though there was little demand for new ones. It is probably no coincidence that the fourteenth century was also the time when Arthurian verse romances (with the exception of *Meliador*) were no longer being composed. Given that we are to some extent at the mercy of chance survivals, it is difficult to be sure that the impression created is an accurate reflection of reality. On the other hand, the total absence of survivors from the early fifteenth century onwards is surely indicative. There is a marked contrast here between Arthurian verse literature and the continued popularity of the *Roman de la rose*, which was still being copied well into the sixteenth century.

In the case of narrative literature, verse increasingly gave way to prose, and by the fifteenth century prose was so much the established medium that there was a fashion for turning earlier verse texts into prose (Doutrepont 1939). Only a small proportion of these *mises en prose* were Arthurian, and the manuscripts of them are far from numerous. Best known are the adaptations of *Erec* and *Cligés*, whose manuscripts were in the Burgundian library by 1467 (Barrois 1830, nos 1277 and 1477) and are now Brussels, Bibliothèque Royale, MS 7235 and Leipzig, Universitätsbibliothek, MS Rep. II 108. The copies of these two texts are written on very similar paper in a fifteenth-century cursive that is not very easy to read. Both are entirely devoid of decoration, but the copy of *Cligés* has spaces for miniatures that have not been executed. Everything indicates that they are drafts rather than finished products. The version of *Cligés* was made, the author says, at the command of a 'prince' and the date given at the end is 25 March [1]454, which could mean either 1454, if the writer started the year on Lady Day (25 March), or more probably 1455, if his year did not change until Easter (which fell on 12 April in 1454, and on 28 March in 1455). This 'princely' command is usually taken to mean that the adaptation was intended for Philip the Good himself, and it is likely that the same was true for the version of *Erec*. However, the fact that neither was ever written up as a fair copy suggests that the duke showed little interest. The binding of the Brussels manuscript is probably the original, having been done by a craftsman known as 'the predecessor of Gohon' (Colombo Timelli 2000, 10–11). This binder was the earliest of a distinctive group working in Lille in the second half of the fifteenth century (Colin 1992), and it is quite likely that Lille is where the adaptation itself was made. The incorporation of the first part of this version of *Erec* into a *Guiron* compilation (preserved by BNF, fr. 358–63 and by the fragments in Bodleian Library, MS Douce 383) indicates that another manuscript (with a text somewhat closer to Chrétien's verse original) was available in Flanders in the 1470s (Middleton 1988; Colombo Timelli 2000). In 1474 there was a manuscript of 'Ereth filz du roy Lach' in the library of the Countess of Montpensier at Aigueperse (Boislisle 1880, 302), doubtless the same manuscript as 'Le chevalier herech filz du Roy lac' that appears in a second inventory of the library in 1507 (BNF, fr. 20598, fol. 356; Le Roux de Lincy 1850, 121, item 155). Since this was amongst the books on paper (a point confirmed by the more detailed description of 1507), it was probably a copy of a prose adaptation, and we could not rule out the possibility that the Count or Countess of Montpensier was responsible for the original commission.

The only non-Chrétien Arthurian text turned into prose in this way was *Floriant et Florete*. This is not mentioned by Doutrepont (1939), but there are two surviving copies, both on paper, in BNF, fr. 1492 and 1493. In the light of what has just been said about the library at Aigueperse it may not be coincidental that it also contained 'Floret et Florete' and 'Le livre de Florent' (Boislisle 1880, 301 and 306). In 1474 both are listed amongst the books on paper, but in 1507 they are described as 'Le livre de Florent Florette ... en pappier' and 'Le Floret ... en parchemyn' (Le Roux de Lincy 1850, 125 and 128, items 215 and 258). The one on paper is likely to have been a prose adaptation, but the one on parchment could have been a copy of the verse original. There was also a 'Floriant de Sécille' at Tours at the end of the fifteenth century (Chéreau 1868, item 81), but since we do not know whether this was on paper or on parchment we have no guide at all as to whether it is more likely to have been in prose or verse.

Almost invariably overlooked in the context of these *mises en prose* is the very early example provided by the prose adaptation of Chrétien's *Charrette* that survives in three manuscripts of the *Lancelot–Grail* Cycle. Instead of the usual prose version of this story, two closely related manuscripts made in Paris at the very beginning of the fifteenth century (BNF, fr. 117–20 and Arsenal MSS 3479–80) and the somewhat earlier BNF, fr. 122 (written in 1345) preserve a prose adaptation that follows Chrétien's text so closely as to borrow phrases verbatim (Hutchings 1938, xliii–xlvii). Another rather different case is the fragmentary prose *Yvain* now in Aberystwyth, National Library of Wales, MS 444-D. This consists of seven discrete episodes separated by traditional interlace formulas. Only the first is related to Chrétien's *Yvain* in that it offers a variant account of Yvain's rescue of a lion from a dragon. The longest episode is a reworking of a narrative associated with the *Chevalier aux deux épées*; though not necessarily drawn directly from this verse text. Other episodes are analogues of material found in prose romances such as the *Queste* and the prose *Tristan*, and there also seems to have been some influence from the compilation of Rusticien de Pise. Three episodes are either original to this text or based on sources now lost (Muir 1964; Lacy 2004). Thus although this eclectic work has been partly created by making prose versions of narratives that are represented in earlier verse texts, it is not a *mise en prose* in the usual sense. Its composite nature, the freedom of its adaptation, the date of the manuscript (fourteenth century rather than fifteenth) and the place of its production (Italy rather than northern France) all suggest a very different literary environment.

By the sixteenth century, prose versions of the verse romances were being made for publication in print rather than manuscript. Such were Claude Platin's *Hystoire de Gyglan* first printed in 1520 (mentioned above as combining *Le Bel Inconnu* and *Jaufre*) and the version of Chrétien's *Perceval* and its Continuations printed in 1530 for Jean Longis, Jean Saint-Denis and Galiot du Pré. The last remnant of a literary (as opposed to an antiquarian) interest in Arthurian verse romance is the work of Pierre Sala in Lyon, who made a verse adaptation of Chrétien's *Yvain* (Suard 1970). This is dedicated to King Francis I (who visited Sala's house in Lyon in 1522), but it should be noted that the only surviving manuscript (BNF, fr. 1638) bears the ex-libris of Jean Sala (Pierre's half-brother), suggesting that the king either never received a dedication copy or never kept it. The fact that this Jean Sala was also the owner of the copy of the *Chanson de Roland* that begins with ten lines from Chrétien's *Yvain* (Lyon, Bibliothèque Municipale, MS 743) seems to be purely coincidental. Pierre's other known work in the Arthurian field is his prose version of *Tristan* (Muir 1958), but it looks as though he also made a verse adaptation of *Erec*, if we may judge from the few lines preserved by Du Verdier (Middleton 1993, 166–8).

All this implies that manuscripts of the verse romances were still available in the late fifteenth and early sixteenth centuries, and that some people continued to show some interest. However, it is revealing that no Arthurian verse romance was put into print except by way of an adaptation into prose. The printers presumably had access to verse manuscripts, and also had an interest in their narrative content, but they judged that the verse form was no longer commercially viable. One printer who certainly knew such a manuscript was Geoffroy Tory. In his *Champ fleury* of 1529 he reports that he has recently seen various works of Old French literature in parchment manuscripts shown to him by René Macé of Vendôme (Tory 1529, Biii). The Arthurian items are the 'Cheualier a lespee' (said to be by Chrétien), 'Perseual' (also by Chrétien) and the 'Mule sans frein' (by 'Paysant de Mesieres'). Since the only surviving copies of the *Chevalier* and the *Mule* are in Bern, Burgerbibliothek, MS 354, which also contains a copy of *Perceval*, this could well be one of the manuscripts that Tory saw. On the other hand, Tory's text presents some difficulties of interpretation, and the only corroborating evidence is the possibility that the attribution of the *Chevalier* to Chrétien stems from the marginal note that is in the manuscript itself. Coincidentally, later in the sixteenth century Bern 354 was owned by another printer, Henri Estienne, whose signature and ex-libris are on the first folio.

By the second half of the sixteenth century, Arthurian verse romances were of no more than antiquarian interest. Several are mentioned by Etienne Pasquier in his *Recherches de la France*, in a passage that was first published in 1596, but he admits that he is taking his information from Tory, and that he has not seen the texts for himself (Pasquier 1617, 726). Only Claude Fauchet had the kind of first-hand knowledge that allowed him to write his *Recueil de l'origine de la langue et poesie françoise* (1581), which remained authoritative for more than 150 years. Fundamental to Fauchet's unrivalled expertise was his own extensive collection of manuscripts (Espiner-Scott 1938a). His manuscript of the *Charrette*, *Yvain* and *Meraugis* survives as Biblioteca Apostolica Vaticana, Reg. lat. 1725, and the fragment of *Meraugis* in Berlin is in a manuscript that was once his. He must also have had access to copies of *Yvain* and *Perceval* that are now lost, because he transcribed extracts from them into a notebook that is now BNF, fr. 24726 (Espiner-Scott 1938b, 261–3). He also records how he found eight stray leaves of parchment in a printer's shop from which he transcribed some lines of *Perceval* into the *Recueil* (Fauchet 1581, 98). Both La Croix du Maine and Du Verdier in their respective *Bibliothèques françoises* of 1585 take their entries on Chrétien from Fauchet (La Croix du Maine briefly, but without acknowledgement; Du Verdier with extensive quotation, explicitly attributed). Despite his reliance on

Fauchet, Du Verdier had in fact seen a manuscript of *Perceval* in Lyon, in the possession of Antoine Guillem, the nephew of François Sala, whose father Jean was the half-brother of the Pierre Sala who had produced the modernized version of *Yvain* (Rigoley de Juvigny 1772–3, III, 559; Middleton 1993, 168).

A feature of the copying of verse romances that distinguishes them from their prose counterparts is the existence of significant numbers of 'modern copies'. Such copies of the prose romances are extremely rare, for reasons that are obvious: the texts were accessible in far more medieval manuscripts and in the various early printed editions, so that the task of copying hundreds of pages can have had few attractions (though there is the exception of Aberystwyth, National Library of Wales, MS 5154). The verse romances, on the other hand, were difficult to find and short enough to transcribe without major difficulty. In the eighteenth century La Curne de Sainte-Palaye had complete or partial copies made of BNF, fr. 375 (copy in Arsenal MSS 3313–18), BNF, fr. 1420 (copy in Arsenal MS 3319), BNF, fr. 2168 (partial copy, without *L'Atre périlleux,* in Arsenal MS 2770) and Bern, Burgerbibliothek MS 354 (copy in BNF, MS Moreau 1720–1). He may also have been involved in procuring the copy of *Perceval* (from Bern 354) that is now Arsenal MS 2987. At the very beginning of the next century Rochegude copied *Jaufre* from both BNF, fr. 2164 and BNF, fr. 12571; *Le Chevalier aux deux épées* from BNF, fr. 12603; *Erec* from BNF, fr. 375; and *Yvain* and the *Charrette* from BNF, fr. 794 (Albi, Bibliothèque Rochegude, MSS 2, 3 and 8: Middleton 1993, 164–5). It is notable that Chrétien's romances are still predominant.

Not very much later, French and German scholars were making transcriptions, which they sometimes freely lent to other colleagues, sometimes kept to themselves for use in proposed editions that did not always appear. The first edition of any romance by Chrétien de Troyes, the *Yvain* published by Lady Charlotte Guest in 1838, was prepared from a transcript made by Villemarqué (of which Lady Charlotte rightly had a very low opinion), and the first edition of *Erec*, by Immanuel Bekker in 1856, was made possible by the transcript that Francisque Michel had given to Moritz Haupt. Similarly, the critical editions of Chrétien's romances by Wendelin Foerster consistently indicate the extent to which he used transcripts made by others whose names are often commemorated in the choice of sigla. Most of these scholarly copies are of nothing more than passing historical interest, but events can occasionally alter their status in dramatic fashion. Thus, after the Turin fire of 1904, the copy of *Gliglois* made by Professor J. Müller for Wendelin Foerster became the only surviving witness to the text (Livingston 1932, 7–11).

The surviving manuscripts of French Arthurian texts in verse seem to have been made for the most part in a quadrant extending eastwards and northwards from about the centre of France (for the localization of Chrétien manuscripts, see

Nixon 1993b, 15–16 and Stones 1993). This quadrant includes Paris, Normandy, the north-east (Artois, Flanders, Hainault) and eastern France (Champagne, Burgundy). There are very few surviving manuscripts of Arthurian verse made anywhere in France outside this quadrant. From the west we have Tours 942 (containing *Cligés*) and perhaps the fragments in Institut de France, MS 6138 (also *Cligés*). From the south we have BNF, fr. 1374 (*Cligés* again); BNF, fr. 2164 (containing *Jaufre*, the one Arthurian romance in Occitan); and the two fragments of *Jaufre* in Nîmes.

Arthurian verse manuscripts were also produced outside France, and there are surviving examples from Italy, and even more from England. From Italy we have the complete copy of *Jaufre* in BNF, fr. 12571; the two *chansonniers* with excerpts from *Jaufre*; the passage from *Cligés* in Florence, Riccardiana 2756; and perhaps the *Roland* manuscript with a few lines of *Yvain* (Lyon, Bibliothèque Municipale, MS 743). The scarcity of copies of Arthurian verse romances from Italy contrasts with the significant numbers of Italian manuscripts of *chansons de geste* and of Arthurian prose romances.

Rather more numerous are the Arthurian verse manuscripts that were written in England. Most important is Cambridge University Library, MS Ee. 4. 26, which contains the only surviving copy of *Yder*. Made in England in the second half of the thirteenth century, it eventually entered the library of Sir Thomas Knyvett of Ashwellthorpe in Norfolk, who died in 1618 (McKitterick 1978, 33 and 162). A second is London, College of Arms, MS Arundel 14, containing Chrétien's *Perceval* (without Continuations) alongside Anglo-Norman lays and historical texts. Its first known owner is William Howard of Naworth Castle in Cumbria, who died in 1640, but the book had presumably been in England from the time of its production in the late fourteenth century. Another possible candidate is the *Perceval* in Florence, Biblioteca Riccardiana, MS 2943, but the evidence is not decisive (Nixon 1993b, 27).

Several other Anglo-Norman manuscripts are represented by surviving fragments. These include the fragments of Thomas's *Tristan*, the fragment of the *Folie Tristan de Berne* in Cambridge, the fragment of the First Continuation of *Perceval* in the Public Record Office, and perhaps the fragment of *Meraugis* in Berlin. There are also Anglo-Norman copies of some of the shorter texts. Most notable is the one manuscript to contain all twelve lays by Marie de France. This is British Library, MS Harley 978, which comes from Reading Abbey in Berkshire. Marie's *Lanval* is also to be found in British Library, MS Cotton Vespasian B. xiv. Another important collection is to be found in Oxford, Bodleian Library, MS Digby 86, but only the *Lai du Cor* falls within our area of interest, the rest being a variety of other works in both French and English. Finally, there is Cologny-Genève, cod. Bodmer 82, containing *Le Donnei des amants*, *Desiré* and *Nabaret*. This manuscript was given to Sir Thomas Phillipps by 'R. B.' (thought to be Robert Benson, Recorder of Salisbury), and there is a suggestion that it had come from Wilton Abbey in Wiltshire.

History and Ownership

Little is known about the early history of the surviving verse manuscripts. This is almost certainly a simple consequence of the date of their production, for the earlier manuscripts of the prose texts are in much the same situation. It is mainly from the later fourteenth century onwards that aristocratic owners commissioned books with their coats of arms incorporated into the decoration, added their ex-libris at the beginning or end, and made catalogues of their libraries. Thirteenth-century books rarely have any clues to their history until they become objects of antiquarian and scholarly interest towards the end of the sixteenth century, and above all when the collectors' market is established from the eighteenth century onwards.

Amongst manuscripts containing works by Chrétien de Troyes there are only nine where anything is known of their history before 1500, and no more than three where there is reliable information before 1400. There are two cases where we know the name of a scribe, and in one of these we also have his address. This is the well-known 'copie de Guiot' (BNF, fr. 794) in which the scribe has added four lines at the end of *Yvain* on fol. 105. Here we find his name 'Guiot' and his place of work 'notre dame del val', which is believed to refer to Provins (Roques 1952, 189). The only other names of scribes are 'Colins li fruitiers' at the end of *Fergus* in Chantilly, Musée Condé, MS 472, fol. 122, and Jean Madoc (or Madot), the nephew of Adam de la Halle, in BNF, fr. 375, fol. 119v. This last is controversial, for the date that accompanies it (2 February 1289) seems to be too early for this manuscript. Consequently, most authorities suppose that the name and the date have been copied from an earlier exemplar. None of these scribes is known as the copyist of other surviving manuscripts, and neither of the first two features in other documents. There was a Jean Madoc at Arras (spelt with final *c* in the only known document), who apparently died shortly before Whitsun 1288, but this may not be the scribe (given that the dates do not quite match), and even if he were the scribe he may not have written the manuscript that we now have (Middleton 1993, 182–3).

The earliest information on ownership is in BNF, fr. 12576, which contains *Perceval* and all Continuations, including Gerbert. This has a note of rents that relate to property in Amiens at the end of the thirteenth century, and we may draw the tentative conclusion that the manuscript was then in the hands of a prosperous burgher of similar social standing to the former mayors of Amiens named in the note. By the early sixteenth century the book was owned by the family of Raisse de la Hargerie, whose nobility was established by this time, but whose earlier generations seem to have been administrators. From a rather similar professional background was Jean Desplancques, *receveur d'Arras* for the Duke of Burgundy in the 1460s, and owner of Mons, Bibliothèque de l'Université de Mons-Hainaut, MS 331/206, which contains *Perceval* with *Bliocadran* and three Continuations. This seems to have been written and illustrated in or near Tournai in the 1280s (Stones 1993, 243–50), and was probably acquired by Jean Desplancques in the region. It was bound by A. Fierlin, probably in Lille, no later than the early sixteenth century (Colin 1992).

A book with early aristocratic connections is BNF, fr. 12560 (containing *Yvain*, the *Charrette* and *Cligés*), which was amongst the property of Margaret of Flanders at the time of her death in 1405 (de Winter 1985, 250–1). Since the book was at Arras (Margaret's principal residence for the latter part of her life), rather than at Paris (the principal residence of her husband Philip the Bold, Duke of Burgundy, at the time of his death a year earlier), it is likely that she had obtained it through inheritance from her father Louis de Mâle, Count of Flanders (d. 1384), or from her grandmother Margaret of France, Countess of Flanders and of Artois (d. 1382). Except for one debatable case, there are no romances of any kind in the inventory of the duke's books at Paris in 1404, and all references to Arthurian romances in Burgundian documents, whether for purchase or refurbishment, are to copies of prose texts (see below, p. 60). By 1400 this manuscript of verse romances was outdated in both form and appearance, being entirely without miniatures at a time when Philip the Bold was vying with his brother Jean de Berry to commission the very finest illustrated books of the day.

The other manuscript of Arthurian verse that is known to have been in the Burgundian library in the Middle Ages is the copy of *Meraugis* that is now in Vienna, Österreichische Nationalbibliothek, MS 2599. This does not appear in inventories of the library until that of 1467 (Barrois 1830, no. 1355), but we should not necessarily take this as evidence of a belated interest in this outmoded text. The book may have been in one of the duke's other residences when the earlier inventories were made, or it may have been acquired for the sake of its impressive appearance. An even later acquisition was BNF, fr. 12603, not obtained until 1511, when Margaret of Austria, Regent of the Netherlands for her nephew the Emperor Charles V, bought a substantial number of manuscripts from Charles de Croy, Prince of Chimay (Debae 1995, XIII). The characteristic ex-libris at the end (see below, p. 72) shows that it was part of the Croy collection in 1486, but there is no way of knowing whether it had been in the family for generations or whether it was a more recent acquisition. It is not very likely that Charles de Croy (or even his father Philippe, or his grandfather Jean who had begun the collection) would have enjoyed the difficulties of reading verse romances written in Old French, but he (or they) may have wished to acquire old manuscripts simply to enhance the collection. If chosen deliberately, it may have been so as to provide material for the kind of modernized prose adaptations that were then fashionable at the Burgundian court.

Other verse manuscripts owned by noble families in the fifteenth century are BNF, fr. 1450, which remained in the family of Matignon until the seventeenth century, and BNF, fr. 1453, which seems to have passed from the families of Orléans de Rere and Tranchelion to the Duke of Bourbon at some time before the death of Jean II in 1488 (Middleton 1993).

Amongst books not containing the works of Chrétien even fewer have a known early history. The manuscript on deposit in Nottingham University Library, Middleton MS L. M. 6, which includes copies of *La Vengeance Raguidel*, *Ille et Galeron* and *Le Roman de Silence*, has a note referring to 'ma dame de Laval', for whom there is no reliable identification (despite various speculations). The probable date of this note suggests that the book was still in France as late as the fifteenth century, but it had come to Yorkshire in England at some time before 1500, to be owned by 'Johannes Bertrem de Thorp Kilton', whose identity is also still under discussion (Cowper 1959; de Mandach 1974).

Although we lack so much information about the ownership of surviving manuscripts, we are not entirely at a loss to know some of the people who possessed copies of the texts in which we are interested. Books of all sorts are mentioned in various documents throughout the Middle Ages, and by the fourteenth century we begin to get catalogues and inventories that are sufficiently detailed to allow the identification of surviving volumes.

Amongst the most important of these inventories are those of the royal collection. The earliest was made in 1373 and there were then several others until 1424, when the library was valued for its purchase by the Duke of Bedford, Regent of France for his nephew King Henry VI. The entries from the various inventories have been amalgamated and published in a classified order by Delisle (1907). From the inventory of 1411, which quotes the first words of the manuscripts' second folio, we can be sure that all three entries for *Perceval le Galois* refer to copies of Chrétien's text: Delisle no. 1151 cites 'se sont angles' (*Perceval*, 138); Delisle no. 1152 cites 'mais c'est en sain' (*Perceval*, 119); Delisle no. 1153 cites 'et lendemain' (*Bliocadran*, 69). None of these corresponds to a manuscript that is now extant. Other Arthurian romances in verse are *L'Atre périlleux* (Delisle no. 1163: '... l'Estre perileux, achevé par messire Gauvain, en ryme', citing as the first words of the last folio 'celle nuit', which corresponds to *L'Atre périlleux*, 6568) and *Escanor* (Delisle no. 1103: 'Du bel Ascanor de la Montangne ...'). The volume containing *Escanor* was taken from the library by the king for the queen on 29 August 1390, so it is not present in the later inventories that give the folio references that would allow its identification. There was also a text (presumed to be Arthurian) that is not known from any surviving copy (Delisle no. 1195: 'Torrez chevalier au Cercle d'or, rymé, bien historié et escript'). This volume was another that was removed from the library, this time by the queen herself on 11 November 1392, and the absence of the volume from later inventories means that we have no folio references. The text it contained may have been the French original of the Dutch *Torec*, and it may be the same text (perhaps even the same manuscript) as that described in successive inventories of the Burgundian library at Malines in 1523 and Turnhout in 1556: 'Le livre du Chevalier chercle d'or et de Parcheval le Galoy' (Michelant 1871, 37) and 'Livre de Chevalier cercle d'or et de Percheval de Galoy' (Gachard 1845, item 89). Although the removal of *Escanor* in 1390 and of *Torec* in 1392 has deprived us of some additional information, it does reveal that the queen, Isabella of Bavaria, was interested in Arthurian verse romances at a later date than might have been expected.

Not all entries in the royal inventories are quite what they seem, and some need to be interpreted with care. Thus, the 'Cligés et Ypomecol, rymé' (Delisle no. 1101) has a second folio reference 'Calabre' that is not from *Cligés*, but would correspond to line 120 of *Ipomedon* (perhaps implying that there were two columns per page of thirty lines each, with the first line used for a title or with the first verse spread over two lines because of a large initial). However, the reference for the last folio given by Delisle from the inventory of 1411 ('fet si ne sens plit') does not seem to be from either *Ipomedon* or *Cligés*. However, this folio reference is given by Douët d'Arcq as 'fet se ne s'emplit' (1867, item 108), though it must be noted that the difference is purely editorial. Despite his title (*Inventaire de . . . 1423*) Douët d'Arcq takes the text of each entry from the inventory of 1411, there being no folio references in that of April 1424 (Delisle 1907, I, 31–2; 34). Nevertheless, the form adopted is extremely helpful, because it can be recognized as a corruption of 'fet cent [*variant*: ces] nes emplir' (*Cligés*, Gregory and Luttrell edn, 6676, less than 120 lines from the end, as required by the presumed format). Thus, 'Cligés et Ypomecol' does represent *Cligés* and *Ipomedon*, but in the opposite order. Other problematic entries are 'Glorion de Bretagne, rymé' (Delisle no. 1112), whose folio references do not suit the unique, late manuscript of *Galeran de Bretagne*, and the 'Merengis rymé, très vieil' (Delisle no. 1141), whose folio references do not suit *Meraugis de Portlesguez*. Other possible evidence for a different *Meraugis* (unless 'Sado' is a corruption of 'Lidoine') is the 'romaunz de Merangys et Sado' that was issued to Queen Isabella, wife of Edward II, in London in March 1327 (London, British Library, Additional MS 60584, fol. 27v, lines 11–12; Vale 1982, 50, with slightly different transcription).

From a very different context is the inventory of Jean de Saffres, a dean of the chapter of Langres, who died in 1365. This includes a number of Arthurian entries in both prose and verse (Carnandet 1857, 471). Those presumed to be in verse are 'romancium dicti *de Cligez*', 'romancium dicti *de Percevaux le Galoix*' and 'romancium dicti *de Beaudoux*' (items 3, 4 and 6). The occurrence of *Perceval* is no surprise; just as it has the greatest number of surviving manuscripts, so it is also by far the most common Arthurian verse text in the inventories. By contrast, *Beaudous* does not occur anywhere else, and *Cligés* is far from common, though there was one in the library of King Martin I of Aragon in 1410 (Massó Torrents 1905, item 281). This is heavily disguised in the published inventory as 'vn altre libre appellat *De Rech* en frances' (*another book called* De Rech *in French*). This title should have been transcribed as *d'Erech*, but there is an older misunderstanding in the inventory itself, for the *incipit* given is 'Cil qui fests de rech', i.e. the first line of *Cligés*: 'Cil qui fist d'Erec et d'Enide' (*he who wrote about Erec and Enide*). In 1474 the library of the Countess of Montpensier at Aigueperse had amongst the books on parchment 'Le livre de Parseval le Galoiz' and a 'Durmas le Galoiz, en ryme' (Boislisle 1880, 299), but by 1507 only the *Perceval* remained, unless *Durmart* is represented by 'Ung petit Livre des Chevaliers de la Table Ronde ... en parchemyn' (Le Roux de Lincy 1850, 121, items 143 and 152).

We have already seen that BNF, fr. 12560 appears amongst the books of Margaret of Flanders in 1405, and that the *Meraugis* in Vienna had entered the Burgundian library before 1467, but it is extraordinary that these are the only examples of Arthurian verse manuscripts in catalogues of this extensive collection until the acquisition of BNF, fr. 12603 from Charles de Croy in 1511. This is almost certainly an anomaly that results in part from the inventories' being restricted to one particular ducal residence on each occasion. It is extremely unlikely that dukes of Burgundy did not possess other Arthurian verse. Indeed, it looks as though they did have a second copy of *Yvain*, if we may judge from the closing line 's'on n'y vient mensoenge adiouster' given in the inventory of 1487 for a volume that ended with 'pluiseurs autres livres' (*several other books*) whose titles are not specified (Barrois 1830, no. 1756; Doutrepont 1906, xxiii). However, the inventory of 1467 records the opening words of the last folio of the same book as 'presques exploittié' (Barrois 1830, no. 1484), which fails to support the identification with *Yvain*, forcing us to suppose either that another text used the same closing line, or that *Yvain* was added to the volume between the making of the two inventories. It is also hard to believe that Philip the Bold never had a copy of the ubiquitous *Perceval*, when he commissioned a tapestry of its subject-matter as a gift for the Duke of York (Dehaisnes 1886, 697 and 727). There was certainly an opportunity for a copy to be in the library, because there are several routes by which Philip the Bold or Margaret of Flanders could have had a share in the inheritance of Matilda, Countess of Artois, who bought a *Perceval* at Arras in November 1308 (Dehaisnes 1886, 183).

The distribution of the manuscripts of verse texts was at one time much wider than the history of the surviving copies would indicate. The survivors are now mostly in France, and those that are elsewhere nearly all reached their present homes after the Middle Ages. Out of the 58 surviving Arthurian verse manuscripts and 46 sets of fragments only 19 (of which 11 are fragments) are likely to have been outside France before 1500, and this figure includes four that were in territories that some definitions might count as part of France: three in the Burgundian Netherlands (as already indicated) and Turin, Biblioteca Nazionale, MS L. IV. 33, which was presumably in Savoy. Only those that were made in England and Italy were outside France in the broader sense.

There is, however, evidence of various kinds that manuscripts now lost were to be found somewhat further afield. There were, for example, at least one or two copies of *Perceval* in Italy. The inventory of the Gonzaga library at Mantua in 1407 includes: 'Princivallis le galoys per versus. Incipit: *Qui petit seme petit cheul. Et finit: se il chierent par chemin.* Continet cart. 315.' (Braghirolli 1880, item 39). The title has been distorted, but the *incipit* identifies the text as Chrétien's *Perceval*, and the *explicit* is that of Manessier's Continuation. The copy of *Perceval* owned by Valentina of Milan may have been brought from Italy on the occasion of her marriage to Louis d'Orléans in 1388, but it is not specifically recorded amongst her books at that time. It was later inherited by her son Charles d'Orléans in 1408 (Champion 1910, lxix, lxxiii and 86). Somewhat surprisingly, given the survival of so much of the Orleans library, this book cannot be identified amongst extant copies.

English bequests and catalogues include a good number of Arthurian titles, but most are likely to be in prose. A possible example of one in verse is in a book in the Benedictine abbey at Peterborough at the end of the fourteenth century. This contained 'Tristrem Gallice' and 'Amys et Amilion Gallice' (Blaess 1973, 343). Since the prose *Tristan* is too long to share a volume, it is likely that both texts were in verse, though whether the *Tristan* was the version by Thomas or Beroul, or some other that has not survived, would be pure speculation. The only document that provides sufficiently precise information to identify texts and manuscripts beyond doubt is the library catalogue of St Augustine's Abbey at Canterbury. Thus, 'Romaunz de per le Galois, 2° f°. *et oreisons*' (James 1903, 373, item 1530) is confirmed as a copy of Chrétien's romance by the opening words of its second folio (*Perceval*, 157). Less certain in its identification is the 'Romance de Perciuall & Gawyn' owned by King Richard II, though this too is likely to have been Chrétien's *Perceval*. It appears in a list of books in 1384–5, but it had previously been recorded in the Issue Rolls of the Exchequer as having been handed over to the *valet de chambre* John Rose in 1379. It could have been the 'romaunz Perceual coaperto de coreo albo' released by command of Queen Isabella to Thomas de Useflete in March 1327 (London, British Library, Additional MS 60584, fol. 27v, line 7; Vale 1982, 50, with slightly different transcription), and it is presumably the 'Perceual & Gauwayn' bequeathed by Isabella to Edward III in 1358, and inherited by Richard II in 1377. However, far from being a 'catalogue' of the royal library at the time, the list of 1384–5 records books that Richard had already discarded (for the text of the lists of 1358 and

1384–5, see Rickert 1932; for a correct interpretation of the documents involved, see Green 1976, especially 237). Evidence that there was once a manuscript of *Erec* in England is provided by the section of this text listing the Knights of the Round Table (ed. Foerster, 1691ff.) that has been copied into British Library, MS Harley 4971, a composite manuscript, whose various parts were written in England in the fourteenth century before finding their way to Bury St Edmunds.

There is also the indirect evidence provided by translations and adaptations. Most notably, Chrétien's romances gave rise to versions in several languages. Thus *Erec*, *Yvain* and *Perceval* all have their counterparts in German, Norse and Welsh, and the latter two also exist in English, whilst a somewhat later German version of *Cligés* is now known only from fragments (Meyer 2000, 107). The *Lanzelet* by Ulrich von Zatzikhoven is not taken directly from Chrétien's *Charrette*, but its author claims to have used a French manuscript. There are German, Norse and English versions of Thomas's *Tristan*, and a Norse version of lays by Marie de France and other writers. Equally important, though less well preserved, are several romances in Middle Dutch. The only one to have survived in an independent form is *Ferguut*, a slightly abridged version of Guillaume le Clerc's *Fergus*, composed in the first half of the thirteenth century (Besamusca 2000, 211–14). However, there must at one time have been others, because versions of them have been included in the *Lancelot* Compilation of about 1320. These are: *Perchevael* (a version of the Gauvain section of *Perceval* combined with episodes from the First Continuation); *Wrake van Ragisel* (a version of *La Vengeance Raguidel* which survives in an earlier fragment as well as in the much-abridged version of the *Lancelot* Compilation); *Lanceloet en het hert met de witte voet* (related to the *Lai de Tyolet*); and *Torec*, which probably reflects the lost French romance of *Torrez* (Besamusca 2000, 200–11).

All these translations and adaptations imply access to manuscripts of the originals. Theoretically, some of the foreign versions could have been done in France and exported later, but it is very much more probable that it was the French manuscripts that travelled abroad for the foreign versions to be made in their own country. Certainly, the documented cases of *Lanzelet* and *Tristrams saga* appear to be of this type, as does Wolfram von Eschenbach's non-Arthurian *Willehalm*.

Manuscripts of Arthurian Prose

Texts and Manuscripts

In considering the manuscripts of Arthurian texts in prose, one of the most significant differences is the sheer number of the survivors (in the region of 450) by comparison with the volumes containing Arthurian verse (58, plus 46 sets of fragments). There is, however, an even bigger change in the ratio of texts to manuscripts, since for most purposes scholars recognize fewer Arthurian texts in prose than in verse. The vast majority of extant manuscripts are classified as copies of only two 'texts', the *Lancelot–Grail* and the prose *Tristan*, but when confronted by the actual contents of these several hundred volumes, it soon emerges that this classification is as much the result of a particular scholarly understanding as of any consistency in the books themselves. Given that the *Lancelot–Grail* is made up of five branches (usually presumed to be by several different authors), it is far from clear that it can legitimately be treated as one text rather than five. In reality, matters are even more complicated than that, because the *Estoire* exists in at least three versions (short, long and mixed), not to mention those manuscripts that have the *Joseph d'Arimathie*, either as an alternative, or in addition, or even embedded within the text of the *Estoire*. Similarly, the *Merlin* has a short and a long version, as well as occurring with or without one or other of its various sequels (Vulgate *Suite*, Huth *Suite du Merlin*, or the *Livre d'Artus* of BNF, fr. 337). Following which, *Lancelot* exists in the early non-cyclic version and in the much extended cyclic version (with an expanded form of the earlier text and several additional sections long enough to be romances in their own right, and sometimes known by separate titles, especially in the case of *Agravain*). Manuscripts of the *Queste* and *Mort Artu* are less subject to such large variations, but the important question here is how they relate to their so-called Post-Vulgate counterparts. And this is still not counting the anonymous abridgement of the whole Cycle represented by New York, Pierpont Morgan Library, MS M. 38 (a manuscript copied by Loys Daymeries at Bruges in 1479) and by the incomplete Arsenal MS 3350 (Bogdanow 1955 and 1976). Nor does it include the modernized adaptation of the cycle made by Guillaume de la Pierre, of which parts can be found in Brussels, Bibliothèque Royale, MS 9246 (*Estoire*) and in BNF, fr. 91 (*Merlin*), these being the two surviving volumes of a manuscript written for Jean-Louis of Savoy, Bishop of Geneva (Bayot 1909, 341–51).

Thus, even without considering differences between individual copies, the term *Lancelot–Grail* can be used to cover any number of texts from one to fifteen, or even more. This is complicated enough, but the term prose *Tristan* is, if anything, even more nebulous. Well-known differences between manuscripts are so considerable that scholars recognize several distinct versions (short, long and mixed). Even then, many manuscripts have individual variants that can be extensive, not to mention those that incorporate substantial portions of the *Lancelot–Grail*, or mix the *Tristan* with *Guiron le Courtois* in the Compilation of Rusticien de Pise. The consequence of all this is that the same codex may be cited as a manuscript of three or four different texts, according to each scholar's particular interest at the time.

A classic example of the difficulties that arise in this way is *Guiron le Courtois*. In one sense this text survives in twenty-six manuscripts (bound in thirty-six volumes) and in various further fragments (Lathuillère 1966 and below, chapter IX). Yet in another sense it survives in none at all. Amongst those that bear witness to its existence there is none that gives the complete text, scarcely any two that contain the same material from *Guiron* (even on the larger scale) and none that does not contain material from other texts, either individually or in combination. These other texts are most often the Compilation of Rusticien de Pise, but also quite frequently the *Lancelot–Grail* or the prose *Tristan*, and occasionally the *Prophecies de Merlin* or a different version of *Guiron* itself. Thus, in the case of what we call *Guiron le Courtois*, every manuscript is a compilation, and many consist of one compilation embedded within another. Added to which, one can say almost exactly the same of the Compilation by Rusticien. Given that its very nature is to combine parts of *Guiron* and *Tristan*, it is no surprise that of the eleven manuscripts considered by Cigni (1992) no fewer than eight are also described by Lathuillère (1966) as copies of *Guiron*. Of the remaining three, BNF, fr. 99 and Chantilly, Musée Condé, MS 647 are invariably included amongst the manuscripts of *Tristan*, leaving only BNF, fr. 1463, probably written within ten or twenty years of the date of composition, and chosen by Cigni as the most authentic representative of the text. Not discussed by Cigni is Berlin, Deutsche Staatsbibliothek, MS Hamilton 581 (Bogdanow 1991b). In principle, both BNF, fr. 1463 and Hamilton 581 contain only the Compilation by Rusticien, and yet both are also listed amongst manuscripts of the Post-Vulgate (Bogdanow 1991a, 132–3 and 135–7).

In the light of these considerations, it is obvious that a comparison of the type made for verse texts between the number of texts and the number of copies would simply be at the whim of our classifications. It is also clear that when considering the prose romances the concept of compilation takes on a meaning that is quite different from the collections of texts in verse. In the case of verse, the texts preserve their integrity; it is the manuscript that is the compilation. Even in the extreme case of BNF, fr. 1450 the beginning and end of each individual text is well defined, despite the changes and omissions brought about by their being inserted into the middle of Wace's *Brut*. In prose compilations, however, sources are amalgamated to produce a continuous text, so that only careful comparison with other copies will reveal the addition of extraneous material and any further modification. The technique of *entrelacement* means that even a text in its purest form moves from one strand of narrative to another at frequent intervals, so nothing could be easier than inserting episodes from a different source, or from one's own imagination. Once a compilation has been made, it may be transmitted by a number of further copies, or it may remain as a more or less isolated example. Thus we have the cases of *Guiron*, Rusticien and the prose *Tristan* with a Grail narrative, where each is represented by several surviving manuscripts (each in turn with its own modifications), but we also have a number of cases where a particular combination of texts is confined to just one or two copies. The best-known example is BNF, fr. 112, studied in detail by Pickford (1959/60*) and in chapter IX, but there are several other cases of some importance. One such is the unusual compilation created by interpolating religious texts into the *Lancelot–Grail* that is now Cologny-Genève, cod. Bodmer 147, described in detail by Vielliard (1974).

Less strictly Arthurian is the *Guiron le Courtois* in Cologny-Genève, cod. Bodmer 96, a compilation that is sometimes attributed to Jean Vaillant of Poitiers (Loomis ed. 1959*, 354–5). However, Vaillant's contribution is probably confined to his abridged adaptation of the *Brut*, said to have been made for Louis II, Duke of Bourbon, during April and May, and finished on 'le samedi jour Saint Jehan euvangeliste' of 1391. A small problem not previously noticed is that the date intended is surely the feast of St John the *Baptist* (24 June), which was indeed a Saturday in 1391, whereas the feast of St John the Evangelist (27 December) would have been a Wednesday. The other copy of this prologue (in BNF, fr. 358) agrees on the year 1391, but omits the more detailed reference. Subject to correcting 'Evangelist' to 'Baptist', the date given is probably reliable, but it may not refer to the whole compilation. The Geneva manuscript itself is often described as being from about 1410–30, but it is in fact slightly later, for there is a passage on fol. 4 that refers to the present year as being 1443. Towards the end of the century this compilation was expanded into the six-volume *Guiron* made for Louis de Bruges (BNF, fr. 358–63). This originally had a companion (made for Engelbert of Nassau) that has been reduced to the fragments that remain in Oxford, Bodleian Library, MS Douce 383. These seventeen leaves (preserved for the sake of their miniatures) contain material from the first and last volumes of the set (Bogdanow 1964, but it is not the case that both volumes were by the same scribe, the hand of the second being measurably smaller than that of the first, and its overall appearance much neater). The original foliation still present on the Oxford fragments enables us to calculate that the amount of text now missing between the surviving leaves is consistently within 1 per cent of the amount that has survived in BNF, fr. 358 and 363 (once due allowance has been made for the different amount of text per page). The two Nassau volumes were still intact when they were described in 1686, and they remained intact until at least 1749 (Renting et al. 1993, item 1318: 'Histoire Guiron le Courtois. premier Volume. MS. en parchemin. Quatriesme et dernier Volume'). The description of these volumes as 'first' and 'fourth and last' does not refer to how the set was bound, but to how the text was divided by the compiler, for the complete set in Paris uses the same terminology. The *explicits* of the six bound volumes (Lathuillère 1966, 70–4) divide the tale into a first volume (BNF, fr. 358), a second volume, parts 1 and 2 (BNF, fr. 359 and 360), a third volume, parts 1 and 2 (BNF, fr. 361 and 362), and a fourth and last volume (BNF, fr. 363). No doubt the Nassau set was treated in the same way, unless we entertain the possibility that the first and last volumes were the only ones to have been made. An additional Arthurian interest of this *Guiron* compilation is that the first part of the prose adaptation of *Erec* (probably done in Lille in the 1450s) has been incorporated into the final volume (Middleton 1988; Colombo Timelli 2000).

From a number of related manuscripts with additional material of this sort, and influenced no doubt by parallels in the works of Malory, which he was then editing, Vinaver and his Manchester colleagues extracted tales that they presented (at least by implication) as if they were separate texts (Vinaver 1942; Pickford 1951; 1959; Bogdanow 1965), but it is far from certain that these tales have the independence that this procedure implies. They do not necessarily occur in the manuscripts as continuous, easily defined sections, often appearing as episodes separated by other material, subject to the usual procedure of *entrelacement*. Even more problematic is the Post-Vulgate *Queste du Graal*. In one sense this is represented by an impressive array of manuscripts (Bogdanow 1991a), but never in a complete and uncorrupted form. Embedded in other compilations, not in one continuous sequence, and often fragmentary, it presents a real challenge to any definition of what constitutes a text. Even if it were once a text, it is not clear what it would mean to make such a claim for what the surviving manuscripts now contain. This is a case of considerable importance that is on the very boundary of our definitions.

Outside the two great cycles, Arthurian prose manuscripts are no more numerous than verse, even when we include texts that are only on the fringes of being Arthurian. Best represented is *Guiron le Courtois* with its twenty-six manuscripts and various fragments, but in addition to the complexities of its text that have already been mentioned, its connection with Arthurian literature is rather tenuous. Similarly, although the cover of the recent edition (though not the title page) confidently describes it as a 'roman arthurien', *Ysaÿe le Triste* is a tale in which most of the action takes place outside the Arthurian realm (Giacchetti 1989). This is preserved in just two manuscripts: Darmstadt, Hessische Landes- und Hochschulbibliothek, MS 2524 and Gotha, Herzogliche Bibliothek, MS 688. The first of these comes from the library of Philip the Good, Duke of Burgundy; it is first recorded in the inventory of 1467 (Barrois 1830, no. 1282), and is still present in 1487 (Barrois 1830, no. 1834). This shortage of copies might give the impression that the text had a very restricted readership, were it not for the fact that there were several printed editions. There was also sufficient continuity of interest for the manuscript now at Gotha (apparently made 1517–25) to be the latest of all surviving Arthurian manuscripts (discounting secondary copies made by scholars in the eighteenth and nineteenth centuries).

Represented by more manuscripts, but even less Arthurian than *Guiron* and *Ysaÿe le Triste*, is *Perceforest*. This is preserved in twenty-four volumes, yet this is largely a reflection of the sheer length of the text. In the Middle Ages it was usually divided into six volumes, but eighteenth-century rebinding has turned one of these sets of six into a set of twelve (Arsenal MSS 3483–94). Thus, the large number of volumes disguises the fact that there were in reality relatively few copies of the text, though it is clear that at least a dozen other volumes have disappeared, and there were also printed editions of 1528 and 1531.

If *Guiron*, *Ysaÿe le Triste* and *Perceforest* can claim to be Arthurian more by their associations than by their substance, the Arthurian credentials of the *Prophecies de Merlin* are much more apparent, but even here the prophecies themselves are often devoted to other things. The narrative framework certainly incorporates the elements we might expect of a chivalric romance, but the text as a whole does not fit easily within the genre. Four of the twelve surviving manuscripts incorporate the prophecies into the text of the Vulgate *Merlin*, and one other combines them with *Guiron le Courtois*. Whether associated with other texts or preserved in isolation, the number of copies is probably a reflection of a general interest in prophecy and of the particular reputation of Merlin himself.

Conversely, a text whose Arthurian credentials are often overlooked is the *Roman de Laurin* (Thorpe 1958). Taken as a whole it is not, of course, an Arthurian romance, being a sequel to *Marques de Rome*, itself a sequel to the *Sept sages de Rome*, but it does contain two lengthy sections that are exclusively Arthurian, in which many familiar figures (such as Arthur, Guinevere, Gauvain, Kay, Lancelot, Perceval, Yvain, Erec and Bohort) make their appearance, but also in which less well known Arthurian characters have significant roles (notably Baudemagu, but also Brandelus, Claudas and Giglain). Given that these sections amount to very nearly half the text (occupying 185 pages out of a total of 386 in Thorpe's edition) it has, in some ways at least, a much better claim to be called Arthurian than *Perceforest*, *Ysaÿe le Triste* or *Guiron*. On the other hand, the copies in which it survives are all manuscripts of the Seven Sages Cycle, so although the text could claim to be Arthurian, the manuscripts are not.

Not fully incorporated into the *Lancelot–Grail* Cycle, but not entirely independent, are the three prose texts attributed to Robert de Boron: *Joseph*, *Merlin* and *Didot-Perceval*. These occur together in just two manuscripts: Modena, Biblioteca Comunale Estense, MS E. 39 and BNF, nouv. acq. fr. 4166. This prose version of *Perceval* appears nowhere else, and it is this in particular that defines these three texts as an alternative cycle. In contrast to this, the *Merlin* is also a constituent of the *Lancelot–Grail* Cycle, and even the *Joseph* is more usually found in manuscripts of the *Lancelot–Grail*, sometimes instead of the Vulgate *Estoire*, sometimes alongside it, sometimes embedded within it.

In the mainstream of Arthurian literature there are really only two texts without some connection to the two great cycles: *Perlesvaus* and *Le Chevalier du Papegau*. One is early and the other late, but each survives in only a few manuscripts. Indeed, in the case of the *Papegau*, there is just one known copy (BNF, fr. 2154, obtained from Cangé in 1733, having previously belonged to various members of the Tournon family). There is a 'Liber militis a papagallo' in the inventory of the Gonzaga library at Mantua in 1407 (item 36), and the next item is also a 'Papagallus' (Braghirolli 1880). Since the *incipits* and *explicits* of these two books are the same in all but one minor variant, it is clear that these were two copies of the same text (one in seventy leaves, the other in sixty). However, neither the *incipit* nor the *explicit* resembles anything in the surviving *Chevalier du Papegau*, though it may not be irrelevant that the Tournons had close connections with Italy, and owned several Arthurian manuscripts that had been made there (see below, p. 69).

The more interesting case is that of *Perlesvaus*, which survives more or less complete in three manuscripts and in a defective copy that lacks the final third (Chantilly, MS 472, a major repository of Arthurian texts in verse, see Chapter XI). Several small sections of the text are preserved in Bern, Burgerbibliothek, MS 113 (which we have also encountered before for its verse romances), and there are three sets of fragments. In addition, a short passage has been incorporated into a version of the *Lancelot–Grail* preserved in two closely related copies completed in Paris in 1404 or very soon afterwards (BNF, fr. 117–20 and Arsenal MSS 3479–80). There is also a translation into Welsh (Lloyd-Morgan 1986). Two of the three principal manuscripts have no documented history until the sixteenth century, but the third (Oxford, Bodleian Library, MS Hatton 82) has much more to tell us. The Bodleian *Summary Catalogue* suggests that it was written in England, but the editors Nitze and Jenkins (1932–7) failed to find any specifically Anglo-Norman linguistic forms, and were led to suppose that it was probably written in northern France, in the middle of the thirteenth century. Later additions, however, are certainly in an English hand (the French poem on the recto of the last leaf and the Latin on the verso both use long-stemmed *r*), and there is reason to believe that the book was in England by 1300, or not very much after. At the head of the first leaf of text there is an ex-libris that reads 'Le seint Graal; le liuer Sire Brian, fiz alayn'. In the edition by Nitze and Jenkins this leaf is designated 'fol. 1', but the foliation on the manuscript itself begins with the four flyleaves, making this first leaf of text fol. 5. The editors insist that the inscription has *seinti*, but this is not really so, since the stroke that represents the final *i* is significantly fainter than the rest. It has probably been imperfectly erased by the writer of this inscription, who probably began by following the wording of the text itself (which has *seintisme*), but then decided to abbreviate so as to have room for the name that follows. It is just possible that the *i* might be a survival from a previous inscription that is no longer legible, but whose existence is implied by the fact that these first words are written upon erasure.

Brian Fitzalan has been identified by Nitze (1935; 1932–7) as the lord of Bedale in Yorkshire who died in 1306. The origins of his family are not documented with complete certainty, but the tradition that he was descended from a younger son of Alan the Black, Duke of Brittany (d. 1146) is unlikely to be correct, though Brian himself or his descendants may have believed it. Whatever its ultimate origins, the family of Brian Fitzalan, lord of Bedale, had been established in northern England for several generations. His grandfather, another Brian Fitzalan, had been sheriff of Northumberland and of Yorkshire. Brian himself was summoned to the Welsh war of 1282 and to the council of Gloucester of 1287. In 1290 he was appointed warden of the castles of Forfar, Dundee, Roxburgh and Jedburgh (in southern Scotland), and in 1292 he was made one of the guardians of Scotland. In 1294 he was summoned to repress the Welsh revolt, and in 1295 he was summoned to Parliament (and again on various occasions until 1305). From 1296 he spent most of his life in Scotland or on the border. It is notable that the available records do not include any period of service in France, his summons to serve beyond the sea (7 July 1297) being immediately superseded, firstly by his appointment as captain of all garrisons and fortresses in Northumberland (12 July 1297) and then by his appointment as guardian of Scotland (14 August 1297). We could not be sure that Brian had never been abroad, but it seems more likely that the manuscript had been brought across the Channel by someone else.

The manuscript itself is an interesting example of cooperation between several scribes working simultaneously and perhaps in some haste. Nitze and Jenkins (1932–7) have identified nine different hands, but what they do not make clear is that most of the transitions take place at the start of a new gathering. Even more revealing are the occasions when the scribe finishing the previous gathering has slightly misjudged the amount of material available to fill the final column. Fol. 28v ends with two blank lines; fol. 36v ends with its last line half blank; fol. 44v has four lines in which letters and words are widely spaced, but still ends with a blank line; on fol. 50v the last line is five letters too long; on fol. 51v the last line consists of only two words, completed by an extended horizontal stroke; on fol. 53 the catchword of fol. 52v has been added before the text in a different hand; fol. 77v ends with two extra lines below the ruling, written in an even smaller hand; fol. 83v has two lines in which letters and words are widely spaced, followed by a line with only one word, and then three blank lines. These procedures (which all correspond to changes of scribe) are clear evidence that the exemplar was divided into quires, and distributed to the various different scribes for each to copy a specified section of the text.

Format and Appearance

In physical appearance, manuscripts of Arthurian prose texts are usually quite different from their verse counterparts. The prose manuscripts are typically larger than the verse, and some are very large indeed. A simple means of gaining an impression of these different sizes is to compare the shelf-marks of those that are in the Bibliothèque Nationale de France. The order of manuscripts in the earlier part of the *fonds français* is still essentially that of the numerical sequence established by Nicolas Clément for his catalogue of 1682, which was arranged in a series of categories that were determined by size. These began with *folio maximo* (as far as modern shelf-mark fr. 151), followed by *folio magno* (to fr. 390), *folio mediocri* (to fr. 888), *folio parvo* (to fr. 1747) and finally *quarto* (to fr. 2423), after which the system becomes more complicated. The merest glance at a list of shelf-marks will show how many of the prose manuscripts are *folio maximo*, whereas verse manuscripts have nothing larger than one *folio magno* (BNF, fr. 375) and after that only one *folio mediocri* (BNF, fr. 794), with both of these being collective manuscripts containing a wide range of texts. A further difference, despite this average increase in size, is that prose manuscripts usually contain either a single text or consecutive texts of the *Lancelot–Grail* Cycle. Copies of the complete Cycle are often divided into several volumes, as are those of *Perceforest*, *Guiron le Courtois* and *Tristan*. The obvious reason for both these differences is that the prose compositions are much longer than the verse, so that the additional space is a practical necessity, though it is also the case that many prose manuscripts, especially the later ones, are written in a larger script and with much more generous margins.

It is also worth remembering that the Middle Ages tolerated far thicker volumes than modern libraries or collectors. Earlier inventories often allow us to know that books now bound as two, three or four volumes were originally single volumes of over 600 leaves. Thus, the four volumes of BNF, fr. 117–20 began life as a single volume in the library of the Duke of Berry, and so did its twin in the collection of the Duke of Burgundy (now Arsenal MSS 3479–80). The four volumes of BNF, fr. 113–16 owned by Jacques d'Armagnac were a single volume until after 1645 (Omont 1908–21, III, 6, item 54), and the three volumes of British Library, Additional MSS 10292–4 were still bound as one in 1686, as were the two volumes of Cologny-Genève, cod. Bodmer 96. These last two items (a complete *Lancelot–Grail* Cycle and a *Guiron* compilation) both come from the collection of the princes of Orange at Nozeroy, where they were items 5 and 28 in the inventory taken in 1686 (their numbers 'cinq' and 'vingt huit' being written on their opening folios, as specified by the inventory itself). The descriptions of 1686 also allow them to be identified in earlier inventories at Nozeroy, the *Lancelot–Grail* being item 5 in 1533 and the *Guiron* being item 15 in 1542 (Lanoë 1998, 475, 480, 486 and 488, without identifications). A similar case is the complete *Lancelot–Grail* Cycle that is now divided between Amsterdam, Bibliotheca Philosophica Hermetica, MS 1 (three volumes), Manchester, John Rylands University Library, MS French 1 (two volumes) and Oxford, Bodleian

Library, MS Douce 215. There is some evidence that this may have been a single volume at one stage, but it was certainly in only two volumes when it disappeared from the Abbey of Sainte-Geneviève in Paris early in the eighteenth century (Kohler 1898, xciii, item 6). It is described as 'deux gros volumes' in the two catalogues of the library preserved in Paris, Sainte-Geneviève, MS 952 (fol. 16) and MS 965 (p. 17), and the first of these also has a note by Mercier de Saint-Léger recording its absence, and another giving its shelf-mark as T 7 (which is what appears on the opening folios of Amsterdam vol. 1 and Douce 215).

On the other hand, we should not suppose that all prose manuscripts were particularly large, nor that they never contained unrelated texts. It is true that no survivor is as small as the smallest of the verse, but quite a few are no bigger than more typical verse manuscripts. For example, nine of the twenty-one surviving manuscripts containing texts from the *Lancelot–Grail* Cycle that were in England during the Middle Ages are no more than 300mm tall (Middleton 2003, n. 43). This proportion of nearly half is not repeated outside England, but there were certainly some smaller manuscripts elsewhere. The sizes given by Micha (1960–3) for copies of the *Lancelot* are an easily accessible guide. His list includes eight of the nine smaller manuscripts that were in England, all now in the British Library: MSS Egerton 2515 (267mm); Lansdowne 757 (225mm); Royal 15. A. xi (185mm); Royal 19. B. vii (300mm); Royal 19. C. xiii (300mm); Royal 20. A. ii (275mm); Royal 20. B. viii (266mm); Royal 20. C. vi (185mm). The ninth (containing the *Estoire* and *Merlin*) is British Library, Additional MS 32125 (250mm). Smaller manuscripts of the *Lancelot* that were in France during the Middle Ages are: BNF, fr. 1430 (289mm); BNF, fr. 12573 (280mm); Aberystwyth, National Library of Wales, MSS 445-D (280mm) and 5018-D (297mm); Escorial, Monasterio Real de San Lorenzo, MS P. II. 22 (289mm); Fribourg, Bibliothèque Cantonale, MS L. 310 (292mm). The dimensions given by Micha for New York, Pierpont Morgan Library, MSS M. 805–06 are in error; the library describes these volumes as measuring 346mm.

There are also some examples of Arthurian prose manuscripts with additional texts (not counting those compilations with interpolated texts that have already been mentioned). A notable case is Berkeley, Bancroft Library, MS UCB 106 (ex Phillipps 3643), which consists mainly of texts in verse, but also contains the *Estoire* and *Merlin*, though there is some room for doubt whether this was the original intention. It is now in two volumes, and although the present division does not fall between the verse and the prose, there are signs that the manuscript was at one time bound in a different order. Equally significant is BNF, fr. 95, whose *Estoire* and *Merlin* are followed by the *Sept sages de Rome* and the *Pénitence Adam*, despite the fact that it is believed to be a companion to New Haven, Yale University, Beinecke Library, MS 229, which contains *Agravain*, the *Queste* and the *Mort Artu* (Stones 1996). Other examples are: BNF, fr. 770, in which an *Estoire* (with embedded *Joseph*), *Merlin* and *Suite* are followed by the *Histoire d'outre-mer et du Roi Saladin*, into which has been interpolated *La Fille du Comte de Pontieu* and the *Ordene de chevalerie*; BNF, fr. 12581, in which the *Queste* is followed by various texts, including a *Tresor* of Brunetto Latini copied in 1284; Arsenal MS 5218, in which the *Queste* is followed by a chronicle; Biblioteca Apostolica Vaticana, MS Reg. lat. 1517, in which *Merlin* is preceded by *Garin de Montglane*; Copenhagen, Kongelige Bibliotek, MS Thott 1087 4°, in which the *Mort Artu* is followed by troubadour poetry; and the former Newcastle 937, in which *Lancelot* was accompanied by a life of Bertrand du Guesclin. This last had been divided into two volumes by 1986 (Tenschert, Catalogue 16, items 6 and 7), but both volumes were still companions when offered for sale in 1995 by Jörn Günther of Hamburg (Catalogue 3, item 11).

Most prose manuscripts contain miniatures, and it is common for them to have extensive programmes of illustration. For obvious reasons it is those with the most lavish illustrations that are best known through the repeated reproduction of their pictures, not only in specialized studies, but also in more popular publications. We must not, however, be misled into supposing that all prose manuscripts were of this type. Even amongst the survivors this is far from the case, and it is a reasonable assumption that cheaper manuscripts will have perished in greater numbers than their more expensive counterparts. This availability of 'untypical' copies is of some importance. We tend to know the history of the lavishly illustrated manuscripts owned by members of the higher aristocracy much better than that of the plainer volumes. This might lead us to associate Arthurian prose literature with a particular social class, whereas in fact it had a much wider distribution. A characteristic side-effect of this is the assumptions that are made about the work of Sir Thomas Malory. More than one attempt to identify the writer of the *Morte Darthur* has thought it necessary to explain how the favoured candidate had access to a substantial library packed with expensive volumes, but this rests upon a misconception. All the French texts that Malory used could be contained in two or three volumes at most, and there is no need for any of them to have been expensive, particularly in England. As we have already seen, nine of the surviving manuscripts of the *Lancelot–Grail* known to have been in England in the Middle Ages are relatively small. Six of these have no more than coloured initials for decoration, and the other three have only one or two miniatures. What is more, even five of the larger manuscripts are without miniatures (Middleton 2003, n. 43). There is every reason to believe that the relevant French texts would have been available without much difficulty to anyone from the landed gentry, and there is every chance that Sir Thomas Malory (whoever he may have been) could have owned his own copies (Meale 1985, 105–8). A much more pertinent question in Malory's case would be to consider how he obtained access to the English alliterative *Morte Arthure*, which really was a rarity.

In France, however, the fifteenth century witnessed a new type of manuscript production, in which outward appearance was very much a prime consideration. The number and quality of the illustrations had always had a major influence upon the price, and those that could afford it might buy more than one copy of the same text if the volumes were sufficiently attractive. Older copies might be replaced by those that were newer, and plainer copies by those that were more prestigious. Kings and dukes might acquire multiple copies as a result of gifts or by inheritance, but except for the production of bibles and service books it is not until the fifteenth century that we encounter situations where the making of a particular book is more important than the copying of a particular text.

This change of emphasis appears in commissions to produce a copy of a text that the patron already owns, in commissions to produce two or three matching copies of a particular text, and in repeated commissions to produce copies of the same text in different formats. The last of these categories is most obviously exemplified by the Duke of Berry and his many Books of Hours, but there are no documented cases amongst Arthurian manuscripts. For the production of matching copies we can turn to Philip the Bold, Duke of Burgundy, who in 1403 paid his agent Jacques Raponde for three copies of the *Fleur des histoires de la terre d'orient* (Cockshaw 1969, no. 55). One of these was for his brother the Duke of Berry, the second for his nephew the Duke of Orleans and the third for Philip himself. As an Arthurian example, it is likely that a similar commission is at the origin of the two matching copies of the *Lancelot–Grail* that are now BNF, fr. 117–20 and Arsenal MSS 3479–80, the first owned by the Duke of Berry, the second by Philip's son, John the Fearless. If this double commission is not fully documented, it is probably because Philip the Bold had died (on 27 April 1404) before the books were ready. The copy owned by Jean de Berry was obtained by him from the Parisian bookseller Regnaut du Montet in January 1405 (Delisle 1907, Berry no. 270), but it is hard to believe that the production of these expensive matching copies was a commercial speculation. It is usually assumed that the Arsenal volumes are the book for which John the Fearless paid his (and his father's) Parisian agent Jacques Raponde in 1406 or 1407, and this is probably so, despite some discrepancies.[4]

The classic example of a bibliophile making new books using texts that he already owned is Jacques d'Armagnac, Duke of Nemours, who seems to have supplied the exemplars for manuscripts that he commissioned (see below, pp. 66–8). One characteristic of these productions is that they often combine existing texts in a new way. This is especially noticeable in the case of Jacques d'Armagnac's Arthurian compilation that is now BNF, fr. 112 (Pickford 1959/60*), but it also applies on a smaller scale to the *Lancelot–Grail* of the dukes of Berry and Burgundy, which is distinguished by the use of the prose adaptation of Chrétien's *Charrette* (instead of the usual prose version of the same story) and by the insertion of a short section of *Perlesvaus*. However, these modifications to the text are probably less important than the physical appearance of the resulting books. The manuscripts that stem from the commissions of known bibliophiles are conceived on the grand scale; they are large, well illustrated and expensive.

Dates and Places of Production

The earliest surviving manuscript of the *Lancelot–Grail* Cycle is thought to be Rennes, Bibliothèque Municipale, MS 255 (containing the *Estoire*, *Merlin* and an incomplete *Lancelot*), but there is a serious possibility that two manuscripts containing the non-cyclic version of the prose *Lancelot* (BNF, fr. 768 and 1430) and one of the manuscripts of the trilogy attributed to Robert de Boron (Modena, Biblioteca Comunale Estense, MS 39) are even earlier. The miniatures of the Rennes manuscript have been studied by Stones (1977), who came to the conclusion that they were painted in the 1220s, and who has since suggested that this could be slightly modified to 'the early 1220s' (1991, 299) or even to '*c.*1220' (1996, 221). Although she has not published a similar study of the Modena manuscript, her opinion of its miniatures (mentioned in various lectures and conference papers) is that they may be as early as the decade 1210–20. For BNF, fr. 1430 and BNF, fr. 768 Stirnemann suggests *c.*1215–25 (1993, 206, 207). Thus, given that we have no exact dates for the composition of the texts involved, and that some of the dates suggested for the texts are later than those proposed for the manuscripts in which they occur, the reliability of these various suggestions becomes an issue of some importance.

Such an early date for the Modena manuscript is wholly incompatible with the conventional view of how and when the prose *Joseph* was written. It is normally supposed that the prose version is an adaptation of the verse *Joseph d'Arimathie* also known as *Le Roman de l'Estoire dou Graal*, whose author seems to have been called Robert de Boron (Nitze edn, 3155 and 3461). A passage at the end of this text (3489–91) appears to invoke as a patron a certain Gautier de Montbéliard, who has been identified with the person of that name who was regent of Cyprus from 1205 to 1210 and who probably died fighting in Palestine in 1212. The most plausible interpretation of this difficult passage suggests that Robert de Boron produced this rhymed version in the East after 1212 (Gallais 1970), making it extremely difficult for there to be a manuscript of the prose version from the decade 1210–20. The difficulty might be alleviated by rejecting the mention of Gautier de Montbéliard, or by reversing the relationship of verse to prose, but even with a date for the prose *Joseph* as early as 1200 a problem would still remain. This is because, by the common consent of those who have studied the manuscript tradition, the copy of the *Joseph* in the Modena manuscript is the most decadent of all those that survive. Such a situation is not impossible in theoretical terms, but it would be extremely unusual for the latest stage of a text's development to be preserved exclusively by the oldest manuscript. Even if we allow that the later manuscripts all derive from even earlier exemplars, it still implies that there were more stages between the original and the Modena text than might have been expected for the supposed time available, or that the deterioration from one copy to the next was on a much greater scale than would have been anticipated. Only if the Modena manuscript were shown to be later than 1250 could we be comfortable with the conventional view of the prose *Joseph* and its manuscript tradition.

Another difficult case is that of the Vulgate *Estoire*, whose recent editor suggests a date of composition 'postérieur à 1220–1225' whilst accepting the date of 'environ 1220' for the Rennes manuscript (Ponceau 1997, I, xiv). If there were no more to it than this, the apparent conflict of dates might be resolved by taking a liberal view of the approximations involved. However, the text of the *Estoire* in the Rennes manuscript is partly from the short version and partly from the long version (Ponceau 1997, I, xxvii–xxviii and xxxi–xxxiii). Thus, whichever version is the earlier, the combination of the two places the Rennes manuscript at two removes from the beginning of the tradition. Only in the highly improbable event of its own unique combination being the original form of the text can this manuscript be close to the date of composition. Consequently, if the manuscript really is as early as 1220, the time needed for the development of whichever version was secondary and the subsequent mixture of long and short forms implies a date of composition that is surely no later than 1215, and probably no later than 1210. Even the mechanical copying of the manuscripts would take several years, without allowing for any delay between successive copies or for the additional time required by such deliberate editorial intervention. However, since it is also normally supposed that the creation of the *Lancelot–Grail* Cycle began with the expansion of the Lancelot section and with the addition of the *Queste* and *Mort Artu* before the incorporation of the *Estoire*, this would place the origins of the Cycle no later than 1200–10, and the non-cyclic *Lancelot* would have had to have been made either at the very beginning of that period or even earlier.

Such a possibility would have profound consequences, not least of which would be the possible role of Walter Map. When the Cycle was supposed to be from later than 1230, the attribution of some of its parts to Walter Map, who died on 1 April 1209 or 1210, did not require serious consideration, but if the Cycle were earlier the least that we should have to allow is that the attribution was made while Walter Map was still alive. This does not make it true, of course, but it does alter its significance. Such a date would also cast a different light upon the reference to the story of the grail in Helinand's chronicle, itself of uncertain date, but presumed to have been written not long after 1204 and certainly before 1227 (Lot 1918, 136–7). Perhaps most significant of all would be the consequences that an early date for the *Lancelot–Grail* Cycle would have for the relationships between the Cycle and a number of early thirteenth-century verse texts, especially the *Perceval* Continuations: either some of the proposed dates would have to be revised, or the direction of influence would have to be reconsidered. The exact dating of manuscripts is always a delicate matter, but it would be difficult to think of another circumstance where a difference of only a decade either way could have such an impact upon our understanding of the literature involved.

Quite apart from raising the possibility that these various prose texts were created in a different political and literary environment, the early dating of any of these four manuscripts would mean that there are surviving copies of Arthurian texts in prose that are no later than the earliest complete copy of any Arthurian text in verse. Only the Sneyd fragments of *Tristan* and the defective copy of *Cligés* in Tours are any earlier. What is more, these manuscripts of the prose texts are already illustrated, long before this becomes the normal practice for manuscripts of Arthurian verse. Indeed, the interval between the time of composition and the earliest manuscripts to contain the prose texts is so short that we could reasonably suggest that manuscripts of the *Lancelot–Grail* Cycle were illustrated from the very beginning. This would not preclude earlier unillustrated copies of the non-cyclic prose *Lancelot*, nor does it deny the existence of unillustrated copies of the Cycle, for there are such examples amongst later survivors. Nevertheless, there is a serious possibility that the idea of creating the Cycle and the idea of presenting it in manuscripts with a developed programme of illustrations were virtually simultaneous. In any event, there is a significant difference in this respect between verse and prose.

There is also a further significance to the fact that the earliest manuscripts of the *Lancelot–Grail* Cycle were already fully illustrated. Since the Rennes manuscript was apparently made in Paris, it is possible that the programme of illustration also had a Parisian origin, and if that were so, there is the prospect that the Cycle itself was a Parisian creation. Indeed, if there really is a close connection between the making of the Cycle and the illustrations that accompany it, the whole project takes on the air of being a business venture by a Parisian *libraire*, an exercise in marketing as much as a literary or artistic creation.

The earliest recorded date on an Arthurian prose manuscript is 'Mil deus Cens et sixante et quatorse, le semedi Apries les octaues de le trinite' (i.e. Saturday 9 June 1274), which appears in the colophon of BNF, fr. 342 (Bruce 1910, 264). This is accompanied by the invitation 'pries pour celi ki lescrist' (*pray for the one who wrote it*) in which the use of the form 'celi' (rather than 'celui') presumably indicates that the scribe was a woman. Although it is possible to find examples of 'celi' as a masculine pronoun, it is unlikely that a male scribe would deliberately choose such a form when referring to himself. Almost as early is Bonn,

Universitätsbibliothek, MS 526, whose colophon gives both the date and the name of the scribe: 'Explicit. Arnulfus de Kayo scripsit istum librum qui est Ambianis. En l'an del Incarnation M. CC. IIII^{xx}. VI el mois d'aoust le jour devant le S. Iehan decolasé' (Frappier 1936, xxv). Loomis (1938, 94) prints this colophon without 'devant' and inexplicably interprets the date as 27 August; Micha (1958, 86) includes 'devant' but gives a self-contradictory date: 'le mercredi 26 août 1286'. As it happens, Wednesday is correct, for the beheading of John the Baptist is commemorated on 29 August, making the date of the colophon 28 August 1286, which was indeed a Wednesday (given correctly in Hutchings 1938, ix). The form 'ambianis' presumably means either that the scribe was a native of Amiens or that he was living and working there at the time. In either case, by this date, 'de Kayo' might well be a family name, so it does not guarantee the scribe's own place of origin (though it was no doubt derived originally from one of the several localities within easy reach of Amiens that are named either Caix or Cayeux). This point is somewhat more than academic, because the manuscript of the *Estoire* (with embedded *Joseph*) in Le Mans, Bibliothèque Municipale, MS 354 has the colophon: 'Explicit. Walterus de Kayo scripsit istum librum' (without date). This manuscript has sometimes been assigned to the second quarter of the fourteenth century, but it is in fact one of a group made in the last three decades of the thirteenth century, and there is a manuscript of the *Image du monde* from 1282 with the colophon: 'Explicit. En l'an de l'incarnation M. CC. IIII^{xx} et II. l'escrit Wautiers dou Kai, foi que jou doi a Deu' (BNF, fr. 14962). The similarities between these colophons (the identical wording of the two in Latin, and even the fact that they are in Latin at all after vernacular texts; and the form of the date in the two that give it) prompt the speculation that there may be connections (of family or place of work) between these scribes. There does not appear to be any connection between 'Arnulfus ... ambianis' and the 'Ernouls damiens' whose name appears in a colophon to the *Lancelot* of Oxford, Bodleian Library, MS Rawlinson Q. b. 6, fol. 187v, as having written 'la branche de Galeholt' [*sic*, not as transcribed in the *Summary Catalogue*]. This manuscript was probably made in Paris in the early decades of the fourteenth century, and the hand is not the same as that of Bonn 526. The elaborate style and layout of the colophon seem to eliminate the possibility of the name's having been copied from an exemplar.

Other dated manuscripts earlier than the fifteenth century are: BNF, fr. 122 (a *Lancelot–Grail* dated 'le lundi prochain devant le jour de paskes flories en mars l'an mille CCCXLIIII' i.e. Monday 14 March 1345 rather than Monday 22 March 1344); and BNF, fr. 335–6 (a *Tristan* 'qui fut fait l'an mille III^{cc} IIII^{xx} et XIX la veille de Pasques grans' i.e. 17 April 1400 rather than 29 March 1399). When converting these dates to modern forms it is normally safe to assume that French documents of the period will follow the practice of the royal chancery and change the year at Easter, but in dates that use Easter itself as a reference it is necessary to make an adjustment for the date on which Easter falls, as well as changing the year. The practice in England (and in the Franche-Comté) was to begin the year on Lady Day (25 March), and this occasionally makes a difference when a date falls between then and Easter. Examples of manuscripts that are not only dated but also signed by the scribe are: BNF, fr. 750, a *Tristan* signed in Latin by Petrus de Tiergevilla (presumably Tiergeville in Normandy) in 1278; Rennes, Bibliothèque Municipale, MS 593, a *Prophecies de Merlin* written by Robin Boutemont in 1303 or 1304 (for the complications in determining the exact date, see Paton 1926–7, I, 4–5); Arsenal MS 5218, a *Queste* written, illustrated and bound by Pierart dou Tielt in 1351; and New Haven, Yale University, Beinecke Library, MS 227, a *Joseph, Estoire, Merlin* and *Suite* completed by the scribe Jehan de Loles, from Hainault, on 'le premier samedi de guillet' of 1357 (Knight 1967–8). In 1357 'the first Saturday of July' was in fact 1 July.

Although we have names and dates on these various manuscripts, we know virtually nothing about the circumstances of their production. Conversely, although they are not signed or dated, there are several associated manuscripts that allow us to understand something of how they were made, and of the personnel employed. These belong to a group identified as having been made in Paris in the first half of the fourteenth century (probably the second quarter) by scribes, artists and pen-flourishers associated with the *libraires* Thomas de Maubeuge (who sold non-Arthurian manuscripts to Matilda, Countess of Artois in 1313 and 1328, and to Guillaume, Count of Hainault in 1323: Dehaisnes 1886, 207, 276, 255), Geoffroy de Saint-Ligier and Richard de Montbaston (Stones 1993, 260–2; 1998; Rouse and Rouse 2000, I, 184–260). These include the *Lancelot* of Arsenal MS 3481 and two copies of the *Estoire, Merlin* and *Suite*: BNF, fr. 105 and BNF, fr. 9123 (which may have spent all its life in Paris, for it is probably one of three Arthurian manuscripts alienated from the Abbey of Sainte-Geneviève early in the eighteenth century). According to Richard and Mary Rouse, the Master of Thomas de Maubeuge shared the illustration of BNF, fr. 9123 with the Fauvel master, who painted all of BNF, fr. 105 and also all of Arsenal 3481, apart from one miniature contributed by Richard de Monbaston. There are similar patterns of collaboration between identifiable scribes and pen-flourishers (Rouse and Rouse 2000, I, 184–7, 214–17 and 235–41; II, 176, 178, 182–9, 197, 198, 199 and 204). More loosely connected is the *Tristan* in Los Angeles, J. Paul Getty Museum, MS Ludwig XV. 5, with a frontispiece by Jeanne de Monbaston and other miniatures by one of the artists of BNF, fr. 12577, which contains *Perceval* and its Continuations (Rouse and Rouse 2000, I, 391, n. 105, and II, 204).

The Rouses also include in this same group a manuscript that they refer to as the *Histoire du Graal* (I, 184), giving the shelf-mark as 'Florence, Laurenziana

MS Ashburnham 121' (I, 372, n. 84). This is said to have been illustrated by the Maubeuge Master, a claim later repeated under the reference 'Florence, Biblioteca Laurentiana Ashburnham 121. *Roman du Graal*' (II, 176). The official shelf-mark of this manuscript in the Biblioteca Medicea Laurenziana is MS Ashburnham 48 (though the Rouses are not alone in using the number 121, for it was MS Libri 121 when owned by the Earl of Ashburnham). It contains a *Queste* (rather than the *Estoire* that one might have supposed from the titles given), but it has a colophon stating that it was made in Avignon in 1319 (sometimes read as 1314). Such claims are not always reliable when found on manuscripts that have passed through the hands of Libri (who had a habit of forging provenances), but in the present case the style of the miniatures themselves is confirmation enough (Stones 1996, 213, 215, 219, etc., n. 59 and figs 8.5 and 8.9).

For the first 100 years or so, the production of verse manuscripts continued alongside the prose, but by the middle of the fourteenth century the copying of Arthurian verse texts seems to have been almost entirely abandoned. The copying of the prose romances, however, continued unabated through the fourteenth and fifteenth centuries until print became the dominant medium. There are even examples of manuscripts of Arthurian prose being produced in the early sixteenth century. The latest datable manuscripts seem to be the *Lancelot* in BNF, fr. 1427 (dated 1504) and the copy of *Ysaÿe le Triste* in Gotha, Herzogliche Bibliothek, MS 688, which has the arms of Louis de la Trémoïlle (who died at Pavia in 1525) and of his second wife Louise Borgia (whom he married in 1517), implying a date of production in the period 1517–25 (Giacchetti 1989). Other manuscripts assigned to the sixteenth century are the copies of *Tristan* in BNF, fr. 24400 and Ghent, University Library, MS 6; the copy of *Guiron le Courtois* in British Library, Additional MS 36673; and possibly the *Merlin* and *Suite* in St Petersburg, National Library of Russia, MS fr. F. pap. XV. 3. We should also remember that in the late 1520s Pierre Sala of Lyon produced a version of *Tristan* that survives in two manuscripts (Muir 1958).

In considering how manuscripts of Arthurian romances gave way to the printed editions there is a difficulty of comparing like with like. The new printed editions were effective in producing a readable copy of the text, but despite the use of woodcuts and the provision for decoration to be added by hand, they were no match for the traditional product as works of art. In earlier centuries this deficiency might not have been so important, but the nature of book buying and of book collecting had been changing. The lavishly illustrated volumes of the fifteenth-century bibliophiles would have had nothing to fear from the new printed editions. The problem is in knowing how many plain copies of the texts were still being made, for it is these that would be in most direct competition with the new medium. The small number that survive are not of the most elaborate type, but not of the plainest either, and these may not be a true reflection of the numbers that were made. For all that we know, they may have been produced in quantity, and may have continued in production alongside the printed editions; they would certainly have been competitive in terms of price and in speed of delivery (assuming that an exemplar were available). Only if the bookseller already had a copy of the printed equivalent in stock could he or she be sure of providing a faster service.

It is popularly assumed that the arrival of printing suddenly made books much cheaper and more numerous, but this was far from the case. Printing presses and type required unprecedented levels of capital investment, and the process of setting type was much slower than writing out the text by hand. Thus, producing a copy of a book in the new way had no advantage at all in either time or cost; it is the ease with which many copies can be made at the same time, for little additional outlay, that eventually tips the balance, provided enough of them can be sold without significant delay. It must also be remembered that printers would not have had sufficient type to set a whole book at once, a consideration that necessitated a decision about the number of copies from the very beginning of the process, with any change of plan proving costly. It is highly probable that early print runs were very short, hence the rarity of incunabula and the constant need for new editions of the titles that proved successful. Be that as it may, there is ample evidence that the Arthurian prose romances enjoyed considerable popularity in their new printed form. Not only did all the major texts soon appear in print, but each soon reappeared in one edition after another until about the middle of the sixteenth century, and to a lesser extent even beyond.

Manuscripts of Arthurian prose were apparently produced over a wider area than their verse counterparts, though we should be careful not to draw too firm a conclusion from the available evidence. What is true is that we have many more examples amongst the survivors of manuscripts that were written outside northern and eastern France, but this may be a reflection of the fact that there are so many more prose manuscripts still extant. It does not, however, seem to be connected with the fact that prose manuscripts continued to be produced over a longer period. It is during the thirteenth and fourteenth centuries that we find them being written in England and Italy, areas where the use of French as a literary language had much declined by the later period. Not surprisingly, the Arthurian prose manuscripts produced in the fifteenth and sixteenth centuries were all written in France.

Copies of various parts of the *Lancelot–Grail* Cycle were made by English scribes and artists (presumably working in England, though perhaps in some cases working in northern France). These are: London, British Library, MSS Royal 19 B. vii, 19 C. xiii, 20 A. ii, 20 C. vi, Egerton 2515, Lansdowne 757 and Additional 32125; Cambridge, Corpus Christi College, MS 45; and BNF, fr. 123 (Middleton 2003). Cambridge, University Library, Additional MS 7071 can

probably be added to the list on the basis of its Anglo-Norman spellings, though
the evidence from its script is less clear-cut.

When considering the production of French Arthurian manuscripts in Italy we
must first bear in mind that two of the prose romances with which we are
concerned were not merely copied but actually composed in Italy. The *Prophecies
de Merlin*, attributed to 'Maistre Richart d'Irlande' and purportedly commissioned by the Emperor Frederick II, was in fact produced by a Venetian working
between 1272 and 1279. Even more significant, especially for the development of
Arthurian literature in Italian, was the Compilation by Rusticien de Pise. This
was composed soon after 1272–4 by the Rustichello da Pisa who in 1298, whilst
in prison in Genoa, wrote the French account of the travels of Marco Polo (Cigni
1992). We might also mention in this context the prose *Yvain* (part adaptation,
part compilation), which is likely to have been put together in Italy, given that the
unique manuscript in Aberystwyth, National Library of Wales, MS 444-D was
made there (Muir 1964; Avril, Gousset and Rabel 1984, 25, n. 25).

The early copy of the Compilation by Rusticien de Pise in BNF, fr. 1463 is one
of a group of manuscripts associated with Genoa at the end of the thirteenth
century (Cigni 1992, 522 and n. 25; 524 and n. 44, based upon Avril, Gousset
and Rabel 1984, 25). The other manuscripts of this group are six copies of
Tristan: Aberystwyth, National Library of Wales, MS 446-E; Florence, Biblioteca
Medicea Laurenziana, MS Ashburnham 50 (sections of *Tristan* and *Guiron*);
London, British Library, MS Harley 4389; Modena, Biblioteca Comunale
Estense, MS E. 59; BNF, fr. 760; Venice, Biblioteca Nazionale Marciana, MS
fr. XXIII; and four copies of various branches of the *Lancelot–Grail*: Berlin,
Deutsche Staatsbibliothek, MS Hamilton 49; BNF, fr. 354; BNF, fr. 16998; and
Venice, Biblioteca Nazionale Marciana, MS fr. XI. To Cigni's list must be added
two copies of *Guiron*: Biblioteca Apostolica Vaticana, MS Reg. lat. 1501 and
Venice, Biblioteca Nazionale Marciana, MS fr. IX; a unique *Queste* in Udine,
Biblioteca Arcivescovile, MS 177; and the prose *Yvain* in Aberystwyth, National
Library of Wales, MS 444-D (Avril, Gousset and Rabel 1984, 25, n. 25).

Other manuscripts made in Italy include copies of all the principal prose
romances. The copy of the *Estoire*, *Merlin* and *Suite* in Oxford, Bodleian Library,
MS Douce 178 has miniatures that were probably painted in Bologna *c.*1270–85.
In addition to those connected with Genoa there are five other Italian copies of
Lancelot (or of parts of it): Florence, Biblioteca Medicea Laurenziana, MS Plut.
89 inf., 61; London, British Library, MS Harley 4419 (Italy or southern France);
BNF, fr. 767 (Tuscany); BNF, fr. 773 (Bologna); and Venice, Biblioteca Nazionale
Marciana, MS fr. XII; though probably not Oxford, Bodleian Library, MS
Douce 199, which is included as Italian by Delcorno Branca (1998, 20), but
whose miniatures were almost certainly painted in France. The *Mort Artu* in
Chantilly, Musée Condé, MS 649 was written for Brexianus de Salis who was

podestà of Modena in 1288, and the partial copy (combined with the death of Tristan) in Oxford, Bodleian Library, MS Douce 189 is also from northern Italy. There are copies of *Joseph* and *Merlin* in Florence, Biblioteca Riccardiana, MS 2759 (written by Nicolaus Merlinus); of *Joseph*, *Merlin* and the *Prophecies de Merlin* in Chantilly, Musée Condé, MS 644; and of *Merlin* and the *Prophecies* in Venice, Biblioteca Nazionale Marciana, MS fr. App. XXIX. Copies of the Post-Vulgate *Queste* and *Mort Artu* are to be found in Oxford, Bodleian Library, MS Rawlinson D. 874 and BNF, fr. 343 (both from the library of the dukes of Milan at Pavia). Commonest of all is *Tristan*, with the six copies from Genoa and the extract in MS Douce 189 that have already been mentioned being joined by eight more: the first part of Aberystwyth, National Library of Wales, MS 5667-E; Cologny-Genève, cod. Bodmer 164; London, British Library, Additional MS 23929 (from the Gonzaga library); Modena, Biblioteca Comunale Estense, MS E. 40; BNF, fr. 755 (from the library at Pavia); BNF, fr. 756–7 (from Naples, with the arms of Carafa); BNF, fr. 12599 (which also includes a fragment of an Italian version of *Guiron* and the 'Folie Lancelot' section of the *Suite du Merlin*); and Biblioteca Apostolica Vaticana, MS Barb. lat. 3536, but probably not MS Pal. lat 1964 (said to be Italian by Loomis 1938, 117, but rejected by Delcorno Branca 1998, 57, n. 13). Finally, there are four further copies of *Guiron*: BNF, nouv. acq. fr. 5243; London, British Library, Additional MSS 12228 and 23930; and Venice, Biblioteca Nazionale Marciana, MS fr. XV (Loomis 1938, 114–21; Avril, Gousset and Rabel 1984; Cigni 1993; Delcorno Branca 1998). There are two other manuscripts that were probably written in France, but whose decoration was completed either in the Holy Land or in southern Italy. The first of these is the *Tristan* in BNF, fr. 750, which was signed by the scribe Petrus de Tiergevilla (presumed to be Tiergeville in Normandy) in 1278. The suggestion made by Loomis (1938, 92) that the illustration is Spanish is to be rejected in favour of the Holy Land or southern Italy (Avril, Gousset and Rabel 1984, 163–4). The second manuscript is the *Estoire*, *Joseph*, *Merlin* and *Suite* in Tours, Bibliothèque Municipale, MS 951. This was probably made in Paris *c.*1290 with paintings by followers of the Hospitaller Master, but the decoration was left incomplete, and further miniatures were added some years later in southern Italy (Folda 1976, 198).

History and Ownership

For manuscripts of Arthurian romances in prose there is a major difference between what we know about those that were made early and those that were made later. For the earlier manuscripts we are in much the same position as we are for manuscripts of the same period containing the texts in verse. As we have seen, there is the occasional date, and there is the occasional name of a scribe, but most manuscripts yield no such information, and there are few with the names of any owners. The earliest recorded commission appears to be Darmstadt, Hessische Landes- und Hochschulbibliothek, MS 2534 (containing the *Estoire*, *Merlin* and *Suite*), which is said to have been made for 'le bon Comte de bloys jadis signeur de byaumont' (fol. 210). This is presumed to be Louis de Châtillon, Count of Blois, who died at Crécy in 1346 (Schmidt 1890). Another early mark of ownership is the note (in mirror writing) on the last folio of BNF, fr. 770 stating that it was lent by 'Pierre des Essars' to the Duke of Normandy. It is usually supposed that the owner of the manuscript was the Pierre des Essars who died at Crécy (Delisle 1868–81, I, 15; Brunel 1923, xxxv, n. 1), but his career has been confused with that of his father (also called Pierre). The father held a number of official appointments, but was most important as the foremost banker and financier in France. He was Argentier du Roi and Receveur de la Reine from 1320, and became Maître des Comptes in 1336, in succession to his brother Martin. Before moving to Paris, Martin had been mayor of Rouen, and both Martin and Pierre were burghers of Rouen as well as burghers of Paris. Towards the end of his career, in October 1346, Pierre was imprisoned for alleged financial irregularities, and condemned to pay a fine of 50,000 livres. Such an enormous cash sum would have been beyond many of the highest in the land, but Pierre paid it in May 1347, and was duly released. He died in 1349 without being restored to the king's favour, but in 1350 the Duke of Normandy, to whom the manuscript had been lent, acceded to the throne as King John II, and by February 1352 Pierre had been pardoned, and the amount of the fine was reimbursed to his heirs in October 1353 (Cazelles 1958, 239–42). As implied by his title, the Argentier did have responsibility for the king's silver, but his principal duty was the procurement of all the cloth required by the king's household (Douët d'Arcq 1851). This would have resulted in frequent journeys to the centres of production in Flanders, and constant dealings with Flemish merchants in Paris. Possibly as a consequence of these connections, Pierre was employed on several diplomatic missions to Flanders and Hainault, and by 1338 he was in receipt of a pension from the Countess of Flanders (Margaret of France, later also Countess of Artois, d. 1382, a possible owner of Arthurian volumes that found their way to the Burgundian library). Pierre's most significant mission was to Binche in Hainault in 1345–6 to assist in the negotiation of the marriage of Louis de Mâle (son of Louis de Nevers, Count of Flanders, and Margaret of France) with Marie de Brabant (Cazelles 1958, 210, in contrast to Anselme 1726–33, VIII, 555, who wrongly describes the prospective marriage as that of Louis de France, second son of the Duke of Normandy, and who attributes the mission to Pierre, the son, who died at Crécy). This marriage was a matter of considerable political importance, because it was designed to frustrate the attempts of King Edward III to create an Anglo-Flemish alliance by offering Louis the hand of his daughter Isabella, and it paved the way for Louis de Mâle (Count of Flanders after the death of his father at Crécy) to commit himself to France in 1347. These contacts with Flanders and Hainault may be relevant to the history of BNF, fr. 770, because it was in this region that the book was made (possibly at Douay or not far distant, probably in the 1280s). Pierre's considerable wealth would have allowed him to buy the most expensive books available, but the only surviving records of his purchases are for some of the liturgical books of Clemence of Hungary, which he bought in 1328, probably intending them for his parish church of St Germain l'Auxerrois (Douët d'Arcq 1874, 62–3). This transaction is almost certainly an act of piety rather than a reflection of his interest in books as such. Nor should we draw much of a conclusion concerning a family interest in books from the fact that one of Pierre's great-grandsons, Antoine des Essars, was the king's librarian for a short time in 1411–12 (Delisle 1907, I, 20–1). More relevant is that Antoine's elder brother Pierre, who was Prévot de Paris until his execution in 1413, exchanged volumes with the Duke of Berry (Delisle 1907, Berry nos 198 and 201).

Having borrowed a copy of the *Estoire* and *Merlin* from Pierre des Essars whilst Duke of Normandy, John continued to show an interest in the *Lancelot–Grail* Cycle after he became king. During his captivity in England he borrowed 'two volumes, of Lancelot and Sang Réal' (i.e. Lancelot and Saint Greal) from Isabella of France, queen of Edward II, which he returned to her on 10 December 1357 (Middleton 2003, 220–1, where 'returned from France' is a slip for 'from the king of France'). It is also highly probable that John was responsible for acquiring some of the Arthurian volumes in the library of his son Charles V. The successive inventories of the royal library, beginning with that made by Gilles Malet in 1373, contain at least thirty copies of Arthurian prose romances (including, as it seems, 15 of various branches of the *Lancelot–Grail*, 12 of *Tristan*, 2 of *Guiron* and 1 of the *Prophecies de Merlin*). It is not possible to be sure of exact numbers, because some entries may be duplicates, and some descriptions leave room for doubt over whether the text is a *Lancelot* or a *Tristan* (Delisle 1907, nos 1081, 1082, 1094, 1113, 1114, 1115, 1116, 1116[bis], 1117, 1118, 1119, 1120, 1124, 1131, 1132, 1133, 1139, 1140, 1142, 1143, 1144, 1145, 1146, 1189, 1190, 1197, 1198, 1199, 1200, 1201 and 1202). Several of these were lent or given away (1118, 1124, 1139 and 1202), and others were borrowed by the king or queen and not returned (1081, 1082, 1094, 1114, 1119, 1131, 1144 and 1199). Consequently, despite a few new arrivals, the library's stock was constantly diminishing (Delisle 1907, I, 131–7; Meale 1985, 94, n. 5). Thus, Delisle's decision to combine entries from different inventories can create a slightly false impression, given that the items listed were not all present at any one time. For the two Arthurian entries to be identified with surviving manuscripts, see note 8.[8]

King John's other three sons were also noted bibliophiles, particularly John, Duke of Berry, and Philip the Bold, Duke of Burgundy. The second of the three,

Louis, Duke of Anjou, certainly had a valuable library, but we are less well informed about its contents because there is no formal inventory. In any event, there are no Arthurian items amongst the known survivors, nor amongst the known books of his descendants: his sons Louis II and Charles, and his grandson René, King of Sicily (Delisle 1868–81, I, 54–6; Lecoy de la Marche 1875, II, 183–90).

The collection with the most surviving Arthurian items is that of Philip the Bold and his successors. However, it looks as though in the early years most of the relevant volumes were acquired by inheritance, rather than by purchase. The references to Arthurian books in Philip's accounts are for repair and refurbishment, implying that the volumes had been in the collection for some time (Cockshaw 1969, nos 17 and 29). The inventory made of the books that were in Paris at the time of his death (on 27 April 1404) contains no romances at all (Arthurian or otherwise), unless 'le livre de gneon' really is a *Guiron le Courtois*, as suggested by de Winter (1985, 44 and 134). This is in contrast to the inventory made a year later in Arras on the death of his wife Margaret of Flanders (on 20 March 1405). It is here that we find a substantial number of romances, in verse and prose, including seven Arthurian items (de Winter 1985, 44–5). As already indicated in connection with the verse manuscript BNF, fr. 12560, it seems likely that many of these books at Arras were part of the inheritances that Margaret had received in 1382 on the death of her grandmother Margaret of France, Countess of Flanders and of Artois, and in 1384 on the death of her father Louis de Mâle, Count of Flanders. On the other hand, the books that were repaired or rebound were apparently dealt with in Paris (Philip's habitual residence, rather than Margaret's), and this is not likely to have been because there were no suitable craftsmen in Arras, which had been a major centre of book production for a considerable time. It is difficult to know what significance to attach to the fact that the books at Arras were in chests. This does not necessarily mean that they were packed for transport, or packed away out of use, because it was quite common in the Middle Ages for books to be kept in chests or boxes. On the other hand, by this date, it is surprising that so large a collection had no items on desks; at the very least, it implies that there was no consideration given to putting choice items on display. What we do not know is whether this was how the books were kept during Margaret's lifetime, or whether these arrangements were for the purpose of the inventory, or in readiness for their removal. It may also be remarked in passing that the surviving copy of the inventory was made by a scribe who did not understand the system of labelling these various chests, because he made several errors of copying, which Dehaisnes (1886) and de Winter (1985) both reproduce without comment.

The inventory of 1405 (edited in de Winter 1985) contains: 114 'le livre des histoires du Saint Gral' (probably an *Estoire*, rather than the *Queste* suggested by de Winter, and probably accompanied by *Merlin*, if it is to be identified with a volume that appears in later inventories); 119 'le roumant du Roy Arthus et Lanselot du lac'; 134 'le livre de Lanselot du Lac'; 157 'le livre du roy Meliandus'; 161 'le livre du Saint Gral et Tristant et Galhaut' (possibly the volume from the Louvre that was given to the duchess on 14 October 1381: Delisle 1907, no. 1118); and 179 'le livre Merlin' (presumably the one repaired by the Parisian *libraire* Martin Luillier in 1388: Cockshaw 1969, no. 17). This *Merlin* may be the one that is recorded in 1322 amongst the property of Robert de Béthune, Count of Flanders (Dehaisnes 1886, 240), since two other items from the same list are identifiable in the inventories of 1405 and 1420. As we have already seen, item 171 is the present BNF, fr. 12560 (containing *Yvain*, the *Charrette* and *Cligés*), but with this exception it is difficult to identify these volumes in later inventories, let alone with any surviving manuscripts. It is not until the inventory of 1420 (after the death of John the Fearless) that we have references for second and last folios that enable us to trace the same item through later inventories, and to connect the entries with surviving volumes (Doutrepont 1906).

The nine Arthurian items in the inventory of 1420 may include the seven from 1405, but there are some discrepancies, and it may be that more than two volumes are new. A *Guiron* (Doutrepont 1906, item 69) and one of the two copies of *Merlin* (Doutrepont 1906, items 102 and 184) must be new, and the *Lancelot* (Doutrepont 1906, item 68, now Arsenal MSS 3479–80) was probably the one made in Paris and paid for in 1406 or 1407 rather than the one already present at Arras in 1405 (unless the volume at Arras had been newly received and not yet paid for). The items from 1420 already present in 1405 are: the volume of Chrétien's romances that is now BNF, fr. 12560 (Doutrepont 1906, item 179 in 1420; de Winter 1985, no. 171 in 1405); the 'gros livre nommé du Saint Greal de Tristan et de Galahad' (Doutrepont 204; de Winter 161); 'Istoire du Saint Greal' (Doutrepont 203; de Winter 114); the 'livre du Roy Meliadus' (Doutrepont 201; de Winter 157); and perhaps the 'Mort du Roy Arthus' (Doutrepont 227), which may be de Winter 119. More revealing than the few additions and the continued presence of the earlier volumes is the interest that seems to have been shown by Margaret of Bavaria, wife of John the Fearless. Of the seven books marked in the inventory of 1420 as having been borrowed by her, three are Arthurian prose romances: *Lancelot*, *Guiron le Courtois* and the 'gros livre nommé du Saint Greal de Tristan et de Galahad' (Doutrepont 1906, items 68, 69 and 204).

In 1435 a book 'faisant mention du gréal' (*mentioning the Grail*) was amongst five taken by order of Philip the Good from the archives of the Counts of Hainault (Mons 1842, 11). The folio references allow us to identify the volume in the inventories of 1467 and 1487 (Barrois 1830, nos 1294 and 1671) and to know that it contained the *Estoire*, *Merlin* and *Suite*: the start of the second folio ('Li maistres a cui') is from the *Estoire* (Ponceau edn, 5.18) and the start of the last folio ('Ceulx de la table reonde') is from the *Suite* (Sommer edn, II, 464, 40). In 1435 it was bound in white leather, but by 1467 this had been replaced by black leather, and it is in this binding that it continued to appear in subsequent inventories until it is recorded as missing in 1749 (Doutrepont 1909, 18, n. 2). In 1435 the book is described as being smaller than the copy of the *Sept sages de Rome* taken from the archives at the same time, but this is not as helpful as we might hope. The volume to which it is compared can be identified in the inventories of 1467 and 1487 (Barrois 1830, nos 1238 and 1641), and is now Brussels, Bibliothèque Royale, MS 9245. This is a large volume of 593 leaves that contains all the sequels as well as the *Sept sages* itself, so an *Estoire*, *Merlin* and *Suite* could hardly fail to be smaller. It is tempting to compare the Grail manuscript with a book that had featured in the inventory of the property of the Count of Hainault in 1304: 'vns grans roumans a rouges couuertures ki parolle de Nascijen de Mellin et de Lanscelot dou Lach' (*a large romance with red covers that speaks of Nascien, Merlin and Lancelot of the Lake*: Mons, Archives de l'État, Cartulaire 19, fol. 120; published with minor editorial differences in Devillers 1871, 452, and in Dehaisnes 1886, 156). However, for this to be the volume of 1435 we should have to suppose that it had been divided into two volumes and that the second (containing *Lancelot*) had been lost. The different colour binding is not an obstacle in itself (as we have seen, bindings could be changed), but it leaves us with no more than speculation. An alternative possibility for this volume of 1304 would be the present BNF, fr. 344, a thirteenth-century copy of the complete *Lancelot–Grail* Cycle. This has the right contents and it can fairly be described as 'a large romance' (since it measures 395 x 292mm and has 548 leaves). It also has the right provenance, for its first folio bears the name of 'M. de Henaut duchesse de Bourb ...' (repeated in a simple code that shifts the vowels to the next letter in the alphabet: 'Mbrkf df hbknbxt dxchfssf df bpx ...'). Marie of Hainault, the daughter of Jean II, Count of Hainault, married Louis I, Duke of Bourbon, in 1310 and died in 1354 (Delisle 1868–81, I, 166; P. Paris 1836–45, II, 365). This could well be 'Le vieil Lancelot, parlant des faictz Merlin' that was later in the Bourbon library at Moulins in 1523 (Le Roux de Lincy 1850, item 64).

The inventory made after the death of Philip the Good (d. 1467) contains over three times as many volumes as that of 1420, though not as many as might be assumed from the numbering of the published text (Barrois 1830, nos 705–1612). To obtain a more accurate count, we need to eliminate the books that are kept in the chapel (nos 1103–50 and 1159–99), the two sections of the inventory that have been copied twice (nos 1151–8 that repeat nos 705–12, and nos 1498–1519 that repeat nos 713–34) and finally no. 1612 (which is not a book). This gives a total of 788 compared to the 181 of 1420 (Doutrepont 1906, items 68–248, not counting the books kept in the chapel, items 1–67, which are from a different section of the inventory). Whether this increase in the size of the library is due entirely to new acquisitions is impossible to say. The dukes had many places of residence in which books might be kept, and the inventory of 1467 may reflect a difference of organization as well as a genuine expansion.

In any event, the number of Arthurian volumes in the new inventory has risen to thirty-three (not counting Barrois 1830, no. 706, repeated as no. 1152, that is described as 'un vielz livre en rime ... parlant de Lancelot du Lac' but is identifiable by its folio references as a copy of *Godefroy de Bouillon*). As might be expected for the fifteenth century, almost all the Arthurian additions are of prose texts, but there is one new volume of Arthurian verse. This is described as 'le livre de Moranges ... en rime' (Barrois 1830, no. 1355), and the folio references allow us to recognize the impressive copy of *Meraugis* that is now in Vienna, Österreichische Nationalbibliothek, MS 2599. The next item in the inventory (Barrois 1830, no. 1356) is none other than the volume containing three of Chrétien's romances first recorded in 1405 (now BNF, fr. 12560). Presumably these two volumes were shelved together at this time because of the similarity of their contents, and this implies that someone had examined the books themselves with some care, for the descriptions that appear in the inventories give no clue to the fact that both volumes contain Arthurian verse romances.

Amongst the prose, half the volumes contain texts that have not been recorded before. There are the recent adaptations from verse (*Erec*: Barrois 1830, no. 1277; and *Cligés*: Barrois 1830, no. 1477), a copy of *Ysaÿe le Triste* (Barrois 1830, no. 1282), twelve volumes of *Perceforest* (Barrois 1830, nos 1000, 1248–52, 1253–8) and what may be a *Prophecies de Merlin* (Barrois 1830, no. 801). The other volumes new to this inventory contain further copies of texts that were already present in 1420. There are several volumes containing various parts of the *Lancelot–Grail* Cycle (Barrois 1830, nos 1234, 1235, 1263, 1264, 1294, 1295, 1315 and 1316), several copies of the prose *Tristan* (Barrois 1830, nos 1237, 1239, 1243, 1244 and 1245) and two copies of *Guiron le Courtois* (Barrois 1830, nos 1241 and 1242). Almost all these volumes continue to appear in later medieval inventories, but there are some notable losses: the doubtful *Prophecies de Merlin*, the complete *Lancelot–Grail* (Barrois 1830, no. 1235), all but one copy of the prose *Tristan* (the survivor probably being Barrois 1830, no. 1244) and six volumes of *Perceforest* (the isolated Barrois 1830, no. 1000, and the five volumes of the copy on parchment, Barrois 1830, nos 1248–52).

By the eighteenth century more and more items are recorded as missing, but there are also quite a few survivors that can be identified with reasonable assurance. The volume containing the *Queste* and *Mort Artu* that is now Brussels, Bibliothèque Royale, MSS 9627–8, is first recorded in the inventory of 1467 (Barrois 1830, no. 1263), its earlier owner having been Humfrey, Duke of Gloucester (a younger brother of King Henry V), who is best known for the much more scholarly books that he gave to the University of Oxford (Sammut

1980, 98). The complete *Lancelot–Grail* Cycle in Arsenal MSS 3479–80 (already mentioned as the twin of BNF, fr. 117–20) is probably the book that features in the payment of 1406–7, and it is certainly in the inventory of 1420 (Doutrepont 1906, item 68) and that of 1467 (Barrois 1830, no. 1235). The copy of *Guiron le Courtois* (Barrois 1830, nos 1241 and 2184–5) is now Arsenal MSS 3477–8, and the copy of *Ysaÿe le Triste* (Barrois 1830, nos 1282 and 1834) is now Darmstadt, Hessische Landes- und Hochschulbibliothek, MS 2524. These last two entered the library in the time of Philip the Good, as did the six volumes of *Perceforest* (now bound as twelve) that are Arsenal MSS 3483–94 (Barrois 1830, nos 1253–8, in which no. 1253 is wrongly described as the sixth volume: the preceding nos 1248–52 are five volumes of *Perceforest* on parchment bound in yellow leather, all now missing; the scribe who copied the surviving text of this inventory was expecting a sixth volume to complete this set, but no. 1253 is not it; this is clearly the first volume of the following set on paper bound in black leather, in which nos 1254–8 have the correct second folio references for the volumes 2 to 6 that they are said to be; the matter would have been settled beyond doubt if the entry for no. 1253 had included a second folio reference, but it does not; this is probably because the volume was not physically present at the time of the inventory, there being a note in the margin saying that it had been borrowed by Monsieur de Saint-Pol).

Given what has been lost as well as what has survived, it is easy to create the impression that Arthurian literature enjoyed considerable popularity at the Burgundian court, but this is not what the evidence really shows. It is true that at its height in the later fifteenth century the collection had more Arthurian volumes than any other in the kingdom, but we must remember to keep this in perspective. After the sale of the royal library in 1425, and its subsequent dispersal, the Burgundian library was much larger than any other in France, and when this is taken into account it emerges that the Arthurian volumes (even with the broadest of definitions) formed only a small proportion of it. The nine Arthurian volumes recorded in 1420 represent 5 per cent of a total of 181, and the thirty-three Arthurian volumes recorded in 1467 represent only 4¼ per cent of a total of 788. Despite the increase in numbers, the proportion has fallen, and there are larger holdings in almost every other sphere.

As for whether the dukes themselves took an active interest in their Arthurian volumes, the evidence is remarkably ambiguous. Take, for example, the expensive *Lancelot–Grail* of Arsenal MSS 3479–80. If this was commissioned by Philip the Bold as one of a pair with BNF, fr. 117–20 for himself and his brother Jean de Berry, it would imply a certain commitment, but the belated payment by John the Fearless does not necessarily show any interest in the matter beyond that of settling his father's debts. In any event, it was later allowed to leave the library in the time of Charles the Bold or Maximilian, for it is in the inventory of 1467

(Barrois 1830, no. 1235), but not in that of 1487. It had in fact passed to Philippe de Croy, Count of Chimay (d. 1482) and then to his son Charles (d. 1527), whose ex-libris (now erased) was to be seen on the volume in the eighteenth century (recorded in notes made by Achille Godefroy in 1746, preserved in Lille, Bibliothèque Municipale, MS Godefroy 93, fol. 96). In 1511 it returned to the Burgundian library amongst the seventy-eight volumes bought from Charles de Croy by Margaret of Austria (Debae 1995, xiii and 30–5). Whether any of the book's owners had a real interest in its Arthurian contents would be a matter of speculation. Even Philip the Bold may have commissioned it more as a work of art than of literature. After all, he (or his wife) already had several copies of the text that would have served just as well for simple reading. Of course, once made, it was an object of value to be inventoried and handed down the generations like all the other valuables.

Another case is that of *Perceforest*, a project to which Philip the Good must have committed substantial sums for the reworking of the older text that produced the version copied by David Aubert into the six volumes of his draft. Yet we should still be cautious. The six volumes of David Aubert's draft, written on paper during the course of 1459 and 1460, were in the library during Philip's lifetime. They are recorded in the inventory of 1467 (Barrois 1830, nos 1253–8, as indicated above), and they continue to appear in later inventories, four volumes being at Ghent in 1485 (Barrois 1830, nos 1629–32) and the two others at Brussels in 1487 (Barrois 1830, nos 2187–8). It seems that they then spent some time in the possession of several members of the Croy family, who added various mottoes and signatures, but by 1536 the volumes were back in Brussels, where they remained until taken by the French in 1748. Apart from the short period that they spent with the Croy family this is very much what we should expect, but the history of the fair copy on parchment is much less straightforward. The three volumes that survive (British Library, MSS Royal 15. E. v, 19. E. iii and 19. E. ii) have paintings that were certainly not done during the lifetime of Philip the Good (d. 1467) and probably not even during that of Charles the Bold (d. 1477), so there is no clear evidence that Philip the Good ever intended to have the draft made into a more expensive fair copy. The three surviving volumes on parchment are not the ones that appear in the Burgundian inventories (Barrois 1830, nos 1248–52), which are now lost.

Earlier in the century Jean de Berry had owned the *Lancelot–Grail* of BNF, fr. 117–20 (Delisle 1907, Berry no. 270), a *Guiron le Courtois* in two volumes (Delisle 1907, Berry no. 272) and the *Tristan* that is now Vienna, Österreichische Nationalbibliothek, MS 2537 (which bears his ex-libris, but does not appear in the inventories). The *Lancelot* is specified as having been bought in January 1405 from Regnaut du Montet in Paris for 300 escus. After the death of Jean de Berry in 1416 it was one of five books that the executors gave in settlement to Bernard,

Count of Armagnac (the husband of Bonne de Berry, Jean's younger daughter). It then descended by inheritance to Bernard's grandson Jacques d'Armagnac, Duke of Nemours, who added his ex-libris and who had the miniatures repainted in a more modern style in the 1460s.

It is notable that Arthurian literature is not much represented amongst the manuscripts that were commissioned by the royal brothers, which is very much in contrast to the habits of Jacques d'Armagnac, Duke of Nemours. Not only did he possess older copies of Arthurian prose texts (though none in verse as far as we know), he also commissioned several new copies of the *Lancelot–Grail* and the prose *Tristan*. His practice of having multiple copies of particular texts may have been influenced by the fact that he maintained separate libraries in both his principal residences (at Carlat and Castres), but there are also indications that he simply wanted to be up to date. Such is the implication of repainting the miniatures of BNF, fr. 117–20.

Manuscripts that belonged to Jacques d'Armagnac are recognizable by a characteristic ex-libris at the end of the text, giving the title, the number of pages, the number of miniatures and the residence at which the book was to be kept, often followed by his autograph signature. Unfortunately, after his execution for treason in 1477, the collection was dispersed, and many of the new owners erased these marks of ownership with varying degrees of thoroughness. Some of the ex-libris remain more or less legible, others are at least partially readable under ultra-violet light, but further suspected examples are beyond recovery.

Amongst older Arthurian manuscripts that were certainly owned by Jacques d'Armagnac the earliest are the copy of *Guiron le Courtois* in Arsenal MS 3325, which may be not much later than 1250, and the incomplete *Tristan* in BNF, nouv. acq. fr. 6579, which is also from the thirteenth century. From about 1300 (except for its last leaf, which was made for Jacques d'Armagnac in about 1460) is the *Tristan* in Vienna, Österreichische Nationalbibliothek, MS 2542. Rather later than these, but still before the time of Jacques d'Armagnac himself, is the *Lancelot–Grail* completed before 1405 that came from Jean de Berry (BNF, fr. 117–20), and later still is the *Lancelot–Grail* in BNF, fr. 113–16, which dates from Jacques's own lifetime, and which originally bore his arms and devices (now replaced by those of Pierre de Bourbon).

Also from the second half of the fifteenth century is the *Perceforest* that is now BNF, fr. 106–9, but this too is more likely to have been an acquisition than a commission. It has an ex-libris of the usual type in each of its four volumes, noting that they are to be kept at Carlat, and recording both the number of leaves and the number of miniatures. The count of the miniatures is rather disconcerting, because the decoration of these volumes has never been completed, and although spaces have been left for the intended illustrations their number does not always correspond to the counts given in each of the four ex-libris. It seems less likely that Jacques d'Armagnac would have accepted a manuscript that he had commissioned in this unfinished state than that he might have taken the opportunity of acquiring one that he encountered by chance. These volumes are probably those that later appear in the inventory of the library of the Duke of Bourbon at Moulins in 1523 (Le Roux de Lincy 1850, item 171: 'Quatre grans volumes de Perceforestz'). The description is far from precise, but the fact that there are only four volumes implies that the set was incomplete, so the correspondence is significant, especially when considering that these Bourbon manuscripts were incorporated into the royal library (as were BNF, fr. 106–9) and that the other incomplete four-volume set in the royal library came from elsewhere (BNF, fr. 345–8, from Louis de Bruges). The other interesting feature of these volumes is that two of them contain leaves from a late fifteenth-century copy of the *Estoire del Saint Graal*, and we may reasonably suppose that these are the remains of another manuscript that had once belonged to Jacques d'Armagnac (though they could be from the library of the dukes of Bourbon, or even from the shop of a later binder).

Several Arthurian manuscripts are known to have been made especially for Jacques d'Armagnac. The first is the copy of *Tristan* written by Micheau Gonnot that is now BNF, fr. 99, but the most interesting is the unique *Lancelot–Grail* compilation in BNF, fr. 112, which contains material not normally found in this Cycle (Pickford 1959/60*; chapter IX). This manuscript was completed by Micheau Gonnot on 4 July 1470, and parts of the text seem to have been derived directly from Jacques d'Armagnac's *Lancelot–Grail* of BNF, fr. 113–16, whilst other sections are closely related to his copies of the prose *Tristan* in BNF, fr. 99 and BNF, nouv. acq. fr. 6579 (Pickford 1965, 249–50). For its connections with Turin, Biblioteca Nazionale, MSS L. I. 7–9, see chapter IX.

The *Guiron le Courtois* in the three volumes of this Turin manuscript may also have belonged to Jacques d'Armagnac, but the attribution relies upon the brief description given by Durrieu (the manuscript itself having been too badly damaged by the fire of 1904 to yield any new information in this regard). Durrieu states that the manuscript was executed for Jacques d'Armagnac, but he does not mention any ex-libris or other signs of ownership, and his assertion may be a conclusion drawn from his identification of the miniatures as the work of Evrard d'Espingues, 'l'un des miniaturistes favoris du malheureux duc de Nemours' (*one of the favourite miniaturists of the unfortunate Duke of Nemours*; Durrieu 1904, 403). This would certainly make the supposition plausible, but it is frustrating not to have more direct evidence.

Another example of the work of Evrard d'Espingues is the *Tristan* in three volumes that is at Chantilly (Musée Condé, MSS 645–7). This was eventually completed for Jean du Mas, seigneur de l'Isle, whose arms and ex-libris are in the manuscript, and who paid Evrard d'Espingues for illustrating a *Tristan* in three volumes in 1479–80 (Thomas 1895). However, there is reason to think that the book may have been begun for Jacques d'Armagnac. Its text is closely related to that of the two older copies (BNF, fr. 99 and BNF, nouv. acq. fr. 6579) that bear his ex-libris and that seem to have contributed to the compilation of his BNF, fr. 112. Both the scribe, Gilles Gassien of Poitiers, and the artist had already been employed by the duke for other manuscripts. What happened to Jacques d'Armagnac's library after his arrest in 1476 and his execution in 1477 is not entirely clear, but much of his confiscated property was given by the king to those who were prominent in his arrest, and many of the manuscripts also reappear in their libraries. Particularly notable in both regards were Pierre de Beaujeu (later Duke of Bourbon), Jean du Mas and Tanguy du Chastel. The Bourbon library was confiscated by King Francis I in 1523 (Le Roux de Lincy 1850); most of the surviving manuscripts from Jean du Mas were acquired by Anne de Montmorency, the Constable of France, and are now in the Musée Condé at Chantilly (Picot 1897, 315–17); most of the books known to have belonged to Tanguy du Chastel (some with the ex-libris of Jacques d'Armagnac) are now divided more or less equally between the Bibliothèque Nationale de France and the Nationalbibliothek in Vienna (incomplete list in Delisle 1868–81, II, 353 and 360), with most but not all of them having been in the sale of the library from Anet.[5] Two of the Arthurian books with an individual history are BNF, fr. 112 and BNF, fr. 113–16. The first of these came into the possession of the family of Montejehan, perhaps through their connection with Tanguy du Chastel, whose daughter and heiress Jeanne later married Louis de Montejehan. Something of the later history of the second emerges from an inscription on fol. 735 of BNF, fr. 116, stating that on 3 June 1496 it was given by Jean de Chabannes, Count of Dammartin, 'à mon fils Monseigneur de Chastillon sur Loin' (i.e. Jacques de Coligny, whose first marriage was to Anne de Chabannes, Jean's only daughter).

The family of Coligny produced military leaders, not book collectors, but its members consistently married into families that possessed Arthurian volumes. Thus, it is characteristic of patterns of ownership at this time that a figure such as Gaspard de Coligny, the Marshal of France who died in 1522, should be only one step away from several important manuscripts without ever having owned one himself (as far as we know). As we have just seen, his elder brother Jacques (d. 1512) had been given the complete *Lancelot–Grail* by his father-in-law in 1496, but two of Gaspard's brothers-in-law were also owners of Arthurian prose romances. After 1514, when Gaspard de Coligny married Louise de Montmorency, his brother-in-law was Anne de Montmorency, who succeeded him as Marshal in 1522, and who became Constable in 1538. In due course, though not necessarily before 1522, Montmorency acquired from the descend-ants of Jean du Mas two copies of the prose *Tristan* (Chantilly, Musée Condé, MSS 645–7 and 648). Somewhat earlier, Gaspard's sister Prégente de Coligny had married Pierre d'Égreville, who was almost certainly one of the owners of Le Mans, Bibliothèque Municipale, MS 354. This copy of the *Estoire* (with embedded *Joseph*) written by Walter de Kayo has the inscription 'pour la librairie d'Esgreville' and the motto 'E non plus' (with both name and motto repeated in several different hands). The same inscription and motto are in London, British Library, MS Stowe 54, which also has the arms of the lords of Égreville (Seine-et-Marne). Given that these additions seem to be from the sixteenth century, the books are likely to have been owned by both Pierre and his son Émond, who did homage for Égreville in 1517, and who succeeded his uncle the Marshal as captain of fifty lances in 1522. After Émond had died (between October 1522 and July 1524) without male heir, the château of Égreville was sold to Anne de Pisselieu, the mistress of King Francis I (*Actes* 1887–1908, V, nos 17533 and 17804; Michel 1879, 278).

After the death of his first wife, Jacques de Coligny married Blanche de Tournon, daughter of Jacques de Tournon (d. 1501) and widow of Raymond d'Agoult (d. 1503). The family of Agoult were almost certainly the owners of the manuscripts that are wrongly supposed to have belonged to the Constable de Lesdiguières, including the *Prophecies de Merlin* that is now BNF, fr. 15211 (Middleton 1993, 143–5), but more importantly the family of Tournon seem to have had at least four Arthurian manuscripts. The unique manuscript of *Le Chevalier du Papegau* has an inscription 'A ma dame Jehanne de Tournon' (possibly Jeanne de Polignac, who married Jacques de Tournon in 1466, but more probably Jeanne de Vissac, wife of Just de Tournon, who succeeded his father Jacques as seigneur de Tournon in 1501). A second inscription 'A ma demoiselle Justine de Tournon' accompanied by the name 'Françoys Armant' refers to Justine, the daughter of Just and Jeanne de Vissac, and to her husband François Allemand, seigneur Des Champs (Heuckenkamp 1896, v–vi; François 1951, 7 and 392, n. 3). Also connected with the family are three Arthurian manuscripts that were written in Italy (Delcorno Branca 1998, 43): Biblioteca Apostolica Vaticana, Reg. lat. 1501 (containing *Guiron le Courtois*), which has the name 'Just de Tournon, sieneur et barun Rebellion' on fol. 89v (Lathuillère 1966, 81); BNF, fr. 756–7 (a prose *Tristan* in two volumes) and BNF, fr. 760 (another prose *Tristan*), which both have notes referring to Arlenc, a lordship belonging to the family of Jeanne de Vissac (Avril, Gousset and Rabel 1984, 47). On the Tournon family's many connections with Italy in the early sixteenth century, see François 1951.

After Jacques d'Armagnac the most important bibliophile of the later fifteenth century was Louis de Bruges, seigneur de la Gruthuyse, who died in 1492. His extensive collection of manuscripts was important in its own right, but it took on even greater significance when, by means that have yet to be clarified, it passed into the possession of King Louis XII to become one of the major constituents of the new royal library that was being created at Blois (Delisle 1868–81, I, 140–6; Van Praet 1831). The Arthurian items are: the *Lancelot* in BNF, fr. 121; the *Lancelot, Queste* and *Mort Artu* in BNF, fr. 122 (dated 1345); the same three texts in BNF, fr. 123 (which was probably made in England); the *Estoire* and *Merlin* in BNF, fr. 749 (which seems to have spent some time in England); the extended *Guiron* compilation in BNF, fr. 358–63; and the *Perceforest* in BNF, fr. 345–8. The manuscripts obtained from Louis de Bruges were added to the collection at Blois (many of the volumes still bear distinctive Blois shelf-marks), and they feature in the inventories of 1518 and 1544 (Omont 1908–21, I). In most cases some effort has been made to replace the arms and devices of Louis de Bruges with those of France, but this has rarely been done thoroughly enough to cause any difficulty in identifying the previous owner.

The basis of the library at Blois was the collection made by previous dukes of Orleans, and inherited by Louis d'Orléans before he succeeded to the crown as Louis XII. This had been at Blois since the fourteenth century, and there are inventories of various kinds from 1417, 1427, 1436, 1440 and 1442, as well as many other documents relating to purchases, commissions, repairs and other matters (Champion 1910). Amongst the Arthurian items can be found a copy of Froissart's *Meliador* (Champion 1910, 45–6), which is often identified with BNF fr. 12557 for no better reason than the presumed scarcity of copies of such a little-known text. In 1399 a copy of *Guiron le Courtois* was repaired for the duchess, Valentina of Milan, and it remained hers (rather than her husband's) until it was inherited by her son Charles d'Orléans, the poet, in 1408 (Champion 1910, 48–9 and lxxiv). A more complex case is the 'grant livre en françois faisant mencion du roy Arthus' (*a large book in French mentioning King Arthur*) that was bound in red leather for the duchess in 1402. This is presumably the volume in red leather recorded as 'Les histoires du roy Artus, du saint Graal' in 1417, 1427 and 1442. The two later inventories also note that it is 'moult vieil' (*very old*) and that it lacks its beginning (Champion 1910, 9–10; Le Roux de Lincy 1843–4, item 71). It is identified by Champion with the *Lancelot* in BNF, fr. 1430, which certainly comes from the Orleans collection since it has the note 'de camera compotor. Bles.' (on which, see Champion 1910, lxvi). This could fairly be called very old in 1427 (given that it is thought to have been written 1215–25), and it is defective at the beginning as specified by the later inventories. On the other hand, it has no Grail text, and at 289 x 200mm it is unlikely to have been called a large book, as it was in 1402. When the library was moved from Blois to Fontainebleau in 1544, the future BNF, fr. 1430 was recorded in the inventory under the title that is written in a sixteenth-century hand on its first leaf: 'Histoire du roy Arthus et de la Table Ronde' (Omont 1908–21, I, 216, item 1257; Champion 1910, 10). However, the inventory describes this manuscript as 'couvert de cuir blanc tout rompu' (*covered in white leather all broken*). Since this binding was already in poor condition it can hardly have been a recent replacement, so the fact that it was white raises a doubt over whether this can be the Orleans volume that was still bound in red in 1442. An alternative candidate for the volume in the Orleans inventories is BNF, fr. 342. This manuscript was in the library at Blois (Bruce 1910, xv), and it is a better match for the descriptions given in the Orleans documents: it has a Grail text (it contains *Agravain*, *Queste* and *Mort Artu*); it is defective at the beginning; it is large (373 x 259mm); and although it is not quite as old as BNF, fr. 1430 (having been written in 1274) it would probably have counted as 'moult vieil' in 1427. Either of these two surviving manuscripts might be the *Lancelot* that Louis d'Orléans (grandfather of Louis XII) bought in 1397 (Champion 1910, 65; Delisle 1868–81, I, 102).

When Louis became king in 1498 he was able to add to the library that he already possessed at Blois the royal collection that had been created by Charles VIII (Delisle 1868–81, I, 94–8). Further significant additions were made after the French capture of Milan in 1499–1500, when the library of the Duke of Milan at Pavia soon yielded many valuable items (Thomas 1911; Pellegrin 1955). Earlier inventories of the ducal library in 1426 (A), 1459 (B) and 1469 (C) include at least ten Arthurian items, some described in sufficient detail to be identifiable (those in A), others indicated by brief titles only (those in B and C). Identifiable items from the inventory of 1426 (edited in Pellegrin 1955) are one manuscript that was made in France, the *Estoire* and *Merlin* in BNF, fr. 95 (A. 198), and three that were made in Italy: the Post-Vulgate *Queste* and *Mort Artu* in BNF, fr. 343 (A. 908); the same texts in Oxford, Bodleian Library, MS Rawlinson D. 874 (A. 943), alienated from the Bibliothèque du Roi at some time during the sixteenth or seventeenth century; and the *Tristan* in BNF, fr. 755 (A. 952). For possible identifications in other inventories, see Delcorno Branca 1998, 41–2.

With these major contributions from Charles VIII, Orleans, Louis de Bruges and Milan, the library at Blois formed the core of what later received the formal title of Bibliothèque du Roi, and in due course Bibliothèque Nationale de France. The collection was moved to Fontainebleau in 1544, and then to Paris in the 1560s, receiving its present accommodation in the Rue de Richelieu in 1721 (Balayé 1988, 41–7, 186–8).

Another fifteenth-century figure who owned several Arthurian manuscripts was Prigent de Coëtivy, Admiral of France, who died in 1450. He seems to have had a much smaller collection than other fifteenth-century bibliophiles, but his library contained a much higher proportion of Arthurian items. Information gathered by Delisle results in a list of nineteen books that are mentioned in various family documents, but no fewer than five of these are Arthurian: 'les Histoires de Josèphe et de Merlin', 'le livre du roy Meliadus de Lionnoys', 'le livre de Tristan', 'le livre de Lancelot' and 'le livre de Guyron le Courtoys' (Delisle 1900, 191–2). Some of these are to be identified with surviving manuscripts that have the ex-libris of Prigent de Coëtivy. The *Meliadus* is probably the copy of the Compilation by Rusticien de Pise preserved in BNF, fr. 340, with miniatures from the workshop of the Egerton Master, who worked for the Duke of Berry (Lathuillère 1966, 60; Meiss 1967, I, 357). There is a copy of *Tristan* in London, British Library, MS Royal 20. D. ii, but this was made too early (*c*.1300) to have been illuminated for Prigent himself, and it is therefore not the one mentioned in a payment to Hancelin for the illumination of a *Tristan*, a *Lancelot* and a *Guiron*. Possible candidates for the other two manuscripts included in this payment are the *Guiron* in BNF, fr. 356–7 and the *Lancelot* represented by groups of fragments sold at Sotheby's (14 July 1981, lot 30; 2 December 1997, lot 65; 6 July 2000, lots 23–6) and at Christie's (3 April 1984, lot 62). Both of these manuscripts have miniatures by the Dunois Master (the artist of the Coëtivy Hours in Dublin, Chester Beatty, Western MS 82), but it is not certain that they were made quite early enough for Prigent's commissions in the 1440s (Avril and Reynaud 1995, 37–8). It is assumed that Prigent's library passed with his other property to his younger brother Olivier, and at least one of the books was later owned by Olivier's daughter Catherine de Coëtivy, whose arms feature on a number of manuscripts at Chantilly (Picot 1897, 318–22), but none is Arthurian.

Later in the century there was the larger and better-known library of Philippe de Croy, Count of Chimay (d. 1482), and of his son Charles (d. 1527). Their collection of some seventy or eighty manuscripts was systematically reviewed in 1486 (the year in which Charles was elevated from Count to Prince of Chimay by the Emperor Maximilian), and each manuscript was provided with an ex-libris at the end, giving a list of contents, the number of miniatures, Charles de Croy's title as Count (or occasionally Prince) of Chimay and finally an autograph signature. Other manuscripts that belonged to Charles de Croy that have an ex-libris of a different type at the beginning are not part of the same process (Middleton 1999, 58–61). Most of the manuscripts of 1486 were sold in 1511 to Margaret of Austria, Regent of the Netherlands for her nephew the Emperor Charles V (Debae 1995, XIII). These included: the verse manuscript BNF, fr. 12603; the *Estoire* in BNF, fr. 12582; the complete *Lancelot–Grail* Cycle in Arsenal MSS 3479–80; the *Guiron* (with Rusticien de Pise) in Arsenal MSS 3477–8; and the *Perceforest* in Arsenal MSS 3483–94. These last three items had previously belonged to the Duke of Burgundy (Doutrepont 1906, item 68 and Barrois 1830, no. 1238; Barrois 1830, nos 1241 and 2184–5; Barrois 1830, nos 1253–8). Some of the Croy mottoes and ex-libris have been erased, but they were recorded by Achille Godefroy in 1746 (Lille, Bibliothèque Municipale, MS Godefroy 93, fols 96, 71 and 44). Apparently not owned by Charles but with his father's motto ('moy seul Chimay') is the *Tristan* in Brussels, Bibliothèque Royale, MSS 9086–7. However, the principal owner of these volumes was Engelbert of Nassau (see

Renting et al. 1993, item 1354, though the ex-libris in fact begins 'Ce livre est au jentil comte de Nassau ...' *This book belongs to the noble Count of Nassau).*

A particularly interesting figure of the early years of the next century is Anne de Graville, whose life story is practically an Arthurian romance in its own right (Montmorand 1917). She was the youngest daughter of Louis Malet, sire de Graville, Admiral of France. In 1507 she incurred the wrath of her father by eloping with her cousin Pierre de Balsac. After acrimonious accusations and several lawsuits, father and daughter were in open conflict for a number of years, and never again on close terms. However, Anne did effect at least a partial reconciliation, and although in theory she had been disinherited, she nevertheless laid claim to a share of her father's estate at the time of his death in 1516. After some dispute she eventually agreed a settlement of the succession with her two elder sisters in 1518, and this allowed her to obtain some of her father's manuscripts. Those acquired in this way are recognizable by a characteristic note written on their flyleaves or opening folios. Such is the copy of *Lancelot* now preserved in Chicago, Newberry Library, MS f21, which bears the inscription 'A madamoiselle Anne de Graville, [de la] succession de feu monseigneur l'Amiral, V^c XVIII' (Saenger 1981). The Roman numeral (often wrongly transcribed in early descriptions of some of these manuscripts) represents the date of the legal agreement between Anne and her sisters (1518). There is a similar note on London, British Library, MS Egerton 989 (containing the prose *Tristan*), a manuscript that had once belonged to the antiquary and collector Francis Douce (d. 1834), who left his books to the Bodleian Library in Oxford. The reason that this volume did not go to Oxford was that Douce had already disposed of it during his lifetime, as appears from a note that is to be found in his copy of the printed *Tristan* of 1489 (Bodleian Library, Douce 224). At the end of this volume there has been inserted a sheet of paper with an eighteenth-century transcription of the end of the story, and in the margin Douce has written: 'The Ms whence this paper was taken agreed in substance with 20 D. II though it neither begins nor ends as that does. The manner of the death of Tristan & Yseult is the same in both. See my M. N. B. II. 116. It also agreed in the latter part with my Ms. of the Mort de Tristan. It was written in 1475 in a wretched hand scarcely legible of the long bastard kind, which induced me to part with it.' The eighteenth-century transcription reproduces the colophon of the manuscript from which it was taken, including its unique date: 'le XXI jour d'Octob. le propre jour des XI^m Vierges l'an M IIII^c. LXXV'. This leaves no doubt that it was made from what is now Egerton 989, a manuscript that fully justifies Douce's comments on its handwriting.[6]

Douce also had another Arthurian manuscript whose ownership by Anne de Graville is indicated by her ex-libris at the end (but without any note of its being inherited from her father). This is Bodleian Library, MS Douce 178 (containing the *Estoire, Merlin* and *Suite*). Anne also owned a copy of the partially Arthurian

Roman de Laurin, for the three volume set of the whole *Sept sages* Cycle that is now BNF, fr. 22548–50 bears her arms. Several of Anne de Graville's manuscripts subsequently came into the possession of Claude d'Urfé, who had married Anne's eldest daughter Jeanne in 1532, and these were incorporated into the library that he established at La Bastie in Forez. The details of what happened to this important collection in later years are not entirely clear; some volumes were certainly alienated as time went on, but it seems that the major part of it stayed in the family until the death of the last marquise d'Urfé in Paris in 1775. Whatever then remained was acquired, in 1777, by the Duke of La Vallière. Many of the d'Urfé manuscripts are therefore described in the La Vallière sale catalogue published by De Bure in 1783, but their provenance is not always indicated. The Chicago *Lancelot* was lot 4004 in the sale that eventually began in January 1784, but the two Douce volumes are not from the same source, nor can they be identified with any certainty amongst entries from the d'Urfé catalogue that is known to have existed in the eighteenth century. Although this catalogue has been lost, the Arthurian entries were copied (at least in part, and probably in their entirety) by the compiler of notes preserved in Paris, Bibliothèque de l'Arsenal, MS 5871. This may or may not have been La Curne de Sainte-Palaye, as suggested by the Arsenal catalogue; the notes are not in his own hand, but he employed several different secretaries at various times, and there are indications that these notes have been copied from elsewhere by someone other than their author. The small number of minor corrections that seem to be in the hand of Sainte-Palaye would not be proof positive that he was the author, but if the notes are not by him they are certainly by someone with similar expertise – which severely limits the field.

   From these preserved catalogue entries it is possible to identify further d'Urfé volumes by matching numbers and descriptions. The unexpected title 'Chronique de Bretagne de ...' that is on fol. 1 of the Chicago *Lancelot* seems to match the description of number LXXV in the catalogue ('Lancelot du Lac ou Chronique de Bretagne'), but this is deceptive. The true correspondence is with number XXXVIII 'Lancelot du Lac', whose opening sentence quoted by the catalogue offers a perfect match for the variants that occur in the Chicago manuscript. In confirmation of this, number LXXV can be identified with the former Phillipps 8230, which is now in a private collection in Japan. Its present owner has kindly informed me that this manuscript has the note 'Num 75' on its first folio. Given that this was lot 4003 in the La Vallière sale of 1784 there is every prospect of a d'Urfé provenance. On the same basis we can identify number LXXIV of the catalogue, described as 'Saingraal. MS. velin, en 2. colonnes, du 13 siecle'. This is lot 3993 from the La Vallière sale, now Oxford, Bodleian Library, MS Douce 303, which has the note 'Nvm 74' in the lower left-hand corner of its first folio. That these notes really do record d'Urfé catalogue numbers is indicated by the fact that several manuscripts that are in d'Urfé bindings have just such a note in this position.[7]

The extracts from the d'Urfé catalogue record a total of six Arthurian manuscripts, plus a printed *Lancelot* in the Vérard edition of 1494. Some of these may be lost, but it is quite likely that several of them are simply unidentified amongst the many survivors. Barring recorded disasters, manuscripts that survive until the eighteenth century have a good chance of reaching our own day. Once it is known that collectors will pay good money for illegible old books, people are more likely to see what they can get for them than to throw them away.

If MS Douce 303 belonged to Anne de Graville before entering the d'Urfé library (far from certain, of course) it would mean that she had owned at least five surviving manuscripts that contain Arthurian prose, including two copies of the *Estoire*. One of these (MS Douce 178) has a number of marginal notes that show it was read with close attention at some time, but whether any of these notes are from the time of Anne's ownership, let alone written by Anne herself, is difficult to say.

Many manuscripts that were in France during the Middle Ages have coats of arms or names that may be those of their owners. A few examples of those that are more or less identifiable must suffice, beginning with the two volumes of a *Lancelot* in New York, Pierpont Morgan Library, MSS M. 805–6. These bear the partially illegible inscription: 'Ce livre est a nous Jehan de Brosse, seigneur de . . . et mareschal de France' (M. 806, fol. 266). This is clearly the Jean de Brosse, lord of Sainte-Sévère and of Boussac, who was made Marshal of France on 14 July 1426, and who died in 1433. His great-great-grandson, Jean de Brosse IV, married Anne de Pisselieu who bought the château of Égreville, whose library had housed Le Mans, Bibliothèque Municipale, MS 354. So it is not out of the question that Anne owned both the Morgan and Le Mans manuscripts.

Another remarkable coincidence involves Le Mans 354 and BNF, fr. 770. These two manuscripts have the same *Estoire* with embedded *Joseph*, and their miniatures were painted in the same workshop, probably in or near Douai, and probably in the 1280s. As we have already seen, by the middle of the next century BNF, fr. 770 had been lent by Pierre des Essars to John, Duke of Normandy, but in the fifteenth century its owner was a 'Jehan de la Riviere segneur de Chande . . s' (as transcribed by Brunel 1923, xxxv, n. 2). The name of the lordship had previously been read by P. Paris (1836–45, VI, 131) as 'Chandenier', but this is rightly rejected by Brunel. Although it would be unwise to insist on the exact spelling on the basis of what can be read, it seems to me that the form is in fact some version of 'Chamlemy' (a variant of Champlemy, a fief in the possession of the family of La Rivière). The ex-libris would then be that of Jean de la Rivière, seigneur de Champlemy, who died in 1468. His father was the Bureau de la Rivière who died at Agincourt, and his mother was Philiberte de Champlemy, making him the first

Jean de la Rivière to hold the lordship of Champlemy. On 4 February 1451 (possibly meaning 1452) he repurchased the lordship of La Rivière from Waleran de Châtillon, son of Jeanne de la Rivière, the eventual heiress of the senior branch of the family (La Chenaye-Desbois, 1863–77, XVII, col. 149). Thus, from 1451/2 Jean would probably have called himself 'seigneur de la Rivière' (the most important of the family lordships) rather than 'seigneur de Champlemy', and the same consideration applies to his son (another Jean) who inherited the titles in 1468. So it is likely that Jean was already the owner of BNF, fr. 770 in October 1449 when he was knighted at the siege of Rouen (Escouchy 1863–4, I, 215). Another of those knighted at the same ceremony was the 'seigneur d'Aigreville'. This will have been Jean, seigneur d'Égreville, who was captain of Montargis from 1447 to 1461 (Dupont-Ferrier 1942–66, IV, no. 15744; wrongly called Pierre in a note in Escouchy, I, 212, but correctly identified as Jean in the Errata, II, 576, and in the Index, II, 455). Since the Le Mans manuscript was certainly in the possession of his descendants in the early sixteenth century, there is every possibility that it was already in the family in 1449 when he and the owner of the closely related BNF, fr. 770 were knighted together before Rouen.

In the later fifteenth century, the *Agravain, Queste* and *Mort Artu* in BNF, nouv. acq. fr. 1119 belonged to Lyonnet d'Oreille, who also owned Arsenal MS 3356 (containing the *Enseignements* of the Chevalier de La Tour Landry, *Mélibée et Prudence*, and Christine de Pizan's *Livre des trois vertus*) and Arsenal MS 3457 (containing the poetry of Charles d'Orléans). Most informative, however, is the copy of *Baudoin de Flandres* that Lyonnet seems to have commissioned (BNF, fr. 1611). This was written by Gilet Leclerc 'es prisons du Roy nostre sire à Troyes' and completed on 8 March 1474 (presumably 1475 by modern reckoning), and there is an ex-libris on fol. 183v in which Gilet describes Lyonnet as 'maistre d'ostel de monseigneur le gouverneur' (Favre 1888–9, cccxvii–cccxviii). The governor at this time was Charles d'Amboise, lord of Chaumont-sur-Loire and Count of Brienne, governor of Champagne and Brie from 1473 to 1481 (whose eldest son, also called Charles, married Jeanne Malet de Graville, who so narrowly missed inheriting the Arthurian manuscripts that went to her sister Anne). It seems likely that Lyonnet was a relative of the Rigaud d'Oreille, seigneur de Villeneuve, who was a page to Charles d'Amboise in 1474. By 1483 Rigaud had become a *maître d'hôtel* to Louis XI, and he was later *bailli* of Chartres in 1496, and then seneschal of Agen and Gascony from 1513 until his death on 15 September 1517 (Dupont-Ferrier 1942–66, I, nos 42 and 2413, II, no. 6656, and III, no. 12233). The paper leaves (fols 216–36) added to BNF, nouv. acq. fr. 1119 in the fifteenth century may be due to Lyonnet.

Also associated with Troyes at this time is the fifteenth-century *Lancelot–Grail* in four volumes that is now Cologny-Genève, cod. Bodmer 105. The arms on fol. 1 of the first volume are those of Le Peley, probably those of Guyot II (d. 1485).

The family was prominent in Troyes during the fifteenth century, and various members were owners of important manuscripts (Vielliard 1975, 67–71; Avril and Raynaud 1995, 186–9; and, for its later history, Middleton 2003, 231–2).

The *Lancelot–Grail* that is divided between Amsterdam, Bibliotheca Philosophica Hermetica, MS 1 (3 vols), Manchester, John Rylands University Library, MS French 1 (2 vols) and Oxford, Bodleian Library, MS Douce 215 has the arms of La Rochefoucauld (probably fifteenth century) on the opening folio of its first volume. Since the whole manuscript (bound in two volumes) was at the Abbey of Sainte-Geneviève in Paris until the early eighteenth century, it presumably passed through the hands of Cardinal François de La Rochefoucauld, who gave manuscripts to the abbey after becoming its abbot in 1619 (Kohler 1898, xxxv–xxxvi). It is described in two catalogues of the library (Paris, Sainte-Geneviève, MS 952, fol. 16, and MS 965, p. 17), and its shelf-mark (T 7) is still visible on the first folios of Amsterdam vol. 1 and Douce 215. It was one of three Arthurian manuscripts that left the abbey shortly before 1720 (Kohler 1898, xciii, without identifications). A second (T 4, according to the catalogue in MS 952) is probaby BNF, fr. 9123 (lot 2351 in the Du Fay sale held in Paris in 1725), and the third (T 3) is New York, Pierpont Morgan Library, MS M. 41. This has the date 15 April 1468 in the frame of the catchword on fol. 182v, and the name of Jean de la Moussaye, seigneur de Lorgeril, on fol. 264 may well be that of its first owner. The date is likely to be suitable, for his daughter Guyonne, wife of Jean de Rohan, died on 22 August 1502 (Anselme 1726–33, IV, 60). This manuscript was probably lot 97 in the so-called Ehrencron sale of 5 September 1718 in The Hague, but since it is not in the catalogue for the Ehrencron sale in Hamburg in 1717 it was presumably acquired elsewhere and added to the Ehrencron manuscripts by the bookseller Abraham de Hondt (a common practice of the time). It was certainly lot 435 in the Peter Le Neve sale of 19 March 1731 in London, when it was sold for £5 18s to Thomas Sclater Bacon, who may have been acting on behalf of its subsequent owner George Vertue, the well-known engraver. It then came into the possession of William Warburton, Bishop of Gloucester, and a later note in the book itself claims that Vertue had given it to Warburton as a present, but its appearance in the Vertue sale catalogue of 18 March 1757 (lot 75) suggests that the bishop bought it on the open market.

There are far too many French inventories with Arthurian prose manuscripts for them all to be mentioned here, but it is worth drawing attention to a few of the most significant. Already cited in connection with texts in verse is the inventory of Jean de Saffres of 1365. This also contained: 21 'romancium Mellini'; 22 'romancium de Lancelot' (exchanged for 'romancium Julii Cesaris'); 27 'romancium dicti Galaad'; 32 'unam peciam Romancii Tritan'; 46 'romancium de Joseph'; 47 'novem quaternos Romancii Lanceloti'; and 52 'romancium Tritani' (Carnandet 1857).

In a *Bible historiale* that belonged in 1341 to Hervé de Léon (Paris, Bibliothèque Sainte-Geneviève, MS 22) a later hand has written a list of the thirty-seven books in the owner's collection. These include: 'Lancelot du Lac'; 'Giron le courtoys'; 'Le sainct Greal'; 'Merlin et ses prophecies'; 'un aultre petit livre du sang Greal'; and 'un petit livre de la table ronde, Greal' (Meyer 1883). The *Bible historiale* bears the name of the *libraire* Geoffroy de Saint-Ligier and is illustrated by the *Fauvel* Master, who contributed to several Arthurian volumes (see above, p. 53, and Rouse and Rouse 2000, I, 206–7). Since the *Bible historiale* itself is a manuscript it has been assumed that the books in the list are also all manuscripts, but the list is late enough for some to have been printed.

There is another important document from the period when manuscripts were giving way to print, but it is not easy to interpret. It is an inventory, usually referred to as the 'Catalogue d'un libraire de Tours' (*Catalogue of a Tours book-seller*), which is preserved, somewhat incongruously, amongst letters and documents mainly connected with Ymbert de Batarnay, seigneur du Bouchage (BNF, fr. 2912, fols 78–83). The list (edited in Chéreau 1868) consists of 185 items described as 'livres en françois escripts à la main, à Tours devant l'ostel Monseigneur de Dunois' (*hand-written books in French, at Tours in front of the hotel of Monseigneur de Dunois*), followed by thirty-four 'Aultres livres en mistaires' (*other books: mystery plays*), nineteen 'Moralités' (*morality plays*) and then twenty-nine items described as 'livres en françois en impression' (*printed books in French*). Amongst the manuscripts are eleven volumes of Arthurian prose romance ('Tristan en trois volumes', 'Lancelot du Lac en trois volumes', 'Merlin', 'Les prophécies Merlin', 'Josephes du Sainct Gréal', 'La queste du Sainct Gréal' and 'Le petit Tristan'). Surprisingly, there are no Arthurian items amongst the printed books. The document has been well known for many years, but there is no satisfactory explanation of what it represents. It is treated as if it were the stocklist of a bookseller, but if this is really so, the number of books involved is quite extraordinary. The amount of capital needed to hold a stock of this size would have been considerable, and this would not even take account of the fact that the list includes very few of the titles that might be expected to constitute a bookseller's most regular sales: law books (for merchants as well as lawyers), medical texts (for laymen as well as doctors) and above all church books (theology at various different levels and service books for both public and private use). The religious texts are almost entirely confined to the plays and to one Book of Hours, followed by the comment 'et plusieurs aultres en grand nombre' (*and several others in great number*). It seems inconceivable that there were enough readers in Tours to justify a stock of this size. After all, in other contexts scholars are quick to stress that extensive libraries are the prerogative of the very wealthy, but if the Tours document represents a real stock, this would have been one of the largest libraries in France (267 items, some in several volumes, plus all those not listed individually). Only the king and the greatest of his magnates could have matched it (a century earlier the inventories of Jean de Berry list 297, as counted by Delisle 1907; in 1523 the library of the Duke of Bourbon at Moulins had 290, as counted by Le Roux de Lincy 1850). Consequently, it is extremely difficult to see how a bookseller could have hoped to make a living if his practice were to maintain his stock at this level. The explanation that makes commercial sense is that he had obtained these books by purchasing one or two ready-made collections, preferably at a bargain price, which he intended to disperse over the next few years. Thus the list may be evidence for the dispersal of one or more important private libraries. This in itself is speculation, and it would be even more speculative to attempt any guess at whose library might be represented. Of course, if the bookseller were slow to discover the economic realities, the list may represent his stock at bankruptcy, resulting from an accumulation of manuscripts that remained unsold, possibly because his clients preferred the new printed editions. Failing that, despite the title that appears to give a commercial address, we might have to assume that the list is not from a bookseller after all.

Outside France, as we might expect, it is in England and Italy that most owners of Arthurian prose romances are to be found. Surviving manuscripts containing texts of the *Lancelot–Grail* Cycle that were in England during the Middle Ages are documented in Middleton (2003), but there are very few examples where we have information about their medieval owners. Some of the manuscripts that were in the royal collection in the eighteenth century when it was given to the British Museum (i.e. those with MS Royal shelf-marks) may well have been in the royal collection before 1500, but it is also likely that some were acquired after the dissolution of the monasteries, or as gifts to Tudor monarchs. One such later acquisition is MS Royal 14. E. iii, which was apparently owned by Sir Richard Roos and bequeathed to his niece Eleanor Hawte (Middleton 2003, 221–2). Amongst the copies of the *Lancelot–Grail* only MS Royal 20. D. iv has a medieval provenance that can be established with reasonable certainty. The arms of Bohun, added in the fourteenth century, suggest ownership by Humphrey de Bohun, Earl of Hereford, Essex and Northampton, but the evidence for the book's having belonged to the earl's second daughter Mary is not reliable. From 1380 to her death in 1394 she was the wife of Henry Bolingbroke, Earl of Derby (who became King Henry IV in 1399), and the arms of Leon and Castille that are also in the manuscript were once thought to derive from the claim to these kingdoms maintained until 1388 by Henry's father, John of Gaunt. However, it is now known that the arms of Leon and Castille are part of the original decoration of *c.*1300 (Sandler 1986, 154–5). On the other hand, even without specific evidence, we might speculate that the transmission of the manuscript to Mary and Henry IV was how it entered the royal collection. An alternative would be to suppose that it had passed to Humphrey de Bohun's elder daughter Eleanor, wife of Thomas of Woodstock, Duke of Gloucester. The advantage of this suggestion is that there was a copy of *Lancelot* amongst the books and other property seized from his castle of Pleshey in Essex after his execution for treason in 1397 (Dillon and Hope 1897, 301). Since Pleshey was part of his wife's inheritance, the books may also have been from her family, and their seizure by the king presumably led to their incorporation into whatever royal library existed at the time.

In the second half of the fifteenth century the copy of *Tristan* that is now British Library, MS Harley 49 received the signature of Richard of York (later to be King Richard III), and the *Tristan* in British Library, MS Royal 20. D. ii (which belonged to Prigent de Coëtivy) has the signature of 'Gorge Nessefeld' (presumably from Nessefeld in Yorkshire). Given that the Christian name George is very rare at this time, one suspects a connection of some kind with the 'Georges Hessefeld' (probably for 'Nessefeld') who was Captain of Vire in Normandy for Henry VI in 1420 (Dupont-Ferrier 1942–66, I, no. 4834). Other signatures on the same manuscript ('G. Hermanuille' and 'Elizabeth Kykeby') remain unidentified. Various other manuscripts have names in them that may or may not refer to their owners, but the people concerned remain unidentified (e.g. British Library, MSS Royal 19. C. xii and 20. D. iii; Bodleian Library, MS Rawlinson Q. b. 6). The *Estoire* on deposit in Nottingham University Library (MS Middleton L. M. 7) has notes that refer to a fourteenth-century bishop of Coventry and Lichfield, which probably means that it was in the diocese at the time, but not necessarily owned by the bishop himself (presumed to have been Roger de Northburgh, 1322–59).

Humfrey, Duke of Gloucester, owned the *Queste* and *Mort Artu* in Brussels, Bibliothèque Royale, MSS 9627–8, though we do not know that he ever took the book to England, and the fact that it entered the Burgundian library at some time before 1467 (Barrois 1830, no. 1263) might suggest that it never left France. Humfrey's elder brother, John, Duke of Bedford, Regent of France for their nephew King Henry VI, acquired the French royal library in 1425, and it is supposed that many of these books were eventually taken to England. Information about particular volumes is almost entirely lacking, though it has been speculated that some were later acquired and returned to France by Louis de Bruges (Delisle 1868–81, I, 145–6). Other evidence of medieval ownership in England comes mainly from inventories and testaments. To the list of *Lancelot–Grail* texts given in Middleton (2003, 220–1) may be added: the 'Tristram et Isolda' in the possession of Queen Isabella at the time of her death in 1358; the copies of *Tristan* left by Elizabeth la Zouche in 1380, by Margaret Courtenay, Countess of Devon in 1391, by Sir John le Scrope in 1405, by Matilda Bowes, of Yorkshire, in 1420, by Thomas, Duke of Exeter, in 1426; and the *Guiron le Courtois* in two volumes left by Maud Clifford, Countess of Cambridge, in 1446 (Meale 1993, 139–40). None of the manuscripts recorded in these documents is identifiable amongst the survivors.

There must also have been various manuscripts available for the translations and adaptations that were made into English. Most important are the works of Sir Thomas Malory, but his are far from alone. There are: the *Merlin* and *Holy Grail* by Henry Lovelich; the anonymous prose *Merlin* of Cambridge University Library, MS Ff. 3. 11; the Scottish *Lancelot of the Laik*; the stanzaic *Le Morte Arthur*; and a number of lesser texts (Newstead 1967). The story of the Grail also exists in Welsh, and in a surprising combination. Probably made in the later fourteenth century in the circle of Hopcyn ap Thomas, *Y Seint Greal* is explicitly in two parts: a translation of the *Queste*, followed by a translation of the much rarer *Perlesvaus*. There is also a fragmentary Welsh version of the birth of Arthur that seems to derive from the French *Merlin* (Lloyd-Morgan 1986; 1991).

The situation in Italy is fairly similar, though the inventories are more detailed, the numbers involved seem to be greater, and more volumes can be identified amongst the survivors. Those brought to France from the library of the dukes of Milan at Pavia have already been listed, and none of those left at Pavia can be identified. The second part of the *Tristan* in Aberystwyth, National Library of Wales, MS 5667-E (written in France) has the arms of the Visconti on its first leaf (fol. 89), but it does not correspond to any item in the only inventory (that of 1426) that gives enough details to allow any identification (Pellegrin 1955, 355). The *Guiron* in British Library, Additional MS 12228 has the arms of Louis of Taranto, King of Naples, and identifications have been suggested for three items in the inventory of the Gonzaga library made in 1407 (Braghirolli 1880): the *Tristan* in Venice, Biblioteca Nazionale Marciana, MS fr. XXIII is probably item 64; the *Tristan* in London, British Library, Additional MS 23929 (still in a Gonzaga binding) is probably item 63; and the *Queste* in Udine, Biblioteca Arcivescovile, MS 177 may be item 40 (Delcorno Branca 1998, 40, n. 67, and 53, n. 11). However, the other Arthurian items in the same inventory have not been identified amongst surviving manuscripts: a *Merlin* (item 17); a *Lancelot* (item 32); two copies of *Guiron le Courtois* (items 33 and 38); what appear to be two copies of the Compilation by Rusticien de Pise (items 31 and 34); and no fewer than seven further volumes of *Tristan*, some being from multi-volume sets (items 35, 60–2 and 65–7).

The inventory of the d'Este library in 1437 (Rajna 1873, 50–4) includes: two copies of *Merlin* (items 6 and 43); three copies of *Lancelot* (items 1, 16 and 45); two volumes described as *Saint Graal*, of which either could be an *Estoire* or a *Queste* (items 20 and 30); two volumes that are presumably copies of the *Mort Artu* (items 28 and 49); a *Tristan* (item 21); and what is probably a *Guiron* (item 17). A later inventory of 1488 (Rajna 1873, 55–6) includes a similar range of items, some of which are likely to be the same as those of 1437 despite the differences in the very brief descriptions: a *Merlin* (item 20); three copies of *Lancelot* (items 1, 8 and 21); two items described as *Saint Graal* (items 16 and 39); four copies of *Tristan* (items 5, 14, 18 and 24); and three copies of *Guiron* (items 11, 19 and 28). There is also a *Lancelot* and *Queste* (item 23), and a *Lancelot, Queste* and *Mort Artu* (item 17). For details of entries in other inventories and of references in other documents, see Bertoni (1918–19) and Delcorno Branca (1998, 35–6, 40–1, notes 68 and 69, and 87–8). None of these Arthurian items has been identified.

In 1240 the Emperor Frederick II, writing from Foligno, acknowledged receipt of a 'liber Palamides', which is usually assumed to be some form of what we now call *Guiron le Courtois* (Lathuillère 1973). Further evidence that manuscripts of the French prose romances were in Italy slightly later in the century is provided by what must have been available to Rusticien de Pise (writing soon after 1271–4) and to the Venetian author of the *Prophecies de Merlin* (writing between 1272 and 1279). Early in the next century we have Dante's famous description of how Paolo and Francesca had read about the kiss of Lancelot and Guinevere (*Inferno*, canto V), and in the course of the fourteenth century, translations, adaptations and independent compositions made the Arthurian stories available in Italian (Delcorno Branca 1998). However, the existence of these Italian versions did not put an end to the copying of the French originals, nor to the acquisition of manuscripts that had been made in France.

Less well documented are Spain and Portugal, but here as elsewhere there were important translations and adaptations of all the texts of the Vulgate and Post-Vulgate Cycles (Entwistle 1925; Loomis ed. 1959*, 406–18). The first of these were made in the thirteenth century, and we can infer the presence of French manuscripts at an early date. More specific evidence for copies of the French prose romances comes from Catalonia in the fourteenth century. Not all the references collected by Entwistle (1925, 90–4) are to books that are known to have been in French; the manuscripts being written for Pere III (Pedro IV of Aragon) in 1336, 1339, 1346 and 1349 (paid for in 1356) are more likely to have been in Catalan, as is the 'Lançalot' sent for binding in 1374, though the documents themselves do not specify a language (Rubío y Lluch 1908–21: II, 57, doc. 59; I, 119, doc. 105; 135, doc. 127; 146, doc. 144; 172, doc. 172; II, 172, doc. 182). For those stated to be in French the earliest reference is for 6 August 1319, when Jaume II bequeathed to his son Ramon Berenguer what is described as a 'liber de Lançalot' (Rubío y Lluch 1908–21, II, 33, doc. 40). However, the *incipit* that is given as 'apres ce che maestres Gauters' identifies the text as the *Mort Artu*. The *Meliadus* in French paid for by Pere III on 27 March 1339 may or may not be the same book as the one described in more detail by the Infant Joan in a letter of 17 October 1383 (Rubío y Lluch 1908–21, I, 117, doc. 101 and 314, doc. 344). The *Lancelot* mentioned in a letter of 20 June 1379 as having been borrowed by the Infant Joan from the Viscount of Roda (on account of its great beauty) is presumably different from the 'Lançalot' (*Mort Artu*) of 1319 (Rubío y Lluch 1908–21, I, 278, doc. 301). Finally, the letter of 1383 also mentions a 'Tristany ystoriat' (*illustrated Tristan*).

As well as the *Cligés* already mentioned amongst the manuscripts of texts in verse, the library of King Martin I of Aragon inventoried in 1410 included a *Prophecies de Merlin* in French (Massó Torrents 1905, item 71), whilst at a some-what later date (1461) Don Carlos, Prince of Viana, son of King John II of Aragon, had copies of several Arthurian prose romances in French: 'del Sant Greal en ffrances'; 'de Giron en ffrances'; 'Tristany de Leonis en ffrances'; and 'un altre libre intitulat Giron en ffrances' (Raymond 1858). The surviving copies of *Lancelot* that are now in Spain may have been there from medieval times, but we do not know their history until a century or so later. The fourteenth-century copy on parchment in Escorial, Monasterio Real de San Lorenzo, MS P. II. 22 is from the library of the Conde-Duque of Olivares (1587–1645), being 'Cax. 24, núm. 13' in the catalogue of *c.*1627 (Andrés 1972–3, no. 633), in which a copy of Chrétien's *Charrette* was 'Cax. 10, núm. 20' (Andrés 1972–3, no. 1100). The fifteenth-century copy on paper in Madrid, Biblioteca Nacional, MS 485 is from the library of Gaspar Galcerán, Count of Guimerá (1584–1638).

In northern Europe, the Arthurian prose romances seem to have left no trace in Scandinavia, even though they must have been available when their verse counter-parts were being turned into sagas. By contrast, at much the same time, there is evidence for at least three, and perhaps as many as five, independent translations into Dutch, of which the earliest may be from not much after 1235. A unique characteristic of these Dutch versions is that the prose originals were repeatedly turned into verse (Besamusca 2000, 191–202). At a later date there were versions in Dutch prose, and it is supposed that it was in part through these that the material passed to Germany (Besamusca 2000, 203). In Germany itself, this interest in the prose romances seems to have been much more restricted than in other countries, and somewhat later in date (Andersen 2000, 155–6, 162).

Evidence for the presence of French manuscripts of the prose romances in German-speaking territory during the Middle Ages is rather scarce. The *Tristan* and the *Mort Artu* in the Biblioteca Apostolica Vaticana (MSS Pal. lat. 1964 and 1967) were amongst the books taken to Rome from Heidelberg in 1623, and could well have been in Germany for some time before that. All but one of the few surviving manuscripts that are now in German libraries are known to have been post-medieval acquisitions. The exception is Bonn, Universitätsbibliothek, MS 526, a copy of the complete *Lancelot–Grail* Cycle written by Arnulfus de Kayo in 1286. At the end of the fifteenth century it entered the library of Wirich VI von Daun zu Oberstein (*c.*1418–1501). In a note written at Oberstein in 1495 Wirich gives a list of its contents and the number of its leaves (in German, on fol. 170). Given that Wirich had been counsellor and chamberlain to King Charles

VIII of France, it seems likely that he had acquired the manuscript whilst in France at the royal court (Beckers 1986, 30–2; 1993, 11, 16; Deighton 1986, 272). He was no doubt more impressed by its many pictures than by a text that was in the French of 200 years earlier, though his note does show that he was familiar with its narrative. Not long afterwards it passed into the library of the Count of Manderscheid-Blankenheim, where it found itself in the company of Gottfried's *Tristan* (with the continuation of Ulrich von Türheim), of *Wigalois* and of the German *Prosa-Lancelot* that are now in the Stadtarchiv at Cologne.

Copied in significant numbers from the twelfth century to the sixteenth, made in France, England and Italy, some of them small enough to be carried with ease, others almost too heavy to lift, some of them extremely plain, others elaborately illustrated, some of them owned by merchants and civil servants, others by kings and princes, the manuscripts of French Arthurian literature present us with a picture of almost infinite variety. With the passing of the Middle Ages they were preserved in greater numbers than those of any other type of vernacular literature, and from the eighteenth century onwards, as soon as the finding and the buying of manuscripts became the province of book collectors rather than scholars and librarians, copies of Arthurian romances were soon amongst the items that were most sought after. Already widely distributed throughout Europe during the Middle Ages, they can now be found even further afield in the United States and Japan, and their present locations are an eloquent testimony to the enduring interest of their contents and of the books themselves.

Notes

[1] Editions of texts are often the best sources of information on individual manuscripts, and bibliographical details can be obtained from the chapters that deal with the texts that they contain.

[2] Detailed information on the manuscripts that contain works by Chrétien can be found in the Catalogue compiled by Terry Nixon (1993b), with what is known of their history being given in the Index of Former Owners and its accompanying Additional Notes (Middleton 1993). The count of sixty-seven includes the small fragment added to BNF, fr. 1429 (mentioned in the description of fr. 1429, but not separately numbered in the Catalogue of Manuscripts) and also the 'fragments' preserved as extracts by Fauchet and Borel (mentioned briefly in the Index of Former Owners). Further information on ownership has come to light since publication. Princeton, University Library, MS Garrett 125 was item 227 in the sale catalogue of the Baron d'Heiss in 1785 (information kindly supplied by William and Meradith McMunn). BNF, fr. 1429 came to Colbert from the collection of Habert de Montmor in 1682, being 'Le Roman du St. Graal' in the list preserved in BNF, MS Baluze 100, fol. 153. The potential ambiguity of the title is not a problem since all the other candidates owned by Colbert can be traced to other provenances, and the wording is in fact that of the seventeenth-century title on the flyleaf of the manuscript itself ('Li Romans du Saint Graal, composé par Chrestiens'). The manuscripts of Nicolas-Joseph Foucault (including BNF, fr. 1450 and the Edinburgh *Perceval*) appear in the sale catalogue of Jean-Jacques Charron, marquis de Ménars (The Hague: Abraham de Hondt, 1720). This sale took place in June 1720, proving

conclusively that Foucault's library was dispersed before his death (on 7 February 1721). The Edinburgh *Perceval* (NLS, Adv. 19. 1. 5) appears in a very rare Foulis catalogue of 1740, and was subsequently borrowed for many years by Bishop Thomas Percy (see Middleton 2006).

[3] None of the arguments advanced for a more precise dating for Thomas, Marie or *Erec* can be considered reliable. For what it is worth, it seems to me that *Erec* may not have been written until the later 1170s. *Caradigan*, a place with no Arthurian pedigree, may have been better known to poets with Welsh or Breton connections after the supposedly well-publicized 'eisteddfod' of 1176, and the name *Yvain de Cavaliot* seems to reflect that of the historical Owein Cyfeiliog, who may have been a more suitable model after he was on good terms with King Henry II, particularly after his loyalty in 1173 (during the revolt of the king's sons) and after his attendance at such gatherings as the Council of Oxford in 1177. We could also suggest that Erec goes unrecognized by Kay and Gauvain because he is wearing a closed helm (usually said to have been introduced *c.*1180, but probably a little earlier). In the end, however, these points are of no great weight, and each could be explained in various different ways.

[4] This question requires a new examination of the documents, which are differently transcribed by almost all who have published them. The record of the payment to Jacques Raponde is apparently dated 21 February 1405 (meaning 1406 by modern reckoning), but it is entered amongst accounts for 1407 (Cockshaw 1969, no. 67). There is also some doubt over the amount, either because there is a discrepancy in the original or because there have been errors of transcription. The payment is sometimes given as 400 francs, sometimes as 400 escus. The difference is relevant because 400 francs would correspond exactly to the 300 escus paid by the Duke of Berry for BNF, fr. 117–20. A further problem is that the description of the book paid for by John the Fearless does not quite match the description of the book in the inventory of 1420 (Doutrepont 1906, item 68), which is undoubtedly the present Arsenal MSS 3479–80.

[5] Much detailed work remains to be done on this sale, but amongst the manuscripts that are identifiable with reasonable certainty there are more than a dozen with the ex-libris of Jacques d'Armagnac. In the original catalogue (Anet 1724) the entries are not numbered, but this deficiency is made good in Bauchart (1886), and some of the manuscripts have these numbers written on them in pencil. Two of the copies of *Tristan* now in Vienna, Österreichische Nationalbibliothek, were in this sale: MS 2542 with the ex-libris of Jacques d'Armagnac was lot 135, and MS 2537 with the ex-libris of Jean de Berry was lot 134.

[6] The leaf with the transcription (and Douce's marginal note) is reproduced in the Scolar Press facsimile of the Douce volume (Pickford 1978, Appendix II). Douce's note is transcribed (not very accurately) by Vinaver (1925). Neither Vinaver, nor Pickford in the Scolar reprint, realized that Douce must be referring to the manuscript that is now British Library, MS Egerton 989, and they have also misread the second letter of Douce's reference, which they both transcribe without explanation (Pickford has 'M. h. B. II. 116'; Vinaver has 'M. H. B. II. 116'). This should in fact be 'M. N. B. II. 116' (as given above), being Douce's standard abbreviation for the volumes that are now Bodleian Library, MSS Douce e. 9–15. These contain Douce's notes on manuscripts in the British Museum (where he was an Assistant Curator from 1807 to 1811), and pp. 116–19 of vol. 2 (MS Douce e. 10) have his comments on MS Royal 20 D. ii (as specified in his note). His 'Ms. of the Mort de Tristan' is Bodleian Library, MS Douce 189, obtained at the Soubise sale of 1789 (probably lot 5351).

[7] I have seen examples, though not all in quite the same style, on MS Douce 329 ('Num 80') and National Library of Scotland, Advocates MS 19. 1. 4 ('Num 91'), both with d'Urfé armorial bindings, both from the La Vallière sale (lots 4175 and 3271). However, there are other d'Urfé manuscripts with no such annotation, and the question of how and when these numbers were added must remain in abeyance until there has been a systematic search of all known d'Urfé manuscripts.

[8] Whilst the present chapter was in the press it was discovered that London, British Library, Additional MSS 10292–4 appear as a single volume in the inventory of 1411 (Delisle 1907, no. 1116), and that BL, MS Royal 14. E. iii was present from 1373 onwards (Delisle, no. 1113), both identified by the references for second and last folios.

Reference List

For items accompanied by an asterisk, see the General Bibliography.

Texts

In the present chapter, references to modern editions of Arthurian texts have been confined to specific contributions made by the various editors, and are therefore cited as studies under the names of those editors. More general bibliographical information on the editions of Arthurian texts can be obtained from the chapters in which the texts themselves are discussed.

Studies

Actes, 1887–1908. *Catalogue des actes de François Ier*, 10 vols, Paris.

Andersen, E. A. 2000. 'The Reception of Prose: The *Prosa*-Lancelot', in Jackson and Ranawake eds 2000*, 155–65.

Andrés, G. de. 1972–3. 'Historia de la biblioteca del Conde-Duque de Olivares y descripcíon de sus códices', *Cuadernos Bibliográficos*, 28, 131–42; 30, 5–73.

Anet, 1724. *Catalogue des manuscrits trouvez après le décès de Madame la Princesse, dans son château royal d'Anet*, Paris.

Anselme, 1726–33. *Histoire généalogique et chronologique de la maison royale de France ...*, *continuée par M. Du Fourny, troisième édition, revue, corrigée et augmentée par les soins du P. Ange et du P. Simplicien*, 9 vols, Paris.

Avril, F., M.-T. Gousset, and C. Rabel. 1984. *Manuscrits enluminés d'origine italienne, 2: XIIIe siècle*, Paris.

Avril, F., and N. Reynaud. 1995. *Les Manuscrits à peintures en France 1440–1520*, Paris.

Balayé, S. 1988. *La Bibliothèque Nationale des origines à 1800*, Geneva.

Barrois, J. 1830. *Bibliothèque protypographique, ou librairies des fils du roi Jean, Charles V, Jean de Berri, Philippe de Bourgogne et les siens*, Paris.

Bauchart, E. Q. 1886. *Les Femmes bibliophiles de France (XVIe, XVIIe & XVIIIe siècles)*, 2 vols, Paris.

Bayot, A. 1909. 'Les Manuscrits de provenance savoisienne à la Bibliothèque de Bourgogne', *Mémoires et documents publiés par la Société Savoisienne d'Histoire et d'Archéologie*, 47, 307–410.

Beckers, H. 1986. '*Der püecher haubet, die von der Tafelrunde wunder sagen*: Wirich von Stein und die Verbreitung des *Prosa-Lancelot* im 15. Jahrhundert', in W. Schröder ed. *Wolfram Studien IX: Schweinfurter 'Lancelot'-Kolloquium 1984*, Berlin, 17–45.

Beckers 1993. 'Literarische Interessenbildung bei einem rheinischen Grafengeschlecht um 1470/80: Die Blankenheimer Schloßbibliothek', in J. Heinzle ed. *Literarische Interessenbildung im Mittelalter: DFG-Symposion 1991*, Stuttgart and Weimar.

Benskin, M., T. Hunt, and I. Short. 1992–5. 'Un nouveau fragment du *Tristan* de Thomas', *Rom*, 113, 289–319.

Bertoni, G. 1918–19. 'Lettori di romanzi francesi nel quattrocento alla corte estense', *Rom*, 45, 117–22.

Besamusca, B. 2000. 'The Medieval Dutch Arthurian Material', in Jackson and Ranawake eds 2000*, 187–228.

Blaess, M. 1973. 'Les Manuscrits français dans les monastères anglais au Moyen Âge', *Rom*, 94, 321–58.

Bogdanow, F. 1955. 'An Arthurian Manuscript: Arsenal 3350', *BBIAS*, 7, 105–8.

Bogdanow 1964. 'The Fragments of *Guiron le Courtois* preserved in MS Douce 383, Oxford', *Med. Aev*, 33, 89–101.

Bogdanow ed. 1965. *La Folie Lancelot: A Hitherto Unidentified Portion of the Suite du Merlin Contained in MSS B. N. fr. 112 and 12599*, Tübingen.

Bogdanow 1976. 'Another Hitherto Unidentified Arthurian Manuscript: New York Pierpont Morgan Library M 38', *BBIAS*, 28, 191–203.

Bogdanow ed. 1991a. *La Version post-vulgate de la Queste del Saint Graal et de la Mort Artu*, vol. 1, Paris.

Bogdanow 1991b. 'A Hitherto Unnoticed Manuscript of the Compilation of Rusticien de Pise', *FSB*, 38, 15–19.

Boislisle, A. de. 1880. 'Inventaire des bijoux, vêtements, manuscrits et objets précieux appartenant à la comtesse de Montpensier, 1474', *Société de l'Histoire de France: Annuaire-Bulletin*, 17, 269–309.

Braghirolli, W. 1880. 'Inventaire des manuscrits en langue française possédés par Francesco Gonzaga I, capitaine de Mantoue, mort en 1407', *Rom*, 9, 497–514.

Bruce, J. D. ed. 1910. *Mort Artu: An Old French Prose Romance of the XIIIth Century, being the Last Division of Lancelot du Lac*, Halle.

Brugger, E. 1904. 'Beiträge zur Erklärung der arthurischen Geographie, I: Estregales', *ZfSL*, 27, 69–116.

Brunel, C. ed. 1923. *La Fille du Comte de Pontieu: conte en prose: versions du XIIIe et du XVe siècle*, Paris.

Busby, K., T. Nixon, A. Stones and L. Walters eds 1993. *Les Manuscrits de Chrétien de Troyes/The Manuscripts of Chrétien de Troyes*, 2 vols, Amsterdam.

Carnandet, J. 1857. 'Bibliothèques de deux chanoines de Langres au XIVe siècle', *Bulletin du Bibliophile*, 13, 463–77.

Cazelles, R. 1958. *La Société politique et la crise de la royauté sous Philippe de Valois*, Paris.

Champion, P. 1910. *La Librairie de Charles d'Orléans*, Paris.

Chéreau, A. 1868. *Catalogue d'un marchand libraire du XVe siècle, tenant boutique à Tours*, Paris.

Cigni, F. 1992. 'Pour l'édition de la *Compilation* de Rustichello da Pisa: la version du ms. Paris, B.N., *fr. 1463*', *Neophil*, 76, 519–34.

Cigni 1993. 'Manoscritti di prose cortesi compilati in Italia (secc. XIII–XIV): stato della questione e prospettive di ricerca', in S. Guida and F. Latella eds. *La filologia romanza e i codici*, 2 vols, Messina, II, 419–41.

Cockshaw, P. 1969. 'Mentions d'auteurs, de copistes, d'enlumineurs et de libraires dans les comptes généraux de l'état bourguignon (1384–1419)', *Script*, 23, 122–44.

Colin, G. 1992. 'Lille, centre de reliure à la fin du Moyen Âge', *Gutenberg-Jahrbuch*, 352–67.

Colombo Timelli, M. ed. 2000. *L'Histoire d'Erec en prose: roman du XVe siècle*, Geneva.

Cowper, F. A. G. 1959. 'Origins and Peregrinations of the Laval-Middleton Manuscript', *NMS*, 3, 3–18.

Debae, M. 1995. *La Bibliothèque de Marguerite d'Autriche: essai de reconstitution d'après l'inventaire de 1523–1524*, Louvain and Paris.

Dehaisnes, C. 1886. *Documents et extraits divers concernant l'histoire de l'art dans la Flandre, l'Artois et le Hainaut avant le XVe siècle*, 2 vols, Lille.

Deighton, A. R. 1986. 'Die Bibliothek der Grafen von Manderscheid-Blankenheim', *Archiv für Geschichte des Buchwesens*, 26, 259–83.

Delcorno Branca, D. 1998. *Tristano e Lancillotto in Italia: studi di letteratura arturiana*, Ravenna.

Delisle, L. 1868–81. *Le Cabinet des manuscrits de la bibliothèque impériale*, 4 vols, Paris.

Delisle 1900. 'Les Heures de l'amiral Prigent de Coëtivy', *BEC*, 61, 186–200.

Delisle 1907. *Recherches sur la librairie de Charles V, roi de France, 1337–1380*, 2 vols, Paris; repr. Amsterdam, 1967.

de Mandach, A. 1974. 'A Royal Wedding-Present in the Making', *NMS*, 18, 56–76.

Devillers, L. 1871. 'Notice sur un cartulaire de la trésorerie des comtes de Hainaut', *Compte rendu des séances de la Commission Royale d'Histoire, ou recueil de ses bulletins*, series 3, 12, 339–468.

de Winter, P. M. 1985. *La Bibliothèque de Philippe le Hardi, duc de Bourgogne (1364–1404): étude sur les manuscrits à peintures d'une collection princière à l'époque du 'style gothique international'*, Paris.

Dillon, Viscount, and W. H. St. John Hope. 1897. 'Inventory of the Goods and Chattels Belonging to Thomas, Duke of Gloucester, and Seized in his Castle at Pleshy, co. Essex, 21 Richard II (1397); with their Values, as Shown in the Escheator's Accounts', *The Archaeological Journal*, 54, 275–308.

Douët-d'Arcq, L. 1851. *Comptes de l'argenterie des rois de France au XIVᵉ siècle*, Paris.

Douët-d'Arcq 1867. *Inventaire de la bibliothèque du roi Charles VI fait au Louvre en 1423 par ordre du regent duc de Bedford*, Paris.

Douët-d'Arcq 1874. *Nouveau recueil de comptes de l'argenterie des rois de France*, Paris.

Doutrepont, G. 1906. *Inventaire de la 'Librairie' de Philippe le Bon (1420)*, Brussels; repr. Geneva, 1977.

Doutrepont 1909. *La Littérature française à la cour des ducs de Bourgogne*, Paris.

Doutrepont 1939. *Les Mises en prose des épopées et des romans chevaleresques du XIVᵉ au XVIᵉ siècle*, Brussels.

Duggan, J. J. 1982. 'The Manuscript Corpus of the Medieval Romance Epic', in P. Noble, L. Polak and C. Isoz eds *The Medieval Alexander Legend and Romance Epic: Essays in Honour of David J. A. Ross*, Millwood, NY, London and Nendeln, 29–42.

Dupont-Ferrier, G. 1942–66. *Gallia Regia: ou état des officiers royaux des bailliages et des sénéchaussées de 1328 à 1515*, 7 vols, Paris.

Durrieu, P. 1904. 'Les Manuscrits à peintures de la Bibliothèque incendiée de Turin', *Revue archéologique*, 4th series, 3, 394–406.

Entwistle, W. J. 1925. *The Arthurian Legend in the Literatures of the Spanish Peninsula*, London, Toronto and New York.

Escouchy, M. 1863–4. *Chronique de Mathieu d'Escouchy*. Ed. by G. du Fresne de Beaucourt, 3 vols, Société de l'Histoire de France 118, 120, 126, Paris.

Espiner-Scott, J. G. 1938a. *Claude Fauchet: sa vie, son œuvre*, Paris.

Espiner-Scott 1938b. *Documents concernant la vie et les œuvres de Claude Fauchet: documents, inédits, bibliothèque de Fauchet, extraits de poèmes copiés d'après des manuscrits perdus*, Paris.

Fauchet, C. 1581. *Recueil de l'origine de la langue et poesie françoise, ryme et romans, plus les noms et sommaire des œuvres de cxxvii. poetes françois vivans avant l'an M. CCC.*, Paris; repr. Geneva, 1972.

Favre, C. 1888–9. Introduction to Jean de Bueil, *Le Jouvencel*. Ed. by L. Lecestre, Paris, I, i–cccxxxii.

Folda, J. 1976. *Crusader Manuscript Illumination at Saint-Jean d'Acre, 1275–1291*, Princeton.

Fontanella Vitale-Brovarone, L. 1988. 'Due frammenti francesi all'Accademia delle Scienze di Torino: L'*Estoire du Graal* e il *Tristano Torinese*', in A. Cornagliotti, L. Fontanella, M. Piccat, A. Rossebastiano and A. Vitale-Brovarone eds *Miscellanea di studi romanzi offerta a Giuliano Gasca Queirazza per il suo 65o compleanno*, 2 vols, Alessandria, I, 291–314.

François, M. 1951. *Le Cardinal François de Tournon, homme d'état, diplomate, mécène et humaniste (1489–1562)*, Paris.

Frappier, J. ed. 1936 . *La Mort le roi Artu*, Paris.

Gachard, L.-P. 1845. 'Notice sur la librairie de la reine Marie de Hongrie, soeur de Charles-Quint, régente des Pays-Bas', *Compte rendu des séances de la Commission Royale d'Histoire, ou recueil de ses bulletins*, 10, 224–46.

Gallais, P. 1970. 'Robert de Boron en Orient', in *Mélanges de langue et de littérature du Moyen Âge et de la renaissance offerts à Jean Frappier*, 2 vols, Geneva, I, 313–19.

Giacchetti, A. ed. 1989. *Ysaÿe le Triste: roman arthurien du Moyen Âge tardif*, Rouen.

Green, R. F. 1976. 'King Richard II's Books Revisited', *The Library*, 5th series, 31, 235–9.

Heuckenkamp, F. ed. 1896. *Le Chevalier du Papegau*, Halle.

Hult, D. F. 1989. 'Steps Forward and Steps Backward: More on Chrétien's *Lancelot*', *Spec*, 64, 307–16.

Hutchings, G. ed. 1938. *Le Roman en prose de Lancelot du Lac: le conte de la charrette*, Paris.

James, M. R. 1903. *The Ancient Libraries of Canterbury and Dover*, Cambridge.

Knight, A. E. 1967–8. 'A Previously Unknown Prose *Joseph d'Arimathie*', *RPh*, 21, 174–83.

Kohler, C. 1898. *Catalogue général des manuscrits des bibliothèques publiques de France: Paris, Bibliothèque Sainte-Geneviève: Introduction*, Paris.

La Chenaye-Desbois, 1863–77. *Dictionnaire de la noblesse, contenant les généalogies, l'histoire et la chronologie des familles nobles de France, par de la Chenaye-Desbois et Badier*, 3rd edn, 19 vols, Paris.

Lacy, N. 2004. 'The Enigma of the Prose *Yvain*', in *Arthurian Studies in Honour of P. J. C. Field*, Cambridge, 65–71.

Langlois, E. 1913. 'Fragments d'un roman de la table ronde', in *Mélanges offerts à M. Émile Picot*, 2 vols, Paris, I, 383–9.

Lanoë, G. 1998. 'La Bibliothèque des Chalon à Nozeroy (1463–1686)', in D. Nebbiai-Dalla Guarda and J.-F. Genest eds. *Du Copiste au collectionneur: mélanges d'histoire des textes et des bibliothèques en l'honneur d'André Vernet*, Turnhout, 467–94.

Lathuillère, R. 1966. *Guiron le Courtois: étude de la tradition manuscrite et analyse critique*, Geneva.

Lathuillère 1970. 'Le Manuscrit de *Guiron le Courtois* de la bibliothèque Martin Bodmer à Genève', in *Mélanges de langue et de littérature du Moyen Âge et de la Renaissance offerts à Jean Frappier*, 2 vols, Geneva, II, 567–74.

Lathuillère 1973. 'Le Livre de Palamède', in *Mélanges de langue et de littérature médiévales offerts à Pierre Le Gentil*, Paris, 441–9.

Lecoy de la Marche, A. 1875. *Le Roi René, sa vie, son administration, ses travaux artistiques et littéraires, d'après les documents inédits des archives de France et d'Italie*, 2 vols, Paris; repr. Geneva, 1969.

Le Roux de Lincy, A. J. V. 1843–4. 'La Bibliothèque de Charles d'Orléans à son château de Blois en 1427', *BEC*, 5, 59–82.

Le Roux de Lincy 1850. 'Catalogue de la bibliothèque des ducs de Bourbon', in *Mélanges de littérature et d'histoire recueillis et publiés par la Société des Bibliophiles François*, Paris, 43–144.

Livingston, C. H. ed. 1932. *Gliglois: A French Arthurian Romance of the Thirteenth Century*, Cambridge, MA.

Livingston 1940–1. 'Fragment d'un roman de chevalerie', *Rom*, 66, 85–93.

Lloyd-Morgan, C. 1986. 'Perceval in Wales: Late Medieval Welsh Grail Traditions', in *The Changing Face of Arthurian Romance: Essays on Arthurian Prose Romances in Memory of Cedric E. Pickford*, Cambridge, 78–91.

Lloyd-Morgan 1991. '*Breuddwyd Rhonabwy* and later Arthurian literature', in Bromwich, Jarman and Roberts eds 1991*, 183–208.

Loomis, R. S. 1938 (Part II in collaboration with L. H. Loomis). *Arthurian Legends in Medieval Art*, New York.

Loomis 1949. *Arthurian Tradition and Chrétien de Troyes*, New York.

Lot, F. 1918. *Étude sur le Lancelot en prose*, Paris.

McKitterick, D. J. 1978. *The Library of Sir Thomas Knyvett of Ashwellthorpe c.1539–1618*, Cambridge.

Massó Torrents, J. 1905. 'Inventari dels bens mobles del rey Martí d'Aragó', *Revue Hispanique*, 12, 413–590.

Meale, C. 1985. 'Manuscripts, Readers and Patrons in Fifteenth-Century England: Sir Thomas Malory and Arthurian Romance', *AL*, 4, 93–126.

Meale 1993. '"… alle the bokes that I haue of latyn, englisch, and frensch": Laywomen and their Books in Late Medieval England', in C. M. Meale ed. *Women and Literature in Britain, 1150–1500*, Cambridge, 128–58.

Meiss, M. 1967. *French Painting in the Time of Jean de Berry: The Late Fourteenth Century and the Patronage of the Duke*, 2 vols, London and New York.

Meyer, M. 2000. 'Intertextuality in the Later Thirteenth Century: *Wigamur, Gauriel, Lohengrin* and the Fragments of Arthurian romances', in Jackson and Ranawake eds 2000*, 98–114.

Meyer, P. 1883. 'Inventaire d'une bibliothèque française de la seconde moitié du XVe siècle', *Bulletin SATF*, 9, 70–2.

Meyer 1910. '*Les Enfances Gauvain*: fragments d'un poème perdu', *Rom*, 39, 1–32.

Meyer, P., and G. Paris. 1897. 'Fragment du *Vallet à la cote mal tailliee*', *Rom*, 26, 276–80.

Micha, A. 1958. 'Les Manuscrits du *Merlin* en prose de Robert de Boron', *Rom*, 79, 78–94.

Micha 1960–3. 'Les Manuscrits du *Lancelot en prose*', *Rom*, 81, 145–87; 84, 28–60, 478–99.

Michel, E. 1879. *Monuments religieux, civils et militaires du Gâtinais (Départements du Loiret et de Seine-et-Marne) depuis le XIe jusqu'au XVIIe siècle*, Lyon, Orleans and Paris.

Michel, F. 1835–9. *Tristan: recueil de ce qui reste des poëmes relatifs à ses aventures composés en françois en anglo-normand et en grec dans les XII et XIII siècles*, 3 vols, London and Paris.

Michelant, H. 1871. 'Inventaire des vaisselles, joyaux, tapisseries, peintures, manuscrits, etc., de Marguerite d'Autriche, régente et gouvernante des Pays-Bas, dressé en son palais de Malines, le 9 juillet 1523', *Compte rendu des séances de la Commission Royale d'Histoire, ou recueil de ses bulletins*, 3rd series, 12, 5–78, 83–136.

Middleton, R. 1988. 'The Prose Adaptation of Chrétien's *Erec et Enide*', summary of unpublished conference paper (Leuven, 1987), *BBIAS*, 40, 348–9.

Middleton 1993. 'Index of Former Owners' and 'Additional Notes on the History of Selected Manuscripts', in Busby, Nixon, Stones and Walters eds 1993, II, 87–243.

Middleton 1999. 'The History of BNF fr. 1588', in *Philippe de Remi, Le Roman de la manekine, Edited from Paris BNF fr. 1588 and Translated by Barbara N. Sargent-Baur, with Contributions by Alison Stones and Roger Middleton*, Amsterdam, 41–68.

Middleton 2003. 'Manuscripts of the *Lancelot–Grail Cycle* in England and Wales: Some Books and their Owners', in C. Dover ed. 2003*, 219–35.

Middleton 2006. 'Chrétien de Troyes at Auction: Nicolas-Joseph Foucault and other Eighteenth-century Collectors', in P. Damian-Grint ed. *Medievalism and "Manière Gothique" in Enlightenment France*, Studies on Voltaire and the Eighteenth Century, 2006:05, Oxford, 261–83.

[Mons] 1842. 'Livres de la trésorerie des chartes de Hainaut, 1435', in *Publications de la Société des Bibliophiles Belges séant à Mons n°. 12*, 11–12.

Montmorand, M de. 1917. *Une femme poète du XVIe siècle: Anne de Graville: sa famille, sa vie, son œuvre, sa postérité*, Paris.

Muir, L. R. ed. 1958. *Pierre Sala: Tristan, roman d'aventures du XVIe siècle*, Geneva.

Muir 1964. 'A Reappraisal of the Prose *Yvain* (National Library of Wales MS. 444-D.)', *Rom*, 85, 355–65.

Newstead, H. 1967. 'Arthurian Legends', in J. B. Severs ed. *A Manual of the Writings in Middle English 1050–1500*, New Haven, 38–79, 224–56.

Nitze, W. A., and T. A. Jenkins eds. 1932–7. *Le Haut Livre du Graal, Perlesvaus*, 2 vols, Chicago; repr. New York, 1972.

Nitze 1935. 'Un ex-libris médiéval', in *Mélanges de littérature, d'histoire et de philologie offerts à Paul Laumonier*, Paris, 51–5.

Nixon, T. 1993a. 'Romance Collections and the Manuscripts of Chrétien de Troyes', in Busby, Nixon, Stones and Walters eds 1993, I, 17–25.

Nixon 1993b. 'Catalogue of Manuscripts', in Busby, Nixon, Stones and Walters eds 1993, II, 1–85.

Omont, H. 1908–21. *Anciens inventaires et catalogues de la Bibliothèque Nationale*, 5 vols, Paris.

Paris, G. 1896. '*Le Donnei des amants*', *Rom*, 25, 497–541.

Paris, P. 1836–45. *Les Manuscrits françois de la Bibliothèque du Roi*, 6 vols, Paris.

Pasquier, E. 1617. *Les Recherches de la France, augmentées par l'autheur en ceste derniere édition de plusieurs beaux placards & passages, & de dix chapitres entiers*, Paris.

Paton, L. A. ed. 1926–7. *Les Prophecies de Merlin*, 2 vols, New York and London.

Pellegrin, E. 1955. *La Bibliothèque des Visconti et des Sforza, ducs de Milan, au XVᵉ siècle*, Paris.

Pickford, C. E. ed. 1951. *Alixandre l'Orphelin: A Prose Tale of the Fifteenth Century*, Manchester.

Pickford ed. 1959. *Erec, roman arthurien en prose publié d'après le ms. fr. 112 de la Bibliothèque Nationale*, Geneva.

Pickford 1965. 'A Fifteenth-Century Copyist and his Patron', in F. Whitehead, A. H. Diverres and F. E. Sutcliffe eds *Medieval Miscellany presented to Eugène Vinaver by Pupils, Colleagues and Friends*, Manchester and New York, 245–62.

Pickford 1978. *Tristan 1489* [Scolar Press facsimile], with an Introductory note by C. E. Pickford, London.

Picot, E. 1897. 'Le Duc d'Aumale et la bibliothèque de Chantilly', *Bulletin du Bibliophile*, 305–48.

Ponceau, J.-P. ed. 1997. *L'Estoire del Saint Graal*, 2 vols, Paris.

Rajna, P. 1873. 'Ricordi di codici francesi posseduti dagli Estensi nel secolo XV', *Rom*, 2, 49–58.

Raymond, P. 1858. 'La Bibliothèque de Don Carlos, prince de Viane', *BEC*, 19, 483–7.

Renting, A. D. et al. 1993. *The Seventeenth-Century Orange-Nassau Library: The Catalogue Compiled by Anthonie Smets in 1686, the 1749 Auction Catalogue, and Other Contemporary Sources, Edited with Introduction and Notes by A. D. Renting and J. T. C. Renting-Kuijpers, with Notes on the Manuscripts by A. S. Korteweg*, Utrecht.

Rickert, E. 1932–3. 'King Richard II's Books', *The Library*, 4th series, 13, 144–7.

Rigoley de Juvigny, J. A. 1772–3. *Les Bibliothèques françoises de La Croix Du Maine et de Du Verdier*, 6 vols, Paris; repr. Graz, 1969.

Ritchie, R. L. G. 1952. *Chrétien de Troyes and Scotland*, Oxford.

Roach, W. ed. 1949–83. *The Continuations of the Old French Perceval of Chrétien de Troyes*, 5 vols, Philadelphia.

Roques, M. 1952. 'Le Manuscrit fr. 794 de la Bibliothèque Nationale et le scribe Guiot', *Rom*, 73, 177–99.

Rouse, R. H., and M. A. Rouse. 2000. *Manuscripts and their Makers: Commercial Book Producers in Medieval Paris 1200–1500*, 2 vols, Turnhout.

Rubío y Lluch, A. 1908–21. *Documents per l'historia de la cultura catalana mig-eval*, 2 vols, Barcelona; repr. as *Documents per a la història de la cultura catalana medieval*, 2 vols, Barcelona, 2000.

Saenger, P. 1981. 'Un manuscrit de Claude d'Urfé retrouvé à la Newberry Library de Chicago', *BEC*, 139, 250–2.

Sammut, A. 1980. *Unfredo duca di Gloucester e gli umanisti italiani*, Padua.

Sandler, L. F. 1986. *Gothic Manuscripts 1285–1385*, A Survey of Manuscripts Illuminated in the British Isles, 5, 2 vols, London and New York.

Schmidt, A. 1890. 'Aus altfranzösischen Handschriften der Gr. Hofbibliothek zu Darmstadt', *ZrP*, 14, 521–39.

Stirnemann, P. 1993. 'Some Champenois Vernacular Manuscripts and the Manerius Style of Illumination', in Busby, Nixon, Stones and Walters eds 1993, I, 195–226.

Stones, M. A. 1977. 'The Earliest Illustrated Prose *Lancelot* Manuscript?', *RMS*, 3, 3–44.

Stones 1991. 'Manuscripts, Illuminated: 1, Introduction; 9, Some Outstanding Manuscripts', in Lacy ed. 1991*, 299–301, 305–8.

Stones 1993. 'The Illustrated Chrétien Manuscripts and their Artistic Context', in Busby, Nixon, Stones and Walters eds 1993, I, 227–322.

Stones 1996. 'The Illustrations of BN, fr. 95 and Yale 229', in Busby ed. 1996*, 203–83.

Stones 1998. 'The Stylistic Context of the *Roman de Fauvel* with a Note on *Fauvain*', in M. Bent and A. Wathey eds *Fauvel Studies: Allegory, Chronicle, Music, and Image in Paris, Bibliothèque Nationale de France, MS français 146*, Oxford, 529–67.

Suard, F. 1970. 'Notice sur le manuscrit B. N. fr. 1638: Pierre Sala et *Le Chevalier au Lion*', *Rom*, 91, 406–15.

Thomas, A. 1895. 'Un enlumineur allemand dans la Marche au quinzième siècle – Evrard d'Espingues et Jean du Mas', *Annales du Midi*, 7, 219–24.

Thomas 1911. 'Les Manuscrits français et provençaux des ducs de Milan au château de Pavie', *Rom*, 40, 571–609.

Thorpe, L. ed. 1958. *Le Roman de Laurin, fils de Marques le sénéchal: Text of MS. B. N. f. fr. 22548*, Cambridge.

Tobin, P. M. O. 1976. *Les Lais anonymes des XIIe et XIIIe siècles: édition critique de quelques lais bretons*, Geneva.

Tory, G. 1529. *Champ fleury*, Paris; repr. with an introduction by J. W. Joliffe, New York and The Hague, 1970.

Vale, J. 1982. *Edward III and Chivalry: Chivalric Society and its Context 1270–1350*, Woodbridge.

Van Praet, J. B. B. 1831. *Recherches sur Louis de Bruges, seigneur de la Gruthuyse*, Paris.

Vernet, A. 1976. 'Les Manuscrits de Claude d'Urfé (1501–1558) au château de La Bastie', *Académie des Inscriptions et Belles Lettres: comptes rendus des séances de l'année 1976*, 81–97.

Vielliard, F. 1974. 'Un Texte interpolé du cycle du Graal (Bibliothèque Bodmer, manuscrit 147)', *RHT*, 4, 289–337.

Vielliard 1975. *Bibliotheca Bodmeriana: manuscrits français du Moyen Âge*, Cologny-Genève.

Vinaver, E. 1925. *Études sur le Tristan en prose: les sources, les manuscrits, bibliographie critique*, Paris.

Vinaver 1942. Introduction to *Le Roman de Balain: A Prose Romance of the Thirteenth Century*, ed. by M. D. Legge, Manchester, ix–xxx.

II

THE ARTHUR OF THE CHRONICLES

Françoise Le Saux and Peter Damian-Grint

Geoffrey of Monmouth

It is established usage when discussing medieval Arthurian texts to distinguish between a 'romance' tradition, the best-known examples of which are the works of Chrétien de Troyes, and a pseudo-historical tradition, originating with Geoffrey of Monmouth's *Historia Regum Britanniae* (*c*.1138).[1] This distinction is based on obvious structural and narrative differences: the romances typically are episodic in nature and focus on the personal adventures of one or several heroes connected with Arthur's court, whereas the pseudo-histories cover the entirety of the history of Celtic Britain, thus placing Arthur within a wider pattern of dynastic succession. They also have a marked annalistic flavour, thanks to the time rubrics that punctuate the narrative, hence the term 'Arthurian (pseudo-) chronicles' commonly used to refer to these works. By present-day standards, the chronicle strand of the Arthurian tradition is not 'real' history, in the sense that much of the material sprung on an unsuspecting and delighted world by Geoffrey of Monmouth is pure fiction, but it was accepted by most of Geoffrey's contemporaries as a convincing and authoritative historical narrative.

There are a number of reasons for the ease with which the *Historia* was granted the authoritative status it so quickly achieved. First, Geoffrey of Monmouth himself was not without credentials. He was a cleric, probably an Augustinian canon active in Oxford between 1129 and 1151, and acquainted with Walter, Archdeacon of Oxford. Indeed, Geoffrey maintains in his preface that it was Walter himself who provided the source of the *Historia*, a 'very ancient book written in the British language'.[2] Geoffrey was made Bishop Elect of St Asaph in Flintshire in 1151, ordained and consecrated in 1152, and in 1153 was one of the bishops witnessing the Treaty of Westminster between King Stephen and Henry, son of the Empress Matilda. He is thought to have died in 1155. We are therefore dealing with a genuine scholar, who enjoyed a good network of ecclesiastical and political connections and whose Welsh origins lent credibility to his claim that he translated Walter's ancient book into Latin. The discovery of the book itself would not have been perceived as implausible, as the existence of a long written tradition in the Celtic languages was known and accepted.

Moreover, the *Historia* is not pure fabrication. It draws from a range of sources, both oral and written, including all the historical sources available at the time, from the classics to the *Historia Britonum* and the works of Gildas and Bede. Even if we cannot accept the claim made by Geoffrey in his introduction that his putative source was 'attractively composed to form a consecutive and orderly narrative' (5), he certainly made extensive use of Welsh genealogies and king-lists (Piggott 1941). The stories relating to different kings and their parentage might well be due to Geoffrey's imagination, but the names at least were genuine, and their order of succession was roughly based on the authority of Welsh documents. In order to create the illusion of chronological coherence, Geoffrey punctuates his narrative with time rubrics which hint at the underlying indebtedness to an annalistic type of source and always refer to well-known events in world history. New and old material is interwoven; references to events and characters mentioned by recognized authorities indirectly validate the narrative of the lesser-known events happening at the same time in Britain. The material specific to Geoffrey, buttressed by this armature of respectability, is made more credible for a reader who finds the *Historia* to be in agreement, or at least not in contradiction with, established knowledge. By the time the truly dubious stories turn up – Vortigern's tower, Merlin's prophecies, the moving of the stones of Stonehenge from Ireland, and of course Arthur's conception, glorious conquests and mysterious end – the reader has already accepted the credentials of the *Historia* and is more likely to enjoy the stories than to question them.

Politically, the *Historia* conferred valuable prestige on the Plantagenet kings, who encouraged the acceptance and dissemination of the work; but this in itself cannot account for its extraordinary popular success. The key to an understanding of the enthusiastic reception of the *Historia* may be found in the opening lines of Geoffrey's prologue:

> Whenever I have chanced to think about the history of the kings of Britain, on those occasions when I have been turning over a great many such matters in my mind, it has seemed a remarkable thing to me that, apart from such mention of them as Gildas and Bede have each made in a brilliant book on the subject, I have not been able to discover anything at all on the kings who lived here before the Incarnation of Christ, or indeed about Arthur and all the others who followed on after the Incarnation. Yet the deeds of these men were such that they deserve to be praised for all time. What is more, these deeds were handed joyfully down in oral tradition, just as if they had been committed to writing, by many peoples who had only their memory to rely on. (5)

Geoffrey is here signalling a gap in the scholarly market, the existence of which is obvious because of the alleged existence of a reliable oral tradition. This lacuna is an injustice to the memory of the great departed, especially of Arthur. Walter, Archdeacon of Oxford, then opportunely comes along with his 'ancient book'.

It is clear that King Arthur is very much the hook with which Geoffrey hopes to catch his audience's attention. We know that tales about Arthur were circulating in Europe at the time, witness the well-known Arthurian archivolt of Modena cathedral, featuring Arthur and his knights apparently attacking a castle to free the captive Winlogee (Guinevere).[3] Geoffrey of Monmouth's achievement is to provide an authoritative, scholarly background for the character of Arthur. From the hero of popular tales he is transformed into a medieval king, presented as belonging to a specific dynasty, fixed in time by certain dates, active in realistic geographical settings and fighting identifiable enemies. He maintains law and order in his realm, protects the Church and distributes lands and ecclesiastical benefices.

Arthur, on one level, is just one king among over a hundred mentioned in the *Historia*. After his death in 542, he is succeeded by another twelve rulers before dominion over Britain passes to the English. Moreover, the salient features of his reign – resisting the enemy within (treacherous relatives as well as the pagan Saxons) and defying the enemy without (the Romans) – are present in the accounts of the lives of other rulers. Belinus and Brennius have already conquered Rome once; the son of the British princess Helen was a Roman emperor; strife within the ruling family is a recurrent feature from Locrinus onwards, and its effects are no less destructive than Mordred's treachery, whilst the struggle against the Saxons remains constant from the moment they are allowed to settle in Britain by Vortigern. However, Arthur's importance is signalled by the fact that his reign is recounted at exceptional length, taking up over one sixth of the *Historia* as a whole; by comparison, succeeding kings seem somewhat colourless. Arthur's rule is recounted in a predominantly epic mode, with lavish descriptions of the pomp and splendour surrounding state events. But what truly makes it stand out is the king's aura of predestined glory.

Essential to an understanding of the Arthurian section is the figure of Merlin.[4] Geoffrey first introduces him as the wonder-child who announces to Vortigern the return to Britain of Aurelius and Uther, Arthur's uncle and his father-to-be; he later prophesies the greatness of Arthur at the death of Aurelius and engineers Arthur's birth through appearance-changing drugs which allow Uther to gain access to the chaste Ygerne, Countess of Cornwall. Whether these circumstances surrounding his conception enhance Arthur's greatness, or constitute an essential weakness, will be a matter of debate for Geoffrey's later readers, but there is a sense in which Arthur's achievements merely confirm the reliability of Merlin, specifically with regard to the political prophecies recorded in Book VII of the *Historia* (§§109–17). These prophecies, in the cryptic and obscure style associated with the genre, had been written and circulated by Geoffrey before the completion of the *Historia*; their strong political associations suggest that the work as a whole might have been intended as a cautionary tale for the Plantagenets, under the guise of history. Arthur could then be read as a warning: even the greatest of kings will be unable to fulfil his destiny if he cannot count on the loyalty of his kin.

As a political fable, the *Historia* failed to have much impact, but it gained swift and almost universal acceptance as history.[5] From the moment the *Historia* was published, it became the definitive history of Celtic Britain. Moreover, it offered a fund of stories and anecdotes, fully crafted in elegant Latin and attractive to a wide audience. Above all, Geoffrey turned Arthur into a respectable historical personage, rather than a figment of the imagination of frivolous story-tellers. These elements combined to make the work an instant best-seller; over 200 manuscripts are still extant. [FLS]

Wace

In 1155, an outstanding French verse translation of Geoffrey's *Historia* was completed by Wace, a Jersey-born cleric active in Caen, one of the most import-ant intellectual and political centres of twelfth-century Normandy. Thought to have been born around 1100, Wace was already an experienced writer when he tackled Geoffrey's immensely popular work. He claims in his later *Roman de Rou* that he was the author of a wide range of poetic works, and from his earlier period we still have three hagiographical poems translated from the Latin: *La Vie de sainte Marguerite*, *La Vie de saint Nicolas* and *La Conception Nostre Dame*; these early works chart the progress of a burgeoning career. Having completed his education, probably in Paris, but possibly in Chartres, the young Wace gained a reputation which won him the support, first of local religious establishments, then, for the *Conception*, of local secular patrons and, finally, for the *Roman de Brut*, of the greatest lord of Normandy, the King of England. The *Brut* was an immediate success, both as a scholarly endeavour – Wace's work was to become *the* French version of Geoffrey's *Historia*, eclipsing previous attempts at recasting the British material in French[6] – and as literature, influencing amongst others Chrétien de Troyes. Henry II rewarded the poet with a prebend at the abbey of Bayeux, in Normandy, where Wace probably died some time after 1174.[7]

Some thirty-two manuscripts of Wace's *Brut* are still extant, of which nineteen are complete or near-complete. In the two oldest manuscripts, both Anglo-Norman (the late twelfth-century Durham Cathedral, MS C. iv. 27 and the early thirteenth-century Lincoln Cathedral, MS 104), the work is copied alongside Gaimar's *Estoire des Engleis* and Jordan Fantosme's *Chronicle*, providing the reader with an overview of the history of Britain from the earliest times; the poem was clearly read as history. Later manuscripts, however, and particularly those produced on the Continent, tend to combine the *Brut* with Arthurian romances, indicating that beyond the Anglo-Norman world it was read as a work of fiction rather than an independent historical work.

The text of the *Brut* combines two versions of the *Historia* with additions from Wace's fund of general knowledge, both scholarly and popular. The first part of his poem, up to the prophecies of Merlin, is based on the 'Variant version', an anonymous rewriting of Geoffrey's *Historia*, which slightly abbreviates the text whilst adding a few details and introducing a more pedagogical and moral tone to the work (Wright edn 1988, l–lxxv). After the prophecies of Merlin, Wace appears to have used both the Variant version and Geoffrey's own, fuller text; this suggests that he wished to include as much information as possible in the Arthurian sections, which he amplifies to a far greater extent than the rest of Geoffrey's narrative. Over 4,000 octosyllabic lines, out of a total of 14,866, are devoted to the reign of Arthur. The importance of Merlin, though, is considerably reduced, through the omission of the entire book containing the prophecies. Wace's explanation suggests that his main concern was with the authority of his text:

> Ne vuil sun livre translater
> Quant jo nel sai interpreter;
> Nule rien dire nen vuldreie
> Que si ne fust cum jo dirreie. (7539–42)

(I do not wish to translate his book, as I do not know how to interpret it; I would not wish to say something that would not turn out as I said.)

Even a slight misinterpretation of this notoriously obscure (and politically sensitive) material might jeopardize his standing as a scholar and the credibility of the *Brut* as a whole.

The passage from Latin to French did indeed bring specific problems. Unlike Welsh, which enjoyed the authority of a language with a long written tradition, French was not perceived as a medium of learning. Moreover, the audience Wace was addressing (the lay members of the Plantagenet court, and, if the English poet Layamon is to be believed, Eleanor of Aquitaine herself) could not be expected to recognize references to, or echoes of, Latin authorities. The procedure of implicit validation adopted by Geoffrey and retained with some adaptations by the redactor of the Variant version was not suitable for a work in the French vernacular aimed at lay readers or listeners. Wace, therefore, had to find an explicit way of affirming both his own authority and that of his work, ensuring that any cultural or literary references were understood, but in such a way that his intended audience would not feel unduly patronized. The narrative persona he creates is both scholarly and endearingly candid about the limits of his knowledge. The expression 'ne sai' (*I do not know*) occurs so frequently that it almost becomes a mannerism. However, the information 'not known' is invariably trivial or technical in nature, with the result that the authority of the narrator is actually enhanced. Where scholarly detail is provided, one notices a principle of pedagogical inclusiveness at work. For example, his frequent, lengthy discussions of linguistic change and its effect on place-names show off his knowledge, but they also create a link with the everyday experience of members of his audience, who would have been well aware of problems of language 'corruption' in an already multi-cultural country.

Greater stress is also placed on events relating to religious history. For example, Wace introduces an entirely new story about Taliesin, who is mentioned only fleetingly in Geoffrey's *Historia*, though he is one of the main protagonists of Geoffrey's later *Vita Merlini*. Wace turns Taliesin into a British Isaiah, prophesying the birth of Christ and responsible for the British responsiveness to the good news of the Gospel. This added vignette is also good story-telling, designed to entertain under the guise of instruction. Wace's readiness to add details and anecdotes to make his work more accessible to the general reader or listener gains momentum in the poem, reaching a climax in the Arthurian section.

Wace's most striking addition is the mention of the Round Table, borrowed directly from popular oral tales:

> Pur les nobles baruns qu'il out,
> Dunt chescuns mieldre estre quidout,
> Chescuns se teneit al meillur,
> Ne nuls n'en saveit le peiur,
> Fist Artur la Runde Table
> Dunt Bretuns dient mainte fable. (9747–52)

(*Because of his noble barons, each of whom thought himself superior to the others, each of whom considered himself the best, without anyone knowing who was the worst, Arthur made the Round Table, about which the Bretons tell many a tale.*)

The point of this, says Wace, was that it put an end to quarrels arising from seating precedence, as the table had no high or low end. The creation of the Round Table is even given a date: it took place when Arthur returned to England after conquering Scotland and Scandinavia and settled down to a glorious peace that was to last twelve years (9730). The stories circulating about Arthur and his knights are presented as a record, albeit imperfect, of this protracted period of peace:

> En cele grant pais ke jo di,
> Ne sai si vus l'avez oï,
> Furent les merveilles pruvees
> E les aventures truvees
> Ki d'Arthur sunt tant recuntees
> Ke a fable sunt aturnees:
> Ne tut mençunge, ne tut veir,
> Ne tut folie ne tut saveir.
> Tant unt li cunteür cunté
> E li fableür tant flablé
> Pur lur cuntes enbeleter,
> Que tut unt fait fable sembler. (9787–98)

(It was in this time of great peace I have mentioned – I do not know if you have heard of it – that the wondrous events occurred and the adventures were experienced that are so often told about Arthur, to the extent that they have been turned into tales: not all lies, not all true, neither all folly nor all wisdom. The story-tellers have told so many tales, the spinners of yarns have recounted so many fables, that they have made everything seem like pure invention, in their attempts to embellish their stories.)

Wace does for Arthurian tales what Geoffrey did for Arthur himself: he gives them credibility and anchors them in time. The fact that the adventures of the Round Table took place during a period of peace rationalizes the contrast between the forceful and energetic conqueror of 'history' and the somewhat shadowy 'roi fainéant' (*weak king*) of romance. Indeed, the account of Arthur's campaign against Rome allows Wace to foreground prominent Arthurian characters such as Kay (Kei), Bedivere (Bedoer) and especially Gauvain (Walwein), whose heroic stature Wace endows with a somewhat gentler nature than his counterpart in Geoffrey of Monmouth. In a light-hearted exchange with Cador of Cornwall, following the Roman ultimatum to Arthur, Gauvain is made an advocate for the virtues of peace, in terms that would not be out of place in any romance:

> Bone est la pais emprés la guerre
> Plus bele et mieldre en est la terre;
> Mult sunt bones les gaberies
> E bones sunt les drueries.
> Pur amistié e pur amies
> Funt chevaliers chevaleries. (10767–72)

(It is good to have peace after war, the land is the fairer and the better for it; it is excellent to be able to indulge in joking and courting the ladies. It is for love and their beloveds that knights perform knightly deeds.)

This little speech is an addition by Wace to the scene found in his Latin source. It acts as a corrective to the warlike enthusiasm of Cador, casting Gauvain in the role of courtly admirer of ladies that is his hallmark in the romance tradition.

Despite his qualified endorsement of popular tales of Arthur, Wace does not succumb to the temptation to interpolate any of them into his narrative, beyond the mention of the Round Table.[8] He follows faithfully the structure and sequence of events of the *Historia*, expanding on descriptions of sea journeys, court events and battle scenes. The evident pleasure taken in the depiction of the pomp and luxury of state occasions is in great part responsible for Wace's reputation as a courtly poet. The Arthur who most inspired Wace was the conqueror of France and victor over Emperor Lucius of Rome; the struggle for self-preservation on British soil and the ensuing consolidation of power of the youthful Arthur are not elaborated to any great extent. This may be interpreted as a desire to undermine further the political undercurrent to Geoffrey's material, or simply as an indication that Wace was trying to make the narrative more continental in outlook. Wace's handling of the characters of Mordred and Guinevere similarly weakens the political dimension of their treason, motivating Mordred's usurpation of Arthur's bed and throne by a long-standing secret love harboured for the queen (11179–89), rather than by the lust for power implied by Geoffrey of Monmouth's account.

More so than in the *Historia*, there is a distance between the narrator of the *Brut* and his material, which is seen most clearly in the aside relating to Arthur's death:

> Arthur, si la geste ne ment
> Fud el cors nafrez mortelment;
> En Avalon se fist porter
> Pur ses plaies mediciner.
> Encore i est, Bretun l'atendent,
> Si cum il dient e entendent
> De la vendra, encor puet vivre.
> Maistre Wace, ki fist cest livre,
> Ne volt plus dire de sa fin
> Qu'en dist li prophetes Merlin;
> Merlin dist d'Artur, si ot dreit,
> Que sa mort dutuse serreit.
> Li prophetes dist verité;
> Tut tens en ad l'um puis duté,
> E dutera, ço crei, tut dis,
> Se il est morz u il est vis. (13275–90)

(*If the story is true, Arthur received a mortal wound to his body. He had himself carried to Avalon to have his wounds tended. He is still there, the British are waiting for him; they say and believe that he will return from there, he may still be alive. Master Wace, who made this book, will not say any more about his end than did the prophet Merlin. Merlin said about Arthur, and he was right, that his death would be doubtful. The prophet spoke truly: it has been doubted ever since, and people, I believe, will be forever uncertain whether he is dead or alive.*)

There is little doubt that this passage is meant to be humorous, poking fun both at the foolish 'Bretun' and the opaqueness of Merlin's prophecies. This superior attitude gives way to open contempt for the Welsh descendants of the ancient British in the closing lines of the poem, where the narrator states:

> Tuit sunt mué e tuit changié
> Tuit sunt divers e forslignié
> De noblesce, d'onur, de murs
> E de la vie as anceisurs. (14851–54)

(*They have completely changed and altered, they are totally different and have degenerated from the nobility, the honour, the customs and the life of their ancestors.*)

Whereas Geoffrey was writing his *Historia* from the assumed perspective of an insider, Wace clearly approaches his subject-matter from the outside, and with an amused distance. This attitude is particularly evident in Wace's later *Roman de Rou*, a verse history of the dukes of Normandy, in which he mentions the disappointment he felt after a visit to the famed forest of Brocéliande in Brittany:

> La alai jo merveilles querre,
> Vi la forest e vi la terre,
> Merveilles quis, mais nes trovai,
> Fol m'en revinc, fol i alai. (6393–96)

(*I went there seeking marvels; I saw the forest, I saw the land; I looked for marvels, but I did not find them. I came back a fool, a fool I went there.*)

The world of Breton romance is firmly identified as being both foreign and untrustworthy. But it is noteworthy that Wace's 'folly' lies in his readiness to believe in the presence of *fées* in Brocéliande; we are not dealing with a blanket condemnation of Arthurian material. The distinction in the *Brut* between the core of historical truth that lies at the heart of Arthurian romances, and the more fabulous aspects of the tales, is still subscribed to by the poet.

Whilst maintaining the trappings of 'serious' history, Wace's *Brut* is a precursor of the later Arthurian romances, which will be indebted to him in three main respects: (i) as a result of his attribution of a kernel of truth to stories of Arthur and the Round Table, this material lent itself to literary reworking in written form; (ii) his well-crafted poetics demonstrated the appropriateness of the octosyllabic couplet for lengthy and complex narratives; (iii) his lively descriptions and expansions in the epic and courtly modes provided a template for future writers. The *Brut* is not an Arthurian romance, but it paved the way for the new genre. [FLS]

Arthur in the *Brut* Tradition

In view of the popularity of Wace's *Brut*, other vernacular histories of Britain composed between the twelfth and the fourteenth centuries are also generally referred to as *Brut*s. Like Wace's *Brut*, they present Arthur as one king among many. The importance they attribute to him changes, though in general it diminishes as time goes on. There is a distinct difference between the early verse *Brut* texts, inspired directly by Geoffrey's *Historia*, and the later prose versions, written in a dry, annalistic style and appearing to owe more to the monastic chroniclers or even to the *Anglo-Saxon Chronicle* than to the historiographical tradition typified by Wace or his contemporaries.

The Verse *Brut* Tradition

The verse *Brut* tradition consists of a small group of works of the late twelfth and early thirteenth centuries. Six texts are known to have survived, five of which have been edited or at least transcribed (Damian-Grint 1994).[9] Although all the surviving texts are fragmentary, in at least two cases, the Royal and Harley *Brut*s, the surviving portions are large enough to give a good idea of the authors' intentions. The tradition divides naturally into two branches according to prosodic form; the majority are in the standard narrative form of octosyllabic couplets, but two are in the less usual, though not unique, form of monorhymed Alexandrine *laisses*.

The Royal *Brut* consists of 6,237 lines in octosyllabic couplets and translates approximately one third of the text of Geoffrey's *Historia*, from just after the beginning up to the conception of Arthur. In BL, MS Royal 13. A. xxi (late thirteenth-century) the Royal *Brut*, composed in the twelfth century, replaces the beginning of Wace's *Brut* (Damian-Grint 1996). Also written in octosyllabic couplets is the 254-line Harley Fragment, which has been considered as a fragment of the same version as the Royal *Brut*. But there is no overlap of material and the evidence is insufficient, although it is not impossible from a stylistic and linguistic point of view.[10] The Royal *Brut*, naturally enough, does not refer to Arthur at all; references to Arthur within the Harley Fragment derive very closely from the Vulgate text of Geoffrey's *Historia* (Damian-Grint 1994, 91).

Also in octosyllabic couplets is the Munich *Brut*, which, unlike all the other verse *Brut* texts, is of continental origin:[11] it appears to have been composed in or near Flanders in the early thirteenth century, and thus within the flourishing vernacular historiographical tradition which also produced several versions of the *Pseudo-Turpin Chronicle* (see Spiegel 1993). Some 4,180 lines of this text survive in a single manuscript, Munich, Bayerische Staatsbibliothek, Codex Gallicus 29, but only the early part of Geoffrey's *Historia* is translated, and again Arthur does not appear.[12]

A separate branch of the same tradition is represented by the Harley *Brut*, which consists of five fragments totalling 3,359 lines in Alexandrine monorhymed *laisses*. The five portions of the text cover just over a quarter of Geoffrey's *Historia*, translating with some gaps from the death of King Lucius up to Arthur's campaign against (coincidentally) the Emperor Lucius. One section of the text, the prophecies of Merlin, is also to be found in two other manuscripts, where it is interpolated into copies of Wace's *Brut* at the point at which Wace himself declares that he will not translate the prophecies from Geoffrey.[13] It has been suggested that the text was composed by Claraton, an English writer known to have translated Geoffrey into French verse, but there is no compelling evidence why it should be this text which should be attributed to him, rather than any of the others, or indeed some other text which has not survived (Damian-Grint 1999a, 63–4). The 136-line Bekker Fragment, which describes the moving of the Giants' Dance to Britain by Merlin, is also in Alexandrine *laisses*; it is very close stylistically to the Harley *Brut*, even to the extent of sharing a number of lines, but the precise nature of the relationship is unclear.

The Harley poet's choice of prosodic form is intriguing. Although Anglo-Norman literature of the period is notable for its extremely wide variation in verse form (ranging from Philippe de Thaon's hexasyllables to fourteen-syllable lines, and from couplets to *laisses* of sometimes hundreds of lines), the octosyllabic couplet is the chosen form for the majority of authors of historiography and other narrative forms, such as saints' lives, which present themselves as non-fiction. The Alexandrine monorhymed *laisse* is found in two other historiographical works, the early sections of Wace's *Roman de Rou* and the *Estoire d'Antioche*, where it has generally been regarded as a deliberately epic form.

Arthur in the Harley *Brut* appears exactly as he appears in Geoffrey. Given the constraints of the metre, the author translates remarkably closely (the Harley *Brut* version of the prophecies of Merlin is almost improbably faithful to the Latin, considering the complexity of the material), and Geoffrey's warrior-king and general is reproduced here with few changes. It may be noted that the author shows slightly more interest in the figure of Arthur than in those of Ambrosius Aurelius and Uther, to the extent of allowing himself a certain degree of amplification in descriptions of court life. He elaborates on Arthur's crown-wearing in Caerleon after his northern campaign and provides, when Arthur arrives in France, a long description of his pavilion at Barfleur.

All the texts of the Anglo-Norman verse *Brut* tradition date from the second half of the twelfth century or possibly the early years of the thirteenth; it is not hard to imagine a flurry of literary activity in the years immediately following the appearance of Geoffrey's work, which enjoyed enormous popularity from the moment of its publication. The three longest texts appear to be the wreckage of ambitious projects: judging from their size in relation to the proportion of Geoffrey's Latin original that they cover (necessarily only the roughest of comparisons), the complete Royal *Brut* could have been almost 16,000 lines, about the same length as Wace's *Brut*, and the Harley *Brut* at least 10,000 lines long. Nevertheless, whatever their authors' intentions, or pretensions, they cannot be regarded in any real sense as rivals to Wace's text, which was the only vernacular version of Geoffrey still being regularly copied well into the thirteenth century.

The reasons for this are various. Of all the twelfth-century translators of Geoffrey's *Historia*, only Wace is known to have had significant patronage; however, the fragments are all missing their prologues and epilogues, where one would expect to find such information, and an argument *ex silentio* is naturally of limited value. As far as the literary qualities of the poems are concerned, there is general agreement that none of the octosyllabic texts measures up to Wace's standards. In his edition of the Royal *Brut*, Bell states (xiv) that it is the work of 'a journeyman in comparison with Wace'. On the other hand, the Harley *Brut* is 'a vigorous and effective work' by a competent poet (Damian-Grint 1999a, 64); however, the fact that it uses a completely different prosodic form may save it from too direct a comparison with Wace. The choice of form may also have dictated the literary fate of the Harley *Brut*. As we have seen, monorhymed

Alexandrine *laisses* were used in other works of historiography of the period, but it was not a common nor, apparently, a popular form (the *Estoire d'Antioche* is preserved in only two manuscripts and no medieval manuscripts of the Alexandrine sections of the *Roman de Rou* survive).[14]

No less important is the portrayal of characters, especially Arthur. Wace's Arthur is a courtly figure, while the Arthur of the Harley *Brut* and the Harley Fragment is essentially Geoffrey's Arthur, a very different king; little effort is made to produce an Arthur closer in character to the figure of Arthurian romance. While it can be argued that this is simply the result of a lack of imagination on the part of the *Brut* poets, it seems more likely that it was a matter of deliberate choice. All the authors of the verse *Brut*s present their texts as *estoires*, works of historiography and not fiction, making heavy use of historiographical terminology and consistently stating that their texts are trustworthy because they are translations of authoritative Latin sources. In keeping with their general strategy of translation, in which close, even literal, word-for-word translation is the norm (Damian-Grint 1999b), their presentation of Arthur as military leader, rather than courtly king, corresponds closely to that of Geoffrey's original, with only minor variations (Damian-Grint 1994, 353–4). But this dry, 'historical' Arthur does not seem to have been what their audiences wanted.

The Prose *Brut* Tradition
The tradition of *Brut* texts in prose is considerably more complex than that of the verse works. The very first version, produced around 1300, used a variety of sources, probably including both the verse *Brut* tradition and Geffrei Gaimar's *Estoire des Engleis*.[15] Immensely popular, the *Brut* text was added to, abbreviated and adapted, the different versions surviving in more than fifty manuscripts. A complete history of the prose *Brut* tradition, and even of the different versions and the relationships between them, remains to be written.

Some of the prose *Brut* texts were commissioned by important patrons – the *Petit Bruit* is dedicated to Henry de Lacy, one of the most eminent barons of Edward I's reign – but they cannot be considered as 'courtly' works. Their style is often dry and annalistic, their construction schematic and their grasp of chronology sometimes unsure. They are presented as the history not of Britain but of England; some versions start with the division of England into five kingdoms and the reign of King Egbert, and attention is frequently concentrated on post-Conquest and even contemporary history. No longer the outstanding figure of British history, Arthur, when he appears at all, is not even the *primus inter pares*; he is overshadowed by such kings as Havelock, Edgar and Edward the Confessor. From here to the somewhat inadequate Arthur of Middle English tradition, the Arthur of *The Avowing of King Arthur* or *The Awntyrs off Arthur*, is a short step.

Although he is no longer the emperor who defeats the Romans and conquers Gaul, as does the Arthur of the verse *Brut* tradition, Arthur in the prose tradition is still a local hero, the conqueror of Scotland, Wales and Ireland. More importantly, perhaps, he has become the hero of Arthurian romance, 'si merveillousement chevalerous qe parmy le mound home parlout de sa nobley et de la graunt genterie qi en luy fuit trové' (*so wonderfully chivalrous that men throughout the world spoke of his noble knights and of his own great nobility*; *Petit Bruit*, 12. 29–30). Some prose *Brut*s find space to mention Arthurian knights – Gauvain, Perceval – by name, but they do not expand on their deeds; it is the atmosphere of romance and chivalry which is required. Indeed, it is used simply as a distinguishing mark; Arthur is 'the chivalric', as Athelstan is 'the fair' and Ethelred is 'the bad'. Arthur thus takes his place in a list, a king with a single quality to distinguish him from all the other kings, who each in their turn have their own label. The Arthur of the prose *Brut* is the undistinguished figure of the chronicles, a sketch rather than a portrait. [PDG]

The Political Arthur

There is no proof that Geoffrey of Monmouth was consciously making a political statement in writing his *Historia*; it has indeed been suggested that the work was intended to be read as a parody, for humorous effect (Flint 1979). However, the writing of history, even in jest, always has political implications. Inasmuch as chronicles and histories are perceived as reflections of the past, they will be used as keys to an understanding, not only of the past, but of the present with its roots in that past, and be invoked to justify future plans and policies. Geoffrey of Monmouth's decision to give his work the form of a *historia* thus suggests concerns above and beyond the desire to gain preferment for an ecclesiastical benefice.[16]

The political circumstances in England when Geoffrey was composing his work were tense. Henry I, who died in 1135, shortly after the publication of the *Prophecies of Merlin* apparently, did not have a direct male heir to succeed him. He had designated his daughter Matilda as heir to the throne, but already during his lifetime it was clear that his choice would be hotly disputed by his nephew Stephen. So the dire consequences of dissension in the ruling family may be interpreted as a warning to Stephen, or indeed, as a warning to the entire royal clan (Tolhurst 1998). Seen in this light, the recurrence of female rulers in the *Historia*, all of them capable and worthy of wielding power, may be read as an indirect way of giving support to Matilda. This dimension would certainly not have been lost on Geoffrey's contemporary readers; for later translators and adapters of his work it would no longer have been relevant, at least until the accession to the throne of Elizabeth I, for whom these strong female rulers would have offered both models and precedents.

On a different level, relations with France were problematic. As Duke of Normandy, the King of England was technically a vassal of the King of France. A history in which kings of Britain repeatedly defeat the French with insulting ease would have been useful propaganda. Wace's *Roman de Rou* attests to an age-old antagonism between Normandy and France, a situation exacerbated by the marriage to Eleanor of Aquitaine of the future Henry II, who thus controlled more territories in France than the king himself. There is, therefore, an ideological divide in the way Geoffrey's image of the past would have been perceived, depending on whether the reader or adapter belonged to the Anglo-Norman or the Île-de-France spheres of influence. It was in the interests of Paris to view the *Historia* as an amusing collection of anecdotes from a distant past, devoid of any connection with the present day; hence the tendency in Continental manuscripts of the *Brut* to link the text with romances rather than histories. Conversely, one observes a keen interest in the material as history by English poets and historians of the thirteenth and fourteenth centuries.

The Anglo-Norman kings were also at a disadvantage compared to their French counterparts, in that they had no Charlemagne. Theirs was a relatively new dynasty and its coming to power was founded on William the Conqueror's forcible subduing of his future subjects. Geoffrey's new history provides Britain with a figurehead equal to Charlemagne, modelled indeed on Alexander the Great. Arthur is not a Norman, but neither, crucially, is he English, and through the putative Trojan ancestry of the British he is made the equal of any hero of classical antiquity. Moreover, through Arthur's blood ties with the kings of Brittany, Geoffrey allows for an alignment of the Celtic, pre-Anglo-Saxon population of Britain with William the Conqueror's Breton allies, who by the late 1130s would have become good Anglo-Norman barons. For Continental writers this dimension would have been secondary to Arthur's entertainment value; but Geoffrey's Anglo-Norman audience was quick to perceive the new legitimacy offered by the character.

Geoffrey's work had political overtones for another section of his readership: the Welsh. The *Historia* gives the Britons a long, successful and cultured past at odds with the image of the boorish Welshman current at the time and immortalized by Chrétien de Troyes's uncouth Perceval. Moreover, Geoffrey's underlying warnings against dissension would have taken on particular resonance within the context of the struggle of the Welsh princes against the Anglo-Norman kings in the early twelfth century. Outbreaks of revolt occurred in different parts of Wales, firstly in 1116, under the leadership of Gruffudd ap Rhys, then in the years following the death of Henry I. The figure of Arthur, under such circumstances, could be viewed as a threat to the Anglo-Norman rulers (Gillingham

1990). So the intended audience of the *Historia* might not have been the Anglo-Normans at all, but Geoffrey's own Welsh people; they did not heed the lesson, however, and the hopes of the uprisings in the 1130s foundered due to divisions among the Welsh princes.

The real power of Geoffrey's creation lies in the fact that he did not invent Arthur. Tales relating to the once and future king were already in circulation around Europe, and Arthur was a household name before the *Historia* was published. For the propaganda value of the Arthurian material to remain strong, it was necessary to ensure that its entertainment value be unimpaired, even as history. Wace and the Anglo-Norman translators and adapters of the *Historia* recognized this and exploited as many of the cues for amplification offered by Geoffrey as their narrative would allow. This means that, to the modern reader, these reworkings of the *Historia* frequently appear to cross the boundary from (supposed) history to fiction, and all too often they are assimilated to romances. But the chronicle format, with its recurrent themes throughout a long succession of reigns, raises questions that are not typically those of romance. With each episode a different light is shed on preceding events, and each colours those that follow. Arthur is no exception: any political or ideological interpretation of his reign has to take account of the context in which he arose. The way in which different writers viewed his predecessors and his successors had a direct bearing on the political or ideological message conveyed by his birth, rule and death. He is an important part of the whole, but still only a part. The sheer number of reigns and combinations of power patterns in the *Historia* made reappropriation relatively simple; a shift in emphasis from one aspect to another can unobtrusively change the flavour of the entire work.

The Anglo-Norman kings seem to have lost interest in the 'historical' Arthur quite rapidly: no royal commissions to update or rework Geoffrey's material were made after Wace's *Brut*. This may have been due to an awareness of the potentially dangerous implications of the character of Arthur, particularly with regard to the widespread belief in Arthur's return. The much-publicized 'discovery' of Arthur's grave in Glastonbury in 1190 can be seen as an attempt to put an end to the legend and relegate the once and future king firmly to the past. Equally, the increasing integration of the English into the ruling circles made the Celtic kings of Britain less politically useful to the crown. The patronage of Arthurian chronicles was taken over by the Anglo-Norman barons, whose specific agendas are reflected in the works they commissioned. The implicit advocacy of a strong royal power found in the *Historia* and retained by Wace in his *Brut* is thus radically undermined in the Anglo-Norman *Brut*s, where greater attention is given to episodes featuring kings such as Belinus or Cassibelaunus, who, in various ways, are shown to be dependent on the good will and support of their barons (Zatta 1998). The increased importance of these episodes (which, crucially, tend to be neglected by readers of all periods interested primarily in the figure of Arthur) results in the loss of some of Arthur's eminence in the Anglo-Norman prose *Brut*s.

The change in the balance of cultures in England during the thirteenth and four-teenth centuries eventually led to the abandonment of Anglo-Norman French as a medium of ideological expression, in favour of English. By the end of the Middle Ages French had become a foreign language, overwhelmingly employed on the Continent and therefore reflecting a different world-view; there the material of the *Historia* was perceived as scholarly, rather than political, as the history of the distant past of an alien people whose interest is subordinated to other narratives. The political Arthur must therefore be viewed as a British phenomenon, for in Britain there was a vested interest in exploiting the prestige and potential for prece-dent of this paragon of kingship, an interest which ensured that the 'chronicle' strand of Arthurian literature retained much of its political charge well into the Tudor period (see Bryan 1999, especially chapter 7). [FLS]

Notes

[1] For a discussion of the date of the *Historia*, see Wright edn 1984, xi–xvi.

[2] Quoted from Geoffrey's introductory dedication to the *Historia* (Thorpe transl., 51); all English translations of the *Historia* are from Thorpe.

[3] A photograph of the Modena archivolt is reproduced in Loomis ed. 1959*, between pages 60 and 61.

[4] Geoffrey's *Vita Merlini*, composed in Latin verse some twelve years after the *Historia*, attests to an enduring interest in the character of Merlin, but also presents a very different vision of the prophet. The wonder-child is now a hermit, a wild man of the forest aspiring to salvation. See *Geoffrey of Monmouth: Vita Merlini*, ed. and transl. by B. Clarke (Cardiff, 1973).

[5] William of Newburgh (1196–7) was one of the few to see through Geoffrey's narrative strat-egies, but his violent rejection of the *Historia* could be the consequence of his personal anti-Celtic agenda.

[6] Gaimar tells us in the prologue to his *Estoire des Engleis* that he had also composed (probably in the 1140s) an *Estoire des Bretuns*, now lost.

[7] 1174 being the date of the latest Bayeux charter in which Wace's name appears. On Wace's life, see Holmes 1967, Blanchet 1959 and Burgess 2002 (*Roman de Rou* transl.), xv–xxl.

[8] This, however, offered the cue for manuscript compilers to include Arthurian romances along-side the *Brut*, e.g. BNF, fr. 1450, in which the five romances of Chrétien de Troyes are inserted into Wace's *Brut*, at the point when the twelve-year peace is mentioned; see Chapter XI.

[9] There is some evidence for the existence of a number of other *Brut*s that have not survived (see Arnold edn of Wace's *Brut*, I, xcviii). It is also possible that the book Gaimar claims to have used as a source for the earlier section (now lost) of his *Estoire des Engleis* may be Geoffrey's (Short 1994, 327–8, 337–40).

[10] See Bell 1963, esp. 201. For Harley *Brut*, fragment 5, see Blakey edn; fragments 1–4 are tran-scribed in Damian-Grint 1994. See also Damian-Grint in Short ed. 1993 (esp. 94–5).

[11] Grout edn. See also Bell 1939; Grout 1985; 1988. On the language of the text, see Jenrich 1881.

[12] Another version is to be found in BL, MS Egerton 3028, but this is simply a heavily condensed version of Wace's text. See Damian-Grint in Short ed. 1993, 92.

[13] The two manuscripts are the Penrose manuscript (BL, Additional MS 45103), fols 86–97, and Lincoln Cathedral, Chapter Library, MS 104, fols 48–57. See Damian-Grint 1994, 375–6.

[14] For manuscripts of the *Roman de Rou*, see Holden edn, III, 19–24, and Burgess transl., xxv–xxvi. The sections written in Alexandrines are preserved only in a seventeenth-century copy (BNF, Duchesne 79).

[15] See Gillingham in Genet ed. 1997, 165–76 (esp. 167–9).

[16] On the political dimension of the *Historia*, see *Arthuriana*, 8: 4 (1998); esp. K. Robertson, 'Geoffrey of Monmouth and the Translation of Insular Historiography', 42–57, and M. Fries, 'The Arthurian Moment: History and Geoffrey's *Historia Regum Britannie*', 88–99.

Reference List

For items accompanied by an asterisk, see the General Bibliography.

Texts and Translations

Geoffrey of Monmouth

The Historia Regum Britannie of Geoffrey of Monmouth. Ed. by N. Wright: *I, Bern, Burgerbibliothek, MS 568* (Cambridge, 1984); II, *The First Variant Version: A Critical Edition* (Cambridge, 1988).

La Geste du Roi Artur selon le Roman de Brut de Wace et l'Historia Regum Britanniae de Geoffroy de Monmouth: édition bilingue. Transl. by E. Baumgartner and I. Short (Paris, 1993).

The History of the Kings of Britain. Transl. by L. Thorpe (Harmondsworth, 1966).

Gaimar

L'Estoire des Engleis by Geffrei Gaimar. Ed. by A. Bell, ANTS 14–16 (Oxford, 1960; repr. New York, 1971).

Wace

Wace, Roman de Brut. Ed. by I. D. O. Arnold, 2 vols, SATF (Paris, 1938–40). [Wace's *Brut*].

La Partie arthurienne du Roman de Brut. Ed. by I. D. O. Arnold and M. M. Pelan (Paris, 1962).

Wace's Roman de Brut: A History of the British. Ed. and transl. by J. E. Weiss (Exeter, 1999; 2nd edn, 2002).

La Geste du Roi Artur selon le Roman de Brut de Wace et l'Historia Regum Britanniae de Geoffroy de Monmouth. Transl. by E. Baumgartner and I. Short (Paris, 1993). Includes the text of the Arthurian section of the *Brut*.

Le Roman de Rou de Wace. Ed. by A. J. Holden, 3 vols, SATF (Paris, 1970–3).

Wace, The Roman de Rou, Translated by Glyn S. Burgess with the Text of Anthony J. Holden and Notes by Glyn S. Burgess and Elisabeth van Houts (St Helier, 2002).

The Brut Tradition

Bekker Fragment. Ed. by S. Lefèvre, 'Le Fragment Bekker et les anciennes versions françaises de l'*Historia Regum Britanniae*', *Rom*, 109 (1988), 225–46.

Brute d'Engleterre abregé. Ed. by E. Zettl, in *Anonymous Short English Metrical Chronicle* (London, 1935).

Brutus, Li rei de Engleterre, Le Livere de Reis de Engleterre. Ed. by C. Foltys (Berlin, 1962).

Harley *Brut*, fragment 5. Ed. by B. Blakey, 'The Harley *Brut*: An Early French Translation of Geoffrey of Monmouth's *Historia Regum Britanniae*', *Rom*, 82 (1961), 44–70.

Harley *Brut*, fragments 1–4. Transcribed in Damian-Grint 1994, Appendix II.

Harley Fragment. Ed. by Damian-Grint, in Short ed. 1993, 87–104.

Munich *Brut*. Ed. by P. B. Grout, Ph.D. thesis, London, 1980.

Rauf de Boun, *Le Petit Bruit*. Ed. by D. B. Tyson, ANTS, PTS 4 (London, 1987). [*Petit Bruit*].

Royal *Brut. An Anglo-Norman Brut (Royal 13, A.xxi)*. Ed. by A. Bell, ANTS 21–2 (Oxford, 1969).

Studies

Bell, A. 1939. 'The Munich *Brut* and the *Estoire des Bretuns*', *MLR*, 34, 321–54.

Bell 1963. 'The Royal *Brut* Interpolation', *Med. Aev*, 32, 190–202.

Blacker, J. 1994. *The Faces of Time: Portrayal of the Past in Old French and Latin Historical Narrative of the Anglo-Norman Regnum*, Austin, TX.

Blanchet, M.-Cl. 1959. 'Maistre Wace, trouvère normand', *MRom*, 9, 149–58.

Bryan, E. J. 1999. *Collaborative Meaning in Medieval Scribal Culture: The Otho La3amon*, Ann Arbor, MI.

Burch North, S. ed. 1988. *Studies in Medieval French Language and Literature Presented to Brian Woledge*, Geneva.

Busby, K., and N. J. Lacy eds 1994. *Conjunctures: Medieval Studies in Honor of Douglas Kelly*, Amsterdam.

Crisafulli, A. ed. 1964. *Linguistic and Literary Studies in Honor of Helmut A. Hatzfeld*, Washington DC.

Damian-Grint, P. 1994. 'Vernacular History in the Making: Anglo-Norman Verse Historiography in the Twelfth Century', Ph.D. thesis, London.

Damian-Grint 1996. 'Redating the Royal *Brut* Fragment', *Med. Aev*, 65, 280–5.

Damian-Grint 1999a. *The New Historians of the Twelfth-Century Renaissance: Inventing Vernacular Authority*, Woodbridge.

Damian-Grint 1999b. 'Translation as *enarratio* and Hermeneutic Theory in Twelfth-Century Vernacular Learned Literature', *Neophil*, 83, 349–67.

Dean, R. J. 1999. 'Chronicles', in *Anglo-Norman Literature: A Guide to Texts and Manuscripts*, London, 1–51.

Flint, V. I. J. 1979. 'The *Historia Regum Britanniae* of Geoffrey of Monmouth: Parody and its Purpose: A Suggestion', *Spec*, 54, 447–68.

Genet, J.-P. ed. 1997. *L'Histoire et les nouveaux publics dans l'Europe médiévale (XIIIe–XVe siècles)*, Paris.

Gillingham, J. 1990. 'The Context and Purposes of Geoffrey of Monmouth's *History of the Kings of Britain*', *ANS*, 13, 99–118.

Grout, P. B. 1985. 'The Author of the Munich *Brut*, his Latin Sources and Wace', *Med. Aev*, 54, 274–82.

Grout 1988. 'The Manuscript of the Munich *Brut* (Codex Gallicus 29 of the Bayerische Staatsbibliothek, Munich)', in Burch North ed. 1988, 49–58.

Holmes, U. T., Jr. 1964. 'The Anglo-Norman Rhymed Chronicle', in Crisafulli ed. 1964, 231–6.

Holmes 1967. 'Norman Literature and Wace', in W. Matthews ed. *Medieval Secular Literature: Four Essays*, Berkeley and Los Angeles, 46–67.

Jenrich, K. 1881. 'Die Mundart des Münchener *Brut*', Ph.D. thesis, London.

Loomis, R. S. 1959. 'The Oral Diffusion of the Arthurian Legend', in Loomis ed. 1959*, 52–63.

Piggott, S. 1941. 'The Sources of Geoffrey of Monmouth', *Antiquity*, 15, 269–86.

Short, I. ed. 1993. *Anglo-Norman Anniversary Essays*, London.

Short 1994. 'Gaimar's Epilogue and Geoffrey of Monmouth's *Liber vetustissimus*', *Spec*, 69, 323–43.

Spiegel, G. 1993. *Romancing the Past: The Rise of Vernacular Prose Historiography in Thirteenth-Century France*, Berkeley and Los Angeles.

Tatlock, J. S. P. 1950. *The Legendary History of Britain: Geoffrey of Monmouth's Historia Regum Britanniae and its Early Vernacular Versions*, Berkeley.

Tolhurst, F. 1998. 'The Britons as Hebrews, Romans, and Normans: Geoffrey of Monmouth's British Epic and Reflections of Empress Matilda', *Arthuriana*, 8: 4, 69–87.

Tyson, D. B. 1979. 'Patronage of French Vernacular History Writers in the Twelfth and Thirteenth Centuries', *Rom*, 100, 180–222.

Zatta, J. 1998. 'Translating the *Historia*: The Ideological Transformation of the *Historia Regum Britannie* in Twelfth-Century Vernacular Chronicles', *Arthuriana*, 8: 4, 148–61.

III

THE TRISTAN LEGEND IN OLD FRENCH VERSE

Tony Hunt and Geoffrey Bromiley

Although the Tristan legend is not always thought of as Arthurian, it belongs to the Celtic *matière de Bretagne* which provided important source material for French Arthurian romances. What were probably, in their original form, the longest versions of the legend in Old French verse, those by Beroul and Thomas, both allot a small role to King Arthur, whilst the thirteenth-century prose romance (see chapter VIII) represents a massive combination of the Tristan legend with that of Arthur.

The early French Tristan material in verse has survived in the form of two fragmentary romances and some shorter, episodic texts. Whether these now diverging remnants derive directly from a once complete and fully developed *Urtext* (original version), or are evidence of an expanding and constantly diversifying body of stories, has been a matter for scholarly debate. Attempts to complete the surviving fragments, at least notionally, have to rely on the evidence of the more complete adaptations of the French romances into medieval German, English and Norse. Nowadays, critics prefer to concentrate on the aesthetic and ideological qualities of the extant works, rather than to speculate on their origins. It has been traditional, but by no means mandatory, for scholars since Bédier to divide the surviving Tristan texts into two groups representing two versions of the story. The 'version commune', or popular version supposedly performed by *jongleurs*, is said to be exemplified by Beroul, Eilhart von Oberg and the *Folie Tristan de Berne*; the 'version courtoise' is primarily exemplified by Thomas's romance, the *Folie Tristan d'Oxford* and foreign adaptations of Thomas: Gottfried von Straßburg's German *Tristan* (*c*.1210), Brother Robert's Norse *Tristramssaga* (1226) and the fourteenth-century English *Sir Tristrem*. More recently, however, the epithets 'épique' and either 'lyrique' or 'cléricale' have been employed to describe the versions by Beroul and Thomas respectively, whilst the later prose romance has more accurately been called a 'version chevaleresque' (Payen edn, vii). The following discussion will treat the influential longer verse romances by Beroul and Thomas, followed by the shorter episodic verse texts, all witnesses to the popularity of the Tristan legend within French Arthurian literature.

Beroul

The fragment of 4,485 lines represented by a single extant manuscript, BNF, fr. 2171, supplies the name 'Berox' (Beroul) in two third-person references (Ewert edn, 1268, 1790) which leave it uncertain whether the reference is to a reciter of the work, to the fictional narrator, to the author or to a source. The intriguing attribution in the Yale manuscript of the Anglo-Norman *Purgatoire de saint Patrice* to a 'Beros'[1] seems less ambiguous, though equally difficult when it comes to identification. Nevertheless, Beroul will continue to serve as a convenient label for the more 'epic' version of the Tristan legend in Old French. Despite its broad correspondence, for the first 3,000 lines, with the version dubbed 'commune' (Frappier 1963) and represented by Eilhart von Oberg, there is no way of objectively resolving the riddle of the authorship of the fragment, which lacks both a beginning and an end. For some (Raynaud de Lage 1958, 1964; Reid 1965) the fragment is the work of two authors, with a change at line 2765. For others (Hanoset 1961; Ménage 1974) it is merely part of a complete version, most of which is lost, but which may have run, according to one calculation (Illingworth 1985, 12), to some 17,000 lines. For another group (e.g. Ribard 1979, 234) its features of repetition, parallelism and cyclical structures suggest a distinct unity, possibly representing almost all of the legend which 'Beroul' chose to treat (with an abrupt ending replacing Tristan in exile and his marriage to the second Yseut).[2] Yet another school of critics would see in the fragment the work of a *remanieur* (reviser) who assembled a series of orally transmitted episodes (Heinzel 1869).

It is generally accepted that medieval poems were not necessarily recited in full and that recorded repertoires often seem to indicate selected episodes rather than complete narratives. An increasing appreciation of the poem's artistry has helped to promote the view that it is a unitary work, an estimate reinforced by critical improvements to the readings offered by the slovenly manuscript copy, which belongs to the second half of the thirteenth century. All attempts at dating the poem, especially from internal allusions, have proved precarious, and a date in the second half of the twelfth century is as far as one can reliably go, unless one regards the reference to Malpertis (4285) as a definite allusion to the *Roman de Renart* and considers, moreover, the 'branch' of that work in which it is located to be firmly dated to the period 1176–80. On linguistic grounds, it seems clear that Beroul came from the western dialect area, possibly from southern Normandy; a period of residence in England is likely, but uncertain.

Beroul's fragment opens with the famous scene, immortalized by medieval iconography, in which King Mark hides in a tree in order to spy upon the lovers' tryst.[3] He is persuaded, however, by Yseut's verbal ambiguity that his nephew and wife are innocent. Another trap set by the evil dwarf Frocin almost enables the king to catch the lovers *in flagrante delicto*, though Tristan escapes punishment by leaping from a chapel and then rescues Yseut, whom Mark had delivered up to the lust of a band of lepers as a fate even worse than burning at the stake. There then ensues a long period of outlawry in the forest of Morrois with only the aid of Governal (Tristan's mentor), Husdent (a dog who hunts without barking) and a bow rigged up to kill game. During a chance meeting, the hermit Ogrin fails to convince the lovers to repent and return to Mark. The latter, tipped off by a forester, finds them in the forest, but noting Tristan's sword lying between his nephew and wife, who are fully clothed, he shows mercy towards them, exchanging swords and rings and leaving his gloves to protect Yseut from the sun. Unfortunately, the lovers interpret his ambiguous signs as hostility, and flee.

One day the love potion (which Beroul seems to imply was the cause of their love, yet it appears to last for only three years) wanes, and the lovers return to Ogrin to seek reconciliation with Mark. Tristan is banished, but Yseut returns to Mark until his barons convince him to procure further proof of her innocence. As a result of an elaborate ruse set up by Yseut and witnessed by King Arthur, the queen is able to swear that no man, apart from her husband and the leper who carried her across a ford at the Mal Pas, had been between her thighs. The leper, however, is Tristan in disguise. After Yseut's verbal defence, the barons continue to spy on the lovers, who meet secretly, and the Beroul fragment breaks off just as Tristan and Yseut have taken their revenge on two of the barons, the dwarf having met his death earlier after revealing that King Mark had horse's ears!

Despite a sometimes extravagantly judgemental narrator, who seems to take moral issues as cut-and-dried (though not necessarily according to conventional values), the poem represents a carefully and sensitively articulated exploration of the conflict of appearances and reality, the problems of reading signs and the challenge of how to access moral truth, all three issues, of course, being linked. The fundamental structure of the work is based on a dialectical opposition which offers a moral paradox. On the one hand, notwithstanding their constant characterization as 'felons', the barons appear to be loyal and acting in accordance with their feudal duty by 'advising' Mark of the adultery between his wife and nephew; conversely, the lovers seem to be totally disloyal in continuing, whilst at the same time denying, their adultery. On the other hand, the barons' true relationship with their lord is shown not to be one of loyalty: they threaten to withdraw from his service and make war on him, and their treatment of Frocin, the dwarf, is both dishonourable in itself and disloyal to Mark; instead the barons are motivated by self-interest, for they wish to rid themselves of Tristan, out of jealousy for his prowess (773–4). They remain totally indifferent to their monarch's reconciliation with the lovers, mediated by Ogrin, who seems to recognize the moral justice of such an arrangement, and the barons continue to demand, by extortion, the exiling of Tristan. Against this, the lovers, who have keenly desired the reconciliation with Mark and the return to normality at court, do all in their power to conceal from him the existence of the potion and its consequences; administered in error on their return from Ireland, the potion suspends all moral responsibility for three years, after which its effects wear off. Tristan and Yseut see clearly that its exculpatory force pales into insignificance compared with the damage which would be caused by confirmation of its reality. Despite Mark's consistent denial to his nephew of an *escondit* (defence), his intended punishment of the queen without trial, and the sadistic brutality of his handing over his wife to the lepers, the lovers display no animosity and make no criticism of him, thus exhibiting extraordinary equanimity.

Mark is faced with a *jeu parti* (625, 3077): an impossible choice between his dependence on the barons and his love for his wife and nephew. Politically and legally, however, he cannot rely on hearsay evidence, which would be inadmissible in court, and must therefore cling to the idea that 'seeing is believing', hence the rhetorical elaboration of the terms *voir* and *savoir*. That in the person of a desperately anxious man this notion may be reversed into 'believing is seeing' is illustrated by the central episode of the poem: the king's discovery of the lovers in the forest (Hunt 1998). Potentially this is the most dramatic, emotional and decisive episode of the whole work. In fact, it takes place with minimal indication of any of these properties. Mark reasons from his observation of the lovers with almost forensic logic. The only sign of emotion comes in an assertion by him that he has taken pity on the lovers (2024), not through any depicted experience. The central irony is obvious: on the one occasion that Mark seeks to behave dispassionately, to be ruled by his head rather than by his heart, he gets everything wrong. He misinterprets the significance of the lovers' posture and the unsheathed sword, whilst they in turn misinterpret the 'demostrance' (2020), involving sword, ring and glove, intended for them. They conclude that he has gone to get reinforcements for a final assault on them rather than recognize his intended meaning, which is to demonstrate that he has had mercy on them. This double misunderstanding at a key moment in the poem seems to establish incontestably that the interpretation of signs is a central concern of the work.

In the courtly world of conspicuous display and exuberant splendour it was perhaps valuable to urge the penetration of outward appearances, or *senblant*. The opening scene of Beroul's fragment depicting Mark in the tree spying on the lovers below in the orchard reveals the king's dependence on appearances in terms which are echoed in the discovery scene; such verbal echoes are a significant part of Beroul's artistry (see 299ff., 2006ff. and cf. 496ff.). He is shown already repenting his previous judgement in language which anticipates his later reaction to King Arthur's criticism of him at the Mal Pas (273, 308, 4172ff.). The irony of his reaction to the events of the orchard scene is expressed in the rhyming of 'veü' (*seen*) and 'deceü' (*deceived*) (265–6).

This mismatch of surface appearances and deeper moral reality leads us to the third theme of the poem: the problem of gaining access to that reality so that it may be recognized. Although to all appearances the lovers are guilty, Beroul implies that the moral reality is different. The crucial element here is the potion. The potion and the concomitant suffering and deprivation it inflicts on the lovers are a disaster: in Yseut's words, 'ce fu pechiez' (*it was a terrible misfortune*, 1415), not only for the lovers, but potentially for Mark, since the straight fact of adultery, however induced, makes Mark's position precarious in the extreme. It follows that it must never be publicly revealed or confirmed. Accordingly, the hermit Ogrin agrees to tell a white lie ('par bel mentir', 2354). He has been forthright to the lovers and tried to insist on repentance, but such a step is of no avail when it comes to suppressing the 'honte' (*shame*) and 'mal' (*harm*) which would befall Mark, whom Ogrin has every right to protect. Yseut is intelligent and principled in rejecting the notion of repentance, since neither of the lovers bears the slightest responsibility for the potion. How or why, then, should Mark be expected to suffer? Given their limited free will, the lovers are blameless and hence recognize no moral imperative to confess to the king. Beroul's strategy is rendered more complicated by his remarkable innovation of limiting the potion's compulsive power to three years. The moral paradox, or opposition of the barons' disloyalty and the lovers' loyalty, risks being annulled. Beroul's decision, though paralleled by Eilhart, can only have been conceived as an attempt to subject the lovers' subsequent behaviour to moral evaluation. Once the effects of the potion have worn off, Yseut tells Ogrin that she and Tristan are no longer having sexual relations (2329–30). Is she telling the truth? Though Beroul provides us with many examples of beneficent deception, he does not depict lying. On the one occasion when there is an unambiguous case of lying, Brengain's pretence that she has fallen out with Tristan, the narrator draws attention to it and indignantly brands her a liar (519ff.). Lying has never been a very productive literary device, whereas the exploitation of ambiguity can have fascinating moral and narrative ramifications, as in the case of Yseut's two ambiguous oaths. The cynical interpretation of the post-potion sequence in Beroul is that the lovers continue to enjoy sexual relations, thus reducing to a lie Yseut's protestation of chastity (2329–30). This interpretation is largely based on an inference, namely that since the lovers' continued meetings are clandestine, the lovers must be guilty. The counter-argument would be that the clandestine nature of the meetings results from the lovers' continuing persecution by the barons, who do not recognize the reconciliation with Mark and continue to seek the banishment of Tristan, come what may. The lovers simply cannot afford to be seen together by such obviously malicious royal advisers.

Against this background the narrator's judgements, favourable to the lovers, hostile to the barons, critical of Mark, will thus bear more penetrating scrutiny than has hitherto been applied. For all the unenviability of Mark's position, it cannot be overlooked that he is roundly criticized for his credulousness concerning the barons by King Arthur (4144ff.), who must surely represent the ultimate authority in the context of courtly romance. Mark's admission that he assented to the barons' demands against his better judgement (4170–80) is morally damaging and can only lead to greater sympathy for the lovers. Beroul looks at human behaviour from the outside, giving due weight to circumstances, and assessing the moral position of the lovers in a situation where deception is their only weapon against injustice. The conflict is essentially an external one, to which Mark holds the key. This is a quite different perspective from that offered by Thomas, who, like a psychologist, examines the inner life of the participants, the unruliness of their will and the confusion of their feelings. The difference between outer conflict and inner conflict is also reflected in the fact that Beroul has no special concept of love (he is much more concerned with justice, infringed at key points by Mark, despite the appeals of Dinas, 1088ff., 1133ff., 2532ff.) whereas Thomas can use his idea of *fin'amor* as at least offering one criterion for the judgement of inner states. In the final analysis, Beroul's version of the legend is a comedy of joint triumph by the lovers, whilst Thomas's romance is a tragedy of failed communication.

On the literary side, it may be said that Beroul mixes all the genres. Whilst the first part of his work has an obviously episodic structure, its brief narrative summaries and calls to attention reflecting the origins of many of his motifs in folklore, the second part, with the introduction of Arthur, exhibits the more leisurely pace of the courtly romance. Yet both parts lack the unifying thread of a quest or a search for identity. Generically, his *Tristran* is a hybrid, which invites us to see beyond the constraints or conventions of a single genre (Busby 1989a). Thematic, lexical and stylistic debts to the love lyric are evident, the barons taking the role of the 'losengeors' (*treacherous flatterers*, 427, 1056), whilst at the same time participating in a feudal nexus of enmity, treachery and revenge, which recalls the epic. The epic also provides precedents for the solidarity between narrator and audience (addressed as *seignors*), repeated phraseology resembling formulaic diction and names like Guenelon, Otran and Bel Joëor (Tristan's horse). Some of the humour, bordering on the scabrous, evokes the mood of the *fabliaux*. By this eclectic mixture of elements Beroul has sought to attract as wide an audience as possible for his version of the celebrated legend, for he is at pains to tackle the problems of reading signs and of dependence on appearances without being constrained by specific generic expectations. Life is depicted in its dramatic, dynamic and unrestrained variety. The guiding intelligence, however, which conceals itself beneath apparent indications of cynicism, frivolity or excitement, is manifested in the tightly controlled network of thematic duplication, lexical repetitions, structural parallels and cyclical patterns (Illingworth

1985). In neither Beroul nor Thomas is there any depiction of ennobling love: Beroul depicts persecuted love and offers a robust defence, emotional and moral, in which even God is implicated. God and the saints are constantly invoked in the poem and Tristan's successful leap from the chapel is attributed to His intervention, an attribution accepted by Ogrin. The vitality of Beroul's account proscribes any association of love with death, and triumph seems always to be within the lovers' reach. Trickery and transgression are assimilated to the idea of moral justice in what is seen as an unjust world, depicted in all its crudeness and violence. Thomas, on the other hand, whose account is much more static, depicts a *self*-destructive love in a psychological sphere from which God is largely absent; he depicts in fact a much bleaker universe than Beroul; the moral landscape is emptier and it is one in which the lovers renounce life. Neither poet can be said in any way to celebrate love or portray its joys. [TH]

Thomas

The *Tristan* of Thomas (the form 'Tristran' is frequently encountered in the manuscripts) is represented by ten fragments (three of which perished in 1870) drawn from six manuscripts, for the most part Anglo-Norman, totalling 3,298 lines.[4] It is estimated that this total constitutes about one quarter of the complete original. The earliest manuscript, Oxford, Bodleian Library, MS French d. 16, which contains the two 'Sneyd' fragments, dates from the end of the twelfth century. The Cambridge, Turin, Strasbourg (now lost), Douce and Carlisle fragments were produced in the thirteenth century. From the textual point of view the copies themselves are disappointingly mediocre, though for the most part beautifully written. They furnish, completely or imperfectly, six narrative episodes from the last third of the romance, the location of which is best indicated by the chapters of the Norse *Tristramssaga* (indicated here by the siglum S), which was based on Thomas and offers the only complete version of the story to survive. The text of Thomas covers the following episodes, four of which survive in single copies: (i) the lovers' exchanges after drinking the potion and the marriage night in which Brengain is substituted for Yseut (S chapter 46); (ii) the lovers' meeting and valediction in the orchard (S chapter 67); (iii) Tristan's reflections on the idea of marriage to Yseut of the White Hands and the wedding (S chapters 69–70); (iv) the Hall of Statues (S chapters 80–2); (v) the Queen's Procession (S chapter 87); (vi) the concluding sequence of events which contains the quarrel between Queen Yseut and Brengain and the latter's interview with Mark (S chapters 89–90); Tristan's visit to the court in disguise and his refuge in the manner of St Alexis (S chapters 90–2); Thomas's digression on his treatment of the story and his fidelity to a poet called 'Breri'; Tristan's and Kaherdin's revenge on their enemies, killing Cariado (S chapter 93); Tristan's meeting with Tristran le Nain (essentially invented by Thomas; there are two Tristans as there are two Yseuts!) and their fight with Estout l'Orguilleux and his brothers, leading to Tristan's injury (S chapters 94–5); Tristan's sending of Caerdin to summon Queen Yseut to his aid (S chapter 96); the queen's voyage (S chapters 97–8) and the lie told by Yseut of the White Hands about the colour of the sails (S chapter 99); the death of the lovers (S chapters 99–101).

The dating of Thomas's *Tristan* has divided scholars into those who favour the 1150s (*terminus ad quem* 1157) and those who propose the 1170s (with possible links to Henry II and Eleanor of Aquitaine) or the 1180s. Linguistically and stylistically conservative features in Thomas have been used to defend the earlier dating, but no argument has proved decisive. Thomas names himself in two places, including the epilogue, but none of his occasional personal statements provides us with factual details. Another contentious issue is Thomas's attitude to love. There has been a move away from Frappier's idea (1964) that Thomas glorifies *fin'amor* and its ideology, a move which has led to two opposing arguments: one is that Thomas displays a negative view of earthly love and wrings his clerical hands in frustration at the sterility of the four protagonists' situations (Hunt 1981); the other is that Thomas has no specific concept of love, but is concerned with the broader issue of the 'unruly will', as expressed by Augustine's *velit* and *potest* and by Thomas's opposition of *voleir* and *poeir* (Adams 1999). Equally divergent are views on the function of the potion. Frappier (1964) believed, on the strength of Tristan's message to the queen in the concluding fragment, that Tristan and Yseut fell in love before drinking the potion, which thus becomes purely symbolic of their 'amur fine et veraie' (*pure true love*, p. 134, l. 1219). However, this view has proved vulnerable to criticism (Cormier 1980).

It is noteworthy that Mark belongs to a generation after King Arthur, rather than being coeval, as in Beroul. He is also depicted as King of England, and there are possibly intended parallels with Henry II. The traditional topography, Tintagel, Caerleon, Logres, is ignored, and London becomes the site of Mark's court. Versions of the *Tristan* incorporating changes such as these were probably superseded in public favour by the prose romances of the thirteenth century, which sought to reunite the worlds of Tristan and Arthur.

There is no doubt that the *Saga* provides an indispensable outline of the events covered by Thomas, who himself seems to have aimed for a simplified, more coherent narrative than some of the other versions in circulation, albeit admitting the occasional deviation, as in the episode dealing with Arthur drawn from Wace, an example of *entrelacement* which the narrator admits is not really part of his story (p. 62, l. 729). There is a particularly detailed correspondence between the Carlisle fragment and chapter 46 of the *Saga*. But the *Saga* poet habitually abbreviates, to the point of near omission, precisely those elements which are uniquely characteristic of Thomas, namely his penchant for psychological dissection and moral commentary. The most striking case is the extensive moral debate which precedes Tristan's marriage to Yseut aux Blanches Mains. It begins with a monologue of 178 lines culminating in his decision to marry, and is followed by fifty lines of narratorial commentary on Tristan's decision. This leads to the debate being opened out by the narrator's *excursus* on 'novelerie' (*fickleness*), to which so many people fall victim. This digression holds a central position in the debate, for it is followed by more narratorial commentary on the specific situation of Tristan and by another monologue of exactly the same length (178 lines) as the one which opened the debate; the structuring of this extensive debate could scarcely be more carefully calculated. In the *Saga* it is summarized in no more than a dozen lines at the end of chapter 69, displaying that same economy of treatment which Thomas applies to straight narrative – here the marriage service, wedding night and nocturnal recreation of the partners – an abbreviating approach which he explicitly acknowledges at the beginning of the episode of the Queen's Procession (p. 80, ll. 5ff.).

Similarly, the Hall of Statues episode, which, like the opening orchard scene, Thomas seems to have invented, despite suggestions redolent of Mariolatry, calls forth a systematic analysis of the amatory sufferings first of Tristan, then of all four protagonists: Mark, Queen Yseut, Tristan and Yseut aux Blanches Mains: 'Entre ces quatre ot estrange amor' (*the love each of the four experienced was a strange one*, p. 72, l. 71). In 133 lines there is a full exploration of the paradoxes of the situation leading to the narrator's agnostic conclusion that he is in no position to judge who suffered most, since he has no experience of his own to go on. There is none of this in the *Saga*. In the last part of Thomas's romance there is a similar pessimistic *divisio* (separation into cases) concerning Queen Yseut, Tristan, Mark and Cariado, amounting to twenty lines; this, equally, finds no echo in the *Saga*. In addition to these passages which place Thomas in the long line of French *moralistes*, there are two *excursus* on envy and anger which show him as a *moralisant*. The first occurs after the passage, based on Wace's *Brut*, describing Tristan's victory over the nephew of Orgillos and the wound he sustains. That is the last Yseut has heard of Tristan, for, as the narrator reports in a twenty-six-line digression on envy (p. 63, ll. 755ff.), people enjoy spreading bad news rather than good news. Another digression, thirteen lines on woman's anger (p. 139, ll. 1323ff.), inspired by *Ecclesiasticus* 25:23, is proleptically placed when Tristan explains to Kaherdin the proposed significance of the black and white sails as his friend departs to summon the queen to Tristan's aid.

It is difficult to avoid the conclusion that Thomas is a pessimistic commentator on the vicissitudes of earthly love and on humans' propensity to create problems whilst believing that they have found solutions. Despite the suffering which she has in common with the others, Yseut aux Blanches Mains is, before the end, blameless, and her misery seems quite unmerited. Thomas's narrator somewhat insensitively turns to conventional misogyny to condemn her lie, though simultaneously retracting his condemnation as not his business (p. 140, ll. 1334–5), just as earlier, in the *excursus* on *novelerie*, he exploited an Ovidian commonplace about the changeability of women, whilst adding 'but what do I know about it?' (p. 45, l. 291). Despite the thoroughgoing analysis of interior states, which is the hallmark of Thomas's *Tristan*, the narrator seems anxious to appear as an outside observer, on the sidelines so far as personal experience of love and secular activities is concerned, notwithstanding the fact that amatory dialogue here finds one of its earliest expressions in Old French literature. After the analysis of the 'estrange amor' experienced by the four protagonists (p. 72, l. 71), it is proposed that lovers should determine the conclusions to be drawn, the narrator arguing that he cannot judge, for it is beyond his experience; opinion should be left to those equipped to make such judgements. The narrator disclaims all knowledge of what pleasure Tristan and Yseut aux Blanches Mains may have enjoyed together in bed.

What, then, attracted Thomas to the Tristan legend? There is more *dolur* (suffering) than *amur* (love) in his poem (the two words are often together at the rhyme, as in the concluding couplet). The lexis is dominated by expressions denoting gloom and melancholy. Thomas's fundamental pessimism cannot be denied; one thinks of the confrontation of Yseut and Cariado and its consequences, of the violent quarrel between Brengain and her mistress and of the unedifying jealousy which leads Yseut aux Blanches Mains to lie about the sails. In addition, Thomas has a strong sense of interpretative rectitude and criticizes the versions of others. In an *excursus* addressed to the audience (*seignurs*), in which he names himself, he begins by affirming his intention not to overload the story with extraneous detail, pointing out that there are many divergent forms of the tale in circulation, for he is himself familiar with a number of oral and written versions. He wishes to follow 'Breri', who knew all the stories relating to the kings and counts of Britain. The Welsh latimer known as 'Bledhericus' (Bledri ap Cadivor, *c.*1075–1133) is a familiar figure from the court at Poitiers (Bullock-Davies 1966). On a point of rationality Thomas is unyielding: he rejects any suggestion that it was Governal who was sent to England to fetch Yseut, for he was too well known and hated by the king to have remained unrecognized. The error seems obvious to Thomas, but he will not argue with those who persist in it: 'La raisun s'i provera ben!' (*the tale* [or *reason*] *will bear me out*, p. 121, l. 884). The only other time Thomas names himself is in his epilogue, where he repeats his claim to have held to the truth. The dialectic which marks so much of Thomas's commentary in the body of the romance seems to survive in the dichotomous pairing, rather than synonymic pairing, as some think, of the 'lovers' to whom the work is addressed. Both those who are happy and those who are troubled in love will draw strength (*confort*), from the example contained in this tale, against 'change', 'tort', 'paine', 'dolur' and 'engins d'amur' (*mutability, wrong, travail, suffering* and *the ruses of love*). These are all key terms exploited in the body of the poem and suggest that Thomas wrote his version of the Tristan and Yseut legend as a negative exemplum, in something of the same spirit in which Heinrich von Freiberg completed Gottfried's poem at the court of Wenzel II a century later.[5]

Whether or not it is agreed that Thomas wrote his poem as a *consolatio*, recording those trials and tribulations inextricably linked with love which are best avoided, it cannot be doubted that he was a cleric, who had studied logic in the schools, and who wrote in the *contemptus mundi* (*contempt for the world*) tradition. His rhetorical virtuosity is remarkable and rivalled only by that of Chrétien in his neo-*Tristan*, *Cligés*. In both, arduous logical reasoning is depicted as ironically unproductive. One critic justly observes of Thomas:

> The language of argument dominates the poem. Abstract terms, learned syntax, and syllogistic reasoning contribute to a general impression of detachment, of intellectual analysis. Multiple repetitions give almost pedantic emphasis to problems and conclusions. (Crane 1986, 150)

In Thomas the use of antithesis is disjunctive and analytic, whereas in Gottfried it is conjunctive and synthetic, an instrument in the German author's transcendental, mystical conception of unity in love. In Thomas opposition tends to duality, towards an isolating style, rather than the unifying one aimed for by Gottfried. Technical devices of repetition and amplification in Thomas follow the example of Wace's *Brut* and the *romans d'antiquité*, but in a more sustained form. The constructions Thomas exploits unremittingly are parallelism and antithesis: 'Fuir deport et querre eschil, / Guerpir joie, sievre peril' (*flee enjoyment and seek out suffering, leave joy and follow pain*, Cambridge, 27–8); parallelism between different speeches: Tristan: 'Tel duel ai por la departie, / Ja n'avrai hait jor de ma vie' (*I am so upset at leaving that I shall never more be joyful*, Cambridge, 29ff.) and Yseut: 'Tel paine ai de la desevranche, / Ja n'avrai mais, amis, deport' (*I suffer such pain at parting that I shall never, my beloved, experience pleasure again*, Cambridge, 43). In Beroul the lovers appear most frequently together; in Thomas they are usually apart. In the opening debate on marriage there are three parallel *résumés* (Sneyd 1, 213ff., 297ff., 349ff.) representing the technique of *interpretatio, frequentatio* or *expolitio*. The various figures of repetition (*annominatio, traductio, anaphora, anadiplosis, chiasmus*) occur with a striking density and the use of contrast (*contentio*), especially in dialectically framed monologues, recalls the *Roman d'Eneas*. Thomas also makes use of logical markers, such as *pur ço*, and the figure of *conclusio*. These techniques are common to both the characters' speeches and the narrator's commentary, which sometimes seem stylistically indistinguishable.

Whilst Beroul caters to a varied audience who, he hopes, will keep up with the plot and enter into the task of reading signs and desiring justice, Thomas is a more reflective analyst, introspective, sceptical and generally diffident about love, anxious to distinguish concupiscence (*voleir*) from the more elevated yearning he calls *desir*, and to subject both to the intellectual control of *raisun*. [TH]

The Episodic Tristan Texts: The *Folies Tristan, Chevrefoil, Tristan Rossignol, Tristan Menestrel*[6]

The *Folie Tristan de Berne* and the *Folie Tristan d'Oxford*, so named because of the locations of the two complete extant manuscripts, share a common scenario. Tristan has been expelled from Mark's court and living for some time in Brittany, whilst Yseut remains in Cornwall, closely guarded by King Mark. Anxious to see the queen again, Tristan decides to visit her and to adopt the disguise of a fool. When he arrives in Cornwall, the people mock him, but eventually he is able to reach the royal court. There, Tristan is interrogated by King Mark and answers in the manner of a fool, but inserts into his responses references to the life he has shared with the queen which would help her to recognize his true identity. The king eventually goes off to hunt, while the plainly disturbed Yseut, after retiring to her private room, has Brengain summon the fool to her. In the queen's presence, Tristan continues to make allusions to their former life together and Yseut, after some initial resistance, is able to acknowledge that the fool is her lover.

In the context of the Tristan legend this episode takes place at a fairly advanced stage: Tristan is in Brittany, associated with Kaherdin, and, as is made explicit in the Bern *Folie* at least, married to the second Yseut (aux Blanches Mains). The Tristan material at this point presents a number of returns by the disguised hero to see Yseut, and this is just one of the variations on this theme. In the Douce fragment of Thomas's poem, for example, Tristan visits Yseut disguised as a leper, and a number of German works (Eilhart's version of the legend, the continuations of Gottfried von Straßburg by Ulrich von Türheim and Heinrich von Freiberg) tell of Tristan's return precisely in the guise of a fool. But what distinguishes our two French *Folie* poems from these other texts is the wealth of allusions made by the hero to the life he previously shared with Yseut, which evoke, both for the queen and for the audience or reader, much of the substance of the story so far.

Notwithstanding their obvious affinity, these are two separate texts. The Anglo-Norman *Folie Tristan d'Oxford* is represented by a single manuscript, dating from the second half of the thirteenth century: Oxford, Bodleian Library, MS Douce d. 6 (significantly in the same manuscript which contains a long fragment of Thomas's romance). The *Folie Tristan de Berne* is again found in its entirety in just one, early fourteenth-century manuscript, Bern, Burgerbibliothek, MS 354 (Rychner 1984), but a fragment of sixty-one lines found in Cambridge (Cambridge, Fitzwilliam Museum, MS 302), which describes the fool's arrival at Mark's court and the early allusions he makes, has also been published (Dean and Kennedy edn); editors now draw upon this fragment to fill lacunae and to correct certain errors in the Bern manuscript, which is universally acknowledged as far from perfect. Modern editors have also inevitably had to concern themselves with the relationship between the two poems. Bédier (1907, vi–vii, 82–3) deemed it possible either that one of the two poems had imitated the other, or that both were independent derivatives of a lost poem, but he was firmly of the view that the Bern *Folie* reflected knowledge of the material in Beroul's poem (or, at least, a poem very similar to Beroul), whereas the Oxford *Folie* drew upon Thomas. Hoepffner (edns 1934 and 1938), seeing no need to envisage the existence of a common archetype, suggested that the Bern *Folie* was directly inspired by Beroul and that it was then followed and imitated by the Oxford *Folie*, which incorporated material drawn from Thomas. Lecoy (edn 1994, 10), however, while recognizing the similarity between the two texts and supporting the view that one was inspired by Beroul and the other by Thomas, was reluctant to commit himself further on the issue of a possible common source and on the question of composition. Demaules, on the other hand, emphasizes (edn, 1313) the closeness of the two poems to Beroul and Thomas, but revives the idea, on new but rather insubstantial grounds, that both poems are representatives of a lost original, recast independently by their authors.

Whatever the exact relationship between the poems, it is nonetheless important that the two texts should be judged on their individual merits; they may share the same scenario, but there are appreciable differences between them. In the Bern *Folie* (*Fb*), the allusions to earlier events do seem to have been inspired by Beroul's poem (*B*), by a version close to Beroul, or, at the very least, by the *version commune*, the 'non-courtly' Tristan texts. In support of this view, one can point specifically to incidents recalled by the 'fool' which are not found in the *version courtoise*: for example, when Tristan finds himself alone with Yseut, he alludes, in quick succession, to the 'Saut Tristran' (*Tristan's Leap*), the handing over of Yseut to the lepers and her liberation from their clutches, and to the hermit Ogrin, a significant figure, but only in Beroul's version of the legend (*Fb*, 457–75). Other minor details might also be invoked: Dinas figures here (*Fb*, 33), but not in Thomas's poem, and the reference to Saint Sanson (*Fb*, 28) recalls the scene in Beroul when Yseut is restored to Mark and is received at the church dedicated to that saint (*B*, 2973). Moreover, the dénouement of the poem, where the dog Husdent is joyfully reunited with his master (*Fb*, 496–528), is again strongly reminiscent of the scene in Beroul in which the dog, released from captivity, joins the lovers in the Forest of Morrois (*B*, 1541–8).

In some quarters the Bern *Folie* has been harshly criticized, notably for the way in which the allusions in the text are presented: the phrase 'un pêle-mêle extraordinaire' (an extraordinary hotchpotch) has even been employed (Hoepffner edn 1934, 10). Critics have pointed to the lack of any chronological order in these allusions, the brusqueness with which they are introduced, the degree of repetition involved and the differing emphasis placed on the allusions. These points are undoubtedly valid, but the aim of the references within the specific context of the Bern *Folie* also has to be borne in mind. Tristan is seeking to convince Yseut of his identity, whilst remaining mindful that in his disguise as a fool he must guard against appearing too obviously rational. After the initial exchanges, there is growing panic on his part as his references fall on deaf ears and he is driven to call on ever-new evidence. This is not at all a cool and calculated exposure of material, but one convincingly dictated by Tristan's developing despair. The allusions fail to convince Yseut, and it is only when he embarks on a different ploy and produces physical evidence in the form of Husdent and the ring given to him by Yseut that Tristan finally wins the day.

At 998 lines, nearly twice as long as the Bern *Folie*, the *Folie Tristan d'Oxford* (*Fo*) continues the same story-line in its essential details, but when the hero alludes to incidents in the life he has shared with Yseut the material evoked reflects Thomas's romance, the so-called *version courtoise*. The features recalled here are: the treachery committed by the seneschal (*Fo*, 715–26), the Petit-Crû incident (*Fo*, 757–62) and the scene in the *verger* (*Fo*, 943–56), all of which belong exclusively to this version, and the author does seem to be striving to be comprehensive and to include as many references as he can. All the allusions are presented in a much more methodical way than in the Bern *Folie*, with the text regularly punctuated by phrases such as 'membre vus?' (*do you remember?*) and 'membrer vus en dait' (*surely you remember*), and no reference is simply thrown away, but is appropriately amplified. Moreover, Tristan's references come in what is close to the chronological order of events in the legend, beginning with the Morholt episode (*Fo*, 329–66) and concluding with the meeting with Yseut in the *verger* which led to their separation and his exile in Brittany. So thorough is this evocation of the lovers' past life that for the reader or audience the interest of the story may well shift from discovering the way in which the narrative unfolds to taking pleasure in recognizing the source of the allusions. The author does have one surprise in store at the dénouement of the tale. Yseut, an uncomprehending figure throughout (Gaffney 1992–5), is not convinced of Tristan's identity by the production of the ring, but feels even greater distress, believing that this evidence confirms that her lover is now dead. Only when Tristan decides to revert to his normal voice, another physical manifestation, is Yseut able to recognize her lover.

If the content is reminiscent of Thomas, so in some ways is the style. To take as an example merely the introductory passage, the first fifty-six lines, the author of the Oxford *Folie*, in the style of Thomas, repeats the same idea in successive couplets (*Fo*, 37–40), he moves between an observation on an individual character and an assessment of human behaviour in general (*Fo*, 43–56), and he may repeat significant rhyme words: *guarir* and *murir* are twice juxtaposed (*Fo*, 5–6, 15–16). Such similarities have even led editors to suggest, not unreasonably, that Thomas himself was responsible for the Oxford *Folie* (Hoepffner edn 1938, 35–9: Demaules edn, 1315). Certainly, when compared with the Bern *Folie*, this text has a greater literary sophistication. The description of the castle of Tintagel (*Fo*, 95–140), strongly influenced by Wace's *Brut* and by other conventional descriptions of towns (Hoepffner edn 1938, 15–18: Demaules edn, 1330–1), and the extended metaphor in which Yseut's love is compared to a dried-up stream (*Fo*, 701–8) suggest a writer fully conversant with the artistic production and practice of his day. It is also important to point out that the relationship between the lovers is different from that in the Bern *Folie*. Tristan remains in control, especially in the latter stages, playing a cruel game with Yseut (Curtis 1976) as he accuses her of being disloyal and of feigning love (*Fo*, 851–6). Similar charges of deceit, pretence and disloyalty are laid against the queen after Husdent is brought upon the scene (*Fo*, 933–8), and it is only when Yseut is in complete disarray, believing that her lover is dead, that Tristan reverts to his normal voice and permits himself to be recognized. It is not recognition that is wrested from Yseut in the first instance, but a demonstration of her continuing loyalty to Tristan. Yseut has had to undergo a test, and it is only when she has passed that test and shown that she is loyal to her lover, even beyond the grave, that Tristan reveals his identity and allows her to recognize him.

The *Folie Tristan* story can be described as having a happy outcome, but for the lovers this happiness is only fleeting. The same is true of the situation in Marie de France's lay of *Chevrefoil*, where the lovers' pleasure at meeting must be related to the essential tragedy of the story, as indicated at the beginning of the lay (8–10). Tristan has spent a year in exile in South Wales, his homeland according to this text. He decides to take the risk of returning to Cornwall and to attempt to see his beloved Yseut. During the day he hides in the forest, at night he takes refuge with local people, until he learns that the king and his court will be spending Whitsun at Tintagel. Knowing which road the members of the royal party must travel along to reach their destination, Tristan plans a meeting with the queen. He takes a hazel branch, squares it off, writes upon it and then places it at a spot where Yseut will notice it as she passes. We are assured that a similar ploy has worked on a previous occasion, and it turns out to be successful again. Yseut separates from her escort and is reunited with Tristan in the forest. But soon, after Yseut has suggested how Tristan might rehabilitate himself and return to court, the lovers must sadly part again. At Yseut's behest, Tristan composes a new lay to commemorate the occasion. If we wish to set this story at a particular point in the lovers' history as reconstructed by modern scholars, it seems to come at an earlier stage than the *Folie* poems: Tristan is not in Brittany, there is no mention of marriage or of a second Yseut, and reconciliation with King Mark remains a possibility. The situation is not unlike that obtaining at the beginning of the Beroul fragment, where the hero has been removed from court because of the activity of slanderers, but there are obviously other reminiscences (Adams and Hemming 1976).

For a work running to a mere 118 lines, *Chevrefoil* has generated a considerable amount of controversy. A paramount concern has been to determine precisely what Tristan carved upon the hazel branch. Line 54, 'De sun cutel escrit sun nun' (*with his knife he wrote his name*), appears quite explicit, but the matter is complicated by a subsequent passage (61–78) where difficulties in interpretation are compounded by uncertainties as to what an authoritative edition should contain. The contentious lines include a message, in some way associated with what was written on the branch, and introduce the distinctive image of the poem. Tristan and Yseut are compared to the hazel and the honeysuckle which, for mutual survival, must remain together: 'Bele amie, si est de nus: / Ne vus sanz mei, ne mei sanz vus!' (*Fair lady, so it is with us: neither you without me nor me without you*, 77–8). Line 61, 'Ceo fu la summe de l'escrit', has been variously understood. It has been taken to refer to the whole of the message in 63–78 (Rychner edn, 279), but it seems difficult to accept that all this could have been contained upon the four surfaces of the branch, and even if Tristan had carved the message in ogam (Cagnon 1970) the limited dimensions of the branch would still render this a very difficult task and a considerable challenge to Yseut's eyesight. The text strongly suggests the existence of a message transmitted earlier by Tristan to Yseut. The 'summe de l'escrit' might indicate that Tristan's name alone was written on the branch and that this alone gave Yseut the information she needed, given the existence of the earlier message (Burgess 1987, 65–9). Alternatively, rather than take *escrit* as referring to the carving on the branch, it may refer to the previous message. If this were the case, 'la summe de l'escrit' would suggest that Tristan's name on the hazel branch was both a recognition signal and also a *résumé*, a symbolic encapsulation of the message contained in 63–78 (Poirion 1986, 114–17).

There is a further, associated issue. After his return to Wales, Tristan composes a new lay, 'pur les paroles remembrer' (*to record the words*, 111). These are less likely to be the words spoken to Tristan by Yseut in the wood at the time of their meeting (Spitzer 1946–7, 88) than to be the words transmitted by Tristan in his earlier message to Yseut, the passage which contains the central image of the hazel and the honeysuckle (67–78). Tristan is being invited to shift this image via the lay from the private to the public domain. This is just one of the creative acts presented in the poem: Tristan carves on the branch and then composes a lay at Yseut's instigation, whilst Marie de France draws upon this lay or its successor and writes it down in rhyme, in accordance with the task she set herself in the prologue she produced for her whole collection. Quite exceptionally for her, Marie seemingly claims to have drawn not only upon an oral, but also a written, source for the *lai*: 'Plusors le me unt cunté e dit / E jeo l'ai trové en escrit' (*Several people have told me the story and I have found it written down*, 5–6). Or is Marie using *trover* with the sense of 'to compose' and stating more predictably that she has set down an oral work in written form? Notwithstanding the difficulties in interpretation posed by the lay of *Chevrefoil*, it clearly suggests within its narrow compass much of the spirit of the legend; it is a distillation, a synecdoche, a *summe* of the whole Tristan story.

Although regularly associated with the other episodic Tristan poems and included with them in the major collections, the *Tristan Rossignol* story differs from the two *Folies* and from *Chevrefoil* in that it has no independent existence, but is found only as part of a larger poem, the *Donnei des amants*. The *Donnei*, surviving in a single manuscript and Anglo-Norman in provenance (Legge 1963, 128), tells how in the spring the poet enters an enclosed garden and there eaves-drops on the conversation (the *donnei* of the title) of two lovers. So impressed is the poet by the arguments and counter-arguments brought forward by the lady and the lover that he decides to pass on what he has heard for the general benefit of all. In lines 453–683 of the *Donnei*, in a bid to persuade his lady to risk all for love, the lover tells the *Tristan Rossignol* story, an illustration of what Queen Yseut was prepared to do for Tristan. He relates how the hero returns secretly from Brittany to visit Yseut, and, at night, in a garden, imitates the song of birds, including that of the nightingale. For Yseut, the birdsong is a signal with its own private significance, just like the *bastun* in *Chevrefoil*. Yseut reacts to the sound by leaving the marital bed and makes her way through the guards set to watch over her by King Mark, who are fortunately all asleep at this time. However, she makes a noise as she attempts to open the door and alerts the dwarf. The ensuing commotion awakens the household, but Mark insists that the very boldness of the queen's behaviour indicates she had nothing untoward in mind. Yseut is then free to join her lover in the garden.

This incident is not recounted elsewhere in any of the extant Tristan material. The same is true of the particular modulation of the *folie* story then related by the lady, in which she describes the humiliation Tristan was prepared to endure for the sake of Yseut. This serves as a riposte to the lover's story and brings this section of the *Donnei* to a close. The *Tristan Rossignol* episode is unusual also in that, as Gaston Paris noted long ago (1896, 536), it is difficult to know to what point in the legend it should be attached: the return from Brittany suggests a rela-tively late stage, but the involvement of the dwarf argues for an earlier position. At the same time, the material seems decidedly familiar, and one may well have a sense of coming upon a collection of commonplaces. Tristan stations himself at night, in a garden, by a stream, beneath a pine tree, exactly as in the opening episode of the Beroul fragment. Again, as in that episode, Mark completely misjudges the situation in refusing to believe that the dwarf has told anything like the truth. But the anecdote also contains quite new material, such as the long *excursus* on the meaning and resonances of the term *gelus* (jealous husband), which breaks up the progress of the narrative. The lover certainly introduces the material as if he were asking his lady to recall a story which she knows already (Busby 1989b, 188), but the material needs to be presented in this way if it is to have the same status as the other illustrative examples put forward in the rest of the *Donnei*. It is quite possible that the author of the *Donnei des amants* built his *Tristan Rossignol* anecdote upon the hero's ability to imitate birdsong, a skill akin to the musical talents he exhibits in other texts, and then developed the story by exploiting familiar motifs.

Although the *Tristan Rossignol* poem is part of a larger entity, it can easily be separated off, acquiring the appearance of an independent tale. With the *Tristan Menestrel* tale, another story embedded within a much longer work, it is clear where it ends: editors agree in marking a pause at l. 4832 in the standard edition of Gerbert de Montreuil's *Continuation de Perceval* (Williams edn, II, 1922), at a moment when the main participants separate from Perceval (Weston and Bédier 1906; Marchello-Nizia edn). However, there is no such consensus over the beginning. If the hint given by the standard edition is taken, it seems logical to begin the sequence at l. 3248, at a point when Perceval resumes the Grail Quest and Mordred, following his defeat by Perceval, comes to the classic Arthurian setting of Caerleon. The story itself lacks any homogeneity. At Arthur's court, a knight with gilded weaponry defeats a number of leading figures and is engaged in combat with Gauvain, when the mysterious knight is revealed to be Tristan. Tristan establishes a friendship with Gauvain, but after a while feels a pressing desire to see Yseut. With twelve knights, all disguised as musicians, he reaches Lancien, and the group is given the task of watching over Mark and his household. In a tournament against the Roi des Cent Chevaliers the cause of Mark's side is considerably boosted when the 'minstrels' finally involve themselves, but the arrival of Perceval and his support for the opposition redress the balance. This phase comes to a close when Gauvain and Perceval disclose their identities to each other and explain the circumstances which led to their present encounter.

As Busby (1983, 152) has rightly intimated, the Tristan material found here is little more than an entertaining diversion within a serious Grail romance. But there is certainly a Tristan tale here, one which is reminiscent of the *Folie* poems. One might in fact say two Tristan tales, for possibly two Tristan stories may lie behind the extant text (Weston and Bédier 1906, 497, 525): the first dealing with Tristan's friendship with Gauvain; the second concerned with Tristan's relationship with Yseut and not too far removed from our *Folie* poems. True, in this text the emotional impact of the story is very much lessened, because the material is scattered over a large number of lines, and there is no attempt to evoke the whole of the legend through the banter of the disguised hero (though a convenient minstrel near the beginning does rehearse Tristan's past experiences, 3614–44). But the action is triggered off, as in the *Folie* poems, by Tristan's desire to see Yseut again, even though he then travels to see her, not as a solitary figure, but as part of a large group. His first meeting with Yseut leads to the usual refusal on the part of the queen to recognize him: his voice may be Tristan's, she admits, but, unlike her lover, this figure apparently no longer has both his eyes. The second stage of the story, typically enough, finds Tristan in the main hall, where he plays the lay of *Chevrefoil* upon his small flute. After some brief soul-searching, Yseut acknowledges that it is her lover who stands before her, her 'loiax amis' (4092); the playing of a composition describing a meeting between the lovers has inspired another meeting. There is a little more. Gerbert must break off from his account of the tournament to present the lovers' customary fleeting moments of pleasure (4199–4207), and, towards the end of the tale, King Mark is persuaded by Gauvain, Yvain and Perceval to cease his antagonism towards Tristan (4736–68). The reconciliation which is hoped for in *Chevrefoil* actually comes about in this text. **[GB]**

Notes

[1] See *Le Purgatoire de saint Patrice par Berol, publié pour la première fois par Marianne Mörner* (Lund, 1917), p. 63, l. 884.

[2] For the suggestion that Tristan, as in the prose *Tristan*, perished at Mark's hand, see Adams and Hemming 1973.

[3] Throughout this volume, the following name forms will be used for characters in all versions of the Tristan legend: Mark, Tristan, Yseut, Yseut aux Blanches Mains (*Yseut of the White Hands*). There is, of course, an element of arbitrariness in these choices from a selection of variant forms.

[4] Some of the 154 lines of the Carlisle fragment are essentially editorial reconstructions; see Benskin, Hunt and Short 1992–5.

[5] See Jackson and Ranawake eds 2000*, 130, 139.

[6] References to the lay of *Chevrefoil* are to the Ewert edition. Unless otherwise stated, references to the other texts considered in this section are to the Marchello-Nizia edition.

[7] See Kelly 1992*, 177.

Reference List

For items accompanied by an asterisk, see the General Bibliography.

Bibliographies

Shirt, D. J. *The Old French Tristan Poems: A Bibliographical Guide* (London, 1980).

Burgess, G. S. *Marie de France: An Analytical Bibliography* (London, 1977; supplement no. 1, 1986; supplement no. 2, 1997). Includes *Chevrefoil*.

Texts and Translations

Early French Tristan Poems. Ed. by N. J. Lacy, Arthurian Archives, 2 vols (Cambridge, 1998).
Tristan et Yseut: les premières versions européennes. Ed. by C. Marchello-Nizia (Paris, 1995).
Tristan et Iseut: les poèmes français, la saga norroise. Ed. by D. Lacroix and P. Walter (Paris, 1989).
Tristan et Yseut. Les Tristan en vers. Ed. by J.-C. Payen (Paris, 1974).

Beroul

The Romance of Tristran by Beroul: A Poem of the Twelfth Century. Ed. by A. Ewert, 2 vols (Oxford, 1939, 1970).
Béroul, Tristran et Iseut: poème du XIIᵉ siècle [with French transl.]. Ed. by H. Braet and G. Raynaud de Lage, 2 vols (Paris and Louvain, 1989).
The Romance of Tristran by Beroul [with English transl.]. Ed. by S. Gregory (Amsterdam and Atlanta, GA, 1992).
Beroul, The Romance of Tristran [with English transl.]. Ed. by N. J. Lacy (New York, 1989).
Beroul, Tristan et Yseut [with French transl.]. Ed. by D. Poirion in Marchello-Nizia edn, 3–121 and 1127–1208 (text and notes).

Thomas

Les Fragments du roman de Tristan par Thomas: poème du XIIᵉ siècle. Ed. by B. H. Wind, TLF 92 (Geneva and Paris, 1960).
Le Roman de Tristan, Thomas. Ed. by J. Bédier, 2 vols (Paris, 1902 and 1905).
Thomas, Tristan [with German transl.]. Ed. by G. Bonath (Munich, 1985).
Thomas of Britain: Tristran [with English transl.]. Ed. by S. Gregory (New York, 1991).
Le Roman de Tristan par Thomas. Ed. by F. Lecoy (Paris, 1991).
Le Roman de Tristan par Thomas suivi de la Folie Tristan de Berne et La Folie Tristan d'Oxford. Ed. by F. Lecoy, transl. and notes by E. Baumgartner and I. Short (Paris, 2003).

The *Folies Tristan*

La Folie de Tristan, version de Berne [with French transl.]. Ed. by M. Demaules in Marchello-Nizia edn, 245–60, 1310–25 and 1343–58 (text and notes).
La Folie de Tristan, version d'Oxford [with French transl.]. Ed. by M. Demaules in Marchello-Nizia edn, 217–43 and 1310–42 (text and notes).
Les Deux Poèmes de la Folie Tristan. Ed. by J. Bédier, SATF (Paris, 1907).
La Folie Tristan de Berne. Ed. by E. Hoepffner (Paris, 1934).
La Folie Tristan d'Oxford. Ed. by E. Hoepffner (Paris, 1938).
Les Deux Poèmes de la Folie Tristan. Ed by F. Lecoy, CFMA 116 (Paris, 1994).
The Anglo-Norman Folie Tristan. Ed. by I. Short (London, 1993).
The Romance of Tristan by Beroul and the Tale of Tristan's Madness. Transl. by A. S. Fedrick (Harmondsworth, 1970).
The Birth of Romance: An Anthology. Four Twelfth-Century Anglo-Norman Romances. Transl. by J. Weiss (London, 1992). For the *Folie Tristan d'Oxford*, see pp. 121–40.
Le Roman de Tristan par Thomas suivi de la Folie Tristan de Berne et de la Folie Tristan d'Oxford. Ed. by F. Lecoy, transl. and notes by E. Baumgartner and I. Short (Paris, 2003).

Dean, R. J., and E. J. Kennedy. 1973. 'Un fragment anglo-normand de la *Folie Tristan*', *MA*, 79, 57–72.

Chevrefoil

Marie de France, Lais. Ed. by A. Ewert (Oxford, 1944 ; repr. with introduction and bibliography by G. S. Burgess, Bristol, 1995).
Marie de France, Le Lai du Chèvrefeuille [with French transl.]. Ed by M. Demaules in Marchello-Nizia edn, 213–16 and 1287–1309 (text and notes).
Les Lais de Marie de France. Ed. by J. Rychner, CFMA 93 (Paris, 1966).
The Lais of Marie de France. Transl. by G. S. Burgess and K. Busby (Harmondsworth, 1986).

Tristan Rossignol

Le Donnei des amants. Tristan Rossignol [with French transl.]. Ed by C. Marchello-Nizia in Marchello-Nizia edn, 967–73 and 1566–9 (text and notes).
Paris, G. 1896. '*Le Donnei des amants*', *Rom*, 25, 497–541.

Tristan Menestrel

Gerbert de Montreuil, La Continuation de Perceval, Tristan Ménestrel [with French transl.]. Ed by C. Marchello-Nizia in Marchello-Nizia edn, 975–1010 and 1570–5 (text and notes).
Gerbert de Montreuil, *La Continuation de Perceval*, vols I and II. Ed. by M. Williams, CFMA 28, 50 (Paris, 1922, 1925); vol. III. Ed. by M. Oswald, CFMA 101 (Paris, 1975).

Studies

Adams, A., and T. D. Hemming. 1973. 'La Fin du *Tristan* de Béroul', *MA*, 79, 449–68.
Adams and Hemming. 1976. '"Chèvrefeuille" and the Evolution of the Tristan Legend', *BBIAS*, 27, 204–13.
Adams, T. 1999. '"Pur vostre cor su jo em paine": The Augustinian Subtext of Thomas's *Tristan*', *Med. Aev*, 68, 278–91.
Baumgartner, E. 1987. *Tristan et Iseut: de la légende aux récits en vers*, Paris.
Benskin, M., T. Hunt, and I. Short. 1992–5. 'Un nouveau fragment du *Tristan* de Thomas', *Rom*, 113, 289–319.
Berkvam, D. D. 1989. 'La "Vérité" déplacée dans le *Chevrefoil*', *Neophil*, 73, 14–22.
Bromiley, G. N. 1986. *Thomas's Tristan and the Folie Tristan d'Oxford*, London.
Bruckner, M. T. 1981–2. 'The *Folie Tristan d'Oxford*: Speaking Voice, Written Text', *Tris*, 7, 47–59.
Bullock-Davies, C. 1966. *Professional Interpreters and the Matter of Britain*, Cardiff.
Burgess, G. S. 1987. *The Lais of Marie de France: Text and Context*, Manchester.
Busby, K. 1983. 'Der *Tristan Menestrel* des Gerbert de Montreuil und seine Stellung in der altfranzösischen Artustradition', *VR*, 42, 144–56.
Busby 1989a. 'Le *Tristan* de Béroul en tant qu'intertexte', in N. J. Lacy and G. Torrini-Roblin eds *Continuations: Essays on Medieval French Literature and Language in Honor of John L. Grigsby* (Birmingham, AL, 1989), 19–37.
Busby 1989b. 'The *Donnei des amants* and Courtly Tradition', *MR*, 14, 181–95.
Cagnon, M. 1970. '*Chievrefueil* and the Ogamic Tradition', *Rom*, 91, 238–55.
Calin, W. 1994. *The French Tradition and the Literature of Medieval England*, Toronto.
Cormier, R. J. 1980. 'Bédier, Brother Robert and the *Roman de Tristan*', in *Études de philologie romane et d'histoire littéraire offertes à Jules Horrent*, Liège, 69–75.
Crane, S. 1986. *Insular Romance: Politics, Faith, and Culture in Anglo-Norman and Middle English Literature*, Berkeley.

Curtis, R. L. 1976. 'The Humble and the Cruel Tristan: A New Look at the Two Poems of the *Folie Tristan*', *Tris*, 2:1, 3–11.

Dannenbaum [Crane], S. 1979. 'Doubling and *Fine Amor* in Thomas' *Tristan*', *Tris*, 5:1, 3–14.

Ferrante, J. M. 1973. *The Conflict of Love and Honor: The Medieval Tristan Legend in France, Germany and Italy*, The Hague and Paris.

Fourrier, A. 1960. *Le Courant réaliste dans le roman courtois en France au Moyen Âge*, Paris.

Frappier, J. 1963. 'Structure et sens du *Tristan*: version commune, version courtoise', *CCM*, 6, 255–80, 441–54.

Frappier 1964. 'Sur le mot "raison" dans le *Tristan* de Thomas d'Angleterre', in A. S. Crisafulli ed. *Linguistic and Literary Studies in Honor of Helmut A. Hatzfeld*, Washington DC, 163–76.

Fritz, J.-M. 1992. *Le Discours du fou au moyen âge, XIIᵉ–XIIIᵉ siècles*, Paris.

Gaffney, P. 1992–5. 'Iseut la (Dumb) Blonde: The Portrayal of the Queen in the *Folies Tristan*', *Rom*, 113, 401–20.

Grimbert, J. T. 1990. '*Voleir* vs. *poeir*: Frustrated Desire in Thomas's *Tristan*', *PQ*, 69, 153–65.

Halvorsen, J. 1983. 'Tristan and Iseult: The Two Traditions', *ZfSL*, 93, 271–96.

Hanoset, M. 1961. 'Unité ou dualité du *Tristan* de Béroul?', *MA*, 67, 503–33.

Heinzel, R. 1869. 'Gottfrieds von Straßburg Tristan und seine Quelle', *ZfdA*, 14, 272–447.

Horrent, J. 1946–7. 'La Composition de la *Folie Tristan* de Berne', *RBPH*, 25, 21–38.

Hunt, T. 1977. 'Abelardian Ethics and Béroul's *Tristran*', *Rom*, 98, 501–40.

Hunt 1979. 'Aristotle, Dialectic, and Courtly Literature', *Viator*, 10, 95–129.

Hunt 1981. 'The Significance of Thomas's *Tristan*', *RMS*, 7, 41–61.

Hunt 1998. 'Béroul's *Tristran*: The Discovery of the Lovers in the Forest', in M. Ailes, P. E. Bennett and K. Pratt eds *Reading around the Epic: A Festschrift in Honour of Professor Wolfgang van Emden* (London, 1998), 233–48.

Illingworth, R. N. 1985. 'Thematic Duplication in Beroul's *Tristran*', *ZrP*, 101, 12–27.

Jodogne, O. 1965. 'Comment Thomas d'Angleterre a compris l'amour de Tristan et d'Iseut', *LR*, 19, 103–19.

Johnson, P. 1972–3. '*Dolor, dolent* et *soi doloir*: le vocabulaire de la douleur et la conception de l'amour selon Béroul et Thomas', *RPh*, 26, 546–54.

Jonin, P. 1958. *Les Personnages féminins dans les romans français de Tristan au XIIᵉ siècle: étude des influences contemporaines*, Aix-en-Provence.

Kjær, J. 1990. 'L'Épisode de "Tristan menestrel" dans la "Continuation de Perceval" par Gerbert de Montreuil (XIIIᵉ siècle): essai d'interprétation', *Revue Romane*, 25, 356–66.

Larmat, J. 1979. 'La Souffrance dans le *Tristan* de Thomas', in *Mélanges de langue et littérature françaises du Moyen Âge offerts à Pierre Jonin*, Senefiance 7, Aix-en-Provence, 369–85.

Legge, M. D. 1963. *Anglo-Norman Literature and its Background*, Oxford.

Ménage, R. 1974. 'L'Atelier Béroul ou Béroul artiste', *Rom*, 95, 145–98.

Noble, P. S. 1982. *Beroul's Tristan and the Folie de Berne*, London.

Poirion, D. 1986. 'Le Message des contes', in D. Poirion ed. *Résurgences: mythe et littérature à l'âge du symbole (XIIᵉ siècle)*, Paris, 99–118.

Pollmann, L. 1988. 'Tristan und Isolde im Kontext der hochhöfischen Literatur Frankreichs (*Folie* und szenische Gestaltung)', in *Studia in honorem prof. M. de Riquer*, 4 vols, Barcelona, III, 471–98.

Punzi, A. 1988. 'Materiali per la datazione del *Tristan* di Thomas', *CN*, 48, 9–71.

Raynaud de Lage, G. 1958 and 1964. 'Faut-il attribuer à Béroul tout le *Tristan*?', *MA*, 64, 249–70 and 70, 33–8.

Reid, T. B. W. 1965. 'The *Tristran* of Béroul: One Author or Two?', *MLR*, 60, 352–8.

Reid 1972. *The Tristran of Beroul: A Textual Commentary*, Oxford.

Ribard, J. 1979. 'Le *Tristan* de Béroul, un monde de l'illusion?', *BBIAS*, 31, 229–44.

Rychner, J. 1984. 'Deux copistes au travail: pour une étude textuelle globale du manuscrit 354 de la

Bibliothèque de la Bourgeoisie de Berne', in I. Short ed. *Medieval French Textual Studies in Memory of T. B. W. Reid*, London, 187–218.

Sandqvist, S. 1984. *Notes textuelles sur le Roman de Tristan de Béroul*, Lund.

Schaefer, J. T. 1993. 'Specularity in the Mediaeval *Folie Tristan* Poems or Madness as Metadiscourse', *Neophil*, 77, 355–68.

Spitzer, L. 1946–7, 'La "Lettre sur la baguette de coudrier" dans le lai du *Chievrefueil*', *Rom*, 69, 80–90.

Telfer, J. M. 1952–3. 'The Evolution of a Mediæval Theme', *DUJ*, 45, 25–34.

Vàrvaro, A. 1972. *Beroul's Romance of Tristran*, transl. by J. C. Barnes, Manchester.

Walter, P. 1990. *Le Gant de verre: le mythe de Tristan et Iseut*, La Gacilly.

Weston, J. L., and J. Bédier. 1906. '*Tristan Ménestrel*: extrait de la continuation de *Perceval* par Gerbert, *Rom*, 35, 497–530.

Wind, B. H. 1960–1. 'Éléments courtois dans Béroul et dans Thomas', *RPh*, 14, 1–13.

IV

CHRÉTIEN DE TROYES

Douglas Kelly

Chrétien de Troyes made highly original contributions to Arthurian literature and his influence was immense. Although Arthur and the Round Table were known to French audiences before he wrote, especially through Wace and oral channels of transmission, Chrétien was the first, as far as we know today, to treat the quest by Knights of the Round Table, the love of Lancelot and Guinevere, and the Grail as holy object. Instead of the conquering warrior, in the tradition of Geoffrey of Monmouth and Wace, Chrétien depicts King Arthur as a less domineering or effective ruler, whose glory derives more from his Round Table knights than from his own initiatives. Some, like Lancelot, Gauvain and Kay, are given distinct characters that survive and evolve throughout the rest of the Middle Ages and beyond; the same is true for Guinevere.

The knight, not Arthur, is central in Chrétien's Arthurian romances. The depiction of love, although socially orientated, is sometimes marked by Tristan and Yseut's experiences and fate. Finally, Chrétien is surely the first author to give the word *roman*, or romance (*Cligés*, 23; *Charrette*, 2), a generic sense, and therefore to have invented a new fictional genre: Arthurian romance with its characteristic themes and motifs.[1] For these reasons, Chrétien can fairly claim to be one of the most original and influential authors in French and, indeed, in European literature.

Although scholars do not agree on the precise dating of his works (Fourrier 1950; Misrahi 1959), Chrétien de Troyes certainly flourished in the second half of the twelfth century. He wrote five Arthurian romances: *Erec et Enide*, *Cligés*, *Lancelot* or the *Chevalier de la charrette* (to avoid confusion with the prose *Lancelot* this romance will henceforth be referred to as the *Charrette*), *Yvain* or the *Chevalier au lion*, and the incomplete *Perceval* or *Conte du Graal*. Several other works have also been attributed to him: *Philomena*, an adaptation of a tale in Ovid's *Metamorphoses* referred to in the prologue to *Cligés*; *Guillaume d'Angleterre*, an adventure romance with hagiographic features; and at least two *chansons* that perhaps make Chrétien the first *trouvère* to adopt the style and manner of the troubadours. The prologue to *Cligés* refers to several other works that are probably lost: a second Ovidian adaptation based on the tale of Pelops in the *Metamorphoses*, French versions of Ovid's *Art of Love* and *Remedy for Love*, and a story entitled 'Dou roi Marc et d'Yseut la blonde' (*Cligés*, 5) (*about King Marc and Yseut the blonde*).[2]

The Author

As Hunt has pointed out (1986, 9), nothing is known about Chrétien, except that he was very well known! The full name 'Chrétien de Troyes' (Chrestiens de Troies) appears only in the prologue to *Erec* (9); the other romances refer to him simply as 'Chrétien'.[3] He may not have been born in Troyes itself, but his French does show some Champenois traits (Woledge 1986–8, I, 17–49). The prologue to the *Charrette* states that he wrote the romance at the behest of Marie de Champagne and that she furnished him with its *matiere* and *san* (1–3, 21–7); these terms are generally taken to refer to the plot's source and its informing idea or context. The epilogue claims that Chrétien entrusted the task of completing the last thousand lines or so to an otherwise unknown, but apparently skilful versifier, Godefroy de Lagny (*Charrette*, 7102–10). Chrétien did not complete his last romance, *Perceval*. According to its prologue, Philippe de Flandre gave Chrétien the 'book' that he then rewrote in French verse (60–6). As Philippe died during the Third Crusade of 1189–92 (Diverres 1990, 23–32), loss of patronage may explain its incomplete state. Or Chrétien, as Gerbert de Montreuil claims in his *Perceval Continuation*, may have died before completing the romance.

Several scholars have questioned these biographical statements. They argue, for example, that Godefroy de Lagny is a fictional continuator of a romance which Chrétien himself completed, and also that the *Perceval* is in fact complete, in the sense that Chrétien either did not intend to effect closure, or that it is structurally or thematically complete as it stands, despite the absence of a conventional dénouement (Dragonetti 1980; Hult 1989a; Zemel 1996). The validity of these interpretations depends on Chrétien's biography, about which we know no more than what is claimed by authorial interventions in the romances.

Marie de Champagne's patronage of the *Charrette* is the most credible of these biographical allusions. The apparent idealization of Lancelot's love for Guinevere is consistent with the justification of adultery ascribed to Marie de Champagne in Andreas Capellanus's *De amore* (but see the reservations in Benton 1961), where the patroness of Chrétien's *Charrette* argues that there is no necessary conflict between adulterous love and conjugal affection. Chrétien's connection to Philippe de Flandre is less clear. Beyond the perhaps coincidental link between the incomplete *Perceval* and Philippe's death in the Holy Land in 1191, their only other possible contact, itself dubious, occurred during failed negotiations in the 1180s for marriage between Philippe and Marie de Champagne, after the death of her husband. Philippe's patronage of the *Perceval*, it has been suggested, came about during those negotiations (Benton 1961, 554; Bezzola 1963, III, 415, esp. n. 1).

Some scholars have linked Chrétien to the troubadours Rigaut de Barbezilh and Bernart de Ventadorn, whom he may have met at the court of Eleanor of Aquitaine (Rossi 1987). On the basis of references to British geography in *Erec* and *Cligés*, other scholars have suggested connections with the Plantagenet court and a sojourn in Britain (Rickard 1956, 107–13; Schmolke-Hasselmann 1980*, 190–200/1998, 232–43; Bullock-Davies 1981; Morris 1988*, esp. 264–74; Carroll 1994; but cf. Broadhurst 1996). Chrétien's social status is uncertain; he has been variously characterized as an ecclesiastic, a low-level cleric, a *trouvère*, and a minstrel or *jongleur*; 'Par lo sornon conoist en l'ome' (*Perceval*, 527) (*through his name one knows the man*), says Perceval's mother to her son. Some scholars have suggested that Chrétien's name implies that he was a converted Jew. Two ecclesiastical dignitaries in Troyes are known to have had the name 'Christianus'; one of these could have been our poet (Kay 1997).

Chrétien's romances offer some evidence that he received a clerical education. His study of the *trivium* may account for the prominence of certain features of medieval grammar and rhetoric in his style, and these arts, basic in the education of clerical authors, have played a prominent part in modern criticism (Hunt 1982, 165–71; Kelly 1992*, chapter 2). Some scholars have focused on the place of logic in his works (Hunt 1977; 1979; Vance 1987*; Maddox 1989). The *quadrivium* (arithmetic, geometry, music and astronomy) is described in Erec's coronation robe (6738–82). But although the assumption of Chrétien's clerical education has been generally accepted, some question not only that education, but even his literacy (Vitz 1999*).

Chrétien's name and reputation gradually slid into oblivion during the thirteenth century. But if his name was forgotten,[4] his influence on the subject-matter, issues and art of Arthurian romance survives well beyond his time.

The Romances

All of Chrétien's romances, except *Perceval*, are some 7,000 lines long. Moreover, all except the *Charrette* divide their narrative into two parts, corresponding to two more or less distinct plots connected by a 'crisis' (Warning in *GRLMA*, IV:l, 25–59; Maddox 1980–1). The second plot is approximately twice as long as the first. The two plots may be linked thematically, for example by the defence of the fountain in *Yvain*, or marriage and ascent to the throne in *Cligés*. Usually, scenes at Arthur's court mark the beginning and the end of the plot, as well as important narrative divisions. The approximate mid-point between the first and last line (*c*.3500) often falls within a significant episode. Each romance introduces a major figure whose identity and significance emerge as the plot progresses and whose name gives each romance its usual title or titles. Certain figures reappear from romance to romance; the most common are Arthur, Gauvain, Kay and Guinevere. Women are less often named; of noble birth, they inspire love and usually marry the titular knights. More importantly, they are the willing or unwilling source of the crises in the plots (Lefay-Toury 1972; Krueger 1993*, 35; Paupert 1995).

In what follows, each romance is briefly summarized in order to identify the major issues raised in its plot as well as any novel features in its narrative composition.

Erec et Enide

The first part of Chrétien's first Arthurian romance interlaces two adventures: the Hunt for the White Stag and the Sparrow-hawk Contest. Each adventure serves to identify the most beautiful woman. Erec does not take part in the hunt. Instead, he acts as escort for Guinevere and encounters a discourteous knight, Yder, who insults the queen by allowing his dwarf to strike both her companion and Erec himself. Being unarmed, Erec follows Yder to a town, where he obtains armour from an impoverished knight and meets the latter's beautiful daughter. He challenges Yder in the Sparrow-hawk Contest and defeats him; the daughter receives the prize. Erec asks for her hand in marriage and goes with her to Arthur's court, where all agree that she should receive the Kiss of the White Stag. When Erec marries her, we learn her name: Enide. After a tournament, the couple departs for Carnant, the court of Erec's father King Lac. This ends the first part.

The second part relates a crisis in the marriage. Because Erec neglects tournaments for his beloved wife, almost everyone accuses him of *recreantise* (failure to act as a knight should, 2462–63, 2551). Enide is deeply troubled by these complaints, fearing that she has caused him to lose his honour, and reveals her concern to her husband one morning in bed. The change in their marriage is dramatic. Although Erec admits that he must do something to rectify the situation (2572–73), he does not embark on a round of tournaments. Rather he sets out 'en aventure' (2763) with Enide.

Erec does not repudiate his wife. However, although he may treat his wife correctly by the standards of the time, he no longer seems to regard her as his beloved: she is still his *feme*, but no longer his *amie* (Sargent-Baur 1979–80). He orders her to remain silent unless he grants her permission to speak. During their quest, they meet and overcome violent threats to both husband and wife. While Erec is always victorious in combat, Enide does not obey her husband's injunction to remain silent when she sees danger. Finally exhausted, Erec collapses, to all appearances dead. A knight with the sinister name of

Count Oringle de Limors – 'the dead one' – forces Enide to marry him; only Erec's speedy recovery saves her.

Their quest shows that Enide's love is as constant as her husband's prowess. Erec pardons whatever wrong she may have done in repeating the slander and she again becomes his *amie* (4929). Whilst returning to Arthur's court, they encounter a final challenge called the Joy of the Court. A knight named Mabonagrain had promised to remain in a magic garden with his beloved until another knight defeated him. Erec, who has always sought joy (5458–65), is victorious. After King Lac's death, Arthur crowns both Erec and Enide at Nantes in Brittany.

The crisis in Erec and Enide's marriage arises from a conflict between love and knighthood: in an aristocratic marriage, what are the relative demands of martial prowess and noble love? Erec's propensity to prefer the company of ladies to that of men is apparent when he escorts Guinevere, rather than participating in the Hunt for the White Stag. Later he is accused of uxoriousness because he lingers in bed with his wife, rather than accompanying his men to tournaments. His stern treatment of Enide during the quest marks a profound change in their relationship. Yet his striking victories counterpoint Enide's own disobedience to his command to keep silent, when she warns him of danger; his victories and her concern for her husband lead to reconciliation, in a love that does not appear to require tournaments or other chivalric activity as proof of worth. Sexual compatibility and mutual affection are sources of worth and prowess.

Cligés

The first part of *Cligés* narrates the love and marriage of Alixandre, son of the Emperor of Constantinople, and Soredamors, Gauvain's sister. Alixandre leaves Constantinople for Arthur's court in order to become a knight. Whilst Arthur is in Brittany, Angrés, Count of Windsor, rebels against Arthur. The latter returns to England and besieges Angrés in Windsor Castle. By clever deception, Alixandre captures Angrés. Interlaced with these events, but separate from them (Nolting-Hauff 1959, 32), is the love story of Alixandre and Soredamors, who give voice to their feelings in lengthy monologues. Guinevere brings about a mutual declaration. They marry and in due course Cligés is born.

After the death of their father, Alixandre's younger brother Alis, believing his elder brother to be dead, is crowned emperor. When Alis learns the truth, he and Alixandre find a compromise: Alis will remain on the throne, but he must not marry, so that Cligés will succeed him. But Alis breaks his word and marries Fénice, daughter of the Holy Roman Emperor. Cligés and Fénice fall in love, but she is unwilling to follow Yseut's example and give her body to two men. Thessala, her governess and a sorceress, helps her to deceive Alis (this is the mid-point of the text) with a potion that causes him to fall asleep each night and merely dream that he makes love to his wife; in this way Fénice will not give Alis an heir. Whilst the Greeks are returning from Cologne, the Duke of Saxony tries to abduct Fénice, but Cligés rescues her.

Later, after triumphs in tournaments in England, Cligés and Fénice confess their love. Fénice again enlists the help of Thessala, who prepares a potion that makes her appear to be dead; Cligés will free her from the tomb and take her to a secret hideaway. However, sharp-eyed doctors from Salerno see through the deception and torture Fénice to make her confess. But a band of women defenestrate the doctors and Fénice is entombed. Cligés rescues her at night and the lovers lead a life of solitary bliss until, unexpectedly discovered, they flee to Arthur's court. Alis dies of jealous rage after learning the truth about his unconsummated marriage. Cligés and Fénice marry and are crowned. Succeeding emperors, fearing Alis's fate, establish the harem.

Deception and treachery are rife in *Cligés*; Angrés betrays Arthur and, in order to capture it, Alixandre deceives the defenders of Windsor Castle. Alis breaks his oath never to marry, but Fénice, refusing to give her body to both her husband and her lover, retains her virginity through deception. When she does 'elope' with Cligés, she still insists on secrecy. But they are betrayed, and she and Cligés become exemplary of secret adulterers.

The *Charrette*

Prior to the *Charrette*, the relation between love and prowess in Chrétien's romances has been problematic. To be sure, Erec fights better in the Sparrowhawk Contest because of Enide, and Cligés, inspired by Fénice, wins her partly by his prowess. Yet absorption by love to the exclusion of prowess causes problems. Erec is accused of being *recreant*, whereas Cligés in effect abandons knighthood in order to love Fénice in seclusion. By contrast, love in the *Charrette* is superior to knighthood, because, in this romance, love itself inspires exceptional chivalric achievements.

An unknown knight, later identified as Meleagant, boasts that he holds many of Arthur's subjects prisoner in Gorre. To liberate them, a knight must defeat Meleagant in a combat for which Guinevere is the prize. The challenge is taken up by Kay, but he is defeated and the queen is abducted. Gauvain and an anonymous knight follow her. In order to learn of the queen's whereabouts, the anonymous knight rides in a cart, a shameful act usually reserved for criminals; as a result he receives the name Knight of the Cart. Gauvain chooses to proceed to Gorre by way of the Underwater Bridge, whilst the Knight of the Cart takes the more dangerous Sword Bridge. Numerous adventures mark the knight's progress (Gauvain's adventures are not narrrated), until he finally crosses the Sword Bridge before the castle where Guinevere and Kay are prisoners.

During the ensuing combat between the Knight of the Cart and Meleagant, Guinevere reveals the knight's true name: Lancelot (the naming takes place in l. 3660, the mid-point of the text). At first, Lancelot is stymied by the sight of the queen; then, inspired by her beauty, he almost defeats his opponent. But Meleagant's father, Baudemagu, intervenes to reschedule the combat at Arthur's court and the prisoners are temporarily freed. Because he hesitated before mounting the cart, Lancelot receives a sharp rebuff for his service from the queen. Later, regretting this lighthearted gesture (4205), she receives him into her bed. Meleagant accuses Guinevere of adultery with Kay, and Lancelot defends her honour. Baudemagu again halts the combat. Meleagant treacherously captures Lancelot, whilst Gauvain is rescued from drowning at the Underwater Bridge. A forged letter, allegedly from Lancelot, claims that he is at Arthur's court.

Meanwhile, the maidens in Logres proclaim a tournament so that they can choose husbands from amongst the best knights. Lancelot gains permission from his jailer's wife to participate incognito. Since he is the best knight in the tournament, the queen recognizes him. At her behest, he does his worst ('au noauz', 5654), then, again following her wish, he does his best ('au mialz', 5879). All the maidens want to marry him, but he slips away at the end of the tournament to return to prison; none of the maidens marries.

Meleagant learns of Lancelot's escapade and imprisons him in a tower (Godefroy de Lagny's part begins here). Since Lancelot cannot come to Arthur's court, it appears that the prisoners and Guinevere must return to Gorre. But Meleagant's sister finds Lancelot and frees him because he helped her during his quest. Lancelot defeats and beheads Meleagant, thereby freeing the prisoners once and for all. The queen plans to reward Lancelot later in a suitable place.

The theme of adultery as found in *Cligés* is not a major issue in the *Charrette*.[5] What is emphasized here is the beneficial influence on knightly prowess of an extraordinary love. Lancelot and Gauvain, for example, are contrasted in the cart episode in which Lancelot acquires his pseudonym. Although Gauvain finds it reasonable to stay on his horse, rather than shame himself by mounting the cart, Lancelot springs into it after the briefest hesitation, because Love, triumphing over Reason, wishes him to do so (365–77). If, as a lover, he sometimes appears foolish or odd, Lancelot's love always helps him to overcome obstacles. He not only achieves the quest for the queen, he is also instrumental in saving Gauvain from drowning at the Underwater Bridge and, more importantly, he releases all Arthur's captive subjects. As Lancelot himself states, love inspires all his chivalric accomplishments (4354–60). But does it also justify adultery with the king's wife?

Yvain

At the beginning of the narrative, Calogrenant relates his shameful defeat at the Marvellous Fountain. Wandering in search of adventures to test his prowess, he had been directed to this marvel by a gigantic herdsman. Pouring water on to a stone next to the fountain, he unleashed a violent storm; after calm returned, the defender of the fountain, Esclados le Roux, took vengeance by defeating Calogrenant in combat. His cousin, Yvain, vowing to avenge him, hastens to the fountain. Mortally wounding Esclados, he pursues him into a castle but is trapped in a gateway. In return for courtesies he once showed her, Lunete, serving-maiden to the lady of the castle, gives him a ring that makes him invisible, and Yvain thus escapes discovery. He sees Laudine, Esclados's beautiful widow, and immediately falls in love with her. Lunete senses this and, unbeknownst to Yvain, succeeds in interesting her in him. After the marriage, the new husband defends the fountain against Kay. Gauvain advises Yvain to avoid uxoriousness by embarking on a round of tournaments. Laudine agrees to a separation, provided Yvain returns within a year.

Yvain fails to keep his word. His wife withdraws her love. Grief-stricken, Yvain goes mad and leads a savage life in the woods. Later, a maiden recognizes him and, using a magic ointment, restores him to his right mind. He rescues a lion from a dragon (mid-point). The lion becomes his companion and Yvain assumes the name Knight of the Lion (4285). In his many adventures he assists women who are in dire straits. On each occasion, the lion assures his victories, except in the final combat against Gauvain (the plot of *Yvain* is linked to that of the *Charrette* by Gauvain's role in both; see *Yvain* 3706–11, 3914–23 and 4734–9). After fighting Arthur's nephew to a draw, Yvain returns to the Marvellous Fountain, where he unleashes storm after storm against Laudine's lands and castle. Lunete tricks her into reconciling 'the Knight of the Lion' with his lady.

Yvain turns on the ambiguous relationship between love and prowess. Yvain keeps tourneying beyond the year allotted to him and thus neglects love for the very tournaments Erec avoided in favour of marital bliss. Yet it is by destructive storms unleashed from the fountain, and by Lunete's deception, that he wins the right to return to his wife: Lunete does not tell Laudine that the knight she must reconcile with his lady is her own husband Yvain. This problematic ending (Chrétien calls it a *jeu de verité* 'play on truth', 6624) is, in fact, a deceptive play on words.

Perceval

Because it is incomplete, *Perceval* poses unusual problems of interpretation. The first part begins in the Waste Forest where the Widow Lady has raised her son, 'Beau Fils'. She wanted to keep him ignorant of knighthood, since her husband and two other sons, all knights, perished because of violent conflict. But a chance encounter with knights awakens in the boy the desire to become a knight. As he rides off, his mother faints, but her son ignores her. We learn later that she died of grief.

The young man is uncouth in the ways of knighthood, chivalry and courtesy. Yet a smiling maiden and a court fool recognize his extraordinary potential when he appears at Arthur's court. Kay rewards them with a slap and a kick. Violence and humour mark Beau Fils's progress and failures. Clumsily following his mother's advice, he ruins the reputation of the Tent Maiden in the eyes of her lover, the Orgueilleux de la Lande, who abuses her in jealous anger. Then he kills a knight who has insulted Arthur and Guinevere. Yet he learns knighthood with phenomenal ease, saves the lovely Blanchefleur from siege and a forced marriage and enjoys her embraces. At the castle of the maimed Fisher King he observes a procession that includes a Grail and a bleeding lance, but fails to ask the required questions (on the *dire/teisir* topos in Chrétien, see Hunt 1994, 156–7): why does the lance bleed? whom does the Grail serve? If he had asked these questions, the Fisher King would have been healed and his land would have been at peace. After leaving the castle, he meets his cousin, who informs him that he failed to ask the Grail questions because of the sin he committed by ignoring his mother's distress, thereby causing her death (3531–3). At the same time, Beau Fils divines his real name, Perceval (3511–15; see Ménard 1995). After restoring the Tent Maiden's honour, he falls into contemplation of three drops of blood that have fallen on to the snow from a wounded goose: the colours remind him of Blanchefleur's lovely complexion. When Sagremor and Kay interrupt his contemplation, he defeats them in combat, breaking Kay's arm and shoulder and thereby avenging the smiling maiden. When the snow melts, Perceval recovers from his rapture and is reunited with Arthur's court. Thus ends the first part of the romance.

The second part begins when a Hideous Damsel announces the disastrous effects of Perceval's failure to ask the Grail questions; wives will now be widowed, lands laid waste, maidens and orphans made disconsolate; many a knight will die (4601–13). Perceval undertakes a quest to redeem himself but, after five years, he has forgotten God. Good Friday penitents direct him to a hermit who is also his maternal uncle. Perceval learns that his mother's prayers saved him from death and prison (6329–31), despite his sin in neglecting her distress (6318–28). He also learns the answer to one Grail question: the Grail serves the host to the Fisher King's father, who is also Perceval's uncle (6341–5). Confession and penance (6286–6312, 6358–9) wipe away Perceval's sin (Köhler 1970*, 231/1974, 263). We hear no more of him in the romance.

The second part of *Perceval* also contains a lengthy Gauvain plot. Gauvain is accused of having treacherously killed the King of Escavalon. On his way to defend himself at Escavalon, Gauvain champions the Pucelle aux petites manches against her abusive sister and then has an erotic encounter with the King of Escavalon's daughter, who does not recognize him. Protected by the hospitality custom, he is granted a one-year reprieve. He can recover his honour by bringing the Bleeding Lance to Escavalon, a lance destined to destroy Arthur's kingdom of Logres (6092–7) (here Chrétien inserts Perceval's Good Friday episode). However, Gauvain's subsequent adventures contain no reference to either the alleged murder or the Bleeding Lance; at the Castle of Ladies he survives the test of the Perilous Bed and discovers Arthur's mother, his own mother, and his sister Clarissant. He must, however, do battle with Clarissant's beloved, Guiromelant, who believes his own father and brother were murdered by Gauvain's father and by Gauvain himself. At this point the narrative breaks off abruptly.[7]

This complex, yet inconclusive, plot offers no clear choice among competing ideals. The principal characters are accused of serious wrongs, although their guilt is never absolute. Perceval causes his mother's death, yet this sin is unintentional. He progresses as knight. Indeed, *Perceval* relates a sort of learning process, an *Entwicklungsroman* in which Perceval matures as time passes and his experience grows (Kellermann 1936, 138; Frappier in Loomis ed. 1959*, 190; Köhler 1970*, 250–2/1974, 286–8). Gauvain, for his part, encounters hatred almost everywhere. He is accused of murder (on Gauvain as murderer, see Le Rider 1978, 226–7). The knight Greoreas seeks vengeance because, as punishment for rape, Gauvain forced him to eat with the dogs for a month with his hands tied behind his back. The sharp-tongued damsel, the Orgueilleuse de Logres, mocks him, hoping that he will kill her. These open-ended plots provide the impetus for later continuations, adaptations and interpolations (see Chapter VI).

Problem Romances

Because of the specific thesis each romance was thought to illustrate, earlier scholarship tended to treat Chrétien's romances as *Thesenromane* (Foerster 1914, 43*–45*); Chrétien would thus be an author engaged in promoting specific social and moral ideals. But since the ground-breaking work of Vinaver there has been a tendency to move away from ascribing a firm social or moral thesis to the romances. Instead, scholars have begun to identify the problems they raise and to relate these issues to audience reception (Vinaver 1971*, 30–1; cf. Nolting-Hauff 1959, 17; Baumgartner 1992, 19–20, 73–9; Pickens 1977; Kay 2001). To be sure, there are statements enunciated by the narrator or by a character in the plot that evoke a definite moral. For example:

> Molt est qui ainme obëissanz,
> Et molt fet tost et volentiers,
> La ou il est amis antiers,
> Ce qu'a s'amie doie plaire. (*Charrette*, 3798–3801)

(He who loves is very obedient, and when he is wholly beholden to his love eagerly does whatever may please her.)

However, Gauvain argues, as if in rebuttal, that great devotion to a beloved wife can make a knight less worthy (*Yvain*, 2484–90).

The close connection between the plots of the *Charrette* and *Yvain* sets up a virtual *jeu parti*: does love make a knight better or worse?[8] The *jeu parti* flourished as a lyric genre in the twelfth and thirteenth centuries (Långfors 1926, I, xi–lx; Zumthor 1972, 264–5; *Genere*). The typical *jeu parti* stages a debate between two speakers who argue for opposing points of view. In the *Charrette* the hero offers Gauvain the choice between the road to the Underwater Bridge and that to the Sword Bridge, an offer identified as a *jeu parti* (695). Similarly, a maiden offers Lancelot lodging if he will sleep in her bed, thus creating a dilemma: should he sleep with the maiden or forgo his night's lodging? The narrator suggests that for many knights the choice would be easy, but not for Lancelot, who wishes to remain loyal to Guinevere. Finally, a *jeu parti* is implicit in Lunete's question: which is the better knight, the one who defeats his opponent in combat or the one who is defeated?

Several lyric *jeux partis* treat problems raised in Chrétien's romances. One, for example, debates the choice between participating in tournaments and staying away for the sake of love or love-making (the central issue in both *Erec* and *Yvain*) (Långfors 1926, I, xlv, civ; cvi debates the difference between lovers before and after marriage); another points to the potential conflict between Lancelot and Arthur because of adultery (Långfors 1926, I, cvii), a conflict which becomes real in the prose *Lancelot*. *Cligés*'s contrast between Yseut's and Fénice's conception of acceptable adultery is an implicit *jeu parti* (on *Cligés* and the Tristan legends, see Weber 1976; Freeman 1979). Erec's *recreantise* contrasts with Mabonagrain's violence. Lunete claims that Laudine is a typical woman because she says the opposite of what she thinks (*Yvain*, 1640–4); is this traditional misogyny, woman's prudence, or the narrator's irony? Or is it Chrétien's (cf. Zaddy 1980; Krueger 1993*, 42–5)? The debate motif is a paradigm for internal monologues and dialogues, in which speakers weigh alternatives (Hilka 1903, 86–92, 124–34; Nolting-Hauff 1959, 30–93; Chênerie 1995). These controversial positions show how Chrétien's romances pose problems to which the answers they provide, far from being definitive, provoke debate among narrative characters whilst challenging audiences and flirting with irony that lightens the earnestness of the debate.

The 'casuistical nature' of Chrétien's plots, their 'moral evaluation … of individual case histories and the circumstances peculiar to them', makes each romance a 'case' (Hunt 1986, 18). Each case is made not so much as a final solution, but as a possible interpretation that, ultimately, no doubt provoked audiences (Vàrvaro 2001). If this is so, then the ideological coherence of Chrétien's *œuvre* is not a critical *desideratum*. Rather, we must identify the issues raised in each romance, in order to appreciate how in one romance the same writer could, for example, make the case for love in marriage, yet seem to undermine that ideal in another. It is noteworthy that, in conflicts such as these, contrasting ideals become alternatives, even irreconcilable solutions to one debatable problem. 'Like so much of *Yvain*', this ending 'is designed to produce *debate*!' (Hunt 1986, 82; his italics).

The views Chrétien chooses to illustrate in a given romance set a context for interpreting the adventures that make up the plot, like the choice between prowess and love for Erec and Yvain, between reason and love for Lancelot, or between Yseut as model and Fénice's adaptation of the Tristan model in *Cligés*. Individual episodes may also turn on dilemmas, such as Enide's debates as to whether to speak or not, or Laudine's on whether or not to marry the man who killed her husband. Combat can illustrate *jeu parti*. The martial game becomes unfair if several knights attack a lone knight, as when Yvain fights Laudine's seneschal and two others. Enide herself exclaims, in respect of a similar confrontation: 'N'est pas igaux partiz cist jeus / D'un chevalier encontre trois' (*Erec*, 2832–3) (*one knight against three is an unfair match*). Might one not say the same of the choice offered to Laudine between destruction of her castle and reconciliation with Yvain?

Scholars have read Chrétien's 'problem romances' by looking for solutions to problems such as these. Solutions there have been, including some second-guessing of Chrétien's intentions, but there is hardly any real consensus. Bruckner (1986–7) confronts this issue head on, by asking why there are so many interpretations of Chrétien's *Charrete*.[9] Why, indeed, are there so many interpretations of all Chrétien's romances? (Maddox 1973; Shirt 1978; Ménage 1980; Maddox 1980–1; Williams 1983; Bertolucci Pizzorusso in Cigni 1992, 9–20; Pensom 1993; Döffinger-Lange 1998). Bruckner's question focuses on the *Charrete*, where Lancelot's love for Guinevere makes him the best knight in the world. The narrative makes the case for this claim in exemplary fashion as Lancelot overcomes great obstacles, even if his love seems at times to shame him or make him appear ineffectual or ridiculous. For example, when absorbed by thoughts of his love, he may become oblivious to dangers that rise up before him. Yet Lancelot triumphs again and again, finally achieving his quest because of his extraordinary love (Chênerie 1986*, 379–81; cf. 394–7 and 573–5 on Lancelot's voluntary and heroic *recreantise*). The shame of riding in the cart is seen as a fault, not only by some of the characters in the plot but even by the queen herself. Her rebuff perplexes even her unquestioning lover (4339–41), since, he reasons, nothing arising out of love can be called blameworthy (4354–60). The issue rebounds when the queen herself regrets her mistreatment (4197–4207); Chrétien models her repentance, contrition and penance on standard religious topoi (Payen 1967 , 379–82).

Lancelot later learns that Guinevere faulted him, not for mounting the cart but for hesitating to do so (4484–9). For her part, the queen atones for her earlier rebuff by receiving Lancelot into her bed. Clearly the love ideal and its illustration in the *Charrette* are not so much the solution to a problem as the problem itself. As Bruckner aptly phrases the issue, 'we cannot measure only the conduct of an individual; we must also measure the norm by which we usually judge his conduct' (1986–7, 177; cf. Baumgartner 1992, 68–9; Schnell 1998). Assessing norms in this way raises questions regarding the norms articulated by Chrétien's plots. A romance may make a case for one of competing norms, as the *Charrette* does on the relation between love and prowess. The divergent conduct of romance protagonists can make the problems more compelling, for Gauvain is not a Lancelot any more than Fénice is an Yseut. Yet each enunciates a norm that stands in greater or lesser opposition to norms illustrated by other characters and other romances. The dénouements do not provide a conclusive summing-up of the meaning or validity of the norm. Conflicting views are never entirely silenced.

Audiences may have their own, different views. As Calogrenant explains, in the process of reception 'parole oïe est perdue / S'ele n'est de cuer entendue' (*words heard are lost if the heart fails to understand them*; *Yvain*, 151–2). The heart is not only the seat of emotions in Old French, it is also the agent of understanding (Brault 1972). Calogrenant wants his public to listen attentively to his 'tale of shame' (59–60) because, he says, his tale is true. For him, its truth is an awareness of his shame. Yet, as we have seen in Lancelot's case, 'shame' depends on how different minds interpret actions.

We must remember that audiences may be quite heterogeneous, and even conflicting. 'Audience' includes two special groups that loom large in the reception of Chrétien's romances. One group is made up of medieval readers or audiences whose reactions are recorded; this includes full-blown adaptations of the romances in French and other languages, such as the rewriting of Lancelot's love and prowess in the prose *Lancelot*. The other group comprises generations of scholars who, since the early nineteenth century, have interpreted and evaluated Chrétien's romances in the light of their own times and their own critical presuppositions. For example, the opinion once expressed, that Chrétien was a *bon bourgeois* disinclined to idealize Lancelot, contrasts with recent feminist readings that critique the ethic by which love inspires prowess (Cross and Nitze 1930; Krueger 1993*, 36–7, 51–66; Gaunt 1995, 91–103). These distinctions oblige us to reconsider the problems raised by Chrétien's romances, as well as modern approaches to them, since the *locus* of problems as perceived by medieval audiences may not be germane today. Chrétien raises issues of marriage and martial prowess that are curious, but not always urgent to modern readers. On the other hand, current psychoanalytic or anthropological approaches would not, and indeed could not, have been intended by medieval authors or publics.

In what follows, Chrétien's art of romance is first delineated using his interventions as guide and his romances as illustration. Then the performance of his romances is discussed, including ways in which medieval audiences might have heard or read them. Finally, the contexts are examined within which Chrétien sets the norms and poses the problems of conduct illustrated by his romances. These three factors mark his achievement and define his legacy for the tradition of Arthurian romance in French and other languages.

Chrétien's Art of Writing Romance

The investigation and reconstruction of presumed sources dominated Chrétien scholarship until the mid-twentieth century.[10] Then came reaction leading to closer reading of his romances in order to appreciate their composition. In the 1970s, modern theoretical approaches reintroduced source study in new contexts, such as intertextuality (Bruckner in Lacy, Kelly and Busby eds 1987–8*, I, 223–65; Wolfzettel ed. 1990*, 1–17; Watanabe 1990) and mythopoetic readings (Walter 1988; Vincensini 1996; Watanabe 2002).

Intertextuality comprises a number of different models that explain relations among texts. It differs from most earlier source study by taking into account the process of adaptation in rewriting sources. The new author perceives a potential inherent, but not yet realized, in an antecedent work and rewrites it in his or her new version (cf. Marie de France's notion of adding the *surplus* of meaning to an earlier work; *Lais*, Prologue, 16; cf. Köhler 1970*, 52–3/1974, 61–2). 'Antecedent' can also refer to motifs and themes already used by the same author in one or more of his or her own earlier works, as in the return in *Yvain* to the love versus prowess issue found in *Erec*. Such 'analogical composition' (Lacy 1980, 110) within this broad sense of intertextuality (which therefore includes intratextuality) may operate by virtual repetition, by greater or lesser resemblance or by contrast; for example, the tournament episode in the *Charrette* reuses features of the entire romance (Bruckner 1993*, chapter 3).

Two aspects of intertextuality must be distinguished: (i) the relationships between texts perceived by the author, but of which the public is unaware (for example, a Latin model adapted for a vernacular public), and (ii) the relationships which audiences are expected to perceive, such as Chrétien's reference in the prologue to *Erec* to other versions of the tale, or the allusions to the *Charrette* contained in *Yvain*. These relationships reflect the art of romance and the reception of romance by the reading and listening audiences.

The prologue to *Cligés* locates Chrétien's art and writings in a scholastic tradition going back to Greece and Rome, but surviving, he believes, in twelfth-century France. In books whose age makes them authoritative and trustworthy he proclaims that we can learn the marvellous deeds of bygone peoples, deeds that reveal the significance of *chevalerie* and *clergie*; these two poles of a common ideal constitute a given civilization's 'honour' (27–39). Such honour can be gained and lost. For example, *chevalerie* and *clergie* left Greece and Rome to settle in France. In Chrétien's romances chivalric honour is an obvious theme. But just as obvious is its problematic nature. What properly determines honourable chivalric conduct? The question reverberates throughout the romances, although no single answer is given.

The art by which Chrétien articulates these problems illustrates his own *clergie*, a notion as broad as *chevalerie*. *Clergie* is transmitted through scholastic traditions, including education in the *trivium* as taught in the best medieval schools. The *trivium* comprised grammar, rhetoric and logic. The pupil mastered these arts by systematic, sustained learning of each formal art, by study of its practice in canonic examples, and by exercises applying various aspects of the art in written compositions and declamations. Having been trained in the art until practice became habitual, the student can then move beyond the classroom to imitate and emulate, and to do so freely and with originality. This is, presumably, what happened in Chrétien's case: he applied his art to writing Arthurian material in French. Traces of his preparation survive in his works, both in the Ovidian adaptations he names in the prologue to *Cligés*, and in allusions to clerical sources such as Macrobius (*Erec,* 6733–5), to the library of Saint-Pierre in Beauvais (*Cligés*, 18–21; on the Beauvais manuscript Chrétien may have known, see Villa 1996) and Latin literature.[11]

In prologues, epilogues and interpolated digressions Chrétien refers to an art of writing romance.[12] Although there is some controversy regarding the precise meaning of these interventions (see most notably Dragonetti 1987), they are useful in defining his conception of narrative composition and as guides for the scholar attempting to interpret his romances and the problems they raise. Furthermore, they may suggest which features of Chrétien's art subsequent generations of romancers adopted, adapted or rejected. Certain terms are critical. They fall into three major groups: *matiere, san* and *aventure merveilleuse*; *sans, painne* and *antancion* applied to composition; and *bele conjointure* as *roman*. To summarize briefly: *matiere* and *san* designate, respectively, the source material Chrétien chooses to rewrite and the meaning given to material chosen for its marvellous features. Applying his critical intelligence (*sans*) and artistic effort (*painne*) to rewriting, Chrétien realizes a purpose (*antancion*) by moulding *matiere* and *san* into a coherent, intelligible whole. This whole, which he calls a *bele conjointure*, comes to be known as a *roman*, a word that for him seems to connote a coherent amalgam of marvellous adventures in a sophisticated narrative.

Matiere, san and *aventure merveilleuse*
In the prologue to the *Charrette*, Chrétien says that Marie de Champagne provided him with both *matiere* and *san* for the composition of the romance

(26–7). It is generally agreed that Chrétien uses the word *matiere* to refer to his sources, an antecedent version or versions of the story he retells or rewrites. No source for any of Chrétien's Arthurian romances is extant, but we do know that the source for the pre-Arthurian *Philomena* mentioned in the prologue to *Cligés* was a tale in Ovid's *Metamorphoses* (*Marques de Rome*, a thirteenth-century prose romance, contains an analogue to *Cligés*). In *Erec* he alludes to a *conte d'aventure* (13), which he says story-tellers are wont to dismember and fragment (*corrompre* and *depecier*, 19–22; on these meanings, see Kelly 1992*, 125–9). This reference gives us a glimpse of itinerant *jongleurs*, who, more or less successfully, hawked about a well-known tale for the pleasure of the high-born. Chrétien refers elsewhere to a 'lai de joie' (*Erec,* 6179–81) and to another lay about Landunet (*Yvain*, 2153–5; cf. Foulet and Uitti 1983–4). Accordingly, the expression *conte d'aventure* corresponds both to the written *conte* about Cligés, which Chrétien claims to have found in a Beauvais manuscript (18–23), and the book which Chrétien claims to have received from Philippe de Flandre (*Perceval*, 64–6). Furthermore, all Chrétien's romances express a *san* through narratorial interventions, such as the explanation of Lancelot's obedience to Guinevere's wishes quoted above (*Charrette*, 3797–3801). Similar interpretative statements by characters in the narrative include diverse rules for knightly decorum in *Perceval*, structural contrasts such as that between the knighthood of Lancelot and Gauvain in the *Charrette*, the issue of love versus knighthood in *Erec* and *Yvain*, and the choice between consent and submission to marriage in *Cligés* and *Yvain*.

Chrétien's allusion to a *conte d'aventure* in Erec implies that adventure is the subject-matter of his romance plots. Adventure in this sense is whatever happens, whether it comes to a person or a place or whether a person goes out seeking it. It includes the play of chance, fortune and destiny in adventures encountered (Ménard 1991; Kelly 1999b). An adventure comes to court in the opening episode in the *Charrette*, when Meleagant challenges Arthur to seek the release of the prisoners in Gorre by making Guinevere hostage for their release. More commonly, however, a knight goes out in search of adventure. This activity takes two forms: wandering about (*errances*) and quest. Calogrenant illustrates the former in *Yvain*. As he puts it: 'Aloie querant aventures, / Armés de toutes armeüres' (*I went in search of adventures, fully armed*, 177–8). Later he tells the herdsman that he is seeking adventures to test his prowess and his courage (360–1). Adventures are, therefore, encounters that test a knight's mettle. On the one hand, the knight merely roams about exposing himself to challenges; on the other hand, a quest has a specific goal or purpose, such as the Knight of the Cart's search for Guinevere in the *Charrette* (on the common features of Chrétien's quests, see Kelly 1971, 334–43; on Erec's intentions, see also Zaddy 1973, 1–14; Lacy 1980, 39–45).

Calogrenant's *errances* reveal another feature of adventure in Chrétien's romances: the adventure as marvel. Calogrenant asks the giant herdsman to direct him to an adventure or a marvel (*Yvain*, 362–4). Not being a knight, the herdsman knows nothing about 'adventure', and apparently has never heard the word before; but 'marvel' does ring a bell and he directs Calogrenant to the Marvellous Fountain (*Yvain*, 365–78; see Köhler 1970*, chapter 3; cf. *Perceval* 4671–6). In Chrétien's romances, narrative focuses on marvellous adventures that, like *Yvain*'s Marvellous Fountain, test prowess. Unlike Wace, who leaves marvellous adventures out of his writings (*Rou*, III, 6373–98; *Brut*, 9785–98), Chrétien makes the marvel and, more specifically, the marvellous adventure in his sources, a defining feature of his romances.

The story-tellers' *conte d'aventure* no doubt provoked wonder. Wonder seems to have been a major component in the medieval romance aesthetic (Poirion 1982*; 1986). Marvellous episodes are commonly recalled in Chrétien's imitators (Schmolke-Hasselmann 1980*, 160–9/1998, 195–205). Marvels comprise anything extraordinary, ranging from the unusual to the supernatural (Carasso-Bulow 1976; Kelly 1992*, 167–76). Chênerie (1986*, 593–8) identifies the marvellous with the supernatural or with enchantment, but also notes its slippage in Chrétien and elsewhere, towards a religious or chivalric context (648–9; see also Dubost in Dufournet ed. 1988, 47–76). The insights of anthropological, psychoanalytic and historical approaches to Chrétien's romances help us to appreciate the aesthetic impact of the marvellous on medieval audiences. *Perceval* especially has been the object of such investigations, focusing, for example, on the Grail and the Castle of Ladies inhabited by the 'living-dead' female relations of Arthur and Gauvain (Dragonetti 1980; Méla 1984; Vincensini 1996; Rey-Flaud 1998 and 1999). It is well to bear in mind that medieval notions of what is historically accurate or scientific may account for the different reception of the marvellous (Schöning 1991, chapter 4). Scholars have not ignored the more supernatural adventures in other romances, such as the *Joie de la cort* in *Erec*, with its invisible wall, the devilish *netuns* in *Yvain* and the otherworldly connotations of the imprisonment in Gorre in the *Charrette*. However, the marvellous in Chrétien's romances designates the extraordinary or unusual more often than it does the supernatural or miraculous. Dragons and giants are rare; when they do appear, they are, paradoxically, relatively small. The dragon in *Yvain* is no larger than an apparently small lion; giants like those in *Erec* and *Yvain* are tall and corpulent, but hardly superhuman in size. The devils in *Yvain* are half-human and can be killed. The lion is tame. The Grail is holy only because it contains the host; it has no apparent power of its own, unlike in later romances. Gauvain's adventure in the Marvellous Bed of the Castle of Ladies is an encounter with automata more than with an enchantment; the lion that attacks him there is merely a lion let loose. Marvellous adventures are therefore extraordinary and unusual. More importantly, they single out the extraordinary and unusual knight or maiden who confronts them. All these factors point to the second feature of marvels: their role in defining a context for the person who achieves marvellous adventures.

Sans, painne and antancïon

If Chrétien receives *matiere* and *san* in the sense of source matter and meaning, by what art does he conjoin them in a romance? In the *Charrette* Chrétien discusses this aspect of his composition. Although he insists on the primacy of Marie de Champagne in the invention of the work (21–3), he says that he has rewritten her *matiere* and *san* using his 'thought', a notion that he clarifies as follows:

> Matiere et san li done et livre
> La contesse et il s'antremet
> De panser, que gueres n'i met
> Fors sa painne et s'antancïon. (26–9)

> (*The countess provides him with matter and meaning, whereas he undertakes to think, for he brings to the task nothing more than his effort and his intention.*)

The terms *painne* and *antancïon* together describe the writer's concentrated effort, or *penser*, to achieve a predetermined goal (Köhler 1970*, 90–1/1974, 105). Marie de Champagne's 'command' ('comandemanz', 22) to write a romance (2) containing her *matiere* and *san* designates that goal. The artist contributes his 'sans' and 'painne' (23) and his 'painne' and 'antancïon' (29), i.e. his skill as artist (on *sans* and *antancïon* as binomal synonyms, see Buridant 1980). What skill or skills does Chrétien use to write *matiere* and *san* into his romances?

When Erec reacts to Enide's criticism of his alleged *recreantise*, both his men and Enide herself wonder why he begins to arm himself:

> Li serjant et li chevalier
> Se prenent tuit *a mervoillier*
> *Por qoi* il armer se fesoit (2649–51, my emphasis, cf. 2676–82)

> (*The men at arms and knights all begin* to wonder why *he had himself armed.*)

Similarly, many wonder why Guinevere receives Lancelot so coldly, including Baudemagu, Kay and Lancelot himself (*Charrette*, 3947–9, 3982–5, 4074–5, 4337–41). When Lancelot later asks her why she did so (4472–5), the queen provides a surprising answer: because he hesitated before mounting the infamous cart. Her action is extraordinary, as is her explanation. Both are examples of the marvellous as source of extraordinary adventures that also reveal narrative meaning. As author and narrator, Chrétien too interrogates marvellous matter. The marvellous in Chrétien's *matiere* introduces a questioning mode consistent with the problem romance and conducive to oppositions such as those in *jeux partis*: the mind 'wonders', as in 'I wonder why', an expression also current in Old French (see the example of *se merveiller por quoi* in lines 2650–1 quoted above).

Let us look more closely at the cart episode in the *Charrette* to see how Chrétien gives meaning to this crucial adventure in Lancelot's quest. The cart may well have been a feature of the *matiere* on which Chrétien drew to write the *Charrette* (Loomis 1949, 204–14; Frappier 1968, 134–6). Chrétien uses two comparisons to explain, for contemporary audiences, the shame attached to the cart (321–44). First, he cites a current proverb: in order to avoid misfortune one should cross oneself when seeing a cart; the cart accordingly signifies a threat. Secondly, Chrétien likens riding in a cart in Lancelot's time to exposing a criminal in a pillory in his own time. Those guilty of treason or murder should not only be punished but publicly shamed as well. Accordingly, honourable knights do not ride in carts. In subsequent adventures many judge Lancelot unfavourably because he mounted the cart. By contrast, Guinevere judges him harshly for hesitating to do so. This virtual *jeu parti* suggests two norms for evaluating the cart episode, a chivalric norm and an amorous one.

The different responses of Gauvain and Lancelot to mounting the cart illustrate the two norms and define two kinds of knighthood. Chrétien expresses the difference by means of a debate in Lancelot's mind, a virtual *jeu parti*, between Reason and Love. Reason argues against mounting the cart, in order to avoid shame. But, according to the narrator, this is only so much talk, for Reason (*raison* can also mean 'language' in Old French as well as 'speech, discourse' in the narrative sense) is only in his mouth and therefore in Lancelot's case is merely lip-service. In his heart Love convinces him to spring into the cart.

Here Chrétien contrasts norms, thereby raising issues important to contemporary aristocratic audiences. Similarly, penitents criticize Perceval for wearing armour on Good Friday, thus contrasting religious duty and knighthood. God is the authority according to whom Perceval should not bear arms on Good Friday: 'Hui ne deüst hom qui Deu croie / Armes porter' (*today no one who believes in God should bear arms*, 6225–6). Bearing arms illustrates Perceval's status as a knight who has forgotten God. Analogously, at the tournament at Noauz in the *Charrette*, some knights do not participate because they are prisoners or crusaders (5770). Gauvain too claims that he cannot participate in the Tintagel tournament because he must undergo a trial by combat, the outcome of which will be decided by God (*Perceval*, 5119–27).

Chrétien's descriptions of contrasting norms are not always as obvious as in these instances. More problematic is the crisis in Erec and Enide's marriage, where the shame attached to *recreantise* is contrasted with the pleasures of love. Similarly, we see in *Yvain* how difficult it is to accommodate chivalry and marriage, fidelity and one's word of honour, in the construction of knighthood. No doubt such dilemmas also inspired diverse reactions among audiences.

Custom is an important factor in rewriting marvels in putative sources, and thus in the adaptation of *matiere* to *san*, or of source matter to chivalric context

(Köhler 1960). Chrétien underscores the importance of custom in his first romance, when Arthur proclaims that he intends to uphold the Custom of the White Stag because his ancestors did so (*Erec*, 1800–10). Similarly, Lancelot submits to the Custom of the Cart for the sake of Guinevere, no matter what the consequences may be. Maddox has proposed a threefold typology of custom (Maddox 1991, 35). There are customs 'that King Arthur must observe', such as the White Stag Custom in *Erec*, and there are also those 'whose abuse the hero ends, but which nonetheless continue to exist' (Maddox 1991, 36), as when Yvain is reinstated as defender of Laudine's fountain. There are, finally, customs 'that are permanently abolished', like the custom of holding inhabitants of Logres in Gorre or the *Joie de la cort* episode in *Erec*. Although the odd and therefore marvellous features of customs may well derive from Chrétien's sources, their definition as custom explains them in a twelfth-century legal context, as when Chrétien compares the shame of riding in a cart to that attached to the pillory.

Chrétien's transformation of Celtic marvels into medieval customs can be troubling. In Lancelot's case, we may ask whether love justifies, and indeed honours, a lover who willingly 'pillories' himself for its sake. Even more problematic is the custom of Logres, which allows the knight to take a maiden by force if he defeats her escort in combat (*Charrette*, 1302–16). In *Yvain* the custom of the Marvellous Fountain provides a disturbing dénouement when Yvain seeks reconciliation with his wife by force, unleashing violent storms on her realm, whilst relying on Lunete to trick Laudine into becoming reconciled with him. The disturbing, yet original, way in which Chrétien treats these features of his *matiere* brings contrasting norms into opposition (cf. Haug 1979; Cheyette and Chickering 2005).

Similarly, the incognito combat between Gauvain and Yvain shows the problematic union of *matiere* and *san* in composition. In this episode, the combatants' armour hides their identity as they duel. According to the narrator, Yvain and Gauvain appear to love and hate each other at one and the same time. Chrétien explains the anomaly by describing a house in which Hate occupies the front room, whereas Love is in a back room, far removed from the action (6023–36). Informing images like the Love–Hate dwelling are present wherever Chrétien conflates matter with meaning. The conventional separation of heart and body in love provides the occasion for a 'scientific' digression on the impossibility of such separation in *Cligés*, 2774–2808. This is, of course, as obvious as the digression on the cohabitation of love and hate in the Yvain–Gauvain combat. But, as a metaphor, it shows two hearts that share the same desire. Its very artificiality underscores the metaphorical character of the image, especially for Chrétien's unschooled aristocratic audiences, more so perhaps than for Latin-educated audiences. He wants them to understand the sense of loss created by separation from a loved one. Having insisted on the impossibility of the heart's physically leaving the living body, he can affirm the metaphorical value of the image, and continue to use it knowingly, not only in other romances but later in *Cligés* itself, when Fénice claims that her heart has left Constantinople to be with Cligés in England (4288–92, 4398–4408).

Chrétien's *antancïon* in articulating *matiere* and *san* can provoke surprise, suspense, wonder and controversy, as in the manipulation (the word is not too strong) practised by author and characters, notably Lunete's manipulation of Laudine's feelings. Laudine herself uses various expressions to refer to that manipulation, most of which suggest trickery or deception. Lunete makes her first appeal for Yvain in the form of a rhetorical question, but one with two implied answers:

> Quant .ii. chevaliers sont ensamble
> Venu as armes en bataille,
> Li quiex cuidiez vous qui miex vaille,
> Quant li uns a l'autre conquis? (1694–7)

(*When two knights fight, which in your opinion is more worthy, when the one has defeated the other?*)

Laudine recognizes that more is at issue than a simple declaration of victory: 'Il m'est avis que tu *m'aguaites*, / Si me veuz *a parole prendre*' (*I think that you are out to* trap me *with a* play on words, 1700–1; my emphasis). In fact, Lunete has set up a *jeu parti*. But the *jeu parti* is not a simple debate, as Laudine herself perceives; it is also a *jeu de vérité*, or deceptive play on words and on names (on *jeu de vérité* as deceptive play on words, see Kelly in Dufournet ed. 1988). Chrétien plays much the same game with his audiences and, like Laudine at the end of *Yvain*, readers must decide for themselves how to respond to such deception (Hunt 1986, chapter 4; Baumgartner 1992, 66–7).

Humour and irony must certainly be taken into account when evaluating the often ambiguous or problematic *san* of Chrétien's romances (Haidu 1968; Ménard 1969; Haidu 1972, esp. 52–3; Green 1979; Ménard in Dufournet ed. 1988; Bouché and Charpentier 1990; Boutet 2000*). Diverse approaches to the subject reveal how subtle, complex and elusive this humour can be. More recent scholarship has raised the issue of individual response and sensitivity, where the same humour makes some laugh and others smile, whilst still others are offended. Why? In part, to paraphrase Pascal, *rire au deçà des Pyrénées, larmes au delà*; one person's wit is another's bad joke or bad taste. Here temporal distance can be just as crucial as geographic distance.

Some have argued that Chrétien himself felt uncomfortable with the choices apparent in the plots commissioned by his patrons. This is especially the case with the *Charrette*. Was not Marie de Champagne's *san* repugnant to him because it idealized adulterous love? More recent readings have questioned this reconstruction of the author and his patroness (McCash 1985), and some have suggested that Chrétien subverted or even inverted the ideas of Marie de Champagne (Krueger 1993*, 54–66).

Such interpretations underscore the fact that neither option available in *jeux partis* may be desirable. Nor is there reason to suppose that they actually express the authors' personal views, or that they were any more sure of what they really thought than is Laudine in her debate with Lunete (on *jeux partis* between women, see Doss-Quinby 1999). *Jeux partis* recalling analogous situations in Chrétien's romances make their ostensible *san* more problematic than authoritative.[13] The principle of the *jeu parti* implies judges in the audience, whose views on the conflict are not reported in the poem. In Andreas Capellanus's *De amore* arbiters resolve debates; among them are identifiable historical names such as Marie de Champagne. Similarly, in Chrétien's romances, exemplary content illustrates meanings that, by emphatic restatement, provoke reaction, and ultimately audience or individual judgement.

Such reception may well be a factor in romances relying on oral recitation, rather then on private reading, a situation that seems to have prevailed in Chrétien's time. It is corroborated by a number of his interventions addressing audiences (Gallais 1964, 483–93). Moreover, audience response is not confined to occasional commentary or debate at the time a romance is read. It occurs when a writer rewrites Chrétien. For example, Hartmann von Aue rewrites the reconciliation between Erec and Enide: whereas in Chrétien Erec pardons his wife, in the German adaptation he asks for her pardon. Both authors articulate the same issue, but evaluate it differently. Correction by rewriting is a standard feature of topical invention and of the *jeu parti* itself. Subsequent chapters in this volume and the other volumes in the series show that Chrétien was frequently rewritten, whether such rewriting focused on the narrative, on the meaning of a whole work or on specific motifs or themes.

Bele Conjointure as *Roman*

Chrétien states that he is drawing from a tale of adventure a very beautiful 'conjointure' (Erec, 13–14). The term *conjointure* has inspired diverse definitions and applications, as scholars seek to explain the word by identifying its sources in ancient and medieval poetic commentary, or by extrapolating its meaning from analysis of his romances (Kelly 1970; Hilty 1975). The combination of two or more entities is a *conjointure*, a fact easily understood, even by audiences unfamiliar with the scholastic tradition from which Chrétien's term *conjointure* may well derive (Kelly 1992*, chapter 1), but entirely conversant with the word's usual meanings in twelfth-century French.[14] The *Erec* passage fits this meaning when Chrétien says that he *draws* his *conjointure* from a tale, thus suggesting that he is lifting parts from the tale or from a number of different versions of a tale, and recombining them in a new version. Although the noun is a hapax in its artistic sense, analogous instances of *conjointure,* such as *conjoindre* or *joindre,* are attested (Buckbee in Kelly ed. 1985, 51–4; Kelly 1992*, 15–21). These examples refer to places where parts of a romance are joined or jointed together. However, such 'jointing' is, of and by itself, aesthetically neutral (Topsfield 1981, 23).

The prologue to *Erec* contrasts Chrétien's tale with other versions of the same tale as related in high courts. As we have seen, Chrétien claims that these versions are 'depecié' (*fragmented*) and 'corrompu' (*incomplete*); but a defective combination is still a *conjointure*. That is no doubt why Chrétien added the important qualification *bele* to his use of *conjointure*. Only his *conjointure* is 'beautiful' because it conjoins matter and meaning in a new, complete whole.

Chrétien's aesthetic of the *bele conjointure* is strikingly illustrated in the first part of *Erec*. After Arthur bestows on Enide the Kiss of the White Stag as the most beautiful woman at court, the narrator abruptly announces that here ends the romance's 'premerains vers' (1840). This expression has often been translated as 'first part' (of the romance), although it does not mark the actual dénouement of the first part, which continues on for some 500 more lines, before ending with the marriage of Erec and Enide. Their marriage marks a true narrative pause analogous to that in Chrétien's other two-part romances, notably *Cligés* and *Yvain*.

In the prologue to *Erec* Chrétien criticizes the story-tellers for their allegedly incomplete versions. We can postulate one such *conte* as being the Hunt for the White Stag, Chrétien's 'premerains vers', that does indeed end when Arthur bestows the kiss on Enide; another, second tale or *vers* about the Sparrow-hawk includes the marriage that Erec promised, as Enide's champion in combat against Yder. Enide links the two *vers* by being the most beautiful woman in each. Since *vers* in Old French can mean not only 'line of verse' but also 'narrative segment', we can interpret the reference to the *premerains vers* as Chrétien's complex intertwining of two tales in the first section of his new *conjointure*, tales that are linked through the themes of knightly prowess and noble beauty (Kelly 1970, 195–8; cf. Maddox 1978, 101–12). Chrétien's other romances suggest similar combinations. For example, *Yvain* may combine a tale about a marvellous fountain with another about a fountain fairy, perhaps the very *lai de Landunet* to which Chrétien alludes (2154). Quests are a concatenation of diverse *vers*, episodes held together by the questing knight (Berthelot 1993). These examples illustrate antecedent matter being conjoined into a whole and complete plot by an artistic mind and intention.

Description of feminine beauty such as Enide's is conventional in Chrétien's romances as well as in those of his contemporaries. These formal catalogues of beautiful features begin with the description of the elegant parting in pure golden hair and continue down the body as far as the narrator is willing to go (*Cligés*, 842–53; Colby 1965; Kelly in Lacy, Kelly and Busby eds 1987–8*, I, 191–221). Yet even here Chrétien can be original. In *Cligés*, the stereotypical description of Soredamors combines the image of the arrow suggested by the analogy between the parting in her golden hair and the groove and feathers in the metaphorical arrow shot into Alixandre's astonished eyes. As Alixandre, in his mind's eye, follows her physical beauty down the arrow shaft, his gaze stops abruptly at her hemline, which leaves him wondering about the hidden part of the arrow shaft and the arrowhead. Elsewhere, Chrétien contrasts physical beauty and ragged dress in his description of both Enide and the *amie* of the Orgueilleux de la Lande in *Perceval*; Laudine's conventional beauty, again from hair to hemline, incites Yvain's love at the very moment when, grief-stricken by the death of her husband, she lacerates that beauty by scratching her face and tearing her hair (1146–65, 1466–94; Accarie 1979; 1998, 14–15; Liborio 1982, 173–5; Press 1987, 15–18; Ferroul 2000).

A *bele conjointure* is also a medium for transmitting knowledge (*Erec*, 15–18), the credibility of which depends on the structural coherence of the plot (Haug 1992, 101–3/1997, 101–3). Description provides that coherence. The art of description is topical invention, a skill acquired in the study of the *trivium*. This 'questioning mode' finds answers in 'its proper place in a sequence of coordinated occurrences' (Vinaver 1963–4, 488; see also 490–5; Zumthor 1972, 352–61; Burns 1987–8) such as a quest or the usual stages in courtship or seduction (*gradus amoris*); the writer's training in this skill formed 'a habit of mind' which, becoming ingrained, 'could easily become a habit of conception' (Vinaver 1963–4, 493). By topical invention, therefore, Chrétien identifies 'places' (*loci*, topoi) in his *matiere* where he can develop a coherent, albeit problematical interpretation of it (*san*).

A brief discussion of scholastic topoi will clarify their use in Chrétien's descriptions.[15] Topoi as used here are common places. Technically, such 'places' are 'common' to persons, things or activities (Haidu 1972, 14–15, uses 'symbolism' and 'sign' in an analogous way). The scholastic tradition identifies the places which are common to persons as the following: name, nature (including native language, native land, age, family, sex), way of life, fortune, character, goals, appetites, judgement, luck, exploits and speech. The author selects the places which are useful for describing a given person (Faral 1924, 77–8).

Take, for example, the *chevalier errant* 'knight errant' (Chênerie 1986*, 103–6). A source may contain a tale about a man's adventures. Chrétien, the author, invents or identifies this person as a young man (age) of noble birth (family; see Ménard 1984, 61–3; Schmid 1986; Kullmann 1992; Bruckner in Kelly ed. 1996*), who has a fortunate encounter (luck) with other men identified as knights (way of life). Although he is Welsh (native land) and uncouth (way of life), the encounter awakens in the young man a desire to become a knight himself (appetite). One sees here a plausible, historically credible illustration of the invention of Perceval. Moreover, since the young man is not named until after his failure at the Grail Castle, we see the naming topos being brought into the invention of the person and his acts. Setting out in search of Arthur's court (goal), the young man begins an itinerary whose goal changes with the circumstances of his progress: return to his mother, return to Blanchefleur, return to the Grail Castle. Having become a knight (way of life), he wanders about in search of his goals – he is a knight errant (see above on *errance*). In addition, like his dress, his name is variously qualified according to his successes and failures on the quest. Because of his uncouth ways, he is Perceval the Welshman (*li Gualois*, 3513) before he visits the Grail Castle, and after his failure there he becomes Perceval the Wretch (*li chaitis*, 3520) (cf. Ménard 1995).

The naming topos is an important feature of Chrétien's art (Schmolke-Hasselmann 1980*, 35/1998, 41; Kelly 1984; Ménard 1995. Cf. Burgess 1984, 40–2). He assigns a specific name to many of his characters, so that the range of problems illustrated by each of them comes to identify a type that the name itself epitomizes and distinguishes. For example, the unique, yet diverse excellence of an Erec, a Perceval or a Lancelot derives from Chrétien's different description of each knight and his actions; the same holds true for women like Enide, Laudine and Guinevere. Moreover, characters change name, or more precisely acquire and set aside pseudonyms like Knight of the Cart (Lancelot), Knight of the Lion (Yvain) and Beau Fils (Perceval). Perceval's mother stresses the importance of the name and *sornon* (name, nickname, pseudonym) in knowing a *preudom*, or noble person (523–6). Attribution of these pseudonyms also marks a crisis or other significant moment in the narrative for the renamed person.

If we compare this analysis of the invention of Perceval in Chrétien's romance with that of other knights, we discover analogous instances of topical invention – that is, of descriptions and narratives that can be explained in terms of common places diversely articulated. These descriptions show how Chrétien articulates stereotypical schemes in novel ways that identify different kinds of knight: Lancelot, the knight as lover, Erec, the knight as husband, Yvain, the knight as defender of the fountain. They also define the roles of secondary characters (Lepri 1991). Yet, lest the audience assume that the knight or lady described illustrates a definitive ideal, each romance offers a problematic dénouement that forces the audience to reflect on the way the knights are idealized (Lefay-Toury 1972, 285–8).

Actions have their common places too. Quests emphasize those of time and place, which Chrétien rewrites in the journey motif as chivalric *errances* and quests (Ménard 1967; Baumgartner 1986; Kelly 1988; Walter in Dufournet ed. 1988, 195–217; Zumthor 1993). They appear in Lancelot's two-step hesitation before the cart, where, alone in the woods without a horse, he hesitates before springing into the cart. Elsewhere, drawing on sources that preserve traces of the Celtic supernatural Other World, Chrétien redefines places using the scholastic model of the *locus amoenus*, or 'pleasance' (Gsteiger 1958). Such a 'place' may be a clearing or orchard, a spring, stream, tomb, cemetery or chapel (Ziltener 1972; Liborio 1982, 175–7). Such places are beneficial (*amoenus*) or malevolent in the chivalric context of each romance. They also have a potential for restatement, not only in Chrétien's own rewriting, as with the different descriptions of the fountain setting in *Yvain* (Baumgartner in Dufournet ed. 1988, 31–46), but also for original or novel rewriting in the epigonal romances that rewrite Chrétien. The quest has common places besides time and place. For example, the adventures encountered may be an obstacle or aid to progress.

In Chrétien's romances we should not expect to find, says Chênerie (1986*, 216–17), a pre-established code of chivalry, for such a code is created by the behaviour of the hero and the value of the code is made absolute by the repetition of this behaviour (cf. Lacy 1980, 27–33). Different *matieres* may, by topical invention, exemplify diverse norms. Hence, a Lancelot is not an Yvain, even though the quest of each knight includes defence of wronged women. Places are common to all these narratives, yet as topoi they are differently enunciated and evaluated in the divergent conduct of knights in the same romance or in succeeding romances. For instance, the decisions made by Gauvain and Lancelot in the cart episode, and the choice of the Underwater Bridge or the Sword Bridge, illustrate different conceptions of knighthood and articulate divergent norms.

Chrétien's last three romances raise interesting questions regarding their *conjointures*. Sargent-Baur (1987) has proposed reading the *Charrette* and *Yvain* as two parts of one romance (cf. Bruckner 1993*, 90–4).[16] She bases her suggestion on two features of these works, both found in *Yvain*. First, it lacks a prologue; there are only digressive 'opening signals' (Uitti in Kelly ed. 1985, 199–204) praising the courtesy of Arthur's time, whilst condemning the villainy characteristic, the narrator argues, of his late twelfth-century world. Secondly, Gauvain is absent in *Yvain* because of his quest for Guinevere and because he accompanies her back to court, events that are narrated in the *Charrette* (*Yvain*, 3702–13, 3914–23, 4730–9). The potential *conjointure* of the two works includes a third component: the last 1,000 lines of the *Charrette* claimed to be written by Godefroy de Lagny.

The incomplete *Perceval* is similarly problematic. Although there seems to be a relatively coherent progression in Perceval's development from ignorant youth to knight worthy of asking the Grail questions, a rationale for the extensive Gauvain narrative, itself incomplete and seemingly fluid as to its potential dénouement, has eluded consensus. Gauvain's goals shift, from his initial promise to relieve the siege of a maiden at Montesclaire (4636–50), to his defence against Guingambresil's accusation that he murdered his father (4705–26), to, finally, the quest for the Bleeding Lance (6122–7) and his wanderings, after his departure from Escavalon, in quest of that lance, which is, however, not mentioned again.

These features of the incomplete romance raise a number of important, but unanswerable, questions about its intended *conjointure*. Did Chrétien intend a conjuncture of Perceval and Gauvain tales, analogous to that which Sargent-Baur suggests for the linking of the *Charrette* and *Yvain*? What meaning did he intend for Perceval's and Gauvain's quests, both in search of the Grail castle, the one to answer the Grail questions, the other to find the Bleeding Lance? Has Chrétien adopted in Gauvain's case a new, centrifugal kind of *conjointure*, which the *Perceval* continuations will emulate (on centrifugal and centripetal intertextuality, see Bruckner in Lacy, Kelly and Busby eds 1987–8*)? These questions point not only to the variety of ways in which *conjointures*, or combinations of diverse material, are possible, but also to the difficulties of making such *conjointures beles*, and of our identifying the criteria that reveal their beauty.

As far as we know, Chrétien de Troyes was the first to use the word *roman* in the sense of 'romance'. In earlier examples the term *roman* designated the French language and, by extension, any work written in that language (Baumgartner 1995, 3–7). Chrétien uses it in this way in the prologue to *Cligés* (3), but then he seems to endow the term with the more specific sense of 'romance', as a kind of narrative (23). Again in the *Charrette* (2) he uses the word *roman* to refer to the kind of narrative poem he writes. Since *Erec* is a *bele conjointure*, he may have understood *roman* in this way too: his *romans* are *beles conjointures*. In coining the expression *bele conjointure*, Chrétien defined a new narrative mode, romance, for future writers in the French and wider European romance tradition that emerged after him, and in large measure, from or in response to his romances.

The beauty of Chrétien's romance *conjointures* resides not only in their topical coherence; Chrétien's language itself, including features of his art such as versification and rhyme, ornamental embellishment and artful syntax, enhances the oral reception of his works. Frappier (1965) noted the originality with which Chrétien (along with Benoît de Sainte-Maure) adapted the rhymed octosyllabic couplet typical of narrative and chronicle in his time by 'couplet breaking' (*brisure du couplet*). This technique modifies traditional couplet composition in French verse, wherein a sentence regularly terminates only on the even-numbered line. Breaking on the uneven line allows for greater flexibility and ease in sentence articulation and embellishment.

Ornamental, or 'rhetorical', embellishment realizes the potential of the French language as a medium for expressing thought, emotion and humour, especially by irony and play on words related to *jeux de vérité* (Huon de Méry lauds Chrétien's 'bel françois'; see Schmolke-Hasselmann 1980*, 29–31/1998, 34–7). It also articulates the *jeu parti* mode of problem romances. The catalogues of tropes and rhetorical figures established by modern critics suggest the highly artificial quality imputed to rhetorical embellishment (Grosse 1881; Bertolucci 1960). However, catalogues obscure the relationship between embellishment and the message that the language communicates (Hunt 1986, 83–91; Monson 1987; for further references, see Kelly bib. 1976/2002, section Fb). There is a relation between the plan of the work, identified by Chrétien as *bele conjointure*, and the articulation of that plan, not only in the conjunction of parts and topical description of persons and actions but also in the quality of the language employed that, sentence by sentence, line by line, and even rhyme by rhyme, articulates meaning. Rhetoric, an oral and written art, is fully realized in romance performance.

Performance: Orality, Writing and the Manuscript

Zumthor's studies of orality in medieval works (1984; 1987) fired interest in the ways Chrétien's romances might have been read aloud or recited (see also Vitz 1999*); the narrator in the work, as distinguished from the author who wrote it, may connote the narrator as reader to an audience. Orality comprises a wider range of phenomena within the medieval context than that of *jongleur;* it is a factor in Latin education, in philosophical reflection on the word and in private reading (Zink 1981; Stuip and Vellekoop 1993). Like *jongleurs,* clerics were active in the secular world; some clerics became minstrels and *jongleurs,* such as those criticized by Chrétien in *Erec* (Faral 1910). In all these cases they may have read to, or improvised for, diverse audiences. The casual story-teller also transmitted material, either as a latimer serving as conduit for tales from one language to another (Bullock-Davies 1966) or as someone with a good memory for a stock of stories that could be related informally in prose (Chênerie 1986*, 515; Gerritsen 1995; 158–61). The ability to tell stories was valued in the courtier (Roussel 1994, 23–4). In romance, knights relate their adventures at court, much as Calogrenant is obliged to do in *Yvain.*

   None of these possibilities resolves the question of how Chrétien 'performed' his own works, although they do suggest how others might have performed them in specific instances. His prologues refer only to high courts, where one might hear professional story-tellers whose performances he castigates in *Erec,* as well as hearing his own romances whose *bele conjointure* he proclaims.[17] We lack further documentary evidence about how his romances were actually presented to such audiences. At best, we know how specific works might have been received in the diverse circumstances outlined in the preceding paragraph. In *Yvain,* a young woman reads a romance to her parents (5360–8). In the Occitan romance *Flamenca* people listen to episodes of works whilst, as it were, strolling from one story-teller to the other (Duggan 1989). Chrétien's romances could themselves be divided into shorter pieces for recitation, especially for audiences already familiar with them. Yet in *Erec* Chrétien seems to favour the performance of the work as a whole, the *bele conjointure* he contrasts with the story-tellers' piecemeal versions. There is, nonetheless, evidence for both kinds of performance in the scholastic milieu, on festive occasions such as the wedding in *Flamenca*, or during tournaments (Delbouille 1932, lxxi–lxxii). There is also evidence of *mimes* acting out what a reader read to the audience (Kelly 1999a, 112, n. 123). Yet uncertainties abound. How did readers enunciate the lines they read or recited? How did *mimes, jongleurs* or clerics gesture? What were their facial expressions?[18]

Recent studies have gone beyond merely proclaiming the rather obvious likelihood that, because of a largely illiterate aristocracy, most of Chrétien's romances were first known aurally. Fundamental is the recognition that the manuscript is different from the printed book and, indeed, the modern edition (Vielliard 1998). Manuscript production, including layout, illustration, lettering, punctuation and special marks, has been scrutinized for clues on oral presentation; such aspects as syntax, versification and other written features can suggest how they were read aloud.[19] Moreover, performance has been interpreted not only as oral but also as visual, because of manuscript layout, illustration and contents. Manuscripts that transmit romances to us have therefore received closer scrutiny (see Busby, Nixon, Stones and Walters eds 1993); each manuscript being unique, the notion of the manuscript as 'performance' has emerged (Huot 1987). Codicological research has investigated manuscript production, audiences and intertextual relationships among manuscripts (Busby 2002*). All these factors relating to the interpretation of texts within manuscripts point to different kinds of audiences, either readers or listeners. There was clearly the intimate circle, such as that depicted in *Yvain*, or the solitary reader like Laudine in the same romance; larger audiences are suggested by those depicted in some manuscript illustrations or the festive crowds at marriages, tournaments and public holidays, as in *Flamenca*. Whether read privately or publicly, or read aloud or to oneself, the manuscript collection is solid evidence that audiences could recognize allusions, adaptations and other kinds of rewriting and retelling, because the manuscripts they read, or had read to them, contained the different works linked through intertextual allusions (see chapter XI). It is obviously erroneous to restrict these features of transmission to one option or another. Rather, using the evidence available in romances and their manuscripts, one discovers the multiple ways that Chrétien's romances might have been read or recited, and how, if at all, different kinds of transmission determine or even alter reception (Hindman 1994; Hunt in Busby, Nixon, Stones and Walters eds 1993, I, 27–40; Uitti 1987; Hult 1998, 7–11).

Recent debate about philological methodologies has focused attention not only on manuscripts but also on the critical editions we read today. Despite some 150 years of editing, no definitive edition of Chrétien's complete works exists. Indeed, there is considerable disagreement among editors as to what a truly critical edition should be. Both student and scholar should be aware of the problems of editing Chrétien, as well as of the editorial principles used to prepare each edition (Foulet and Speer 1979; Hult 1991. See, for example, Hult 1986; 1989b; Uitti and Foulet 1988).

Social and Moral Issues: The Problematic Blend of Ideal and Reality

During the last twenty years or so, emphasis has moved from Chrétien's art of fiction to the way in which his fictions may mirror contemporary moral and social issues. These issues define the contexts in which his romances locate problems. When aristocratic audiences listened to them in the Middle Ages, to what extent did these narratives correspond to their world (Ménard 2000)? How well may we modern readers recover and evaluate their experience? How do these medieval issues relate to modern or current controversies and values?

Köhler defined the world-view in Chrétien's romances in terms of ideal and reality, or, more specifically, a blend of the two. Chênerie (1986*, 3), echoing Marc Bloch, insists that any attempt at interpretation must give equal weight to the authentic and the imaginary. The problems Chrétien raises suggest how a given social or moral reality might be corrected in a desirable way. The following problematic contexts have recently received attention for the interpretation of social and moral ideals and realities in his romances: the three orders, lineage and marriage, knighthood, chivalry, courtesy and love, and, finally, religion. They reflect the uncertain, often ambiguous relation of ideal to reality, both in the twelfth century and as we perceive them today. All impinge on gender issues. But, as will be apparent, Chrétien treats gender itself principally for men and women of royalty or high nobility, and his depiction reflects opinions and prejudices of those social strata.

The Three Orders

Duby has demonstrated the importance of the three orders in the twelfth-century world-view (Duby 1978, 325–70; cf. Batany 1978). This social hierarchy divided society into three distinct orders, the ecclesiastical order, or those who pray (*oratores*), the nobility, or those who fight to conquer and defend (*bellatores*), and those who work so that the two higher orders can carry out their assigned tasks (*laboratores*). As Duby has noted, the hierarchy is adumbrated in Chrétien's romances. Perhaps its most obvious, if incomplete, statement is found in the prologue to *Cligés*, where the first two orders are evoked in the translation of *clergie* and *chevalerie* from Greece through Rome to France.

Chrétien seems to adapt this social hierarchy by replacing Wace's conquering Arthur with a more domestic ruler (Köhler 1970/1974*, chapter 1) whose principal resource is the seemingly inexhaustible largesse with which he maintains his court. The Knights of the Round Table pursue honour there, rather than in their own lands. Arthur dominates a court, not a kingdom, and his prestige is enhanced by his knights' presence at court. The scattering of the court (*Perceval*, 812–16), or the absence of many knights (*Perceval*, 3938–41), is unsettling. In Chrétien's romances there is no significant feudal relation of vassal to lord. A seat at the Round Table is the only fief Arthur's knights desire (Chênerie 1986*, 80–2). This is apparent when Yvain neglects the lands he married Laudine to defend, or when, even after his coronation, Erec stays at Arthur's court, rather than at his own. Alixandre is willing to allow his younger brother Alis to reign whilst he remains in Britain, provided that Cligés succeeds Alis. Sometimes, when action is required, a certain hesitancy or *recreantise* among Knights of the Round Table creates a vacuum filled by the principal knight, as when Guinevere's abduction in the *Charrette* seems to stymie the court, or when no one responds to the Red Knight's challenge in *Perceval*. Both these events include an insult to Queen Guinevere and thus, through her person, to the court. Insult to the queen is a motif near the beginning of all Chrétien's romances except *Cligés*.

Chrétien's romances describe the ideals and the trials of aristocrats, but they show far less interest in the labouring classes. One does find peasants, harriers, heralds, fools, servants, serfs, giants, scullions, coal men, etc., however (for references, see Ollier 1989), and scholars have certainly argued that the plight of the 300 women forced to do sweatshop labour in *Yvain*'s Pesme Avanture is evidence for Chrétien's social conscience. Yet, as others have noted (Frappier 1969, 123–8; Pioletti 1979; 1980; Chênerie 1986*, 448–51), Chrétien calls the seamstresses 'dameiseles' (5223, 5793; cf. *Yvain*, 5230–1: 'beles et gentes / Fussent mout', *all would have been very beautiful and noble*, had they not been in prison). Nobility is an attribute they share with the lion (cf. *Yvain*, 3375); they are noble, like the women Yvain defends or protects. Chrétien evinces social consciousness only within the hierarchy of the three orders, according to which aristocratic young women do not work and are therefore unjustly subjugated to a task only suited to ignoble working women. In *Perceval* the desire of the burghers of Escavalon to avenge their lord's alleged murder by Gauvain shows a lack of judgement regarding honourable conduct (5984–96; Duby 1978, 336–7). Chrétien notes not only the error made by the burghers, but also ambiguities in Gauvain's own conduct in this part of the romance (Voicu 1990).

Indifference to ignoble labourers is evident in another episode in *Yvain*. The gigantic herdsman has animal-like features and Calogrenant doubts at first that he possesses reason or language. When asked who he is, the herdsman answers: 'Je sui uns hom' (*I am a man*, 328). Calogrenant finds this answer insufficient; he therefore asks for more precision. 'Ques hom es tu?' (*What kind of man are you?*, 329). His question evokes social distinctions of which the 'man' is unaware, just as his ignorance of the word *aventure* (365–6) separates him from knights who, in Chrétien's romances, seek out adventures.

Calogrenant's query, 'Ques hom es tu?', also points to subdivisions within each of the three orders. Occasionally in Chrétien's romances there are workers who, unlike the herdsman, function within the social hierarchy. Field workers and traders appear in *Erec* and *Perceval,* as does the twelfth-century commune in the latter romance. Servants supply the needs of knights on quest or at court. The same subservient role obtains for the clergy. In Chrétien's romances these orders and trades are evaluated as good or bad, in so far as they support or fail to support the guardians of *chevalerie* (Lepri 1991, 63–9).

Lineage and Marriage

Lineage was another important topic for aristocratic audiences. However, unlike later prose romancers, especially those in the Grail tradition, Chrétien develops neither the vertical line of descent nor the horizontal line characteristic of medieval genealogies (Bloch 1983*; Schmid 1986; Kullmann 1992; Duggan 2001, chapter 2). Fathers are often named, like Erec's father Lac, Alixandre (the name of both Cligés's father and his grandfather), Yvain's father Urien and Laudine's father Landunet. The only mother named is Soredamors. Yet Fénice must have had at least one child, as her descendants establish the harem, but her mother-hood is not a motif in the romance. We know Laudine principally as 'de Landuc, / La dame' (*Yvain* 2153–4); her name is not found in all *Yvain* manuscripts (Woledge 1986, I, 135–8; Foulet and Uitti 1983–4). Perceval's mother is only the 'Widow Lady'. Many have wondered why men are given proper names more often than women. Perhaps titles like *dame* or *demoiselle* mattered more to medieval ladies than personal names (see Duplat 1974, and in general Grisay, Lavis and Dubois-Stasse 1969; Lebsanft 1988). Lineage itself matters only when it is threatened, as in the strife between Alixandre and his brother Alis over Cligés's accession to the throne, a concern that also weighs heavily in Fénice's decision not to consummate her marriage with Alis.

However, marriage is a major source of difficulties. *Yvain* is an obvious example. Laudine must remarry in order to protect her domain, not her succession. Abduction, rape and forced marriage are not uncommon threats. Because the Dame de Noroison refuses to marry Alier, this would-be husband lays waste her lands until Yvain defeats him. Similar threats to Enide in the Galoain and Limors episodes underscore the precarious position of the wife in Chrétien's romances. In all of them the threat of forced marriage, including abduction, looms when women turn down suitors. Forced marriage is a motif in *Erec* (Galoain and Limors), in *Cligés* (the Duke of Saxony), in *Yvain* (Alier) and in *Perceval* (Clamadeu); real or potential rape is a motif in the custom of Logres, the abduction of Guinevere in the *Charrette*, and in the punishment of Greoreas in *Perceval* (on the motif in current scholarship, see Gravdal 1991, chapter 2; Vitz 1997; Sylvester 1998). The Harpin de la Montagne episode in *Yvain* also shows the threat to a knight's lineage, both by the capture and torture of sons and by a daughter who, if exchanged for them, would be surrendered to gang rape by Harpin's scullions.

Scholars have long recognized marriage as a primary motif in Chrétien's romances (Noble 1982). Yet marriage was a controversial topic in the twelfth century, and the controversy focused on differing views of consent to marriage. Spousal consent, especially the woman's consent to marriage, was a contentious issue that on occasion opposed clergy and aristocracy (Duby 1981; Shirt 1982; Kelly 1999a, chapter 5). The Church introduced consent as part of the sacrament of marriage, itself a new sacrament in Chrétien's time. However, consent conflicted with the traditional parental role in deciding spouses for children, whether son or daughter. One *jeu parti* argues both sides of the issue (Långfors 1926, cxxxix).

Although Chrétien nowhere proclaims ecclesiastical authority for consent, he does very much problematize consent in the aristocratic context, either by actually making consent to marriage an issue, as he does in *Cligés* and *Yvain*, or by ignoring the father's approval, as in *Erec*, where, for his marriage to Enide, the young prince seeks Arthur's blessing not his father's. Although a petty nobleman impoverished by war, Enide's father profits by his daughter's marriage when Erec, again on his own initiative, gives his wife's parents two fine castles, a virtual dowry for their daughter (on the dowry given to the wife in medieval marriages, see Duby 1981, 97–8, 104–15). The traditional domination of man over woman is also at issue, both in Erec's reaction to Enide's questioning his knighthood and in the Orgueilleux de la Lande's abuse when he doubts his *amie*'s fidelity in *Perceval*.

The subject of marriage leads to the vexed question of 'courtly love'. But before discussing this notion in Chrétien's romances, let us first examine the theme of knighthood, with which love has a problematic relationship.

Knighthood

Chrétien's romances present knighthood as a noble calling (Sargent-Baur 1983–4; Flori 1996; for more general studies, see Hunt 1981; Chênerie 1986*; Barbero 1987). The knight (*chevalier*) was not just a horseman (*cavalier*). He was trained and dubbed because, by birth and blood, he possessed an outstanding potential for combat (Flori 1979). Liberation from feudal obligations associated with joining the Round Table in Chrétien's romances makes permanent the temporary military service a vassal owed his lord. Hence, the Round Table promotes an ideal quite divorced from feudal reality. In Wace's *Brut* King Arthur was a conqueror, aided and abetted by the Knights of the Round Table; in Chrétien the focus is on the quests which enable individual knights to gain prominence and distinguish themselves from one another. The only quest Arthur undertakes in Chrétien's romances is for Perceval, and the court accompanies him (*Perceval*, 4068–93). The Round Table may remain implicitly a table of equals, as in Wace, but it does not obscure the diverse talents and achievements of its major figures. From its inception it creates an explicit hierarchy of knights (*Erec*, 1683–97; see Köhler 1970*, 89–93/1974, 103–8; Schmolke-Hasselmann 1980,

50–1/1998, 59–61). Knights sit at the Round Table, but never at Arthur's 'high table', which is not the same as, but superior to, the Round Table (Schmolke-Hasselmann 1982*). Some scholars have linked Chrétien's knights to the group of young, landless knights, or *iuvenes*, who serve a lord in the hope of winning land or a wife (Köhler in *GRLMA*, IV: 1, 88–91). The case of Enide illustrates an inversion of the *iuvenis* model, since she rather than Erec raises her status and that of her family through marriage (*Erec*, 525–36). Yet the major Knights of the Round Table are princes and high aristocrats (Ménard 1976; Chênerie 1986*, 31–3, 37–9, 49–55). They prefer Arthur's court to the kingdom or the feudal lands they already possess or will inherit, a choice that medieval audiences might have found unrealistic.

In these romances the Arthurian knight confronts the violence and injustice that surrounds and even penetrates Arthur's court. Meleagant proposes combat there, with Guinevere as hostage. Enide's father has been ruined by wars (*Erec*, 515–17) and Arthur himself has been at war at the beginning of *Perceval* (808–10). Perceval's father and brothers died through violence (400–49; on violence in *Perceval*, see Baumgartner 1999, 59–80, and Sargent-Baur 2000, 165–88). But war is a major motif only in *Cligés*, where Angrés's rebellion against Arthur leads to a siege with some skirmishes. The conflict is actually brought to a conclusion by Alixandre's stratagem whereby he and twelve Greek knights capture Windsor Castle. This achievement is more like a quest adventure, where combat takes place between two knights or between small groups of knights, and the obstacles represent the rebellious conduct that the knight's achievements ideally correct.

Another source of debate in the twelfth century was the tournament. In Chrétien's day tournaments were poorly regulated, violent confrontations that could degenerate into virtual gang warfare (Benson 1980; Parisse in *Turnier* 1985, 175–211; Chênerie 1986*, 327–46; Neumeyer 1998; and, in the context of ideal and reality, Baldwin 1990). For this reason the Church condemned them as part of its policy of the Truce or Peace of God, and it did so more than once in the twelfth and thirteenth centuries by interdiction and excommunication, apparently with little success. Tournaments occur in all of Chrétien's romances, but they do not present such a starkly negative (and thus realistic) picture of the actual conflict. The contrast might well have coloured reception of his romances, and indeed the meaning of exemplary narrative about tournaments, in which knights such as Erec and Yvain choose between love and tourneying (Schmolke-Hasselmann 1980*, 65–72/1998, 72–88; Ferlampin-Acher 1995). Henry II forbade tournaments in England (Keen 1984, chapter 5; Barker and Keen in *Turnier*, 214–19), a fact surely present in the minds of audiences when Cligés goes there to test his mettle against knights of the Round Table. Yet, in all of his romances except *Perceval,* Chrétien suppresses the mortal or even extremely violent features of contemporary tournaments. In the Gauvain section in *Perceval* a tournament held at Tintagel between Meliant de Lis and Thibaut de Tintagel shows a lord waging virtual siege warfare against a vassal whose possessions he could destroy (4821–7). In this context it is noteworthy that, although Erec's *recreantise*, according to his own men, lies in neglecting tournaments, he does not tourney again, even after his reconciliation with Enide.

Women in Chrétien's romances are keenly interested in tournaments. Meliant calls for the tournament at the request of his beloved, Thibaut's elder daughter. In the *Charrette*, maidens request a tournament in order to find husbands (on women spectators, see Chênerie 1986*, 337, 439–41; Santina 1999, chapter 7). Tournaments are problematized in terms of a choice between love and tourneying in *Erec* and *Yvain*. A *jeu parti* (Långfors 1926, xlv) offers an interesting assessment of the issue analogous to, but not identical with, the cases in *Erec* and *Yvain*. Here, each of two women loves a knight; the first encourages her beloved to refrain from tournaments because of their violence, whereas the second wants hers to frequent them in order to enhance his worth. At issue is the danger of unnecessary death vis-à-vis the knight's role as warrior. But Chrétien nowhere depicts the consequences of violence as clearly as does Marie de France in *Chaitivel*, where three protagonists are killed and the fourth wounded in such a way that he cannot love (but see Le Rider 1978, 242–5).[20]

Chivalry, Courtesy and Love

In Chrétien's world of questing knights, chivalry and courtesy prevail, by and large, over villainy (Köhler 1970*, 61–5/1974, 72–6). Yet there are anomalies. For example, in *Perceval* Kay's propensity to discourteous slander turns to physical abuse; there too Gauvain is twice accused of murder. Although *Perceval* sets out three lists of chivalrous and courteous maxims, one by Perceval's mother (*Perceval*, 491–558), another by Gornemant (1592–1646), and the last by Perceval's hermit uncle (6365–97; see Chênerie 1986*, 472–83; Kelly 1993*, 121–5), Perceval fails at first to comprehend the rationale for the lessons in chivalry, given to him by his mother and by Gornemant. He ignores these lessons when he fails to assist his widowed mother and applies them literally, clumsily and without discrimination when he forces kisses on the Tent Maiden, kills the Red Knight and does not speak when he meets Blanchefleur or observes the Grail and the Bleeding Lance. Perceval must learn chivalry and courtliness (*corteisie*) by experience as well as by precept. Courtliness brings us to the vexed matter of 'courtly love' in Chrétien's romances.

Gaston Paris coined the expression *amour courtois* 'courtly love', inferring from the *Charrette* a code of conduct for lovers that includes adultery (Paris 1883, 519–20). Paris's ideas were given wide prominence by C. S. Lewis (1936, chapter 1; see also McCracken 1998).[21] Although the modern expression 'courtly love' has become universal, there is little agreement on its meaning or significance, apart from an obviously widespread assumption that it can be defined and that it relies on a code of conduct or etiquette (cf. Kay in Krueger ed. 2000*, 81–96). The acceptance of such a definition and code based on the examples from the *Charrette*, the troubadours and the Tristan poems has contributed to the equally widespread belief that 'courtly love' is an adulterous love, a belief that has provoked surprise at the emphasis on conjugal love and its problems in Chrétien's romances (cf. Chênerie 1986*, 451–72). Indeed, this view lent support to the once generally held, and still occasionally heard, conviction that Chrétien himself found morally repugnant the adulterous, and therefore courtly, love idealized in the *Charrette* in order to promote prowess and chivalry, and that this explains his unwillingness to complete this romance.

There is no code of love in Chrétien's romances, or anywhere else in his time, if one means by code a set of rules tantamount to a formal etiquette for lovers (Schnell 1985, 137). On the other hand, the modern expression 'courtly love' can translate a number of expressions common in the twelfth century, including in Chrétien's romances: *fin'amor*, *bone amor*, *amor par amors*, and others, including *amor* standing alone (Frappier 1967; Ferrante 1980). The finesse of such love depends not on prescribed rules of conduct but on the mind capable of analysing its own feelings and obligations, and then acting accordingly within given social and moral demands and constraints. Although in one of his lyrics Chrétien contrasts the sense of free choice with the love of Tristan and Yseut, love in his romances is subject to wide emotional fluctuation, from madness (Yvain) to ecstasy (Lancelot), from love–hate (Laudine) to total absorption (Perceval before the drops of blood in the snow). This love seeks sexual gratification, but is also restrained by the concept of noble behaviour in the selection of the beloved and in the conduct appropriate to the relationship with him or her. Chrétien treats love in marriage in its relation to prowess and tournaments, to fidelity and constancy and to the notion of honour.

In Gaston Paris's definition of courtly love, adultery touches on moral issues such as consent. If the Church and aristocratic custom differed on the issue of consent to marriage or participation in tournaments, they were united in their opposition to adultery. Biblical condemnation of adultery is consistent with biblical condemnation of lust, even in marriage. Yet adultery's assumed potential to 'pollute' the womb (Duby 1981, 42) is not an issue in the *Charrette*, nor is it a factor in Fénice's decision to avoid consummation with Alis. Chrétien does not broach the subject of conception, even though both ecclesiastical and aristocratic traditions condoned sexual intercourse for purposes of reproduction. The role of continence does not concern Chrétien's couples so much as the relation between martial prowess and love-making in *Erec*, *Yvain* and the *Charrette*. Love-making occurs for love and pleasure, but not for lineage.[22] In Chrétien's romances 'courtly love' can be a noble and ennobling love characterized by reflection on its quality in the face of specific social or moral obstacles and demands, whether these are idealized or accurate mirrors of contemporary realities. Because of their equally noble qualities Erec and Enide are worthy of each other, despite the contrasts between his wealth and her poverty (*Erec*, 1500–9; cf. *Yvain*, 1802–6, 1815–19 and 2121–6; *Perceval*, 1827–32). Hence, matters of honour, courtliness, chivalry and other abstract notions colour much of Chrétien's descriptions of love (Rohr 1962). The moral or religious constraints of the time do not impinge significantly on marvellous adventures in his romances before *Perceval*, a crucial text in the harmonization of religion and knighthood, or *clergie* and *chevalerie*.

Religion

In the prologue to *Cligés*, *clergie* figures in the transfer of culture from past to present. There, just as chivalric knighthood replaces imperial power, thus signalling the emergence of knighthood as a noble calling, so *clergie* evokes the wide range of clerical functions in Chrétien's day. Although scholars often equate *clergie* with the learning represented by the seven liberal arts, as well as other, more advanced disciplines, and although the *translatio studii* theme does have this sense, clerical learning is rarely evoked in Chrétien's romances. When he describes the *quadrivium* depicted on Erec's coronation robe, he is describing the handiwork of fairies, not announcing a renaissance of Greek or Latin culture at Arthur's court. Although the knight is certainly prominent in his romances, the cleric is not; no knight is learned and no cleric is a knight (although Lancelot can read, *Charrette*, 1863–4). It is therefore important to keep separate the art of writing acquired by Chrétien in the schools and the use he made of it 'devant rois et devant contes' (*before kings and counts*; *Erec*, 20).

In Chrétien's romances the clergy serves a largely supportive function. Princes of the Church perform marriages and bless the marriage bed; priests recite Mass and clerics read letters. Monks hardly appear. Although Lancelot learns in a monastery cemetery that he will rescue the queen and other prisoners in Gorre, the revelation carries no suggestion of sin in connection with his adulterous love for Guinevere that makes his achievement possible.[23] The solitary hermit is some-what more prominent than monks. A hermit helps Yvain in his madness, but offers no moral counsel. When Perceval's uncle, a hermit, explains his sin to him, he introduces to Chrétien's romances a new standard for knightly conduct (Winkler 1958, 123–8).

The emphasis placed on religion in *Perceval* is exceptional (Winkler 1958, 172–3; Sargent-Baur 2000). The prologue emphasizes Christian charity, and the Grail is a sacred object because it contains the host, although Chrétien does not associate it with Christ's blood or the Last Supper, as in the Robert de Boron tradition. Of the two questions Perceval fails to ask when he sees the Grail, the first, 'whom does the Grail serve?', is answered by Perceval's hermit uncle: it serves the hermit's father (and therefore Perceval's grandfather) with the host; this man leads a life so saintly that he survives on the host alone. The second question, 'why does the Lance bleed?', is not answered in the romance. We are told that the lance will some day destroy Logres, Arthur's kingdom, but not why it is important that Gauvain should find it and bring it to Escavalon to atone for allegedly killing Guingambresil's suzerain. Perceval's failure to ask the two questions and, consequently, to heal the maimed Fisher King results from his sin: he ignored his mother's fainting, followed by her death, after his departure for Arthur's court. Here sin intrudes for the first time into Chrétien's romances as a significant factor in evaluating conduct (on *caritas* and Perceval's chivalry, see Sargent-Baur 2000).

Erec, Lancelot and Yvain must deal with alleged faults as knights; in *Perceval* the accusation that Gauvain is a murderer is made in a knightly context in which sons and vassals of the victim seek vengeance.[24] There is no suggestion that sin explains his alleged murders, as is the case later in the Vulgate *Queste*. Only Perceval's *pechié* is a sin in the religious sense. He begins to comprehend this when the Hideous Damsel castigates his conduct. He sets out to right the wrong by seeking the Grail Castle in order to ask the unasked questions; for more than five years he wanders about. But whilst he defeats some sixty knights, he fails to find the castle and, moreover, he forgets God. His encounter with the Good Friday penitents leads to confession at his uncle's hermitage. Redemption begins, perhaps redemption that might have allowed him to realize the smiling maiden's prediction that Perceval 'de chevalerie / Avra tote la seignorie' (*will completely master knighthood*, 1017–18).[25] Although Perceval sins by ignoring his mother's distress, her prayer before dying saves his life (6328–34), making atonement for sin and redemption possible (Payen 1967, 398–400). In Grail romances after Chrétien, the significance of the Grail and the knight's sin and redemption loom ever larger, raising moral doubts about issues like killing, love and adultery that Chrétien's romances tend to ignore.

This is not to say that scholars have ignored the moral or religious implications of the plots and characters in Chrétien's romances. By reading them as allegories, some have discerned a second level of signification alongside their more literal meanings. For example, some see Lancelot as a Christ figure who actually realizes a messianic mission by freeing the prisoners in Gorre (Ribard 1972; Borsari 1983, chapter 4). Others read a moral allegory into the same romance; Lancelot's love is lust, and therefore medieval audiences, accustomed to moral allegory, will have readily interpreted the romance in this context. Similar approaches uncover allegories in his other romances (Robertson Jr 1951; 1962; 1972; Artin 1974; Diverres 1990). Since Chrétien does not explicitly enunciate these moral contexts, unlike, for example, the authors of later Grail romances, the validity of these interpretations rests on the historical likelihood of the allegorical or moral model for reading them. Are these common patterns coincidental or intended? We confront once more not only audience awareness of the moral or religious allegories that scholars have perceived in his romances, but also the potential of each work for the kinds of interpretation found in later rewritings of Grail romances (Piraprez 2000). Audiences were able to discover the allegorical potential of the moral or religious implications of the literal narrative, and such audiences included rewriters who drew explicit allegorical readings from antecedent material (Tuve 1966). They are part of Chrétien's legacy.

Chrétien's Legacy[26]

Chrétien de Troyes is today recognized as a major European author. He discovered in Arthurian material a marvellous source of inspiration and invention. Indeed, probably no European writer has, by his or her original accomplishments, been a model for so many generations of rewriting, even, at least indirectly, up to modern times (see Lacy in chapter XIV). The quest by Round Table knights, Lancelot and Guinevere's love and the Grail are not only marvellous subjects in his telling, they had a rich potential for those kinds of retelling and rewriting characteristic of both oral and written traditions of his time. The notion of *bele conjointure*, a truly original coinage, led to awareness of romance as a narrative mode and genre. Chrétien's interventions articulate an art of romance that was influential in focusing audience expectation and interpretation of his own and subsequent romances in French and other European languages.

On the level of interpretation, the quest, love and the Grail raised intriguing questions. How did audiences reconcile Erec's and Yvain's conduct in love and tourneying, or the love of Lancelot and Guinevere in a world that contains the Holy Grail? Although romancers after Chrétien sought to authorize different answers to such questions, Chrétien himself seems to have opted for contrasting norms in his romances, allowing audiences to resolve or reconcile differences in broad social and moral contexts. One sees the problem of reconciling love and prowess in *Erec* and *Yvain*, even though the choices made may seem mutually exclusive.

Chrétien treats equally compelling issues for his time, such as consent in love and marriage, and violence and the moral implications of knighthood as an ideal. The *jeu parti* mode articulates such issues and a potential for original reinterpretation that is also a part of Chrétien's legacy, despite the final lines of *Yvain*:

> Onques plus dire n'en oï,
> Ne ja plus n'en orés conter
> S'on n'i velt mençogne ajoster. (6806–8)

(*I never heard any more told, nor will you hear more related unless someone wishes to add on lies.*)

Even when later authors no longer articulate the problems in the way he does, the issues he treats and the ways audiences may confront them are not so foreign to Chrétien's modern readers as their medieval surface may lead one to surmise.

Chrétien's legacy is transmitted in manuscripts. This medium has enjoyed a revival of interest in their role in his legacy. Yet manuscripts inevitably raise the question of manuscript editing. A printed edition is not a handcrafted manuscript, but an edited version or versions of the text. Such editing involves interpretation, and interpretation is guided by the questions we ask of the manuscripts. Traditionally, the purpose of the edition has been to recover what the first author wrote. Various theories have been advanced as to how to recreate that first version (Foulet and Speer 1979, chapter 1). More recently, the charge of corruption levelled against manuscripts, corruption because they alter the author's original version, and other factors such as layout, the place of the manuscript in a collection and the significance of variants, have suggested that a manuscript can be altered and yet remain of interest, precisely because of the reasons why it was altered, and the effects of such alterations on audience reception (Hindman 1994).

In her ground-breaking study of epigonal romances, Schmolke-Hasselmann (1980*, 116–17/1998, 142–3) demonstrated the detailed, often profound ways in which these works rewrite and reinterpret Chrétien as model.[27] The modern interpreter is confronted with a problem in evaluating such emulation. To what extent was such rewriting evident to medieval audiences? Since the horizon of expectation, or the way in which past readings prepare expectations for future readings, actually varies from person to person, we are obliged to adopt a prudent view of the possible scope of intertextual reception that we can know and evaluate. If the author of *Durmart le Galois* corrected *Erec* (Schmolke-Hasselmann 1980*, 146–8/1998, 177–80), appreciation of the adaptation would be different for those ignorant of *Erec* from that of those who knew his romance (assuming that they did reflect on the differences). Scholars must be cautious in assigning intertextual links that may never have occurred to contemporary audiences. This applies especially to Latin allusions for audiences ignorant of Latin.[28]

Chrétien's romances disappeared from view in the late Middle Ages, to be rediscovered in the eighteenth century (Busby 1998). Scholarly reception has today restored Chrétien's writings to the prominence they once had. First seeking his sources, then assessing his artistic quality and achievements, scholars now draw on his romances to illustrate current theoretical or methodological controversies on matters of language and interpretation. There have emerged as well important sociological, psychoanalytical, mythopoetic, feminist and other readings, to cite the most prominent today. No doubt Chrétien and his audiences would have been baffled by some of these readings. Yet such readings assist us in understanding how rich his marvellous adventures are, as they acquire additional meanings in ways that neither he nor his immediate audiences could have imagined.

Notes

[1] For convenience, references are to *Chrétien de Troyes, Romans*, 1994; the texts printed here have been compared with other editions (see Kelly bib. 1976 and 2002, section A).

[2] Other works have been ascribed to Chrétien, but with little general approval (Wilmotte 1930; Owen 1971; Gallais 1991).

[3] *Philomena* names its author as 'Crestiiens li Gois' (734). Chrétien's full name appears in the *Chevalier à l'épée*, *Didot-Perceval*, Gerbert de Montreuil's *Perceval* Continuation, *Hunbaut* and the *Tournoiement Antechrist*; Wolfram von Eschenbach names him as 'von Troys meister Cristjân' (van Coolput in Lacy, Kelly and Busby eds 1987–8*, I, 333–7). On the problematic status of Chrétien's name, see Nykrog 1996, 42–4; Kay 1997.

[4] The latest reference to Chrétien by name is found in *Claris et Laris*, 627. This romance is dated 1268 (see Combes in chapter X). On Chrétien's reputation and that of his romances in the Middle Ages, see Schmolke-Hasselmann 1980*, 29–34/1998, 34–40; Pickford 1981; Van Coolput in Lacy, Kelly and Busby eds 1987–8*, I, 91–114, 333–42; Hult 1998.

[5] Only Meleagant raises this issue when he accuses Guinevere and Kay of adultery (4820–57). Nowhere in Chrétien's romances is Lancelot's adulterous love condemned, as it will be in the prose *Lancelot*.

[6] This is the first known mention of the Grail in literature. The form Chrétien meant it to take is not clear from the text, but it seems to be some sort of platter for serving fish; it is later described as holy because it contains the host which feeds the father of the Maimed King (*Perceval*, 6346–54; see Frappier 1972, 5–12). Chrétien's Grail does not have the shape of a chalice common in Grail romances after him.

[7] Did Chrétien intend a romance of about 14,000 lines, or twice as long as his others? See Kellermann 1936, 11–13.

[8] On *jeu parti* and Chrétien's romances, see Remy 1964; Neumeister 1969, 176–80; Schnell 1985, 124–5; Hunt 1986, 82–3; Hunt 1994, 156. Cf. Frappier 1968, 224–6. In one of his *chansons* Chrétien adumbrates a *jeu parti* by rejecting Tristan's potion-induced love in favour of a conscious choice to love. In his other *chanson*, Love unleashes 'tençon et bataille' (*dispute and war*) against her champion, much as Yvain unleashes storms against Laudine from the Marvellous Fountain.

[9] See also Duggan 1977; Lacy 1980, 38–66; Hunt 1986, 18–24; Grimbert 1988; Krueger 1993*, chapter 1; Nykrog 1996, 45–7, 49–51.

[10] See the contents of Loomis ed. 1959*, in which Frappier's chapter marks a reaction to this approach, a reaction begun by Kellermann in 1936. For a current overview of Chrétien's Celtic background, see Duggan 2001, chapter 5.

[11] The source of such allusions can be difficult to evaluate; for example, those to 'Lavine' in *Erec* may be to the *Aeneid* or to its French adaptation, the *Roman d'Eneas* (Kelly 1999a, 196–201). On the relationship between Latin and vernacular in Chrétien's rewriting, see Hunt 1978 and Comes 1996.

[12] Much has been written on such interventions in Chrétien's romances. See Hunt 1972; 1994; Ollier 1974. More generally, see Gallais 1964–70; Hunt 1970; Badel 1975; Zink 1981; Halász 1992; Haug 1992/1997, chapters 5–7; Kelly 1992*.

[13] Cf. Långfors 1926, poem xix (physical abuse) and poem cxiii (deceiving the beloved).

[14] The diverse meanings of *conjointure*, which may have occurred to Chrétien's contemporary audiences, suggest ways in which we can understand Chrétien's concept today. For example, its pharmaceutical sense may have (even unbeknownst to his non-Latinate audiences) suggested blending Ovidian models with the new *matiere*; see Freeman 1979, 91–127.

[15] The art of topical invention can be discussed only briefly here. However, further study of it in Chrétien's romances would reveal its usefulness for the study of intertextuality, source and influence, and adaptation; see Liborio 1982.

[16] Baumgartner (1992) reads the two romances together. On later manuscript cycles that conjoin romances in an analogous manner, see Walters, chapter XI.

[17] Maddox (1978, 25–6) bases his approach to interpreting the romance on the presupposition that it was written for group rather than for individual reading.

[18] Manuscript illuminations can offer clues; see Schmitt 1990. Cf. de Riquer 1999.

[19] This research is in its early stages. But see Parkes 1992; Brandsma in Kelly ed. 1996*, 145–60; Marnette 1998. According to Roques (1952), the Guiot manuscript contains scribal indications for reading aloud.

[20] A similar problem emerges in Gautier d'Arras's *Ille et Galeron* after Ille loses an eye in a tournament (see Chapter X).

[21] In the Matter of Britain, besides the Tristan and Yseut texts, only Marie de France's *Lais* treat and, occasionally, justify the adultery of *mal-mariées*.

[22] The Burgundian adaptation of *Erec* changes this feature in Chrétien's romance (see Wallen 1982).

[23] This contrasts remarkably with the cemetery scene in the prose *Lancelot* where Lancelot learns that his love disqualifies him from the Grail Quest.

[24] Audiences, of course, might have thought of their actions as sinful or socially unacceptable; but the narrator does not call them sins, as he does Perceval's neglect of his mother. Some have noted the role of medieval Christian audiences in the reception of apparently secular works; see most recently (with additional bibliography) Ribard 1997.

[25] On these transformations in Perceval's character as a result of his adventures, see Payen 1967, 391–403, and Köhler 1970*, 195–205/1974, 224–34.

[26] On Chrétien's thematic legacy in French verse romance, see Schmolke-Hasselmann 1980/1998* and Chênerie 1986*. For a general discussion, see Lacy, Kelly and Busby eds*, 1987–8 and Green 2002; for English romance, see Barron 1987, and for German romance Haug 1992/1997 (esp. chapters 5 and 6) and Jones and Wisbey 1993.

[27] On prose romances, see Bogdanow 1966, chapter 1; Baumgartner in Lacy, Kelly and Busby eds*, 1987–8, I, 167–90.

[28] Such allusions may tell us how Chrétien rewrote antecedent models, but not how such audiences might have appreciated his rewriting. A good basis for examining the reception of his works is the *recueil* (see Walters, chapter XI).

Reference List

For items accompanied by an asterisk, see the General Bibliography.

Bibliography

Kelly, D. *Chrétien de Troyes: An Analytic Bibliography* (London, 1976; Supplement No. 1, London, 2002).

Editions and Translations

Edition Used

Chrétien de Troyes, *Romans suivis des chansons avec, en appendice, Philomena*. General ed. M. Zink (Paris, 1994). Includes a modern French translation.
This edition reprints the romances and poems printed separately in the Lettres Gothiques series: *Erec et Enide*, ed. and transl. by J.-M. Fritz (Paris, 1992); *Cligès*, ed. and transl. by C. Méla and O. Collet, *suivi des chansons courtoises*, ed. and transl. by M.-C. Gérard-Zai (Paris, 1994); *Le Chevalier*

de la charrette ou Le Roman de Lancelot, ed. and transl. by C. Méla (Paris,1992); *Le Chevalier au lion ou le Roman d' Yvain*, ed. and transl. by D. F. Hult (Paris, 1994); *Le Conte du graal ou le Roman de Perceval*, ed. and transl. by C. Méla (Paris, 1990).

Other Editions

Les Romans de Chrétien de Troyes, édités d'après la copie de Guiot (Bibl. nat. fr. 794), 1, *Erec et Enide* (ed. by M. Roques, CFMA 80, Paris, 1952); 2, *Cligés* (ed. by A. Micha, CFMA 84, 1957); 3, *Le Chevalier de la Charrete* (ed. by M. Roques, CFMA 86, 1958); 4, *Le Chevalier au lion (Yvain)* (ed. by M. Roques, CFMA 89, 1960); 5–6, *Le Conte du Graal (Perceval)* (ed. by F. Lecoy, CFMA 100, 103, 1972–5).
Chrétien de Troyes, Le Roman de Perceval ou Le Conte du Graal. Ed by W. Roach, TLF 71 (Geneva and Paris, 1959).
Chrétien de Troyes, Erec et Enide, ed. and transl. by C. W. Carroll with introduction by W. W. Kibler; *Lancelot, or, The Knight of the Cart*, ed. and transl. by W. W. Kibler; *The Knight with the Lion, or Yvain (Le Chevalier au lion)*, ed. and transl. by W. W. Kibler; *The Story of the Grail: Li Contes del Graal, or Perceval*, ed. by R. T. Pickens and transl. by W. W. Kibler; *Philomena et Procne*, in *Three Ovidian Tales of Love*, ed. and transl. by R. J. Cormier (New York and London, 1981–90).
Chrétien de Troyes, Œuvres complètes. General ed. D. Poirion (Paris, 1994).
Chrétien de Troyes, Cligés. Ed. by S. Gregory and C. Luttrell (Cambridge, 1993).
Chrétien de Troyes, Le Roman de Perceval ou Le Conte du Graal: édition critique d'après tous les manuscrits. Ed by K. Busby (Tübingen, 1993).
'The Princeton *Charrette* Project', http://www.princeton.edu/~lancelot
Chrétien de Troyes, Philomena, in *Trois Contes du XIIᵉ siècle français imités d'Ovide*. Ed. and transl. by E. Baumgartner (Paris, 2000).
Chrétien, Guillaume d'Angleterre. Ed by A. J. Holden, TLF 360 (Geneva, 1988).
Les Chansons courtoises de Chrétien de Troyes. Ed. by M.-C. Zai (Bern and Frankfurt, 1974).

Translations

Owen, D. D. R., *Arthurian Romances* (London, 1987).
Kibler, W. W., with C. W. Carroll, *Arthurian Romances* (Harmondsworth, 1991).
Staines, D., *The Complete Romances of Chrétien de Troyes* (Bloomington, IN, 1990).
Cline, R. H., *Erec and Enide, Cligès, Lancelot, or The Knight of the Cart, Yvain, or, The Knight with the Lion, Perceval, or, The Story of the Grail* (Athens, GA, 1975–2000).
Raffel, B., *Erec and Enide, Cligès, Lancelot: The Knight of the Cart, Yvain: The Knight of the Lion, Perceval: The Story of the Grail* (New Haven, CT, 1987–99).
Translations of the CFMA editions: *Erec et Enide*, transl. by R. Louis (Paris, 1954); *Cligès*, transl. by A. Micha (Paris, 1957); *Le Chevalier de la charrette*, transl. by J. Frappier (Paris, 1962); *Le Chevalier au lion: Yvain*, transl. by C. Buridant and J. Trotin (Paris, 1971); *Le Conte du Graal (Perceval)*, transl. by J. Ribard (Paris, 1991).

Studies

Accarie, M. 1979. 'Faux Mariage et vrai mariage dans les romans de Chrétien de Troyes', *Annales de la Faculté des Lettres et Sciences Humaines de Nice*, 38, 25–35.
Accarie 1998. 'Vérité du récit ou récit de la vérité: le problème du réalisme dans la littérature médié-vale', *Razo*, 15, 5–34.
Artin, T. 1974. *The Allegory of Adventure: Reading Chrétien's Erec and Yvain*, Lewisburg, PA.

Badel, P. Y. 1975. 'Rhétorique et polémique dans les prologues de romans au Moyen Âge', *Littérature*, 20, 81–94.

Baldwin, J. W. 1990. 'Jean Renart et le tournoi de Saint-Trond: une conjonction de l'histoire et de la littérature', *Annales*, 45, 565–88.

Barbero, A. 1987. *L'aristocrazia nella società francese del medioevo: analisi delle fonti letterarie (secoli X–XIII)*, Bologna.

Barron, W. R. J. 1987. *English Medieval Romance*, London and New York.

Batany, J. 1978. 'Du *bellator* au *chevalier* dans le schéma des "trois ordres" (étude sémantique)', in *La Guerre et la paix: frontières et violences au Moyen Âge*, Paris, 23–34.

Baumgartner, E. 1986. 'Temps linéaire, temps circulaire et écriture romanesque (XIIe–XIIIe siècles)', in T. Bellenger ed. *Le Temps et la durée dans la littérature au Moyen Âge et à la Renaissance: actes du colloque organisé par le Centre de Recherche sur la Littérature du Moyen Âge et de la Renaissance de l'Université de Reims (novembre 1984)*, Paris, 7–21.

Baumgartner 1992. *Chrétien de Troyes: Yvain, Lancelot, la charrette et le lion*, Paris.

Baumgartner 1995. *Le Récit médiéval, XIIe–XIIIe siècles*, Paris.

Baumgartner 1999. *Chrétien de Troyes: Le Conte du Graal*, Paris.

Baumgartner 2003. *Romans de la Table Ronde de Chrétien de Troyes: Erec et Enide, Cligès, Le Chevalier au Lion, Le Chevalier de la Charrette de Chrétien de Troyes*, Paris.

Benson, L. D. 1980. 'The Tournament in the Romances of Chrétien de Troyes and *L'Histoire de Guillaume le Maréchal*', *SMC*, 14, 1–24, 147–52.

Benton, J. F. 1961. 'The Court of Champagne as a Literary Center', *Spec*, 36, 551–91.

Berthelot, A. 1993. 'The Romance as *conjointure* of Brief Narratives', *Esp*, 33, 51–60.

Bertolucci, V. 1960. 'Commento retorico all'*Erec* e al *Cligés*', *SMV*, 8, 9–51.

Bertolucci Pizzorusso, V., in F. Cigni ed. 1992. *Bibliografia degli studi italiani di materia arturiana (1940–1990)*, Fasano, 9–20.

Bezzola, R. R. 1944–63. *Les Origines et la formation de la littérature courtoise en Occident (500–1200)*, 3 vols, Paris.

Bogdanow, F. 1966. *The Romance of the Grail: A Study of the Structure and Genesis of a Thirteenth-Century Arthurian Prose Romance*, Manchester.

Borsari, A. V. 1983. *Lancillotto liberato: una ricerca intorno al 'fin amant' e all'eroe liberatore*, Florence.

Bouché, T., and H. Charpentier. 1990. *Le Rire au Moyen Âge dans la littérature et dans les arts*, Bordeaux.

Brault, G. J. 1972. 'Chrétien de Troyes' *Lancelot*: The Eye and the Heart', *BBIAS*, 24, 142–53.

Broadhurst, K. M. 1996. 'Henry II of England and Eleanor of Aquitaine: Patrons of Literature in French?', *Viator*, 27, 53–84.

Bruckner, M. T. 1986–7. 'An Interpreter's Dilemma: Why are there so many Interpretations of Chrétien's *Chevalier de la Charrette*?', *RPh*, 40, 159–80.

Bullock-Davies, C. 1966. *Professional Interpreters and the Matter of Britain*, Cardiff.

Bullock-Davies. 1981 'Chrétien de Troyes and England', *AL*, 1, 1–61.

Burgess, G. S. 1984. *Chrétien de Troyes: Erec et Enide*, London.

Buridant, C. 1980. 'Les Binômes synonymiques: esquisse d'une histoire des couples de synonymes du Moyen Âge au XVIIe siècle', *Bulletin du Centre d'Analyse du Discours*, 4, 5–79.

Burns, E. J. 1987–8. 'Quest and Questioning in the *Conte du Graal*', *RPh*, 41, 251–66.

Busby, K. 1998. 'Roman breton et chanson de geste au XVIIIe siècle', in *Echoes of the Epic: Studies in Honor of Gerard J. Brault*, Birmingham, *AL*, 17–48.

Busby, K., T. Nixon, A. Stones, and L. Walters eds. 1993. *Les Manuscrits de Chrétien de Troyes/The Manuscripts of Chrétien de Troyes*, 2 vols, Amsterdam and Atlanta, GA.

Carasso-Bulow, L. 1976. *The Merveilleux in Chrétien de Troyes' Romances*, Geneva.

Carroll, C. W. 1994. 'Quelques observations sur les reflets de la cour d'Henri II dans l'œuvre de Chrétien de Troyes', *CCM*, 37, 33–9.

Chaurand. J. 1973. 'Quelques réflexions sur l'hyperbole dans *Le Chevalier de la Charrete*', in *Études de langue et de littérature du Moyen Âge offertes à Félix Lecoy par ses collègues, ses élèves et ses amis*, Paris, 43–53.

Chênerie, M.-L. 1995. 'Le Dialogue de la dame et du chevalier dans les romans de Chrétien de Troyes', in D. Quéruel ed. *Amour et chevalerie dans les romans de Chrétien de Troyes: actes du Colloque de Troyes (27–29 mars 1992)*, Paris, 107–19.

Cheyette, F. L., and H. Chickering. 2005. 'Love, Anger and Peace: Social Practice and Poetic Play in the Ending of *Yvain*', *Spec*, 80, 75–117.

Colby, A. M. 1965. *The Portrait in Twelfth-Century French Literature: An Example of the Stylistic Originality of Chrétien de Troyes*, Geneva.

Comes, A. 1996. 'Tra parodia e critica letteraria: *Cligès, miles gloriosus* e la distinzione *cuer-cor*', *SMV*, 42, 119–28.

Cross, T. P., and W. A. Nitze. 1930. *Lancelot and Guenevere: A Study on the Origins of Courtly Love*, Chicago.

De Riquer, I. 1999. 'Interpretación de la indumentaria en las traducciones de las novelas de Chrétien de Troyes', in *Traducir la Edad Media: la traducción de la literatura medieval románica*, Granada, 103–34.

Delbouille, M. 1932. Introduction to *Jacques Bretex, Le Tournoi de Chauvency*, Liège and Paris.

Diverres, A. 1990. 'The Grail and the Third Crusade: Thoughts on *Le Conte del Graal* by Chrétien de Troyes', *AL*, 10, 13–109.

Döffinger-Lange, E. 1998. *Der Gauvain-Teil in Chrétiens Conte du Graal: Forschungsbericht und Episodenkommentar*, Heidelberg.

Doss-Quinby, E. 1999. '*Rolan, de ceu ke m'avez / Parti dirai mon samblant*: The Feminine Voice in the Old French *jeu-parti*', *Neophil*, 83, 497–516.

Dragonetti, R. 1980. *La Vie de la lettre au Moyen Âge: le Conte du Graal*, Paris.

Dragonetti 1987. *Le Mirage des sources: l'art du faux dans le roman médiéval*, Paris.

Duby, G. 1978. *Les Trois Ordres ou l'imaginaire du féodalisme*, Paris.

Duby 1981. *Le Chevalier, la femme et le prêtre: le mariage dans la France féodale*, Paris.

Dufournet, J. ed. 1988. *Le Chevalier au lion de Chrétien de Troyes: approches d'un chef-d'œuvre*, Paris.

Duggan, J. J. 1977. 'Ambiguity in Twelfth-Century French and Provençal Literature: A Problem or a Value?', in *Jean Misrahi Memorial Volume: Studies in Medieval Literature*, Columbia, SC, 136–49.

Duggan 1989. 'Oral Performances of Romance in Medieval France', in *Continuations: Essays on Medieval French Literature and Language in Honor of John L. Grigsby*, Birmingham, *AL*, 51–61.

Duggan 2001. *The Romances of Chrétien de Troyes*, New Haven.

Duplat, A. 1974. 'Étude stylistique des apostrophes adressées aux personnages féminins dans les romans de Chrétien de Troyes', *CCM*, 17, 129–52.

Faral, E. 1910. *Les Jongleurs en France au Moyen Âge*, Paris.

Faral 1924. *Les Arts poétiques du XIIᵉ et du XIIIᵉ siècle: recherches et documents sur la technique littéraire du Moyen Âge*, Paris.

Ferlampin-Acher, C. 1995. 'Les Tournois chez Chrétien de Troyes: l'art de l'esquive', in D. Quéruel ed. *Amour et chevalerie dans les romans de Chrétien de Troyes: actes du Colloque de Troyes (27–29 mars 1992)*, Paris, 161–89.

Ferrante, J. 1980. '*Cortes'Amor* in Medieval Texts', *Spec*, 55, 686–95.

Ferroul, Y. 2000. 'Réalités sexuelles et fiction romanesque', in D. Buschinger ed. *Les 'realia' dans la littérature de fiction au Moyen Âge: actes du Colloque du Centre d'Etudes Médiévales de l'Université de Picardie-Jules Verne, Saint-Valery-sur-Somme, 25–28 mars 1999*, Amiens, 40–9.

Flori, J. 1979. 'Pour une histoire de la chevalerie: l'adoubement dans les romans de Chrétien de Troyes', *Rom*, 100, 21–53.

Flori 1996. 'La Notion de chevalerie dans les romans de Chrétien de Troyes', *Rom*, 114, 289–315.

Foerster, W. 1914. *Kristian von Troyes: Wörterbuch zu seinen sämtlichen Werken*, Halle/S.

Foulet, A., and M. B. Speer. 1979. *On Editing Old French Texts*, Lawrence, KS.

Foulet, A., and K. D. Uitti. 1983–4. 'Chrétien's "Laudine": *Yvain*, vv. 2148–55', *RPh*, 37, 293–302.

Fourrier, A. 1950. 'Encore la chronologie des œuvres de Chrétien de Troyes', *BBIAS*, 2, 69–88

Frappier, J. 1965. 'La Brisure du couplet dans *Erec et Enide'*, *Rom*, 86, 1–21.

Frappier 1967. ' "D'amors", "par amors"', *Rom*, 88, 433–74.

Frappier 1968. *Chrétien de Troyes: l'homme et l'œuvre*, Paris.

Frappier 1969. *Étude sur Yvain ou le Chevalier au lion de Chrétien de Troyes*, Paris.

Frappier 1972. *Chrétien de Troyes et le mythe du Graal: étude sur Perceval ou le Conte du Graal*, Paris.

Freeman, M. A. 1979. *The Poetics of translatio studii and conjointure in Chrétien de Troyes's Cligés*, Lexington, KY.

Gallais, P. 1964–70. 'Recherches sur la mentalité des romanciers français du Moyen Âge: les formules et le vocabulaire des prologues', *CCM*, 7, 479–93; 13, 333–47.

Gallais 1978. 'Métonymie et métaphore dans le *Conte du Graal'*, in *Mélanges de littérature du Moyen Âge au XXᵉ siècle offerts à Mademoiselle Jeanne Lods par ses collègues, ses élèves et ses amis*, 2 vols, Paris, I, 213–48.

Gallais 1991. 'Et si Chrétien était l'auteur de *Liétart*? L'argument de la versification', *PRIS-MA*, 7, 229–55.

Gaunt, S. 1995. *Gender and Genre in Medieval French Literature*, Cambridge.

Genere = Il genere 'tenzone' nelle letterature romanze delle origini, Ravenna, 1999.

Gerritsen, W. P. 1995. 'Een avond in Ardres: over middeleeuwse verhaalkunst', in *Grote Lijnen: Syntheses over Middelnederlandse Letterkunde*, Amsterdam, 157–72 , 220–3.

Gravdal, K. 1991. *Ravishing Maidens: Writing Rape in French Literature and Law*, Philadelphia.

Green, D. H. 1979. *Irony in the Medieval Romance*, Cambridge.

Green 2002. *The Beginnings of Medieval Romance: Fact and Fiction, 1150–1220*, Cambridge.

Grimbert, J. T. 1988. *Yvain dans le miroir: une poétique de la réflexion dans le Chevalier au lion de Chrétien de Troyes*, Amsterdam.

Grisay, A., G. Lavis, and M. Dubois-Stasse. 1969. *Les Dénominations de la femme dans les anciens textes littéraires français*, Gembloux.

Grosse, K. 1881. 'Der Stil Crestien's von Troies', *Französische Studien*, 1, 127–260.

Grundmann, H. 1952. '*Sacerdotium-regnum-studium*: zur Wertung der Wissenschaft im 13. Jahrhundert', *Archiv für Kulturgeschichte*, 34, 5–21.

Gsteiger, M. 1958. *Die Landschaftsschilderungen in den Romanen Chrestiens de Troyes: literarische Tradition und künstlerische Gestaltung*, Bern.

Haidu, P. 1968. *Aesthetic Distance in Chrétien de Troyes: Irony and Comedy in Cligés and Perceval*, Geneva.

Haidu 1972. *Lion-queue-coupée: l'écart symbolique chez Chrétien de Troyes*, Geneva.

Halász, K. 1980. *Structures narratives chez Chrétien de Troyes*, Debrecen.

Halász 1992. *Images d'auteur dans le roman médiéval (XIIᵉ–XIIIᵉ siècles)*, Debrecen.

Haug, W. 1979. 'Strukturalistische Methoden und mediävistische Literaturwissenschaft', *Wolfram-Studien*, 5, 8–21.

Haug 1992. *Literaturtheorie im deutschen Mittelalter: von den Anfängen bis zum Ende des 13. Jahrhunderts. Eine Einführung*, 2nd edn, Darmstadt; 1997. Transl. as *Vernacular Literary Theory in the Middle Ages: The German Tradition, 800–1300, in its European Context*, Cambridge.

Hilka, A. 1903. *Die direkte Rede als stilistisches Kunstmittel in den Romanen des Kristian von Troyes: ein Beitrag zur genetischen Entwicklung der Kunstformen des mittelalterlichen Epos*, Halle/S.

Hilty, G. 1975. 'Zum *Erec*-Prolog von Chrétien de Troyes', in *Philologica romanica Erhard Lommatzsch gewidmet*, Munich, 245–56.

Hindman, S. 1994. *Sealed in Parchment: Rereadings of Knighthood in the Illuminated Manuscripts of Chrétien de Troyes*, Chicago and London.

Hult, D. F. 1986. 'Lancelot's Two Steps: A Problem in Textual Criticism', *Spec*, 61, 836–58.

Hult 1989a. 'Author/Narrator/Speaker: The Voice of Authority in Chrétien's *Charrete*', in *Discourses of Authority in Medieval and Renaissance Literature*, Hanover, NH and London, 76–96, 267–9.

Hult 1989b. 'Steps Forward and Steps Backward: More on Chrétien's *Lancelot*', *Spec*, 64, 307–16.

Hult 1991. 'Reading it Right: The Ideology of Text Editing', in M. S. Brownlee, K. Brownlee and S. J. Nichols eds *The New Medievalism*, Baltimore and London, 113–30.

Hult 1998. *Manuscript Transmission, Reception and Canon Formation: The Case of Chrétien de Troyes*, Berkeley.

Hunt, T. 1970. 'The Rhetorical Background to the Arthurian Prologue: Tradition and the Old French Vernacular Prologues', *FMLS*, 6, 1–23.

Hunt 1972. 'Tradition and Originality in the Prologues of Chrestien de Troyes', *FMLS*, 8, 320–44.

Hunt 1977. 'The Dialectic of *Yvain*', *MLR*, 72, 285–99.

Hunt 1978. 'Chrestien and the *Comediae*', *MS*, 40, 120–56.

Hunt 1979. 'Aristotle, Dialectic, and Courtly Literature', *Viator*, 10, 95–129.

Hunt 1981. 'The Emergence of the Knight in France and England, 1000–1200', *FMLS*, 17, 93–114.

Hunt 1982. 'Rhetoric and Poetics in Twelfth-Century France', in B. Vickers ed. *Rhetoric Revalued: Papers from the International Society for the History of Rhetoric*, Binghamton, NY, 165–71.

Hunt 1986. *Chrétien de Troyes: Yvain (Le Chevalier au lion)*, London.

Hunt 1994. 'Chrétien's Prologues Reconsidered', in *Conjunctures: Medieval Studies in Honor of Douglas Kelly*, Amsterdam, 153–68.

Huot, S. 1987. *From Song to Book: The Poetics of Writing in Old French Lyric and Lyrical Narrative Poetry*, Ithaca, NY.

Jones, M. H., and R. Wisbey eds 1993. *Chrétien de Troyes and the German Middle Ages: Papers from an International Symposium*, Cambridge and London.

Kay, S. 1997. 'Who was Chrétien de Troyes?', *AL*, 15, 1–35.

Kay 2001. *Courtly Contradictions: The Emergence of the Literary Object in the Twelfth Century*, Stanford.

Keen, M. H. 1984. *Chivalry*, New Haven, CT and London.

Kellermann, W. 1936. *Aufbaustil und Weltbild Chrestiens von Troyes im Percevalroman*, Halle; repr. Darmstadt, 1967.

Kelly, D. 1970. 'The Source and Meaning of *conjointure* in Chrétien's *Erec* 14', *Viator*, 1, 179–200.

Kelly 1971. 'La Forme et le sens de la quête dans l'*Erec et Enide* de Chrétien de Troyes', *Rom*, 92, 326–58.

Kelly 1976, 2002. See above (Bibliography).

Kelly 1984. 'Les Fées et les arts dans la représentation du Chevalier de la Charrette', in D. Buschinger ed. *Lancelot: actes du Colloque des 14 et 15 janvier, Université de Picardie, Centre d'Etudes Médiévales*, Göppingen, 85–97.

Kelly ed. 1985. *The Romances of Chrétien de Troyes: A Symposium*, Lexington, KY.

Kelly 1988. 'Le Lieu du temps, le temps du lieu', in *Le Nombre du temps: en hommage à Paul Zumthor*, Paris, 123–6.

Kelly 1999a. *The Conspiracy of Allusion: Description, Rewriting, and Authorship from Macrobius to Medieval Romance*, Leiden.

Kelly 1999b. 'Forlorn Hope: Mutability *topoi* in some Medieval Narratives', in *The World and its Rival: Essays on Literary Imagination in Honor of Per Nykrog*, Amsterdam, 59–77.

Köhler, E. 1960. 'Le Rôle de la coutume dans les romans de Chrétien de Troyes', *Rom*, 81, 386–97.

Kullmann, D. 1992. *Verwandtschaft in epischer Dichtung: Untersuchungen zu den französischen chansons de geste und Romanen des 12. Jahrhunderts*, Tübingen.

Lacy, N. J. 1980. *The Craft of Chrétien de Troyes: An Essay in Narrative Art*, Leiden.

Lacy, and J. T. Grimhert eds 2005. *A Companion to Chrétien de Troyes*, Cambridge.

Långfors, A. I. E. 1926. *Recueil général des jeux-partis français*, 2 vols, SATF, Paris.

Lebsanft, F. 1988. *Studien zu einer Linguistik des Grüßes: Sprache und Funktion der altfranzösischen Grußformeln*, Tübingen.

Lefay-Toury, M.-N. 1972. 'Roman breton et mythes courtois: l'évolution du personnage féminin dans les romans de Chrétien de Troyes', *CCM*, 15, 193–204, 283–93.

Lepri, A. 1991. 'I personaggi minori nei romanzi di Chrétien de Troyes', in *Lingua, immagini e storia*, Bologna, 7–94.

Le Rider, P. 1978. *Le Chevalier dans le Conte du Graal de Chrétien de Troyes*, Paris.

Lewis, C. S. 1936. *The Allegory of Love: A Study in Medieval Tradition*, Oxford.

Liborio, M. 1982. 'Rhetorical *Topoi* as "Clues" in Chrétien de Troyes', in B. Vickers ed. *Rhetoric Revalued: Papers from the International Society for the History of Rhetoric*, Binghamton, NY, 173–8.

Loomis, R. S. 1949. *Arthurian Tradition and Chrétien de Troyes*, New York.

McCash, J. H. 1985. 'Marie de Champagne's "cuer d'ome et cors de fame": Aspects of Feminism and Misogyny in the Twelfth Century', in G. S. Burgess and R.W. Taylor eds *The Spirit of the Court: Selected Proceedings of the Fourth Congress of the International Courtly Literature Society (Toronto 1983)*, Cambridge, 234–45.

McCracken, P. 1998. *The Romance of Adultery: Queenship and Sexual Transgression in Old French Literature*, Philadelphia.

Maddox, D. 1973. 'Critical Trends and Recent Work on the *Cligés* of Chrétien de Troyes', *NM*, 74, 730–45.

Maddox 1978. *Structure and Sacring: The Systematic Kingdom in Chrétien's 'Erec et Enide'*, Lexington, KY.

Maddox 1980–1. 'Trois sur deux: théories de bipartition et de tripartition des œuvres de Chrétien', *Œuvres et critiques*, 5:2, 91–102.

Maddox 1989. 'Opérations cognitives et scandales romanesques: Méléagant et le roi Marc', in *Hommage à Jean-Charles Payen: 'Farai chansoneta novele'. Essais sur la liberté créatrice du Moyen Âge*, Caen, 239–51.

Maddox 1991. *The Arthurian Romances of Chrétien de Troyes: Once and Future Fictions*, Cambridge.

Marnette, S. 1998. *Narrateurs et points de vue dans la littérature française médiévale: une approche linguistique*, Bern.

Méla, C. 1984. *La Reine et le Graal: la conjointure dans les romans du Graal, de Chrétien de Troyes au Livre de Lancelot*, Paris.

Ménage, R. 1980. '*Erec et Enide*: quelques pièces du dossier', in *Mélanges de langue et de littérature françaises du Moyen Âge et de la Renaissance offerts à Monsieur Charles Foulon, II, M Rom*, 30, 203–21.

Ménard, P. 1967. 'Le Temps et la durée dans les romans de Chrétien de Troyes', *MA*, 73, 375–401.

Ménard 1969. *Le Rire et le sourire dans le roman courtois en France au Moyen Âge (1150–1250)*, Geneva.

Ménard 1976. 'Le Chevalier errant dans la littérature arthurienne: recherches sur les raisons du départ et de l'errance', in *Voyage, quête, pèlerinage dans la littérature et la civilisation médiévales*, Aix-en-Provence, 289–310.

Ménard 1984. 'Problèmes et mystères du *Conte du graal*: un essai d'interprétation', in J. De Caluwé and H. Braet eds *Chrétien de Troyes et le Graal*, Paris, 61–76.

Ménard 1991. 'Problématique de l'aventure dans les romans de la Table Ronde', in Van Hoecke, Tournoy and Verbeke eds 1991*, II, 89–119.

Ménard 1995. 'La Révélation du nom pour le héros du *Conte du graal*', in D. Quéruel ed. *Amour et chevalerie dans les romans de Chrétien de Troyes: actes du colloque de Troyes (27–29 mars 1992)*, Paris, 47–59.

Ménard 2000. 'Réflexions sur les coutumes dans les romans arthuriens', in *'Por le soie amisté': Essays in Honor of Norris J. Lacy*, Amsterdam, 357–70.

Misrahi, J. 1959. 'More Light on the Chronology of Chrétien de Troyes?', *BBIAS*, 11, 89–120.

Monson, D. A. 1987. 'La "Surenchère" chez Chrétien de Troyes', *Poétique*, 70 (vol. 18), 231–46.

Neumeister, S. 1969. *Das Spiel mit der höfischen Liebe: das altprovenzalische partimen*, Munich.

Neumeyer, K. 1998. *Vom Kriegshandwerk zum ritterlichen Theater: das Turnier im mittelalterlichen Frankreich*, Bonn.

Noble, P. S. 1982. *Love and Marriage in Chrétien de Troyes*, Cardiff.

Nolting-Hauff, I. 1959. *Die Stellung der Liebeskasuistik im höfischen Roman*, Heidelberg.

Nykrog, P. 1996. *Chrétien de Troyes: romancier discutable*, Geneva.

Ollier, M.-L. 1974. 'The Author in the Text: The Prologues of Chrétien de Troyes', *YFS*, 51, 26–41.

Ollier 1989. *Lexique et concordance de Chrétien de Troyes d'après la copie Guiot, avec introduction, index et rimaire*, Montreal.

Owen, D. D. R. 1971. 'Two More Romances by Chrétien de Troyes?', *Rom*, 92, 246–60.

Paris, G. 1883. 'Études sur les romans de la Table Ronde. Lancelot du Lac II: Le *Conte de la charrette*', *Rom*, 12, 459–534.

Parkes, M. B. 1992. *Pause and Effect: An Introduction to the History of Punctuation in the West*, Aldershot and Berkeley.

Paupert, A. 1995. 'L'Amour au féminin dans les romans de Chrétien de Troyes', in D. Quéruel ed. *Amour et chevalerie dans les romans de Chrétien de Troyes: actes du colloque de Troyes (27–29 mars 1992)*, Paris, 95–106.

Payen, J.-C. 1967. *Le Motif du repentir dans la littérature française médiévale (des origines à 1230)*, Geneva.

Pensom, R. 1993. 'Zumthor and After: A Survey of Some Current Trends in the Reading of Old French Literature', *Med. Aev*, 62, 294–306.

Pickens, R. T. 1977. *The Welsh Knight: Paradoxicality in Chrétien's Conte del Graal*, Lexington, KY.

Pickford, C. E. 1981. 'The Good Name of Chrétien de Troyes', in *An Arthurian Tapestry: Essays in Memory of Lewis Thorpe*, Glasgow, 389–401.

Pioletti, A. 1979. 'Lettura dell'episodio del "Chastel de Pesme-Aventure" (*Yvain*, vv. 5101–5805)', *MR*, 6, 227–46.

Pioletti 1980. 'La Condanna del lavoro: gli "ordines" nei romanzi di Chrétien de Troyes', *Le forme e la storia*, 1, 71–109.

Piraprez, D. 2000. 'Chrétien de Troyes, allégoriste malgré lui? Amour et allégorie dans *Le Roman de la rose* et *Le Chevalier de la charrette*', in J. Dor ed. *Conjointure arthurienne: actes de la 'Classe d'Excellence' de la Chaire Franqui 1998, Liège, 20 février 1998*, Louvain-la-Neuve, 83–94.

Poirion, D. 1986. 'Théorie et pratique du style au Moyen Âge: le sublime et la merveille', *Revue d'Histoire Littéraire de la France*, 86, 15–32.

Press, A. R. 1987. 'Death and Lamentation in Chrétien de Troyes's Romances: The Dialectic of Rhetoric and Reason', *FMLS*, 23, 11–20.

Remy, P. 1964. 'Jeu parti et roman breton', in *Mélanges de linguistique romane et de philologie médiévale offerts à M. Maurice Delbouille*, 2 vols, Gembloux, II, 545–61.

Rey-Flaud, H. 1998. *Le Sphinx et le Graal: le secret et l'énigme*, Paris.

Rey-Flaud 1999. *Le Chevalier, l'autre et la mort: les aventures de Gauvain dans Le Conte du Graal*, Paris.

Ribard, J. 1972. *Chrétien de Troyes, Le Chevalier de la charrette: essai d'interprétation symbolique*, Paris.

Ribard 1997. 'Pour une lecture allégorique et religieuse des œuvres littéraires médiévales', in J.-C. Vallecalle ed. *Littérature et religion au Moyen Âge et à la Renaissance*, Lyon, 15–26.

Rickard, P. 1956. *Britain in Medieval French Literature, 1100–1500*, Cambridge.

Robertson, D. W., Jr. 1951. 'Some Medieval Literary Terminology, with Special Reference to Chrétien de Troyes', *SP*, 48, 669–92.

Robertson 1962. *A Preface to Chaucer: Studies in Medieval Perspectives*, Princeton.

Robertson 1972. 'The Idea of Fame in Chrétien's *Cligés*', *SP*, 69, 414–33.

Rohr, R. 1962. 'Zur Skala der ritterlichen Tugenden in der altprovenzalischen und altfranzösischen höfischen Dichtung', *ZrP*, 78, 292–325.

Roques, M. 1952. 'Le Scribe Guiot et le manuscrit français 794 de la Bibliothèque Nationale', *Académie des Inscriptions et Belles Lettres: comptes rendus*, 21–2.

Rossi, L. 1987. 'Chrétien de Troyes e i trovatori: Tristan, Linhaura, Carestia', *VR*, 46, 26–62.

Roussel, C. 1994. 'Le Legs de la rose: modèles et préceptes de la sociabilité médiévale', in A. Montandon ed. *Pour une histoire des traités de savoir-vivre en Europe*, Clermont-Ferrand, 1–90.

Santina, M. A. 1999. *The Tournament and Literature: Literary Representations of the Medieval Tournament in Old French Works, 1150–1226*, New York and Canterbury.

Sargent-Baur, B. N. 1979–80. 'Erec's Enide: "sa fame ou s'amie"?', *RPh*, 33, 373–87.

Sargent-Baur 1983–4. 'Promotion to Knighthood in the Romances of Chrétien de Troyes', *RPh*, 37, 393–408.

Sargent-Baur 1987. 'The Missing Prologue of Chrétien's *Chevalier au Lion*', *FS*, 41, 385–94.

Sargent-Baur 2000. *La Destre et la senestre: étude sur le Conte du Graal de Chrétien de Troyes*, Amsterdam.

Schmid, E. 1986. *Familiengeschichte und Heilsmythologie: die Verwandtschaftsstrukturen in den französischen und deutschen Gralromanen des 12. und 13. Jahrhunderts*, Tübingen.

Schmitt, J.-C. 1990. *La Raison des gestes dans l'Occident médiéval*, Paris.

Schnell, R. 1985. *Causa amoris: Liebeskonzeption und Liebesdarstellung in der mittelalterlichen Literatur*, Bern and Munich.

Schnell 1998. 'The Discourse on Marriage in the Middle Ages', *Spec*, 73, 771–86.

Schöning, U. 1991. *Thebenroman–Eneasroman–Trojaroman: Studien zur Rezeption der Antike in der französischen Literatur des 12. Jahrhunderts*, Tübingen.

Shirt, D. J. 1978. 'Chrétien's *Charrette* and its Critics, 1964–74', *MLR*, 73, 38–50.

Shirt 1982. '*Cligés* – A Twelfth-Century Matrimonial Case-Book?', *FMLS*, 18, 75–89.

Stuip, R. E. V., and C. Vellekoop eds 1993. *Oraliteit en schriftcultuur*, Hilversum.

Sylvester, L. 1998. 'Reading Rape in Medieval Literature', *StMed*, 10, 120–35.

Topsfield, L. T. 1981. *Chrétien de Troyes: A Study of the Arthurian Romances*, Cambridge.

Turnier = Das ritterliche Turnier im Mittelalter: Beiträge zu einer vergleichenden Formen- und Verhaltensgeschichte des Rittertums, Göttingen, 1985.

Tuve, R. 1966. *Allegorical Imagery: Some Mediaeval Books and their Posterity*, Princeton.

Uitti, K. D. ed. 1987 *The Poetics of Textual Criticism: The Old French Example*, in *Esp*, 27:1.

Uitti and A. Foulet. 1988. 'On Editing Chrétien de Troyes: Lancelot's Two Steps and their Context', *Spec*, 63, 271–92.

Vàrvaro, A. 2001. 'Elaboration des textes et modalités du récit dans la littérature française médiévale', *Rom*, 119, 1–75.

Vielliard, F. 1998. 'Le Manuscrit avant l'auteur: diffusion et conservation de la littérature médiévale en ancien français (XIIᵉ–XIIIᵉ siècles)', *TL*, 11, 39–53.

Villa, C. 1996. 'Per *Erec*, 14: "une molt bele conjointure"', in *Studi di filologia offerti a D'Arco Silvio Avalle*, Milan, 453–72.

Vinaver, E. 1963–4. 'From Epic to Romance', *BJRL*, 46, 476–503.

Vincensini, J.-J. 1996. *Pensée mythique et narrations médiévales*, Paris.

Vitz, E. B. 1997. 'Rereading Rape in Medieval Literature: Literary, Historical, and Theoretical Reflections', *RR*, 88, 1–26.

Voicu, M. 1990. 'Une émeute communale au XIIᵉ siècle ou "le monde bestourné"', *Analele Universității București: limbi și literaturi străine, 39, 62–68.*

Wallen, M. 1982. 'Significant Variations in the Burgundian Prose Version of *Erec et Enide*', *Med. Aev*, 51, 187–96.

Walter, P. 1988. *Canicule: essai de mythologie sur Yvain de Chrétien de Troyes*, Paris.

Watanabe, K. 1996. 'L'Ironie dans l'œuvre de Chrétien de Troyes: de l'approche rhétorique à l'approche mythologique', *Pespectives médiévales*, 22, 80–4.

Watanabe 2002. *Introduction à l'étude des romans de Chrétien de Troyes: de l'approche rhétorique à l'approche mythologique*, Tokyo (in Japanese).

Weber, H. 1976. *Chrestien und die Tristandichtung*, Bern, 1976.

Williams, H. F. 1983. 'Interpretations of the *Conte del Graal* and their Critical Reactions', in R. T. Pickens ed. *The Sower and his Seed: Essays on Chrétien de Troyes*, Lexington, KY, 146–54.

Wilmotte, M. 1930. 'La Part de Chrétien de Troyes dans la composition du plus ancien poème sur le Gral', *Académie Royale de Belgique: Bulletins de la Classe des Lettres et des Sciences Morales et Politiques*, 5th series, 16, 40–64, 97–119.

Winkler, M. 1958. *Der kirchliche Wortschatz in der Epik Chrétiens von Troyes*, Munich.

Woledge, B. 1986–8. *Commentaire sur Yvain (Le Chevalier au lion) de Chrétien de Troyes*, 2 vols, Geneva.

Zaddy, Z. P. 1973. *Chrétien Studies: Problems of Form and Meaning in Erec, Yvain, Cligés and the Charrette*, Glasgow.

Zaddy 1980. 'Chrétien misogyne?', in *Mélanges de langue et de littérature françaises du Moyen Âge et de la Renaissance offerts à Monsieur Charles Foulon, II, MRom*, 30, 301–7.

Zemel, R. 1996. 'Perceval en geen einde', *Voortgang*, 16, 7–26.

Ziltener, W. 1972. *Studien zur bildungsgeschichtlichen Eigenart der höfischen Dichtung: Antike und Christentum in okzitanischen und altfranzösischen Vergleichen aus der unbelebten Natur*, Bern.

Zink, M. 1981. 'Une mutation de la conscience littéraire: le langage romanesque à travers des exemples français du XIIe siècle', *CCM*, 24, 3–27.

Zumthor, P. 1972. *Essai de poétique médiévale*, Paris.

Zumthor 1984. *La Poésie et la voix dans la civilisation médiévale*, Paris.

Zumthor 1987. *La Lettre et la voix de la littérature médiévale*, Paris.

Zumthor 1993. *La Mesure du monde: représentations de l'espace au Moyen Âge*, Paris.

V

ARTHUR IN THE NARRATIVE LAY

Matilda Tomaryn Bruckner and Glyn S. Burgess

Often referred to as Breton lays, narrative lays (*lais*) are predominantly short stories of love and adventure in verse. The existence of analogous genres such as the *fabliau* and the *dit* makes it difficult to establish a definitive corpus of extant lays, but there is general agreement that the twelve poems found in London, British Library, MS Harley 978, normally attributed to an author known as Marie de France, are not only lays but the very model of the genre. Marie's poems, known collectively as the *Lais*, occur in the Harley manuscript in the following order: *Guigemar, Equitan, Le Fresne, Bisclavret, Lanval, Les Deus Amanz, Yonec, Laüstic, Milun, Chaitivel, Chevrefoil* and *Eliduc*.[1] In addition, there are eleven lays by unknown authors which are commonly designated as anonymous Breton lays. In alphabetical order they are: *Desiré, Doon, Espine, Graelent, Guingamor, Lecheor, Melion, Nabaret, Trot, Tydorel* and *Tyolet*. A further dozen or so poems, some anonymous, others with named authors, are also generally classed as lays: *Amours, Aristote, Conseil, Cor, Espervier, Haveloc, Ignaure, Mantel, Narcisus, Oiselet, Ombre* and *Piramus et Thisbé*.[2]

Whatever their category, the lays vary greatly in theme and tone, and they have been variously classified as realistic, supernatural, courtly, classical, didactic, parodic, etc. (Damon 1929; Williams 1964; Donovan 1969). It could also be said that the lays in the first two categories are more specifically Breton, either because they themselves claim to be Breton in origin or inspiration or because their themes relate more to Celtic material than that of many of the poems in the third group.[3] This chapter will begin by examining the *Lais* of Marie de France, with particular reference to *Lanval* and *Chevrefoil*, the two Arthurian lays in her collection, then proceed to a discussion of the anonymous lays, especially the specifically Arthurian lays, *Melion, Tyolet* and *Trot*, and those with links to the Lanval story, *Graelent, Guingamor* and *Desiré*. The *Lai du Cor* and the *Lai du Cort Mantel*, the only Arthurian lays amongst those remaining, will be discussed at the end of this chapter.

Marie de France

At first glance, looking for Arthur in the *Lais* of Marie de France leads to a partial and selective reading. Twelve lays are included in the Harley manuscript, the only manuscript to present them as a collection assembled by the author and introduced by a General Prologue, in which they are offered to an unnamed but 'noble' king. Among the twelve, a single tale, *Lanval*, operates directly in the Arthurian context.[4] Another lay, *Chevrefoil*, may claim an unstated connection, since, by the second half of the twelfth century, stories involving Tristan and Yseut have moved, in Hoepffner's expressive phrase (1959, 119), into the Arthurian orbit. Discrete and apparently isolated tales (*Lanval* occupies fifth position, *Chevrefoil* next to last), these two lays can nevertheless guide us through a network of associations to a more comprehensive reading of the *Lais*, one which highlights its most essential and critical features. Reading for Arthur will thus appear in this chapter as a clearly delimited task, as well as a more general challenge to ask questions leading to the heart of Marie's collection of short tales.

When it comes to identifying the author and her works, there are no simple answers to the basic questions of who, what, where and when. The very name we use to designate 'Marie de France' has been constructed after the fact, using information provided in her writing. This is one of the first and enduring characteristics of her works, which pose the necessity, as well as the difficulty, of aligning historical personages and literary productions, a demand that requires us to adopt her story-telling impulse as our own. The data constitute a series of puzzle pieces, which fit together in a variety of designs without any one achieving definitive status. Literary historians generally associate three works signed 'Marie', which are all translations of one sort or another: the *Lais*, the *Fables* and the *Espurgatoire seint Patriz*.[5] Efforts to identify Marie and date her works depend on such matters as patrons, language, style and literary references. In the *Fables* (widely disseminated in more than twenty-five manuscripts, including Harley 978), an epilogue includes Marie's name along with her place of origin: 'Marie ai nun, si sui de France' (*Marie is my name and I am from France*, Brucker edn, l. 4), a phrase which led Claude Fauchet, in his *Recueil de l'origine de la langue et poesie françoise*, published in 1581, to coin her current name. Originally from the Continent, Marie of France would now be writing for a francophone public in England. She claims to have translated the fables from an English collection and names as her patron a Count William, whom she praises as the flower of chivalry, learning and courtliness (*curteisie*). He has variously been identified as William of Mandeville (Earl of Essex from 1167, d. 1189, a patron of the arts and esteemed by Henry II), William Marshal (Earl of Pembroke from 1189, first preceptor to the Young King and an outstanding knight), William

Longsword (illegitimate son of Henry II and Rosamund Clifford, Earl of Salisbury from 1196), and William of Gloucester (d. 1183, friend of Henry II, son of the scholar and literary patron Robert of Gloucester). Each one presents tantalizing possibilities for making connections with candidates for the historical Marie and the patron of her *Lais*, who is usually recognized as Henry II (1154–89), but sometimes identified with Henry the Young King (crowned in 1170 but predeceased his father in 1183).

The chronological ordering and dating of Marie's works by modern critics generally take these possible identifications into account: the *Lais* between 1160 and 1189 (as demonstrated by their manuscript transmission, some individual lays appear to have been composed and disseminated over a period of years before the collection was put together),[6] the *Fables* between 1167 and 1189, or possibly later if dedicated to William Longsword or William Marshal (the latest editor dates them between 1189 and 1208, Brucker edn, 1–3), and the *Espurgatoire* after 1190. Including this last work in Marie's repertoire has raised further questions about her probable period of literary production. The *Espurgatoire* is a translation from the *Tractatus de Purgatorio sancti Patricii*, composed in England by Henry of Saltry and variously dated, depending on the identity of his patron, Hugh or Henry, abbot of Sartis. If the former, a date *c*.1190 seems likely for Marie's *Espurgatoire* (Pontfarcy edn, 10); if the latter, Henry's *Tractatus* must have been written between 1208 and 1215, so Marie's translation would move well into the thirteenth century. But a more reasonable period of literary activity, which corresponds well to what is known about Marie as author, would be the period 1160 to 1190 (Burgess in Ewert edn 1995, ix).

Based on this limited knowledge, we can piece together who she might have been. Some candidates proposed have been eliminated from current consideration (e.g. Marie de Champagne and Marie de Compiègne), but four women in particular continue to compete for the honour: (i) Marie, the abbess of Reading, suggested primarily because of her connection with the abbey where the Harley manuscript, containing both the *Lais* and the *Fables*, may have been copied; William Marshal and William of Mandeville were both closely associated with this abbey; (ii) Marie, abbess of Shaftesbury, the illegitimate daughter of Geoffrey Plantagenet, and thus Henry II's half-sister; she was born in France and lived in England between 1181 and 1216. The abbey of Shaftesbury, patronized by Marie's nephew William Longsword, was founded by King Alfred, and in the epilogue to her *Fables*, the author Marie claims that it was King Alfred who translated a Latin collection into English (although no such version has been found) and thus provided the text for her translation from English to French; (iii) Marie, Countess of Boulogne, the daughter of King Stephen of England and Marie de Boulogne. Abbess of Romsey in Hampshire, she was compelled by Henry II to marry Matthew of Flanders (which made her the sister-in-law of

Hervé II, whose father, Guiomar of Léon, may have provided the name for Guigemar, the hero of the first lay in Marie's collection); she returned to the religious life between 1168 and 1180; (iv) Marie of Meulan, born *c*.1150, the daughter of Waleran II, Count of Meulan, and Agnes of Montfort; her father was one of the Beaumont twins, a flamboyant man who participated with gusto in the contemporary play of power and politics (Grillo 1988; Pontfarcy 1995). If this last Marie is our author, her interest in twins (which will become apparent below) may have stemmed from family experience. She would have been raised in the French Vexin, which corresponds to her described origin, as well as to her detailed knowledge of the town of Pitres and its surroundings featured in *Les Deus Amanz*. This Marie married Hugh of Talbot, whose family held lands in south-west England, where some of the events in the last two lays in the collection, *Chevrefoil* and *Eliduc*, take place.

If the historical Marie continues to elude us, her portrait as an artist emerges from the works themselves. Well educated, plurilingual, familiar with both written and oral literary traditions (from the classics to contemporary Latin and vernacular works), she wrote for an aristocratic audience and demonstrates an intimate knowledge of court life with all its pleasures and tensions. In his *Vie seint Edmund le rei* (*Life of St Edmund the King*, *c*.1170), Denis Piramus bears disapproving witness to the popularity of a 'dame Marie' whose rhymed lays, not at all true, are often read out loud at court, praised and enjoyed by counts, barons, knights and especially ladies.[7] It is indeed as the author of the *Lais* that Marie is most appreciated by the modern public. In the General Prologue which introduces her collection, she establishes her credentials as a writer who has mastered the art of rhetoric as taught in the schools. Looking back to written traditions in Latin, Marie situates herself within the renewable process of glossing and interpretation, while at the same time looking forward as a Modern keen to stake out a claim for her own unprecedented literary project. Others had produced translations from the Latin, whereas Marie laboured late into the night to give birth to something different. To the oral lays of the Bretons, musical compositions commemorating past adventures, she gave a new form and shape as narrative in rhyme and writing. From those individual pieces she made a collection in honour of the noble king, in whose heart all good things take root; if it pleases him to accept them as a gift, she will in turn receive great joy.

The process of courtly exchange, the transformation of Breton lays for new publics, the appropriate role of artists and kings, men and women, such is the general frame which Marie gives to her Arthurian matter. Aware that her daring may seem presumption, especially since she has made no secret of writing as one of the twelfth century's rare female authors, Marie boldly ventures into new territory and nowhere more outrageously than in *Lanval*.[8] Her gamble clearly paid off: based on the number of manuscripts, translations and imitations, *Lanval* was one of her most popular lays.[9] In this medium-length tale, narrated in 648 lines, she has refashioned the common matter of a story which can also be glimpsed through the anonymous lay of *Graelent*. Her most striking innovations are linked to the surprising identities she gives to her characters through naming. Probably anonymous in her source, the king whose ingratitude opens the story has in Marie's version become Arthur, and his unnamed queen, now implicitly identified with Guinevere, operates in a scenario based on the well-known plot of Potiphar's wife. The hero of the tale, known elsewhere with a recognizably Breton name, has here been identified by a name with no known literary precedents (Koubichkine 1972; Rychner edn 1966, 254), while his lady remains anonymous, her potential identity as Arthur's sister Morgan unclaimed and her functional identity as fairy never acknowledged in Marie's text (O'Sharkey 1971).

Lanval's plot develops dramatically, and in three movements. When Arthur distributes gifts to his deserving knights, Lanval is forgotten. He is a king's son, but serving in a distant court he has no one to save him from poverty and disfavour. Alone in a meadow one day, he is invited to a lady's tent; she has come from far away for love of him. If he agrees to keep their love a secret, he can enjoy her favours and wealth in abundance; if he fails to keep his word, he will never see her again. Their union formally engaged, the lady sends Lanval back to Arthur's court, where he continues to enjoy her secret visits and distributes gifts to all, unrestrainedly. He thus comes to the attention of the queen, who offers him her love. Rebuffed, she accuses him of homosexuality and he ripostes by telling her that he loves a woman who is above all others; her poorest servant is more beautiful and more worthy than the queen. Humiliated, she tells Arthur that Lanval has propositioned and insulted her. Lanval defends himself against the sexual charge, but he confirms the truth of his boast. The king orders a trial, and, to buttress his claim, Lanval must produce evidence before the court. Disconsolate that, having revealed their love, he has now lost the power to summon his lady, Lanval awaits the day of judgement without hope. The Count of Cornwall summons the accused to produce his lady as guarantor of the truth, but Lanval replies that he cannot do so. As the king presses for a decision, two maidens approach the court; they are so beautiful that Gauvain is sure that one must be Lanval's beloved, but Lanval does not recognize them. This is repeated with two more maidens, until finally Lanval's lady herself appears, so ravishingly beautiful that the judges have no hesitation in granting the truthfulness of Lanval's boast. He is acquitted, and as the lady rides off to Avalon Lanval jumps on to the back of her horse and disappears with her.

While some critics have speculated that Marie gratuitously named her king to capitalize on Arthur's popularity, others (e.g. Hoepffner 1930; 1935, 58–9; Walkley 1983) have looked for greater significance in that choice, given the economy of Marie's style and the subtlety of an art based on exploiting what the

General Prologue calls the 'surplus of meaning' associated with written texts
(9–22). Marie's audacious gesture at the very least requires us to ask the question:
what difference does it make if the king is Arthur or not? Of course, no single
answer will exhaust that query. At the most obvious level, Arthur's name introduces a set of possible associations that inevitably come into play as the public
reacts to Lanval's story. Hoepffner (1930, 20–5) has documented how carefully
Marie establishes her Arthurian setting with proper names, geography and
history, thereby firmly placing her work in relation to Geoffrey of Monmouth
and his French translator Wace, as well as in relation to some form of the Tristan
story. She establishes herself as a reader of contemporary historians and
romancers, including the romances of antiquity, *Eneas* and *Thèbes*, whose
descriptions of luxury items, such as tents, and portraits of beautiful ladies on
horseback, also embellish her narrative.[10]

This alignment of texts corroborates the dating of Marie's *Lais* to the latter
half of the twelfth century, but does it help to resolve one of the most unsettling
and unsettled issues in their dating: the relationship between the works of Marie
and those of Chrétien de Troyes, the first Arthurian romancer? In the view of
Jackson (1979), Marie counts on her audience's knowledge of competing traditions representing Arthur as hero, but also as the weak king pictured in Chrétien's
romances. The fit between Marie's lay and Chrétien's romances is uncanny, yet
most scholars would probably agree with Hoepffner (1930, 25) that Marie's
Arthurian world seems to respond to a stage of elaboration earlier than Chrétien.
Whether or not they knew each other's work, they interacted with many of the
same materials and reinvented them, each with characteristic and distinctive
boldness.

In Wace's *Roman de Brut* Arthur is repeatedly presented as the king who
distributes gifts to each man according to his service. Marie's picture of Arthur as
gift-giver thus initially appears to confirm the traditional view, but then turns it
upside down by offering an exception which overturns the rule: in *Lanval* Arthur
rewards counts, barons and knights of the Round Table with rich gifts, women
and lands, 'fors a un sul ki l'ot servi' (*except for one knight who had served him*,
18). Lanval is forgotten, despite his service, and envy prevents the other knights
from reminding the king. Later, faced with the queen's accusations, Arthur
threatens to have Lanval burned or hanged, and he generally shows himself to be
a weak king, somewhat lacking in judgement. Marie's assessment of Arthur and
his court is calibrated precisely to evoke and then to respond negatively to Wace,
providing a contradictory image that turns the anonymous king of her source
into Arthur's bad twin.[11] Indeed, repeated gestures of twinning gone askew
become a powerful tool in the narrative to reshape the common story-matter.
Commentary and interpretation emerge implicitly from these alignments: as
shared elements bring the potential 'twins' together, imperfect matches inevitably

highlight their difference. In Marie's collection, the thematic of twinning has already come to the surface in *Le Fresne*, the third lay, where twins literally born and doubled among the characters are built figuratively into both the narrative architecture and the semantic discourse of the tale. As we shall see, there is in the *Lais* a tendency to pull stories into each other's orbit through varying degrees of twinning, which operates at all levels, within, between and beyond the twelve assembled lays.

The folklore of twins brings out two kinds of doubling: the duality of good and bad, as well as the complementarity of the two halves necessary to form a whole.[12] Readers/listeners who first encountered Marie's Arthur may have been shocked to see him act so ungenerously, but they would recognize the tendency of Guinevere's fame to bifurcate: Wace's *Brut* sketched out her reputation for vice as well as virtue, setting up the adulterous triangle of king, queen and nephew which (re)appears in Tristan stories and is reprised with significant changes in *Lanval*. The textual traditions which develop as romances expand and elaborate these early stories continue to furnish positive and negative visions of the major Arthurian figures, including Arthur as hero, in counterpoint to Arthur as 'roi fainéant'. The kinds of contradiction which characterize Gauvain in the *Perceval* Continuations, or Lancelot and Guinevere in the Vulgate Cycle, reflect an essential part of the human character quite familiar to Marie and her public.

Consider in this respect the accounts of Waleran of Meulan's ruthlessness, combined with his apparently genuine piety, his love of power and wealth and his deathbed transformation into a monk. Waleran may or may not have been Marie's father, but he and his brother Robert, the Beaumont twins, certainly function as exemplars of a set of players who cross the Anglo-Norman connection at the time of Henry I, Stephen and Henry II. Waleran, the first-born, inherited the father's patrimony and was the charismatic, impulsive one; Robert, the second son, was more thoughtful, a careful administrator, more cautious but devoted to his twin.[13] They resemble the kind of people represented in the *Lais*, as well as the public who received them, from the 'noble king' on down. If that king was Henry II, as seems likely, *Lanval*'s characterization of Arthur provides an instructive commentary on his patronage of Arthurian literature as political propaganda, his bid to identify his reign with that of the autochthonous Britons. In the contrasting figures of Arthur and Lanval, a king and the son of a distant king, Marie offers an important lesson concerning largesse, the courtly virtue *par excellence* (Flori 1990). Arthur's presence in the collection thus calls attention to the theme of appropriate kingship as it reappears in negative and positive models across the selection of lays offered to the king (Jonin 1982): *Equitan*, *Bisclavret*, *Les Deus Amanz*, *Yonec* and *Eliduc*.

If Lanval's story has floated into Arthur's orbit, it is no less true that the king's story has floated into Lanval's. Arthur notices Lanval too little; the queen notices him too much, precisely when he begins to function as a king should, distributing rich gifts, acquitting prisoners, rewarding *jongleurs* (209–11). Her proposal would push Lanval further into the king's place, into his very bed; this unnamed Guinevere is indeed an evil twin, deprived of her compensating virtues. But, in a sense, both king and queen are unfaithful, each in their respective domains. Are they twins of each other, setting the (im)moral tone of a court unworthy of the Arthurian ideal? Doubling takes on increasing energy as the plot turns. The queen offers her love as forthrightly as the lady of the tent, but with contradictory results; the trial staged as a beauty contest disproves their twin-like status and reveals the true beauty. When Lanval takes off for Avalon at the end, he imitates Arthur at the end of his life. According to Wace (*Brut*, 13277–94), the mortally wounded Arthur was transported to Avalon by boat in order to have his wounds cured – hence the Bretons' uninterrupted wait for Arthur's return.[14] Lanval, we are told quite emphatically by the narrator, was never heard from again, after he was 'ravished', carried off on his lady's horse (644–6). As always, Marie gives the Arthurian orbit a new spin.

Marie saves for the end this dramatic introduction of the fairy mistress's faraway place. Avalon (641), described as a most beautiful island (643), is also a name that plays upon the hero's own: they are anagrams of each other, scrambled mirror images brought together by the lay's final twist.[15] In this play of names, different orders of reality are momentarily twinned. Just as Marie matches up her fictional world and the experience of her medieval public (especially in her elaborate description of the trial with its carefully noted juridical terms and procedures[16]), she establishes within the world of *Lanval* different spheres, real and marvellous, which both separate and intersect. History and fiction, the Other World and Arthur's world, fairyland and storyland are matched and unmatched, as they inscribe an implicit commentary, the surplus of meaning that needs to be drawn out from a text orchestrated in writing. In light of the Lanval/Avalon connection, Koubichkine (1972, 471) suggests that the hero cannot be fully himself in a world where Arthur forgets him as if he did not exist; the incompatibility of Arthurian and other worlds would thus offer a critique of Arthur's court and courtliness (477; cf. Sienaert 1978, 99–100, 106). On the other hand, Poe stresses the lay's lexical playfulness as a cue for signalling irony at all levels of the text: *Lanval*'s meaning takes on humorous overtones, 'pok[ing] gentle fun at certain paradigms of courtly literature' (1983, 309–10).

Whatever its significance, the negative match of the king and queen is certainly complemented by the positive match of the two foreigners, Lanval and his lady. The constant theme of the lays is love; their constant concern, coupling. Couples good and bad, successful and unsuccessful, twos frequently struggling in a threesome populate the collection and set up parallels and contrasts that couple and uncouple the twelve lays in an unending game of permutation and combination

(Frey 1964). The fit between Lanval and his lady is warranted by their distant origins, but we may further notice how they exchange gender roles within the twosome. As Burns (2002*, 170–6) points out, this lady who takes the initiative in love fulfils the role of feudal lord, enrobing Lanval in costly textiles rather than in armour, generously supplying all the wealth necessary for his largesse and speaking out in court, as would a knight, to defend him against the queen's charge. And, of course, at the end of this story it is not the queen who is kidnapped by a traitorous nephew, as in the catastrophic ending of Arthur's story, but Lanval himself taken off to Avalon: 'La fu ravi li dameiseaus!' (*There was the young man carried off*, 644).

Marie connects both Lanval and Avalon to the Breton story-tellers: Lanval in the prologue (4), Avalon in the build-up to what passes ironically for an epilogue in the last two lines (642). We can gauge in this gesture both her subtlety and boldness as author. After all, she has not only taken an anonymous king's story and given it to Arthur, while moving elements of Arthur's own story to the eponymous hero, she has also simultaneously dispossessed a Breton hero of his story and given it to Lanval, whose name appears as if from nowhere to give her as great a margin of poetic licence as she is willing to claim (Rychner edn 1966, 254). Without engaging the issue of precedence or even contact, we must still wonder about the mystery of sounds and situations which connect the works of Marie and Chrétien through the myriad echoes between Lanval and Lancelot, not quite twins certainly, but both of them lovers caught in triangles which occupy an Arthurian space. For subsequent readers, if not for the authors themselves, these two stories remain in orbit around each other, creating a provocative push and pull as common elements bring out all the more strongly their specific difference. Here, as elsewhere in her collection, the mobility of stories and the power of naming, characteristically intertwined in Marie's art, connect the fruits of her literary production to the seeds sown widely among her contemporaries, predecessors and followers.

It will come as no surprise, then, to discover with *Chevrefoil* (treated in depth in chapter III) that she has once again taken material circulating among other story-tellers and matched it with a new set of heroes (Rychner edn 1966, 276). Lovers who can live only as long as they remain intertwined like the honeysuckle and the hazel are perfect twins for Tristan and Yseut, two beings who form a single soul.[17] Here we can begin to see how Marie explores the other face of twinning, the resonance between two parts necessary to make a harmonious whole. And we can see further into her art of composing lays as she reveals in the final product the very process of composition. In the shortest lay of her collection, whose brevity (118 lines) is emphasized when compared to the last and longest lay, *Eliduc* (1,184 lines), Marie has concentrated the story of Tristan and Yseut into a single episode and a single powerful image. Within that small compass she has reserved a fifth of the space for the prologue and epilogue which traditionally open and close each lay, marking its link to the oral tradition from which she has borrowed in order to give it new life. The weight of the story which explains and presents this tale of reunion in exile seems no less important than the tale itself (for summary, see chapter III).

No explicit mention of Arthur appears in Marie's brief account of the lovers' forest encounter, but a number of small details set the scene for a possible Arthurian connection, and, more specifically, set up pointed lexical echoes with *Lanval*: a court that meets at Pentecost, the use of Cornwall as name and location. More generally, anticipations of Tristan and Yseut's story have appeared earlier in the collection, through reinventions of well-known motifs: *Lanval*'s triangle of queen, king and lover; bloody sheets discovered in *Yonec*; in *Les Deus Amanz*, which immediately follows *Lanval*, the magic potion reconfigured for young lovers who die in each other's arms on a mountain top, where many a good herb grows from the undrunk *beivre*. Pulled into the orbit of Arthurian matter by common themes and materials, Tristan and Yseut's story has likewise moved into the orbit of the *Lais*, most especially on the heels of the Arthurianized *Lanval*.[18] Two unnamed queens are matched in the interplay: a bad one, unfaithful and unworthy of love, and a good one (perhaps an unfaithful wife, but one whose love for Tristan is faithfully served when she promises to seek his reconciliation with King Mark). Marie's situational ethics are always on the side of loyal love, which may or may not coincide with marriage in the permutations of her stories, as in the vagaries of twelfth-century society.

In the context of the *Lais* there are multiple orbits of stories in relation to each other; no single story or configuration dominates for long. *Chevrefoil*'s foray into vegetable symbolism suggests another lead to follow. The tree names given to the twin sisters Le Fresne (Ash) and La Coudre (Hazel) seem to prepare and play off against the plants chosen to represent the lovers here. Many of the lays crystallize around a particular emblem – the bird reliquary in *Laüstic*, the belt and knot in *Guigemar*. These emblems show another facet of Marie's art, her characteristic wrapping of metaphor and metonymy to encapsulate the truth of the adventures she recounts. The double figure of the twin, seen earlier, returns in another form in these rhetorical tropes. At the most obvious level, an object which stands in a metaphorical relationship to a character is its twin in another dimension, a substitute, the same. Thus, when the barons in *Le Fresne* discuss possible marriage partners for their lord, they contrast the positive features of the fertile Hazel with the barren Ash (his current mistress). What they do not know is that both women are equally fertile and suitably noble, twin sisters separated at birth, Le Fresne only differentiated by her abandonment and named metonymically after the tree in which she was found. When her true identity is revealed, metonymy appears to recuperate and trump metaphor, as her sister's marriage to

Gurun is dissolved so that the lovers can unite in equal marriage, instead of in unequal concubinage. In *Chevrefoil* the hazel reappears to claim a primary role in the couple. The metaphors for Tristan and Yseut, their twins in the plant world, twist round each other metonymically: they stand side by side in a necessary relationship to each other, according to the definition of metonymy, which appears, at first blush, different from twinning. Juxtaposition does not necessarily require, or imply, identity or sameness, but in this case these are not simply parts standing for the whole, they are two parts of the same whole, two identities forming one, complementary sides of a single self; their juxtaposition is not accidental, but essential to their continued existence. Metaphor and metonymy entwine again, as each lay finds its own pattern, each set of lovers its difference (Sankovitch 1988).

Once honeysuckle wraps round the hazel, the two can live together, but if separated, both die (68–76): 'Bele amie, si est de nus: / Ne vus sanz mei, ne mei sanz vus' (*Fair beloved, so it is with us: neither you without me nor me without you*, 77–8). With these words in direct speech we clearly hear Tristan speaking to the queen, but where and how we hear them is one of the great points of scholarly dispute that occupies much of the critical tradition devoted to this popular lay. To signal his presence to the queen, Tristan squares off a hazel branch and inscribes his name on it (54). The following twenty-four lines report in third-person narrative the complete message he conveys to the queen. Gradually the narrator's voice blends with that of the character, indirect speech becomes free and finally shifts into the two lines of direct quotation given above, Tristan's eloquent and powerful summary of their love. What remains unclear in the way Marie reports the message is whether Tristan carves all these words in the wood, implies them by the mere presence of his name inscribed on hazelwood, or has already sent them to the queen on a previous occasion (see chapter III). At this point, we are reminded of the passage in Marie's General Prologue where she raises the issue of glossing to bring out the surplus of meaning: is it hidden in the written word by the original author, to be discovered or invented by later generations of readers/writers? Each interpretation has had its defenders; we are caught up again and again in the very activity anticipated in Marie's written text, embroiled in figuring out the messages caught in writing when she transposes the oral tales of the Bretons.[19]

The uncertainty of what is said, what is implied, what remains spoken and what is written, resurfaces in the epilogue, when Marie reports Tristan's decision to compose a musical commemoration, 'un nuvel lai' (*a new lay*, 113), because of the joy he had in seeing the queen and 'to remember the words' (111). Tristan, as a composer of lays, is an obvious figure for Marie herself. Though she works in the written word, rather than in music, she implicitly twins her own and Tristan's artistic activities by connecting them in her epilogue. Placed after *Chaitivel*, the lay of *Chevrefoil* is the second consecutive lay to end with an account of the poem's composition and with the role of Marie herself in transmitting both their multiple names and the stories to be commemorated.[20] 'Marie de France' and her writing are as entwined as the honeysuckle and the hazel. Whoever the historical Marie may have been, her literary twin continues to live as long as we continue to read her in her own words.

Chevrefoil's position as the next-to-last lay reminds us that Arthurian connections are not allowed to frame Marie's whole collection; they operate from within the arrangement, one of the orbits circulating among the lays through a series of multiples, fleeting twins that momentarily foreground certain links or leave them in the shadow until another lay pulls them back into view. Once we place *Lanval* and *Chevrefoil* within the larger context of the *Lais*, what also stands out is the way Marie has brought into relationship – still fragmented and discontinuous as befits the nature of the collection – two of the great commonplaces of medieval literature associated with the figure of Arthur: the queen and her lover, the lovers Tristan and Yseut. However uncertain the links between Marie's and Chrétien's works at the moment of composition, subsequent readers of the *Lais* cannot fail to find intimations of Lancelot refracted through Lanval. Whatever the state of the Tristan legend available to Marie in the oral and written versions mentioned briefly in the prologue to *Chevrefoil*, her single episode encapsulates the heart of the lovers' story, while at the same time anticipating, in the echoes that extend it through the *Lais*, the elaboration through doubling typical of romance versions outside the collection. Marie has mapped out these commonplaces not only by putting the lays into writing, but most especially by gathering them together in a collection arranged by her authorial vision.[21] In so doing, she accumulates for her short tales the kind of weight associated with those rival works signalled in the General Prologue, translated from Latin into the vernacular ('romaunz', 30). She certainly knew and used lengthy and important works such as Wace's *Brut*, the *Thèbes* and the *Eneas*, but for contemporary and subsequent audiences she just as surely anticipates the Arthurian romance tradition which is developing so strongly under the impetus of Chrétien's romances.

Using association and fragmentation as boldly as does Chrétien in his corpus, Marie has prepared the way for the kind of cycle-building characteristic of prose romances in the thirteenth century, but she has done so through brevity and concentration, her own distinctive approach. She has seen the value of exploiting the 'matter of Britain' on both large and small scales. Though she may seem to work in an ephemeral, insignificant form, when she takes oral tales told by anonymous Breton story-tellers and tells them in her own voice, authorized by her own name, she gives them and herself a posterity available only in writing. Her collection thus claims the attention of a wide readership over space and time. Whatever the uncertainties of her historical identity, we may recognize even today the 'lady Marie' whose name, according to Denis Piramus, was already synonymous with pleasurable lays enjoyed by courtly publics in the twelfth century. In the prologue to *Guigemar*, which in Harley 978 functions as an extension of the General Prologue, Marie signs her work:

> Ki de bone mateire traite,
> Mult li peise si bien n'est faite.
> Oëz, seignurs, ke dit Marie,
> Ki en sun tens pas ne s'oblie. (1–4)

> (*Whoever has good material for a story is grieved if the tale is not well told. Hear, my lords, the words of Marie, who in her own time does not squander her talents.*)

Conscious of the moment to seize, and conscious of her own worth in relation to the worthy stories she has to tell, Marie establishes in the letter of her text the art of not forgetting one's self ('pas ne s'oblie').[22] [MTB]

The Anonymous Lays

The poems considered in this section are principally the eleven anonymous 'Breton' lays published by Tobin in 1976.[23] None of these lays can be dated with precision, but the likely period of composition is from the later twelfth century to the early years of the thirteenth century. They are found in several manuscripts, the most important of which is *S* (Paris, BNF, nouv. acq. fr. 1104), which contains eight of the lays, the exceptions being *Melion*, *Nabaret* and *Trot*. There has been a good deal of discussion concerning the origin of these lays and their relationship to those of Marie de France. The most famous formulation of this relationship is that of Lucien Foulet (1905, 319): 'L'histoire des lais français commence et s'arrête à Marie' (*The history of French lays begins and ends with Marie*). In Foulet's view, the authors of these lays used or consciously imitated Marie, and in some cases imitation went as far as plagiarism (19). But, although there are some clear borrowings from Marie, there is also material which must have come directly from other, perhaps older sources (Illingworth 1975). A more fruitful approach is to examine the poems as we have them, in order to see how their themes and story-patterns are combined to create appealing tales for an eager public.[24]

Eight of the lays in Tobin's collection possess a structure which is similar to that of a lay by Marie de France. A man, usually a knight, forms a relationship with a woman and their *aventure* is recounted in the poem, i.e. the story revolves around the difficulties they encounter in attempting to preserve their relationship, whilst coping with the obligations which bind them to society. In the anonymous lays it is not uncommon for a mortal to have a supernatural lover (*Desiré*, *Graelent*, *Guingamor*, *Tydorel*). In *Doon*, *Melion* and *Tyolet* both hero and heroine manifest elements of the supernatural, but to a great extent the characters in these lays are presented as human. In three of the lays, *Lecheor*, *Nabaret* and *Trot*, a different thematic structure appears (see Burgess and Brook edn). *Lecheor* tells how lays recounting noble deeds of love and prowess are composed at an annual ceremony, but in the year concerned one of the courtly ladies present identifies a woman's 'con' (*cunt*) as the inspiration for all chivalric deeds; this becomes the subject of the new lay. *Nabaret* is very brief (48 lines). A knight married to a lady of high lineage accuses her of dressing to please other men. He even goes as far as enlisting the help of her parents in order to keep her in line, but she counters with a quip: 'He should let his beard grow long and have his whiskers braided; that is the way for a jealous man to avenge himself' (38–40). In both these lays there is a significant element of comedy.

Trot is, along with *Melion* and *Tyolet*, one of only three strictly Arthurian lays amongst the eleven.[25] The hero Lorois is a brave knight attached to Arthur's Round Table, but in this lay Arthur has no part to play once the story begins. Lorois's home is the castle of Morois (probably Moray or Murray in Scotland) and the adventure takes place in a nearby forest. Out riding one morning, he encounters several groups of riders, both male and female. The groups are distinguished both by their appearance (elegant dress and happy countenances on the one hand, ragged dress and evident suffering on the other), and by the gait of their horses. The contented ladies are accompanied by their equally contented beloveds and they ride ambling horses which carry them along evenly and smoothly. These women, Lorois learns, have served love well, but those who have neglected love ride alone on emaciated and exhausted horses whose trotting motion, hence the title of the lay, causes them great pain as they advance (Burgess 1998). Lorois relates this story at court as a warning to other ladies not to treat love with scorn and derision.

Arthur plays a more significant, but still not thoroughly influential role, in *Tyolet*, the first part of which recalls Perceval's meeting with a group of knights at the beginning of Chrétien's *Perceval*. Tyolet is a young man who lives in the forest with his widowed mother. He has been taught by a fairy to whistle in such a way that wild animals are attracted to him. One day his mother asks him to kill some game, but on this occasion he is unsuccessful until he suddenly catches sight of a large stag. Instead of responding to his whistle, the animal leads him towards a dangerous stretch of water, which it then crosses. At that moment Tyolet spots a roe deer, which does respond to him. He kills it, but whilst he is skinning it the stag he had been chasing is suddenly transformed into a knight on horseback. Tyolet converses with the knight and asks him a number of naive questions concerning his function and his armour. One question is: 'What sort of beast are you?' In his reply the knight describes only the external trappings of knighthood, but Tyolet is fired with enthusiasm to become a 'knight-beast' (*chevalier beste*, 155, 189, 205, etc.). The knight tells him to go home and explain things to his mother, who will give him his father's armour.

In spite of her misgivings, his mother duly gives Tyolet the armour and advises him to go to Arthur's court. On his arrival, Arthur invites him to dismount and eat with him, and Tyolet tells him who he is and why he has come. As he is about to eat, a beautiful girl, daughter of the King of Logres, suddenly enters, followed by a white brachet with a bell round its neck. She announces that she will give her love to, and take as her husband, the man who can bring her the white foot of the stag which lives in the forest guarded by seven lions; the brachet will act as guide. A number of Arthur's knights attempt this feat, but none is successful; they are afraid to cross a broad, deep river in which the water is black, hideous and raging (379–81). When Tyolet tries, he crosses the river, whistles to attract the stag and removes its foot. The animal's cries attract the seven lions, but Tyolet manages to kill them all, before falling wounded and exhausted at their side. At this point a knight arrives on the scene, and, unwisely, Tyolet recounts the adventure to him and gives him the white foot. This knight departs, then returns, striking Tyolet and leaving him for dead. At Arthur's court he claims the maiden's hand. The king, however, notices that the brachet has not returned and orders a delay of eight days. When the dog returns, Gauvain follows it and finds Tyolet. Gauvain asks a maiden to take Tyolet to a doctor and returns to court to relate what has happened. The knight denies everything, but Tyolet arrives and accuses him of attempting to kill him. The knight asks for mercy and Tyolet pardons him. Tyolet then marries the girl and goes to her country, where they reign as king and queen.[26]

In this lay Arthur and his court are amongst the elements which unite a bipartite text.[27] The knight whom Tyolet meets seems to be a member of the court, and whilst Tyolet is in conversation with him 200 other knights pass by, having carried out a mission on behalf of the king (197–205). The second part begins at the court of King Arthur; Tyolet is aware of the court's reputation, for he praises it for its *afetement* (good manners), *cortoisie* (courtliness) and *ensaignement* (learning) and claims that it is with Arthur that he will learn *sens* (wisdom), *cortoisie* and *chevalerie* and how to distribute largesse (303–10). Recognizing his potential, Arthur agrees to retain Tyolet at court (314). Later in the story, Arthur's prescience in delaying the award of the maiden's hand in marriage, and Gauvain's participation in the rescue of Tyolet, confirm Arthur's court as a place of justice. At the end of the narrative, he gives the maiden to Tyolet. Although the latter does not remain with Arthur, his departure does not imply the criticism of Arthur's court one detects in *Lanval*.

It is in *Melion* that Arthur has a truly decisive role to play in the launching and conclusion of the narrative. *Melion* opens at Arthur's court, where Melion vows only to love a woman who has never loved, or even spoken of, another man. For this he is ostracized by the ladies at court, and he sinks into a state of gloom, until he is rescued by Arthur, who provides him with a rich castle by the sea.

Melion delights in the forest situated around his new home, and during a hunting expedition he encounters a beautiful woman whom he marries and with whom he has two children. On a later hunt, accompanied by his wife, he catches sight of a huge stag and asks his wife to take a look at it. She replies that she will never eat again, if she does not have part of this stag. Melion then reveals that he can transform himself into a wolf, if she touches his head with the white stone in his ring (there is also a red stone to restore his human form). But whilst he is away catching the stag, his wife returns to Ireland, taking with her his squire. Melion pursues her and is finally rescued from his permanent state as a wolf, thanks to the help provided by King Arthur. The wife confesses what she has done and gives the ring to Arthur. Duly transformed into human shape, Melion wants to use the ring to turn his wife into a wolf, but Arthur recommends that she be spared this fate for the sake of their beautiful children.[28]

In this tale Arthur resolves Melion's first crisis, albeit one of his own making, by setting up the circumstances in which he can live an enjoyable life and meet his wife. When things go wrong once more, it is again Arthur's intervention which helps to resolve the difficulty. We can also note that there are two images of Arthur in this text: the courtly Arthur, who presides over a successful court, and the warrior Arthur, who sails to Ireland to put an end to the activities of warring factions there (337–40), an intervention further motivated by his own need for assistance from the Irish in his war against the Romans (341–2). But also fundamental to the thematic structure of *Melion* is the werewolf motif, already used by Marie de France in *Bisclavret*. Like Bisclavret, Melion is condemned by his wife to a lengthy and possibly permanent bestial state, and he is rescued thanks to the human qualities he retains and to the intervention of a king. As an agent of transformation, clothing in *Bisclavret* is replaced in *Melion* by a ring with white and red stones.[29] Another link with Marie's lays is the way in which Melion's wife comes for him ('D'Yrlande sui a vos venue', *I have come to you from Ireland,* 109), just as did Lanval's *amie* ('Pur vus vienc jeo fors de ma tere; / De luinz vus sui venu[e] quere', *For you I come forth from my land; from afar I have come to seek you,* 111–12). Similarly, in *Tyolet* the hero is clearly the husband chosen by, and for, the princess of Logres (the wives of both Melion and Tyolet are further linked by their concern to possess part of a stag).

It is noticeable that the depiction of Arthur in these three lays is entirely positive. In *Trot* it is stated that Arthur knows how to honour a good knight and to distribute rich gifts (10–12). Arthur's largesse is also mentioned in *Melion* ('E qui dona les riches dons / As chevaliers e as barons', *And who gave rich gifts to the knights and the barons,* 3–4). In *Melion* Arthur is further described as 'cil ki les terres conqueroit' (*he who conquered lands,* 2). In *Tyolet* he is said to have been a man of 'grant pris' (*great reputation*) and to have had with him bold, fierce knights, superior to those of the present day (6–12). By situating a tale in the time of King Arthur ('Al tans que le rois regnoit', *in the time the king reigned; Melion*, 1; 'Jadis au tens q'Artur regna / Que il Bretaingne governa', *Formerly, in the time when King Arthur reigned who governed Britain*; *Tyolet*, 1–2), or linking it with the Round Table (*Trot*, 9), the authors immediately lend a degree of authenticity and distinction to their heroes' adventures. One expects that justice will prevail, and that any contribution Arthur makes will be to the benefit of the heroes. This contrasts with the image of Arthur conveyed in Marie de France's *Lanval*.

If we treat the anonymous lays as a single corpus, their themes and motifs can be compared with those found in Marie's *Lais*. As in the *Lais*, the chivalric activities of hunting, tournaments and war loom large in the thematic structure of the poems (Burgess 1992). Hunting is fundamental to the structure of *Desiré*, *Guingamor*, *Melion* and *Tyolet*. Tournaments or individual jousts are central to *Doon* and *Espine*, and war is important in *Desiré* (259–62) and *Melion*. In *Tydorel* the hero's ability to prevent war illustrates his fitness to rule (115–20, 226–31). Such activities allow the plot to advance and help the hero to seek his fame ('querre son pris', *Desiré*, 77; *Doon*, 146; *Espine*, 207; cf. *Guigemar*, 51; *Milun*, 311). As in Marie, the female characters, whether mortal or supernatural, are beautiful, worthy, wise, noble and of good breeding ('cortoise e bele', *Doon*, 10; *Guingamor*, 75; *Tyolet*, 400; 'noble e bele', *Lecheor*, 43; *Tyolet*, 526; 'preus e cortoise', *Espine*, 23; 'sage e bien aprise', *Guingamor*, 496; 'sages e ensaingnies', *Lecheor*, 55). Like Lanval's *amie*, Graelent's lady is more beautiful than any woman on earth ('En tut le secle n'ot plus bele', *Lanval*, 550 / 'Il n'a si bele en tot le monde', *Graelent*, 222). Descriptions are generally very close to those found in Marie (e.g. *Tyolet*, 696–8: 'Fleur de lis ou rose novele / Quant primes nest el tans d'esté / Trespassoit ele de biauté'; *Lanval*, 94–6: 'Flur de lis [e] rose nuvele, / Quant ele pert al tens d'esté, / Trespassot ele de biauté').[30] Guillet-Rydell (1975) has been able to show how, like Marie de France, the anonymous authors exploit the theme of marriage, which legitimizes unions and stabilizes society. Marriage can be the reward for success in a specific test (*Doon*, 159–60; *Espine*, 496; *Tyolet*, 699–701) or crown a sequence of events (*Desiré*, 733–44). Adultery, or suspicion of adultery, provides a new twist to the story (*Melion*, *Tydorel*) or even creates humour (*Nabaret*). A number of these lays exploit the father–son relationship (Suard 1980a).

Readers of Marie's *Lais* find her interest in the theme of love particularly appealing, as she handles human emotions, even human psychology with great subtlety. Love, or the search for a harmonious relationship, is just as central to the anonymous authors, even if their emphases seem different, centring perhaps on plot rather than passion. But *Trot*'s insistence that love must be served and honoured, Graelent's lengthy prescription for perfect love ('Love demands chastity in deed, word and thought ... true love exists between two people, two bodies and two hearts', 83–44, 91–2), or the fact that Doon's lady retains or even develops love for him in spite of his absence of around twenty years (275–8), could form part of one of Marie's lays just as easily as of an anonymous lay. When things get difficult for her heroes, Marie is not averse to making use of magic or marvellous elements to provide a solution (especially in *Guigemar*, *Lanval* and *Yonec*). Magic is even more prevalent in the anonymous lays. Tobin (1980) has listed a number of magic or marvellous motifs: (i) supernatural beings; (ii) the crossing of a frontier between the real world and the Other World; (iii) magic animals which guide the hero to this Other World; (iv) the function of time, which in the Other World can take on a different rhythm or meaning (*Guingamor*, 554–5; *Trot*, 26, 97–8, 187–8); (v) the taboo or *geis* (an injunction by a supernatural being not to reveal a secret or perform a certain action: *Graelent*, 302–4; *Tydorel*, 111–12; *Desiré*, 231–7; *Guingamor*, 564–7; *Espine*, 425–6); (vi) magic bushes or gardens connected to supernatural beings or happenings (the *ente* 'grafted tree': *Espine*, 263; *Tydorel*, 29–31, 40–2; the bush beside the ford in *Espine*); (vii) fairies possessed of wondrous beauty (*Graelent*, *Guingamor*), women who come for the hero or unleash a challenge (*Desiré*, *Graelent*, *Guingamor*, *Tyolet*).

Tobin designates these motifs as Celtic, and she states that the writers of the lays, in their attempt to produce the level of realism demanded by courtly society, often fail to understand their original meaning and confuse disparate legends and myths. But more important is the function of magic and the marvellous in the lays. In *Tyolet*, for example, the movement, unity and coherence of the text are created by the fairy who taught Tyolet how to whistle, by the animal which leads him to his encounter with the *chevalier beste* (this takes place at a river, which acts as the frontier with the Other World) and by the princess who comes for a man capable of completing the challenge involving the white foot of a stag and who takes him away to dwell in her kingdom. Magic, combined with the presence and actions of King Arthur himself, moves the text forward and permits Tyolet to realize his potential and advance swiftly to the point at which he has achieved a young knight's social aspirations: a positive response from Arthur's court and marriage to an heiress. Tyolet leaves the court to dwell in his beloved's kingdom, not because he has been unable to identify himself with Arthur and his world, like Lanval, but because he himself is destined to exercise royal power.[31]

There are also magical elements in *Melion*. These include Melion's vow, the woman who comes for him and marries him, her desire to possess part of the stag, his ability to transform himself into a wolf by means of a ring. These features again advance the story, but in this case they create more problems than they solve. It is Arthur who provides a solution and saves the day for Melion, preserving both his human and his social status. In this lay the characters have almost thrown off their non-human characteristics, and it is a surprise when the marvellous puts in an appearance. Similarly, in *Doon* the hero's horse clearly has magic properties, and we are surprised when Doon suddenly reveals his gift of prophecy and tells his wife that she is pregnant with a son (177–84).

The *Lanval* Story

Another feature of the anonymous Breton lays is the presence of the *Lanval*-type story in which a hero's happiness is threatened by his lord's wife, either before or after he forms a relationship with a fairy mistress. The fairy imposes a *geis* on the hero: if he reveals the love, he will lose her. This theme is found in *Graelent* and *Guingamor* and to a certain extent in *Desiré*. In *Graelent* the wife of the King of Brittany offers Graelent her love, but he rejects her; she in turn persuades her husband to deprive him of his pay. Graelent leaves court and comes across a fairy bathing in a fountain; they become lovers. When he returns to court, the king forces all other knights to praise his wife's beauty. Unable to do so, Graelent states that his beloved is far more beautiful. The king orders him to produce this lady, but by breaking his oath of secrecy he has lost her. She finally takes pity on him, and when she arrives at court Graelent is duly vindicated. They leave court together, but his problems are not yet over. He is almost drowned trying to catch up with her as she crosses a river, again a frontier with the Other World. She eventually rescues him, and henceforth they will dwell together in her land. Graelent's horse remains on the riverbank and continues to grieve for its master.

In *Guingamor* the queen offers the hero her love whilst her husband, his uncle, is out hunting. He rebuffs her and she determines to rid herself of him to prevent her disloyalty from coming to the king's attention. She encourages Guingamor to undertake the hunt for a white boar, a dangerous adventure which she hopes will ensure that he never returns. He comes to a castle and finds a spring in which he sees a maiden bathing. He seizes her clothes, but she calls out to him and offers him her love. He remains with her for what he thinks is three days, but turns out to be 300 years. Wishing to see his uncle again, he returns to his own land; the *geis* in this case takes the form of an injunction not to eat anything whilst away. He meets a charcoal-burner who tells him his uncle died centuries ago, and, forgetting what he had been told, he eats a wild apple and shrivels up. In order to return to his beloved, he has to be rescued by her serving maidens.

In *Desiré* the hero is born to a hitherto childless couple from Calatir in Scotland, who make a pilgrimage to St Giles in Provence. He grows up and goes to Brittany and Normandy in search of adventure; on his return, he meets a fairy with whom he falls in love. She offers him love and wealth and gives him a ring, which will disappear from his finger if he reveals her existence. When confessing to a hermit, Desiré does reveal the secret and the ring duly disappears. But after he has grieved for a year, the fairy takes pity on him. There follows a complex series of adventures, during which he discovers that he has a son and a daughter. Desiré and his beloved eventually marry and she takes him to her own land. Before they depart, the boy is dubbed a knight by the king and the girl is taken as the king's own bride. During the course of the story other magic motifs a re present (the fountain, the fairy's magic castle, etc.). Unlike *Graelent* and *Guingamor*, *Desiré* uses only the kernel of the Lanval story, which it places in a different narrative programme.

The relationship of *Graelent* and *Guingamor* to *Lanval*, the order of compos-ition of these three lays and the question of whether *Guingamor* was composed by Marie de France herself have preoccupied scholars since the nineteenth century. Scholars such as Gaston Paris (1879), Schofield (1896), Foulet (1905; 1908) and Kusel (1922) have argued that *Guingamor* was, or may well have been, composed by Marie, but others such as Hoepffner (1931), Segre (1959), Weingartner (1971–2) and Illingworth (1975) argue against this. Segre and Illingworth see the order of composition as *Lanval, Graelent, Guingamor*. Illingworth thinks that the author of *Graelent* based much of his work on *Lanval* and on other lays by Marie, but that it also contains 'a nucleus of genuine Celtic tradition independent of Marie's *lais*' (38). In his view the author of *Guingamor* made use not only of *Graelent* and Marie's lays, but also of Celtic themes independent of Marie.[32]

Unlike Marie, the authors of *Graelent* and *Guingamor* did not associate their works specifically with King Arthur and his court. Here the ruler is the King of Bretai(n)gne (*Graelent*, 9; *Guingamor*, 5), but the distinction is not clear-cut. In *Tyolet* the king who 'Bretaingne governa' (3) is Arthur, whereas in *Tydorel* (4) the lord 'qui Bretaingne tint' (5) is not named. It may be that when, as in *Lanval* (4) and *Tyolet* (3–4), the author makes it clear that the action is set in Britain, the king can be specified as Arthur, but when the action takes place in Brittany (*Graelent*, 9; *Guingamor*, 5; *Tydorel*, 4, 19, 235) the ruler remains nameless.

The *Lai du Cor* and the *Lai du Mantel*

The *Lai du Cor* is preserved in a single manuscript, Oxford, Bodleian Library, MS Digby 86, dating from between 1272 and 1282. The language of the author, who gives his name as Robert Biket (589), is close to standard Continental usage, but certain Anglo-Norman features suggest an insular background (Erickson edn, 22).[33] The poem itself seems to date from *c*.1200 (Erickson edn, 23), although earlier (Hoepffner 1959, 114) and later (Rider 1985, 196) dates have been proposed. The poem is unusual in that it uses a six-syllable rather than the tradi-tional eight-syllable line.

One Whitsuntide King Mangoun of Moraine (Moray in Scotland) sends to Arthur's court at Caerleon a drinking-horn made by a fairy. This horn has two functions: it can expose both a wife's infidelity and her husband's jealousy. If either is the case, the husband becomes drenched with wine as he drinks. Arthur is the first to try to drink, and he is furious when he fails to do so successfully. Interpreting the failure as signifying adultery on his wife's part, he lunges at her with a knife and has to be restrained by his knights. However, he is cheered to discover that the other knights who make the attempt are equally unsuccessful. Finally, a knight named Garadue (Caradoc) passes the test and Arthur gives the horn to his wife and rewards him with the lordship of Cirencester. The author states that he received the story from an abbot, and that the horn, which could be seen on feast days at Cirencester, was later put on display at Caerleon.

The *Lai du Cor* differs from most of the lays discussed above, because of the comic or burlesque elements it contains; it has therefore sometimes been classed as a *fabliau*. But the poem is called a lay (583), and in spite of its humour it treats themes of importance to court society (e.g. honour, power, loyalty). Although failure to drink successfully can be triggered by either husband or wife, and the horn thus tests purity of thought and deed on both sides, there are clear links to the well-established tradition of chastity tests with a horn or a mantle (Erickson edn, 4–9). But the novelty is that the repeated failure of Arthur's knights creates a new form of courtly unity, a new form of community spirit based on shared dishonour. Garadue's success leads to the acquisition of land, which is any knight's ideal, but it condemns him and his wife to remain outside Arthurian society (Rider 1985).

A similar tale is found in a text known by various names: the *Lai du Mantel, Le Conte du Mantel, Le Mantel mautaillié* or the *Lai du Cort Mantel*. Extant in five manuscripts (one of which is BNF, nouv. acq. fr. 1104), this text has often been regarded as a *fabliau*; it is probably of Norman provenance. Here a mantle replaces the horn as the testing device, and on this occasion the test concerns more specifically the chastity of women; it will shrink if worn by a woman who has been unfaithful, and only fit a woman who is perfectly chaste. *Mantel* is sometimes thought to be later than the *Lai du Cor*, and perhaps to have been influenced by it (Hoepffner 1959, 116), but the texts are probably more or less contemporary (Bennett edn, xxiii); they share the same Arthurian setting and the same hero, Caradoc, whose beloved wears the garment successfully.

The preceding discussions of Marie's lays, as well as the various categories of mostly anonymous lays which follow in her wake, bear ample testimony to the way this short narrative form operates in relation to a constellation of narrative 'genres' of varying length, from short *récits* to short romance and beyond. As a medieval narrative type, which flourished primarily from the end of the twelfth to the end of the thirteenth century, the lay appears distinctive in character, yet at the same time open to hybridizing mixes that play on combinations of different materials and different horizons of expectation (Marie's *Equitan*, for example, partakes of both *fabliau* and lay). Any attempt to define the character of the lay needs to take into account the following characteristic: specificity at the genre's centre, shifting boundaries at the periphery. Not surprisingly, the term *lai*, as used by medieval authors and scribes, does not always facilitate the efforts of modern critics to define and delimit the corpus of lays (Payen 1975; 1980). The give-and-take among short tales with different emphases, orientations and diction, like the interaction between lays and the larger narrative canvas offered by romance, not only feeds authorial invention; it also guides audience reception, when a sophisticated public can be expected to recognize and appreciate the literary allusions in play (Schmolke-Hasselmann 1980). When, for example, the *Lai du Cor* is inserted into the *Livre de Caradoc* of the First *Perceval* Continuation, or the *Lai du Mantel* into *La Vengeance Raguidel*, not only do the transpositions reveal the resources of brevity used within the amplifications of romance but they also invite readers to appreciate how retelling involves remotivation and reorientation to integrate the 'new' version into the larger frame of the romance narrative.

Likewise, the transformation of short tales into romance-length narrative may act as a reminder of the affinities, as well as of the differences between these narrative types: the romances *Ille et Galeron* and *Galeran de Bretagne*, based respectively on Marie de France's *Eliduc* and *Le Fresne*, demonstrate the elasticity of her materials and the narrative forms which reshape them, as their centre of gravity shifts from Marie's female characters to the chivalric exploits of romance heroes. As argued above, the creative tension between romance and lay already operates within Marie's collection. Although she ostensibly rejects the model of translation from the Latin epic tradition ('romanced' with Ovidian overlays), she in fact enters implicitly into a kind of rivalry with romancers, by organizing her twelve lays into a collection whose accumulated scope gives the individual tales the added weight of *amplificatio* through the game of intertextual play. Her links with the romance tradition, as well as with the anonymous lays, remind us on another level that the *matière de Bretagne* continues to offer a rich reservoir of motifs, characters, situations and themes, which easily cross boundaries between lay and romance. The stories which surface in Marie's work and the anonymous lays, as well as in the romances of Chrétien and others, emerge from a large pool of orally circulating tales, many tied to the figure of King Arthur. In Wace's memorable words, so many marvels and adventures have been told about Arthur that it is no longer possible to distinguish truth from lie, folly from wisdom:

> Tant unt li cunteür cunté
> E li fableür tant flablé
> Pur lur cuntes enbeleter,
> Que tut unt fait fable sembler. (*Brut*, 9795–8)

(*The story-tellers have told so many stories and the spinners of yarns have recounted so many fables, that they have made everything seem like pure invention, in their attempts to embellish their stories.*)

This complaint recalls Denis Piramus's critique of Dame Marie, whose tales were not entirely true. Both Denis and Marie give testimony to the immense popularity of Breton tales, so intertwined and compelling that writers and story-tellers, as well as readers medieval and modern, continue to find themselves pulled into their intersecting orbits. **[GSB]**

Notes

[1] Titles of lays, which in some cases vary from edition to edition, are taken from the edition of the *Lais* by A. Ewert, as are quotations from the text.

[2] For further information concerning these lays, see Baader 1966 and Donovan 1969. For bibliography, see Burgess bib.1995.

[3] The expression 'narrative lays' has been preferred in this chapter to 'Breton lays', because of the difficulty in deciding, in some cases, whether the terms *breton* and *Bretaigne* refer to Britain or to Brittany (or to both).

[4] The Harley manuscript (*H*) contains the General Prologue followed by twelve lays. The *Strengleikar*, a Norse translation made for Hákon Hákonarson, King of Norway (Cook and Tweitane edn), contains twenty-one lays from Old French, including all of Marie's except *Eliduc* (*Chaitivel* and *Lanval* are incomplete). Four other French manuscripts give one or more of Marie's lays: BNF, nouv. acq. fr.1104 (*S*) has nine; BNF, fr. 2168 (*P*) *Guigemar*, *Lanval* and the end of *Yonec*; BL, MS Cotton Vespasian B xiv (*C*) just *Lanval*; BNF, fr. 24432 (*Q*) just *Yonec*.

[5] Objections have been raised, however, regarding Marie de France's authorship of the *Espurgatoire* (see Burgess in Ewert edn 1995, vi–vii). But Mickel (1974, 143–4) discusses a fourth work also signed 'Marie', the *Vie seinte Audree*, and McCash (2002) argues strongly in favour of its acceptance as a work by Marie de France.

[6] On the dating and the order of composition of the lays, see Burgess 1981; 1987, 1–34.

[7] *La Vie seint Edmund le rei, poème anglo-normand du XIIe siècle*, ed. by H. Kjellman (Göteborg, 1935; repr. Geneva, 1974), ll. 35–48.

[8] In the Harley manuscript the two adjectives which modify the author in the General Prologue (55–56) are both masculine in form: they are emended to feminine forms by modern editors, but their problematic presence is a useful reminder that some scholars have called into question Marie's identity as author of all the *Lais* (Baum 1968), or as a woman author (Huchet 1981). Nevertheless, there have been multiple efforts to explore *écriture féminine* or look for feminist points of view in her *Lais* (Freeman 1984; Arden 1992; Rosenn 1992; Kinoshita 1993–4). Griffin (1999) discusses the notion of fixed authorship for the lays.

[9] *Lanval* is found in four manuscripts: *H* (fols 154v-159v), *S* (fols 6v-10r), *P* (fols 54r-58v) and *C* (fols 1r-8v). There are two translations (in Norse and Middle English) and imitations include Jean Renart's *Guillaume de Dole* and a German poem, *Peter von Staufenberg* (Hoepffner 1935, 70–1; Burgess 1995, 172–3). For the text of all four manuscripts, as well as of the Norse version, see Rychner edn 1958.

[10] See the notes in Rychner edn 1966 and Burgess in Ewert edn 1995, xxiv–xxv, xxxi–xxxii. Proper names are particularly powerful markers for aligning texts, as the titles of the lays given in prologues and epilogues continually remind us. There are two variants on the king's name given in *Guigemar*. MS *H* identifies him as Hoilas (27), a name which Marie perhaps found in Wace's *Roman*

de Brut, where Hoeël, the King of 'Bretaigne la menor', is Arthur's nephew (ed. by I. D. O. Arnold, 2 vols, SATF, 1938–40, 9140–1). MS *P* gives 'Artus' for the king's name (Burgess in Ewert edn 1995, p. 166), thus making P's version another Arthurian lay. In *H*, when Marie locates the action in Brittany during the kingship of Hoilas, she gives a clue for readers familiar with Wace's *Brut* that the story operates in the time of King Arthur. On Marie and naming, see Bruckner 1993*.

[11] Cf. the highly negative view of Arthur in Jonin (1982).

[12] See, for example, J. Chevalier and A. Gheerbrant, *Dictionnaire des symboles* (Paris, 1969), 439. I would like to thank Kate Loysen for this reference.

[13] D. Crouch, *The Beaumont Twins: The Roots and Branches of Power in the Twelfth Century* (London, 1986).

[14] Later versions place Arthur's sister Morgan in the boat which carries him to her Elysian isle. See, for example, R. S. Loomis, 'The Legend of Arthur's Survival', in Loomis ed. 1959*, 64–8, and V. Greene, 'Qui croit au retour d'Arthur?', *CCM*, 45 (2002), 321–40.

[15] See Koubichkine 1972, 467–88. Poe (1983, 309 and n. 28) goes further in recognizing the hero's name as a palindrome when spelled Launval, as in MS *C* (with *u* and *v* interchangeable in medieval usage).

[16] See Francis 1939 and Rychner edn 1958, 78–84. Eccles (1998) analyses the precision of Marie's legal vocabulary in the light of the Assize of Clarendon, which would date *Lanval* definitively as post 1166.

[17] On doubling in the Tristan story, see M. T. Bruckner, 'The Representation of the Lovers' Death: Thomas' *Tristan* as Open Text', *Tris*, 9 (1984), 49–61, and S. Dannenbaum [Crane], 'Doubling and *fine amor* in Thomas' *Tristan*', *Tris*, 5 (1979), 3–14.

[18] Burgess (in Ewert edn 1995, 183) gives a summary of critical views concerning which Tristan stories Marie might have known. See also Bromiley, chapter III.

[19] The number of studies devoted to the General Prologue is substantial (Burgess bib. 1977 and Supplements). See especially articles by Spitzer 1943–4, Hunt 1974, Braet 1978, Foulet and Uitti 1981–2, Burch 1998, and Rychner edn 1966 (236–7).

[20] In the preceding lay, *Chaitivel*, the failure of the characters to achieve specific identity motivates the alternative titles. In *Chevrefoil*, by contrast, the famous lovers will be recognized in whatever language their lay is identified. On the issue of how Marie shapes her collection through her authorial presence, despite the lack of any closing movement comparable to the General Prologue, see Bruckner 1993*.

[21] Other collections, such as that in manuscript *S*, as well as the independent circulation of lays like *Lanval*, make us realize how in the Harley collection reader reception is invited and guided by the General Prologue. On the *Lais* as a collection, see Maddox 2000.

[22] The word *oblier* is also the last word of the entire collection, as the four-line epilogue to *Eliduc* returns to the important topos of remembering.

[23] See the introduction to this chapter. In 1879 G. Paris had published five lays from BNF, nouv. acq. fr. 1104: *Tyolet, Guingamor, Doon, Lecheor* and *Tydorel*. In 1928 Grimes published *Desiré, Graelent* and *Melion*.

[24] Smithers (1953) points in particular to three patterns: (i) a mortal in unhappy circumstances falls in love with a fairy (*Graelent, Guingamor, Lanval*); (ii) a supernatural being fathers a son and gives the mother instructions (*Desiré, Doon, Tydorel, Yonec*); (iii) the son brings his parents together after an armed combat with his father (*Doon, Milun*).

[25] Arthur is also mentioned in the lay of *Haveloc* (ed. by A. Bell, Manchester and New York, 1925). This lay begins with an account of Haveloc's father, who was killed when Arthur crossed the sea to Denmark (27–40, see also 51 and 605). The *Lai de l'ombre* (ed. by F. Lecoy, Paris, 1979) contains allusions to Gauvain (61), Lot (Gauvain's father, 60), Tristan (105, 124, 457) and Yseut (125).

[26] In addition to Arthur and Gauvain, other Arthurian knights are mentioned by name in *Tyolet*

(629–31): Lodoer, who is first to attempt the quest (perhaps for Bedoer), Kay, Yvain (said to be the son of Morgan the Fay) and Urien (presented as Yvain's father) (629–31).

[27] Some writers, such as G. Paris (edn), have stressed that the two parts are fundamentally disparate, whereas others (e.g. Braet 1980) think that the author has effectively unified the two parts.

[28] In addition to Arthur himself, the other Arthurian knights mentioned in *Melion* are: Gauvain (353, etc.), Yder (355, etc.) and Yvain (354).

[29] For a comparison between *Bisclavret* and *Melion*, see Ménard 1984. See also L. Foulet 1905, 40–5.

[30] See also *Graelent*, 215–22, 593–5, *Melion,* 91–8, *Equitan,* 31–6 and *Eliduc,* 1012–16. For the presentation of female characters, see Gosman 1984, Kallaur 1988 and Régnier-Bohler 1980.

[31] For discussion of Celtic or Other-World themes in the lays, see Bromwich 1960–1, Tobin 1980, De Caluwé 1983 and Jodogne 1960–1.

[32] Rychner (edn 1966, 253–4) argues for retaining both Segre's analysis of *Graelent* as imitator of *Lanval* and Hoepffner's view of a common model for both (1955).

[33] M. D. Legge states that the author is unlikely to have been Anglo-Norman, but that he 'probably worked in England' (*Anglo-Norman Literature and its Background*, Oxford, 1963; repr. Westport, CT, 1978, 133).

Reference List

For items accompanied by an asterisk, see the General Bibliography.

Bibliography

Burgess, G. S. *Marie de France: An Analytical Bibliography* (London, 1977; Supplement No.1, 1986, Supplement No. 2, 1997).
Burgess, G. S. *The Old French Narrative Lay: An Analytical Bibliography* (Cambridge, 1995).

Texts and Translations
Marie de France
Lais

Marie de France: Lais. Ed. by A. Ewert (Oxford, 1944; reissued with introduction and bibliography by G. S. Burgess, London, 1995).
Les Lais de Marie de France. Ed. by J. Rychner, CFMA 93 (Paris, 1966).
Lais de Marie de France. Ed. by K. Warnke and transl. by L. Harf-Lancner (Paris, 1990).
Lais de Marie de France, présentés, traduits et annotés. Ed. and transl. by A. Micha (Paris, 1994).
The Lais of Marie de France. Transl. by G. S. Burgess and K. Busby (Harmondsworth, 1986; 2nd edn 1999).
Marie de France, Le Lai de Lanval. Ed. by J. Rychner, TLF 77 (Geneva, 1958).

Fables

Marie de France, Les Fables: édition critique accompagnée d'une introduction, d'une traduction, de notes et d'un glossaire. Ed. and transl. by C. Brucker (Louvain, 1991, 2nd edn 1998).

Espurgatoire Seint Patriz

Marie de France, L'Espurgatoire Seint Patriz: nouvelle édition critique accompagnée du De Purgatorio sancti Patricii (éd. de Warnke), d'une introduction, d'une traduction, de notes et d'un glossaire. Ed. by Y. de Pontfarcy (Louvain, 1995).

Saint Patrick's Purgatory: A Poem by Marie de France. Transl. by M. J. Curley (Binghamton, NY, 1993). Includes Warnke's text.

Anonymous Lays

Paris, Gaston, 'Lais inédits de *Tyolet*, de *Guingamor*, de *Doon*, du *Lecheor* et de *Tydorel*', *Rom*, 8 (1879), 29–72.
Les Lais anonymes des XIIe et XIIIe siècles: édition critique de quelques lais bretons. Ed. by P. M. O'H. Tobin, PRF 143 (Geneva, 1976).
The Lays of Desiré, Graelent and Melion: Edition of the Texts with an Introduction. Ed. by E. M. Grimes (New York, 1928; repr. Geneva, 1976).
Le Coeur mangé: récits érotiques et courtois des XIIe et XIIIe siècles. Transl. by D. Régnier-Bohler (Paris, 1979).
Lais féeriques des XIIe et XIIIe siècles. Ed. and transl. by A. Micha (Paris, 1992).
Three Old French Narrative Lays: Trot, Lecheor, Nabaret. Ed. and transl. by G. S. Burgess and L. C. Brook, Liverpool Online Series, Critical Editions of French Texts 1, 1999 (*www.liv.ac.uk/sml/LOS/index.htm*).

Cor and *Mantel*

The Anglo-Norman Text of Le Lai du Cor. Ed. by C. T. Erickson, ANTS 24 (Oxford, 1973).
Mantel et Cor: deux lais du XIIe siècle. Ed. by P. E. Bennett, Textes Littéraires 16 (Exeter, 1975).

Strengleikar

Strengleikar: An Old Norse Translation of Twenty-One Old French lais: Edited from the Manuscript Uppsala De la Gardie 4–7-AM 666b, 4°. Ed. and transl. by R. Cook and M. Tveitane (Oslo, 1979).

Studies

Arden, H. 1992. 'The *Lais* of Marie de France and Carol Gilligan's Theory of the Psychology of Women', in Maréchal ed. 1992, 212–22.
Baader, H. 1966. *Die Lais. Zur Geschichte einer Gattung der altfranzösischen Kurzerzählungen*, Frankfurt.
Baum, R. 1968. *Recherches sur les œuvres attribuées à Marie de France*, Heidelberg.
Baumgartner, E. 1975. 'A Propos du *Mantel mautaillié*', *Rom*, 96, 315–32.
Bloch, R. H. 2003. *The Anonymous Marie de France*, Chicago.
Braet, H. 1978. 'Marie de France et l'obscurité des anciens', *NM*, 79, 180–4.
Braet 1980. 'Le Lai de *Tyolet*: structure et signification', in *Études de philologie romane et d'histoire littéraire offertes à Jules Horrent*, Liège, 41–6.
Braet 1981. 'Tyolet/Perceval: l'invention du père', *Incidences*, 71–7; transl. into English as 'Tyolet/Perceval: The Father Quest', in *An Arthurian Tapestry: Essays in Memory of Lewis Thorpe*, Glasgow, 299–307.
Bromwich, R. 1960–1. 'Celtic Dynastic Themes and the Breton Lays', *Ét. Celt*, 9, 439–74.
Bruckner, M. T. 1993. 'Textual Identity and the Name of a Collection: Marie de France's *Lais*', in Bruckner 1993*, 157–206.
Burch, S. L. 1998. 'The Prologue to Marie's *Lais*: Back to the *littera*', *AUMLA*, 89, 15–42.
Burgess, G. S. 1981. 'The Problem of Internal Chronology in the *Lais* of Marie de France', *ZfSL*, 91, 133–55.

Burgess 1987. *The Lais of Marie de France: Text and Context*, Athens, GA, and Manchester.

Burgess 1992. 'Chivalric Activity in the Anonymous Lays', in G. Angeli and L. Formisano eds *L'Imaginaire courtois et son double,* Naples, 271–91.

Burgess 1998. 'The Lay of *Trot*: A Tale of Two Sittings', *FSB*, 66, 1–4.

Buschinger, D. ed. 1980. *Le Récit bref au moyen âge: actes du colloque des 27, 28 et 29 avril 1979, Université de Picardie*, Amiens and Paris.

Damon, S. F. 1929. 'Marie de France: Psychologist of Courtly Love', *PMLA*, 44, 968–96.

De Caluwé, J. 1983. 'L'Autre Monde celtique et l'élément chrétien dans les lais anonymes', in *The Legend of King Arthur in the Middle Ages: Studies Presented to A. H. Diverres by Colleagues, Pupils and Friends*, Cambridge, 56–65.

Donovan, M. J. 1969. *The Breton Lay: A Guide to Varieties*, Notre Dame, IN.

Eccles, J. 1998. 'Marie de France and the Law', in L. Duffy and A. Tudor eds *Les Lieux interdits: Transgression and French Literature*, Hull, 15–30.

Flori, J. 1990. 'Aristocratie et valeurs "chevaleresques" dans la seconde moitié du XIIe siècle: l'exemple des *Lais* de Marie de France', *MA*, 96, 37–65.

Foulet, A., and K. D. Uitti. 1981–82. 'The Prologue to the *Lais* of Marie de France: A Reconsideration', *RPh*, 35, 242–9.

Foulet, L. 1905. 'Marie de France et les lais bretons', *ZrP*, 29, 19–56, 293–322.

Foulet 1908. 'Marie de France et la légende de Tristan', *ZrP*, 32, 161–83, 257–89.

Francis, E. A. 1939. 'The Trial in *Lanval*', in *Studies in French Language and Mediaeval Literature Presented to Professor Mildred K. Pope*, Manchester, 115–24.

Freeman, M. 1984. 'Marie de France's Poetics of Silence: The Implications for a Feminine *Translatio*', *PMLA*, 99, 860–83.

Frey, J. A. 1964. 'Linguistic and Psychological Couplings in the *Lays* of Marie de France', *SP*, 61, 3–18.

Gosman, M. 1984. 'Le Statut descriptif de la dame aimée dans les lais dits féeriques', in D. Buschinger and E. Crépin eds. *Amour, mariage et transgressions au Moyen Âge: actes du colloque des 24, 25, 26 et 27 mars 1983, Université de Picardie, Centre d'Études Médiévales*, Göppingen, 203–13.

Griffin, M. 1999. 'Gender and Authority in the Medieval French *laï*', *FMLS*, 35, 42–56.

Grillo, P. 1988. 'Was Marie de France the Daughter of Waleran II, Count of Meulan?', *Med. Aev*, 57, 269–74.

Guillet-Rydell, M. 1975. 'Nature et rôle du mariage dans les lais anonymes bretons', *Rom*, 96, 91–104.

Hoepffner, E. 1930. 'La Géographie et l'histoire dans les *Lais* de Marie de France', *Rom*, 56, 1–32.

Hoepffner 1931. 'Marie de France et les lais anonymes', *SM*, n.s. 4, 1–31.

Hoepffner 1935. *Les Lais de Marie de France*, Paris; repr. 1971, 1995.

Hoepffner 1955. 'Graëlent ou Lanval?', in *Recueil de travaux offert à M. Clovis Brunel*, 2 vols, Paris, II, 1–8.

Hoepffner 1959. 'The Breton Lais', in Loomis ed. 1959*, 112–21.

Hofer, S. 1953–4. 'Bemerkungen zur Beurteilung des *Horn*- und des *Mantellai*', *RF*, 65, 38–48.

Hofer 1957. 'Untersuchungen zum *Mantellai*', *ZrP*, 73, 469–85.

Huchet, J.-C. 1981. 'Nom de femme et écriture féminine au Moyen Âge: les *Lais* de Marie de France', *Poétique*, 48, 407–30.

Hunt, T. 1974. 'Glossing Marie de France', *RF*, 86, 396–418.

Illingworth, R. N. 1975. 'The Composition of *Graelent* and *Guingamor*', *Med. Aev*, 44, 31–50.

Jackson, W. T. H. 1979. 'The Arthuricity of Marie de France', *RR*, 70, 1–18.

Jodogne, O. 1960–1. 'L'Autre Monde celtique dans la littérature française du XIIe siècle', *Académie Royale de Belgique, Bulletin de la Classe des Lettres et des Sciences Morales et Politiques*, 5th series, 46, 584–97.

Jonin, P. 1982, 'Le Roi dans les *Lais* de Marie de France: l'homme sous le personnage', in *Essays in Early French Literature Presented to Barbara M. Craig*, York, SC, 25–41.

Kallaur, M. 1998. 'Une reconsidération du portrait dans les lais médiévaux', in K. Kupisz, G. -A. Pérouse and J. Debreuille eds *Le Portrait littéraire*, Lyon, 15–23.

Kinoshita, S. 1993–4. 'Cherchez la femme: Feminist Criticism and Marie de France's *Lai de Lanval*', *RomN*, 34, 263–73.

Koubichkine, M. 1972. 'A propos du *Lai de Lanval*', *MA*, 78, 467–88.

Kusel, P. 1922. *Guingamor: ein Lai der Marie de France*, Berlin.

McCash, J. H. 2002. '*La Vie seinte Audree:* A Fourth Text by Marie de France?', *Spec*, 77, 744–77.

Maddox, D. 2000. 'The Specular Encounter in Fictions of Reciprocity: The *Lais* of Marie de France', in Maddox 2000*, 24–82.

Maréchal, C. A. ed. 1992. *In Quest of Marie de France, a Twelfth-Century Poet*, Lewiston, Queenston and Lampeter.

Maréchal ed. 2003. *The Reception and Transmission of the Works of Marie de France, 1174–1974*, Lewiston, Queenston and Lampeter.

Ménard, P. 1984. 'Les Histoires de loup-garou au Moyen Âge', in *Symposium in honorem Prof. M. de Riquer*, Barcelona, 209–38.

Mickel, E. J., Jr. 1974. *Marie de France*, New York.

O'Sharkey, E. M. 1971. 'The Identity of the Fairy Mistress in Marie's *Lai de Lanval*', *Trivium*, 6, 17–25.

Payen, J.-C. 1975. 'Le Lai narratif', in *Typologies des sources du moyen âge occidental*, fasc. 13, Louvain, 31 63.

Payen 1980. 'Lai, fabliau, exemplum, roman court: pour une typologie du récit bref au XIIe et XIIIe siècles', in Buschinger ed. 1980, 7–23.

Poe, E. W. 1983. 'Love in the Afternoon: Courtly Play in the *Lai de Lanval*', *NM*, 84, 301–10.

Pontfarcy, Y. de. 1995. 'Si Marie de France était Marie de Meulan . . .', *CCM*, 38, 353–61.

Régnier-Bohler, D. 1980. 'Figures féminines et imaginaire généalogique: étude de quelques récits brefs', in Buschinger ed. 1980, 73–96.

Ribard, J. 1973. 'Essai sur la structure du lai du *Chèvrefeuille*', in *Mélanges de langue et de littérature médiévales offerts à Pierre Le Gentil*, Paris, 721–4.

Rice, J. 1984. 'Conventional and Unconventional Character Description in the *Lais* of Marie de France', *NM*, 85, 344–52.

Rider, J. 1985. 'Courtly Marriage in Robert Biket's *Lai du Cor*', *Rom*, 106, 173–97.

Rosenn, E. 1992. 'The Sexual and Textual Politics of Marie's Poetics', in Maréchal ed. 1992, 225–42.

Sankovitch, T. 1988. 'Marie de France: The Myth of the Wild', in T. Sankovitch ed. *French Women Writers and the Book: Myths of Access and Desire*, Syracuse, NY, 15–41.

Schmolke-Hasselmann, B. 1980. 'L'Intégration de quelques récits brefs arthuriens (*Cor, Mantel, Espee*) dans les romans arthuriens du XIIIème siècle', in Buschinger ed. 1980, 107–29.

Schofield, W. H. 1896. 'The Lay of *Guingamor*', *Harvard Studies and Notes in Philology and Literature*, 5, 221–43.

Segre, C. 1959. '*Lanval, Graelent, Guingamor*', in *Studi in onore di Angelo Monteverdi*, 2 vols, Modena, II, 756–70.

Sienaert, E. R. 1978. *Les Lais de Marie de France: du conte merveilleux à la nouvelle psychologique*, Paris.

Smithers, G. V. 1953. 'Story-Patterns in some Breton Lays', *Med. Aev*, 22, 61–92.

Spitzer, L. 1943–4. 'The Prologue to the *Lais* of Marie de France and Medieval Poetics', *MP*, 41, 96–102.

Suard, F. 1980a. 'Le Fils dans les lais anonymes', in Buschinger ed. 1980, 57–73.

Suard 1980b. 'Le Projet narratif dans *Lanval, Graelent* et *Guingamor*', in *Études de langue et de littérature françaises offertes à André Lanly*, Nancy, 357–69.

Tobin, P. M. O'H. 1980. 'L'Élément breton et les lais anonymes', in *Mélanges de langue et de littéra-ture françaises du Moyen Âge offerts à Monsieur Charles Foulon, II. M. Rom.*, 30, 277–86.

Walkley, M. J. 1983. 'The Critics and *Lanval*', *NZJFS*, 4, 5–23.

Weingartner, R. 1971–2. 'Stylistic Analysis of an Anonymous Work: The Old French *lai Guingamor*', *MP*, 69, 1–9.

Williams, H. F. 1964. 'The Anonymous Breton Lays', *Research Studies*, 32, 76–84.

Williman, J. P. 1972. 'The Sources and Composition of Marie's Tristan Episode', in *Studies in Honor of Tatiana Fotitch*, Washington, 115–27.

VI

PERCEVAL AND THE GRAIL: THE CONTINUATIONS, ROBERT DE BORON AND *PERLESVAUS*

Rupert T. Pickens, Keith Busby and Andrea M. L. Williams

We do not know whether Chrétien de Troyes simply abandoned his *Perceval* (perhaps on the death of his patron, Philippe de Flandre) or whether he died before he was able to complete his work.[1] He may even have never intended to finish the romance, possibly in the expectation of engendering a body of Continuations. We do know, however, that the *Perceval* quickly spawned attempts to continue, complete and rewrite it. As in the tradition of the medieval epic cycle, it also contained the seeds to produce texts recounting prior events, not unlike *enfances*, such as the epigonal prologues, the *Elucidation* and *Bliocadran*. This chapter will examine: (i) the two prologues; (ii) the four texts collectively known as the Continuations; (iii) three works attributed to Robert de Boron, the *Estoire dou Graal*, *Merlin* and the *Didot-Perceval*, and (iv) *Perlesvaus*.

The Prologues: The *Elucidation* and *Bliocadran*

Among the epigonal 'pre-histories' generated by, and in response to, Chrétien's *Perceval* are two minor texts, both dating from the early thirteenth century: the *Elucidation*, edited by Potvin (1866), Thompson (1931) and Hilka (1932, 493–8) and *Bliocadran*, edited by Potvin (1866), Wolfgang (1976) and Hilka (1932, 430–54). Both serve as prologues in manuscripts of Chrétien's poem and one or more of its Continuations.

The *Elucidation* is found in MS *P* of *Perceval*,[2] where it precedes a truncated version of Chrétien's prologue (Busby edn, 61–8; Thompson edn, 477–84). *Bliocadran*, which in this manuscript follows Chrétien's prologue, also occurs independently in the London manuscript (*L*) of *Perceval*,[3] where it was crudely interpolated at the end of Chrétien's prologue, after the narrative had already been copied (Wolfgang edn, 54–5; Busby edn, xx). In addition, fourteenth-century German translations of the *Elucidation* and *Bliocadran* in the Alsatian dialect are incorporated into Philipp Colin and Claus Wisse's *Der Nüwe Parzival* (composed 1331–6, see Jackson and Ranawake eds 2000*, 168–72), an edition of Wolfram von Eschenbach's work also augmented by the First and Second Continuations and Manessier's conclusion (Thompson edn, 13–16; Gentry

1991); thus, their French source was a manuscript related to *P*. Finally, the *Elucidation* and a truncated version of *Bliocadran* introduce the 1530 prose *Perceval* (Hilka edn, 493ff.), printed anonymously in Paris by Bernard Aubry (Thompson edn, 9).

Bliocadran as a 'prologue' is not an *exordium* in the rhetorical or poetic sense, but a 'prequel' with a pre-history to Chrétien's poem that supplies patrilineal information, complementing, and responding to, the matrilineal emphasis in Perceval's genealogy given by his mother (Busby edn, 409–88) and in subsequent accounts by his cousin (3582–3612) and uncle (6392–6431). The *Elucidation*, which consistently precedes *Bliocadran* (except in *L* where the latter appears as an after-thought), functions, however, as an extended *exordium* whilst introducing prediegetic matter. For, like the 'rhymed table of contents' with which it is often compared (Thompson 1959, 208 and n.), it also self-consciously anticipates a global Grail romance embracing *Bliocadran*, Chrétien's *Perceval*, the First Continuation, certain aspects of the Second Continuation, and perhaps Manessier, which either includes or is augmented by multiple branches that also 'muevent del Graal' (*spring from the Grail*, 382).

The *Elucidation*

The *Elucidation* begins with an *exordium* designed to introduce an extended *Perceval* such as that found in *P*, including narratives attributed to seven *gardes* 'guards' (17, 345)[4] constituting the story's seven branches, also called *gardes* (344, etc.) or *souviestemens* (341, 343).[5] Maistre Blihis (12, cf. 'bon mestre', 449) is mentioned as an authority on the Grail's secrets and perhaps as a source. Thompson (edn, 67–79) considers all passages having to do with the 'guards' and with Maistre Blihis, including the prologue (1–22, 339–82, 343–56), to be interpol-ations on the grounds that they refer to events outside the *Perceval* and the First and Second Continuations; lines 327–38 are likewise interpolated because they are redundant.[6] Maistre Blihis has been identified with known real and fictional story-tellers of Grail matter, including the knight Blihos Bliheris, a master story-teller in his own right (170–82) who informs Arthur's court about King Amangon's atrocity and its aftermath (161–212) (Weston 1920, 189–209; Gallais 1988–9).[7]

Confusion abounds throughout the textual tradition as to the meaning of a key word in the *Elucidation*, i.e. *pui(s)*, which designates the dwelling-places of the maidens who offer hospitality to wayfarers and the water sources that dry up after King Amangon commits an atrocity that brings disaster to Logres and ultimately prompts the Grail Quest. Weston (1920, 172 and n. 17), supported by Colin and Wisse, who translate *pui(s)* as 'Berg' and 'Gebirge', insists that the maidens live in hills (*pui* from Lat. *podium*), perhaps 'hills' in the sense of fairy mounds, whilst Thompson describes the maidens as living in wells (*puis* from Lat. *puteus*) (Thompson edn, 37–50; 1959, 208; Wolfgang in Lacy ed. 1991*, 131). More recently, Meneghetti distances herself somewhat from the latter by stating that the maidens dwell '*auprès des* puits' (Meneghetti 1987–8, 57, my emphasis), i.e. *by* wells rather than *in* wells, but her reading does not account for the fact that hospitable maidens 'come out' of *puis* to greet visitors (44–5, 87–8, etc.).

The author's meaning turns out to be 'wells', and in *P* occurrences of *pui* ('hill[s]') instead of *puis* ('well[s]') are scribal errors. Yet the bilingual Strasbourgeois, translating for Colin and Wisse, who could not read French (Thompson edn, 14; Gentry 1991), similarly 'misread' the text in the 1330s, and the Middle French *mise en prose* defines the word in a complementary way: 'caves que l'ancienne Hystoire appelle aultrement puys qui estoient en celles forestz entaillees par ouvraige merveilleux' (Hilka edn, 493), i.e. caves cut into rocky hillsides. The later witnesses find that 'hills' makes sense and 'wells' does not. In consideration of their testimony, the inescapable conclusion is that the concept of maidens living in wells results from a north-eastern French author's own misunderstanding of a source with distant Celtic roots. In parallel texts, benevolent other worldly creatures come through tunnels from (within) hills. In Marie de France's *Yonec*, the lady's lover, a shape-shifter like the *Elucidation*'s Rich Fisher (220–2, cf. 280–96), lives inside a *hoge* (345–56, 450–2, Ewert edn), a hill or a mound (Tobler-Lommatzsch) or perhaps a high place overlooking water (Godefroy), and in the *Itinerarium Kambriae* (Dimock edn, 74–5), Gerald of Wales tells of a boy passing through a tunnel to visit a fairy kingdom inside a river's 'ripas concavas', high-vaulted shores ('overhanging banks', Thorpe transl., 135), just the kind of description that may have inspired the Middle French translation of *puis* as 'caves'. Thompson (edn, 39–41) provides other parallel texts. Humans may encounter fairy maidens in fountains, springs or lakes, but not in watery pits, the ultimate *puis* being hell itself.

Thompson (41) fails to substantiate his claim that hospitable maidens live specifically in wells elsewhere, but he does cite one Irish tale in which a well serves as the entrance to a mound. Even so, while the meaning of 'Ja li damages ne sera / Recovrés a nul jor del monde' (*never will the damage ever be repaired*, 190–1) is clear, it remains difficult to understand what is meant by Arthur's project to 'recover' or 'repair' the *puis* (*recovrer* in 124, 137, 198) except in reference to them as sources of water. Despite suspicions that the *Elucidation*'s author did not fully understand the material with which he was working, we have of course no choice but to take the text in *P* at face value.

Meneghetti (1987–88, 57) divides the *Elucidation*, excluding the prologue and epilogue, into fifteen movements falling into three main sections, but she omits reference to nearly a third of the text (239–382). I follow Meneghetti's outline in general terms with necessary modifications as noted.

Part 1. (#1) Maidens in the kingdom of Logres live in wells and give wayfarers food and drink (29–62). (#2) King Amangon and his knights rape them and steal their golden cups, symbols of their hospitality (63–86). (#3) Thereafter, the maidens no longer appear to offer hospitality (32–3, 87–8). (#4) The kingdom is struck by drought and famine (23–31, 89–98). (#5) The court of the Rich Fisher, who used to spread wealth throughout the kingdom, is no longer to be found (99–115). (#6) While the kingdom is still rich, Arthur's knights hear about the adventure and set out to avenge the maidens; they kill offenders, but fail to find the maidens (116–44); (#7) In their search, they fight knights riding with maidens on their horses (145–51). (#8) Gauvain defeats Blihos Bliheris, who tells Arthur's court that the knights and maidens are offspring of the well-maidens and the men who raped them (152–93). (#9) In order to rescue the well-maidens, and restore prosperity, Arthur's knights must find the Rich Fisher's court (194–212). (#10) Arthur's knights start out on their quest of the Rich Fisher (213–24).

Part 2. (#12) Eventually Gauvain finds the Rich Fisher in his court; the joy and increase he brings to the kingdom will be recounted later (225–30).[8] (#11a) But before that, a very young Perceval visits there (230–5).[9] (#11b) Perceval comes to the Round Table and surpasses all in knighthood; he is held in contempt at first, before setting out for knightly conquest (236–47). (#11c) He asks whom the Grail served, but not why the lance bleeds; he asks about a corpse there, but not about the broken sword, half of which lies on the bier (248–57). (#11d) Other marvels include a silver cross, censers and food served by a floating Grail (258–314).[10] (#11e) A great wonder occurs that Perceval himself will recount later in the text (315–22). Thus Perceval may be one of the 'guards' who will narrate one of the seven branches. (#11f) At the point when the great knight (Perceval? Gauvain?) finds the Rich Fisher's court a third time, the narrator will explain the function of the wells and the Grail mysteries point by point (323–39), as happens during Perceval's third Grail visit in Manessier. (#11g) In reverse order, the seven branches constituting the 'natural stories' springing from the Grail (381–2) are anticipated one by one.[11] (#13) 'This adventure' (Gauvain's partial success, or Perceval's?) brings joy to the people and restores water and prosperity to the land (383–400).

Part 3. (#14) Arrogant descendants sired by Amangon and his men construct castles (the Castle of Maidens, the Perilous Bridge, the Proud Castle) and pit themselves against the Round Table (401–28) (Meneghetti attaches #14 to the middle part). (#15a) They wage war against Arthur, who vanquishes them after four years (429–64). (#15b) Henceforth Arthur's court devotes itself to hunting and games of love (465–74). *P* continues with a transitional couplet, indicating that readers have only heard a sample of Chrétien's work (475–6), and the last verses of Chrétien's prologue (61–8).

Many difficulties remain. It is by no means clear, for example, whether it is Perceval or Gauvain who is finally to bring Logres back to life. The narrator emphasizes Gauvain by presenting his successful Grail quest first (#12), but delays giving details (until the First Continuation?). In any case, the summary six-line account diminishes his importance by comparison with eighty-six lines devoted to the prior visit by Perceval (#11), which will recur in Chrétien. Perceval's visit in the *Elucidation* in effect transfers to him Gauvain's adventure in the First Continuation and perhaps, as it becomes a partial success, also its benefits. Which knight is destined to visit the Grail Castle three times, the last of which is to provoke the revelation of Grail secrets, as well as the narrations of the seven guards? Indeed, after the digression on the seven guards, the return to the main topic with 'Ceste aventure' (*this adventure*, 383) harks back to the closer of the two already referred to: the fuller account concerning Perceval. Yet scholars tend to see Gauvain as the ultimate victor (Weston 1920, 115, etc.; Meneghetti 1987–8; but Thompson edn, 61–2, is indecisive).

Thompson (1959, 209), who is concerned primarily with sources, finds the *Elucidation* to be a text hopelessly botched by clumsy composition and inept interpolation. Meneghetti (1987–8, 63), who views it as confused and confusing, thinks that any conclusion in regard to it is hazardous. She detaches the *Elucidation* from the texts it appears designed to introduce. For her it is a transparent rewriting of Chrétien's *Perceval*, one which appears as 'une tentative – assez bien construite, d'ailleurs – de restauration culturelle et même idéologique' (*a fairly well-constructed attempt at cultural, and even ideological, restoration*). It resolves the ambiguities and ambivalences inherent in Chrétien's conflicted kingdoms and reflects the renewed unified culture shaped by Philip Augustus (68). The vast territory separating these positions provides ample room for exploring anew this narrative concerning Perceval, rewritten to introduce both Chrétien's *Perceval* and a whole body of Continuations generated by it.

Bliocadran

Bliocadran follows the conclusion of Chrétien's prologue in *P* and is interpolated after the whole of that prologue in *L*. The *Elucidation* provides a chronological framework of about twenty-five years for the adventures it recounts and anticipates. Events in *Bliocadran* take place within about sixteen years, up to the time Perceval, aged fourteen, is poised to discover knighthood. Thus, in terms of the *Elucidation*'s chronology, *Bliocadran* opens well after King Amangon's atrocity and closes somewhat before Perceval's first Grail visit, during a period of time the *Elucidation* passes over in silence. Thus *Bliocadran*'s 'realism', that is, an absence of the *merveilleux breton*, contrasts all the more starkly with the otherworldly qualities, which in fact it demystifies, that pervade the *Elucidation*.

Scholars have speculated about the *Bliocadran* author's reasons for proposing an alternative to the advice of Perceval's mother in Chrétien (Busby edn, 409–88) either that he was a redactor who intended to produce a version of *Perceval* without her speech, or perhaps it did not appear in his exemplar (Thompson

1959, 210), or else that he found his source wanting in explaining the mother's motivations and sought to provide a counterpoise to it (Wolfgang edn, 9). Whatever the case, the paternal biography it invents, wherein the father receives a name while the mother remains anonymous, and its realism devoid of mystical or other worldly concerns, provides a clear variant to Perceval's genealogy as found in Chrétien, which is grounded in British history, sacred history, Grail history and the *merveilleux breton*. *Bliocadran*'s 800 straightforward lines far outweigh in bulk, if not poetic richness, the mother's forty-line speech in Chrétien and the seventy-one lines of the cousin's and uncle's speeches combined. In juxtaposition with Chrétien's *Perceval*, the two perspectives are not complementary, but absolutely opposed. Wolfgang (edn, 8–9) argues convincingly that such a dialect-ical confrontation is not a deterrent in medieval reading practices, even in the face of contradictory assertions. Indeed, her insight is consonant with Meneghetti's view of the *Elucidation* as an 'interpretive response' to problems raised in the text it introduces (1987–8, 56).

Wolfgang (edn, 81–3) divides *Bliocadran* into seven episodes: (#1) Twelve brothers in Wales are the most honoured and most accomplished knights in the country. Eleven are killed in tournaments and battles. The twelfth, Bliocadran, inherits an important fief. He seeks to return to the tournaments, but his wife and vassals persuade him to stay with them (1–52). (#2) Two years later, when Bliocadran's wife is pregnant with their first child, a messenger arrives. After enjoying his host's hospitality, he informs him about a tournament organized by the King of Wales against the Cornish. When Bliocadran responds that he and his men will fight, his wife and vassals again beg him to remain, but this time he leaves (53–160). (#3) At the tournament, Bliocadran and his knights join the front ranks of the Welsh. Bliocadran defeats his adversary in the first round, but is later wounded and dies. His knights bury him with great ceremony (161–243). (#4) His wife gives birth to her first son three days after he leaves. She sends a messenger to inform her husband, but he arrives too late. Bliocadran's knights instruct him not to tell their lady what has happened. They will all return a week later. Unable to face their lady, however, they engage an abbot to break the sad news. After a long period of mourning, she finds comfort in her son (244–456). (#5) Seven months later, she determines to keep her son from any knowledge of knighthood. She will take him to the Waste Forest in secret. After having her men swear fealty to her son with the promise to acknowledge him when he returns, and against the people's wishes that she stay, she leaves with her son, on the pretence of making a pilgrimage to St Brendan in Scotland (457–655). (#6) Instead, she makes her way to Calfle on the Welsh coast, where she meets all who are to accompany her. They travel for several days, enter the forest and wander for two weeks before finding the ideal place to establish their community under the leadership of her steward and his sons (656–724). (#7) Fourteen years later, her son can ride and hunt with the javelin. He knows nothing of the world outside the Waste Forest. She warns him against devils covered with iron, whom he may ward off by making the sign of the cross and repeating the creed. After hunting in the forest all the next day, he returns home and his mother asks him what has happened. She asks no more when he answers that he found sport and pleasure (725–800).

Clearly, the last episode is written with the opening of Chrétien's narrative foremost in mind. It demonstrates the causes of Perceval's appearance to Arthur's knights as a witless *naïf*, and it portrays him learning from his mother the words he repeats when he sees, and then becomes acquainted with, Arthur's knights. Moreover, in addition to endowing Perceval with flesh-and-blood parents, *Bliocadran* as a whole gives new perspectives on, and new emphasis to, important themes that recur in Chrétien's text, such as genealogy itself, deferred action, departure in the midst of joy, postponed speech and dissimulation.

Thompson (1959, 210) finds five contradictions between *Bliocadran* and Chrétien's *Perceval*, three of which are valid: (i) Bliocadran is killed in a tournament, not wounded in a war and then impoverished; (ii) Perceval is an only child, not the youngest and sole survivor of three sons; (iii) his mother, not his father, leads their household into exile.[12] *Bliocadran* in fact offers many more contradictions that are just as significant: (i) The name of Perceval's father is given; (ii) the *émigrés* discover the place to build their manor in the Waste Forest; it is not a working domain already belonging to Perceval's father; (iii) Bliocadran is not, like the Fisher King, 'parmi les jambes navrez' (*wounded between the legs*, Busby edn, 436), and he is not carried on a litter; (iv) Bliocadran is a vassal of the King of Wales, not Utherpendragon and afterwards, presumably, Arthur; (v) Bliocadran is not oppressed in the wars following Uther's death and Arthur's coronation and so is not connected with British history (as narrated by Wace); (vi) consequently, the exile of Perceval's family is not linked chronologically to the founding of Ygerne's Roche de Canguin castle; (vii) Perceval has no brother serving the King of Escavalon, whom Gauvain is accused of murdering. As a response to Perceval's genealogy according to his mother, *Bliocadran* provides, in context with it, and against it, a richer reading of the *Perceval* than Chrétien's text alone, as Wolfgang argues, but the stark alternatives the response offers are bleak and one-dimensional. **[RTP]**

The Continuations

There have been a number of theories as to how Chrétien might have intended to complete his *Perceval*, some more fanciful than others, but the most likely is that there would have been some kind of encounter between Perceval and Gauvain, in which Perceval would have established his spiritual and physical superiority over Arthur's principal knight, before eventually returning to the Grail castle and passing the test he had previously failed.

   Chrétien's dual structure offered the continuators a ready-made vehicle for prolonging the text. Despite multiple authorship and considerable differences of style and intent, the four Continuations in existence by *c.*1225, or shortly thereafter, essentially maintain the alternation of Gauvain and Perceval as central figures, adding others, while never quite losing sight of the Grail Quest. The manuscript transmission of the Continuations is complex and for many years formed an obstacle to serious scholarship, but the modern state of critical editions is now, relatively speaking, satisfactory, thanks in large part to the work of Roach (Busby 1987–8). There are four basic Continuations, which appear in the following order in the manuscripts: the First Continuation (*Continuation-Gauvain* or Pseudo-Wauchier), the Second Continuation (*Continuation-Perceval* or Wauchier de Denain), the Continuation of Gerbert de Montreuil and the Continuation of Manessier. In the most complete manuscripts, the total number of lines taken up by Chrétien's romance and its prequels and sequels is about 75,000 lines.

The First Continuation

Although four manuscripts do present Chrétien's *Perceval* without the Continuations, in the majority of copies the First Continuation follows without any evident demarcation between the two; one of these four (London, College of Arms, Arundel XIV, or its model at some stage in the transmission) even shows evidence of having been copied from a manuscript which contained various of the Continuations, in an apparent attempt to re-establish the limits of the original, unfinished, romance (Busby 1993b). Most medieval readers or listeners, however, might even have remained unaware that Chrétien's part was over until the mention of one or other of the continuators by name at some later point. Certainly, the modern scholarly parameters of each Continuation would not have been defined so strictly in the Middle Ages, or experienced so acutely, and the medieval view of Chrétien's whole *Perceval* romance, together with the Continuations, is more likely to have been either that of a single Grail romance or of a collection of adventures related more or less loosely to the theme of the Grail Quest. The four manuscripts which appear to contain Chrétien's text alone indicate that his part in the *Perceval* compilation ends after nine thousand lines (*Perceval*, 9234), just as Gauvain's messenger arrives at Arthur's court to request

the king to join him at the Château des Merveilles. The First Continuator consequently pursues the adventures of Gauvain.

Of the four principal texts, the First Continuation is the one to pose the
most complex problems with respect to textual transmission, existing as it does in
three discernible redactions, generally called Short, Long and Mixed. These
redactions also have interpolations, omissions and *remaniements* of various
episodes. It is usually thought that the Short Redaction is the earliest of the three
(before 1200) and that the Mixed and Long show influence of other texts known
to have been composed after that date, including perhaps one or more of the
other Continuations.[13] The First Continuation also contains some of the most
extraordinarily imaginative narrative in the entire corpus of Arthurian romance,
which makes the critical neglect it has suffered all the more culpable.[14]
Medievalists may not find a complex and disorderly text to their liking and may
prefer to concentrate on works circumscribed by prologue and epilogue, by
beginning and end. However, the existence of Roach's editions long ago rendered
the texts accessible, and may even, it could be argued, have imposed a neatness on
them unsupported by the manuscript transmission.[15]

Dominated for long episodes by the *merveilleux*, the Short Redaction may
preserve very old material from Arthurian tradition; much of it is certainly less
'courtly' than what is found in Chrétien, whose own measured and restrained use
of the mysterious is jettisoned in favour of a more fantastic and spectacular presentation of Gauvain's adventures. The beginning of the First Continuation
picks up the narrative thread of Gauvain's conflict with Guiromelant. Arthur
and Gauvain are reunited with their mothers in the Château des Merveilles and
the combat between Gauvain and Guiromelant takes place, the latter being
reconciled as a result of Clarissant's appeal to them; only Brun de Branlant
among Guiromelant's followers does not accept the reconciliation (I, 1–5 – references are to sections and episodes in Roach edn). Arthur sets out to besiege
Brun's castle, beginning the next major series of episodes of the Short Redaction.
During the siege of Branlant, Gauvain is wounded, and while out riding in order
to test his fitness, he encounters the Pucelle de Lis, whom he seduces. The
damsel's father challenges Gauvain and is killed, as is one of her brothers;
Gauvain's combat with a second brother, Bran de Lis, is interrupted, on the
condition that it will be resumed whenever the two meet again. Brun de Branlant
finally submits to Arthur (II, 1–7).[16] The narrative then switches to Carados of
Nantes, who marries Arthur's niece Ysave de Carahés; a son (actually engendered
by the enchanter Elïavrés), also named Carados, is born (III, 1–16). The Carados
section appears to be loosely related, if at all, to the Grail romance in which it
appears. The lineage of Arthur provides a kind of cohesion, but once any notions
of organic unity are discarded, the First Continuation begins to appear as a
repository of Arthurian tales.[17]

From the Carados section at least two motifs occur elsewhere in Arthurian romance, and another achieves a measure of celebrity in the manuscripts in which it is preserved. During the ceremonies in which Carados is made a knight a stranger arrives at Arthur's court and challenges the company to exchange blows with him, thus setting the stage for the so-called beheading test, best known from *Sir Gawain and the Green Knight* and other late Middle English versions (III, 4–5, but see *Perlesvaus* below). The section concludes with another stranger bringing to court a drinking-horn, from which only a man whose wife is faithful to him can drink without spilling the contents (III, 16). This 'chastity test' is known in a number of variants, such as the *Lai du Cor*, or the *Lai du Mantel* (in which the horn is replaced by a magic mantle fitting only faithful women; see chapter V). The other episode in question is that in which Elïavrés causes a serpent to attach itself to Carados's arm; the serpent is removed when Carados and his *amie* Guignier stand naked opposite each other in tubs of vinegar and milk respectively. The serpent leaps from Carados's arm to Guignier's breast, where it is killed. Guignier's nipple, cut off in the process, is later restored in gold (III, 11–14). This episode is the subject of miniatures in a number of the illuminated manuscripts (Rossi 1980; Busby 1993a; Doner 1996).

The next major section of the First Continuation re-establishes the link with Chrétien's *Perceval* when Arthur proposes rescuing Girflet, imprisoned for the last four years in the Chastel Orguellous (IV, 1–2). On the way to the Chastel, Gauvain encounters Bran de Lis and is obliged to relate to Arthur and his companions the details of his encounter with the Pucelle (IV, 3–5). This has the dual function of resuming an earlier narrative thread and summarizing it for those among the audience who might have missed or forgotten the episode in question; the audience of the text coalesces with Gauvain's audience within the text itself. This also suggests strongly that medieval listeners or readers experienced the text by episodes and not necessarily in sequence. The apparently fragmentary nature of the narrative in the First Continuation requires us to read it in a different way. It may well be that, despite periodic links to the main theme and reminders of Chrétien's host romance, the First Continuation in particular represents earlier forms of medieval narrative, before Chrétien had transformed this kind of *matière* by means of the precepts of Latin rhetoric and the arts of poetry. One of the most charming episodes from the whole corpus of Continuations occurs in this section, namely that in which the Pucelle de Lis holds her son up between his father and uncle as the pair resume their interrupted combat; the child innocently reaches out to touch the shining swords (IV, 7). After the reconciliation between Gauvain and Bran de Lis, Arthur's party continues on to the Chastel Orguellous. With Bran's help, the Chastel is finally conquered; Gauvain defeats its master, the Riche Soudoier, although he is convinced to feign defeat briefly so as not to upset the latter's *amie* unduly (IV, 8–15). Returning home by way of the Chastel de Lis, they learn that Gauvain's young son has been kidnapped; a search for the child proves futile (IV, 16). Here again, kinship ties seem to constitute the thread that links the various episodes and also to furnish provision for future adventures: if Gauvain's son has been abducted, he will surely reappear at some future point.

However, the search for the child is not pursued in the short term, as the next section of the narrative returns to the Grail when Gauvain visits the Fisher King. The author of the First Continuation seems to have understood that the Grail is not something that can be sought, that the Grail Castle is not a location that can be found, save by accident or *aventure* (Roach 1966). Or, in other words, if we are dealing with a relatively direct form of transmission of oral sources, it is implicit in the tales themselves that the Grail and related phenomena are unexplained manifestations of the *merveilleux*. There seems to be little here of the notion, so clear elsewhere, that success in the Grail adventure is dependent on matters of spirituality, guilt and innocence. After a stranger is mysteriously killed at Arthur's court, Gauvain assumes his armour and horse and sets out to accomplish his mission, despite having no knowledge of what this might be (V, 1–2). Here is the true definition of *aventure*: something which the individual, convinced that it will befall him sooner or later, invites by arbitrary roaming. A storm portends Gauvain's arrival at a chapel where a black hand emerges from behind the altar and extinguishes the light. At nightfall the next day, the horse leads Gauvain down a causeway to a mysterious castle where the Grail appears, dispensing food to all those present. Some elements of the episode appear to be archaic, others derived from Chrétien's text or its latent potential (a corpse on a bier with a broken sword, a bleeding lance, etc.), while others still appear to be new developments, additions or interpretations of the original romance (the lance is that of Longinus, the Grail is the receptacle used by Joseph of Arimathea to catch Christ's blood, and so on). Gauvain fails to join the two parts of the broken sword, thereby effectively precluding any further revelations. When he awakens the next morning, Gauvain is far from the castle, but vows not to rest until he finds it again. If he is unsuccessful with respect to the Grail, he is at least reunited with his son, whom he encounters guarding a ford, and with whom he fights until identities are revealed. Gauvain, his son and the latter's *amie* return to Arthur's court (V, 3–8).

The next section deals largely with the adventures of Guerrehet, brother of Gauvain, of whom he could be viewed as an avatar. Like so many episodes of the First Continuation (and of romance generally), the Guerrehet section opens with a mysterious arrival at court. Often this narrative device takes the form of a challenger, but here it is a boat drawn by a swan, on which is the body of a dead knight, a broken lance protruding from it (VI, 1). The dead knight must be avenged with the tip of the broken lance. Any failed attempt to avenge the knight is enigmatically linked to the shame incurred by Guerrehet in the garden, an adventure related in the next section of text (VI, 2–6). While looking for Gauvain, Guerrehet is defeated by the Petit Chevalier, to whom he promises to return in a year's time to fight again, or else become the slave-labourer of the wounded master of the castle; insults and humiliations are heaped upon him before he returns to Arthur's court in the swan-boat. The dead knight is now revealed as Brangemuer, son of a mortal and a fairy, whose death was necessary before he could return to his mother's kingdom (VI, 7–8). There are certain thematic parallels here with Grail episodes from Chrétien's text and earlier in the First Continuation, although it is difficult to know to what extent these would have been apparent to a medieval audience. In fact, Chrétien's *Perceval* and the First Continuation share so many motifs that it almost seems as if the Continuation was itself the source from which Chrétien's romance was constructed and remodelled.

The fundamental textual difference between the Short Redaction on the one hand, and the Mixed and Long Redactions on the other, is the presence in the latter of a number of episodes (I, 6–10 in Roach's division). These seem to constitute a retrospective attempt to strengthen the ties between the First Continuation and Chrétien's text, and they certainly indicate an awareness of the desirability of doing so on the part of redactors and scribes.[18] Episode I, 5, which in the Short Redaction described the marriage of Clarissant to Guiromelant and the reconciliation of the latter and Gauvain, ends somewhat differently in the Mixed and Long Redactions and enables the interpolation of the supplementary material. Here, Gauvain leaves court in anger after discovering that Clarissant has married his enemy even before the reprise of their combat. His aimless departure creates the narrative space in which he rescues the Damsel of Montescleire, wins the Espee as Estranges Renges and is reconciled with Guingambresil and the King of Escavalon; at this point, the Mixed and Long Redactions rejoin the Short. Equally noteworthy are the appearance of a maiden who had been wronged by Greoreas (I, 6) and a failed visit to the Grail Castle (I, 7). Gauvain's encounter with Dinasdarés, who accuses him of having killed his father (I, 9), clearly reduplicates the Guiromelant and Guingambresil episodes from Chrétien, the second of which it obstructs, but with which it finally merges in resolution (I, 10). If those responsible for the additional episodes had an eye to the unresolved details of Chrétien's text, they also seem to have understood and implemented certain of his narrative methods, creating an extraordinary textual and narrative interplay, in which *Perceval* and the Continuation appear as mutual sources and inspiration.

If we are to look for elements linking the sections of the First Continuation, they are discernible, but may be no more than inherent in the matter of romance: family ties (Gauvain and Arthur; Gauvain and his son; Gauvain and his brother; Arthur and his niece Ysave; King Carados and his son Carados); the supernatural (Carados, the Grail theme, the swan-boat in the Guerrehet section); affairs of the heart (Clarissant and Guiromelant, Gauvain and the Pucelle de Lis, Ysave and Carados); adventures, quests, matters of vengeance and rebellion, and so on. Even the periodic efforts made to relate the Continuation to the original romance, while apparently revealing a concern for a kind of unity, may be more of an acknowledgement of indebtedness to Chrétien and attempts to control, to restore to the orbit of the Grail, an unruly and exuberant narrative. Although efforts to read Chrétien and the First Continuation in an uninterrupted sequence are probably anachronistic and unmedieval, a basic awareness of the Grail context may be posited. And while Roach's division of the narrative into episodes generally corresponds to narrative breaks, sometimes supported by the placement of decoration in the manuscripts, it does not imply sequential reading of large sections of texts. It is much more likely that readers read or audiences requested and listened to favourite episodes, perhaps even shortish sections of them. Such an approach (especially when it includes the other Continuations) acknowledges both the structural integrity of the long compilation as defined by the codex and the quasi-independence of the individual tales within it.

The Second Continuation
If the dividing-line between Chrétien's romance and the First Continuation is clear enough on stylistic grounds alone, the traditional break between the First and Second Continuations, accepted by Roach in his series of editions, has been questioned by Corley (1987), who would prolong the work of the first continuator by some 900 lines (to Second Continuation 20530, the end of the Guiot manuscript, BNF, fr. 794). Such a concern is legitimate but was probably not an issue for medieval readers or listeners, at least not until Wauchier de Denain claims authorship of the Second Continuation (31421). Only then, and only incidentally, is the matter of what can be attributed to whom of much significance. The supposed authorship of Wauchier had generally been doubted until the work of Vial (1978) and Corley (1984), who confirm its stylistic similarities to other works known to have been written by him. It is difficult to know whether the attribution to Wauchier would have meant anything to medieval readers or listeners, as his name can hardly have resounded with the same echoes as those of, say, Chrétien de Troyes.[19]

The Second Continuation is usually thought to have been written just after the Short Redaction of the First Continuation, although its narrative links to the former are somewhat tenuous, albeit not entirely lacking. Towards the end, a tournament is held at the Chastel Orguellous (##23–4 – references are to episode numbers in Roach edn); Gauvain meets his son, Guinglain, and relates to him a lengthy account of his visits to the Chapel of the Black Hand and the Grail castle (#32); Perceval also visits the same Chapel of the Black Hand (#34) on his approach to the Grail castle. If the traditional division between First and Second Continuations is maintained, however, the second continuator can be seen to secure his work to the Grail compilation simply by rejoining Perceval's wanderings. In manuscripts containing the Mixed and Long Redaction of the First Continuation, Perceval's adventures are located temporally after his departure from his uncle's hermitage in Chrétien, although in the manuscripts of the Short Redaction the link is made by a huntsman who reproaches Perceval with having failed to ask questions of the Fisher King. By returning to Perceval for the majority of his text, the second continuator re-establishes Chrétien's structure of alternating heroes and the basic comparison of Gauvain and Perceval,[20] and the Second Continuation is linked to Chrétien quite clearly on several occasions: the introductory passage mentioned above (including a verbatim quotation from *Perceval*); the Mont Dolerous (##1, 25, 27; cf. *Perceval*, 4724); the appearance of a brother of the Chevalier Vermeil (#8); Perceval's return to Blanchefleur at Beaurepaire (#15), to his mother's home (#18), to his Hermit Uncle (#19) and to the Grail Castle (##34–5). The theme of the Grail Quest or the quest for the Bleeding Lance is a constant reminder of the subordination of worldly adventures to the spiritual: the Lance (#2), and especially reminders concerning Perceval's unsuccessful visit to the Fisher King are prominent (##3, 6, 8, 19, 22, 26, 28, 33–5).

The traditional demarcation between the First and Second Continuations seems to be supported by a change in the nature of the *merveilleux,* beginning with Roach's episode 1. There is something more restrained and disciplined, more courtly, about the supernatural of the Second Continuation: the Ivory Horn (##1–2) evokes wonder, but is merely a splendid example of its kind; the Magic Chessboard (##4, 26) is indeed supernatural, but its basic function is still that of a chessboard; the giant (#12) is a typical ogre of romance; the same can be said of the white stag hunted by Perceval (#5, etc.) and the lion in the castle of Abrioris (#9); the Castle of Maidens (#20) is a standard feature of the genre, as is the knight imprisoned in the tomb (#25); the Glass Bridge (##22–3) may have been inspired by well-known episodes from Chrétien's *Charrette*. These manifestations of the *merveilleux* may be compared with the Grail in both Chrétien and the First Continuation, which remains largely mysterious (particularly Gauvain's Grail visit in the latter text and the episodes in the Chapel of the Black Hand), and also with the Carados sequence and the adventures of Guerrehet (Busby 1998).

The Second Continuation, while by no means dull and certainly worthy of greater scholarly attention than it has received, is perhaps most remarkable for its conventional nature. It is in many ways a better reflection of romance and its evolution at the turn of the twelfth and thirteenth centuries than other parts of the compilation, being composed for a large part of numbers of stock themes, motifs and other narrative elements. Despite being part of a Grail romance, it is largely secular in nature and shows no influence of the doctrinally specific *Queste del Saint Graal*, confirming that its date of composition was almost certainly *c.*1200 rather than *c.*1225. Indeed, the spirit of the various components of the verse Grail romance in these long manuscripts is precisely what best differentiates them the one from the other: Chrétien, spiritual and mystical; the First Continuation, wildly supernatural, exuberant and archaic; the Second Continuation, secular and conventional; Manessier, rational and reassuring; Gerbert de Montreuil, solemn and sermonizing.

Although visible in both parts of Chrétien's romance, the technique of interrupted quests seems to be fundamental to the structure of the Second Continuation (Bozoky 1980), and it is this repeated pattern which enables the author to prolong Perceval's adventures and incorporate many of the conventions of romance. Perceval's plan to go to the Mont Dolcrous (#1) interrupts his search for the Grail Castle and has not been carried out by the time the Second Continuator ceases writing. The arrival of the Sire du Cor at Arthur's court (#2) functions as a catalyst to spur Arthur and the knights to leave in search of Perceval. At the castle of the Magic Chessboard, Perceval falls in love with the damsel (apparently forgetting his commitment to Blanchefleur), a love which will only be granted if he brings her the head of a white stag (#4). Another damsel steals the brachet, which the damsel had lent to Perceval, and the head of the stag which he had succeeded in killing (#5). Perceval is thus obligated to pursue the brachet and stag's head, thereby interrupting his journey to the Mont Dolerous, which had itself caused him to defer his attempt to return to the Grail castle. Perceval now has three objectives: the Grail Castle, the Mont Dolerous and the stag's head and brachet.[21]

In episode 7, Perceval kills a knight who had murdered a young man, but forgets to inquire of an old knight (the brother of the Chevalier Vermeil), who nevertheless informs him that the second damsel had stolen the stag's head and hound because of his failure at the Grail Castle (#8); the old knight also indicates a castle where the damsel can be found. Perceval initially thinks he has been misled, but the castle finally appears. The old knight does in fact seem to have misled Perceval, as the inhabitant of the castle, Abrioris, defeated in combat by Perceval, knows nothing of the fate of the brachet (#9) and is sent with his *amie* to surrender to Arthur (#10). These are all standard incidents of romance: the encounter with strangers, hospitality scenes, combats and the sending of defeated opponents back to court, all of which deal with the transmission of information, reliable or unreliable, enabling the hero to move on, and providing a means of informing Arthur's court of his progress.

The encounters proliferate: after finding a dead knight and his *amie* in the forest (#11, narrative thread not pursued), Perceval comes to another deserted tower where he slays a giant and frees a damsel (#12), defeats the White Knight at the custom of the Gué Amorous and sends him to surrender to Arthur (#13), and meets Gauvain's son, the Biau Desconeü and his *amie* (#14), who also give Perceval news of Gauvain. All of these episodes illustrate the function of the romance custom, both as a means of confirming the hero's prowess and of maintaining contact between its widely dispersed constituent members.

This most recent accumulation of adventures (##9–14) deflects Perceval from previous tasks which continue to obstruct each other, in a self-perpetuating narrative that creates only an illusion of progress towards the ultimate goal of the Grail. Indeed, the next part of the Continuation (#15) sees Perceval return to Blanchefleur at Beaurepaire, in a rewriting of Chrétien's own episode, but one in which prosperity and optimism have been restored to the country. If Perceval had earlier apparently forgotten his promise to Blanchefleur (cf. #4), it is now restated, but specifically dependent on his resolving the issue of the stag's head and brachet and learning the truth about the Grail and the Lance (23121–40, beginning of #16); of the Mont Dolerous there is no mention at this point. Episodes 16 and 17 form yet another variation of the motif of the defeated opponent sent to Arthur's court. Perceval encounters the Biau Mauvais and his ugly *amie*, Rosete, vanquishing the former and sending the couple to report to Arthur, who is now at Caradigan. Kay mocks Rosete, who later regains her beauty and the Biau Mauvais becomes a member of the household.

During Perceval's visit to his Hermit Uncle, made during his sojourn at his mother's home (##18–19), the narrative of Chrétien's romance becomes further integrated into that of the Second Continuation, as Perceval recounts his acquisition of the red armour, his failed visit to the Fisher King, the events at the Chessboard Castle, the affair of the stag's head and the brachet, his killing the lion and his subsequent defeat of Abrioris. Convention and the narrative require that Perceval refuse his sister's invitation to stay and that he accomplish, before returning, 'iceste euvre que j'ai amprise' (*the task which I have undertaken*, 24207).

The Castle of Maidens (#20) appears to be a kind of secular equivalent of the Grail Castle, somewhat like the castle of the Magic Chessboard, although it also clearly has overtones of the Château des Merveilles from Chrétien's *Perceval*. Like the giant's tower and Abrioris's castle, to Perceval the Castle of Maidens also at first appears deserted. Near a brass table is a steel hammer attached to a silver chain. Perceval strikes the table with the hammer three times and is rewarded with food and hospitality by the lady of the castle and her 300 maidens. Had he not struck the table after the warning to desist, he would have received neither food nor entertainment. The function of the castle is clearly to test a knight's prowess; it is also supernatural and has disappeared when Perceval wakes up the next morning under an oak tree. The intertextual associations of this episode are multiple: in addition to the Château des Merveilles, the table and hammer recall the water and the stone from *Yvain*, and the castle's disappearance strongly resembles that of the Grail Castle in episodes I, 7 and V, 6 of the First Continuation.

The narrative of the Second Continuation characteristically alternates between Wauchier's own invention and reminders of Chrétien or the First Continuation. This alternation is responsible both for a basic coherence and for the constant deferral, postponement and entangling of a number of different narrative threads. Perceval recovers the head of the stag and the brachet from Garsallas and Criseuz (#21) at the same time as the custom of the Black Knight and the tomb is explained to him; Garsallas and Criseuz are also sent to Arthur's court, found this time at the unlikely sounding 'Tinpincarantin' and variants (25420). The recovery of the stag's head and the brachet now requires Perceval to return to the Chessboard Castle; this he does (#27) only after a near miss with the Grail, which a damsel claims was the origin of a bright light in the forest. The same damsel lends Perceval her white mule, which she says will lead him to the Grail Castle if he wears a ring she also gives him (#22). The road to the Chessboard Castle, and then the Grail Castle, is anything but direct and is filled with a profusion of the kind of adventures which characterize this Continuation. Nevertheless, the narrative now turns on itself as Perceval begins to retrace his steps.

The first part of his road is the glass bridge leading to the land of Briol de la Forest Arsee, from whom Perceval learns that he must prove himself the best knight in the world by taking part in a tournament at the Chastel Orguellous, which can only be reached by means of another, unfinished, bridge (#23). This part of his trajectory brings Perceval briefly into contact with Arthur and his knights before he returns to Briol's castle, whence he departs the next day with the ring, the white mule, the stag's head and the brachet (#24). Before he finds the damsel who had lent him the ring and the mule, Perceval frees a knight imprisoned in a tomb, who advises him go to the Mont Dolerous to increase his renown even further (#25). The brachet now leads Perceval back to the Castle of the Magic Chessboard, where the damsel explains its origin. Perceval promises to return after he has visited the Fisher King, to whose castle the damsel directs him (#26). It is no surprise that other events intervene before the objective is reached.

For the second time, Perceval ignores directions to the Grail Castle; as he had earlier spurned the path pointed out by the ferryman in episode 3, he now does the same with indications provided by the Damsel of the Chessboard Castle. On both occasions, this is a narrative expedient for expanding the romance, another adventure impeding direct progress towards the immediate goal, and perhaps a way of suggesting either that Perceval does not yet understand the significance of the Grail or that he understands only too well that he must prove himself in other knightly activities before returning to the Fisher King. Arguably, the latter is more likely to be the case, as the encounter with Bagomedés, maltreated by Kay, spurs Perceval on to the Mont Dolerous, where Kay and three other knights have already failed to tie their horses to the pillar (#27). It now seems clear that Perceval is working his way through his objectives in reverse order: the return of the stag's head and brachet (just accomplished), the Mont Dolerous (imminent) and the Grail (coming closer).

After Bagomedés's return to Arthur's peripatetic court, now at Caradigan, the knights resolve to go in search of Perceval. Lancelot, Yvain and Gauvain eventually come to a crossroads. There is obviously the potential here for the kind of development which characterizes the prose cycles and which is articulated by means of *entrelacement*, but the author says he will relate only the adventures of Gauvain. This choice is essentially determined by the acknowledgement of Chrétien's dual structure and the subsequent alternation of Perceval and Gauvain as principal protagonists. While the transitional formulae (29190–208 and 31414–20) are not those of prose romance, they are of the kind used by Chrétien to position the Hermit episode in Gauvain's adventures, and they anticipate the more familiar 'Or dist li contes' (*now the story relates*) variety, which is to become the norm within a quarter of a century.

The episode of the Petit Chevalier and his sister reflects perfectly the ambiguous nature of Gauvain in Arthurian romance. After having made love to the girl (who had been enamoured of him for some time), he and her brother proceed to a tournament in the Blanche Lande where only Gauvain, incognito among Arthur and his knights, is able to carry the shield destined for a peerless knight loved faithfully by his *amie* (##29–30). The Petit Chevalier and the Pansif Chevalier of episode 31 are two in a sequence of 'odd' characters defined by a paradox or apparent physical or mental deficiency of some kind. The Pansif Chevalier is reunited by Gauvain with his *amie*, who had been abducted by Brun de la Lande; Brun is sent to Arthur's court at Cavalon, where, as is customary, he becomes a member of the household. In the context of the Continuation as a whole, these last three episodes are not especially significant, but they serve to reintroduce Gauvain as an alternate protagonist and to underline the conventional nature of non-Grail romance. And the last two episodes (like episode 17) ensure that we do not forget the boastful and arrogant Kay. In a sense, the set of paradoxically defined characters, which also includes the Biau Desconeü and the Biau Mauvais (##14, 16–17), act as so many personified component elements of Arthurian knighthood, whose very principles they question.

Gauvain now encounters his son, Guinglain, the same Biau Desconeü whom Perceval has previously met (#14). This meeting is essentially the occasion for narrative recapitulation, as Gauvain relates to Guinglain several of his adventures from the First Continuation: the mysterious death of the knight he was escorting to Guinevere, the Chapel of the Black Hand and the events at the Grail Castle, the latter in some detail. He returns to the present by saying that he is looking for Perceval, of whom Guinglain is able to give him recent news. After helping Arthur defeat the invader King Carras, Gauvain and Guinglain both decide to remain with the king, whose court is seriously depleted of knights (#32).

The Gauvain adventures come to an end as the narrative returns to Perceval. A mysterious child in a tree refuses to answer questions about the Fisher King, but encourages Perceval to proceed to the Mont Dolerous where he is deemed to be the best knight in the world.[22] A damsel explains to Perceval the origin of the custom of the Mont Dolerous, an explanation that links it (and the Grail, to which it is clearly a prelude) to the origins of the Arthurian kingdom: it has been created by Merlin so that Utherpendragon might know the best knight in the land (#33). As Perceval leaves the Mont Dolerous, a maiden on a white mule (probably the same as in episodes 22 and 25) indicates the path that will lead to the Fisher King. This time Perceval takes the path indicated, which leads him through a storm, past an illuminated tree, to the Chapel of the Black Hand where the body of a dead knight lies on the altar. The next day four hunters tell him he is close to the Fisher King's castle, and a maiden, calling the tree and the chapel a 'senefiance', says that he will soon learn the truth about the Grail and the Lance; she divulges no information about the child in the tree (#34).

The successful quests to return the stag's head and brachet, and his triumph at the Mont Dolerous, together with the manifestations of the *merveilleux* (the tree and the Chapel of the Black Hand) clearly indicate that Perceval is near to the Grail Castle. The Fisher King promises to explain to Perceval, after he has eaten, the significance of what he has witnessed. The meal is interrupted by a procession in which Perceval sees the Grail, the Lance and the broken sword. His confusion and reticence once more render him mute, but when he finally asks the Fisher King to explain the significance of the Grail, the Lance and the sword, the King replies that Perceval's neglect of God precludes him from telling him. Perceval learns only that the broken sword can be joined by a 'prodom' who excels in both chivalry and piety. As a small crack still remains after Perceval's attempt at reuniting the pieces, he is clearly not in the state of perfection required if he is to receive explanations of all the mysteries he has seen. The Fisher King nevertheless offers Perceval the lordship of his castle. Here, the text of the Second Continuation ends (#35). Perceval's failure to reach perfection obviously opens the way for subsequent Continuations.

This extended summary of the narrative of the Second Continuation may give a glimpse into the nature and complexities of the text as well as into its place in the compilation. It is at once episodic and fragmented, yet joined to the Grail story in general, and even somewhat coherent within itself. Frequent recapitulations of their adventures by the protagonists, and allusions to earlier parts of the compilation, might suggest the need on the part of audiences to establish their bearings at intervals, and to remind themselves of the overall context, whilst appreciating the individual episodes. If discovering the secrets of the Grail is to be Perceval's final achievement, it has also become clear that this would preclude further story-telling and foreclose the romance. It is therefore not surprising that authors, including Wauchier de Denain, are reluctant to have Perceval succeed at the Fisher King's castle. Failure is here a narrative stratagem.

Manessier's Continuation

In most of the manuscripts of the Continuations, an author who names himself as Manessier (42657–61) claims to have completed the romance for Jeanne de Flandre (42643–4), and to have started his work 'au soudement de l'espee' (*at the joining of the sword*), which would clearly indicate Roach's episode 35 of the Second Continuation. Moreover, the London manuscript (*L*) ends and the Bern copy (*K*, Burgerbibliothek 113) adds an independent conclusion at the same point ('Et Percevaux se reconforte', 32594), while a new hand takes over in BNF, fr. 1429 (*Q*), and the twin copies *T* and *V* (BNF, fr. 12576 and nouv. acq. fr. 6614) insert between the Second Continuation and that of Manessier the Continuation of Gerbert de Montreuil. All the indications are that Manessier's Continuation was written between 1214 and 1227, most likely towards the end of that period (Ivy 1951; Salmeri 1984). The case for a later, rather than an earlier date can be made largely on the basis of visible influences of the *Lancelot–Grail* Cycle, particularly the *Lancelot* proper and the *Queste del Saint Graal*. Principal among these are the prominence of characters such as Dodinel le Sauvage and Sagremor li Desreés (*Lancelot*), the fight between Perceval and Hector (*Lancelot*), the dispute between Lionel and Bohort (*Queste*) and the temptations of Perceval (*Queste*). The influence of the prose cycle on Manessier is confirmed in Corley 1986.

Manessier's Continuation, however, is also anchored firmly in the verse Grail tradition of Chrétien and the first two Continuations. The explanations given to Perceval by the Fisher King are quite specific: the Lance is that of Longinus; the Grail, the vessel in which Joseph of Arimathea caught the drops of Christ's blood and which sustained him during forty years in prison; Joseph himself built the Grail Castle. The Fisher King is descended from Joseph, and the maiden who carried the Grail is the King's daughter; the maiden who bore the 'tailleor' (*trencher, platter*) is the daughter of the Fisher King's brother Goondesert. Perceval vows to avenge the latter, who had been killed by Partinal with the sword whose parts Perceval has just joined together, albeit imperfectly. Further explanations follow about the illuminated tree and the Chapel of the Black Hand, where Perceval must also do battle (#1 – references are to episode numbers in Roach edn). It is already clear at the beginning of Manessier's work that he is more concerned with clarifying than with mystifying, that his *merveilleux* is explicable rather than impenetrable, as has been the case particularly with Chrétien and the First Continuation. There is thus a distinct progression in the course of the

compilation as a whole, a movement away from the enigmatic and the bewil-
dering, in the direction of reason and reassurance.

Perceval encounters Sagremor, with whose help he rescues a damsel. During
the rescue, he is seriously wounded in the thigh, necessitating a month's recuper-
ation; his sword is also broken during the combat (#2). This forced respite creates
for Manessier the narrative space in which he is able to follow the adventures
of Sagremor (##3–5) and Gauvain (##6–11) before returning to Perceval. The
transitions between the three sets of adventures are effected by formulae at once
similar and dissimilar to those used in the prose romances. In essence, they fulfil
the same purpose, but are not yet the voice of 'li contes', representing rather
a first-person narrator whose function is to transmit the contents of the 'estoire'.

Sagremor's adventures are largely secular in nature: he pursues and defeats a
robber knight and his accomplices (#3), lifts a siege at the Castle of Maidens (#4)
and rescues a maiden from two knights attempting to ravish her (#5); the wounds
he receives during this last deed oblige him to remain in bed for six weeks. In
contrast with the Castle of Maidens episode from the Second Continuation
(#20), there is nothing *merveilleux* at all about Sagremor's visit (other than his
exceptional prowess). The gravity of Sagremor's wounds and the requisite rest-
period repeats the motif from episode 2 (used there in connection with Perceval),
and likewise enables Manessier to switch heroes again.

Gauvain's first adventure in Manessier picks up narrative threads from the
First Continuation (with reprise in the Second), namely the murder of the
stranger he had been escorting to the queen, the events at the Chapel of the Black
Hand and his visit to the Grail Castle. The opening of the sequence, in which
Gauvain recalls the events, constitutes yet another of the periodic narrative
summaries which must have served as reminders to readers and listeners of the
wider context of the compilation. A damsel now arrives at court, claiming that
she is the sister of the murdered knight, whose name was Silimac. She reproaches
Gauvain for his failure to avenge her brother's death and to complete the latter's
mission (which had been to avenge the death of the knight whose body lay on a
bier at the Grail Castle). Gauvain failed to inquire of this knight's identity as he
fell asleep listening to the Fisher King telling him about the Lance and the Grail;
this was due to his sinfulness. Gauvain vows to resume the double vengeance
quest (#6). This entire succession of Gauvain adventures is in fact dominated by
the Silimac affair, which it explains in detail and largely resolves; its origin in the
First Continuation determines the nature of its *merveilleux*, somewhat distinct
from that which characterizes most of Manessier (West 1970–1).

On his quest to avenge Silimac, Gauvain frees Dodinel le Sauvage from prison,
killing one of Dodinel's accusers in the process; three nephews of the latter are
defeated by Gauvain before he and Silimac's sister are able to continue their
journey (#7). It is possible to see episodes such as this as providing the

background necessary for the understanding of the kind of accusation levelled against Gauvain (by Guingambresil, Greoreas and Guiromelant, for example) in Chrétien's *Perceval*. Whether this is a conscious effort on Manessier's part or not, it at least suggests that medieval audiences might not have been as shocked as modern readers by the violent side of one of the Arthurian court's most distinguished members. Gauvain and Silimac's sister arrive at her castle to find it besieged by King Margon, whose son Cargrilo was in love with her and who had also captured and hanged another knight with whom she was in love. By way of revenge, the girl had hurled Cargrilo to his death from a catapult. It was while returning to help his sister against Margon that Silimac had been murdered in Gauvain's company by Kay. Gauvain defeats Margon and promises to arrange a duel with Kay. On his way to surrender at Arthur's court, Margon liberates his sister, the Dame de Malohaut, from Gorgari. Upon arrival at court, he is made a member of the Round Table and is henceforth known as the Roi des Cent Chevaliers (#8).

Lineage is one of the cohesive elements of romance in general and it serves as such in Chrétien's *Perceval* and most of the Continuations, as knights encounter their own sons, brothers, sisters, uncles and aunts, and as new acquaintances are revealed as being related to old ones (Salmeri 1984, 127–35). Examples are too numerous to cite, but the next damsel Gauvain encounters on his way to fight Kay is a niece of Silimac, who still blames Gauvain and Guinevere for the death of her uncle; she is disabused of the notion by her aunt, now said to be called the Sore Pucelle, and Silimac is revealed as the lord of the Chastel de la Roche (#9). Gauvain proceeds to Arthur's court, where he defeats Kay, staining with the latter's blood a banner previously given to him by the Sore Pucelle; Kay is spared only after Arthur pleads with the Sore Pucelle. Gauvain departs for further unspecified adventures (#10) and two months later encounters his brother Agravain, who reassures him that Kay has recovered from his wound. No one, including Agravain, was able to identify Kay's accuser and vanquisher. A week after defeating a band of five knights, Gauvain and Agravain return to Arthur's court. The narrator now turns again to Perceval (#11).

Perceval survives an attack by the Devil in the Chapel of the Black Hand and learns from a hermit that Queen Branguemore, who had originally had the chapel built, is buried in the adjacent cemetery, where he and Perceval bury the now charred body that had lain on the altar. By ensuring that no one was killed by the Black Hand that day, Perceval had brought the 'avanture' to an end; the priest urges Perceval to do penance and save his soul (#12). This episode is in many ways representative of Manessier's work: while it relates to adventures from the First and Second Continuations, and bears the mark of their own *merveilleux*, its open revelation of the Devil, the priest's urgings and the general monastic setting lend it a more contemporary aspect, showing clearly the influence of texts such as the *Queste*. More diabolical temptations follow: a black horse, which appears when Perceval is robbed of his own horse, plunges into a river when he makes the sign of the cross; a false Blanchefleur disappears into thin air as he is reminded by the hilt of his sword to cross himself. An old man in a boat reveals the devilish nature of the manifestations and gives Perceval a white horse on which to continue his adventures (#13). These last two episodes both take place in an apocalyptic atmosphere of fire, rain, thunder and lightning.

Perceval defeats the Knight of Lindesores (#14) before rescuing the *amie* of Dodinel le Sauvage from a would-be abductor; both vanquished opponents are sent to Arthur's court. A damsel arrives with the news that Blanchefleur is being harassed by Aridés d'Escavalon, thus obligating Perceval to go to her aid; he will rejoin Arthur's court at Pentecost (#15). En route, Perceval visits a smith in order to have a nail extracted from his horse's foot. The smith turns out to be Tribüet, who promises to mend Perceval's broken sword (#16). Perceval defeats Aridés, who refuses to surrender either to Blanchefleur or Tribüet but agrees to give himself up to Arthur. Perceval leaves Blanchefleur in order to reach Arthur's court by Pentecost (#17). Perceval's sword is mended symbolically in a sequence of episodes which rejoins Manessier's text to that of Chrétien and the earlier Continuations, not only through the figures of Blanchefleur and Tribüet, but also through Aridés's refusal to surrender to Blanchefleur or Tribüet. This clearly re-uses the motif from sections of Chrétien's romance where Enguigeron and Clamadeu in quick succession refuse to surrender to Blanchefleur or Gornemant de Goort before making their way to Arthur. The various prisoners indeed arrive at Arthur's court one after the other, bringing news of Perceval and his prowess in defeating each of them; all are made members of the Round Table (#18). Partly as a result of Perceval's remonstrations and partly because he has himself been wounded, the Biau Mauvais becomes valiant and helps Perceval prevent two maidens from being cast on a pyre (#19).

Perceval's failure to return to Camelot, as promised at Pentecost, provokes the departure of twenty-five knights in search of him (#20). This multiple quest is the framework into which Manessier introduces the story of Bohort and Lionel, which appears in a recognizably similar form in the *Queste* (##21, 23–4), although it is here devoid of the detailed allegorical significance attributed to it there. Nevertheless, shared elements, such as the Devil disguised as a saintly hermit and a direct intervention by the voice of God, strongly suggest a close connection between the two versions. It is not exactly clear whether *La Queste del Saint Graal* influenced Manessier (in my view the more likely possibility, cf. also Corley 1986) or vice versa, or whether both are derived from a common source. In any event, the two versions present the potential for interesting comparisons. Another feature shared by the prose romances and the series of Continuations, which in manuscripts *T* and *V* also contain Gerbert de Montreuil, is an encyclopaedic tendency, a visible desire on the part of authors, manuscript planners, and presumably audiences, to have something resembling a *summa arthuriana*. While the Grail compilations do not go quite that far, the tenuous relationship of some parts of Manessier and Gerbert in particular to the Grail theme and the obvious 'newness' of some of the material (compared with, say, much of the First Continuation) do illustrate the process of accretion which characterizes much later Arthurian romance.

The performance of Perceval and the Biau Mauvais at a tournament organized by King Baudemagus underlines Perceval's present status as a hero in the ascendant. The Biau Mauvais will henceforth be known as the Biau Hardi. He and Perceval separate, but will meet again at Arthur's court at Pentecost (#25). The encounter between Perceval and Hector, in which the near-fatal wounds they inflict on each other in an incognito combat are cured only by a vision of the Holy Grail borne by an angel (#26), is likewise related in the prose *Lancelot* and once more shows the assimilation of later prose and verse romance. Any study of the Bohort–Lionel episodes and the *Queste* should consider these analogues also.

Before arriving at the Fisher King's castle, Perceval defeats and kills the unrepentant Partinal, murderer of the Fisher King's brother, Goondesert (#27). Perceval takes Partinal's head to the Fisher King who, miraculously cured, has it impaled on a stake and displayed atop a tower. After the Grail, Lance and *tailleor* have passed before them three times during their meal, Perceval and the Fisher King discuss their family relationships: Perceval's mother was the king's sister and they are therefore uncle and nephew. Perceval refuses to accept the Fisher King's crown and lands while the king is alive and departs for Arthur's court (#28). This appears as a false climax, for, although Perceval seems to have achieved all his goals and quests, especially healing the Fisher King, the resolution of the romance is postponed briefly while he carries out the promise to be at Arthur's court at Pentecost. Essentially, this is little more than a tying up of loose ends, a farewell to the world before Perceval takes over at Corbenic.

Perceval's impending arrival at Arthur's court at Pentecost is announced the preceding day by six defeated opponents, Salandre des Isles and his five sons. Wearing the Fisher King's black armour, Perceval finally arrives to great rejoicing and all the knights relate their recent adventures. The Bohort–Lionel conflict, the death of Calogrenant and various adventures of Perceval are described in some detail, constituting the last of the many narrative summaries found throughout the course of the Continuations. Arthur has the adventures written down and sealed in an 'aumaire' (*library*) in Salisbury. After eight days of celebrations, a damsel arrives with letters announcing the death of the Fisher King and summoning Perceval to be crowned his successor at Corbenic (#29). In Arthur's presence, Perceval is crowned on All Saints' Day, and all witness the procession of Grail, Lance and *tailleor* every day for a month and a day. Arthur and his company then depart, leaving Perceval to reign in peace for seven years, after which he withdraws to a hermitage in the forest, leaving his kingdom to King Maronne, who had married the daughter of the Fisher King. The Grail, Lance and *tailleor* follow Perceval to the hermitage, where he becomes successively acolyte, subdeacon, deacon and priest. At his death on Candlemas Eve, ten years after entering the hermitage, he is received into Heaven with the Grail, Lance and *tailleor*, none of which is ever seen again by a living person. Perceval is buried beside the Fisher King (#30). Manessier concludes by a dedication to Jeanne de Flandre, indicating where he took over (at the moment of the joining of the sword) and claiming Arthur's book in Salisbury as his source.

Manessier's closure of the tale is quasi-definitive, as the objective of the quest is achieved and the objects symbolizing it removed to Heaven. Corbenic has been desacralized with Perceval's departure to the hermitage and the accession of Maronne. Although there are, as I have suggested, similarities between Manessier's Continuation and the *Lancelot–Grail* Cycle, the closure of the Grail romance by Manessier does not appear to have the kind of ramifications for the Arthurian world that the *Queste* has in the latter. Here, there is no Armageddon, no implication that Arthurian chivalry has been discredited or that the post-Grail world falls into internecine strife and anarchy. If Manessier is drawing on the prose cycle, he is rewriting it with a view to rehabilitating the values of knighthood by showing them to be in the service of the spiritual rather than at odds with it. This view of Arthurian adventure is reflected by the preservation of Arthur's book in the cathedral city of Salisbury, sanctifying the secular at the same time as the book becomes identified with the manuscripts preserving the Continuations themselves and their sources. Romance is indeed the 'secular scripture'.

Gerbert de Montreuil's Continuation

The nature of Manessier's conclusion meant that any further expansion of the Continuations had to be by means of interpolation, rather than extension of the narrative. While it might have been possible simply to have claimed that he was telling after the event what the three earlier continuators had left unsaid, Gerbert de Montreuil's strategy (or that of an early scribe) is to insert his Continuation between the Second Continuation and that of Manessier, bringing the length of the compilation in manuscript *T* (BNF, fr. 12576) to over 75,000 lines; *V* (BNF, nouv. acq. fr. 6614) is fragmentary.[23] The associations of Wauchier de Denain, Manessier and Gerbert de Montreuil with Flanders and the north-east, combined with Chrétien's original dedication to Philippe de Flandre, make of *Perceval* and the Continuations a strongly regional work, reflecting the extraordinary cultural and literary life of this area throughout the Middle Ages. Manuscripts *T* and *V* are also markedly north-eastern, copied by the same scribe, probably in or around Arras in the 1270s or shortly thereafter.

Like Wauchier de Denain, Gerbert de Montreuil is recognized as the author of other works, in his case primarily the *Roman de la Violette*, dedicated to Marie de Ponthieu (1199–1250, m. Simon II de Dammartin *c*.1212). Manessier, too, judging from his dedication to Jeanne de Flandre (d. 1244, r. 1214–27 during the imprisonment of her husband, Ferrand of Portugal), was a professional poet working in the setting of a court. It is therefore clear that the cultural context of at least four parts of the compilation (Chrétien's *Perceval*, the Second Continuation and those of Manessier and Gerbert) is strictly central rather than peripheral in any sense. We know of no other work by Manessier, but if Wauchier's other known works are hagiographical in nature, Gerbert's *Roman de la Violette* is in the mainstream of courtly narrative, exhibiting also direct knowledge of the lyric tradition. Indeed, Gerbert's Continuation is probably more conventional than any of the others and shows an even stronger tendency than Manessier to incorporate material from outside the immediate context of the Grail Quest. It differs, however, in the strongly moralizing tone found in many of its episodes, which resembles that of, say, the Vulgate *Queste*. Gerbert's Continuation dates from *c*.1225–30, not much later than Manessier, and is more or less contemporary with the *Roman de la Violette*.[24]

Gerbert's Continuation is interpolated at Second Continuation 32594 and the transition back to Manessier is effected by the repetition of the last fourteen lines of the Second Continuation (32581–94). As with the other Continuations, there are clear attempts to recall Chrétien and other parts of the compilation, as well as to incorporate apparently extraneous matter as a means of expanding the narrative.[25] Stephens (1996) has also argued that Gerbert is responding to what he perceives as deficiencies or lacks in Manessier. Gerbert begins at the point when Perceval has just failed to rejoin perfectly the two parts of the broken sword, but has just been offered the lordship of his castle by the Fisher King (Second Continuation, #35). Perceval's failure is now attributed fairly and squarely to his sins (including that relating to his mother's death) and a heavenly voice instructs him to return to his maternal home; he wakes up the next morning far from the castle. Unable to enter a garden surrounded by a black and white wall, Perceval strikes the door with his sword, breaking the latter in two once more. An old man tells Perceval that he will never enter the earthly paradise (and through it the celestial one) or discover the truth about the Grail, until his sword is mended by the smith who made it. The old man gives Perceval a letter which restores the sanity of those upon whose head it is placed (1–286, #1); Perceval hangs it around his neck (Sturm-Maddox 1994). When he looks back, the garden has disappeared, just as the Grail Castle had done. Perceval is hailed as a saviour at Cotoatre, home of Tribüet the Smith, where he nevertheless has to resist sexual temptation in the person of a damsel named Escolasse. After killing two serpents, he meets the smith who indeed restores the sword to its original condition

(287–909, #2). Perceval liberates two damsels from Sagremor and Agravain, who have both become insane after visiting the Mont Dolerous. The letter brings the pair to their senses, and all five proceed to the house of Gaudin au Blanc Escu, where they stay the night (910–1187, #3).

A number of features call for comment here, particularly as they are of significance generally in Gerbert. The most obvious, perhaps, is the persistence of the need of continuators to join their text to Chrétien's romance and to the other Continuations (here through the themes of his mother's house, Tribüet and the sword, and the Mont Dolerous). Secondly, Gerbert emphasizes the nature and importance of Peceval's sin, although his restoration to prosperity of the Fisher King's country implies that his ultimate success is practically a foregone conclusion. In this case, the continuation can best be seen as an extended examination of the function of knighthood in general, and Perceval's embodiment of, and transcendence of, this function (Sturm-Maddox 1992). The emphasis on repair and restoration may be seen as a metaphor for the progress of the narrative, towards the making whole of an unfinished text, as Leupin (1982, but cf. Larmat 1974) has suggested may be the case of the broken sword and its text in other Continuations. We might extend this kind of reading to include the healing letter, suggestive of the power of the written word to restore reason and humanity.

Perceval's election is confirmed by his visit to Arthur's court and by his successful attempt to sit in the Siège Périlleux (Perilous Seat), a motif best known from the prose romances, where the seat is destined for Galahad. Perceval's success also liberates the six knights who had previously attempted to sit in the chair, and who had been swallowed up by the earth. The episode is the occasion for yet another narrative recapitulation, as Perceval tells Arthur about his two visits to the Fisher King and rejoins Chrétien's romance through the reminder of Kay's broken arm and collarbone; there is furthermore a direct allusion to *Erec*, perhaps reminding audiences that Chrétien's Grail romance is as much part of an *œuvre*, as it is the first text of the verse Grail compilations (1188–1612, #4). Another figure from Chrétien's romance, Perceval's female cousin, here called Ysmaine, now reappears, seeking him, in the hope that he might help her make her false lover Faradïen keep his promise and marry her; incognito, Perceval does so before sending the pair to Arthur's court (1613–2482, #5). The sign of the cross reveals that a damsel claiming to be the daughter of the Fisher King and to be in love with Perceval is a diabolical temptation (2483–2586, #6).

A series of episodes follows in which Perceval once again meets in turn his sister, his Hermit Uncle, Gornemant de Goort and Blanchefleur; all episodes draw the narrative back into the close orbit of Chrétien's romance. In the midst of this sequence, however, is interpolated the long episode usually known as 'Tristan menestrel' (3248–4832, the last part of #9). Through verbal similarities between his text and Chrétien's, Gerbert provides a reminder of the latter's opening scenes essentially through Perceval's eyes, but Perceval resolves to remove his sister from the forest, despite its apparent prosperity (2587–731, #7). Together with his sister, Perceval visits his mother's grave and his Hermit Uncle, who delivers a sermon on the duties of a Christian knight (2732–95, #8). Next day, Perceval continues his quest for the Grail and the Lance, taking his sister with him. He defeats Mordred, who attempts to carry off his sister, and sends him back to Arthur's court. The description of the Castle of Maidens shows a detailed knowledge of episode 20 of the Second Continuation, and Perceval continues to relive his childhood by informing the lady of the castle how his mother used to call him 'biaus fieus' and he called her 'mere'. It is not clear when the Fisher King told Perceval that his father's name was Gales li Chaus (3072–73), but this episode is the occasion of further revelations about his lineage: the lady of the castle reveals that she is his mother's cousin, and that his mother was called Philosofine (3181). The two cousins had brought the Grail from over the sea, but it had been taken by angels for safe-keeping to the Fisher King; one of the maidens tells Perceval that their lady is 'dame sainte Ysabiaus' (3243). In a sense, Gerbert is here 'demystifying' Chrétien's text, although the revelations are almost as mysterious as the enigmas themselves.

There follows the episode of 'Tristan menestrel', which draws into the context of a Grail romance material that is fundamentally extraneous and originally non-Arthurian, although contemporaneous; the integration of the Tristan story into the Arthurian world is being realized elsewhere, notably in the Prose *Tristan*. Although 'Tristan menestrel' is usually referred to as an interpolation, it is in fact quite well integrated into the Continuation. During the festivities which follow Mordred's return to court, a knight arrives and challenges the company; he defeats Girflet, Lancelot and Yvain before being recognized as Tristan during his joust with Gauvain. Together with a group of Arthur's knights, they visit Cornwall disguised as minstrels and Tristan reveals himself to Yseut, with whom he is reunited. They help Mark in a tournament against the Roi des Cent Chevaliers, during which Perceval appears, exhausted but still able to defeat the mocking Kay, and then Agravain, Cligés, Lancelot and Tristan. He helps Gauvain and Yvain to convince Mark to forgive Tristan, who remains in Cornwall. Gauvain leaves to rescue the damsel of Montescleire while Perceval continues on his Grail Quest (2796–4868, #9). 'Tristan menestrel' is itself something of an intertextual performance and its integration into the Continuation extends the ramifications of its narrative beyond the traditional boundaries of the Tristan matter (Busby 1983; Kjær 1990; see chapter III).

In an extraordinary metamorphosis, Gornemant de Goort, at whose castle Perceval now arrives, is transformed into an avatar of the Fisher King ('je n'ai pooir de mon cors', *I have no power over my body*, 5054), and his country is transformed into a waste land which Perceval liberates from the persistent attacks by hordes of devil-knights sent by the Roi de la Gaste Cité. He obtains two casks containing a miraculous balm, with which he resuscitates Gornemant's four sons, mortally injured during the attacks (4869–6031, #10). Gornemant and his sons accompany Perceval on his visit to Blanchefleur's castle of Beaurepaire, which is now flourishing, in contrast to the lamentable state it was in when Chrétien described it. Perceval marries Blanchefleur in order to avoid further temptations of the flesh, but their love is not consummated, as both agree that virginity is the supreme condition, which they should maintain (6032–6244 and 6245–7014, ##11–12). Gerbert names himself here (6358, 6998, 7001, 7008, 7016), tells us that Chrétien died before completing his romance (6984–7) and claims to have related the adventures 'selonc la vraie estoire' (*according to the true story*, 7001) contained in a book.

Perceval leaves Blanchefleur in order to resume his Grail Quest and frees Rohais from the clutches of her abductor, Dragoniaus li Cruels, whom he sends to Carduel. He accompanies Rohais back to where her *ami* Arguisiaus de Carhais is lying wounded, but is unable to heal him because he had forgotten the two casks of balm; the pair are advised to go to Beaurepaire to ask Blanchefleur to administer the remedy. Perceval frees Semiramin from Parsamant and four of his followers, and reunites him with his *amie* Roseamonde de Nobles Vals, before coming to a cross, where a letter tells him that the road on the right leads to the safety of Durecestre whereas that on the left is 'la Voie Aventureuse' (8263). Perceval chooses the latter and immediately encounters two knights covered in burns (7015–8331, #13). Near another cross being struck by two hermits, Perceval witnesses the Beste Glatissant devoured by its fawns (Bozoky 1974; Roussel 1983); in a hermitage he successfully passes a test preliminary to the Grail by removing a white shield with a red cross (containing a fragment of the True Cross) from around the neck of a damsel. The Hermit King gives Perceval allegorical explanations of the cross and the Beste Glatissant, but Perceval forgets to ask about the shield (8332–8905, #14). The shield protects Perceval from its fire-spitting counterpart belonging to the Chevalier au Dragon, who is besieging the Pucele au Cercle d'Or in Montesclaire (Larmat 1979). Perceval defeats him, thereby also avenging the death of the *ami* of Claire, the Pucele as Dras Envers, also known as the Pucele au Char; during the struggle, however, a maiden absconds with Perceval's shield. It is characteristic of Gerbert's Continuation that rather than behead his defeated opponent, Perceval delivers to him a stern sermon on repentance before giving him the opportunity to make a deathbed confession to a priest. This moralizing tone, achieved largely through lengthy digressions on good and evil, the respective duties of knights and priests, sin and repentance, bring Gerbert's Continuation into the orbit of the *Queste*, while frequent links back to Chrétien and the other Continuations assure its foundation in the verse compilation. Other intertextual links may suggest that Gerbert also knew *Perlesvaus* (8906–10148, #15; see Saly 1998).

In the chapel of an abbey, a priest celebrates Mass and offers the host to a wounded king. A monk tells Perceval the story of Evalac's conversion by Joseph of Arimathea and baptism as Mordrain. Joseph was guardian of the Grail, Philosofine (Perceval's mother) of the *tailleor*, and an unnamed lady of the Lance. The pagan King Crudel imprisoned all three until Mordrain liberated them, killing Crudel in the process. Mordrain, however, is too eager to approach the Grail and is punished for his temerity; he is the wounded knight in the chapel and has been there for 300 years. Perceval has to leave before he learns whether he has healed Mordrain (10149–613, #16). Gerbert is here probably rewriting material from *L'Estoire del Saint Graal* and the *Queste*, which both contain the Evalach–Mordrain story, although the knight in question there, of course, is Galahad; Mordrain is clearly a double of the Fisher King.

Gerbert now takes up a long-forgotten thread from Chrétien's *Perceval*. If one constituent of the poetics of continuation is the completion of interrupted adventures, another is the narrative capital to be made by the retrospective motivation of the unexplained. Chrétien's art of mystification, or the poetics of early romance, does not require explanation of the Chevalier Vermeil's aggressive behaviour at Arthur's court, but that is precisely what Gerbert now provides. Perceval arrives unknowingly at the castle belonging to the Chevalier Vermeil's daughter and four sons (Leander, Evander, Enardus and Meliadas). An ivory coffin which has arrived drawn by a swan is opened by Perceval and contains the corpse of the Chevalier Vermeil and a letter claiming that only the murderer could have opened it. After a lengthy and interrupted combat with Leander, in which he uses their young nephew as a human shield, Perceval is assaulted by the four wicked knights who had originally urged the Chevalier Vermeil to claim Arthur's lands; Perceval defeats them with the help of a minstrel and they are thrown into prison and executed the next day. Recognizing that Perceval was not entirely responsible for their father's death, the brothers forgive him and release their prisoners, including Gauvain. The latter will go to Montesclaire to liberate the damsel and Perceval will continue his quest for the Grail and the Lance. The tale now leaves Perceval and turns to an adventure of Gauvain (10614–12380, #17).

In addition to maintaining the alternation of heroes, this particular adventure provides a shocking contrast with the edifying nature of Perceval's ascent towards moral and spiritual perfection. Bloeisine, the daughter of Urpin, welcomes Gauvain with open arms, but intends to kill him with a knife concealed under her pillow because he had killed one of her brothers, Brun de l'Essart. Gauvain is attacked in turn by the girl's cousins and brothers, who refuse his offer to go into exile for three years to atone for the murder. Unwittingly, Gauvain arrives at Urpin's castle, where he is obliged by a custom of the house to relate truthfully his recent adventures. Bloiesine, who is now in love with Gauvain, takes him into her 'prison' for the night, and the next morning she lets herself be used as a human shield to help him escape. Gauvain wins the subsequent combat with Urpin, whom he spares at Bloeisine's request. That evening Gauvain learns from the Pucele as Dras Envers that Perceval has lifted the siege of Montesclaire, and the next day he is met by Arthur and 4,000 of his knights and their ladies, who had come to free Gauvain from Urpin's prison. The tale now returns to Perceval (12381–14078, #18).

After listening to another sermon from another hermit, Perceval is deceived into freeing a demon in the form of a serpent from beneath a tombstone, to where it returns after having laid waste a city and the surrounding land (14078–571, #19). Perceval now encounters and defeats the melancholic Lugarel, whose *amie* had been killed while he was out hunting. Lugarel is spared at the request of a damsel, who disappears as suddenly as she had arrived. A dishevelled and naked damsel, up to her neck in water, tells Perceval that her *ami* has punished her thus for claiming that Perceval was a better knight than he. Perceval defeats and kills the knight Brandin Dur Cuer, and frees the damsel Dyonise de Galoee, but abandons her after she unsuccessfully incites a *vallet* to kill him (14572–15267, #20). Underlining the theme of deceitful women, Perceval is drawn into an ambush by Felisse de la Blanclose, but defeats a band of brigands before destroying their lair. He receives hospitality first from a couple who had been harassed by the brigands and then from two hermits, one of whom delivers the obligatory sermon before he departs. Perceval's next encounter is with Madiex, Cil a le Cote Maltaillie, whom he defeats and sends to surrender to Arthur. The next day he meets the brother of a giant he had killed earlier and dispatches him with his spear (recalling the death of the Chevalier Vermeil). Madiex arrives at court, where news of Perceval prompts many knights to leave in search of him. Perceval defeats Kay and Goullains li Chaus before continuing his quest for the Grail, *tailleor* and Lance. The narrative switches between Perceval and Madiex are also effected by narrative formulae in a first-person narrator's voice which usually refers to 'li contes' (15268–16855, #21).

Perceval falls asleep on his horse. After he has woken up, a wooden hand attached to a cross indicates which of three paths he is to follow. The path leads him to his final destination, where the Fisher King inquires where he had stayed the night before. Perceval also tells him of the knight in the chapel, the serpent which came out of the tomb and the child in the tree, the significance of which is still unclear to him. He now witnesses the Grail procession, including the Grail, Lance and a broken sword, the pieces of which he succeeds in joining. The Fisher King pronounces Perceval worthy to learn the truth about all these matters and Perceval can hardly refrain from bursting into song (16856–17086, #22). At this point, manuscripts *T* and *V* repeat the last fourteen lines of the Second Continuation before proceeding with Manessier. The conclusion to Perceval's adventures and the romance is thus illusory, for it is deferred for over 10,000 lines.

Conclusion

In a sense, Chrétien's *Perceval* and its four Continuations are so many articulations of the coexistence, the conflicts and the interrelationship between the secular and the spiritual, and between chivalry and theology, the former in the service of the latter, but ultimately and always subservient to it. This might be the basic theme of the compilation, if it is necessary to seek one, and the later texts, particularly Gerbert, and some episodes interpolated into the Mixed and Long Redactions of the First Continuation are relatively explicit doctrinally. The first two Continuations, however, seem to follow Chrétien in retaining and even propagating a kind of curious ineffability, informed by both the *merveilleux arthurien* and the *merveilleux chrétien*. Structurally, although all of the continuators demonstrate a concern with anchoring their own contribution in the Grail romance as a whole, the kind of analysis that is possible for Chrétien's earlier romances, and even to some degree for *Perceval*, is of doubtful value. Something similar may be true of the kind of ethical and moral concerns on which Chrétien's romances are centred: although we may evaluate the protagonists' behaviour to some degree, the conflict between love, marriage and knighthood does not seem to be a basic concern of the continuators. Such issues may have been regarded as already explored by Chrétien and superseded by the basic question of how Perceval is to prepare himself spiritually to succeed in his Grail quest. Manessier and Gerbert do, however, explore the nature of knighthood and its function in a Christian society. Although Gerbert especially takes pains to stress Perceval's frustrated preoccupation with the Grail quest, it is difficult not to feel that the continuators are more often than not caught up in the joy of story-telling, paradoxically pressured by that same lack of closure which assures the furtherance of the text.

To date, modern scholarship on the Continuations has concentrated largely on issues of character presentation, narrative structure, sources and relationships between the different parts of the compilation and other Arthurian romances. It has not been particularly prolific and is consequently an area offering a good deal of potential. It has been necessary to provide long narrative summaries of the texts here because they are still relatively neglected. If the rehabilitation or legitimacy of the *Lancelot–Grail* and the post-Chrétien epigonal romances as objects of study has been established in recent decades, the same cannot be said of the Continuations. Now that we are beginning to understand better the mechanics of medieval narrative composition and the transmission of texts in manuscript, and to read them on their own terms rather than by the received norms of modern scholarship, a re-examination of the corpus of continuations of Chrétien's *Perceval* could prove extraordinarily fruitful. **[KB]**

Robert de Boron (the *Estoire dou Graal, Merlin* and the *Didot-Perceval*)

Two works by Robert de Boron systematically and creatively amplify brief secondary narrative accounts sown throughout Chrétien's *Perceval*: the verse *Estoire dou Graal* (edited by Nitze in 1927 and by O'Gorman in 1995) and *Merlin* (edited by Nitze in 1927). Both works are preserved in a single manuscript, *R* (Paris, BNF, fr. 20047) and both were put into prose very early as *Joseph d'Arimathie* (edited by O'Gorman in 1995) and *Merlin* (edited by Micha in 1979).[26] Robert's narratives link Grail history and Perceval's genealogy to biblical and to British history (Pickens 1988, 20–4) and include references to Perceval's genealogy (*Perceval*, 408–88, 3507–33, 3583–3611, 4646–83, 6392–6431), accounts of sacred history (*Perceval*, 567–94, 6253–6300) and stories relating to Uther Pendragon, Ygerne and her daughter who is Gauvain's mother (*Perceval*, 442–50, 8721–63). Another work attributed to Robert de Boron represents an effort to complete Chrétien's *Perceval*: the *Didot-Perceval* (Roach edn).[27] This romance rewrites Chrétien's text as a necessary complement to the *Joseph* and *Merlin* by incorporating material from the Second Continuation and from Wace's *Brut* (Roach edn, 33–125; Pickens 1988; 1984, 500–9). The *Joseph, Merlin* and the *Didot-Perceval* constitute a prose trilogy which, despite its problematic history of transmission and transformation, scholars tend to agree in attributing to Robert de Boron, at least in its inception.[28]

Robert de Boron, who wrote at the turn of the thirteenth century in the borderland between Imperial Burgundy and the Franche-Comté, is arguably the most important of the epigonal writers of French romance following Chrétien de Troyes (Becker 1935; Hoepffner 1951; 1956; Micha 1980, 215–28; Pickens 1988). The *mises en prose* of the two works ascribed to him with certainty were executed shortly after 1200. The *Joseph d'Arimathie* and the prose *Merlin*, along with their verse antecedents, constitute what is known as the Little Grail Cycle or the Robert de Boron Cycle, which in two manuscripts is augmented by the *Didot-Perceval*. This cycle is significant if for no other reason than that it turns Chrétien de Troyes's ambiguous grail into the Holy Grail, as Christ's wine cup of the Last Supper, in which Joseph of Arimathea and Nicodemus collected Christ's blood, and because it documents the translation of the Grail from the Orient to Britain in a westward migration paralleling the *translatio imperii* from Troy to Britain (Gowans 1996), documented in Geoffrey of Monmouth's *Historia Regum Britanniae* (Wright edn) and, more to the point, Wace's *Brut* (Arnold edn). Furthermore, just as British history is construed as being a modern continuation of Trojan history, as opposed to that of Continental kingdoms which derive their power from Rome, so, through the Grail, British history also has a privileged connection with the history of human redemption.

Also of prime importance is the fact that, for the first time, Robert introduces into the biography of King Arthur a highly developed Merlin (Tolstoy 1985, 1–20; Walter 2000, 15–30), a wizard divinely inspired, yet full of mischief, who pursues specific missions ordained by God, whereas in Wace, as in Geoffrey of Monmouth, a more one-dimensional seer, having served the three sons of King Constant, disappears from history with Arthur's conception. Robert's Merlin promotes the cause of the Grail by laying claim to the infant Arthur, arranging for his upbringing and setting the stage for the revelation of his kingship. Unlike Wace, who, following Geoffrey of Monmouth, evinces little interest in Merlin's origins, Robert confronts his diabolical parentage and unambiguously portrays him as God's instrument in the blending of British history with that of the New Testament and the early Church. Robert's Merlin, moreover, produces the book in which that conjunction is recorded, the *Estoire dou Graal* (*History of the Grail*), the source which Robert purportedly translates and which Merlin dictates to his priestly scribe Blaise. That Robert's work is as potent as Chrétien's unfinished *Perceval* in generating continuations and rewritings is demonstrated in the fact that the *Estoire* and *Merlin*, or rather their *mises en prose*, are the bases from which derive the two introductory romances of that immense thirteenth-century compendium, the *Lancelot–Grail* or Vulgate Cycle (see chapter VII), which in turn stands as the progenitor of nearly all subsequent texts that treat the Arthurian matter (Kibler 1994*). Robert's *Merlin* itself generates continuations, e.g. that in the Huth *Merlin*[29] which pertains to the Post-Vulgate Cycle (see Bogdanow, chapter IX), but most especially the vast Continuation, found in the great cyclical manuscripts (Sommer edn, II, 88–466), upon which depends the prose *Lancelot*, and, in fact, the rest of the Vulgate Cycle (see Pickens, chapter VII).

L'Estoire dou Graal

Prologue. The *Estoire* opens *ex abrupto* with two accounts of biblical history. One focuses on prophecies of Christ's sufferings. Its amplification enumerates Old Testament figures in hell awaiting Christ's Incarnation, narrates the Virgin Mary's Immaculate Conception and her life, and concludes with Christ's conception, birth and ministry (#1: 1–192 – line numbers following an episodic division refer to the verse *Estoire* in O'Gorman edn).

Joseph of Arimathea and the Grail. Extra-biblical material directly related to the Grail is insinuated into sacred history in a recapitulation of Christ's ministry. A follower of Christ, Joseph, is a knight in Pilate's service. Meanwhile, Judas's jealousy and greed alienate him from his companions and he conspires with

Caiaphas to betray Jesus. After the Jews arrest Jesus, Joseph stays behind and discovers the vessel 'ou Criz feisoit son sacrement' (*in which Christ made his sacrament*, 396). Jesus is delivered to Pilate for trial. Pilate finds him innocent, but finally yields to demands to condemn and crucify him. Joseph asks Pilate for the body and receives it in payment for his service. As he and Nicodemus prepare it for burial, Joseph collects the blood in the vessel (#2: 193–592). When their arrest is ordered, Nicodemus flees, but Joseph is imprisoned. Christ visits him and brings him the vessel for comfort. He must keep it and then entrust it to three others, one for each Person of the Trinity. It is a means of salvation and Joseph will be remembered whenever a sacrament is performed with it. The Last Supper is the prototype for the Mass and the service of the vessel. Robert's narrator discusses his source (929–36) and associates Joseph's vessel with the Grail (#3: 593–960). Meanwhile, Vespasian, son of the emperor Titus, is struck with leprosy (in Robert the names of father and son are reversed). A pilgrim saw Christ heal the sick; perhaps an object owned by him could cure Vespasian. Titus sends messengers to Pilate; they persuade Veronica to give them her veil with its imprint of Jesus's face, and it heals Vespasian. Vespasian and Titus travel to Judaea to avenge Jesus's death. Vespasian finds Joseph in prison and liberates him. Only Jews who convert are saved from retribution (#4: 961–2306). Joseph departs for faraway lands with all his kin, including his sister Enygeus and her husband Bron (Hebron). Their community prospers, but then suffers famine because some are guilty of lust. Christ tells Joseph how to discover which are the sinners by inviting the community to the Grail table. Some sit, leaving an empty place representing Judas's seat at the Last Supper; they are filled with grace. The sinners remain standing, feeling nothing. As they leave in shame, they ask the vessel's name. It is called the Grail because it gives pleasure (*agree*, 2661) to those who see it, like the delight a fish feels when it slips from the hand that has caught it and swims away. Henceforth the Grail service will take place daily at the hour of terce. Robert names his work *L'Estoire dou Graal* (2684) because it tells the truth about the Grail. Moÿse asks to join the elect. [Joseph prays to know Moÿse's true nature. Christ instructs Joseph to invite him to sit at the Grail table. He takes the empty seat and instantly plunges into a chasm.][30] The Holy Spirit tells Joseph that Moÿse tricked the elect and fell into hell (#5: 2307–2842).

Bron and the westward Migration. Joseph instructs Bron and Enygeus's twelve sons in God's service. Eleven take wives. The twelfth, Alain, does not marry and becomes Joseph's disciple and leader of the others. The Holy Spirit commands Joseph to teach him the Grail's history and service: Alain's son will become Grail-keeper. Alain must lead his brothers and sisters-in-law westward as far as they can go and exalt God's name throughout the land. Thus the Grail is associated with the evangelization of Britain. The following day the elect will see a light that will bring them a letter for Petrus, who is destined to go westward to the

Vales of Avalon. There he must await Alain's son to learn Moÿse's fate. Robert names himself; his book abbreviates the story (3155–64). The light appears at the next Grail service and the letter is given to Petrus, who departs. Bron invests Alain with lordship over the elect and they migrate to foreign lands where Alain preaches. Joseph entrusts the vessel and teaches the Grail's secrets to Bron, who catches fish used in the Grail service, and therefore must be known as the Rich Fisher. He must await his grandson and give him the Grail. Petrus and Bron leave and Joseph dies in the land of his birth (#6: 2843–3460).

Epilogue. Robert projects four narrative branches ('parts') that derive from the *Estoire dou Graal*, which he is the first to write about. They concern Alain, Petrus, Moÿse and Bron,[31] and he hopes to bring them together in one account if he can find the proper sources, but a fifth branch must be told first, upon which depends the meaning of the other four (#7: 3461–3514). The *Merlin* follows in *R* without interruption.

Merlin

Merlin's conception and early childhood. Satan and his devils scheme to spawn a man in his image to counter Christ's redemption. A woman gives a devil control over all she and her husband possess. He kills their livestock and their son, and provokes her to hang herself; her husband dies of grief, leaving three daughters. The youngest is seduced at the devil's behest and buried alive for her sin. When a worthy priest (Blaise) comforts her sisters, the devil seeks to destroy them. The younger sister sinks into debauchery (the verse text in *R* ends here, line 504, due to the loss of the remaining gatherings), but the elder, whose piety is strengthened, is violated by an incubus as she sleeps. She confesses to the priest that she may have been deflowered by a devil (#1: 1–504, §4, 31–§7).[32] She is brought to justice and is locked in a tower to await her child's birth and her punishment. When Merlin is born, he possesses a devil's natural knowledge of things past and present, but God also endows him with knowledge of the future (#2: §§8–11). Court is convened and the mother's sentence is pronounced, but the child Merlin proves her innocence and recounts the true story of his conception and the grace he enjoys. He has the judge and other witnesses tell their stories to Blaise, who will henceforth serve as Merlin's scribe. Merlin dictates the events of the *Estoire* and his own early life. He also foretells events connected with Vortigern's tower and the composition of Blaise's book (#3: §§12–16, see #5 below).

Merlin's entry into pre-Arthurian history. King Constant is succeeded by his weak son, Moine, who is attacked and routed by pagan Saxons. Moine's men treat with his seneschal, Vortigern, who is declared king after they kill Moine, whose brothers, Pendragon and Uther, flee to the Continent. When the people revolt, Vortigern enlists Saxons to quell the uprising. He marries the sister of the Saxon leader Hengist (#4: §17–§19, 19). Vortigern builds a defensive tower that keeps collapsing. His clerks consult the stars and find no cause, but read that a fatherless boy will succeed. They trick Vortigern into sending messengers to kill him. Merlin makes his identity known to two messengers and gains their confidence by demonstrations of clairvoyance. He sends Blaise to Northumberland to finish his work. Eventually, he will show him the Grail, in the place where Joseph's descendants have gone; Blaise's book will be called *Li Livres dou Graal*. Taking leave of his mother, Merlin goes to the king. He exposes the clerks, who forswear astrology as devilry. The tower falls because of two dragons that live beneath it. Workmen dig down to the dragons, which begin fighting. As Merlin predicts, the red dragon is killed by the white one's fiery breath. The former represents Vortigern and his faithlessness, the latter signifies Constant's two sons, who are on their way by sea to Winchester (#5: §19, 19–§32). The brothers land on the day foretold and Vortigern perishes when they burn the castle. Pendragon is declared king. When the Christians are harassed by Hengist, Uther besieges his castle and Pendragon searches for Merlin in Northumberland. Merlin informs him that Hengist has been killed by Uther. Merlin dictates these events to Blaise, while Pendragon rejoins his brother. At the siege, Merlin takes the form of a certain lady's serving boy and hands Uther a letter she purportedly wrote to him; he is overjoyed. At length, Merlin admits to several other instances of shapeshifting. He will serve both Pendragon and Uther and, although he must leave them from time to time, he will always be mindful of them. He leads negotiations with the Saxons, who sail from Winchester harbour in ships provided by the king (#6: §§33–40).[33] Merlin correctly predicts how one of Pendragon's barons will die by breaking his neck, drowning and hanging. The astonished king orders a book to be written, *Li Livres des prophecies de Merlin*, in which are to be inscribed all his words. This book will not duplicate Blaise's work, for the one records direct speech and the other is a narrative (#7: §41–§44, 22).

Merlin correctly predicts that Saxons will attack to avenge Hengist's death and one of the brothers (Pendragon) will die in battle. The Saxons are all slaughtered. Uther is crowned in London (#8: §44, 23–§46). He takes the surname Pendragon because a dragon appeared in the sky to announce the battle. Then Merlin magically transports great stones from Ireland and stands them up on the Christians' burial ground near Salisbury, where they are still seen. He explains to Uther the origins of his powers and relates the institution of the Grail table and the westward migration. To represent the Trinity, the king must establish another table, later identified as the Round Table (see #13 below), at Carduel.[34] Merlin chooses Uther's fifty worthiest knights to sit at the table, drawing attention to the empty seat. The elect feel a pleasure such as that experienced at the Grail table (#9: §47–§49, 68; see *Estoire*, #4). Merlin explains that the one to take the empty seat and fulfil the Grail adventures will not be conceived in Uther's time. Merlin leaves to stay with Blaise. His enemies at court question his pronouncements about the vacant place; a knight takes the seat and immediately melts away. Uther refuses to let others undergo the test (#10: §49, 68–§51).

King Arthur. As Merlin commanded, Uther begins holding obligatory court at Carduel at Christmas, Pentecost and All Saints. At an extraordinary court, he falls in love at first sight with Ygerne, wife of the Duke of Tintagel; she avoids him, but dares not refuse his gifts. At Pentecost, Uther lavishes gifts on her and her distress increases. At the next court, the duke makes her accept a golden goblet from Uther; that night Ygerne tells her husband of Uther's advances. Angry, but fearful, the duke and his party slip away. Uther challenges him. Abandoning the rest of his lands, the duke lodges his wife at Tintagel and himself in another invincible castle. Merlin promises that Uther will sleep with Ygerne. Through Merlin's magic, Uther takes on the likeness of the duke, and Ulfin and Merlin take on those of his companions, Jordan and Bretel. They ride into Tintagel, where Ygerne receives Uther in her bed (#11: §§52–65). When word arrives that the duke has been killed, Uther and his companions rush away. Merlin claims as his reward the male conceived that night. The duke has been killed and his castle taken. After Merlin departs to dictate to Blaise, Uther makes peace with Ygerne and her vassals. She weds Uther and her daughter marries King Lot of Orkney, while the duke's bastard daughter, Morgan the Fay, marries King Neutre of Garlot. Meanwhile, Ygerne confesses to Uther that the night the duke was killed she lay with another man in his form.[35] To hide her shame, they agree to give the child to Antor to raise; Antor's wife will give her own son Kay to a peasant to nurse (hence his harsh behaviour) and will nurse the baby herself. When the child is born, Merlin delivers him to Antor, who must baptize him Arthur (#12: §§66–76). Much later, Ygerne grows old and dies, and Uther dies in Logres[36] after putting down a rebellion. After prophesying that God will choose the new king at Christmas, Merlin goes to Blaise (#13: §77–§81,14).[37] Antor has raised Arthur as agreed. Kay was knighted at All Saints. At Christmas, Antor brings both to Logres, where all barons and prelates gather. On Christmas morning, a great stone is found bearing an anvil with a sword stuck through it. The one who withdraws the sword will be the king chosen by Christ. All who attempt the test fail, but Arthur easily takes the sword later when Kay has him fetch his sword and he cannot find it. Kay boasts to Antor that he has succeeded, but soon admits the truth. When all witness Arthur's success, the archbishop declares him king, but disgruntled barons force him to hold further trials at Candlemas and Easter. Finally, on Easter Eve, the archbishop admonishes all to accept God's will. On Sunday, Arthur succeeds again and all consent to crown him at Pentecost. He demonstrates his essential nobility in cheerful acts of generosity. On Whitsun Eve, Arthur is knighted and keeps vigil. He forgives his detractors and one last time removes the sword. The crowd take him to the altar to be crowned. Thereafter he holds the kingdom of Logres in peace for a long time (#14: §81, 14–§91, 58).[38]

The *Didot-Perceval*

Perceval's first Grail quest. Arthur's fame is so great that all worthy knights serve him. Alain, grown old and feeble, sends his son Perceval to Arthur's court. Perceval departs without taking his mother's leave. Arthur knights him, and for the first time he learns about knighthood and courtesy (#1, B–R: B; *D* 1–24, *E* 10–29).[39] Sagremor, Yvain son of Urien, Yvain of the White Hands, Dodinel and the four sons of King Lot, Mordred, Guerrehet, Gaheriet and Gauvain, arrive at court and are soon followed by Lancelot. At Merlin's instruction, Arthur reinstitutes the Round Table at a Pentecost court. After Mass, he seats his twelve best knights[40] at the Round Table, with one seat left vacant. All knights except Perceval joust and the twelve peers surpass all others. Perceval fights the next day, defeating Sagremor, Kay, Yvain and Lancelot. The knights proclaim him worthy of taking the vacant seat. Arthur invites him to join his household, but in spite of Arthur's protests, he takes the seat. Amid earthquakes, darkness and smoke, the stone beneath the seat splits and a chasm opens. A voice berates Arthur for ignoring Merlin's command and denounces Perceval's foolhardiness. Joseph's vessel is in the house of the Fisher King, Bron, who is now crippled. He cannot be healed, or the stone rejoined, until one of those seated in the hall proves himself to be the greatest knight in the world, visits the Fisher King and asks whom the Grail serves (#2, B–R: C; *D* 25–220, *E* 29–252). Perceval meets a maiden weeping over a dead knight. After the knight had rescued her from a giant, they found revellers in a tent who became sad and warned them against the Orguelleus de la Lande, who later killed the knight. Perceval vows to go to the tent himself and meets the Orguelleus, who challenges him. Eventually, Perceval forces him to beg for mercy. Perceval sends him to Arthur and the maiden to the queen (#3, B–R: D; *D* 220–445; *E* 253–456). Perceval arrives at a castle, where a magic chessboard defeats him three times. He makes to throw the pieces into a stream, when a maiden scolds him. He falls in love with her at once, but she will not hear him until he brings her the head of a white stag that runs in the forest nearby. He hunts with her hound, which soon leads to his quarry. No sooner does Perceval kill the stag and take its head than an old woman steals the hound. She will return it after he fights a ghostly knight, who, near defeat, flees back into his tomb. As they struggle, Perceval sees another knight take the hound and the stag's head. The hag refuses to tell him about either knight (#4, B–R: E[1]; *D* 446–606; *E* 456–632). Perceval chances upon the castle where he was born in the Gaste Forest and finds his sister. When he tells her that he is searching for the Grail Castle, she informs him that the Fisher King is his grandfather and that their mother died of grief when Perceval left home. She then takes him to a hermit, their father's brother, to confess the sin of killing their mother. The hermit has told her about Joseph and the Grail; the Grail is to pass to Perceval.

He counsels Perceval to keep from sin and avoid killing knights. Perceval escorts his sister home (#5, B–R: F; *D* 606–776, *E* 632–810).

Perceval meets a knight, the Handsome Coward, with a hideous lady, Blond Rosette. When Perceval laughs at her, the knight challenges him and is defeated. Perceval spares him and sends him with his lady to Arthur's court. She is mocked, but eventually grows beautiful (#6, B–R: G; *D* 776–902, *E* 810–965). Perceval is challenged at a ford by a knight, Urbain, whose fairy lover, the Queen of the Black Thorn, lives in an invisible castle. Perceval defeats him and hears his story. A gloom descends and a voice curses Perceval, who is attacked by monstrous birds. When he kills one of them, its body turns into that of a woman. The birds were Urbain's lady and her attendants who were trying to help Urbain escape. The dead woman is his lady's sister, who is now happy in Avalon (#7, B–R: H; *D* 902–1007, *E* 966–1114). At a crossroad, Perceval sees two children playing in a tree beside a cross. One tells Perceval to take the right-hand branch of the road, where something will help him in his quest for the Fisher King. Tree, children and cross disappear (#8, B–R: J; *D* 1007–26, *E* 1115–45). A voice from a shadow, speaking as Merlin on behalf of Christ, tells Perceval to do as the child instructed. If he proves worthy, he will fulfil God's prophecy to Joseph (#9, B–R: K; *D* 1027–40, *E* 1146–64). Perceval sees three men fishing in a boat on a river. One, his grandfather Bron, invites him to spend the night. At the castle, Bron is already waiting for him in the hall. During the first course of their meal, they see a maiden carrying two silver carving platters, followed by a youth holding a lance with three drops of blood coming from its tip. They disappear into another room. At the sight of another youth bringing in Joseph's vessel, the Grail,[41] all bow and strike their breasts in contrition. Later, the procession returns. Perceval yearns to ask about the Grail, but fears offending his host. If he had asked whom the Grail served, the Fisher King would have been healed. Next morning, the castle is deserted and the gate stands open for him to leave (#10, B–R: L; *D* 1040–1106, *E* 1165–1269). Perceval sees a maiden weeping disconsolately. She curses him for failing to heal his grandfather, to make himself the keeper of Christ's blood or to release Britain from all enchantments and evils (#11, B–R: M; *D* 1107–33, *E* 1270–1303). Perceval finds a maiden standing with her palfrey beside a tree, where his stag's head hangs; he takes the head. While she protests, he sees his lady's hound chasing a deer. As he makes to seize the dog, he is challenged by a knight who was hunting with it. Perceval defeats him. The hag who took his stag's head is the sister of the lady of the Chessboard Castle and the fairy-lover of the Tomb Knight. Perceval takes the stag's head to his lady, who forgives his delay and offers him her castle. He leaves because he has vowed not to stay two nights in the same place before finding the Fisher King (#12, B–R: E²; *D* 1133–1239, *E* 1303–1447).

Perceval's second Grail quest. Perceval wanders seven years, sending many defeated knights to King Arthur, but, unable to find the Fisher King's castle again, he goes mad and forgets God. On Good Friday, his memory is restored when he meets a band of penitent knights and ladies, who reprove him for wearing armour. God leads him to the hermitage of his uncle, who hears his confession. Two months later, he renews his quest (#13, B–R: N; *D* 1229–59, *E* 1447–1507). A tournament will take place after Pentecost at the White Castle. Perceval goes there to meet Arthur's knights. In disguise, he defeats Meliant de Lis and Kay, and fights Gauvain to a draw (#14, B–R: O; *D* 1259–1469, *E* 1508–1770). Returning to the castle with his host, Perceval meets Merlin, who reproaches him for breaking his vow. He points the way to the Fisher King's castle and promises to bring Blaise to stay with Perceval after he has found the Grail (#15, B–R: P; *D* 1469–95, *E* 1770–1822). Perceval arrives at the Fisher King's castle and is taken to Bron. During their meal, the Grail procession passes,[42] and without hesitation Perceval asks whom these things serve. Bron is healed. He explains that the Bleeding Lance is Longinus's spear and that the Grail contains the blood Joseph collected from Christ's wounds. Obeying the voice of the Holy Spirit, Bron teaches Perceval secret words Joseph learned from Christ in prison and gives him the Grail; he dies three days later. Perceval remains at the Fisher King's castle and enchantments throughout the world are broken. That same day, as Arthur and his companions sit at the Round Table, they hear a great noise and the broken stone is fused. Merlin dictates these events to Blaise and informs him that they are to join Perceval at the Fisher King's castle (#16, B–R: Q; *D* 1495–1570, *E* 1822–1922).

The *'Mort Artu'*. With the end of enchantments and adventures, Arthur and his knights seek adventure abroad. After entrusting his lands and the queen to Mordred, Arthur lands in Normandy, whose duke surrenders at once, and takes France when he kills King Frollo in single combat. Arthur is crowned king of France and returns to Britain (#17, B–R: R; *D* 1571–1696, *E* 1922–2167). Messengers from Rome come to Carduel to reassert the emperor's claims over Britain; they condemn Arthur for Frollo's death and demand tribute, but he declares his rights to Rome, twice conquered by British kings. The emperor raises an army reinforced with pagans and heads towards Brittany. Meanwhile, again entrusting Britain to Mordred, Arthur gathers his fleet at Dover. He lands at Calais and advances to Paris, where the emperor turns to meet him. After failed attempts at negotiation and prolonged fighting, Arthur kills the emperor in battle. He will be crowned emperor in Rome (#18, B–R: S; *D* 1697–1914, *E* 2168–2540). But Mordred has betrayed him by marrying the queen and seizing his crown, so Arthur rushes back to Britain. Mordred meets them on the shore with an army of Saxons. Kay, Sagremor, Bedivere, Lot and Gauvain are killed before getting ashore, but Arthur lands and defeats the Saxons. Mordred flees to Winchester, where Arthur defeats him again. He finds protection from a Saxon king in Ireland. In a final battle, Arthur kills Mordred and the Saxon, but is struck by a lance in the chest. He is taken to Avalon, where Morgan tends his wounds. The Britons wait for him at Carduel for forty years before electing another king. He has been seen hunting in the forests thereabouts (#19, B–R: T; *D* 1914–57, *E* 2541–2652).

Conclusion. Merlin dictates to Blaise, then informs him and Perceval that God has commanded him to build a dwelling outside the castle. He will live there, in his *esplumoir* (*E*) or *esplumeor* (*D*) ('moulting cage'),[43] unseen by anyone, until he dies at the end of time, after which he will enjoy life everlasting (Nitze 1943). He prays God to be merciful to all those who hear his book or have it copied (#20, B–R: U; *D* 1958–80, *E* 2652–74).

We know a little less about Robert de Boron than we do about Chrétien de Troyes himself (Giffin 1965; Gallais 1970; Pickens 1995; O'Gorman 1996). He was associated with Gautier de Montfaucon, Count of Montbéliard in Imperial Burgundy not far from Belfort, in whose court he wrote the *Estoire* around the year 1200. The village of Boron, from which he hailed, lies within twelve miles of Montbéliard. Robert's use of Wace and Chrétien de Troyes, and especially of a large number of Latin sacred and theological texts (O'Gorman 1979), shows that he was a man of learning and culture. As Robert was in service to Gautier de Montfaucon when he finished the verse *Estoire dou Graal*, he certainly wrote prior to 1202, when Gautier left for the Fourth Crusade, never to return, dying in 1210.

Confusion about Robert's social status arises because of the way his very name appears in the manuscript of the verse *Estoire*, where he names himself twice. Once he appears as 'Messires Roberz de Beron' (O'Gorman edn, 3461),[44] and *messire* occurs in all subsequent references to him by other writers and in all texts attributed to him. The title implies that he was of the knightly class and that he might have held Boron as a fief; the military association is strengthened by the fact that, in naming his patron, Robert stresses that he is with him in time of peace ('en peis', 3490), when a knight might well have the leisure to write (Micha edn, §23, 63–4; *Merlin*, #5). However, another title is found earlier in the *Estoire* manuscript: 'Meistres Roberz . . . de Bouron' (3155). The term *meistres* refers to a *clerc* who, like Maistre Wace,[45] has had formal training in Latin and follows a career involving him with the written word. The two titles, *messires* and *meistres*, are contradictory: they imply mutually exclusive vocations, unless one were to imagine Robert as an incongruous *clerc guerrier*, although Micha (1968, 467) accepts with baffling equanimity the implications of both designations together. But everything we know about the very tradition of writing in vernacular romance, and what we know or can surmise about the authors who name themselves, lend added weight to arguments in favour of Robert's clerkly status (Uitti 1975).

In the Middle Ages Robert was considered a prime authority on the history of the Grail, and his name and the works attributed to him were disseminated throughout the medieval Francophone world and beyond in what appears to have been a remarkably large number of manuscripts, some sixty of which survive along with fragments of others (O'Gorman edn, 4–12; Micha 1958). Yet only part of one work in one manuscript, the verse *Estoire dou Graal*, and a fragment of another, the verse *Merlin*, in the same manuscript, can be fully attributed to him with certainty; this manuscript, MS *R* (BNF, fr. 20047) dates from the end of the thirteenth century (O'Gorman edn, 4–6).[46] The other three score or so manuscripts contain prose adaptations in various redactions of the *Estoire* and/or the *Merlin*.

The two manuscripts of the *Didot-Perceval* offer no evidence that a verse original of the trilogy's conclusion ever existed. As the *Didot-Perceval* does not mention Robert's name, it can be attributed to him only by inference. Significantly, however, two other manuscripts (*A*: BNF, fr. 747, Micha's base; *B*: BL, Add. 10292) announce in Robert's name his intention to follow the *Merlin* with a text, not provided, that resembles the *Didot-Perceval*, though not perfectly (§91, 59–69; see Micha 1980, chapter 1), just as Robert projects, at the conclusion of the *Estoire-Joseph*, the subsequent branches of his Grail history. These facts, which pertain to four of the fourteen manuscripts to transmit both the *Joseph* and the prose *Merlin*, strengthen the case for Robert's authorship of the *Didot-Perceval* in some form.

In all probability, Robert de Boron did not produce the *mises en prose*.[47] Rather they represent a second-generation *translatio* of his work. The invention of the prose *Joseph* and the prose *Merlin* is a signal literary and cultural milestone, for they are amongst the earliest examples of prose narrative fiction in French. Indeed, as there is no evidence of a verse original, the *Didot-Perceval* may well be one of the earliest narratives to be composed and written in prose. Although the survival of medieval manuscripts is to a large degree a matter of chance, it is patently obvious merely from their numbers that Robert's romances in verse were not nearly so popular, and were not considered to be nearly so momentous, as the prose adaptations. It would thus seem that the very act of *mise en prose* itself produced an explosion in Robert de Boron's popularity and an increased awareness of his stature as an authority.

As important as it is, and despite monumental efforts in the area of textual history by scholars such as Roach, Micha and O'Gorman, the significance of Robert de Boron's work has not been well understood or widely appreciated until very recently. Robert's standing has now improved, thanks to a wave of important scholarly work such as Gowans 1996, Evdokimova 1999, Bazin-Tacchella 2000, Trachsler 2000, Walter 2000, Baumgartner 2001, Bryant transl., and others.[48] Robert's relative obscurity has been due in large part to the vicissitudes of manuscript transmission and textual *translatio*. Nevertheless, although his skills in versification are certainly not those of a Chrétien de Troyes, he has few peers in the scope of his poetic vision or, a prime concern in medieval poetics, in his inventive use of sources.

Robert's verse romances and the second-generation prose adaptations had a tremendous influence on Arthurian literature to come, particularly on the Vulgate Cycle: the Vulgate *Merlin*, where Robert's contribution will be discussed in detail in chapter VII, the Vulgate *Estoire del Saint Graal* and the *Queste del Saint Graal*. From Robert's *Joseph* onwards, the Grail will always be referred to as *saint* and will always be identified with Christ's cup. Moreover, as we have seen, the *Joseph* connects Grail history with the history of human redemption and, via Joseph of Arimathea and his family, it makes Great Britain the preordained haven for the Grail-keepers. Robert's *Estoire* seeks to place Grail history, as Chrétien de Troyes reveals it and Robert interprets it, within the context of sacred history, for it translates and incorporates several authoritative texts, including the Bible and apocryphal works (James edn, de Santos Otero edn) such as the *Gospel of Pseudo-Matthew*, the *Protevangelium of James* and the *Gospel of Nicodemus* (or *Acts of Pilate*), as well as a *Cura sanitatis Tiberii* and *Vindicta Salvatoris*, which recount, in turn, the healing powers of Veronica's veil and the destruction of Jerusalem (see Micha 1968, O'Gorman 1979). Accordingly, the *Estoire* opens with references to the Old Testament Prophets and the confinement of all dead souls to hell, and continues the history of redemption with the Immaculate Conception and birth of Mary (*Pseudo-Matthew, James*),[49] the Annunciation and the birth of Christ. It then moves to an account of Christ's trial before Pilate (*Pilate, Nicodemus*), the Crucifixion, the descent from the Cross, the Harrowing of Hell, the Resurrection (*Nicodemus* as well as canonical accounts), the healing of Vespasian (*Cura, Vindicta*) and the imprisonment and liberation of Joseph of Arimathea thanks to the intervention of Titus and Vespasian (*Vindicta*).

Similarly, the *Merlin* succeeds in conjoining Grail history with British history, also in harmony with Chrétien's *Perceval*. The sacred texts Robert employs to create a context for early Grail history, especially those pertaining to the Virgin Mary and the conception and birth of Christ, provide parallels that are developed in the *Merlin*, which Robert deliberately opens (§§1–16) with a series of episodes that mirror the beginning of the *Estoire* (11–614). In negative correlation with the *Estoire*, the *Merlin* begins with devils discussing the Harrowing of Hell; they complain about how Christ came to release the prophets who had been their prisoners (cf. *Nicodemus*). They plan revenge and hatch their plot to produce an Anti-Christ by having an incubus impregnate a young, pious virgin (cf. *Protevangelium*, canonical Gospels).[50] She gives birth to a precocious boy she names Merlin. He is saved from the devils thanks to her prayers and the ministrations of her chaplain, who makes clear to her the nature of the being who raped her. Eventually, she is brought to trial for fornication, but is acquitted when the boy turns the tables on the judge by proving to him that his own mother cuckolded his father with a priest. Unlike the analogous episodes in the *Estoire*, the opening events in the *Merlin* are not known to have any full-blown precedents. Robert invents the latter as an overt inversion of authoritative sacred history – with a corresponding result, however, that, contrary to the devils' vengeful purposes, Merlin is redeemed and accorded the grace to retain his diabolical powers and to use them in God's service in Britain.

Just as significantly, Robert extends his invention by rewriting large sections of material found in Geoffrey of Monmouth's *Historia Regum Britanniae* and Wace's *Brut*: passages devoted to Vortigern, Pendragon and Uther. Although he was obviously competent in Latin, Robert's source is most certainly the *Brut* because of its emphasis on Arthurian matter as well as details not found in Geoffrey's *Historia* that recur in Robert's *Merlin*. For example (cf. #11), Geoffrey does not name the man whose form Merlin takes in helping Uther to seduce Ygerne (Wright edn, §137), but in Wace it is Bretel (Arnold edn, 8714), as in Robert (§64, 11). But Robert also inventively brings Merlin into the Arthurian world. Robert's use of Wace in the *Merlin* is discussed in detail in chapter VII below.

In conclusion, let us look at the contribution of the *Didot-Perceval* to Arthurian literature. This text provides a conclusion to Perceval's biography that satisfies in many ways the logic of Chrétien's romance by Perceval's triumphant return to the Grail Castle, although it ignores Chrétien's Gauvain section and much else, not to mention the First (*Gauvain*) Continuation. However, the outcome in the *Didot-Perceval* is wholly determined by the new forces the author sets into play, principally in terms of his rewritten Grail history and of the dynamics of Merlin's roles as the means whereby destinies are accomplished and as instigator of the writing down of Robert's source. The *Didot-Perceval* also reintroduces the *Brut* into Robert's trilogy, as the standard for measuring historical fact, by incorporating Wace's 'Mort Artu' (##17–19) following the cessation of the 'enchantments' and 'adventures' with Perceval's succession as Grail King:[51] Arthur and his knights must go to foreign lands in search of them, and they find them in France. Thus the *Didot-Perceval* explicitly situates the Perceval adventures during the Pax Arthuriana, from the rise of young King Arthur's court, in accordance with the *Merlin* conclusion and including Perceval's retirement to the Grail Castle, to its end with the war against Rome. Indeed, Perceval's success is the cause of Arthur's decline. The *Didot-Perceval* brings closure not only to Chrétien's *Perceval*-cum-Second Continuation, but also to the entirety of Grail history. **[RTP]**

Perlesvaus

Perlesvaus, or *Li hauz livres du Graal* (*The Noble Book of the Grail*) as it is named in the three complete surviving manuscripts,[52] is a prose Grail romance dating from the first half of the thirteenth century. Extensive research and critical debate have so far failed to fix anything approaching a precise date,[53] and in particular it has yet to be determined whether *Perlesvaus* pre- or post-dates the other great prose Grail romance of its period, *La Queste del Saint Graal*. *Perlesvaus*, like the *Queste*, is a significant work partly because it is one of the earliest romances to recount the successful completion of the Grail adventures. It follows the tradition of Chrétien de Troyes and his continuators in making the knight Perceval, or in this case Perlesvaus (*perd-les-vaus*, so named because his father had been dispossessed of certain of his territories, 42 – references are to page numbers in Nitze edn), the Grailwinner. The Quest for the Grail is set here in the context of those antecedent narratives, for at the start of *Perlesvaus* we are told that the eponymous hero has already visited the Grail Castle once and failed to ask the questions that would have resulted in the Grail adventures being brought to a successful conclusion.[54]

There have been two modern printed editions of the text, by Potvin in 1866 and Nitze and Jenkins in 1937.[55] The latter edition, though extremely useful, is unfortunately once more out of print and difficult to find. More readily available are Bryant's English translation and Marchello-Nizia's abridged version in French.

Perlesvaus is quite a substantial text, divided by the author into eleven branches (all three extant manuscripts agree on this number), and it displays a highly complex internal structure, both in broad terms of narrative interlace (whereby the tale follows different strands, thus charting the progress of various characters on the Quest) and in terms of what have been described by critics (Nitze edn, II, 165–9; Lacy 1989, 169–78) as linking and analogy, forms of interlace which operate at the level of detail and involve groups of, or individual, figural and other elements, within and across episodes. It is unquestionably the case that repetitions and variations on a theme provide the building-blocks for this romance, as they do for others of the period (Burns 1985, 139–40; Williams 2001, 186).

Perlesvaus is, however, an unusual Arthurian romance in that King Arthur himself plays a considerable role in the adventures, rather than merely providing a base, through the setting of the court, from which knights errant depart and to which they return (or not, as the case may be) at the conclusion of their individual quests. Indeed, the opening of *Perlesvaus* is not quite what a reader familiar with Arthurian tradition might expect, departing as it does from the Arthurian romance topos of court celebrations being interrupted by the occurrence of an *aventure*; this departure is achieved in a very bold and arresting manner.

Branch 1 begins with King Arthur at Carduel for the feast of the Ascension. The queen is unhappy, lamenting the lack of adventures at court compared to former times (in the context of the Grail romances, where the adventures have symbolic significance and represent stages along the path to spiritual perfection, a lack of adventures invariably reflects unworthiness of the character or characters concerned). The queen suggests that Arthur should ride out to the Chapel of St Augustine, and it emerges that finding the Chapel is an adventure in itself. She persuades Arthur, against his better judgement, to take a squire with him on this *aventure*, and the king chooses a certain Cahus (27). On the eve of their departure, Cahus sleeps outside Arthur's chamber and dreams that the King has set off without him (it should be noted here that dreams, visions and voices play a crucial role in this text; indeed we are told in the Prologue that the narrator recorded the story in writing, it having been transmitted to him via 'la voiz d'un angle' (*the voice of an angel*, 23). Cahus follows the tracks of Arthur's horse, but the trail goes cold outside a chapel, which the squire enters, and in it he finds a bier on which lies the dead body of a knight, with four candles burning in candlesticks of gold at each of its four corners. Cahus takes one of the candlesticks, stowing it in his trousers, then rides off into the forest, where he encounters a giant who is 'noir et let' (*black and ugly*, 29) and armed with a fearsome double-bladed knife. The giant demands that Cahus return the candlestick, which he refuses to do, whereupon the giant stabs the squire, pushing the knife into his side, up to the hilt. At this moment Cahus wakes and cries out. Hearing the scream, the king, queen and chamberlain enter the antechamber and find the squire lying mortally wounded, with a knife in his side. He also has the candlestick, still secreted in his hose. Thus the hapless squire's dream has been 'molt ledement averez' (*realized in a most unpleasant way*, 30).

This bloody and disquieting opening episode sets the tone for the rest of the work. Many of the adventures recounted are striking, original and frequently very violent.[56] The subsequent *branches* describe three principal Grail quests: those of Gauvain, Lancelot and Perlesvaus, with King Arthur himself later completing a pilgrimage to the Grail Castle.

In branches 2 to 6 inclusive, the narrative follows the fortunes of Gauvain. After various adventures (including an encounter with Joseus, Perlesvaus's cousin) and an unsuccessful visit to the Grail Castle (both related in branch 5, 89, 91–2), Gauvain returns there in branch 6, having won the Sword of John the Baptist, possession of which is a prerequisite for him to gain admission (112–18). Unfortunately, however, once in the presence of the Grail and the Lance, Gauvain is so distracted by the sight of three drops of blood falling on to the white tablecloth[57] that he forgets to ask the crucial questions as to the purpose of the Holy Vessel and is thus a failure in the Quest (118–21). Although in many ways a worthy knight (for instance he has succeeded in converting Gurgaran, from whom he won the Sword, to Christianity), Gauvain lacks the spiritual perfection required to achieve the Grail. The end of branch 6 takes up Lancelot's narrative thread briefly: he attempts (unsuccessfully at this stage) to find the Grail Castle and in the Waste City becomes involved in a Beheading Game (137–8) which is resolved later on in the tale (see p. 285).

Lancelot's exploits are more fully recounted in the eighth branch (branch 7 being devoted to several of Perlesvaus's lesser adventures). Here he finally reaches the Grail Castle, but is not permitted even to see the Holy Vessel because of his sinful love for Queen Guinevere (166–71). Thus, like Gauvain, but for rather different reasons, Lancelot is unsuccessful in the Quest. In fact, the text clearly suggests that Lancelot has further to go on the path to spiritual perfection than does Gauvain, who did at least see the Lance and the Grail, even if he failed to ask the questions that would have brought the adventures to an end.

The narrative thread now returns to Perlesvaus, who encounters his devilish uncle, the king of the Chastel Mortel (signifying evil incarnate), for the first time (178), and then, after several adventures in which he has the opportunity to prove his prowess and his spiritual worth, the hero learns from his sister Dandrane that the Fisher King (another uncle, keeper of the Grail Castle and a mirror image of his wicked brother), has died. His untimely death has given the king of the Chastel Mortel the opportunity to seize the Castle, and the Grail has vanished (225).

Branch 9, however, describes the successful outcome of Perlesvaus's Quest: he defeats several enemies, retrieves the sacred relic of the Golden Circlet (which is the Crown of Thorns encased in a reliquary, 254), and returns to the Grail Castle. On seeing his nephew triumphant, the king of the Chastel Mortel despairs and commits suicide by throwing himself from the battlements (267). Perlesvaus has thus regained control of the Grail Castle on behalf of the Church Militant, and in a sense the main goal of his quest has been achieved. There is no longer any necessity (nor, indeed, possibility, now that the Fisher King is dead) for the questions to be asked regarding the purpose of the Grail. At this point, then, the focus of the narrative returns to King Arthur.

In branch 9 Arthur is told by a voice that he must go on a pilgrimage to the Grail Castle (270). As he is about to depart, he learns that his son Loholt has been treacherously killed by Kay. The latter flees to Brittany, there forming an alliance with Brian of the Isles (274) – the two men begin a plot against Arthur, the consequences of which are developed in the subsequent branches. This section of the text ends with the reporting of the passing of Guinevere, who has died of grief at the loss of her son Loholt (302).

Branch 10 is principally concerned with Arthur's successful journey to the Grail Castle: he is rewarded with a vision in which the Grail appears under five different guises (304–5). In the latter part of the branch, Brian of the Isles, now Arthur's new seneschal, manages to turn Arthur against Lancelot (353–5).

The final branch, number 11, describes the dénouement of the remaining unresolved elements of the tale. Perlesvaus finally frees his mother from her enemies, and succeeds in converting Jandree, a pagan queen, to Christianity (375–7). Lancelot and Arthur are reconciled. Perlesvaus visits the mysterious Castle of the Four Horns (387–91), wins a golden chalice at a tournament (399), and visits the Grail Castle for the last time before sailing away to an undisclosed destination. His mysterious destiny is susceptible of multiple interpretations: for example, it may recall that of Arthur in the *Mort Artu* (like Arthur, Perlesvaus makes his exit in a ship), or it may be intended to reinforce the notion that we are to read his character as a type of Christ. Perlesvaus's cousin, Joseus, remains at the Grail Castle, but after his death the edifice falls into ruins with the exception of the chapel, which we are told remains intact to this day (408).

Throughout the many vicissitudes of the narrative, there is one constant theme: that of the struggle between the New Law and the Old, the latter including not only those of the Jewish faith, but all non-Christians. The enemies of the Church are dealt with and mercilessly dispatched (if not converted, as in the case of Queen Jandree) by protagonists representing the New, or Christian Law, sometimes with almost shocking cruelty (see, for instance, the defeat and subsequent torture of the Sire des Mores in branch 8, 234–5).

It is perhaps surprising that a text as rich as *Perlesvaus* has attracted relatively few detailed studies of any length. It is undeniably a complex and difficult work, but it is also one of the masterpieces of its period.[58] Thus far, critical studies of *Perlesvaus* have tended to focus on two main problematics: on the one hand, the dating of the text and its relationship to other Arthurian romances, and on the other hand the narrative's structure. As mentioned above, critical opinion remains divided on the former matter, with Carman (1936), Nitze (edn), Frappier (1954), Kelly (1974), Berthelot (1989) and others favouring an early date, antecedent to the *Lancelot–Grail*, and Lot (1918, 136–8), Bruce (1924/1928*), Foulet (1959), Bogdanow (1984, 44–51), Zink (1992, 185) and others supporting a date later than the Vulgate Cycle.

One of the editors of the text, Nitze, also undertook the first serious academic study of *Perlesvaus*. The second volume of his 1972 edition contains notes on the manuscripts, possible links between this romance and Glastonbury Abbey (the text itself claiming a connection, 409), as well as material on dating and likely sources. There is also a brief section on style and structure, but the latter must be of central concern to the critic, given the nature, length, and complexity of the narrative. T. E. Kelly's 1974 study is the first, and to date the only, work of criticism to tackle the issue head-on and in any kind of detail. He provides a close analysis of many of the episodes and concludes that the narrative can usefully be divided into two sections: the first comprising the adventures until and including Perlesvaus's conquest of the Grail Castle and the second containing the defeat of the Black Hermit and Perlesvaus's withdrawal from the world (75). This bipartite structure, he claims, reflects the duality of the work's main themes: God and man, divine intervention and human response (181). More recently, E. Kennedy (1998) has written an illuminating examination of the place of interlace in the structure of *Perlesvaus*, comparing and contrasting it with narrative technique in the *Lancelot*, and there have been other useful studies on structural issues in connection with specific episodes, notably by Berthelot (1994). Much in this domain, however, is still uncharted territory, and as Lacy (1996, 157) states: 'The most productive studies remaining to be done surely involve not simply the selection of motifs, but also their uses and the effects achieved by their modification and recombination'.

It will no doubt be difficult to produce a definitive study of the myriad motifs in *Perlesvaus* and their function in the narrative in terms of structure. However, such a study would help to elucidate the place of this text within the wider context of French Arthurian romance. *Perlesvaus* can be shown to have had direct influence on at least two later narratives. The character of Brian of the Isles plays a significant role in the thirteenth-century romance *Meriaduc*, and the Anglo-Norman prose romance *Fouke le Fitz Waryn*[59] contains an entire episode from *Perlesvaus*.

No doubt the dating of the text will continue to be of central concern to critics, as well as problems of categorization. Berthelot (1994, 31) summarizes the enigma of *Perlesvaus* thus:

> *A priori*, le Graal ne se distingue pas aussi clairement qu'on pourrait le souhaiter des autres merveilles du royaume de Logres; en mettant les choses au mieux il y a toujours un résidu de merveilleux païen qui contamine les épisodes les plus aisément récupérables par l'allégorèse du plus orthodoxe des ermites.

My own view is that the relationship between *Perlesvaus* and the other Grail romances, the *Queste* in particular, is analogous to that between the so-called 'version commune' and the 'version courtoise' of the *Tristan*, but further detailed study will be necessary to provide sound arguments in support of this theory. Irrespective of its precise date and position in the Arthurian tradition, *Perlesvaus* is unquestionably one of the most striking and multifaceted of the extant Grail romances. **[AMLW]**

Notes

[1] This information is given to us by Gerbert de Montreuil in his Continuation, written *c.*1225 (6986). Gerbert's proximity to cultural circles in the north-east, where the roots of romance lie, suggests that his information was reliable (Baldwin 2000). It has also been claimed that Chrétien wrote himself into a corner and was unable to find a satisfactory outcome to the romance. While the notion of the old poet's powers failing him is not inconceivable, the accomplished state of the

extant part of the romance does not support this view and argues strongly in favour of composition and revision by episodes or instalments.

[2] Mons, Bibliothèque de l'Université de Mons-Hainaut MS 331/206 (formerly 4568). In addition to the *Elucidation*, *Bliocadran* and Chrétien's *Perceval*, P contains the First (short version) and Second Continuation and Manessier's conclusion.

[3] London, British Library, Additional MS 36614. In addition to *Bliocadran*, L contains Chrétien's *Perceval*, the First (short version) and Second Continuations followed by *La Vie de sainte Marie l'Égyptienne*.

[4] The seven guards are story-tellers who have found the Rich Fisher's court (339–46): they 'governent par tout le mont / Tous les bons contes c'on a dit' (*have mastery throughout the world over all the good stories that have been told*, 18–19).

[5] An Old French *hapax legomenon*. Godefroy ventures the guess that it may mean 'travestissement'.

[6] Thus, in Thompson's view, ninety of 400 lines are interpolated.

[7] Blihos Bliheris also appears in *Erec et Enide*, *Le Bel Inconnu*, *Les Merveilles de Rigomer*, *La Vengeance Raguidel*, and Gerbert de Montreuil's Continuation. See West 1969*, 20–1.

[8] Doubtless a reference to Gauvain's Grail visit in the First Continuation. Meneghetti presents ##11 and 12 in chronological, not narrated, order.

[9] Meneghetti excludes the details of Perceval's visit (11b–11e) and the future narrations and explanations (11e–11g).

[10] As in the First Continuation. Thus Gauvain's partial success in the First Continuation is here transferred to Perceval (in anticipation of the Second Continuation?).

[11] Each for one of the seven times (?) the Rich Fisher's court is found (340–1). They are not all easy to identify: (7th) the Bleeding Lance as the Lance of Longinus (353–6); (6th) a great strife (357–8); (5th) Huden (Tristan's dog?) (359–60); (4th) a dead knight in a boat drawn by a swan (361–4); (3rd) a hawk that wounded Amangon's son (365–9); (2nd) Lancelot's loss of strength (370–4); (1st) the adventure of the shield (375–80). For details, see Thompson edn, 67–78.

[12] Two other differences noted by Thompson are not contradictions, but accretions to Chrétien's account: (i) Bliocadran has eleven brothers; (ii) the steward, his family, and other servants accompany the exiles. In any event, Thompson (1959, 210) observes that the mother's genealogical discourse is 'not essential for the rest of Chrétien's romance', and so *Bliocadran* could just as well take its place.

[13] For an overview, see Roach 1956 and the introductions to his editions of the First Continuation, Second Continuation and Manessier, which are those referred to here.

[14] The scholarly neglect of the Continuations in general is the justification for the rather lengthy narrative summaries which form a susbstantial part of this chapter. See, however, Gallais's authoritative and exhaustive study (1988–9).

[15] Leupin (1979) has also suggested that the disorder of the First Continuation (particularly as it appears in MS *T*) reflects the nature of medieval narrative composition.

[16] The Pucelle de Lis episode has been the object of some scholarly attention. See Gallais 1964b and Doner 1993. On the presentation of Gauvain in the Continuations generally, see Busby 1980*.

[17] Frappier sensed something of the kind when he referred to the First Continuation as a 'chapelet de lais ou de fabliaux courtois que seule relie la permanence du décor arthurien' (1958, p. 331). On the other hand, one could dispute the use of the terms 'lais' and 'fabliaux' and point out the frequent links to Chrétien.

[18] The continuators' concern with reading and linking up with Chrétien and with each other has been termed by Bruckner 'the poetics of continuation' (1993, 1996, 1999, 2000). See also for traces of Chrétien's æsthetics in the Continuations, Grigsby 1987–8b.

[19] Wauchier's other works are primarily hagiographical or pseudo-hagiographical. Recent editions include *L'Histoire des moines d'Égypte suivie de La Vie de Saint-Paul le Simple*, ed. by

M. Szkilnik, TLF 427 (Geneva, 1993) and *La Vie mon signeur seint Nicholas le beneoit confessor*, ed. by J. J. Thompson, TLF 508 (Geneva, 1999).

[20] If Corley is correct, the idea of returning the narrative to Perceval would be attributable to the First Continuator. It is curious that the last line of BNF, fr. 794 (*A* 10268/*E* 20530), 'Percevax molt s'an desconforte', anticipates (or echoes and contradicts?) the last line of the Second Continuation itself (*E* 32594), 'Et Percevaux se reconforte.'

[21] The story of the hound (*brachet*) has been examined by Luttrell (1989).

[22] The 'child in the tree' motif with its variant of an illuminated tree also appears in Manessier's Continuation, the *Didot-Perceval* and *Durmart le Galois*. It has been studied most recently by Saly (1989).

[23] It is possible, of course, that the interpolation was carried out by a scribe or planner of MSS *TV*.

[24] Gerbert de Montreuil, *Le Roman de la Violette ou de Gerard de Nevers*, ed. by D. L. Buffum, SATF (Paris, 1928). See also Baldwin 2000, 7–11, 59–60. The only monograph devoted to Gerbert's Continuation is Cocito 1964. Gerbert does not actually call himself 'de Montreuil' in the Continuation, but stylistic and other evidence renders the identification with the author of *Le Roman de la Violette* quite secure. See François 1932.

[25] The Williams–Oswald edition of Gerbert has no convenient episode divisions such as those found in Roach's editions of the other Continuations; I have given line numbers from the edition, preceded by episode numbers taken from De Riquer and De Riquer 1989.

[26] Gowans (2004) presents evidence, often compelling, suggesting that the *Joseph* and *Merlin* were originally written in prose; the *Joseph* by Robert, the *Merlin* by an anonymous continuator. She proposes that *R* represents the later work of an unknown versifier.

[27] So called in honour of Ambroise Firmin Didot, once owner of the Paris manuscript, which is one of two bearing witness to the text: Paris, BNF, nouv. acq. fr. 4166, and Modena, Biblioteca Estense, E. 39. The Modena text, much fuller than that of the Didot manuscript, is also in Cerquiglini 1981a.

[28] Roach, for one, was convinced that the *Didot-Perceval* 'is a much-interpolated and rewritten version of a fairly faithful prose rendering of Robert's original "branches" dealing with Perceval and the last days of Arthur' (Roach edn, 16, also 113–25). Micha is also 'strongly inclined' to ascribe the supposed original to Robert (Micha 1980, 10–29). Pickens (1984, 494–5), argued that the *Didot-Perceval* could not be by Robert de Boron; more recently, after examining the trilogy in light of different assumptions about *translatio* and rewriting, I have concluded that undeniably it is consistent with Robert's modes of rewriting his sources and with the spirit of the *Estoire* and *Merlin* (Pickens 1988, esp. 20). In O'Gorman 1996, Robert's authorship of the *Didot-Perceval* is a given. In any event, there is no evidence that the *Didot-Perceval* ever existed in verse form.

[29] So called in honour of the bibliophile Henry Huth, who owned one of the two manuscripts to transmit this Continuation (London, British Library, Add. 38117; the other is Cambridge, University Library, Add. 7071).

[30] A lacuna occurs following 2752 in the manuscript (*R*: Paris, BNF, fr. 20047), due to the loss of a bifolium, which must have contained about 128 lines. Material in square brackets is taken from the edition of the prose *Joseph d'Arimathie* in O'Gorman edn, ll. 1115–62.

[31] A reference to the *Didot-Perceval* or a text like it.

[32] After the fragmentary beginning, references are to paragraphs and line numbers in the prose text of Micha 1979. The opening episode and the one following are a vast amplification of three short passages in direct speech from the *Brut* (Arnold edn): the boy Merlin's defence against a tormenter (*Brut*, 7373–84) (cf. #5 below), the confession Merlin's mother makes to Vortigern (7414–34), and the explanation of incubi made by Vortigern's clerk Magant (7439–56).

[33] In *Brut*, 7929–62, Merlin has nothing to do with the surrender and departure of the Saxons, who are not sent abroad by the king, but given unoccupied lands in Britain.

[34] This reflects the three generations of Joseph's lineage in the *Estoire*, which also represent the

Trinity. Christ alludes to the Round Table in the prose *Joseph* (349–61), but not in the verse *Estoire* (cf. 893–928). Here Merlin is depicted as inventing the Round Table himself; he does not say that the Round Table was prophesied by Christ. This fact leads Micha to conclude that the *Merlin*, which does not contradict the *Estoire*, was committed to prose before the *Joseph* (Micha 1956–7). It is noteworthy that this Round Table seats fifty, whereas, according to the Modena manuscript, the Round Table as Arthur re-establishes it seats thirteen (*Didot-Perceval*, #2).

[35] Robert thus introduces the theme of Arthur as fatherless child like Merlin (esp. §86, 29–44) and, implicitly, thanks to parallels with the beginning of the *Estoire*, with Christ himself.

[36] In the *Merlin*, Logres is a city that, as in the Vulgate Cycle, is associated with London.

[37] Robert is uninterested in Uther's subsequent deeds as recounted by Wace (*Brut*, 8823–9004).

[38] There is no equivalent in the *Brut*, but Robert hugely amplifies 9009–14.

[39] Episodes correspond to those in Roach edn, 18–32, following Brugger 1930 (=B–R); they are represented by capital letters, from B to U. These indications are followed by line references to Roach's edition of the Didot (*D*: Paris, BNF, nouv. acq. fr. 4166) and Modena (*E*: Biblioteca Estense, E. 39) manuscripts. As Roach demonstrates (edn, 13–15), following Brugger 1930, Episode A concludes the *Merlin*.

[40] These are Gauvain and the eight companions just mentioned plus Kay, Erec and Urgans. The Round Table that Uther Pendragon founds in the *Merlin* seats fifty knights (*Merlin* #9).

[41] In Chrétien's *Perceval*, the Grail procession has the order: Bleeding Lance (a youth), cande-labra (two youths), Grail (a maiden), one carving platter (a maiden) (Busby edn, 3191–3231).

[42] The scene is greatly abbreviated, but the procession has the same order as in Chrétien (n. 41 above): Lance, Grail, carving platters.

[43] Perhaps a reference to Merlin's shape-shifting.

[44] 'Messires Roberz de Beron / Dist, se ce [i.e., the story of 'li Boens Pescherres' (3456)] savoir volum, / Sanz doute savoir couvenra / Conter la ou Aleins ala, / Li fiuz Hebron, et qu'il devint' (3461–5) (*My lord Robert de Boron says that, if we wish to know about this [the story of the Good Fisher], it will doubtless be necessary to tell where Alain, son of Bron, went and what became of him*).

[45] In the third part of the *Rou*, Maistre Wace (Holden edn, III, 158) observes that he served three king Henrys (Henry I, Henry II, and the Young King) as 'clerc lisant' (179–80); also in the *Brut* (Arnold edn, 7, 3823, 13282, 14866).

[46] *R* was copied in Lorraine, probably at Metz. Its medieval compiler apparently sought to place Grail history in context with natural history, for the *Estoire* is preceded by Gossuin de Metz's popular, encyclopaedic *Image du monde* in verse (author's first edition 1246). Unfortunately, a bifolium of the *Estoire* text, that is, the inner leaves of gathering 18, following v. 2752, is lost, along with 124 to 128 lines. All but the first eight folios of the original *Merlin* (504 verses) was lost before the book received its present binding, along with anything that may have come thereafter. At an average of 31–2 lines per page, the original length of the *Estoire* must have been some 3,640 lines instead of the 3,514 in modern editions; a rough estimate of the total length of the verse *Merlin*, based on the number of lines in the verse fragment as compared to the number of lines in the prose version, is some 7,800 lines.

[47] But Gowans (2004) asserts that the prose versions are original.

[48] By contrast Schmolke-Hasselmann 1980/1998* mentions Robert de Boron only twice, in passing reference to his verse romances and the *mises en prose*, although she acknowledges the importance of prose romances in general.

[49] O'Gorman, observing that the material in *Estoire*, 45–80 taken specifically from Pseudo-Matthew is not found in the prose *Joseph*, suggests that it may have been interpolated in *R* (O'Gorman edn, 341, n. 45). The point does not diminish the significance of the parallelism that compares and contrasts Merlin's conception and birth with Christ's.

[50] In fact, the identity of Merlin's otherworldly father as an incubus conjoins inversion of the orthodox account of the Annunciation with use of Wace's *Brut* (see chapter VII).

[51] The *Didot-Perceval* marks the end of enchantments and adventures in Britain (*D*: 1571–2; *E*: 1923–4) which begin, according to what the Fool tells Arthur in Chrétien's *Perceval* (Busby edn, 1257–9), with Perceval's departure from Carduel: 'Ore aprochent vos aventures; / De felenesses et de dures / En verrez avenir sovent' (*Now your adventures are about to begin. You will frequently see them happening, dreadful and arduous ones*).

[52] Oxford, Bodleian Library, MS Hatton 82; Brussels, Bibliothèque Royale de Belgique, MS 11145; Chantilly, Musée Condé, MS 626. There are also several extant fragments.

[53] See Carman 1936; Nitze edn (esp. II, 73–89); Frappier 1954, 194; Foulet 1959; T. E.Kelly 1974, 9–15; Lloyd-Morgan 1984; E. Kennedy 1986, 8–9.

[54] It must be said, however, that certain elements of the *Perlesvaus* fit ill with Chrétien de Troyes's version and with the Continuations. For instance, in *Perceval* we are told that Perceval's mother is dead; in the *Perlesvaus*, she is very much alive and plays a significant role in the narrative.

[55] References are to the Nitze and Jenkins edn; the text itself is contained in vol. 1.

[56] It seems unfortunate that various critics, following Bruce (1928*, II, 18), have dismissed *Perlesvaus* as a highly derivative text. A detailed reading suggests that the opposite is true: witness for instance the episode recounting the death of Loholt, son of Arthur and Guinevere (pp. 216ff., 272ff.).

[57] This is clearly a motif derived from Chrétien de Troyes's *Perceval*.

[58] According to Berthelot, *Perlesvaus* is 'un roman absolument unique, qui constitue un des chef-d'œuvre de la littérature romanesque médiévale, et est écrit dans une prose magnifique' (1989, 112).

[59] Ed. by E. J. Hathaway, P. T. Ricketts, C. A. Robson and A. D. Wiltshire (Oxford, 1975). The extant text dates from the fourteenth century, but the passage concerned, relating to Arthur and Cahus's dream, is in verse and presumably retained from the original thirteenth-century verse romance.

Reference List

For items accompanied by an asterisk, see the General Bibliography.

Texts and Translations

The Prologues

The Elucidation: A Prologue to the Conte del Graal. Ed. by A. W. Thompson (New York, 1931) [*Elucidation*].

Bliocadran: A Prologue to the Perceval of Chrétien de Troyes, Edition and Critical Study. Ed. by L. D. Wolfgang. *Beihefte zur Zeitschrift für romanische Philologie* 150 (Tübingen, 1976) [*Bliocadran*].

See Chrétien de Troyes (ii) below (Other Editions).

The Continuations

The Continuations of the Old French Perceval of Chrétien de Troyes. Ed. by W. J. Roach (Philadelphia, 1949–83). I: The First Continuation, Mixed Redaction of MSS. *TV* (1949); II (with R. H. Ivy, Jr.): The First Continuation, Long Redaction of MSS. *EMQU* (1950); III, i: First Continuation, Short Redaction of MSS. *ALPRS* (1952); III, ii: Glossary to the First Continuation by L. Foulet (1955); IV: The Second Continuation (1971); V: The Third Continuation by Manessier (1983).

Gerbert de Montreuil, *La Continuation de Perceval*. (i) Ed. by M. Williams, 2 vols, CFMA 28, 50 (Paris, 1922–5); (ii) ed. by M. Oswald, CFMA 101 (Paris, 1975) [Gerbert].

Première Continuation de Perceval: Continuation-Gauvain. Ed. and transl. by C.-A. van Coolput-Storms (Paris, 1993).

Robert de Boron

Robert de Boron, Joseph d'Arimathie: A Critical Edition of the Verse and Prose Versions. Ed. by R. O'Gorman (Toronto, 1995).

Robert de Boron, Merlin: roman du XIIe siècle. Ed. by A. Micha, TLF 281 (Paris and Geneva, 1979).

The Didot-Perceval According to the Manuscripts of Modena and Paris. Ed. by W. Roach (Philadelphia, 1941).

Les Prophéties de Merlin: cod. Bodmer 116. Ed. by A. Berthelot (Cologny-Genève, 1992).

Merlin and the Grail: Joseph of Arimathea, Merlin, Perceval: The Trilogy of Prose Romances Attributed to Robert de Boron. Transl. by N. Bryant (Woodbridge, 2001).

Le Roman du Graal: manuscrit de Modène. Ed. by B. Cerquiglini (Paris, 1981).

Lancelot: roman en prose du XIIIe siècle. Ed. by A. Micha, 9 vols, TLF 247, 249, 262, 278, 283, 286, 288, 306, 315 (Geneva, 1978–83).

Le Roman de l'Estoire dou Graal. Ed. by W. A. Nitze, CFMA 57 (Paris, 1927).

Merlin, roman en prose du XIIIe siècle, publié … d'après le manuscrit appartenant à M. Alfred H. Huth. Ed. by G. Paris and J. Ulrich, 2 vols, SATF (Paris, 1886).

The Story of Merlin. Transl. by R. T. Pickens, in N. J. Lacy ed. *Lancelot–Grail: The Old French Arthurian Vulgate and Post-Vulgate in Translation* (New York and London, 1993), I, 165–424.

The Vulgate Version of the Arthurian Romances. Ed. by H. O. Sommer, 8 vols (Washington, 1908–16).

The Post-Vulgate, Part I: The Merlin Continuation, Part II: The Quest for the Holy Grail, Part III: The Death of Arthur. Transl. by M. Asher, in N. J. Lacy ed. *Lancelot–Grail: The Old French Arthurian Vulgate and Post-Vulgate in Translation* (New York and London, 1993–6), IV, 167–277, V, 1–312.

Perlesvaus

Le Haut Livre du Graal: Perlesvaus. Ed. by W. A. Nitze and T. A. Jenkins, 2 vols (New York, 1932 and 1937; repr.1972) [*Perlesvaus*].

Perlesvaus: Le Haut Livre du Graal. Transl. by C. Marchello-Nizia, in D. Régnier-Bohler ed. *La Légende arthurienne: le Graal et la Table Ronde* (Paris, 1989), 117–309. Heavily abridged French translation.

The High Book of the Grail: A Translation of the Thirteenth Century Romance of Perlesvaus . Transl. by N. Bryant (Cambridge, 1978 ; repr. in paperback 1996).

See Chrétien de Troyes (i) below (Other Editions).

Other Editions

The Apocryphal New Testament: being the Apocryphal Gospels, Acts, Epistles and Apocalypses with other Narratives and Fragments. Ed. by M. R. James, 2 vols (Oxford, 1924).

Chrétien de Troyes: (i) *Chrétien de Troyes, Perceval le Gallois ou Le Conte du Graal.* Ed. by C. Potvin, 6 vols (Mons, 1866–71; repr. in 3 vols, Geneva, 1977; vol. 1 contains the *Perlesvaus*); (ii) *Der Percevalroman (Li Contes del Graal) von Christian von Troyes.* Ed. by A. Hilka (Halle, 1932) (*Elucidation*, 493–8, *Bliocadran*, 430–54); (iii) *Chrétien de Troyes, Le Roman de Perceval ou Le Conte du Graal.* Ed. by K. Busby (Tübingen, 1993).

Los Evalgelios apócrifos. Ed. by A. de Santos Otero, Biblioteca de Autores Cristianos 148 (Madrid, 1963; 10th edn, 1999).

Geoffrey of Monmouth: (i) *Geoffrey of Monmouth, The Vita Merlini.* Ed. and transl. by J. J. Parry (Urbana, 1925); (ii) *The Historia Regum Britannie of Geoffrey of Monmouth. I, Bern, Burgerbibliothek, MS 568).* Ed. by N. Wright, 2 vols (Cambridge, 1984–5).

Geraldi Cambrensis opera. Ed by J. F. Dimock (London, 1888; repr. 1964), vol. 6.

Gerbert de Montreuil, Le Roman de la Violette ou de Gerard de Nevers. Ed. by D. L. Buffum, SATF (Paris, 1928).
Jehan Bodel, La Chanson des Saisnes. Ed. by A. Brasseur, TLF 369 (Geneva, 1989).
Marie de France, Lais. Ed. by A. Ewert (Oxford, 1944).
La Mort le roi Artu: roman du XIIIᵉ siècle. Ed. by J. Frappier, TLF 58, 3rd edn (Geneva, 1964).
La Queste del Saint Graal. Ed. by A. Pauphilet, CFMA 33 (Paris, 1923).
La Vie mon signeur seint Nicholas le beneoit confessor. Ed. by J. J. Thompson, TLF 508 (Geneva, 1999).
Wace: (i) *Le Roman de Brut de Wace*. Ed. by I. Arnold, 2 vols, SATF (Paris, 1938–40); (ii) *Le Roman de Rou de Wace*. Ed. by A. J. Holden, 3 vols, SATF (Paris, 1970–3).
Wauchier de Denain, *L'Histoire des moines d'Égypte suivie de La Vie de Saint-Paul le Simple*. Ed. by M. Szkilnik, TLF 427 (Geneva, 1993).

Studies

Asher, M. 1995. 'Introduction, *The Post-Vulgate*', in N. J. Lacy ed. *Lancelot–Grail: The Old French Arthurian Vulgate and Post-Vulgate in Translation*, New York and London, IV, 163–6.
Baldwin, J. W. 2000. *Aristocratic Life in Medieval France: The Romances of Jean Renart and Gerbert de Montreuil, 1190–1230*, Baltimore.
Baumgartner, E. 2001. *Le Merlin en prose: fondations du récit arthurien*, Paris.
Bazin-Tacchella, S. 2000. *Le Merlin de Robert de Boron* (with T. Revol and J.-R.Valette), Neuilly.
Becker, P.-A. 1935. 'Von den Erzählern neben und nach Chrestien de Troyes', *ZrP*, 55, 257–92.
Beer, J. M. A. 1992. *Early Prose in France: Contexts of Bilingualism and Authority*, Kalamazoo, MI.
Berthelot, A. 1989. *Histoire de la littérature française du Moyen Âge*, Paris.
Berthelot 1994. 'L'Autre Monde incarné: Chastel Mortel et Chastel des Armes dans le *Perlesvaus*', in Buschinger and Spiewok eds *König Artus und der heilige Graal*, Greifswald, 27–37.
Bogdanow, F. 1966. *The Romance of the Grail: A Study of the Structure and Genesis of a Thirteenth-Century Arthurian Prose Romance*, Manchester and New York.
Bogdanow 1984. 'III. Le Perlesvaus', in *GRLMA**, IV:2, 43–67.
Bogdanow 1996. 'Post-Vulgate Cycle', in Lacy ed. 1996c*, 364–6.
Bozoky, E. 1974. 'La Bête Glatissante et le Graal: les transformations d'un thème allégorique dans quelques romans arthuriens', *Revue de l'Histoire des Religions*, 186, 127–48.
Bozoky 1980. 'Quêtes entrelacées et itinéraire rituel (regard sur la structure de la deuxième continuation du *Perceval*', in *Mélanges de langue et de littérature françaises du Moyen Âge et de la Renaissance offerts à Monsieur Charles Foulon*, 2 vols, I, Rennes, 49–57.
Bruckner, M. T. 1993. 'The Poetics of Continuation in Medieval French Romance: From Chrétien's *Conte du Graal* to the *Perceval* Continuations', *FF*, 18, 133–49.
Bruckner 1996. 'Rewriting Chrétien's *Conte du Graal* – Mothers and Sons: Questions, Contradictions, and Connections', in Kelly ed. 1996*, 213–44.
Bruckner 1999. 'Knightly Violence and Grail Quest Endings: Conflicting Views from the Vulgate Cycle to the *Perceval* Continuations', *M&H*, new series, 26, 17–32.
Bruckner 2000. 'Looping the Loop Through a Tale of Beginnings, Middles, and Ends: From Chrétien to Gerbert in the *Perceval* Continuations', in *'Por le soie amisté': Essays in Honor of Norris J. Lacy*, Amsterdam and Atlanta, GA, 33–51.
Brugger, E. 1930. 'Der sog. *Didot-Perceval*', *ZfSL*, 53, 389–459.
Burns, E. J. 1985. *Arthurian Fictions: Rereading the Vulgate Cycle*, Columbus, OH.
Busby, K. 1983. 'Der *Tristan Menestrel* des Gerbert de Montreuil und seine Stellung in der altfranzösischen Artustradition', *VR*, 42, 144–56.
Busby 1987–8. 'William Roach's Continuations of *Perceval*', *RPh*, 41, 298–309.
Busby 1993a. 'Text, Miniature, and Rubric in the Continuations of Chrétien's *Perceval*', in Busby, Nixon, Stones and Walters eds 1993, I, 365–76.

Busby 1993b. 'The Text of Chrétien's *Perceval* in MS London, College of Arms, Arundel XIV', in I. Short ed. 1993. *Anglo-Norman Anniversary Essays*, London, 75–85.

Busby 1998. '"Estrangement se merveilla": l'autre dans les *Continuations* de *Perceval*', in *Miscellanea Mediaevalia: mélanges offerts à Philippe Ménard*, 2 vols, Paris, I, 279–97.

Busby, K., T. Nixon, A. Stones, and L. J. Walters eds 1993. *Les Manuscrits de Chrétien de Troyes / The Manuscrits of Chrétien de Troyes*, 2 vols, Faux Titre 71–2, Amsterdam and Atlanta, GA.

Carman, J. N. 1936. *The Relationship of the Perlesvaus and the Queste del Saint Graal*, University of Kansas Humanistic Studies 5, no 4.

Cerquiglini, B. 1981. *La Parole médiévale: discours, syntaxe, texte*, Paris.

Cocito, L. 1978. *Gerbert de Montreuil e il poema del Graal*, Genoa.

Corley, C. 1982. 'Réflexions sur les deux premières continuations de *Perceval*', *Rom*, 103, 235–58.

Corley 1984. 'Wauchier de Denain et la deuxième continuation de *Perceval*', *Rom*, 105, 351–9.

Corley 1986. 'Manessier's Continuation of *Perceval* and the Prose *Lancelot* Cycle', *MLR*, 81, 574–91.

Corley 1987. *The Second Continuation of the Old French Perceval: A Critical and Lexicographical Study*, London.

De Riquer, M., and I. De Riquer. 1989. *El cuento del grial de Chrétien de Troyes y sus continuaciones*, Madrid.

Doner, J. 1993. 'Gauwain and the Pucelle de Lis', *RPh*, 46, 453–63.

Doner 1996. 'Scribal Whim and Miniature Allocation in the Illustrated Manuscripts of the *Continuation-Gauvain*', *Med. Aev*, 65, 73–95.

Dubost, F. 1994. 'Le *Perlesvaus*, livre de haute violence', in *La Violence dans le monde médiéval*, Senefiance 36, Aix-en-Provence, 1994, 177–99.

Evdokimova, L. 1999. 'Vers et prose au début du XIII⁀e siècle: le *Joseph* de Robert de Boron', *Rom*, 117, 448–73.

Fauchet, C. 1581. *Recueil de l'origine de la langue et poesie françoise, ryme et romans*, Paris; repr. Geneva, 1972.

Foulet, J. 1959. 'Sur la chronologie et la langue des oeuvres du XIII⁀e siècle', *Rom*, 80, 515.

François, C. 1932. *Étude sur le style de la continuation du Perceval par Gerbert et du Roman de la Violette par Gerbert de Montreuil*, Liège.

Frappier, J. 1954. 'Le Graal et la chevalerie', *Rom,* 75, 165–210.

Frappier 1958. 'Le Personnage de Gauvain dans la première continuation de *Perceval (Conte du Graal)*', *RPh*, 11, 331–44.

Gallais, P. 1964a. 'Formules de conteur et interventions d'auteur dans les manuscrits de la *Continuation-Gauvain*', *Rom*, 85, 181–229.

Gallais 1964b. 'Gauwain et la Pucelle de Lis', in *Mélanges de linguistique romane et de philologie médiévale offerts à M. Maurice Delbouille*, 2 vols, Gembloux, II, 207–29.

Gallais 1967. 'Bleheri, la cour de Poitiers et la diffusion des récits arthuriens sur le continent', in *Moyen Âge et Littérature comparée: actes du VII⁀e congrès national de la Société Française de Littérature Comparée*, Paris, 47–79.

Gallais 1970. 'Robert de Boron en Orient', in *Mélanges de langue et de littérature du Moyen Âge et de la Renaissance offerts à Jean Frappier*, 2 vols, Geneva, I, 313–19.

Gallais 1988–9. *L'Imaginaire d'un romancier français de la fin du XII⁀e siècle: description raisonnée, comparée et commentée de la Continuation-Gauvain, première suite du Conte du Graal de Chrétien de Troyes*, 4 vols, Amsterdam.

Gentry, F. G. 1991. 'Colin, Philipp, and Claus Wisse', in Lacy ed. 1991*, 97.

Giffin, M. E. 1965. 'A Reading of Robert de Boron', *PMLA*, 80, 499–507.

Gowans, L. 1996. 'The Grail in the West: Prose, Verse and Geography in the *Joseph* of Robert de Boron', *NFS*, 35, 1–17.

Gowans 2004. 'What Did Robert de Boron Really Write?', in *Arthurian Studies in Honour of P. J. C. Field*, Cambridge, 15–28.

Grigsby, J. L. 1987–8a. 'Heroes and their Destinies in the Continuations of Chrétien's *Perceval*', in Lacy, Kelly and Busby eds. 1987–8*, II, 41–53.

Grigsby 1987–8b. 'Remnants of Chrétien's Æsthetics in the Early *Perceval* Continuations and the Incipient Triumph of Writing', *RPh*, 41, 379–93.

Grimbert, J. T. 1990–1. 'Testimony and "Truth" in *Joseph d'Arimathie*', *RPh*, 44, 379–401.

Hoepffner, E. 1951. 'L'*Estoire dou Graal* de Robert de Boron', in R. Nelli ed. *Lumière du Graal: études et textes*, Paris, 139–50.

Hoepffner 1956. 'Robert de Boron et Chrétien de Troyes', in *Les Romans du Graal aux XIIᵉ et XIIIᵉ siècles, Strasbourg, 29 mars–3 avril 1954*, Paris, 93–106.

Ivy, R. H., Jr. 1951. *The Manuscript Relations of Manessier's Continuation of the Old French Perceval*, Philadelphia.

Kelly, T. E. 1974. *Le Haut Livre du Graal: Perlesvaus, a Structural Study*, Geneva.

Kennedy, E. 1986. *Lancelot and the Grail: A Study of the Prose Lancelot*, Oxford.

Kennedy 1998. 'Structures d'entrelacement contrastantes dans le *Lancelot* en prose et le *Perlesvaus*', in *Miscellanea mediaevalia: mélanges offerts à Philippe Ménard*, 2 vols, Paris, II, 745–57.

Kjær, J. 1990. 'L'Épisode de "Tristan ménestrel" dans la "Continuation de Perceval" par Gerbert de Montreuil (XIIIᵉ siècle): essai d'interprétation', *Revue Romane*, 25, 356–66.

Lacy, N. J. 1989. 'Linking in the Perlesvaus', in G. Mermier ed. *Contemporary Readings of Medieval Literature, Michigan Romance Studies*, 8, 169–78.

Lacy 1996. 'Motif Transfer in Arthurian Romance', in Kelly ed. 1996*, 157–68.

Larmat, J. 1974. 'Le Péché de Perceval dans la *Continuation* de Gerbert', in *Mélanges d'histoire littéraire, de linguistique et de philologie romanes offerts à Charles Rostaing*, 2 vols, Liège, I, 541–57.

Larmat 1979. 'Perceval et le Chevalier au Dragon, la Croix et le Diable', in *Le Diable au Moyen Âge*, Senefiance, 6, Aix-en-Provence, 293–305.

Leupin, A. 1979. 'Les Enfants de la mimésis: différence et répétition dans la première continuation du *Perceval*', *VR*, 38, 110–26.

Leupin 1982. 'La Faille et l'écriture dans les continuations du *Perceval*', *MA*, 88, 237–69.

Lloyd-Morgan, C. 1984. 'The Relationship between the *Perlesvaus* and the *Prose Lancelot*', *Med. Aev*, 53, 239–53.

Loomis, R. S. 1963. *The Grail: From Celtic Myth to Christian Symbol*, Cardiff and New York.

Lot, F. 1918. *Étude sur le Lancelot en prose*, Paris.

Luttrell, C. 1989. 'The Arthurian Hunt with a White Bratchet', *AL*, 9, 57–80.

Lynde-Recchia, M. 2000. *Prose, Verse, and Truth-Telling in the Thirteenth-Century*, Lexington, KY.

Meneghetti, M.-L. 1987–8. 'Signification et fonction réceptionnelle de l'*Elucidation* du *Perceval*', in Lacy, Kelly and Busby eds 1987–8*, II, 55–69.

Micha, A. 1956–7. 'L'Origine de la Table du Graal et de la Table Ronde chez Robert de Boron', *RPh*, 9, 173–7.

Micha 1958. 'Les Manuscrits du *Merlin* en prose de Robert de Boron', *Rom*, 79, 78–94, 145–74.

Micha 1960 and 1963. 'Les Manuscrits du *Lancelot en prose*', *Rom*, 81, 145–87; 84, 28–60.

Micha 1964 and 1966. 'La Tradition manuscrite du *Lancelot en prose*', *Rom*, 85, 293–318, 478–517; 87, 194–233.

Micha 1968. '"Matière" et "sen" dans l'*Estoire dou Graal* de Robert de Boron', *Rom*, 89, 457–80.

Micha 1978. 'L'Influence du *Merlin* de Robert de Boron', *TLL*, 16, 395–409.

Micha 1980. *Étude sur le Merlin de Robert de Boron*, PRF 151, Geneva.

Nitze, W. A. 1943. 'The *Esplumoir Merlin*', *Spec*, 18, 69–79.

Nitze 1953. 'Messire Robert de Boron: Enquiry and Summary', *Spec*, 28, 279–96.

O'Gorman, R. 1971. 'La Tradition manuscrite du *Joseph d'Arimathie* en prose de Robert de Boron', *RHT*, 1, 145–81.

O'Gorman 1979. 'A Note on the Orthodoxy of Robert de Boron', *NM*, 80, 387–90.

O'Gorman 1996. 'Robert de Boron', in Lacy ed. 1996c*, 385–6.

Pickens, R. T. 1984. '"Mais de çou ne parole pas Crestiens de Troies . . .": A Re-Examination of the *Didot-Perceval*', *Rom*, 105, 492–510.

Pickens 1988. 'Histoire et commentaire chez Chrétien de Troyes et Robert de Boron: Robert de Boron et le livre de Philippe de Flandre', in Lacy, Kelly and Busby eds 1987–8*, II, 17–39.

Pickens 1994. 'Autobiography and History in the Vulgate *Estoire* and in the *Prose Merlin*', in Kibler ed. 1994*, 98–116.

Pickens 1995. 'Robert de Boron', in W. W. Kibler and G. A. Zinn eds *Medieval France: An Encyclopedia,* New York and London, 803–4.

Roach, W. J. 1956. 'Les Continuations du *Conte du Graal*', in *Les Romans du Graal, dans la littérature des XIIᵉ et XIIIᵉ siècles, Strasbourg, 29 mars–3 avril 1954*, Paris, 107–17.

Roach 1966. 'Transformations of the Grail Theme in the First Two Continuations of the Old French *Perceval*', *PAPS*, 110, 160–4.

Rossi, M. 1980. 'Sur l'épisode de Caradoc de la *Continuation-Gauvain*', in *Mélanges de langue et de littérature françaises du Moyen Âge et de la Renaissance offerts à Monsieur Charles Foulon, II*, *M Rom*, 30, 247–54.

Roussel, C. 1983. 'Le Jeu des formes et des couleurs: observations sur la beste glatissante', *Rom*, 104, 49–82.

Salmeri, F. 1984. *Manessier: modelli, simboli, scrittura*, Catania.

Saly, A. 1989. 'L'Arbre illuminé et l'arbre à l'enfant', *PRIS-MA*, 5, 81–93.

Saly 1998. 'Le *Perlesvaus* et Gerbert de Montreuil', in *Miscellanea mediaevalia: mélanges offerts à Philippe Ménard*, 2 vols, Paris, II, 1163–82.

Séguy, M. 1992–5. 'L'Ordre du discours dans le désordre du monde: la recherche de la transparence dans la quatrième continuation', *Rom*, 113, 175–93.

Spiegel, G. M. 1993. *Romancing the Past: The Rise of Vernacular Prose Historiography in Thirteenth-Century France*, Berkeley and Oxford.

Stephens, L. 1996. 'Gerbert and Manessier: The Case for a Connection', *AL*, 14, 53–68.

Sturm-Maddox, S. 1992. '*Tout est par senefïance*: Gerbert's *Perceval*', *AY*, 2, 191–207.

Sturm-Maddox 1994. '*Letres escrites i a*: The Marvelous Inscribed', in *Conjunctures: Medieval Studies in Honor of Douglas Kelly*, Amsterdam and Atlanta, GA, 515–28.

Szkilnik, M. 1986. 'Écrire en vers, écrire en prose: le choix de Wauchier de Denain', *Rom*, 107, 208–30.

Thompson, A. W. 1959. 'Additions to Chrétien's *Perceval*: Prologues and Continuations', in Loomis ed. 1959*, 206–17.

Tolstoy, N. 1985. *The Quest for Merlin*, London.

Trachsler, R. 2000. *Merlin l'enchanteur: étude sur le Merlin de Robert de Boron*, Paris.

Uitti, K. D. 1975. 'The Clerkly Narrator Figure in Old French Hagiography and Romance', *MR*, 2, 394–408.

Vial, G. 1978. 'L'Auteur de la deuxième continuation du *Conte du Graal*', in *Mélanges d'études romanes du Moyen Âge et de la Renaissance offerts à Monsieur Jean Rychner par ses collègues, ses élèves et ses amis*, Strasbourg, 519–30.

Vial 1987. *Le Conte du Graal, sens et unité: la première continuation, textes et contenu*, Geneva.

Walter, P. 2000. *Merlin ou le savoir du monde*, Paris.

West, G. D. 1970–1. 'Grail Problems, I: Silimac the Stranger', *RPh*, 24, 599–611.

Weston, J. L. 1920. *From Ritual to Romance*, Cambridge; repr. Princeton City, NJ, 1993.

Williams, A. M. L. 2001. *The Adventures of the Holy Grail: A Study of La Queste del Saint Graal*, Oxford.

Zink, M. 1992. *Littérature française du Moyen Âge*, Paris.

VII

LANCELOT WITH AND WITHOUT THE GRAIL: *LANCELOT DO LAC* AND THE VULGATE CYCLE

†Elspeth Kennedy (ed.), Michelle Szkilnik, Rupert T. Pickens, Karen Pratt and Andrea M. L. Williams

Lancelot with and without the Grail

The *Lancelot–Grail* Cycle, which, to judge from the number of surviving manuscripts, was, like the prose *Tristan* and the *Roman de la Rose*, a medieval 'bestseller', consisted in its final version (the Vulgate Cycle) of the following parts:

(i)   *L'Estoire del Saint Graal*
(ii) *Merlin* and its *Suite* (a prose version of the *Merlin* of Robert de Boron and a Continuation)
(iii) *Le Lancelot* proper (a modern, not a medieval title) which begins 'En la marche de Gaule' with an account of the events that led to Lancelot being carried away by the Lady of the Lake and contains all the adventures of Lancelot and some of those of other Arthurian knights up to the beginning of the Grail Quest
(iv) *La Queste del Saint Graal* or *Les Aventures del Saint Graal*
(v)   *La Mort le roi Artu*.[1]

However, it is generally agreed that the romance was not planned from the beginning in these terms. The contrasts and contradictions within a closely interlacing structure have fascinated scholars for years. In the late nineteenth and early twentieth century Brugger (1906–10) argued that the Cycle was preceded by one combining a Lancelot romance with a Perceval quest; Bruce (1918–19) emphasized what he saw as the disunity of the work and ascribed a major role to interpolators and *remanieurs*. Lot (1918), whilst admitting that the *Merlin* (and its Continuation) was a later addition, maintained that all the other branches of the Cycle were by a single author and stressed its unity. Frappier (1954–5; 1961, appendix; 1978a) believed that the romance from 'En la marche de Gaule' to the end of the *Mort Artu* was planned by an 'architect' directing a team of writers. Micha (1961; 1973) too argues eloquently for the unity of the Cycle. Both scholars maintain that the *Estoire* and *Merlin*, which was provided with a Continuation to link up with the beginning of the *Lancelot* in many, but not all manuscripts containing this part of the Cycle, are later additions (see the section on the date of the Cycle below). I would, however, suggest that the manuscript tradition indicates a first stage in the development of the prose *Lancelot*, in which the tale of Lancelot does not yet incorporate a Grail Quest. All manuscripts give the same version of Lancelot's adventures from the opening 'En la marche de Gaule' until Lancelot and Galehot become Knights of the Round Table and leave Arthur's court (*LK*, 1–572; *LM*, 7 and 8). At that point the manuscripts divide into two main versions. The first of these is the non-cyclic or pre-cyclic version of the journey to the lands of Galehot, the False Guinevere episode and Lionel's first adventure as a knight, a version which ends the romance with the death of Galehot and Lancelot's decision to become a permanent member of Arthur's court (*LK*, 572–613; *LM*, 3, 2–69). The second is the cyclic version of these same episodes, but in a form that prepares the way for a Grail Quest to be achieved by the son of Lancelot (*LM*, 1, 1–389).[2] These versions will be compared below. The non-cyclic version is to be found, except for the last folio, in the oldest surviving manuscript of the prose *Lancelot*, BNF, fr. 768, and in full in Rouen, Bibliothèque Municipale, MS 06 and Florence, Biblioteca Medicea Laurenziana, MS Pl. 89. inf., 61, and is found in part in fourteen other manuscripts.[3] In the part of the text common to cyclic and pre-cyclic manuscripts, the allusions to the Grail Quest (including the characters connected with it in the twelfth- and early thirteenth-century tradition) all refer to it as an adventure already told and as part of an existing tradition (E. Kennedy 1986). This is clearly illustrated by a passage listing the three most beautiful women: Guinevere, Helene sans Per and the daughter of Pellés. The third of these is described as the daughter of the maimed king and the sister of Perceval/Perlesvaus:

> Et l'autre fu fille au roi mehaignié, ce fu li rois Pellés qui fu peres Perlesvaus [Perceval in a number of manuscripts], a celui qui vit apertement les granz merveilles del Graal et acompli lo Siege Perilleus de la Table Reonde et mena a fin les aventures del Reiaume Perilleus Aventureus, ce fu li regnes de Logres. Cele fu sa suer . . . (*LK*, 33)

> (*And the other was the daughter of the maimed king, that was King Pellés, father of Perlesvaus [or Perceval], of him who saw openly the great marvels of the Grail and achieved the Perilous Seat of the Round Table and brought to a successful conclusion the adventures of the Perilous Adventurous Realm, that was the kingdom of Logres. She was his sister...*)

This is the reading of the majority of manuscripts. It seems to combine allusions to Chrétien de Troyes and to Robert de Boron: in Chrétien, Perceval is named as the Grail hero and in Robert de Boron is to be found the Perilous Seat (*Merlin*, 185–94). This is in clear contradiction with what happens in the *Queste*, where it is Galahad who is destined to sit in the Perilous Seat and to be the only one of the three Grail heroes to look inside the Grail and to 'see' what is beyond the reach of human senses. Yet this is the reading common to the majority of manuscripts from a wide range of groups and must have been the original reading of the ancestor of the extant manuscripts (*LK*, 2, 89–90; E. Kennedy 1970; cf. Frappier

1961, 454; Lot 1918, 120, n. 15; Micha 1964, 297–8). As can be seen from a study of the variants, the inconsistency with the *Queste* is perceived by a number of scribes, including that of London, British Library, Additional MS 10293 (the base manuscript for the editions of both Micha (*LM*, 7, 59) and Sommer for this part of the text), who names 'Galaat' as the knight who sat in the Perilous Seat and saw the Grail 'apertement' (*openly*) and identifies Pellés as his grandfather (E. Kennedy 1993). The uncorrected allusions to the Grail in the part of the text common to all manuscripts before there is a division into pre-cyclic and cyclic versions would fit in, therefore, with the whole pattern of allusions outwards to the wider Arthurian context to be found in the tale of Lancelot up to his installation as a Knight of the Round Table.

The version to be found in BNF, fr. 768 and its related manuscripts, which brings the story to an end with the death of Galehot, would indeed seem to represent the first stage in the development of the prose tale of Lancelot (cf. Micha 1987, 57–83). The second stage incorporates a prose version of Chrétien's *Charrette*, adding other adventures (including some preparing the way for a Grail Quest), a *Queste* with Galahad as the main Grailwinner and a *Mort Artu*. In the third stage, an early history of the Grail (the *Estoire*) is specially written to prepare the way for the Galahad *Queste*, but also looks forward to other events in the Cycle (compare the building of Solomon's boat in *Estoire*, 283–90 and *Queste*, 220–6; the history of the Croix Noire in *Estoire*, 479–84; *LM*, 2, 320–4). At this stage too was added a *Merlin* based on the prose version of Robert de Boron's work, to be followed by a Continuation preparing the way for the *Lancelot* with episodes looking forward to the war that led to the death of Lancelot's father (for example *S*, II, 444–50, 465–6). In stage three, alongside correlation there is also contradiction: for example, that between the version of the birth of Merlin to be found in the account of Lancelot's childhood, where Merlin is an unredeemed child of a devil, useful only to give the Lady of the Lake lessons in magic and then imprisoned by her, and that given in the *Merlin*, where he is a prophet of the Holy Grail. This and other such contradictions do not pass unnoticed, so that even after the third and final stage in the structural development of the Cycle is reached, scribes often attempt to smooth away such contradictions, though frequently removing one form of inconsistency only to create another (E. Kennedy 1970, 525–7; 1986, 111–55, 309). An interesting feature of a manuscript such as BNF, fr. 113–16, is the attempt to bring some Tristan adventures into the Lancelot story, as opposed to setting the Tristan story in the context of the *Lancelot–Grail* Cycle, as happens in the prose *Tristan* (Baumgartner 1975, 118–32). Those manuscripts that link up with the prose *Tristan* prepare the way for the Reader's Digest type of compendium of Arthurian romance to be found in a fifteenth-century manuscript such as BNF, fr. 112, which contains some chunks of the *Lancelot–Grail* in unshortened form as well as summaries of parts of the text, alongside material from other romances (Pickford 1959/60*). The trend has therefore been towards the gradual inclusion within Lancelot's story of as many of the main Arthurian themes and characters as possible.

The Date of the Cycle

Most scholars would place the composition of the Cycle comprising the *Lancelot* proper, the *Queste* and the *Mort Artu* between 1215 and 1230; the *Estoire* and the *Merlin* and Continuation would have been added later (Lot 1931; Frappier, *Mort Artu* edn).[4] However, Stones (1977) has dated to the early 1220s the manuscript Rennes, Bibliothèque Municipale, 255, which contains the *Estoire*, *Merlin* (without Continuation) and *Lancelot* up to the middle of the interpretation of Galehot's dreams in the cyclic version of the events leading towards the death of Galehot. Significantly, this interpretation includes the prophecy of a new Grailwinner, son of Lancelot. This suggests that a cyclic version that included the *Estoire* and *Merlin* might be dated to at least the early 1220s. The manuscript BNF, fr. 768, which gives the pre-cyclic version ending with the death of Galehot, has been dated between 1215 and 1225 (Stirnemann 1993, 207). In my view this version predates the *Perlesvaus*, and was probably written early in the thirteenth century (E. Kennedy 1986, appendix 1); Bogdanow (1984) and Lloyd-Morgan (1984) would date the *Queste* after the *Perlesvaus*.

The General Structure of the Cycle

After an overconcentration by critics such as Brugger and Bruce on lost early cycles and on narrative fragmentation, Lot, Frappier and Micha have all emphasized the unity of the Cycle, sometimes in somewhat post-medieval terms of literary criticism, although Frappier and Micha would admit that the *Estoire* and the *Merlin* were added later and created their own links with what was to follow. Burns (1985a) has taken a different approach. She retreats from the search for a continuous referential plot-line or coherent narrative development, but has rightly emphasized the importance of the pattern of repetition in a continued rewriting of the text. However, I would suggest that if a medieval text is approached according to its own terms, and if its particular patterns of pairing and contrast, of references forwards and backwards, are observed, and if the distinctions that are made between the allegorical and the non-allegorical (distinctions clearly marked within the text) are taken into account, then the terms 'amorphous' and 'rambling' (used by Burns) seem also to be a post-medieval imposition on a work that requires a different kind of reading.

Because of the immense length of the Cycle in its 'final form' (a term to be wary of in relation to much medieval vernacular literature) scholars have tended to concentrate upon a particular part of the text without always placing it within a wider context; no one branch should ever be read in isolation from the whole. The references to what the tale has told and what the tale will tell or not tell are significant, as can be the recurrence of similar episodes that may serve to make links, to emphasize certain themes. It must be admitted that some parts of the Cycle are more successful at creating meaningful patterns than others, but this is a complex work in which different kinds of truth are explored. Lancelot remains the central figure for much of the Cycle, but there are subtle or more obvious shifts in the way he himself and his relationship with Arthur and Guinevere are presented as the narrative progresses. There is no single voice to be believed without question; earlier events are continually being reinterpreted. 'Li contes' can introduce new information that leads to a reinterpretation of the past, but it is not the sole voice of authority. Nor should the interpretation of earlier episodes given by men of religion and true for the time of the Grail adventures necessarily still be valid after the end of the *Queste*. As in that other great romance that developed in more than one stage and was widely read for centuries, the *Roman de la Rose*, there is a tension between various possibilities, no single answer is given, and we oversimplify at our peril (E. Kennedy 1996a). [EK]

L'Estoire del Saint Graal

The anonymous prose text, the *Estoire del Saint Graal*, has always belonged to the *Lancelot–Grail* Cycle; conceived as part of a whole, it was never an independent romance. Occupying the first position in the internal chronology of the Cycle, it recounts the *translatio* of the Grail from the foot of the Holy Cross to the shores of Great Britain, which is subsequently christianized. Evidently inspired by Robert de Boron's verse *Estoire dou Graal*, otherwise known as *Joseph*, it considerably expands the story in order to account not only for the existence of the Grail, but also for many characters and places found in the *Lancelot–Grail* Cycle.

In a long prologue (##1–30), the narrator, a hermit living in the year 717, explains how, on the night before Good Friday, Christ gave him a small book. Whilst reading it, the narrator was taken in spirit to heaven, where he was given access to the mystery of the Holy Trinity. Having returned to his senses, he locked the book in a box containing the host, but on Easter day, the book was missing.

After a long quest, the narrator retrieved it and was ordered to make a copy of it. His transcription is in effect the *Estoire del Saint Graal*.

The narrative proper contains three main sections:

After recounting Joseph of Arimathea's devout attitude towards Christ's body (which he buries after having collected drops of his blood in the Grail) and his subsequent imprisonment and liberation after forty-two years (##31–57), the first section deals with the conversion of the kingdom of Sarras, where Joseph was sent with some companions and the Grail. This part introduces the main characters: Joseph's son Josephé, whom Christ himself will anoint as the first bishop of his new people; Evalach-Mordrain, King of Sarras, who will defeat his enemy Tholomer thanks to Josephé's help and will subsequently convert to Christianity; his brother-in-law Seraphe-Nascien and the wives of Seraphe and Evalach (##58–285).

The second section focuses on the perilous adventures of various characters: Mordrain is taken to la Roche de Port Peril, the former lair of the pirate Forcaire, who was defeated by Pompey (##286–374); Nascien is brought to the Turning Island (##375–472); Chelidoine, Nascien's son, arrives at a deserted shore, where he encounters and converts King Label (##473–528). Finally, messengers sent in search of Nascien are shipwrecked on Hippocrates's island, whose exemplary story is included (##529–99). All of them (except pure Chelidoine) are in turn tempted by the devil and visited by Christ. Fortified in their new faith by their hardships, these heroes are reunited, before being sent on a new mission (##600–14). This middle section introduces Solomon's 'nef' (*ship*) and David's sword, and includes the story of the Tree of Life.

The last section describes the arduous yet successful evangelization of Great Britain, after Josephé's, Joseph's and their companions' miraculous crossing of the sea on Josephé's shirt (##615–60). It establishes most of the places and motifs of major importance to the Vulgate Cycle, providing the etiological back-ground to many episodes contained in the other branches: Mordrain's blinding for having looked into the Grail (##751–3); the episode of la Croix Noire (the black cross, ##758–65); Moÿse's punishment for having dared to sit in the empty seat at the Grail Table (##766–71); Alain's multiplication of the fish, after which miracle he will be called the Rich Fisher King and will be entrusted with the Grail (##775–9); the first sighting of the stag with the four lions (##792–802); Chanaam's burning tomb as well as most of the perilous cemeteries visited later by Galahad and Lancelot (##810–28, ##870–3); the foundation of Orcanie (##833–63); the making of a cross on the shield that will be Galahad's (##874–6); the construction of Corbenic where the Grail will be kept (##883–4); King Lambor's murder with David's sword, a crime which will turn Wales and the kingdom of la Terre Foraine into a waste land (##890–1).

This strange text has long suffered from scholarly contempt. Lot (1918, 278) described it as weak and boring; Frappier (1961, 56) commented on its literary mediocrity. These very severe judgements by two respected scholars explain why until very recently no one had chosen to edit or analyse the *Estoire*. Three editions of the text had been published: two in the nineteenth century (Furnivall and Hucher) and one at the beginning of the twentieth (Sommer). But all are hard to find and all are unsatisfactory. This is all the more surprising since the text was obviously very popular throughout the Middle Ages; two versions (a long and a short) exist, in forty-four extant manuscripts dating from the thirteenth to the fifteenth century. There are also a number of fragments dispersed in several manuscripts and two sixteeenth-century printed editions. Besides being the first part of the *Lancelot–Grail* Cycle, the *Estoire* was probably reused to form the first part of the Post-Vulgate *Roman du Graal*, see chapter IX). It was also translated and adapted into other languages, notably Portuguese and Spanish.

In the last decade of the twentieth century, however, scholars rediscovered this very original work and began to re-evaluate its qualities. In 1997, Ponceau published a new edition, based on two manuscripts: Amsterdam, Bibliotheca Philosophica Hermetica, MS 1 (fols 1a–63d) for the first half, and, for the second half, Rennes, Bibliothèque Municipale, 255 (fols 43f–100e), a representative of the long version that Ponceau (edn, xxviii), Micha (*LM*, 1, xiv) and most other scholars now deem to be the original one.[5] An English translation has been provided by Chase (Lacy transl. I, 1993), but to date there is no translation into modern French of the long version, only of the short (see *Le Livre du Graal,* Poirion and Walter edn, vol. 1).

Nothing is known about the author of the *Estoire*; some scholars have suggested that the author might be from Corbie (Picardy) or Meaux (near Paris), and Ponceau does not refute these hypotheses (edn, xi, nn. 3 and 4). As in many other parts of the Cycle, the name of Robert de Boron is given several times as the person who translated from Latin into the vernacular the book first transcribed by a hermit who acquired the story from Christ himself (Ponceau edn, §§613, 757). Ponceau (1998) clearly demonstrates what many scholars had stated earlier: the *Estoire* and the *Queste* were not written by the same person (Szkilnik 1991b), and it is now generally accepted that the *Estoire* was added to an existing Cycle.

What has mainly fascinated scholars in this unusual text is the long and elaborate prologue in which the narrator, who presents himself as a hermit living in a remote place, explains how he happened to receive a book written by Christ, which contains the story we are going to read. Leupin (1979; 1982) was the first scholar to produce an enlightening study of the prologue and to question the *locus* from which the discourse originates (Szkilnik 1991a, esp. chapter 3; Kelly 1988). Other scholars, such as Burns (1985b) and Chase (1994), have examined narratorial interventions in this branch of the Cycle. The linguistic approach deployed by Bertin (Combes and Bertin 2001), who looks at the use of indirect speech, of the pronoun *on* and of the adverbs *car* and *or*, also yields interesting conclusions. Bertin notes that the *Estoire* repeatedly employs the phrase *ci endroit* (in the formula *Ci endroit dist li contes*) instead of *or*, thus replacing temporal narrative markers characteristic of earlier texts with spatial ones. The *Queste* offers the more traditional *or dist li contes*. Bertin, who, as is now generally accepted, assigns a later date of composition to the *Estoire* than to the *Queste*, interprets this replacement as indicative of the new type of relationship between prose texts and their audiences that will develop at the end of the thirteenth century: oral communication being replaced by silent reading (Combes and Bertin 2001, esp. 116–21).

All these studies testify to a persistent trend in Arthurian scholarship: a pronounced interest in narrative techniques and the processes involved in the composition of romances and cycles. In this respect, the *Estoire* is especially important, since the prologue, in addition to many shorter narratorial interventions throughout the text, demonstrates that the author conceived of his work not simply as the chronological origin of the whole Cycle, but also as some sort of fixed reference point that would lend cohesion to stories connected, yet dispersed (Szkilnik 1991a). However – and this is another intriguing aspect of the *Estoire* – the narrative seems to have trouble preserving its own cohesion. What threatens it is not its use of interlace in itself, for the *Estoire* follows in turn different heroes in a way familiar to readers of the prose *Lancelot*, and no less skilfully. However, it also includes stories such as those of Pompey and the pirate Forcaire, or Hippocrates's misadventures with women, narratives that are supposedly meant to account for a detail in the main story: for example, a dark and frightening cave on the island to which Mordrain is taken, the presence of a beautiful old mansion on another island. Yet these sub-plots evolve into independent tales, told for their own sake. Their tone at times even clashes with the atmosphere of the episode in which they are included. Hippocrates's involvement with a Gallic beauty and his subsequent humiliation appear to belong more to the genre of *fabliau* (Szkilnik 1991a, 120–2). Yet this is recounted in the midst of a dire adventure experienced by King Label's daughter and two messengers sent to find Nascien. Even if one could find connections with the main story (for example, it is possible to read Hippocrates's downfall as an *exemplum*), the disproportionate treatment of these sub-plots is such that one suspects the narrator developed them for the sheer pleasure of telling a good story. Thus the *Estoire* exhibits a characteristic that later romances, such as *Perceforest*, will exploit to a much greater extent.

The *Estoire* is a work about conversion, about the eradication of pagan creeds and the expansion of the Christian faith. This aspect sets it apart from the other branches of the Cycle, although the conversion of heathens, and more specifically Saracens, is central to the account of the history of the Croix Noire in *LM*, 2, 320–4, a topic picked up and explored further in the *Estoire*. Yet this aspect has not received all the attention it deserves, despite the work of scholars such as Chase (1995). The *Estoire*'s main protagonists are, in some cases, Christians from the start, Joseph and his son Josephé, for example, but most of them are new converts, examples being Evalach-Mordrain, Seraphe-Nascien and his son Chelidoine, and King Label and his daughter. Thus the atmosphere of the text is strikingly epic. The Saracens play a major role, whether they embrace *en masse* the new faith or die during great battles against Christ's heroic knights.

Christian proselytization is the other remarkable theme of this branch. Some heroes specialize in preaching to the pagans: Joseph of Arimathea is the first one to lecture Evalach about the mysteries of the Christian faith, explaining to him both the Holy Trinity, Christ's virginal Conception and Birth, the Redemption and other obscure points. But soon, he is replaced in that role by his son Josephé, whom Christ himself appoints as first bishop. Josephé then becomes the most vehement and gifted preacher, the one to whom everyone else defers when confronted with incredulous pagans, the one who relentlessly harangues his own followers, in turn scolding, comforting or explaining. Chelidoine is also invested with this evangelizing mission: although still a young boy, he converts Label, King of Persia, and later initiates Duke Ganor in the tenets of the Christian faith, thus preparing his subsequent conversion by Josephé. These long sermons might seem boring or exasperating to modern readers, yet they deserve careful analysis. Whilst in some way they recall the lessons given by hermits in the *Queste*, especially when Josephé, for example, glosses a vision detail by detail, they are also very different in that they usually take place in front of a big audience, sometimes even in some sort of debate against 'clers de la loi sarrasine' (*doctors of the pagan law*). The moral is geared towards one individual, but also towards a whole group that is expected to convert, and it is often accompanied by a miraculous intervention; for example, the incredulous pagan doctor who dares to contradict the Christians is either stunned or dies on the spot, and an injured man is healed by touching Evalach's shield. The mass conversion that ensues is usually followed by the destruction of pagan idols and the purification of temples turned into churches. Seen in the thirteenth-century context of the Crusades, of the reconquest of the Holy Land, of renewed attempts at converting Muslims, the work takes on a much more combative tone. The recurring description of Josephé and his disciples entering pagan cities or castles, barefoot and poorly attired, brings to mind the Franciscan friars and their missions to the Muslims, for example, St Francis's mission to the Egyptian Sultan al-Kamil, which took place in 1219. Scholars agree that the *Queste del Saint Graal* was written under Cistercian influence. It would be of great interest to examine whether the *Estoire* was influenced by another monastic order. Whatever the case, the difference between the two texts is striking; whilst the *Queste* deals with individual salvation in terms of a quest for a glimpse of the divine (even if each character is representative of a type), the *Estoire* is concerned with the conversion of whole peoples, whether by persuasion or by force. It describes an expansion, a conquest marked by the erection of Christian monuments, churches, abbeys and crosses. It is a militant text, as close in some ways to the *Perlesvaus* as it is to the *Queste*. In depicting the conquest of Brittany in that manner, it also expands references already in the prose *Lancelot* to the conversion of pagans and Saracens by Joseph (*LM*, 2, 253, 321–4, 329–38). Care is therefore being taken to link the *Estoire* to the Cycle as a whole, not just to the *Queste*.

The *Estoire* has another feature in common with the *Perlesvaus:* the use of the *merveilleux* that borders on the fantastic. This aspect has been justly emphasized by Dubost (1991*). One of the headings that the hermit reads in the book given by Christ is 'Chi est li commenchemens des Paours' (*Here begin the Terrors*; Ponceau edn, 6). The whole work is indeed shrouded in a climate of fear and foreboding. Most characters are uncertain about what is awaiting them, and the audience is also unsure about where the narrator is leading them. This is especially true in the numerous episodes where the protagonists, brought to some desert island, experience temptations and frightening situations in order to test their faith. Dubost (1991*, I, 303) states that the *Estoire* is one of the medieval texts most marked by what he calls the 'fantastique de l'île' (*the fantastic nature of islands*). Since readers, denied superior knowledge by the narrator, are forced to adopt the point of view of the character, they share the hero's puzzlement in the face of supernatural adventures. Whilst in the *Queste* the reader soon learns to decipher the meaning of events, thanks to the lessons given by obliging hermits, in the *Estoire* some adventures frustrate interpretation. The narrator himself seems to hesitate between two kinds of explanation: realistic (or at least pseudo-realistic) and supernatural ones, thus fostering the fantastic. If sometimes, as in the *Queste*, a character (who in the *Estoire* is rarely a hermit) glosses an event or a vision, we are frequently given no explanation of the fearful sight. A good example is the strange bird which steals Mordrain's bread on the Island of Port Peril. The precise description of this *serpolion* and of its habits is all the more interesting in that it does not lead to an allegorical interpretation (Szkilnik 1991a, 100–5). The *serpolion* reminds the reader of two other strange animals, two *bestes diverses*: the narrator's guide in the prologue and the monster hunted by Queen Sarracinte's brother. Both are described as fantastic animals. Dubost (1991*, I, 519) sees the latter as encoding an incestuous desire and the former as emblematizing the monstrous transgression of which this or any author is guilty. But he insists that the narrator, while suggesting these interpretations, does not impose them and thus maintains an unsettling feeling of uncertainty.

Far from being a negligible text, written by a mediocre author who was trying to compete with his more gifted predecessors, the *Estoire* deserves more critical attention. Conceived as a retelling of the *enfances* of the Grail, its goal was to perfect the symmetry of the Vulgate Cycle by providing a new beginning to balance the *Mort Artu* at the end. As a latecomer, it was able to fill in the gaps, supply extra explanations where needed, assure the cohesion of the whole and reflect on the entire project. The *Estoire* is indeed a key text in our understanding of how cycles were formed and evolved. [MS]

Merlin and its *Suite*

The Vulgate *Merlin* (Sommer edn, II) consists of two major sections. The *Merlin* proper (II, 1–88, about one fifth of the total), the text of which resembles more or less that of the early thirteenth-century *mise en prose* of Robert de Boron's verse *Merlin* (see chapter VI), is followed by a *Suite Merlin*, or Merlin Continuation (II, 88–466, four times longer), which is designed to link Robert's text to the prose *Lancelot*, the Grail material that accrues to it, much of which also derives from Robert de Boron, and the concluding *Mort Artu*. Thus, although the *Merlin* proper, in its independent form, was undoubtedly the earliest of the components of the Vulgate Cycle to be composed, the Vulgate *Merlin* as a whole was perhaps the latest. As we shall see, the *Merlin* proper is not fully reworked stylistically to mesh flawlessly with the other branches, nor does it reflect the degree to which the Continuation is tailored to conform with them.

The Merlin proper. Merlin is conceived by an incubus and successfully defends his mother in court (#1, *S*: 3–20).[6] Merlin explains why Vortigern's tower will not stand (#2, *S*: 20–35). Merlin supports the reigns of Pendragon and Uther and establishes the Round Table (#3, *S*: 35–58). King Uther falls in love with Ygerne and Merlin uses magic to bring about Arthur's conception. Uther marries Ygerne after her husband, the Duke of Tintagel, is killed and he wins the loyalty of the duke's vassals (#4, *S*: 58–80). Arthur, raised without knowledge of his lineage, is crowned after he pulls the sword from the stone as a sign that he is a divinely ordained king (#5, *S*: 80–8).

The Suite: Rebellion of Uther's barons. Led by the Six Kings (Aguisant of Scotland; his father Caradoc, a knight of the Round Table; Lot of Orkney and Lothian; Neutre of Garlot; Urien of Gorre; Yder [of Cornwall]), Uther's barons refuse to pay Arthur homage even after Merlin and the Duke of Tintagel's men swear that Arthur is Uther's son. The kings rebel, along with the knights of Uther's Round Table. Arthur, armed with Excalibur and aided by Merlin, routs them. Merlin has Arthur summon the brother kings, Ban of Benoyc and Bohort of Gaunes, from Brittany to fight alongside the rebellious King Leodagan of

Carmelide against the Saxons led by King Rion (#5 continued, *S*: 88–101). The brothers recognize Arthur's legitimacy and pay him homage (#6, *S*: 101–9). Meanwhile, the Six Kings reorder their forces, gather more allies and attack Arthur, who again defeats the rebels (#7, *S*: 109–21). Merlin teases Arthur when the former appears in camp in the guise of a birdcatcher (#8, *S*: 121–4).

Saxon threats. The Six Kings and their allies fortify the borderlands to defend the kingdom against Saxons, who have invaded Orkney and Cornwall. Meanwhile, Galescalain, King Neutre's son by one of Arthur's half-sisters (identified as Morgan in #5, *S*: 73), determines to be knighted by his uncle (#9, *S*: 124–8). His cousins Gauvain,[7] Agravain, Guerrehet and Gaheriet, King Lot's sons by another of Arthur's half-sisters, learn this and long to go with him (#10, *S*: 128–31). (Their half-brother Mordred was sired by Arthur, not knowing the lady was his sister, when he was elected king.) The rebel kings disperse to strengthen their various fortifications. Sagremor, stepson of King Brandegorre, an ally of the Six Kings, leaves Constantinople to receive arms from Arthur. Meanwhile, the Saxons overrun Logres (#11, *S*: 131–3). Galescalain and Lot's sons leave together for Arthur's court. They find the countryside laid waste, attack retreating Saxons and defeat them when forces from the city of Logres (London) join them (##12–13, *S*: 133–41). Arthur and his allies anonymously join forces with King Leodagan and his supporters to face the Saxons at Carhaix. The Knights of the Round Table are overpowered and Leodagan taken prisoner (#14, *S*: 141–5). Leodagan's daughter, Guinevere, watches from a window as Arthur and his men rescue her father and lead the rout of the Saxons. She is distinguished from another Guinevere, a half-sister fathered by Leodagan the same night as she, by her crown-shaped birth mark (#15, *S*: 145–9). As Arthur stands out in individual combats, the Saxons are defeated, but King Rion sends to Denmark for reinforcements (#16, *S*: 149–56).

Arthur and Guinevere's love. As Guinevere serves Arthur, whose identity remains hidden, they fall in love. Leodagan approves because he recognizes Arthur as superior to himself (#17, *S*: 156–9).

Continued Saxon threats and the advancement of the young heroes. Merlin informs the victors that another battle against the Saxons has been won by Lot's sons, Galescalain and Sagremor, on the plain before Logres. Meanwhile, King Tradelmant of North Wales and the King of the Hundred Knights defeat the Saxons at Arundel (#18, *S*: 159–64). In Scotland, King Aguisant and his cousin attack a Saxon train hauling away plunder; they are nearly overwhelmed when the enemy regroup, but are rescued by Urien, his sons Yvain, from another of Arthur's half-sisters, and Yvain the Bastard, his nephew Baudemagu and Bademagu's son Meleagant. They slaughter the Saxons, and Urien and Baudemagu claim the plunder. When news of their cousins' victory at Logres arrives, the two Yvains wish to be knighted by Arthur. In the Welsh Marches, King Neutre forces the Saxons to withdraw after a hard battle (#19, *S*: 164–71). Kings Caradoc, Belinant and Brandegorre force the Saxons to retreat from South Wales. Meanwhile, Brandegorre's son, Dodinel the Wildman, hears about the exploits of Arthur's nephews, and he and Caradoc's son, Kay of Estral, vow to join them (#20, *S*: 171–4). Saxons invade Northumberland, ruled by King Clarion, who summons the aid of Duke Escant of Cambenic (#21, *S*: 174–8). At Carhaix, Merlin informs Arthur and the brother kings that the Saxons have attacked Yder in Cornwall, Lot in Orkney and Loonois (Lothian) and Clarion in Northumberland. Lot's sons and their companions need Merlin's help. Meanwhile, Sagremor and his friends arrive from Constantinople and prepare to face a Saxon contingent near Camelot, which Lot's sons have come to defend. Disguised as a peasant, Merlin convinces Lot's sons to join Sagremor. After heavy but indecisive fighting, they all withdraw to Camelot (##22–3, *S*: 178–86). Clarion and Escant drive the Saxons out of Northumberland, while Gauvain raises an army and heads towards Arundel. The two Yvains and their companions join Yder's forces to defend Cornwall, facing the enemy at a bridge (#24, *S*: 187–91).

Moves toward reconciliation. Disguised as a runner, Merlin purports to deliver to Gauvain a letter from Yvain asking for help. Gauvain and his companions rush to Cornwall to join the fight with Agravain in the lead. The combined forces decimate the Saxons. The young heroes move to Arundel, defended by Kay of Estral, Kehedin, and others who seek to join Arthur. The combined troops drive the Saxons to their stronghold. Merlin, in the form of an old man, convinces the young companions to withdraw to Arundel and await Arthur. Meanwhile, as Lot flees his devastated lands with his wife and the infant Mordred, the queen is taken prisoner during a Saxon skirmish. Near Arundel, as Gauvain and his companions ride through the forest at Merlin's behest, Lot's squire, who has escaped with Mordred, informs them of the kidnapping. From afar Gauvain sees his mother being manhandled by Saxons; he leads his companion into their ranks and crushes them. Merlin flies to Gaul to incite Leonce of Payerne and Pharian to prepare to defend Ban's and Bohort's lands against the Roman consul Pontius Anthony, King Claudas of the Land Laid Waste and King Frollo of Germany. Later, he sees and falls in love with Viviane, who will bring about his downfall. In exchange for her promise of love, he begins to teach her magic. The rebellious kings meet at Lancaster to plan a final campaign against the Saxons.

Meanwhile, Merlin returns to Carhaix and promises success in Gaul and Britain. Leodagan begs Arthur to lead the defence against Rion and his giants, and, at Merlin's urging, offers him Guinevere in marriage. When Merlin reveals Arthur's identity, Leodagan and the Knights of the Round Table swear fealty to him. Various knights shine in an extended battle. Arthur wounds Rion, whose sword (Marmiadoise) he wins and begins to use. The Saxons are routed, with

Merlin's help, and retreat. Meanwhile, Bohort arms his British castle at Charroie (##25–31, *S*: 191–243). When Arthur and his companions return to Carhaix, Merlin instructs him to withdraw to Bredigan with Ban, who summons his brother. On his way, after his brother Guinebal prepares the magic adventures that await Lancelot in the Forest of No Return, Bohort is challenged by the rebellious King Amant, whom he kills in single combat. Amant's knights swear fealty to Arthur at Bredigan. Gauvain and his brothers and companions join them there and Arthur knights them (#32, *S*: 243–56).

Events on the Continent.[8] At Merlin's behest, Arthur leads his allies to Gaul, where Pontius Anthony, Frollo and Claudas besiege Ban's castle at Trebe. They are defeated and flee after an extended battle in which Arthur and Lot's sons stand out. Queen Elaine, Ban's wife, conceives a child (Lancelot), and both have wondrous, disturbing dreams concerning their son and his (Galahad) (#33–4, *S*: 256–79). Merlin interprets their dreams, then visits Viviane, whom he continues to teach magic. Meanwhile, Arthur's companions plunder Claudas's lands. Merlin travels to Rome, where his powers serve the emperor Julius Caesar and the warrior maiden Avenable, whom Caesar marries (#35, *S*: 279–91).

Marriage and reconciliation amid disasters in Britain. Meanwhile, the rebellious kings mount their campaign against the Saxons and are defeated (#36, *S*: 292–8). Arthur and his faithful knights and barons return to Carhaix for Arthur's marriage to Guinevere. The rebels regret opposing Arthur, as they learn of his successes. Lot does not know how he can honourably make peace, especially as his wife and sons are under Arthur's sway. He plans to kidnap Guinevere and exchange her for his queen. Meanwhile, the False Guinevere's kinsmen plot to substitute her for Arthur's bride on their wedding night. At jousting to celebrate the wedding, Gauvain and the young knights best the Knights of the Round Table. The plotters are foiled thanks to Merlin, but they will betray Guinevere again. Leodagan refrains from executing the False Guinevere for love of her putative father, his seneschal Cleodalis. She is imprisoned in a faraway abbey, but will be freed by Bertelay the Red in vengeance against Arthur and Leodagan. Arthur orders preparations for high court to be held at Logres (##37–8, *S*: 298–315). Along the way, Arthur's retinue is ambushed by Lot and his knights. Gauvain and his companions rescue Arthur when Lot unhorses him. Gauvain attacks his father and brings him to the ground, then makes peace between him and Arthur, who accepts his allegiance. Gauvain and his companions are made the Queen's Knights. Guinevere employs four scribes to write down all their adventures. In a protracted tournament gone awry, Gauvain and his companions trounce the Knights of the Round Table, but are overwhelmed when Lot and his knights join the fray. They are rescued by Yvain and his friends just arriving at Logres. Eventually peace is made when the Knights of the Round Table beg to make amends and recognize Gauvain as their master. News about the Grail prompts quests for the best knight in the world, who is predicted to find it (#39, *S*: 315–35). Ban and Lot recommend that Arthur seek reconciliation with the remaining rebellious kings in order to drive out the Saxons. Lot and his sons will serve as Arthur's ambassadors (#40, *S*: 335–9). As they head for Arestel, in Scotland, where Lot means to assemble the rebels, they are attacked by Saxons, but escape after inflicting great losses (#41, *S*: 339–46). The son of King Pellés (Eliezer), intent on being Gauvain's squire, leaves for Arthur's court, where his cousin (Perceval) is training to become a knight. He and his squire are attacked by Saxons and kill them. He joins Lot and his sons on their way to Arestel and enters Gauvain's service (##42–4, *S*: 346–64). Later, Lot and his companions encounter Saxons near Cambenic and join Duke Escant's forces to crush them. The rebellious kings gather at Arestel and agree to band with Arthur to fight the Saxons on Salisbury Plain on All Saints' Day (#45, *S*: 365–74). In Brittany, Merlin bids Leonce of Payerne, Pharian and others to join forces with them, while Arthur summons his barons throughout Logres (#46, *S*: 374–83). The rebellious kings meet Arthur on Salisbury Plain. Arthur wins them over with his charm and courtesy. Gauvain knights Eliezer. Merlin leads the combined forces to Clarence, besieged by Saxons. After a great battle the Saxons are driven to the sea, where half of the survivors are slain as the others escape by ship (##47–8, *S*: 383–401).

Final victory over the Saxons. After leaving Camelot on their way to Brittany, Ban and Bohort happen upon the Castle of the Fens, where Agravadain the Black offers hospitality. Bewitched by Merlin, Ban and Agravadain's daughter sleep together and conceive a son (Hector de Maris) (#49, *S*: 401–7). Meanwhile, as Arthur and his barons celebrate their victory, he is challenged by King Rion, who has again attacked Carmelide. Arthur leads his forces to Carhaix, where he kills Rion and ends the Saxon menace (##50–1, *S*: 407–19).

Victory over Rome and the coming adventures in Britain. Near Jerusalem, Merlin interprets the dream of a Saracen king, Flualis, which foretells his military defeat and conversion to Christianity. Merlin visits Viviane, whom he continues to teach magic. When he returns to Arthur, messengers arrive from the Roman emperor Lucius, who lays claim to Britain and summons Arthur to Rome at Christmas (#52, *S*: 420–7).[9] After landing in Gaul with a vast army, Arthur slays a devilish giant at Mont-Saint-Michel.[10] Then he advances to the Aube, where he is joined by King Ban and King Bohort, to face the Romans, who are reinforced by Saracens. Gauvain leads an embassy to Lucius that goes awry when a skirmish develops into a great battle; the Romans and Saracens are overwhelmed. On Merlin's advice, Arthur does not chase them into Italy, but leads his army to the Lake of Lausanne, where he kills a devil cat and defeats the army of King Claudas (##53–5, *S*: 427–45). At the Castle of the Fens, Agravadain's daughter gives birth to Hector. Meanwhile, Flualis's dream is fulfilled (#56, *S*: 445–9). After Arthur's victories on the Continent, Merlin visits Blaise one last time and returns to Viviane, who imprisons him by magic in the Forest of Brocéliande. In response to Arthur's grief over Merlin's disappearance, the Queen's Knights make individual quests for him (#57, *S*: 449–53). Arthur knights a hideous dwarf, Evadeam, son of King Brandegorre, whom a beautiful maiden brought to court. Later, he is restored to his natural size and beauty when Gauvain passes by him and his lady and blesses them. Gauvain succeeds in the quest for Merlin when he finds him as a disembodied voice lamenting his foolishness in love. Soon afterwards, Gauvain discovers that he has become a dwarf when he is taunted by knights assaulting a lady. After he defeats the knights and swears an oath that he will always help ladies and greet them before they greet him, he too is restored to his natural state. All knights, including Evadeam, return to Arthur's court and dictate their adventures (##58–9, *S*: 453–8). Queen Elaine gives birth to Galahad (also called Lancelot). King Bohort's wife gives birth to Lionel and, a year later, to Bohort. King Bohort dies shortly after his second son is born. Shortly thereafter, Ban is attacked and overwhelmed by Claudas and his Roman supporters. Ban's holdings are reduced to the castle of Trebe, which he will soon lose (#60, *S*: 465–6).

One textual problem not apparent in the foregoing summary concerns the nature of the relationship between the beginning of the Vulgate Continuation and the ending of the text from which the *Merlin* proper derives.[11] On the basis of available editions (notably *S*, II; and Micha edn 1979), the place where Robert de Boron's *Merlin* ends and the Vulgate Continuation begins is not self-evident. The overwhelming majority of manuscripts conclude Robert's *Merlin* with a brief account of Arthur's coronation that ends: 'Einsis fu Artus esliz et fait roi dou roiaume de Logres et tint la terre et le roiaume en pais' (*Thus was Arthur chosen and made king of the kingdom of Logres, and he held the land and the kingdom in peace*, §91, 57–8). The Vulgate Cycle proceeds with the common Vulgate Continuation. However, the two manuscripts that transmit the *Didot-Perceval* (*D*: Paris, BNF, nouv. acq. fr. 4116 and *E*: Modena, Estense E. 39, see chapter VI) conclude Robert's *Merlin* with an episode in which Merlin informs Arthur and the barons of the new king's royal birth and, moreover, associate the Round Table with the Grail service and the table of the Last Supper (Micha edn 1979, 293–302, Roach edn, 281–307). Following Roach (edn, 11–15) and Brugger (1930, 411), Micha (edn 1979, 293; 1980, chapter 1) argues convincingly that the Didot and Modena material following 'Einsis fu Artus esliz et fait roi' represents the authentic conclusion to Robert's *Merlin*. From another perspective, Maddox (2000*, 124–8) has demonstrated that the narrative logic of Robert's *Merlin*, as a specular romance, in fact requires the completion of the motif of Arthur as fatherless son with a revelation to Arthur of his origins.

These indications suggest not only that the original ending to Robert's *Merlin* may have been lost in most of the manuscripts, but also that the opening of the first episode in the Vulgate *Merlin* Continuation (corresponding roughly to *S*: 88–98) is an amplification of that ending in which, however, the matter pertaining to the Grail has been dropped. There can be no mistake as to whether or not the early Vulgate compilers were confused about the transition from Robert's work to their own. In a strong textual tradition representing twenty-one of the manuscripts that transmit the *Merlin* proper with the Vulgate Continuation, the division is clearly signalled by a flourished initial, a blank space or a miniature following 'Einsis fu Artus esliz et fait roi ...' In eleven of twelve other, closely related manuscripts, however, the transition is seamless (Micha 1958, 154).

Several conclusions may be drawn. To begin with, the amplification, which is at the same time highly recapitulative of matter in the *Merlin* proper (Merlin's biography, Arthur's conception and birth, etc.) and anticipatory of matter in the Vulgate Continuation (the rise of Arthur's nephews, Arthur's relations with the brother kings, etc.), as well as being narrational (particularly of the private and public reception of Merlin's accounts by Arthur and the barons), serves to link Robert's text to the Vulgate's story of the Six Kings' rebellion and its effects. The consequence of this amplification and the addition of the Vulgate Continuation is that the ending of Robert's *Merlin*, as preserved in the Didot and Modena manuscripts, becomes redundant. Finally, in the Vulgate Cycle the separation between the *Merlin* proper and the Continuation becomes blurred as Robert's work is absorbed, albeit imperfectly, by the *Lancelot–Grail*, which officially regards Robert not as its authoritative source, but as a translator of a parallel text which the Vulgate compilers seek to suppress (Pickens 1994).

Robert's *Merlin* underwent other kinds of transformation in its accommodation with the style and content of the Vulgate Cycle. When Merlin dictates Grail history to Blaise, the details in the group of twenty-one manuscripts are consistent with Robert's *Joseph d'Arimathie*, whilst details in the version of the *Merlin* proper found in the group of ten closely related manuscripts are made to conform with the rewritten matter (Micha 1958, 153–4), either by adding material, such as references to Nascien, an invention of the Vulgate *Estoire* (e.g. §16, 61–71, esp. §16, 67–70 *variants*), or by deleting material, such as anticipatory allusions to Grail material previously recorded by Blaise, which may or may not constitute the *Didot-Perceval* (e.g. §23, 58–65 *variants*). Furthermore, as the *Merlin* Continuation includes Agravain among the number of King Lot's sons, he appears in the list in the Vulgate *Merlin* proper (*S*: 73, §75, 5 *variant*). In Robert's *Merlin* Lot has three sons besides Mordred: Gauvain, Guerrehet and Gaheriet (§72, 4–5); Agravain does not appear in the *Didot-Perceval* (#2) either. In addition, the Vulgate *Merlin* proper is adorned with formulae characteristic of the Vulgate Cycle as a whole, formulae that serve to introduce textual divisions: 'En ceste partie dist li contes que ...' (*In this part the story says that ...*, *S*: 3, 20), 'Chi dist le contes que …' (*Here the story says that* …, *S*: 35), etc. The make-over remains incomplete, however, for the accompanying closing formulae typical of the Vulgate Cycle elsewhere, for example, 'Si sen taist ore li contes que plus nen parole i chi endroit anchois vous dirons del roy artu …' (*Now the story falls silent about them and does not say anything more right here; rather, we shall tell you about King Arthur* …, *S*: 113), have not been inserted in the rewriting.

Elsewhere in the Vulgate Cycle, including the *Merlin* Continuation, not only do the formulae occur with far greater frequency than in the *Merlin* proper, but the opening formula is also nearly always preceded by a closing formula that marks the interruption of the preceding narrative strand. These paired formulae signal interlacing, a distinctive structuring principle of the Vulgate Cycle in general, that does not characterize either the *Merlin* proper or Robert de Boron's work as a whole.

Among other inconsistencies that stand between the *Merlin* proper and the Continuation are the number and identity of Arthur's half-sisters. In Robert de Boron, as in the *Merlin* proper, Ygerne has two small daughters, who are betrothed when she and Uther Pendragon marry. King Lot of Orkney has one, who will become the mother of Gauvain, Guerrehet, Gaheriet and Mordred (the Vulgate adds Agravain); the other, Morgan the Fay, a bastard, will wed King Neutre of Garlot, who sees to her education, described in detail (§72, 1–14). In the *Brut*, Wace does not mention any daughters except Enna (or Anna), born to Ygerne and Uther after Arthur, who marries King Lot (Arnold edn, 8819–22). She is the mother of Gauvain and, implicitly, of Mordred as well (13015–17). The Vulgate mentions a third daughter in passing (*S*: 73, §72, 6–7 *variant*). Early in the *Merlin* Continuation, however, the number of daughters grows to five. As Merlin informs Arthur of his heritage, he specifies, without naming them, that Ygerne had three daughters by the Duke of Tintagel and two by her unnamed first husband: one has married Lot, another Neutre, another Urien and another, now deceased, Caradoc (Caradan), father of King Aguisant of Scotland, while the fifth is young enough still to be at school (*S*: 96). In anticipation of later events, Merlin mentions Lot's sons by name, including Agravain as well as Mordred, whom Arthur fathered whilst a squire, Galescalain, son of Neutre, and Yvain, son of Urien. The conjoining of Robert's *Merlin* and the Vulgate Continuation is thus far from perfected, and the individuality of Robert's work stands out all the more despite the Vulgate compilers' efforts to obliterate his name.

Nevertheless, the Vulgate, in the *Merlin* proper, maintains intact Robert de Boron's project of blending Grail history and British history, as recorded by Geoffrey of Monmouth and more particularly in Wace's *Brut*, which is most certainly his source (see chapter VI). In the Continuation, moreover, the Vulgate *Merlin* also protracts Robert's model and reinforces a historical framework that is necessary, not only for the exploits of the young King Arthur, but also for the remainder of the entire Cycle. Robert's method of rewriting Wace in the light of Grail history is evident in the *Merlin* proper:

(i) 'Merlin's Conception and Childhood Deeds' (#1) is in large part an amplification of two passages in the *Brut*'s Vortigern history: the confession Merlin's mother makes to Vortigern (*Brut*, 7414–34) and a description of incubi by Vortigern's clerk Magant (*Brut*, 7439–56).[12] The *Merlin* amplification is designed to parallel the opening of Robert's *Estoire*.

(ii) The Vortigern section (#2) corresponds much more closely with the *Brut*. Differences include the concretization of Wace's speculation about Merlin's conception in, and the transfer of Merlin's mother to, the opening section; the identity of the foreign invaders; the nature of Vortigern's treachery; the identity of King Constant's sons; the location of Vortigern's tower; and Robert's invention of Blaise.

(iii) 'The Reigns of Uther and Pendragon' (#3) also follows the *Brut*. Differences include Merlin's role in the defeat of Hengist and the Saxons' eventual surrender and departure; Merlin's shape-shifting; the baron's three deaths; the role of Vortigern's son; the Round Table (essential in the *Merlin*, where it reflects the tables of the Last Supper, and the Grail service and its significance is elaborately established; mentioned in passing in the *Brut*, where Arthur founds it himself).

(iv) 'Uther and Ygerne' amplifies the *Brut* through Uther's marriage to Ygerne (*Brut*, 8551–822) and continues with the account of Uther's last days (*Brut*, 8823–9004). In the *Brut*, Merlin disappears when Uther invades Tintagel, whilst Robert does not dwell on Uther's last days. Other differences include the identity of Arthur's sisters (see above) and the time of Arthur's conception: Uther and Ygerne's first night together (Robert), either then (*Brut*, 8733–6) or their wedding night (*Brut*, 8814–15).

(v) 'The Sword and the Stone' rewrites and amplifies Wace's brief account of Uther's death and Arthur's succession:

> Li esvesque s'antremanderent
> Et li barun s'antr'assemblerent;
> Artur, le fiz Uther, manderent,
> A Cilcestre le corunerent.
> Jovencels esteit de quinze anz,
> De son eage fors et granz. (*Brut*, 9009–14)

(*The bishops convened and the barons gathered. They summoned Arthur, Uther's son, and crowned him at Silchester. He was a youth of fifteen years, big and strong for his age.*)

Similarly, the Continuation takes up the main thrust of Wace's account of the early days of Arthur's reign: his successful war against pagan Saxons, as well as Picts and Scots, with the support of his Breton and Cornish allies, Cador and Hoel (*Brut*, 9033–368). This war concludes with a successful campaign in

Scotland and a display of generosity by the king (*Brut*, 9369–526). The *Brut* also demonstrates Arthur's political and moral ascendancy in terms of his expulsion of foreign invaders and the distribution of fiefs among his loyal supporters who were dispossessed by the Saxons, among whom Lot, Urien and Aguisel (Aguisant), three of the six kings who later rebel against Arthur, stand out (*Brut*, 9605–40). Finally, Arthur's triumph culminates with his marriage to Guinevere (*Brut*, 9641–58). Wace's history thus provides the basis of one of the Continuation's most important narrative strands, which the Vulgate text elaborates by compounding the numbers of Saxon forces and expanding the theatres of war. More significantly, the Continuation creates a vastly more complex plot, a plot rendered all the more intricate thanks to the techniques of interlace and intra- and extra-diegetical anticipation within the Vulgate *Merlin* and without to other branches of the Cycle, by intertwining important new narrative strands with the war against the Saxons. These new strands are: (i) the plottings of rebellious vassals, three of whose leaders figure in the *Brut* as Arthur's favoured allies (Lot, Urien and Aguisant), but in the *Merlin* are rather associated with Uther's generation; (ii) the emergence as knights of Arthur's youthful nephews, rebels' sons who gravitate to the king implicitly through the attraction of their mothers' blood; (iii) the concomitant weakening of Uther's knights and allies who have revolted; (iv) Arthur and Guinevere's love and marriage; (v) mounting conflict between Arthur and his Breton allies on the one hand, and, on the other, the Roman emperor and his vassals in Gaul; (vi) the rise of Arthur's Breton allies, the brother kings Ban and Bohort; (vii) the further rise of Merlin as instigator and orchestrator of the king's triumphs; and (viii) the extension of Merlin's and Blaise's roles as narrator and scriptor of Arthurian history as an essential moment in Grail history.

Multiple climactic moments in the development of these and other narrative strands stretch – and here we are forced to oversimplify – from Arthur's first expedition to the Continent (##33–4) until his marriage with Guinevere (##37–8), the ensuing reconciliation of Arthur with the rebellious vassals (##39–48) and the final victory over the Saxons (##49–51), to Arthur's second continental campaign and his victory over Frollo, Claudas and their Roman allies (##52–5). This development again imitates the structure of Wace's *Brut*, where, having driven out the Saxons, Arthur marries Guinevere (*Brut*, 9641–58) and, after conquering Ireland and Iceland (9659–730), introduces in Britain the twelve-year-long Pax Arthuriana (9731–10619), which is followed by the conquest of France over Frollo and Arthur's grants of fiefs to his knights. The movement in Wace culminates in Arthur's second coronation at Caerleon, where the celebration is disrupted by the arrival of messengers from the Roman emperor Lucius, an event that leads to a second, victorious campaign in France. The *Merlin* Continuation further borrows from the *Brut* the challenge issued by Lucius, who both seeks retribution for

Arthur's defeat of Frollo and lays claim to Britain by right of Julius Caesar's conquest (#52, *Brut*, 10639–710), and also adapts (11279–598) the singular adventure of Arthur's slaughter of the Giant of Mont-Saint-Michel, who imprisons, rapes and murders the daughter of his Breton ally, Hoel (#53).

In the *Merlin* Continuation, Arthur's second campaign against the Romans in France, whilst indecisive, because Merlin thwarts the pursuit of Lucius into Italy, is nevertheless a rousing success, rather like the first in Wace. In the *Brut*, as in the *Didot-Perceval*, which also imitates Wace, the triumph turns out to be illusory, for in both texts the Continental campaign introduces 'Mort Artu' sequences, as Arthur's departure leads to Mordred's treason. Such, however, would be out of the question at this stage in the *Merlin* Continuation, which pointedly makes it clear in the kidnapping of King Lot's wife that Mordred is a babe in arms (#27). The innovation in the Continuation's rewriting of Wace comes fully into focus as the Vulgate *Merlin* transforms Wace's 'Mort Artu' (as well as that of the *Didot Perceval*, perhaps) into an unmitigated success: the Giant of Mont-Saint-Michel episode heralds, not destruction, but victory. As the Vulgate *Merlin* was incorporated into the Cycle after the *Queste* and the *Mort Artu* had been completed, the transformations that have been observed were wrought in reaction to the fact that the *Mort Artu* itself preserves the essence of Wace's and Robert de Boron's conclusions. For it rewrites their version of the second campaign against the Romans as a postscript to Arthur's war against Lancelot, which sets Mordred's treason into motion (Frappier edn of the *Mort Artu*, §§134–75). Thus, between the moment of Arthur's victory in France in the *Merlin* Continuation and the moment of the Roman emperor's death in the Vulgate *Mort Artu*, the *Lancelot–Grail* Cycle opens up a narrative space in British history as recounted by Wace, and in British and Grail history as recounted by Robert de Boron, into which to insert the *Lancelot*, the *Queste* and their aftermath.

In this way the Vulgate Cycle imitates, or perhaps initiates, the procedure manifest in that important *Brut* manuscript (Paris, BNF, fr. 1450) in which the works of Chrétien de Troyes are inserted into the *Brut* (Huot 1987; see chapter XI). According to Wace (9787–98) it is during the period of twelve years' peace that the marvellous adventures associated with Arthur took place (see chapter II). This is precisely the time of Chrétien's romances as well as that of the *Didot-Perceval*. In adapting and adopting Wace, the Vulgate Cycle's 'translator(s)', not unlike Robert de Boron before them, would make the same veracity claim for their own work as Wace did for his *Brut*. For at the deepest level of narrative invention in their *translatio*, they make explicit the truth hidden within Chrétien's *Charrette* and *Perceval* as well as within Robert's de Boron's trilogy.

As the Vulgate *Merlin* concludes, following the climactic moments during which the narrative strands identified above reach a pinnacle of Arthurian accomplishment, certain strands spiral even higher, while others fade into decline. In the romance's multifaceted resolutions: (i) the Saxons are driven from Britain; (ii) the rebellious vassals receive their lands from Arthur as fiefs and serve him faithfully; (iii) Arthur's nephews are incorporated into the Round Table fellowship and initiated into the privileged Queen's Guards. Arthur introduces a policy promoting adventure as a function of the Knights of the Round Table as well as its inscription in the annals of the court; (iv) Uther's old guard is gradually eclipsed; (v) Arthur's marriage to Guinevere remains a demonstrable mark of his triumph; (vi) the conflict in Gaul between Arthur and the Romans is resolved in Arthur's favour, but Claudas and his Roman supporters continue to harass Ban and Bohort; (vii) the brother kings' stars rise as Lancelot is born to Elaine, King Ban's wife, and Lionel to Bohort's queen. However, they are still under attack by Claudas. Bohort eventually dies and Ban's holdings are reduced to a single castle. The Vulgate *Merlin* ends on a note of disaster as it foretells Ban's betrayal by his trusted seneschal. The remaining strands likewise lead to negative outcomes; (viii) Merlin is weakened by his love for Viviane, and she finally imprisons him by exercising the magic he has taught her. His disembodied voice eventually fades to nothingness; (ix) consequently, Merlin no longer functions as the author of Arthurian and Grail history, and Blaise falls from sight as its recorder. Blaise and Merlin are replaced by a new, secular means of writing history, as knights returning from adventure dictate their stories to court scribes. Robert de Boron, who, like the old guard, has already been eclipsed, will eventually be replaced, but only in the last two branches of the Cycle, by Walter Map as translator. The stage is set for the prose *Lancelot*. **[RTP]**

The Prose *Lancelot*

Lancelot's Childhood and Early Adventures

The prose tale of Lancelot in its earliest form begins with an account of Lancelot's loss of his father, kingdom and name, of his childhood in the land of the Lady of the Lake and that of his cousins Lionel and Bohort. It then narrates his knighting at Arthur's court, his first sight of Guinevere, who immediately becomes the inspiration for all his achievements, and the adventures that lead to his becoming a Knight of the Round Table. This account is common to manuscripts giving the pre-cyclic and the cyclic versions. Its two main themes, related to the central character Lancelot, are the making of a name and the love theme, the latter including Lancelot's love for Guinevere and Galehot's love for his fellow knight Lancelot. These themes are set within the context of Arthur's kingdom, of feudal service and of the role of the knight within society (E. Kennedy 1994b).

The identity theme is a recurring one in twelfth- and early thirteenth-century romance (for example, in Chrétien's *Erec* and *Perceval* and in *Le Bel Inconnu*). A young man has to discover who he is and make his name through his exploits as a knight, or an older knight has to prove his right to a reputation won in the past or recover a good name he has lost. In the prose romance, unlike some of the verse romances, the hero's baptismal name Galahad and his pseudonym Lancelot are announced at the beginning, but the boy himself, taken as a baby by a fairy (the Lady of the Lake) into what appears to be a lake, does not know his name or his parentage.[13] He first learns his name when he raises the slab of a tomb at the Dolorous Garde, but continues to operate under a series of pseudonyms, such as the White, Red or Black Knight. It is only when Guinevere is able to call him by his own name, in the scene leading up to the first kiss, that the name Lancelot becomes regularly used in the narrative, and it is only after Lancelot has saved Arthur from the Saxons that he is welcomed at Arthur's court under his own name before he becomes a Knight of the Round Table.

The theme of the making of a name, here in terms of a reputation, is continued in relation to the young knight Hector, who, while Lancelot remains withdrawn from the action, far away in the distant land of Galehot, represents the young man who has to prove his worth as knight and lover, in one case in an episode (*LK*, 442–65; *LM*, 8, 272–311) reminiscent of Perceval's visit to Beaurepaire in Chrétien's romance (Roach edn, 1706–2937). The theme is explored in different terms in relation to Gauvain, who is chosen incognito as an unworthy substitute for himself by a dwarf whose lady, la dame de Roestoc, wants Gauvain as her champion in a judicial duel. On the way to the battle, the unrecognized Gauvain has to *watch* Hector go through a series of tests (here against an increasing number of knights) before he himself wins the judicial duel (*LK*, 371–90; *LM*, 8, 154–85), much as Lancelot, as a youth just knighted, had to undergo tests on the way to his battle for the Lady of Nohaut (*LK,* 166–77; *LM*, 7, 287–304).[14]

The theme of Lancelot as the lover of Guinevere has elements in common with Chrétien's *Charrette*. Lancelot's adoration of her manifests itself both actively, in splendid deeds inspired by love, and passively, in a series of lover's trances (E. Kennedy 1978). The lover's monologues found in Chrétien are missing from the prose romance, but would be evoked for the early thirteenth-century reader by the constant interplay with Chrétien's romance (E. Kennedy 1995). Lancelot achieves eloquence only once in relation to his love during this stage in the development of his tale in prose, that is in the scene leading up to the first kiss, when in his first confession of love to her he tells the queen what effect her words 'biaus douz amis' had upon him on his first visit to Arthur's court (*LK*, 345–6; *LM*, 8, 111). This avowal of love will be recalled and transformed in the cyclic romance into a reluctant confession of the sinfulness of his love (*Queste*, 66). The progress of this love in visual and physical terms is also represented on a divided shield, depicting a knight on one half and a lady on the other, which is brought to Arthur's court *after* the first kiss. The top of the shield has come together and the lips of knight and lady are joined, but below they are still divided (*LK*, 402–3; *LM*, 8, 205–7). When, during the war against the Saxons, Lancelot and Guinevere's love is consummated, the division in the shield disappears (*LK*, 547; *LM*, 8, 444).

All Lancelot's exploits are achieved under the inspiration of his love, both those he achieves as an individual knight and those he achieves in great tournaments or in great battles against invaders. While Lancelot is withdrawn from the action when Galehot has taken him away to his own distant lands, his exploits as an individual knight inspired by love are echoed by those of Hector, also a young lover inspired by his love for his lady, but Hector's lady, unlike Lancelot's, is reluctant to see her knight set out on adventure (*LK*, 375, 400–1, 405; *LM*, 8, 160, 203, 211). The love theme is also explored in relation to some of the adventures undertaken against knights who do not recognize the important contribution of a woman's beauty compared with knightly prowess. For example, Persides maintains that his prowess as a knight is greater than the beauty of his wife Helyenne sans Per, named as one of the three most beautiful women (*LK*, 33; *LM*, 7, 59). He is defeated by Hector, champion of Helyenne (*LK*, 519–24; *LM*, 8, 398–406). There is also an interesting contrast made between the achievements of Lancelot (all inspired by his love for Guinevere) who is rated as the greatest knight, and those of Gauvain, whose deeds are not inspired by a single great love and who is ranked the second greatest knight. This is made clear in the episode in which Agravain's leg is healed by Lancelot's blood as the best knight and his arm by Gauvain as the greatest knight after Lancelot (*LK*, 416–17, 539; *LM*, 8, 227–9, 432).

Lancelot's friendship for Galehot represents another important form of love, the comradeship between two great warriors (Frappier 1973). At Lancelot's request, Galehot sacrifices his ambition to conquer Arthur; he also arranges the meeting at which Guinevere and Lancelot kiss for the first time, even though he knows that Lancelot's love for the queen is greater than his emotional bond with Galehot and may eventually separate them. In contrast, Galehot's love for Lancelot is clearly far stronger than any love he might feel for his *amie* the Lady of Malohaut.

It is important to note that Lancelot's love is presented in all manuscripts containing the account of his exploits up to his installation as a Knight of the Round Table in very positive terms and is not morally condemned. Although the Lady of the Lake, when she comes to heal Lancelot, who is out of his mind, refers to 'li pechié do siegle' (*the sins of this world*) in connection with earthly love, she describes it as the most honoured 'folie' of all (*LK*, 557; *LM*, 8, 461). The emphasis throughout this part of the text is on the contribution that Lancelot, inspired by his love, makes to the land of Arthur, a king who had been unable to come to the aid of his vassal Ban, Lancelot's father.

The Arthurian context operates both in terms of what is related in the romance and of the existing tradition within which it is set and to which reference is made.

During these adventures, before Lancelot has been recognized at court, Arthur appears in two different ways, both of which have their counterpart in existing tradition: firstly, the active Arthur of chronicle tradition, who is under great pressure from external opponents in the early years of his reign; secondly, the passive Arthur, reminiscent of Arthur's role in much of Chrétien, a king who tends to fall into broodings when he sees that events are beyond his control. The presentation of Arthur is carefully balanced, so that membership of the Round Table, over which he presides, can appear a worthy goal for Lancelot. He is compared favourably with Claudas, who had seized the land of Lancelot and his two cousins, but is not so perfect that he does not need Lancelot's help. Arthur is unable to protect his vassal Ban, as a *rendu*, a former knight now in a religious order, points out. He is also reproached for his inadequacies as a king by a *preudomme* who appears at court after Arthur's first battle with Galehot.[15]

During Lancelot's childhood the pattern of the interlace is mainly based on switches between three different locations: (i) the lands of Benoyc and Gorre, once the kingdoms of Lancelot's father Ban and of his brother Bohort, where the relationship between lord and vassal is an important theme; (ii) the abbey in which the widowed queens, mothers of Lancelot and of his two cousins, Lionel and Bohort, take refuge; (iii) the Lake in which Lancelot and eventually his two cousins are brought up and prepared for knighthood. The pattern of the interlace after Lancelot has come to court is different and prepares the way for that to be found in the following branches of the Cycle up to the beginning of the *Mort Artu*. The switches are between the narrative threads of the knights seeking adventure away from Arthur and his court, and the activities of Arthur, whether presiding at court in various locations or engaged in wars that require the return of his knights, for example the war against Galehot (*LK*, 276–82, 304–27; *LM*, 8, 2–12, 47–85) or that against the Saxons (*LK*, 539–68; *LM*, 8, 431–82). What is noticeable is that the only character whose narrative thread has no gaps in it is Lancelot. Until he has been welcomed under his own name at Arthur's court (*LK*, 566–9; *LM*, 8, 478–85), his characteristic narrative pattern shifts between the following: a series of individual adventures away from court interspersed with periods of withdrawal from the action through imprisonment or illness, and periods of involvement under several different names in events that bring Arthur and his knights together to perform feats of arms in tournaments or wars (against Galehot and against the Saxons). In contrast, Arthur's narrative thread is never followed continuously, and this is true throughout the Cycle. That of Gauvain is followed more consistently than that of any other knight except Lancelot, but only on those quests for the unknown knight (Lancelot using a series of names: White, Red or Black Knight) that turn out to be successful. On unsuccessful quests, Gauvain's adventures are not told (*LK*, 299; passage missing from *LM*). The adventures of Hector are followed without a gap once he enters the narrative; he fulfils the role of the young knight, both as a lover and one with a reputation (a name) to make, who is active while Lancelot is hidden in the land of Galehot, Hector being successful in his quest for Gauvain, who is seeking Lancelot. The other knights only figure at Arthur's court, or in tournaments or wars, or when their adventures cross or follow the paths of Lancelot, Gauvain or Hector.

The adventures of other knights are therefore recounted only in so far as they are relevant to the tale of Lancelot, as is explained (*LK*, 365–6; *LM*, 8, 144). His tale up to his installation as a Knight of the Round Table is presented as part of an Arthurian literature existing outside the story being narrated here. Thus, there is a series of references to an Arthurian past found in earlier texts by Wace, Chrétien de Troyes and Robert de Boron, and in the First and Second *Perceval* Continuations. It is important to note that at this point none of these references look forward to Grail adventures yet to come; they all allude to the Grail as a story already told (E. Kennedy 1986, 143–55). There are a number of brief allusions to Arthur's wars contemporary with the account of Lancelot's childhood up to his first arrival at Arthur's court; after that, Lancelot himself will be involved in any battles Arthur has to fight, but there are some references to conflicts between other great lords, with which knights seeking Lancelot may become temporarily involved and which set events within a wider background (for example *LK*, 477; *LM*, 8, 330). References to an Arthurian future not yet told are much more limited (*LK*, 407; *LM,* 8, 214); they mainly refer to events related later in the narrative leading up to Lancelot's installation at the Round Table (E. Kennedy 1986, 216–17).

The interplay between earlier Arthurian verse romance and a number of episodes in this stage of Lancelot's story is important in relation to the thematic structure of the text and appears to assume a considerable knowledge of existing Arthurian tradition on the part of the audience, as, for example, in relation to the theme of the Fair Unknown discussed above. It is at the point after Lancelot and Galehot, now both Knights of the Round Table, leave Arthur's court to return to the land of Galehot, that the manuscripts divide into two distinctive versions of the text: the pre-cyclic version, ending with the death of Galehot and Lancelot's integration into Arthur's kingdom (*LK*, 572–613; *LM*, 3, 1–69); and the cyclic version (beginning in *LM*, 1, 1), which prepares the way for adventures of the Grail yet to come, and for the replacement of Lancelot as the greatest Arthurian knight by a new hero, his son Galahad, who will surpass his father during the adventures of the Grail, but will leave this world after he has looked inside the holy vessel.

The Pre-cyclic Version of the Journey to Galehot's Lands, the False Guinevere Episode and the Death of Galehot
The pre-cyclic version is to be found in whole or in part in seventeen manuscripts (see n. 3). It continues two of the main themes to be found in the account of

Lancelot's life up to his installation as a Knight of the Round Table. The first of these is the love theme, evoked as soon as the two friends Lancelot and Galehot leave Arthur's court. Both have left ladies they love behind them, and Lancelot would have preferred to stay at court; Galehot is aware that Lancelot's love for Guinevere will override his friendship for himself, and that he will eventually lose him as a companion in spite of the great sacrifice he has made for Lancelot. His thoughts on this are so painful that he faints. When they continue their journey, he shows Lancelot a great castle in which he would have worn a crown were he to have conquered Arthur's kingdom. This castle then crumbles before their eyes, and many of his other castles collapse. Then Galehot has a strange dream and sends for Arthur's wise clerks to interpret it; they tell him that he will die within three years because of his love for Lancelot. The accusation against Guinevere that she is not the true queen brings the two companions back to Arthur's court. Lancelot's love for the queen keeps him there, Galehot has to return to his own lands, hears a false rumour of Lancelot's death and dies. Throughout this version there is no condemnation of Lancelot and Guinevere's love as sinful, and Guinevere comforts him for the death of his friend.

The identity theme is also explored in relation to Guinevere. She is accused of being an impostor by a False Guinevere and a knight called Berthelai. Arthur, under the influence of magic, accepts the False Guinevere as the true queen, but Guinevere's right to her name is proved by Lancelot, and the king has to renounce the impostor immediately. Again Lancelot's love for Guinevere is presented in positive terms. The queen, when accused of imposture, asks herself if she is being punished for some sin she has committed (*LK*, 595; *LM* 3, 39), but the love for Lancelot is not mentioned with reference to this, and indeed it is that love that enables Lancelot to defeat the three knights, and it is the love of Guinevere that helps to console Lancelot for the death of his friend. The identity theme also recurs in relation to Lancelot's cousin Lionel in a very abbreviated version of the making of a name motif: Lionel kills a crowned lion, thus proving his right to his name (*LK*, 610–12; *LM*, 3, 64–7).

The Cyclic Version of Events from the Journey to Sorelois up to the Quest
In the cyclic version of the departure of Lancelot and Galehot from Arthur's court, of the False Guinevere episode and of the events leading up to the death of Galehot, very important changes are made. The identity theme in the False Guinevere episode is still pursued, but here for the first time there is an admission by Guinevere, when Arthur has renounced her in favour of the impostor, that her love for Lancelot is sinful and that she is now perhaps being punished for it (*LM*, 1, 151–2). Lancelot defends the queen's identity in a judicial battle against three knights, but Arthur, still influenced by magic, exiles her, and she leaves with Galehot and Lancelot. It is only when the False Guinevere and her fellow

conspirator fall ill, and before they die finally confess to their deception, that Arthur is forced to admit his mistake.

What represents an even more fundamental change is that a Grail Quest yet to come, with a new Grailwinner descended from Lancelot (himself unworthy to achieve this adventure because of his adulterous love), is foretold by Arthur's clerks in their interpretations of Galehot's dreams and of the collapse of his castles (*LM*, 1, 52–6). When Arthur welcomes Guinevere back, as in the pre-cyclic version, Lancelot remains at court and Galehot returns to his own lands, but here, unlike the pre-cyclic version, a long series of adventures, set off by the abduction of Gauvain by Caradoc, then follow. Lancelot, Yvain and the Duke of Clarence go in quest of Gauvain. Lancelot's two companions fail at a succession of adventures, in contrast with Lancelot, who succeeds at all of them and finally achieves the rescue of Gauvain. Love as an inspiration for great deeds is picked up in the adventure of the Val sans Retor, also called the Val as Faus Amans, which Lancelot, as a true lover, brings to an end. It is followed by yet another withdrawal of Lancelot from the action by imprisonment, this time by Morgan. Here the beneficent magic of the Lady of the Lake is contrasted with the more hostile magic of Morgan, whose jealousy for Guinevere provides a recurring theme throughout the Cycle. Finally, the foretelling by the clerks of Galehot's death (*LM*, 1, 57–8) is fulfilled when he hears a false rumour of Lancelot's death and pines away, as in the pre-cyclic version (*LM*, 1, 388–9), but here Lancelot hears of his friend's death only much later (*LM*, 2, 212).

The cyclic version has already, in relation to Galehot's dreams, looked forward to a Grail Quest yet to be told within the Cycle. It continues the process of incorporation of earlier Arthurian tradition within the romance, but now this is done by providing a new prose version of stories and themes from twelfth-century verse romance, whereas in the account of Lancelot's childhood and early adventures it was achieved by references outwards to what is told elsewhere or by interplay with earlier romances in relation, for example, to the theme of making or remaking a knight's name. Thus, a version of the episode of the Knight of the Cart, where Lancelot rescues Guinevere from the land of Gorre, to which Meleagant has abducted her, is now included within the romance (*LM*, 2, 1–108). As in Chrétien's work, Lancelot is able to cross the Sword Bridge under the inspiration of his love for the queen, but, through a new and important narrative pattern of adventures, this success through earthly love is contrasted with failure at a different and more spiritual type of test precisely because of this love. This is well illustrated by the scene at the cemetery, where Lancelot, as the knight destined to free the prisoners in the land of Gorre and inspired by his love for Guinevere, can raise the slab of the tomb of Galahad (*LM*, 2, 33), son of Joseph of Arimathea, and included in the list of great knights by the Lady of the Lake in her discourse on chivalry to the young Lancelot (*LK*, 146; *LM*, 7, 256).

However, Lancelot fails to raise the slab of the tomb of Symeu (father of
Moÿse), destined to be raised only by the knight who will end the enchantments
of the 'Roialme Aventureus' and achieve the Perilous Seat at the Round Table
and the Grail Quest (*LM*, 2, 32). This is a new version of the reference early in
Lancelot's childhood, where the name of the knight who is to achieve all this is
Perceval. This pattern of success at one adventure through the inspiration of love,
but failure at another linked with the Grail is to continue as the Adventures of
the Grail (the *Queste*) approach. Once these start, Lancelot's earthly love can
bring him only failure. The Cart as a symbol of dishonour that only a true lover
such as Lancelot would mount (strongly emphasized by Chrétien) is somewhat
weakened in the prose romance when Gauvain, Arthur, Guinevere and the whole
court climb into it at the end of the episode (cf. *LM*, 2, 385–6, in which Gauvain
rides in a cart as a symbol of degradation after he has failed to respond to the
Grail).

From the end of the Charrette episode onwards, a similar narrative pattern
illustrates the power of love to inspire achievement of certain earthly adventures,
but the need for another form of inspiration in relation to the Grail adventures. A
number of episodes present positive achievements inspired by Lancelot's love.
For example, Lancelot ends the Carole Magique, which has imprisoned within it
those knights who have not achieved the status of true lover. Only Lancelot can
free them from this (*LM*, 4, 286–7). However, there is another occasion where
Lancelot through love is able to achieve something that would otherwise be
beyond his powers, but this very achievement helps to prepare the way for the
Mort Artu. That is the episode with echoes from the Tristan story in which
Lancelot, imprisoned by Morgan, is inspired by his love to produce a series of
paintings of past events, some of which portray scenes that illustrate his love for
Guinevere (*LM*, 5, 52, 61–2). Morgan sees these as a weapon to use against
Guinevere (*LM*, 5, 52–4) and does so in the *Mort Artu* (Frappier edn, §§51–4),
where she shows them to Arthur. On the other hand, it is again Lancelot's love for
the queen that enables him to escape from Morgan by pulling apart the bars, just
as he had done in both Chrétien and the prose *Charrette*, although there to reach
Guinevere.

The combination of Lancelot's love bringing both success and failure, characteristic of the prose *Charrette* and once again preparing the way for the *Queste*, is
also to be found. For example, Guinevere talks to Lancelot of the inscription that
Gauvain found in the Gaste Chapele (*LM*, 2, 367; *LM*, 5, 2); it concerns the
adventure to be achieved only by the ill-fated knight who by his wretched *luxure*
would fail at the Grail adventures, i.e. the son of the Roine Doloreuse, Lancelot's
mother. Guinevere is grieved that Lancelot has bought her love so dearly. He
replies that it is his love for her that gave him the strength to achieve his great
deeds (*LM*, 5, 2). Later he combines failure and success when he cannot cool a

boiling fountain, but can draw a head from it, and he can raise a tomb slab and put his grandfather Lancelot beside his wife in a tomb (*LM*, 5, 118–22).

Another important preparation for the creation of a new Grail hero who will replace Lancelot as greatest knight is to be found in the episode in which Lancelot comes to Corbenic, sees the Grail procession and is then deceived into engendering Galahad in the daughter of Pellés because he believes that he is lying with Guinevere (*LM*, 4, 209–11). This is to be contrasted with Bohort's one night that cost him his virginity (he is the only one of the three Grailwinners to lose it) through the spell put on him by a magic ring, but whose firm intention to remain chaste is strongly emphasized (*LM*, 2, 196–8). As one of the future three Grailwinners, Bohort is given a greater number of successful adventures than his brother Lionel; he also appears as a better knight than Gauvain, until then the best knight after Lancelot, but unable to achieve as much as the latter because he lacks the inspiration of true love. Bohort, on his visit to Corbenic before the beginning of the *Queste*, sees the Grail and suffers less shame than any of the other knights. In *LM*, 6, 171–2, the very young Galahad is brought to Camelot, but does not stay there. Lancelot, who has been healed of madness by the Grail at Corbenic (*LM*, 6, 219–25), returns there (*LM*, 6, 242) to say goodbye to Galahad, who goes to a nunnery to await the beginning of the Grail adventures. The young Perceval appears at Arthur's court only as the beginning of the *Queste* approaches, is knighted and is taken by a damsel, speaking for the first time, to the seat at the Round Table next to the Perilous Seat (*LM*, 6, 191).

In addition to scenes looking forward to Grail adventures to come, there are a number of allusions to the early history of the Grail that mainly link up with Robert de Boron's work and developments from that, as for example in the early *Perceval* Continuations, where the Grail and Joseph of Arimathea come to Britain. For example, the history of the Croix Noire is linked to Joseph of Arimathea's arrival in Britain and the conversion of the Saracens who then lived there (*LM*, 2, 320–39). When these references were first put in the romance, they were not designed to link up with an early history of the Grail already forming part of the Cycle but to existing external tradition. However, a number of them are picked up in the *Estoire*, as, for instance, the history of the Croix Noire (*Estoire*, 482–4).

There are also preparations for the final branch of the Cycle, the *Mort Artu*, in addition to Lancelot's paintings and Morgan's plans to make use of these. For example, there is a reference forward (*LM*, 6, 15) to the episode in which Agravain and Mordred tell Arthur that Lancelot is his wife's lover, thus helping to bring death and destruction to themselves, Arthur and the Knights of the Round Table (*Mort Artu*, §§109–10). There is also a prophecy of the final battle between Mordred and Arthur depicted in the *Mort Artu*. This is to be found in the explanation given by a hermit, about to be killed by Mordred, of one of

Arthur's dreams. In it a serpent inflicts fatal wounds on Arthur, but is killed by the king (*LM*, 5, 221–2). This foretelling is picked up in *LM*, 6, 60–1, where Lancelot tells Guinevere about it.

References to the past are also used to link up with earlier events. For example, memories of the war between Claudas and the men of Benoyc and Gaunes, described in the account of Lancelot's childhood, are explored further in *LM*, 6, 45. It is noticeable that Arthur is given a more positive and active role in, for example, his battle against Frollo (*LM*, 6, 161–4), but there are no longer recurring references to the wars he is fighting or those of his barons that are not part of the tale of Lancelot before the latter becomes a knight and is centrally involved in the affairs of Arthur's kingdom. There are also many instances of knights (for example, Lambegues and Banin) from earlier parts of the story reappearing, with references back to their earlier activities or particular characteristics. Another element, first found in the account of Lancelot's early adventures, but given even greater emphasis in the rest of the Cycle, is the promise made by a knight setting off from Arthur's court on a quest that he will give a truthful account of his adventures on his return. This account is then recorded by Arthur's scribes in a great book. In the later branches of the Vulgate Cycle a summary of these reports is given in the actual narrative, including references to what knights do not tell, in spite of their oath to do so, sworn before they set out.

The pattern of the interlace from the cyclic version of the False Guinevere episode onwards (*LM*, 1–6) is less tightly organized than the account of Lancelot's adventures up to his installation as a Knight of the Round Table, where relevance to the tale of Lancelot is the criterion for inclusion or exclusion of material. The completeness of the information provided by the tale, including the knights' reports of their adventures, becomes more problematic. The interlace pattern is not necessarily to be regarded as inferior, but reflects a change in the presentation of the narrative (Perret 1982; Chase 1983; 1986; E. Kennedy 1986, 156–235; 1994; 1996b; Micha 1987, 85–142; Brandsma 1996). Possible new authorship at this stage in the development of the Cycle is not necessarily the major factor in this change; more central would seem to be the new thematic developments linked with a preparation for a Grail Quest, in which the main hero until now and many other worthy knights, including Gauvain, are destined to fail, failures from which much can be learned. There are more narrative strands, but also more silences, more breaks in continuity, more later additions in terms of extra information that can modify what we have already been told. The account of all earlier events may need to be reinterpreted, particularly in relation to the Grail Quest now to come (E. Kennedy 1996a). The justifications for inclusion or exclusion of material are still predominantly made in the third person and never with the name of an author given.[16] The tale, which is presented as largely based on reports made by the knights on their return to court, is given as the principal authority, and the reference to Mestre Gautiers Map in the colophon that precedes the opening of the *Queste* occurs only in some manuscripts (Baumgartner 1981, 29).

Thus in the long account of events in the tale of Lancelot from his abduction into the Lake up to the eve of his son Galahad's knighting and replacement of his father as the greatest knight, the presentation of Lancelot's earthly love as an inspiration for his achievement in chivalry changes considerably. However, this usually finds expression not in terms of a break with the past, but of a reinterpretation of the past. Such reinterpretations may not necessarily be valid once the Grail adventures have ended, and the very narrative pattern itself seems to imply more than one level of truth, but throughout, the links between past, present and future are constantly maintained. [EK]

La Queste del Saint Graal

The penultimate branch of the *Lancelot–Grail* Cycle, *La Queste del Saint Graal*, or, as the manuscripts themselves have it, *Les Aventures del Saint Graal*, was probably composed *c*.1220. There are over fifty extant manuscripts and fragments of this section of the tale (Trachsler 1996*, 564), and three printed editions have appeared, the most widely available being Pauphilet's edition, originally published in 1923. The *Queste* develops many of the themes and characters found in antecedent Arthurian texts, particularly, of course, those described in the *Lancelot* proper, in which a Grail Quest with a new hero is prepared for from the beginning of the account of Galehot's dreams in the cyclic version (*LM*, 1, 52–6). In fact, it is arguably the case that Lancelot, although he fails to achieve the Grail Quest, remains the main focus of the narrative in this part of the 'history' of the Round Table and its knights.

Despite the fact that the *Queste* forms an integral part of the *Lancelot–Grail* whole, there is very strong evidence to suggest that this section of the Cycle was composed by someone other than the author of the *Lancelot* proper and indeed that of the *Mort Artu*, the conclusion to the tale, which immediately follows the *Queste* in the sequence: the preoccupations of the latter, in particular its emphatically didactic tone, and the portrayal of certain of the main characters, differ markedly from those of the rest of the Cycle. It seems that the author of this particular segment was heavily influenced by Cistercian doctrine, although he also knew a great deal about knighthood, and it has also been shown that there are significant Templar elements to be found in the narrative (Pratt 1995; Nicholson 2001*).

Beyond the immediate influence and importance of the antecedent elements of the Cycle itself, there are several other Grail romances with which the author of the *Queste* was undoubtedly familiar. Notable amongst these are Chrétien de Troyes's *Perceval* and its first two Continuations, and Robert de Boron's verse *Estoire dou Graal* or *Joseph*. The dating of the *Didot-Perceval* and *Perlesvaus* with respect to the *Queste*, and the relationship (if any) between those three texts, are rather more problematic issues (Bogdanow 1984; Lloyd-Morgan 1984).

In essence the *Queste* recounts the attempt by Arthur's knights to undertake the Quest for the Holy Grail and bring it to a successful conclusion, this being defined not as the recovery of a sacred relic but rather as reaching an understanding of the significance of the Holy Vessel. The narrative opens in a fashion typical of Arthurian romance: it is the eve of the feast of Pentecost, and all the knights are making their way to the court of Camelot for the festivities. Lancelot, however, is first summoned to an abbey and asked to knight a fair youth whom he does not seem to recognize, this youth being Galahad, Lancelot's virgin son by the daughter of King Pellés (see *LM*, 4, 209–11). It is not long before Galahad appears at court, taking his rightful place at the Round Table and thereby immediately achieving the adventure of the Perilous Seat, in which only the best knight in the world could sit and remain unharmed. During his brief presence at Camelot, Galahad also brings to a conclusion the adventure of the Sword in the Floating Stone, further confirming his status as the greatest of the Knights of the Round Table, surpassing even his father Lancelot, who himself acknowledges the superiority of his son.[17]

Shortly after Galahad's arrival, the Holy Grail makes its first appearance in the narrative, feeding all the Companions of the Round Table equally, providing each of them with his favourite food. The Grail, covered with a white samite cloth and with no apparent means of support, moves through the Great Hall at Camelot (Pauphilet edn, p. 15). This veiling of the Grail has crucial symbolic significance, and contributes to the definition of the Quest as declared by Gauvain:

> [D]e tant sont il [the knights] engignié qu'il nel porent veoir apertement, ançois lor en fu coverte la vraie semblance. Por coi je endroit moi faz orendroit un veu, que le matin sanz plus atendre enterrai en la Queste en tel maniere que je la maintendrai un an et un jor et encor plus se mestiers est; ne ne revendrai a cort por chose qui aviegne devant que je l'aie veu plus apertement qu'il ne m'a ci esté demostrez ... (p. 16)

> (*They* [the knights] *are so deceived that they could not see it clearly: its true form was hidden from them. So here and now I swear an oath on my own account: that in the morning without further delay I shall embark upon the Quest in such a way that I shall pursue it for a year and a day and longer if need be; nor shall I return to court, no matter what occurs, until I have seen it more clearly than it has been shown to me here.*)

All the Companions swear to follow the Quest, and the narrative pattern henceforth becomes that of interlacing the various knights' adventures, a technique developed throughout the *Lancelot*, but here adapted with the specific purpose of inviting the reader to make comparisons between the characters and their relative progress in the *aventures* of the Grail. After the Quest has begun, each of the adventures encountered by the characters is a test of spiritual worth, and what emerges is a new hierarchy amongst the Knights of the Round Table, based not on the traditional values associated with Arthur's court, but on the highest Christian virtues.

Of the three knights who achieve the Quest, Galahad does so most completely, being the only one deemed worthy of looking inside the uncovered Grail (277–8). In theological terms, he can be seen as representing the doctrine of Predestination, but also functions, at times, as a type of Christ or saviour figure, as for instance in the Castle of the Maidens episode (46–51). Perceval, the other virgin knight amongst the Grailwinners, is successful because of his simple, even naive, faith and is redeemed through Grace. Bohort, being a reformed sinner (he lost his virginity, albeit by enchantment, in an episode recounted in the *Lancelot* (*LM*, 2, 196–8)), endeavours to raise himself spiritually through deeds, and embodies the notion of salvation through effort (Matarasso 1979; Williams 2001).

Each of the three successful knights undergoes a series of tests in the form of *aventures*. The trials faced by Galahad tend to be of two types: the disenchanting of marvellous objects, or the defeat of enemies of God. Under the first category we find episodes such as the Sword in the Floating Stone (5–6; 11–12); the Shield (27–34); the Tomb (35–40); the Ship of Solomon (200–28) and the Broken Sword (266). The second kind of episode includes adventures such as the Castle of the Maidens (46–51), the Château Carcelois (229–34) and the Castle of the Leprous Lady (237–45).

The tests undergone by Perceval are mostly to be found in a long section of the narrative devoted exclusively to his adventures (71–115), and all involve a challenge to the strength of his faith in God. For example, following an unprovoked attack by twenty anonymous knights, Perceval finds himself without a horse, and is offered an immensely powerful jet-black steed by a mysterious maiden (91–3). Although the sight of the horse fills him with foreboding, Perceval accepts the gift, and the demonic stallion carries him away, many leagues distant, to an island that will provide the setting for the temptation of the flesh that almost proves his undoing (104–10). The naive knight is just about to succumb to the charms of a temptress when Providence intervenes in the form of the fortuitous presence of the cruciform sword, reminding Perceval of his determination to remain chaste.

The trials with which Bohort is presented are, in some ways, more complex than those faced by either Galahad or Perceval, for they involve conflicts of interest on an apparently human level and dilemmas that challenge some of the fundamental tenets of chivalry. For instance, at one point Bohort is forced into making an extremely difficult choice: in one direction he sees his brother Lionel being utterly humiliated by two knights who have bound him (naked except for his breeches) to a pack-horse and are thrashing him with thorny switches; in another, he sees a young maiden being carried off into the forest by a knight whose intention is rape (175–7). Bohort decides to make the maiden's rescue his first priority: this is later revealed, by a holy man, to have been the correct course of action, but not before a false cleric has almost succeeded in persuading Bohort that his choice has led to the death of his brother Lionel; this is not in fact the case: Lionel reappears in the narrative shortly afterwards (188–93), takes Bohort to task for having left him for dead, and issues a challenge of a fight to the death, thus providing yet another test for the more virtuous brother. Like Perceval, Bohort is tempted carnally (180–2), but this time there is an interesting twist to the situation: the 'maiden' in question threatens suicide if Bohort refuses her advances; furthermore, she claims that twelve of her retinue will likewise cast themselves from the top of her tower should the knight turn her down. The knight remains unmoved, and the ladies do indeed jump from the ramparts, but once Bohort has crossed himself, both tower and ladies disappear in an infernal din, revealing all to have been a temptation of devilish origin.

Although not entirely successful in the Grail adventures, the character of Lancelot is central in the *Queste*, both to the hierarchy and to the narrative. In terms of the hierarchy, he represents a state between that of the Grailwinners and that of the unredeemed sinners. Lancelot's adulterous love for the queen prevents him from being one of the chosen three,[18] but he does eventually confess, repent and, after a painful struggle, in both the emotional and the physical sense, he is rewarded with a partial Grail vision (253–6). In narrative terms, it is arguable that, despite not fully achieving the Quest, Lancelot remains the central focus of this part of the Cycle. He is undoubtedly the most complex and subtle of the characters who embark upon the Grail adventures, and more narrative time is devoted to his personal quest than to that of any other individual knight.

A significant theme of the *Queste* is the way in which those characters who in earlier Arthurian tradition represented the flower of chivalry are, in the new spiritual context of the Grail Quest, brought low by their inability to cope with the different nature of the challenges offered by the *aventures del Saint Graal*. Three knights in particular are represented in this way: Gauvain, who was previously regarded as second only to Lancelot in greatness (see *LK*, 416–17, 539; *LM*, 8, 227–9, 432), Hector, Lancelot's brother, and Lionel, the brother of Bohort. All fail in the Quest through a lack of faith, and through an attachment to the worldly trappings of chivalry that is incompatible with a state of high spiritual awareness, let alone perfection.[19]

The *Queste* ends with the three chosen knights taking the Grail from Arthur's realm of Logres to the holy city of Sarras, located 'es parties de Babiloine' (*in the region of Babylon*, p. 279), and it is here that Galahad looks inside the unveiled Grail and sees 'les merveilles de totes autres merveilles' (*the marvel of all marvels*, p. 278) just before he dies. The Grail is then definitively removed from the world of mortals:

[U]ne mein vint devers le ciel [...]. Et elle vint droit au seint Vessel et le prist, [...] et l'enporta tot amont vers le ciel, a telle eure qu'il ne fu puis hons si hardiz qu'il osast dire qu'il eust veu le Saint Graal. (p. 279)

(A hand came down from heaven and went straight to the Holy Vessel, then took it and carried it right up into heaven, and from that hour onwards there was no man bold enough to claim that he had seen the Holy Grail.)

Finally, Bohort alone returns to Arthur's court (Perceval having lived out his few remaining days in a hermitage) and recounts the *aventures* to Arthur's clerks, who record them in writing in the time-honoured manner.

To date, most of the scholarly criticism devoted to the *Queste* has tended to focus on one or more of the following areas: the meaning of the Holy Grail itself, the use of metaphor, intertextuality and structure. The first major study of the *Queste* was undertaken by Pauphilet during the preparation of his edition. His *Études sur la Queste del Saint Graal*, first published in 1921 (two years before his edited text appeared), is mainly concerned with the principles by which the edition was established and with an analysis of the religious dimension of the symbolism in the narrative. Pauphilet (1921, 24) originally suggested that the Grail is intended as a representation of the figure of God Himself, but later (1950, 195) stated that he was persuaded by Gilson's point of view, which was that the Grail embodies the Grace of the Holy Spirit (Gilson 1925). Lot-Borodine (1951), developing this idea further, concludes that the Grail *is* the Holy Spirit and that, in Sarras, Galahad beholds the revelation of the Mystery of the Trinity. Hamilton (1942), on the other hand, claims that the Holy Vessel symbolizes the sacrament of the Eucharist. Matarasso (1979, 181–2) correctly cautions against trying to define too closely a symbolic meaning for the Grail, stating that all the scenes in which it appears must be taken into account to avoid twisting the text to fit a particular interpretation. My own view (Williams 2001) is that we must not forget that the narrative itself keeps reminding us that the Holy Vessel represents 'ce que langue ne porroit descrire ne cuer penser' (*what the tongue cannot describe nor the heart imagine*, 278) – the whole point about the Grail Quest is that it has a dimension which is ultimately ineffable from a human perspective.

As far as metaphoric elements in the *Queste* are concerned, Pauphilet (1921) paved the way for others to analyse the influence of Scripture on the narrative, and the extent to which its symbolism is specifically Christian. This is an approach most fully developed by Matarasso (1979), who, in addition to very useful material on the spiritual aspects of the new model of chivalry embodied by Galahad, also provides detailed lists of specific biblical references and allusions found within the text. Baumgartner (1981) pays particular attention to the Tree of Life episode and its function and importance in the narrative.

In addition to the links between the *Queste* and Scripture, critics have done a certain amount of work on possible sources within secular literature, folk-tales and the like. Of these, the most cautious (and therefore the most useful) is the study by Frappier (1978b) on the possible pre-Christian origins of the Grail motif. As mentioned above, much more identifiable and established are links with earlier Arthurian texts.

Central to any study of the *Queste* must be the issue of structure and how it is related to metaphor. The narrative has a complex structure, characterized by interlace and by the repetition of themes and symbolic elements from one episode to another, although linked scenes are frequently separated by many pages. Various critics have attempted to tackle this issue: Cornet (1969), in a study of three particular episodes, has much to say on the link between narrative structure and metaphor; Baumgartner (1980), in an article on the knights' adventures, demonstrates that the concept of *aventure* has a particular meaning in the context of the Grail Quest, and that each knight is granted a vision of the Grail commensurate with his particular level of spiritual understanding. Burns (1985a), in an extensive study of the *Lancelot–Grail* Cycle, also devotes considerable space to the problem of linking the structural and the symbolic, and Williams (2001) claims that structure and symbolism provide the keys to understanding the *Queste*'s central theme and relates this notion to the didactic function of the narrative.

One of the most striking features of the narrative technique used by the author of the *Queste* is the interplay between the metaphoric and homiletic modes: a pattern is established in the early part of the text whereby the knights experience adventures whose symbolic significance they (and, it must be said, the reader) do not always grasp. These adventures are at least partially explained (to characters and readers) within the narrative by explicit exegesis, sometimes in the form of inscriptions and the like, but more often by a figure of authority such as a cleric, with direct interventions on the part of the narrator being rare. As the Quest develops, we find that the homiletic passages become less frequent, and it is increasingly left to the reader to interpret the metaphorical dimension of the adventures. Thus the reader is placed in a position analogous to that of the characters engaged on the Quest, with each attaining a level of achievement appropriate to the extent of his understanding of spiritual matters; in this way, the essentially didactic nature of the text is revealed (Williams 2001).

There still remains much to be done in terms of editorial and critical work on the *Queste*. It is high time that a new scholarly edition was produced: for various reasons Pauphilet consulted only about half the total number of manuscripts available to us today, and Bogdanow and Berrie's 2006 edition in the Lettres Gothiques series is a welcome addition. Furthermore, the vexed question of the relative dating of the *Queste*, the *Perlesvaus* and the *Didot-Perceval* still remains unresolved, as do issues concerning the possible textual links between these three works.

The *Queste del Saint Graal* is a highly significant work within the Arthurian canon. It is the earliest extant Grail romance which can be said with any certainty to attempt a detailed and extensive interweaving of the dual (pseudo-Celtic and Christian) tradition associated with the Vessel. Of the antecedent texts, Chrétien's *Perceval* introduces a largely Celtic object, the status of the passage in which Perceval's hermit-uncle provides a retrospective Christianizing interpretation of the Grail procession remaining in some doubt (Frappier 1951, 181). Robert de Boron's *Estoire dou Graal*, on the other hand, concentrates on the alleged role of the Grail during and after the passion of Christ, although the surviving prose version of his *Merlin* does present the Round Table as the third of the Three Tables, after those of the Last Supper and the Grail.[20] Furthermore, and perhaps more importantly, the *Queste* is also the first text to portray the character of Galahad, the Perfect Knight, who achieves the Adventures of the Holy Grail most completely. [AMLW]

La Mort le roi Artu

La Mort le roi Artu constitutes the last branch (though not the latest to be composed) of the *Lancelot–Grail* Cycle and, in relating the deaths of Arthur and Lancelot (as well as those of Guinevere and Gauvain), it attempts to impose closure on the biographies of Arthurian literature's most famous protagonists (Trachsler 1996*, esp. chapter 3). It continues the fiction of authorship on which the *Queste* ends by claiming that Walter Map was commissioned by King Henry (II of England) to commemorate in writing the post-Quest adventures of Arthur's knights up to the fatal wounding of the legendary king. A further link with the preceding branch is provided by Bohort, the only one of the elect three to survive the Quest. He, as the Grailwinner destined to return to Arthur's court at Camelot, brings news of his companions' saintly deaths after their final vision of the Grail. However, it is clear from the beginning of the *Mort Artu* that the spiritual allegory of the didactic *Queste* has been left behind and we have returned to the more secular, courtly world of the *Lancelot* proper.[21]

In relating the demise of the Arthurian world, the anonymous, probably clerical, author of the *Mort Artu* has fused the romance tradition of adultery between the queen and her lover, inherited from Chrétien's *Charrette* and the earlier branches of the Vulgate Cycle, with the pseudo-chronicle narrative of Arthur's death exemplified by Geoffrey, Wace and the *Mort* section of the *Didot-Perceval*. He has thereby produced a generically hybrid work with two heroes: Lancelot, the product of romance imagination, and Arthur known from pseudo-history and romance. Whilst the king is the eponymous protagonist of the last branch, Lancelot is the hero of the whole Cycle, which, in the conclusion to the

Mort Artu, is called 'l'*Estoire de Lancelot*' (§204). Drawing on the Tristan legend (and especially on a version similar to that of Beroul) in his portrayal of the psychological distress and political conflict created by the gradual revelation of the queen's adultery, the prose romancer produces a complex work in which various reasons for Arthur's downfall are suggested. A victim, in Wace's *Brut,* of his nephew Mordred's treachery, in the form of alliances with Arthur's pagan foes and adultery with the willing Guinevere, Arthur now suffers not only from Mordred's attempts to usurp his throne and claim his wife, but also from the repercussions of Guinevere's adulterous passion for Lancelot, the king's greatest knight. Yet the *Mort Artu* also presents Arthur as contributing towards his own downfall, for Mordred turns out to be his illegitimate son by incest with his sister, Gauvain's mother (not named in this romance). Moreover, the king is at times unduly vengeful, allowing Gauvain's thirst for revenge over the deaths of his brothers to influence him, making him prefer personal and family honour over the well-being of his kingdom.

Any attempt to interpret the *Mort Artu* must take into account its careful structure. The organizing principle of the first half of the romance is interlace: the interweaving and juxtaposition of events taking place simultaneously in different locations and narrated from the perspective of different characters. This technique (as well as the nature of many of the early episodes: quests for Lancelot incognito, Guinevere's jealousy and rejection of her lover, her need for a champion, tournaments and woundings) is reminiscent of the *Lancelot* and allows the reader to be privy to information not available to the protagonists, thereby creating in the *Mort Artu* dramatic irony, with sometimes comic and sometimes tragic effect. However, although some interlace remains, in the second half of the work the plot becomes more linear and the pace more rapid as the Arthurian protagonists rush inexorably towards their demise.

The final branch of the Vulgate Cycle begins on a note of censure. There being no authentic adventures left after the Grail Quest (during which Gauvain's sinful state resulted in the unwitting murder of many Knights of the Round Table, whilst Lancelot was hindered by his adultery, *Mort Artu,* §§3–4), Arthur resorts to promoting the dangerous pseudo-adventure of the tournament, an activity strongly criticized by thirteenth-century churchmen, though defended by other writers as useful for training knights. Although Lancelot, fighting incognito, wins the Winchester tournament, he is wounded by his cousin Bohort and this prevents him from returning to Arthur's court. Meanwhile, Guinevere, hearing that her champion has worn the sleeve of the demoiselle d'Escalot, who trapped Lancelot into this act of courtesy by asking him for a boon (§14), has become insanely jealous (not for the first time in the Vulgate Cycle), especially as Gauvain, who tried to woo the demoiselle himself, is spreading rumours that Lancelot is in love (§§31, 36, 44).

From the beginning of the *Mort Artu* ill-motivated courtiers have schemed to reveal the queen's adultery to Arthur and further proof is supplied by his sister Morgan, who shows him pictorial evidence for the adulterous liaison (§§48–54). This episode is already prepared for by the *Lancelot*, which narrates Morgan's imprisonment of Lancelot, during which time he depicts his chivalric adventures and love for the queen in words and pictures on the walls of her castle. In the *Mort*, however, Arthur's suspicions are somewhat allayed when, on returning to Camelot, he finds that Lancelot has been absent for longer than one might expect of a lovesick knight (§62). In fact, his absence is due to Guinevere's jealous rejection of him, which she regrets when a complicated plot to poison Gauvain ends with the death of another knight, Gaheris, and when the latter's brother Mador de la Porte falsely accuses her of murder (§§62–3). While the queen is waiting for a champion, the body of the demoiselle d'Escalot arrives in a boat with a letter accusing Lancelot of causing her death from unrequited love (§§70–3). At the eleventh hour, Lancelot returns to defend the queen successfully in a judicial combat fought on the grounds of intention, and after such a long separation, their adulterous passion intensifies (§85). When the lovers are subsequently caught almost red-handed (§90), and Lancelot and his men, in rescuing Guinevere from the stake, kill three of Gauvain's brothers (§§94–6), a chain reaction of revenge is set in motion, which Lancelot's magnanimous gestures fail to stop. After a period with Guinevere in the castle of Joyeuse Garde (the winning of which is related in the *Lancelot*) Lancelot returns her at the pope's instigation to Arthur (§119), who nevertheless pursues Lancelot to Gaul, leaving the kingdom in the hands of Mordred. A second judicial combat (§§151–7), this time between Gauvain and Lancelot, the former accusing the latter of killing his brothers treacherously, results in a fatal head-wound for Gauvain. The ill-timed arrival of the Romans, against whom Arthur's favourite nephew insists on fighting, brings about his death (§172). The final nail in Arthur's coffin, is, however, provided by Mordred, who attempts to usurp the throne by claiming that Arthur is dead and by trying to force the queen to marry him (§§134–40). His treachery fulfils the hermit's prophecy in the *Lancelot* (*LM*, 5, 220) and Arthur is reminded (§164) of the frightening dream he had on the night of Mordred's conception (*LM*, 5, 220–1). Ignoring Gauvain's advice from the next world to call on Lancelot's help (§176), Arthur kills his illegitimate son during a bloody battle on Salisbury Plain, a disaster prophesied by Merlin years earlier (§§178–91). Mortally wounded by Mordred, the king orders his sword Excalibur to be thrown into the lake (symbolic perhaps of his wish that Lancelot du Lac should replace him as king), accidentally kills Lucan in a last desperate embrace (§192) and, having failed to be healed by Morgan's magic, is apparently given a Christian burial.[22] After Arthur's death has been avenged on Mordred's sons by Lancelot and his kin, Lancelot, Hector and Bohort end their days in the service of God, thus securing their salvation, as does Guinevere, who has already died in a nunnery.

For those critics who emphasize the unity of ethos of the *Lancelot–Grail* Cycle, claiming either that the last three branches are the work of a single author (Micha 1987) or were supervised closely by an 'architect' (Frappier 1954–5), the *Mort Artu* constitutes the apocalyptic finale following the 'Old Testament' *Lancelot* and the 'New Testament' *Queste*, an interpretation strengthened by the later addition to the Cycle of the *Estoire* (Lagorio 1978). Reading the *Mort* from the moral perspective of the preceding branch, they argue that Bohort returns to a fallen world, whose feudal/courtly/chivalric values are found wanting and whose protagonists are all tainted by sin, a situation prophesied in Gauvain's dream in the *Queste* (Pauphilet edn, 149–57). Factors which lead modern scholars to conclude that there is something rotten in the kingdom of Camelot include (i) Arthur's reliance on morally dubious tournaments; (ii) Lancelot and Guinevere's return to sinful adultery after the abstinence of the *Queste*; (iii) two judicial combats in which, according to Bloch (1974, 1977), Lancelot's might is relied upon more than his right (though Bloch underestimates the importance of intention in deciding who is in the right); (iv) the incest that produced Mordred; (v) Gauvain's thirst for revenge; (vi) general conflict at court between different factions. They therefore argue that sin accounts for the demise of Arthurian civilization, failure and death being perceived as forms of divine punishment. Nevertheless, many characters, Gauvain, Guinevere and especially Lancelot, achieve salvation, and the romance concludes on a positive, spiritual note, as Lancelot and his closest kin end their days in a hermitage. So, the worldly values of *cortoisie*, Christian *chevalerie* and kingship, with which Arthur has been associated in both chronicle and romance since Geoffrey's *Historia*, are eclipsed by the spiritual, monastic values of worldly renunciation, repentance and devotion to God, all guaranteeing individual salvation. The *Mort Artu* can therefore be interpreted as a moral exemplum on the *contemptus mundi* theme, presenting ultimately an 'Augustinian' approach to secular history.[23]

Such a reading of the *Mort Artu* is consonant with the ethical position of the *Queste* and is supported by the general structure of the romance, which describes the flawed protagonists' descent from success and happiness to disaster. However, unlike the *Queste*, which offers a moral commentary on the protagonists' actions through the numerous interventions of hermits, the *Mort Artu* provides neither an intrusive, judgemental narrator nor the authoritative interpretation of events by any of the characters. Narratorial interventions in the first person are rare; the romance is narrated by 'li contes' (*the tale*), leaving the reader/audience to interpret events largely unaided. However, there is evidence in the text, some lexical and some structural, to suggest that the *Mort Artu*'s author is encouraging a more humane, less morally judgemental response to its protagonists and their actions, than that provided by the author of the *Queste*.

In some respects the *Mort Artu* shares the amorality of classical tragedy (Pratt 2004, chapter 2). Lancelot's *hamartia* or false step is not only his faithful love for Guinevere, already present in the *Lancelot*, but also his fateful decision to grant the demoiselle d'Escalot a boon. Thus, he triggers an unstoppable series of events which results in the downfall of a whole civilization. The greater victim of the *peripeteia* (ironic reversal), though, and the character most deserving of our fear and pity, is Arthur, who does contribute to his own fate, but unwittingly, and whose faults in no way justify the harshness of his demise. Such a reading depends, however, on a more secular approach to Arthurian history than that promoted by the *Queste*. Indeed, in juxtaposing these last two branches, the Vulgate Cycle highlights a key hermeneutic problem: how to interpret the events of the past and the romance texts that commemorate them (see Kunstmann and Dubé 1982 for references to the *Mort Artu* as 'estoire').

The challenges of interpretation are dramatized within this highly ambiguous text as the reader witnesses its protagonists struggling to understand the events leading to the extinction of the Arthurian world. In the prologue, the narrator claims he will show *how* Arthur met his end; he offers few answers, however, to the question *why*, yet it is this question that preoccupies the protagonists (and readers) of the *Mort Artu*. The author offers, mainly through the direct speech of his characters, two sets of explanatory factors, which can be summarized as human culpability and sheer bad luck. Together they contribute to an ethically complex work, which defies facile moral judgements and allows scope for different reader responses.

At various points in the narrative the protagonists blame either themselves or others for the multitude of disasters which befall them. Each of the main characters seems to be flawed in some way, and yet they are also endowed with compensatory qualities and often act in mitigating circumstances. In fact, the ethically charged terms *pechié* (sin) and *orgueil* (pride) occur infrequently in the *Mort Artu*, and are rarely applied by the narrator to his protagonists (Kunstmann and Dubé 1982). A notable exception is Lancelot's adultery, which is called a sin by the narrator in paragraph 4, yet it should be borne in mind that the early paragraphs of the *Mort Artu* constitute a sort of bridging passage with the preceding *Queste*, after which the strongly moral tone dissipates. From then on, Lancelot is presented as a loyal, courteous lover, a magnanimous Christian knight and a good friend to both Arthur and Gauvain, who is forced against his will into fighting them. Gauvain's character is also mixed (Adler 1950), his early moderate advice, his bravery, popularity, charity to the poor counterbalancing his *desmesure* (lack of moderation) after the loss of his brothers. Thus, his anger and revenge are depicted as being born of deep grief and distress (Greene 2002, chapter 5). Similarly, the figure of Arthur receives complex treatment: many characters rightly express criticism of his intransigent pursuit of Lancelot and concern for personal honour, both under the influence of Gauvain. Yet, two further criticisms of Arthur voiced by modern scholars are perhaps less justified. The first is the charge of royal weakness, a refusal to accept and punish what is obvious, namely the queen's adultery (MacRae 1982). However, in mitigation one must not forget that Arthur does not share the omniscience of the work's readers. The structure of the narrative emphasizes the fact that Arthur is the victim of dramatic irony. Struggling to interpret conflicting evidence, the king is, in my view, rightly slow to act on allegations which, although correct, are made by ill-intentioned courtiers reminiscent of the evil barons in Beroul's *Tristran*. Even Morgan's pictorial evidence of Lancelot's love is suspect, given the supernatural atmosphere surrounding her castle (§§48–54). The author's emphasis on the malign motivations of those characters who tell the truth about the adultery, Agravain, Mordred and Morgan, not only makes us more sympathetic towards Arthur's personal and political dilemma (not easily resolvable by simply punishing Guinevere), but also problematizes and relativizes many of the values promoted by Arthurian romance: loyalty, truth, love and honour.

The second charge against Arthur is his incest with his sister (Archibald 1989). Interestingly, this specific term is not used; instead Mordred is simply the king's illegitimate son and explicit moral condemnation of his father is thereby avoided. Moreover, the circumstances of the incest are not explained until later in Arthurian tradition, when the *Suite Merlin* is added to the Vulgate Cycle. Although there are references to Mordred's parentage in the *Lancelot*, the prophecies involving a serpent issuing from Arthur's belly and then attacking him may be scribal interpolations, inserted once the author of the *Mort Artu* had decided to enhance the pathos of Arthur's death by making him the victim of his own son. On the other hand, if the incest was integral to the conception of the whole Vulgate Cycle, its function is still open to interpretation: is it a sin punishable by God and thus provoking moral condemnation or an instrument of fate eliciting our sympathy for its hapless victim?

The ambiguity concerning human responsibility for Arthur's demise is further complicated by the interlacing of allusions to character flaws with frequent mention, made by both the narrator and the protagonists, of *mescheance* or *mesaventure*; both terms imply that bad luck, misfortune and unfortunate timing cause or at least contribute to the abrupt end of Arthurian civilization (Lyons 1983; Pratt 1991; 2004). Thus, the lovers might not have renewed their passion so violently had Lancelot not been trapped into wearing the demoiselle d'Escalot's sleeve, provoking Guinevere's uncontrollable jealousy and anger. The separation resulting from this and from Lancelot's series of unfortunate woundings leads to the lovers' abandonment of any courtly discretion, hence to discovery. The good fortune enjoyed by Lancelot in the *Lancelot*, enabling him to love Guinevere and serve Arthur and his kingdom, has certainly run out by the time he kills Gaheriet unknowingly, thus earning Gauvain's wrath. It is also bad luck that the Romans decide to attack Arthur just when Gauvain has incurred a serious head-wound.

By compressing the plot inherited from his chronicle sources, the author of the *Mort Artu* has Arthur receive news of Mordred's treachery on the very day that he has defeated the Romans. Arthur is thus given no time to reflect and is precipitated headlong towards his death. In this way it is implied that the Knights of the Round Table, though flawed, are also tragic victims of a force beyond their control. The choice then confronting the reader is whether this force should be seen as providential, fulfilling the divine will, or whether it emanates from a more pagan source, represented in the text by the goddess Fortuna. Again, no clear answers emerge, either from the narrator or from the characters. While God is frequently invoked when the Knights of the Round Table feel they have been fortunate, there is a tendency to blame Fortuna, the evil stepmother, for the disasters which befall them (§§190: 5–8; 192: 21–4, etc.). The narrator remains silent on this point of interpretation, except when relating Arthur's dream on the eve of the battle of Salisbury. When Fortuna knocks Arthur from the top of her wheel, her behaviour is described as treacherous, and the narrator further comments that Arthur thus foresaw the 'mescheances' (*misfortunes*) which were to befall him. However, Fortuna's own explanation to Arthur is that 'tel sont li orgueil terrien qu'il n'i a nul si haut assiz qu'il ne le coviegne cheoir de la poesté del monde' (*such is worldly pride* [or *such are the vanities of this world*] *that there is no one, however highly placed, who can avoid falling from the heights of human power*, §176). However, the phrase 'tel sont li orgueil terrien' is tantalizingly ambiguous, as the translation above indicates. Is Fortuna justly punishing Arthur for the sinfulness of his rule, thus adopting the role of handmaiden of God as presented in the later books of Boethius's *Consolation of Philosophy*? Or is she the pagan Fortuna, as understood by Boethius's narrator and the many medieval readers of the *Consolation* who focused on the figure as depicted in Book 2: an amoral goddess who capriciously withdraws her favours from Arthur, irrespective of his merits? Is she in fact merely pointing out the unfair rules of worldly power, the natural rise and fall of civilizations, the cyclical nature of secular history as symbolized by her wheel? The *Mort Artu* refuses to supply answers to these binary questions, perhaps even preferring a 'both/and' to the traditional 'either/or' of dialectic (Adler 1950).

Despite its final paragraphs, which concentrate on individual salvation, the majority of the work functions like a secular tragic narrative. Characters of high social status, but not wholly good nor wholly evil, set in motion a chain reaction leading to their demise. They contribute to their fates, but are also the victims of bad luck and chance events, the tragic outcome being out of all proportion to their initial faults. Sometimes two 'goods' or two laudable intentions are placed in conflict and lead to disastrous consequences. Although it gestures from time to time towards the *contemptus mundi* genre, the *Mort Artu* also commemorates, especially in the actions of Lancelot, but even in Gauvain, Arthur and many of the Knights of the Round Table, the more laudable aspects of Arthurian civilization (Lyons 1983). So, unlike the *Queste*, whose didacticism encourages a strongly judgemental response, the *Mort Artu* encourages a mixture of wonder and admiration for Arthurian virtue, fear at the intransigence of some of its protagonists, and both fear and pity for the frailty and humanity which its heroes share with us. Indeed, as Greene (2002) argues, the *Mort Artu* is an Art of Courtly Death, whose protagonists provide us with mirrors in which to contemplate our own demise.

This subtle and moving work, often studied in isolation, but only to be fully appreciated when read as the final branch of the whole Vulgate Cycle, has recently generated much scholarly interest. Critics reflecting modern preoccupations with death (Planche 1997; Greene 2002), ethics (Kay 1997), closure (Lacy 1994; Trachsler 1994; 1996), narrative structure (Lacy 1977; Zuurdeeg 1981; Delcourt 1998), reading and writing (Colliot 1973; Solterer 1985), textual criticism (Leonardi 2003) have found fertile material for analysis in the *Mort Artu*, while the existence of a concordance (Kunstmann and Dubé 1982) has generated fascinating semantic studies on the themes of loyalty and treason (Szkilnik 1994), love (Santucci 1992; Andrieux-Reix 1994), truth and knowledge (Terry 1990; Delcourt 1998) and the meaning of the term *preudome* (Chênerie 1977). From these analyses the author of the *Mort Artu* emerges as a gifted practitioner of Old French prose (Rychner 1970), a sensitive investigator of human psychology and a sympathetic observer of the human condition in all its complexity (Pratt 2004). Yet his attempt in the last branch of the Vulgate Cycle to impose closure on the whole of Arthurian history was short-lived. Despite his (somewhat traditional) claim at the very end of the *Mort Artu* that any continuator would be a liar (§204), the authors of the prose *Tristan* and the Post-Vulgate *Roman du Graal* soon took up the challenge, expanding yet further Arthur's narrative universe. **[KP]**

Notes

[1] See the Reference List to this chapter for editions of the various versions and branches mentioned here and for the sigla used to indicate these edited versions. The last part of the *Lancelot* proper (*LM*, 4–6; *S*, 5) is sometimes known as the *Agravain* because it opens with Agravain's departure from Gauvain and his companions on an adventure which rapidly leads to imprisonment. However, the title is misleading (*LM*, 4, introduction) and is therefore not used in this chapter.

[2] From the beginning of *LM*, 1 there are two versions of the cyclic romance: the long, on which Micha's edition is based, and the short, of which Micha gives extracts in *LM*, 3 and in appendices to other volumes. Sommer's edition is based on a manuscript (London, BL, Additional MS 10293) giving the short cyclic version from *S*, 4, 5 onwards. For the short version of the *Estoire*, see the introduction to Ponceau's edition. There is no marked difference between long and short versions in

LK, 1–571; *LM*, 7 and 8; *S*, 3. The short cyclic version is generally considered to be a little later than the long; see, for example, *LM*, 1, 14, and Ponceau edn, xxviii.

[3] For a list of the manuscripts giving the pre-cyclic version in whole or in part, see *LK*, 2, 29–30. A further *Lancelot–Grail* manuscript, in Amsterdam, Bibliotheca Philosophica Hermetica, MS 1, has since become accessible. It belongs to the same general group as BNF, fr. 110 and 113–16, and as BL, Additional MS 10293, which joins the group only at the beginning of the journey of Lancelot and Galehot away from Arthur's court.

[4] Ponceau, the editor of the *Estoire* (edn, xi–xii), puts forward a different view, namely that only the *Lancelot*, by which he seems to mean the whole of *LM*, preceded the *Estoire*, and that the *Queste* and the *Mort Artu* were written later. He proposes to discuss this in a forthcoming study. It should be pointed out, though, that the Rennes manuscript, to which he appears to attach particular importance in relation to this theory, does already look forward to a Grail Quest and a Grailwinner, son of Lancelot, thus preparing the way for the *Queste*.

[5] Basing her conclusions on the evidence of manuscript illumination, Stones (1977) dates the manuscript to the early 1220s. Mentré (1986) suggests more cautiously that it dates from the thirteenth century, or even the beginning of the fourteenth.

[6] Episodes (indicated by #) correspond to chapters in Lacy transl., vol. 1; *S* introduces page numbers in Sommer edn, vol. 2.

[7] Throughout the Vulgate *Merlin* Continuation Gauvain's name appears as a diminutive (Gawainet), as do occasionally the names of his brothers and cousins.

[8] Cf. Wace's *Brut*, 9799–946, where Arthur leads an expedition to Europe first to win back King Lot's lands in Norway and conquers Denmark before moving south into Gaul.

[9] Beginning with the summons to Rome, the *Merlin* is again shaped by Wace (*Brut*, 10620ff., Arnold edn). In the *Didot-Perceval* (see chapter VI), which closely follows Wace, the episode opens the 'Mort Artu' section and Mordred's treason.

[10] *Brut*, 11279–608; not in the *Didot-Perceval*.

[11] Two other, non-Vulgate, manuscripts (London, British Library, Additional MS 38117, the Huth Manuscript, and Cambridge, University Library, Additional MS 7071 (which transmits a superior text) bear an idiosyncratic continuation, the *Suite Huth*, otherwise known as the Huth *Merlin*, that pertains to the Post-Vulgate Cycle (Paris and Ulrich edn; Asher in Lacy transl.; Bogdanow 1966 and 1996).

[12] As E. Kennedy shows (1986, 112–15), the passage from Wace sheds light on the depiction of Merlin in the prose *Lancelot* as the source of the Lady of the Lake's knowledge of necromancy, but it is Wace read through the filter of Robert's *translatio*.

[13] For the boy brought up without a name in a lake by a fairy, see Ulrich von Zatzikhoven's Middle High German romance *Lanzelet*, which seems to have shared a source with the prose romance. There is a reference to a fairy bringing up Lancelot in a lake in Chrétien's *Charrette* (Roques edn, 2342–50); there are also parallels with Perceval's childhood without a name in a 'gaste forest' in Chrétien's *Perceval*. The magical element is not given undue prominence in the prose romance (E. Kennedy 1986, 111–42; Poirion 1984). For the importance of customs in the prose *Lancelot*, see Maddox 1994; and for Lancelot's education in the lake, see Frappier 1949.

[14] The tests undergone on Gauvain's journey to Roestoc recall the series in *Erec*, linked by Brugger (1943, 323, n. 2) and Luttrell (1974, 87–92, 264–8) to the narrative pattern of the Tale of the Fair Unknown.

[15] For reproaches addressed to Arthur, see *LK*, 54–5, 283; *LM*, 7, 96–8; *LM*, 8, 13–14. For praise of Arthur, see *LK*, 34–5; *LM*, 7, 61–3. See also E. Kennedy 1986, 79–110.

[16] There is an occasional use of a first-person formula as, for example, in the explanation of the name Croix Noire, *LM*, 2, 320–1; these formulae occur more frequently in the *Estoire*, where the nature of the material demands a different type of narrative voice.

[17] The sword's pommel is engraved with an inscription declaring that it could only be removed

from its block of floating red marble by 'li mieldres chevaliers del monde' (*the best knight in the world*; *Queste*, p. 5).

[18] Note that, whilst we are told at the beginning of the *Lancelot* proper (*LK*, 1; *LM*, 7, 1) that Lancelot's baptismal name was Galahad (Galaaz), it is only in the cyclic version's account of the interpretation of Galehot's dreams that we learn that Lancelot was originally supposed to be the Grailwinner, but, because of his sinful love for Guinevere, was unable to fulfil that destiny (see *LM*, 1, 52–6).

[19] Gauvain's failure and exit from the Quest is marked by the defeat and injury he suffers at the hands of Galahad (196–7); Hector is refused entry to Corbenic (pp. 259–61) on the grounds that he is too proud, a vice symbolized by his approach made on horseback; and Lionel disappears from the narrative after God calls a halt to his unworthy combat against his brother Bohort (p. 193).

[20] See Robert de Boron's *Merlin* (Micha edn, pp. 183–6, an account on which the author of the *Queste* appears to have drawn (74–8).

[21] Only the first four paragraphs of the *Mort* share the ethos of the *Queste*, although the tone of religious didacticism returns at the end. There is some confusion amongst scribes over where one branch ends and the other begins. Yet of the forty-six extant MSS containing the *Mort*, the latter follows the *Queste* in all but nine, which offer the *Mort* alone.

[22] At least Girflet sees a tomb purportedly belonging to Arthur, and this is confirmed by a hermit (§194).

[23] For the distinction between 'Boethian' and 'Augustinian' approaches to history, see Pratt 1991; 2004, chapter 3.

Reference List

For items accompanied by an asterisk, see the General Bibliography.

Texts and Translations

Complete Vulgate Cycle and Related Texts

The Vulgate Version of the Arthurian Romances, Edited from Manuscripts in the British Museum. Ed. by H. O. Sommer, 8 vols (Washington, 1908–16) [*S*].

Lancelot–Grail: The Old French Arthurian Vulgate and Post-Vulgate in Translation. Ed. by N. J. Lacy, 5 vols (New York and London, 1993–6).

Le Livre du Graal. General editor P. Walter, I: *Joseph d'Arimathie: Merlin, les premiers faits du roi Arthur*. Ed. by D. Poirion et al. (Paris, 2001); II: *Lancelot (De 'la Marche de Gaule' à 'la première partie de la quête de Lancelot'*. Ed. by D. Poirion et al. (Paris, 2003).

The Didot Perceval, According to the Manuscripts of Modena and Paris. Ed. by W. Roach (Philadelphia, 1941).

Robert de Boron, *Le Roman du Graal: manuscrit de Modène*. Ed. by B. Cerquiglini (Paris, 1981).

L'Estoire del Saint Graal

L'Estoire del Saint Graal. Ed. by J.-P. Ponceau, 2 vols, CFMA 120–1 (Paris, 1997) [*Estoire*].

Seynt Graal or the Sank Ryal: The History of the Holy Graal. Ed. by F. J. Furnivall, 2 vols (London, 1861–3).

Le Saint Graal, ou Le Joseph d'Arimathie, première branche des romans de la Table Ronde, publié d'après des textes et des documents inédits. Ed. by E. Hucher, 3 vols (Le Mans, 1875–8).

Merlin

Robert de Boron, *Merlin: roman du XIIIᵉ siècle*. Ed. by A. Micha, TLF 281 (Geneva and Paris, 1979) [*Merlin*].

*Merlin, roman en prose du XIIIᵉ siècle, publié ... d'après le manuscrit appartenant à M. Alfred H.
   Huth*. Ed. by G. Paris and J. Ulrich, 2 vols, SATF (Paris, 1886) [Huth *Merlin*].

The *Lancelot* proper, Prose *Lancelot*

Lancelot: roman en prose du XIIIᵉ siècle. Ed. by A. Micha, 9 vols, TLF 247, 249, 262, 278, 283, 286,
   288, 307, 315 (Geneva and Paris, 1978–83) [*LM*].
Lancelot do Lac: The Non-cyclic Prose Romance. Ed. by E. Kennedy, 2 vols (Oxford, 1980) [*LK*].
Lancelot of the Lake. Transl. by C. Corley (Oxford, 1989). English translation of parts of *LK*.
Lancelot du Lac, I. Ed. by E. Kennedy and transl. into French by F. Mosès (Paris, 1991).
Lancelot du Lac, II. Ed. by E. Kennedy and transl. into French by M.-L. Chênerie (Paris, 1993).
Lancelot du Lac, III. Ed. by F. Mosès and L. Le Guay, and transl. into French by F. Mosès (Paris,
   1998).
Lancelot du Lac, IV. Ed. by Y. G. LePage and transl. into French by M.-L. Ollier (Paris, 2002).
Lancelot du Lac, V. Ed. by Y. G. LePage and transl. into French by M.-L. Ollier (Paris, 1999).

La Queste del Saint Graal

La Queste del Saint Graal: roman du XIIIᵉ siècle. Ed. by A. Pauphilet, CFMA 33 (Paris, 1923) [*Queste*].
The Quest of the Holy Grail. Transl. into English by P. M. Matarasso (Harmondsworth, 1969).
La Quête du Saint-Graal. Transl. into French by E. Baumgartner (Paris, 1979).
La Quête du Saint Graal. Ed. by F. Bogdanow and transl. into French by A. Berrie (Paris, 2006).

La Mort le roi Artu

La Mort le roi Artu: roman du XIIIᵉ siècle. Ed. by J. Frappier, TLF 58, 3rd edn (Geneva, 1964).
   [*Mort Artu*]
*Mort Artu: An Old French Prose Romance of the XIIIth Century, Being the Last Division of Lancelot
   du Lac*. Ed. by J. D. Bruce (Halle/S., 1910).
The Death of King Arthur. Transl. into English by J. Cable (Harmondsworth, 1971).
From Camelot to Joyous Guard: The Old French La Mort le roi Artu. Transl. into English by J. N.
   Carman (Lawrence, KA, 1974).

Studies

Adler, A. 1950. 'Problems of Aesthetic versus Historical Criticism in *La Mort le roi Artu*', *PMLA*,
   65, 930–43.
Andrieux-Reix, N. 1994. 'D'amour, de vérité, de mort: signes et enseignes', in Dufournet ed. 1994,
   9–24.
Archibald, E. 1989. 'Arthur and Mordred: Variations on an Incest Theme', *AL*, 8, 1–27.
Baumgartner, E. 1975. *Le Tristan en prose: essai d'interprétation d'un roman médiéval*, Geneva.
Baumgartner 1980. 'Les Aventures du Graal dans la première *Continuation*', in *Mélanges de langue
   et littérature françaises du Moyen Âge et de la Renaissance offerts à Monsieur Charles Foulon*, 2
   vols, Rennes, I, 23–8.
Baumgartner 1981. *L'Arbre et le pain: essai sur la Queste del Saint Graal*, Paris.
Baumgartner ed. 1994. *La Mort le roi Artu*, Paris.
Baumgartner E., and N. Andrieux-Reix. 2001. *Le Merlin en prose: fondations du récit arthurien*,
   Paris.
Bloch, R. H. 1974. 'From Grail Quest to Inquest: The Death of King Arthur and the Birth of
   France', *MLR*, 69, 40–55; repr. in Baumgartner ed. 1994, 107–24.
Bloch 1977. *Medieval French Literature and Law*, Berkeley and London.
Bogdanow, F. 1966. *The Romance of the Grail: A Study of the Structure and Genesis of a Thirteenth-
   Century Arthurian Prose Romance*, Manchester.
Bogdanow 1984. 'Le Perlesvaus', *GRLMA**, IV: 2, 43–67.

Bogdanow 1991. 'Post-Vulgate Cycle', in Lacy ed. 1991*, 364–6.

Bogdanow 1996. 'Post-Vulgate Cycle', in Lacy ed. 1996c*, 364–6.

Brandsma, F. 1996. 'The Eyewitness Narrator in Vernacular Prose Chronicles and Prose Romances', in Lacy ed. 1996*, 57–69.

Bruce, J. D. 1918–19. 'The Composition of the Old French Prose *Lancelot*', *RR*, 9, 241–68, 353–95; 10, 48–66, 97–122.

Brugger, E. 1906–10. 'L'Enserrement Merlin: Studien der Merlinsage', *ZfSL*, 29, 56–140; 30, 169–239; 31, 239–81; 33, 145–94; 34, 99–150; 35, 1–55.

Brugger 1930. 'Der sog. *Didot-Perceval*', *ZfSL*, 53, 389–459.

Brugger 1943. 'Der "Schöne Feigling" in der arthurischen Literatur, IIIa', *ZrP*, 63, 275–328.

Burns, E. J. 1985a. *Arthurian Fictions: Rereading the Vulgate Cycle*, Columbus, OH.

Burns 1985b. 'The Teller in the Tale: The Anonymous *Estoire del Saint Graal*', *Assays*, 3, 73–84.

Chase, C. J. 1983. 'Sur la théorie de l'entrelacement: ordre et désordre dans le *Lancelot* en prose', *MP*, 80, 227–41.

Chase 1986. 'Multiple Quests and the Art of Interlacing in the 13th-century *Lancelot*', *RomQ*, 33, 407–20.

Chase 1994. '"Or dist li contes": Narrative Interventions and the Implied Audience in the *Estoire del Saint Graal*', in Kibler ed. 1994*, 117–38.

Chase 1995. 'La Conversion des païennes dans l'*Estoire del Saint Graal*', in Wolfzettel ed. 1995*, 251–64.

Chênerie, M. -L. 1977. 'Le Motif de la *merci* dans les romans arthuriens des XIIe et XIIIe siècles', *MA*, 83, 5–52.

Chênerie 1994. 'Preudome dans *La Mort Artu*: étude sémantique et stylistique', in Dufournet ed. 1994, 67–83.

Colliot, R. 1973. 'Les Épitaphes arthuriennes', *BBIAS*, 25, 155–75; repr. in Baumgartner ed. 1994, 148–62.

Combes, A., and A. Bertin. 2001. *Écritures du Graal: XIIe-XIIIe siècles*, Paris.

Cornet, L. 1969. 'Trois épisodes de la *Queste del Graal*', in *Mélanges offerts à Rita Lejeune*, 2 vols, Gembloux, II, 983–98.

D'Arcy, A. M. 2000. *Wisdom and the Grail: The Image of the Vessel in the Queste del Saint Graal and Malory's Tale of the Sankgraal*, Dublin.

Delcourt, D. 1998. 'La Vérité dans *La Mort le roi Artu*: couverture, détours, et labyrinthe', *MR*, 22, 16–60.

Dufournet, J. ed. 1984. *Approches du Lancelot en prose*, Paris.

Dufournet ed. 1994. *La Mort du roi Arthur, ou, le crépuscule de la chevalerie*, Paris.

Frappier, J. 1949. '"L'Institution" de Lancelot dans le *Lancelot en prose*', in *Mélanges de philologie romane et de littérature médiévale offerts à Ernest Hoepffner*, Paris, 269–78; repr. in id. *Amour courtois et Table Ronde* (Geneva, 1973), 169–79.

Frappier 1951. 'Le Cortège du Graal', in R. Nelli ed. *Lumière du Graal*, Paris, 175–221.

Frappier 1954–5. 'Plaidoyer pour l'"architecte", contre une opinion d'Albert Pauphilet sur le *Lancelot en prose*', *RPh*, 8, 27–33.

Frappier 1961. *Étude sur La Mort le roi Artu: roman du XIIIe siècle*, 2nd edn, Geneva.

Frappier 1973. 'Le Personnage de Galehaut dans le *Lancelot en prose*', in *Amour courtois et Table Ronde*, Geneva, 181–208.

Frappier 1978a. 'Le Cycle de la Vulgate *Lancelot en prose* et *Lancelot-Graal*', in *GRLMA**, IV: I, 536–89.

Frappier 1978b. 'La Légende du Graal: origine et évolution', in *GRMLA**, IV: 1, 292–331.

Gilson, E. 1925. 'La Mystique de la grâce dans *La Queste del Saint Graal*', *Rom*, 51, 321–47.

Greene, V. 2002. *Le Sujet et la mort dans La Mort Artu*, Saint-Genouph.

Hamilton, W. E. M. C. 1942. 'L'Interprétation mystique de la *Queste del Saint Graal*', *Neophil*, 27, 94–110.

Huot, S. 1987. *From Song to Book: The Poetics of Writing in Old French Lyric and Lyrical Narrative Poetry*, Ithaca, NY.

Kaeuper, R. W. 2000. 'The Societal Role of Chivalry in Romance', in Krueger ed. 2000*, 97–114.

Kay, S. 1997. 'Adultery and Killing in *La Mort le roi Artu*', in N. White and N. Segal eds *Scarlet Letters: Fictions of Adultery from Antiquity to the 1990s*, Basingstoke, 34–44.

Kelly, D. 1988. 'Le Patron et l'auteur dans l'invention romanesque', in E. Baumgartner and C. Marchello-Nizia eds *Théories et pratiques de l'écriture au Moyen Âge: actes du colloque, Palais du Luxembourg-Sénat, 5 et 6 mars 1987*, Littérales 4, Paris, 25–39.

Kennedy, E. 1970. 'The Scribe as Editor', in *Mélanges de langue et de littérature du Moyen Âge et de la Renaissance offerts à Jean Frappier*, 2 vols, Geneva, I, 523–31.

Kennedy 1978. 'Royal Broodings and Lovers' Trances in the First Part of the Prose *Lancelot*', in *Mélanges de philologie et de littératures romanes offerts à Jeanne Wathelet-Willem, MRom*, Liège, 301–14.

Kennedy 1986. *Lancelot and the Grail: A Study of the Prose Lancelot*, Oxford.

Kennedy 1993. 'Le *Lancelot* en prose (MS 45)', in N. Wilkins ed. *Les Manuscrits français de la Bibliothèque Parker: Parker Library, Corpus Christi College, Cambridge: actes du Colloque, 24–27 mars, 1993*, Cambridge, 23–38.

Kennedy 1994a. 'Variations in the Patterns of Interlace in the *Lancelot–Grail*', in Kibler ed. 1994*, 31–50.

Kennedy 1994b. 'The Knight as Reader of Arthurian Romance', in Shichtman and Carley eds 1994*, 70–90.

Kennedy 1995. 'Chrétien de Troyes comme intertexte du *Lancelot* en prose', in D. Quéruel ed. *Amour et chevalerie dans les romans de Chrétien de Troyes*, Besançon, 279–86.

Kennedy 1996a. 'Who is to be Believed? Conflicting Presentations of Events in the *Lancelot–Grail* Cycle', in Kelly ed. 1996*, 169–80.

Kennedy 1996b. 'Rupture de la linéarité temporelle dans la technique narrative du cycle *Lancelot–Graal*', in *'Ensi firent li ancessor': mélanges de philologie médiévale offerts à Marc-René Jung*, Alessandria, 387–98.

Kunstmann, P., and M. Dubé. 1982. *Concordance analytique de la Mort le roi Artu*, 2 vols, Ottawa.

Lagorio, V. M. 1978. 'The Apocalyptic Mode in the Vulgate Cycle of Arthurian Romances', *PQ*, 57, 1–22.

Lacy, N. 1977. 'Spatial Form in the *Mort Artu*', *Symp*, 31, 337–45; repr. in Baumgartner ed. 1994, 100–6.

Leonardi, L. 2003. 'Le Texte critique de la *Mort le roi Artu*: question ouverte', *Rom*, 121, 133–63.

Leupin, A. 1979. 'Qui parle? Narrateurs et scripteurs dans la *Vulgate* arthurienne', *Digraphe*, 20, 81–109.

Leupin 1982. *Le Graal et la littérature: études sur la Vulgate arthurienne en prose*, Lausanne.

Lloyd-Morgan, C. 1984. 'The Relationship between the *Perlesvaus* and the Prose *Lancelot*', *Med. Aev*, 53, 239–53.

Lot, F. 1918. *Étude sur le Lancelot en prose*, Paris.

Lot 1931. 'Sur la date du *Lancelot* en prose', *Rom*, 57, 137–46.

Lot-Borodine, M. 1951. 'Les Grands Secrets du Saint-Graal dans la *Queste* du Pseudo-Map', in R. Nelli ed. *Lumière du Graal*, Paris, 151–74.

Luttrell, C. 1974. *The Creation of the First Arthurian Romance: A Quest*, London.

Lyons, F. 1983. '*La Mort le roi Artu*: An Interpretation', in P. B. Grout, R. A. Lodge, C. E. Pickford and E. K. C. Varty eds *The Legend of Arthur in the Middle Ages*, Cambridge, 138–48.

MacRae, D. 1982. 'Appearances and Reality in *La Mort le roi Artu*', *FMLS*, 18, 266–77.

Maddox, D. 1994. 'Coutumes et "conjointure" dans le *Lancelot* en prose', in *Conjunctures: Medieval Studies in Honor of Douglas Kelly*, Amsterdam and Atlanta, GA, 293–309.

Matarasso, P. 1979. *The Redemption of Chivalry: A Study of the Queste del Saint Graal*, Geneva.

Maurice, J. 1995. *La Mort le roi Artu*, Paris.

Mentré, M. 1986. 'Remarques sur l'iconographie des romans arthuriens: à propos de quelques exemples', *CCM*, 29, 231–42.

Micha, A. 1958. 'Les Manuscrits du *Merlin* en prose de Robert de Boron', *Rom*, 79, 78–94, 145–74.

Micha 1961. 'Études sur le *Lancelot* en prose: II. L'Esprit du *Lancelot-Graal*', *Rom*, 82, 357–78.

Micha 1964. 'La Tradition manuscrite du *Lancelot* en prose', *Rom*, 85, 293–318.

Micha 1973. 'Sur la composition du *Lancelot* en prose', in *Études de langue et de littérature du Moyen Âge offertes à Félix Lecoy par ses collègues, ses élèves et ses amis*, Paris, 417–25.

Micha 1980. *Étude sur le 'Merlin' de Robert de Boron: roman du XIIIᵉ siècle*, Geneva.

Micha 1987. *Essais sur le cycle Lancelot-Graal*, Geneva.

Pauphilet, A. 1921. *Études sur La Queste del Saint Graal attribuée à Gautier Map*, Geneva.

Pauphilet 1950. *Le Legs du Moyen Âge: études de la littérature médiévale*, Melun.

Perret, M. 1982. 'De l'espace romanesque à la matérialité du livre: l'espace énonciatif des premiers romans en prose', *Poétique*, 50, 173–82.

Pickens, R. T. 1994. 'Autobiography and History in the Vulgate *Estoire* and in the *Prose Merlin*', in Kibler ed. 1994*, 98–116.

Planche, A. 1997. 'Les Mots de la mort et du malheur dans *La Mort le roi Artu*', in *De l'Aventure épique à l'aventure romanesque: hommage à André de Mandach*, Bern, etc., 269–80.

Poirion, D. 1984. 'La Douloureuse Garde', in Dufournet ed. 1984, 25–48.

Ponceau, J.-P. 1998. 'L'Auteur de l'*Estoire del Saint Graal* et celui de *La Queste del Saint Graal* sont vraisemblablement distincts', in *Miscellanea Mediaevalia: mélanges offerts à Philippe Ménard*, 2 vols, Paris, II, 1043–56.

Pratt, K. 1991. 'Aristotle, Augustine or Boethius? *La Mort le roi Artu* as Tragedy', *NFS*, 30, 81–109.

Pratt 1995. 'The Cistercians and the *Queste del Saint Graal*', *RMS*, 21, 69–96.

Pratt 2004. *La Mort le roi Artu*, London.

Rychner, J. 1970. *L'Articulation des phrases narratives dans la Mort Artu (formes et structures de la prose médiévale)*, Geneva.

Santucci, M. 1992. 'Propos sur la structure de la *Mort Artu*', *Travaux de Littérature*, 5, 7–17.

Solterer, H. 1985. '"Conter le terme de cest brief": l'inscription dans *La Mort le roi Artu*', in Foulon ed. 1985*, II, 558–68.

Stirnemann, P. 1993. 'Some Champenois Vernacular Manuscripts and the Manerius Style of Illumination', in Busby, K., T. Nixon, A. Stones and L. Walters eds. 1993, *Les Manuscrits de Chrétien de Troyes/The Manuscripts of Chrétien de Troyes*, Amsterdam and Atlanta, GA, I, 195–226.

Stones, A. 1977. 'The Earliest Illustrated Prose *Lancelot* Manuscript', *RMS*, 3, 3–44.

Suard, F. 1997. 'Hasard et nécessité dans *La Mort le roi Artu*', in *De l'Aventure épique à l'aventure romanesque: hommage à André de Mandach*, Bern, etc., 281–94.

Szkilnik, M. 1991a. *L'Archipel du Graal: étude de L'Estoire del Saint Graal*, Geneva.

Szkilnik 1991b. 'L'*Estoire del saint Graal*: réécrire la *Queste*', in Van Hoecke, Tournoy and Verbeke eds 1991*, 294–305.

Szkilnik 1994. 'Loiauté et traïson dans la *Mort le roi Artu*', *Op. cit.*, 3, 25–32.

Terry, P. 1990. 'Certainties of the Heart: The Poisoned Fruit Episode as a Unifying Exemplum in *La Mort le roi Artu*', *Romance Languages Annual*, 1, 328–31.

Trachsler, R. 1994. 'Au-delà de la *Mort le roi Artu*: ce dont parle le conte quand le roi a disparu', *Op. cit.*, 3, 33–41.

Williams, A. M. L. 2001. *The Adventures of the Holy Grail: A Study of La Queste del Saint Graal*, Oxford.

Zuurdeeg, A. D. 1981. *Narrative Techniques and their Effects in La Mort le roi Artu*, York, SC.

VIII

THE PROSE *TRISTAN*

†Emmanuèle Baumgartner (translated by Sarah Singer)

The prose *Tristan* was composed between 1230 and 1235, possibly by the writer who, in the prologue, adopts the rather enigmatic pseudonym Luce del Gast. However, a second author, who goes by the pseudonym Hélie de Boron, also signed the work (Curtis 1983; Baumgartner 1985). In the epilogue of some manuscripts Hélie presents himself as the brother-in-arms and relative of Robert de Boron, who is mentioned elsewhere as the author of the verse *Joseph* (Baumgartner 1988; see chapter VI). It is, however, difficult to establish the respective contributions of Luce and Hélie to a text which has inappropriately been called by critics the *Tristan en prose*. Did Hélie continue a text originally begun by Luce, which could have been an early prose version of the verse Tristan material? More probably, did Hélie revise and amplify the whole of Luce's text? This theory is supported by references made by Hélie to Luce's 'book' throughout the text and the fact that, in those manuscripts with an epilogue containing his name, Hélie presents himself as the author of a 'livre entier' (*entire book*) in which he has assembled

> tout ce que lessa missire Luces de Gaut, qui premierement ancomença a translater, et mestre Gautier Map, qui fist le propre livre de Lancelot, et missire Robert de Borron.
>
> (*all that was left by my lord Luce de Gaut, who first began the translation, by Master Gautier Map, who wrote the book centred on Lancelot [the 'Lancelot proper'], and by my lord Robert de Boron*).[1]

What is certain, however, is that the *Tristan*, as it stands today, was composed after the *Lancelot–Grail* Cycle, that its author or authors knew at least the whole of the *Lancelot–Queste–Mort Artu* and that they were influenced in particular by the *Lancelot* proper (see chapter VII).

The prose *Tristan*, or rather the various versions of it which were produced from around 1230 to the end of the Middle Ages (the printed versions of the fifteenth and sixteenth centuries show how interest in this text continued well into the sixteenth century), was for a long time known only through the very meticulous *Analyse* (plot summary) provided by Löseth in 1890. After the pioneering monograph by Vinaver (1925) critical interest developed slowly. But, thanks to Curtis's three-volume edition of the beginning of the text (1963; 1976; 1985),[2] to Blanchard's 1976 edition of an important passage from manuscript BNF, fr. 772 and to the nine-volume TLF edition of the remainder of the text, supervised by

Ménard (1987–97), this romance has now secured its rightful place within literary studies. The prose *Tristan*, or, as it was more aptly referred to in the Middle Ages, 'le livre (ou le roman) du bon chevalier Tristan de Leonois' (*the book, or the romance, of the good knight Tristan of Leonois*) clearly follows in the footsteps of the twelfth-century verse narratives treating the ill-fated passion of the lovers of Cornwall. Yet under the influence of the prose *Lancelot*, it places increasing emphasis on the heroic career of Tristan the knight. It is also a constantly expanding textual space, in which authors from the thirteenth to the fifteenth centuries experimented with romance composition in a variety of new ways, for the most part successfully.

The main sources on which the prose *Tristan* drew indiscriminately were the twelfth-century verse romances, which provided the basic plot and the original cast of characters (Vinaver 1925, 5–20; Baumgartner 1975, 101–17). However, from the outset the prose author's explicitly new conception of his source material changes its original orientation. Whereas Beroul, Thomas and the *Folies* focus on the love relationship between Tristan and Yseut, and the physical and emotional obstacles they have to overcome to stay together, the prose author emphasizes his hero's prowess right from the beginning. He sets out to demonstrate that Tristan rivals Lancelot and Galahad as one of the best three knights in the Arthurian world. Indeed, his aim is to tell his readers:

> ce que li latins devise de l'estoire de Tristan, qui fu li plus soveriens chevaliers qui onques fust ou reaume de la Grant Bretaigne, et devant le roi Artus et aprés, fors solement li tres bons chevaliers Lancelot dou Lac. Et li latins meïsmes de l'estoire del Saint Graal devise apertement que au tens le roi Artus ne furent que troi bon chevalier qui tres bien feïssent a prisier de chevalerie: Galaaz, Lanceloz, Tristan. (Curtis edn, I, §39)

> (*what the Latin says about the story of Tristan, who, before and after the reign of King Arthur, was the most excellent knight who ever lived in the kingdom of Great Britain, apart from the very good knight Lancelot du Lac. And the Latin of the story of the Holy Grail itself says clearly that at the time of King Arthur there were only three good knights who well deserved to be esteemed for their chivalry: Galahad, Lancelot and Tristan.*)

Thus the narrator presents his project: to make Tristan the rival of the best knights in the world by including him in the heroic trinity which will henceforth dominate the Arthurian world, whilst at the same time raising the Tristan material to the same level as the Arthurian material. His aim will be to unite the world of love and chivalric adventures, represented by Lancelot and Tristan, with the mystical world of Galahad and the Grail. He has no intention of providing a continuation to the *Lancelot–Grail* Cycle, but rather to add to it, or more precisely to introduce Tristan's story into the fictional world already established around Arthur, Lancelot, the Knights of the Round Table, the Grail and its quest.

As in the verse narratives, Tristan's destiny is definitively linked to that of Yseut by the love potion, which will cause suffering and death, as the narrator explicitly declares:

Ha! Diex, quel boivre! Com il lor fu puis anious! Or ont beü; or sont entré en la riote qui jamés ne faudra tant com il aient l'ame el cors. Or sont entré en cele voie dont il lor covendra sofrir engoisse et travail tot lor aaige. Diex, quel duel! Il ont beü lor destrucion et lor mort. (Curtis edn, II, §445)

(*Oh! Lord, what a drink! What strife it later caused them! Now they have drunk, and they have embarked on tribulations which will not cease while their souls remain in their bodies. They have embarked upon the road of suffering and toil which will last as long as they live. Lord, what sorrow! They have drunk their destruction and their deaths*).

From Yseut's marriage to Mark until Tristan's departure for Brittany the prose version follows the verse originals fairly closely. In fact, for a long time the prose *Tristan* was read with the sole aim of identifying vestiges of the verse romances.[3] Yet the prose author clearly changes the tone and spirit of his sources and makes many additions. A technique he frequently employs is to repeat pre-existing episodes two or three times, as for example with the motif of the ambush prepared for Tristan by Mark and the evil Audret.[4] The difference between the verse and the prose versions is even greater, however, when Tristan, wounded by a poisoned arrow, leaves for Brittany, Mark having abducted the queen after the lovers' stay in the forest of Morrois. Tristan is healed by Yseut aux Blanches Mains (*Yseut of the White Hands*), whom he ends up marrying, although the marriage is never consummated. The narrative then goes on to describe the chivalric adventures of Tristan and his new companion, Kaherdin. The hero's first attempt to return to Cornwall is compromised by Kaherdin's illicit passion for Queen Yseut. Yet Kaherdin is rejected by her and dies of love, whilst Tristan, thinking he has been betrayed, sinks into madness. Yseut heals him after Mark has found him in the forest of Morrois, but the king exiles his nephew to the kingdom of Logres. Tristan's numerous adventures with his new companion, the very sceptical Dinadan, his constant rivalry with another creation of the prose romancer, the Saracen knight Palamedes (Queen Yseut's melancholic suitor), the tournaments in which he takes part with ever-increasing glory, all confirm his chivalric excellence. The high point is his reception at the Round Table, where he symbolically occupies the seat of the Morholt. Arthur succeeds in reconciling uncle and nephew, who both return to Cornwall. However, despite Tristan's success in saving Cornwall from Saxon invasion a second time, Mark twice imprisons his nephew. Tristan manages to escape – the details of his two imprisonments and liberation vary markedly from one version to another – and he finally flees with Yseut to Logres. The lovers enjoy a period of perfect bliss alone in the castle of Joyeuse Garde, which Lancelot has offered to them as a refuge. Following the great tournament of Louvezerp, at which Tristan wins the prize, Yseut convinces him to take part in the Quest for the Holy Grail. Mark, however, takes advantage of the Quest to carry off Yseut once more. Tristan returns to his mistress in Cornwall, but as he is playing a lay on his harp to Yseut in her chamber, Mark wounds him with a poisoned lance (originally given to the king by Morgan the Fay), and after an emotional farewell to the Arthurian world and knight-errantry, Tristan dies, suffocating Yseut in his arms (Harf-Lancner 1998).

In his rewriting of the verse *Tristan* poems there is a strong link between the prose romancer's increasing emphasis on Tristan's chivalry in the Arthurian world, and the changes made to the character of King Mark. Tristan's uncle, unlike Arthur, becomes the bad king of a Cornwall populated by cowardly knights, who are the laughing-stock of the knights of Logres. The episode featuring the wife of Séguradés (Curtis edn, I, §§353–80), who prefers Tristan to Mark, signals the beginning of the enmity between Tristan and his uncle, who is now jealous both of his nephew's glory and exploits (namely his victory over the Morholt) and of his success with women. The tension between the two men is, of course, exacerbated when Mark can no longer ignore, or put an end to, the love between Tristan and Yseut, or prevent the couple from escaping to the forest of Morrois. The king promptly ends this idyllic interlude by recapturing his wife. Thus, throughout the romance, Mark plays the part of the traitor; he relentlessly tries to harm his nephew, whom he fears as much as he hates, and he repeatedly tries to kill him, imprison him and banish him from Cornwall. He even pursues him deep into the kingdom of Logres. Whereas in the verse romances Tristan is torn between his passion for the queen and his loyalty to his uncle and king, in the prose text he can possess Yseut without the slightest remorse. Hence his numerous attempts to steal her away from Mark, culminating in their escape from the sinister kingdom of Cornwall so that they can live together in Logres. Mark's killing of Tristan, in an ending markedly different from that found in the verse sources, not only puts an end to the adulterous relationship between the lovers, but also destroys the paragon of Arthurian chivalry which Tristan has finally become; his death is long mourned by Arthur and his knights.

The modern reader's preference for the twelfth-century French verse *Tristan* poems (including the German adaptations by Eilhart von Oberg and especially Gottfried von Straßburg) over the French prose *Tristan* is not surprising. Indeed, it took some time for critics and the occasional modern reader to recognize, let alone appreciate, the aesthetic choices made by the thirteenth-century authors of the first prose romances. Thanks to Vinaver's seminal study, *A la recherche d'une poétique médiévale* (1970), critical interest was at last kindled in the carefully thought-out innovations made by the prose romancers, and only then did we begin to appreciate a new type of fictional writing, which drew essentially on the resources of literary prose. Yet, from the thirteenth century onwards, the prose *Tristan* outshone in popularity its verse rivals, and it is on this prose romance that the Italian, Spanish, Portuguese, English versions and other narratives on the lovers of Cornwall are based (Delcorno Branca 1968; 1998; Heijkant 1989; Roubaud-Bénichou 2000). The sheer number of (sometimes very beautifully) illuminated manuscripts of the romance – the iconography of the *Tristan* deserves to be studied more systematically – also testifies to the interest which this work aroused, especially in the aristocratic circles of the later Middle Ages. Payen (1973) suggests that this lasting success is no doubt due to the very clear chivalric orientation which the hero's career takes in the prose romance. The amplification of heroic adventures diverts our attention away from the subversive character of the lovers' fatal passion, induced by the love potion and subject to the desires of the flesh, a passion which already in the verse narratives was in conflict with courtly representations of love. The number of romances written in the wake of the *Tristan*, such as *Guiron le Courtois*, the *Prophecies de Merlin*, the compilation of Rusticien de Pise and later *Ysaÿe le Triste*, suggests that this success is linked to the prose romancer's predilection for the narration of adventures. The reader is swept along by a succession of interlacing episodes, repeated motifs, echoes and correspondences, reminiscent of the self-generating narrative of the serialized novel. These lengthy and complex Arthurian prose romances, with which their readers satisfied their need for sentimental and heroic escapism, were probably the 'consumer literature' of the Middle Ages.

Until recently, scholars have tended to divide the various versions of the *Tristan* found in the numerous extant manuscripts (about eighty-two manuscripts or fragments have been listed, but further fragments are still being discovered) into two main families.[5] Vinaver (1959, 339) distinguished between the relatively short 'First Version', composed between 1225 and 1235, and an expanded 'Second Version', which he dated to the second half of the thirteenth century. It is this long or 'vulgate' version which is given in most of the extant manuscripts (notably Vienna, Österreichische Nationalbibliothek MS 2542, which serves as the base manuscript (*A*) for Ménard's TLF edition), whilst BNF, fr. 757 is the best representative of the short version (CFMA edition). The 'first' version (henceforth V.I) is indeed a short version with specific characteristics, the most striking being the absence of the text of the *Queste del Saint Graal*, which is included in the 'vulgate' and of which only a rewritten version of the initial scene of the Pentecost of the Grail has been preserved (Van Coolput 1986, 120–51). However, as studies on the manuscript tradition have shown, nothing suggests that V.I is an older, earlier version of the *Tristan*.[6] It is now seen as a different, abbreviated version of the long version (henceforth V.II).[7] In the latter, there are inconsistencies (in the form of substantive variants and interpolations) not only between families of manuscripts, but even within the families (see the introductions to the TLF volumes). Moreover, V.II soon found itself in competition with versions which exploited still further the techniques of compilation, the transference of motifs and characters from one text to another, or the invention of narrative elements based on tried and tested models (Baumgartner 1975, 63–87). It may be in reaction to this practice that the sixteenth-century printed versions of the romance are based on BNF, fr. 103, a late manuscript offering a much abbreviated form of the *Tristan* and also containing passages taken from the verse *Tristan* poems (including a version of the death of the lovers very close to that of Eilhart).

Vienna, MS 2542 itself (*A*), to which critics generally refer for the 'vulgate' version (V.II), provides a good example of the art of variation practised by the copyists of the *Tristan*, as well as demonstrating the impossibility of classifying these different versions precisely. The scribe of this manuscript does not provide Hélie's epilogue and considerably shortens the prologue and the beginning of the narrative (Löseth 1890, §§1–41, Curtis edn I, §§1–468). He also systematically suppresses details found in other manuscripts of the same family, such as BNF, fr. 335–6. Last, but not least, from Ménard's sixth volume onwards the scribe includes extensive passages from the *Lancelot*, passages found in manuscripts of the later versions V.III and V.IV. Whatever its other merits, manuscript *A* appears to be a free adaptation of V.II; in it the reader can enjoy, apart from the long version of the *Tristan*, some exciting narrative taken from the 'Agravain' section of the *Lancelot* (see chapter VII, n. 1), as well as a sequel to the story of Bohort's illegitimate son, Helian le Blanc, a story which the prose *Lancelot* leaves incomplete (Baumgartner 1993).

As a general rule, the *Tristan* strives to offer a complete, encyclopaedic version of the Arthurian legend, thus reflecting its conception (particularly obvious in the later manuscripts) of a Round Table which gradually accommodates all the knights of Arthurian literature, including those from the Tristan tradition. The *Lancelot–Grail* had already begun the process of cyclification, but in that Cycle the component narratives retain their autonomy and specificity while being assembled into a more or less coherent whole. In contrast, those manuscripts containing the complete *Tristan* offer a more homogeneous text, in which the two worlds created around Tristan and the *Lancelot–Grail* sometimes coexist and sometimes overlap.

The *Tristan* occupies a peculiar position in relation to the time-scale established by the *Lancelot–Grail*. The former begins with the story of Sadoc, the eleventh and recalcitrant son of Bron, who is himself the brother-in-law of Joseph of Arimathea (Baumgartner 1990a, 15–18). In this way Tristan is linked, along with Lancelot and Galahad, to the founding narrative of the discovery of the Grail by Joseph of Arimathea. Similarly, whereas the *Mort Artu* imposes clear closure on the *Lancelot–Grail* Cycle, the fictional chronology of the *Tristan* is almost indefinitely prolonged by the addition of various endings provided by the different manuscripts. BNF, fr. 757 ends with the death of the lovers, the mourning of Arthur's court and Hélie's epilogue, whereas the 'vulgate' concludes with the return of Bohort to court, after the completion of the 'aventures du Saint Graal' (TLF edn, IX, §143), and just before the beginning of the 'Mort Artu'. BNF, fr. 24400, a very late manuscript, recounts Dinadan's failed attempt to take revenge on Mark, and thus expands the limits of the *Tristan* material beyond those of the *Lancelot–Grail* (Trachsler 1996*, 195–236). As for the pre-Arthurian period, this narrative space, filled almost to overflowing in the *Lancelot–Grail* by the *Estoire del Saint Graal* and the *Merlin*, is filled in the *Tristan* by the tragic and somewhat scandalous story of Mark's and Tristan's ancestors, which in many ways foreshadows that of the protagonists (Van Coolput 1986, 18–38). Finally, when the *Queste* is interlaced in the 'vulgate' versions of the *Tristan* with fragments of a different quest-narrative, more chivalric than mystical,[8] it no longer functions as a spiritual conclusion to the romance. Rather, this is another way of expanding from the inside a narrative limited by the boundaries of the Tristan story, and is as such an essential element in the technique of compilation fundamental to the prose *Tristan*.

The term 'compilation' still has negative connotations for modern critics. Yet the concept, expressed by the terms *acomplir* and *compiler* (Baumgartner 1990c and 1994b), is used by the authors of the *Tristan* themselves to define as accurately as possible, through the image of the crown found in Hélie's epilogue, the aesthetic of completeness which guided those who wrote and redrafted the various prose versions. To compile is to attempt to complete the 'entire' work, and the aim was to reunite within one text, and therefore in one manuscript, what was later (until the time of Paulin Paris) correctly given the title 'Les Romans de la Table Ronde' (*The Romances of the Round Table*). In the *Lancelot–Grail* Cycle, to complete the Grail Quest means to exhaust a fixed supply of adventures and their associated narratives. In the 'vulgate' *Tristan*, however, the Quest becomes a powerful story-producing machine. It tears Tristan away from the pleasures of Joyeuse Garde, from the stasis produced by consummated love, to launch him on a series of new adventures and to bring him face-to-face with the new hero, Galahad. This confrontation had in fact been announced, as we have seen, in Luce's prologue.

The addition of episodes not found in the *Queste del Saint Graal*, but present in the Post-Vulgate *Queste*,[9] generates yet further narratives. It is understandable that such an unusual addition to the original Tristan material would quickly necessitate narrative interventions and announcements of future events in order to justify and prepare the reader for the inclusion of the Quest. This might explain the skilful interpolation of episodes from the *Lancelot* early in the manuscript tradition of the prose *Tristan*, as exemplified by Vienna, MS 2542 (TLF edn, VI, 12–23). However, the effect created by modifying the text of the Vulgate *Queste* in order to interlace it with the *Tristan*, and then combining this material carefully with episodes from the Post-Vulgate *Queste*, was not simply to amplify and expand the narrative. This process also subtly changed the meaning of the 'aventures du Saint Graal', removing the spiritual dimension from the Quest, which Tristan soon admits he had embarked upon mistakenly. So this example of compilation has two consequences: it incorporates texts which are alien to the Tristan material and offers the reader an approach which contradicts that of the *Queste*, contrasting in pointed fashion the mystical and somewhat degraded world of the Grail Quest with the deliberately worldly ethos of the *Tristan* (Van Coolput 1986, 116–87). It is thus an effective way of introducing disparities and dissonance into the narrative, effects also produced by the inclusion of micro-narratives, by the appearance of characters such as Palamedes, Kaherdin and above all Dinadan (all of whom challenge Arthur's world), and by the frequent presence within the prose text of lyrical passages in which characters directly express the pains and pleasures of love.

The manuscripts of V.IV (*c*.1400?) exploit the technique of compilation even more extensively, by including or inventing the story of Alixandre l'Orphelin, a young hero who appears as Tristan's double; a complete version of this narrative can be read in the enormous, late manuscript BNF, fr. 112 (Pickford 1959/60*, 124–25). It features at length the tournament at Sorelois (in which Tristan does not even take part), provides a different version of the hero's two imprisonments and even includes a fragment of the compilation of Rusticien de Pise. It should also be noted that BNF, fr. 758 (fourteenth century) provides the whole of the 'Mort Artu', whilst BNF, fr. 24400 (sixteenth century), the latest in date of the *Tristan* manuscripts, prolongs the narrative right up to the deaths of all the *Tristan* and *Lancelot* characters, the sole survivor being, ironically, King Mark.

The use made by the prose *Tristan* of texts and fragments of the *Lancelot–Grail* Cycle fits with a more general tendency in this romance to exploit all available forms of literary discourse. Hence the inclusion of brief narratives freely inspired by Arthurian verse romances and equally freely incorporated into the main story-line. Lamorat, an invention of the *Tristan*, becomes the hero of the enchanted horn motif (originally linked to Caradoc); the episode of Dinas the seneschal and his faithful dogs, descendants of the no less faithful Husdent, combines the Tristan tradition with the misfortunes of Gauvain in the *Chevalier à l'épée* or the *Vengeance Raguidel* (Baumgartner 1980; 1990b). The mini-romance of 'Brunor le Vallet à la cote maltaillée' (*Brunor with the ill-fitting tunic*) was inspired by the *Bel Inconnu* or even by *Jaufre* (Curtis 1988). These rather comical and often misogynous insertions, which are further developed in the later prose versions, mostly provide an ironic counterpoint to the courtly ethic and chivalric behaviour normally observed by the protagonists. However, the heroes are sometimes rehabilitated later in the narrative: Lamorat becomes the lover of the Queen of Orcanie (the mother of Gauvain and his brothers) and the hero of a sad story of love, revenge and death, which echoes the destiny of Tristan and even of Palamedes. As for Brunor, he reappears later (TLF edn, VII) in the guise of the brilliant knight with the scarlet shield, a poet, brother to Dinadan and admirer of Yseut. The inclusion of tournament scenes is also part of this practice of including short narratives.[10] Since Chrétien's *Charrette*, the tournament in which the knight/lover takes part has become a canonical, compulsory motif. Yet the frequency and length of the *Tristan* tournaments, the technical precision of the descriptions and the continued amplification of these model sequences from the 'vulgate' to V.IV (which includes the very long episode of the Sorelois tournament), tend to turn these tournaments into semi-autonomous episodes, which are reminiscent of texts such as the *Tournoi de Chauvency* or episodes from the *Roman du Chastelain de Couci et de la Dame de Fayel*. It would no doubt be useful to examine more closely these micro-narratives, which, by decentring the action, focusing on secondary characters and rewriting existing motifs, progressively destabilize the main narrative thrust inherited from earlier models.

The fact that the story of Tristan and Yseut has been transferred from the world of love to the world of chivalry, and that the lovers are separated for longer periods, reduces the number of exchanges between them. These forced and often prolonged separations give rise to another feature of the prose *Tristan*: the insertion of lyrical passages in verse or poetic prose, monologues, laments, letters in verse or prose, lays in which forbidden love is debated (on the model of the *jeu parti*), sung about and lamented, thus instigating a new discourse of love. Now that we have a complete edition of the romance, we are in a position to analyse the thematic diversity of these lyric insertions. Although love remains the main subject, the insertions highlight the relationship between the purely lyrical outbursts expressing the joys and torments of love and their narrative contexts. Examples of this are: the 'lai mortel' which Tristan composes under the influence of jealousy, just before entering a long period of madness (Curtis edn, III, §§867–71); Yseut's 'lai mortel', which she composes and sings before attempting to commit suicide and which summarizes in a few stanzas the heroic and amorous story of the lovers so far (ibid., §§930–4); and even the 'lai' composed by Tristan after the Louvezerp tournament (TLF edn, VII, §168) in celebration of the fact that he has at last won love and glory.

The master of the love song is, of course, Tristan himself. He was already a poet and musician in the twelfth-century verse narratives, enchanting Mark, his court and the young Yseut by playing his harp and singing, or composing the lay of *Chevrefoil*. Revolving around Tristan, the composer of lyrics, the world of the prose romance becomes imbued with a poetic and musical atmosphere, in which physical jousts sometimes lead to verbal jousts. Yseut becomes a *trobairitz* (female troubadour), as she had already been in Thomas. More innovatively, the prose *Tristan* creates a series of male lovers, enamoured of the queen (Kaherdin, Palamedes, Hélys, Brunor) or of some other great lady (Méléagant and Lamorat), all of whom celebrate or lament in long monologues or lays the sufferings induced by love. This introduces into the narrative a profusion of first-person performers, whose 'real' presence within the story lends an air of authenticity to the general expression of emotion. Links between the main narrative and singing are created by the use of very ornate, rhythmical prose, enriched by comparisons and rhetorical effects; prose monologues by amorous knights often precede an explosion of lyrical expression. This ornate prose is also found in most of the letters, and in the exchanges and debates which constitute throughout the text a semi-theoretical discussion on passion and its effects (Baumgartner 1990a; Ménard 1999). Whether it takes the form of verse or prose, the language of love in the *Tristan* introduces a new rhythm and a different tone into the 'normal' prose, providing the narrative with a multifaceted poetic discourse.

By turning Tristan into a character who can write, speak and sing about his destiny, Luce, who presents himself as an English knight who is 'amoreus, gais et envoisiez' (*amorous, happy and joyful*), and Hélie, who in the epilogue expresses his return to writing as a form of regeneration, invent a hero who combines two characteristics in an original way: the knight-lover is now capable of recreating, through his poetry, his own experience of love, an experience whose authenticity is guaranteed by the narrative itself. Unlike the emperor Conrad in Jean Renart's *Guillaume de Dole*, or the hero of the *Chastelaine de Vergy,* Tristan and his doubles do not sing the songs of other *trouvères*. They perform the lay, the lament or the farewell poem which they themselves have just composed whilst riding or sitting by the numerous fountains at which they seek refreshment. Moreover, prose monologues mark the birth of lyrical expression in the heart of the lovers and testify to its necessity. This device is reminiscent of the play between *cansos, vidas* and *razos* in the songbooks of certain troubadours. We know that this innovation on the part of the *Tristan* was particularly well received; from then on there are not many romances, Arthurian or otherwise, that do not practise the art of lyric insertion as another way of expressing, within the narrative, the joys and torments of love.

The introductions to the different volumes of the Ménard edition provide a useful complement to the numerous articles devoted fairly recently to the prose *Tristan*. The former feature detailed analyses of the motifs and characters that make up the 'système arthurien du monde' (*Arthurian world system*), which, as the romance progresses, both evolves and is challenged, notably by the likes of Kaherdin, and later, Dinadan, or by the anti-chivalric behaviour of Brehus sans Pitié or even Gauvain (Trachsler 1994). Here, I shall concentrate on the *Tristan*'s principal features. A common, but somewhat restrictive, practice in Arthurian texts is the reuse of characters and of the same temporal and spatial background as a context for the narrative, a technique introduced by Chrétien de Troyes in *Erec*. Again, the *Tristan* employs this device in a very complex manner. There is a doubling of textual locations: Mark's Cornwall is the chivalric and courtly antithesis of Arthur's Logres. In addition to characters who have already been modified and reorientated from the verse *Tristan*s, the prose romance integrates into the world of Tristan specifically Arthurian characters, who, for the most part, are imported from the *Lancelot–Grail*. The role of a careful reader thus consists in seeing how these characters, whether primary or secondary in the original text, function in the target text, noting for instance the changing image of the royal couple Arthur/Guinevere, of Lancelot and his kin, and of Galahad, who loses much of his mystical aura. In more general terms, it is interesting to note how the Arthurian world is perceived by 'aliens' such as Tristan, Yseut, Mark and Kaherdin, or by the newcomers Dinadan and Palamedes, whose response is a mixture of admiration, criticism and hostility, but above all fascination. Some of them, especially Tristan, accept the rules unthinkingly. Others, led by Dinadan, discuss, ridicule and reject the ways and customs which regulate the kingdom of Logres, enshrined in the narrative motifs invented by Chrétien and which have already become romance commonplaces by the time of the prose *Lancelot*. In this constant questioning it is difficult not to see the authors of the *Tristan* adopting a critical attitude to their inherited material, thereby establishing complicity with their readers (Milland-Bove 1999).

Following in the footsteps of the *Lancelot*, the *Tristan* also makes systematic use of the repetition, with variation, of the same motif or similar narrative sequences, a very useful technique for prolonging the narrative or effortlessly multiplying the adventures. There is thus a profusion of (more or less amusing) cases of mistaken identity, of perilous fords, bridges and crossroads to be negotiated; numerous evil customs need to be eradicated, while hospitality is accepted at one's own risk and peril; damsels 'under escort' are passed from one knight to another; there are friendly or tense encounters, and conversations in the depths of the forest or next to springs. The true originality of the *Tristan*, however, lies in the doubles the authors have created around Tristan, knights who are direct rivals in both love and chivalric prowess, such as Kaherdin and especially Palamedes, or who are made more or less in Tristan's image, like Lamorat, the lover of the queen of Orcanie, or even Alixandre l'Orphelin. This technique is not only useful for prolonging the narrative; it also has an ethical purpose.

The last rule of love expounded by Andreas Capellanus in his *De amore* states that nothing prevents a woman from being loved by two men or a man from being loved by two women.[11] Unlike the *Lancelot*, in which no knight is sufficiently worthy to act as a rival to Lancelot in respect of his love for Guinevere, the *Tristan* explores the possibility of worthy rivals by multiplying Yseut's knightly admirers. Palamedes, the Saracen knight whose prowess equals Tristan's and who is often more generous than his rival both in chivalry and love, spontaneously (no love potion is needed in his case) falls in love with the young Yseut in Ireland (before Tristan takes any notice of the girl) and his passion will plague him until almost the end of the romance (TLF edn, IX, §§118 and 130–3). Kaherdin, who is madly in love with Yseut, dies singing about his sweet death once he realizes that

Yseut will never love him (Rabeyroux and Roland 1990; Toury 1990). At least he achieves poetic creation, as does the young Hélys, who recites to Tristan the virtues of love, however impossible (TLF edn, VI, §§133–40). The prose authors certainly invented these Tristan doubles, the knights in love with Yseut, in order to multiply the narrative opportunities for adventure and conflict between Tristan and his rivals. Tristan's prolonged madness is induced by the jealousy he feels when he believes that Yseut prefers Kaherdin to him. Many adventures come from the continuous rivalry between Tristan and Palamedes, whether in love or in arms. Yet this is also a way of reflecting on the idealized interdependence of love and prowess, which is the foundation of the Arthurian world and its courtly ethos, and a way too of emphasizing its fragility and limitations. The *Tristan* preserves the exemplary relationship between Tristan and Yseut, a union forged by love for the goodness of the knight and the beauty of the lady. Around the couple, however, the bonds between love and prowess gradually dissolve. What happens when a knight in love loses all hope, when Yseut does not fulfil the hopes of Palamedes, who is as good a knight as Tristan? It would be difficult for Palamedes to admit that one's right to be loved does not depend on prowess. Kaherdin, a lesser knight, has no alternative but to allow himself to die. Others, like Brunor or Hélys, resign themselves to never being loved, whatever their merits. Love in the *Tristan* is no longer the reward for prowess, and in the end only the outspoken Dinadan expresses this clearly, continuously denouncing the perverse effects of passion and the absurdity of chivalric customs.

What becomes of the knight-errant's *raison d'être* if, as Kaherdin and then Dinadan point out at every possible opportunity, a knight's function in this world is to fight in battles which are as deadly as they are pointless and to respect ridiculous and outdated customs in order to demonstrate his prowess? Under the influence of the love potion, Tristan never questions his love for Yseut and has no doubts about the mission of a knight-errant, except during the Grail Quest, the true meaning of which escapes him. He is born in sadness, yet he is destined to bring joy to the world; he is the knight who must risk all in adventure in order to bring peace, freedom and justice wherever he goes. Yet he is surrounded by knights, all speaking with one voice (except for Lancelot, who still respectfully attempts to protect a courtly world under threat), all questioning the meaning of their lives and expressing or demonstrating the dire consequences of love. Likewise, they all denounce chivalric practices, which are now either meaningless and can be transgressed with impunity, or they can be turned to individual advantage by knights such as Brehus, a veritable highwayman, or, more dramatically, by Gauvain and his brothers, who have now become hardened murderers.

In Luce's prologue, the *Tristan* is presented as a 'translation' of 'le grant livre del latin ... qui devise apertement l'estoire del Saint Graal' (*the big book in Latin, which clearly recounts the story of the Holy Grail*), a book which the prose author has read and reread before setting to work to 'translater une partie de ceste estoire' (*translate a part of this story*; Curtis edn, I, 39). Hélie's epilogue also depicts a tired 'translateur', who is about to have another look at the 'livre de latin' (*Latin book*) in order fully to exploit its material and finish the 'livre entier' (*entire book*) which his lord King Henry has commissioned from him (Baumgartner 2001). The representation of the process of translating a source book, a narrative already fixed in writing, had by that time become a fairly common motif, found, for instance, in the prose *Merlin* and the epilogue of the *Queste del Saint Graal.* There are, however, few Arthurian prose romances which, whilst preserving the fiction of a written source on whose authority the production of a new book rests, allow the narrator to express himself so clearly, to exercise his authority and control, and to underline the fictional nature of his narrative. Hélie is selective in his use of his source material, carefully warning his reader of what is to come. He rejects all that seems superfluous to him or that belongs to a different story. He thus emphasizes how much the content and the organization of his work, as well as his omissions, depend ultimately on his own will and on the way in which he conceives of his work. When he was writing *Madame Bovary*, Flaubert wrote:

> La prose est née d'hier, voilà ce qu'il faut se dire. Le vers est la forme par excellence des littéra-tures anciennes. Toutes les combinaisons prosodiques ont été faites, mais celles de la prose, tant s'en faut.

> (*Prose was born only yesterday, this is what one needs to bear in mind. Poetry is the form* par excellence *of ancient literature. All possible metrical combinations have been tried, but those in prose are far from exhausted.*)[12]

Is not the main contribution of the prose *Tristan* to have shown, as early as the thirteenth century, that the writer of newly born prose is conscious of the limits he can and must impose on material which has been inherited, brought together, remodelled or even invented according to the needs of the narrative? In the thirteenth century, prose, or at least prose romances, do not question the truth of the text. Instead, from the prose *Merlin* to the *Tristan*, prose becomes, through its novel use of chronology, the complexity of its syntax and its emphasis on careful narrative structure, the expression of an autonomous, self-referential textual world, in which the author is all-powerful. The prose *Tristan* marks an important stage, perhaps even the culmination, of a process begun by Chrétien de Troyes, whereby a new fictional space, the imaginary space of Arthurian romance, is created in the likeness of the real world. The insistent presence of the narrator, the play of repetition, intertextual allusions, the casual way in which the compiler assembles disparate narratives plundered from a variety of sources and expands or contracts the narrative space as he sees fit, these are all characteristics which point to what one might call the arbitrary nature of the text. The other vital innovation made by the author or authors of the *Tristan* is to show how adaptable and flexible prose writing can be, how it can accommodate all types and modes of narrative and even rival the lyric genre in celebrating and deploring love. When Hélie states in his epilogue that he must get back to work to 'crown' his book, he is not admitting that he has failed. He is calling for a renewal in the writing of fiction, and his call was immediately heard. With its dark forests of chivalric adventure, its clear springs and agreeable conversations on love, the prose *Tristan* genuinely opened up new avenues and created new spaces in the world of romance, a fictional world epitomized, since its founding father Wace, by the image of the Round Table.

Notes

[1] The epilogue appears in BNF, fr. 104, 760, 1628; Modena, Biblioteca Estense, MS E. 59 and Oxford, Bodleian Library, MS Douce 189. The spelling is that of BNF, fr. 1628.

[2] Curtis's edition, the first two volumes of which were reprinted in 1985, corresponds to Löseth 1890, §§1–92.

[3] See Bédier edn, II, 190–3 and 321–95 for the relevant passages based on BNF, fr. 103.

[4] See Curtis, II, §§513–15, 532–3, 534–7: these are three ambush scenes which end with the lovers escaping into the Morrois (§§ 544–53).

[5] Among the recent inventories and studies on the manuscripts and their classification, see Pickford 1959/60*; Vielliard 1973, 84–92 on Bodmer 164; Willard 1985; Field 1989; Chênerie 1998, as well as the introductions to the various volumes of the Curtis and TLF editions.

[6] See vol. 1 of the Blanchard and Quereuil edition of BNF, fr. 757. For a different opinion, see Bogdanow, chapter IX.

[7] On the use of this version in Italy and the reasons for its use, see Heijkant 1989.

[8] On this different quest narrative, see Bogdanow, chapter IX.

[9] On the two quests inserted into the *Tristan*, see Bogdanow 1990 and 2000; Harf-Lancner's introduction to volume IX of the TLF edn, 25–38.

[10] On the importance of tournaments in the *Tristan*, see the introductions and bibliography to vols II and V of the TLF edition, as well as L. Leonardi, 'Il torneo della Roche Dure nel *Tristan* in prosa', *CN*, 57 (1997), 209–51.

[11] See *Andreas Capellanus on Love*, ed. by P. G. Walsh (London, 1982), 285, rule 31.

[12] Letter to Louise Colet, *Correspondance*, ed. by J. Bruneau (Paris, 1980), II, 79.

Reference List

For items accompanied by an asterisk, see the General Bibliography.

Texts and Translations

Le Roman de Tristan en prose. Ed. by R. L. Curtis, 3 vols (Cambridge, 1985).

Le Roman de Tristan en prose: les deux captivités de Tristan. Ed. by J. Blanchard (Paris, 1976).

Le Roman de Tristan en prose, publié sous la direction de P. Ménard, 9 vols, TLF 353, 387, 398, 408, 416, 437, 450, 462, 474 (Geneva): I, ed. by P. Ménard (1987); II, ed. by M.-L. Chênerie and T. Delcourt (1990); III, ed. by G. Roussineau (1991); IV, ed. by J.-C. Faucon (1991); V, ed. by

D. Lalande and T. Delcourt (1992); VI, ed. by E. Baumgartner and M. Szkilnik (1993); VII, ed. by D. Quéruel and M. Santucci (1994); VIII, ed. by B. Guidot and J. Subrenat (1995); IX, ed. by L. Harf-Lancner (1997).

Le Roman de Tristan en prose (version du ms fr. 757 de la Bibliothèque Nationale de Paris), 4 vols, CFMA (Paris): I, ed. by J. Blanchard and M. Quereuil (1997); II, ed. by N. Laborderie and T. Delcourt (1999); III, ed. by J.-P. Ponceau (2000); IV, ed. by M. Léonard and F. Mora (2003).

Le Roman de Tristan: poème du XIIe siècle, par Thomas. Ed. by J. Bédier, 2 vols (Paris, 1902–5).

Studies

Baumgartner, E. 1975. *Le Tristan en prose: essai d'interprétation d'un roman médiéval*, Geneva.

Baumgartner 1980. 'Récits brefs et romans en prose: l'exemple du *Tristan*', in D. Buschinger ed. *Le Récit bref au Moyen Âge: actes du colloque des 27, 28 et 29 avril 1979, Université de Picardie, Centre d'Études Médiévales*, Paris, 27–38.

Baumgartner 1985. 'Luce del Gat et Hélie de Boron: le chevalier et l'écriture', *Rom*, 106, 326–40.

Baumgartner 1987. 'Les Techniques narratives dans le roman en prose', in Lacy, Kelly and Busby eds 1987–8*, I, 167–90.

Baumgartner 1988. 'Masques de l'écrivain et masques de l'écriture dans les proses du Graal', in M.-L. Ollier ed. *Masques et déguisements dans la littérature médiévale*, Montreal and Paris, 167–75.

Baumgartner 1990a. *La Harpe et l'épée: tradition et renouvellement dans le Tristan en prose*, Paris.

Baumgartner 1990b. 'Des femmes et des chiens', in T. Bouché and H. Charpentier eds *Le Rire au Moyen Âge dans la littérature et dans les arts*, Bordeaux, 43–51.

Baumgartner 1990c. 'Compiler/accomplir', in Dufournet ed. 1990, 33–49.

Baumgartner 1993. 'Histoire d'Helain le Blanc: du *Lancelot* au *Tristan* en prose', in *'Et c'est la fin pour quoy sommes ensemble': hommage à Jean Dufournet, professeur à la Sorbonne Nouvelle: littérature, histoire et langue du Moyen Âge*, 3 vols, Paris, I, 139–48.

Baumgartner 1994a. 'La Préparation à la *Queste del Saint Graal* dans le *Tristan* en prose', in *Conjunctures: Medieval Studies in Honor of Douglas Kelly*, Amsterdam and Atlanta, GA, 1–14.

Baumgartner 1994b. 'Le Roman de *Tristan* en prose et le cercle des bretthes estoires', in Besamusca, Gerritsen, Hogetoon and Lie eds 1994*, 7–20.

Baumgartner 2001. 'Sur quelques constantes et variations de l'image de l'écrivain (XIIe–XIIIe siècle)', in M. Zimmerman ed. *Auctor et auctoritas: invention et conformisme dans l'écriture médiévale*, Paris, 391–400.

Bogdanow, F. 1966. *The Romance of the Grail: A Study of the Structure and Genesis of a Thirteenth-Century Arthurian Prose Romance*, Manchester.

Bogdanow 1990. 'L'Invention du texte, intertextualité et le problème de la transmission et de la classification de manuscrits: le cas des versions de la *Queste del Saint Graal Post-Vulgate* et du *Tristan en prose*', *Rom*, 111, 121–40.

Bogdanow 2000. 'Un nouvel examen des rapports entre la *Queste Post-Vulgate* et la *Queste* incorporée dans la deuxième version du *Tristan en prose*', *Rom*, 118, 1–32.

Chênerie, M.-L. 1998. 'Étude et édition des fragments du *Tristan* en prose', *BBIAS*, 50, 231–64.

Curtis, R. L. 1969. *Tristan Studies*, Munich.

Curtis 1983. 'Who Wrote the Prose *Tristan*? A New Look at an Old Problem', *Neophil*, 67, 35–41.

Curtis 1988. 'A Romance within a Romance: The Place of the *Roman du Vallet a la Cote maltailliee* in the *Prose Tristan*', in *Studies in Medieval French Language and Literature presented to Brian Woledge in Honour of his 80th Birthday*, Geneva, 17–35.

Delcorno Branca, D. 1968. *I romanzi italiani di Tristano e la Tavola ritonda*, Florence.

Delcorno Branca 1998. *Tristano e Lancillotto in Italia. Studi di letteratura arturiana*, Ravenna.

Delcourt, T. 1988. 'Un fragment inédit du cycle de la *Post-Vulgate*', *Rom*, 109, 247–79.

Dubost, F. 1991. 'Trois géants, trois époques, un "roman": le géant poseur d'énigmes, le Géant de Cornouailles et Taulas de la Montagne dans le *Tristan en prose*', *PRIS-MA*, 7, 57–72.

Dufournet, J. ed. 1990. *Nouvelles recherches sur le Tristan en prose*, Geneva.

Field, P. J. C. 1989. 'The French Prose *Tristan*: A Note on Some Manuscripts, a List of Printed Texts, and Two Correlations with Malory's *Morte Darthur*', *BBIAS*, 41, 269–87.

Harf-Lancner, L. 1996. 'Gauvain l'assassin: la récurrence d'un schéma narratif dans le *Tristan en prose*', in *Tristan–Tristrant: mélanges en l'honneur de Danielle Buschinger à l'occasion de son 60ᵉ anniversaire*, Greifswald, 219–30.

Harf-Lancner 1998. 'Une seule chair, un seul cœur, une seule âme: la mort des amants dans le *Tristan en prose*', in *Miscellanea Mediaevalia: mélanges offerts à Philippe Ménard*, 2 vols, Paris, I, 613–28.

Heijkant, M.-J. 1989. *La tradizione del Tristan in prosa in Italia e proposte di studio sul Tristano Riccardiano*, Nijmegen.

Huot, S. 2003. *Madness in Medieval French Literature*, Oxford.

Le Vot, G. 1988. 'Les Lais lyriques du *Tristan en prose* et leur musique', in A. Gier et al. eds. *Narrativa Breve, Medieval Romanica*, Granada, 89–110.

Löseth, E. 1890. *Le Roman en prose de Tristan, le roman de Palamède et la compilation de Rusticien de Pise: analyse critique d'après les manuscrits de Paris*, Paris; repr. Geneva, 1974.

Ménard 1993. 'Chapitres et entrelacement dans le *Tristan en prose*', in *'Et c'est la fin pour quoy sommes ensemble': hommage à Jean Dufournet, professeur à la Sorbonne Nouvelle: littérature, histoire et langue du Moyen Âge*, 3 vols, Paris and Geneva, II, 955–62; repr. as 'L'Entrelacement dans le *Tristan en prose*' in Ménard 1999, 163–9.

Ménard 1994. 'Les Pièces lyriques du *Tristan en prose*', in C. Lachet ed. *Les Genres insérés dans le roman: actes du colloque international du 10 au 12 décembre 1992*, Lyon, 35–46; repr. in Ménard 1999, 141–61.

Ménard 1999. *De Chrétien de Troyes au Tristan en prose: études sur les romans de la Table Ronde*, Geneva.

Milland-Bove, B. 1999. '"La dameisele (…) qui sa seror desheritoit": enjeux d'une récriture dans le *Tristan* en prose', *Rom*, 117, 78–97.

Payen, J.-Ch. 1973. 'Lancelot contre Tristan: la conjuration d'un mythe subversif (réflexions sur l'idéologie romanesque au Moyen Âge)', in *Mélanges de langue et de littérature médiévales offerts à Pierre Le Gentil*, Paris, 617–32.

Rabeyroux, A., and V. Roland 1990. 'La Mort du trouvère: Kahedin et la mise en scène du lyrisme', in Dufournet ed. 1990, 191–205.

Ribard, J. 1993. 'Figures du chevalier errant dans le Tristan en prose', in *'Et la fin pour quoy sommes ensemble': hommage à Jean Dufournet, professeur à la Sorbonne Nouvelle: littérature, histoire et langue du Moyen Âge*, 3 vols, Paris and Geneva, III, 1205–16.

Roubaud-Bénichou, S. 2000. *Le Roman de chevalerie en Espagne: entre Arthur et Don Quichotte*, Paris.

Suard, F. 1993. 'Le Récit à distance de soi-même dans le *Tristan en prose*', in *'Et c'est la fin pour quoy sommes ensemble': hommage à Jean Dufournet, professeur à la Sorbonne Nouvelle: littérature, histoire et langue du Moyen Âge*, 3 vols, Paris and Geneva, III, 1297–1305.

Toury, M.-N. '"Morant d'amours": amour et mort dans le tome I du *Tristan en prose*', in Dufournet ed. 1990, 173–90.

Trachsler, R. 1994. 'Bréhus sans Pitié: portrait-robot du criminel arthurien', in *La Violence dans le monde médiéval*, Senefiance 36, Aix-en-Provence, 525–42.

Traxler, J. 1994. 'Courtly and Uncourtly Love in the *Prose Tristan*', in D. Maddox and S. Sturm Maddox eds. *Literary Aspects of Courtly Culture*, Cambridge, 161–9.

Van Coolput, C.-A. 1986. *Aventures quérant et le sens du monde: aspects de la réception productive des premiers romans du Graal cycliques dans le Tristan en prose*, Louvain.

Van Coolput 1987. '"Por deviser comment": l'évolution de la formule dans le Tristan en prose',
    Tris, 11:2, 10–20.

Vielliard, F. 1973. *Bibliotheca Bodmeriana: manuscrits français du Moyen Âge*, Geneva.

Vinaver, E. 1925. *Études sur le Tristan en prose: les sources, les manuscrits, bibliographie critique*,
    Paris.

Vinaver 1959. 'The *Prose Tristan*', in Loomis ed. 1959*, 339–47.

Vinaver 1970. *A la recherche d'une poétique médiévale*, Paris.

Walworth, J. 1995. 'Tristan in Medieval Art', in Grimbert ed. 1995*, 255–99.

Willard, C. 1985. 'Codicological Observations on Some Manuscripts of the Complete Version of
    the *Prose Tristan*', in Foulon et al. eds 1985*, II, 658–67.

IX

REWRITING PROSE ROMANCE: THE POST-VULGATE *ROMAN DU GRAAL* AND RELATED TEXTS

Fanni Bogdanow and Richard Trachsler

The Post-Vulgate *Roman du Graal*

The Vulgate Cycle of Arthurian prose romances, which in its final form consisted of five branches, the *Estoire del Saint Graal*, a *Merlin* and *Suite*, the *Lancelot*, the *Queste del Saint Graal* and the *Mort Artu* (see chapter VII), was rewritten shortly after its composition by a writer who combined it with themes derived from the First Version of the prose *Tristan* (see chapter VIII). This new Arthuriad, spanning the time from the early history of the Grail down to the destruction of Arthur's kingdom, used to be called the 'pseudo-Robert de Boron Cycle', but is now known as the Post-Vulgate *Roman du Graal* [*P-V*] (Bogdanow 2003).

The *P-V* has not survived in French in its complete form in any one manuscript, but has had to be reconstructed from fragments of varying lengths, some of which have been discovered only recently, and also from Portuguese and Castilian translations, as well as from redactional information supplied by the writer himself. This evidence suggests that the original *P-V* Arthuriad consisted of three parts. The first two comprised a redaction of the *Estoire del Saint Graal* and the prose rendering of Robert de Boron's *Merlin*, followed by a *Suite du Merlin* partly dependent on the Vulgate *Suite*, but mostly distinct from it. The final section included the *P-V*'s own version of the *Queste* and *Mort Artu*, both freely adapted from the corresponding Vulgate narratives.

The section from which scholars first deduced the existence of a cycle parallel to the Vulgate Cycle was the *Suite du Merlin*, originally known from the following sources: (i) the early fourteenth-century Huth codex (British Library, Additional MS 38117), edited by G. Paris and J. Ulrich in 1886 [the Huth *Merlin*]; (ii) two early editions of the Castilian *Baladro del sabio Merlín* printed in Burgos in 1498 (*Baladro*, Bohigas edn) and Seville in 1535 (vol. 1 of *La Demanda*, Bonilla y San Martin edn); (iii) Malory's English adaptation. No manuscript of the Castilian *Baladro* has yet been discovered, though a small section of the Castilian *Merlin* proper has been preserved in MS 1877 of the Salamanca University Library (*Spanish Grail Fragments*, Pietsch edn, I, 3–54), and in 1979 a fragment of a Galician–Portuguese translation of the *Suite* section was discovered by A. J. Soberanas. Both the Huth *Merlin* and the two extant editions of the

Baladro are incomplete at the end: the former breaks off shortly after the beginning of the triple adventures of Gauvain, Yvain and the Morholt (Huth *Merlin*, II, 254), whilst *Baladro* editions omit the latter section of the Huth *Merlin* (II, 198–254), completing the narrative instead with a more detailed account of Merlin's death (Bogdanow 1962a). A fragment discovered by Wechssler (1895) in BNF, fr. 112 (*Livre II*, fols 17b-58b) and published in 1913 by Sommer [*Abenteuer*] includes the final portion of the Huth codex, yet also continues the narrative further by completing the triple adventures of Gauvain and his two companions. Another manuscript of the *Suite* did not come to light until 1945, when Vinaver correctly identified the fourteenth-century Cambridge University Library manuscript, Additional 7071, which continues beyond the end of the Huth codex, but breaks off earlier than the BNF, fr. 112 fragment (Vinaver 1949). Finally, yet more recently, short fragments of the *P-V* have been discovered in Italian libraries: the Siena fragment (Micha 1957; Bogdanow 1960b; 1966, 228–41) dates from the thirteenth century and covers a portion of the Huth and Cambridge manuscripts, whilst other fragments found in Imola and Bologna date from the fourteenth century and correspond to certain sections of the BNF, fr. 112 narrative (Longobardi 1987a and b; 1992a; cf. Bogdanow 1998; Bogdanow, *P-V* edn, IV, 2, 572–8; 591–640).

The *P-V* writer, anticipating the fate of his work, announces in the *Suite* section (Huth *Merlin*, I, 280; Cambridge MS, fol. 264a) that he has divided his 'book' into three equal parts: the first part, we are told, ends 'au commenchement de ceste queste' (*at the beginning of this quest*, that is at the end of Balain's quest of an invisible knight); the second part comes to its conclusion 'el commenchement dou Graal' (*at the beginning of the Grail Quest*) whilst the third part 'finishes after Lancelot's death at the very point where it relates King Mark's death'. He justifies giving the contents of his Arthuriad at this point by adding that if the 'story of the Grail' is dismembered by any of its later scribes, the attentive reader would be able to tell if the narrative was complete or if certain sections were missing.

For a long time the only versions of the *Mort Artu* that were known to include an account of King Mark's death were the redactions which in the Portuguese *A Demanda do Santo Graal* and the two early printed editions of the Castilian *La Demanda del Sancto Grial* (Toledo 1515 and Seville 1535) follow on after the end of the *P-V Queste*. Although not identified as such, the original French version of the *Demanda* account of Mark's death, preserved in one of the manuscripts of Rusticien de Pise's *Roman du Roi Artus et des chevaliers errans*, BNF, fr. 340, and preceded in this codex by the *Demanda* version of Guinevere's death, was known since 1891 from Löseth's *Analyse* (1890), but not identified as such until 1907 by Sommer. A further French redaction, somewhat more detailed, but clearly related to BNF, fr. 340 and the *Demandas*, came to light some eighty-four years later:

i.e. the text included in Cologny-Genève, cod. Bodmer 105 (see Bogdanow, *Queste P-V*, III, 506–28, §§701–14). This volume, a codex of the last three branches of the Vulgate Cycle, inserts in its version of the *Mort Artu* not only the account of Mark's death, but also certain other sections of the *P-V Mort Artu* of which previously no French manuscript was known.

The Portuguese and Castilian *Demandas* are both translated, though not independently of each other, from the French *P-V Queste–Mort Artu* which, like the *Suite* section, no longer survives intact, but has had to be reconstructed from textual fragments incorporated in various manuscripts. Two of these (see Wechssler 1895) are BNF, fr. 112 (*Livre IV*), compiled by Micheau Gonnot in the fifteenth century (see below), and BNF, fr. 343, copied in the fourteenth century by an Italian scribe. The latter codex combines the first two-thirds of the Vulgate *Queste* with a substantial section of the last third of the *P-V*, whilst BNF 112, in addition to one of the episodes which it shares with BNF, fr. 343, incorporates several others, both from earlier and later parts of the narrative.

Another incident (that of the Olivier vermeil) derived from the *P-V Queste* was inserted by the scribe of a late fifteenth-century codex of the Vulgate Cycle, BNF, fr. 116, between the end of the Vulgate *Queste* and the beginning of the Vulgate *Mort Artu*, whilst yet further episodes were incorporated into a codex of *Guiron le Courtois*, Turin, Biblioteca Nazionale, MS L. I. 7–9 (Bogdanow 1965; *Queste P-V*, I, 126–8) as well as into certain manuscripts of Rusticien de Pise's compilation, the *Roman du Roi Artus et des chevaliers errans* (Bogdanow 1967; *Queste P-V*, I, 128–37). Moreover, substantial sections from the second half of the *P-V Queste*, combined with the first half of the Vulgate *Queste*, were incorporated into the Second Version of the prose *Tristan* and have survived in some twenty-two manuscripts of the latter, including BNF, fr. 772 (Bogdanow 2002). In 1984 a codex which had been in the Bodleian Library in Oxford since 1755, MS Rawlinson D. 874, was identified as a manuscript of the *P-V Queste* closely related to BNF, fr. 343, but continuing beyond the point where the latter breaks off (Bogdanow 1985; Lloyd-Morgan 1985; *Queste P-V*, I, 108–12). A number of further fragments of the *P-V Queste*, which are likely to be from the same codex and some of which cover sections previously unknown in French, have in recent years come to light in the State Archives in Bologna (Longobardi 1987a; 1992a; 1993; *Queste P-V*, I, 5–10, 101–8; IV, 2, 503–72, 641–723). Finally, portions of the *P-V Mort Artu* have survived in the two French manuscripts mentioned above (BNF, fr. 340 and Bodmer 105) as well as in two small strips from the same codex as the Bologna *P-V Queste* fragments (Longobardi 1989; 1992a; *Queste P-V*, I, 10–13; 200–3).

G. Paris (1887) was the first to realize that the Portuguese *A Demanda* represented the third part of the tripartite *Livre* announced in the Huth *Suite du Merlin*. Whilst neither the Vulgate *Queste* nor the Vulgate *Mort Artu* has references to such subdivisions, *A Demanda* and its French source, the *P-V Queste–Mort Artu* in its surviving portions, refer to the tripartition of the *Livre* and mention that the *Queste* is the third part (Bogdanow 2003, 40; *Queste P-V*, III, 307, §581). Furthermore, there are in the *Suite* certain references to future events in the *Queste–Mort Artu* which correspond only to incidents related in the equivalent sections of the *P-V*. Thus, in the *Suite*, our writer not only announces King Mark's death, which is subsequently related in the *P-V Mort Artu*, but at the point where he first introduces the newly crowned Mark states that he was to marry Yseut, 'as this very story will show clearly in connection with an event of which the *Graaus* speaks' (Huth *Merlin*, I, 230). The Vulgate *Queste* makes no mention of King Mark, but in the *P-V Queste* Mark invades Logres during the Grail Quest in the hope of recovering Yseut, who had taken refuge with Tristan in the Joyeuse Garde (*Queste P-V*, III, 82–125, §§445–72). Similarly, the reference in the *Suite* to the Beste Glatissant as 'one of the adventures of the Grail' (Huth *Merlin*, I, 160) is of relevance only in the *P-V Queste*, where the Beste is finally slain and its origin is related. On the other hand, in the *P-V Queste* alone, at the point where Galahad heals Pellean, the Maimed King, the latter explains that it was the 'Chevalier as deus espees' who had caused the wound (*Queste P-V*, III, 321, §590), an obvious reference to the scene where Balain, 'the Knight with the Two Swords' struck in the *Suite* the Dolorous Stroke (Bogdanow 1966, 241–9). As for the allusions to the feud between Gauvain and Pellinor's lineage in the *P-V Queste* (II, 313, §221; III, 257, §548), these too are only of relevance in the context of the *P-V* Arthuriad, where in the *Suite* section we are told the origin of this feud: in the war between Arthur and King Lot, King Pellinor slew Lot, where-upon the latter's son Gauvain, then aged eleven, swore to avenge his father's death on Pellinor and his lineage (Huth *Merlin*, I, 261; II, 11).

In the Vulgate Cycle, the *Queste* is preceded by the *Lancelot*. But what in the original *P-V* Cycle followed the end of the triple adventures of Gauvain, Yvain and the Morholt (the *Abenteuer* section), long considered to be the end of the *P-V Suite*? According to Wechssler (1895), whose theories were accepted with some modification by G. Paris (1895), Brugger (1906–10) and Vettermann (1918), the original 'pseudo-Robert' Cycle, which they wrongly believed predated the Vulgate Cycle, went through three successive redactions. It was assumed that the first of these, [*A*], consisted of six branches, one of which corresponded to the *Lancelot*; the second one, [*B*], omitted the *Lancelot*, whilst the third one, [*C*], additionally omitted the *Estoire del Saint Graal*. Moreover, they argued that the compilers of the second and third redactions shortened the remaining sections so that the Cycle would fall into three equal parts. Bruce (1924/1928*, I, 458–79), whilst realizing that the so-called 'pseudo-Robert' Cycle was dependent on the Vulgate, nevertheless followed Wechssler in thinking that this Cycle had under-gone two successive abridgements and that in the process of shortening the Cycle some *remanieur* had omitted the *Lancelot*. But there is no evidence to support any of these conjectures (Bogdanow 1966). In fact, the question of the form and structure of the original *P-V Roman du Graal* can only be resolved by taking at face value the evidence provided by the extant *P-V* manuscripts.

At various points in the narrative the *P-V* writer not only states that he has divided his *livre* into three equal parts, but also that, although the substance of the 'Grant Hystoire de Lanscelot' was not irrelevant to his own work, he has excluded it from his composition, as its inclusion would have made the middle part three times as long as the other two. Thus at the point where, in the *Suite*, he refers to the ring that the Lady of the Lake gave to Lancelot, our author states explicitly that this fact is narrated in the 'Great Story of Lancelot', which he is omitting because its inclusion would spoil the symmetry of his work (Bogdanow 2003, 42; Cambridge MS, fol. 279c; Huth *Merlin*, II, 57).

But if the *Lancelot* proper formed no part of the Post-Vulgate Cycle, it is equally apparent that the *Suite* cannot have ended originally with the *Abenteuer* section. There is a considerable chronological gap between the end of the *Abenteuer* and the beginning of the *P-V Queste*: the Grail knights, Galahad and Perceval, have not yet been born, whilst Lancelot, who is to be Galahad's father, is still a small boy. Moreover, there are also in the *P-V Suite* a number of references to later incidents not related before the end of the *Abenteuer* section, but which the writer mentions retrospectively in the *P-V Queste*. In fact a considerable portion of the missing narrative has survived in two manuscripts, a thirteenth-century codex of the prose *Tristan*, BNF, fr. 12599, and *Livre III* of BNF, fr. 112. First published in 1965 under the title *La Folie Lancelot* [*Folie*], this narrative has made it possible to understand how the *P-V* writer was able to exclude the *Lancelot* and yet avoid a break in continuity: in order to provide a transition to the *P-V Queste*, he extended the *Suite* by adapting certain incidents from the *Agravain* section of the *Lancelot* (see chapter VII, n. 1), combining these with his own inventions and a number of episodes derived from the First Version of the prose *Tristan*. The *Folie* begins with an incident announced in the *Abenteuer* (93): Gaheriet's slaying of his mother. This is then followed by episodes such as Lancelot's madness and his stay in the Isle de Joie, Perceval's youth, the death of two of Pellinor's sons, Lamorat and Drian, predicted in the *Suite* (Huth *Merlin*, I, 261) as well as Erec's early exploits, which are concluded in the *P-V Queste*. However, the *Folie* is in itself incomplete and does not completely fill the gaps preceding and following it. Many of these lacunae can now, however, be filled by fragments preserved in libraries in Imola and Bologna (Longobardi 1992a; Bogdanow 1998, 33–64; *Queste P-V*, IV:2, 511–46, 614–40). Probably deriving from the same codex as the other *P-V* fragments in these libraries, this new series includes, among other incidents, Pellinor's death, announced in the *Suite* (I, 261), and Lancelot's departure from the Isle de Joie with Galahad aged sixteen. This episode is adapted from the *Agravain*, but interwoven with other episodes that develop themes introduced both in the *Suite* and the *Folie*, such as those relating to the Chastel Tugan and Erec (*Queste P-V*, IV:2, 527–44). Finally, a sixteenth-century codex of the Castilian prose *Lancelot*, MS 9611 in the Biblioteca Nacional in Madrid contains a further portion of *P-V* narrative, some of which coincides textually with one of the new French fragments (Bogdanow 1999; *Queste P-V*, IV:2, 724–51).

The first part of the *P-V* Arthuriad ends, to judge from the redactional indications in the Huth and Cambridge manuscripts, at the point where in the *Suite* section Balain sets out in quest of the Invisible Knight (Huth *Merlin*, I, 280). In both these codices, as well as in the Castilian *Baladro*, the *Suite* is preceded by the prose rendering of Robert de Boron's *Merlin*, and indeed is presented as a continuation of the latter. Further, in the Cambridge codex (fols 202d–230a) and in Malory, but neither in the Huth codex nor in the *Baladro*, an account of Arthur's wars against the rebel kings, based on the Vulgate *Merlin*, is inserted between the end of the *Merlin* and the beginning of the *Suite* proper. Though not absolutely certain, it is highly probable that this section dealing with Arthur's early wars formed an integral part of the original *P-V* Arthuriad (Vinaver 1949; Bogdanow 1966, 31–9; but cf. Wilson 1952). What is incontrovertible, however, is that originally an account of the early history of the Grail, an *Estoire del Saint Graal*, and not as in the Huth codex, the prose rendering of Robert's *Joseph* must have preceded the *Merlin*. This is evident from the fact that there is in the *P-V Queste* a specific reference to an incident related 'in the first part of our book' which figures only in the *Estoire del Saint Graal* (compare *S*, 1, 242.6–7 with *Queste P-V*, III, 290, §569). The allusion is to the episode where Mordrain, on approaching too closely the ark containing the Holy Vessel, lost his sight and the use of his body, and was told that he would not be healed until the coming of Galahad.

However, this is not the only evidence suggesting that for the writer of the *P-V* the *Estoire* formed an integral part of his composition. The unique codex of a Portuguese translation of the *Estoire*, the *Josep Abarimatia* of MS 643 in the Torre do Tombo, Lisbon, significantly bears the subtitle 'a primeira parte da Demanda do Santo Graal', whilst the Salamanca codex of the Castilian *P-V* fragments contains an extract from the *Libro de Josep Abarimatia* just before its *Merlin* section. To judge from the Portuguese *Josep*, the *P-V Estoire* differed only slightly from the versions preserved by the extant Vulgate *Estoire* manuscripts. The few divergences are, however, significant: they reveal the *P-V* writer's deliberate attempt to strengthen the links between the *Estoire* and the *P-V* versions of the *Suite du Merlin* and the *Queste*. Thus, whereas according to the Vulgate *Estoire* manuscripts the blow of a single sword will inaugurate in Arthur's time marvels and adventures (Rennes, Bibliothèque Municipale, MS 255, fol. 75a–b;

S, I, 226.13–14), according to the Portuguese *Josep* these marvels will be caused by the blow of a lance (Lisbon, MS 643, fol. 232v), a clear reference to Balain's Dolorous Stroke in the *P-V Suite*. Elsewhere, the reference to this later event is even more precise. In speaking of King Pellean, the Maimed King, the Vulgate *Estoire* manuscripts explain that he received his wound in a battle in Rome (Rennes, MS 255, fol. 98c; *S*, I, 290.28–30). The Portuguese *Josep*, however, announces that it will be the Knight with the Two Swords who will strike the fatal blow with the Avenging Lance and that this blow will not only maim the king, but inaugurate the adventures of Logres 'as this story will relate' (Lisbon, MS 643, fol. 304v).

Early scholars not only failed to recognize the structure of the *P-V Roman du Graal*, but condemned those of its constituent parts at their disposal as a 'labyrinth of fantastic adventures' (Bruce 1923/1928*, I, 464; cf. Huth *Merlin*, I, xlviii). In reality, the *P-V* is a creative reinterpretation of the Vulgate, the work not of a 'barbare maladroit', as Pauphilet claimed (1907, 606), but of a writer who attempted to produce a more homogeneous and closely knit whole, of which Arthur and the history of his kingdom, rather than Lancelot, was the central character. The 'double esprit' so characteristic of the Vulgate – the clash between the exaltation of courtly love in large portions of the *Lancelot* and the religious mysticism of the *Queste*, followed by a resurgence of the love theme in the *Mort Artu* (Bogdanow 1984a; 1984c; 1986b) – is absent from the *P-V*. Our author not only dispensed with the greater part of the *Lancelot* proper, but radically revised both the *Queste* and the *Mort Artu* sections. The Vulgate *Queste*, written by a man steeped in the mystical theology of St Bernard (Bogdanow 1986a), is essentially a treatise on grace, with almost every line intended for doctrinal exposition (Gilson 1925). For the *P-V* author, in contrast, the *Queste* is part of the history of Arthur's kingdom. Hence he does not confine himself to the adventures of the Vulgate Grail Knights, but adds incidents relevant to the fortunes of Logres. Moreover, to give his work a wider appeal, he cuts out or shortens some of the theological disquisitions. Yet the *P-V* is by no means secular in outlook. The Grail remains a symbol of grace and the Final Scene at Corbenic constitutes the high point of the narrative. Moreover, although the characters may not always be as assiduous in their religious practices as in the Vulgate, there are many references to prayer and confession, and sin by all standards is condemned. Lancelot not only repents of his love for Guinevere as in the Vulgate, but in a passage peculiar to the *P-V*, Count Hernoul expresses his deep sense of guilt for not having revealed to Arthur Lancelot's love for Guinevere, which he refers to as 'folie', 'traïson', 'vilennie' and 'pechié' (*Queste P-V*, III, 59–60, §429). Similarly, in additional episodes which develop the love theme, the sinful nature of illicit love is underlined. Thus the unrequited feelings of King Brutus's daughter for Galahad are described as 'folle amour' (*Queste P-V*, II, 142, rubric); Tristan and Yseut's relationship is belittled (*Queste P-V*, II, 494, §370; Bogdanow 1994a), and whilst Palamedes (the Saracen and Tristan's rival for Yseut's affections) will convert and be rewarded as one of the twelve chosen knights to participate in the Final Scene at Corbenic, Tristan, unrepentant of his love, will be denied this honour. Furthermore, although in the *P-V Mort Artu*, as in the *Vulgate*, Lancelot will relapse into his sinful ways, the anti-courtly spirit of the preceding section will continue to be reflected in the *P-V Mort Artu*, where our author deliberately suppresses most of the Vulgate scenes in which Lancelot and Guinevere appear alone (Bogdanow 1966, 146, 214–15).

As for the *Suite du Merlin,* far from leading into a *Lancelot*, it has the same ascetic, anti-courtly overtone as the other branches. Here too, there is a constant preoccupation with sin. Tor, about to leave home, is reminded by his mother not to forget his Creator, but to protect his soul so as to render it to Him intact (Huth *Merlin*, II, 135). Gaheriet, before his fight with the giant Aupartis, does penance as a hermit had suggested (*Abenteuer*, 121). Arthur, on the point of facing Lot's army, is advised by Merlin to confess all his sins, as this would help him more than anything else (Huth *Merlin*, I, 249). Moreover, the damsels of the Roche aux Pucelles, the author stresses, desist from doing too much harm by their enchantments 'for fear of sinning' (*Abenteuer*, 80). Above all, unlawful love, as in the *Queste,* is severely condemned. Though subsequently ashamed of his 'mesfait' (*misdeed; Folie*, 4.162.2–4; 5.202–6), Gaheriet not only defends the murder of his mother, the Queen of Orkney, as a just punishment for a queen who 'par maleureuse luxure' (*through her wretched debauchery*) brought shame to her children and her whole lineage, but expresses the hope that his action 'will be a lesson for the noble ladies who commit such great disloyalties' (*Folie*, 5.172–5). Similarly, Gauvain's relationship with Arcade is referred to as 'pechié grant et orrible' (*a great and terrible sin, Abenteuer*, 32), and Morgan, once beautiful, is said to have become ugly when the devil entered her heart and she was filled with *luxure* (Huth *Merlin*, I, 166). As for the episodes taken over from the *Lancelot* in the *Folie* section, these in no way idealize Lancelot. Rather they serve to explain the circumstances leading up to Galahad's conception, whilst stressing the pathetic and humiliating consequences for Lancelot of his relationship with Guinevere, his madness and his exile from court (Bogdanow 1966, 60–87).

Structurally, too, the *P-V Roman du Graal* forms a more coherent whole than the Vulgate Cycle. Unlike the latter, which evolved in stages, the *P-V Roman du Graal* was from the outset conceived as a complete work. The *P-V Queste* runs without interruption into the *P-V Mort Artu*, and many of the discrepancies in the Vulgate Cycle between the *Estoire* and the other branches have been avoided (Bogdanow 1966, 156–70, 199). Above all, *pace* Bruce (1923/1928*) and G. Paris (Huth *Merlin*, I, xlviii), the author of the *P-V Roman du Graal* was not content to pile up a series of disparate adventures. Instead, he presents a coherent narrative in which the principal events of Arthur's reign are skilfully motivated. This is achieved in a manner characteristic of thirteenth-century writers, not psychologic- ally, but structurally, by supplying the antecedents of the incidents to be elucidated (Vinaver, *Le Roman de Balain*, introduction; 1949; 1956). Hence the *P-V Suite du Merlin*, instead of being limited largely to a series of Arthur's wars, as is its Vulgate counterpart, consists of long sequences of events, which are completed in the later portions of the narrative. One of the most notable of these is the opening episode of the *Suite* proper, Arthur's begetting of Mordred, which is presented as the initial link in a chain of events leading up to the death of Arthur and the downfall of his kingdom (Bogdanow 1966, 144–5). Similarly, the series of episodes culminating in Balain's Dolorous Stroke and its tragic conse- quences, i.e. the adventures of Logres, prepare for and are counterbalanced by the coming of Galahad. He is the chosen knight, who will not only end these adventures, but will, in the Final Scene at Corbenic, heal the Maimed King wounded by Balain's fatal stroke (Bogdanow 1966, 129–37).

Moreover, the structural unity of the *P-V Roman du Graal* is closely linked to the asceticism of the work, which is itself reflected in the author's conception of Arthur and his kingdom. For our writer, Arthur is the *roi aventureux,* the king of chance and mischance, and his kingdom is the *roiaume aventureux* (Huth *Merlin*, II, 97; *Queste P-V*, III, 469, §679). Arthur and the knights of his kingdom are doomed to commit unintentionally, through mischance, sinful acts, which they and the whole country will subsequently have to expiate. Thus it is by chance that Balain arrives at the Grail Castle in his search for the invisible knight Garlan, who has slain his companion; and it is by chance that Balain, needing a weapon to defend himself when his sword breaks in combat against Garlan's brother King Pellean, enters the Grail Chamber and, unaware of the sin he is committing in touching the Holy Lance, seizes it and strikes with it the Dolorous Stroke that is to incur divine vengeance (Bogdanow 1966, 129–37). Similarly, when Arthur begets Mordred on Lot's wife, he is unaware that she is his half-sister, but never- theless, though his sin of incest is unintentional, he and his kingdom will pay for it. Indeed, this has been divinely decreed, as Arthur himself recognizes after the battle on Salisbury Plain, shortly before his death (*Queste P-V*, III, 457–8, §672, cf. Vulgate *Mort Artu*, Frappier edn, §192).

Yet this is not the final mischance to befall Arthur and his kingdom. After the king's death and that of Lancelot, King Mark in the *P-V* version invades Arthur's kingdom for the second time to avenge the shame he suffered when he first invaded Logres during the *P-V* Grail Quest. And though Mark eventually dies, he succeeds in destroying not only Camelot, but also the symbol of Arthur's former glory, the Round Table. Yet this final tragedy could have been avoided if Arthur's behaviour had not turned Mark's early loyalty into hatred, for Arthur had allowed Tristan and Yseut to take refuge at Joyeuse Garde, and it was in order to regain Yseut that Mark had invaded Arthur's kingdom during the *Queste* (*Queste P-V*, III, 82–133, §§445–74).

If, in the *P-V*, sins committed not only deliberately but also in ignorance must be expiated, this is because our author is applying to his narrative one of the Old Testament teachings that Bernard of Clairvaux reaffirmed in his *Treatise on Baptism*, contesting Abelard's assertion that one cannot sin in ignorance.[1] Our author's conception of Arthur's kingdom as the *roiaume aventureux* not only explains the kind of incidents the author chooses to narrate; it also accounts for the tripartition of the work. Far from being arbitrary, as critics have assumed, the divisions indicated correspond to the three phases in the history of Logres. The first part, which deals with the history of Logres before the beginning of the 'adventures of the Grail', naturally includes the early history of the Grail (the *Estoire del Saint Graal*), as well as the events leading up to Arthur's reign (the prose rendering of Robert de Boron's *Merlin*). It ends, as is logical, at the point in the *Suite du Merlin* when Balain sets out on the adventures which are to lead him to the Grail Castle, where he is to strike the Dolorous Stroke that begins the adventures of the Grail. The second part, which includes the remainder of the *Suite* narrative (including the *Folie*), shows us Logres labouring under the consequences of the Dolorous Stroke. The third part starts equally logically, with news of the arrival of the long-awaited deliverer, the Good Knight Galahad, who, as Balain's counterpart, will end the adventures of Logres. However, as Arthur and his realm have yet to pay for the king's sin of incest, this final section includes not only the *Queste,* but also its sequel, Arthur's death at the hands of his incestuous son Mordred, and the destruction of the kingdom.

The author of the *P-V Roman du Graal* calls his whole work the *Estoire dou Graal* (Huth *Merlin*, I, 280; II, 61, 137), or the *Haute Escriture del Saint Graal* (Huth *Merlin*, II, 57), or the *Contes del Saint Graal* (*Folie*, 21.928), a title that clearly reflects the importance of the Grail in his conception of the Arthurian world. The date of the *P-V* can be fixed fairly precisely. Since our author drew both on the Vulgate Cycle (written *c.*1215–30) and the First Version of the prose *Tristan* (written *c.*1225–35), the year 1225 must be considered as the *terminus a quo*.[2] On the other hand, as the Second Version of the prose *Tristan*, compiled probably early in the second half of the thirteenth century, made in its turn use of the *P-V*, the latter was evidently composed before 1250. But an even more precise *terminus ad quem* is supplied by a reference in the *Palamedes* to the final episode of the *P-V*, the destruction of Camelot by King Mark (BNF, fr. 350, fol. 6a). Assuming that this reference was also in the *Palamedes* mentioned by Emperor Frederick II in his letter to the *secretus* of Messina dated 5 February 1240 (see Trachsler below), the *P-V Roman du Graal* was written most probably no later than 1235–40.

As regards the relationship of the *P-V* Cycle to the *Perlesvaus* (see Williams, chapter VI), there can be no doubt that the latter was composed before the *P-V*

Arthuriad. For while the *Perlesvaus* is the source of a reference in the *Chevalier aux deux épées* (Micha in Loomis ed. 1959*, 380), the latter is the source of an incident in the *P-V Suite du Merlin*. The details in question are the following. The *Deux épées*, like the *Perlesvaus*, states that Perceval's (or 'Perlesvaus's') family home is the Vaus de Camaalot – compare 'Et Perceval le fil Alain, / Le Gros des Vaus de Kamelot' (*Le Chevalier aux deus épées*, 2604–5)[3] with 'Gais li Gros de la Croiz des Ermites fu peres Julain le Gros des Vax de Kamaalot' (*Perlesvaus*, I, 24, 42–3).[4] The *P-V* author also develops in his *Suite* section the theme of the Knight with the Two Swords from the *Deux épées*. In the latter (1149–1309) a damsel called Lore arrives at Arthur's court with a sword girded round her waist, which only the best knight in the world can unfasten. Similarly, in the *P-V Suite* a female messenger from the Dame de l'Isle d'Avalon arrives at Arthur's court with a sword girded round her, which only the best knight in the country will be able to undo (Huth *Merlin*, 1, 213–17). In both cases, though for different reasons, the damsel had first been to King Rion's/Ris's court. The knight who succeeds in the adventure, Meriadeuc in the *Chevaliers*, Balain in the *P-V Suite*, is henceforth called the 'Chevalier as deus epees'.[5] The fact that the *P-V* thus clearly drew on the *Chevalier aux deux épées* means that just as the *Perlesvaus*, itself composed after the Vulgate, furnishes the *terminus a quo* for the *Deux épées*, so the *P-V* furnishes the *terminus ad quem* of 1240 for the *Deux épées*.[6]

Finally, as in the case of the Vulgate Cycle, we do not know the name of the compiler or compilers of the Post-Vulgate *Roman du Graal*. But whereas the writers of the *Agravain*, *Queste* and *Mort Artu* branches of the Vulgate Cycle attribute to themselves the name Gautier Map, the Post-Vulgate redactor, like the redactors of the Vulgate *Estoire del Saint Graal* and the Vulgate *Merlin*, adopts the name Robert de Boron – the author of the late twelfth-century verse redaction of the *Estoire dou Graal–Merlin*. [FB]

The Arthurian Material in Maistre Richart d'Irlande's *Prophecies de Merlin*

Between 1272 and 1279 a Venetian, writing in French and referring to himself by the pseudonym 'Maistre Richart d'Irlande', composed a long series of prophecies attributed to Merlin and now known as the *Prophecies de Merlin*. At the time of Paton's preliminary study (1913) and her edition in 1926 (henceforth *PP*), the *Prophecies* were known from thirteen manuscripts, including Cologny-Genève, cod. Bodmer 116, published subsequently by A. Berthelot in 1992 (henceforth *PB*). Since 1926 a number of other manuscripts have come to light: five fragments preserved in Dijon, Bibliothèque Municipale, MS 2930 identified by Vermette (edn); several fragments from three different manuscripts preserved in the State Archives of Bologna, another in the Archiginnasio of Bologna and a further four in the State Archives of Imola, all identified by M. Longobardi (1989 edn; 1993 edn); and finally four others in the State Archives of Modena identified by Bogdanow (1962–3 edn; 1972 edns).[7] In addition, there are fifteenth- and sixteenth-century printed editions of the *Prophecies*, of which the first, the 1498 edition, was reprinted by C. E. Pickford (1975 edn). In content, this printed text contains material not found in any of the manuscripts (Paton 1913, 124; *PP*, I, 39–46). There are also three non-French versions, which include some material derived from the *Prophecies*, two in Italian and one in Spanish. Of the Italian versions, the older one, the *Storia di Merlino* of Paolino Pieri (Sanesi edn) has survived only partially in a fifteenth-century manuscript in the Biblioteca Riccardiana in Florence. The other one, the *Historia di Merlino*, referred to also as the *Vita di Merlino con le sue profetie*, whose redactor claims it is a translation from the French written on 20 November 1379, is known from a manuscript in the Biblioteca Palatina of Parma, as well as a number of early printed editions (Gardner 1930, 191–216; Paton edn, I, 46–50). The Spanish *Profecias del sabio Merlino*, a short narrative of only a few pages, has been inserted between the end of the Spanish version of the *P-V Suite du Merlin* and the beginning of the Spanish *Demanda* (Bonilla y San Martin edn, 155–62).

Maistre Richart d'Irlande was of course not the first writer to conceive the idea of presenting Merlin as a prophet. We owe both this theme and the title to Geoffrey of Monmouth who, by incorporating in his *Historia Regum Britanniae* a series of Merlin's prophecies under the title *Prophetiae Merlini* (see chapter II), began a tradition which was to flourish throughout the Middle Ages (Zumthor 1943). Subsequent to Geoffrey, the theme of Merlin the prophet was continued first by Wace in his *Roman de Brut*, followed by Robert de Boron in his *Merlin*, then the Vulgate and Post-Vulgate Continuations of the *Merlin*, as well as the *Livre d'Artus* (see below). In the latter, we are told that while Merlin was residing at court *maistre Helyes* wrote down his prophecies both of the events which had already occurred and of those which were yet to take place. 'And they were all put in writing in a separate book which is still called the *Prophecies de Merlin*. And Blaise himself wrote them down in his book together with the story he had begun' (*S*, VII, 163.4–8).[8]

While Geoffrey's *Prophetiae* deal largely with Arthurian events, the prophecies uttered by Merlin in Richart d'Irlande's work refer mainly to political events that occurred in Italy and the Holy Land in the twelfth and thirteenth centuries. As in the earlier works, Merlin is presented as having dictated the prophecies to his scribes, but Blaise is no longer the sole scribe. After the latter's death, Merlin entrusted the task first to maistre Antoine, Bishop of Galles (*PB*, 38, 123), then to Tholomer (*PB*, 39), and finally to the Sages Clers de Gales (*PB*, 124; cf. *PP*, II, 301–27). However, the author of the *Prophecies*, who had strong moral scruples to judge from his condemnation of evil-doers as well as the corruption of the priesthood and monastic life,[9] was obviously well acquainted with thirteenth-century Arthurian prose romances. At various points he alludes to specific events in them. Not only, as one might expect, does he refer to Merlin's birth, explain his gift of prophecy (*PP*, I, 207–8; *PB*, 38, 123, 315–16, 354) and mention the incident where Merlin exculpates his mother before the judge (*PP*, I, 208; *PB*, 123, 258), but he also alludes to numerous other Arthurian events. These include from the *Estoire del Saint Graal* the incidents when Joseph of Arimathea takes Christ down from the cross and when Joseph's son Josephé is consecrated bishop in the city of Sarras (*PB*, 116), and the conversion of England thanks to the teachings of Joseph and his son (*PB*, 354).

Perhaps one of the most notable predictions about Arthur concerns his future greatness: his reputation for prowess, nobility, courtesy and largesse will spread throughout the world (*PP*, I, 155) and he will conquer many lands (*PP*, I, 116–17). Allusions to specific events related in the prose *Lancelot* include the Dame du Lac's nurture of Lancelot (*PB*, 93), whom she takes to be knighted to Arthur's court, where he falls in love with Guinevere (*PP*, I, 197; *PB*, 115, 118); the knighting of Bohort (*PB*, 241); Galehot's intention to lay waste 'Great Britain', from which he is deterred only by Lancelot's intervention (*PP*, I, 89; *PB*, 55); Arthur's war against Claudas de la Desierte and his determination to avenge King Ban's death (*PB*, 332); Arthur's conquest of a number of countries including Gaul (*PB*, 68); Arthur's excommunication until he takes back his wife Guinevere (*PB*, 301–02, 323); Lancelot and Galehot's friendship (*PB*, 169); the machinations of the False Guinevere aided by Bertelai li Vieus (*PB*, 136, 246–8, 268, 298–9; *PP*, I, 236); Lancelot saving the life of the genuine Guinevere falsely accused (*PB*, 136; *PP*, I, 236); Lancelot beheading Baudemagu's son Meleagant 'ensi com li livres de Lancelot le divise' (*just as the book of Lancelot relates it*; *PB*, 329); Lancelot's imprisonment by Morgan (*PB*, 348); Lancelot and Guinevere's future love and the conception of Galahad: 'a knight who will descend from the lineage of Celydoyne signifying the leopard of Benoyc will go to the kingdom of Logres and give his heart to the crowned serpent of Logres', but 'he will beget a lion [Galahad] on another white serpent [Pellés's daughter] thinking that it is the crowned serpent' (*PB*, 98–9).

References to events in the *Queste* include the prediction that Bohort will be one of the three successful Grail Knights (*PP*, I, 223), and that Lancelot will succeed only partially 'pour les pechiés de luxure qui se herbergera en lui' (*because of the sins of lechery which will reside in him*): it will be his offspring Galahad who will achieve all he will fail to do: 'qui metra a fin tout ce a quoi il avra falli' (*PP*, I, 193; *PB*, 113). As for the latter, he will be crowned the King of Sarras before his translation to heaven: 'and this lion [Galahad] will have wings and fly over the sea and become king of the land [Sarras] over which formerly Evalac ruled' (*PB*, 99). Other references to the Grail Quest are to the 'estranges aventures' that will take place in Arthur's time in the kingdom of Logres and in Great Britain 'pour la venue del Saint Graal' (*because of the arrival of the Holy Grail, PB*, 55); the coming of the Grail to Arthur's court at Whitsuntide (*PB*, 395); Perceval's journey along the road to Corbenic 'ou li sains Graaus estoit' (*PB*, 214). Even more precise predictions to events in the *Queste* are the details concerning Perceval and his sister, and the mention of Arthur's distress when the Grail Quest begins, for he fears that the companions will never return to court (*PB*, 376). Perceval, correctly identified as the son of King Pellinor of Listenois (*PB*, 137; *PP*, I, 237) will remain a virgin to the end and will be present when the Grail Quest is achieved. His sister, who will also remain a virgin, will be buried in the place in Sarras where formerly Josephé was bishop. She will die so that she can save the life of another. But before her death she will fulfil the prophecy formerly uttered by Solomon's wife that the hangings on the good sword that formerly belonged to King David will be made of what is dearest to her (*PB*, 137; *PP*, I, 237; cf. the reference to Solomon's boat 'ou l'espee as estranges renges estoit mise', *in which the sword with the extraordinary belt was placed, PB*, 110; *PP*, I, 189). Nor does the writer forget to announce, in the form of Merlin's predictions, the final destinies of Arthur, Lancelot and Bohort. As related in the *Mort Artu*, ladies in a boat will take Arthur dead or alive 'hors de cestui païs', namely out of Logres to the island of Avalon (*PB*, 331; cf. 339). As for Lancelot and Bohort, they will end their days as hermits (*PB*, 401).

Other references recall events related in the prose *Tristan*: Tristan's birth (*PB*, 111; *PP*, I, 192); Perceval's freeing of Tristan from prison (*PB*, 357); Governal being made King of Loenois, the land given to him by Tristan (*PB*, 383); Tristan's death by a poisoned arrow ('ja est forgiez li glavez et envenimez qui le metra a mort', *the sword which will kill him has already been made and tipped with poison, PP*, I, 192; *PB*, 112). Other prophecies share details with the prose *Tristan* and *Guiron le Courtois*: the mention of Palamedes's brother Saphar (*PB*, 179, 198, etc.) and of the Morholt's son Golistan (*PB*, 155, etc.). Yet other details refer to characters common to the *Guiron* and the Compilation of Rusticien de Pise, notably Dinadan, son of the Bon Roi (Chevalier) Sans Peur (*PB*, 195, 198, etc.) and Segurant le Brun (*PB*, 73, etc.; cf. *PP*, II, 279–95). A number of other details are common to the prose *Tristan* and the *P-V Roman du Graal*: Mark's treachery (*PB*, 343); Tristan finding refuge in Lancelot's castle, the Joyeuse Garde (*PB*, 383); Palamedes's father identified as Esclabor le Mescouneu (*PB*, 187; *PP*, I, 227, 383); and Palamedes, known as the Chevalier a la Beste Glatissant (*PB*, 262; cf. 166), being of the 'Saracen' faith (*PB*, 189), is requested to accept Christianity (*PB*, 195). As for the intriguing reference made by Mark that he knows that the Quest for the Holy Grail will begin soon (*PB*, 384), this can only be an allusion to the incident in the *P-V Queste* and the prose *Tristan*, when Mark, in order to recover Yseut, invades Logres during the *Queste*.

It is particularly interesting that certain details in the *Prophecies* can only have been derived from the *P-V Roman du Graal*. In preparing for the incident in which Galahad will draw the sword reserved for him from a stone slab, the *Prophecies*, like the *P-V Suite du Merlin*, explains that Merlin placed the sword in a slab which would arrive at Camelot when the Grail Quest was about to begin (*PB*, 122; *PP*, I, 206; II, 31; Huth *Merlin*, II, 59). Similarly the account of Merlin's entombment was clearly influenced by the corresponding *P-V* narrative. Just as in the latter Niviene fastened the lid on Merlin's tomb so firmly 'par conjuremens et par force de parole' (*by means of magic and the power of her words*) that no one could ever again open it (Huth *Merlin*, II, 197), so in the *Prophecies* she secures the lid so firmly by magic that it was impossible ever again to raise it (*PB*, 92; *PP*, I, 168–9). The prediction of the final destruction of Arthur's kingdom and of the Round Table appears also to point to the Post-Vulgate. Merlin tells Meliadus (who in the *Prophecies*, but in no other Arthurian text, is presented as Tristan's brother) that Arthur's court will be destroyed on account of the sin of lechery and that the Round Table will likewise be destroyed on account of his brother's (i.e. Tristan's) lechery (*PP*, I, 193; *PB*, 115). In the *P-V Mort Artu* King Mark, after the death of Arthur, Lancelot, Galahad, Tristan and the other distinguished Knights of the Round Table, decides to invade Arthur's kingdom for a second time, having failed the first time to take revenge for the refuge offered to Tristan and Yseut in Logres. On the second occasion Mark succeeds in destroying not only the Joyeuse Garde, but also the greater part of Camelot, including the Round Table (*P-V*, III, 510, §703, 1–2).

The writer of the *Prophecies*, moreover, does not limit himself to mere references to Arthurian events. He also includes in his work detailed adventures of Arthurian characters, including Perceval, Arthur's sister Morgan, Sebile l'Enchanteresse, 'evil' King Mark, to mention but a few, as well as two series of extended incidents adapted from earlier works: the adventures of Alixandre l'Orphelin, derived from the prose *Tristan* but interwoven in the *Prophecies* with other events (*PB*, 159–63, 281–5, 290–4, 325–9, 340–1, 358–66, 377); the Tournament of Sorelois organized by Galehot in honour of Guinevere, derived in part from the prose *Lancelot* and the prose *Tristan* (*PB*, 163–80, 184–5). These incidents have, however, been preserved only in certain of the *Prophecies* manuscripts: both the story of Alixandre and the Tournament are found in Cologny-Genève, cod. Bodmer 116; Paris, BNF, fr. 350; London, British Library, Additional MS 25434 and MS Harley 1629; and partially in some of the Modena fragments, the other manuscripts having omitted them. In addition, a revised redaction of the *Alixandre*, derived from a late version of the *Prophecies*, is incorporated in two manuscripts of *Guiron le Courtois*, BNF. fr. 362 and Turin, Biblioteca Nazionale, MS L. I. 9, whilst the version figuring in BNF, fr. 112 (see below) is identical with that of the Turin *Guiron* (Bogdanow 1965). The Tournament figures also in BNF, fr. 112 and 362, but not in the Turin codex.[10]

The name attributed to the author of the *Prophecies de Merlin*, Maistres Richart d'Irlande, is found in a passage near the beginning of the work (*PP*, I, 76–7; *PB*, 48–9). In order to strengthen the authenticity of his work, our writer claims to have translated Merlin's prophecies from the original Latin version at the request of the Emperor Frederick of Rome (1212–50). But this claim has no foundation in fact, for, as Paton (*PP*, II, 4–24, 33) has indicated, historical events as late as 1272 are mentioned, which means that the *Prophecies* must have been compiled at least two decades after Frederick's death. **[FB]**

The *Livre d'Artus*

Shortly after its composition, the Vulgate Cycle of Arthurian prose romances, which in its final form consisted of five branches, was in part remodelled by certain anonymous *remanieurs*. The name *Livre d'Artus* (henceforth *LA*, published by Sommer as volume VII of his Vulgate edition)[11] has been given by critics to the revised section of the Vulgate *Merlin* Continuation which in Paris, BNF, fr. 337 (dated *c.*1280), replaces the Vulgate version from the point where, after King Lot's departure with his four sons on their mission to negotiate a truce with the rebel kings, the writer explains Morgan's hatred for Guinevere: the queen had revealed Morgan's affair with Guiomar (MS 337, beginning of fol. 115a; *S*, II, 339.1–4; VII, 3.20–4). The so-called *LA* then follows (middle of fol. 115a–fol. 294d; *S*, VII, 3.24–323.47).

Though MS 337 is incomplete both at the beginning and at the end – it begins with the Vulgate *Merlin Suite* (*S*, II, 88.19) and breaks off where Arthur holds court at the 'Chastel as Dames' – the *LA* is by no means an isolated fragment, but was clearly integrated into a cycle almost identical with the Vulgate Cycle. This is evident from the writer's method of composition. Anxious to link up the various sections of his Arthuriad, he includes in the *LA* references both to the portions of the narrative which would have preceded it and those which would have followed it. Not only do the opening words of the *LA* follow on without a break after the final section derived from the Vulgate *Suite* (MS 337, fol. 115a; *S*, VII, 3.24), but certain allusions leave us with no doubt that, like the completed Vulgate Cycle, the *LA* Arthuriad began originally with a version of the *Estoire* followed by the prose *Merlin* and the greater part of its Continuation (*S*, I–II, 339.1–4), whilst other allusions indicate that the *LA* was followed by the *Lancelot*, and by versions of the *Queste* and *Mort Artu*.

Numerous events link the *LA* with the *Estoire*: Nascien, son of the Bele Damoisele de la Blanche Nue and one of the seventeen knights who went to the aid of

Agloval (as distinct from Mordrain's brother-in-law Nascien d'Orberique), was descended on his mother's side from the lineage of 'Joseph of Arimathea, who had the Grail in his care and brought it from Sarras to Logres' (*S*, VII, 241.37–9; cf. I, 13.27–8; 19.18–19); the maimed kings Alain and Pellinor were wounded by the same lance as Joseph of Arimathea (*S*, VII, 244.26), a reference to the incident in the *Estoire* where Joseph was wounded in the hip by an angel (*S*, I, 77.13–19); after a hermit has told Nascien the story of Christ's life, based on the *Gospel of Nicodemus* (*S*, VII, 247.27–260.37), the *LA* recalls briefly Joseph of Arimathea's early life: his imprisonment by Cayphas, his delivery by Titus's son, his departure from the Holy Land with all of his lineage, taking the Holy Grail and going first to Sarras, where his son Josephé is consecrated bishop by Christ himself, and then to 'la Bloie Bertaigne' (Great Britain) where they convert many of the inhabitants. As for Mordrain, he gives up his crown and follows Joseph and Nascien to Britain (*S*, VII, 260.39–261.1, echoing events in the *Estoire*). Further details recall his fate as mentioned both in the *Estoire* and the *Queste*. Notably there are references to Mordrain's maiming and blinding as punishment for a sin he committed 400 years earlier and to the fact that sustained solely by a holy wafer, he will not be able to die until the coming of the Good Knight who will end the adventures of the Grail (*S*, VII, 241.44–242.2; cf. I, 241.26–242.7; *Queste*, Pauphilet edn, pp. 85, 262–3). Other themes begun in the *Queste* and partially elucidated in the *Estoire* are explained and brought to an end in the *LA*. For example, the *Estoire* (*S*, I, 114–21) had explained why Mordrain's brother-in-law Nascien had been carried on a cloud to the Isle Torneant (cf. *Queste*, pp. 205–7). The *LA* adds the explanation as to how and why the Isle Torneant was established by Merlin (*S*, VII, 299.17–302.29) and how the adventure is brought to a successful conclusion by Gauvain and four companions (*S*, VII, 303.3–310.4).

The same processes are seen in the linking of the *LA* to the Vulgate *Merlin* sections (henceforth *VM*), as well as to the branches that follow it. Whilst introducing new incidents and characters, our writer not only prolongs Merlin's role as Arthur's counsellor, but reintroduces the theme of Arthur's wars with the Saxons, the 'mescreanz' (*unbelievers*), during which, as in the *VM*, Arthur benefits from Merlin's advice and is aided by his foster-father Antor and the latter's son Kay, by Pharien (*S*, VII, 15.17–19, etc.), Bohort of Gaunes, Leonce of Payerne (*S*, VII, 11.42–3, etc.), the kings Karados, Brangorre, Belinant de Sorgales and many others (*S*, VII, 15.20–1, etc.). Named amongst the Saxons who invaded Arthur's realm, first in the *VM* and then in the *LA*, is the ugly gigantic Hardogabran.[12] And in order to recall the theme of the rebel kings who from the beginning of the *VM Suite* had refused to acknowledge Arthur, the *LA* not only presents them as taking part in the fight against the *mescreanz*, but states that they do less well than Arthur for 'this was God's will as they did not wish to make peace with Arthur' (*S*, VII, 15.28). Included among the Vulgate rebel kings who fight against the Saxons are Belinans, King of Sorgales and Neutre, the father of Galeschin, who after joining in the battles against the Saxons near Clarence (*S*, VII, 11.17, 15.22, 26.1, 27.8–9) is later one of Arthur's companions in the adventure of the Isle Torneant (*S*, VII, 229.4–311.9). And before that, Merlin, anxious to bring about peace between Arthur and the rebel kings, goes on four occasions to the rescue of the rebel kings in their fight against the Saxons, warning them on each occasion, however, that they will not be successful until they do homage to Arthur (*S*, VII, 15.34–41). *VM* motifs brought to a conclusion in the *LA* include that of the statue of the Laide Semblance placed originally as a boundary mark by Judas Machabeus and which *li ancien* had announced would not be removed until 'the adventures of the kingdom of Logres began to end' (*S*, II, 231.33–6). After two attempts, and thanks to the advice of the Sage Dame de la Forest Aventureuse (a character first mentioned in the *VM*, where she is called 'la Sage Dame de la Forest Sans Retour', *S*, II, 148.16; 218.6), Grex, named only in the *LA*, finally succeeds in removing the statue from one of the rivers in 'Libe' (Libya), the kingdom of the Sage Dame's niece, whom he subsequently marries (*S*, VII, 150.3–158.38).

It is not surprising that the author of the *LA* should have kept the greater part of the original *VM Suite*, which includes incidents essential to his Arthuriad: the theme of the rebel kings and the wars against the Saxons; the incestuous conception of Mordred in ignorance (*S*, II, 128.26–129.33; MS 337, fol. 20b–c); Arthur's search for a wife and his wedding (*S*, II, 216.30–217.33; MS 337, fol. 59b); the reference to Kay's malicious tongue, a fault acquired from his wet-nurse (*S*, II, 104.1–12; MS 337, fol. 8a); the mention of King Lot's five sons, of whom Gauvain will be the best knight and the most loyal, and who will, along with his cousin, King Urien's son Yvain li Granz, serve Arthur until his death (*S*, II, 96.30–97.1; MS 337, fol. 4a–b).

References forward to the *Lancelot* are no less striking. These include the mention of Claudas's legitimate son Dorin and the death of Claudas's wife (*S*, VII, 60.37–9; 128.18–20; cf. III, 26.27–9); Claudas's love affair with Pharien's wife (*S*, VII, 128.24–44; cf. III, 22.33–5); Lancelot's birth and his baptismal name Galahad (*S*, VII, 140.27–37; cf. III, 3.8–10); the birth of Lionel and Bohort to King Bohort and Queen Elaine (VII, 140.45–141.8); the announcement that Lancelot would vanquish Alibon at the Guez la Roine and the explanation that this ford, first mentioned in the *Lancelot*, was named after Queen Guinevere, as she was the first to cross it during Arthur's war against the Saxons (*S*, VII, 122.15–18; cf. III, 141.32–142.41; 143.10–153.7); the early exploits of Brandus (Brandis) des Illes (Yles), lord of the Dolorous Garde and the Dolorous Chartre, who in the *Lancelot* escapes with his life when Lancelot vanquishes the knights guarding the Dolorous Garde (*S*, III, 151.1–6). In the *LA*, Brandus invades Arthur's kingdom and sends his captives to the Dolorous Chartre, whereupon

Arthur besieges the castle. A Saxon king, Oriol, comes to his aid; the siege is lifted, but thanks again to Merlin, the Saxons are defeated (*S*, VII, 116.5–117.36; 120.39–123.19; 126.25–38). Another incident serving to prepare for events in the *Lancelot* concerns the character called Alier/Alyer. In the *Lancelot* we are told briefly that when Alier, formerly a knight but now a hermit, learned that his son's enemies were *mescreans*, worse than Saracens, he left the hermitage dressed in his clerical robes to combat the enemies of Christianity (*S*, III, 359.27–40). The *LA*, which sometimes assigns to Alier the title *de Raguindel* (*S*, VII, 145.7; 240.8) or *de Thaningues* (VII, 22.5; 199.15; 203.13; VII, 200.4), relates how Alier, originally one of the rebel kings, takes part in the Saxon wars first near Clarence (VII, 22.5–29.22) and then near the Pui de Malohaut. He is accompanied by fourteen of his sons, who have all been knighted by Arthur (*S*, VII, 145.7–9), the fifteenth, as well as a daughter, both little children, having remained behind at Thaningues (*S*, VII, 199.35–6). After the death of his fourteen sons near the Pui de Malohaut (*S*, VII, 200.51–201.1; 201.41), Alier, overcome by grief, entrusts his baby son to the care of the lady of Roestic and enters a hermitage in the depths of the forest 'entre Norgales et Sorelois' (*S*, VII, 199.17–204.34).

Yet other details in the *LA* anticipate the role of Galehot, the son of la Bele Jaiande des Longtaines Isles, who in the *Lancelot* invades Arthur's kingdom, but at Lancelot's request makes peace with Arthur, is made a Knight of the Round Table and later dies of grief when he hears of Lancelot's presumed death (*S*, IV, 144.31–155.28). In the *LA*, no doubt to prepare for his role as a distinguished warrior and a loyal friend, Galehot is referred to as the most courtly man alive (*S*, VII, 50.27–8; cf. *S*, VII, 145.28). Descended from the lineage of giants, he has already at the age of fourteen sworn to conquer thirty kingdoms (*S*, VII, 145.12–19), yet knows how to honour a person he respects (*S*, VII, 145.19–29). There are also references to Galehot's future invasion: in the account of the battle near the Pui de Malohaut, the author mentions that in the same place there was subsequently the 'conflict between Arthur and Galehot's men in which the Companions of the Round Table suffered so much' (*S*, VII, 201.41–3; cf. VII, 261.18–19).

The *LA* also provides an explanation for Perceval's mother's loss of all of her children except Agloval and Perceval, a situation mentioned in the *Lancelot* (*S*, V, 383.17–18). When Perceval was still learning to walk, King Rion's uncle, King Agripe (*S*, VII, 235.15–17), invaded their land and fourteen of Agloval's brothers were killed (*S*, VII, 239.41–3). Agloval himself only survived because he was aided by seventeen of his companions, one of whom was Nascien, son of 'la bele Damoisele de la Blanche Nue' (*S*, VII, 239.46–242.37).

But significant above all is that certain themes referred to in both the *VM* and the *Lancelot* are brought to a conclusion. The most notable of these is that of Merlin's love affairs with Morgan and Niviene, the Damsel of the Lake. The theme is first mentioned briefly in the *Lancelot* (*S*, III, 21.1–38) and is further developed by the authors of the Vulgate and Post-Vulgate *Suite du Merlin* (Bogdanow 1966, 180–3). Like the *P-V Suite*, but independently of it, the *LA* endeavours to explain how Niviene came to entomb Merlin. Despite Merlin's interest in her, Niviene is introduced by her cousin Lunete to Brandus des Illes, with whom she falls in love. However, Merlin cannot do without her, and so, on Brandus's advice, Niviene decides to rid herself of him (*S*, VII, 127.11–12).

Neither the Post-Vulgate nor the majority of the Vulgate *Lancelot* manuscripts mention Merlin's fate following his entombment. The only exceptions are the *LA* and one of the *Lancelot* manuscripts, BNF, fr. 754. Following his entombment, at the point where the *Lancelot* states that no more was ever heard of Merlin (*S*, III, 21.37–8), MS 754 adds the words 'until Perlesvaux, who saw the great marvel of the Grail, freed him [Merlin] after Lancelot's death, as the story will relate later' (*S*, III, 21 n. 7; MS 754, fol. 14b). Now in the section where the *LA* speaks of Merlin's eventual fate at the hands of Niviene, a short passage significantly recalls MS 754's addition: 'in order to free Merlin, the Lord sent on earth a chaste and loyal servant of the lineage of King David, as Gautier Map, at the request of the good King Henry, will relate later, provided that he, Map, is able to translate it from Latin or find it in the vernacular' (*S*, VII, 127.21–5).

The fact that the *LA* shares with MS 754 a reference to Merlin's eventual delivery cannot be a coincidence: it suggests that our writer must have had at his disposal a codex of the *Lancelot* closely related to MS 754. And since, in both the *LA* and MS 754, it is a Grail hero who would free Merlin, there can be no doubt that the writer of the *LA*, like the *Lancelot*, intended his composition to be part of a larger whole which included a Grail Quest. But perhaps no less significant is the fact that the *LA*, unlike MS 754, explains why Merlin would finally recover his freedom. Although as a result of his conception Merlin's body belonged to the devils who wished to destroy him through love of a woman, the Lord – whilst not approving of carnal sin – nevertheless did not wish to lose Merlin's soul on account of the many good deeds he had accomplished (*S*, VII, 127.17–21). Hence, after allowing Merlin's body to suffer for a while, He sent him the chaste knight who was to deliver him.

No less important are the links with the *Queste*, certain of which refer both forward to the *Queste* and back to the *Estoire*, for example the Isle Torneant and Mordrain and his brother-in-law Nascien d'Orberique, mentioned above. Equally significant are the details concerning the second Nascien, son of the Bele Damoisele de la Blanche Nue, who came to Agloval's aid in defence of his mother's home against Agripe. In order to provide a history for the hermit Nascien in the *Queste* (13.9; 19.14), the *LA* identifies the hermit as this Nascien, explaining that after the end of the conflict with Agripe he gave up his career as a knight and retired from the world (*S*, VII, 261.12–14). Although the *Lancelot*, in contrast to the *VM*, does not assign the name Nascien to the wise man who counselled Arthur at the time of his war with Galehot (cf. *S*, III, 215.32–216.39; II, 222.2–3), the *LA* identifies as Nascien both this counsellor and the hermit who used to visit the young Galahad while he was living in a convent (cf. *S*, VII, 261.17–22; *S*, V, 407.37–9; 408.32–4).

Another reference foreshadows the scene in the *Queste* when Lancelot remains in a stupor on seeing a wounded knight borne on a litter healed by the Grail (*Queste*, 59.3–27; 60.1–10; 61.8–20); in the *LA* a knight is healed in similar circumstances witnessed by Nascien and his companions. This Nascien, who is the son of the Bele Damoisele de la Blanche Nue and who later becomes a hermit, immediately recognizes the Grail, dismounts from his horse, kneels and utters a prayer (*S*, VII, 245.3–26). His companions, though, like Lancelot in the *Queste*, fail to react, the *LA* explaining that their sins have prevented them from recognizing the Grail here and elsewhere for what it is (*S*, VII, 245.28–32).

In order to prepare for the fact that Bohort, but not Lancelot, will be one of the three Grail heroes, the *LA* mentions that Bohort, the best knight of his lineage except for Lancelot, saw more Grail adventures than Lancelot (*S*, VII, 141.5–7). Similarly, in order to explain why Arthur's nephew Gauvain fails in the Grail Quest, the *LA* states that this was on account of his sinful lechery and because he was not of the chosen lineage (*S*, VII, 245.39–42).

But not all the references to the Quest correspond in every respect to incidents in the Vulgate *Queste*. The Grail, we are told, will never be seen by anyone until the coming of the knight who will end the perilous adventures of the Grail; he must be virgin in body and mind and will have two companions of his lineage, one of whom will be a virgin and the other chaste (*S*, VII, 147.13–16). These three will be together until their death from the time they find the Grail, and after the death of two of them, the Grail, in the presence of the third one – Bohort – will ascend to Heaven (*S*, VII, 147.17–20, cf. *Queste*, 279.1–7). As for Perceval, the *LA* accounts for his second place in the hierarchy of the three chosen Grail heroes by linking it with the infirmity of his father, here named Pellinor and not Pellehen as in the Vulgate *Queste* (201.14). We are told, in an account unique to the *LA*, that Pellinor, having refused to believe in the Grail miracles, suffered a double punishment: not only was he himself struck through both thighs by a fiery lance descending from heaven and had as his only recreation fishing in a river (*S*, VII, 243.24–36), but his son Perceval will not be Guardian of the Grail until after the death of Galahad (*S*, VII, 243.36–9). However, these statements concerning Perceval and Bohort do not fit the Vulgate *Queste* narrative. In the latter, not only does Perceval never have the Grail in his care, but it is in the joint presence of both Perceval and Bohort that, immediately after Galahad's death, a hand takes the Grail and the Lance up to Heaven (cf. *Queste*, 279.1–7).

There are further discrepancies between the *LA* and the Vulgate *Queste*. Most notable are the references to Pellinor and the other maimed kings and their eventual healing. The *Queste* has only two maimed kings: Mordrain, who passes away peacefully in Galahad's arms (262.23–263.22), and King Parlan, who is called the Maimed King (209.9–10), and who is healed in the Final Scene at Corbenic when Galahad anoints his legs with drops of blood from the Holy Lance (271.32–272.1). As for King Pellés, though always identified in the prose *Lancelot* as Galahad's grandfather, he is on one occasion referred to as the Maimed King (*S*, III, 29.4) while on another he is said to be his son (*S*, V, 303.5–13). The *Queste*, which assigns the name Pellés to three characters, Galahad's grandfather (20.3–4; 138.12–15; 259.13–22; cf. *S*, III, 29.4), Galahad's uncle and Eliezer's father (266.14–16), and a relative of Perceval (81.7), never presents him as the Maimed King.

According to the *LA*, however, which here follows in part the account of the *VM Suite* preserved in MS 337 (fol. 18b; *S*, II, 125.9–15), there are, besides Mordrain, whose destiny we have already mentioned, three other maimed kings: Perceval's father King Pellinor; a second Pellinor, who at one point is said to be the cousin of Perceval's father (*S*, VII, 243.34–6), but elsewhere is referred to as the brother of Perceval's mother (*S*, VII, 237.4–5); and finally Alain, the brother of the second King Pellinor and of King Pellés, all three of whom were *cousin germain* of Perceval's father (VII, 146.7–9). As to the fate of these three last-named maimed kings, the *LA* is quite explicit. Unlike the Vulgate *Lancelot* (cf. BNF, fr. 120, fol. 510d and *Folie*, p. 250, n. 82. 16–20), the *LA* assumes Perceval's father to be still alive when Perceval sets out for Arthur's court. For Perceval's mother, in answer to Agloval's questions about his father, claims that he will not recover until the Grail adventures begin (*S*, VII, 237.2–4). And King Pellinor, having been struck by the Vengeful Lance, is informed by the divine voice that, although he will regain his health the same day as his cousin Pellinor, he will die immediately thereafter (*S*, VII, 243.24–34). In the meantime, as in Chrétien's *Perceval*, the only recreation that he, like his cousin King Alain, will be able to enjoy is fishing (*S*, VII, 243.34–6; cf. VII, 146.10–12).

The author of the *VM*, no doubt under the influence of Chrétien's *Perceval* or the *Didot-Perceval*, had already announced that the Maimed King Alain would not be healed until the best knight in the world asked him why he was ill and what the Grail was (MS 337, fol. 18b; cf. *S*, II, 125.12–15). The *LA* similarly states that Alain, Pellinor and Pellinor's cousin, Pellinor du Chastel de Corbenic (the brother of Perceval's mother) will not recover from their wounds until the knight stays in their dwelling and asks who is served by the Holy Grail (*S*, VII, 147.20–6).

Now the theme of 'asking questions', like that of the Maimed King's recreation, has no place in the Vulgate *Queste*. These and the other inconsistencies between the Vulgate and the *LA* raise a question impossible to answer: did the author, like the writer of the Post-Vulgate *Roman du Graal*, intend to remodel the Vulgate *Queste* in order to fit in with his conception of the Cycle as a whole? But regardless of the particular version of the *Queste* that would have been included in the *LA* Cycle (if we may give it that name), there can be no doubt that the quest narrative in that Cycle would, as in the Vulgate and Post-Vulgate Cycles, have been concluded by a version of the *Mort Artu*. As Sommer points out (VII, 163, n. 3), one of the prophecies uttered by Merlin clearly looks forward to the closing events of Arthur's reign. On account of Guinevere, a great battle will take place in which the knight whom Arthur had loved most (Mordred) will kill Arthur and he him (*S*, VII, 163.19–20).

Although the author of the *LA* is anonymous, he follows the tradition initiated by Robert de Boron in his *Merlin* and continued by the compiler of the *VM Suite* in claiming at numerous points in the narrative that Merlin's master, Blaise, whom Merlin visited at regular intervals, wrote down the story exactly as Merlin dictated it to him (*S*, VII, 148.6–9).[13] **[FB]**

Guiron le Courtois (Palamède)

For readers familiar with the *Lancelot–Grail* Cycle or the prose *Tristan*, the vast prose romance entitled *Guiron le Courtois* can be considered to tell the story of the 'fathers' of famous Arthurian protagonists. Characters such as Ban, Lac, Urien and Lot, known to everyone since the romances of Chrétien de Troyes, are joined by some new figures from the preceding generation, such as Meliadus, the father of Tristan, Guiron le Courtois or King Pharamond of France (the latter having been taken from other literary traditions). The action takes place when chivalry was young, that is to say at the end of Utherpendragon's reign and the beginning of Arthur's. Throughout the work, the reader recognizes the *dramatis personae* of Arthurian tradition, augmented by newly invented characters whose attributes and exploits help to explain, in a retrospective manner, certain qualities of the 'sons'.

Guiron le Courtois is one of the last Arthurian texts to remain unedited. The outline of the text is given by Lathuillère (1966) and two sixteenth-century editions are easily accessible, both published by Pickford, *Meliadus de Leonnoys* (1980) and *Gyron le Courtoys* (1977), but they do not of course reflect the medieval text very accurately, being the result of a selection made by the early publishers, who separated the bulk of the romance into two thematic 'parts', each focusing on one major character. *Meliadus* thus roughly covers the first part of the romance, *Gyron* the second.[14]

Since there is no modern edition, the text is one of the least well known, such that an overall interpretation may still seem premature. The reasons for the delay in producing studies of *Guiron* are multiple and complex; over thirty lengthy manuscripts and several fragments are known and others are constantly being discovered (Bogdanow 1967; 1969b; 1994c; Longobardi 1988a, 1988b; 1992b; 1996; Benedetti and Zamponi 1995). The manuscripts divide into no fewer than ten, sometimes strongly diverging, versions. These versions, in turn, range from what appear to be fragments, where certain adventures are unfinished, to more or less complete romances. Certain manuscripts even resemble anthologies or digests.[15] Although additions of 'new' material and omissions or substitutions of episodes are an issue, the nature of each version cannot be analysed simply on quantitative grounds, since the differences also concern structure and composition. The difficulty in defining the contours of *Guiron* is further increased by the fact that parts of the romance are found inserted in very different manuscript contexts, as if *Guiron* was considered to be freely at the disposal of other writers. Episodes of *Guiron* are found accompanying the *Prophecies de Merlin*, the prose *Tristan*, in Rustichello of Pisa's (Rusticien de Pise's) Compilation and even alongside a prose rendering of *Erec et Enide* (see n. 21 and chapter I). The quest to define the romance of *Guiron le Courtois* thus tends to become a mirage, the best example of medieval textual *mouvance*. A detailed examination of the extant versions does permit us to identify a state of the text which may be fairly authentic, but this version, as it has come down to us, is probably itself unfinished and thus attracted continuators and other *remanieurs*.[16] The result is for modern readers a very puzzling narrative, not free of internal contradictions and unresolved mysteries.

Some general considerations may help to elucidate the specific form of *Guiron* and explain why it appears so different from other prose romances. As early as 1230, the Arthurian 'chronotope' was largely saturated by vast cyclical ensembles. The *Lancelot–Grail* Cycle and the prose *Tristan* recount the 'invention' of the Grail, back in apostolic times in the East, and its arrival in Britain, the western limit of the then known world. These romances proceed to relate the adventures of the Knights of the Round Table, the death of these heroes and the demise of Arthur's realm. Every inch of land seems to have been visited, every moment in the life of the Arthurian characters covered, everything has been said. Moreover, the entire construction of these vast cycles – especially the *Lancelot–Grail* – seems hermetically 'sealed' in a genealogical scheme, in which every single aspect of the families of the Grail keepers or the Grail heroes is both sufficient and indispensable to the economy of the romance. The task of the writer becomes more and more difficult: how is one to compose an Arthurian romance without repeating what others have previously written or, even worse, contradicting the established tradition?

Certain Arthurian verse romances illustrate one of the possibilities: into the familiar background of Arthur's court, a fresh character arrives and occupies the centre of the story for a couple of years. Instead of adopting this method of filling in the gaps in Arthurian history, *Guiron le Courtois*, like *Ysaÿe le Triste* and *Perceforest* (see chapter XII), prefers a genealogical structure that widens the chronological frame, favouring an episodic rather than a linear approach. These three texts simply add, either before or after Arthur, the tale of one or more generations. *Perceforest* presents itself as a pre-Arthurian chronicle, leading up to the time of Merlin and his protégé, whereas *Ysaÿe le Triste* recounts the story of the sons of the great warriors of the Round Table after the death of Arthur. Both texts have a concise plot and a very uniform manuscript tradition. It may therefore be tempting to link *Guiron*'s extraordinarily fluctuating textual tradition, where each scribe seems to have used the extant material as a sort of quarry for his own purposes, to the characteristics of the plot itself. In *Guiron le Courtois*, there is no love potion, no Grail, and therefore no powerful and rigid 'vector', forcing the events to be depicted in a necessary order. The plot of the romance

> consists mainly of ambushes, imprisonments, abductions, unrelated to any larger scheme. Meliadus, Guiron and their friends are ready for any adventure of love or battle which comes their way, but seem to be guided only by whim. The lack of guiding principle and controlling pattern made it easy for scribes to omit, rewrite, or add episodes, according to their own taste or the taste of their patrons. (Pickford in Loomis ed. 1959*, 349)

Even if it is true that the readership around 1230 was probably more interested in continuations than conclusions, and thus was less concerned with internal coherence and overall design than we are, it is easy to see that one major objective of *Guiron le Courtois* is constant throughout the romance: the author literally lays the foundations for the fictional universe of the *Lancelot–Grail* and the prose *Tristan*. For instance, he shows the moment when Brehus sans Pitié becomes evil. He describes how famous traditions are inaugurated and well-known monuments are built, thereby linking his text to the great models and referring to them in order to legitimize all the minor customs and obscure towers and bridges he freely invents (Trachsler 2001). The large number of 'independent' stories the characters tell each other as soon as they meet is an effective way of inventing new facts and of pretending that they are already part of Arthurian memory. Thanks to this technique, *Guiron* skilfully positions itself at the centre of the literary tradition, establishing credible filiations not only with the *Tristan* and *Lancelot* texts, but also with the epic world. In one instance, Ogier le Danois is presented as a descendant of the Arthurian knight Ariohan, and on another occasion Charlemagne visits a monument built by Arthur.

It is not surprising then that the author of *Guiron le Courtois* also participates in this intertextual game, calling himself Hélie de Boron and claiming to be a companion of Robert de Boron. This is most certainly a pseudonym, but it is a significant one (see Baumgartner 1988). If the authorship of this work remains anonymous, there is slightly more to be said concerning its date. The composition of the romance is traditionally fixed with the help of a historical document (Lathuillère 1973). On 5 February 1240, the Emperor Frederick II wrote to his secretary to inform him that he had safely received fifty-four quaternions of the *liber Palamidis* (Pickford in Loomis ed. 1959*, 348). Despite some doubt as to the identification of the book of Palamedes, it is today largely accepted that our romance existed in some form before 1240 in Italy. How long before is difficult to say and depends on the dates one is willing to ascribe to the sources the author used. Since he draws on the *Lancelot–Grail* Cycle (including the *Mort Artu*) and the prose *Tristan*, a date around 1235 is generally accepted. It would be wise to remember, however, that all these texts are currently undergoing redating and may be a decade older than assumed (see chapter VII).

The emperor's letter raises the question of the title of the romance. Some critics indeed prefer *Palamède* to *Guiron*, for the author in his prologue (which may not be authentic) hesitates and wonders what would be the more appropriate name for his book (Bogdanow 1968). He then argues that it should be called the book of Palamedes, for that is the will of his lord, King Henry, who believes Palamedes is the most courtly of all Arthurian knights. Apart from the rubricator of Paris, BNF, fr. 355, who writes: 'Ci endroit commence le livre de Meliadus et de Guiron le courtois et de Palamedes' (*here begins the book of Meliadus and of Guiron le courtois and of Palamedes*), and thus places the oriental knight in the third position after Guiron and Tristan's father (Lathuillère 1973, 445), we have no scribal indication that the title *Palamedes* really applied to the romance. Palamedes in fact has only a minor role in the romance, and the titles supplied most commonly by rubricators and scribes focus logically on Guiron and Meliadus, just as did those chosen by the sixteenth-century printers.

The legacy of *Guiron le Courtois* was considerable. The romance seems to have been especially appreciated in Italy, since several manuscripts were copied there (Bubenicek 1997) and Rustichello/Rusticien used certain parts for his compilation (Cigni 1992). Some episodes of the romance were also translated into Italian as early as the thirteenth century (see Cigni 1999 on Paris, BNF, fr. 12599); Boiardo and Ariosto too were familiar with the text (Rajna 1900; Limentani 1962; Lathuillère 1966, 164–69) and Luigi Alamanni (Hauvette 1903, 302–32, 357–400) even produced a rhymed transposition of the romance. In France, *Guiron* was printed several times at the beginning of the sixteenth century, before falling into oblivion until the revival of medieval literature in the eighteenth century and the publication of the outline of the romance in the *Bibliothèque Universelle des Romans* in 1776 (Ménard 1997*). **[RT]**

Rustichello of Pisa (Rusticien de Pise) [17]

Rustichello of Pisa is first of all a name that occurs, with some variants, in the prologue to a French Arthurian Compilation and in the prologue to Marco Polo's *Devisement du Monde*. In the latter, one reads that the Venetian explorer asked a certain *Rustaciaus* (or *Rusta pisan*) to write down in order ('fist retraire par ordre') the contents of Marco's story, when they were both in prison in Genoa in 1298 (Ménard edn, I, 118). Little can be said about the circumstances in which Rustichello was captured, but we know that the prisoners were set free in 1299; we then lose track of Rustichello, since any attempt to identify him with contemporary persons by the same name recorded in Pisa has hitherto been unsuccessful (for more on Rustichello, see Ménard edn, I, 19–24).

On the basis of the striking resemblance between the two prologues (Bertolucci-Pizzorusso 2002), it is generally accepted that the 'author' of the Arthurian Compilation and the scribe of the Venetian traveller are the same person. Indeed, the difficulties raised by the two prologues are very much the same: the exact nature of the collaboration between Rustichello and Marco Polo, especially the character of the 'sources' Rustichello had at his disposal and the question of the language in which they were written, is as much discussed as the problems raised by the prologue of his Arthurian Compilation. Here is the relevant passage as it appears in one of the oldest Franco-Italian manuscripts:

> Et sachiez tot voirement que cestui romainz fu treslaités dou livre monseingneur Odoard, li roi d'Engleterre, a celui tenz qu'il passé houtre la mer en servise nostre Sire Damedeu pour conquister le saint Sepoucre. Et maistre Rusticiaus de Pise, li quelz est imaginés desovre, conpilé ceste romainz, car il en treslaité toutes les tresmervillieuse novelles qu'il truevé en celui livre et totes les greingneur aventures; et traitera tot sonmeemant de toutes les granz aventures dou monde. Mes si sachiez qu'il traitera plus de monseingneur Lanseloth dou Lac et de monseingneur Tristain, le fiz au roi Meliadus de Leonois, que de nul autre, por ce que san faille il furent li meillor chevaliers que fussent a lour tenz en terre. Et li maistre en dira de cist deus plusor chouses et plusor batailles que furent entr'aus que ne trueverés escrit en trestous les autres livres, pour ce que li maistre le truevé escrit eu livre dou roi d'Engleterre. (Cigni edn, 233).

> (*And know truly that this romance was translated from the book belonging to milord Edward, the King of England, at the time when he went overseas in the service of Our Lord God to win back the Holy Sepulchre. And Master Rusticiaus of Pisa, who is painted above, produced this romance, for he translated from the book all the marvellous stories and the most impressive adventures which he found in it; and he will treat briefly in this compendium all the great adventures of this world. But let it be known that he will treat milord Lancelot du Lac and milord Tristan, son of King Meliadus of Leonois, more fully than any other, for without doubt they were the best knights in the world living at the time. And the master will tell you many things about these two and describe many battles they fought against each other which you will not find written in any other book, for the master found them written in the book belonging to the King of England.*)

If one assumes that the passage is not merely a variation on the *Buchtopos*, these few lines provide not only the name, but also a date for the composition of the Compilation. It is traditionally accepted that the English king is Edward I and that Rustichello was handed the book he 'translated' some time around 1272, when the king, on his way back from the Crusade, was travelling through Italy. The exact circumstances in which an encounter between the compiler and the king or someone of his entourage may have taken place are not known, since there is no record of Edward having stopped in Pisa. Rustichello may of course have come into contact with the monarch virtually anywhere en route between Charles of Anjou's Sicilian court, where he disembarked, and Milan, which was his last stop in Italy. It is also possible that Rustichello himself travelled to the Holy Land, where he may have received the book, for instance at Acre, a centre of vernacular book production (Ménard edn, 23–4).

Even if nothing is known about the actual relationship between Rustichello and Edward, the well-documented interest of the English monarch in Arthurian matters makes him a likely candidate for carrying a book containing new material on the Knights of the Round Table, especially during this period. A good case in point is that Edward and his wife Eleanor of Castile are known to have been in Amiens in 1279, where the queen probably ordered Girart d'Amiens to write *Escanor*, one of the last Arthurian romances to be composed in verse, and one echoing Edward's territorial ambitions in Wales. If one turns to the manuscripts containing Rustichello's Compilation, it soon becomes apparent that, just as for *Guiron le Courtois*, the text can vary in length and content (Cigni edn, 369–70; Cigni 1993; 2000). This is most likely the result of the work's plot, which is made up of different, fairly autonomous, episodes. Dipping into the (by then) immense reservoir of Arthurian texts, Rustichello composed his *florilegium* (Cigni edn, 10) of the most beautiful and extraordinary adventures not only of Arthur's, but also of Utherpendragon's knights. This manner of composing a romance, by producing rather loosely linked narrative 'blocks' is presumably not a sign of incompetence on Rustichello's part, as earlier critics assumed. In fact this style announces the Italian *cantari*, which are essentially episodic and which abandon completely the continuous narrative beginning with the Grail's 'invention' and culminating in the fall of King Arthur used by the original French prose romancers.

This does not mean that Rustichello fails to arrange his *matière* in a chronological, if not cyclical manner: in what seems to be the most authentic redaction, he starts off his compilation with the story of Banor, the Vieux Chevalier, a miraculous survivor of Utherpendragon's times, who arrives at Arthur's court to provoke and defeat the younger generation, starting with Palamedes and ending with Karados and Yon of Ireland, not to mention Tristan, Lancelot and Arthur himself. The Compilation ends with Tristan's death, thus covering a time-span running from the beginning of the Arthurian world to one of the most significant events of the chivalric universe, and the point at which the prose *Tristan* breaks off. Five other episodes have been placed within these chronological limits: Tristan and Lancelot at the Perron Merlin, largely based on the prose *Tristan*, followed by the adventures of the Knight with the Red Shield, taken from the same source. There then follows a series of adventures involving Perceval, inspired, perhaps, by the prose *Lancelot*, into which Rustichello inserted the story of the war between the kings of Ireland and North Wales, as it appears in the prose *Tristan*. He then moves on to the story of Galehot and his arrival in Arthur's realm, before concluding with Tristan's death. Some of the episodes selected by Rustichello are real highlights of Arthurian narrative material, yet the author did little to create any narrative links between them. They follow one another barely in chronological order, held together by rather obvious transitions between the branches. The continuous presence of the characters of Lancelot and Tristan and the theme of their rivalry do form a kind of unifying thread throughout the entire compilation, but the individual episodes tend towards autonomy. A literary study of Rustichello's work centred on this new kind of aesthetics still remains to be written.

Like *Guiron le Courtois*, Rustichello's Compilation seems to have met with some success during the late Middle Ages. Vérard uses the opening episode in his edition of *Gyron le Cortoys, avec la devise des armes de tous les Chevaliers de la Table Ronde* (no date, but probably 1501), and Denys Janot incorporates several other episodes into his edition of *Meliadus de Leonnoys* from 1532. In Italy, numerous echoes can be traced in the vernacular production of romances or *cantari*, and there is evidence of a fairly similar reception in Spanish print (Cigni edn, 365–8). More surprising, perhaps, than these references is the existence of a Serbo-Russian version (see Muir 1979; Sgambati 1977–9) and a Greek verse-adaptation, the latter unfortunately only fragmentary (Garzya 1981). [RT]

Micheau Gonnot's Arthuriad Preserved in Paris, BNF, fr. 112 and its Place in the Evolution of Arthurian Romance[18]

Jacques d'Armagnac, duc de Nemours, comte de la Marche, who was executed in 1477, was one of the most remarkable fifteenth-century bibliophiles. We owe to him an impressive collection of manuscripts, including several of Arthurian prose romances, a number of which, including Paris, BNF, fr. 112, dated 1470, were transcribed by Gonnot.[19] Although in its present form MS 112 consists of three parts bound in one, originally it comprised four main sections, *Livre I* having been lost, most probably when the work was rebound in the seventeenth century. *Livre II*, with which the volume now opens, consists of 230 vellum leaves numbered 1–248, *Livre III* of 301 and *Livre IV* of 230, numbered 1–233.

At first sight it would appear that the 112 compilation is a manuscript similar to those of the Vulgate *Lancelot–Grail* Cycle, for, like a number of the latter, each of its sections is preceded by a rubric referring to the whole as *Le Livre de Lancelot du Lac*. In reality, manuscript 112 includes, in addition to portions of the Vulgate *Lancelot* and *Queste*, the whole of the Vulgate *Mort Artu*. Further, it preserves a large portion of the version of *Guiron le Courtois* found in Turin, Biblioteca Nazionale, MSS L. I. 7–9 (Bogdanow 1965), sections of the prose *Tristan*, as well as material derived from the Post-Vulgate *Roman du Graal* (*P-V*) notably portions of the *P-V Suite du Merlin* (see *Abenteuer*, Sommer edn), including the *Folie Lancelot* (Bogdanow edn 1965) and certain incidents from the *P-V Queste* (Bogdanow edn 1991–2001). And to prepare the reader for the fact that his compilation narrates much more than just the adventures of Lancelot, Gonnot specifies in the rubric at the beginning of *Livre II* that the volume includes also the adventures of that other great hero, Tristan: 'Et si parleray du tres vaillant Tristan, tres beau chevalier messier Tristan de Leonnoys' (*And I shall speak here of most valiant Tristan, the very handsome knight messire Tristan de Leonois*; MS 112, II, fol. 1rb).

Pickford, to whom we owe the only complete study of the MS 112 Arthuriad and who, with the exception of the Turin *Guiron* and the *Folie Lancelot* section, identified most of the other incidents, assumed that Gonnot had a double aim: on the one hand, to give the impression by means of skilful links that his compilation was a single long romance narrating the adventures of the main Arthurian knights, whilst in reality he sought to offer the reader a series of short, self-contained tales, each dealing with some of the incidents that befell these characters (Pickford 1959/60*, 200–1, 291–3).

However, it is doubtful whether Gonnot's aim was to produce an anthology of Arthurian tales. A closer examination of our compiler's sources and the use he made of these would, in fact, suggest the reverse. Far from seeking to offer the reader a collection of short stories, Gonnot clearly sought to produce a unified history of Arthur's kingdom from its earliest days down to the death of Arthur and his greatest knights. But whereas the writers of the thirteenth-century Vulgate Cycle of Arthurian romances did not include in their composition any of the characters of the twelfth-century *Tristan* verse romances, Gonnot, following the example of the writers of the thirteenth-century prose *Tristan*, of the *P-V Roman du Graal* and of the *Palamède–Guiron* romances (see Trachsler above), sought to widen the Arthurian background by including in his Arthuriad material from these works. However, unlike the writers of these romances, Gonnot did not himself compose the bulk of his narrative.[20] Rather, in order to produce his Arthuriad, he selected from his sources a series of incidents which he combined in such a way as to form a coherent, closely knit whole.

Hence, it is not surprising that, contrary to Pickford's assumption, Gonnot in the first part of his *Livre II* did not select extracts from the Vulgate *Lancelot* and prose *Tristan*, but made extensive use of a volume similar to Part III of the version of *Guiron le Courtois* preserved in Turin, Biblioteca Nazionale (MSS L. I. 7–9), which contains a redaction of *Guiron* distinct from any of the versions summarized by Löseth (1890; 1905, 29–32) in his *Analyses* of the Paris and British Library manuscripts. Like MS 112, the Turin *Guiron* (written after 1275, the probable date of its most recent source, Rusticien de Pise's Compilation) originally formed part of Jacques d'Armagnac's library.[21] It is probable that the manuscript used by Gonnot was not the Turin codex itself, but rather the Turin scribe's exemplar. For there is evidence that Gonnot had at his disposal a manuscript of the Turin version of *Guiron* which contained certain episodes omitted by the scribe of MS L. I. 9 (Bogdanow 1965). This common source of MSS 112 and L. I. 9 may well also have been in Jacques d'Armagnac's library.

That Gonnot should deliberately have chosen for a substantial portion of his *Livre II* and for a section of his *Livre III* a manuscript of *Guiron* similar to Part III of the Turin version (MS L. I. 9) is not surprising. For in this version material from the Vulgate *Lancelot* and the prose *Tristan* has already been skilfully interlinked with *Palamède–Guiron* themes. But Gonnot did not make a straightforward copy of the whole of Turin Part III. For although seeking, like the writer of the latter, to produce a unified whole, his aim was not the same. Anxious to produce a closely knit Arthuriad and not a history of the Brun–Guiron family, he selected from the Turin version only those incidents that fitted into his overall plan, changing where appropriate the order of events, inserting episodes from other sources and modifying or adding references to link the different sections of the narrative. Thus Turin, MS L. I. 9 begins with two incidents derived from the *P-V Quest*: Esclabor's account of how the Beste Glatissant killed eleven of his twelve sons (Turin, fol. 1ra; *P-V*, II, §§125–6) and the story of the birth of this monster (Turin, fols 1rb–3va; *P-V*, III, §§604–9), motifs to be used later in the MS 112 Arthuriad (II, fol. 176va–b and IV, fols 150va–152va). Gonnot, in contrast, begins his *Livre II* with a narrative which chronologically one would expect to find at this point, namely a heavily abbreviated account of the early life of Lancelot up to the point where he is knighted (MS 112, II, fols 1ra–7vb) and of Tristan's ancestry and youth up to Tristan's arrival at King Mark's court (MS 112, II, fols 8ra–9vb; 16ra–17ra, fols 10r–15v having been lost). These accounts of Lancelot's and Tristan's youth ultimately derive from the prose *Lancelot* and the prose *Tristan*, with which they are in parts identical. However, Gonnot copied them, with certain changes, from the Turin *Guiron*, where these incidents had already been skilfully combined, but were related at a later point in the narrative (Turin, fols 6va–23vb). Thus, when the Vulgate *Lancelot*, MS 112 and Turin describe Bannin/Banny/Bany (MS 112, II, fol. 7vb; Turin, fol. 13va; Vulgate *Lancelot*, *S*, III, 108.33), MS 112, following the Turin version, announces that the story will now turn to another matter of direct relevance to the book. This matter is the ancestry of Tristan, who, with the exception of Lancelot, was one of the best two knights of his time (MS 112, II, fols 7vb–8ra; Turin, fol. 15va).

Having named Tristan's father as Meliadus of Leonois, the author of the Turin version, as anxious as Gonnot to produce a unified whole, links this part of his narrative to the preceding portions by referring the reader for Meliadus's exploits back to the 'first two books' (*aux deux livres precedens*). But as Gonnot divided his Arthuriad into four books, not three, and presumably, unlike the Turin writer, did not include in his first book any of Meliadus's adventures, he naturally omits the Turin reference to the preceding two books. Clearly wishing, however, to interlink the various sections of his Arthuriad, he keeps the Turin version's transition from Lancelot's to Tristan's early life, which reminds the audience of facts concerning Joseph of Arimathea, whose life-story figures in the Vulgate *Estoire del Saint Graal* (MS 112, II, fol. 8ra; Turin, fol. 15va).

In the opening section of his *Livre II*, Gonnot similarly ensures the unity of his Arthuriad. He keeps the reference at the beginning of the *Lancelot*, a branch of the Vulgate Cycle incorporated most probably into Gonnot's now lost *Lancelot*, announcing that the story will later relate why Lancelot's baptismal name was Galahad (MS 112, II, fol. 1va; cf. *S*, III, 3.9–10), but subsequently, when referring again to Ban's infant son, follows the Turin codex, not the Vulgate, in repeating that he will explain later why the child was called Lancelot, despite the fact that his baptismal name was Galahad (MS 112, II, fol. 2ra; Turin, fol. 10rb: badly damaged; *S*, III, 7.29–32; cf. *LM*, VII, 10, §16.1–5).

Moreover, instead of including an account, as does the Vulgate *Lancelot*, of the birth of Merlin who, prior to his entombment by the Dame du Lac, had taught the latter all she knew of the art of magic (*S*, III, 19.29–21.38), Gonnot, like the Turin version, refers to an earlier portion of the narrative, no doubt the now lost *Livre I*, and so reinforces the link with that section (MS 112, II, fol. 2vb).[22]

Nor is this all. In the opening pages of the narrative in *Livre II*, where the text, along with the Vulgate *Lancelot*, mentions how, after the death of King Raymon/Aramons and Utherpendragon, Arthur, now king of Logres, went to the aid of King Ban and King Bohort, who were being attacked by Claudas, MS 112 adds 'ainsi que vous avés oÿ cy dessus' (II, fol. 1d; cf. *S*, III, 4.13–17; *LM*, VII, 3, §4.5–11).[23] And even more precise are the references a few lines further on. Having mentioned that Arthur, after aiding the two kings, returned to Logres 'ainsi que l'istoire a devisé au premier livre' (MS 112, II, fol. 1vb), both MS 112 and the Vulgate *Lancelot* state that Poince Anthoine helped Claudas in his renewed war against Ban. But at this point MS 112, like the Turin volume, refers the reader once more to the *premier livre* – a clear reference, like the one to Merlin's birth, to a part of the narrative in the now lost *Livre I* (MS 112, II, fol. 1vb).

As already mentioned, Gonnot, attempting to produce a unified whole, does not make a straightforward copy of the whole of the Turin exemplar. Where appropriate, in order to strengthen the links between the various sections of his Arthuriad, he inserts episodes from other sources. It is thus no coincidence that following the account of Tristan's early life, Gonnot inserts (MS 112, fols 17rb–58rb) a series of incidents that do not figure in the Turin *Guiron*, the so-called triple adventures of Gauvain, Yvain and the Morholt copied from a manuscript of the *P-V Suite du Merlin*. This set of incidents (edited by Sommer in *Abenteuer*) begins with a reference back to Arthur's departure from Morgan, who had deceived him 'par enchantement' (MS 112, II, fol. 17rb; *Abenteuer*, 1), an incident related at an earlier point in the *P-V Suite*. At first sight such a reference may seem surprising in the context of Gonnot's Arthuriad. But there is no reason for excluding the possibility that his lost *Livre I* included relevant portions of the preceding sections of the *P-V Suite*. And this would not be the only justification for inserting the triple adventures into his *Livre II*. For there are in this section incidents which at the same time link up with the preceding narrative and look forward to later portions of the MS 112 Arthuriad. One such notable anticipatory reference is to the Morholt's death resulting from his combat with Tristan in the Isle Sanxon when he came to claim tribute from Cornwall (MS 112, II, fol. 19va; *Abenteuer*, 9; cf. MS 112, II, fol. 36ra and fol. 58rb; *Abenteuer*, 64, 134). This reference not only links the narrative with the account of Tristan's early life during which in MS 112, as in the Turin *Guiron*, the Morholt heard news of his death (Turin, fol. 24ra–b; MS 112, II, fol. l6ra), but reinforces the link with a later portion of the MS 112 narrative, the Morholt's fatal combat adopted from the Turin version (MS 112, II, fols 7lva–74ra: Turin, fols 300rb–302va). Other equally notable references are to the coming of the Good Knight in the *Queste* section, to the death of Gauvain and his brothers Agravain, Gaheriet and Guerrehet in the *Mort Artu* section, as well as to the death of Arthur at the hands of his own son and the destruction of Arthur's kingdom.

After the triple adventures of Gauvain, Yvain and the Morholt, MS 112 returns to the Turin *Guiron*, incorporating from this version the delivery of Danain le Roux, the lord of Malohaut (MS 112, II, fols 58va–61rb; Turin, fols 3rb–6rb), who, according to the narrative in Part II of the Turin version, and perhaps also in MS 112 *Livre I*, had been imprisoned in the Vallee de Faus Soulas. But even if the MS 112 compilation did not include the account of how Danain le Roux came to be incarcerated, the account of his delivery is of double significance from the point of view of the overall structure of Gonnot's Arthuriad. Firstly, it brings in the theme of Palamedes's quest for the Beste Glatissant (MS 112, II, fol. 58va; Turin, fol. 3rb illegible) so important in MS 112, *Livre IV*: it is Palamedes, who, in the words of the text, is destined to kill the Beste Glatissant (MS 112, II, fol. 59d; Turin destroyed at this point) and who in quest of this creature comes one day to the Forest des Deux Voies and frees Danain by doing battle on thirty-six successive days, first with the knights of the Tours des Chevaliers and then with Danain himself. Secondly, the episode looks forward to an important theme incorporated into both the Turin and MS 112 narratives from the prose *Lancelot*: Galehot's love for the Dame de Malohaut. After his delivery, Danain, accompanied by Palamedes, returns to Malohaut, falls ill and dies within a month, so leaving the Dame de Malohaut free to love Galehot (MS 112, II, fol. 61ra; Turin, fol. 6ra). And indeed, subsequently, in MS 112, as in the prose *Lancelot*, the Dame de Malohaut and Galehot, encouraged by Guinevere, reveal their love for each other (MS 112, II, fol. 102vb; Turin, fol. 308va; cf. *S*, III, 267.18–26), the theme of their mutual love recurring intermittently until the death of the Dame de Malohaut following that of Galehot (MS 112, III, fol. 1va; *S*, IV, 156.22–5).

Gonnot's desire to produce a unified Arthuriad is likewise evident from his treatment of the incidents following Danain le Roux's death. In the Turin *Guiron* the account of Tristan's youth is followed by a considerably shortened version of a further portion of the prose *Lancelot*, namely Lancelot's departure for Great Britain with the Dame du Lac and their arrival at Lavenor (Turin, fols 23vb–24rb). This narrative, skilfully linked to Lancelot's earlier life-story by the rubric 'Comment la Dame du Lac enmena Lancelot a la court du roy Artus pour estre fait chevalier' (*How the Lady of the Lake brought Lancelot to Arthur's court to have him dubbed a knight*; MS 112, fol. 61rb) is taken over by Gonnot (MS 112, II, fol. 61rb–va). But in order to reinforce the unity of his Arthuriad, Gonnot follows the Turin version only up to the point where the Dame du Lac says farewell to Lancelot at Lavenor (MS 112, II, fol. 61va; Turin, fol. 24rb). For here the Turin version (fols 24rb–259vb) inserts a lengthy account of the deeds of the knights of the older generation, adapted from the account preserved in Paris, Bibliothèque de l'Arsenal, MS 3325 (fols 48ra–234va) and skilfully presented as a 'book' which Licanor, the lord of Lavenor, allows Lancelot and his guests to read (Bogdanow 1965, 50–2). Omitting this section, Gonnot passes straight on to the account of the knighting of Lancelot, his first acquaintance with Guinevere and his successful combats at the Dolorous Garde, which in the Turin codex follow the end of the Arsenal manuscript's interpolation (Turin, fols 259d–265d; MS 112, II, fols 61vb–67vc). But while this narrative is ultimately based on the prose *Lancelot* (*S*, III, 119.111–189.17), Gonnot here again adopts the Turin version rather than the Vulgate account. For the Turin version includes references which, not only in the latter, but also in the MS 112 Arthuriad, serve to interlink the narrative as a whole. For instance, at the point where the Vulgate *Lancelot* states that no knight ever came to the Dolorous Garde who was not killed or imprisoned there (*S*, III, 143.34–6), the Turin–112 redaction adds that the only exception was the Bon Chevalier Sans Peur (MS 112, II, fol. 64ra; Turin, fol. 262ra). And when the Dolorous Garde is finally captured, the Turin and MS 112 version adds that this event took place on the very day that Tristan killed the Morholt (MS 112, II, fol. 65ra; Turin, fol. 263rb), thereby linking these events.

But before the Morholt's fatal combat with Tristan (MS 112, II, fols 71ra–78ra; Turin, fols 300rb–305vb; 320ra), significantly already announced previously on more than one occasion, Gonnot, still following the Turin version, inserts the same account as the latter of Lancelot's delivery of Guiron from prison (MS 112, II, fols 67vb–71rb; Turin, fols 296ra–300rb), this incident also being linked to Lancelot's conquest of the Dolorous Garde both in the Turin version and the MS 112 Arthuriad. When Guiron is freed after Lancelot's successful combat first with Helin le Roux's three sons and then with Helin himself, Lancelot does not at first reveal his name, but Helin suspects who he is, for, as he tells Lancelot himself, he had heard that Guiron would only be freed by the knight who would bring about the conquest of the Dolorous Garde (MS 112, II, fol. 70va; Turin, fol. 299vb, in part damaged).

Gonnot, of course, never forgets, unlike the writer of the Turin version, that his overall aim was not to record the history of the Guiron family, but that of the Arthurian kingdom. Hence Gonnot changes or adds references. After Guiron's delivery and that of his son Galinant, Gonnot, still following the Turin version, mentions that Galinant, who had unhorsed near a fountain Tristan, Gauvain and Blioberis, as well as the knight 'de qui Dynadam se moquoit tant' (*whom Dinadan mocked so much*, MS 112, II, fol. 71rb; Turin, fol. 300rb), was killed by Palamedes. But whereas the Turin codex adds 'ainsi que nous dirons cy aprés a la fin de nostre livre' (*as we shall relate later at the end of our book*; fol. 300rb), the MS 112 (II, fol. 71rb) refers the reader for details to the *Grant Histoire de Guyron* and the *Grant Hystoire de messire Tristan de Leonois*, explaining that 'these do not form part of our present narrative'.

As in the Turin version, a few days later Lancelot departs from Helin without revealing his identity. But before continuing thereafter with the Turin version of the Morholt's fatal battle with Tristan and the latter's subsequent voyage to Ireland where he and Palamedes first became rivals for Yseut's love, followed by Tristan's return to Mark's court (Turin, fols 300rb–303vb (fols 304r–305v are missing); 320ra; MS 112, II, fols 71ra–78ra), Gonnot gives a short account of Guiron's last years spent as a hermit in the Cave des Bruns, referring the reader once more for further details to the *Grant Histoire de Guiron* (MS 112, II, fol. 71va).

Following the account of Tristan's return to Cornwall, Gonnot, like the Turin codex, resumes narration of Lancelot's adventures. Carefully linking this section to Lancelot's earlier deeds by referring back to his delivery of Guiron 'ainsi que ouÿ avés ça devant' (*as you have heard earlier*, MS 112, II, fol. 78a), Gonnot gives the same abridged version as the Turin codex of the prose *Lancelot*'s account of

Lancelot's return to the Dolorous Garde, his ending of the remaining enchantments, followed by Gauvain's successful combat with the Chevalier de la Porte (MS 112, II, fol. 78ra–vb; Turin, fols 320ra–321ra; cf. *S*, III, 189.19–194.29). The latter episode is incomplete in MS 112 owing to the loss of folios 79–87, but with folio 88 the volume rejoins the Turin codex with Arthur's symbolic dream and his war with Galehot, *le sire des Lointaines Isles*. Thereafter, still as in the Vulgate, but in an identically slightly shortened version, Turin and MS 112 relate how Lancelot and Galehot, after enjoying the love of Guinevere and the Dame de Malohaut respectively, go together to Sorelois and Arthur sends Gauvain and forty knights in quest of Lancelot.[24]

At this point Gonnot's version diverges from the Turin text. The latter, picking up from Part II of the Turin version of *Guiron* the theme of the Bon Chevalier Sans Peur's imprisonment by Nabon le Noir in the Val du Servage, relates how Nabon finally lets his prisoner go when he realizes he has lost his senses (Turin, fols 31va–317vb). MS 112 (II, fols 105rb–175ra), on the other hand, first has a further series of incidents from the prose *Lancelot* (*S*, III, 222.23-IV, 72.8) followed by a number of Palamedes's adventures not found elsewhere (II, fols 175ra–178vb). Then MS 112 (II, fols 178d–183a) gives the same account as the Turin codex of the Bon Chevalier Sans Peur's delivery and his death two years later when, on his return to Estrangorre, he is killed by Ferrant and Briandan while sitting unarmed by a fountain. But Gonnot, apparently ignoring the fact that, unlike the writer of the Turin *Guiron*, he had not previously mentioned the Bon Chevalier's imprisonment, nevertheless on introducing the account of the knight's delivery refers, like the Turin codex, to the *second livre*: 'comme vous avez oÿ ainsi que fait mencion le second livre' (*as you have heard and as the second book mentions*; MS 112, II, fol. 179ra; Turin, fol. 311va).

This oversight is, however, significant, for it confirms that the Turin *Guiron*'s exemplar is the source of MS 112. As for Palamedes's adventures, which in the 112 codex precede the Bon Chevalier's delivery, these too are of significance. In order to ensure the overall unity of his Arthuriad, Gonnot not only introduces these adventures by referring back to Palamedes's departure from the tournament in Ireland related earlier in the narrative (MS 112, II, fol. 175ra referring to fols 74va–77rb), but also stresses Palamedes's unrequited love for Yseut, whom he had first met in Ireland (MS 112, II, fols 175ra–b; 178ra–vb). For the same reason, he reintroduces a theme which, like a unifying thread, runs through his composition: Palamedes's quest of the Beste Glatissant (MS 112, II, fols 175rb–76va). And no less significantly, this series includes an allusion to Galehot's love for the Dame de Malohaut, whom Palamedes finds as a guest in Galehot's castle (MS 112, II, fol. 178ra–b). Finally, this series ends with a forward reference to the Tournament of Sorelois (MS 112, II, fol. 178vb), which in MS 112, but not in the Turin *Guiron*, follows the delivery of the Bon Chevalier

(MS 112, II, fols 183vb–197vb) and is deliberately linked to Guinevere's stay at Galehot's castle in Sorelois where she sought refuge after Arthur, deceived by the false Guinevere, had abandoned her: Galehot, to cheer Guinevere up, arranged the tournament together with Lancelot (MS 112, II, fol. 183vb).

In the Turin *Guiron* (fols 282va–283va) the Bon Chevalier's death is followed immediately by the account, adapted from the prose *Tristan*, of how the Bon Chevalier's youngest son, Brunor le Noir (later named the Chevalier a la Cote Mal Taillee), avenged his father's death. But Gonnot, obviously wishing to inter-link firmly the various parts of his Arthuriad, relates this incident in his *Livre III*, introducing it with a clear reference back to the circumstances of the Bon Chevalier's death in his *Livre II* (MS 112, III, fols 51ra–56rb). And with the structure of his composition in mind, Gonnot omits the first three incidents, which in the Turin *Guiron* follow Brunor's vengeance – the death of Leodogan, Ariohan and Lac (Turin, fols 283va–287ra), incidents which in the Turin *Guiron* complete themes begun in Parts I and II of the latter, but are of no direct relevance for the MS 112 Arthuriad. Instead Gonnot passes straight on to the following two episodes in the Turin version, the adventures of Tristan's cousin Alixandre l'Orphelin and the death of Ludinas, the Bon Chevalier de Norgales.

In the prose *Tristan*, from which the Turin writer adapted the Alixandre story, but not in the Turin and MS 112 version, the narrative is in two sections, Alixandre's early exploits being separated from the events culminating in his death by a portion of the Tournament of Sorelois. The Alixandre story being thus presented as a single narrative is for Pickford (1959/60*, 126, 187) proof that Gonnot wished to present the reader with a series of unconnected tales. But it was the Turin compiler and not Gonnot who combined the two portions of the Alixandre story. Moreover, the narrative is not treated as a self-contained episode. Like all the other portions, it is carefully linked to the preceding and following parts. Both the initial rubric and the opening section reintroduce King Mark and underline the treacherous side of his character, thereby preparing the reader for incidents in Gonnot's last two *Livres*. Thus, for instance, in *Livre III*, in a section adapted from the prose *Tristan*, there are references to Mark's disloyal treatment of Tristan (MS 112, III, fols 124vb–125ra; cf. Löseth 1890, §§251–2) whilst both in *Livre III* and *IV* there are references to Mark's assassination of his own brother Perneham (MS 112, III, fols 119d–120a; MS 112, IV, fol. 160ra) with which the Alixandre story began in *Livre II* (fol. 197vb). As for Alixandre's death, this is linked both in the Turin codex and in MS 112 to the Tournament of Sorelois: it was following the tournament (MS 112, II, fol. 204vb; Turin, fol. 294vb) that Lancelot after his departure from Sorelois encountered Alixandre and engaged with him in the battle that was to prove fatal for the latter.

In both Gonnot and the Turin *Guiron* Alixandre's death is followed by Lancelot's encounter with Ludinas, the Bon Chevalier de Norgales, accompanied by his one remaining son, Suffort, and thirty knights. The Bon Chevalier de Norgales attacks Lancelot, but he and Suffort are killed and the thirty knights vanquished (MS 112, II, fols 206vb–208ra; Turin, fols 351rb–vb, 350ra–vb). Now this episode, too, is of significance for the overall structure of the MS 112 Arthuriad. For not only is it linked to the tournament of Sorelois, but it prepares for an incident in *Livre IV*, the war between the kings of Ireland and Norgales incorporated from the prose *Tristan* (MS 112, IV, fols 61b–84d; Löseth 1890, §§492, 492a). Both in MS 112 and in Turin we are told that the Bon Chevalier de Norgales, encountering Lancelot by chance, attacked him because he wished to avenge the death of his son Yvain, whom Lancelot had wounded mortally in the tournament of Sorelois (MS 112, II, fols 206d–207a; Turin, fols 351rb–vb, 350ra–vb). The King of Norgales, on learning of the death of the Bon Chevalier de Norgales and Suffort, is all the more distressed as Lancelot is a companion of his lord Galehot, so he would not be able to take vengeance on Lancelot (MS 112, II, fols 207vb–208ra; Turin, fol. 350vb). Moreover, as mentioned above, this incident is also closely linked to the account of the war between the kings of Ireland and Norgales in 112, *Livre IV*. As both MS 112 and Turin explain at the beginning of the episode the Bon Chevalier de Norgales's sister had married the King of Norgales, to whom he had given as a wedding gift a castle called Marchot. During the lifetime of the Bon Chevalier, no one dared to question the ownership of this castle, but long after his death a dispute was to break out over this castle between the kings of Ireland and Norgales. And this dispute, as both texts announce, will be related at the end of the 'derrier livre' (*last book*; MS 112, II, fol. 206vb; Turin, fol. 351va).

The Turin *Guiron* passes on from the account of Suffort's death to an episode borrowed from Rusticien's Compilation, which serves to reintroduce the theme of the valour of the knights of the older generation, notably those of Branor le Brun. From here the Turin codex returns to Guiron and relates how, following his delivery by Lancelot, the two knights subsequently encounter each other again, but not recognizing each other, they engage in a combat and Guiron, severely wounded, retires as a hermit to the Cave des Bruns. The volume ends with the adventures leading up to the episode where Guiron's son, Galinant, mortally wounded by Palamedes, is taken by Arthur to Camelot for burial.

Gonnot, who had inserted a brief reference to the last days of Guiron and the latter's son Galinant following their rescue by Lancelot (MS 112, II, fol. 71rb–va), does not reproduce the Turin version's detailed account, but passes from Suffort's death back to the Arthur–Guinevere theme from the point where he and the Turin *Guiron* had left it, namely Guinevere's exile in Sorelois on account of the False Guinevere. Gonnot now follows the prose *Lancelot* in describing the pope's excommunication of Arthur up to Lancelot's imprisonment by Morgan; Gauvain and Yvain's quest of Lancelot; the latter's return to

Sorelois, where he is overcome with grief on not finding Galehot there; the latter's quest for Lancelot (MS 112, II, fols 208ra–236rb; *S*, IV, 72.8–154.30). At this point, Gonnot turns to the prose *Tristan* (MS 112, II, fols 236va–247va; cf. Löseth, 1890, §§34–63) as his source, incorporating episodes vital for the later portions of his Arthuriad, notably Tristan's voyage to Ireland to request Yseut's hand in marriage for King Mark and how Tristan and Yseut drank the love potion intended for Yseut and Mark. Included are also Tristan's combat with Galehot's father, Brunor, the journey which Brunor's daughter made, taking the heads of her father and mother to her brother Galehot, and the latter's combat with Tristan, all incidents which, though derived from the prose *Tristan*, link up with the Galehot theme from the earlier portions of Gonnot's Arthuriad. The last incident in this section adopted from the prose *Tristan* includes a reference to Tristan's marriage to Kahedin's sister (MS 112, II, fol. 247rb) prior to the chance arrival of the three of them in the Val du Servage, of which Nabon le Noir, a cruel giant, was the lord. Tristan mortally wounds Nabon in combat and the valley is henceforth called La Franchise Tristan. But in order to link this episode to the preceding narrative, notably the Bon Chevalier Sans Peur's incarceration in the Val du Servage (MS 112, II, fols 178vb–179ra) and the Bon Chevalier de Norgales's combat with Lancelot (MS 112, II, fols 206d–208a), Gonnot recalls that Nabon kept prisoner all those who came to the Val du Servage with the exception of two knights, Brunor le Noir, known also as the Bon Chevalier Sans Paour, whom he finally set free as he had lost his senses, and Ludinas, the Bon Chevalier de Norgales (MS 112, II, fol. 247rb).

The final episode in Gonnot's *Livre II* (fols 247vb–248ra), based on the prose *Lancelot* (*S*, IV, 154.31–155.18), brings to its conclusion the Galehot theme: when on his return to Sorelois Galehot finds Lancelot's bloodstained bed empty, he goes in search of him, but still suffering from a previous wound and refusing to eat or drink, he dies some fifteen days later in an abbey (MS 112, II, fols 247vb–248rb).

With his *Livre III* Gonnot continues his Arthuriad, making extensive use of both the prose *Lancelot* and the prose *Tristan*, but nevertheless aiming to produce a unified whole. Thus after a Prologue, in which he stresses that in his first and second *livres* he recorded the valiant deeds of the *chevaliers errans* and Companions of the Round Table, but especially those of Lancelot and Tristan, he begins his *Livre III* with an episode which not only follows on from the end of his *Livre II*, but also continues a theme begun in *Livre II*, that of the Dame de Malohaut's love for Galehot. As in the prose *Lancelot*, after mentioning Galehot's grief at not having been able to find Lancelot, there is a reference to the Dame de Malohaut who, as we mentioned earlier, died of grief on hearing of Galehot's death (MS 112, III, fol. 1ra–va; *S*, IV, 155.19–156.28). From here on Gonnot follows the greater part of the Vulgate *Lancelot* narrative, but at appropriate points inserts relevant material from the prose *Tristan*, alluding where possible to earlier incidents. For instance, after having related how Lancelot, after various adventures, brought Galehot's body back to the Joyeuse Garde (MS 112, III, fols 1va–51rb; *S*, IV, 156.29–296.18), Gonnot turns to the prose *Tristan* for some of Lamorat's adventures and those of the Chevalier a la Cote Mal Taillee who avenged his father's death (MS 112, III, fols 51rb–56rb). But Gonnot links the further adventures of these two knights by referring to the earlier incidents in *Livre II*. Thus he recalls how, thanks to Tristan's successful combat with Nabon le Noir, all the latter's prisoners, including Lamorat, had been freed from the Val du Servage (MS 112, III, fol. 51rb). And similarly he recalls, in the words of the Chevalier a la Cote Mal Taillee, how the latter's father, the Bon Chevalier Sans Peur, had been attacked and fatally wounded by Ferrant and Briadans (MS 112, III, fol. 52ra).

Thereafter Gonnot continues to interweave material from the prose *Lancelot* and the prose *Tristan*, adding where appropriate references to Utherpendragon, Lac, Guiron, Galinant, Meliadus and Pellinor (MS 112, III, fol. 52ra). No less significant from the point of view of the overall structure is that Gonnot uses the *P-V Roman du Graal* as his source for the series of events from Gaheriet's slaying of his mother (MS 112, III, fol. 21va) up to Lancelot's madness and return to Arthur's court. This section of the *P-V*, known as *La Folie Lancelot*, not only skilfully combines themes from the prose *Tristan* and the prose *Lancelot*, but includes incidents which prepare for events in the Quest section, notably the adventures of King Lac's son Erec. This was of importance for Gonnot. For in his *Livre IV*, anxious to continue themes from the earlier portions of his Arthuriad, he could not simply make a straightforward copy of the Vulgate *Queste*. Hence he combined certain portions of the Vulgate *Queste* and the prose *Tristan* with sections of the *P-V Queste*, including all the Erec adventures. The author of the *P-V Roman du Graal* concludes his Arthuriad with an account of King Mark's death (*P-V*, III, 518–28, §§707–14). Gonnot, too, wishing to round off themes begun earlier, reports King Mark's death. But he does not adopt for this incident the *P-V* version. Consistent in his portrayal of Mark as a villain, he places an account of his death, distinct from the *P-V* version, in the *Queste* section and not at the end of the *Mort Artu*. After referring to Mark's treachery in killing not only his brother Perneham, but also Tristan and Dinas (MS 112, IV, fols 16ra–b, fols 162ra–b), he relates how Dinas's two sons surprise Mark sitting by a fountain. Determined to avenge their father's death, they tie Mark to a tree where the following day he is devoured by a bear (MS 112, IV, fols 162rb–163ra).

Gonnot was a skilful scribe-compiler who knew what his aim was: to produce a comprehensive and unified history of the Arthurian kingdom which included the most memorable events not only of the Vulgate and Post-Vulgate Cycles, but also of the prose *Tristan* and *Guiron le Courtois*. And like his predecessors he knew that one of the most important literary techniques for this purpose was to have themes running intermittently throughout the whole Arthuriad until each of the threads reached an appropriate conclusion. [FB]

Notes

[1] See 'S. Bernardi Abbatis, ad Hugonem de Sancto Victore epistola seu tractatus, de baptismo alliisque quaestionibus ab ipso propositis', in Migne, *Patrologia Latina*, 182, 1041–2.

[2] For the dating of these works, see chapters VII and VIII.

[3] *Li Chevaliers as deus espees*, ed. by W. Foerster (Halle/S., 1877; repr. Amsterdam, 1966).

[4] *Le Haut Livre du Graal: Perlesvaus*, ed. by W. A. Nitze and T. A. Jenkins, 2 vols (New York, 1937; repr. 1972). Further references in *Perlesvaus*, I, 42, 457–8, 460–2; I, 148, 3169–70.

[5] *Deux épées*, 1164–5; *Suite du Merlin*, Roussineau edn, I, §104.14–16; the folio is missing in the Huth manuscript (Paris and Ulrich edn, I, 222).

[6] With regard to Rusticien de Pise's *Roman du roys Artus*, this was clearly composed after the *P-V*, for it borrowed from the latter the episode of Dalides (Bogdanow 1967; *Queste P-V*, 1, 128–37).

[7] Modena fragment II will be published by Bogdanow.

[8] *S* refers to the edition of the Vulgate Cycle by Sommer.

[9] *PP*, I, 65–6, 78, 80–1, 84–5, 101–2, 229–31; II, 25–6, 272–6, 366–7; *PB*, 259–60, 273–6, 285–7.

[10] Apart from in the *Prophecies* manuscripts, the Alixandre tale figures in four manuscripts of the prose *Tristan*: BNF, fr. 99; Chantilly, Musée Condé, MS 646; New York, Pierpont Morgan Library, MS M. 41; St Petersburg, National Library of Russia, MS fr. v. xv. 2.

[11] Sommer's theory according to which the *LA* was part of a compilation composed *before* the Vulgate Cycle (*S*, VII, 2: 'The Structure of *Le Livre d'Artus*') and based on a narrative, now lost, which was also the source of the Vulgate *Merlin* Continuation, was rightly rejected by Bruce (1923/1928*, I, 445 n. 5; cf. Whitehead in Loomis ed. 1959*, 336). However, Bruce (1919, 263–4, 265, n. 58), noticing that the *LA* related in detail certain episodes referred to briefly in the prose *Lancelot*, assumed wrongly that the former was one of the sources of the *Lancelot*.

[12] *S*, II, 113.6, 126.20, 176.30, etc.; VII, 3.30–1, 4.2, 4.10, 13.17–46, 14.6, etc.

[13] Cf. *S*, II, 179.7–8 (BNF, fr. 337, fol. 42b); II, 293.8 (BNF, fr. 337, fol. 93a); II, 207.15–23 (BNF, fr. 337, fols 54d–55a); II, 315.1–6 (BNF, fr. 337, fol. 104).

[14] Venceslas Bubenicek is currently preparing an edition of the beginning of the text.

[15] The changing form, but also the changing 'ideology' of the romance has been examined by Lathuillère and Bogdanow in several of their studies of different manuscripts (Bogdanow 1967; 1969b; 1994; Lathuillère 1979; 1980a; 1980b). See also Löseth 1890; 1905; 1924.

[16] See Lathuillère in *GRLMA**, IV:1, 610–14, but compare Bogdanow 1964a, who succeeds in reconstructing an original outline for the romance by using extant fragments like pieces of a puzzle.

[17] *Rusticien*, the form sometimes used by French critics, is the result of the Picard form of the suffix *-ellus* in *Rusticiaus* being misread as *Rusticians*.

[18] For a fuller account, see Bogdanow 2005.

[19] Like all but one of the volumes copied by Gonnot, MS 112 bears on the last folio the date when the copyist completed his work: '*Aujourduy IIIIe jour de jullet l'an mil CCC soixante dis a esté escript ce darnier livre par Micheau Gantelet prestre demeurant en la ville de Tournay*'. A 'C' has been effaced and the date is 1470, not 1370. As for the words *Gantelet* and *Tournay*, written over words in part effaced, these have probably been substituted for *Gonnot* and *Crozant*. Though now partly erased, Gonnot's signature is still visible in *Livre II*, fol. 248r and *Livre IV*, fol. 233r.

[20] The only sections of MS 112 for which no sources have hitherto been found are: (i) *Livre II*, fols 175ra–178vb (Palamedes's love for Yseut; an explanation of why he hunts the Beste Glatissant;

his delivery of a damsel; his conversation with Galehot, who announces the tournament to be held in honour of Guinevere; Pickford 1959/60*, 301–2); (ii) *Livre III*, fols 172va–177ra (Bohort's combat with the Duke of Clarence and a number of other knights; Pickford 1959/60, 308); *Livre IV*, fols 160ra–163ra (episodes leading up to Tristan's and Mark's death in a version peculiar to MS 112).

[21] The *Palamède–Guiron* romances evolved in stages. We do not know if the *Guiron* was ever available to medieval readers in its original form, but certain later writers endeavoured to reinterpret and complete the work. One of these writers was Rusticien de Pise/Rustichello of Pisa (see above), for whom the *Guiron* was essentially the story of Tristan's father Meliadus. Rusticien took over the whole of Part I of the *Guiron* (Redaction *B*), expanding the narrative both backwards and forwards. Another more extensive *remaniement* of the *Guiron* is the version preserved in manuscripts Paris, BNF, fr. 358–63. For the anonymous writer of this version, the *Guiron* was primarily the story of Guiron le Courtois, whose name he replaced by that of Palamedes in the prologue. As for the version of which portions have survived in Turin, Biblioteca Nazionale (MSS L. I. 7–9), its redactor in his turn derived some of his material from Rustichello's Compilation.

[22] Although this part of the Turin codex (fol. 6ra) is badly damaged, a few words are still legible, suggesting it had a reading similar to that of MS 112.

[23] Again the Turin codex is damaged at this point.

[24] MS 112, II, fols 88ra–105rb; Turin, fols 321rb–vb, 318–19, 323, 322, 327, 326, 324–5. 266–81, 306–11rb (cf. *S*, III, 194.29–275.28). The lacuna in MS 112 corresponds to Turin, fols 321rb–vb, 318–19, 323, 322, 327, 326, 324–5 (*S*, III, 194.29–222.22).

Reference List

For items accompanied by an asterisk, see the General Bibliography.

Texts and Translations

The Post-Vulgate Cycle and Micheau Gonnot's Arthuriad

La Version Post-Vulgate de la Queste del Saint Graal et de la Mort Artu: troisième partie du Roman du Graal. Ed. by F. Bogdanow, 5 vols, SATF, vols I, II, IV,1 (Paris, 1991); vol. III (Paris, 2000); vol. IV, 2 (Paris, 2001) [*P-V*].

Merlin, roman en prose du XIIIe siècle, publié avec la mise en prose du Merlin de Robert de Boron d'après le manuscrit appartenant à M. Alfred H. Huth. Ed. by G. Paris and J. Ulrich, 2 vols, SATF (Paris, 1886) [Huth *Merlin*].

Erec, roman arthurien en prose, publié pour la première fois d'après le ms. fr. 112 de la Bibliothèque Nationale. Ed. by C. E. Pickford, TLF 87 (Geneva and Paris, 1959; 2nd edn 1968).

La Suite du roman de Merlin. Ed. by G. Roussineau, 2 vols, TLF 472 (Geneva, 1996).

Le Roman de Balain: A Prose Romance of the Thirteenth Century. Ed. by M. D. Legge, introduction by E. Vinaver (Manchester, 1942).

Die Abenteuer Gawains Ywains und Le Morholts mit den drei Jungfrauen. Ed. by H. O. Sommer, Beihefte zur *ZrP*, 47 (Halle/S., 1913). Contains an edition of a fragment of the *P-V Suite du Merlin* preserved in MS 112, *Livre II*, fols 17rb–58rb [*Abenteuer*].

Les Enchantemenz de Bretaigne. An Extract from a Thirteenth-Century Prose Romance, La Suite du Merlin. Ed. by P. C. Smith, University of North Carolina Studies in the Romance Languages and Literatures 146 (Chapel Hill, NC, 1977). Contains an edition of fols 314c–341a of the Cambridge manuscript.

The Tale of Balain from the Romance of the Grail, a 13th-century French Prose Romance. Transl. by D. E. Campbell (Evanston, 1972).

La Folie Lancelot: A Hitherto Unidentified Portion of the Suite du Merlin Contained in Mss B.N. fr. 112 and 12599. Ed. by F. Bogdanow, Beihefte zur *ZrP*, 109 (Tübingen, 1965) [*Folie*].

Bogdanow, F. *The Romance of the Grail, a Study of the Structure and Genesis of a Thirteenth-century Arthurian Prose Romance* (Manchester, 1966). Contains an edition of 'The Establishment of the Round Table at Camelot' based on Siena MS (228–41); an edition of 'The Dolorous Stroke' based on the Cambridge MS (241–9); an edition of 'The Final Scene at Corbenic' based on BNF, fr. 343 (250–61); an edition of 'Guenevere's Death and Mark's Second Invasion of Logres' based on BNF, fr. 340 (261–70).

Lancelot–Grail. The Old French Arthurian Vulgate and Post-Vulgate in Translation. Ed. by N. J. Lacy, 5 vols (New York and London, 1993–96). Contains IV, *The Post-Vulgate*, part I: *The Merlin Continuation*, introduction and translation by M. Asher (161–277); V, *The Merlin Continuation* [end, 1–109]; part II: *The Quest for the Holy Grail*, transl. by M. Asher (111–289); part III: *The Death of King Arthur*, transl. by M. Asher (291–312); chapter summaries for *The Post-Vulgate* by D. S. King (362–80).

The *Prophecies de Merlin*

Les Prophécies de Merlin. Ed. by L. A. Paton, 2 vols (New York and London, 1926–27). An edition based on Rennes, Bibliothèque Municipale, MS 593 [*PP*].

Les Prophesies de Merlin (cod. Bodmer 116). Ed. by A. Berthelot (Cologny-Genève, 1992) [*PB*].

Merlin 1498, 3 vols (Ilkley, Yorkshire and London, 1975), III: *Les Prophecies de Merlin.* A facsimile reprint, with an introduction by C. E. Pickford, of the three-vol. work published by Antoine Vérard (Paris, 1498).

Les Prophesies de Merlin, roman en prose du XIIIe siècle. Ed. by N. Koble (Paris, dissertation, 1997).

Bogdanow, F. 1962–3. 'A New Fragment of the *Tournament of Sorelois*', *RPh*, 16, 268–81. An edition of the Modena fragment I.

Bogdanow 1972a. 'Some Hitherto Unknown Fragments of the *Prophécies de Merlin*', in *History and Structure of French. Essays in the Honour of Professor T. B. W. Reid*, Oxford, 31–59. An edition of the Modena fragment III.

Bogdanow 1972b. 'A New Fragment of *Alixandre l'Orphelin*', *NMS*, 16, 61–8. An edition of the Modena fragment IV.

Longobardi, M. 1989. 'Altri recuperi d'archivio: le *Prophécies de Merlin*', *SMV*, 35, 73–140. An edition of the fragments of the *Prophecies* in Bologna.

Longobardi 1993. 'Dall'Archivio di Stato di Bologna alla Biblioteca Comunale dell'Archiginnasio: resti del *Tristan en prose* e di *Les Prophécies de Merlin*', *SMV*, 39, 57–103. There is a *P-V* fragment on pp. 63–5; the *Prophecies* are on pp. 75–103.

O'Gorman, R. F. 1962. 'A Vatican Grail Manuscript', *Man*, 6, 36–42.

Vermette, R. 1981–2. 'An Unrecorded Fragment of Richart d'Irlande's *Prophéties de Merlin*', *RPh*, 34, 277–92. An edition of fragments 5, 7, 8, 9, 10 of Dijon, Bibliothèque Municipale, MS 2930.

The *Livre d'Artus*

The Vulgate Version of the Arthurian Romances, Edited from Manuscripts in the British Museum. Ed. by H. O. Sommer, 8 vols (Washington, 1908–16). [*S*]. VII: *Le Livre d'Artus of the MS no. 337 at the Bibliothèque Nationale, ff. 115a to 294d.*

Guiron le Courtois

Meliadus de Leonnoys, c.1532. Ed. by C. E. Pickford (London, 1980). A facsimile edition of the first part of the romance based on D. Janot's edition of *c.*1532.

Gyron le Courtoys, c.1501. Ed. by C. E. Pickford (London, 1977). A facsimile edition of the second part of the romance based on A. Vérard's edition of *c.*1501.

Anthologie de Guiron le Courtois: édition et traduction d'épisodes choisis. Ed. by R. Trachsler, with the collaboration of S. Albert, M. Plaut and F. Plumet, Gli Orsatti 22 (Alessandria, 2004). An edition and translation into modern French of §§7, 14, 18, 20, 56, 64–5, 69, 75, 95, 108–9, 112–15 of Lathuillère's digest. The text is based on Paris, BNF, fr. 350; corrections and a small selection of variants according to BNF, fr. 338 and fr. 355.

Rustichello of Pisa (Rusticien de Pise)

Il Romanzo arturiano di Rustichello da Pisa. Ed. by F. Cigni, foreword by V. Bertolucci Pizzorusso (Pisa, 1994).

Related French Texts

The Vulgate Version of the Arthurian Romances, Edited from Manuscripts in the British Museum. Ed. by H. O. Sommer, 8 vols (Washington, 1908–16). [*S*].

Lancelot: roman en prose du XIIIᵉ siècle. Ed. by A. Micha, 9 vols, TLF 247, 249, 262, 278, 283, 286, 288, 307, 315 (Geneva and Paris, 1978–83). [*LM*].

Alixandre l'Orphelin: A Prose Tale of the Fifteenth Century. Ed. by C. E. Pickford (Manchester, 1951). Edition based on a MS of the prose *Tristan*, New York, Pierpont Morgan Library, MS M. 41.

Sir Thomas Malory, *Le Morte Darthur.* Ed. by H. O. Sommer, 3 vols (London, 1891). III: *The Adventures of Alysaunder Le Orphelin*, 295–312. Edition based on British Library, Additional MS 25434.

La Queste del Saint Graal: roman du XIIIᵉ siècle. Ed. by A. Pauphilet, CFMA 33 (Paris, 1923) [*Queste*].

La Mort le roi Artu: roman du XIIIᵉ siècle. Ed. by J. Frappier, TLF 58, 3rd edn (Geneva, 1964) [*Mort Artu*].

Le Roman de Tristan en prose, publié sous la direction de P. Ménard, 9 vols, TLF 353, 387, 398, 408, 416, 437, 450, 462, 474 (Geneva): I, ed. by P. Ménard (1987); II, ed. by M.-L. Chênerie and T. Delcourt (1990); III, ed. by G. Roussineau (1991); IV, ed. by J.-C. Faucon (1991); V, ed. by D. Lalande and T. Delcourt (1992); VI, ed. by E. Baumgartner and M. Szkilnik (1993); VII, ed. by D. Quéruel and M. Santucci (1994); VIII, ed. by B. Guidot and J. Subrenat (1995); IX, ed. by L. Harf-Lancner (1997).

Marco Polo. *Le Devisement du Monde: édition critique.* Ed. by P. Ménard, 3 vols to date, TLF 533, 552, 568 (Geneva, 2001–4).

Related Texts in Other Languages

The Portuguese Book of Joseph of Arimathea. Ed. by H. H. Carter (Chapel Hill, 1967).

Livro de José de Arimateia: estudo e ediçao do cod. antt 643, Faculdade de Letras de Lisboa. Ed. by I. de Castro (Lisbon, 1984). An edition of the first 48 folios of MS 643.

El Baladro del sabio Merlín segun el texto de la edicion de Burgos de 1498. Ed. by P. Bohigas, Selecciones Bibliofilas, 2nd series, 3 vols (Barcelona, 1957–62) [*Baladro*].

La Demanda del Sancto Grial. I: *El Baladro del sabio Merlín con sus profecias.* II: *La Demanda del Sancto Grial con los maravillosos fechos de Lanzarote y de Galaz su hijo.* Libros de Caballerias 1: *Ciclo arturico.* Ed. by A. Bonilla y San Martin, Nueva Biblioteca de Autores Españoles 6 (Madrid, 1907). An edition of the 1535 Seville edition [*La Demanda*].

Spanish Grail Fragments: el Libro de Josep Abarimatia, la Estoria de Merlin, Lançarote. Ed. by K. Pietsch, 2 vols (Chicago, 1924–5). An edition of the Salamanca MS 1877.

Soberanas, A. J. 1979. 'La Version galaïco-portugaise de la *Suite du Merlin*: transcription du fragment du XIVᵉ siècle de la Bibliothèque de Catalogne, ms 2434', *VR*, 38, 174–93.

A historia dos cavalleiros da Mesa Redonda e da Demanda do Santo Graal. Ed. by K. Reinhardstöttner (Berlin, 1887). An edition of folios 1–70 of the Vienna MS.

A Demanda do Santo Graal. Ed. by A. Magne, 3 vols (Rio de Janeiro, 1944; 2nd revised edn, I, 1955; II, 1970; glossary I, 1967) [*A Demanda*].

A Demanda do Santo Graal: texto modernizado com base em cópia do século XV e nas edições Magne de 1944 e 1955–70. Ed. by H. Megale (São Paulo, 1988; repr. 1989) [*A Demanda*].

A Demanda do Santo Graal. Ed. by J. M. Piel, completed by I. Freire Nunes, introduction by I. de Castro (Moeda, 1988) [*A Demanda*].

A Demanda do Santo Graal. Ed. by I. Freire Nunes (Moeda, 1995) [*A Demanda*].

La Storia di Merlino di Paolino Pieri. Ed. by I. Sanesi (Bergamo, 1898).

Paolinio Pieri, *La Storia di Merlino*. Ed. by M. Cursietti (Rome, 1997).

Studies

Balaguer, P. B. 1925. *Los Textos españoles y gallego-portugueses de la Demanda del Santo Grial*, Revista de Filologia Española 7, Madrid.

Baumgartner, E. 1975. *Le Tristan en prose: essai d'interprétation d'un roman médiéval*, Geneva.

Baumgartner 1988. 'Masques de l'écrivain et masques de l'écriture dans les proses du Graal', in M.-L. Ollier ed. *Masques et déguisements dans la littérature médiévale*, Montreal and Paris, 167–75.

Baumgartner 1998. 'La Musique pervertit les moeurs', in *Miscellanea Mediaevalia: mélanges offerts à Philippe Ménard*, 2 vols, Paris, I, 75–89.

Bayard, M.-J. 1985. 'La Place de la femme dans le *Livre d'Artus*: un exemple de la transposition littéraire des structures sociales dans les romans en prose du XIIIe siècle', in Foulon et al. eds 1985*, I, 44–58.

Benedetti, R., and S. Zamponi 1995. 'Frammenti di *Guiron le Courtois* nell'Archivio Capitolare di Pistoia', *Lettere Italiane*, 47, 423–35.

Berthelot, A. 1993. '*Cartengles, Feragus, Mingles* et *le dragon de Babyloine:* les variations du Bestiaire apocalyptique dans les *Prophesies de Merlin*', in *Fin des temps et temps de la fin dans l'univers médiéval*, Senefiance 33, Aix-en-Provence, 53–65.

Berthelot 1994a. 'Légende arthurienne et histoire contemporaine dans les *Prophesies de Merlin*', in D. Buschinger and W. Spiewok eds *Die kulturellen Beziehungen zwischen Italien und den anderen Ländern Europas im Mittelalter*, WODAN 28, Greifswald, 15–23.

Berthelot 1994b. 'La Dame du Lac, Sebile l'enchanteresse, la dame d'Avalon … et quelques autres', in D. Buschinger ed. *Europäische Literaturen im Mittelalter: Festschrift Wolfgang Spiewok*, WODAN 30, Greifswald, 9–17.

Berthelot 1995. 'De Niniane à la Dame du Lac: l'avènement d'une magicienne', in *L'Hostellerie de pensée. Études sur l'art littéraire au Moyen Âge offertes à Daniel Poirion par ses anciens élèves*, Paris, 51–7.

Berthelot 1996a. 'Merlin du substrat celtique à la réalité politique du XIIIe siècle', in D. Buschinger and W. Spiewok eds *Le Héros dans la réalité, dans la légende et dans la littérature médiévale*, WODAN 63, Greifswald, 1–9.

Berthelot 1996b. 'Le Graal nourricier', in *Banquets et manières de table au Moyen Âge*, Senefiance 38, Aix-en-Provence, 451–66.

Berthelot 1997a. 'Brehus sans pitié ou le traître de la pièce', in M. Faure ed. *Félonie, trahison, reniements au Moyen Âge: actes du troisième colloque international de Montpellier, Université Paul-Valéry (24–26 novembre 1995)*, Montpellier, 386–95.

Berthelot 1997b. 'Magiciennes et enchanteurs: comment apprivoiser l'autre "faé"', in *Chant et enchantement*, Toulouse, 105–20.

Berthelot 1999. 'Merlin magicien?', in *Magie et illusion au Moyen Age**, 51–64.

Bertolucci-Pizzorusso, V. 2002. 'Pour commencer à raconter le voyage: le prologue du *Devisement du monde* de Marco Polo', in E. Baumgartner and L. Harf-Lancner eds *Seuils de l'œuvre dans le texte médiéval*, 2 vols, Paris, I, 115–30.

Bogdanow, F. 1955. 'The Rebellion of the Kings in the Cambridge MS of the *Suite du Merlin*', *UTSE*, 34, 6–17.

Bogdanow 1958. 'The Character of Gauvain in the Thirteenth-century Prose Romances', *Med. Aev*, 27, 145–61.

Bogdanow 1959. 'The *Suite du Merlin* and the Post-Vulgate *Roman du Graal*', in Loomis ed. 1959*, 325–35.

Bogdanow 1960a. 'Pellinor's Death in the *Suite du Merlin* and the *Palamedes*', *Med. Aev*, 29, 1–9.

Bogdanow 1960b. 'Essai de classement des manuscrits de la *Suite du Merlin*', *Rom*, 81, 188–98.

Bogdanow 1961. 'A Hitherto Unidentified Manuscript of the *Palamède*: Venice, St Mark's Library, MS fr. XV', *Med. Aev*, 30, 89–92.

Bogdanow 1962a. 'The Spanish *Baladro* and the *Conte du Brait*', *Rom*, 83, 383–99.

Bogdanow 1962b. 'A New Fragment of Tristan's Adventures in the *Pays du Servage*', *Rom*, 83, 259–66.

Bogdanow 1962–3. 'A New Fragment of the *Tournament of Sorelois*', *RPh*, 16, 268–81.

Bogdanow 1963–4. 'A Hitherto Neglected Continuation of the *Palamède*', *RPh*, 17, 623–32.

Bogdanow 1964a. 'Arthur's War against Meliadus: The Middle of Part I of the *Palamède*', *Research Studies*, 32, 176–88.

Bogdanow 1964b. 'The Fragments of *Guiron le Courtois* Preserved in MS Douce 383, Oxford', *Med. Aev*, 33, 89–101.

Bogdanow 1965. 'Part III of the Turin Version of *Guiron le Courtois*: A Hitherto Unknown Source of MS BN. fr. 112', in *Medieval Miscellany Presented to Eugène Vinaver by Pupils, Colleagues and Friends*, Manchester, 45–64.

Bogdanow 1966. *The Romance of the Grail: A Study of the Structure and Genesis of a Thirteenth-century Arthurian Prose Romance,* Manchester and New York.

Bogdanow 1967. 'A New Manuscript of the *Enfances Guiron* and Rusticien de Pise's *Roman du roi Artus*', *Rom*, 88, 323–49.

Bogdanow 1968. Review of R. Lathuillère, *Guiron le Courtois: Étude de la tradition manuscrite et analyse critique*, *CCM*, 11, 76–9.

Bogdanow 1969a. 'Morgain's Role in the Thirteenth-century French Prose Romances of the Arthurian Cycle', *Med. Aev*, 38, 123–33.

Bogdanow 1969b. 'The Fragments of Part I of the *Palamède* Preserved in the State Archives of Modena', *NMS*, 13, 27–48.

Bogdanow 1970. 'A Note on the Second Version of the Post-Vulgate *Queste* and *Guiron le Courtois*', *Med. Aev*, 288–90.

Bogdanow 1972. 'An Attempt to Classify the Extant Texts of the Spanish *Demanda*', in *Studies in Honour of Tatania Fotitch*, Washington, DC, 213–26.

Bodganow 1973. 'The Transformation of the Role of Perceval in Some Thirteenth-century Prose Romances', in *Studies in Medieval Literature and Languages in Memory of Frederick Whitehead*, Manchester and New York, 47–65.

Bogdanow 1974–5. 'Old Portuguese *seer em car teudo* and the Priority of the Portuguese *Demanda do Santo Graal*', *RPh*, 28, 48–51.

Bogdanow 1975. 'The Relationship of the Portuguese and Spanish *Demandas* to the Extant French Manuscripts of the Post-Vulgate *Queste del Saint Graal*', *Bulletin of Hispanic Studies*, 52, 13–32.

Bogdanow 1976. 'Another Manuscript of a Fragment of the Post-Vulgate *Roman du Graal*', *BBIAS*, 28, 189–90.

Bogdanow 1980. 'Old Portuguese *o bem*: A Note on the Text of the Portuguese *Demanda do Santo Graal*', in *Études de philologie romane et d'histoire littéraire offertes à Jules Horrent*, Liège and Gembloux, 27–32.

Bogdanow 1983. 'The Spanish *Demanda del Sancto Grial* and a Variant Version of the Vulgate *Queste del Saint Graal*. 1. The Final Scene at Corbenic', in *Homenagem a Manuel Rodrigues Lapa, Boletim de Filologia*, 28, Lisbon, 45–80.

Bogdanow 1984a. 'The *double esprit* of the Prose *Lancelot*', in G. R Mermier and E. Du Bruck eds *Courtly Romance: A Collection of Essays*, Detroit, 1–22.

Bogdanow 1984b. 'Le *Perlesvaus*', in *GRLMA**, IV:2, 43–67, 177–84.

Bogdanow 1984c. 'The Changing Vision of Arthur's Death', in J. H. M. Taylor ed. *Dies Illa: Death in the Middle Ages*, Liverpool, 107–23.

Bogdanow 1985a. 'A Hitherto Unknown Manuscript of the Post-Vulgate', *FSB*, 16, 4–6.

Bogdanow 1985b. 'Theme and Character: The Two Faces of King Mark', in Foulon et al. eds. 1985*, I, 89–109.

Bogdanow 1985c. 'The Post-Vulgate *Mort Artu* and the Textual Tradition of the Vulgate *Mort Artu*', in *Estudios romanicos dedicados al Prof. Andres Soria Ortega*, 2 vols, Granada, I, 273–90.

Bogdanow 1985d. 'Textual Criticism and the Portuguese *Demanda do Santo* Graal', in *Homenaje a Álvaro Galmés de Fuentes*, 3 vols, Oviedo and Madrid, II, 301–12.

Bogdanow 1986a. 'An Interpretation of the Meaning and Purpose of the Vulgate *Queste del Saint Graal* in the Light of the Mystical Theology of St. Bernard', in *The Changing Face of Arthurian Romance: Essays on Arthurian Prose Romances in Memory of Cedric E. Pickford*, Arthurian Studies 16, Woodbridge, 23–46.

Bogdanow 1986b. 'La Chute du royaume d'Arthur: évolution du thème', *Rom*, 107, 504–19.

Bogdanow 1986–87. 'The Spanish *Demanda del Sancto Grial* and a Variant Version of the Vulgate *Queste del Saint Graal*. 2. A Hitherto Unnoticed Manuscript of the Variant Version of the Vulgate *Queste del Saint Graal* and Galaad's Final Adventures in the Spanish *Demanda*', *Boletim de Filologia*, 31, 79–131.

Bogdanow 1987. 'Un nouveau témoin de la *Queste Post-Vulgate*: version du *Tristan en prose* (Bibliothèque Bodmer, manuscrit 147)', in D. Buschinger ed. *Tristan et Iseut: mythe européen et mondial. Actes du colloque des 10, 11 et 12 janvier 1986*, Göppingen, 59–74.

Bogdanow 1990. 'L'Invention du texte, intertextualité et le problème de la transmission et de la classification de manuscrits: le cas des versions de la *Queste del Saint Graal Post-Vulgate* et du *Tristan en prose*', *Rom*, 111, 121–40.

Bogdanow 1991. 'A Newly Discovered Manuscript of the Post-Vulgate *Queste del Saint Graal* and Its Place in the Manuscript Tradition of the Post-Vulgate', in *Studia in honorem prof. M. de Riquer*, 4 vols, Barcelona, IV, 347–70.

Bogdanow 1994a. 'L'Amour illicite dans le *Roman du Graal Post-Vulgate* et la transformation du thème de la *Beste Glatissant*', in D. Buschinger and W. Spiewok eds *Les Perversions sexuelles au Moyen Âge*, WODAN 46, 17–28.

Bogdanow 1994b. 'La Recherche des antécédents littéraires: un remaniement méconnu de la *Queste du Saint Graal Vulgate*, nouvelle source de la *Post-Vulgate*', in *Perceval-Parzival, hier et aujourd'hui: recueil d'articles assemblés par D. Buschinger et W. Spiewok pour fêter les 95 ans de Jean Fourquet*, Greifswald, 25–37.

Bogdanow 1994c. 'Une compilation arthurienne méconnue: le ms LV. 30 de la Bibliothèque Nationale de Turin', in D. Buschinger ed. *Europäische Literaturen im Mittelalter: Festschrift Wolfgang Spiewok*, WODAN 30, Greifswald, 19–31.

Bogdanow 1996. 'Robert de Boron's Vision of Arthurian History', *AL*, 14, 19–52.

Bogdanow 1998. 'The Importance of the Bologna and Imola Fragments for the Reconstruction of the *Post-Vulgate Roman du Graal*', *BJRL*, 80, 33–64.

Bogdanow 1999. 'The Madrid *Tercero Libro de don Lançarote* (ms 9611) and its Relationship to the Post-Vulgate *Roman du Graal* in the Light of a Hitherto Unknown French Source of One of the Incidents of the *Tercero Libro*', *Bulletin of Hispanic Studies*, 76, 441–52.

Bogdanow 2000a. 'Un nouvel examen des rapports entre la *Queste Post-Vulgate* et la *Queste* incorporée dans la deuxième version du *Tristan en prose*', *Rom*, 118, 1–32.

Bogdanow 2000b. 'The Italian Fragment of the *Queste del Saint Graal* Preserved in the Biblioteca Nazionale Centrale, Florence, and its French Source', *Med. Aev*, 69, 92–5.

Bogdanow 2002. 'Intertextuality and the Problem of the Relationship of the First and Second Versions of the Prose *Tristan* to the Post-Vulgate *Queste del Saint Graal*, Third Part of the Post-Vulgate *Roman du Graal*', *Arthuriana*, 12: 2, 32–68.

Bogdanow 2003. 'The *Vulgate Cycle* and the *Post-Vulgate Roman du Graal*', in Dover ed. 2003*, 33–51.

Bogdanow 2005. 'Micheau Gonnot's Arthuriad Preserved in Paris, Bibliothèque Nationale, MS f. fr. 112 and its Place in the Evolution of Arthurian Romance', *AL*, 22, 20–48.

Bruce, J. D. 1919. 'The Composition of the Old French Prose Lancelot', *RR*, 9, 241–68, 353–95.

Brugger, E. 1906–10. 'L'Enserrement Merlin: Studien zur Merlinsage', *ZfSL*, 29, 56–140; 30, 169–239; 31, 239–81; 33, 145–94; 34, 99–150; 35, 1–55.

Brugger 1924–5. Review of H. O. Sommer, *The Structure of Le Livre d'Artus*, *ZfSL*, 47, 319–60.

Brugger 1935–7. 'Kritische Bemerkungen zu Lucy Allen Patons Ausgabe der *Prophecies Merlin* des Maistre Richart d'Irlande', *ZfS*, 60, 36–68.

Brugger 1936a. 'Die Komposition der *Prophecies Merlin* des Maistre Richart d'Irlande und die Verfasserfrage', *Archivum Romanicum*, 20, 359–448.

Brugger 1936b. 'Verbesserungen zum Text und Ergänzungen zu den Varianten der Ausgabe der *Prophecies Merlin* des Maistre Richart d'Irlande', *ZrP*, 56, 563–603.

Brugger 1937–8. 'Das arthurische Material in den *Prophecies Merlin* des Maistre Richart d'Irlande, mit einem Anhang über die Verbreitung der *Prophecies Merlin*', *ZfS*, 61, 321–62, 486–501; 62, 40–73.

Bubenicek, V. 1993. 'Du bûcher à l'exposition au froid: avatar d'un motif hagiographique. *Guiron le Courtois* et la *Suite du Merlin*', in *Lorraine vivante: hommage à Jean Lanher*, Nancy, 285–99.

Bubenicek 1997. 'A propos des textes français copiés en Italie: variantes "franco-italiennes" du roman de *Guiron le Courtois*', in B. Combettes and S. Monsonégo eds *Le Moyen Français. Philologie et linguistique: approches du texte et du discours. Actes du VIIIᵉ congrès international sur le moyen français*, Paris, 47–69.

Bubenicek 1998. 'A propos des textes français copiés en Italie: le cas du roman de *Guiron le Courtois*', in G. Ruffino ed. *Atti del XXI congresso internazionale di linguistica e philologia romanza, Università di Palermo, 18–24 settembre 1995*, 6 vols, Tübingen, VI, 59–67.

Bubenicek 1999. 'Quelques figures de rois-chevaliers errants dans le roman en prose de *Guiron le Courtois*', *Bien dire et bien aprandre*, 17, 49–61.

Bubenicek 2000. 'Correspondance poétique de Meliadus pendant la guerre qui l'oppose à Arthur', in *Guerres, voyages et quêtes au Moyen Âge: mélanges offerts à Jean-Claude Faucon*, Paris, 43–72.

Busby, K. 1984. 'Quelques fragments inédits de romans en prose', *CN*, 44, 125–66.

Busby 1991. 'L'Intertextualité du *Livre d'Artus*', in Van Hoecke, Tournoy and Verbeke eds 1991*, 306–19.

Cigni, F. 1992. 'Pour l'édition de la *Compilation* de Rustichello da Pisa: la version du ms Paris, B.N., fr. 1463', *Neophil*, 76, 519–34.

Cigni 1993. 'Manoscritti di prose cortesi compilati in Italia (secc.: XIII–XIV): stato della questione e prospettive di ricerca', in S. Guida and F. Latella eds *La filologia romanza e i codici: atti del convegno, Messina, Università degli Stufi; Facoltà di Lettere e Filosofia, 19–22 dicembre, 1991*, 2 vols, Messina, II, 419–41.

Cigni 1999. '*Guiron, Tristan* e altri testi arturiani: nuove osservazioni sulla composizione materiale del MS Parigi BNF, fr. 12599', *SMV*, 45, 31–69.

Delisle, L. 1868–81. *Le Cabinet des manuscrits de la Bibliothèque Nationale*, 4 vols, I, 86–91.

Delisle 1905. 'Note complémentaire sur les manuscrits de Jacques d'Armagnac, duc de Nemours', in *BEC*, 66, 255–60.

Field, P. J. C. 1991. 'A New Episode from the *Livre d'Artus*', *BBIAS*, 43, 253–6.

Frappier, J. 1965–6. 'Les Romans de la Table Ronde et les lettres en France au XVIᵉ siècle', *RPh*, 19, 178–93; repr. in *Amour courtois et Table Ronde*, Geneva, 1973, 265–81.

Freymond, E. 1892. 'Zum Livre d'Artus', *ZrP*, 16, 90–127.

Freymond 1895. 'Beiträge zur Kenntnis der altfranzöischen Artusromane in Prosa', *ZfSL*, 17, 1–128.

Fritz, J.-M. 1990. 'Daguenet ou le bouffon amoureux', in D. Poirion ed. *Styles et valeurs: pour une histoire de l'art littéraire au Moyen Âge*, Paris, 37–73.

Gallais, P. 1969. 'Scénario pour l'affaire Sagremor', *Mélanges offerts à Rita Lejeune*, 2 vols, Gembloux, II, 1025–38.

Gardner, E. G. 1930. *The Arthurian Legend in Italian Literature,* New York; repr. 1971.

Garzya, A. 1981. '*Matière de Bretagne* a Bisanzio', in *Letterature comparate: problemi e metodo. Studi in onore di Ettore Paratore*, Bologna, 4 vols, III, 1029–41.

Gilson, E. 1925. 'La Mystique de la grâce dans la *Queste del Saint Graal*', *Rom*, 51, 321–47.

Guichard-Tesson, F. 1996. 'Jeux de l'amour et jeux du langage', *MF*, 38, 21–44.

Haffen, J. 1984. *Contribution à l'étude de la Sibylle médiévale: étude et édition du ms B.N. fr. 25407, fol. 160v–172v: le Livre de Sibile*, Paris.

Harding, C. E. 1988. *Merlin and Legendary Romance*, New York and London.

Hauvette, H. 1903. *Un exilé florentin à la cour de France au XVIe siècle: Luigi Alamanni, sa vie et son œuvre (1495–1556)*, Paris.

Huet, G. 1911. 'Le Château tournant dans la suite du *Merlin*', *Rom*, 40, 235–42.

Ihring, P. 1999. 'Merlin und die literarische Sinnbildung. Zur erzählstrukturellen Funktion prophetischer Rede in der Artusdichtung zwischen Mittelalter und Renaissance', in F. Wolfzettel and P. Ihring eds *Erzählstrukturen der Artusliteratur: Forschungsgeschichte und neue Ansätze*, Tübingen, 47–65.

Kennedy, E. 1970. 'The Scribe as Editor', in *Mélanges de langue et de littérature du Moyen Âge et de la Renaissance offerts à Jean Frappier*, 2 vols, Geneva, I, 523–31.

Kennedy, E. D. 1993. 'Malory's "Noble Tale of Sir Launcelot du Lake", the Vulgate *Lancelot,* and the Post-Vulgate *Roman du Graal*', in *Arthurian and Other Studies Presented to Shunichi Noguchi*, Cambridge, 107–29.

Kinter, W. L., and J. R. Keller. 1967. *The Sibyl: Prophetess of Antiquity and Medieval Fay,* Philadelphia.

Lathuillère, R. 1966. *Guiron le Courtois: étude de la tradition manuscrite et analyse critique*, Geneva.

Lathuillère 1970. 'Le Manuscrit de *Guiron le Courtois* de la bibliothèque Martin Bodmer, à Genève', *Mélanges de langue et de littérature du Moyen-Âge et de la Renaissance offerts à Jean Frappier*, 2 vols, Geneva, II, 567–74.

Lathuillère 1973. 'Le Livre de Palamède', in *Mélanges de langue et de littérature médiévales offerts à Pierre Le Gentil*, Paris, 441–9.

Lathuillère, 1978–84. 'Le *Roman du Graal* postérieur à la *Vulgate* (Cycle du Pseudo-Robert de Boron)', in *GRLMA**, IV:1, 615–22; IV:2, 166–7.

Lathuillère 1979. 'Un exemple de l'évolution du roman arthurien en prose dans la deuxième moitié du XIIIe siècle', *Mélanges de langue et littérature du Moyen Âge offerts à Pierre Jonin*, Senefiance 7, Aix-en-Provence, 387–401.

Lathuillère 1980a. 'L'Évolution de la technique narrative dans le roman arthurien en prose au cours de la deuxième moitié du XIIIe siècle', *Études de langue et de littérature françaises offertes à André Lanly*, Nancy, 203–14.

Lathuillère 1980b. 'Le Texte de *Guiron le Courtois* donné par le manuscrit de Paris, B. N. n. acq. fr. 5243', in *Études de philologie romane et d'histoire littéraire offertes à Jules Horrent*, Liège, 233–8.

Limentani, A. 1962. *Dal Roman de Palamédes ai cantari di Febus el Forte*, Bologna.

Lloyd-Morgan, C. 1985. 'Another Manuscript of the Post-Vulgate *Quest*: MS Rawlinson D. 874', *BBIAS*, 37, 292–8.

Longobardi, M. 1987a. 'Un frammento della *Queste* della Post-Vulgata nell'Archivio di Stato di Bologna', *SMV*, 33, 5–24.

Longobardi 1987b 'Frammenti di codici in antico francese dalla Biblioteca Comunale di Imola', *CN*, 47, 223–55. There is a fragment corresponding to *Abenteuer*, 92–8 on pp. 239–55.

Longobardi 1988a. 'Frammenti di codici dall'Emilia Romagna: primo bilancio', *CN*, 48, 143–8.

Longobardi 1988b. 'Nuovi frammenti del *Guiron le Courtois*', *SMV*, 34, 5–24.

Longobardi 1989. 'Altri recuperi d'archivio: le *Prophécies de Merlin*', *SMV*, 35, 73–139. There is a fragment of the *P-V Mort Artu* on pp. 112–14.

Longobardi 1992a. 'Nuovi frammenti della *Post-Vulgata*: la *Suite du Merlin*, la Continuazione della *Suite du Merlin*, la *Queste* e la *Mort Artu* (con l'intrusione del *Guiron)*', *SMV*, 38, 119–55.

Longobardi 1992b. 'Due frammenti del *Guiron le Courtois*', *SMV*, 38, 101–8.

Longobardi 1993. 'Frammenti di codici dall'Emilia Romagna: secondo bilancio', in S. Guida and F. Latella eds *La filologia romanza e i codici: atti del convegno, Messina, Università degli Stufi, Facoltà di Lettere e Filosofia, 19–22 dicembre 1991*, 2 vols, Messina, II, 405–18.

Longobardi 1996. '*Guiron le Courtois*: restauri e nuovi affioramenti', *SMV*, 42, 129–68.

Löseth, E. 1890. *Le Roman en prose de Tristan, le roman de Palamède et la compilation de Rusticien de Pise: analyse critique d'après les manuscrits de Paris*, Paris; repr. Geneva, 1974.

Löseth 1905. *Le Tristan et le Palamède des manuscrits français du British Museum: étude critique*, Christiania.

Löseth 1924. *Le Tristan et le Palamède des manuscrits de Rome et de Florence*, Kristiania.

Megale, H. 1986. 'In Search of the Narrative Structure of *A Demanda do Santo Graal*', *Arthurian Interpretations*, 1, 26–34.

Megale 1991 'Le Texte portugais de la *Demanda do Santo Graal:* les éditions de 1944 et de 1955–70', in Van Hoecke, Tournoy and Verbeke eds 1991*, 436–61.

Meneghetti, M. L. 1987. 'Palazzi sotterranei, amori proibiti', *MR*, 12, 443–56.

Micha, A. 1957. 'Fragment de la Suite-Huth du *Merlin*', *Rom*, 78, 37–45.

Michon, P. 1996. *A la lumière du Merlin espagnol*, Publications Romanes et Françaises 214, Geneva.

Muir, L. 1979. 'The Serbo-Russian *Tristan* and the French *Prose Tristan*', *BBIAS*, 31, 217–27.

Newstead, H. 1948. 'The Besieged Ladies in Arthurian Romance', *PMLA*, 63, 803–30.

Nitze, W. A. 1943, 'The Esplumoir Merlin', *Spec*, 18, 69–79.

Paris, G. 1887. Review of Karl von Reinhardstöttner, *Historia dos cavalleiros da Mesa Redonda e da demanda do Santo Graal*, *Rom*, 16, 582–6.

Paris 1895. Review of E. Wechssler, *Ueber die verschiedenen Redaktionen des Robert von Borron zugeschriebenen Graal-Lancelot-Cyclus*, *Rom*, 24, 472–3.

Paton, L. A. 1903. *Studies in the Fairy Mythology of Arthurian Romance*, Boston; 2nd edn revised by R. S. Loomis, New York, 1960.

Paton 1913. 'Notes on Manuscripts of the *Prophecies de Merlin*', *PMLA*, 28, 121–39.

Pauphilet, A. 1907. 'La *Queste du Saint Graal* du MS. Bibl. Nat. fr. 343', *Rom*, 36, 591–609.

Pickens, R. T. 1984. '*Mais de çou ne parole pas Crestiens de Troies ...* A re-examination of the *Didot-Perceval*', *Rom*, 105, 492–510.

Pickford, C. E. 1965. 'A Fifteenth-century Copyist and his Patron', in *Medieval Miscellany Presented to Eugène Vinaver by Pupils, Colleagues and Friends*, Manchester, 245–62.

Pickford 1966. 'Morgain la Fée in the *Prophéties de Merlin*', *BBIAS*, 18, 169.

Pickford 1980. 'Antoine Vérard: éditeur du *Lancelot* et du *Tristan*', in *Mélanges de langue et de littérature françaises du Moyen Âge et de la Renaissance offerts à Monsieur Charles Foulon*, 2 vols, Rennes, I, 277–85.

Rajna, P. 1900. *Le fonti dell'Orlando Furioso*, Florence.

Sgambati, E. 1977–9. 'Note sul Tristano Bielorusso', *Ricerche Slavistiche*, 24–6, 33–53.

Sommer, H. O. 1907. 'The Quest of the Holy Grail Forming the Third Part of the Trilogy Indicated in the *Suite du Merlin*, Huth MS', *Rom*, 36, 369–402, 543–90.

Sommer 1914. *The Structure of Le Livre d'Artus and its Function in the Evolution of the Arthurian Prose Romances*, London and Paris.

Struss, L. 1984. '*Le Didot Perceval*', in *GRLMA**, IV:2, 21–41.

Susong, G. 1994. 'Les Impressions arthuriennes françaises (1488-1591) et la grande rhétorique', *MF*, 34, 189–203.

Thomas, A. 1906. 'Jacques d'Armagnac, bibliophile', *Journal des Savants*, 633–44.

Thompson, R. H. 1979. 'The Perils of Good Advice: The Effect of the Wise Counsellor upon the Conduct of Gawain', *Folklore*, 90, 71–6.

Trachsler, R. 1994. 'Brehus sans Pitié: portrait-robot de criminel arthurien', in *La Violence dans le monde médiéval*, Senefiance 36, Aix-en-Provence, 525–42.

Trachsler 2001, 'A l'origine du chant amoureux: à propos d'un épisode de *Guiron le Courtois*', in *'Chanson pouvez aller pour tout le monde': recherches sur la mémoire et l'oubli dans le chant médiéval. Hommage à Michel Zink*, Orleans, 133–50.

Van Coolput-Storms, C.-A. 1999. 'Souillure, indignité et haine de soi: l'impossible rachat dans la *Demanda do Santo Graal*', in H. Megale and H. Osakabe eds *Textos medievais portugueses e suas fontes: matéria da Bretanha e cantigas com notação musical*, São Paulo, 57–75.

Vettermann, E. 1918. *Die französische Balaain-Erzählung im Huth Ms.*, Beihefte zur *ZrP*, 60, 85–193.

Vinaver, E. 1949. 'La Genèse de la *Suite du Merlin*', in *Mélanges de philologie romane et de littérature médiévale offerts à Ernest Hoepffner*, Paris, 295–300.

Vinaver 1956. 'The Dolorous Stroke', *Med. Aev*, 25, 175–80.

Vinaver 1959. 'The Prose *Tristan*', in Loomis ed. 1959*, 339–47.

Vinaver 1970. 'La Fée Morgain et les aventures de Bretagne', in *Mélanges de langue et de littérature du Moyen Âge et de la Renaissance offerts à Jean Frappier*, 2 vols, Geneva, II, 1077–83.

Wechssler E. 1895. *Über die verschiedenen Redaktionen des Robert von Borron zugeschriebenen Graal-Lancelot-Cyclus*, Halle/S.

Williams, H. F. 1959. 'Apocryphal Gospels and Arthurian Romance', *ZrP*, 75, 124–31.

Wilson, R. H. 1952. 'The Rebellion of the Kings in Malory and in the Cambridge *Suite du Merlin*', *UTSE*, 31, 13–26.

Wilson 1957. 'The Cambridge *Suite du Merlin* Re-examined', *UTSE*, 36, 41–51.

Zumthor, P. 1942. 'La Délivrance de Merlin: contribution à l'étude des romans de la Table Ronde', *ZrP*, 62, 370–86.

Zumthor 1943. *Merlin le Prophète: un thème de la littérature polémique de l'historiographie et des romans*, Lausanne.

X

ARTHURIAN VERSE ROMANCE IN THE TWELFTH AND THIRTEENTH CENTURIES

Douglas Kelly (ed.) and Contributors

Almost all twelfth- and thirteenth-century Arthurian verse romances seem to take Chrétien's romances as models to emulate, rewrite or correct (Schmolke-Hasselmann 1980/1998*; Lacy, Kelly and Busby eds 1987–8*; Lachet ed. 1997). However, of the romance subjects Chrétien de Troyes probably invented, the quest by Knights of the Round Table, Lancelot and Guinevere's love, the Grail, only the first is significant in the Arthurian verse romances composed by his successors. In this they differ from contemporary prose romances, which combine these subjects with the intention of exploring the problems arising from their combination. In the epigonal verse romances the marvellous also seems to recede in importance (Chênerie 1986*, chapter 7; cf. Cirlot 1991, 393) and, as the titles of these romances indicate, new protagonists appear alongside those made famous by Chrétien. But familiar names can play new roles, notably in the case of Gauvain and Kay. Other innovations include the appearance of the Grail in Norway in *Sone de Nansay*, and in the *Roman de Silence* a woman becomes a knight until Merlin sees through her disguise, whilst in *Floriant et Florete* a wife fights courageously alongside her husband as they make their way to Arthur's court.

Motifs and themes common in Chrétien's romances reappear, especially those from *Erec* and *Perceval*:[1] e.g. the Hunt for the White Stag, the Sparrow-hawk Contest, *recreantise* and customs such as hospitality, the abduction of maidens accompanied by a knight and challenges issued at court on a given feast day. The threat of forced marriage looms large, a common result being war against women who refuse a proposal. Although Gauvain rarely marries, he often assists in uniting those who do wish to do so; this includes obliging knights to wed when they fail to keep their promises. In the second half of the thirteenth century, prose romance begins to influence the verse romances, notably in multiple quests such as those found in *Rigomer* and in *Claris et Laris*, and by the introduction of some characters. By the end of the thirteenth century, Arthurian verse romances cease to be composed.[2]

The number of surviving manuscripts for twelfth-century romances is greater than for their epigones; indeed, the latter are dwarfed alongside Arthurian prose romance of the same century. Most verse romances other than Chrétien's survive

in only one manuscript (see chapter I). Schmolke-Hasselmann has suggested that
these romances were composed principally for British publics; if true, this may
explain their relatively limited transmission (1980*, chapters 2:2–3/1998, chapters
8–9). In modern times, some were destroyed or badly damaged in the disastrous
Turin library fire of 1904. Many survive in manuscript compilations (see chapter
XI).

Until recently, these sometimes astonishingly diverse romances have not been
subject to close reading, or have not even enjoyed much general attention.
Although the late nineteenth and early twentieth centuries produced a number of
studies comparing them with Chrétien's romances, works of reference such as
Loomis ed. 1959* and *GRLMA** treat them by and large as 'miscellaneous'
works, regarding them as the inferior epigones of greater twelfth-century masters
such as Chrétien de Troyes, the Tristan verse romancers and Marie de France.
Many, especially the longer ones, are still neglected. Most of the verse romances
were edited in the late nineteenth or early twentieth century, but many of these
editions are hard to find today, or they survive in a deteriorated state. Moreover,
many were prepared by methods of textual criticism that do not meet current
standards. Editions published or forthcoming have begun to correct this problem,
thus making these romances accessible once more to broader scholarly scrutiny.

Chrétien's rise to critical prominence in the middle of the twentieth century
tended to eclipse these romances. However, the publication in 1980 of Schmolke-
Hasselmann's *Der arthurische Versroman* offered a correction to received scholarly
opinion concerning their 'miscellaneous' character. The English translation of
this volume (1998) will no doubt spur greater interest; the Foreword by Keith
Busby, a critical summary of verse romance scholarship since 1980, is essential
reading. Chênerie's *Le Chevalier errant**, published in 1986, is an important study
of the themes and motifs, and Trachsler's annotated bibliography and review of
scholarship will facilitate study of these romances (1997*, 19–22, 25–31, 59–63;
see also Busby and Grossweiner 1996). Trachsler's research has also broadened
the scope of investigation into the realms of intertextuality (including topical
historical allusions) and of the history of medieval French literature. The originality of these romances can now be appreciated, especially the way in which they
redefine and rewrite Chrétien's concept of adventure, and in their remarkably
diverse treatment of Gauvain, who from an exponent of ideal knighthood now
becomes an alleged murderer, philanderer and misogynist lover. In many ways,
the diverse representation of Arthur's nephew is characteristic of the diverse,
sometimes quite original characterization of the knights and ladies who populate
these works. An especially interesting development is the problem of identity,
especially that of Gauvain. Topoi[3] such as appearance (including portraits),
name, gender, age and even death are sources of original, often problematic
invention (Van Coolput-Storms 1994; Maddox 2000*; Cirlot 2001; Corbellari

2001). Motifs are also invested with new meaning. Several recent studies include Arthurian verse romances in their analysis of motifs such as secrecy, silence and the sword (Cirlot 1991, 395; James-Raoul 1997*; Le Nan 2002*).

The originality of these romances is evident in other ways too. First, Gautier d'Arras and the author of *Galeran de Bretagne* extend the range of the Matter of Britain in the twelfth and thirteenth centuries, perhaps reflecting the influence of Marie de France or the anonymous lays. However, Chrétien's influence is paramount, not so much because his achievements impose constraints or limitations on his successors (although there is some evidence of this, Schmolke-Hasselmann 1980*, 29–34/1998, 34–40), but also because his art of narrative composition suggested how the new writers might innovate (Warning in *GRLMA**, IV:1, 25–59; Schmolke-Hasselmann 1980/1998*; 1983; Kelly 1992*; Mora 2001). Thus, adaptations and corrections were common in recycling Chrétien's themes and motifs (Mauritz 1974; Bozóky 1984*; Halász 1992), and these adaptations derive as much from a desire to write new stories as from a serious questioning of Chrétien's achievements (Schmolke-Hasselmann 1981*; Adams in Lacy, Kelly and Busby eds 1987–8*, I, 141–65; Lacy in *ibid.*, I, 33–56; Cirlot 1991). For example, Chrétien's implicit *jeu parti* mode that contrasts romances such as *Erec* and *Yvain* – does love or the tournament make the better knight? – is apparent in his successors, as when Meraugis and Gorvain Cadruz debate the relative merits of courtliness and beauty in love. Gauvain too offers a potential contrast with the new knights introduced to the fellowship of the Round Table in these romances. Parody is also a factor in rewriting, as are comedy and even farce (see Ménard 1969; Gravdal 1989; Baumgartner 1990). Perhaps most significant is the way in which each author rewrites known characters or describes new ones on a vertical axis defined by degrees of excellence (Vitz 1989, chapter 1). In this way, given attributes may enhance or degrade the stereotypical views of a particular knight or lady as variable human specimens of a perceived ideal type. The nature of stock figures varies from romance to romance; for example, Lancelot becomes an idle kitchen scullion in *Rigomer*; Kay in *Escanor*, rendered more courtly by the fact that he falls in love, contrasts dramatically with the felonious seneschal of *Yder*. Thus, in these romances new characters are often brought into the Arthurian pantheon, but new meanings are not infrequently attached to traditional characters.

The most intriguing adaptations occur in the depiction of the character of Gauvain.[4] Although Chrétien foregrounds him in all his romances, he is not a titular knight in any of them. Perhaps this perceived failure to write a Gauvain romance inspired a distinct group of romances that make Arthur's nephew the main protagonist or a major actor in their plot, whilst probing anew qualities and defects in his character and actions that Chrétien had already suggested. In *Rigomer*, for example, Gauvain alone among more than fifty Round Table

Knights, including Lancelot, achieves the redoubtable quest to terminate the enchantments of Rigomer Castle; yet the same romance also casts aspersions on his character. In other romances his alleged murder of fellow knights or other innocent persons, a motif borrowed from Chrétien, raises serious questions concerning the quality of his chivalry. Gauvain's name, and therefore his identity, is also at issue in the *Atre périlleux*. On the other hand, his role as an attractive sexual partner who remains celibate admits of more positive adaptations: he marries in *Beaudous* and *Floriant*, and he is willing to marry, until rejected in *Gliglois,* betrayed in *Rigomer* or spurned in the *Chevalier à l'épée*. These romances also blend misogynist motifs into their apparent comedy (Baumgartner 1990; De Looze 1995).

Three major features characterize the verse romances' adaptation of the *conjointure* principle inherited from Chrétien, largely because of Gauvain's prominence (Cirlot 1991, 393–5). For example, Gauvain's reputation does not have to emerge through a crisis; when called into question, it needs merely to be restored. Moreover, the absence of a quest for identity tends to deprive quests of a goal, thus permitting the return of *errances* in place of the goal-orientated quest and creating a more centrifugal or random narrative (Bruckner in Lacy, Kelly and Busby eds 1987–8*, I, 223–65; Lacy 1993). Finally, the doubling of knights, either through the introduction of Gauvain's son or another, new protagonist, tends to juxtapose narratives, rather than subordinate them, as is usual in Chrétien and the prose romances (except, perhaps, in *Perceval*; Meneghetti 1984). This juxtaposition leads to the extensive use of interlace in the second half of the thirteenth century (Kelly 1969; Combes 1992–5, 164–8), as well as to the multiplication of motifs beyond what was typical in Chrétien (Lacy 1993). Interlace introduces more new or recycled names from Arthurian tradition, whilst multiplying, lengthening and complicating the plots. However, unlike the prose romances that probably inspired this use of interlace, the hierarchy of knights suggested by the titles is more imposed than justified by careful moral or social standards.

All Arthurian verse romances use octosyllabic rhyming couplets, with occasional insertions of prose or other kinds of verse. Studies of versification and rhyme are rare, as are those of related topics such as rhetorical embellishment, orality and performance, unless by performance one understands manuscript layout (Huot 1987; Busby 2002*). The borrowing of passages from earlier romances occurs in *Fergus*, *Floriant et Florete* and *Claris et Laris*; recent studies suggest that more than plagiarism is at work in these instances (Kelly 1992*, 292–301). Social and moral issues have been explored in the context of audiences, especially conservative, French-speaking audiences in Britain, for which a number of verse romances may have been written and whose concerns they seem to mirror (Schmolke-Hasselmann 1980*, chapter 2:3/1998, chapter 9). Yet their tendency to cover contemporary reality with an idealized patina complicates interpretation of their social and moral relevance (Chênerie 1986*, 79; cf. Cirlot 1991, 394–5; Accarie 1998; Ferroul 1999).

Since serious study and evaluation of thirteenth-century Arthurian verse romances is relatively recent, it is still too early for a thorough assessment of their significance (Trachsler 1997*, 307–8; Busby in Schmolke-Hasselmann 1998*). Much remains to be done. It is important, therefore, to consider not only what progress has been made in the study of each romance treated below, but also the implications of such progress for the other romances in the corpus. In this way, their originality and variety may emerge more clearly, as will a better appreciation of what they have in common and what, separately, they have to offer.

Given these constraints, instead of attempting somewhat prematurely to offer a sophisticated typology of the verse romances, this chapter groups them rather superficially. Most verse romances can be termed Arthurian because of their close or distant connection with Arthur's court. However, some which are not strictly speaking Arthurian, but belong nevertheless to the Matter of Britain, are included, in conformity with the scope of the present volume. Except for their length, the romances belonging to the Matter of Britain are more akin to narrative lays; they have been included as they use motifs typical of both the Matter of Britain and Arthurian romance. But in addition, their inclusion corresponds to a recent tendency to look outside the Arthurian tradition for influences, intertextual links and innovations in genre and narrative (Berthelot 1991; Sturm-Maddox and Maddox 1993; Kay 1995; Trachsler 2000, esp. on *Sone* and *Silence*, 108–26).

The Breton romances are treated first. These narratives are related in subject matter to Breton lays and are therefore part of the Matter of Britain. The second group of romances makes Arthur's nephew Gauvain the principal protagonist. The third group focuses on Gauvain's sons, introducing a new generation of Round Table knights by making the traditionally celibate hero a father; Gauvain himself remains prominent. The next group links new, unrelated knights to Gauvain, continuing Chrétien's practice of introducing fresh heroes and heroines into the romance corpus. The fifth group reflects later thirteenth-century developments, where Gauvain is no longer a major protagonist. However, the number of knights whose adventures are related multiplies, so that verse romance becomes defined by the multiple quest. The proliferation of quests produces narrative diversity, but the technique of interlace allows authors to integrate the various quests into a coherent narrative. A final group of hybrid romances with loose connections to the Matter of Britain or to Arthur himself concludes the chapter.

The individual sections are identified by the title of the romance treated. Many romances are anonymous, so names of authors and narrators (on their diverse narrators, see Berthelot 1991; Halász 1992) are discussed within each section. The contributions are roughly tripartite. Treatment of factual matters such as title, manuscripts, editions and attribution is followed by a plot summary and finally by a discussion of issues of interpretation raised by modern scholarship. [DK]

Breton Romances[5]

Ille et Galeron

Gautier d'Arras wrote two romances: *Eracle* and *Ille et Galeron*. He worked in the same milieu as Chrétien de Troyes and is regarded as one of Chrétien's principal literary rivals and also as the creator of an alternative romance aesthetic (Pierreville 2001). Cowper (edn, x–xiv) identified the poet with a certain Gualterus de Atrebato who appears as a witness on numerous documents associated with the court of Philippe d'Alsace; but this evidence is by no means conclusive. Gautier was almost certainly a *clerc* familiar with court life (Renzi 1964), writing for a courtly audience. He was acquainted with a broad range of vernacular literature, including troubadour lyric poetry, *chansons de geste*, *romans antiques*, Wace's *Brut* and narrative *lais*.

Ille is linked to Arthurian material through its Breton location and its intertextual relationship with Marie de France's *Eliduc*. The hero, Ille, is introduced as the son of Eliduc; his story is a careful reworking of the 'man with two wives' folktale that underlies Marie's *lai*. Critical opinion has been divided over whether *Ille* represents a direct response to *Eliduc* or a parallel rewriting of similar Celtic source material. The number of similarities in incidental detail, as well as in plot outline, indicates that Marie's poem was probably Gautier's starting-point. The modifications made to the story-line by Gautier can therefore be read as a critique of the *lai*, thus giving an interesting insight into the reception of Breton material in the last third of the twelfth century.

Ille survives in two manuscripts, which differ markedly in length, and present different versions of the central episode of the hero's loss of an eye in combat. In the longer version found in BNF, fr. 375 (*P*) Ille is injured as a result of an ill-judged joust in a tournament; in the shorter version, preserved in the Wollaton manuscript at the University of Nottingham (*W*), he is injured whilst besieging a castle during the course of a war. Both versions may well be by Gautier (Fourrier 1960, 179–313); the evidence suggests that *W* is probably a revision of *P*. *P* is dedicated to the Empress Beatrice of Burgundy, wife of Frederick Barbarossa; *W* contains at the end an additional dedication to Thibaut V, Count of Blois, which suggests that the revised version was prepared for a new patron. Both versions were composed between 1167 (the date of Beatrice's coronation) and 1191 (the death of Thibaut V). Though Fourrier argued for a date of composition in the late 1170s or early 1180s, most critics now follow Calin (1959) in dating *Ille* to the early 1170s.

The outline of the story is broadly the same in both manuscripts. Dispossessed as a boy by his father's enemy Hoel, Ille returns to Brittany as a knight, defeats Hoel and is made seneschal by Duke Conain. He falls in love with the duke's sister Galeron and marries her, despite opposition from her rejected suitors. Having lost an eye in combat, Ille flees to Rome, convinced that Galeron will reject him because of the loss; there he once again rises to the rank of seneschal and the emperor's daughter Ganor falls in love with him. Unable to discover the whereabouts of Galeron, who had set out from Brittany to find him, Ille agrees to marry Ganor.

On the wedding day Galeron reappears and offers to become a nun in order to allow the marriage to take place; Ille refuses and returns to Brittany with her, much to Ganor's distress. Later, Galeron does enter a convent in fulfilment of a vow made in childbirth. Hearing that Ganor is under attack from the Emperor of Constantinople, whose hand she has refused, Ille, torn between his former love for Galeron and his growing tenderness towards Ganor, returns to Rome. He defeats the invaders, rescues Ganor from treacherous barons who were plotting to hand her over to the Greeks, marries her and becomes emperor himself.

One of *Ille*'s most remarkable features is its complete rejection of the *merveilleux*: Gautier explicitly criticizes the fantastic elements in some *lais*, which make them difficult to take seriously (934–6). Despite its Celtic setting, Gautier's Brittany is very different from the atemporal land of mystery and magic associated with the *lais* (Renzi 1967). Geography, topography and action are firmly grounded in contemporary reality, and the romance also contains a number of allusions to historical events of the later twelfth century. A concern with psychological realism informs the portrayal of the hero's social inferiority complex (Rauhut 1978), the analysis of the process of falling in love and the contrasting portraits of the two female protagonists. Gautier restructures the story of the man with two wives, so that the hero's relationships take place in series rather than in parallel: the centre of gravity of his romance is the love between husband and wife, not the illicit passion found in Marie's *Eliduc*. The roles of the two women are transformed: Gautier replaces passive victims with active heroines and introduces the notion of feminine *aventure* (Wolfzettel 1990a). Contemporary debates about love and marriage are reflected in the motif of Ille's disfigurement (which closely parallels one of the 'cases' in Andreas Capellanus's *De amore*), and in the assumption that a husband is free to remarry if his wife enters a nunnery (Schnell 1982). Love is also closely interwoven with broader social and political concerns (Wolfzettel 1990b and 1992); both love and political success are linked to personal merit rather than to wealth or rank (Leone 1991). Ille's rise to power in Brittany and Rome, two realms brought to the brink of collapse by weak leadership, represents the renewal of political authority through a return to the fundamental values of prowess and *cortoisie* (Castellani 1990).[6]

Gautier's style and narrative technique have often been compared, sometimes unfavourably, with those of Chrétien de Troyes (Renzi 1964; Nykrog 1973; Offord 1979; Leone 1991; Pierreville 2001). King (1996) notes that both his romances are composed of poetic tableaux designed to lend visual power to the narrative. Particularly striking in *Ille* are the skilful handling of metaphor, complex combinations of rhetorical devices in internal monologues, lively and well-constructed scenes of combat (Burgess 1989) and the almost total absence of descriptions of people and places. Repetition is an important structuring device, ranging from the use of alliteration and anaphora to the doubling of plot elements, such as weak rulers and journeys between Brittany and Rome (Batany 1974; Pierreville 1994). Also worthy of note are the consistent use of proverbial expressions (Schulze-Busacker 1985, 64–75) and the narrator's moralizing interventions, many of which point to the major themes of proper knightly conduct in war, peace and love. [PE]

Galeran de Bretagne

The plot of *Galeran de Bretagne* unfolds by and large in a Breton setting. The titular hero is the son of Count Alibran of Brittany, but, as Jean Dufournet has noted, the romance departs from and, indeed, rejects marvellous motifs familiar in the Matter of Britain tradition (Dufournet transl., 10). The one brief reference to Arthur compares the king's combat with a cat (*chapelu*) to a character's anger during a chess game (5070–1). In fact, the romance turns away from a world that is obviously imaginary, whilst multiplying allusions to the contemporary, early thirteenth-century world.

The one extant manuscript (BNF, fr. 24042) lacks the beginning; in addition, there is a lacuna after line 1128. The loss of the first folio would be all the more unfortunate if it identified a patron. The author's language is Franco-Picard, from a region not too far from the Île-de-France (Foulet edn, xiii–xix, xxx–xxxi), and in the last line he names himself as Renans. Langlois (1926–8, I, xxvi, 1–7) first suggested identifying this Renans with Jean Renart. Foulet accepted this identification and corrected the manuscript reading 'Renans' to 'Renars' (7798; see the note on p. 255). But this attribution has been widely contested; scholars generally agree in naming the author Renaut. More recent studies have demonstrated convincingly that Renaut and Jean Renart are different authors (Lejeune-Dehousse 1935, 24–34; Hoepffner 1936; Lindvall 1982). Similarities between *Galeran* and Jean Renart's writings are now attributed to the latter's influence. The identification of Renaut with Renaut de Bâgé, author of the *Bel Inconnu* (Guerreau 1982) has also been rejected (*Bel Inconnu*, Fresco edn, xii–xiii). In view of these factors, the date proposed by Foulet, between 1195 and 1220, is inaccurate. *Galeran* certainly follows *L'Escoufle*, *Meraugis de Portlesguez* (Renaut knows the character Lidoine) and *Folque de Candie* (there is an allusion to the Saracen princess Anfelise). Lejeune dates the romance to 1205–8 (*GRLMA**, IV:2, 193), but Dufournet believes that *Guillaume de Dole* also influenced Renaut, which, if true, would place the date of composition between 1216 and 1220 (Dufournet 1996, 9).

A noble lady named Gente gives birth to twin girls. Fearful of being accused of infidelity, she entrusts a young valet with the task of abandoning one of her daughters in a place where she will be cared for properly. To this end, Gente puts the little girl in a sumptuous cradle together with valuable effects that reveal her noble birth: a marvellous pillow filled with phoenix down and a precious covering embroidered by Gente herself. The valet deposits the child in the forked trunk of an ash tree outside a convent. She receives the name Fresne from the tree in which she is found and is brought up by the abbess and her chaplain, Lohier, together with the abbess's nephew, the young Galeran, son of the Count of Brittany.

The children fall in love, eventually confessing their feelings to each other. Their idyllic life continues for a time, thanks to the chaplain's discretion and good will. Yet clouds soon darken the young couple's happiness. Although Galeran promises to marry Fresne, after his parents' death he must leave her to return to Brittany in order to succeed his father. Meanwhile, the abbess learns of the young couple's love. Outraged at the prospect of a mismatch if Galeran marries Fresne, she drives Fresne from the convent. Taken in by a burgess in Rouen, Fresne earns her keep by needlework. But Galeran has not forgotten her. Trained as a knight at the court of the Duke of Lorraine in Metz, he resists marriage until, during a tournament in Rheims, he meets her twin, Flourie. Struck by her resemblance to Fresne (5530–1), Galeran consents to marry her, but not without heartbreak at the thought of losing Fresne. News of the impending marriage reaches Fresne, and just as the marriage is about to be celebrated, she appears, clothed in the splendid attire she sewed from the cloth that her mother had embroidered and placed in her cradle. Gente immediately recognizes her lost daughter by the cloth and weeps joyously at having recovered her. Galeran marries Fresne, whilst Flourie withdraws into a convent.

The basic motifs of *Galeran* are such that it is difficult to interpret their social and moral relevance. The birth of twins, an abandoned child and recognition by means of familiar objects are also found in Marie de France's *Le Fresne*, to which Renaut shows his indebtedness by borrowing the heroine's name. But to this backdrop, he adds another element, that of the thwarted love of two children. Early in the romance (516–17), he alludes to the story of *Floire et Blancheflor*, and he also draws abundantly on the fate of the young lovers in Jean Renart's *L'Escoufle*. Finally, he adapted the motif of 'the man with two wives' found in

Marie de France's *Eliduc*, Gautier d'Arras's *Ille et Galeron* and Thomas's *Tristan*. Galeran voices his tribulations in long monologues that echo Tristan's doubts and hesitations before marrying Yseut of the White Hands; his delight in sensual play with his beloved's image embroidered on a sleeve recalls the way Tristan withdraws into the *Salle aux images* in search of intimate contact with Queen Yseut's likeness (Peron 1992; Van Coolput-Storms 1994, 105–6; Grimbert 2005).

Intertextuality is clearly important in *Galeran* (Hoepffner 1930; 1936, 208–29; Grossel 1996). But if this feature of the romance seems particularly attractive today, it was not always so. Branded a common plagiarist by Wilmotte (1928), Renaut certainly exploits the works he knows. Yet he does so with skill and originality, bequeathing to posterity a romance that is richly rewarding, subtle, interesting and of great charm.

Certainly, Renaut suffers somewhat from comparison with Jean Renart, a brilliant forebear who fascinated him, but from whom he differs markedly. Both evidently belong to the same romance tradition that rejects the marvellous characteristic of Arthurian romances in favour of realistic features, with descriptions of towns peopled with craftsmen and burgesses, geographical realism (Brittany, Normandy, Champagne, Lorraine) and details of daily life, especially of beautiful objects such as embroidery. Psychological analyses reveal the characters' complexity through lively dialogue and monologue (Lyons 1965a, 62–82; 1965b; Lejeune, *GRLMA**, IV:1, 439; *Galeran*, Dufournet transl., 10–15). But Renaut is more of a moralist than Jean Renart. With marked religious sensibility (Hoepffner 1936, 220–4), he depicts characters brought up in a courtly tradition, anxious to enter marriage undefiled, attentive to social distinctions and disdainful of stooping to actions incompatible with their nobility.

The originality of *Galeran* is evident first and foremost in the way it distinguishes constantly between surface and interior, body and heart, portrait and person, shape and essence, illusion and truth. The plot tells how its protagonists overcome a painful transition during which objects and persons seem to mirror one another. Individuals are torn between mutually contradictory forces, before achieving a happy resolution of their problems. Indeed, the principal characters reject illusions, which enables them to grasp the reality that finally unites them (Plasson 1973, 680). [CVCS]

Arthurian Romances: Gauvain Romances

Le Chevalier à l'épée and *La Mule sans frein*

Gauvain entered French literature in a largely supportive role. He was a model knight with whom individual heroes could be compared and against whom their accomplishments or failures could be measured. In Chrétien's first four romances he is a prominent but not a leading character, so it is not surprising that he should have been promoted to centre stage elsewhere. This happens in two short works, *Le Chevalier à l'épée* and *La Mule sans frein*. Both by their length and their relatively straightforward language and technique, they seem intended for recitation in a single session. Copied consecutively in a single manuscript, Bern, Burgerbibliothek, MS 354, they are linguistically very close to Chrétien and datable to the late twelfth or early thirteenth century. Although their authorship is uncertain, they could have been by the same poet. This raises an intriguing possibility.

Each addresses its public in a way reminiscent of Chrétien's prologues, where he justifies his work and identifies himself in the third person; this he does in all his romances except *Yvain*, where he leaves his name until the end. The poet of the *Chevalier* speaks of the impossibility of recounting all of Gauvain's virtues. Yet that will not deter him from having his say:

> Trop ert preudon a oblïer.
> Por ce me plest a reconter
> Une aventure tot premier
> Qui avint au bon chevalier. (25–8)

(*He was too worthy a man to be forgotten; and so I am happy to be the very first to relate an adventure which befell the good knight.*)

This makes little sense unless the author is naming himself as Chrétien and declaring his intention to repair his understandable omission. Such appears to have been the interpretation of the person who later copied Chrétien's name into the margin of the manuscript. His authorship was in fact generally accepted up to the late eighteenth century. In his German adaptation in 1777 Christoph Martin Wieland names Chrétien as its author.

The prologue to the *Mule* is closely based on that of *Erec*, with the line 'Por ce dist Crestïens de Troies' replaced by 'Por ce dist Paiens de Maisieres', a possible pseudonym in which the antonym of Chrétien is coupled with a place-name found in southern Champagne. With both short romances thus ascribed, directly or indirectly, to the master, it must be concluded that either he was their author, or that one or two of his followers used not only a good deal of his material but also his name to promote their Arthurian stories. If by Chrétien himself, these texts might be thought of as 'pot-boilers', produced towards the end of his career. And if the *Perceval* has come down as essentially the conflation of two substantial fragments, one on Perceval and one on Gauvain, then the prologue to the *Chevalier* might reflect Chrétien's regret at not yet having brought the latter to a conclusion.

Le Chevalier à l'épée

Leaving court dressed like a dandy, Gauvain loses his way in the forest. A knight gives him hospitality there and in the morning precedes him to his home. Once there, Gauvain is denied nothing, including the company that night of the man's beautiful daughter. Despite the girl's own warnings and the inopportune interventions of an enchanted sword, he survives with only two slight wounds. Next morning the amazed host recognizes him as Gauvain and gives him his daughter in marriage. Much later, whilst leaving the castle with the girl, Gauvain goes back to fetch her beloved hounds. When he returns, a knight appears and challenges him for his wife. Unimpressed by Gauvain's qualities as a husband, she chooses to leave with the stranger. Her dogs, however, when put to the same test, opt for Gauvain's company. He slays the objecting knight, but, when his wife tries to make her peace, he abandons her with a misogynistic tirade and returns to court with his sorry tale.

Around 1155 Wace had departed from his source to have Gauvain sing the praises of peace, notably because it gave ample opportunity for *drueries* ('love-making'; *Brut*, 10767–72). This, or something similar, could have inspired the portrayal of Gauvain the philanderer in verse romances such as the *Chevalier*. Since it shows close knowledge of most of Chrétien's works, it could be based on an encounter in the *Perceval*, where the king of Escavalon sends the hero ahead to enjoy the love of his sister, but to ill effect. This material would then have been combined with two widespread motifs, the perilous bed and the seduction test, as well as with the faithful-dog motif of the final episode.[7] In this well-told story, the poet's purpose is not to develop Gauvain's character, but to burlesque his qualities as a philanderer, and hence bring into focus the picture of him created in the *Perceval*. Apparent inconsistencies, as in the character of the daughter turned wife, may be read in this context.

La Mule sans frein

A girl arrives at court on a mule lacking a bridle, which, she claims, has been wickedly taken from her. If any knight should restore it, she would be entirely his. Her mule will guide him on the journey. Kay volunteers and heads for the forest, where terrifying beasts kneel in honour of the mule and its owner. He passes first a stinking valley full of fire-breathing dragons, then a wintry plain and a beautiful spring, before arriving at a black gulf spanned by a plank. Terrified and filled with shame, he returns to court. Gauvain volunteers for the search. Before he leaves, the mule's owner honours him, unlike Kay, with a kiss. He follows Kay's route up to the 'devil's bridge', which he crosses before coming to a castle surrounded by stakes with heads on all but one; the castle spins like a top. He manages to enter, though the mule loses part of its tail, and is greeted by a dwarf who promptly disappears. A black churl emerges from a cellar and then, after dinner, challenges him to a 'beheading test'. He does behead the churl, but is spared the return stroke next day. He similarly survives an attack by two lions and then an assault by a wounded knight. On finally slaying two dragons, he is received by a lady, the quester's sister. Gauvain rejects the offer of her hand, but she gives him the missing bridle. When Gauvain leaves the castle, he is honoured as a saviour before returning to court. There the maiden, on receiving her bridle, greets him with many kisses before leaving.

The *Mule* not merely has its prologue developed from Chrétien's *Erec* but contains apparent reminiscences of all his romances. It begins with Kay typically failing to achieve an adventure, then shows Gauvain performing it with success up to the point where the owner of the bridleless mule thanks him effusively, then departs as mysteriously as she arrived. Gauvain had already declined her sister's hand, so is left with his recollections, but no permanent attachment. The *Mule*'s various adventures also carry allusions to its own sources, such as the references to the testing bridge of Hell as found in the *Charrette* and the story of Christ's Harrowing of Hell drawn on by *Cligés*, the honouring of the mule by the wild beasts and a number of elements from an early version of the Fair Unknown motif. Important sections are devoted to the beheading test and the whirling fortress, which seem to have figured in a lost legend of Celtic provenance known to Chrétien. Complex as the *Mule*'s sources appear to have been, there is no need to look beyond Chrétien's lifetime for their occurrence. It is indeed likely that his contemporaries would have found other aspects of this engaging tale to stir their memories, including a story of a disinherited sister, of which Chrétien's extant romances give us no more than glimpses.

Though only surviving in a single manuscript, the *Chevalier* and the *Mule* were more widely disseminated in the Middle Ages and may often have been thought of as a pair. Both were used extensively in Heinrich von dem Türlîn's *Crône* (*c.*1220). Rather later, perhaps, the author of *Hunbaut* drew liberally from them, as it seems did the poet of the *Chevalier aux deux épées*. On the other hand, Raoul (de Houdenc?) used the *Chevalier* alone in his *Vengeance Raguidel*, whilst an apparent echo from the same text appears in the *Queste del Saint Graal*.

It was, however, towards the end of the fourteenth century that these two texts surely underwent their most exciting transformation. That was when an anonymous English poet combined their plots and greatly expanded them into *Sir Gawain and the Green Knight*. It has been argued that this poet used a text (presumably French) to which the *Chevalier* and the *Mule* were collaterally related. But a number of close verbal parallels makes such a remote connection unlikely. A comparison of the English and French texts, together with other acknowledged sources, leads to the conclusion that the poet of *Sir Gawain* manipulated them with his own native genius (see Owen's edn of the *Chevalier* and the *Mule*, Part II). [†DDRO]

The *Enfances Gauvain*

The *Enfances Gauvain* survives in a fragment of 712 lines (Paris, Bibliothèque Sainte-Geneviève). Dating probably from the 1230s, this is a version of a story, variants of which occur elsewhere, namely in *Perlesvaus* and the Latin *De ortu Walwanii*, with traces of the tradition found in Geoffrey of Monmouth's *Historia Regum Britanniae* and Wace's *Brut*.

In this particular version, Gauvain is the son of Arthur's sister Morcadès and her page Lot. The child is entrusted to a knight called Gauvain le Brun, who names the boy after himself and sets him adrift in a cask; after the boy is rescued by a fisherman, he is brought to Rome and educated by the pope. Although the fragmentary state of the text makes it difficult to be categorical, this treatment of Gauvain would seem to bear little relationship to the ironic and burlesque treatment of him visible in other verse romances of the period; it may represent a conscious anachronism that attempts to restore him to the heroic status he enjoyed in Wace, and which had been generally eroded in both verse and prose romances.

The popularity of heroes often generates 'prequels', as well as sequels and continuations, to a body of existing tales in which they are prominent, the *Elucidation* and *Bliocadran* prefixed to Chrétien's *Perceval* being obvious examples. The structure in which adult exploits precede the tale of a hero's birth and boyhood deeds is an ancient one, common in both classical and Celtic mythology, as well as in the Old French epic, of which it is practically a defining feature (Wolfzettel 1973–4). The genealogical structure, essentially an expedient for capitalizing on the popularity of particular subject-matter, can also be effected by adding the deeds of ancestors, including parents, and of immediate descendants. The *Bel Inconnu* and some episodes in the First *Perceval* Continuation present adventures of Gauvain's son, but the huge amount of attention paid to Gauvain in romances of the twelfth and thirteenth centuries practically guaranteed the existence of an *Enfances Gauvain*. [KB]

La Vengeance Raguidel

Dating from the first third of the thirteenth century, perhaps *c.*1220–30 (Schmolke-Hasselmann 1980*, 16/1998, 17), *La Vengeance Raguidel*, by a certain Raoul, survives in two complete manuscripts, two fragments and some scattered lines transcribed by Pierre Borel (see chapter I). The complete manuscripts are Chantilly, Musée Condé, MS 472, executed between 1250 and 1275, and Nottingham, University Library, MS Middleton LM. 6, dating from the second half of the thirteenth century. The Chantilly manuscript is written in Picard, but Friedwagner argues that *Raguidel* was originally composed in a dialect of the south-western border of the Île-de-France (see also Pallemans 1992). BNF, nouv. acq. fr. 1263, is a thirteenth-century fragment corresponding to lines 3488–3637 (Meyer 1892); the BNF fragment, fr. 2187, corresponds to lines 1–29.

The question of the authorship of the romance preoccupied early critics. Originally, it was thought that *Raguidel* was the work of two different authors and that the second, who names himself in lines 3356 and 6178, could be Raoul de Houdenc, author of *Meraugis*. Micha rejected this idea, claiming that Raoul was the sole author of *Raguidel*, but that he was not the same person as the author of *Meraugis* (Micha 1944–5). Atanassov (2000, 72, n. 49) has recently revived the debate, agreeing that Raoul is the sole author of *Raguidel*, but suggesting that he may also have written *Meraugis*. More recently, Roussineau, after careful examination of the issues and the evidence, has argued convincingly that 'Raoul' should be identified with the Raoul de Houdenc who wrote *Meraugis* (*Raguidel* edn, pp. 9–26). These studies also raise the issue of *Raguidel*'s intertextual relation to prior tradition, especially to Raoul de Houdenc and Chrétien de Troyes (Adler 1960). When, in the *Tournoiement Antechrist*, Huon de Méry discusses his own relationship to these two illustrious forebears, is he also referring to *Raguidel*?

Raguidel opens with King Arthur celebrating Easter at Caerleon. As is customary at such feasts, the king refrains from eating until news of a new adventure reaches his court. When none arrives, Arthur orders the knights to begin without him. Later, a ship arrives bearing the corpse of Raguidel; a lance pierces his chest and his fingers have five rings. Letters found on the corpse request that a knight of the Round Table avenge his death by removing the lance and rings. Gauvain succeeds in drawing the lance from the body, but he cannot remove the rings. An unknown knight does remove them, but then leaves the court. Kay sets off in pursuit, but is defeated. Arthur then orders Gauvain to pursue the knight. His nephew does not know for whom he is looking, nor where to find him; moreover, he forgets to take the lance with which he is to punish the murderer.

A peasant leads Gauvain to the Castle of Madoc, the Black Knight. Madoc observes the custom of decapitating all his visitors and displaying their heads outside the castle. After defeating him, Gauvain demands an explanation for the beheading custom. Madoc explains that he hopes in this way to avenge himself on Gauvain. Without revealing his identity to the Black Knight, Gauvain obliges him to put an end to the custom. The prize of the combat is the hand of the lady of Gautdestroit, but Gauvain, to the dismay of Madoc and the lady, abandons her.

Meanwhile, the lady of Gautdestroit is holding Gaheriet, Gauvain's brother, in her prison in the hope of luring Gauvain. Pretending to be Kay, Gauvain is received by the lady. She shows him her chapel, where a decapitation machine is in place to avenge herself on Gauvain because he has scorned her love; after this she intends to commit suicide in order to be reunited with her beloved in death. Gauvain secretly frees Gaheriet and they flee the castle; he returns to Arthur's court for the lance he forgot earlier. On his way, he delivers Ydain from the hands of Licoridon and then, when they kiss, falls in love with her. Gauvain spends the night with her, whilst Gaheriet enjoys the solaces of one of Ydain's friends.

Meanwhile, at Arthur's court the 'ill-fitting cloak' has revealed that all men there are cuckolds, except for Carduel Briefbras. When Gauvain arrives with Ydain to fetch the lance, he arouses Kay's sarcasm. Gauvain retaliates by calling attention to the inconstancy of Kay's *amie*, provoking a misogynist outburst from the seneschal. Then a deformed knight appears asking the king for a boon. The knight, Druydain, whose name means 'Ydain's lover', claims that Ydain was destined for him. In a month's time, at a tournament to be held at Baudemagu's court, Gauvain will fight him for her.

Ydain departs with Gauvain. A knight catches up with them, claims Ydain and convinces Gauvain to let Ydain choose her companion. This *jeu parti* angers Ydain because of what she considers to be Gauvain's indifference, so she chooses the unknown knight. Gauvain now voices sympathy for Kay's misogyny. When Ydain asks her new companion to fetch her greyhounds from Gauvain, he proposes another *jeu parti* for the dogs. When the animals choose to remain with Gauvain, the unknown knight challenges him, but is defeated and killed. Ydain claims that she was merely testing Gauvain's love for her. When they reach Baudemagus's court, Gauvain easily defeats Druydain but surrenders Ydain to him, together with the warning never to believe her.

Next, Gauvain finds the vessel that brought Raguidel's body to Caerleon. The ship transports Gauvain to Scotland where he meets a lady who has vowed to wear her clothes inside out and sit backwards on her horse until she meets Gauvain, the knight destined to avenge Raguidel's death. Yder, the knight who removed Raguidel's rings, loves Trevilonete, daughter of Guengasouin, who will give her only to the knight who kills him. With the lance Gauvain wounds Guengasouin, who is always accompanied by an enormous bear. Yder kills the bear, then Gauvain kills Guengasouin, presenting his head to Raguidel's *amie*. Yder beseeches Gauvain for Trevilonete, but Arthur's nephew claims her for himself. However, when Trevilonete announces that she can love only Yder and the barons decide that she should go to him, Gauvain relinquishes his claim. Yder and Trevilonete go to court to vouch for Gauvain's avenging of Raguidel's death.

Questions of authorship are related to the problem of *Raguidel*'s composition. Micha, echoing Gaston Paris, has argued that the romance contains three distinct plots: Vengeance (1,874 lines), Gautdestroit (2,863 lines) and Ydain (1,441 lines) (*GRLMA**, IV:1, 383; cf. Micha 1944–5, 347–8), and that these three parts are loosely juxtaposed rather than integrally related to each other in a true *conjointure*. Atanassov believes that Raoul unifies these three parts through parody. For example, Raoul creates the figure of the Dame de Gautdestroit to parody the avenging of Raguidel's murder (Atanassov 2000, 10), whilst the Mantel episode parodies the Arthurian court, a place where infidelity prevails. Atanassov views

Gauvain as a true hero who must confront the image of him that many idolize (2000, 18). In this way, Gauvain's adventure becomes a semantic one, dramatizing the relation between the signifier and the signified.

In arguing that *Raguidel* represents a new type of *conjointure*, Atanassov rejects Busby's psychological interpretations of late Gauvain verse romances as well as Schmolke-Hasselmann's view that Raoul uses parody in order to reveal deeper moral significance (1980*, 106–15/1998, 129–41). Yet, Atanassov is perhaps too hasty in rejecting these interpretations. Raoul does parody Gauvain as an ideal knight and lover. Gauvain, who is neither ready for, nor capable of, true love, also fails as a knight. This adapts the idealized, but less colourful Gauvain of earlier Arthurian romances through parody and ironic exaggeration of his conventional features and his weaknesses (Schmolke-Hasselmann 1980*, 114/1998, 139). For example, Raguidel's mistress, wearing her clothes inside out and riding her horse backwards until Raguidel's murder is avenged, becomes an image of the medieval parody, or a poetics of reversal (*contrefaçon* or *bestornement*, 4996–7). We might extend this to other romances in Chantilly, Musée Condé, MS 472. For example, the *Atre périlleux* compares the sparrow-hawk maiden to Enide. This recalls Raoul's implied comparisons between Enide and Ydain, another maiden associated with a sparrow-hawk (Schmolke-Hasselmann 1980*, 112/1998, 137).

Raguidel's comedy constantly enlivens its parodic intent. Gauvain's diminished status as knight and lover receives humorous treatment when he is confused with Kay in order to hide his identity from the lady of Gautdestroit. In *Raguidel* he is a bungler who forgets the lance he needs to achieve his quest. Yder pre-empts half of his challenges by removing the rings from Raguidel's corpse. As a lover, this knight, who scrupulously avoids permanent attachment, falls in love with a woman who abandons him quickly for another, better-endowed knight. Trevilonete shows that faithful women do exist; she loves Yder, despite the fact that he is not as good a knight as Gauvain, thus making the latter's sudden misogyny appear mean-spirited.

The dénouement is particularly telling. Despite Kay's sarcasm, Yder and Trevilonete pledge to vouch in court for Gauvain's version of the vengeance. Once there, Yder confirms Gauvain's story and identifies himself as the one who removed the rings from the corpse. Raguidel's *amie* also vouches for Gauvain's story. Yet, although the story is repeated in this way, no one gets it right, not even the author, because, as he claims, he bases his story on the retellings of Gauvain and the two unreliable eyewitness-participants in the plot. (See chapter XI for further discussion of the view that *Raguidel* endows semantic drama with ethical concerns.) **[LJW]**

L'Atre périlleux

The mid-thirteenth-century *Atre périlleux* survives in three manuscripts: Chantilly, Musée Condé, MS 472 (*c*.1250–75); BNF, fr. 2168 (end of the thirteenth century) and BNF, fr. 1433 (*c*.1315–30) (see chapter I). At least one other manuscript of the romance has been lost (Delisle 1907, II, 190; Trachsler 1997*, 85).

The narrator claims in the prologue that his lady asked him to relate a story about the good knight Gauvain. The complex plot begins when a beautiful woman arrives at court and asks for a boon from Arthur: she wants to become his cup-bearer and have his best knight designated as her defender. Whilst all are still at table, an arrogant knight named Escanor abducts her. After some hesitation, Gauvain pursues them. Incognito, Gauvain encounters three weeping maidens and a blinded knight, who inform him that Gauvain has been slain and dismembered by three knights. Resuming his pursuit of Escanor, Gauvain stops at the 'âtre périlleux' (*perilous cemetery*), where he frees a young woman from bondage as a devil's sex slave. After pursuing Escanor for three days and two nights, Gauvain finds and kills him.

Gauvain rescues a maiden who has lost her lover's favourite sparrow-hawk. When he climbs a tree to retrieve the bird, the lover returns. Concluding that Gauvain is a rival, he takes Gauvain's horse Gringalet, leaving him stranded with the woman. Raguidel of Angarde arrives on the scene and gives Gauvain a horse in return for a future boon, taking the sparrow-hawk as pledge (BNF, fr. 1433 inserts here a 666-line episode not found in other manuscripts: Woledge edn, pp. 212–33; Black edn and transl., 388–421. In it Gauvain defeats Brun Sans Pitié and delivers a maiden whom Brun mistrusts for doubting his prowess). Then another knight, Espinogre, appears and relates how a maiden scorned him, but he is nevertheless abandoning her for another woman. Gauvain defeats him in order to enforce his loyalty to his first love. Together with Espinogre and the sparrow-hawk maiden, Gauvain encounters Cadrés, who must rescue his beloved from a rival and twenty friends. Because of the sparrow-hawk maiden's hunger and thirst, Gauvain discourteously steals food and drink from the chatelaine of a nearby castle, a woman whose seven brothers are away hunting. Raguidel reappears and demands as his boon that Gauvain abduct and bring to him the chatelaine with her seven brothers. In response to the chatelaine's cries, the eldest of her brothers, Codrovain, appears; he is also the sparrow-hawk maiden's jealous lover. Codrovain loses the ensuing battle with Gauvain and must return Gringalet, give his sister to Raguidel in marriage and make peace with his own *amie*.

Gauvain, Raguidel, Espinogre, Cadrés and six of the brothers liberate Cadrés's beloved by defeating the twenty knights holding her. Gauvain and Espinogre now seek the three maidens who lamented Gauvain's supposed death and dismemberment. They encounter Tristan-qui-ne-rit, who tells them where to find Gauvain's two alleged murderers, Gomeret and the Orgeuilleux Fé. Gauvain defeats them, after which Gomeret restores the sight of the young man they blinded and brings back to life the Courtois de Huberlant, the knight killed in Gauvain's place because his arms resembled those belonging to Gauvain. Everyone then returns to Arthur's court, where Gauvain officiates at the weddings of Espinogre, Cadrés and Raguidel.

The *Atre* sums up prior romance tradition, whilst depicting a hero who has lost his name. Traditional motifs included in the *Atre* are a false death, Gauvain loved for his reputation, Kay keeping a promise that leads to his dishonour, the kidnapping of a cup-bearer, marriage promised by a woman to a suitor if he proves himself superior to Gauvain, and Gauvain's fairy mother. Girart d'Amiens may have borrowed the name of his hero Escanor from the *Atre*; and in *Claris et Laris* the liberation of a woman prisoner of the devil is analogous to that in the *Atre*.

The *Atre* is one of the Gauvain romances in which Arthur's nephew is a main character rather than a foil to the protagonist. Although critics are divided as to whether the work's protagonist attains the status of a true hero, his reputation appears to have been rehabilitated by the end of the romance, which depicts 'an admirable Gauvain who can lay claim to the status of true hero' (Busby in Lacy, Kelly and Busby eds 1987–8*, II, 105); Schmolke-Hasselmann contends that, even if its comic elements contain deliberate criticism, it is not directed against Gauvain (1980*, 105/1998, 128). Yet Gauvain's rehabilitation is also undercut through irony (Walters 2000). The Latin rhetorical tradition defines *ironia* as giving 'false praise' of someone when criticism is intended (Gaunt 1989, 9; Walters 2000). Such irony is evident, for example, in the ambiguous depiction of Gauvain as knight and as lover, and in particular as a disinterested defender of women. To be sure, he performs exploits that ensure the happiness of other couples; yet his ambivalence towards women and his championing by the misogynist narrator undermine his position as defender of the institution of marriage. His reputation is further compromised by his adventures with the sparrow-hawk maiden and the discourteous chatelaine. These adventures, with their lingering suggestions of lechery, impotence, chivalric ineptitude and cowardice, make it difficult to accept Gauvain unreservedly as a 'marriage broker'.

When Gauvain is deprived of his name, becoming 'cil sans nom', he begins a quest to recover his identity (Combes 1992–5). The romance thematizes the problem of judging Gauvain, a character whom Chrétien's *Erec* depicts as the best knight of the Round Table, but whose image has undergone much re-evaluation by the time the *Atre* was written. Critics have recently begun to study the linguistic and semantic connotations of Gauvain's quest; like *Raguidel*, the *Atre périlleux* sanctions the thirteenth-century tendency to transform the elect protagonist into a new figure with new meaning (Morin 1995; Atanassov 2000, 126).

The division of opinion among critics reflects a debate implicit within the romance itself with regard to Gauvain's status as exemplary knight and lover. This concern is also implicit in the romance's title, repeated many times over the course of the work (*Atre*, 792, 937, 960, 1121, etc.) and emphasized in the rubrics in two of the three surviving manuscripts. Is this knight whom Chrétien 'forgot', according to the *Chevalier à l'épée*, a worthy continuator of the Arthurian tradition, or is he not? When Gauvain frees the young woman from the devil's embrace in the episode that gives the romance its title, the cemetery is said to lose its name (*Atre*, 1443; Cirlot 2001, 46–51). Thus, the loss of the *Atre*'s name is a function of Gauvain's regaining his good name. Yet the romance reconfigures Gauvain's place in Arthurian tradition, metaphorically placing him, in his customary status as Arthur's nephew, as the representative Arthurian knight standing at a crossroads in the romance tradition. The continual deconstruction and reconstruction of a collective Arthurian memory is epitomized in all three surviving manuscript collections containing the romance (see chapter XI). [LJW]

Arthurian Romances: Romances about Gauvain's Sons

Le Bel Inconnu

This romance survives in a single codex, Chantilly, Musée Condé, MS 472. Little is known about the author, who names himself 'Renals de Biauju' in line 6249 of the epilogue and entitles his romance *Li Biaus Desconeüs*; the usual title today is the *Bel Inconnu*. Until 1982 the author's name was taken to apply to a member of the house of Beaujeu, a powerful family in the French Mâcon region; however, Guerreau's analysis (1982, 73–4) of both genealogical records and linguistic traits of the area provides persuasive evidence that the author in fact belonged to the rival house of Bâgé. This is also the family to which belongs the blazon sported by the hero of the work: an ermine lion upon an azure field. Since Renaut was a common name in the Bâgé family, it is impossible to determine which member of the family wrote the *Bel Inconnu*; nor is it possible to date the romance more precisely than to the period 1191 to 1213. The earlier of these dates, taken to be the point at which Chrétien de Troyes ceased to write, is derived from references throughout Renaut's romance to Chrétien's *œuvre*; the later date is based on the quotation in *Guillaume de Dole*, thought to have been composed by 1213, of a song attributed to Renaut. But whether this is the same *cançon* as the one referred to by the poet in line 3 of his romance is not known. Indeed, if Renaut wrote a number of songs (Colby-Hall 1984, 120), the reference in the romance could be to another poem post-dating *Guillaume de Dole*. All we can say today is that Renaut de Bâgé appears to have been writing around 1213 and that the *Bel Inconnu* would fit into the period from 1191 to 1225.

The prologue announces that Renaut wrote the *Bel Inconnu* for the lady he loves (4–6); additional references to this (fictional?) love, both in insertions and in the epilogue, relate the narrator's love story to that of the Bel Inconnu (the Fair Unknown). The plot begins one August at Arthur's court at Caerleon with the sudden arrival of a nameless young man (on the significance of this summer festival, see Walter 1996). Since he does not know his name, he is designated by the court as the Fair Unknown, with reference both to his appearance and to his courtly conduct. He requests and receives the king's boon. A young woman, Helie, arrives, requesting the assistance of Arthur and his court for her mistress who can be rescued only by a knight able to accomplish the ordeal of the Fier Baisier (Gruesome Kiss). The Fair Unknown requests permission to undertake the mission as the boon promised to him by Arthur. The king reluctantly agrees, despite the misgivings of his knights and the obvious scorn of Helie.

The party's journey is punctuated by a series of encounters, quite obviously calqued on episodes from Chrétien's romances, in which the hero repeatedly demonstrates his prowess. The most significant of these occurs at the castle of the Isle d'Or, where, having defeated the knight who was defending the causeway, the hero is introduced to the castle's mistress, the beautiful Pucele as Blances Mains (Maid of the White Hands). He believes his desire for the maiden, or fairy, as she proves to be, is reciprocated when she visits his bed that night, clad only in her chemise. The maiden, however, is not prepared to submit to any advances and in the morning the hero departs without taking leave, unsatisfied by the previous night's events. The party arrives at the castle where, amidst ominous signs of desolation and evil foreboding, the hero must undergo the trial of the Fier Baisier. The trial consists of kissing the bright red lips of a serpentine creature. When the young knight confronts the hideous creature, he has the perspicacity to realize, from its demeanour, that it means him no harm. He duly kisses the monster and refrains from killing it. A voice is then heard telling him of his name and lineage: he is Guinglain, son of Gauvain and Blanchemal la Fee. Exhausted, the hero falls asleep and wakens to find the beautiful Blonde Esmeree beside him. She had been transformed by the spell of Mabon, a wicked magician, into the monster whom he kissed. Because his kiss freed her, Guinglain should now marry her and become lord of her lands. He agrees, subject to the approval of Arthur, whom the lady, Blonde Esmeree, goes to petition.

Guinglain is left in a quandary, for his heart belongs to the Pucele, to whom he now surreptitiously returns. She initially rebuffs him by way of punishment for his earlier desertion, but finally grants him access to her chamber and to her love, after subjecting him to a series of terrifying illusions. Blonde Esmeree, meanwhile, enlists the support of King Arthur in calling a tournament to entice Guinglain back to her. Guinglain attends the tournament, deserting the Pucele a second time, is victorious and marries Blonde Esmeree. The romance concludes with an epilogue in which the poet affirms that his hero's heart belongs truly to the Pucele and that he will bring the two back together if his own lady grants him the favour of her 'bel sanblant' (*welcoming expression*, 6255, 6266).

The *Bel Inconnu* was a relatively neglected text in the early part of the twentieth century, when scholars tended either to denigrate the romance's complex, bipolar structure involving two rival heroines, or to view it simply as an inferior reworking of Chrétien (G. Paris 1886; Schofield 1895; Boiron and Payen 1970). Later work, however, opens up discussion of the romance as a play upon the thematics and conventions of Old French literary forms, paving the way for a number of more probing analyses (Sturm 1971a; 1971b; 1972; Haidu 1972; Freeman 1983; Guthrie 1984; Perret 1988; 1999). The figure of King Arthur provides a useful case study through which the principal themes of this recent critical interest may be explored.

Arthur and his court represent one of a series of axes around which the aspirations of the hero revolve. It is possible, however, to read this aspirational focus on a variety of levels. At the simplest level, Arthur represents within the narrative the goal towards which the hero's political and social ambitions are directed: the Bel Inconnu approaches Arthur in his quest for the adventure which leads to the revelation of his name, affirmation of his prowess and the acquisition of a wife and lands. On a more complex level, Arthur also provides the key element on which intertextual play is centred: surrounded by references to the works of Chrétien, Renaut's Arthur typifies the courtly romance genre which Chrétien had perfected, and to which the hero may also aspire (Bruckner in Lacy, Kelly and Busby eds 1987–8*, I, 224–65). On a different level again, the success of the hero in the Arthurian world provides wish fulfilment within the text for the house of Bâgé, whose economic and political power was beginning to diminish in the early thirteenth century (*Bel Inconnu*, Fresco edn, xi). Renaut allows all these layers of meaning to coexist, along with other constructions of meaning from the text deriving from the inclusion within his romance framework of elements from *lai* and lyric conventions, and from the blurring of the intra- and extra-diegetic by the references to the poet-narrator's own lady (Guthrie 1984; De Looze 1990). He simultaneously invites his audience to use the cues he provides to construct meaning from his text, and thwarts such attempts by the inclusion of signals suggesting contradictory meanings.

In this way the *Bel Inconnu* sets up a locus within which the processes of narrative composition, reception and reading are explored. The resultant plot marks a significant development on the first generation of Arthurian romances, as the basic elements of the form are problematized and destabilized; yet, potentially unstable as Renaut's text is, it retains narrative cohesion and sense. There are other romances, both before and after the *Bel Inconnu*, in which some scholars see the process of deconstruction leading to narrative collapse: Hue de

Rotelande's *Ipomedon* and the later, anonymous *Joufrois de Poitiers* are good examples (on the latter text and its relation to *Le Bel Inconnu*, see Grigsby 1968).

The *Bel Inconnu* successfully combines a playful interpretation of the raw materials of Old French narrative with a fidelity to the tradition from which they are derived: the result is a beguiling exposition of medieval *inventio*. [PS]

Beaudous

Robert de Blois, the author of *Beaudous*, flourished in the second third of the thirteenth century. He probably composed the romance in about 1250 in the Francien dialect (Micha 1946–7; Fox 1950, 45 and 85). Some 4,600 lines long, it survives in a single manuscript, BNF, fr. 24301, dating from the last third of the thirteenth century. The prologue names the author, who describes himself as a moralist writing in order to correct contemporary moral decline. He hopes, there-fore, that *Beaudous* will both please and instruct. The author promises to name his patron at the end of the romance, but unfortunately the last leaf is missing from the manuscript. We do know, however, that Robert enjoyed significant protection. A passage in Paris, Bibliothèque de l'Arsenal, MS 5201, containing Robert's other works, resembles that in BNF, fr. 24301; it names Hue Tyrel, lord of Poix (1230–60), and his son Guillaume, who succeeded his father and died in 1302 (Fox 1950, 43–4). Another manuscript, BNF, fr. 2236, replaces Hue's name with those of Thierry, Count of Forbach, and Jean de Bruges, both of whom lived in the thirteenth century (Langlois 1926–8, II, 176–8).

The romance relates the chivalric and amorous exploits of Gauvain's son Beaudous. At Pentecost, Arthur's court learns that Gauvain's father, the King of Ireland, has passed away and that Gauvain is to be crowned as his successor on St John's Day, as Arthur wishes, at which time the court will reassemble. The next episode derives largely from Chrétien's *Perceval*. The titular hero, who lives away from court with his mother, the Maid of Wales, wishes to go to Britain in search of renown. The Maid of Wales consents, dubbing him herself before his depart-ure and lecturing him on his duties as a knight. But unlike that of Perceval, Beaudous's career will be faultless. Preserving his anonymity under the pseudo-nym the Knight of the Two Swords, he encounters a messenger, a woman riding a white mule and searching for someone who can draw the sword she bears. His success in this test shows that he is destined to wed Beauté, daughter of the King of the Islands.

Beauté is besieged by King Madoine, an uncouth suitor whom she despises. Beaudous is successful in several adventures that establish his reputation. Beauté and he form a perfectly matched couple. Moreover, Beauté divines her beloved's real name: 'Tant estes biaus et dous, / Bien dussiez avoir nom Biausdoz' (*You are so beautiful and sweet that your name should be Beaudous*, 2328–9). A spectacular combat between Madoine and Beaudous brings the siege to a conclusion. The defeated suitor is dispatched to Arthur's court, where he confirms our hero's renown. Beaudous wins a tournament by unhorsing the best Round Table knights. The plot concludes as the court prepares to reward Gauvain and his son in a double marriage and coronation, Beaudous with Beauté and Gauvain with the Maid of Wales.

Beaudous is one of those Arthurian romances that have been described as 'optimistic', because they are aimed at an aristocratic audience intrigued by exemplary conduct and familiar with the genre's conventions (Schmolke-Hasselmann 1981, 283–5). Beaudous easily overcomes all obstacles; he undergoes no inner crisis and his destiny appears clearly set out. Arthurian values are not questioned; the Round Table still seats the flower of knighthood, especially Gauvain (428, 671–2). The plot relates a largely conventional nuptial quest, drawing on time-honoured motifs such as a shield attached to a tree as a challenge, play on the hero's name, a three-day tournament with a daily change of armour in order to appear incognito and a marvellous sword. Robert reveals a certain literary culture by drawing not only on *Perceval*, but on *Cligés* and *Yvain* as well (Fox 1950, 47–50; Walters 1993b, 179–80). A special fondness for proverbs suits his moralizing intentions.

Robert went as far as to interpolate most of his poetic works into the plot of *Beaudous*. These include: religious poems; an *Enseignement des princes*, which also lauds King Arthur; *Floris et Lyriopé*, a romance about Narcissus's parents; some love poems; and finally a *Chastoiement des dames*. These interpolations fill no less than eighty-four folio pages in the manuscript. They are placed in the mouth of the Maid of Wales when she admonishes her son upon his departure for Arthur's court. His mother pointedly states that her son is not the only person to whom she directs her admonitions (poem iv: 7–10), implying that the romance's audience can profit from them too. In fact, her words resonate with concerns expressed by Robert de Blois in his prologue.

At the same time, the larger audience she addresses justifies arranging her counsel in two branches, one for men and another for women. Despite the tensions and inconsistencies revealed by the interpolations in Robert's instruction (Krueger 1993*, 164–6), the recycling of these moralizing poems in the romance's Arthurian context links them to the celebration of marriage as an institution in the dénouement (Walters 1993b, 186–9). [CVCS]

Arthurian Romances: New Protagonists with Gauvain

Gliglois

Gliglois is somewhat eccentric within the corpus of post-Chrétien verse romances. Written about 1230, this anonymous 2,942-line romance survived in Turin,

Biblioteca Nazionale, MS L. IV. 33, but it was lost in the disastrous fire of January 1904. The edition is based on transcriptions made by scholars in the 1870s (Lacy 1980). The poem is unusual, in the first instance because of its length, which falls between the usual 6,000 or 7,000 lines typical of an episodic romance and the approximately 1,000 lines of texts such as *Le Chevalier à l'épée* and *La Mule sans frein*.

Gliglois relates the rivalry of Gauvain and his young squire Gliglois for the hand of the aptly named Beauté (also the name of the heroine in *Beaudous*). Whilst a number of romances of this period favourably contrast their heroes with Gauvain as suitors for the same woman (e.g. *La Vengeance Raguidel* and *Le Chevalier à l'épée*), and whilst Gauvain's reputation as a lover is a major theme in Arthurian romance generally, the treatment accorded to it in *Gliglois* is unique (Lacy 1980). Gliglois wins the hand of Beauté simply through devotion and patience, whereas Gauvain appears content to rely on his traditional appeal and status as one of the great Arthurian knights.

Gliglois is entirely free of the kind of *merveilleux* so characteristic of Arthurian verse romance, to the extent that it has often been described as 'realistic'. Most of the narrative takes place in and around various courts, and the only major event is a tournament at which Gliglois distinguishes himself. The treatment of the love theme is traditional in that both Gauvain and Gliglois appear to suffer the usual torments, but there are undeniable suggestions that Gauvain's feelings for Beauté are formal, even routine, whilst those of Gliglois appear genuine and spontaneous. Most of the amorous interest is explored by means of dialogue and inner monologue, some of which may recall Chrétien's *Cligés*, and Gliglois himself is torn between his love for Beauté and his loyalty to his master, Gauvain; love prevails. The irony of this romance is double: it was Gauvain's reputation that caused Gliglois's father to send him to Arthur's court to seek the former's service, and Gauvain's decision to have Gliglois wait on Beauté that enables her to become aware of the young man's virtues: 'In this romance we see the fickle affection of the great Gawain rejected in favour of a young, unknown and naive squire who is capable of true love. Heartfelt and sacrificial love carries the day against *amour-vanité*' (Schmolke-Hasselmann 1980*, 97/1998, 119).

Although the basis of the romance is the demythification of Gauvain's reputation, the treatment is without the kind of critical or burlesque edge so common elsewhere, and certainly without the harsh criticism of Arthur's nephew that comes to dominate prose romance. Even the final tournament fails to pit Gauvain against Gliglois physically, and Gauvain in the end gracefully, if reluctantly, accepts the outcome of their rivalry. Implicit in *Gliglois* are generational conflicts, of old and new orders and of reputation versus merit. In this sense, the romance is yet another examination of issues treated in different ways in other texts, and as a Gauvain romance it explores another possibility inherent in the figure. Like that of Arthur himself, the figure of Gauvain held the potential for articulating different concerns for different authors and their audiences. **[KB]**

Le Chevalier aux deux épées

Also known as *Meriadeuc*, this anonymous verse romance of 12,353 lines was probably written in the first third of the thirteenth century. It survives in one manuscript, BNF, fr. 12603, which was produced in Arras and has been dated to the late thirteenth or early fourteenth century (Nixon in Busby, Nixon, Stones and Walters eds 1993, II, 69–70; Trachsler 1994). Predominantly Francien, the romance contains enough Picard features to have convinced its editor that the author came from an area of the Île-de-France bordering on Picardy (*Deux épées*, Foerster edn, lxi–lxii).

The *Deux épées* opens at Arthur's court during Pentecost. King Ris d'Outre Ombre has laid siege to Caradigan. His messenger demands Arthur's submission and his beard, but Arthur refuses. Meanwhile, at Caradigan, Ris promises to grant the wish of anyone bold enough to retrieve his coat from the altar of the *Gaste Chapelle* and to put in its place a *pasture* (fetlock fetter). A woman, Lore, the Dame de Caradigan, alone offers to retrieve the coat. Successful, she demands and receives as prize the restoration of her realm. She wears a talismanic sword she took from the grave of Bléheris, whose burial she witnessed in the Gaste Chapelle. Only a knight whose qualities equal those of Bléheris will be able to remove the sword. She goes to Arthur's court, where she requests that she be married to the knight who can perform this act. Gauvain is absent; his squire, whose name, Meriadeuc, is revealed only at the end of the romance, unsheathes the sword, but departs without marrying Lore. Since his name is unknown, Kay names him 'the Knight of the Two Swords'. The court soon learns that this young knight has defeated King Ris.

Gauvain returns to court to learn that Arthur has promised to send him in search of Meriadeuc on Lore's behalf. This promise frames the rest of the narra-tive. Before his departure, the unarmed Gauvain is attacked by Brien des Illes. The Queen of the Isles has promised to marry him if he demonstrates that he is a better knight than Gauvain. The unarmed Gauvain is seriously wounded and Brien leaves him for dead. But Gauvain recovers and leaves court to seek vengeance and find Meriadeuc. Several comic episodes ensue, because Gauvain's hosts believe he is dead. Among these is that of the Demoiselle du Port, whose love Gauvain wins. But in bed she refuses to make love because she has been saving her virginity for Gauvain. When he identifies himself, she departs immedi-ately to seek verification at Arthur's court. Gauvain then arrives at Les Illes where he and Meriadeuc disrupt Brien's coronation; they depart together. Later, learning that Gauvain had earlier slain his father Bléheris, Meriadeuc mistakenly assumes that he must take vengeance on Gauvain; they part company.

At the same time, near the Lac as Jumelles, Meriadeuc comes upon a spring next to which lies a sword. Its blade is covered in blood that cannot be removed. Keeping the sword, he is brought to his mother, the lady of the Lac as Jumelles. She eventually recognizes her son and recounts the story of Bléheris's demise. A rash boon had obliged Gauvain to champion Brien de la Gastine (a character distinct from Brien des Illes); Bléheris mistook Gauvain for Brien and fought him, but was mortally wounded. Meriadeuc departs, electing to carry only two of his three swords. He encounters Melye, cousin of Bléheris, who holds her dead husband, another victim of Brien, in her lap. Meriadeuc agrees to bury him in the Gaste Chapelle, where he retrieves the *pasture* left on the altar by Lore. In the ensuing episodes Meriadeuc avenges the victims of Brien and eventually beheads him.

Meanwhile, in pursuit of Meriadeuc, Gauvain, incognito, restores to the lady of the Lac as Jumelles the lands she lost after Bléheris's death; for this she pardons him for the death of her husband. When Meriadeuc arrives, she also reconciles him with Gauvain. Together the two knights proceed to the Fontaine des merveilles, where they encounter a wounded knight who can be healed only by the sword that wounded him. The sword that Meriadeuc found earlier beside the spring proves to be the required weapon. When a second stroke is delivered, the blood on the sword vanishes, revealing Meriadeuc's name.

Arthur, who had been searching for Meriadeuc, is invaded by Rous du Val Perilleus. Gauvain and Meriadeuc arrive, defeat Rous and send him as a prisoner to Arthur's court, shackled in Ris's *pasture*. The two reach Caradigan on Ascension Day. Meriadeuc is reunited with Lore, and Gauvain with the Damoisele du Port who, now convinced that he is indeed Gauvain, is eager to consummate their love. The romance ends with the coronation of Meriadeuc and Lore, who wears a robe embroidered with scenes from all of Arthurian history.

Verse romance from this period is sometimes thought to have originated among French-speaking families living in Britain (Schmolke-Hasselmann 1980*, 206–7/1998, 249–50). This hypothesis raises the question of whether the blend of dialects in the manuscript should be attributed to scribal transmission, rather than to the author. Its intended audience seems to have consisted of connoisseurs well acquainted with the Arthurian tradition (Schmolke-Hasselmann 1980*, 183, 284/1998, 224, 279). Clear echoes of passages from Wace's *Brut* and Chrétien's *Erec*, *Yvain* and *Perceval* confirm the importance of adaptation in the composition of this romance (Thedens 1908; Lacy 2003) and account for the dense web of intertextual allusions that characterize its relationship with twelfth-century romance. Early commentators considered *Deux épées* to be unoriginal, but the subtle changes introduced into the traditional material (Busby 1980*, esp. 99–101, and in Lacy, Kelly and Busby eds 1987–8*, II, 93–109) suggest that their disparagement is unjustified (Micha, *GRLMA**, IV:1, 393; Atanassov 2000,

81–105). The role of rewriting in medieval composition, and in particular the concept of 'motif transfer' (Lacy 1996*), opens the door for a reassessment of the romance's composition. In some passages the density of borrowed material may belie a parodic intent (Rockwell 2000). Brief, occasional references to *realia* in the text, identified in historical studies that were very broad in their scope, accounted for most of the early critical commentary on this work. Until recently, very few scholars focused on *Deux épées* in detail (Colliot 1986; Trachsler 1997*, 122–3). Scholars have now addressed from various perspectives the significance of names and naming in the romance, with special emphasis on its relation to this motif in *Perceval* (Atanassov 1984; Kelly 2000; Rockwell 2000). To date no one has revisited Micha's suggestion that the source of the talismanic sword in this romance is the golden bough in Virgil's *Aeneid* (Micha 1976). [PVR]

Hunbaut

Hunbaut is an incomplete romance that breaks off in the middle of a phrase in Chantilly, Musée Condé 472 (*Hunbaut*, 3618). It was probably written between 1250 and 1275 (Szkilnik 2000) in the dialect of western Picardy. As Busby states (1994, 53), *Hunbaut*, unlike most Arthurian verse romances, is openly didactic. Indeed, one passage was interpolated into a manuscript of the *Chastoiement d'un pere a son fils*, a French version of the *Disciplina clericalis*, transforming the passage into an even more didactic piece by omitting all references to Arthur. In the prologue, the poet-narrator castigates his audience, claiming that no one tries to write well these days because public support is lacking. The public needs the moral edification he provides. Moreover, he praises his own talent, denigrates his rivals and claims to be in friendly rivalry with Chrétien (Busby 1994, 52–3, notes similarities with the prologue to *Erec*). He then announces his intention to write a romance about Gauvain.

The didactic stance of the *Hunbaut*-poet is reflected in the protagonist's function as Gauvain's counsellor. Arthur sends Gauvain on a mission to subdue a king who refuses him homage; he also sends Gauvain's sister with him, who, he maintains, will be a great help when he is attacked (172–3). Hunbaut argues that Arthur has erred in sending his nephew, so Arthur has him join the brother and sister. After they leave Gauvain's sister alone at a crossroads, Gorvain Cadrus abducts her in order to make her his *amie*. A number of adventures mark the progress of Hunbaut and Gauvain, including a sexual adventure for Gauvain, a food fight and a beheading contest. The *Hunbaut* author refers to this last adventure as a *jeu parti*, thus suggesting once again that he is engaged in friendly competition with Chrétien.

The plot returns to Gauvain, who meets his brother Gaheriet. Together they encounter a number of young women of dubious morals, who demand a kiss; although the women appear to be prostitutes, Gauvain forces other knights to respect the kissing custom. Yet, why did he defend women's honour in this way, if the women are dishonourable? Comedy here, as elsewhere in the romance, seems to diminish the worth of Arthurian knights and ladies. Meanwhile, Arthur and all his knights set out in search of Gauvain's sister. They encounter the Lady of Gautdestroit, who has fallen in love with Gauvain without having set eyes on him (she also appears in *Raguidel*, Busby 1994, 64) and keeps a statue that is a perfect likeness of him. Although Kay mocks Gauvain's reputation, all marvel at the statue's resemblance,[8] whilst Kay mutters that the real Gauvain is little better than a womanizer. This episode points once again to the disparity between Gauvain's image as courtly ideal and the real person. However, Gauvain finds his sister with her abductor Gorvain Cadrus (another name from *Raguidel* and *Meraugis*), who promises to marry her. Gorvain also accuses Gauvain of having killed one of his relatives, but Gauvain defeats him, and Gorvain returns to court to confess that he had abducted Arthur's niece. Arthur welcomes Gorvain to the Round Table and here the plot breaks off in the manuscript.

If, as Busby suggests, this is a didactic romance, its lessons are more often than not negative ones. Gauvain's conduct is of dubious exemplarity. He fails to clear himself of the murder charge. The author implies that his reputation is based on physical strength, rather than on moral superiority. Gauvain is not faulted for leaving his sister unprotected, nor is Gorvain blamed for abducting and apparently dishonouring her. Although two episodes make light of the custom of forcing knights to marry women they dishonour, the fact that Gorvain should not have abducted her at all is glossed over, as is the fact that, if he does marry her, the new wife will have acquired an abusive husband.

Hunbaut needs to be re-examined for its close intertextual connections with other romances in addition to Chrétien's, such as *Meraugis*, *Raguidel*, *Fergus* and the *Atre périlleux*. Apart from these romances, there are scarcely any references to it. Both Busby (1994) and Szkilnik (2000) argue that the group *Fergus–Hunbaut*, the only two romances to share a quire in the Chantilly manuscript, can both be seen as 'continuing' *Perceval*, though Chrétien's romance is not in this compilation. It seems likely that poets responded to each other's innovations by alternately building up and deflating Gauvain in thirteenth-century romance (see chapter XI). These factors suggest that *Hunbaut* may have been written expressly for inclusion in its manuscript compilation. **[LJW]**

Meraugis de Portlesguez

Written between 1200 and 1215, the 5,938-line *Meraugis de Portlesguez* is preserved in five manuscripts, three complete and two fragmentary (see chapter I and *GRLMA*, IV:2, 192). In the prologue, preserved in one manuscript only, the author identifies himself as Raoul de Houdenc. He was greatly admired and respected in his time; Huon de Méry equates him with Chrétien de Troyes and praises his style (Schmolke-Hasselmann, 1980*, 29–30/1998, 34–5). Lacy (1998, 817) points out that in modern times 'Meraugis is acknowledged to be an important romance, but it appears to be more praised than read'. Indeed, few scholarly works have been devoted to Meraugis in its own right (Kundert-Forrer 1960; Fernández Vuelta 1992). However, the new edition and translation by Szkilnik (edn) should remedy this situation. Like other Arthurian verse romances, Meraugis is often compared to Chrétien's romances. There have also been attempts to relate it to Raoul's other works; as well as La Vengeance Raguidel, two allegorical poems, the Roman des eles and the Songe d'enfer, have also been attributed to him (Busby 1985).

The young knight Meraugis and his friend Gorvain Cadruz attend the Lindesores tournament; there, both fall in love with the same woman, Lidoine. However, Gorvain loves Lidoine for her beauty, whilst Meraugis loves her for her cortoisie. Indeed, a virtual jeu parti ensues as each claims that his kind of love is superior and, therefore, that he alone is worthy of Lidoine. They bring the matter to Arthur's court. Queen Guinevere and the ladies are judges, and they give Lidoine to Meraugis, arguing that inner qualities rank higher than appearance. Gorvain challenges this decision, announcing that he will fight Meraugis in order to win Lidoine for himself. Lidoine, whilst not partial to either knight at first, accepts the ladies' judgement, but wants to test Meraugis's knightly qualities for a year. Then – coup de foudre – she falls in love with Meraugis.

Together Meraugis and Lidoine leave court in search of Gauvain, who has not been heard of for some time. They encounter numerous adventures that reveal Meraugis's prowess and courage, as well as his youth and inexperience which cause him to create difficulties by questioning customs he does not understand. In the Cité sans Nom (the city without a name), he is obliged by a custom to cross over to an island in order to fight with a knight. The knight is Gauvain, who has been a prisoner there since defeating the former lord of the island. Through a trick devised by Meraugis (he locks up the lady of the island and dresses in her attire), the two knights escape, but forget to fetch Lidoine who is waiting for them in the Cité. She decides, therefore, that Meraugis must be dead. When Lidoine is abducted by a lord who wants to marry her to his son, she summons Gorvain Cadruz to the rescue. Meanwhile, Meraugis has learned of her plight. He succeeds, thanks to another trick, in reclaiming her, once more depriving Gorvain of his expected prize. Meraugis defeats Gorvain, but then renews his friendship with his old friend. All's well that ends well.

This short summary hardly does justice to the complex plot of this problematic romance. Not only does Raoul cast his new story in the familiar Arthurian spatial and temporal framework, he also recycles numerous Arthurian stock scenes and characters familiar from Chrétien (Schmolke-Hasselmann 1980*, 117–18/1998, 144). He even models his style on Chrétien's: its sophistication and *préciosité*, especially the use of rhetorical questions and the breaking of the octosyllabic couplet, are typical of Chrétien's often highly polished verse style. Raoul's prologue itself is a good example of his playful manner. He accumulates many opening topoi: the qualities required in a good poet; the worth of his subject-matter; attacks against the hack rhymester ('rimeour de servanteis', 11–12) reminiscent of Chrétien's dismissal of bad *jongleurs* in the prologue to *Erec*; humility mixed with praise of his own tale which, he proclaims, will be remembered as long as the world endures; a definition of the audience that, he insists, must be as courteous as the tale. Borrowing words and phrases from Chrétien in this way, Raoul presents himself as a faithful, yet innovative disciple of his great model. He also suffuses the prologue with irony. By repeatedly inserting references to his story (*conte, conter, raconter* and *mesconter*), Raoul draws attention to his skill as a deft rhetorician. His subtle play on words demonstrates that what matters most is his skill in retelling stories.

It is largely along these lines that modern scholars have dealt with this puzzling romance. In the wake of Schmolke-Hasselmann's study of Arthurian verse romance after Chrétien, critics have investigated the dialogue that Raoul initiates with his predecessor, even looking for signs of rebellion against Chrétien's powerful influence (Busby 1991). Raoul's ironic slant shows that, whilst apparently complying with the conventions of romance, he can also question them.

Two interpretative approaches, complementary rather than contradictory, have been explored. On the one hand, *Meraugis* is read as a disguised poetological statement, critical of the narrative potential of Arthurian *matière*. In her analysis of its authorial voice, Krueger suggests that Raoul ingeniously recycles old devices and situations (Lacy, Kelly and Busby eds 1987–8*, I, 115–40). Yet Meraugis's multiple and complex adventures do not sketch a chivalric itinerary as much as they reveal Raoul's concern with romance aesthetics. This is evident in parallels between Meraugis's cunning and Raoul's own deft composition. What Raoul retains from Chrétien is more his rhetorical mastery than his ideals. For example, he indirectly redefines the adjective *cortois* (courteous, courtly): such an audience is one that is highly educated in Arthurian tradition, for only Arthurian connoisseurs can fully appreciate Raoul's clever rewriting. The hero's early failures, his bewilderment on many occasions, and later his refusal of custom, may reflect the author's questioning of narrative conventions (Blumenfeld-Kosinski in Lacy, Kelly and Busby eds 1987–8*, II, 79–92). If in the end both Raoul and Meraugis accept the traditional Arthurian framework – Arthurian scenes enclose and frame quests and other adventures – questions may still linger in the minds of the perceptive audience he envisions. These questions may undermine belief in Arthurian romance as an intermediary between ideal and reality in medieval society.

On the other hand, *Meraugis* has elicited critical reflection on Raoul's ideology. Does it probe courtly love in the opening debate on beauty versus *cortoisie*? How seriously are we to take the verdict of the queen and her ladies? This *jeu parti* gives new meaning to Chrétien's material by reflecting on the interplay between appearances and representation, interplay that introduces an ironic perspective on courtly ideals more familiar in clerical writing than in Arthurian romance, according to Fernández Vuelta (1990), who compares *Meraugis* to certain developments in Andreas Capellanus's *De amore*. The romance is also unsettling because the ideal it seems to foster is somewhat conventional, not to say conservative. In the first part women are given narrative as well as social power, but are returned to a submissive role in the second. Is this Raoul's way of condemning the excesses of *fin'amor* by proposing a more solid basis for love and marriage (Schmolke-Hasselmann 1980*, 124/1998, 157–8)? Or does he merely condone the prevailing social order and consequently mock women's attempt to alter the imbalance (Lacy 1998, 825)? Yet this apparent social conservatism (or is it prudence?) seems to clash with Raoul's sophisticated narrative strategies, his brilliant and innovative reshaping of Arthurian material. Or so it seems to those modern readers who link artistic originality to social advancement.

The episode that best illustrates this tension, and one often commented on, is Meraugis's rescue of Gauvain. In this highly comical passage, both Raoul and Meraugis show their skill in treating traditional motifs in entirely new ways. Gauvain's retention on the island near the Cité sans Nom recalls that of Mabonagrain in *Erec*, but differs from it as well in that Gauvain is not in love with the lady whose prisoner he is, and is strangely resigned to complying with a custom he denounces as unjust. Thus the audience is invited to compare Gauvain's passivity to Meraugis's ingenuity, that is, to contrast the old ways of Arthurian romance with the new ones inaugurated by *Meraugis*. However, Meraugis's harsh treatment of the ladies, his thoughtless abandoning of Lidoine and his ambiguous disguise as a woman suggest misogynist undertones to the whole episode that seem more at home in a *fabliau* (Busby 1998; Lacy 1998, 822–3). This humorous, and at times farcical tone seems to aim at deflating the audience's idealistic expectations as much as it exhibits irreverence towards Chrétien. Or is it complicity? Did a sagacious reader of Chrétien such as Raoul know that Chrétien did not always expect to be taken too seriously? [MS]

Arthurian Romances: New Protagonists without a Major Role for Gauvain

Yder

Yder is usually dated to the end of the twelfth or the first decades of the thirteenth century. The rhymes suggest an author from western France, perhaps from the modern department of La Manche (Gelzer edn, xl). The romance survives in an Anglo-Norman manuscript of the second half of the thirteenth century, Cambridge University Library, MS Ee. 4. 16. It may have been written in England for an Anglo-Norman audience by an author hailing from the Continent (Schmolke-Hasselmann 1980; Adams edn, 13), because its numerous insular place-names are more diversified than traditional place-names in Arthurian literature (Schmolke-Hasselmann 1980*, 200/1998, 243–4). The last lines claim that it was written only for kings and queens, clerics and knights who delight in beautiful subjects, and for ladies and damsels who are courteous and beautiful (6762–9).

The beginning is lost, as the first gathering is missing in the manuscript. Some 1,000 lines long, it can be reconstructed from allusions in the extant text (Adams edn, 1). The plot relates Yder's double quest for his father, who abandoned his pregnant mother twenty-five years earlier, and for queen Guenloïe, whom he loves and hopes to win, both by glorious exploits and by his moral qualities. Yder's five halts at Arthur's court are brief because of the king's discourtesy (Schmolke-Hasselmann 1980*, 46/1998, 54). Instead, Yder joins Tallac de Rougemont, a rebellious vassal to whom Arthur has laid siege. Yder shines in combat before Guenloïe, unhorsing Kay three times in succession; angered at his discomfiture, Kay treacherously wounds the young hero. Guenloïe cares for Yder in an abbey. Still further trials await him: combat with a bear that enters Guinevere's chamber; battle with an unknown knight, Duke Nuc, who turns out to be his own father; and the defeat of two terrifying giants. The thought of his lady constantly sustains him and with the final exploit he gains Guenloïe's love. The romance ends with the double marriage of Guenloïe and Yder (whom Arthur crowns king) and of his parents.

This lively tale holds the reader's attention by virtue of its economically related adventures, its spirited dialogues and interior monologues, and its amusing passages and realistic details. Above all, the author excels in depicting the devastating effects of jealousy, a folly he calls an illusion and a great vice (5143–67). This is especially obvious in Kay and Arthur. For example, the king, piqued by Guinevere's insistent, albeit innocent praise of Yder, indiscreetly asks the queen whom she would marry if he were to die. Although she is, of course, reluctant to play this game, Arthur heavy-handedly perseveres until he receives the expected, but feared answer; the unfortunate Yder will pay for being named. Obsessed with eliminating the young man, Arthur relies on Kay's absolute unscrupulousness to advance his plot. The treacherous seneschal serves poisoned water to the young hero.[9] Unlike Yder, who upholds loyalty and the *covenant* (i.e. keeping one's word of honour as a condition for mutual confidence and harmonious human relations), Arthur is besmirched with *vilanie* (Schmolke-Hasselmann 1980*, 76–85/1998, 92–103), the first signs of which are his unceremonious conduct and his neglect of the basic principles of decorum. The king no longer guarantees the ideals underpinning Arthurian society and, therefore, is unable to assure harmony. The final reconciliation scene is possible only because Yder is endowed with a talent for resolving conflicts by negotiation.

The unfavourable light cast on Arthur in *Yder* has led to its being called an anti-Arthur romance (Schmolke-Hasselmann 1980*, 76/1998, 92). Although Gauvain and Guinevere enjoy positive evaluation, the romance inaugurates a process of disillusionment with Arthurian ideals. Anti-monarchical criticism in Arthurian romance after Chrétien de Troyes becomes more virulent. In *Yder*, even King Arthur, who had once served to restore an ideal past, makes his conduct conform to present reality and, by doing so, dissipates any lingering illusions regarding its true features (Rieger 1989, 370). For the romance's audiences in Britain this disappointing present was perhaps the reign of King John (1199–1216) (Schmolke-Hasselmann 1981, 292).

Yder has attracted critical attention for another reason: it recalls the origins of the Arthurian legend; an Isdernus appears in the Modena archivolt. Dated about 1120–40, this archivolt was fashioned before the *Historia Regum Britanniae* could have become known in Italy. Isdernus appears in the archivolt together with Winlogee, who is probably Arthur's wife; but her name also resembles Guenloïe's. Arthur and his barons, including Isdernus, liberate her (Stiennon and Lejeune 1963). Was there a link between Yder and a tale about the abduction of Arthur's wife, or even a love story about her and another knight, such as that in a plot echoed in Chrétien's *Charrette* (Webster 1951, 85–6)? From 1140 onwards a version of the abduction of Arthur's wife by King Melwas was in circulation, as we can observe in the *Vita Gildae* by Caradoc of Llancarfan (Faral 1929*, II, 411–12). Several decades later, the *Folie Tristan de Berne* refers to Yder's suffering on account of Guinevere and alludes to a combat between Yder and a bear. It is tempting to connect these elements, although it has proved difficult to assemble them into the *Ur-Yder* that some have conjectured. The trials imposed on Yder have also been linked to combat with a bear in an Indo-European warrior initiation rite attested among early Germanic peoples, and, in an Iranian analogue, victory over the three-headed Indra (Grisward 1978). *Yder* is also profoundly concerned with sovereignty and the qualities required for the exercise of power (Morin 1995). [CVCS]

Fergus

About a generation after Chrétien's death, the tradition he started was remarkably exploited in *Fergus* by the self-styled Guillaume le Clerc (Owen 1997). This romance survives in two manuscripts: Chantilly, Musée Condé, MS 472, and BNF, fr. 1553. The former, an earlier manuscript, runs to 7,012 lines. Recent research has made it plain that Guillaume le Clerc was in close touch with Scotland's aristocracy, and it was for them and any others conversant with contemporary French literature that he composed his romance. He appears to have been a native French-speaker, but not in the service of any named patron. To his detailed knowledge of the vernacular romances, from which on occasion he was able to quote, he brought some knowledge of the epic genre, including *Roland* and its Latin derivative, and also of figures from classical legend. One of William the Lion's subjects seems therefore to be outstandingly qualified for the authorship of *Fergus*.

A possible candidate is William (Guillaume) Malveisin, who is thought to have come to Scotland in the 1180s to pursue a career as a royal clerk (Ash 1972; Watt 1977). He progressed from being archdeacon of Lothian to royal chancellor and bishop, first of Glasgow, then of St Andrews (1202–38), the diocese that included Lothian. He thus achieved the frequently declared ambition of the young Fergus to become not a knight but a counsellor to the king. Malveisin was later credited with lost Latin works on St Ninian and Glasgow's patron St Kentigern or Mungo, by whom both Fergus and his mother swear. One notes, in the romance's happy outcome, some divine intervention rare in Arthurian romances other than those devoted to the Grail. For example, Galiene's intended suicide is prevented by a divinely inspired voice alerting her to Fergus's presence (5772–7). Malveisin's authorship would also fit the date of 1207, to which the text could contain a clue (Owen 1997, 148). Certainty is impossible, but he may well have been the *Fergus*-poet.

The plot begins as Arthur calls his knights to hunt a white stag. After a chase through the Scottish forests, Perceval catches up with the stag in the wilds of Galloway. There the party is seen by young Fergus, as he ploughs the lands of his father Soumilloit, a wealthy peasant of the district; his mother is of high nobility. Inspired to seek service with Arthur, Fergus follows Perceval to Carlisle, where he is knighted and girt with Perceval's own sword. Setting out to tackle Arthur's enemy, the Black Knight, he comes to Liddel Castle, where the owner's beautiful niece Galiene falls in love with him. He spurns her advances, however, before he has accomplished his mission. But having defeated the Black Knight and sent him to submit to Arthur bearing the trophies from the neck of his marble lion, Fergus returns to Liddel to find that the offended Galiene has secretly left. Belatedly overcome by the pangs of love, he leaves in a frantic search for her, undergoing numerous trials. Beside a wonderful spring he learns from a prescient dwarf that he will recover her only after obtaining the shining shield guarded by a giant hag at Dunnottar Tower. This he achieves. He then discovers that Galiene, now mistress of Lothian after her father's death, is besieged in Roxburgh by a hostile king and his nephew. He rides incognito to her rescue and raises the siege, before winning the honours at a tournament arranged by Arthur in nearby Jedburgh. There he is reunited with Galiene; they are wed in Roxburgh, to rule as lord and lady of Lothian.

Guillaume makes no attempt to conceal his sources, the deft manipulation of which is not the least of his literary skills (for sources, see Owen transl., Appendix A). He tells the resulting story in fluent, economical verse designed for a listening audience. His achievement is to have composed an extended travesty of the Grail legend as it existed before its systematic christianization by others of the post-Chrétien generation. In doing so, he shows an intimate knowledge of the master's romances other than the *Charrette*, having quickly established that his naive hero is to usurp the place of Perceval (Zemel 1994); and in elaborating Fergus's adventures, he draws liberally on the First, and especially the Second *Perceval* Continuation. Fergus's eventual success is assured when he wins the shining shield, the talismanic substitute for the Grail.

The romance is a purely literary construct, and such folkloric elements as are traceable have already passed through the source texts (Loomis 1949, 115–16, 291, 301–5, 365–6). Its main interest therefore lies in an assessment of its author's outlook and purpose. Despite his parodic and generally light-hearted approach, he does not overplay the humour (Freeman 1983; Owen 1984). He enjoys the caustic give-and-take of argument, often giving his characters' gibes a legalistic slant; and a favoured trick is to reverse features in his models, as when he replaces the radiant Grail-maiden with the hairy hag at Dunnottar. However, behind Guillaume's sophisticated wit are potential debating points that suggest a serious dimension to the romance.

The key to this less flippant side lies in his unparalleled treatment of places and people. It has often been noted that no other Arthurian romance has such a precise geographic setting; and this lies exclusively in the territory ruled or claimed by the Scottish monarch of its day. Fergus's Galloway home could well have been inspired by the primitive Mote of Urr near the Solway Firth. A close examination of his itinerary shows it to reflect a first-hand knowledge of the territory. Finally, as lord of Lothian, Fergus receives Tweeddale as a bonus (Schmolke-Hasselmann 1980*, 208–10/1998, 251–4).

Guillaume has, then, abandoned the typically vague Arthurian geography for a setting designed to draw a Scottish audience into the action. Within this more realistic scene he has introduced characters and their occupations: from ploughing teams and their equipment to border reivers, ferrymen and leather merchants on the one hand, to prosperous landowners and court officials on the other. Certain proper names narrow the period to the reign of William the Lion. The historical Fergus of Galloway died in 1161, five years before William came to the throne; but his descendants still frequented the court in the following century, as did Galiena de Mowbray, the lady with Lothian connections, after whom Guillaume apparently named his heroine. Those attached to the royal circles, where French was the favoured language, would have readily identified other prominent characters there, such as the lord of Liddel or the chamberlain especially noted for his chivalry. They might even have drawn mental parallels between King William and Arthur himself; and oblique references to events of his reign, like the English occupation of Roxburgh or the arranged marriage there of his natural daughter, could have helped to stimulate discussion.

The author was a man of considerable sophistication and verbal skills. He addressed a Scottish public with access to a body of literature that has otherwise left little trace in the country's records. On the simplest level Guillaume reminded them of Perceval's quest for a mysterious platter. Far more intriguing, though, was the way in which he manipulated his sources to call into question some of the conventions that dominated contemporary Continental romance. Central to these was the chivalrous pursuit of *fin'amor*, leading to an ideal marriage without regard for arranged matches. He was thus inviting his public to pursue one of their known debates on the place of women in society, and not merely within Scotland. In this and other ways a close reading of *Fergus* has invaluable light to shed for historians, as well as for students of literature, on an inadequately documented period when the country was actively engaged on the European political and cultural scene.

Guillaume le Clerc produced not only a well-crafted and entertaining romance, but also one that is socially challenging. No insular copies have survived: it has come down to us in two manuscripts from the north-east French region and a fairly free fourteenth-century Dutch version (Zemel 1991; Besamusca 2000, 211–24). It has left its clear mark on *Huon de Bordeaux* and *Aucassin et Nicolette*. Not the least of its merits is its claim to be Scotland's earliest extant literary fiction. [†DDRO]

Durmart le Galois

Durmart, a 16,000-line romance, survives in a unique thirteenth-century manuscript, Bern, Burgerbibliothek, MS 113. There is general agreement that the poem was probably written about 1220 (Wolfzettel 1985, 670). Its anonymous author is thought to be of Picard origin (Gildea edn, II, 85). Whilst there is no single identifiable source for the romance, there are many echoes of Chrétien's romances, most obviously in the use of the Sparrow-hawk Tournament at the beginning of Durmart's adventures; the candle-tree adventure appears to derive from the Second *Perceval* Continuation. Durmart's association with the seneschal's wife recalls the situation of Marie de France's *Equitan*, and the danger of marriage between an elderly man and a young woman is used in *Guigemar* and *Yonec*. Thematic parallels have also been noted with *Meraugis de Portlesguez* (Kirchrath 1884; Blumenfeld-Kosinski in Busby, Lacy and Kelly eds, 1987–8*, II, 79–92), *Le Bel Inconnu* and *Yder* (*Durmart*, Gildea edn, II, 29–68). *Durmart* has been described as an anti-*Erec* because Erec marries a girl inferior in rank to him (Schmolke-Hasselmann 1980*, 139–48/1998, 170–80), whilst the poet's drawing attention to the fact of their differences in rank (8453–8) implies that he attributes Erec's *recreantise* to this error of judgement. Durmart's father tells him early on that the son of a king should love a high-born, royal damsel (862–3), which resonates with the author's announcement that *Durmart* is a 'roial conte d'aventure' (*a royal tale of adventure*, 12). The romance has also been seen as influencing, in varying degrees, *Garin de Monglane*, *Le Chevalier aux deux épées*, *Claris et Laris* and *L'Atre périlleux* (*Durmart*, Gildea edn, II, 69–84; Lyons 1971).

Durmart divides into three parts of unequal length: a short, introductory episode (1–920), the main story, consisting of Durmart's quest for and eventual marriage to the Queen of Ireland (921–15540) and a final brief section in which Durmart and his wife visit the pope in Rome and rescue him from pagan attack (15540–16000). In the first section the King of Wales sends his son Durmart to be trained for knighthood by his seneschal. Durmart promptly falls in love with the seneschal's young, attractive wife; her elderly husband withdraws to allow them to conduct an adulterous relationship, in defiance of the admonitions and condemnation of Durmart's father. The relationship lasts for three years, until Durmart, now eighteen years old, realizes the unacceptability of his situation and behaviour. He abandons his mistress, and, within a few months, completes his training as a knight. As he approaches the city where he is to be dubbed by his father, a pilgrim tells him of the young and beautiful Queen of Ireland, who would prove an ideal wife for him. Durmart is immediately smitten with love for her and determines to find and marry her.

The dubbing ceremony over, there follows a lengthy *errance*, forming the main story and consisting of a series of adventures during which Durmart proves his prowess and the endurance of his love for the queen, all the while upholding the highest chivalric standards. Unbeknown to him, he actually accompanies her in the early episodes, until he inadvertently loses his way. It is at this point in the story that he learns that the object of his love is in fact the damsel he has already accompanied and championed in the Sparrow-hawk Contest. Eventually he seeks her in Ireland, where she is being besieged at Limerick by Nogant, her liegeman, who was supposed to have championed her in the Sparrow-hawk Contest, but who is now afraid that she would reveal his cowardly behaviour in running away from that challenge. Arthur and his knights assist Nogant in the siege, but Durmart defeats them and finally marries the queen. As in the case of Enide, it is at the time of her marriage that we learn the queen's name: Fenise.

The appearance of a miraculous candle-tree early in his adventures warns Durmart to heed the advice given him the next time the vision appears, which it does after his marriage. A voice instructs him to seek his salvation by confessing to the pope in Rome. There, Durmart defeats the pagan armies attacking Rome and learns from the pope the significance of the candle-tree. He is now a perfect

Christian knight, and he and his wife live out their days as exemplary rulers over their lands in Ireland.

Some attention has been paid to the structure of this romance in relation to traditional Arthurian romances and to the type of episodes it contains (Southworth 1973). Its tripartite structure represents three stages in the hero's moral ascendancy. Initially, he sins both against Christian teaching and the social rank into which he was born. To form a liaison with a woman of inferior rank is unbecoming for a prince, a fact that Durmart eventually recognizes, and it is significant that, as soon as he enters the regenerate phase, the goal of his long quest is his equal in rank and that he intends to marry her, not simply bed her. Once happily married, and properly integrated into the social framework for which his birth has destined him, a further dimension of the defence of the Church is added. The two appearances of the candle-tree link this progression, whilst the pope's explanation of the eschatological significance of the tree marks Durmart out for privileged knowledge.

The relationship between the hero and the Arthurian world is especially interesting. Durmart remains from first to last an independent knight. He sends all his conquered knights to his mother, rather than to Arthur, and consistently declines invitations to join Arthur's household. In fact, despite being a cousin to Arthur, he sees no need or desire to be judged by Arthurian society (Schmolke-Hasselmann 1980*, 140/1998, 170); indeed, 'the successful development of Durmart as the model hero is in no way linked to his acceptance by the Arthurian court' (Blumenfeld-Kosinski in Lacy, Kelly and Busby eds 1987–8*, II, 88). He is more a simple visitor to, or independent ally of, Arthur's court (Wolfzettel 1985, 679). Moreover, there is no direct contact with the court until over halfway through the poem, when Durmart's quest is well under way. By this time he has already championed his unknown beloved in the Sparrow-hawk Contest, and lost sight of her after going to free the knight of a damsel who had healed him of his wounds. He has also delivered Guinevere from the lustful hands of Brun de Morois, who had abducted her, thereby assuming Lancelot's traditional role. When he does go to Arthur's court, he simply tries to learn the whereabouts of the Queen of Ireland. On the way, he delivers prisoners from the aggressive knights of the Roche Brune. He is then declared the winner in a tournament against Arthur's knights, but does not stop to claim his prize. It is only four months later, during the Christmas festivities, that he actually reaches Arthur's court (8929–10406), where he proves his worth by sitting with impunity on the Perilous Seat. Whilst there, he also demonstrates his prowess by fighting the Green Knight, but then takes leave. Arthur's court is, however, present at the siege of Limerick, but only because Nogant lied about Fenise in requesting the king's aid, and because Arthur hoped that, by assisting Nogant, there might be some territorial gains for himself in Ireland. In the ensuing conflict Durmart easily defeats various Arthurian knights. Nor is it Arthur who eventually resolves the conflict, but Durmart's father, who is present alongside Arthur and who recognizes his son in their brilliant adversary. Although the wedding takes place in the presence of Arthur and his knights, they are really no more than honoured guests among others, even though Arthur does crown Durmart king of Ireland.

The marginalizing of Arthur and his court allows emphasis to be placed on independence and lineage. Arthur himself stresses the importance of lineage when he tells Durmart that he is bound to be a good knight because he comes from distinguished stock (9720–2). Wolfzettel discerns in this a political motive, relating to the situation in France since the time of Philip Augustus, when kings were attempting to centralize power and ally themselves with the growing townships; he sees the poem therefore as a plea to assert traditional feudal values such as the independence and autonomy of lineage (Wolfzettel 1985, 681). *Durmart* is therefore a model of a decentralized feudalism, an ancestral romance in which the highest nobility sets an example by upholding its traditional standards. One should always strive to be worthy whilst despising 'perece' (*idleness*, 10386), even as one grows older (15736–8).

A profoundly moralizing romance, *Durmart* openly promotes a conservative ideology (Wolfzettel 1985, 671), whilst addressing itself to the high nobility in general (15958). Wolfzettel concludes that it is not only anti-*Erec*, but also anti-Arthurian (1985, 681). Southworth, on the other hand, despite a detailed analysis of the poem, sees it as rather superficial (1973, 175); because the hero undergoes no psychological crisis during his adventures, she finds them rather monotonous and even somewhat platitudinous (1973, 108). **[LCB]**

Floriant et Florete

Floriant et Florete is an anonymous Arthurian verse romance of 8,278 lines. The title is given by the explicit of the only extant manuscript, New York, Public Library, MS 122, which dates from the fourteenth century. The romance itself is generally dated to the second half of the thirteenth century. On linguistic grounds, its author hails from eastern France or northern Burgundy. These observations, though not without foundation, require further investigation.

For an Arthurian romance the setting is unusual, as the action is situated almost entirely in the Mediterranean region. During a stag hunt, Elyadus, King of Sicily, is murdered by his seneschal Maragoz, who is in love with the queen. Maragoz offers to marry her in order to maintain peace in the land, but the virtuous queen rebuffs him, fleeing from Palermo to Monreale, where Omer, a reliable vavassor, helps her resist the treacherous Maragoz. On the way to Monreale, she gives birth to Floriant, whom Morgan the Fay immediately abducts and takes to her abode in Mongibel. There she raises and educates the child.

Morgan sends the young man to Arthur's court in a magic boat. On his way, Floriant accomplishes several exploits, sending all freed prisoners or defeated enemies to Arthur. The king decides to hold a tourney in order to attract Floriant to his court. The young knight participates and succeeds brilliantly. A letter from Morgan reveals his name and parentage as well as Maragoz's siege of Monreale. The Knights of the Round Table embark for Sicily with Floriant in order to help his mother; Maragoz obtains the aid of the Emperor of Constantinople, the island's suzerain. At the end of the first battle involving the two gigantic hosts, Floriant sees Florete, the emperor's daughter, and she him. Immediately they fall in love. However, since they cannot meet, they endure their passion without knowing that it is reciprocated.

Finally Florete, following the advice of her friend Blancadine, the daughter of the King of Hungary, sends a messenger to enquire of Floriant's love. Floriant, Florete, Gauvain and Blancadine have secret rendezvous in an orchard; however, an evil dwarf discovers them and informs the emperor. Infuriated, the emperor attacks Arthur's army, but is soon forced to come to terms. Informed about Maragoz's treachery, he settles for a duel between the seneschal and Floriant. Maragoz is defeated and quartered. The two couples, Floriant and Florete, and Gauvain and Blancadine, are married in Palermo with great celebration. Arthur's knights, including Gauvain and his bride, return to London, whilst Floriant and Florete remain in Sicily. Florete gives birth to a son who is named Froarz.

For three years, Floriant devotes himself exclusively to Florete. One day, by chance, he overhears a conversation in the street, in which a woman criticizes his inactivity as a knight. He therefore decides to leave Sicily in quest of adventures in Britain. Florete accompanies him; they travel under the pseudonyms of Li Biaus Sauvages and La Plaisans de l'Ille. En route, they defeat and kill a dragon together. After numerous other adventures, Floriant and Florete reach London at almost the same time as a messenger from Constantinople, who informs them of the emperor's death. The couple set out for Constantinople; later they transfer their residence to Palermo. Two years later, a white stag that Floriant is hunting leads him to Morgan's castle in Mongibel. The fairy tells him he is about to die, although he will survive for ever in Mongibel. When Floriant laments Florete's absence, Morgan sends for her and the couple are reunited for ever.

As critics have long noted, *Floriant* is highly derivative. But resemblances between texts may easily be exaggerated and they do not necessarily indicate direct relationships. Nevertheless, from a structural standpoint, *Floriant* resembles the romances of Chrétien de Troyes, from which the author also borrows entire blocks of text that he inserts verbatim into his own romance (Busby 1995). He also draws on non-Arthurian romances and other generic traditions, notably the *chanson de geste* (Micha in *GRLMA**, IV:1, 396–7; Bouchet 1999). It would be mistaken, however, to attribute these borrowings to a lack of imagination; it seems more accurate to see in them the mark of the writer's intertextual aware-ness. The literary tradition is not simply repeated, but reassessed. The reuse of traditional motifs and themes, the highly formulaic style, with the same lines recurring in different parts of the romance, as well as the narrator's recounting of his own love story, are part of a literary project that could be recognized and appreciated by a public of connoisseurs.

A most interesting feature in this context is the Sicilian setting *Floriant* shares with *Guillaume de Palerne* (McKeehan 1926), but which also echoes a twelfth-century tradition associating Arthur, and especially Morgan, with Mount Etna (Graf 1893; Pioletti 1989; Sturm-Maddox 2000a). Modern critics alternate between intertextual analyses of the reprise of (local) Arthurian folklore and an approach in which the Arthurian universe is seen as the reflection of an external political environment.[10] To date no thorough, systematic investigation of the historical elements present in the text has been undertaken, and possible echoes of contemporary events are thus variously interpreted. It may prove useful to take a closer look at Sicilian history in the thirteenth century, and especially its relation to the kingdom of Hungary, which may figure prominently in the romance, perhaps because at least twice in the thirteenth century it was ruled by Angevin kings.

As with other Arthurian verse romances preserved in single manuscripts, *Floriant* raises the question of the actual diffusion of the text. Two manuscripts of a fifteenth-century *mise en prose* have come down to us, and on the grounds of textual criticism it seems unlikely that they both depend on the New York manu-script.[11] **[RT]**

Arthurian Romances: Multiple Quest and Interlace Romances

Claris et Laris

Claris et Laris derives its title from the *explicit* to the unique thirteenth-century copy of the romance, BNF, fr. 1447. Its 30,369 lines make it one of the longest Arthurian verse romances. *Claris* can be dated with some precision because the prologue (46–7) refers to the fall of Antioch in May 1268 as a recent event. It is unlikely that the work was widely known in the Middle Ages, since its existence is revealed only by the one manuscript that preserves it.

There is little evidence as to the author's identity; on linguistic grounds one can presume that he hailed from Lorraine. The prologue suggests that he was a cleric with some interest in current events; it gives a sombre account of losses in the Orient due to greed (51–2). The prologue also states that the author was tempted to write a chronicle, but abandoned the project for fear of angering his contem-poraries by telling the truth (79–82; but cf. 23477–512). Instead, he wrote an Arthurian romance.

Claris relates the exploits of Claris and Laris, but the doubling of the two young knights does not correspond strictly to a bipartite structure, which alternates between the quest model, or sequence of adventures, and that of territorial conquest, or sequence of sieges. Amplification of adventures provides narrative dynamism, whereas love-matches and marriages punctuate and interlace with the quests and sieges. King Arthur also plays an important role. At first the object of admiration from afar, he emerges in the course of the narrative as an ideal king who unfailingly supports defensive wars that are quickly transformed into conquests.

The young Lydoine is married to Ladon, the hundred-year-old King of Gascony. Her brother Laris is Claris's companion. Claris falls in love with the queen, but opts to leave for Arthur's court with Laris. The two knights seek out adventures on their way to test their prowess (449–8228), in one of which the fay Madoine in the forest of Brocéliande falls in love with Laris. After they reach Arthur's court, the King of Spain besieges Ladon. Claris and Laris return to Gascony with a few of Arthur's knights. They drive out the invader, and after Claris confesses his love to Lydoine they return to Britain. En route, Madoine abducts Laris, and Claris sets out in search of him, together with ten other knights, including Gauvain, Yvain and Kay (8473–13356). The narrator interlaces the separate adventures of all eleven knights. They achieve their quest after a year and Laris is once again free. During the ensuing celebration, Laris falls in love with Yvain's sister Marine. When Ladon dies, the King of Spain again invades Gascony and abducts Lydoine. Arthur intervenes with an army to liberate her and triumphs after a full-blown siege; then he entrusts the conquered land to Claris, who marries Lydoine; he also decides to unite Laris and Marine. After some new adventures, the knights reach Camelot where they learn that Tallas, King of Denmark, and his father Salahadin are besieging Marine and her father King Urien. Arthur and his army put the Danish king to flight, but not before the Danes have captured Laris. Thirty knights, divided into three groups of ten, set out to liberate Laris. Thanks again to interlace, each knight's quest is related (20478–899). After the deaths of Tallas, Salahadin and their ally the King of Russia, Arthur ultimately triumphs. Laris receives the conquered lands and Marine's hand, but not without some interference from Madoine. One task remains: the liberation of Claris's father, King of Germany, besieged by the King of Hungary. Victory ends the romance, leaving Laris king of a vast realm.

The author knew Arthurian literature quite well. Although we do not know his actual sources, scholars have for some time noted the influence of Chrétien's romances, the *Perceval* Continuations and other verse narratives such as the *Bel Inconnu*, *Meraugis* and the *Atre périlleux* (*Claris*, Alton edn, 817–21; Klose 1916). Although Gauvain is not a major figure in the romance, motifs characteristic of Gauvain romances are common (Schmolke-Hasselmann 1980*,

167–8/1998, 203–4). Rewriting is evident in lines of verse literally lifted from antecedents, as well as in the recycling of commonplace adventure motifs, such as combat with one or more knights or with a monster, discovery of an empty castle in a 'terre gaste' (*waste land*) and an enchanted setting. Some motifs appear transformed, as when Claris and Laris come upon a version of the *pesme aventure* episode from *Yvain*, in which men are victims (2325–2496), or when Brandelis, like Chrétien's Perceval at the Grail Castle, is mute instead of questioning Merlin (22155–262). The anonymous author uses interlace, as in thirteenth-century prose romance, in order to organize two of the most elaborate quests in medieval literature.

After Klose (1916) had set out the anonymous author's debts to his predecessors, *Claris* was long neglected in critical scholarship. It receives only passing, usually unfavourable comment in a few general studies. Bruce (1924*, II, 275) finds it 'mediocre and interminable', whereas Micha faults its unpolished, uninspired artistry (*GRLMA**, IV:1, 395). Although the plot is not stylistically distinguished, and at times seems repetitive, it does have an identifiable structure and narrative interest (Kelly 1969). Today *Claris* is approached in two different ways: either as a reservoir of romance and folklore motifs or as a marvel of narrative virtuosity.

The first approach is less text-specific than the second. By studying motifs such as the maiden plunged into a fountain, or the providential boat, or by enumerating the occurrences of the forest of Brocéliande or of *fabliau* features, scholars focus on one or two examples from among the hundreds found in the romance (Milin 1991; Morales 1991; Pearcy 1991; Demaules 1995). 'A *summa* of all Arthurian motifs', the romance does indeed resemble an inventory of all kinds of adventures (Schmolke-Hasselmann 1980*, 168/1998, 204). However, by treating discrete adventures rapidly and separately, thus using the romance merely to support an independent argument, these studies fail to interpret *Claris*'s narrative whole.

The second approach concentrates on *Claris*'s narrative structure. Its complex plot deploys almost perfectly the principle of 'multiple quests' to integrate numerous adventures into a coherent scheme (Kelly 1969). By distributing the adventures among a significant number of knights, eleven in the first set, thirty in the second, the author gives every questing knight a place in the plot, and the simultaneity of the adventures in the interlace scheme remains intact. In each of the two sets of multiple quests referred to here, the narrative brings about closure, as Claris's quest 'cuts across' the quests of the other knights, thus conjoining them again after the initial separation (Kelly 1969, 262). The theme of *compagnonnage* gives additional significance to the romance by focusing on the knight as he assists the others and achieves the multiple quest (Kelly 1983, 413). Kay and Dodinel function comically in this scheme as counter-examples.

Much remains to be done on the major features of multiple quests, as well as on the *Claris* author's adaptation of interlace. His adaptation threatens the technique's integrity, for example by manipulating the formal switches like so many keys in order to move from one agent to another, all the while reserving only a few sequences for each knight, and sometimes allowing him only one episode before imprisonment immobilizes him. In this way, multiplicity thins the narrative more than in most interlaced plots. Such thinning by short, self-contained narrative elements, detached from what precedes and follows (Bruce 1924*, II, 275), impedes the smooth operation of interlace. Still, *Claris* is suitable for the investigation of narrative codes in Arthurian romance (Bozóky 1978).

Besides its intriguing narrative structure, *Claris* offers other issues for study. For example, it devotes considerable attention to siege warfare (about 6,500 lines). One could investigate the narrative variety of these episodes and their relation not only to other romances but also to chronicles, crusading epic and romances of antiquity. The motif of wars of conquest appears not infrequently in the plot. Expressions like 'nostre gent' (*our army*) or 'nostre baron' (*our barons*) invite audiences to identify with Arthur's knights as model conquerors. At the end of the romance, the King of Britain rules a wide realm. This romance, described as evoking a world that is the antithesis of contemporary evil (Kelly 1983, 416), offers in its way a positive response to the sombre picture of the world the author evokes in his prologue. [AC]

Rigomer

Rigomer, or the *Merveilles de Rigomer* (on the title, see Carapezza 2001, 85, n. 30), an incomplete romance 17,271 lines long, survives in Chantilly, Musée Condé, MS 472, dated 1250–75. The romance itself has been dated to the first half of the thirteenth century (Vesce transl., xix–xv) and its production localized in the Tournai-Cambrai (Hainault) region. *Rigomer*'s third section (15923–17271) was also copied separately in Turin, Biblioteca Nazionale, MS L. IV. 33. This manuscript was edited, but only summarily described, before it was destroyed in the 1904 fire.[12] It is referred to as 'the Turin episode of *Rigomer*' or the 'Quintefeuille episode', after the name of a castle in the narrative. Carapezza argues that this episode was an integral part of a romance originally composed of three parts, each treating a different knight, first Lancelot, then Gauvain, and finally King Arthur (Carapezza 2001, 100, quoting Walters 1994, 31). He also views the Turin episode as a continuation typical of multiple-quest narratives (112) that recast a variety of texts.[13] The 'Jehans' mentioned in lines 1 and 6430 is taken to be the author of an earlier work treating Gauvain's quest to liberate Rigomer castle. Then the anonymous author of the version in the Turin manuscript rewrote Jehan's work. Vesce (transl., xiii–xiv) and Lacy (1993) also argue that Jehan is not the author, but that the anonymous author contrasts his more truthful version of the story with the fanciful poem that Jehan once wrote. Whereas this version contains a great deal of *carole* and *fable*, its narrator assures his audience that he will not let them 'mençoigne entendre' (*hear lies*, 6449). The romance, as we have it, pastes together, as it were, its multifarious adventures, linking them by a weak, but coherent narrative thread (Carapezza 2001, 77–9, n. 2).

The discussion in the prologue of *desroi* ('foolishness') and *sens* ('sense') becomes a leitmotiv in the romance (on this feature of the Chantilly manuscript, see chapter XI) as it explores issues of wisdom in king and vassal. Arthur himself is a knight who evinces more sense than foolishness. In the first, or Lancelot part (18–6402), a maiden leaves Arthur's court after accusing his knights of growing fat and lazy whilst waiting for adventures to come to them. A great exploit awaits them in Ireland: the deliverance of Dionise, the lady of Rigomer Castle, from a spell that prevents her from marrying. Two knights who ride after the maiden bungle their attempts to bring her back. Then Lancelot makes his way to Rigomer, only to fall victim to a spell that makes him lose his memory. His days are taken up with the lowly tasks of a kitchen scullion.

In the second, or Gauvain part of the romance (6403–15916), Arthur's nephew frees both Lancelot and Dionise. It begins when a second maiden announces Lancelot's imprisonment to Arthur's court. Gauvain sets off with a party of other knights to rescue him. Their exploits combine the heroic and the less than heroic. For example, Sagremor attempts to rape a passing maiden, whilst Cligés triumphs over a 'living dead' figure who takes Cligés's place in a tomb in a perilous cemetery. Meanwhile, Gauvain is captured and thrown into a dungeon. Lorie de Roche Florie, Gauvain's fairy companion, brings about his release by promising to help his female jailer to marry her beloved.

Gauvain is unmolested by the enchantments on the way to Rigomer. Not only does a serpent let him cross a bridge unharmed, a damsel also proclaims him to be Rigomer's long-awaited liberator. Gauvain frees Lancelot and the other prisoners by removing gold rings from their fingers. These rings signify their enthralment by erotic love defined as appetite. Noble (1996) argues that this differs from love as a form of magic that works for Christian ends, as in Lorie's case. Gauvain cannot claim the promised reward for his success, the hand of the lady of Rigomer and with it the crown of Ireland, because Lorie keeps him for herself. After promising to arrange a suitable match within a year for the disappointed Dionise, Gauvain returns to Britain and Lorie to Roche Florie.

At Arthur's court, a distraught maiden requests help against Miraudiaus, who intends to force her to marry him. While the damsel's appointed defender, Midomidas, is waiting for Miraudiaus, Lancelot arrives on the scene, dressed as an idiot (which is appropriate, given his prior development). When Miraudiaus sees a scar that identifies his new opponent as Lancelot, he declares himself defeated on the strength of Lancelot's reputation. Gauvain matches Midomidas with Dionise, and Miraudiaus becomes a member of the Round Table. The Arthur part, or Turin or Quintefeuille episode, follows (15917–17271). In it Arthur helps a young woman regain her inheritance.

This unusual romance evokes a complex network of responses, as irony alternates with slapstick, with sophisticated literary parody and even with satire. In *Rigomer* the exemplary status of Arthur's court is at issue. One by one, Arthur's knights, traditionally idealized, are undermined, with the author focusing first on Lancelot, then on Gauvain and finally on the king himself. In the opening lines of the prologue the narrator claims that, of all Arthur's knights, only Gauvain matches the king with as much sense and even less confusion. Gauvain proves himself superior to Lancelot by ridding Rigomer of its enchantments rather than succumbing to them. Moreover, the author transfers Gauvain's reputation for flightiness with women to Lancelot. Lancelot appears to be the paragon of chivalry when he rescues a young woman about to be raped. But he refuses the princess's hand and her kingdom, gets her pregnant and abandons her, consoling her with eloquent but empty promises. The enchantments of Rigomer castle reveal Lancelot to be a creature of appetite, who bends rhetoric to serve his desires. After a year spent in the kitchens, he is paunchy from surviving on kitchen scraps and barely able to speak.

Yet Gauvain is subject to the same loss of prestige as Lancelot. When Miraudiaus suspects that Gauvain is championing the lady he is trying to force into marriage, he claims to be grievously ill. When Gauvain arrives, Miraudiaus offers to make his imprisonment bearable if Gauvain fails to show up for battle at the appointed time. Gauvain agrees. Miraudiaus declares that Gauvain has miraculously cured him, then he orders his beautiful sisters and servant girls to grant Arthur's nephew sexual favours. Gauvain eagerly accepts his generosity.

Minor characters, including women, also oscillate as exemplary figures. For example, Lorie, Gauvain's fairy mistress, appears both as a 'dangerous figure from the otherworld' and as 'an ally of the church and ... a Christian saint' (Noble 1996, 289). *Rigomer* plays on the shortcomings and sins of its traditionally ideal protagonists, showing that all of them, Arthur included, have proverbial feet of clay.

Although *Rigomer* is meant to be humorous, it also invites a moral response. Gauvain's reaction to the sight of Lancelot's degeneration is mixed. He first laughs at the spectacle of the former flower of chivalry reduced to an inarticulate scullion grown fat and sloppy; he is then reduced to tears. What message does this convey to the audience? After enjoying many comic moments, one may reflect on the more serious significance of this scene. To those who look beyond its value as entertainment the romance can communicate a moral lesson on ideal knighthood (Walters 2005). [LJW]

Escanor

In the late thirteenth-century romance *Escanor*, the author is identified in the prologue as Gerardinz or Gerars (4, 50). In the epilogue he is called Girars (25910) and, even more explicitly, Girardins d'Amiens (25900). Girart d'Amiens, as he is usually known today, also composed other literary works: *Charlemagne*, a biography of the emperor written in dodecasyllabic rhymed *laisses*, and *Meliacin*, an octosyllabic non-Arthurian romance in which the motif of the flying wooden horse, also employed in Adenet le roi's *Cleomadés*, is prominent. All these 'signed' works may reflect the self-consciousness of an author who is convinced of his worth, a somewhat paradoxical fact in the light of the rather low esteem in which Girart d'Amiens is held by modern critics. Nonetheless, the little that can be gathered from his works suggests that he was amongst the more successful writers of his period. The dedicatees named in his prologues indicate that Girart wrote for the highest nobility: *Charlemagne* is dedicated to Charles de Valois, brother of Philippe le Bel, King of France, and *Meliacin* seems to be connected to the same milieu. As for *Escanor*, the prologue and the epilogue mention explicitly Eleanor of Castile, wife of Edward I of England, thus establishing a link with this royal family.

Only one nearly complete manuscript of *Escanor* survives (BNF, fr. 24374). However, a reference in the inventory of Charles VI's library, along with two seemingly distinct series of fragments, all now lost, indicate wider reception (see chapter I). Girart's two other works, *Meliacin* and *Charlemagne*, both enjoy wider manuscript diffusion, which seems to confirm the reputation Girart enjoyed in his own day. Five manuscripts of *Meliacin* survive and two of *Charlemagne*. The date of the composition of *Escanor* can be determined fairly well. The romance is dedicated to Eleanor of Castile, who became Queen of England in 1274, when Edward acceded to the throne; she died in 1290. If one accepts the view that *Escanor* is partly a *roman à clé*, the presence within the romance of a king of Scotland bearing the arms of the historical king Alexander III (1241–86), and a king of Wales bearing the arms of Llywelyn ap Gruffydd, narrows the time even more. The latter was notoriously rebellious against English domination. However, he was on good terms with the English court during the short interval between 1277 and 1282; since he is depicted favourably in the romance, its composition probably falls within that period. It has also been suggested that the character of Escanor de la Blanche Montagne is an incarnation of Llywelyn ap Gruffydd, whose domain was the region around Mount Snowdon which the royal army rarely penetrated; the stiff resistance met by Arthur's troops on entering Escanor's dominion may reflect Edward's victorious campaign of 1277 against Llywelyn. It thus seems reasonable to date the romance in the years around 1280.

Escanor is one of the longer Arthurian verse romances; it contains nearly 26,000 lines and, if one counts the loss of a whole quire and two leaves in the first third of the text, it may well have numbered more than 27,000 lines. In spite of its length and a compositional technique drawing heavily on interlace, the outline of the plot is clear (for a more detailed summary, see Trachsler edn and Bruce 1924*, II, 276–85).

King Canor of Northumberland, seeking a valiant husband for his only daughter Andrivete, proclaims a tourney at Baubourc, where Kay, Arthur's seneschal, not only wins the prize but also the heart of the young lady. Unfortunately, he leaves without having declared his love. After Canor's death, Aiglin, his evil brother, does his best to force Andrivete to marry a low-born man whom he can easily dominate. Andrivete manages to escape and Kay convinces Arthur to raise an army to fight Aiglin. The latter's defeat permits Kay and Andrivete to marry.

Into this first plot the story of Gauvain and Escanor le Bel de la Blanche Montagne is interwoven. Whilst away from court, Gauvain is unjustly accused of murder by Escanor le Bel. Not knowing who has discredited him, Gauvain grows increasingly disturbed as the day for the duel draws near. Therefore, his squire Galatinet tries to help him by ambushing Escanor when he comes to court. He attacks the King of the Blanche Montagne, badly wounding him. Naturally, Gauvain is suspected, and Escanor le Grand, uncle of Escanor le Bel, tries to avenge his nephew by capturing Gauvain, but succeeds only in capturing Girflet, who is sent to the Queen of Traverses, Escanor le Bel's sister. Soon she and Girflet become lovers. When Arthur's army marches against Traverses to liberate the imprisoned knight, a duel takes place between Escanor and Gauvain; fortunately, the young Felinete intervenes to stop the combat and prepare the marriage between Girflet and Escanor's sister. After the reconciliation of Gauvain and Escanor before Traverses and the victory against Aiglin, a double marriage seals Arthurian dominion over hitherto independent kingdoms.

In Northumberland the news of his young wife's illness reaches Escanor le Bel. He returns home, but arrives only after her death. He retires from the world in despair, spending two years in a hermitage before dying a saintly death. His uncle, his sister, Girflet and an abbot set out to find him. When they reach the hermitage, they are informed of their friend's perfect death. Girflet and the Queen of Traverses decide to become hermits themselves, but after his wife's death Girflet returns to Arthur's court.

Escanor's close resemblance to contemporary events has led some critics to read it as a kind of propaganda piece for the English king, Edward I. Indeed, Arthur's most trustworthy men, Gauvain, Girflet and Kay, pacify through marriage or military conquest notoriously rebellious populations located on the margins of the Arthurian realm (Schmolke-Hasselmann 1984; Trachsler edn, 56–65). This pro-English message may well be one of the reasons why Girart chose not to write in prose (by 1280 the 'modern' form of Arthurian romance) but in verse; octosyllabic romances of the Round Table were mostly perceived as pro-English, whereas the prose romances, with their 'Continental' hero Lancelot, may have had pro-French overtones.

Whilst *Escanor* may mirror historical events, a political reading of this kind does not fully account for Girart's literary project (Trachsler edn, 65–7). He is well aware of the earlier literary tradition regarding, for instance, Kay and Gauvain (Busby 1980*; Noble in Busby, Kelly and Lacy eds 1987–8*, II, 143–50). He nevertheless deliberately transforms the legacy of Chrétien de Troyes, showing the king's nephew to be hesitant and frightened at the idea of having to face Escanor le Bel in a duel. Kay, traditionally a misogynous boaster, turns out to be not only enterprising, but also successful in what he does, under the influence of his love for the fair Andrivete (Schulze-Busacker 1984). Of course, Girart may have had access to sources now lost that presented a more heroic picture of Kay than the one common in the continental French texts (Noble 1984; Gowans 1988*); but one can also see Girart as drawing on 'stock' characters and situations in a ludic manner. The public he was writing for was most certainly able to appreciate the ironic use of the legacy of earlier writers. This tradition includes, of course, Chrétien de Troyes, but most certainly the *Huon de Bordeaux* Cycle as well (as Esclarmonde, the name of the fairy in love with Brien des Illes, suggests), and, most of all, the Arthurian prose romances.

By its length and its use of interlace, *Escanor* resembles the prose *Lancelot* or the prose *Tristan* more than, for example, *Erec* or *Yvain*. Certain characters such as Dinadan, Lambegues or Sinados, who otherwise appear only in prose romances, strengthen this impression (Trachsler 1993). Several features connect *Escanor* thematically to the prose romances. For example, the hatred of Escanor le Bel for Gauvain is linked to Escanor le Grand's enmity for the king's nephew, the individual characters thus being entrapped in a conflict between clans recalling similar conflicts in the *Lancelot–Grail* Cycle and the prose *Tristan*. Escanor's retreat to the hermitage in the final section of *Escanor*, which runs to over 2,000 lines, seems to echo the end of the *Mort Artu*. But all these factors may also be read as Girart's attempt, albeit somewhat artificially, to introduce more depth into the traditionally sunny universe of Arthurian verse romance and thus to reform the genre from within. [RT]

Intertextual Innovations

Gendered Narrative in *Le Roman de Silence*
The 6,706-line work known as the *Roman de Silence*, but which its author calls in line 1657 a story 'De Cador, de s'engendreüre'[14] (*about Cador and his offspring*), survives in a single late thirteenth-century manuscript, Nottingham University

Library, MS Middleton LM. 6, accompanied by the *Roman de Troie, Ille et Galeron*, a fragment of the *Roman d'Alexandre*, the *Chanson d'Aspremont*, the Arthurian *Vengeance Raguidel* and several *fabliaux*. Since the manuscript appears to be an anthology rather than a planned compilation, *Silence*'s codicological context reveals little about its generic characteristics as perceived by its thirteenth-century copyist. It does, however, represent the tastes and reading experience of its slightly later medieval owner. The *Silence* section contains fourteen small miniatures, eleven of which illustrate scenes from the romance, whilst three (by a different illuminator) depict mythological animals. The first historiated initial, introducing the *titulus* '[M]aistres Heldris de Cornüälle' (1; reproduced in Thorpe edn), portrays the author in non-clerical garb, despite the appellation 'master' (1, 6684) and mention of a Latin source (1660–2). In fact, the identity of Heldris, known only for *Silence,* is obscure: Frappier (*GRLMA**, III, 467–74) sees him as a secular cleric, whilst Thorpe (edn, 14), prefers a wandering *jongleur*. His date, on linguistic grounds the second half of the thirteenth century, and his provenance are also matters for scholarly debate. Heldris demonstrates no particular familiarity with the geography of either Cornwall or Finistère, but may have been connected with the Cornish Duchy. He could, however, have hailed from France (La Cornouaille in Maine-et-Loire), as his language is Francien with Picard features (Thorpe edn, 12–17, 35–59). Alternatively, Heldris may be a pseudonym based on Cheldricus, the enemy of Cador, Duke of Cornwall, mentioned in Geoffrey of Monmouth's *Historia*. Some feminist critics even speculate that Heldris was the *nom de plume* of a female author (Roche-Mahdi edn, xi, n. 2; Brahney 1985, 61). This unusual hypothesis is the result of *Silence*'s apparently very modern treatment of gender issues, which late twentieth-century critics have found fascinating (Gallagher 1992; Psaki 1997; 2001).

After narrating at some length the courtship of Cador and Eufemie, Heldris tells the story of their daughter, Silence, brought up as a boy in order to inherit his/her family's land. Despite the conflict between her female essence and masculine upbringing, personified in the debating figures of Nature and Nurture (2257–2350), Silence is very successful as a man, both in the rather unisex role of minstrel and, more surprisingly and unusually, in the highly masculine performance of chivalry. However, s/he falls victim to the sexual voraciousness of the queen Eufeme, who, like the wife of Potiphar, twice tries to punish the youth's unresponsiveness to her advances. Silence successfully passes her second punitive test, achievable only by a woman, when she captures Merlin (the romance's principal Arthurian link) by offering him cooked meat and wine. However, she thereby reveals her true sex. Further revelations by Merlin result in the deaths of the queen and her male lover, disguised as a nun. Despite the incestuous nature of King Ebain's marriage to his great-niece Silence, both the 'natural' gender order and the political order are restored at the end, for the English king retracts his prohibition on female inheritance, thus conveniently acquiring Cornish land through his wife.

Some scholars, emphasizing the positive depiction of Silence as a man, suggest that, although the narratorial commentary is ultimately gender-normative, the narrative structure indicates a protofeminist authorial stance (Brahney 1985; Lasry 1985; Psaki transl., xxxi–xxxii, on the unstable and unreliable narrator). *Silence* thus demonstrates that gender and the biological justification for different gender roles are cultural constructs (Krueger 1993*, chapter 4). Other critics view Heldris's portrayal of the eventual triumph of nature over nurture as a misogynist's attempt to repress his anxiety about women (Gaunt 1990). Queer theorists extend authorial anxiety to the presentation of sexual orientation, arguing that cases of female and male cross-dressing introduce the possibility of homosexual and lesbian desire (Perret 1985; McCracken 1994; Waters and Blumreich in Psaki ed. 1997). Lacanian/deconstructionist critics, on the other hand, read this *texte de jouissance* as a metaphor for poetic practice and the link between language and desire (Cooper 1985; Bloch 1986; Allen 1989). To support this view, they cite the extensive word-play on linguistic terms; for example, Nature creates by writing (1918, 1931), characters' names evoke types of speech (Silence, Eufeme, Eufemie) and Silentius becomes Silentia (2074–82) by losing the suffix *us*, i.e. she returns to her natural state by losing the 'habit' or 'custom' (Old French *us*) which has gendered her masculine. Scholarly concentration on the political aspects of *Silence* has demonstrated fruitfully that, as its authorial title implies, the romance raises important questions regarding female inheritance and power struggles between barons and the monarchy (Kinoshita 1995). Throughout, Heldris treats these serious issues humorously; Silence, for all her success as a musician and knight, is a figure of fun, a phallically challenged 'male', whose troubling gender is eventually normalized through laughter (Pratt 2003).

Histories of Arthurian romance have often suppressed the *Roman de Silence*, claiming that its Arthurian credentials are slight. Although it contains three references to King Arthur (109, 6154, 6156), and Silence's final adventure resembles the Grisandole episode in the Vulgate *Merlin*, the events narrated in *Silence* are not contemporary with Arthur. Moreover, the tale of Merlin's capture is derived from a common source, not directly from the prose *Merlin* (Lecoy 1978, thereby challenging Thorpe's specific *terminus post quem* of 1230). However, Heldris's familiarity with Arthurian literature is unquestionable, for Silence's claim to be a descendant of Gorlois of Cornwall (6145) is probably based on Geoffrey of Monmouth or Wace (though not the *Merlin*, in which Ygerne's first husband is called Hoel). A further challenge to Thorpe's classification of *Silence* as Arthurian romance was provided by Schmolke-Hasselmann, who excluded it from her study of Arthurian verse romance, on the grounds that it possessed few

Arthurian characteristics and that an Arthurian chivalric romance could not have a female protagonist (1980*, 4/1998, 4). Yet the point about *Silence* is that it deliberately inverts the norms of Arthurian romance, troubling its categories of gender and genre. Moreover, it enters into witty dialogue with Chrétien de Troyes. Heldris's portrayal of the timorous courtship of Silence's parents recalls not only the Tristan legend and the *Roman d'Enéas*, but also *Cligés*; the gendered nature/nurture debate mirrors ideas present in *Perceval* and the problematization of female speech evokes the *plaisir/taisir* binary of *Erec* (Pratt 2003). *Silence*'s main claim to Arthurian status rests, however, on the fact that the unconventional story of its heroine is simply the pretext for the final Merlin episode, in which the Arthurian *sage* triumphantly unveils through laughter the reality behind the appearances (Trachsler 2000, 118–26). **[KP]**

Tournament Narratives in *Sone de Nansay* and the *Roman du Hem*

Both *Sone de Nansay* and the *Roman du Hem* date from the second half of the thirteenth century. Although quite different from each other in some ways, both exalt the genealogy of middle nobility and share with Arthurian literature an interest in court life, especially tournaments, including the pastimes and entertainment associated with them.

Sone de Nansay
The sole surviving manuscript of *Sone de Nansay* is Turin, Biblioteca Nazionale, MS L. I. 13, which dates from the first half of the fourteenth century. Although this copy was severely damaged in the 1904 fire, the romance can still be recovered in part, because it occupies the central portion of the codex. Its prologue is in prose and the interpolated 'Lai d'Odée' (15983–16142) contains 162 decasyllabic lines gathered in eighteen stanzas that change their rhyme (ababbaabb) every two stanzas. Today, *Sone* contains 21,324 lines; 2,400 lines from the original are lost because of a missing quire. The title derives from the statement 'Explicit de Sone de Nansay'. The anonymous romance has been dated after 1263, when Haakon IV, King of Norway, led an expedition against the Scotland of Alexander III. The titular hero is son of a count of Brabant. The history of this region also offers useful clues for dating, notably the withdrawal of Henry, the elder son of Henry III, into a monastery in 1267. Scattered references appear to allude to the historical context of the Crusades prior to the fall of Acre in 1291. According to the prose prologue, the lady of Beyrouth, chatelaine of Cyprus, gave the matter of the plot to a cleric named Branque. The more or less explicit links between the prologue and the rest of the romance (Lachet 1992, 41–52) support the hypothesis according to which the author's name is indeed Branque. He probably hailed from the Walloon town of Nivelle.

The romance begins by relating Sone's genealogical background. Count Assel de Brabant marries Aélis, daughter of Count Ernoul de Flandre. One of their two sons, Henri, marries Ydoine, daughter of the Duke of Malone (Malines?). They also have two sons. The elder, Henri, remains a dwarf, whereas the younger son, Sone, is the protagonist of the romance. Sone falls in love with Yde de Donchéri, but she spurns his suit, despite her apparent love for him. To forget her, he devotes himself to knighthood, undertaking a long journey to Norway to help its king repulse incursions by the Irish and Scots. There he sees the Grail. It is found on an island off the Norwegian coast where Joseph of Arimathea left it (Lachet 1992, chapter 7; Trachsler 2000, 112–17). Back in France, Sone shines in various tournaments. He then returns to Norway, marries Odée, daughter of the recently deceased king, and is crowned king. Following the wishes of the pope, he also becomes emperor in order to defend Christianity against the Saracens. Before his death he witnesses the crowning of his sons: Houdiant as King of Norway, Margon as King of Sicily and Henry as King of Jerusalem. Milon, the youngest son, is elected to the papal see.

The plot follows, therefore, a strict chronological sequence. In order, its five major phases are: Sone's childhood (1–2914), his first exploits (*enfances*, 2915–8208), his victories (8209–16572), his marriage and coronation as King of Norway (16573–18006) and his coronation as emperor (18007–21231) (Lachet 1992, chapter 2).

In spite of the Grail episodes, *Sone* is not, strictly speaking, an Arthurian romance. There is no Grail quest and no Arthurian knight appears. It is rather an adventure romance meant to entertain by love themes, psychological introspection and description of costumes, places and settings, especially tournaments, battles and sieges. The key motif is Sone's social ascent. As an ancestor of Godefroi de Boulogne, he fits into the genealogy of both the prologue and the plot. No less important to the narrative economy is Norway, an exotic country that enters medieval French literature in this romance as a virtual *locus amoenus*. This northern kingdom has even drawn the Grail into its paradise. Norway's idealized court life also contrasts with the author's contemporary world, which he believes to be in decline.

Early criticism tended to fault the romance as dull, long-winded and monotonous (Lachet 1992, 5–7, 136–55). The unjustified neglect has been remedied in large measure by Lachet's monograph (see also Virdis 1997; Lachet 2000). Normand's thesis (1975) includes a summary, analysis of sources, motifs, conventional devices and the principal psychological portraits. [FC]

Roman du Hem

The *Roman du Hem* has been described as news-reporting in verse of exceptional historical value (Henry edn, xii). Its subject is an actual tournament that began on 9 October, probably 1277, at Hem, a village on the river Somme. Its 4,624 lines in Franco-Picard dialect survive in BNF, fr. 1588, a manuscript probably copied in Picardy at the end of the thirteenth or the beginning of the fourteenth century and thus close in time to the actual event (Stones and Middleton 1999). It was common in England, France and Cyprus to stage tournaments in imitation of romances. Often the participants disguised themselves as knights of the Round Table. This happens in *Hem*.

The author's name, Sarrasin, appears four times in the text. He seems to have been a literate minstrel serving a patron, but the name is too common in his time for closer identification. In an otherwise unclear passage (107–9), the author mentions the year 1277 when the tournament probably took place. The *Hem* was in all likelihood written shortly thereafter. A *terminus ante quem* may be provided by the serious wound inflicted on Robert de Clermont during a tournament at Compiègne in 1279 in honour of the King of Sicily; Sarrasin would surely have mentioned this misfortune in referring to this knight's joust, if the wound had occurred prior to the Hem tournament.

After a conventional complaint contrasting contemporary decadence with bygone glory, the prologue imputes the decline of prowess and largesse to Philippe III's prohibition of tournaments. Two young lords from the Artois, Huart de Bazentin and Aubert de Longueval, decide to restore the tradition in order to inspire French knights to go on crusades. Sarrasin promises an account of the event worthy of Chrétien de Troyes's *Perceval* (472–87). 'Guinevere' will preside over all activities. She arrives at Hem on the eve of 9 October. During the banquet 'Soredamors' beseeches her aid against a knight who has imprisoned her beloved. At dawn the following day, 'Kay' begins the jousts. These are recounted in succession up to the end of the narrative. Dances and other entertainments occupy the evenings. The tournament is, therefore, a virtual masquerade using disguises to link Arthurian fame with contemporary restoration of the tournament.

Hem resembles Jacques Bretel's *Tournoi de Chauvency*, which dates from 1285. Both 'tournaments' inaugurate a tradition of tournament narratives that will survive in France into the fifteenth century (*GRLMA** IV:1, 477–8; cf. Stanesco 1988, 71–102). Chrétien de Troyes is no doubt a major influence on Sarrasin, as attested by the presence of knights and ladies disguised as Guinevere, Arthur, Soredamors, Kay, Lancelot and Perceval, as well as by the use of the theme of the Knight of the Lion. Surprisingly, Arthurian prose romance seems to have had less influence on this work (Lachet 1992). **[FC]**

Allegorical Narrative in *Le Tournoiement Antechrist*

Huon de Méry's *Tournoiement Antechrist*[15] is a short poem of about 3,544 lines in which Arthurian elements blend with allegorical features. We know Huon de Méry only by what little his poem tells us. At the beginning, he declares himself to be a knight who had participated in Louis IX's campaign in 1234 against Pierre I Mauclerc. At the end of his text, he states that he retired to Saint-Germain in Paris (3520–1). His itinerary leading from the sword to the pen, from erotic wounding by Love to God and the Church, may of course be completely fictitious, illustrating a spiritual project of no documentary value (Gelzer 1913; Jung 1971, 274). Huon de Méry is more safely defined by his vast culture, more redolent of monastic training than of a university education (Jung 1971, 278), than he is by the autobiographical details in the poem. Moreover, the *Tournoiement* contains passages reflecting the viewpoint of a *jongleur* claiming his reward, which would hardly suit the image of a knight that Huon gives himself. Busby (1983) argues that Huon is speaking *pro domo* when he mentions professional entertainers. We are somewhat better informed on the date of composition, since the military campaign of 1234 establishes a *terminus a quo* and also provides a reasonable date for the period during which Huon wrote his poem; for no one would refer long after the event to a minor campaign such as that against Pierre Mauclerc. The internal chronology of the romance suggests that the events described take place in 1236 (Ruhe 1989, 64). The adventure starts 'la quinte nuit de mai' and ends, three days later, on Ascension Day, that is 8 May 1236.

   The prologue recalls how once, whilst in the forest of Brocéliande, the narrator wished to see the marvellous fountain described by Chrétien de Troyes in *Yvain*. He rides through the forest for four days, and finally reaching his destination he twice pours water on the marble slab (*perron*), unleashing the famous tempest. The next morning Bras-de-Fer, a horrible Moor and chamberlain of the Anti-Christ, arrives and drags the narrator to the city of Despair. There he watches first the infernal dinner served to the Anti-Christ and his followers, and then, the following day, a tournament in which the troops of God (which include personified virtues, angels, biblical characters and Arthurian knights) do battle with the Anti-Christ's army (pagan gods, personified vices and sins of all kinds). Inserted into the account of the tournament is the narrator's love-adventure. Struck through the eye by Venus's arrow, he has an erotic vision. Having recovered, the narrator presents himself before Reason in order to establish whether the responsibility for his injury should be borne by Venus, the eye or the heart. According to Reason, it is the heart's fault. Meanwhile, the tournament comes to an end with the temporary victory of God's forces. The narrator is invited to the city of Hope, where a banquet given by Largesse is taking place. Since he cannot enter God's palace, the narrator retires to the convent of Saint-Germain-des-Prés.

Some twelve manuscripts of the *Tournoiement* have come down to us from the thirteenth and fourteenth centuries.[16] They differ considerably in certain passages. This diversity shows that the poem encountered a certain amount of success in the Middle Ages that critics have only recently begun to appreciate. Probably the most interesting feature of the *Tournoiement* lies in its overt presentation as a synthetic project (Trachsler 2000, 311–24). In lines 3534–44 Huon names his two masters, Chrétien de Troyes and Raoul de Houdenc, and thus places his *Tournoiement* under the aegis of these two great authorities of his time, each of whom he cites as the ultimate reference in a specific genre: Arthurian verse romance and allegorical poetry. Huon de Méry conjoins these two traditions in his own poem.

The novelty of the *Tournoiement* lies in this double and simultaneous artistic patronage of Chrétien and Raoul. The legacy of Chrétien de Troyes is easy to trace (Grebel 1883). The entire first movement, with its journey to Brocéliande, is a *reprise* of the opening of *Yvain*. Chrétien is named (103) after the narrator claims to have seen more birds in the trees than did Calogrenant (95). On the other hand, the intertextual relationship becomes slightly comical when the narrator twice pours water on the slab, doubling the dose and thus the violence of the storm (Ruhe 1989, 71). Huon names Chrétien no less than five times, creating an *imitatio Christiani* so flagrant that one modern critic has called Huon's poem a 'Tournoiement anti-Chrétien' (Ruhe 1989, 73). Raoul de Houdenc is also present, but not as the author of *Meraugis*; rather his allegorical poems the *Songe d'enfer* and the *Roman des eles* determine the mode of the entire poem.

Huon's story is situated in the recent past or even the present, given the fact that he sets out to tell his own story (Jung 1971, 288). This explains why he abandons the dream-frame of the *Songe d'enfer*. Huon has produced a fictitious allegorical autobiography loaded with Arthurian themes and motifs. The narrator, assuming the role of Calogrenant and Yvain, is injured on his brow. He is no mere spectator who, like Raoul in the *Songe d'enfer*, travels to hell without leaving his bed. And because he chooses his two masters, Raoul and Chrétien, to guide his writing, and especially because he explicitly pays tribute to the latter, Huon de Méry does not awaken at the end of his story to admit the unreal character of his adventure. The *Tournoiement* undoubtedly shows how Arthurian material can be adapted to allegorical models. [RT]

Fragments and Lost Romances

A number of Arthurian narratives survive in fragments that tell us little other than the fact that they exist (Schmolke-Hasselmann 1980*, 7/1998, 8; Trachsler 1997*, 43–4, 234–9). They are too brief and had too little apparent influence to permit modern scholars to attempt reconstructions such as those undertaken for the Tristan poems. Others, lost today, are known through probable adaptations in other languages (e.g. the source of Ulrich von Zatzikhoven's *Lanzelet*). The existence of others is more controversial; some have claimed a French source for the Middle Dutch *Walewein* and the Occitan *Jaufre*, but the existence of such sources is considered unlikely today (Besamusca 2000, 214; see also chapter XIII). Allusions to names in extant romances may also be to lost works, but it is more likely that they refer to oral traditions, such as those that were sources of *matière* for the earliest romancers. [DK]

Notes

[1] See the index to Schmolke-Hasselmann 1980*, 160–9/1998, 195–205; Chênerie 1986*. There are Arthurian motif indexes by Ruck 1991* and Guerreau-Jalabert 1992*. Cf. Vincensini 2000.

[2] Froissart's *Meliador* is an exception. Verse romance survives otherwise only in Coudrette's *Melusine* (beginning of the fifteenth century) and in romances that alternate prose and verse, such as Thomas de Saluzzo's *Livre du chevalier errant* and René d'Anjou's *Livre du cuer d'amours espris*. Some verse romances were, of course, still being copied in the fifteenth century.

[3] On the use of topos in this sense, see chapter IV, pp. 158–60; Vitz 1989, 31.

[4] See Schmolke-Hasselmann 1980*, chapter 1:4/1998, chapter 4; Busby 1980* and Busby in Lacy, Kelly and Busby eds 1987–8*, II, 93–109; Cirlot 1991, 391–5; Morin 1995.

[5] Trachsler 1997* does not include these romances or those illustrating textual innovations.

[6] See also the 'Roman' dénouements to *Durmart* and *Sone de Nansay*.

[7] The dogs episode is likely to have derived from a lost *fabliau*-type tale; see *Chevalier à l'épée*, Armstrong edn, 63–7; Micha, in Loomis ed. 1959*, 364; *Gauvain Romances*, Johnston and Owen edn.

[8] In a prior scene with the host's daughter, Gauvain tells Hunbaut he is not 'de fust' (*of wood*, 882); here Gauvain's statue is 'de fust' (3112).

[9] Kay's blackened character recalls his role in *Perlesvaus*, where he murders Loholt, the son of Arthur and Guinevere. Arthur's degradation is also one of *Perlesvaus*'s distinctive features.

[10] On the first tendency, see Castets 1886 (esp. 76–84); Harf-Lancner 1984, 277–9; Stanesco 1995, 349. On the second, see Martin 1892; Lejeune 1958 (esp. 331); Sturm-Maddox 2000a.

[11] See the introduction to *Floriant 2*, Levy edn.

[12] This episode was transcribed before the destruction of the codex, but editions differ with respect to the readings of certain passages (Trachsler 1997*, items 92, 785–7).

[13] For example, the *Pèlerinage de Charlemagne* and Welsh legends of the Chapalu, a ferocious cat referred to in *Galeran de Bretagne*, and perhaps, *Yvain* (Carapezza 2001, 108).

[14] See Roche-Mahdi's edition, which incorporates most of F. Lecoy's proposed corrections to Thorpe's *editio princeps* (Lecoy 1978).

[15] Orgeur (1994) reprints the Wimmer edition of the *Tournoiement* without the critical apparatus but with a French translation. Bender's edition is unreliable.

[16] The identification of *Tournoiement* manuscripts is perhaps incomplete. The following have been identified: Paris, BNF, fr. 1593; fr. 12469; lat. 2381 (a miscellany containing ll. 2203–3262); fr. 24432; fr. 25407; fr. 25566; Rheims, Bibliothèque Municipale, MS 1275; London, British Library, MS Harley 4417; Oxford, Bodleian Library, MS Douce 308; Turin, Biblioteca Nazionale, MS L. V. 32 (largely destroyed in the 1904 fire); Vienna, Nationalbibliothek, MS 2602; Stockholm, Kungliga Biblioteket, MS Vu22. On these manuscripts, see Busby 2002*, 480, 552, and 578.

Reference List

For items accompanied by an asterisk, see the General Bibliography. Title abbreviations used in the chapter appear in square brackets.

Texts Cited

[*Atre*]: *L'Atre périlleux: roman de la Table Ronde*. Ed. by B. Woledge, CFMA 76 (Paris, 1936).

[*Beaudous*]: *Robert de Blois, Sämmtliche Werke*, vol. 1, *Beaudous. Ein altfranzösischer Abenteuerroman des XIII. Jahrhunderts*. Ed. by J. Ulrich (Berlin, 1889).

[*Bel Inconnu*]: (i) *Renaut de Bâgé, Le Bel Inconnu (Li Biaus Descouneüs; The Fair Unknown)*. Ed. by K. Fresco, transl. by C. P. Donagher, music by M. P. Hasselman (New York and London, 1992); (ii) *Renaut de Beaujeu, Le Bel Inconnu: roman d'aventures*. Ed. by G. P. Williams, CFMA 38 (Paris, 1929).

[*Chevalier à l'épée*]: (i) *Two Old French Gauvain Romances: Le Chevalier à l'épée and La Mule sans frein*. Ed. by R. C. Johnston and D. D. R. Owen (Edinburgh and London, 1972), 30–60; (ii) *Le Chevalier à l'épée: An Old French Poem*. Ed. by E. C. Armstrong (Baltimore, 1900).

[*Claris*]: *Li Romans de Claris et Laris*. Ed. by J. Alton (Tübingen, 1884; repr. Amsterdam, 1966).

[*Deux épées*]: (i) *Li Chevaliers as deus espees, altfranzösischer Abenteuerroman*. Ed. by W. Foerster (Halle/S., 1877; repr. Amsterdam, 1966); (ii) *Li Chevaliers as deus espees: A French Verse Romance from the Thirteenth Century*. Ed. by R. T. Ivey (Lewiston, NY, 2006); (iii) *Le Chevalier as deus espees*. Ed. by P. Rockwell (Cambridge, 2006).

[*Durmart*]: *Durmart le Galois, roman arthurien du treizième siècle*. Ed. by J. Gildea, 2 vols (Villanova, PA, 1965–6).

[*Enfances Gauvain*]. Ed by P. Meyer in 'Les Enfances Gauvain: fragments d'un poème perdu', *Rom*, 39 (1910), 1–32.

[*Escanor*]: (i) *Girart d'Amiens, Escanor: roman arthurien en vers de la fin du XIIIᵉ siècle*. Ed. by R. Trachsler, TLF 449, 2 vols (Geneva, 1994); (ii) *Der Roman von Escanor von Gerard von Amiens*. Ed. by H. Michelant (Tübingen, 1886).

[*Fergus*]: (i) *Guillaume le Clerc, The Romance of Fergus*. Ed. by W. Frescoln (Philadelphia, 1983); (ii) *Fergus, Roman von Guillaume le Clerc*. Ed. by E. Martin (Halle/S., 1872).

[*Floriant*]: (i) *Floriant et Florete: édition bilingue*. Ed. by A. Combes and R. Trachsler (Paris, 2003); (ii) *Floriant et Florete*. Ed. by H. F. Williams (Ann Arbor, MI, 1947).

[*Floriant 2*]: *Le Roman de Floriant et Florete ou le Chevalier qui la nef maine*. Ed. by C. M. L. Levy (Ottawa, 1983).

[*Galeran*]: *Jean Renart, Galeran de Bretagne: roman du XIIIᵉ siècle*. Ed. by L. Foulet, CFMA 37 (Paris, 1925; repr. 1975).

[*Gliglois*]: (i) *Le Roman de Gliglois*. Ed. by M.-L. Chênerie, CFMA 143 (Paris, 2003); (ii) *Gligois: A French Arthurian Romance of the Thirteenth Century*. Ed. by C. H. Livingston (Cambridge, MA, 1932).

[*Hem*]: *Sarrasin, Le Roman du Hem*. Ed. by A. Henry (Paris, 1938).

[*Hunbaut*]: (i) *The Romance of Hunbaut: An Arthurian Poem of the Thirteenth Century*. Ed. by M. E. Winters (Leiden, 1984); (ii) *Hunbaut: altfranzösischer Artusroman des XIII. Jahrhunderts*. Ed. by J. Stürzinger (Dresden, 1914).

[*Ille*]: (i) *Gautier d'Arras, Ille et Galeron*. Ed. and transl. by P. Eley (London, 1996); (ii) *Ille et Galeron par Gautier d'Arras*. Ed. by F. A. G. Cowper, SATF (Paris, 1956); (iii) *Gautier d'Arras. Ille et Galeron*. Ed. by Y. Lefèvre, CFMA 109 (Paris, 1988); (iv) *Œuvres de Gautier d'Arras*. Ed. by E. Löseth, vol. 2 (Paris, 1890).

[*Meraugis*]: (i) *Raoul de Houdenc. Meraugis de Portlesguez: roman arthurien du XIIIᵉ siècle, publié d'après le manuscrit de la Bibliothèque du Vatican: édition bilingue*. Ed. and transl. by M. Szkilnik (Geneva and Paris, 2004); (ii) *Raoul de Houdenc, Meraugis de Portlesguez: altfranzösischer Abenteuerroman*, in vol. 1 of *Raoul de Houdenc. Sämtliche Werke*. Ed. by M. Friedwagner (Halle, 1897).

[*Mule*]: *Two Old French Gauvain Romances: Le Chevalier à l'épée and La Mule sans frein*. Ed. by R. C. Johnston and D. D. R. Owen (Edinburgh and London, 1972), 61–89.

[*Raguidel*]: (i) *Raoul de Houdenz, La Vengeance Raguidel*. Ed. by G. Roussineau, TLF 561 (Geneva, 2004); (ii) *La Vengeance Raguidel*, in vol. 2 of *Raoul de Houdenc, Sämtliche Werke*. Ed. by M. Friedwagner (Halle/S., 1909).

[*Rigomer*]: (i) *Les Mervelles de Rigomer: altfranzösischer Artusroman des XIII. Jahrhunderts, von Jehan*. Ed. by W. Foerster and H. Breuer (Dresden and Halle/S., 1908–15); (ii) *Jehan, Les Mervelles de Rigomer: Chantilly, Musée Condé Ms. 472 (626)*. Rev. edn by T. E. Vesce (New York, 1995).

[*Silence*]: (i) *Le Roman de Silence*. Ed. and transl. by S. Roche-Mahdi (East Lansing, MI, 1992); (ii) *Heldris de Cornuälle, Le Roman de Silence: A Thirteenth-Century Arthurian Verse Romance*. Ed. by L. Thorpe (Cambridge, 1972).

[*Sone*]: *Sone von Nausay*. Ed. by M. Goldschmidt (Tübingen, 1899).

[*Tournoiement*]: (i) *Huon de Méry, Li Tornoiemenz Anticrit*. Ed. by G. Wimmer (Marburg, 1888); repr. without critical apparatus, with French transl., by S. Orgeur (Orleans, 1994); (ii) *Li Torneiment Anticrist by Huon de Méri: A Critical Edition*. Ed. by M. O. Bender (University, MS, 1976).

[*Yder*]: (i) *The Romance of Yder*. Ed. and transl. by A. Adams (Cambridge, 1983); (ii) *Der altfranzösische Yderroman*. Ed. by H. Gelzer (Dresden, 1913).

Other Texts Cited

[Andreas Capellanus]: *Andreas Capellanus: On Love. Edited with an English Translation*. Ed. and transl. by P. G. Walsh (London, 1982).

[*Brut*]: *Wace, Le Roman de Brut*. Ed. by I. Arnold, SATF, 2 vols (Paris, 1938–40).

[*Crône*]: *Diu Crône von Heinrich von dem Türlîn*. Ed. by G. H. F. Scholl (Stuttgart, 1852).

[Malory]: Sir Thomas Malory, *The Tale of the Sankt Greal*, in vol. 2 of *The Works of Sir Thomas Malory*. Ed. by E. Vinaver, 3 vols, 2nd edn (Oxford, 1967); 3rd edn, revised by P. J. C. Field (Oxford, 1990).

[*Sir Gawain*]: *Sir Gawain and the Green Knight*. Ed. by J. R. R. Tolkien and E. V. Gordon, 2nd edn, revised by N. Davis (Oxford, 1967).

Translations

La Légende arthurienne: le Graal et la Table Ronde, D. Régnier-Bohler ed. 1989*. Includes complete or partial French translations of *Le Chevalier à l'épée, Hunbaut, La Demoiselle à la mule* [= *Mule*], *L'Atre périlleux, Gliglois, Méraugis de Portlesguez* and *Rigomer*.

Three Arthurian Romances: Poems from Medieval France. Caradoc, The Knight with the Sword, The Perilous Graveyard. Transl. by R. G. Arthur (London, 1996).

[*Atre*]: *The Perilous Cemetery (L'Atre périlleux)*. Ed. and transl. by N. B. Black (New York and London, 1994).

[*Chevalier à l'épée*]: *From Cuchulainn to Gawain: Sources and Analogues of Sir Gawain and the Green Knight*. Transl. by E. Brewer as 'The Knight of the Sword' (Cambridge, 1973), 28–42; rev. edn by E. Brewer as *Sir Gawain and the Green Knight: Sources and Analogues* (Woodbridge, 1992), 109–26.

[*Deux épées*]: *The Knight of the Two Swords: A Thirteenth-Century Arthurian Romance*. Transl. by R. G. Arthur and N. L. Corbett (Gainesville, FL, 1996).

[*Fergus*]: Guillaume le Clerc, *Fergus of Galloway: Knight of King Arthur*. Transl. by D. D. R. Owen (London, 1991).

[*Galeran*]: Renaut, *Galeran de Bretagne*. Transl. by J. Dufournet (Paris, 1996).

[*Ille*]: Gautier d'Arras, *Ille et Galeron*. Transl. by J. C. Delclos and M. Quereuil (Paris, 1993).

[*Mule*]: *From Cuchulainn to Gawain: Sources and Analogues of Sir Gawain and the Green Knight*, transl. by E. Brewer as 'The Girl with the Mule, or the Mule without a Bridle' (Cambridge, 1974), 59–74; rev. edn by E. Brewer as *Sir Gawain and the Green Knight: Sources and Analogues* (Woodbridge, 1992), 42–58.

[*Rigomer*]: *Jehan: The Marvels of Rigomer – Les Mervelles de Rigomer*. Transl. by T. E. Vesce (New York, 1988).

[*Silence*]: *Heldris de Cornuälle: Le Roman de Silence*. Transl. by R. Psaki (London, 1991).

Studies

Accarie, M. 1998. 'Vérité du récit ou récit de la vérité. Le problème du réalisme dans la littérature médiévale', *Razo*, 15, 5–34.

Adams, A. 1978. 'La Conception de l'unité dans le roman médiéval en vers', *SN*, 50, 101–12.

Adler, A. 1960. 'Sur quelques emprunts de l'auteur de *La Vengeance Raguidel* à Chrétien de Troyes', *RJ*, 11, 81–8.

Allen, P. L. 1989. 'The Ambiguity of Silence: Gender, Writing, and *Le Roman de Silence*', in J. N. Wasserman and L. Roney eds. *Sign, Sentence, Discourse: Language in Medieval Thought and Literature*, Syracuse, NY, 98–112.

Ash, M. 1972. 'The Administration of the Dioceses of St Andrews 1202–1328', Ph.D. thesis, University of Newcastle.

Atanassov, S. 1984. 'Gauvain: malheur du nom propre et bonheur du récit', in D. Coste and M. Zéraffa eds *Le Récit amoureux*, Seyssel, 11–21.

Atanassov 2000. *L'Idole inconnue: le personnage de Gauvain dans quelques romans du XIIIᵉ siècle*, Orleans.

Batany, J. 1974. '"Home and Rome", a Device in Epic and Romance: *Le Couronnement de Louis* and *Ille et Galeron*', *YFS*, 51, 42–60.

Baumgartner, E. 1990. 'Des femmes et des chiens', in T. Bouché and H. Charpentier eds. *Le Rire au Moyen Âge dans la littérature et dans les arts*, Bordeaux, 43–51.

Baumgartner 1995. *Le Récit médiéval, XIIᵉ–XIIIᵉ siècles*, Paris.

Bauschke, R. 1993. 'Auflösung des Artusromans und Defiktionalisierung im *Bel Inconnu*. Renauts de Beaujeu Auseinandersetzung mit Chrétien de Troyes', in V. Mertens, F. Wolfzettel et al. eds *Fiktionalität im Artusroman*, Tübingen, 84–116.

Berthelot, A. 1991. *Figures et fonction de l'écrivain au XIIIᵉ siècle*, Montreal and Paris.

Besamusca, B. 2000. 'The Medieval Dutch Arthurian Material', in Jackson and Ranawake eds 2000*, 187–228.

Billington, S. 2000. *Midsummer: A Cultural Sub-Text from Chrétien de Troyes to Jean Michel*, Turnhout.

Bloch, R. H. 1986. 'Silence and Holes: The *Roman de Silence* and the Art of the trouvère', *YFS*, 70, 81–99.

Boiron, F., and J.-C. Payen 1970. 'Structure et sens du "Bel Inconnu" de Renaut de Beaujeu', *MA*, 76, 15–26.

Bouchet, F. 1999. 'Les Eléments épiques dans *Floriant et Florete*', in '*Plaist vos oïr bone cançon vallant?' Mélanges offerts à François Suard*, 2 vols, Lille, I, 87–99.

Boutet, D. 1992. *Charlemagne et Arthur ou le roi imaginaire*, Paris.

Bozóky, E. 1978. 'Roman arthurien et conte populaire: les règles de conduite et le héros élu', *CCM*, 21, 31–6.

Brahney, K. J. 1985. 'When *Silence* was Golden: Female Personae in the *Roman de Silence*', in G. S. Burgess and R. A. Taylor eds *The Spirit of the Court: Selected Proceedings of the Fourth Congress of the International Courtly Literature Society (Toronto 1983)*, Cambridge, 52–61.

Brucker, C. 1998. 'Aventure: discours et structure dans le roman médiéval aux XIIIe et XIVe siècles', in *Miscellanea Mediaevalia: mélanges offerts à Philippe Ménard*, 2 vols, Paris, I, 227–47.

Burgess, G. S. 1989. 'The Theme of Chivalry in *Ille et Galeron*', *MR*, 14, 339–62.

Busby, K. 1983. 'Plagiarism and Poetry in the *Tournoiement Antéchrist* of Huon de Méry', *NM*, 84, 505–21.

Busby 1985. '*Le Roman des eles* as Guide to the *sens* of *Meraugis de Portlesguez*', in G. S. Burgess and R. A. Taylor eds *The Spirit of the Court: Selected Proceedings of the Fourth Congress of the International Courtly Literature Society (Toronto 1983)*, Cambridge, 79–89.

Busby 1991. 'Chrétien de Troyes and Raoul de Houdenc: "Romancing the *conte*"', *FF*, 16, 133–48.

Busby 1994. '*Hunbaut* and the Art of Medieval French Romance', in *Conjunctures: Medieval Studies in Honor of Douglas Kelly*, Amsterdam and Atlanta, GA, 49–68.

Busby 1995. 'The Intertextual Coordinates of *Floriant et Florete*', *FF*, 20, 261–77.

Busby 1998. '"Plus acesmez qu'une popine": Male Cross-Dressing in Medieval French Narrative', in K. J. Taylor ed. *Gender Transgressions: Crossing the Normative Barrier in Old French Literature*, New York and London, 45–59.

Busby, T. Nixon, A. Stones, and L. Walters eds. 1993. *Les Manuscrits de Chrétien de Troyes/The Manuscripts of Chrétien de Troyes*, 2 vols, Amsterdam and Atlanta, GA.

Busby and K. A. Grossweiner 1996. 'France', in Lacy ed. 1996a*, 121–209.

Calin, W. C. 1959. 'On the Chronology of Gautier d'Arras', *MLQ*, 20, 181–96.

Carapezza, F. 2001. 'Le Fragment de Turin de *Rigomer*: nouvelles perspectives', *Rom*, 119, 76–112.

Castellani, M. M. 1990. 'La Cour et le pouvoir dans les romans de Gautier d'Arras', *Bien dire et bien aprandre*, 8, 19–34.

Castets, F. 1886. 'Recherches sur les rapports des chansons de geste et de l'épopée chevaleresque italienne', *RLR*, 30, 61–237.

Cirlot, V. 1991. 'La estética postclásica en los *romans* artúricos en verso del siglo XIII', in *Studia in Honorem Prof. M. de Riquer*, 4 vols, Barcelona, IV, 381–400.

Cirlot 2001. 'El juego de la muerte en la cultura caballeresca', *BSCC*, 77, 37–57.

Colby-Hall, A. 1984. 'Frustration and Fulfillment: the Double Ending of the *Bel Inconnu*', *YFS*, 67, 120–34.

Colliot, R. 1986. 'Problèmes de justice dans *Li chevaliers as deus espees*: Gauvain, meurtrier par procuration', in *La Justice au Moyen Âge (sanction ou impunité?)*, Aix-en-Provence, 125–37.

Combes, A. 1992–5. '*L'Atre Périlleux*: cénotaphe d'un héros retrouvé', *Rom*, 113, 140–74.

Cooper, K. M. 1985. 'Elle and L: Sexualized Textuality in *Le Roman de Silence*', *RomN*, 25, 341–60.

Corbellari, A. 2001. 'De la représentation médiévale: fantasme et ressemblance dans l'esthétique romanesque du Moyen Age central', *Poétique*, 127, 259–79.

Corbett, N. 2001. 'Power and Worth in *The Knight of the Two Swords*', in *Philologies Old and New: Essays for Peter Florian Dembowski*, Princeton, 319–37.

Delisle, L. 1907. *Recherches sur la librairie de Charles V*, 2 vols, Paris; repr. Amsterdam, 1967.

De Looze, L. 1990. 'Generic Clash, Reader Response, and the Poetics of the Non-Ending in *Le Bel Inconnu*', in K. Busby and E. Kooper eds *Courtly Literature, Culture and Context: Selected Papers from the 5th Triennial Congress of the International Courtly Literature Society, Dalfsen, The Netherlands, 9–16 August, 1986*, Amsterdam and Philadelphia, 113–23.

De Looze 1995. 'Feminine "Contre diction" of the Masculine in *Le Chevalier à l'épée*', in Wolfzettel ed. 1995*, 183–95.

Demaules, M. 1995. 'Gauvain et la sirène', in *L'Hostellerie de pensée: études sur l'art littéraire au Moyen Âge offertes à Daniel Poirion*, Paris, 129–39.

Dragonetti, R. 1987. *Le Mirage des sources: l'art du faux dans le roman médiéval*, Paris.

Dufournet, J. ed. 1996. *Le Chevalier et la merveille dans Le Bel Inconnu ou le beau jeu de Renaut*, Paris.

Fernández Vuelta, M. del Mar. 1990. '*Meraugis de Portlesguez*: el *jeu-parti* y la ficción novelesca', *AnFil*, 13, 51–68.

Fernández Vuelta 1992. *Raoul de Houdenc: la identidad de un autor y su obra*, dissertation, Barcelona University.

Ferroul, Y. 1999. 'Le Mythe du courage individuel et de l'exploit singulier', in *'Plaist vos oïr bone cançon vallant?' Mélanges offerts à François Suard*, 2 vols, Lille, I, 251–60.

Foulet, L. 1925. '*Galeran* et Jean Renart', *Rom,* 51, 76–104.

Fourrier, A. 1960. *Le Courant réaliste dans le roman courtois en France au Moyen-Âge*, Paris.

Fox, J. H. 1950. *Robert de Blois, son œuvre didactique et narrative*, Paris.

Freeman, M. A. 1983. '*Fergus:* Parody and the Arthurian Tradition', *FF*, 8, 197–215.

Gallagher, E. J. 1992. 'The Modernity of *Le Roman de Silence*', *University of Dayton Review*, 21, 31–9.

Gaunt, S. 1989. *Troubadours and Irony*, Cambridge.

Gaunt 1990. 'The Significance of Silence', *Paragraph*, 13, 202–16.

Gavino, E. 1994. 'L'eroe alla prova: i protagonisti di Gautier d'Arras tra etica del dovere e pratica dell'esistere', *L'Immagine Riflessa*, new series 3, 341–59.

Gelzer, H. 1913. 'Huon de Méry. Ein Beitrag zum Beginn des literarischen Subjektivismus in Frankreich', *GRM*, 5, 261–73.

Graf, A. 1893. 'Artù nell'Etna', in *Miti, leggende e superstizioni del Medio Evo*, 2 vols, Turin, II, 303–35; repr. Milan, 2002.

Gravdal, K. 1989. *Vilain and Courtois: Transgressive Parody in French Literature of the Twelfth and Thirteenth Centuries*, Lincoln, NE.

Grebel, M. O. L. 1883. '*Le Tornoiment Antéchrist par Huon de Méry in seiner literarhistorischen Bedeutung*, Leipzig.

Grigsby, J. L. 1968. 'The Narrator in *Partonopeu de Blois, Le Bel Inconnu* and *Joufroi de Poitiers*', *RPh* 21, 536–43.

Grimbert, J. T. 2005. 'The Reception of the Tristan Legend in Renaut's *Galeran de Bretagne*', in *'De sens rassis': Essays in Honor of Rupert T. Pickens*, Amsterdam and New York, 215–27.

Grisward, J. H. 1978. 'Ider et le Tricéphale: d'une "aventure" arthurienne à un mythe indien', *Annales*, 33, 279–93.

Grossel, M. G. 1996. 'Jeux de reflets autour d'une même thématique: le *Bel Inconnu, Galeran de Bretagne* et les œuvres de Jean Renart', *Speculum Medii Ævi*, 2, 15–32.

Guerreau, A. 1982. 'Renaud de Bâgé: *Le Bel Inconnu*, structure symbolique et signification sociale', *Rom*, 103, 28–82.

Guthrie, J. S. 1984. 'The *Je(u)* in *Le Bel Inconnu*: Auto-Referentiality and Pseudo-Autobiography', *RR*, 75, 147–61.

Haidu, P. 1972. 'Realism, Convention, Fictionality and the Theory of Genres in *Le Bel Inconnu*', *Esp*, 12, 37–60.

Halász, K. 1992. *Images d'auteur dans le roman médiéval (XIIᵉ–XIIIᵉ siècles)*, Debrecen.

Harf-Lancner, L. 1984. *Les Fées au Moyen Âge: Morgane et Mélusine: la naissance des Fées*, Paris.

Hoepffner, E. 1930. 'Les Lais de Marie de France dans *Galeran de Bretagne* et *Guillaume de Dôle*', *Rom*, 56, 212–35.

Hoepffner 1936. 'Renart ou Renaut ?', *Rom*, 62, 196–231.

Huot, S. 1987. *From Song to Book: The Poetics of Writing in Old French Lyric and Lyrical Narrative Poetry*, Ithaca, NY.

Jung, M.-R. 1971. *Études sur le poème allégorique en France au Moyen Âge*, Bern.

Kay, S. 1995. *The chansons de geste in the Age of Romance: Political Fictions*, Oxford.

Kelly, D. 1969. 'Multiple Quests in French Verse Romance: *Mervelles de Rigomer* and *Claris et Laris*', *Esp*, 9, 257–66.

Kelly 1983. '*Tout li sens du monde* dans *Claris et Laris*', *RPh*, 36, 406–17.

Kelly 2000. 'The Name Topos in the *Chevalier aux deux épées*', in *'Por le soie amisté': Essays in Honor of Norris J. Lacy*, Amsterdam and Atlanta, GA, 257–68.

King, D. S. 1996. 'Romances Less Traveled: Gautier d'Arras's *Eracle* and *Ille et Galeron* Reconsidered', dissertation, Washington University.

Kinoshita, S. 1995. 'Heldris de Cornuälle's *Roman de Silence* and the Feudal Politics of Lineage', *PMLA*, 110, 397–409.

Kirchrath, L. 1884. *Li Romans de Durmart le Galois in seinem Verhaeltnisse zu Meraugis de Portlesguez und den Werken Chrestiens de Troies*, Marburg.

Klose, M. 1916. *Der Roman von Claris und Laris in seinen Beziehungen zur altfranzösischen Artusepik des XII. und XIII. Jahrhunderts, unter besonderer Berücksichtigung der Werke Crestiens von Troyes*, Halle/S.

Kundert-Forrer, V. 1960. *Raoul de Houdenc, ein französischer Erzähler des XIII. Jahrhunderts*, Zurich.

Lachet, C. 1992. *Sone de Nansay et le roman d'aventures en vers au XIIIᵉ siècle*, Geneva.

Lachet ed. 1997. *L'Œuvre de Chrétien de Troyes dans la littérature française: réminiscences, résurgences et réécritures*, Lyon.

Lachet 2000. '*Sone de Nansay*, une somme romanesque', in M.-E. Bély, J.-R. Valette and J.-C. Vallecalle eds *Sommes et cycles (XIIᵉ–XIVᵉ siècles)*, Lyon, 13–24.

Lacy, N. J. 1980. '*Gliglois* and Love's New Order', *PQ*, 59, 249–56.

Lacy 1993. '*Les Merveilles de Rigomer* and the Esthetics of "Post-Chrétien" Romance', *AY*, 3, 77–90.

Lacy 1996. 'Motif Transfer in Arthurian Romance', in Kelly ed. 1996*, 157–68.

Lacy 1998. '*Meraugis de Portlesguez*: Narrative Method and Female Presence', in *Miscellanea mediaevalia: mélanges offerts à Philippe Ménard*, 2 vols, Paris, II, 817–25.

Lacy 2003. 'Naming and the Construction of Identity in *Li Chevaliers as deus espees*', *RPh*, 56, 203–16.

Langlois, C. V. 1926–8. *La Vie en France au Moyen Âge*, 4 vols, Paris; repr. Geneva, 1970.

Lasry, A. B. 1985. 'The Ideal Heroine in Medieval Romances: A Quest for a Paradigm', *KRQ*, 32, 227–43.

Lecoy, F. 1978. 'Le *Roman de Silence* d'Heldris de Cornualle', *Rom*, 99, 109–25.

Lejeune, R. 1958. 'Rôle littéraire de la famille d'Aliénor d'Aquitaine', *CCM*, 1, 319–37.

Lejeune-Dehousse, R. 1935. *L'Œuvre de Jean Renart: contribution à l'étude du genre romanesque au Moyen Âge*, Liège and Paris.

Leone, C. 1991. 'Chrétien de Troyes, Gautier d'Arras et les débuts du roman', dissertation, Brown University.

Levy, C. 1978. 'Un Nouveau Texte de Jean Renart ?', *Rom*, 99, 405–6.

Lindvall, L. 1982. *Jean Renart et Galeran de Bretagne: étude sur un problème d'attribution de textes: structures syntaxiques et structures stylistiques dans quelques romans d'aventures français*, Stockholm.

Loomis, R.S. 1949. *Arthurian Tradition and Chrétien de Troyes*, New York and London.

Lyons, F. 1965a. *Les Éléments descriptifs dans le roman d'aventure au XIIIᵉ siècle*, Geneva.

Lyons 1965b. 'The Literary Originality of *Galeran de Bretagne*', in *Medieval Miscellany Presented to Eugène Vinaver*, Manchester, 206–19.

Lyons 1971. 'The Wounding of Durmart', *FS*, 25, 129–35.

McCracken, P. 1994. '"The Boy Who Was a Girl": Reading Gender in the *Roman de Silence*', *RR*, 85, 517–36.

McKeehan, I. P. 1926. '*Guillaume de Palerne*: A Medieval "Best Seller"', *PMLA*, 41, 785–809.

Martin, E. 1892. 'Neuere Schriften zur Arthur- und Gralsage', *AfdA*, 18, 248–61.

Mauritz, H. D. 1974. *Der Ritter im magischen Reich: Märchenelemente im französischen Abenteuerroman des 12. und 13. Jahrhunderts*, Bern and Frankfurt.

Ménard, P. 1969. *Le Rire et le sourire dans le roman courtois en France au Moyen Age (1150–1250)*, Geneva.

Meneghetti, M. L. 1984. 'Duplicazione e specularità nel romanzo arturiano (dal "Bel Inconnu" al "Lancelot-Graal"), in *Mittelalterstudien: Erich Köhler zum Gedenken*, Heidelberg, 206–17.

Meyer, P. 1892. 'Fragment de la *Vengeance de Raguidel*', *Rom*, 21, 414–18.

Micha, A. 1944–5. 'Raoul de Houdenc est-il l'auteur du *Songe de Paradis* et de la *Vengeance Raguidel*?' *Rom*, 68, 316–60.

Micha 1946–7. 'Les Éditions de Robert de Blois', *Rom*, 69, 248–56.

Micha 1976. 'L'Épreuve de l'épée', in *Alexandre Micha: de la chanson de geste au roman. Études de littérature médiévale offertes par ses amis, élèves et collègues*, Geneva, 433–46.

Milin, G. 1991. 'La Traversée prodigieuse dans le folklore et l'hagiographie celtiques: de la merveille au miracle', *Ann. Bret*, 98, 1–25.

Mora, F. 2001. 'Remploi et sens du jeu dans quelques textes médio-latins et français des XIIe et XIIIe siècles: Baudri de Bourgueil, Hue de Rotelande, Renaut de Beaujeu', in M. Zimmermann ed. *Auctor et auctoritas: invention et conformisme dans l'écriture médiévale*, Paris, 219–30.

Morales, A. M. 1991. 'Los habitantes de Brocelandia', *Med*, 9, 8–17.

Morin, L. 1995. 'De la souveraineté dans le *Roman d'Yder*: la déloyauté d'Arthur et l'excellence d'Yder', *PRIS-MA*, 11, 185–98.

Noble, P. 1984. 'The Unexpected Hero: The Role of Kay in *Escanor*', in G. Mermier ed. *Courtly Romance: A Collection of Essays*, Detroit, 161–8.

Noble 1996. 'The Role of Lorie in *Les Merveilles de Rigomer*', *BBIAS*, 48, 283–90.

Normand, K. 1975. 'A Study of the Old French Romance of *Sone de Nansay*', dissertation, University of Pennsylvania.

Nykrog, P. 1973. 'Two Creators of Narrative Form in Twelfth-Century France: Gautier d'Arras – Chrétien de Troyes', *Spec*, 48, 258–76.

Offord, M. H. 1979. 'Étude comparative du vocabulaire de *Cligès* de Chrétien de Troyes et d'*Ille et Galeron* de Gautier d'Arras', *Cahiers de Lexicologie*, 34, 36–52.

Owen, D. D. R. 1984. 'The Craft of Guillaume le Clerc's *Fergus*', in L. A. Arrathoon ed. 1984*, 47–81.

Owen 1997. *William the Lion 1143–1214: Kingship and Culture*, East Linton.

Pallemans, G. S. 1992. 'Parody and Renewal in *La Vengeance Raguidel*', dissertation, Florida State University.

Paris, G. 1886. 'Études sur les romans de la Table Ronde: Guinglain ou le Bel Inconnu', *Rom*, 15, 1–24.

Pearcy, R. J. 1991. 'Fabliau Intervention in Some Mid-Thirteenth-Century Arthurian Verse Romances', *AY*, 1, 63–89.

Peron, G. 1980. 'Il dibattito sull'amore dopo Andrea Cappellano: "Meraugis de Portlesguez" e "Galeran de Bretagne"', *CN*, 40, 103–21.

Peron 1992. 'Image et amour dans *Galeran de Bretagne*', in D. Buschinger and W. Spiewok eds *L'Image au Moyen Âge*, Amiens and Greifswald, 243–55.

Peron 1998. 'La "mère amère": du *Fresne* de Marie de France à *Galeran de Bretagne*', *Bien dire et bien aprandre*, 16, 217–27.

Perret, M. 1985. 'Travesties et transsexuelles: Yde, Silence, Grisandole, Blanchandine', *RomN*, 25, 328–40.

Perret 1988. 'Atemporalités et effet de fiction dans *Le Bel Inconnu*', in *Le Nombre du temps en hommage à Paul Zumthor*, Paris, 225–35.

Perret 1999. 'Proverbes et sentences: la fonction idéologique dans *Le Bel Inconnu* de Renaud de Beaujeu', in *'Plaist vos oïr bone cançon vallant?' Mélanges offerts à François Suard*, 2 vols, Lille, II, 691–701.

Pierreville, C. 1994. 'Le Couple et le double dans les romans de Gautier d'Arras', in M.-M. Castellani and J.-P. Martin eds *Arras au Moyen Âge: histoire et littérature*, Arras, 97–109.

Pierreville 2001. *Gautier d'Arras, l'autre Chrétien*, Paris.

Pioletti, A. 1989. 'Artù, Avallon, l'Etna', *Quaderni Medievali*, 28, 6–35.

Plasson, A.M. 1973. 'L'Obsession du reflet dans "Galeran de Bretagne"', in *Mélanges de langue et de littérature médiévales offerts à Pierre Le Gentil*, Paris, 673–89.

Pratt, K. 2003. 'Humour in the *Roman de Silence*', *AL*, 19, 87–103.

Psaki, F. R., ed. 1997. *Le Roman de Silence*, *Arthuriana*, special issue, 7:2.

Psaki ed. 2001. *Essays on Le Roman de Silence*, *Arthuriana*, special issue, 12:1.

Putter, A. 1995. *'Sir Gawain and the Green Knight' and French Arthurian Romance*, Oxford.

Rauhut, F. 1978. 'Das Psychologische in den Romanen Gautiers von Arras', in E. Köhler ed. *Der altfranzösische höfische Roman*, Darmstadt, 142–69.

Renzi, L. 1964. *Tradizione cortese e realismo in Gautier d'Arras*, Padua.

Renzi 1967. 'Le Décor celtisant dans "Ille et Galeron" de Gautier d'Arras', *CCM*, 10, 39–44.

Rieger, D. 1989. 'Le Motif de la jalousie dans le roman arthurien: l'exemple du roman d'*Yder*', *Rom*, 110, 364–82.

Rockwell, P. V. 1994. 'Twin Mysteries: "ceci n'est pas un Fresne". Rewriting Resemblance in *Galeran de Bretagne*', in *Conjunctures: Medieval Studies in Honor of Douglas Kelly*, Amsterdam and Atlanta, GA, 487–504.

Rockwell 2000. '*Appellation contrôlée*: Motif Transfer and the Adaptation of Names in the *Chevalier as deus espees*', in *'Por le soie amisté': Essays in Honor of Norris J. Lacy*, Amsterdam and Atlanta, GA, 435–52.

Ruhe, E. 1989. 'Die Turnierkunst des Huon de Méry', *ZrP*, 105, 63–80.

Sansone, G. E. 1996. '*Ille et Galeron*: un anagramma al crocevia', *Studi testuali*, 4, 113–21.

Schmolke-Hasselmann, B. 1980. 'King Arthur as Villain in the Thirteenth-Century Romance *Yder*', *RMS*, 6, 31–43.

Schmolke-Hasselmann 1981. 'Der französische höfische Roman', in *Neues Handbuch der Literaturwissenschaft*, vol. 7: *Europäisches Hochmittelalter*, Wiesbaden, 283–322.

Schmolke-Hasselmann 1984. 'Ausklang der altfranzösischen Artusepik: *Escanor* und *Meliador*', in K. H. Göller ed. *Spätmittelalterliche Artusliteratur*, Paderborn, Munich, Vienna and Zurich, 41–52.

Schnell, R. 1982. 'Von der kanonistischen zur höfischen Ehekasuistik: Gautiers d'Arras *Ille et Galeron*', *ZrP*, 98, 257–95.

Schofield, W. H. 1895. *Studies on Libeaus Desconus*, Boston.

Schulze-Busacker, E. 1984. '"Gauvain li malparlier" – le rôle de Gauvain dans le *Roman d'Escanor*', in J. Ribard et al. eds *Lancelot, Yvain et Gauvain*, Paris, 113–23.

Schulze-Busacker 1985. *Proverbes et expressions proverbiales dans la littérature narrative du Moyen Âge français: recueil et analyse*, Paris.

Simons, P. 1996. 'The "Bel Sanblant": Reading *Le Bel Inconnu*', *FS*, 50, 257–74.

Southworth, M. J. 1973. *Étude comparée de quatre romans médiévaux: Jaufre, Fergus, Durmart, Blancandrin*, Paris.

Stanesco, M. 1988. *Jeux d'errance du chevalier médiéval: aspects ludiques de la fonction guerrière dans la littérature du Moyen Âge flamboyant*, Leiden and New York.

Stanesco 1995. 'L'Enfant aimé des fées', in *Lancelot – Lanzelet, hier et aujourd'hui pour fêter les 90 ans d'Alexandre Micha*, Greifswald, 341–51.

Stiennon, J., and R. Lejeune 1963. 'La Légende arthurienne dans la sculpture de la cathédrale de Modène', *CCM*, 6, 281–96.

Stones, A., and R. Middleton. 1999. A. Stones, 'The Manuscript, Paris BNF fr. 1588, and its Illustrations'; R. Middleton, 'The History of Paris BNF fr. 1588', in B.N. Sargent-Baur ed. *Philippe de Remi, Le Roman de la Manekine*, Amsterdam and Atlanta, GA, 1–68.

Sturm, S. 1971a. 'The *Bel Inconnu*'s Enchantress and the Intent of Renaut de Beaujeu', *FR*, 44, 862–9.

Sturm 1971b. 'The Love-Interest in *Le Bel Inconnu*: Innovation in the *Roman Courtois*', *FMLS*, 7, 241–8.

Sturm 1972. 'Magic in *Le Bel Inconnu*', *Esp*, 12:1, 19–25.

Sturm-Maddox, S., and D. Maddox, eds 1993. 'Genre and Intergenre in Medieval French Literature', *Esp*, 33: 4, 3–109.

Sturm-Maddox 2000a. 'The Arthurian Romance in Sicily: *Floriant et Florete*', in *Conjointure arthurienne: actes de la 'Classe d'Excellence' de la Chaire Francqui 1998*, Louvain-la-Neuve, 95–107.

Sturm-Maddox 2000b. 'Arthurian Evasions: The End(s) of Fiction in *Floriant et Florete*', in *'Por le soie amisté': Essays in Honor of Norris J. Lacy*, Amsterdam and Atlanta, GA, 475–89.

Szkilnik, M. 2000. 'Un exercice de style au XIIIᵉ siècle: *Hunbaut*', *RPh*, 54, 29–42.

Thedens, R. 1908. *Li Chevaliers as deus espees in seinem Verhältnis zu seinen Quellen, insbesondere zu den Romanen Crestiens von Troyes*, Göttingen.

Toury, M.-N. 1998. '*Le Bel Inconnu*, un roman de l'ironie', in *Miscellanea Mediaevalia: mélanges offerts à Philippe Ménard*, 2 vols, Paris, II, 1399–1407.

Trachsler, R. 1993. 'De la prose au vers: le cas de Dynadan dans l'*Escanor* de Girart d'Amiens', in G. Hilty ed. *Actes du XXᵉ Congrès International de Linguistique et Philologie Romanes. Université de Zurich (6–11 avril 1992)*, 5 vols, Tübingen and Basel, V, 399–412.

Trachsler 1994. 'Le Recueil Paris, BN fr. 12603', *CN*, 54, 189–211.

Trachsler 2000. *Disjointures-Conjointures: étude sur l'interférence des matières narratives dans la littérature française du Moyen Âge*, Tübingen and Basel.

Van Coolput-Storms, C. A. 1994. 'Autoportraits de héros', in *Conjunctures: Medieval Studies in Honor of Douglas Kelly*, Amsterdam and Atlanta, GA, 97–111.

Vincensini, J.-J. 2000. *Motifs et thèmes du récit médiéval*, Paris.

Virdis, M. 1997. 'Stranieri e terre straniere nel *Sone de Nansay*', in *Lo straniero*, 2 vols, Rome, II, 367–87.

Virdis 2001. *Gloser la lettre: Marie de France, Renaut de Beaujeu, Jean Renart*, Rome.

Vitz, E. B. 1989. *Medieval Narrative and Modern Narratology: Subjects and Objects of Desire*, New York.

Walter, P. 1996. *Le Bel Inconnu de Renaut de Beaujeu: rite, mythe et roman*, Paris.

Walters, L. 1993a. '"A Love that Knows no Falsehood": Moral Instruction and Narrative Closure in the *Bel Inconnu* and *Beaudous*', *SAR*, 58:2, 21–39.

Walters 1993b. 'Manuscript Context of the *Beaudous* of Robert de Blois', *Man*, 37, 179–92.

Walters 1994. 'The Formation of a Gauvain Cycle in Chantilly Manuscript 472', *Neophil*, 78, 29–43.

Walters 2000. 'Resurrecting Gauvain in *L'Atre périlleux* and the Middle Dutch *Walewein*', in *'Por le soie amisté': Essays in Honor of Norris J. Lacy*, Amsterdam and Atlanta, GA, 509–37.

Walters 2005. 'The King's Example: Arthur, Gauvain, and Lancelot in *Rigomer* and Chantilly, Musée Condé 472 (anc. 626)', in *'De sens rassis': Essays in Honor of Rupert T. Pickens*, Amsterdam and New York, 699–717.

Watt, D. E. R. 1977. *A Biographical Dictionary of Scottish Graduates to A.D. 1410*, Oxford.

Webster, K. G. T. 1951. *Guinevere: A Study of her Abductions*, Milton, MA.

Wilmotte, M. 1928. 'Un curieux cas de plagiat littéraire: le poème de *Galeran*', *Académie Royale de Belgique: Bulletin de la Classe des Lettres et des Sciences morales et politiques*, 5th series, 14, 269–309.

Wolfzettel, F. 1973–4. 'Zur Stellung und Bedeutung der *Enfances* in der altfranzösischen Epik,' *ZfSL*, 83, 317–48, and 84, 1–32.

Wolfzettel 1985. 'Idéologie chevaleresque et conception féodale dans *Durmart le Galois*: l'altération du schéma arthurien sous l'impact de la réalité politique du XIIIᵉ siècle', in C. Foulon et al. eds 1985*, II, 668–86.

Wolfzettel 1990a. 'La Découverte de la femme dans les romans de Gautier d'Arras', *Bien dire et bien aprandre*, 8, 35–54.

Wolfzettel 1990b. 'La Recherche de l'universel. Pour une nouvelle lecture des romans de Gautier d'Arras', *CCM*, 33, 113–31.

Wolfzettel 1992. 'Rom und die Anfänge des altfranzösischen Romans: Liebe, Religion und Politik bei Gautier d'Arras', in B. Schimmelpfennig and L. Schmugge eds *Rom im hohen Mittelalter*, Sigmaringen, 139–63.

Zemel, R. M. T. 1991. *Op zoek naar Galiene: over de Oudfranse 'Fergus' en de Middelnederlandse Ferguut*, Amsterdam.

Zemel 1994. 'The New and the Old Perceval: Guillaume's *Fergus* and Chrétien's *Conte du Graal*', *BBIAS*, 46, 324–42.

XI

MANUSCRIPT COMPILATIONS OF VERSE ROMANCES

Lori J. Walters

Introduction

In the thirteenth century, techniques for manuscript compilation reached a high degree of sophistication. Despite their length, complex prose compilations such as the *Lancelot–Grail* Cycle and the prose *Tristan* became the preferred form for romance composition. This preference continued into the late Middle Ages when writers such as Micheau Gonnot and Rusticien de Pise recombined earlier prose romances to produce even longer and more complex compilations (Pickford 1959/60*; Lacy in Krueger ed. 2000*, 167–82). However, as prose romance emerged during the century, verse was gradually abandoned, perhaps discredited as falsifying the truth (Köhler 1962, 214–17; Baumgartner 1995, 71–5). Although copies of Chrétien's romances survive in relatively large numbers, the verse romances of his successors are most commonly preserved in only one manuscript, usually a compilation (see chapter I). Indeed, before verse romance disappeared almost entirely from the corpus of medieval French literature, compilations of verse romances enjoyed a certain prominence in the thirteenth century. There are approximately twenty such collections, depending on how fragments are counted (Schmolke-Hasselmann 1980*, 179/1998, 221).

Research into these compilations has flourished recently as scholars focus more on post-Chrétien verse romance (Huot 1987; Short 1988; Huot in Krueger ed. 2000*, 60–77; Busby 2002*). Busby, who devotes an entire two-volume study to reading verse romances in their manuscript context, touches on subjects that will be dealt with here, in particular the scribe Guiot of BNF, fr. 794 (Busby 2002*, I, 93–108) and the epigonal Arthurian romances (I, 405–37). The reader should also consult Busby for further examples of verse compilations (Walters 2003b). This chapter will thus serve the dual function of reviewing the latest scholarship on the manuscript context of verse romances and of suggesting avenues for future research. The focus here will be on two major leitmotivs which emerged in chapter X, the importance of Chrétien's romances and of his richly ambiguous character Gauvain as models for later verse romances. These tendencies are apparent not only in later texts, but also in the manuscript compilations which contain them. These leitmotivs will be examined in three compilations (each containing from nine to eleven textual units) whose importance has long been recognized: BNF, fr. 794, transcribed *c.*1230 (Roques 1952, 184; Stirnemann 1999, 66) in Champagne by the copyist and compiler Guiot; BNF, fr. 1450, transcribed *c.*1240 in Picardy by a single anonymous scribe-compiler; and Chantilly, Musée Condé, MS 472 (= Ch), transcribed by several scribes *c.*1250–75 in Flanders/Hainault (Tournai?). It is impossible to determine if Ch's compiler was also one of the copyists. The term 'compiler' is used here to refer to a function rather than to a person; one person may in fact have exercised several functions: compiler, scribe, editor, illuminator, planner, workshop head, bookseller, etc. (see Rouse and Rouse 2000). For a variety of reasons, I believe that the compilers of all three compilations were men, and will thus refer to each one using the masculine singular pronoun. In all three cases under study, the compiler may have been working with a planner and/or for a patron; these possibilities will be discussed when appropriate.

The earliest Old French manuscripts tend to contain a single work, with the first thematic or genre-based collections dating from the beginning of the thirteenth century. From then on, more voluminous manuscripts appear, transmitting a wide variety of text types and genres (Vàrvaro 2001, 9–16). Manuscripts such as BNF, fr. 794, BNF, fr. 1450 and Ch reveal a desire for completeness on the part of manuscript producers, who tried to provide 'a full and true history of the major chivalric heroes and their adventures' (Nixon in Busby, Nixon, Stones and Walters eds 1993, I, 25). Nixon connects such large-scale collections of literary works to the development of princely or royal courts with true literary interests (Busby, Nixon, Stones and Walters eds 1993, I, 17–25); they did so, according to Taylor (1994; 1996) to construct and preserve a certain vision of their literary and/or historical heritage (see below, next section). BNF, fr. 794 and BNF, fr. 1450 are the only surviving collections to contain all five Chrétien romances transmitted as a group. The Annonay fragments testify to the existence of an earlier collection, *c.*1205–20, executed in Champagne. Although no trace of the *Charrette* remains, the collection may well have originally contained this romance along with the other four romances (Busby, Nixon, Stones and Walters eds 1993, II, 20–2). Ch is matched by only one other collection that contains three Chrétien romances, BNF, fr. 12560, although in its original state this collection may have included another of his romances (Nixon in Busby, Nixon, Stones and Walters eds 1993, II, 36).[1]

Large verse collections can run the gamut from true miscellanies (one-volume libraries rather than unified books) to carefully orchestrated compositions (Huot 2000, 68). In the three compilations studied here, the compiler comes to resemble a second author who shapes the total collection according to the structure of a typical romance with a beginning, middle and end (Walters 1985; Bruckner 1993*). In every case, each in a different but related way, the compiler 'completes'

Chrétien by augmenting this author's depiction of Arthur's court with related material. Gauvain's role becomes increasingly important as one passes from BNF, fr. 794 to Ch (roughly from 1230 to 1275). A feature of compilations is their concentration on one hero in order to unify the collection. In picking up on Chrétien's special treatment of Gauvain, a character whose story he failed to complete, all three compilers can be viewed as self-styled continuators of a tradition epitomized by Chrétien.

Models Underlying Compilation: Plenitude and *remembrance*

Two models will help to clarify the structure and underlying logic of our three target compilations. Taylor (1994; 1996, 93–123) identifies a paradigm implicit in the complex compilations in prose and verse that multiplied exponentially, beginning roughly in the mid-thirteenth century and culminating in the prose compilations that came to dominate fourteenth-century romance production to the virtual exclusion of verse compilations. Taylor's model is bipartite: 'reciprocal or sequential cyclicity' views historical events as discontinuous: 'human history consists of a series of virtually discrete cycles each of which has its own organic pattern of birth, maturity, and destruction'; 'linear or organic cyclicity', on the other hand, 'stresses continuity' by positing 'a central, surviving core which runs intact, and above all purposeful, across mutabilities' (Taylor 1996, 100). The two parts of Taylor's model are mutually dependent; each is the corresponding function of the other. It helps us to think in terms of surface versus deep structure, a series of meaningless events versus the meaningful patterns governing the existence of the human organism. Taylor's two-part model ultimately derives from St Augustine, Orosius and the Bible (1996, 101).

The organic metaphor of the body politic complements Taylor's discussion of the relationship between genealogy and plenitude. One way in which royal persons, who symbolically represent the country they govern, receive divine legitimization for their rule is through the fortuitous continuation of their line. The principle is related to the notion of *translatio studii et imperii*, which postulates the transference of political and cultural supremacy from one country to the next as a result of divine disapproval of a country's use of its power. The compilers of BNF, fr. 794 and BNF, fr. 1450 harness the potent *translatio* statement made by Chrétien in his prologue to *Cligés* to supply the structural principle of their entire compilations. Both collections trace the purposeful movement of generations in their sometimes hidden but nonetheless relentless march to fuel the ever-improving kingdom of 'France' (*Cligés*, 36). Both are splendid examples of 'linear cyclicity', revealing the order behind apparent accident. The compilers of each collection integrate Arthur's kingdom into 'an ordered vision of world history, an ideological continuity' (Taylor 1994, 64), based upon typological models and the eschatological patterns of biblical history.

The notion of plenitude, defined as 'a sense of narrative completeness which is predicated on a conception of time as circular and which attempts to integrate any particular fictional construct into a larger universal history conceived against the same overarching temporal scheme' (Taylor 1994, 62), explains the impulse to completeness that can be seen in the development of large verse romance collections. Manuscripts containing works by Chrétien range from those limited to a single romance to those that transmit all five, usually as part of a larger grouping (see chapter I). Eight manuscripts of *Perceval* contain Manessier's conclusion to the quest, whilst two of these eight also include Gerbert de Montreuil's Continuation; five of the eight contain an extensive pictorial cycle (Walters 1999). These and other factors suggest that the aim of manuscript producers was to offer a 'full picture' of Chrétien's Arthurian world. They could do this in various ways: by adding new knights to the Round Table, by enhancing the role of Gauvain, by completing Chrétien's Grail story through the provision of continuations and conclusions to his *Perceval* (see chapter VI; Walters 1994a; 1998; 1999) or by creating iconographic programmes which unified a number of originally separate texts (Walters 1991).

Plenitude complements *remembrance*, the medieval term used for the process of re-membering in both senses of the word that takes place in texts and in the assembling of individual textual units in larger groupings. It is related to a branch structure, whether explicitly or not. The Old French term 'branche' designates a subdivision of a text or books in a larger composition (Walters 1994b, 135). Authors and compilers of verse and prose cycles alike often referred to the divisions of their works as 'branches'. Two works included in Ch are examples of branch structure: the vast verse cycle of *Le Roman de Renart* (c.1170–1250) and the early thirteenth-century *Perlesvaus*, the first prose compilation to organize itself in branches (Kelly 1974, 44–5). *Remembrance* is a function of the materiality of the codex as organic structure with branches radiating out from a central trunk, an arborial metaphor popularized by Hugh of Saint-Victor in his influential twelfth-century *Didascalicon* (IV, 16, p. 118). The organic metaphor is well suited to book production, which involves a range of organic processes, from the wholesale incorporation of entire passages from earlier texts, long dismissed as plagiarism, to the constitution of the book itself as a physical object composed of folios, quires, etc. usually made of stretched and dried animal skins (Jager 2000, 52). The metaphor builds upon analogies between textual transmission and lineage, and between the well-ordered compilation and the body politic, which becomes apparent in deftly organized compilations such as the three in question. *Branches* support *remembrance*, a notion that recurs throughout Old French narrative (Rockwell 1995, 103–228).

Remembrance expresses the transformation from personal to public memory, and the transmission and dissemination of that memory (*translatio*) in the manuscript book. Chrétien alludes to this process when he ends the prologue to his first extant romance, *Erec*, with a brilliant rhetorical flourish that associates his own name and his story with the maintenance of public memory, one secular in scope but grounded in Christian ideology. By leaving the *Charrette* and *Perceval* unfinished, he encouraged the perpetuation of this memory in verse cycles such as the four *Perceval* Continuations and in prose cycles like the *Lancelot–Grail* and *Perlesvaus*. The *Perlesvaus* author draws examples from the matter of Britain that bring to mind the spiritual truths of Christianity (Kelly 1974, 94). In the prologue to Branch 1, which additionally functions as the prologue to the branches to follow, he first casts Arthur as a virtuous ruler, and then as one who no longer upholds Christian values. The Ch compiler implicitly builds upon the *Perlesvaus*'s ethical considerations and its branch structure to give order and meaning to its eleven textual units, ten of them verse romances.[2]

Memory and Ethics in *L'Atre périlleux*

The moral dimensions of memory-keeping are thematized in *L'Atre périlleux*, the second work in Ch. This late thirteenth-century romance is unusual in giving Gauvain star billing as the romance's sole protagonist, as opposed to his more typical role as foil to other characters. The *Atre* treats Gauvain's declining reputation in late romance by having him become 'the knight without a name' when a Gauvain surrogate is dismembered and killed in his place. Gauvain's symbolic dismembering and subsequent re-membering is characteristic of the movement of an Arthurian memory which increasingly takes on ethical overtones. Manuscripts that preserve the *Atre* develop moral aspects of Gauvain's character. The *Atre* heads BNF, fr. 2168, a manuscript Woledge (1954; 1975) places at the end of the thirteenth century. Its twenty-two texts include *Aucassin et Nicolette*, the *Image du Monde* by Gautier de Metz, several of Marie de France's fables, a passage from a prose life of Charlemagne and a collection of anonymous lays and *fabliaux*. The choice and layout of these works indicates a didactic intent. To cite four examples: rubrics announce the lesson to be drawn from each of Marie's short fables; the 'Lucidaire en roumans' begins with the line (fol. 215) 'Souventes fois m'avoient requis nostre deciple' (*our disciples/pupils had often asked me*); fol. 220 contains the rubric, 'Del Incarnation Jhesucrist'; the prose life of Charlemagne begins with a large blue and red initial similar to ones found in Ch. This collection headed by the *Atre* adds a didactic dimension to romance.

The *Atre* also opens BNF, fr. 1433 (*c*.1315–30). This codex is a 'super romance' which fuses separate texts by the same or different writers into a new 'single' text

(Walters 1991; Uitti 1997, 3). Its compiler has substituted the *Atre* for the *Charrette* in Chrétien's original textual coupling *Charrette/ Yvain* and further integrated the two romances through an extensive pictorial cycle that provides commentary on the two romances seen as parts of the 'whole book' (Nichols and Wenzel 1996). The compiler could be attempting to rehabilitate Gauvain's reputation through manuscript layout and illumination (Walters 1991; Busby 2002*, I, 437), or he could be employing a previously rehabilitated Gauvain to represent a model knight, such as the depiction of him in the *Atre*, which predates BNF, fr. 1433 by at least twenty-five years. Among the twelve scenes illustrated in the bifolium frontispiece are two from the episode concerning the King of the Red City, an interpolation absent from the other two manuscripts of the *Atre*. The first illustration shows a woman left naked in a cold stream by a jealous king because she claimed that Gauvain was Arthur's best knight; in the second, Gauvain defeats the king in combat. These illustrations show dramatically Gauvain's role as defender of women in need. In BNF, fr. 1433 Gauvain's knightly service to women contributes to the restoration of the reputation he loses at the beginning of the *Atre*. Portraying a rehabilitated Gauvain in compilations of French and Middle Dutch texts appears to have been a trend in early fourteenth-century Picardy and Brabant (Besamusca 2003).

The compiler exploits the bifolium's iconography to create the image of Gauvain as a model knight. The illuminations cast him as one who accomplishes heroic exploits, rather than one in need of redemption. It is significant that Gauvain figures only in one picture in *Yvain*, found in the bottom right register on fol. 104, in which he fights a battle with Yvain after the two friends fail to recognize each other. In a second image in the same compartment, in which they are reconciled, they appear to be doubles of each other. A similar effect is created by the collection as a whole, where Gauvain and Yvain are assimilated to each other through their identical heraldic devices, a rampant lion, thus making them avatars of the same exemplary knight. Since the device depicts the lion of Flanders, the compiler, working in Picardy, may be associating the two knights in order to create an image of an exemplary Flemish knight for political purposes. Thirteenth-century manuscript producers thus attempted to comment on the declining reputation of Chrétien's eminently popular Gauvain by bringing together previously existing material on him, through textual conjoining of the *Charrette/ Yvain* type and through iconographic 'glossing'. This is also the case for Ch, the third collection containing the *Atre* (see p. 472, below). The three manuscript collections containing the *Atre* thus embody a major theme of thirteenth-century verse romance: the deconstruction and reconstruction of a collective memory with ethical import.

The remainder of this chapter treats three outstanding examples of compilers whose verse-romance collections testify to their importance as organizers and transmitters of an evolving 'Christian' memory. In a phrase echoed throughout the early French tradition, their aim was to commit to public memory those things worthy of note, storing them up against the ever-present dangers of forgetfulness and assuring their continued relevance to a monarchy and a public increasingly enamoured of vernacular lore.

Chrétien and Gauvain in BNF, fr. 794

BNF, fr. 794 contains three units (Roques 1952; Nixon in Busby, Nixon, Stones and Walters eds 1993, II, 29; Meyer edn of Guiot, 11; Vàrvaro 2001, 13–14): (i) *Athis et Prophilias*, a non-Arthurian romance set in a Graeco-Roman world; (ii) the *Roman de Troie* by Benoît de Sainte-Maure, Wace's *Brut*, Calendre's *Empereurs de Rome*, Chrétien's *Perceval*, its First Continuation and a fragment of the Second Continuation; (iii) Chrétien's *Erec, Charrette, Cligés* and *Yvain*. The scribe who copied all three units names himself Guiot in a colophon at the end of *Yvain*. However, this is not the present order of works, which is (iii), (i), (ii), an order established by the second half of the thirteenth century, when a verse table of contents was added to the front flyleaf (Nixon in Busby, Nixon, Stones and Walters eds 1993, II, 29). Based upon the typical placement of a colophon at the end of a scribe's transcription of a text, it is reasonable to believe that the scribe Guiot was the compiler of the first ordering, and that another compiler reordered the collection several decades after Guiot's work.

BNF, fr. 794 is the single compilation that provides our fullest extant picture of Chrétien, since it is the only one that includes the most complete text of all five of his romances. BNF, fr. 1450 lacks several prologues (see below), as well as Godefroy de Lagny's colophon in the *Charrette*; Ch omits Godefroy's colophon, as well as many of Chrétien's verses that precede it (*pace* Huot 2000, 67), and it does not include *Cligés* or *Perceval*. Huot's comment (2000, 66) that BNF, fr. 794 contains no rubrics that identify Chrétien's authorship, albeit correct, does not support her case against Chrétien's authority *per se*, because there are no rubrics identifying any of the compilation's other authors, who instead name themselves in their texts.[3] The named writers, as they appear in the original, chronological, order of the compilation, are: Alexandre (de Bernai), Benoît de Sainte-Maure, Wace, Calendre, Chrétien de Troyes, Godefroy de Lagny and Guiot (who is included in the list because he names himself; he may well have been an author in his own right; Walters 1985; Busby edn of *Perceval*, x). Significantly, Chrétien is named in each of his romances, and owing to the multiple references in the *Perceval* Continuations, there are three times as many occurrences of his name in BNF, fr. 794 as there are references to any other author. If Huot (2000) is correct in seeing Chrétien as only one author among many in BNF, fr. 794, her point risks obscuring the aura of authority that accrues to an author who is named much more frequently than his colleagues.

BNF, fr. 794 is in fact remarkable for the respect Guiot accords to authorial identity, and to Chrétien's in particular (*pace* Busby 2002*; Walters 2003b). Godefroy de Lagny, whose name, significantly, does not appear in our two other target compilations, connects his own authority to Chrétien's in BNF, fr. 794 by saying that he completed the work 'par le boen gré Crestïen' (Roques edn, 7106–7) which implies that he worked with Chrétien's consent and was perhaps even commissioned by him. Despite all the critical ink that has been spilled about this line's ironic overtones, on the face of it Godefroy would seem to be expressing his pride in bringing the ideas of an illustrious predecessor to fruition. Godefroy's wording implies that Chrétien had authorized his continuation, just as Marie de Champagne had authorized Chrétien's composition of the *Charrette*. Moreover, Guiot may have viewed himself as next in line to Godefroy as Chrétien's continuator and as a writer working for, or inspired by, Marie de Champagne. Whereas Busby (2002*, I, 93–108) views Guiot as a 'willful scribe' set on reducing Chrétien's authority, others see him involved in a collaborative project in which he does more to perpetuate Chrétien's authority than to diminish it (Stirnemann 1999, 66; Walters 2003b).

In bequeathing to us our most complete picture of Chrétien, BNF, fr. 794 also gives us the 'full story' about Gauvain, complete with Wace's prehistory of the character. In the *Brut*, the text occupying the third position in the original ordering, Gauvain appears under the name 'Walwein' as Arthur's 'good nephew' (as opposed to the traitor Mordred, the 'bad nephew') and as a military chief renowned for his valour. In a passage that Wace has introduced into his adaptation of Geoffrey of Monmouth's *Historia*, Walwein responds to Cador's call to war against the Romans by lauding the advantages of peace (Weiss edn, 271, n. 1). Among its many benefits, it gives knights and ladies 'time for romance' (Putter 1994). The episode could well be at the root of Gauvain's ambiguous representation in Chrétien's later romances, since in advocating the pleasures of peacetime, Arthur's general/nephew also opens the door to its temptations. BNF, fr. 794 evidences a special interest in Gauvain, as shown on fol. 388v, where a multicoloured lettrine sets off the honorific 'Monseigneur .G.', indicating the esteem in which Gauvain was held (C. Ruby, private consultation). As part of a perhaps conscious desire to supply more of the 'whole truth' concerning Gauvain, Guiot includes all of the First Continuation, which focuses on Gauvain. Guiot often creates a more flattering portrait of Gauvain than had Chrétien. For example, in his best-known omission from *Perceval*, he modifies a passage he found demeaning in the original (Busby 2002*, I, 98). Later writers, obviously wishing to capitalize on Chrétien's considerable authority, augment and nuance not only his own portrait of Gauvain, but also that produced by Chrétien continuators such as Guiot.

The second order of BNF, fr. 794, which displaced Chrétien's original four romances from the last to the first position in the codex, established his primacy in the codex as its titular head, but in his role as a writer at the service of a courtly patroness. From the middle of the thirteenth century onwards, viewers opened the 433-folio manuscript book to find *Erec*. As they read on to the next text, the *Charrette*, they came upon its initial letter on fol. 27, which displayed a small, but brilliantly coloured image of a noblewoman. The picture presumably depicts Countess Marie de Champagne, whose gestures suggest that she is dictating her desires to Chrétien. This initial, the only historiated letter in the entire compilation, is a type of 'author or authorizing portrait' that complements Chrétien's avowal that he composed the work by closely following the dictates of his patroness (Huot 2000, 69). Marie's portrait establishes Chrétien as a vital link in a line of vernacular authority emanating from her court in Troyes in Champagne (Chrétien de Troyes–Godefroy de Lagny–Guiot de Provins). Guiot's colophon localizes his own activity to the collegiate house of Notre-Dame-du-Val in Provins, which Marie de Champagne founded in 1196 (Roques 1952, 189–90). Since Marie endowed the church with thirty-eight prebends, and was entitled to award nineteen to clerics of her choice, it is likely that Guiot was a canon at Notre-Dame-du-Val who owed his living to Marie (Putter 1995, 251). Thus around 1230 the scribe-compiler Guiot continued Chrétien in accordance with Marie de Champagne's pronounced religious interests towards the end of her life, when she commissioned the *Eructavit,* a poetic adaptation of the Forty-Fourth Psalm, and an adaptation of Genesis. Like Chrétien, the *Eructavit* poet addresses Marie as 'ma dame de Champaigne', and his work bears clear overtones of Chrétien's romances, particularly *Erec* (Powell 2002, 92). The person who re-ordered the compilation around the turn of the century would, like Chrétien and Guiot before him, be following Marie's inspirational gestures, with the hope that his work would encourage others to do the same.

BNF, fr. 794 has much to tell us regarding authorship. It suggests that writers derive their authority by conforming to the desires of a royal figure. In the *Charrette* Chrétien celebrates the actions of 'mainte bele dame cortoise, / bien parlant an lengue françoise' (*many beautiful courtly ladies speaking eloquently in the French language*, 39–40) who further the royal cause. In moving these statements, set off by Marie's image, to near the front of BNF, fr. 794, the second compiler foregrounds the countess's ongoing legacy to the developing kingdom of 'France' rather than to 'Engleterre' (*Cligés*, 33, 16). The alliance between the royal house and writer-counsellors such as the three active compilers of BNF, fr. 794, BNF, fr. 1450 and Ch was strengthened by the *roi christianissimus* Louis IX, whose reign (1228–70) spanned *grosso modo* the time when they were all produced. The *Eructavit* epilogue refers to Marie as 'la jantis suer le roi de France' (*the King of France's noble sister*, Jenkins edn, 2079). Since she was in fact only Philip Augustus's half-sister, the statement shows how authors in Marie's employ strengthened her connections to the royal crown, undoubtedly in conformity with her own desires, if not at her express request.

Chrétien and Gauvain in BNF, fr. 1450

The original ordering of BNF, fr. 794, including Guiot's colophon, gives BNF, fr. 794 a pattern that is repeated in BNF, fr. 1450. Both manuscripts place Chrétien's Arthurian romances alongside other Arthurian or Graeco-Roman material in a 'historiographical' sequence (Walters 1985; Huot 1987; Uitti 1997, 4) tracing a *translatio studii et imperii* (transfer of culture and power) from Greece and Rome to Arthur's realm and France. BNF, fr. 1450 (Walters 1985; Vàrvaro 2001, 12–13) contains, in the following order: *Troie, Eneas*, the first part of Wace's *Brut, Erec, Perceval* and its First Continuation, *Cligés, Yvain*, the *Charrette*, the second part of the *Brut* and *Dolopathos* (whose ending is missing). *Dolopathos*, an adaptation in Old French verse of a Latin prose text, structures its intercalated tales in a manner analogous to the way in which Chrétien's romances have been inserted into the *Brut* in this manuscript (Walters 1985). Chrétien's works have been copied into the *Brut*'s narrative at the point in Arthur's reign when twelve years of peace enable the creation of the Round Table (see chapter II). To facilitate insertion, the compiler has edited some texts, most notably by eliminating the prologues to *Erec* and *Perceval,* and perhaps the prologue to the *Charrette* (since its opening folios are missing, it is impossible to know for sure). He has also composed two transitional lines to introduce Chrétien's romances. In describing the adventures that took place during the time of the great peace, adventures that story-tellers have made appear to be fictitious, he adds, diverging from Wace's text, 'Mais ce que Crestiens tesmogne / Porés ci oïr sans alogne' (*but you can hear Chrétien's testimony here without delay*). He also alters the final lines of Godefroy's epilogue (thereby omitting his name) to create a seamless link with his remaining transcription of the *Brut* (Walters 1985, 304, n. 1, 306). The scribe-compiler-editor of BNF, fr. 1450 appropriates Godefroy's voice for himself in order to lead back into the *Brut*, after having interpolated all five Chrétien romances within its textual fabric (Walters 1985; Huot 1987).

BNF, fr. 794 provides a point of comparison for understanding the manipulation of Chrétien by the anonymous scribal compiler of BNF, fr. 1450. On the one hand, the latter omits two (possibly three) prologues in which Chrétien names himself and constructs a powerful authorial persona, a gesture that appears to reduce Chrétien's authority. On the other hand, he accentuates Chrétien's authority by referring to him by name, and by interrupting the transcription of the *Brut* to intercalate all five Chrétien romances inside Wace's text as a powerful textual witness to the story-telling that took place during the twelve years of peace instituted by Arthur. In citing Chrétien in such a manner in a compilation in which his romance *Cligés* occupies its vital centre, the compiler affirms the notion of an author corpus at the service of *translatio* in an even stronger manner than had Guiot. This could be because its compiler, writing about a decade after Guiot, and hailing from Picardy rather than from Champagne, wanted to make a clearer political statement than had Guiot, though its meaning remains to be discovered.

The scribal compiler of BNF, fr. 1450 takes Godefroy's place as Chrétien's continuator. In citing Chrétien's authority as a veracious witness to Arthur's reign, he comes to resemble the *Brut*'s narrator, who affirms his status as truth-teller in the prologue and epilogue. The scribal compiler thus joins his voice to Wace's and to Chrétien's in a common effort to tell the truth about the newly flourishing and rapidly expanding kingdom of 'France', an effort the compiler foregrounds through his ordering of the collection. Our modern idea that history and fiction belong to two separate categories differs from the medieval conception which saw them as both contributing to an authorial process that strove to make sense of human events (Taylor 1996, 99). The scribal compiler of BNF, fr. 1450 becomes the interpreter of the texts he transmits, mining them and refashioning them so that they reveal somewhat obscured but nonetheless constant patterns.

One such pattern concerns lineage. Like BNF, fr. 794, BNF, fr. 1450 locates its 'founding moment' in the one most favoured by European countries, the apogee of the city-state of Troy (Taylor 1996); it likewise charts dynastic history from its Trojan origins down to the thirteenth century. BNF, fr. 1450's compiler implies that Gauvain plays an important part in French dynastic history. He is never far from centre stage in this compilation, since the compiler intercalates all five of Chrétien romances precisely at the moment when he plays a crucial role in Wace's *Brut*. The compiler also highlights Gauvain's generative function at the Round Table by placing, as the third and middle text of the five inserted romances, *Cligés,* whose eponymous hero is Gauvain's nephew. Moreover, the first half of the romance is devoted to the story of Cligés's parents, Soredamors, Gauvain's sister, and Alixandre, Emperor of Constantinople. Beneath its charming surface *Cligés* reveals an anxious concern with questions of agnatic lineage. The positioning of Gauvain and his nephew Cligés at the centre of a collection whose guiding idea is an ethically orientated *translatio* heightens Gauvain's importance as a figure whose actions and choices pull moral weight. BNF, fr. 1450 gives a 'full picture' of the Arthurian world and undoubtedly functions as a mirror designed to provide reflection upon contemporary events and personalities and/or to explore some of the enduring preoccupations and dilemmas of contemporary society.

Gauvain in Chantilly 472

Ch is singled out by Schmolke-Hasselmann (1980*, 180/1998, 220) as the most important compilation of Arthurian verse romance to survive into modern times. Ch includes more late verse romances than any other compilation. The codex comprises in the following order: *Rigomer*, *L'Atre périlleux*, *Erec*, *Fergus*, *Hunbaut*, *Le Bel Inconnu*, *La Vengeance Raguidel*, *Yvain*, the *Charrette*, part of the prose *Perlesvaus* and several branches of the *Roman de Renart*. Three of these works are unknown elsewhere: *Rigomer* (except for the Turin episode, on which, see chapter X), *Hunbaut* and the *Bel Inconnu*. The seemingly haphazard transcription of some romances 'suggests careful planning of a possibly unfinished manuscript rather than loss of text' (Busby 2002*, I, 406). The running heads, which were all present in the original, untrimmed collection, provide the strongest evidence that someone subordinated the individual parts to an overall conception of the total collection. Ch is the product of an active compiler who has organized texts and groups of texts (*Fergus* and *Hunbaut* are the only two texts to share the same quire; Nixon in Busby, Nixon, Stones and Walters eds 1993, II, 40) into a well-ordered 'whole book' (see Carapezza 2001).

The Chantilly collection centres on Gauvain (Walters 1994a, 1994b, 1998; Hasenohr 1999; Carapezza 2001; Besamusca 2003, 166–9). His adventures alternate with those of other knights on the level of the individual text and on that of the manuscript as a whole. Gauvain figures prominently in each and every romance, either as one of several major questing knights (*Rigomer*) or as the sole protagonist (*Atre*). In *Fergus* the protagonist seeks to take over Gauvain's role as the king's counsellor; in *Hunbaut*, Gauvain and the protagonist exchange roles as the king's favoured adviser, but that role is subject to serious undermining, and in *Raguidel* Gauvain is once again a major quester. Thus Ch's compiler continues Chrétien by giving us a full picture of Gauvain as he emerges in the thirteenth century. He even goes so far as to include substitutes for the two Chrétien romances missing from his compilation, *Cligés* and *Perceval* (Busby 2002*, I, 411). Throughout all its constituent texts, Gauvain remains the primary focus of its readers' attention, whether they crave a swashbuckling story of love and adventure or a moral tale.

Gauvain is a prominent presence in the works situated at the beginning, middle and end of Ch. Located at the head of the manuscript, *Rigomer* provides a fitting introduction to the collection by promoting Gauvain over all other knights, including the supposedly peerless Lancelot. Gauvain is alone among over fifty knights to succeed in bringing to an end the enchantments of Rigomer Castle. But *Rigomer* sets the tone of the collection by subjecting Gauvain to the same sort of undermining as Lancelot. Ch holds Arthurian verse romance and its heroes up to serious scrutiny. *Rigomer*'s prologue, in opposing 'desroi' and 'sens' (fol. 1r; Foerster and Breuer edn, 10–11), begins a reflection on wisdom and folly in both king and vassal, with a focus on the figure of Arthur's nephew and chief adviser, a reflection pursued throughout the collection. The *Bel Inconnu*, a 'son of Gauvain' romance, is Ch's centre-piece. In the romance's midpoint episode (3139ff.) the protagonist, known up to that stage only as the 'fair unknown', accomplishes the heroic exploit of the Fier Baisier (*Proud, Fearsome or Gruesome Kiss*) and is rewarded with knowledge of his parentage: he is the son of Gauvain and of Blanchemal the fairy. The *Bel Inconnu*'s midpoint episode, which highlights Gauvain's biological and literary paternity, also occupies Ch's metaphorical centre, its 'heart of hearts'. At the end of Ch there are two works: *Perlesvaus*, which imposes closure on the Arthurian world, and the *Renart* material. The *Renart* branches function as a comic counter-cycle to the Arthurian material and are included as an exploration of the 'animal Gauvain' (Busby 2002*, I, 410).

Manuscript layout and decoration integrate *Perlesvaus* and the *Renart* material into the total compilation. The presence of these two texts has long posed a problem for the interpretation of Ch as a coherent work. If we abandon our modern assumption that the prose *Perlesvaus* and the *Renart* beast fables do not belong with Arthurian verse romance and see them instead as building-blocks in a larger construction united by common themes (Walters 1998), they yield their meaning. Each text implicitly becomes a 'branch' of the total compilation. The term 'branche' appears in the introduction to divisions 2–8 of *Perlesvaus* and in the *explicit* to one section of the *Renart* ('Explicit li branche / De la bataille de Rx et de Y', fol. 259r). Although to modern eyes the branches of the *Renart* are the collection's most striking anomaly, they take their place in the overall design of the decorated manuscript book. Each part begins with a large blue and red initial letter similar to the ones that mark out the opening of all previous works. The running head 'De Renart' assimilates the fox to the other male characters ('D'Erec', 'De Fergus', 'De Gunbaut'); moreover, this is the only collection that accords him the honorific title of 'dant Renart'. Given that the compiler has eliminated the substantial prologue to the *Charrette*, whilst retaining the shorter ones to other romances (the longest being the forty-five-line *Hunbaut* prologue), the inclusion of the seventy-seven-line prologue to *Perlesvaus* is significant. The prose romance thus acquires extra authority by appearing to impose its principle of 'branch composition' on the entire collection.

Rewriting Verse Romance in Prose: *Perlesvaus* in Chantilly 472

As one of the few manuscripts to combine verse and prose romances, Ch testifies to the movement from verse to prose taking place in the thirteenth century. Busby has noted that 'the producers of the illustrated and rubricated Chrétien manuscripts have re-written the master's verse in the likeness of prose' (Busby 1999b, 141; see also Combes 1992–5; Trachsler 2000, 189). Extending Busby's astute observations, one can say that Ch rewrites all its verse texts by borrowing themes and techniques from prose romance. The move from verse to prose in this collection is shown in several ways. The *Bel Inconnu*, which we recall is unique to Ch, shifts the verse romance preoccupation with the uncle–nephew relationship (Arthur–Gauvain) to one of agnatic lineage (Gauvain–Guinglain). The major shift, however, comes when the compiler includes *Perlesvaus*, a Grail romance, amongst other Arthurian works which all lack an explicit religious message. *Perlesvaus* begins with a lengthy, heavily sermonizing prologue, complete with a scene depicting Christ's deposition and burial. In including *Perlesvaus*, the compiler introduces the compilation's commanding metaphor of the perilous cemetery into a new and decidedly Christian context. The compiler insists on the metaphor by breaking off his narrative – or by choosing to include a version that breaks off – at line 5195, around the middle of the longest version. This is soon after Dandrane, Perlesvaus's sister, has passed through another (the same?) dangerous burial ground, where she obtains Christ's shroud, a relic needed to defend her family against its enemies. Ch as a whole can be read as inviting moral reflection upon material that first appears to be merely entertaining. In terms of its themes, it progressively reformulates Arthurian chivalry within a Christian system (Walters 1998).

By heading Ch with *Rigomer* and its sharply critical view of Arthurian verse romance, the anonymous compiler prepares the way for the more doctrinally Christian recasting of Arthurian themes carried out in prose by the anonymous *Perlesvaus* author. The latter, after recounting how the Roman soldier Joseph of Arimathea unexpectedly honoured Christ's crucified corpse with a decent burial, relates how King Arthur was stricken with a crisis of will that endangered his stellar reputation. Prompted by a tearful outburst by Queen Guinevere, Arthur sets out on a pilgrimage to St Augustine's chapel to renew his Christian faith and revitalize his court. Arthur's major champions set out on parallel quests, and, significantly, it is Gauvain's quest that dominates the branches present in Ch. *Perlesvaus* returns to the impasse or malaise that stymies Arthur's court in most of the verse romances in Ch, but with much more force than in any of them. When Arthur becomes depressed and abandons his characteristic largesse, there is a precipitous decline in adventures. Although Arthur at least partially redeems himself, the question of who will carry on his legacy arises. Like the *Bel Inconnu*, *Perlesvaus* deals with the issue of agnatic lineage, in this case by elaborating on Chrétien's passing reference to Arthur and Guinevere's son, Loholt (*Erec*, Roques edn, 1700). In Branch 8, the last branch of *Perlesvaus* included in Ch, Kay mistakenly kills Loholt. The narrative is at an impasse. It asks who will be the standard-bearer of Arthurian chivalry now that Arthur's only son is dead.

The Hero at a Crossroads: The Transformed Gauvain of Chantilly 472

In Ch, Gauvain becomes the knight and prince surrogate who may be able to rescue Arthur's kingdom from disunity and the resulting threat of civil war and foreign invasion. These are dangers that plague the history of the classical and Breton ancestors whose stories figure in BNF, fr. 794 and BNF, fr. 1450, and which would continue to haunt the medieval French monarchy, most pointedly in its age-long disputes with England that would culminate in the Hundred Years War. As opposed to the compilers of BNF, fr. 794 and BNF, fr. 1450, who include texts dealing with Greece and Rome, Ch's compiler highlights the urgency of the issue by limiting his focus to Arthur and his knights. His concentration on Arthur's court is apparent from his inclusion of *Rigomer* as lead text, since it is one of the few romances in which the king also sets out on a quest. Arthur's quest, which Carapezza (2001, 102–6) describes as a *mise en roman* of the satirical *Pelèrinage de Charlemagne*, does little to further the king's reputation for heroism.

Besides discrediting Arthur, Ch's compiler eliminates two other potential saviour-figures, Lancelot and Perlesvaus. The first to go is Lancelot, whose status, like Arthur's, is demoted in *Rigomer* (chapter X). Ch's truncated version of the *Charrette* leaves readers with an image of the valiant Lancelot reduced to Guinevere's ridiculous and impotent puppet. Gauvain too receives a metaphorical beating in *Rigomer*, but he comes off superior to Lancelot and Arthur, as he does in *Perlesvaus*. There Gauvain discovers that, although his deeds and intentions are pure, he will not ultimately succeed in the *Perlesvaus*'s Grail quest. In the scene in the Grail Castle in which Gauvain gazes at the drops of blood flowing from the lance, the negative connotations of these same drops, which also symbolize his inadvertent role in the death of the wife of Marin le Jaloux (a direct result of his reputation as a womanizer), indicate that he will not ultimately be successful in his search for the Grail. After the Grail vision, Gauvain plays against an invisible opponent on a magic chessboard, but he breaks up the game when he realizes that he is headed for defeat. He does not succeed because he cannot escape his poor reputation. In the long version Perlesvaus goes on to pursue a successful quest for the Grail.

But the short version of *Perlesvaus* included in Ch prepares Gauvain's future resurrection as the eagerly awaited 'bon chevalier' (*Atre*) or 'bel inconnu' of Ch, in which Gauvain displaces Perlesvaus. At the point where the transcription breaks off, Perlesvaus's status as the saviour of the kingdom is left in doubt. In the perilous cemetery a bodiless voice had announced to Dandrane the Fisher King's death and the taking of her mother's lands by the King of the Chastel Mortel. It leaves her with the ominous warning that Perlesvaus is the only one to be able to save the kingdom. In the final scene the characters stand at a critical juncture. Dandrane does not recognize her brother Perlesvaus standing before her, and the story never progresses to the point, located a little further on in the longer versions, in which Perlesvaus would have opened the tomb that announced him as the kingdom's saviour (Nitze and Jenkins edn, 5222ff.). In the version of *Perlesvaus* included in Ch, Perlesvaus remains a 'bel inconnu'.

Ch's compiler manipulates the text of *Perlesvaus* found elsewhere in order to introduce his conception of the Arthurian world as a place of *recreantise* in need of regeneration. The compiler proposes a recast version of Gauvain as the model of the saviour of the kingdom in place of Lancelot or Perlesvaus. In this new, reformulated and very ethically grounded version of the Arthurian universe which leaves Lancelot and Perlesvaus virtual unknowns when their stories break off, Gauvain becomes the knight with the greatest potential to save the kingdom. He can take the place of the chaste Perlesvaus on the moral level because his quest to rescue Guinevere – which he pursues in *Yvain* and the *Charrette,* works eight and nine in the compilation – is pure and disinterested, unlike Lancelot's. He can take his place on the rhetorical level as well. Gauvain, by virtue of his linguistic talents, is superior to Perlesvaus, who according to the narrator had no way with words. Gauvain is Ch's only true 'bon chevalier', as he is called in the prologue to the *Atre,* a romance in which he is promoted to the unusual status (for him) of sole protagonist. When *Perlesvaus* breaks off in Ch, Gauvain, who is on a quest for the lance that pierced Christ's side at the Crucifixion, has recently advised Perlesvaus about his duty to rescue his mother and her kingdom. These features make Gauvain a John the Baptist figure, whose mission was to announce the coming of the Messiah (Bryant transl., v; Carman 1946, 64–5).

Gauvain's son Guinglain functions as the prefiguration of Gauvain in his new incarnation as a model knight, the new 'bel inconnu' announced by Ch. At the end of the *Bel Inconnu* Guinglain stands at a crossroads, confronted with a choice that gives him the possibility of going beyond his father's ambiguous status to become a figure of Arthurian legitimacy. The fact that the work bears an *explicit* suggests that Guinglain will stay with his lawfully wedded wife. Guinglain functions as a precursor of the ideal Christian knight. Gérard de Liège, Cistercian abbot of Val-Saint-Lambert, in his macaronic *Quinque incitamenta ad deum amandum ardenter, c.*1250, writes that Jesus, despite all his prowess and beauty, remains for many people 'li biaus descouneüs' (Newman 2003, 153). Jesus is the 'fair unknown' because people fail to realize his true identity as their saviour. The ideal Christian knight of Ch is the Gauvain-yet-to-come, the Gauvain prefigured by his son Guinglain. This may seem strange, until we remember that a fictional character can give metaphorical birth to a new vision of his literary father, as implied by the notion of plenitude (Taylor 1996, 117). A text deals with metaphorical truth, which only becomes literally true when readers apply its metaphors to their own lives. Gauvain will become the progenitor of the kingdom's saviour if readers use him correctly as an exemplary figure to improve themselves and their society.

If Ch's implicit branch structure coalesces around the figure of Gauvain (Busby 2002*, I, 413), it is because the compiler wants him to be seen as the forerunner of the ultimate 'branch', a term applied to the Messiah as a lineal descendant of David (Frye 1982, 150). Gauvain is a prefiguration of the Messiah-yet-to-come, the ruler as a latter-day avatar of the biblical King David. Ch poses over and over again the question of the identity of the saviour of the Arthurian kingdom and repeatedly suggests that he will come from Gauvain's line. (The father–son duo of Gauvain–Guinglain in Ch in many ways is the verse equivalent of the *Queste del Saint Graal*'s father–son duo of Lancelot and Galahad.) Gauvain's presence is especially conspicuous in Ch's beginning, middle and end works, and his persona casts light upon many figures outside the text, among them the knight, lover, prince and lay or clerical royal counsellor. Gauvain in effect becomes symbolic of the potentially redeemable 'body politic'.

A Transformed Chrétien: The 'Christian' Compiler of Chantilly 472

Ch exhibits a particularly sophisticated case of 'motif transfer' (Lacy 1996). In his own way the compiler is a 'bel inconnu', an anonymous but nonetheless powerful presence, who transforms Arthurian verse into Arthurian prose values. He brings about this transformation by appropriating for himself the authority of the many authors of the verse romances in the collection in order to ally himself with the authority of the anonymous *Perlesvaus* author. The latter connects his use of prose with scriptural authority, which he refers to as 'l'autoritez de l'escriture' (fol. 214r). The compiler also marshals the sermonizing tone of *Perlesvaus* and its decoration to transform the *Renart* into a series of exempla designed to reinforce the spiritual message of *Perlesvaus*, which becomes the message of the entire compilation. The decoration of the *Renart* corresponds more closely to the decoration of *Perlesvaus* than to that of the verse romances. The medium-size ornamental letters and small initials of *Perlesvaus* seem to radiate out into the *Renart* that follows. The moral reading of the *Renart* material becomes evident in the presence of the large initial letter 'F' that begins the first line of the 'Confession Renart'. This initial letter is larger than the 'S' that marks the beginning of the *Renart* branches (fol. 244r), and it is one of the two largest in the codex, the other being the initial letter 'J' heading *Rigomer*. The verse heading the 'Confession Renart' reads: 'Fous est qui croit sa fole pensee' (*whoever believes his foolish thought is a fool*, fol. 259r), echoing the discussion of wisdom and folly in the prologue to the first romance in Ch, *Rigomer*. Thus, in the compiler's hands, the *Renart* branches occupying the final position in the codex become moral tales designed to reinforce comically the lessons that a thoughtful reader could derive from the rest of the collection. It is as if the moral tone of *Perlesvaus* transforms the *Renart* into a negative exemplum of its Christian message. In Ch, Renart's false confession has the potential to transform itself into a true one in the reader's heart. The *Renart*'s comic, at times even raucous, tone softens the didactic lesson directed at Ch's readers, inciting them, through the therapeutic pill of laughter, to purge themselves of their 'bestial' tendencies.

Arthur's court, and the vernacular tradition that has transmitted the image of that court, find themselves at a serious juncture in Ch. The compiler responds to this cry for a renewal of Arthurian values by following in the wake of the *Perlesvaus* author's proposed redirection of romance along more canonical Christian lines. By placing *Rigomer* at the head of his collection, the compiler points the way to the higher level of meaning encoded in verse romance by means of *Rigomer*'s critical view of the tradition epitomized by Chrétien. In the *Perlesvaus*, as in prose romance generally, Chrétien disappears as named author. The Ch compiler implies that in order for Chrétien to remain true to his name, a name that defines his identity as representative Christian writer, he had to 'die' in verse romance and be resurrected in a reconfigured form in prose.

The Ch compiler appropriates for himself the Christian authority of the *Perlesvaus* narrator, which is coterminous with the disembodied and anonymous voice of the 'conte'. He thus tries to improve on Chrétien's message by using his texts to channel romance into more doctrinally Christian avenues, associated more with prose than with verse. Ch's compiler encourages his audience to read romance as though it were sacred scripture. To paraphrase St Augustine, the reader is implicitly enjoined 'to take the gold out of Egypt', to mine Arthurian romance for its intimations of divine truth. In the hands of Ch's compiler, romance becomes the potential vehicle of tropological and typological readings, thus giving readers the opportunity to change their own lives.

In staging his revision of Arthurian romance in Ch, the compiler himself becomes a participant in the prototypical Christian incarnational drama in which the dynamics of sin and redemption are part and parcel of the workings of the divine *Verbum*. Set forth ever so eloquently in the opening words of St John's Gospel is the idea that the universe is nothing more, nor less, than a divine word-game. (We wonder if it is mere coincidence that Ch opens on the name 'Jehan'.) Rather than detracting from the compilation's serious message, its comic touches reinforce it. They are the 'hooks' that fix the reader's attention so that the compiler can transform the tragedy of the Fall into the 'divine comedy' that awaits the redeemed human soul. The Ch compiler builds upon the light-hearted details he finds in the collection's constituent texts. Nothing is more playful than Renaut de Bâgé's use of the persona of 'Renals de Biauju', whose name designates him as 'the good game-player'. The metaphor of game-playing appears again in *Hunbaut*, where the narrator persona represents himself as engaged in a friendly game of dice or cards with his predecessor, and somewhat stridently requests that no one accuse him of pillaging Chrétien's work to create his own (86–90; fol. 123v). In an ironic twist on the *Hunbaut* poet's self-portrait, Ch's compiler actually does 'rob blind' all the authors of the texts he seems to assemble so innocently for his readers' enjoyment. Moreover, in Ch's crowning touch, 'Renals', the name of the *Bel Inconnu*'s narrator figure, resurfaces with a slightly different spelling in the name of the wily fox Renart, whose riotous adventures bring the compilation to an end. Playfulness radiates throughout the collection, rendering the compiler's essentially sermonizing intent more palatable to his readers.

One of the compiler's primary means of educating his readers is the creation of a double portrait for Gauvain. By exploiting for didactic ends this character's ambiguous representation in prior tradition, he comes to mimic the stance of the *Perlesvaus* author. In Ch, Gauvain can be 'read' *in bono* as an ideal figure or *in malo* as the 'counterfeit Gauvain', as he is called in *Perlesvaus*. At times he is promoted as a saint, at other times as a *fabliau* trickster or the medieval equivalent of a soap-opera leading man. *Rigomer* sets the tone for the collection by first hailing Gauvain as the saviour sent to earth to perform miracles, and then as a demon from hell, who savagely hacks men to pieces as if they were animals (fol. 38r). In Ch, Gauvain becomes a pure sign, a coin that can be flipped to one side or the other (Rockwell 1995, 46), a sign that the compiler asks his readers to interpret in relation to themselves and their society. Ch's compiler thus endows semantic drama with ethical concerns (see chapter X on *Raguidel*). Gauvain becomes the most commanding guide for the reader's path to self-improvement. Ch not only enters into a dialogue with earlier tradition, its dialogue invites readers to compare their image with those presented by the many faces of Gauvain, by the other Arthurian knights and by Renart, who all reflect Gauvain's multiple personae. Gauvain's mercurial but magnetic figure provides the human knot that ties together the compilation's many textual members in one complex but unified corpus.

If Gauvain's redemption in the *Atre*, as in all the verse romances in Ch, remains fundamentally ambiguous (Walters 2000), his characterization nonetheless proves more positive than that of Arthur or Lancelot. In Ch, Lancelot's sins of treason and adultery far outweigh Gauvain's transgressions (Walters 2005a; 2005b). True to *Rigomer*'s opening statement, Gauvain's political astuteness tempers Arthur's boorish behaviour and ignorance. Arthur's counsellor, like all Arthurian knights, may have failings, but he does offer the king some good advice in the course of the romance. Gauvain's depiction in Ch is similar to his portrayal in the *Lancelot–Grail* Cycle, where his failure is the failure of one of the very best earthly knights. The compiler uses Gauvain to fix his readers' interest and engage their sympathies. Ch's anonymous compiler proves to be an astute psychologist and preacher. He understands that his flawed and all-too-human character Gauvain is a more effective means of realizing his didactic ends than the Vulgate's perfect – and perfectly boring – Galahad.

Finally and most importantly, Ch's emphasis on Gauvain's verbal abilities at the service of Arthurian exemplarity provides reflection on the compiler's own role in the book-making process. The compiler does his part to reorientate an evolving vernacular poetics towards its proper function as a tool for the establishment of the City of God on earth. In editing and re-ordering Ch's eleven texts, the compiler accomplishes an act of re-creation that looks forward to the restoration of the time of peace and harmony that had existed in Eden before the Fall. Carruthers (1998, 60–115) compellingly refers to this as 'remembering heaven', the process of exploiting the spoken and written word with the ultimate goal of realizing a vision of a just human society that approaches the perfect human community for ever present in the eternal mind of God. Ch's compiler allies himself with an ongoing and vigorous process of creating a vital Christian public memory in the vernacular, in which writers and book-makers strive to improve the individual and society through language, the skill that above all others distinguishes human beings from beasts.

Remembering Gauvain: The Compiler and 'Christian' Memory

BNF, fr. 794, BNF, fr. 1450 and Ch are high points in a trend to associate Gauvain and his Old French popularizer, Chrétien, with ideas about memory. The *Atre* treats the collective reputation of Arthur's court in its metaphorical dis-membering and subsequent re-membering of a Gauvain surrogate. The theme, current throughout the Old French tradition, receives its apotheosis in Ch. There Gauvain's fragmentation in the *Atre* goes hand in hand with Chrétien's fragmentation in the total collection, where the compiler separates *Erec* from *Yvain* and the *Charrette*, and removes the *Charrette*'s prologue, Godefroy's colophon, and many of Chrétien's own lines preceding the colophon. If Chrétien had been whole and entire in BNF, fr. 794, he is subjected to fragmentation and dispersal at the hand of Ch's compiler, who then metaphorically resurrects him for more doctrinally Christian purposes. The movement from death to resurrection and back again, seen in individual romances marked by Chrétien's influence and in compilations containing romances by Chrétien and his epigones, symbolizes the constant deconstruction and subsequent reconstruction of an evolving public memory by authors and compilers working in a society founded upon Christian values.

Our three compilers were keepers, shapers and transmitters of a dynamic 'Christian' memory. A manuscript is a memory place, a place to consult information, to take away a bit of knowledge, or to read the whole history of a civilization. A manuscript resembles a graveyard but, like the one depicted in *Perlesvaus*, it should ideally prepare a resurrection of Christ, figured as the divine Logos. The written word needs to be repeatedly given new meaning by readers who apply its lessons to real-life situations. The carefully crafted collections of our three compiler-historians reflect ideological structures and incite further reflection on some of the major recurring dilemmas of their time. As cogs in a constantly evolving system, these three collections constitute, each in its own way, a sort of medieval Zeitgeist, or communal 'mind on the move'.

Individual texts and entire compilations were designed to incite reflection on problems facing the body politic, with the reader in the position of judge in a type of *jeu parti* structure. Compilations treat persistent problems facing the monarchy, many centring on questions of genealogy and lineage (Taylor 1996). Loholt's death in Ch raises the spectre of a kingdom without a legitimate heir, one of the abiding concerns plaguing dynastic succession, whether of the Capetians or the Carolingians. This fear resurfaced in the twelfth century when Philip Augustus's parents Louis VII and Adèle de Champagne tried in vain for several years to produce a male heir; this was especially serious since Louis's first two wives had also failed to give him a son. Philip's birth was celebrated as a miracle, as shown by the illustration of the event figuring in the royal vernacular *Grandes Chroniques de France* (Hedeman 1991, 20–2, fig. 7),[4] commissioned by King Louis IX from the monks at Saint-Denis.

Ch treats problems more particular to Louis IX's reign. Many of the events in Ch seem to relate to issues concerning Louis IX's real and symbolic body (Kantorowicz 1957), which would support a date of *c.* 1271–5 for Ch, around the time when the monk Primat presented the first copy of the *Grandes Chroniques* (1274) to Louis's son and heir Philip III, le Hardi (ruled 1270–85). When Louis died in Tunis on his second, failed Crusade, his body was dismembered and boiled, as was the custom when the king died far from France; the various organs were then distributed to leaders of foreign countries or buried in spots in France (Le Goff 1996, 300, 310). The notion of a body being both a whole and an assemblage of important parts also applies to a codicological body like Ch, whose heart, like Louis's or any king's, held special import. The dismembering and distribution of Louis's body parts reflected the hope that the fragmentation of power experienced after the death of this saintly king, who had proven ineffectual in his second crusade, would be remedied by his progeny. Memory-keeping, then, was a practice and a duty; it shored up royal legitimacy and assured dynastic continuity.

Our three compilations, produced during the reign of Louis IX, whom Le Goff (1996, 402–31) dubs the 'king of the mirror of princes', are mirrors reflecting the individual and corporate body politic. They provide reflection on current issues rather than proposing pat solutions for them. King Arthur was only one model in a long line of kings that included Charlemagne and Alexander. Their images were used as positive or negative exempla to educate various publics to their social responsibilities. The same was true of Gauvain, the focus of our three manuscript books. Ch's compiler assembles the bits and shards of Gauvain's ambiguous reputation in thirteenth-century romance to create an ethical mirror designed to improve the individual and corporate body politic. The didactic impulse is connected to the exemplary use of the figure of Gauvain in all three compilations which include the *Atre*. Narratives like the *Bel Inconnu* and *Beaudous* extend the exemplary portrait of Gauvain to include his sons. Gauvain's fundamentally ambiguous representation in later romance texts becomes a mirror for the audience's self-improvement at the hands of the monk Robert de Blois, author of *Beaudous* (Walters 1993a; 1993b), and of Ch's preacher-like compiler, who may have been a Franciscan. Gauvain's role as Arthur's wise counsellor qualified him to serve not only as Chrétien's mirror image, but also as the compiler's.

King and counsellor are each other's doubles as models of wisdom and eloquence. The king is a 'patron' in several senses of the word. As God's representative on earth, he sets the commanding 'patron' (*pattern*) for the entire body politic. Kings were often literary patrons; Louis IX, as we saw, was responsible for commissioning the vernacular *Grandes Chroniques* de France, a 'défense et illustration' of the genealogy of the kings of France designed to strengthen royal legitimacy. Louis was represented in later copies as one of the favoured models of the wise king, along with Charlemagne, Clovis and Charles V. Louis even composed works himself, probably in his own hand (Le Goff 1996), with the aim of assuring the perpetuation of his intellectual heritage. He composed an *Enseignemenz* for his son Philip, the future Philip III, who would succeed him in Tunis after his death, and for his daughter Isabelle, who in 1255 married Thibaut V, Count of Champagne and Navarre, an event that signalled the incorporation of Champagne within the royal orbit. Louis was a king brought up on John of Salisbury's famous dictum: 'an uneducated king is a crowned ass', whose lessons were reinforced by the *Eruditio regum et principum*, a Latin mirror for princes composed expressly for Louis by Guibert de Tournai (1200–84), a leading thirteenth-century Franciscan theologian (Le Goff 1996, 409–16).

Guibert was one of Louis's major advisers, and may have accompanied Louis to the Holy Land on his first crusade. He occupied a Franciscan chair at the University of Paris from 1257 to 1261. Guibert may have been the third author of the *Roman de la Rose* who wrote under the pseudonym of 'Gui de Mori' (a play on his given name of Guibert de Moriel-Porte) and who enriched Faux Semblant's speech with level-headed defences of the mendicants (Walters 1994c; 2001).[5] Using Renart to teach a lesson, which the compiler does in Ch, is not as strange as it at first seems; Guibert drew upon the *Renart* and the bestiaries in composing his sermons (Welter 1927, 136, n. 42; Zink 1976). It is easy to see a mendicant behind the 'sermonizing fox' of Ch, produced near, or in, Guibert's native Tournai. Following the logic of reversal found throughout the texts in Ch, the trickster fox is transformed from his traditional negative representation to a positive one, as the compiler exploits the trickster's own tricks to out-trick him. Like the Evangelists' animal emblems, Ch's 'sermonizing fox', the fox-turned-preacher, marks the victory of the spirit over the flesh and of truthful rhetoric over its corrupted form, source of the Fall.

'Chrétien', the author figure who imprints his image on our three compilations as well as throughout the texts of the romance tradition, transcends the status of an individual in the modern sense to become the interpreter of the Christian message for his own times. Chrétien fits into a line of truth-seekers that includes St Augustine and Wace, as implied by Guiot and BNF, fr. 1450's anonymous compiler. The French monarchy chose as its guiding light *The City of God*, because, so recounts Charlemagne's biographer Einhard, St Augustine was the king's favourite author and *The City of God* his favourite work. More than 500 years after Charlemagne's death, the treatise found itself at the top of the list of works that the 'Wise King' Charles V had adapted into the vernacular for the greater good of all, as Christine de Pizan documents in that king's biography (Book 3, chapter 12; Walters 2003a). *The City of God* served as the French monarchy's primary blueprint for a Christian society evolving towards its destiny to be an ideal place of truth and justice for all, provided, of course, that it remained a moral leader among Christian nations. *The City of God* exerted its influence on the imagination of writers and compilers of verse and prose romances. Book 16, chapters 39–40 mention a certain Galaad, Manasseh's grandson and the great-grandson of Jacob, renamed Israel (meaning 'seeing God'). St Augustine's Galaad occupies a key position in the lineage of Israel, the Old Testament Promised Land, to which monarchical ideologues repeatedly compared the kingdom of France. It is surely no coincidence that the hero of the *Lancelot–Grail* is named Galahad and that the author of the final *Perceval* Continuation calls himself Manessier. *The City of God* proved to be a fertile source when supporters of the monarchy, writers like Chrétien and his epigones, and manuscript compilers like the three treated in this chapter reflected upon the major dilemmas facing the nascent French 'nation' (Walters 2002). Especially seminal was St Augustine's meditation (*City* 22, 21) on St Paul's famous dictum (1 Cor. 15:44): 'it is sown an animal body, it shall rise a spiritual body'. For our three compilers 'Crestïens' was a seed to be sown in the minds of their readers, a nutritive kernel endowed with the force necessary to help them reshape their animal selves into more spiritual bodies, thereby transforming their entire society in the process.

Notes

[1] Vatican City, Biblioteca Apostolica Vaticana, MS Reg. lat. 1725 may have originally had three as well (Nixon in Busby, Nixon, Stones and Walters eds 1993, II, 63), and BNF, fr. 375 contains *Guillaume d'Angleterre*, ascribed to a 'Crestïen', as well as *Erec* and *Cligés* forming part of an extensive collection with some 'historical' texts like *Troie* and Wace's *Rou* (Nixon in Busby, Nixon, Stones and Walters eds 1993, II, 64).

[2] A versified table of contents that identifies its individual texts as 'branches' heads the second part of BNF, fr. 375 (Walters 1985, 317–20; Nixon in Busby, Nixon, Stones and Walters eds 1993, II, 64–6). BNF, fr. 375 has analogies with Ch, because it too includes just one work in prose, in the case of BNF, fr. 375, a genealogy of the counts of Boulogne.

[3] Works have no titles, but each has an *explicit* in text ink (Nixon in Busby, Nixon, Stones and Walters eds 1993, II, 29). The table added to the second compilation refers to works by title, rather than by author (see Nixon in Busby, Nixon, Stones and Walters eds 1993, II, 385).

[4] Figure 7 identifies Louis VII's queen as Alix, whereas she was Adèle de Champagne. Alix was the name of one of the two daughters Louis had with his first wife, Eleanor of Aquitaine.

[5] This is consistent with revised dates for the Gui de Mori *remaniement*: 1245 for his revisions of Guillaume de Lorris; 1280 for his revisions of Jean de Meun (Walters 2001).

Reference List

For items accompanied by an asterisk, see the General Bibliography.

Texts and Translations

Wace's Roman de Brut. A History of the British: Text and Translation. Ed. and transl. by J. E. Weiss (Exeter, 1999; 2nd edn, 2002).

Chrétien de Troyes, *Erec et Enide*. Ed. by M. Roques, CFMA 80 (Paris, 1952).

Chrétien de Troyes, *Cligés*. Ed. by A. Micha, CFMA 64 (Paris, 1957).

Chrétien de Troyes, *Le Chevalier de la Charrete*. Ed. by M. Roques, CFMA 86 (Paris, 1958).

Chrétien de Troyes, *Le Roman de Perceval ou Le Conte du Graal*. Ed. by K. Busby (Tübingen, 1993).

La Copie de Guiot: fol. 79v–105r du manuscrit f. fr. de la Bibliothèque Nationale: li chevaliers au lyeon de Crestien de Troyes. Ed. by K. Meyer (Amsterdam, 1995).

Renaut de Beaujeu, *Le Bel Inconnu: roman d'aventures*. Ed. by G. P. Williams, CFMA 38 (Paris, 1929).

The Romance of Hunbaut: An Arthurian Poem of the Thirteenth Century. Ed by M. Winters (Leiden, 1984).

[*Rigomer*]: (i) *Les Merveilles de Rigomer: altfranzösischer Artusroman des XIII Jahrhunderts, von Jehan*. Ed. by W. Foerster and H. Breuer (Dresden and Halle/S., 1908–15); (ii) Jehan, *Les Merveilles de Rigomer: Chantilly, Musée Condé Ms. 472 (626)*. Rev. edn by T. E. Vesce (New York, 1995).

[*Perlesvaus*]: (i) *Le Haut Livre du Graal: Perlesvaus*. Ed. by W. A Nitze and T. A. Jenkins, 2 vols (Chicago, 1932–7; repr. New York, 1972); (ii) *The High Book of the Grail: A Translation of the Thirteenth-Century Romance of Perlesvaus*. Transl. by N. Bryant (Cambridge, 1978).

The Didascalicon of Hugh of St. Victor: A Medieval Guide to the Arts. Transl. by J. Taylor (New York, 1991).

Eructavit: An Old French Metrical Paraphrase of Psalm XLIV. Ed. by T. A. Jenkins (Dresden, 1909).

Studies

Baumgartner, E. 1995. *Le Récit médiéval, XIIe–XIIIe siècles*, Paris.

Besamusca, B. 2003. *The Book of Lancelot: The Middle Dutch Lancelot Compilation and the Medieval Tradition of Narrative Cycles*. Transl. by T. Summerfield, Cambridge.

Busby, K. 1987. 'Diverging Traditions of Gauvain in some of the Later Old French Verse Romances', in Lacy, Kelly and Busby eds 1987–88*, II, 93–109.

Busby 1994. '*Hunbaut* and the Art of Medieval French Romance', in *Conjunctures: Medieval Studies in Honor of Douglas Kelly*, Amsterdam and Atlanta, GA, 49–68.

Busby 1999a. 'Fabliaux and the New Codicology', in *The World and its Rival: Essays on Literary Imagination in Honor of Per Nykrog*, Amsterdam and Atlanta, GA, 137–60.

Busby 1999b. 'Rubrics and the Reception of Romance', *FS*, 53, 129–41.

Busby, K., T. Nixon, A. Stones, and L. Walters eds 1993. *Les Manuscrits de Chrétien de Troyes/The Manuscripts of Chrétien de Troyes*, 2 vols, Amsterdam and Atlanta, GA.

Carapezza, F. 2001. 'Le Fragment de Turin de *Rigomer*: nouvelles perspectives', *Rom*, 119, 76–112.

Carman, J. N. 1946. 'The Symbolism of the *Perlesvaus*', *PMLA*, 61, 42–83.

Carruthers, M. 1990. *The Book of Memory: A Study of Memory in Medieval Culture*, Cambridge.

Carruthers 1998. *The Craft of Thought: Meditation, Rhetoric, and the Making of Images, 400–1200*, Cambridge.

Combes, A. 1992–5. '*L'Atre périlleux*: cénotaphe d'un héros retrouvé', *Rom*, 113, 140–74.

Dagenais, J. 1994. *The Ethics of Reading in Manuscript Culture: Glossing the Libro de buen amor*, Princeton.

Frye, N. 1982. *The Great Code: The Bible as Literature*, Toronto.

Hasenohr, G. 1999. 'Les Recueils littéraires français du XIIIe siècle: public et finalité', in R. Jansen-Sieben and H. van Dijk eds. *Codices Miscellanearum*, special issue 60, Brussels, 37–50.

Hedeman, A. D. 1991. *The Royal Image: Illustrations of the Grandes Chroniques de France, 1274–1422*, Berkeley.

Hindman, S. 1994. *Sealed in Parchment: Rereadings of Knighthood in the Illuminated Manuscripts of Chrétien de Troyes*, Chicago.

Huot, S. 1987. *From Song to Book: The Poetics of Writing in Old French Lyric and Lyrical Narrative Poetry*, Ithaca, NY.

Huot 2000. 'The Manuscript Context of Medieval Romance', in Krueger ed. 2000*, 60–77.

Irvine, M. 1994. *The Making of Textual Culture: 'Grammatica' and Literary Theory 350–1100*, Cambridge.

Jager, E. 2000. *The Book of the Heart*, Chicago.

Kantorowicz, E. H. 1957. *The King's Two Bodies: A Study of Mediaeval Political Theology*, Princeton.

Kelly, T. E. 1974. *Le Haut Livre du Graal, Perlesvaus: A Structural Study*, Geneva.

Köhler, E. 1962. *Trobadorlyrik und höfischer Roman: Aufsätze zur französischen und provenzalischen Literatur des Mittelalters*, Berlin.

Lacy, N. J. 1986. 'The Character of Gauvain in *Hunbaut*', *BBIAS*, 38, 298–305.

Lacy 1996. 'Motif Transfer in Arthurian Romance', in Kelly ed. 1996*, 157–68.

Le Goff, J. 1996. *Saint Louis*, Paris.

Newman, B. 2003. *God and The Goddesses: Vision, Poetry and Belief in the Middle Ages*, Philadelphia.

Nichols, S. G., and S. Wenzel eds 1996. *The Whole Book: Cultural Perspectives on the Medieval Miscellany*, Ann Arbor, MI.

Olson, G. 1982. *Literature as Recreation in the Later Middle Ages*, Ithaca, NY.

Powell, M. 2002. 'Translating Scripture for *Ma Dame de Champagne*: The Old French "Paraphrase" of Psalm 44 (*Eructavit*)', in R. Blumenfeld-Kosinski, D. Robertson and N. B. Warren eds *The Vernacular Spirit*, New York, 83–103.

Putter, A. 1994. 'Finding Time for Romance: Mediaeval Arthurian Literary History', *Med. Aev*, 63, 1–16.

Putter 1995. 'Knights and Clerics at the Court of Champagne: Chrétien de Troyes's Romances in Context', in S. Church and R. Harvey eds *Medieval Knighthood V: Papers from the Sixth Strawberry Hill Conference 1994*, Woodbridge, 243–66.

Rockwell, P. V. 1995. *Rewriting Resemblance in Medieval French Romance: 'Ceci n'est pas un graal'*, New York.

Roques, M. 1952. 'Le Manuscrit fr. 794 de la Bibliothèque Nationale et le scribe Guiot', *Rom*, 73, 177–99.

Rouse, R. H., and M. A. Rouse. 2000, *Manuscripts and their Makers: Commercial Book Producers in Medieval Paris 1200–1500*, 2 vols, Turnhout.

Scheidegger, J. R. 1989. *Le Roman de Renart ou le texte de la dérision*, Geneva.

Short, I. 1988. 'L'Avènement du texte vernaculaire: la mise en recueil', in E. Baumgartner and C. Marchello-Nizia eds *Théories et pratiques de l'écriture au Moyen Âge*, Paris, 11–24.

Stirneman, P. 1999. 'Une bibliothèque princière au XIIe siècle', in *Splendeurs de la Cour de Champagne au temps de Chrétien de Troyes*, exhibition catalogue, Troyes, 36–42.

Szkilnik, M. 2000–1. 'Un exercice de style au XIIIe siècle: *Hunbaut*', *RPh*, 54, 29–42.

Taylor, J. H. M. 1994. 'Order from Accident: Cyclic Consciousness at the End of the Middle Ages', in Besamusca, Gerritsen, Hogetoorn and Lie eds 1994*, 59–73.

Taylor 1996. 'The Sense of a Beginning: Genealogy and Plenitude in Late Medieval Narrative Cycles', in D. Maddox and S. Sturm-Maddox eds 1996*, 93–123.

Trachsler, R. 2000. *Disjointures–conjointures: étude sur l'interférence des matières narratives dans la littérature française du Moyen Âge*, Tübingen and Basel.

Uitti, K. D. 1997. 'Background Information on Chrétien de Troyes's *Le Chevalier de la Charrette*', in *The Charrette Project*, http://www.princeton.edu/~lancelot.

Vàrvaro, A. 2001. 'Elaboration des textes et modalités du récit dans la littérature française médiévale', *Rom*, 119, 1–75.

Walters, L. J. 1985. 'Le Rôle du scribe dans l'organisation des manuscrits des romans de Chrétien de Troyes', *Rom*, 106, 303–25.

Walters 1991. 'The Creation of a "Super Romance": Paris, Bibliothèque Nationale, fonds français, MS 1433', *AY*, 1, 3–25 + plates.

Walters 1992. 'The Poet-Narrator's Address to his Lady as Structural Device in *Partonopeu de Blois*', *Med. Aev*, 61, 229–41.

Walters 1993a. '"A Love that Knows no Falsehood": Moral Instruction and Narrative Closure in the *Bel Inconnu* and *Beaudous*', *SAR*, 58:2, 21–39.

Walters 1993b. 'The Manuscript Context of the *Beaudous* of Robert de Blois', *Man*, 37, 179–92.

Walters 1994a. 'The Formation of a Gauvain Cycle in Chantilly MS 472', *Neophil*, 78, 29–43; repr. in Busby and Thompson eds 2006*, 157–72.

Walters 1994b. 'Chantilly MS. 472 as a Cyclic Work', in Besamusca, Gerritsen, Hogetoorn and Lie eds 1994*, 135–9.

Walters 1994c. 'Gui de Mori's Rewriting of Faux Semblant in the Tournai *Roman de la Rose*', in Kelly ed. 1996* , 261–76.

Walters 1998. 'Parody and Moral Allegory in Chantilly MS 472', *MLN*, 113, 937–50.

Walters 1999. 'Female Figures in the Illustrated Manuscripts of *Le Conte du Graal* and its Continuations: Ladies, Saints, Spectators, Mediators', *BJRL*, 81:3, 7–54.

Walters 2000. 'Resurrecting Gauvain in *L'Atre périlleux* and the Middle Dutch *Walewein*', in *'Por le soie amisté': Essays in Honor of Norris J. Lacy*, Amsterdam and Atlanta, GA, 509–37.

Walters 2001. 'Who was Gui de Mori?', in *'Riens ne m'est seur que la chose incertaine': études sur l'art d'écrire au Moyen Âge offertes à Eric Hicks*, Geneva, 133–46.

Walters 2002. 'Christine de Pizan, Primat, and the *noble nation françoise*', *Cahiers de Recherches Médiévales*, 9, 237–46.

Walters 2003a. 'Constructing Reputations: *fama* and Memory in *Charles V* and *L'Advision-Cristine*', in T. Fenster and D. Lord Smail eds *Fama: The Politics of Talk and Reputation in Medieval Europe*, Ithaca, 118–42.

Walters 2003b. Review of K. Busby, *Codex and Context*, *Spec*, 78, 1260–3.

Walters 2005a. 'The King's Example: Arthur, Gauvain, and Lancelot in *Rigomer* and Chantilly, Musée Condé 472 (anc. 626)', in *'De sens rassis': Essays in Honor of Rupert T. Pickens*, Amsterdam and New York, 699–717.

Walters 2005b. "De-membrer pour remembrer": l'œuvre chrétienne dans le ms. Chantilly 472', in M. Mikhaïlova ed. *Mouvances et jointures: du manuscrit au texte médiéval*, Orleans, 253–81.

Welter, J.-T. 1927. *L'Exemplum dans la littérature religieuse et didactique du Moyen Âge*, Paris and Toulouse; repr. Geneva, 1973.

Woledge, B. 1954 and 1975. *Bibliographie des romans et contes en prose française antérieurs à 1500*, Geneva; Supplement *1954–1973*, Geneva.

Zink, M. 1976. *La Prédication en langue romane avant 1300*, Paris.

XII

LATE MEDIEVAL ARTHURIAN LITERATURE

Jane H. M. Taylor (ed.), Peter F. Ainsworth, Norris J. Lacy, Edward Donald Kennedy and William W. Kibler

By the very end of the Middle Ages, it seems, there were those who were uncomfortable with the historical Arthur, so uncomfortable in fact that the Burgundian memorialist Olivier de La Marche, writing around 1470, felt that the issue needed to be faced. After a page of agonized deliberations, he concludes, with due intellectual ponderousness, that it is inconceivable that so much valuable time, so many 'grans et solempnelz volumes' (*lengthy and serious volumes*), could have been devoted to 'choses frivoles trouvées et non advenues' (*frivolous things which had been invented, but never happened*) (*Mémoires*, Beaune and d'Arbaumont edn, I, 120). Olivier's views should not surprise us: he had spent his life in the service of a ducal court where things Arthurian were at a considerable premium, and like Waurin, whom E. D. Kennedy discusses later in this chapter, he was no doubt reluctant to discount a hero so admired by his patrons.

Indeed, the dukes of Burgundy were enthusiastic patrons of Arthuriana in all its forms (Doutrepont 1909). Their great libraries contained the whole range of Arthurian romances in many volumes (Barrois 1830; Middleton, chapter I) and they may well have commissioned or bought further manuscripts. They seem certainly to have commissioned new prose adaptations of old romances,[1] and perhaps extended versions of older romances, to titillate jaded appetites (Pickford 1959/60*). Moreover, their courtiers played Arthurian games, with *pas d'armes* and tournaments organized along Arthurian lines,[2] and their heralds invented imaginary coats of arms for imaginary heroes.[3] When their memorialists wanted standards against which to measure the magnificence of their hospitality, or the valour of their chivalry, it was to the Arthurian world that they automatically turned,[4] and when the dukes and their courtiers were in search of elegant furnishings, they commissioned tapestries with Arthurian motifs (Vaughan 1975, 163). Very soon after the last Valois duke, Charles the Bold, was killed so unexpectedly, and so young, at the battle of Nancy in 1477, rumours circulated persistently that he was only sleeping and would soon return (Weightman 1989, 103), just like the Arthur of the romances, which, again according to Olivier de La Marche (Beaune and d'Arbaumont edn, II, 217), he took great pleasure in having read to him.

The dukes of Burgundy were not alone in their devotion to things Arthurian. As Ainsworth shows, Gaston de Foix reacted with enthusiasm to Froissart's studious pastiche, the *Roman de Meliador*; was he nostalgically drawn to this last, and surprising, verse romance? Other magnates were passionate devotees of Arthuriana: René d'Anjou, for instance, in 1447, organized a dramatic restaging of 'the taking of the Joyeuse Garde at Saumur, complete with a procession led by two lions from his menagerie'.[5] No library was complete without its Arthurian compilations, often with the sumptuous decoration which shows how much the romances were valued. Moreover, as Kibler shows below, many a late epic or romance, however apparently far removed from a British Celtic twilight, would draw on the dramatic possibilities of a fairyland visit, or a dramatic entrance by Morgan the Fay or Merlin.

Arthur and his Round Table, then, had become ubiquitous. They had by this date been enshrined among the Nine Worthies,[6] the chivalric pantheon, and had thus become a sort of byword for knightly excellence. In his biography of Bertrand du Guesclin (*c.*1380), Cuvelier invents a scene in which the Black Prince exhorts his men to valour by urging them to emulate, along with heroes like Roland and Oliver and Charlemagne,

> Li ducs Lions de Bourges, et Guion de Cournans,
> Perceval le Galois, Lancelot et Tristans,
> Alixandre et Artus, Godefroi li sachans,
> De coi cil ménestrelz font ces nobles rommans.[7]

(*Duke Lion of Bourges and Guion of Cournans, Perceval the Welshman, Lancelot and Tristan, Alexander and Arthur, Godfrey the Wise, about whom these minstrels compose these noble romances.*)

Arthur and his men, it seems, were to be classed with Roland and Oliver, Julius Caesar and Alexander the Great (Tyson 1981).

Whence, then, this universal popularity? Clearly, sheer readability is an important factor: it is remarkable that so much of the production of the early printers consists of costly editions not just of mainstream romances, but also of many of those romances, little known today, to which this section alludes: at least two editions of *Perceforest*, five of *Ysaÿe* (Woledge 1954). As Kibler shows below, an ornamental role is very much the one that Arthurian motifs play in the late *chansons de geste*. But it is surely not *just* that the romances were readable that explains why they were so universal. If the dukes of Burgundy founded orders of chivalry to emulate and rival the Round Table,[8] they were presumably capitalizing, as did Edward I and III in England (Vale in Barron ed. 1999*, chap. 8), on the political advantage to be gained from aligning oneself with Arthur. Arthur and his court constituted, it seems, a political tool of considerable value; Froissart's *Meliador* can be plausibly read as an inspiration to the Crusade (Dembowski 1983), and it is not implausible to see a number of these late romances as much more than simply escapist or frivolous. They are inspirational productions that focus, at the behest perhaps of their readers and patrons, on an

ideal which may be particularly desirable in a period of arduous ideological questioning: the universal image of the charismatic leader who transcends everyday
reality, the brotherhood in which there subsists a purer sense of unity and
destiny.[9] Arthur and his court, in other words, are signifiers open to a broad
variety of signifieds, and it may be that the popularity of the romances devoted
to them derives from just that flexibility. [JHMT]

Arthurian Nostalgia: Jean Froissart's *Meliador*

One way to approach Froissart's romance, that exercise in creative anachronism,
is suggested by a short sequence that occurs early in the third book of his
Chroniques. At the end of a long ride westwards from Pamiers, Froissart reaches
his destination, Orthez, in November 1388, bringing with him some greyhounds
from his patron Guy of Châtillon as a gift from the latter to the Count of Foix-
Béarn; but it is the writer's own gift to Gaston III that is here thrown into
prominence: a manuscript volume containing his romance of *Meliador*. Woven
into its narrative, he informs us, are the (seventy-nine) lyric compositions penned
by Wenceslas of Bohemia, Duke of Luxembourg and Brabant, under whose
patronage the poem had taken on its present guise. Count Gaston, we learn, is
soon enjoying a reading from *Meliador* each night after supper (*Chroniques*,
Livre III, Ainsworth edn, chapter 13).

Whilst an initial version of *Meliador*, without Wenceslas's poems, seems to
have been in existence by the mid- to late 1360s, the most intensive period of association between Froissart and Wenceslas was 1373–83 (Dembowski 1983, 47,
51–2, 57–8). Froissart's *Dit dou Florin* (305–9) informs us that Wenceslas did not
live to see the romance completed; his poems may therefore have been incorporated between the mid-1370s and the years following his death in 1383. In any
case, for reasons to be discussed, the *Meliador* known to modern readers through
Longnon's 1899 edition was almost certainly different from that read aloud
to Gaston Fébus; completed in all probability by 1389–90, it incorporates at
least one new episode based on material ostensibly gathered during the visit to
Orthez.

The passage from Book III mentioned above reflects the poet-chronicler's
perceptions of how *Meliador* was received by a live audience. Two sections from
his *Dit dou Florin* (ll. 293–309, 349–89) inform us that the romance was read at a
rate of seven folios per sitting, and that as a reward for each night's reading,
Froissart received the dregs of the count's wine. Upon completion of the entire
reading, he received eighty Aragonese florins, and the manuscript was returned
to him: 'mon livre qu'il m'ot laissié / Ne sçai se ce fu de coer lié' (*my book, which
he had returned to me – willingly or not, I do not know*).

We do not know how Froissart dealt in performance with Wenceslas's lyrics, and we can only speculate as to whether he held his audience entirely spellbound throughout a reading lasting no less than ten weeks. His claim that Fébus derived nothing but 'solas' (*delight*) from the experience should perhaps be taken with a pinch of salt. However, Fébus appears to have refrained from any inclination to curtail the performance, and it would seem that Froissart did not leave Orthez until he had read right to the end of *Meliador*, even if Fébus evinced no desire to retain the manuscript. That this first audience stayed the distance should give us pause for thought before we dismiss the romance, as too many critics have done, as irremediably long-winded.

Meliador might never have made its way back into the public domain had it not been for two discoveries by Longnon. Earlier scholars had speculated that the work must have disappeared soon after Froissart returned home with it in 1389. In 1891, Longnon came across some parchment in the bindings of two seventeenth-century legal registers, on which were written 516 lines of verse, some of it barely legible. He compiled from these a list of proper names, which included 'Artus roy de Bretagne', 'Camel de Camois', 'Hermondine' and, most significantly, 'Melyador, le chevalier au soleil d'or' (Longnon 1891; BNF, nouv. acq. lat. 2374, fols 36–9 = MS *A*). Two years later Longnon noticed that BNF, fr. 12557 was listed in the catalogue as the 'Roman de Camel et d'Hermondine', its early nineteenth-century binding bearing the unhelpful title 'Roman du roy d'Artus'. So emerged from years of loss to Froissart scholars the 'Roman de Meliador'. Longnon's edition was published between 1895 and 1899, the first monograph devoted to it (by Dembowski) appearing only as recently as 1983.

MS *B* (BNF, fr. 12577) was copied *c*.1400; it comprises 226 folios in bi-columnar format. The text is incomplete: Longnon adopted a lineation such that two lacunae where folios had been excised were assigned to (what should have been) lines 5396–5530 and 28469–604. The text of MS *B* also ends abruptly, at line 30771, before the romance has finished dealing with the adventures of Sagremor and Sebille, and in advance of the great tournament which would almost certainly have provided the climax. The plot runs as follows:

Princess Hermondine, only daughter of the King of Scotland, is loved by an impetuous and brutal knight, Camel de Camois, who, in addition to his passionate nature, suffers from a mysterious and shameful somnambulism. Her cousin and confidante Floree, knowing of Camel's affliction and wishing to protect her young friend from his attentions, proposes a quest competition to determine who is the most courtly and valorous knight in the world. Although the initial idea is Floree's, it will be proclaimed jointly by the King of Scotland and King Arthur. The quest is to last exactly five years (2841–2); knightly performances are to be judged by twelve electors, six designated by the King of Scotland and six by King Arthur. The first prize will be the hand of the beautiful Hermondine, together with her inheritance, the realm of Scotland. The history of this five-year quest provides the armature for the interlaced narratives that make up the romance (see Dembowski 1983, 63).

Despite its title, *Meliador* deploys a collective protagonist: 'the hierarchy of young Arthurian knighthood' (Dembowski 1983, 62). If Meliador is the supreme champion, Froissart appears to have been intent on marshalling a veritable champions' league of knights whose individual levels of achievement remind one of the degrees of chivalric aspiration discussed by Geoffroi de Charny in his *Book of Chivalry*. Like the jousts at St Inglevert in Book IV of the *Chroniques* (*c*.1395–1400), those of the romance may be rebarbative to the modern reader, but on closer inspection turn out to portray subtle shades of skill and prowess. The romance's ideology is to this extent congruent with that of the *Chroniques*, especially in the earlier redactions of Book I (*c*.1373–8), which celebrate the earlier military achievements of Edward III's reign, marking it out as a new Golden Age of chivalry. *Meliador*'s prologue takes its audience back to another glorious dawn – that of Arthurian chivalry and the very beginnings of Arthur's court:

> En ce temps que li rois Artus
> Qui tant fu plains de grans vertus,
> De sens, d'onneur et de larghece,
> Regnoit au point de sa jonece,
> Et qu'il commençoit a tenir
> Grans festes et a retenir
> Chevaliers pour emplir ses sales. (Longnon edn, 1–7)

(In those early days of the youthful King Arthur, so possessed of every signal virtue, of wisdom, honour and generosity, when he began to hold great feasts and to retain knights to fill his halls.)

Meliador is the latest extant Middle French Arthurian romance to have been composed in verse, whilst its action takes place a good ten years before the appearance at Arthur's court of heroes such as Lancelot, Meliadus, Lot or Guiron (Trachsler 1997*, 166). That Froissart chose not to embroider upon the exploits of heroes already celebrated by Chrétien and his imitators may in part be accounted for by a desire to trace the very origins of the chivalric ideal. The early Arthurian world conjured up in *Meliador* certainly owes something to Froissart's enthusiasm for the spirited martial and courtly activity of the early years of Edward III's reign, and to the inspirational prowess of the captains who served under him at the decisive victories of Sluys (1340), Crécy (1346) and Poitiers (1356), their loyalty cemented by enrolment into Edward's post-1348 'Arthurian' Order of the Garter.

In the first section of *Meliador*, all the resources of chivalry are employed to stave off the premature marriage of Hermondine, heiress of the King of Scotland. Not yet fourteen years old, but under strong pressure to marry,

Hermondine finds herself the unwilling object of the attentions of sundry knights: chivalrous, moderately chivalrous or downright unsuitable. The most alarming suitor of all is Camel de Camois, his persistence aggravated by an unnatural propensity to sleepwalk. It is more than probable that the portrayal of Camel was inspired by an anecdote recounted to Froissart on his way to, or at Orthez, namely the even more supernatural story of Pierre de Béarn, whose somnambulism and associated violence alienated him from his wife (*Chroniques*, Livre III, Ainsworth edn, chapter 14; see Dembowski 1983, 167, n. 82 for a discussion of this possible influence and for parallels between the self-styled solar Fébus, who associated himself with Phoebus Apollo yet rose each day much later than common mortals to dine at midnight in a banqueting hall illumined by the brilliance of a myriad torches, and Meliador, 'le chevalier au soleil d'or'). By dint of his insistent pursuit of the heroine, Camel represents, it may be argued, the embodiment of a threat from the uncouth and less than courtly here-and-now to foreclose on the timeless vision of this great chivalric quest.

In the introduction to his edition Longnon observes that a Scots herald mentioned in the poem bears on his shield arms representing Hermondine that are strongly Marian in connotation. A major theme of *Meliador* is surely the preservation for as long as possible of the heroine's integrity and nubile status. *Meliador* may thus be seen as precisely the kind of romance identified by Denis de Rougemont in *L'Amour et l'Occident* (see chapter XIV) as offering readers the perverse appeal of an (almost) unending deferment of sexual and marital consummation. But the deferment also has to do with the need to single out from amidst other potentially convincing suitors the ideal candidate for Hermondine's hand and inheritance, and this is a matter that cannot be rushed.

That the romance is more than a protracted erotic tease or series of variations on the themes and motifs of the tournament is confirmed by the not inconsiderable bibliography that it has recently precipitated. Whilst Diverres (1969; 1970) sought to clarify the relationship between the romance's topography and the geography of fourteenth-century Britain, subsequent critics (Lods 1980; Taylor 1987–8; 1990) have focused on the 'dialogue' between the romance and its embedded lyrics. Others have examined the migration of themes and narrative developments from the romance to the chronicles, or vice versa (Harf-Lancner 1980; Zink 1980b; Ainsworth 1990b). References in *Meliador* to painting techniques have generated controversy (Zink 1980b; Van Coolput and Vandenbroeck 1991), whilst the theme of poetry as currency, literary or pecuniary, forms the basis for two important essays (Cerquiglini-Toulet 1991; Zink 1993).

More recently scholars have turned their attention to that late subsection of the romance and its interlaced plot known from the name of its protagonist as the 'roman de Sagremor' (Kibler 2000), seeking to evaluate its depiction of an uncouth fictional 'Ireland' against a background of near-contemporary expeditions to subdue and conquer the real Ireland, a topic engaged with some thirty years earlier, albeit from a different perspective, by Diverres (1970). Froissart underscores the youth and chivalric promise of his Irish prince, supplanted for the moment by the unchivalrous Bondigal. Sagremor, moreover, is the only knight in the romance who will eventually experience 'the privilege of entering into the truly Arthurian Other World, the land of faerie' (Dembowski 1983, 84). Upon meeting Meliador, Sagremor is instructed to go to Arthur's court as an apprentice in order to learn all he can about true chivalry, for there he will encounter figures such as Kay, Gauvain, Agravain and Yvain. With Bondigal eager to keep his realm free of courtliness and knight-errantry, it is not implausible to argue with Dembowski (1983, 85) that the section missing from the end of *Meliador* would have provided us (amongst other things) with an example of chivalry's conquest of Ireland, land of the uncouth, by Sagremor, the embodiment of chivalric youth and its potential, brought through training at Arthur's court to the very peak of knightly achievement. The 'Irish' theme was a live issue as early as 1365–7 (the final two years of Lionel of Clarence's unsuccessful campaign) – unless, as Dembowski has argued, for 'Ireland' we should read 'Prussia' and the activities of those guests of the Teutonic Knights who embarked with them on their crusading forays against the pagans of Lithuania and the neighbouring Baltic lands (cf. Henry, Earl of Derby's expedition of 1390–1; Dembowski 1983, 139–44, and 184, n. 46). This is a reading which we personally find unnecessary, since the Ireland (Land-beyond-the-Pale) of *Meliador*, seized by the uncouth usurper Bondigal, already does sterling service as an exemplar of the pre-Arthurian land awaiting reconquest, redemption and civilization at the hands of the temporarily supplanted heir to the Irish crown, Sagremor, polished and trained through contact with the paragons of Arthur's idealized court.

Finally, rather than labelling *Meliador* as old-fashioned, tiresomely nostalgic, anachronistic or resolutely conservative, we may be nearer the mark if we recognize with Zink that it represents to some extent the emergence of a new poetic sensibility, best expressed in the lyrical interludes *between* the episodes of the quest proper, where verse 'is felt as the natural mode of effusiveness, of self-expression, and of a subjective outlook on the world' (1998a, 171). To this extent at least, *Meliador* looks forwards, rather than backwards to a remote and sterile Arthurian past. [PFA]

Arthurian Burgundy: The Politics of Arthur

During a period of just over a century in the course of the late Middle Ages, the dukes of Burgundy amassed impressive libraries, acquiring by various means earlier manuscripts and commissioning copies or adaptations, often gathered into sumptuous codices, of many epics, romances, chronicles and other works. Philip the Bold (1342–1404), John the Fearless (1371–1419), Philip the Good (1396–1467) and Charles the Rash (1433–77) were indefatigable collectors, and eight inventories of their libraries between 1404 and 1504 (Barrois 1830; Doutrepont 1909) provide an invaluable record of the texts collected, even though certain of the titles are sufficiently general to leave doubt as to the precise content or the identity of the works.

Although their greater interest was in classical subjects, notably the stories of Troy and of Jason and the Golden Fleece, the dukes of Burgundy appear to have owned a fair number of Arthurian titles. The only examples of verse romances for which we have evidence are Chrétien's *Yvain*, *Charrette* and *Cligés* in BNF, fr. 12560, owned by Margaret of Flanders, wife of Philip the Bold, and the *Meraugis* now in Vienna, Österreichische Nationalbibliothek, MS 2599. Prose romances were better represented in Burgundy. According to successive inventories, the following texts were available: the *Lancelot–Grail* Cycle, the prose *Tristan*, *Guiron le Courtois*, *Ysaÿe le Triste* and *Perceforest* (for further details, see chapter I).

Of particular interest, however, are two works which may have been commissioned by Philip the Good: prose adaptations of Chrétien de Troyes's *Erec* and *Cligés*.[10] Both are physically unimposing codices on paper and may have been prepared as preliminary copies, perhaps intended to be subsequently executed in more elaborate form if they met with the duke's favour. It should be noted that neither prosification names Chrétien as author. The manuscript of the Burgundian *Cligés* (Leipzig, Universitätsbibliothek, MS Rep. II 108) is dated within the text as 26 March 1454, and the *Erec* was doubtless composed at roughly the same time, i.e. during the decade 1450 to 1460 (Colombo Timelli edn, 9).[11] We have no indication as to who may have prepared the prose texts, and scholarly opinion is divided on the question of common authorship.[12]

These two works are by no means simple prosifications (*mises en proses*) and modernizations of Chrétien's romances; they are also adaptations and, in effect, interpretations of their models. Episodes may be omitted, invented or materially altered.[13] Wallen (1972, 302) has argued that many of the modifications were determined by the identity of the intended patron or audience. The innovations, she suggests, frequently serve to glorify Philip the Good and his succession, and the *Cligés* in particular is 'a document of political flattery'. A number of other departures from Chrétien's works clearly have as their purpose to rationalize the text, clarifying episodes or events that were left mysterious by Chrétien or that were simply no longer understood three centuries later. Taylor (1998, 183), studying both Burgundian adaptations, speaks of the 'acculturation' of the text, 'a process whereby the socio-culturally unfamiliar is recast in familiar terms, so that the reader can understand systems and phenomena in a source text as corresponding to his own ideologies, preconceptions and behaviour patterns'.

This familiarizing or rationalizing process is perhaps most evident in the *Erec*, where the prosifier attempts to clarify or elucidate the central enigma of Chrétien's romance: the reasons for Erec's harsh treatment of Enide and her reaction to that treatment. In the prose work, the result is to recast that enigma as an unambiguous test of Enide's love and to cast her in the role of patient Griselda, the dutiful wife who will obey her husband's every wish and command (Willard 1991b, 91). The text can thus be seen as a 'manual of wifely conduct' (Lacy 1994, 278). Moreover, Wallen (1972, 61–91) emphasizes in particular the character flaw that leads Enide to question Erec's prowess and thus leads him, in turn, to doubt her love. The result of this focus is an interpretation of the prose romance as an anti-Enide reading of Chrétien (cf. Colombo Timelli edn, 33).

Certain of these observations about the Burgundian *Erec* are applicable also to the *Cligés*: it has clearly been designed and executed to appeal to the tastes of its particular audience. However, as noted, similar approaches do not necessarily demonstrate common authorship. The *Cligés* generally respects the structure and narrative offered by its model but, like the *Erec*, repeatedly truncates, adds and modifies material. Most obvious to readers who compare the prose with its verse model will doubtless be the prosifier's treatment of the extended monologues that characterize Chrétien's *Cligés*. The verse text is a highly rhetorical romance incorporating a number of long soliloquies examining the nature and effects of love, and it must be supposed that the Burgundian author would have found those monologues tedious – or at least that he would have expected his audience to have little patience with them. He tends therefore to abridge them drastically, effacing much of the psychological subtlety of the original and consequently placing greater emphasis on adventures and warfare.[14] He also modifies Chrétien's ambiguous conclusion, in which the lovers achieve happiness but future generations suffer because of their deceptions. The prose author makes no mention of any negative consequences of their actions, preferring merely 'to provide the happiest ending possible – and in the shortest time possible' (Lacy 1998, 203).

Neither of the Burgundian compositions is a masterpiece. Willard (1991a, 403), Lacy (1998, 205), Colombo Timelli (edn, 20) and others have recognized their deficiencies, most notably the deletion of fascinating monologues, the frequent transformation of dialogue into narrative, and a flat, unengaging style that often sounds more like textual summary than literary composition or adaptation. Yet, these same critics and others have argued against a wholesale condemnation of the prose texts, emphasizing that they are instructive, both as examples of the prosifying methods of their age, and as invaluable witnesses to the literary tastes of the dukes and court of Burgundy in the mid-fifteenth century. [NJL]

Arthurian History: The Chronicle of Jehan de Waurin

The fifteenth-century French prose chronicle of the history of Britain and England, the *Recueil des croniques et anchiennes istories de la Grant Bretaigne* by Jehan de Waurin (the name is sometimes spelt Jean de Wavrin or Wauvrin), is an enormous work, covering in its final version the years from the legendary founding of Albion to 1471 and consisting of 2,388 pages of text in its five-volume nineteenth-century edition in the Rolls Series.[15] Its Arthurian section is derived primarily from Geoffrey of Monmouth's *Historia Regum Britanniae*, but, as Fletcher (1906, 225–30) pointed out years ago, it has affinities with French prose Arthurian romances both in style and content.

The Fleming Jehan de Waurin, born *c*.1394, was an illegitimate member of a noble family of Artois. He fought for John the Fearless, Duke of Burgundy, and his English allies against the French at Agincourt and elsewhere. Probably during this period of fighting on the side of the English he developed an interest in the history of England. After the treaty of Arras in 1435, which ended in the Anglo-Burgundian alliance, he concluded his career as a soldier but served two later dukes of Burgundy, Philip the Good and Charles the Bold, as councillor and chamberlain, and went on at least one diplomatic mission (Gransden 1982, 288–9). He began working on his chronicle probably *c*.1446. In his introduction he claims that no one in Britain had written of their kings and princes 'seulement en aulcuns petis livres de chascun roy a par soy' (2) (*except only in some little books concerning each king apart*, 2). The first version of his book, completed in 1455, covered the history of Britain from its founding to the death of Henry IV in 1413. After Edward IV's accession in 1461 he extended the history, first to 1443, and later to Edward's restoration to the throne in 1471. His association with the ducal court at Burgundy undoubtedly encouraged this project and may account too for ways in which his Arthurian section differs from that of many of his predecessors; 'history' was the pre-eminent secular genre at the court, but it was also, as Morse (1980, 48) points out, an 'umbrella term which sheltered narratives of widely varying truth content', and there was often no clear distinction between a chronicle and a historical romance.[16]

Scholars have known since the nineteenth and early twentieth centuries the major sources that Jehan de Waurin drew upon, and for much of his chronicle he was primarily a copyist of other writers' works (Visser-Fuchs [1997], 92). The Arthurian section follows almost exactly the content of an anonymous French prose adaptation of Wace's *Brut* (for the pre-Arthurian section) and Geoffrey's *Historia* as found in two early fifteenth-century manuscripts in the Bibliothèque Nationale de France, fr. 2806 and fr. 5621 (Hardy and Hardy edn, lxiii–lxiv; Fletcher 1906, 226). Much of the Arthurian section of this version closely follows Geoffrey of Monmouth, but it adds many details not in the original, such as the burial of 'Vorcimer' at St Paul's in London and the assurance that Arthur is triumphant in heaven because of his chivalrous campaigns against the pagans (see Hardy and Hardy edn, 211, 338).

More substantive changes occur near the end in the accounts of the adultery of Mordred and Guinevere and of Arthur's final battle. At that point the author remarks that he must depart from Geoffrey of Monmouth's book. Geoffrey, he claims, had said nothing about Arthur's battle against Mordred because Geoffrey was a descendant of Mordred's father, King Lot (Loth) of Scotland; he therefore did not want to bring disgrace upon his own family after Arthur had been so generous to Lot (436–7). All this, of course, is nonsense. Since Geoffrey does indeed tell of Arthur's final battle, the author must have been anticipating readers of French who knew little of Geoffrey's Latin account. The work to which the author says he turns for the final part of the Arthurian story is a book written by 'Gaultier de Oxenee, qui lavoit pourtraitee en langue brete, lequel fut homme scientifficque et tres expert en histoires' (438) (*Walter of Oxenee, who was a learned man, and skilled in history, and who described it in the Breton language*, 396). This is the book that Geoffrey of Monmouth claims was his source, a book supposedly written by Walter, Archdeacon of Oxford, which most scholars believe never existed. A shortcoming of this source, the author points out, is that Walter told the story very briefly (438), and this presumably gave him licence to supplement it.

Although he does not mention the source of his other information, the changes made in the conclusion indicate that he derived it from the final branch of the French Vulgate Cycle, the *Mort Artu*. For example, in Geoffrey of Monmouth's *Historia,* as Arthur prepares to march into Rome to be crowned emperor he learns that his nephew Mordred, whom he had appointed regent of Britain, has usurped the throne and committed adultery with Guinevere. In Jehan de Waurin's chronicle, however, the condemnation of Guinevere found in Geoffrey's *Historia* and other chronicles is absent; the blame is transferred solely to Mordred, who forces her to become his wife. Mordred 'embrase du feu luxurieux ... avoit conjoinct par force la royne Geneviere' (436) (*inflamed with lawless passion ... had forcibly contracted a matrimonial alliance with the Queen Guenever*, 394). Seduced and violated by Mordred's contemptible passion (437), she becomes Mordred's victim rather than a willing conspirator as in the other chronicles. This emphasis on Mordred's overwhelming passion for Guinevere, Mordred's attempt to force her to marry him and the reader's consequent sympathy for the queen, as well as other changes to the end of the story (Guinevere being falsely told that Arthur is dead, Arthur killing Mordred and the detail of the sun shining through the wound when he withdraws his sword, Arthur crushing a knight in a fatal embrace, the appearance of Girflet, here spelled Gifflet, as Arthur's final companion, to whom Arthur gives his sword,

with the suggestion of the well-known story of Girflet being ordered to throw
Excalibur into the water) would all have been suggested by the *Mort Artu*.

Jehan's chronicle attributes three possible fates to Arthur:

(i)   while his two remaining knights, wounded and worn out, slept, 'le noble roy Artu
      sesvanuy, sicque on ne sceut oncques quil devint' (447). (*King Arthur vanished, so that it
      was never known what became of him*, 404);

(ii) some say that he was carried to the island of Avalon to be healed of his wounds (447);

(iii) 'Aulcuns veullent dire que quant le roy Artus apercheut que tous ses compaignons
      estoient mors exepte Gifflet, quil lappella, et sen alerent tous deux sur le rivage de la mer,
      puis baisa Artus Gifflet et ... sy sen entra en une nef quil trouva illec toute preste,
      laquelle sy tost comme le roy Artus fut dedens entres sy se esquippa parmy la mer sy
      impetueusement que Gifflet ne sceut quelle devint en petit espace' (447–8). (*Others will
      have it that, when King Arthur perceived that all his companions were dead except for
      Gifflet, he called him, and they went together to the sea shore, where Arthur kissed Gifflet
      ... and then entered a ship which he found there ready, and which, as soon as King Arthur
      got into it, skimmed along the sea so rapidly that in a little while Gifflet did not know what
      had become of it*, 404.)

The source of the first of these accounts of Arthur's fate, that he vanished and no
one knew what had become of him, is unknown to me, although it would be easy
to find analogues in stories of abductions by figures from the Celtic Other
World;[17] the statement that he was taken to Avalon follows Geoffrey of
Monmouth; the detailed account of his getting into a boat that moved away so
quickly that Girflet did not know what had become of it is derived from the *Mort
Artu*.[18] The author also adds that the story of the 'Saint Graal' presents another
ending that the author will not mention (447). This is probably a reference to the
conclusion of the *Mort Artu*; three days after Arthur was taken away in the boat,
Girflet learns from a hermit that the ladies in the boat brought his body to a
chapel to be buried (*Mort Artu*, §194). As it does in many of the chronicles, the
story of Mordred's usurpation gives the author the opportunity to denounce
treachery, but the changes to the ending were made by an author who wanted his
work to remind readers of prose romances.

Gransden (1982, 288) describes Jehan's chronicle as 'chivalric historiography',
the type of chronicle written for knights who would also have been readers of
romance. Thus Jehan was probably interested in incorporating a version of the
Arthurian chronicle that would be suitable for this type of reader. He himself has
long been thought to be interested in the prose romances: Doutrepont (1939,
428–30) and Naber (1990, 459–64) have shown that he collected manuscripts of
historical romances such as *Ogier le Danois*, *Othovien*, *Apollonius de Tyr*, *Istoire de
Jason*, *Histoire de Thèbes* and a *Destruction de Troie*, and Doutrepont believes that
Jehan commissioned the *mise en prose* of a number of verse romances. Visser-
Fuchs ([1997], 98–102) suggests that Jehan's account of the founding of Britain by
Albinia and her sisters may have been copied from the Arthurian prose romance
Guiron le Courtois or from an earlier romance that the author of Guiron had used.

This combination in a narrative of elements from chronicle and romance was nothing new in Arthurian romances, but rather uncommon in Arthurian chronicles. Elspeth Kennedy (1996, 88) has discussed the influence of chronicles and other genres on the Vulgate Cycle, and authors of prose romances often tried to avoid giving the impression that they had written fiction, claiming authority for their works as historical documents that made important truths about the past available to their audiences (Hanning 1985, 349). However, although the authors of the prose romances were willing to borrow freely from the chronicles to give their works more authority, the chroniclers in England, with the notable exception of John Hardyng (E. D. Kennedy 1989b), generally did not borrow much more than minor details from the romances, but instead usually followed closely Geoffrey of Monmouth's *Historia*. Although there were some memorable protests against Geoffrey's veracity (Fletcher 1906, 179–82; Chambers 1927, 106–8), many of the English chroniclers appear to have accepted his work as a true account and generally did not attempt to add much from the romances. Admittedly, the fourteenth-century English chronicler Robert Mannyng of Brunne, following a suggestion in Wace's *Brut*, attempts to account for some of Arthur's adventures in the French verse romances by indicating that they took place during a twelve-year period of peace during which the chronicles had little to say about Arthur. He also writes that the adventures in the prose romances took place during nine years when Arthur ruled in France after his conquests, when the chronicles said little about his activities (Putter 1994; Johnson 1991). Even though Mannying tries to place the romance adventures within the chronological framework of the chronicles, he does not attempt to retell any of them and remains relatively faithful to the chronicle version of the Arthurian story that Geoffrey's *Historia* had established.

Jehan de Waurin, by contrast, wrote on the Continent, where Geoffrey's account of Arthur's conquest of Europe had not been taken seriously by most chroniclers.[19] Thus the readers on the Continent for whom Jehan was compiling his chronicle might have been expected to tolerate the inclusion of material familiar to readers of romance more readily than readers in England, and he might also have expected even English readers to accept by the fifteenth century a less orthodox version, since many in England then doubted the truth of the Arthurian story.[20] When, some time prior to 1455, Jehan incorporated the Arthurian material into his chronicle, he would have had no way of knowing that perhaps his most important reader would be an Englishman, Edward IV, who was interested in the political potential of Arthurian chronicles because of his Welsh ancestry (E. D. Kennedy 1989a, 2676–7; Allan 1979, 172–8).

When Jehan de Waurin began writing his chronicle, he intended to cover English history only to the death of Henry IV in 1413, but he later extended the history to 1471, possibly with the hope of writing a work that would appeal to the

English king: he included in it French versions of two of Edward IV's pieces of propaganda: *The Historye of the Arrivall of Edward IV* and *The Chronicle of the Rebellion in Lincolnshire* (Visser-Fuchs 1992). After the Lancastrians had forced Edward to flee into exile between October 1470 and March 1471, Edward took refuge in the Low Countries and probably during this period of exile he began to collect manuscripts, particularly of chivalric literature. One of the manuscripts he commissioned was Jehan de Waurin's chronicle.[21] This copy of the chronicle included a dedication to the king, in which Jehan expresses sympathy with Edward's struggles against those who had attempted to usurp his throne.[22] Jehan's version of the Arthurian story would probably have been welcomed by Edward; the account of Arthur as a whole followed the main details of the story that had been presented by Geoffrey of Monmouth, but it added to the conclusion echoes of chivalric romance, with which Edward was apparently familiar. It was also a story about the evils of usurpation and treason, which, as Jehan's dedication to Edward points out, the king had experienced at first hand.

Jehan de Waurin's chronicle, completed in 1471, was written at about the same time as a far better known version of the Arthurian story, Sir Thomas Malory's *Morte Darthur,* completed in 1469–70. Malory wrote his book while a prisoner of Edward; Jehan dedicated his to the king. Malory adapted the French prose romances for English readers accustomed to Arthurian chronicles and made modifications that would have reminded them of these works. Jehan, by contrast, included a version of the chronicle story that would remind readers accustomed to the French romances of the chronicle tradition. Both writers wished to present the old stories in ways that would appeal to contemporary readers. One produced a classic, the other a chronicle known today only to relatively few specialists.
[EDK]

Arthurian Fictions

The *Roman de Perceforest*

The *Roman de Perceforest*, which is divided into six books, has survived in just four manuscripts: *A.* Paris, BNF, fr. 345–8 (Books 1, 2, 3, 5); *B.* Paris, BNF, fr. 106–9; (Books 1–4); *C.* Paris, Arsenal MSS 3483–94 (the only complete manuscript, sometimes, and rather confusingly, labelled *A* in Flutre 1948–70); *D.* London, BL, Royal MSS 15. E. v, 19. E. iii, and 19. E. ii (Books 1–3). If there is one thing on which all readers and commentators agree, it is that *Perceforest* is positively gargantuan: longer by far than the leisurely prose *Tristan*, longer even than the Vulgate Cycle in its entirety. Its size is a function, largely, of its sheer ambition: it promises a universal history tracing the evolution of Britain from its most remote beginnings, with Geoffrey of Monmouth's Brutus, to the very advent of Arthur. To do so involves some historical sleight-of-hand: the writer uses a 'dovetail technique' (Taylor 1987–8, 271), opens up an unexpected chronological gap in Geoffrey's *Historia Regum Britanniae* (Lods 1951, 16–18; Taylor 1987–8; Trachsler 2000, 241–52), interpolates his own history, and then closes the brackets with some narratorial awkwardness by returning to Geoffrey's Utherpendragon.

The pseudo-historical premise of *Perceforest* rests on one of Geoffrey's more obscure kings of England and Scotland, the unremarkable but rather aptly named Pir (punning on the word *pire*, meaning 'worse'). Pir's reign has, it seems, been debilitating: England is dissolving into anarchy as local warlords rape and pillage, and the few surviving barons who have remained committed to the rule of law, but who are powerless to reimpose it, have gathered to pray to Venus for her help. As they do so, a ship appears on the horizon: it carries Alexander the Great, driven out into the Atlantic by a providential storm, and destined by the gods to become emperor and overlord of Britain. He nominates kings for England and Scotland from among the young knights of his entourage whose kingdom, Gadres, he has conquered (Flutre 1953, 45–61): Betis for England and Gadifer for Scotland. He also assists in the process whereby true chivalry and righteous rule are reborn in Britain, by inventing the tournament, and by ensuring that the anarchy which has swamped the country under the evil Darnant l'Enchanteur is replaced by a firm and just government. It is during this process that Betis, purging the forests (especially the forest of Darnantes) of malefactors, acquires the sobriquet 'Perceforest' (Taylor 1997).

The advent of Betis and Gadifer heralds a new age of peace and prosperity: cities, towns and castles are founded, orders of chivalry instituted, primitive peoples made good citizens. But the era is too good to last; soon, Gadifer, almost fatally wounded in a hunting accident, withdraws into a magic retreat in the forests of Scotland under the tutelage of his queen, the Reine Fée, and Perceforest's son Betidés makes the tragic mistake of marrying the treacherous Cerse la Romaine, who betrays the kingdom to the invading Romans under Julius Caesar. In the great battle of the Franc Palais, Caesar massacres the British; all the heroes of Alexander's era are killed, with the exceptions only of Perceforest himself, Gadifer, and some of their most faithful adherents who withdraw to the Île de Vie, where they will await the promised Coming of the Saviour (Szkilnik 1999b).

And yet, not all the seeds of chivalry have vanished. The cities, towns and castles fall into decay, and their inhabitants revert to living in mud huts, dressed in skins, but the heroes of antiquity have left sons and grandsons who will regenerate the kingdom and beat back the descendants of Darnant. Out of the tragedy of Britain comes a new chivalric society, if possible even more glorious than the preceding one, a society which will lead the country towards the new Christian era. The last great heir of Perceforest's Britain, Gallafur, will put an end to all the enchanted adventures of the kingdom, and live not only to hear the good news of the Incarnation, but to carry it to the patient survivors on the Île de Vie (Szkilnik 1999b). At this news Perceforest, Gadifer and their associates can die content. Meanwhile, the knowledge of Perceforest's Britain slips from all public consciousness as the Danes invade, and as the writer of *Perceforest* wrenches fiction back to conventional 'history', he picks up the thread of Geoffrey's 'authentic' line of kings that will lead eventually to Arthur, the distant descendant of Alexander the Great, Gadifer and Perceforest.

Most readers will by now have dismissed the romance as a farrago of unlikelihoods, yet the writer goes to quite remarkable lengths to insist on the authenticity of what he has invented. That no one has heard of Perceforest, that no one has realized that Alexander the Great made it to Britain, is, he claims, because the invading Danes had forbidden all mention of such things (VI, Arsenal 3494, fol. 330r). Why this carefully concealed history (Gaullier-Bougassas 2000) should have come to light in the French-speaking world is explained with similar inventiveness: the deeds of Perceforest's Britain had been scrupulously recorded in a great manuscript which, as the Danes approached, had been concealed in an *aumaire* (*chest*) in what is now the abbey of Wortimer, on the Humber; a reforming abbot repairing his monastery had discovered the mysterious manuscript written, naturally enough, in Greek, had had it translated by a shipwrecked Greek who happened to know Latin, had handed it to the Count of Hainault (who happened, after the marriage of his daughter Philippa to Edward III, to be on a tour of England) and he, in his turn, had had it translated into French by a monk from the abbey of Saint-Landelin in Hainault (Taylor edn, pp. 120–4). There is no trace of irony: nothing seems to suggest that these meticulous truth-guarantees (Taylor 1987–8; Berthelot 1991) should be taken other than at face value; on the contrary, the fact that the writer translates, or copies a translation of, Geoffrey's *Historia* as a prologue to his romance (Taylor 1987–8; Szkilnik 1998b), that he or a later adapter lards his account with authentically historical events such as the death of Alexander the Great or the invasion of Julius Caesar, that he makes such convoluted efforts to reconcile the 'unimpeachable' Geoffrey with the dynasties he has invented, and even that he names authorities like Orosius and Dares Phrygius, all suggest that his masquerade is meant to be taken with some seriousness.

The artifice which attaches the romance to the court of Hainault[23] raises some interesting questions of dating and authorship. The *terminus post quem* is provided by the fact that the romance is attached firmly to Jacques de Longuyon's *Voeux du paon*, which was written in 1313;[24] the *terminus ad quem* derives from a certain number of factors. The first relates to the count to whom the discovery of the Greek manuscript is credited: he is Guillaume I of Hainault, and the phrasing of references to him suggests that the chapter, which need not of course mean the romance as a whole, was written after his death in 1337. Roussineau (1985) has argued convincingly that certain details in the account of the founding of the Order of the Garter in 1344 make it clear that the founders knew, and were duplicating, details of the Franc Palais in *Perceforest*. There is thus no reason to doubt that the romance was, originally, the work of a cleric at the court of Hainault (Taylor edn, 23–4; Roussineau edn, IV/i, ix–xiv; Roussineau, thesis, 63–7). If this is the case, however, there remains a problem, in that we currently possess two rather different versions of the romance, both preserved in Burgundian manuscripts which date from more than a century later than the conjectural date for the composition of the 'Hainault version'.

Roussineau's *version courte*, represented by manuscripts *A* and *B*, seems to have abbreviated the romance somewhat, whilst the *version longue*, represented by manuscripts *C* and *D* (the latter being the *grosse* or fair copy of the former and deriving from the prolific workshop of David Aubert (Straub 1995)), seems to have amplified it considerably. Which of these versions more closely represents that produced for the court of Hainault? Roussineau (edn IV/i, xvi–xx; thesis, 121–78) has suggested, rather audaciously, that neither need be regarded as the *version ancienne*; it is his contention that both the longer and the shorter versions result from a characteristically Burgundian *remaniement* (reworking), done in the fifteenth century, of an older version of *Perceforest*; a study of the lexis of the romance (Baldinger 1988) would seem to support this rather tempting hypothesis.[25] And if the Burgundian hypothesis (that is, that the two versions of the romance as we have it derive from a Burgundian *remaniement*) is correct, it is not difficult to see the attraction of this vast work in a court whose library contains Arthurian romances and commissioned Arthurian *mises en prose* and which, in particular, possessed copies of the Vulgate Cycle and of the prose *Tristan* (see chapter I).

Despite its brevity, the plot summary provided above nevertheless brings out just how crucially *Perceforest* depends on both of these sources.[26] In order to read the *Roman de Perceforest* adequately, one must know the Vulgate and the *Tristan* in considerable detail. How, otherwise, is it possible to understand the significance of the fact that Lancelot is descended from Lyonnel du Glat, the greatest knight of Perceforest's England, and from Gadifer's grand-daughter Lyonnette; Yseut from Gadifer I; Guinevere from a hero called the Chevalier au Dauphin, also known as the Dieu des Desiriers (I, BNF, fr. 345, fol. 384vff.); Merlin from a turbulent knight known as Passelion, and so on? How to account for the curious name Louvezerp given to one of the more chivalric of the English knights, other than by recognizing that it is the name of a noted tournament in the prose *Tristan*? The writer works to a sense of the genealogically apposite (Taylor 1996, 115): a pseudo-biological retrogression to ancestors and antecedents which will seem appropriate, and which will account 'genetically'[27] or onomastically for what happens under Arthur.

What this produces is what Vinaver (1949, 297) calls a 'prolongement rétroactif' (*prequel*) of the Arthurian prose romances, a 'prolonging' which operates teleologically towards a narrative end, knowledge of which is shared by the writer and his readers. On the broadest level it 'explains' Arthur himself: no longer is he the random, even inexplicable, product of Geoffrey's string of more or less minor monarchs; rather, his authority and his personality derive, ultimately, from Alexander the Great, who, it emerges, during his lengthy stay in England conceived a passion for the Dame du Lac, Sebille, and engendered a son, Alexandre Remanant de Joie. A family tree (somewhat simplified) is indispensable here, to show how the writer of *Perceforest* contrives to insert Alexander into the more canonical *Historia Regum Britanniae* (Berthelot 1991):

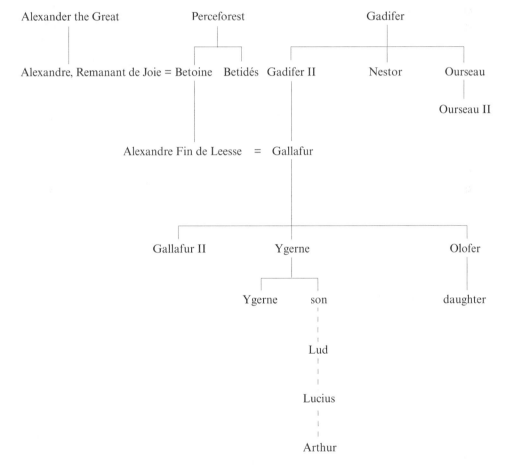

From Alexander and the dynasties he founds and sanctions, Arthur can, plausibly, inherit just those qualities, just those ideological commitments, which make his own reign so remarkable: his unimpeachable chivalry, his firm political and military grip on the kingdom of Britain, his remarkable generosity.

Consider, for instance, Arthur's chivalry. This quality, it turns out, is no accident since it is in Britain, and for Britain, that that most characteristic showcase of chivalry, the tournament, is invented (Lods 1951, 218–33). Pir's reign has reduced the barons of England to a state of such abjection that Alexander is puzzled as to a remedy. One day, meditating in his tent, he is reminded of the time when he had himself lowered in a glass barrel to the bottom of the sea (Gaullier-Bougassas 1996) and saw, he remembers, fish called 'chevaliers de mer' (*knights of the sea*) mock-battling on the ocean floor.[28] Inspired, he invents the tournament 'pour introduire [les chevaliers en terre] es armes et les membres amolier et aprendre a eulx deffendre au besoing' (*to initiate knights living on land to arms and to train their limbs and teach them to defend themselves when necessary*; Taylor edn, pp. 167–9). What this shows, and the point is an important one, is that to make Alexander Arthur's ancestor is not mere name-dropping: Alexander is the indispensable originator of an ideology whose fullest fruition will come under his descendant – indispensable, because only he, with his extraordinary experience, could have been so inspired.

But it is the ingenuity with which the writer interweaves the cycle of the *romans d'antiquité* with the Arthurian cycle in a purposeful, historical panorama, that most interestingly illuminates his practice (Trachsler 2000, 253). Take, for instance, the fact that it is not just Alexander who is Arthur's ancestor, but also Gadifer and Perceforest, who derive ultimately from the *Fuerre de Gadres* (Armstrong and Foulet edn), but more immediately from Jacques de Longuyon's *Voeux du paon*. The premise of this latter, little-known romance is that Alexander, having conquered Gadres and its lord Gadifer du Lairis, is persuaded to be generous to the latter's two sons, and in particular to promise them kingdoms of their own under his suzerainty (Flutre 1953, 45–61). Our writer seems ingeniously to have noted that this promise is never fulfilled (Trachsler 2000, 244) and makes this the premise of his own dovetail. Thus, he is able to merge the matter of Rome with the matter of Britain. It is, for instance, to the elder son, Betis (later Perceforest) that we owe an institution which is the precursor of Arthur's own Round Table: the order of the Franc Palais (Roussineau 1985), which brings together the most valiant of the knights of Britain. Or take the extraordinarily complex and inventive devices whereby Salvation History (Taylor 1973) and the history of the Grail (Trachsler 2000, 275–81) are imbricated with the history of Perceforest and his dynasty. Gallafur II, the last of the 'Perceforestian' kings of England, who was, prophetically, born with a book in his hand, plunges himself into philosophy and meditation. Pious by nature, he is the king towards whom Alain le Gros, arriving in England carrying the Grail, is naturally drawn (VI, Arsenal 3494, fols 368v–369r; Flutre 1970, 220–6). Britain is anticipating the 'good news', which is, after all, what the venerable warriors on the Île de Vie are waiting for, and which has been consistently promised by all the sages of the romance: Dardanon, an escapee from Troy who has, through years of study, learned to read the heavens and the Reine Fée, who was taught by Aristotle himself. Gallafur is naturally drawn to convert, and his conversion cures his leprosy and gives him a new name: Alfasen 'qui estoit a dire en leur langaige rengeneré' (*which in their language meant reborn*; VI, Arsenal 3494, fol. 371r). 'Alfasen' is, of course, comfortingly reminiscent of the name 'Arfasan/Alphasan' borne by the first king of England to be converted to Christianity by the Grail-bearers in the *Estoire del Saint Graal* (Ponceau edn, II, 559–60). What the writer has done (Trachsler 2000, 275–9) is ingeniously to channel *Perceforest* back into the Vulgate – ingeniously, because this conversion is not the self-interested move that it is in the *Estoire*, where Alphasan becomes Christian in order to be cured of leprosy, but rather the rational decision of a meditative and philosophical mind, arrived at in a Britain which is also ripe for conversion. In other words, this is again a purposeful shaping of the history of Britain: a fully thought-out merger of several *matières* into a new and adroit *conjointure* (narrative whole).

This process necessarily requires a permanent authorial vigilance. What, for instance, is to happen to Julius Caesar, whose perfectly 'historical' invasion of Britain must cut across our author's invented history? The writer is not daunted; rather, and unexpectedly, he contrives to merge his Arthurian romance with the *Fet des Romains* (Flutre 1969, 363–70). It turns out that Julius Caesar's assassination is the result of a personal vendetta: his brutality, in the great battle of the Franc Palais, demands vengeance, and Gadifer I's grandson, known as Ourseau II, who has been brought up, for complex reasons, in Rome, discovers his ancestry and orchestrates revenge on Julius Caesar, killing him with *greffes* or sharp blades fashioned from the lance-head which had killed Nestor, Ourseau II's uncle and Gadifer's beloved son (Roussineau edn, IV/ii, 980–1015; V, BNF 348, fols 41–2; Flutre 1969, 363–70; Trachsler 2000, 261–5). No problems of chronology, in other words, or of competing histories, will be allowed to derail our writer's firmly teleological vision.

The writer of *Perceforest* has a very particular view of world history (Lods 1951; Berthelot 1993; Trachsler 2000). The ways in which his own invention contributes to it may well explain its appeal to a Burgundian court whose library was especially rich in history and chronicle, and whose dukes took a particular interest in them (Doutrepont 1909). The writer conceives of history (Taylor 1992; 1994; 1996) as an organic process of birth, growth, apogee, decline and death in which each *civilisation* gives rise to the next; thus the Trojan civilization has, by the advent of King Pir, become decadent and ripe for the reigns of Alexander, Perceforest and Gadifer, but equally their civilization will tire:

> Le fruit qui avoit esté vert es coeurs et courages des chevaliers jennes et gaillars commença a amoindrir. Car viellesse les amaty et fist changier couleur et saveur tellement qu'en la Grant Bretaigne et par toutes les terres voisines il commença ainsi comme un nouveau siecle. (Roussineau edn, IV/i, 482)

(The fruit that had been new and green in the hearts and minds of gallant young knights had begun to fade. For old age wearied them and made them change colour and savour so much that in Great Britain and all neighbouring countries it seemed that a new age was beginning.)

His conception of universal history, in other words, and of the place of Perceforest's Britain within it, is analogous to one which was common currency in medieval historiography: the model of the Six Ages, and of what is known as the theory of *translatio imperii* (Taylor 1996, 102–8; Trompf 1979). His historical model is, in a sense, ameliorative: Perceforest and Alexander create a kingdom and a lineage which will be worthy of Arthur, in ways that Geoffrey visibly had not.

Many readers will, however, feel that this nicely systematized reading of the romance is a misleading one, and that it is being forced too determinedly into a procrustean bed of purpose and finality. For most readers, it is not the fact of a well-ordered history that predominates, not the overarching structure, but rather the author's astonishingly fertile narrative imagination. Around the earnest pseudo-historical framework described here swirl quests and tournaments, enchanters and dwarfs, ladies and damsels in distress. Book III, for instance, sees twelve tournaments, identically patterned (Taylor 1987–8), which produce twelve identically patterned marriages for the twelve daughters of the hermit Pergamon, who had fled Troy and settled in the forests of Britain; Book V sees a series of twelve identically patterned tournaments, the winners of each of which will receive the prize of a red rose. There are astonishing comic interludes where, for instance, certain heroes and heroines are transformed into animals: Le Tors becomes a raging bull (Roussineau edn, III/ii, 37–9); Estonné a bear (Roussineau edn, II/i, 320–9); Liriope a greyhound (Roussineau edn, III/ii, 68–74). There are grotesque and caricatural moments: a remarkable description, for instance, of a witches' sabbath (Roussineau edn, II/i, 216–21; Ferlampin 1993); a vivid and carefully circumstantial description of the Beste Glatissant (Roussineau edn, III/ii, 214–21, and his notes), which derives from the Vulgate Cycle and from the prose *Tristan*; a burlesque episode which has Le Bossu shipwrecked on l'Île de la Singesse and obliged to fend off the alarming attentions of a female monkey (Roussineau edn, IV/i, 63–8). There are lyric interludes; like the prose *Tristan*, this romance is studded with lyric pieces (Lods edn; Huot 1991). There are charming little romances: Neronés, for instance, dresses variously as a shepherd and a squire, and allows herself to be buried alive out of devotion for her love, the Chevalier Doré (Roussineau edn, III/ii, 208–14; 243–56; Szkilnik 1999a). There are little folk-tales: an early version of the story of the Sleeping Beauty (Roussineau edn, III/iii, 78–93; Lods 1951, 283–95), a Tale of the Rose which describes how a husband wagers on his wife's virtue with two rather unscrupulous colleagues, who end up condemned by the virtuous wife to spin for their supper.[29] There is, in other words, a proliferation of episodes of all sorts, from the lyrical to the comic to the epic.

It would be easy to see the romance as mere accumulation: easy, but mistaken, since the writer is clearly pursuing narrative and pseudo-historical aims which go well beyond mere entertainment. Take, for instance, the enchanters just mentioned, and, in particular, King Aroés of the Roide Montaigne (Roussineau edn, III/ii, 79–129; Taylor 1978; Szkilnik 1992–5; Delcourt 1994). He is marked out by vaulting, even megalomaniac, ambition: he wishes to be worshipped as a god, a 'souverain dieu' (Roussineau edn, III/ii, 113). To this end he has his subjects called together in the middle of the night, and gives them a vision of his heaven, where the sick are to be cured and the virtuous rewarded, and of his hell, where those who displease him will be punished; this is, of course, a hallucination (the illusion is created by light from burning torches playing on 'fioles plaines d'eaues' (*phials full of water*; Roussineau edn, III/ii, 108)). But this extraordinary episode, enthusiastically described by the author – the chiaroscuro night-scenes on the island, the elaborate strategy that Gadifer II, wrapped in a bale of cloth, is forced to adopt to reach the Roide Montaigne and undo the illusion in a final apocalyptic dénouement – is not simply gratuitous entertainment; it is a political fiction, an illustration of how kingship may be misused in the service of evil.

Similarly, even the most apparently gratuitous events may be seen as feeding into a larger and much more ambitious scheme. This is illustrated by the *luiton* or goblin, Zephir (Berthelot 1996; Szkilnik 1998). He first appears, disingenuously enough, in Alexander's dream as an old man dressed in a black cape (Taylor edn, I/i, 133), who comforts the emperor as the great storm drives him to England. Thereafter, Zephir becomes a sort of tutelary genius of Britain (extraordinarily, since he claims to be one of the angels deposed along with Lucifer; Roussineau edn, II/i, 74) and he takes the reader on a quite remarkable tour of hell, during which we are introduced to Lucifer himself (Roussineau edn, IV/ii, 739–43). Zephir's main role in *Perceforest* might, at first sight, seem to be comic: he specializes in shape-shifting, and in different guises amuses himself by leading some of the heroes of the romance into embarrassing or uncomfortable predicaments. But contrary to expectation, Zephir has a vital function in the romance as what one critic (Dubost 1991*, 721) aptly calls the 'entremetteur du destin' (*fate's go-between*): it is he who ensures that Merlin's progenitors, Passelion and Gaudine, meet and conceive in auspicious circumstances (Roussineau edn, IV/ii, 704–23). Now, Zephir himself shares certain characteristics with Merlin, including, of course, his shape-shifting; the point, however, is surely to note that the *luiton* who becomes in some sense a tutelary deity of Perceforest's Britain, is also responsible for Merlin's birth. He is thus doubly a 'prefiguration' of Merlin himself (Berthelot 1996; Szkilnik 1998) and a promoter and token of overarching ideological structure.

This, then, is an extraordinary romance – extraordinarily inventive, extraordinarily coherent. Readers may occasionally find the writer's meanders difficult to follow; he, however, works to a strongly realized narrative thread and with a strong sense of ideological and politico-religious commitment. **[JHMT]**

Ysaÿe le Triste

This sizeable romance exists in just two manuscripts: *A*, Gotha, Ducal Library, MS 688 (called *G* by Zeidler 1901, Bianciotto 1985; 1996) and *B*, Darmstadt, Hessische Landes- und Hochschulbibliothek, MS 2524 (called *D* by Zeidler 1901, Bianciotto 1985; 1996). It enjoyed, however, some considerable popularity in the Renaissance, as the number of early printed editions (five are known) would suggest (Bianciotto 1996). The manuscript tradition is difficult to determine; it seems, however, that *A* is considerably emended and has, in particular, been pruned of most of its dialectal traits (Bianciotto 1985), and that a similar operation has been undertaken, independently, in the *editio princeps* for Galiot du Pré in 1522, which has also, unfortunately, stripped the romance of most of its lyric insertions, particularly the longer and more interesting ones (Bianciotto 1996). The romance is anonymous; it is clear, however, from a careful study of the lyrics in the Darmstadt manuscript (Giacchetti 1989, 14–18), that the author is of Picard, and probably Walloon, origin. The question of the date is also a knotty one. The older of the two manuscripts, *B*, was, it seems from the *explicit*, copied in 1449 by a certain Amoury de Noyelle, 'demourant adont a Douay' (*then living in Douai*); it formed part of the library of the dukes of Burgundy in 1467 and 1487 (Barrois 1830, nos 1282 and 1834). Early commentators such as G. Paris (1901) thought it indisputably a product of the fourteenth century, primarily on linguistic grounds (*B* conserves traces of noun-declension), but also because they felt the literary climate of this latter period more conducive to such romances. Later commentators have been less certain, in spite of the fact that the Darmstadt manuscript is strongly dialectal (Giacchetti 1989, 14–18; Bianciotto 1985). Giacchetti (edn, 26) suggests the very early fifteenth century, principally (Giacchetti 1963–4) because of analogies he detects between what is said in the romance and the political situation in England in the early years of the century; he is supported by Bianciotto (1985; 1996; Capin 2004) because of consonances, morphological and lexical, between the language of *B* and other manuscripts securely datable to that period.[30]

The premise of the romance is disconcerting: it is that Tristan and Yseut have produced a son,[31] Ysaÿe, baptized *le triste* partly etymologically, from his father's name, partly because of the sad circumstances of his birth: just before the deaths of both his parents (Victorin 2002). The boy is brought up by a hermit, under the protection of the fairies of the forest; he acquires a faithful squire and 'mentor', the hideous dwarf Tronc. When Ysaÿe and Tronc emerge into the wider world, the battle of Salisbury has destroyed Arthur's kingdom. Ysaÿe's ambition becomes the restitution of the rule of law in Britain, and much of the first half of the romance is occupied by campaigns intended to do precisely that. Meanwhile, however, Marthe, niece of the King of Blamir, impressed by Ysaÿe's growing reputation, has fallen in love with the hero from afar, and Ysaÿe has himself smuggled into the king's palace in disguise; Marthe alone guesses his identity, and they conceive a son, Marc l'Essilié, only to be separated once again for Ysaÿe to undergo a series of adventures: the usual ferocious combats, imprisonment by the viperish Venisse and other picaresque escapades. Marc, meanwhile, a child 'qui ja n'ara peur' (*who will never be afraid*, 160), is born in a flurry of portents and soon becomes insufferably badly behaved. However, before long he is abandoned by his mother Marthe, who disguises herself as a minstrel and goes in search of Ysaÿe, who, on losing Tronc to a ruse, goes mad.

On reaching adulthood Marc sallies forth to exert the same sort of political control as his father had over the unruly barons of Britain. But suddenly the Saracens invade; Ysaÿe has been restored to reason, and he and Marc together annihilate their fleet and their army. Ysaÿe assumes a kingly role, but Marc, with Tronc, is determined to leave to seek a name for himself, in spite of the fact that he has fallen in love with the beautiful Orimonde. He sails to see the *merveilles de Bretagne*: the Chastel des Luittons (redolent of Merlin), the Forest de Darnantes, where the tomb of Darnant l'Enchanteur (see the summary of *Perceforest* above) still provokes tempests, an enchanted tree where a fairy, Oriande, explains to Marc that Tronc is the son of Julius Caesar and Morgan the Fay. Marc triumphs in a series of chivalric adventures, more or less extraordinary, and amorous adventures, more or less burlesque, in which Tronc finds himself often the butt of practical and other jokes. Finally, however, the network of journeys at last brings together Ysaÿe and Marthe, Marc and Orimonde; their marriages are magnificently celebrated, and Tronc, though remaining a dwarf, is revealed to be the son of Julius Caesar and Morgan, renamed Aubron (cf. the Auberon of *Huon de Bordeaux*), and transformed into the most beautiful creature in the world (*YT*, §623). The dynasty reigns long and gloriously, 'mes le gent mirent plus leur entente a mettre en memoire les fais du roy Clovis' (*but people began to be more committed to keeping alive the memory of the deeds of King Clovis*; *YT*, §623), and thus this glorious neo-Arthurian interlude is lost to history.

There can be no doubt, of course, that *Ysaÿe le Triste* is heavily indebted to Arthurian prose romance and especially to the prose *Tristan*; to borrow Szkilnik's expression (1995), the shadows of Lancelot, Morgan the Fay (Victorin 1998) and Merlin (Szkilnik 1998a) loom everywhere. More particularly, though, the romance is related to, and indeed to a degree based on, *Perceforest*. Marc's childhood, turbulent, not to say obstreperous (*YT*, §§298–9), cannot but remind us of the equally belligerent childhood of Passelion in *Perceforest* (Szkilnik 1997); Tronc, in *Ysaÿe le Triste*, must surely remind us of the Zephir of *Perceforest* (Szkilnik 1998a); one wonders if the Neronés of *Perceforest* has not given rise to the Marthe of *Ysaÿe le Triste*, both of them being disguised as men, and searching for their lovers with the aid of song and lyric (Szkilnik 1999a; Victorin 2002); and is it merely a coincidence that Marc l'Essilié is said to be the reincarnation, the *restor*, of Alexander the Great (*YT*, §281; Szkilnik 1996)? But the relations between the two romances would repay a proper investigation, not least because this in turn might be very revealing of narrative strategies in these late romances, and of the circulation of romances in the latter part of the Middle Ages.

The summary given above of *Ysaÿe le Triste* has the disadvantage of all summaries of these vast late-medieval prose romances: it conventionalizes them, and gives the impression of something far more ordered and directed than the romance can ever appear to be upon reading. It is true, however, that certain guiding threads can be defined, the major thread being ideological. *Ysaÿe* shares with *Perceforest* a surprisingly strong sense of political process – surprisingly, because both romances mask seriousness of purpose behind a plethora of episodes and adventures, often burlesque and frequently melodramatic. As he leaves the forest, where he had grown up under the tutelage of the hermit and the *fées*, Ysaÿe discovers that since Arthur's death at the battle of Salisbury the kingdom has dissolved into anarchy: 'ly chevaliers du païs et especiaument les nouviaux fais ont levé tant de mauvaises coustumes cy avant qu'a mervelles, pour ce qu'i n'y ot personne puis qui presist le couronne, quant ly Rois Artus morut' (*the knights of this country, and especially the most recently dubbed, have initiated an extraordinary number of bad customs, because there has been no king to control them since King Arthur died*; *YT*, §37). Having had himself dubbed knight – a rather macabre episode – with Lancelot's disinterred right hand (Szkilnik 1995), Ysaÿe dedicates himself, as had Perceforest, to restoring the rule of law under God's grace by defeating, one after the other, a string of unruly robber barons (*YT*, §§37–93): 'qui poroit le torte voye ramener a droite, ce serroit boine paine ce me samble' (*if there were someone who could make the twisted road straight, it would be effort well spent, I think*; *YT*, §44). They are made to recognize Ysaÿe's sovereignty; those who have most transgressed, particularly against women (again, there are strong echoes here of *Perceforest*), are at best banished, at worst put to death, and full restitution is made to the women themselves. Ysaÿe becomes, ultimately, a wise and just ruler and the champion of Christendom (*YT*, §621).

What *Ysaÿe* also shares with *Perceforest*, on the other hand, is a disconcerting instability of tone (Victorin 2002). There are, for instance, some extraordinarily primitive and savage moments: adversaries beheaded with a casual brutality (*YT*, §§71–2), the two sisters who eat the hearts of their enemies raw (*YT*, §35).[32] Tronc, on the other hand, is a creature of broad comedy. He takes a malign delight in disguise and in plunging his victims – Marc from time to time, but principally his enemies – into burlesque adventures; at the same time, he himself is the constant victim of beatings. But he is also a creature of craft and cunning, and his role in the romance is a vital one: it is he who nurtures Ysaÿe (born into the political vacuum after the battle of Salisbury) in the ways of chivalry, and if Ysaÿe, like a Lancelot or an Yvain, founders into madness, it is because of the loss of his mentor Tronc. It is he, also, who saves Marc on numerous occasions from the dangerous consequences of his own rashness and thoughtlessness, and it is he, finally, who is largely instrumental in the series of neat resolutions which fill the final few pages of the romance: the Saracens defeated, Marthe saved from burning, Marc united, rather reluctantly, with Orimonde, the lady he had seduced and left.

But most people who read the romance will be struck, principally, by its exuberant narrative inventiveness: Tronc trapped by the compassionate instincts which make him take pity on a beggar (*YT*, §§293–4); Marc's childhood escapades (*YT*, §§298–9); Marthe disguised as a boy minstrel (whose *lais* and *chansons* are remarkably talented), escaping with tact and determination from a *dame* who has fallen in love with her (*YT*, §277), or undressed by sailors uncon- vinced by her disguise (*YT*, §§271–3). This, like so many of these late-medieval romances, lends itself to excerpting (Victorin 2002, 379–86); it is a tribute to the writer's narrative control that it remains nevertheless so coherent. [JHMT]

Le Chevalier du Papegau

The little prose romance called *The Knight of the Parrot* is contained in only one manuscript, BNF, fr. 2154. It is written in a late fifteenth-century, or early sixteenth-century hand and there is no clue as to dating. Heuckenkamp (edn, xxix–lvi) and Charpentier and Victorin (edn, 12–20), having compared the *Papegau* exhaustively with Wirnt von Grafenberg's *Wigalois*, conclude that the German and French romances share a common source, and date the *Papegau* to the end of the fourteenth century, as does Taylor (1987–8); Busby (1991, 87) suggests the possibility of a later, fifteenth-century date. Heuckenkamp (1896, lvii) detects linguistic traces of Occitan influence, but locality is no easier to determine than date. The romance reworks episodes from a number of romances: from Chrétien's *Erec* and *Charrette*, from *Durmart* and *Meraugis*; many of the other episodes in the *Papegau* have analogues across the range of Old French Arthurian romance, and there are distant hints of the triadic structure so charac- teristic of Celtic narrative (Bromwich, Jarman and Roberts eds 1991*, 80–2, 214–20). We should probably imagine a writer particularly well versed in the Arthurian repertoire.

Yet he was not slavishly wedded to its conventions: the premise of the romance is a challenge to all our Arthurian preconceptions. In the purest tradition of Arthurian romance,[33] a damsel arrives at Arthur's court one Pentecost, begging that a knight be detailed to lend succour to her lady who is under attack from an oppressor. But this time it is not a young hothead who proposes himself, not some anonymous knight in search of a reputation: rather, it is Arthur himself who leaves the governance of the kingdom to Lot and rides off in the damsel's service. He meets adventures of all sorts, in which he naturally acquits himself with perfect chivalry; in particular, in combat against an exceptionally redoubtable champion, he wins the parrot which becomes his emblem, and which, like Dinadan in the prose *Tristan* (see chapter VIII), provides a permanent and somewhat sardonic running commentary on subsequent events. Arthur, who is not yet married to Guinevere, also makes an amorous conquest, La Dame aux Cheveux Blons, and finally, after a 'sabbatical' lasting precisely a year, he returns triumphant to Camelot and to his royal destiny.

Meanwhile, a welter of baroque adventures of all sorts have befallen him. He encounters combat against a monstrous knight, a sort of centaur, whose armour and horse are an integral part of him; a battle against an army of spectres, from which he is saved only by the scent of a flower from a magic tree; a perilous bridge, defended by a wheel mounted with razor-sharp knife-blades; a dwarf driven to despair by his monstrous son, who was suckled by a unicorn and whose appetites cannot be assuaged. However, this is not just a matter of picaresque adventures, and Arthur is not just another folklore champion; rather, and this is a major preoccupation of late-medieval writers of romance, he is already the instrument of justice and good government. This is exemplified by the interesting little episode of an adversary called Lion Sans Mercy (Heuckenkamp edn, 5–10; Charpentier and Victorin edn, 82–3), who is described, luridly, as guilty of the worst crime imaginable. Our imaginations are fired, until we realize that this worst of crimes consists in his imposing on all the lords and knights of the country an act of homage 'par force et sans droit et sans raison' (*by force, without justice or justification*; Heuckenkamp edn, 5; Charpentier and Victorin edn, 82). Arthur's contempt: 'tu as moult malement gardé l'ordre de chevalerie; car chevalerie veult rayson et droiture a toutes gens' (*you have not adhered as you should to the order of knighthood; for knighthood demands reason and justice for all*; Heuckenkamp edn, 9–10; Charpentier and Victorin edn, 90) is symptomatic of what the author clearly conceives of as his political and ideological mission: the freeing of those labouring under an unjust 'servaige' or 'asservissement' (*servitude* or *subjection*), and the installing of a just society.

Ought we to class under the same heading what seems to be the author's dismay at an amorous *servaige*? In the course of the romance Arthur is solicited by a beautiful lady, the Dame aux Cheveux Blons (Heuckenkamp edn, 29; Charpentier and Victorin edn, 131), who dares to demand that he make a fool of himself for her sake in a tournament. Arthur, having sworn that he will accede to her request, reluctantly does so, but later, furious, he accuses her of being a 'maulvaise putain, plaine de toute maulvaistié' (*a wicked whore, full of all manner of wickedness*; Heuckenkamp edn, 35; Charpentier and Victorin edn, 140), and drags her round the room by the hair (Taylor 1994b; Walters 2000). I cite this in such detail because the result shows just how far, ideologically, we have moved from the world of perfect courtesy and submission in which Chrétien's *Lancelot* operates, to a more pragmatic world where chivalric reputation and victory count for far more than mere sensibility.

That said, it is important not to give the impression that this is a grimly serious romance; on the contrary, it is marked by a narrative verve and inventiveness, by pace and humour which make it one of the more attractive and readable of these late-coming productions. **[JHMT]**

Arthurian Ornament: Arthurian Material in the Late Epic

What testifies to the continuing popularity of, and fascination with, Arthurian material in the late Middle Ages is the way in which Arthurian characters and motifs begin to make sporadic appearances in the epic genre – in what are some-times referred to as *chansons d'aventure*, the second generation of *chansons de geste* where epic and romance merge with each other (Trachsler 2000). Auberon, the fairy adjuvant of the eponymous hero of *Huon de Bordeaux* (*c*.1260), the earliest of these adventure poems, is presented as the son of Morgan the Fay and Julius Caesar (Kibler and Suard edn, ll. 17 and 10690). When he first appears before Huon (ll. 3266–71), Auberon raises a storm that recalls in its very details the one provoked by Calogrenant and Yvain at the storm-making fountain in Chrétien's *Yvain*. Auberon's horn and cup, like the Grail, are inexhaustible in their bounty and allow one to distinguish good men from evil.[34] Although Auberon has most likely a Germanic rather than Celtic pedigree, the anonymous author of *Huon de Bordeaux* was well acquainted with Arthurian literature, particularly the *Lancelot–Grail* Cycle, which was at the height of its popularity when *Huon* was composed, and drew widely upon it for his presentation of Auberon and his magical powers (Rossi, 323–82). Like Merlin, Auberon is a magician of pagan origins who has been Christianized. In *Esclarmonde*, one of the continuations of *Huon de Bordeaux*, Arthur appears to challenge Huon for control of Auberon's kingdom, which has become his own. Every year, on the feast of St James, the two battle it out, but neither can defeat the other (Schweigel edn, 1–3481).

In a version of the *Bataille Loquifer* preserved in eight manuscripts and composed shortly after *Huon*, the epic hero Rainouart is transported by three fairies, led by Morgan, to Avalon where, under the scrutiny of Arthur, Roland [*sic*!], Yvain, Perceval and Gauvain, he must defeat the monster Chapalu, who

has a cat's head on a horse's body, and restore it to human form by letting it drink
blood from his heel. That night Morgan comes to Rainouart's bed and they
conceive a son, the demon Corbon. Two weeks later, with Morgan's help,
Rainouart returns from Avalon to resume his epic adventures (Barnett edn,
3600–3962; Sturm-Maddox and Maddox 1994). This episode has been likened to
Morgan's imprisonment and wooing of Lancelot in the *Lancelot* proper. Her
negative traits may have been influenced by the Vulgate *Merlin* (Suard 1981).

This episode directly influenced several of the late continuations of *Ogier le
Danois*. One of the most celebrated paladins of Charlemagne's court, Ogier the
Dane appears already in the *Chanson de Roland* and was doubtless the hero of a
lost twelfth-century epic. The earliest poem now preserved, the *Chevalerie Ogier*,
dates only to the early thirteenth century and makes him a rebellious vassal
whose son was killed by Charlemagne's offspring. An early fourteenth-century
remaniement in decasyllables adds about 17,000 lines to the *Chevalerie*'s original
13,800.[35] This continuation consists of three main parts, modelled on *Huon de
Bordeaux* and the *Bataille Loquifer*: Ogier's adventures in the East, Ogier and
Morgan the Fay (about 2,200 lines), and Ogier's return to France. After
conquering Babiloine (Cairo) and imprisoning the sultan, Ogier wishes to return
to France, but is the sole survivor of a shipwreck beyond the Red Sea. Alone and
stranded after a magnetic mountain attracts the nails of his ship and holds it fast,
Ogier wanders the land until he enters the earthly paradise. Hungry, he eats an
apple that restores his youth. In a splendid boat he finds Morgan, who gives him
a ring that will assure him eternal youth and leads him to Arthur's castle, Avalon,
whose adamantine pillars shine like the sun (cf. the *Bataille Loquifer*, 3678–700).
Morgan offers her love, but first Ogier has to undergo a series of tests organized
by Arthur: he must kill a lion and defeat the monster Chapalu, who turns out to
be a knight enchanted by fairies. Ogier forgets his homeland and weds Morgan;
they have a son, Meurvin, whose adventures are recounted in an early prose
printed book from 1540 (Suard 1984). One day Morgan informs Ogier that he
has spent 200 years in Avalon, that Charlemagne and all his peers are dead, and
that France has a new king, Philippe, a descendant of Hugues Capet. She gives
him a magical white horse, Papillon, which can carry him back, but which he will
lose if ever he pronounces Morgan's or Arthur's name. Still profiting from eternal
youth, Ogier valiantly serves the new king, but eventually Morgan returns to
carry him back to 'Faerie' (Togeby 1969, 134–47).

Morgan and Arthur reappear, accompanied by Auberon, in *Tristan de
Nanteuil*, an early fourteenth-century *chanson d'aventure* (Taylor 2001). This
Tristan, like his Arthurian predecessor, derives his name from his mother's
suffering: 'Nez fustes en tristresse, pour ce vous appellon / Tristan' (*'You were born
in sadness, therefore we call you Tristan'*) says the fairy Gloriande after he saves
her from a dragon (Sinclair edn, 8432–3). Gloriande reveals to the orphaned

Tristan for the first time his true parentage, then takes him to Arthur's home in fairyland (8537), where he is welcomed by Auberon and Morgan, Gloriande's cousin. There Tristan succeeds in sounding a magic horn that can only be blown by the bravest of the brave, which Arthur then offers him with the admonition to carry it always in battle, for its bearer will never be wounded. Eight days in Arthur's land seem like only two hours to Tristan; as he leaves to pursue his adventures and find his parents, the castle vanishes into the air. Lines 1651–9 tell of Arthur fighting a great cat that had been nourished on the milk of a siren; this is undoubtedly Chapalu.

The fourteenth-century crusade epic, *Le Bâtard de Bouillon*, has a similar adventure in fairyland (Cook edn, 3291–3689). Having passed the Red Sea, Baudouin de Bouillon and twelve companions press on into 'Faërie / ... le terre Artus et Morgue la jolie' (3309–10; *Fairyland ... the land of Arthur and lovely Morgan*). One companion, Hugue de Tabarie, discovers in a tent an ivory horn that can only be sounded by the best knight in the world. When he succeeds in blowing it, Arthur, Morgan and the fairy Oriande appear. Arthur leads them into an orchard filled with music, a sweet aroma and a thousand fairies. In a smaller orchard protected by two automata, Hugue passes another test and picks the red rose that has bloomed for 200 years in anticipation of the bravest knight in the world. Arthur then sends the companions on their way after giving King Baudouin a horse and hauberk for his bastard son.

Lion de Bourges, another fourteenth-century poem, has a variant on this episode. As Lion is traversing the Ardennes Forest, he is challenged, first by a dwarf, who unhorses him, then by a giant, whom he defeats. Both are in fact Auberon, who invites Lion into a castle, where he is fêted by 'Morgue la fee et Artus son baron / La belle Gloriande et le roy Auberon' (*Morgan the Fay and Arthur her lord, lovely Gloriande and King Auberon*; Kibler et al. edn, 20950–1). He stays there enchanted for six years, which seem to him only four days. Much later in the poem King Arthur presents armour to Lion, on condition that he returns it within a year (an echo of Laudine's injunction to Yvain?), and pays a visit to himself and Morgan. After many more adventures Lion comes, true to his word, to fairyland ('en faierie', 34097), into which he disappears for ever. The analogies here with the Isle of Avalon, to which Arthur was carried by Morgan at the end of the *Mort Artu*, are patent.

In *Mabrien*, a fifteenth-century prose continuation of the epic material of *Renaud de Montauban* and the *Quatre Fils Aymon*, Arthur, Gloriande and Morgan, along with two other fairies and a second king, are present at the birth of Mabrien and offer him special gifts to guide his life.[36] During one of his later adventures Mabrien, after being shipwrecked against the magnetic mountain (cf. *Ogier*), arrives in 'Terre Faee', where King Arthur now reigns in the company of Morgan, Gloriande and other fairies. Before entering Arthur's palace, Mabrien finds suspended from a tree a shield, on which is written: 'No one can bear this shield unless he is braver than all others and filled with loyalty and nobility' (Verelst edn, p. 229). He defeats sixteen champions to prove he is the best knight of all and gain entry to Arthur's castle, Aymant, where he is fêted for a month, though he thinks it is only a day. He then uses his new shield to rescue and win the love of Gracienne, who bears him a son. They remain together in fairyland for a year, which seems like only five days, before Mabrien realizes he has tarried too long.

In the wake of *Huon de Bordeaux*, the hero's adventure in fairyland became practically *de rigueur* in the later *chansons de geste*. These adventures are all cut from the same mould and serve a common purpose: as qualifying experiences for the hero. They allow the author to confirm in the Other World what is already manifest in this one, and often to relaunch the hero on his quest (Suard 1981). The Arthurian world evoked is that of Avalon after Arthur's disappearance, whether or not it is explicitly named. Except in *Lion de Bourges* it is located vaguely in the east and sometimes upon an island. The characters are invariably Arthur and his sister Morgan, with accompanying fairies, but, except in *La Bataille Loquifer* and *Ogier*, no other Knights of the Round Table. Arthur himself assumes magical powers in these works, replacing in this sense Merlin, who is never explicitly evoked. Arthur is no longer the head of the Round Table, but the master of an ethereal kingdom populated with fairies and spirits. [WWK]

Notes

[1] New prose adaptations of old romances continued into the Renaissance with Pierre Sala's adaptation of Chrétien's *Yvain* in 1522 and a *mise en prose* of Chrétien's *Perceval* in 1530 (Frappier 1961).

[2] For example, the *Arbre d'Or* held to celebrate the wedding of Margaret of York and Charles the Bold in 1468, described in La Marche (Beaune and d'Arbaumont edn), I, 11–122.

[3] See Michel Pastoureau, 'Introduction à l'héraldique imaginaire (XIIe-XVIe siècle)', *Revue Française d'Héraldique et de Sigilligraphie*, 30 (1978), 19–25.

[4] See, for instance, the account of the wedding of Margaret of York and Charles the Bold given by a Flemish-speaking Burgundian, Simon Mulart, in P. C. Boeren, *Twee Maaslandse Dichters in Dienst van Karel de Stout* (The Hague, 1968).

[5] See *The Book of the Love-Smitten Heart by René of Anjou*, ed. and transl. by S. Viereck Gibbs and K. Karczewska (London, 2001), xv.

[6] See P. Meyer, 'Les Neuf Preux', *Bulletin de la SATF*, 9 (1883), 45–54.

[7] *La Vie de Bertrand du Guesclin, par Cuvelier*, ed. by E. Charrière (Paris, 1839), 10716–19.

[8] On the Order of the Golden Fleece, see Vaughan 1970, 160–2. Jean le Bel explains that Jean de France created his Order of the Star in direct emulation of Arthur and his Round Table: *Chronique*, ed. by J. Viard and E. Déprez, 2 vols (Paris, 1904–5), II, 204.

[9] These terms are from Max Weber; see Charles Lindholm, *Charisma* (Oxford, 1990).

[10] It is not certain that both were commissioned. Colombo Timelli (*Erec* edn, introduction),

noting that the prologue makes no mention of a commission or a patron, suggests the possibility that the prosifier worked on his own initiative, hoping to offer Philip the finished work. On the other hand, a good many prosifications of the period do not name a patron, and the adapter's silence does not constitute proof. For extensive bibliography on the vogue of prosifications (*mises en prose*) during the fifteenth and sixteenth centuries, see Colombo Timelli edn, 17; Doutrepont 1939; Pickford 1959/60*. Until recently, the only editions, by Foerster in 1884 and 1890, left a good deal to be desired. Now we have the excellent edition of *Erec* by Colombo Timelli, with an edition of *Cligés* to follow.

[11] The complete *Erec* is extant in Brussels, Bibliothèque Royale, MS 7235 (*B*); Colombo Timelli (edn, 9–15 and *passim*) also describes and edits two fragments, *P* (Paris, BNF, fr. 363) and a single page in *O* (Oxford, Bodleian Library, MS Douce 383).

[12] For a succinct summary of views on the question of one prosifier or two, see Colombo Timelli edn, 9–10, n. 4.

[13] There are numerous stylistic differences as well. Colombo Timelli (edn, 38, 40–1) points out that the prosifier generally suppresses or summarizes Chrétien's passages of dialogue, but tends to amplify monologues. The loss of dialogue, she notes, decreases the liveliness of the narrative but accelerates its progress.

[14] Charity Willard (1991a, 402–3) suggests that by the time of the prosification, 'the older concept of *fin'amour* had become detached from ideals of chivalry'. She adds that the Burgundian romance, 'without the charm of Chrétien's style, and especially without the analyses of love, seems faded'.

[15] Quotations are from vol. 1 of this edition. The parts from Albinia to 688 and from 1399–1431 were translated by W. Hardy and E. L. C. P. Hardy as *A Collection of the Chronicles and Ancient Histories of Great Britain, Now Called England*. Translations are from the first volume. The part from 1325–1471 was also edited by L. E. E. Dupont.

[16] See also Field 1991, 164, and Salter 1988, 22–3.

[17] One occurs in the account of Lancelot's abduction by Morgan the Fay and three other fairies in the Vulgate *Lancelot*, retold as the first episode of Malory's 'Tale of Lancelot' (253–9). Another would be the Middle English romance *Sir Orfeo*, ed. by A. J. Bliss (Oxford, 1954), 18.

[18] The author of the *Mort Artu* wrote: '[E]t la nef se fu eslongniee de la rive en pou d'eure plus qu'une arbaleste ne poïst trere a uit foiz; et quant Girflet voit qu'il a einsi perdu le roi, il descent seur la rive, et fet le greigneur duel del monde' (*La Mort le roi Artu*, ed. by J. Frappier, 3rd edn, Geneva, 1964, §193). (*In a short time the ship had travelled from the shore more than eight times the distance one can shoot from a cross-bow; and when Girflet saw that he had thus lost the king, he dismounted on to the shore and suffered the greatest grief in the world*, transl. by J. Cable, 225).

[19] Fletcher (1906, 171–7, 221–35) lists only nine Arthurian chronicles produced on the Continent, most by Flemings, like Jehan de Waurin, who were allies of the British, and by Bretons, who considered the story to be part of their heritage.

[20] In the 1485 preface to Malory's *Morte Darthur* Caxton writes that many people 'holde oppynyon that there was no suche Arthur and that alle suche bookes as been maad of hym ben but fayned and fables' (*Works*, cxliv).

[21] Kekewich (1971, 482, 486) suggests that the Seigneur de Gruthuyse of Bruges probably encouraged Edward IV to develop his own library as well as a taste for the works of chivalry that were then popular in Burgundy. Edward's wife, Elizabeth Woodville, owned at least three of the prose Arthurian romances including the *Estoire del Saint Graal*, *La Queste del Saint Graal* and *La Mort le roi Artu*. See also McKendrick 1990.

[22] Hardy and Hardy edn, appendix 3, 610. See also Mahoney 1996, esp. 104–7.

[23] It should be noted that the writer shows far more specialized knowledge of Hainault and the Low Countries than he does of Britain; a major theme of Book II of the romance is the conquest of what is known as the 'Selve Carbonniere', described later in Book IV (Roussineau edn, IV/i, 407–8) as marshland always subject to tides.

[24] The date 1313 for the *Voeux du paon* is both a *terminus post quem* and a *terminus ad quem*. A manuscript was bought by Mahaut d'Artois on 9 September 1313, but surviving copies refer to the death of the Emperor Henry on his return from Rome on 24 August 1313. Unless the reference to Henry's death was added in that short time-scale, we need to assume two versions, neither of which needs to have been written in 1313.

[25] Research in progress by Janet van der Meulen (University of Leiden), for her doctoral thesis on literary culture at the court of Hainault–Holland, suggests further refinement of this contention. She will argue, on plausible grounds, that the 'Hainault' version of the text consisted of Books I–IV, but without the prologue translated from Geoffrey, and that the latter, along with Books V and VI, are Burgundian accretions.

[26] For other, sometimes more detailed, summaries, see Flutre, 1948–70; Lods 1951; Trachsler 2000 and the *résumés* published by modern editors of the text.

[27] These scare-quotes indicate that the Middle Ages clearly did see family inheritance as accounting for broad-brush traits within families (Taylor 1996).

[28] For this episode, see *The Medieval French Roman d'Alexandre*, ed. by E. C. Armstrong et al., vol. 2 (Princeton, 1937), republished by L. Harf-Lancner (Paris, 1994), 389–520.

[29] The story exists in a number of different versions: see *Le Lai de la Rose* (G. Paris edn); Lods 1951, 80–2; Roussineau thesis, 1564–70.

[30] Bianciotto wonders (1996, 630) if there was not 'une école dialectalisante' which particularly enjoyed archaisms and dialects, and which flourished around Douai in the early fifteenth century.

[31] Unknown to previous history because 'li romans ne voloit parler de villonnie qu'il i conchust contre l'onneur [d'Yseut]' (*the romance did not wish to impute any misdeed contrary to Yseut's honour, YT*, 1).

[32] It is conceivable that this cold-bloodedness is an accurate reflection of the anarchies of the Hundred Years War; it is reminiscent of the bloodthirstiness which marks the *Perlesvaus* (see chapter VI).

[33] For a summary of the romance in German, see Heuckenkamp edn, vii–xxvii. For the traditional motifs of Arthurian romance, see A. Adams, 'The Shape of Arthurian Verse Romance (to 1300)', in Lacy, Kelly and Busby eds 1987–8*, I, 141–65. For a detailed discussion of folklore episodes in the romance, see Charpentier and Victorin edn, 37–56.

[34] The moral function of the cup, which refuses sustenance to those who are not in a state of grace, has been likened to that of the drinking horn in the *Lai du Cor*, from which cuckolds cannot drink. See Ruelle edn, p. 74 and Rossi 1975, 334.

[35] An edition of the decasyllabic version based on MS *P* (BNF, fr. 1583) is currently being prepared by T. K. Salberg of the University of Oslo.

[36] Verelst edn, pp. 214–63. Compare the scene in Adam de la Halle's *Jeu de la feuillee*, in which Morgan, with her fairy companions Arsile and Maglore, also offers gifts to her hosts.

Reference List

For items accompanied by an asterisk, see the General Bibliography.

Texts and Translations

General and Burgundian

L'Histoire d'Erec en prose: roman du XVe siècle. Ed. by M. Colombo Timelli, TLF 524 (Geneva, 2000).

Mémoires d'Olivier de La Marche: maître d'hôtel et capitaine des gardes de Charles le Téméraire. Ed. by H. Beaune and J. d'Arbaumont, 4 vols (Paris, 1883–8).

Pierre Sala, *Le Chevalier au Lion*. Ed. by P. Servet (Paris, 1996).

René d'Anjou, *The Book of the Love-Smitten Heart by René of Anjou*. Ed. and transl. by S. Viereck Gibbs and K. Karczewska (New York and London, 2001).

Froissart

Froissart, *Meliador: roman comprenant les poésies lyriques de Wenceslas de Bohème, duc de Luxembourg et de Brabant*. Ed. by A. Longnon, 3 vols, SATF (Paris, 1895–99; repr. 1965).

Froissart, *Le Dit dou Florin*, in A. Fourrier ed. *Jean Froissart, Dits et débats*, TLF 274 (Geneva, 1979), 175–90.

Froissart, *Chroniques. Troisième Livre. Bibliothèque Municipale de Besançon MS 865*. Ed. by P. F. Ainsworth, TLF (Geneva), vol. 1, forthcoming.

Froissart, Jean, *Chroniques*. Ed. by P. F. Ainsworth and A. Vàrvaro (Paris, 2004). Vol. II contains extracts from Books III and IV of the chronicles.

Waurin's Chronicles

Jehan de Waurin, *Recueil des croniques et anchiennes istories de la Grant Bretaigne, à present nommé Engleterre*. Ed. by W. Hardy and E. L. C. P. Hardy, 5 vols, Rolls Series 39 (London, 1864–91).

Jehan de Waurin, *A Collection of the Chronicles and Ancient Histories of Great Britain, Now Called England*. Transl. by W. Hardy and E. L. C. P. Hardy, 3 vols, Rolls Series 40 (London, 1864–91).

Jehan de Waurin, *Anchiennes Cronicques d'Engleterre par Jehan de Wavrin*. Ed. by L. E. E. Dupont, 3 vols (Paris, 1858–63).

The Death of King Arthur. Transl. by J. Cable (Harmondsworth, 1971).

Malory, Sir Thomas. *Works*. Ed. by E. Vinaver; 3rd edn, rev. by P. J. C. Field, 3 vols (Oxford, 1990).

Roman de Perceforest

Book I: *première partie*. Ed. by J. H. M. Taylor (Geneva, 1979). [Taylor edn]; *seconde partie*, see MS *A*, BNF, fr. 345. [I, BNF 345].

Book II: vol 1. Ed. by G. Roussineau (Geneva, 1999). [Roussineau edn, II/i]; vols 2–3. Ed. by G. Roussineau (Geneva, 2001 and forthcoming), meanwhile see MS *A*, BNF, fr. 346. [II, BNF 346].

Book III: vols 1–3. Ed. by G. Roussineau (Geneva, 1988–93). [Roussineau edn, III/i, ii, or iii].

Book IV: vols 1–2. Ed. by G. Roussineau (Geneva, 1987). [Roussineau edn, IV/i or ii]. Book IV is also edited more completely in Roussineau's doctoral thesis for the Université de Paris-Sorbonne, 1982: 'Édition critique et commentaire de la quatrième partie du *Roman de Perceforest*' (microfiche, Atelier de Reproduction des Thèses de Lille). [Roussineau thesis]

Book V: see MS *A*, BNF, fr. 348. [V, BNF 348].

Book VI: see MS *C*, Arsenal 3493–4). [VI, Arsenal 3493].

La Treselegante, Delicieuse, Melliflue et tres plaisante Hystoire du tresnoble, victorieux et excellentissime roy Perceforest (…) (Paris: N. Cousteau for Galiot du Pré, 1528).

La Treselegante, Delicieuse, Melliflue et tres plaisante Hystoire du tresnoble, victorieux et excellentissime roy Perceforest (…) (Paris: Gilles de Gourmont, 1531).

Le Lai de la Rose a la Dame Leal. Ed. by G. Paris, *Rom*, 23 (1894), 117–40.

Les Pièces lyriques du Roman de Perceforest. Ed. by J. Lods (Geneva, 1953).

The Medieval French Roman d'Alexandre. Vol. 4: *Le Roman de Fuerre de Gadres d'Eustache*. Ed. by E. C. Armstrong and A. Foulet, Elliott Monographs 39 (Princeton, NJ, 1942).

Ysaÿe le Triste

Ysaÿe le Triste. Ed. by A. Giacchetti, Publications de l'Université de Rouen 142 (Rouen, 1989) [*YT*].

Ysaÿe le Triste. Transl. by A. Giacchetti, Publications de l'Université de Rouen 193 (Mont-Saint-Aignan, 1993).

Le Chevalier du Papegau

Le Conte du papegau. Ed. and transl. by H. Charpentier and P. Victorin (Paris, 2004).
Le Chevalier du Papegau. Ed. by F. Heuckenkamp (Halle, 1896).
The Knight of the Parrot. Transl. by T. Vesce (New York and London, 1986).
Le Chevalier au Papegau. Modern French translation by D. Régnier-Bohler in Régnier-Bohler ed.
  1989*, 1079–1162.

Arthurian Material in Late Epic

Le Bâtard de Bouillon: chanson de geste. Ed. by R. F. Cook, TLF 187 (Geneva, 1972).
La Bataille Loquifer. Ed. by M. Barnett (Oxford, 1975).
Esclarmonde, Clarisse et Florent, Ide et Olive: drei Fortsetzungen der Chanson von Huon de
  Bordeaux. Ed. by M. Schweigel, Ausgaben und Abhandlungen aus dem Gebiete der romanis-
  chen Philologie 83 (Marburg, 1889).
Huon de Bordeaux. Ed. by P. Ruelle, Université Libre de Bruxelles, Travaux de la Faculté de
  Philosophie et Lettres 20 (Brussels and Paris, 1960).
Huon de Bordeaux: chanson de geste du XIIIe siècle, publiée d'après le manuscrit de Paris BNF fr.
  22555 (P). Ed. by W. W. Kibler and F. Suard (Paris, 2003) contains a modern French translation.
Lion de Bourges: poème épique du XIVe siècle. Ed. by W. W. Kibler, J.-L. G. Picherit and
  T. S. Fenster, TLF 285 (Geneva, 1980).
Mabrien: roman de chevalerie en prose du XVe siècle. Ed. by P. Verelst (Geneva, 1998).
Tristan de Nanteuil: chanson de geste inédite. Ed. by K. V. Sinclair (Assen, 1971).

Studies

Ainsworth, P. F. 1990a. Jean Froissart and the Fabric of History: Truth, Myth and Fiction in the
  Chroniques, Oxford.
Ainsworth 1990b. 'Knife, Key, Bear and Book: Poisoned Metonymies and the Problem of translatio
  in Froissart's Later Chroniques', Med. Aev, 59, 91–113.
Allan, A. 1979. 'Yorkist Propaganda: Pedigree, Prophecy and the "British History" in the Reign of
  Edward IV', in C. Ross ed. Patronage, Pedigree and Power in Later Medieval England, Gloucester
  and Totowa, NJ, 171–92.
Baldinger, K. 1988. 'Beiträge zum Wortschatz des Perceforest (ca. 1340; ca. 1450)', ZrP, 104,
  259–63.
Barrois, J. 1830. Bibliothèque protypographique, ou librairies des fils du roi Jean, Charles V, Jean de
  Berri, Philippe de Bourgogne et les siens, Paris.
Baumgartner, E. 1992. 'Écosse et Écossais: l'entrelacs de la fiction et de l'histoire dans les
  Chroniques et le Meliador de Froissart', in J. Dufournet, A. C. Fiorato and A. Redondo eds
  L'Image de l'autre européen, XVe–XVIIe siècle, Paris, 11–21.
Beardsmore, B. 1990. 'Les Éléments épiques dans le roman Ysaÿe le Triste', Actes du XIème congrès
  international de la Société Rencesvals (Barcelone, 22–27 août 1988), in Memorias de la Real
  Academia de Buenas Letras de Barcelona, 21, 2 vols, I, 43–52.
Berthelot, A. 1991. 'Le Mythe de la transmission historique dans le Roman de Perceforest', in
  D. Buschinger ed. Histoire et littérature au Moyen Âge: actes du colloque du Centre d'Études
  Médiévales de l'Université de Picardie (Amiens, 20–24 mars 1985), Göppingen, 39–47.
Berthelot 1993. 'Apogée et décadence: les reduplications de l'âge d'or arthurien dans le Roman de
  Perceforest', in Apogée et déclin: actes du colloque de l'URA 411, Provins, 1991, Paris, 139–54.
Berthelot 1996. 'Zéphyr, épigone "rétroactif" de Merlin, dans le Roman de Perceforest', MF, 38,
  7–20.
Bianciotto, G. 1985. 'L'Effacement des traits dialectaux dans une tradition manuscrite: le cas limite
  des copies d'Isaïe le Triste', in Actes du IVe colloque international sur le moyen français,
  Amsterdam, 387–409.

Bianciotto 1996. 'Le Roman d'*Isaïe le Triste*: les imprimés', in *'Ensi firent li ancessor': mélanges de philologie médiévale offerts à M.-R. Jung*, 2 vols, Alessandria, II, 623–39.

Blons-Pierre, C. 1994. 'Jeux et enjeux de la violence dans un roman arthurien du Moyen Âge tardif: *Ysaÿe le Triste*', in *La Violence dans le monde médiéval*, Senefiance 36, Aix-en-Provence, 37–53.

Busby, K. 1991. *Le Chevalier du Papegau*, in Lacy ed. 1991*, 87.

Capin, D. P. 2004. 'Le Conservatisme de la langue, gage du caractère littéraire du texte et témoin d'une nouvelle conception de l'acte d'écriture: le cas d'*Ysaÿe le Triste*', *Med. Aev*, 73, 66–92.

Cauchies, J.-M. ed. 1998. *A la cour de Bourgogne: le duc, son entourage, son train*, Turnhout.

Cerquiglini-Toulet, J. 1991. 'Fullness and Emptiness: Shortages and Storehouses of Lyric Treasure in the Fourteenth and Fifteenth Centuries', in D. Poirion and N. F. Regalado eds *Contexts: Style and Values in Medieval Art and Literature*, YFS, special issue, 224–39.

Chambers, E. K. 1927; repr. 1964. *Arthur of Britain*, Cambridge.

Colombo Timelli, M. 1997. 'Entre *histoire* et *compte*: de l'*Erec* de Chrétien de Troyes à la prose du XVe siècle', in C. Thiry ed. *'A l'heure encore de mon escrire': aspects de la littérature de Bourgogne sous Philippe le Bon et Charles le Téméraire*, LR, Special Number, 23–30.

Colombo Timelli 1998. 'Syntaxe et technique narrative: titres et attaques de chapitre dans l'*Erec* bourgugnon', *FCS*, 24, 208–30.

Croenen, G. online bibliography (Froissart), *www.liv.ac.uk/~gcroenen/biblio.htm*.

Delcourt, D. 1994. 'Magie, fiction, et phantasme dans le *Roman de Perceforest*: pour une poétique de l'illusion au Moyen Âge', *RR*, 85, 167–78.

Dembowski, P. F. 1983. *Jean Froissart and his Meliador: Context, Craft, and Sense*, Lexington, KY.

Diverres, A. H. 1969. 'Froissart's *Meliador* and Edward III's Policy towards Scotland', in *Mélanges offerts à Rita Lejeune*, 2 vols, Gembloux, II, 1399–1409.

Diverres 1970. 'The Irish Adventures in Froissart's *Meliador*', in *Mélanges de langue et de littérature du Moyen Âge et de la Renaissance offerts à Jean Frappier*, 2 vols, Geneva, I, 235–51.

Diverres 1988, 'The Two Versions of Froissart's *Meliador*', in *Studies in Medieval French Language and Literature presented to Brian Woledge in Honour of his 80th Birthday*, Geneva, 37–48.

Doutrepont, G. 1909. *La Littérature française à la cour des ducs de Bourgogne: Philippe le Hardi, Jean sans Peur, Philippe le Bon, Charles le Teméraire*, Paris.

Doutrepont 1939. *Les Mises en prose des épopées et des romans chevaleresques du XIVe au XVIe siècle*, Brussels; repr. Geneva, 1969.

Ferlampin, C. 1993. 'Le Sabbat des *vieilles barbues* dans *Perceforest*', *MA*, 99, 471–504.

Field, R. 1991. 'Romance as History, History as Romance', in M. Mills, J. Fellows and C. Meale eds *Romance in Medieval England*, Cambridge, 163–73.

Fletcher, R. H. 1906. *The Arthurian Material in the Chronicles, especially those of Great Britain and France*, Boston; 2nd edn by R. S. Loomis, New York, 1966.

Flutre, L.-F. 1948–70. 'Études sur le *Roman de Perceforêt*', Rom, 70 (1948–49), 474–522; 71 (1950), 374–92, 482–508; 74 (1953), 44–102; 88 (1967), 475–508; 89 (1968), 355–86; 90 (1969), 341–70; 91 (1970), 189–226.

Frappier, J. 1961. 'Sur le *Perceval en prose* de 1530', in *Fin du Moyen Âge et Renaissance: mélanges de philologie française offerts à Robert Guiette*, Antwerp, 233–47.

Gaullier-Bougassas, C. 1996. 'La Réécriture inventive d'une même séquence: quelques versions du voyage d'Alexandre sous la mer', *Bien dire et bien aprandre*, 14, 7–19.

Gaullier-Bougassas 2000. 'Alexandre le Grand et la conquête de l'ouest dans les *Romans d'Alexandre* du XIIe siècle, leurs mises en prose au XVe siècle et le *Perceforest*', Rom, 118, 83–104, 394–430.

Giacchetti, A. 1963-4. '*Ysaÿe le Triste* et l'Écosse', *BBIAS*, 15, 109–19; 16, 121.

Giacchetti 1973. 'Une nouvelle forme du lai apparue à la fin du XIVe siècle', in *Études de langue et de littérature du Moyen Âge offertes à Félix Lecoy par ses collègues, ses élèves et ses amis*, Paris, 147–55.

Gransden, A. 1982. *Historical Writing in England*, II: *c.1307 to the Early Sixteenth Century*, London.

Hanning, R. 1985. 'Arthurian Evangelists: The Language of Truth in Thirteenth-Century French Prose Romances', *PQ*, 64, 347–65.

Harf-Lancner, L. 1980 'La Chasse au blanc cerf dans le *Méliador*: Froissart et le mythe d'Actéon', *M Rom*, 30, 143–52 (vol. 2 of *Mélanges de langue et de littérature françaises du Moyen Âge et de la Renaissance offerts à Monsieur Charles Foulon*).

Huot, S. 1991. 'Chronicle, Lai, and Romance: Orality and Writing in the *Roman de Perceforest*', in A. N. Doane and C. B. Pasternak eds *Vox Intertexta: Orality and Textuality in the Middle Ages*, Madison, WI, 202–23.

Johnson, L. 1991. 'Robert Mannyng's History of Arthurian Literature', in *Church and Chronicle in the Middle Ages: Essays Presented to John Taylor*, London and Rio Grande, 129–47.

Kekewich, M. 1971. 'Edward IV, William Caxton, and Literary Patronage in Yorkist England', *MLR*, 66, 481–87.

Kelly, D. 1978. 'The Fourteenth Century: *Meliador* and the *Voir-Dit*', in D. Kelly, *Medieval Imagination: Rhetoric and the Poetry of Courtly Love*, Madison and London, 243–53.

Kennedy, Elspeth. 1996. 'Intertextuality between Genres in the *Lancelot–Grail*', in Lacy ed. 1996b*, 71–90.

Kennedy, E. D. 1989a. 'Chronicles and Other Historical Writing', in A. E. Hartung ed. *A Manual of the Writings in Middle English, 1050–1500*, vol. 8, New Haven.

Kennedy 1989b. 'John Hardyng and the Holy Grail', *AL*, 8, 185–206; repr. 2001 in J. P. Carley ed. *Glastonbury Abbey and the Arthurian Tradition*, Cambridge, 249–68.

Kibler, W. W. 2000. 'Sagremor dans le *Méliador* de Froissart', in *'Si a parlé par moult ruiste vertu'. Mélanges de littérature médiévale offerts à Jean Subrenat*, Paris, 307–11.

Lacy, N. J. 1993. 'Convention and Innovation in *Le Chevalier du Papegau*', in *Studies in Honor of Hans-Erich Keller*, Kalamazoo, MI, 237–46.

Lacy 1994. 'Motivation and Method in the Burgundian *Erec*', in *Conjunctures: Medieval Studies in Honor of Douglas Kelly*, Amsterdam and Atlanta, GA, 271–80.

Lacy 1998. 'Adaptation as Reception: The Burgundian *Cligès*', *FCS*, 24, 198–207.

Lecoy de la Marche, A. 1875. *Le Roi Réné: sa vie, son administration, ses travaux artistiques et littéraires*, 2 vols, Paris.

Lods, J. 1951. *Le Roman de Perceforest: origines, composition, caractères, valeur et influence*, Geneva and Lille.

Lods 1980. 'Les Poésies de Wenceslas et le *Méliador* de Froissart', in *Mélanges de langue et littérature françaises du Moyen Âge et de la Renaissance offerts à Monsieur Charles Foulon*, 2 vols, I, Rennes, 205–16.

Longnon, A. 1891. 'Un fragment retrouvé du *Meliador* de Froissart', *Rom*, 20, 403–16.

McKendrick, S. 1990. '*La Grande Histoire Cesar* and the Manuscripts of Edward IV', in P. Beal and J. Griffiths eds *English Manuscript Studies 1100–1700*, Oxford, II, 109–38.

Mahoney, D. B. 1996. 'Courtly Presentation and Authorial Self-Fashioning: Frontispiece Miniatures in Late Medieval French and English Manuscripts', *Med*, 21, 97–160.

Morse, R. 1980. 'Historical Fiction in Fifteenth-Century Burgundy', *MLR*, 75, 48–64.

Naber, A. 1990. 'Les Goûts littéraires d'un bibliophile de la cour de Bourgogne', in K. Busby and E. Kooper eds *Courtly Literature: Culture and Context. Selected Papers from the 5th Triennial Congress of the International Courtly Literature Society, Dalfsen, The Netherlands, 9–16 August, 1986*, Amsterdam, 459–64.

Paris, G. 1901. Review of Zeidler 1901, *Rom*, 30, 446.

Putter, A. 1994. 'Finding Time for Romance: Medieval Arthurian Literary History', *Med. Aev*, 63, 1–16.

Rossi, M. 1975. *Huon de Bordeaux et l'évolution du genre épique au XIIIᵉ siècle*, Paris.

Roussineau, G. 1985. 'Éthique chevaleresque et pouvoir royal dans le *Roman de Perceforest*', in Foulon et al. eds 1985*, II, 521–35.

Salter, E. 1988. *English and International: Studies in the Literature, Art and Patronage of Medieval England*, Cambridge.

Smith, N. 1994. 'The Man on a Horse and the Horse-Man: Constructions of Human and Animal in *The Knight of the Parrot*', in D. Maddox and S. Sturm-Maddox eds *Literary Aspects of Courtly Culture: Selected Papers from the Seventh Triennial Congress of the International Courtly Literature Society, University of Massachusetts, Amherst, USA, 27 July–1 August 1992*, Cambridge, 241–8.

Straub, R. 1995. *David Aubert, 'escripvain' et 'clerc'*, Amsterdam and Atlanta, GA.

Sturm-Maddox, S., and D. Maddox. 1994. 'Renoart in Avalon: Generic Shift in the *Bataille Loquifer*', in *Shifts and Transpositions in Medieval Narrative: A Festschrift for Elspeth Kennedy*, Cambridge, 11–22.

Suard, F. 1981. 'La *Bataille Loquifer* et la pratique de l'intertextualité au début du XIIIᵉ siècle', in *VIII Congreso de la Société Rencesvals*, Pamplona.

Suard 1984. '*Meurvin* et *Mabrian*, deux épigones de la *Chevalerie Ogier de Danemarche* et de *Renaut de Montauban*', in *Guillaume d'Orange and the chanson de geste: Essays Presented to Duncan McMillan in Celebration of his Seventieth Birthday by his Friends and Colleagues of the Société Rencesvals*, Reading, 151–66.

Szkilnik, M. 1992–5. 'Aroés l'illusionniste (*Perceforest*, 3ᵉ partie)', *Rom*, 113, 441–65.

Szkilnik 1995. 'L'Ombre de Lancelot dans *Ysaÿe le Triste*', in *Lancelot-Lanzelet, hier et aujourd'hui: mélanges offerts à Alexandre Micha*, Greifswald, 363–9.

Szkilnik 1996. 'Le *Restor* d'Alexandre dans *Ysaÿe le Triste*', in D. Kelly ed. 1996*, 181–95.

Szkilnik 1997. 'Passelion, Marc l'Essilié et l'idéal courtois', in E. Mullally and J. Thompson eds *The Court and Cultural Diversity: Selected Papers from the eighth Triennial Congress of the International Courtly Literature Society, The Queen's University of Belfast, 26 July–1 August 1995*, Cambridge, 131–8.

Szkilnik 1998a. 'Deux héritiers de Merlin au XIVᵉ siècle: le *luiton* Zéphir et le nain Tronc', *MF*, 43, 77–97.

Szkilnik 1998b. 'Le Clerc et le ménestrel: prose historique et discours versifié dans le *Perceforest*', *Cahiers de Recherches Médiévales*, 5: special issue: *Le Choix de la prose (XIIIᵉ–XVᵉ siècles)*, ed. by E. Baumgartner, 88–105.

Szkilnik 1999a. 'Des femmes écrivains: Néronès dans le *Roman de Perceforest*, Marte dans *Ysaÿe le Triste*', *Rom*, 117, 474–506.

Szkilnik 1999b. 'Les Morts et l'histoire dans le *Roman de Perceforest* (1)', *MA*, 105, 9–30.

Taylor, J. H. M. 1973. 'Reason and Faith in the *Roman de Perceforest*', in *Studies in Medieval Literature and Languages in Memory of Frederick Whitehead*, Manchester and New York, 303–22.

Taylor 1978. 'Aroés the Enchanter: An Episode in the *Roman de Perceforest* and its Sources', *Med. Aev*, 47, 30–9.

Taylor 1987–8. 'The Fourteenth Century: Context, Text, Intertext', in Lacy, Kelly and Busby eds 1987–8*, I, 267–332.

Taylor 1990. 'The Lyric Insertion: Towards a Functional Model', in K. Busby and E. Kooper eds *Courtly Literature: Culture and Context. Selected Papers from the 5th Triennial Congress of the International Courtly Literature Society, Dalfsen, The Netherlands, 9–16 August, 1986*, Amsterdam, 539–48.

Taylor 1992. 'Arthurian Cyclicity: The Construction of History in the Late French Romances', *AY*, 2, 209–23.

Taylor 1994a. 'Order from Accident: Cyclic Consciousness at the End of the Middle Ages', in Besamusca, Gerritsen, Hogetoorn and Lie eds 1994*, 59–73.

Taylor 1994b. 'The Parrot, the Knight, and the Decline of Chivalry', in K. Busby and N. J. Lacy eds

Conjunctures: Medieval Studies in Honor of Douglas Kelly, Amsterdam and Atlanta, GA, 529–44.

Taylor 1996. 'The Sense of a Beginning: Genealogy and Plenitude in Late Medieval Narrative Cycles', in Maddox and Sturm-Maddox eds 1996*, 93–123.

Taylor 1997. 'Perceval/Perceforest: Naming as Hermeneutic in the *Roman de Perceforest*', *RomQ*, 44, 201–14.

Taylor 1998. 'The Significance of the Insignificant: Reading Reception in the Burgundian *Erec* and *Cligès*', *FCS*, 24, 183–97.

Taylor 2001. 'The Lure of the Hybrid: *Tristan de Nanteuil: chanson de geste arthurien* [sic]?', *AL*, 18, 77–87.

Togeby, K. 1969. *Ogier le Danois dans les littératures européennes*, Munksgaard.

Trachsler, R. 2000. *Disjointures–conjointures: étude sur l'interférence des matières narratives dans la littérature française du Moyen Âge*, Tübingen and Basel.

Trompf, G. W. 1979. *The Idea of Historical Recurrence in Western Thought: From Antiquity to the Reformation*, Berkeley, CA.

Tyson, D. B. 1981. 'King Arthur as a Literary Device in French Vernacular History Writing of the Fourteenth Century', *BBIAS*, 33, 237–57.

Van Coolput, C.-A., and P. Vandenbroeck. 1991. 'Art et littérature: sur la description de quelques toiles peintes dans deux textes hennuyers du XIVᵉ siècle', *Revue du Nord*, 73, 5–31.

Vaughan, R. 1970. *Philip the Good: The Apogee of Burgundy*, London.

Vaughan 1975. *Valois Burgundy*, London.

Victorin, P. 1998. 'La Reine Yseut et la Fée Morgue, ou l'impossible maternité dans *Ysaïe le Triste*', in A. Petit ed. *La Mère au Moyen Âge, Bien dire et bien aprandre*, 16, Lille, 261–75.

Victorin 1999. 'La Fin des illusions dans *Ysaÿe le Triste*, ou quand la magie n'est plus qu'une illusion', in *Magie et illusion au Moyen Âge**, 569–78.

Victorin 2002. *Ysaïe le Triste: une esthétique de la confluence. Tours, tombeaux, vergers et fontaines*, Paris.

Vinaver, E. 1949. 'La Genèse de la *Suite du Merlin*', in *Mélanges de philologie romane et de littérature médiévale offerts à Ernest Hoepffner*, Paris, 295–300.

Visser-Fuchs, L. 1992. 'Edward IV's "Memoir on paper" to Charles, Duke of Burgundy: The So-Called "Short Version of the Arrivall"', *NMS*, 36, 167–227.

Visser-Fuchs [1997]. 'Jean de Wavrin and the Foundation of Britain', in E. Kooper ed. *Current Research in Dutch and Belgian Universities and Polytechnics on Old English, Middle English and Historical Linguistics: Papers Read at the Seventeenth and Eighteenth Research Symposiums Held in Utrecht in December 1995 and 1996*, Utrecht, 91–105.

Wallen, M. 1972. 'The Art of Adaptation in the Fifteenth-Century *Erec et Enide* and *Cliges*', dissertation, University of Wisconsin.

Wallen, M. 1982. 'Significant Variations in the Burgundian Prose Version of *Erec et Enide*', *Med. Aev*, 51, 187–96.

Walters, L. J. 2000. 'Parody and the Parrot: Lancelot References in the *Chevalier du Papegau*', in *Translatio studii: Essays by his Students in Honor of Karl D. Uitti for his Sixty-fifth Birthday*, Amsterdam and Atlanta, GA, 331–44.

Weightman, C. 1989. *Margaret of York, Duchess of Burgundy, 1446–1503*, Gloucester, NY.

Weis, K. 1984. '*Le Chevalier du Papegau* und der themengeschichtliche Umkreis des Liedes von Ecke', in G. R. Mermier ed. *Courtly Romance: A Collection of Essays*, Detroit, 273–99.

Willard, C. C. 1991a. 'The Misfortunes of *Cligès* at the Court of Burgundy', in Van Hoecke, Tournoy and Verbeke eds 1991*, 397–403.

Willard 1991b. 'Chrétien de Troyes, Burgundian Adaptations of', in Lacy ed. 1991*, 91–2.

Woledge, B. 1954. *Bibliographie des romans et nouvelles en prose française antérieurs à 1500*, Geneva.

Wolfzettel, F. 1991. 'La 'Modernité' du *Meliador* de Froissart: plaidoyer pour une revalorisation historique du dernier roman arthurien en vers', in Van Hoecke, Tournoy and Verbeke eds 1991*, 376–87.

Zeidler, J. 1901. 'Der Prosaroman *Ysaÿe le Triste*', *ZrP*, 25, 175–214.

Zink, M. 1980a. 'Froissart et la nuit du chasseur', *Poétique,* 11, 60–77; repr. in id., *Les Voix de la conscience: parole du poète et parole de Dieu dans la littérature médiévale* (Caen, 1992), 117–34.

Zink 1980b. 'Les Toiles d'Agamanor et les fresques de Lancelot', *Littérature*, 38, 43–61.

Zink 1993. 'Le Temps, c'est l'argent: remarques sur le *Dit du florin* de Jean Froissart', in *'Et c'est la fin pour quoy sommes ensemble': hommage à Jean Dufournet*, 3 vols, Paris, III, 1455–64.

Zink 1998a. '*Meliador* and the Inception of a New Poetic Sensibility', in D. Maddox and S. Sturm-Maddox eds *Froissart across the Genres*, Gainesville, FL, 155–75.

Zink 1998b. *Froissart et le temps*, Paris.

XIII

THE ARTHURIAN TRADITION IN OCCITAN LITERATURE

Simon Gaunt and Ruth Harvey

The Lyric Tradition

Following the sudden death of his protector, Duke William X of Aquitaine, in April 1137, the troubadour Marcabru (*fl. c.*1130–49) declares that 'Puois lo Peitavis m'es faillitz, / Serai mai cum Artus perdutz' (*since the Poitevin has failed me, I will ever more be lost like Arthur*, IVb, 59–60).[1] In a controversial passage of a song dating probably from *c.*1149, Cercamon berates a promiscuous and treacherous lady who nevertheless seeks the heart of Tristan: 'E tal enqer lo cor Tristan / Qe Dieus tan falsa non fetz sai' (*and such a woman seeks the heart of Tristan, for God never made one more false here*, Gaunt 1989, 75), and it may be that Marcabru also alludes obliquely to the Tristan legend when, of an avaricious flatterer, he says:

> Cest vest la blancha camiza
> E fai son seinhor sufren,
> E ten si dons a sa giza. (XI, 62–4)

(This very same man puts on the white shift, makes a cuckold of his lord and holds Madam as he pleases.)

The allusion here is to an episode of the legend, similar to that called 'Bringvain livrée aux serfs' by Bédier, in which Yseut's 'white shift' symbolizes her virginity, given to Tristan; Marcabru uses it as a metaphor for adulterous sexual intercourse (Gaunt 1986 and Raimbaut d'Aurenga XXVII, 25–52, quoted below).

What conclusions have been drawn from these early allusions? Seeking to assert the richness and precocity of the medieval Occitan literary tradition, several influential scholars have argued that the *matière de Bretagne* was known and established in Occitania from the mid-twelfth century and that early references to it in the troubadour lyric were not all pale echoes of the literature of the French-speaking world, but might rather indicate the existence of narrative versions in Occitan which have been lost. To support the latter hypothesis it was argued that the nature of some of the troubadour allusions suggests that Occitania knew versions of the legends apparently different from those which survive in French (Lejeune 1959; Gallais 1967; Pirot 1972). These views have, however, been significantly undermined over the years by new documentary evidence concerning the periods of activity or cultural contacts of individual troubadours, and/or by more plausible reinterpretations of the existing evidence. What does the overall picture look like now?

It is clear from the above examples that, by a relatively early date, knowledge of some elements of the *matière de Bretagne* had reached Poitou at least, and this conclusion is supported by analysis of cartulary evidence, which shows that from *c.*1100 boys were being baptized with the names 'Arthur' and 'Gauvain' in central western France, northern Italy and Flanders (Gallais 1967, summarized in Pirot 1972, 519–21). However, while this may indicate a new fashion, a response to new oral tales (perhaps introduced by the likes of Breri, see chapter III), it remains true that the legends did not take firm root in Occitania at that time, any more than they did in Flanders. Written narrative versions are conspicuous by their absence from the Occitan literary corpus, and these three lyric allusions to Arthur and Tristan are geographically and chronologically isolated.

It is not until *c.*1170 that further evocations of Tristan appear. The most developed treatment by far is found in the works of Raimbaut d'Aurenga (d. 1173):

> De midonz fatz dompn'e seignor
> Cals que sia.il destinada.
> Car ieu begui de la amor
> Ja.us dei amar a celada.
> Tristan, qan la.il det Yseus gen
> E bela, no.n saup als faire;
> Et ieu am per aital coven
> Midonz, don no.m posc estraire.
>
> Sobre totz aurai gran valor
> S'aitals camisa m'es dada
> Cum Yseus det a l'amador,
> Que mais non era portada.
> Tristan! Mout presetz gent presen:
> D'aital sui eu enquistaire!
> Si.l me dona cill cui m'enten,
> No.us port enveja, bels fraire.
>
> Vejatz, dompna, cum Dieus acor
> Dompna que d'amar s'agrada.
> Q'Iseutz estet en gran paor,
> Puois fon breumens conseillada;
> Qu'il fetz a son marit crezen
> C'anc hom que nasques de maire
> Non toques en lieis. – Mantenen
> Atrestal podetz vos faire!
>
> Carestia, esgauzimen
> M'aporta d'aicel repaire
> On es midonz, qe.m ten gauzen
> Plus q'ieu eis non sai retraire. (XXVII, 25–52, Pattison edn)

(*Whatever may be the fate, I make a lord and master of my lady. Because I drank love, for ever I must love you secretly. Tristan, when gentle and beautiful Yseut gave it to him, could not help himself in the matter; and I love my lady, whom I cannot renounce, in a similar way. I shall surpass all in worth if such a shift as Yseut gave her lover is given to me, for it was never worn before. Tristan! You prized greatly the courteous gift: such a one as I am seeking! If she whom I am courting gives it to me, I bear you no envy, fair brother! See, lady, how God aids a lady who takes pleasure in loving. For Yseut was in great fear, then she was soon helped; for she made her husband believe that no man born of woman had ever touched her. You can quickly do the same! Carestia, bring me joy from that place where the lady is who keeps me more joyous than I myself can tell.*)

Following Roncaglia's demonstration that the individual addressed in the *tornada* (final short strophe) by the *senhal* (nickname) *Carestia* is in all probability Chrétien de Troyes himself (Roncaglia 1958), study of the Tristan legend in the lyric has explored the various ways in which features of the story were exploited in intertextual dialogues which debated and developed different views of the nature and ethics of *fin'amor*, the role played by a lover's free choice, by supernatural forces and by the satisfaction or non-satisfaction of carnal desire (Meneghetti 1984, 139–46; Rossi 1987; Girolamo 1989, 120–41). Chrétien's poem 'D'Amors qui m'a tolu a moi' (Zai edn) is a contribution to this debate, which also involved Bernart de Ventadorn, who declares that he suffered greater pain in love than did Tristan for Yseut:

> Plus trac pena d'amor
> De Tristan l'amador
> Que.n sofri manhta dolor
> Per Izeut la blonda, (44, 45–8)[2]

(*I have more pain in love than Tristan the lover, who suffered so much for Yseut the blonde.*)

Bernart also exploited the *senhal* 'Tristan', very possibly as a nickname for Raimbaut d'Aurenga.[3] Such readings indicate that the first Occitan public for these pieces would have been familiar enough with the legend to be able to savour the nuanced uses to which it was put in courtly debate, although the fact that Raimbaut gives something of a plot-summary in the poem quoted above may equally suggest that the story was a novelty for his audience. Given that none of these love songs is securely datable, it does not seem possible to establish conclusively the sequence of these exchanges: witness the different sequences so far advanced by scholars (Borghi Cedrini 1998). However, this cluster of compositions involving Raimbaut does indicate the influence of specific personal relations between the troubadours and the literary culture of northern France, rather than the existence of an indigenous Occitan tradition.

Some approximate figures may help to indicate the general proportion of Arthurian features in the Occitan lyric landscape (contrast the table in Lejeune 1959, 396). Out of some 2,500 surviving troubadour compositions and 2,100 by *trouvères*, the following table gives the number of poems containing one or more references to the literary characters from the *matière de Bretagne* identified as such in Chambers (1971) and Petersen Dyggve (1934) (the epic and classical names are included here for the purposes of comparison):

Name of character	Troubadours	*Trouvères*
Arthur	18	5
Tristan	29	21
Yseut	13	7
Gauvain	13	2
Yvain	3	2
Erec	5	0
Enide	3	0
Perceval	4	0
Lancelot	3	1
Guinevere	0	1
Charlemagne	15	2
Roland	31	3
Alexander	29	3
Narcissus	4	6
Piramus	5	5

The number of *trouvère* references may appear small by comparison, but we should remember that it was for the same northern-French audiences that the narratives themselves were intended, whereas the lyric references are the principal evidence for knowledge of the *matière de Bretagne* in Occitania. Few of these, however, represent more than brief name-dropping.

The allusions to Arthur are almost entirely proverbial, connected with the theme of the 'Bretons' wait' for their legendary, lost king, and as such they could be exploited in various contexts dealing with delay, patience, hopelessness and vanished exemplary individuals. Explicit references to narratives concerning Arthur do not appear in Occitan until some forty or fifty years after Marcabru's allusion.[4] In his lament for the late Count Geoffrey of Brittany (1186), Bertran de Born plays on the theme of the 'Bretons' wait' to suggest that, if God were to let Arthur, rather than Geoffrey, leave Heaven and return to lead his people, He would be keeping the better man:

> S'Artus, lo segner de Cardoil,
> Cui Breton atendon oi mai,
> Agues poder qe tornes sai,
> Breton i aurian perdut
> E Nostre Segner gazagnat. (22, 33–6)[5]

(If Arthur, the lord of Cardeuil [Carlisle], whom the Bretons wait for henceforth, had the power to return to this world, the Bretons would have lost in the exchange, and Our Lord would have won.)

Bertran had frequent personal contact with the Plantagenets, especially with the sons of Henry II, and is known to have attended the royal Christmas court in

Normandy in 1182 (Gouiran edn, I, 39–40). Once again, the influence of a northern literary tradition on Occitan cultural references could hardly be clearer.

Just as evocations of Charlemagne and Roland occur mainly in the *sirventes* (political or satirical songs) of the troubadours, which are vehicles for social and political comment, allusions to Tristan and Yseut are found overwhelmingly in love-songs. They are the archetypal lovers against whose exemplary passion, devotion and sufferings those of the poet-lover of the *canso* (love song) are measured in hyperbole. Pons de Capduelh, for example, declares that his lady should indeed grant him her love, 'for I am a better *fin'aman* to her than was Tristan to Yseut' (XXIII, 14–15, Napolski edn). Similarly, Guilhem Augier Novella claims to have 'drunk from the same pitcher as did Tristan' (V, 26–7, Calzolari edn). In contrast, the figures of Lancelot and Guinevere seem quite unknown in Occitania in the twelfth century, and Lancelot is hardly mentioned thereafter.

Explicit references in the lyric to other Arthurian characters which suggest familiarity with narrative sources occur at the end of the twelfth century. Raimbaut de Vaqueiras compares his own joy favourably to that of Perceval, 'when at Arthur's court he despoiled the Red Knight of his armour' (X, 17–19, Linskill edn). Composed in northern Italy by a troubadour from Provence, this song's debt to Chrétien de Troyes's romance is evident, and it is not isolated, for in this milieu and at this time his fellow poets were also parading their awareness of the latest fashionable literary material from the north of France. Aimeric de Peguilhan mentions Gauvain and Yvain (10, 14–15, Shepard and Chambers edn), a song attributed to Giraut de Borneil refers to the Harpin de la Montagne episode in Chrétien's *Yvain* (LII, 25–32),[6] and it is to this period also that belongs Rigaut de Berbezilh's comparison of his tongue-tied wonderment before his lady to that of Perceval, who gazed on the vision at the Fisher King's castle and failed to ask what purpose the lance and the Grail served:[7]

> Atressi con Persavaus
>   El temps que vivia,
> Que s'esbait d'esgardar
> Tant qu'anc non saup demandar
>   De que servia
> La lansa ni.l graus. (X, 1–6)

(Just like Perceval in the time when he was alive, who was so astonished in his contemplation that he could not ask what purpose the lance and the grail served.)

In our view, the references in Occitan lyric to versions of the legends once thought to be different from those which survive in the literature of northern France are imprecise, rather than clearly indicative of a different southern tradition,[8] and some are after all best explained as vague references to French material. Bertran de Paris's late thirteenth-century evocation of Yvain as the 'first tamer of birds' (33–4, edn in Pirot 1972) may well refer to the Magic Fountain in

Chrétien's romance or to another Yvain, and Uc de Saint-Circ's reference to Gauvain's relations with the 'fair unfortunate stranger' (I, 35–40) appears to be an allusion to Chrétien's *Perceval*.[9] In 'Qui comte vol apendre' Arnaut Guilhem de Marsan singles out Arthur as worthy of emulation for his devotion to, and expertise in, love (281–90), and Yvain as a trend-setter in male fashions, he being the first to wear gloves and zibeline furs (233–50), but these features hardly constitute evidence for the existence in Occitania of stories different from those known in northern France, and their inclusion here, in a work of instruction, accords well with the *ensenhamen*'s (didactic poem's) focus on the courtly pre-occupations of polite society.[10]

With very few exceptions, all the allusions to Arthurian material in the trouba-dour lyric bear traces of the influence of, and contacts with, northern France. It may be that, as Lejeune argued, Eleanor of Aquitaine and her family played an important role in the diffusion of this material.[11] The vast majority of the refer-ences date from the final years of the twelfth century onwards, and there is little indication that different versions of the legends were known in Occitania.

This is a picture supported by the three surviving *sirventes-ensenhamen*. Addressed supposedly to a *joglar* (minstrel), these tongue-in-cheek compositions constitute long lists of literary works which the performers do not know. Guerau de Cabrera's 'Cabra, juglar', the earliest of the three pieces, has played a key role in forming views of awareness of Arthurian material in the land of troubadour poetry. It was thought to be the work of Guerau III and to date from before 1159, thus indicating a truly astounding, precocious and extensive knowledge of literary works in Catalonia at that time.[12] In fact, it was composed by Guerau IV de Cabrera, almost certainly in the years following 1194 and in all probability in Provence, using materials available there (Cingolani 1992–3).

In this context, the relative paucity of Arthurian material in this repertory is all the more striking. Guerau alludes to a vague 'conte d'Artus' (58), to Tristan and Yseut's transgressive love (185–6), to Gauvain (187–9) and to Erec who 'won the sparrow-hawk in a foreign country' ('[E]rec / com conquistec / L'esparvier for de sa reion', 73–5), this last apparently a reference to Chrétien de Troyes's romance.[13] In a list of over 200 lines, just four items belong to the *matière de Bretagne*. Guiraut de Calanson's parodic response to 'Cabra, juglar' gives only one – obscure and uncertain – evocation of Lancelot in its 240 lines.[14]

Even given that, read literally, the *sirventes-ensenhamen* focus critically on the hapless performer's comprehensive ignorance, so that it seems slightly perverse to use these works as evidence for knowledge of the works they mention, the number of Arthurian legends they do not know is tiny compared to the quan-tities of epic, classical and biblical tales which dominate the lists. By the late thirteenth century, Bertran de Paris can add King Mark, Caradoc and 'Merlin li Engles' to the Arthuriana in his own list, but the same proportions obtain.

From both the lyric references and the repertories there emerges a consistent picture of a slight and superficial knowledge of, and interest in, the Arthurian legend in medieval Occitania, in contrast to that of Tristan. Such knowledge as there is can plausibly be traced to influences from northern France towards the end of the twelfth century. [RH]

The Narrative Tradition

The Occitan narrative corpus confirms the picture that emerges from the lyric tradition and the *ensenhamens*: the Arthurian tradition does not establish itself in Occitania as it does in northern France, England and Germany. Indeed, only three full-length romances survive in Occitan: *Jaufre*, *Flamenca* and *Blandin de Cornouaille*, of which only *Jaufre* is an Arthurian romance.[15] As we have seen, some earlier scholars such as Lejeune (1959) and Pirot (1972, 435–525) argued on the basis of references to Arthurian figures in the troubadour lyric and the *ensenhamens* that a substantial corpus of Arthurian material in Occitan once existed. Although *Jaufre* is the only extant Arthurian romance in Occitan, the survival of a fragment of a *Roman de Merlin* (Cornagliotti 2005), supposed Arthurian elements in the fourteenth-century *Blandin de Cornouaille*,[16] and references to Arthurian texts in later medieval library inventories in Occitan-speaking areas, were similarly used as supporting evidence for a lost Occitan corpus of Arthurian romances (Lejeune 1959, 393–4). But the *Merlin* fragment is isolated, *Blandin* has not a single Arthurian character,[17] and it is not clear that the references to Arthurian texts in Occitan libraries refer to texts in Occitan, rather than to texts in French. In *Flamenca* (probably composed *c.*1270), there is famously a list of all the stories performed by *jongleurs* at Flamenca's wedding and this includes Arthurian stories, but, as with the lists in the *ensenhamens*, stories that can be identified as Arthurian are far outnumbered by stories from the Old French epic tradition and from classical sources.[18] In any case, the fact that *Flamenca* is set in northern France surely undermines its value as evidence for Occitan tastes or for lost Occitan texts; on the contrary, it may in fact offer an Occitan perspective on northern-French tastes. Attempts to argue for an extensive lost corpus of Occitan romances often amount to special pleading for Occitan culture. In fact, Baumgartner (1978, 642–3), basing her conclusions solely on the surviving texts, notes that there is scant evidence for an Occitan romance tradition in the twelfth and thirteenth centuries. Perhaps, *pace* Lejeune, we should take seriously medieval sources that suggest that French was deemed more suitable for narrative genres, and Occitan for lyric genres.[19]

Indeed, Huchet (1991) argues that Occitan culture identifies romance as an alien genre, imitated infrequently only to be subjected to amused critical examination.

For Huchet (1991, 206), Arthurian material in particular is identified as part of a hostile foreign culture, which Occitania countered with its own romances. Huchet limits his investigation to texts he defines as romances, but the ambivalent cultural exchange he posits has an obvious parallel in the small surviving corpus of Occitan *chansons de geste*, since the two most substantial texts, *Daurel et Beton* and *Girart de Roussillon*, both express hostility to the French and also, arguably, to French culture, but in a literary form that is itself identified as French (Gaunt 2002). In other words, a consistent picture emerges in Occitania of certain narrative forms being tainted by their ostensible 'Frenchness'. However, the value of *Jaufre*'s play on genre as part of an anti-French agenda would depend on its date of composition, which has proved controversial among modern scholars.

The dating of *Jaufre* rests upon the poet's praise for a king of Aragon (56–94 and 2613–36), whom he does not name but identifies merely as God's 'novels cavalies' (69) (*new knight*) and as having been crowned young (79). This king is taken to be either Alfonso II (reigned 1162–96, crowned at the age of ten) or Jaime I (reigned 1213–76, crowned at the age of five); the composition of *Jaufre* is accordingly dated variously as either *c.*1170–80 or *c.*1220–30.[20] The controversy surrounding the dating of *Jaufre* is, however, further complicated by references in lyrics by the troubadours Giraut de Borneil (*fl.* 1162–99) and Peire Vidal (*fl.* 1183–1204) to a Jaufre who may or may not be the hero of the romance (Pirot 1972, 498–506), and by an epilogue which occurs in only one manuscript of *Jaufre*. This epilogue may or may not suggest that the romance is the work of two writers (10945–54), thus raising the possibility that the surviving text is an early thirteenth-century *remaniement* of a twelfth-century text.[21] A firm dating of *Jaufre* is not possible, but the matter is nonetheless of some importance to the history of the development of the Arthurian tradition, since, as we shall see, there are very close and striking parallels between *Jaufre* and the romances of Chrétien de Troyes, particularly *Perceval*. Thus, if *Jaufre* dates from *c.*1170–80, we would need to accept that Chrétien was strongly influenced by, and chose to imitate, a somewhat obscure Occitan text; on the other hand, if *Jaufre* dates from *c.*1220–30, we would have further evidence for the influence of Chrétien in the early part of the thirteenth century, before the prevalence of prose romance.

The balance of probabilities nonetheless tips in favour of the third decade of the thirteenth century (Baumgartner 1978, 634). The King of Aragon is not clearly identified, so no dating can rest upon these references; on the other hand, the allusions in Giraut de Borneil and Peire Vidal are almost certainly *not* to the hero of our romance (Chambers 1971, 157, whose view is corroborated by more recent editions). As R. G. Arthur (transl., xvi–xvii) has pointed out, scholars arguing for the earlier dating always do so within the context of special pleading designed to show the precocity, richness and influence of Occitan literary culture, whereas those who are more concerned with interpreting the romance itself always argue for the later dating. Not only are the style and tone of *Jaufre* typical of the later period (Schmolke-Hasselman 1980/98*, 19), but the later dating makes better sense of the romance's relationship to Chrétien's corpus. Furthermore, if, as Huchet and others have suggested, there is an attempt in *Jaufre* to criticize and undermine the ideological underpinning of northern-French romance (Huchet 1991, 187–96; Jewers 2000), it makes better sense to see the text as dating from the period after the Albigensian crusade, when hostility to the French and French culture in Occitania was rife. As for the argument concerning dual authorship, the text shows no obvious signs of *remaniement*; on the contrary, as Baumgartner has argued (1978, 634), it has a perceptible unity of conception and a uniform style throughout. Thus, as Huchet suggests (1991, 153), and Lee has recently argued in some detail (2003), the apparent distinction suggested in the epilogue between 'the one who began the romance' and 'the one who finished it' (10949–50) is a textual game that is far from unprecedented in medieval literature. Indeed, Lee (2003) persuasively contends that the author of *Jaufre* deliberately plays parodically and ambiguously on the supposed dual authorship of Chrétien's *Charrette*.

Jaufre narrates the story of a young man who appears at Arthur's court asking to be dubbed and to be allowed to undertake an adventure on the king's behalf. Mocked by Kay for his youth and inexperience, Jaufre sets out in pursuit of Taulat, a wicked knight who has insulted Arthur and his queen. As he follows Taulat, Jaufre vanquishes a series of foes, some of whom he spares, whilst others are killed. After each adventure either his vanquished opponent(s) or people he has liberated from his vanquished opponent(s) are sent back to Arthur's court to narrate Jaufre's exploits. In the midst of these adventures, Jaufre finds himself at a place called Monbrun, with whose mistress, Brunissen, he falls in love, despite being baffled by the frenetic lamentations to which the entire population abandons itself periodically throughout the night; indeed, when he asks the reason for this odd behaviour, he receives a beating. Despite being in love with Brunissen, Jaufre sneaks away from Monbrun, since he regards it as his duty to pursue Taulat.

At his next port of call, the castle of one Augier d'Essart, Jaufre discovers that his quest for Taulat and the histrionics of the people of Monbrun are linked. For the last seven years, Taulat has held the lord of the land, Melian de Montmelior, prisoner. Once a month Melian is forced to climb a hill while being soundly whipped by Taulat; he is then allowed to recover for a month before the torture begins again. The people of Monbrun and the surrounding land have agreed to lament his plight at various points throughout the day and night until their lord is delivered. Augier explains that Taulat will return in a week's time for the ritual torture of Melian, and so Jaufre resolves to be there waiting for him. He takes advantage of the week's wait to vanquish a bandit black knight and a giant, but when Taulat returns he quickly beats him in individual combat and sends him for judgement to Arthur, who decides he should be treated for seven years as he has been treating Melian.

Jaufre, meanwhile, returns to Monbrun and to Brunissen. After some protracted courtly manoeuvring, Jaufre and Brunissen become betrothed, a match that is sanctioned by Melian. Their wedding is to take place at Arthur's court, but as Jaufre, Brunissen, Melian and their retinue make their way there, Jaufre, who has answered the call of a damsel in distress, disappears into a lake, an incident that leads to elaborate laments from his companions, who believe him dead. But Jaufre is alive; he has been kidnapped by the fairy of Gibel, whose supernatural land is entered through the bottom of the lake; she had previously sought help at Arthur's court, since she has been under attack from the wicked Felon d'Auberue, but she found no one there to help her, hence her ruse. As he thinks this is the only way to get back to Brunissen, Jaufre agrees to fight Felon, whom he duly humbles before returning to the real world to marry Brunissen and live happily ever after. During their wedding festivities, the fairy of Gibel appears to reward Jaufre richly before he returns to Monbrun with Brunissen and Melian, who is persuaded to forgive Taulat rather than to punish him as had been agreed.

This brief plot summary passes over many of the details of this complicated and lengthy romance of almost 11,000 lines; it can nonetheless be seen that *Jaufre* is made up of disparate elements of the Arthurian tradition, without it being a direct adaptation of any surviving French source. Indeed, if the character of Jaufre himself bears some relation to a minor character in northern-French texts (Girflet, son of Do), the text has no surviving analogues and has some elements that set it apart from the mainstream Arthurian tradition.[22] As far as we can tell, *Jaufre* is, then, a unique and independent work, probably from an area of Occitania that borders upon Catalonia, which makes its debt to Chrétien's corpus all the more striking.

The author of *Jaufre* clearly knew Chrétien's Arthurian romances well (Baumgartner 1978, 627, 632–4; Hunt 1987; Jewers 1997, 188–90; Jewers 2000; Lee 2003; Limentani 1977, 78–101). Among elements that suggest this are the following: (i) the quest to avenge the insult at Arthur's court recalls the *Charrette* and *Perceval*; (ii) thinking that Jaufre is dead, Brunissen, like Guinevere in the *Charrette*, confesses the true extent of her feelings; (iii) Brunissen and Jaufre's monologues when they fall in love are reminiscent of those of Alixandre and Soredamors in *Cligés*; Brunissen at one point specifically compares herself to Fénice (7610), who is not generally a well-known Arthurian figure; (iv) Jaufre is warned against the dangers of uxoriousness for a young knight (10, 212–18), which recalls *Erec* and *Yvain*; indeed, the episode with the fairy of Gibel can be read as a caution against being uxorious (Baumgartner 1978, 629); (v) Brunissen actively tries to stop Jaufre helping others once she has decided she wants to marry him. This contrasts with Enide's behaviour in *Erec* once her husband's *recreantise* has been revealed; (vi) Gauvain's absence at key moments is noted (e.g. 5071, 6321), which is reminiscent of his equivocal role in *Yvain*; (vii) the forbidden question in Monbrun (asking why everyone laments) reverses the motif of the compulsory question in the Fisher King's castle in *Perceval*; (viii) Jaufre's quest is motivated by a desire to avenge mockery by Kay, which is reminiscent of the hero setting out in *Yvain* (and *Perceval*); (ix) *Jaufre* may play on dual authorship, like Chrétien's *Charrette* (Lee 2003). But the most striking parallels, as many scholars have noted (Limentani 1977, 78–101; Baumgartner 1978, 623–34), concern the specific description of Kay in *Perceval* (Méla edn) and his description in *Jaufre*:

Et Kex parmi la sale vint,	Ab tant Qecs per la sala venc,
Trestoz desafublez, et tint	Desenvoutz et en sa man tenc
En sa main destre un bastonet,	Un baston parat de pomier.
O chief ot chapel de bonet ...	E anc nu-i ac pros cavalier ...
(*Perceval*, 2733–5)	(*Jaufre*, 123–6)

(*And Kay came into the room, lightly attired, and in his right hand he held a staff, and on his head he had a light hat ... / And at that point Kay came into the room, dishevelled, and in his right hand he held a staff decorated with apple wood. And there never was such a bold knight ...*)

The close parallels here suggest that the author of *Jaufre* had written copies of Chrétien's romances before him as he worked and that the specific verbal echoes of his northern-French predecessor are deliberate. But his imitation is obviously parodic, since his irony at the expense of Arthur and the ideals of the Arthurian world is pushed well beyond the delicate, tongue-in-cheek ambiguity at which Chrétien excels. The author of *Jaufre* is not a particularly elegant writer; indeed, his apparent nonchalance about the niceties of style occasionally suggests that he took little trouble over the texture of his work.[23] On the other hand, he does have a real sense of comedy, and one of the pleasures of reading *Jaufre* is that parts of the text are wickedly funny (see particularly Jewers 2000). Thus, for example, the comic representation of Arthur and his court unpicks the ideals of Arthurian romance in a manner that far exceeds the irony of a writer like Chrétien.

Arthur, in *Jaufre*, is twice made to look a total fool. As with many Arthurian romances, the text opens with a court scene, which finds Arthur forlornly waiting for an adventure. When Kay declares he is hungry and that it is perhaps time to eat (141–2), Arthur testily retorts that he cannot eat until the requisite adventure has materialized (144–53). So Arthur rides out to look for an adventure. He instantly encounters an apparently supernatural horned beast. By the time the Knights of the Round Table catch up with him, they find him dangling from the beast's horns over the edge of a high rock. Much lamenting and exaggerated expressions of grief culminate in Kay's claim that the loss of Arthur is the loss of 'valor' (*worth*) personified (358–74). Yet as if Kay's premature lament for

Arthur's death were not sufficient to underline just how ridiculous the king's plight is, his knights decide they will undress and place their clothes in a heap at the bottom of the rock to break his fall. The description of their deliberations and resultant nakedness is truly hilarious (387–406).

The prologue to *Jaufre* had described Arthur as the most glorious king who had ever lived and his court as still unsurpassed. Arthur dangling from the horn of a giant beast while his knights run around helplessly in a state of undress is hardly commensurate with this.[24] That we are dealing here with high farce is confirmed by what follows: the beast is suddenly transformed into the court magician, who has contrived the whole episode in order to supply Arthur with an adventure so that everyone can eat (428–32). Everyone agrees it has been a jolly jape, but if the incident is clearly comic, its implications for how we might view Arthur's court are serious.

Arthur's 'adventure' here is artificially manufactured. Far from being the defender of the weak and the rescuer of damsels in distress, he is portrayed devoting himself to what amounts to rather frivolous games. Indeed, when Taulat appears at his court shortly after this and kills a knight at the queen's feet while offering an insolent challenge, Arthur simply bows his head in shame (592–3) and Jaufre, the newcomer at court, is the only knight present who wishes to do anything in response. Later in the text, the fairy of Gibel, finding no one to defend her at Arthur's court (6295–6335), has to kidnap Jaufre herself. Moreover, the episode with the magician is repeated during Jaufre's wedding festivities (only this time the magician becomes a giant bird) as if to highlight the inward-looking, frivolous tendencies of Arthur and his court.

Neither Arthur nor his court is socially useful in *Jaufre*; on the contrary, the impotence of Arthur and his entourage is constantly emphasized, often rather wittily. Thus, as Jaufre sends people back to Arthur to narrate his exploits, the reader gradually realizes that the king's court is shrinking. The first defeated opponent finds the court breaking up (1580), the liberated prisoners of Jaufre's second foe find the king with twenty-one knights (2090), those released from captivity by his third adventure discover the king 'tot escarit' (*completely aban-doned*) with only twelve remaining knights (2907–9), and finally when Taulat arrives to throw himself on Arthur's mercy, he finds the great king 'privadamenz' (*by himself*, 6294) being harangued by the fairy of Gibel for being unable to help her (Weaver 1971, 41). If Arthur's court is the site where Jaufre wishes to register his chivalric success, its authority visibly diminishes as the text progresses. Fittingly, at the end of the romance Arthur is unable to reward Jaufre appropri-ately for his great deeds of prowess: it is, rather, the fairy of Gibel who does so, while Arthur receives a gift from Jaufre, a magnificent bird brought back from the fairy's magical realm; it is as if the knight were empowering the king, rather than vice versa (Jung 1991).

The poet's wit and propensity for comedy are also to the fore in his treatment of the hero's quest. When he sets out in pursuit of Taulat, Jaufre vows, with an obvious echo of Arthur's unwillingness to eat before having an adventure, not to eat until he has found his foe (638); to this he later adds a vow not to sleep. His privations are dwelt upon insistently (1307, 1344, 1661, 2185–6, etc.). As his quest progresses, he becomes so tired and weak from hunger and lack of sleep that he has difficulty staying mounted and riding in a straight line (3025–33). This immediately precedes his arrival in Monbrun, where he desperately tries to sleep in Brunissen's garden, only to be woken repeatedly by her men as a result of her displeasure at his having disturbed the birds, whose songs she enjoys. Jaufre's inability here to pay attention to the birdsong – a conventional precursor of the onset of love – is not without irony: when he needs to sleep, he does not do so and this hampers his chivalric efficiency; when he should be staying awake, he falls asleep. A little later, as he falls in love with Brunissen, his feelings prevent him from eating and sleeping (6688–9).

Jaufre is thus often portrayed as vaguely absurd and ridiculous. Similarly, Brunissen is often treated in a comic mode. For example, when she thinks Jaufre has drowned (when in fact he has been kidnapped by the fairy of Gibel), she rushes dementedly towards the lake in which he has disappeared followed by 500 frantic ladies; she attempts to drown herself, only to be dragged out by her hair. Between swoons she then intones a perfectly structured formal *planh* (lament), but this is underscored, of course, by dramatic irony, since the reader realizes that Jaufre cannot be dead.

Jaufre also generates a good deal of comedy through its structure and pacing. As Fleischman argues (1981), the two episodes with the magician at Arthur's court ought to form a framing device, with the second episode marking closure, particularly since Taulat has been defeated and Jaufre's love for Brunissen seems to be reciprocated. But the romance continues for another thousand lines after this, and the kidnapping of Jaufre by the fairy of Gibel foils any expectations of neat closure. The structure of *Jaufre* is deliberately awry and this means that Arthur's court is deliberately, but unexpectedly, decentred by the plot, which, with its accumulation of apparently random adventures, sometimes resembles a shaggy-dog story rather than a tightly constructed romance. The humour generated by this is enhanced by the fact that the ostensible climax, Jaufre's defeat of Taulat, is dispatched with remarkable brevity, little intensity and still less drama (5841–6132). When this is considered alongside the narrator's tendency to delay the action and wander off the point with asides, eulogies of the King of Aragon, or apparently irrelevant laments on the loss of courtly virtues, it is hard not to see in the writing a deliberate deflation of the heroic dynamic and high style of romance narrative (Kay 1979; Fleischman 1981, 115).

In short, *Jaufre* offers a humorous, but highly critical, rereading of the romance tradition, particularly of Chrétien de Troyes's romances. At its heart is a repeated episode of ritual torture that turns out not only to be pointless, but also to be bereft of significance in that ultimately it does not even seem to merit punishment. The image of the tortured Melian and of his rescue by Jaufre thus becomes a *mise en abyme* or critical reflection of romance itself: the central issue of this romance would seem to be the equivocal redemption, carried out in the name of a worthless king, of a pointless and repetitive series of own goals scored by the chivalric classes. This raises the question of whether the text should be read in relation to class rather than cultural differences, and it has been suggested that *Jaufre* inscribes the sceptical view of the southern urban classes on courtly society's preoccupations, at least as they surface in romance.[25] The poet's unusual attention to realistic detail (for example, in relation to what the characters eat, or to fabrics) and the supposedly uncourtly, brutal violence that Jaufre dishes out to some of his opponents are taken as evidence for the urban/urbane provenance of the text.[26] It is difficult to refute such a hypothesis, but any convincing reading of this text must take account of its clear relation to Chrétien's Arthurian romances. How an Occitan writer in the 1220s acquired such a detailed knowledge of Chrétien's works, why he chose to write such an extensive parody of them, and whether his (presumably Occitan) audience would have appreciated what he had done are questions to which we are unlikely ever to have firm answers. *Jaufre* may share with *Flamenca* (the other surviving full-length romance in Occitania) a wicked sense of humour and parody, thereby instantiating a particular Occitan trajectory for romance (Jewers 2000), but it is unique both as an Occitan Arthurian romance and as a particularly wicked parody within the broader genre of Arthurian verse romance. The most likely explanation for its singularity in our opinion is a cultural antipathy in Occitania to an Arthurian tradition associated with northern-French culture. [SG]

Notes

[1] Each poet is quoted from the editions listed by author under Texts and Translations in the Reference List.

[2] Some see the poetic network as extending to include other troubadours such as Gaucelm Faidit, Arnaut Daniel, northern-French *trouvères* and perhaps even romances; see Jung 1986; Rossi 1987 and 1992.

[3] See Pattison edn of Raimbaut d'Aurenga, 24–5; Roncaglia 1958; Meneghetti 1984, 139. For the *senhal*, see Bernart's poems 29, 61; 43, 57; 4, 63; 42, 53. Other troubadours also used 'Tristan' as a nickname; see, for example, Bertran de Born, 25, 49–52 and the note (Gouiran edn).

[4] Cf. Bernart de Ventadorn, 23, 38, who refers to 'esperansa bretona'; Bernart's period of activity is conventionally put at *c.* 1150–70, but none of his songs is securely datable.

[5] Bertran is quoted from Gouiran edn, with an emendation to line 34. The following lines make the same point with reference to Gauvain.

[6] The attribution is nonetheless very uncertain; see Sharman edn of Giraut, 24.

[7] The dating of Rigaut was for a long time the subject of vigorous controversy; for full references and a more balanced, better-documented conclusion, see Guida 1990, 87–108.

[8] See, for example, Gauvain's evocation as a solitary hunter, 'Cabra juglar', 187–9, edn in Pirot 1972.

[9] See Jeanroy and Salverda de Grave edn of Uc, 169–70; and Pirot 1972, 480.

[10] For the date of Arnaut's work – not before 1180 and probably later – see Guida 1999.

[11] See Lejeune 1954 and 1959, 397, though a systematic study of troubadour contacts and centres of lyric patronage which may permit an evaluation of this remains a *desideratum*.

[12] Pirot's 1972 study is an exhaustive survey of critical work on the relevant literary history published before 1972 and is still invaluable, but care is needed in consulting it because of the ramifications of his thesis regarding the early date of composition of 'Cabra juglar'.

[13] The vague reference to 'Cardueill' (160) may also be to Arthurian material.

[14] 'Lanselot' (or 'laniolet') conquered 'gen landa', or 'Islanda' (variously interpreted as 'Island', 'Ireland' or 'Oriande': see Pirot 1972, 482–5), but the manuscript evidence is not clear.

[15] An exhaustive list of all surviving texts in Occitan that could count as romances, including fragments and short narratives, is given by Huchet 1991, 13. The texts of both *Jaufre* and *Flamenca* may be found with facing modern French translation in the Lavaud and Nelli edn, from which quotations here are taken; but for *Jaufre*, see also Brunel 1943 and Lee edn 2006; for an English translation, see Arthur transl., which has an excellent introduction. For an exhaustive analytic bibliography of publications relating to *Jaufre* before 1996, see Trachsler 1997*, 217–33.

[16] For parallels between *Blandin* and Arthurian romance, see van der Horst edn, 67–71. Huchet's reading of the text (1991, 196–206) rests upon the assumption that *Blandin* is an Arthurian romance from which Arthurian elements have been significantly erased.

[17] There is also nothing to suggest that the work is set in a distant Arthurian past.

[18] See *Flamenca*, 599–709. The Arthurian material includes two *lais* called *Cabrefoil* and *Tintagoil* (599–600), what looks like the complete surviving Arthurian works of Chrétien together with *Tristan* (665–78) and *Le Bel Inconnu* (679), and then various narratives that are harder to identify, but which involve Guiflet (Girflet), Calobrenan, Kay and Mordret (682–90).

[19] See Marshall edn of Raimon Vidal, 6: 'La parladura francesa val mais et [es] plus avinenz a far romanz et pasturellas, mas cella de Lemosin val mais per far vers et cansons et serventes' (*The French language is better and more seemly for composing romances and pastourelles, but that of the Limousin [Occitan] is better for composing lyrics and songs and sirventes*). The *Razos* date from 1190 to 1223.

[20] For the earlier dating, see Lejeune 1948 and 1953; also Pirot 1972, 498–506. For the later dating, see notably Rémy 1950; also Schmolke-Hasselmann 1980/98*, 19, 71–2. An excellent synthesis of the arguments concerning the dating of *Jaufre* is to be found in Arthur transl., x–xvii.

[21] See de Riquer 1955, who thinks the earlier version of *Jaufre* must date from 1169–70 at the latest, and the *remaniement* from *c.*1200.

[22] For example, Arthur's wife is called Guilalmer in *Jaufre*, 499, 2870, etc., a name that is not attested in any other source.

[23] For example, in lines 5000–36, 20 lines begin with 'E'.

[24] For a stimulating reading of this episode as a *mise à nu* of Arthurian romance, see Huchet 1991, 187–93.

[25] This is certainly the view of two recent commentators: Jewers 1997, 196–7, and Fraser 1995. Fraser argues that scholars have overplayed the parodic thrust of *Jaufre*; she prefers to read the text as satire and does not regard the references to Chrétien as central to understanding the text.

[26] See in particular Fraser 1995, but these qualities are commented upon by others. Examples of Jaufre's uncourtly behaviour would be his summary execution or dismembering of some of his opponents, or his harsh treatment of Kay when he returns to Arthur's court.

Reference List

For items accompanied by an asterisk, see the General Bibliography.

Texts and Translations

Aimeric de Peguilhan: *The Poems of Aimeric de Peguilhan.* Ed. and transl. by W. P. Shepard and F. M. Chambers (Evanston, IL, 1950).

Arnaut Guilhem de Marsan, 'Qui comte vol apendre', in *Testi didattico-cortesi di Provenza.* Ed. by G. E. Sansone, Biblioteca di Filologia Romanza 29 (Bari, 1977), 119–80.

Bernart de Ventadorn: *The Songs of Bernart de Ventadorn.* Ed. by S. G. Nichols, J. A. Galm et al., University of North Carolina Studies in the Romance Languages and Literatures 39 (Chapel Hill, NC, 1962).

Bertran de Born: *L'Amour et la guerre: l'œuvre de Bertran de Born.* Ed. by G. Gouiran, 2 vols (Aix-en-Provence, 1985).

Blandin de Cornouaille: introduction, édition diplomatique, glossaire. Ed. by C. H. M. van der Horst (The Hague and Paris, 1974).

Chrétien de Troyes: *Les Chansons courtoises de Chrétien de Troyes.* Ed. by M.-C. Zai (Bern and Frankfurt, 1974).

Chrétien de Troyes: *Le Conte du Graal, ou, le roman de Perceval.* Ed. by C. Méla (Paris, 1990).

Flamenca: Les Troubadours: l'œuvre épique. Ed. by R. Lavaud and R. Nelli (Bruges, 1960), 619–1063.

Giraut de Borneil: *The 'Cansos' and 'Sirventes' of the Troubadour Giraut de Borneil: A Critical Edition.* Ed. by R. V. Sharman (Cambridge, 1989).

Guilhem Augier Novella: *Il trovatore Guilhem Augier Novella.* Ed. by M. Calzolari (Modena, 1986).

Jaufre: Les Troubadours: l'œuvre épique. Ed. by R. Lavaud and R. Nelli (Bruges, 1960), 15–617.

Jaufre: roman arthurien du XIIIe siècle en vers provençaux. Ed. by C. Brunel, SATF (Paris, 1943).

Jaufre: An Occitan Arthurian Romance. Transl. by R. G. Arthur (New York and London, 1992).

Jaufre: www.rialc.unina.it/jaufre-i.htm. Ed. by C. Lee (2000).

Jaufre. Ed. by C. Lee (Rome, 2006).

Marcabru: A Critical Edition. Ed. by S. Gaunt, R. Harvey and L. Paterson (Woodbridge, 2000).

Pons de Capduelh: *Leben und Werke des Trobadors Ponz de Capduoill.* Ed. by M. von Napolski (Halle, 1879).

Raimbaut d'Aurenga: *The Life and Works of the Troubadour Raimbaut d'Orange.* Ed. by W. T. Pattison (Minneapolis and London, 1952).

Raimbaut de Vaqueiras: *The Poems of the Troubadour Raimbaut de Vaqueiras.* Ed. by J. Linskill (The Hague, 1964).

Raimon Vidal: *The Razos de Trobar of Raimon Vidal and Associated Texts.* Ed. by J. H. Marshall (Oxford, 1972).

Rigaut de Berbezilh. Liriche. Ed. by A. Vàrvaro, Biblioteca di Filologia Romanza 4 (Bari, 1960).

Uc de Saint-Circ: *Poésies de Uc de Saint-Circ.* Ed. and transl. by A. Jeanroy and J. J. Salverda de Grave, Bibliothèque Méridionale 15 (Paris, 1913).

Studies

Baumgartner, E. 1978. 'Le Roman aux XIIe et XIIIe siècles dans la littérature occitane', in *GRMLA**, IV:I, 627–44.

Borghi Cedrini, L. 1998. 'L'enigma degli psedonimi nel *débat* tra Raimbaut d'Aurenga, Bernart de Ventadorn e Chrétien de Troyes', in U. Floris and M. Virdis eds *Il segreto. Atti del convegno di studi, Cagliari, 1–4 aprile 1998*, Rome, 49–75.

Chabaneau, C. 1882. 'Fragments d'une traduction provençale du roman de Merlin', *RLR*, 22, 105–15.

Chambers, F. M. 1971. *Proper Names in the Lyrics of the Troubadours*, University of North Carolina Studies in the Romance Languages and Literatures 113, Chapel Hill.

Cingolani, S. 1992–3. 'The *Sirventes-ensenhamen* of Guerau de Cabrera: A Proposal For a New Interpretation', *Journal of Hispanic Research*, 1, 191–200.

Cornagliotti, A. 2005. 'Les Fragments occitans du *Merlin* de Robert de Boron', in *Études de langue et de littérature médiévales offertes à Peter T. Ricketts à l'occasion de son 70ème anniversaire*, Turnhout, 5–16.

Fleischman, S. 1981. '*Jaufre* or Chivalry Askew: Social Overtones of Parody in Arthurian Romance', *Viator*, 12, 101–29.

Fraser, V. 1995. 'Humour and Satire in the Romance of *Jaufre*', *FMLS*, 31, 223–33.

Gallais, P. 1967. 'Bleheri, la cour de Poitiers et la diffusion des récits arthuriens sur le continent', in *Actes du 7e congrès national de la Société Française de Littérature Comparée (Poitiers, 27–29 mai 1965)*, Paris, 47–79.

Gaunt, S. 1986. 'Did Marcabru Know the Tristan Legend?', *Med. Aev*, 55, 108–13.

Gaunt 1989. *Troubadours and Irony*, Cambridge.

Gaunt 2002. '*Desnaturat son li Frances*: Language and Identity in the Twelfth-Century Occitan Epic', *Tenso*, 17, 10–31.

Girolamo, C. di. 1989. *I trovatori*, Turin.

Guida, S. 1990. 'Problemi di datazione e di identificazione di trovatori. I. Rigaut de Berbezilh. II. Sifre e Mir Bernat. III. Guillem Augier', in G. Tavani and L. Rossi eds *Studi Provenzali e Francesi, 86–87*, L'Aquila, 87–126.

Guida 1999. 'Cartulari e trovatori; 1. Arnaut Guilhem de Marsan; 2. Amanieu de la Broqueira; 3. Guilhem Peire de Cazals; 4. Amanieu de Sescas', *CN*, 59, 71–127.

Huchet, J.-Ch. 1991. *Le Roman occitan médiéval*, Paris.

Hunt, T. 1987. '*Texte* and *Prétexte*: *Jaufre* and *Yvain*', in Lacy, Kelly and Busby eds 1987–8*, II, 125–41.

Jewers, C. A. 1997. 'The Name of the Ruse and the Round Table: Occitan Romance and the Case for Cultural Resistance', *Neophil*, 81, 187–200.

Jewers 2000. *Chivalric Fiction and the History of the Novel*, Gainsville, FL.

Jung, M. R. 1986. 'A propos de la poésie lyrique d'oc et d'oïl', in M. R. Jung and G. Tavani eds *Studi Provenzali e Francesi, 84–85*, L'Aquila, 5–36.

Jung 1991. '*Jaufre*: "E aiso son novas rials"', in *Il miglior fabbro . . . .: mélanges de langue et de littérature occitanes en hommage à Pierre Bec*, Poitiers, 223–34.

Kay, S. 1979. 'The Uses of Time in the Romances of *Jaufre* and *Flamenca*', *MR*, 6, 37–62.

Lee, C. 2003. 'L'Auteur de *Jaufre* et celui du *Chevalier de la Charrete*', in R. Castano, S. Guida and F. Latella eds *Scène, évolution, sort de la langue et de la littérature d'oc: actes du 7e congrès international de l'Association Internationale d'Études Occitanes*, 2 vols, Rome, I, 479–91.

Lejeune, R. 1948. 'La Date du roman de *Jaufré*: à propos d'une édition récente', *MA*, 54, 257–95.

Lejeune 1953. 'A propos de la datation du roman de *Jaufré*. Le Roman de *Jaufré*, source de Chrétien de Troyes?', *RBPH*, 31, 717–47.

Lejeune 1954. 'Rôle littéraire d'Aliénor d'Aquitaine et de sa famille', *CN*, 14, 5–57.

Lejeune 1959. 'The Troubadours', in Loomis ed. 1959*, 393–9.

Limentani, A. 1977. *L'eccezione narrativa: la Provenza medievale e l'arte del racconto*, Turin.

Meneghetti, M. L. 1984. *Il pubblico dei trovatori: ricezione e riuso dei testi lirici cortesi fino al XIV secolo*, Modena.

Petersen Dyggve, H. 1934. *Onomastique des trouvères*, Helsinki.

Pirot, F. 1972. *Recherches sur les connaissances littéraires des troubadours occitans et catalans des XIIe et XIIIe siècles: les 'sirventes-ensenhamens' de Guerau de Cabrera, Guiraut de Calanson et Bertrand de Paris*, Barcelona.

Rémy, P. 1950, 'A propos de la datation du roman de *Jaufré*', *RBPH*, 28, 1349–77.

Riquer, M. de. 1955. 'Los problemas del *roman* provenzal de *Jaufré*', in *Recueil de travaux offert à M. Clovis Brunel*, 2 vols, Paris, II, 435–61.

Roncaglia, A. 1958. 'Carestia', *CN*, 18, 121–37.

Rossi, L. 1987. 'Chrétien de Troyes e i trovatori: Tristan, Linhaura, Carestia', *VR*, 46, 26–62.

Rossi 1992. 'La "Chemise" d'Iseut et l'amour tristanien chez les troubadours et les trouvères', in G. Gouiran ed. *Contacts de langues, de civilisations et intertextualité: actes du IIIe congrès international de l'Association Internationale d'Études Occitanes, Montpellier, 20–26 septembre 1990*, 3 vols, Montpellier, III, 1119–32.

Weaver, T. P. 1971. 'The Return of Arthur: A Study of the Provençal Arthurian Romance *Jaufre*', dissertation, Yale University.

XIV

ARTHUR IN MODERN FRENCH FICTION AND FILM

Joan Tasker Grimbert and Norris J. Lacy

Introduction

Throughout the first half of the sixteenth century, and even beyond, Arthurian romances retained their popularity, and a good many of them were republished a number of times. Frappier (1973) cites as material proof of an enduring taste for the legend the frequent re-editions of romances throughout the century. As regards the Tristan material, he mentions, for example, the prose *Tristan*, *Ysaÿe le Triste*, *Guiron le Courtois* and *Meliadus de Leonnoys*. In addition, Pierre Sala's *Tristan* (1525–9), composed at the request of François I, drew inspiration from these and other prose romances, as did Jean Maugin's *Nouveau Tristan* (1554). A number of earlier Arthurian texts were reworked, condensed, modernized or, in some cases, joined with other romances to constitute new cycles. An example of this reconstitution of earlier cycles is offered by *L'Hystoire du Sainct Greaal* (1516), a compilation that inserts *Perlesvaus* into a sequence including the *Estoire del Saint Graal*, the *Queste del Saint Graal* and a portion of the *Lancelot* proper. Although most of the modernized or recast romances were presented in prose, there are exceptions: around 1520 Pierre Sala, for example, composed, in addition to his *Tristan* romance, a new verse redaction of *Yvain*.

Arthurian themes were praised and embraced by some major sixteenth-century authors (e.g. the Pléiade poets Pierre de Ronsard and Joachim Du Bellay), but by that time the legend had come to be valued largely as history or pseudo-history, that is, as evidence of France's national or linguistic heritage, and not as imaginative literature possessing intrinsic interest. Later in the century some writers, including Montaigne, condemned Arthurian literature as fit only for the amusement of children. The continued publication of Arthuriana implies, however, that popular interest in the legend persisted, even though the stories of Arthur and the Round Table were disparaged by writers seeking to reject the past and forge a new literary aesthetic.

In any event the prestige and appeal of the Arthurian legend waned in France in the late sixteenth and the early seventeenth centuries, and this eclipse lasted well into the nineteenth century. During the seventeenth century, writers produced several serious texts that included chivalric stories and Arthurian figures, generally presented as models of comportment for young people.[1] Few of these texts have any significant connection with the romances of the Middle Ages. Other compositions of the time have even less to do with the legend. During this period by far the most popular Arthurian character was Merlin, who was the subject of light comedies, ballets and children's songs. Both during the seventeenth century and particularly during the eighteenth, there were efforts to present Arthurian stories to the reading public, usually in abridged or simply summarized form. In the eighteenth century, the Bibliothèque Universelle des Romans (BUR) published summaries or adaptations of a number of Arthurian texts, including the prose *Lancelot* and several of Chrétien de Troyes's romances (Busby 1998). In 1776 the Comte de Tressan produced his abridged retelling of the prose *Tristan*, which appeared in successive editions, and in 1869 Alfred Delvau assured the continuing popularity of that romance in the following century by including it in his collection of chivalric romances. Until well into the nineteenth century, these 'travestied' summaries (Glencross 1995, 48), which not only condensed but also modified and modernized events of the texts (and, in some cases, invented new characters or episodes), offered the only access, even for many scholars, to Arthurian literature.[2]

The nineteenth century saw a decided quickening of interest in Arthuriana (Glencross 1995, 58–88). A good many historians and other scholars discussed medieval literature, and partial translations or adaptations, or simply summaries, of early works continued to be published (Glencross 1995, chapters 2 and 4). However, the increased attention and access to Arthurian material did not bring immediate approbation, either public or scholarly. Arthurian texts were often thought either to embody unacceptable standards of morality, or to suffer by comparison with the *Chanson de Roland,* which was commonly taken to be an exemplary element of the French national heritage (the Oxford manuscript was discovered by Francisque Michel and edited by him in 1836).

As a result, very few Arthurian texts were published before the middle of the nineteenth century, and those that were edited by serious scholars most often presented the text in Old French, without benefit of either translation or glossary (Glencross 1995, 77). The most active editor of Arthurian material was Michel, who edited Robert de Boron's *Estoire dou Graal* under the title *Roman du Saint-Graal* (1841) as well as the verse Tristan texts of Beroul and Thomas and the two *Folie Tristan* poems (1835–9). Even by 1850 only one of Chrétien's romances, the *Charrette*, had been edited (see Tarbé edn, Jonckbloet edn and Glencross 1995, 78).

Presentations of Arthurian matter in a form accessible to the general reading public were rare. When Arthurian romances were published, and especially during the first half of the nineteenth century, they were in most cases significantly truncated summaries or disjointed excerpts. Prose romances were even more thoroughly neglected than were those in verse. In fact, Paulin Paris

(1868–77) was virtually the only major scholar to give the prose texts serious attention, both in essays and, notably, in his extensive, though still substantially abbreviated, retelling of prose romances in five volumes. Despite the deficiencies of his presentation, his efforts were significant for bringing to the fore a vast body of important material, most of it devoted to the Grail.

The composition of original Arthurian material began in earnest only after the mid-point of the nineteenth century. This statement is applicable both to treatments of the Tristan legend in particular and to the elaboration of other Arthurian subjects. Yet, despite this chronological correspondence, the fortunes and development of the Tristan material deviated so dramatically from that of other Arthurian subjects as to necessitate the two separate but complementary treatments set out here, beginning with 'non-Tristan' subjects. [NJL]

Arthur in Modern French Fiction and Film (exclusive of the Tristan Material)

It is virtually impossible to establish distinct and comprehensive categories within which modern French Arthurian compositions can be treated. The extraordinary variety, originality, and in some cases eccentricity, of much Arthurian literature in modern France require us to discuss tendencies, rather than unambiguous groupings. We can, however, discern two broad categories, as well as a number of marginally Arthurian texts and others that defy all efforts at categorization. The larger and more amorphous of the two major categories consists of works that, instead of renarrating the Arthurian legend or part of it, simply appropriate an Arthurian character or theme for use in the elaboration of a personal, philosophical or political statement (Lacy 2000, 125). The second and more familiar category comprises texts that retell part or all of the Arthurian story as it became known to French authors through Tennyson (Bowden 1930), Wagner or, more recently, medieval French sources. In both of these broad categories, the figure and work of Richard Wagner loom large, and modern French Arthurian literature includes a number of works that are strongly, and sometimes entirely, inspired by Wagnerian themes. Some, indeed, are devoted to the composer himself rather than to those themes. Finally, as suggested, there are a good many French Arthurian works that simply frustrate all efforts at categorization.

Arguably, the first modern French Arthurian composition of originality and literary import is Edgar Quinet's *Merlin l'enchanteur* (1860).[3] Quinet's massive text is an allegorical epic, with Merlin's exile representing both the author's own disillusion and the political and moral decadence Quinet perceived in a dispirited France suffering under Louis-Napoléon (Glencross 1995, 163–72; Lacy 1996, 377–8). Merlin undertakes voyages or pilgrimages, during which he meets significant personages from both the historical and the literary past. Eventually, as France is awakening from its torpor, Merlin undertakes the conversion of Satan, whose fall symbolically anticipates that of the Second Empire.

The Pre-Symbolist poet Paul Verlaine offers a further example of the appropriation of the legend, i.e. of using a motif to crystallize personal experience. Imprisoned for two years (1873–5) after shooting his friend Arthur Rimbaud, Verlaine expressed his remorse and pain by conceiving of his prison as a magical Arthurian castle in which he conducts a quest to forge a new identity (Dakyns 1996, 168). His ordeal is reflected in a number of his poems, most notably in his 1881 collection *Sagesse*. Furthermore, Verlaine is also among a group of poets who were powerfully influenced by Wagner. Gabriel Mourey, Stuart Merrill, Edouard Schuré and others published numerous pieces that either interpreted some Wagnerian themes or images in poetic form or simply offered 'homage to Wagner'. Verlaine's own contribution to this body of poetry included a 'Parsifal' sonnet that emphasized the Grail hero's efforts to resist temptation and remain pure.[4]

Other authors who exemplify the tendency towards the appropriation of Arthurian motifs or characters for personal or philosophical purposes include Jules Laforgue, Guillaume Apollinaire, arguably Jean Cocteau, Théophile Briant and perhaps also René Guénon. Laforgue's *Lohengrin, fils de Parsifal* uses Arthurian (or, more precisely, Wagnerian) themes as a basis for a satirical treatment of modern love and marriage (Baudry 1998*, 60–75, 91–4, 99–105). In *L'Enchanteur pourrissant*, Apollinaire's first prose composition, we follow a procession or pilgrimage of characters, representing Celtic, Christian, Greek and other mythologies, past the grave of Merlin, who is presented as an Anti-Christ. This simple structure offers Apollinaire what some critics have taken as an opportunity both to attack Christianity and to exorcize the remnants of his own faith. Apollinaire, like Quinet, also appears to have identified Merlin with himself (as a 'fatherless child') and with his own destiny (Forsyth 1972).

Cocteau's *Les Chevaliers de la Table Ronde* presents Merlin's spell as a kind of intoxication, whereas Galahad, the pure knight, is the agent of 'detoxification', countering Merlin's magic. It has been traditional for critics to see the play as a reflection of the author's admitted struggle against opium addiction. That interpretation, however, may be an oversimplification, and Jones (1999, 694) has recently argued that a simple biographical reading, although by no means inadmissible, misses much of the point: that Cocteau wishes to 'engage readers and spectators in an intricate game of identity, authenticity, and embodiment'.

A highly eccentric treatment of Arthurian themes, exploited for largely philosophical purposes, is offered in Briant's novel *Le Testament de Merlin*. Briant recounts the story of the magician but transforms it, having Merlin (here the founder of the chivalric system) eventually kill Mordred and return the sword to the lake before retiring to the forest, where he offers his revelations of esoteric truths to a young friend.

In *Le Roi du monde* René Guénon's project was to examine the entire history of the Grail, beginning with its origin in the emerald that dislodged from Lucifer's forehead at the time of his fall. It was entrusted to Adam and later to the Druids. The Grail quest is the primary function and justification of the Arthurian court. Montsalvat, at the centre of the world, represents the Land of Immortality, which is identified with the earthly paradise. Although Guénon traces the history of the Grail, his emphasis remains on a mystical vision of that history and of the redemptive power of the Vessel.

Like a number of the works discussed here, a 1991 novel by Breton author Philippe Le Guillou entitled *Immortels: Merlin et Viviane* proves difficult to classify. It presents the effects of Merlin's meeting with Viviane and might, to an extent, be considered a retelling of part of the Arthurian story. However, Le Guillou also uses Merlin as a mouthpiece for the exposition of esoteric principles. The author's intent here, as in several essays, is to 're-enchant' adventure and past tradition, countering the loss of wonder. He attempts to revivify the *matière de Bretagne*, which includes his native Brittany in particular, as well as the Celtic lands across the Channel.

Alongside these sometimes radical reinterpretations or appropriations of the Arthurian matter, we also have a number of comparatively full, if occasionally idiosyncratic, 'retellings' of the king's story.[5] Retellings are a renarration of part or all of the Arthurian legend that are set in a historical context, even if the intent is to modernize or modify the spirit of the story. From this point of view, Briant's and perhaps even Guénon's may, with effort, be interpreted as retellings. However, in contrast to Barjavel's work (see below), these two compositions appear remarkably personal and esoteric. The distinction is not always obvious, but it turns on the question of whether an author wishes to *tell* the Arthurian story or instead *use* it as a structure on which may be overlaid a philosophical, political or other vision.

Retellings of the Arthurian story are strikingly common in modern English-speaking traditions, but far less so in French. The causes for this difference in focus are complex and elusive, but, whatever the reasons, writers in English have been much more intent on recasting the legend of Arthur, either as historical fiction or as an effort to renew the mythic appeal of the Arthurian story. In contrast, French authors, rather than renew a historical narrative (of a British king, after all), have been more prone to seize on images, on symbols and on elements of the story that can crystallize a variety of philosophical concerns.

Nonetheless, modern French retellings of the Arthurian story include some outstanding and important literary creations, as well as some notable failures. Apart from the scholarly or semi-scholarly presentations of medieval Arthurian texts, the earliest of the memorable accomplishments in this category may well be two Parsifal works by Julien Gracq (Baudry 1998*, 60–75, 91–4, 99–195).

Strongly evident in these works is the influence of Wagner, which was prevalent during the later nineteenth century and discernible in writers such as Pierre Benoit.[6] Gracq's *Au Château d'Argol* of 1939 and *Le Roi Pêcheur*, a play composed in 1945 and presented in 1948, place more emphasis on Amfortas, the Grail King, than on the youthful Parsifal; the latter composition in particular draws from Wolfram von Eschenbach as well as from Wagner. In *Au Château d'Argol* Gracq inverts conventional motifs, having the blood from Amfortas's wound flow into the Grail, for example, rather than following tradition and having the blood from the Grail used to heal that wound. Gracq was powerfully influenced not only by Wagner and by Wolfram, but also by Breton themes: a number of his other works incorporate images of the Waste Land or of the forest of Brocéliande.

Other retellings include texts by Boris Vian, Romain Weingarten, René Barjavel, Michel Rio, Jean-Pierre Le Dantec, Jacques Roubaud and Florence Delay. The first of these, by Vian, is *Le Chevalier de neige*, a drama, staged in 1953, and later an opera, both with music by Georges Delerue. The 'Chevalier de neige' is Lancelot, so-called because of his white armour. Drawing from Jacques Boulenger's version of Arthurian material (see n. 5), Vian omits the Grail quest and concentrates on the human passions involved in the love affair of Lancelot and Guinevere, her condemnation and her rescue by Lancelot, the latter's war with Arthur, Mordred's treason and Arthur's departure for Avalon.

Weingarten's *Le Roman de la Table Ronde, ou le livre de Blaise* has the story told from the point of view of Blaise, Merlin's master and scribe. Weingarten offers a reasonably full and straightforward account of Arthurian events from the birth of Merlin to the death of the king, though the latter is narrated in a curiously perfunctory and anticlimactic manner. The novel also de-emphasizes the Lancelot–Guinevere–Arthur triangle and does not include the story of Tristan and Yseut.

For many tastes, one of the most successful and appealing of the retellings is Barjavel's *L'Enchanteur*. Merlin is the central figure of the novel, and Barjavel's focus remains on the magician's connection to the Grail and the quest. Merlin, we are told, had established the Round Table and initiated the Grail quest, and he had served as Perceval's tutor, preparing him for the quest. We learn the history of the Grail, which had been fashioned by Eve to receive the blood from Adam's side; it was broken after the Fall and repaired before the Last Supper. Although a brief summary suggests a serious and perhaps pious narrative, Barjavel makes Merlin into a fully 'human' and fallible character, often torn between his devotion to the quest and the erotic interests in Viviane (and sexual frustration) that threaten to compromise the quest.

Michel Rio also concentrates on the magician and on many of the familiar Arthurian events in his 1989 *Merlin*. In this instance, however, it is Merlin himself who, now one hundred years old, looks back and reflects on Arthurian history and on his own relationship with Viviane. Rio extended his exploration of Arthuriana with two novels, the first devoted to Morgan, the second to Arthur himself (Rio 1999; 2001). Both of them offer allusions to, or retellings of, Arthurian events, but Rio shows himself to be particularly interested in his characters and in their response to elements of the Arthurian story.

Memory had also been the theme of Jean-Pierre Le Dantec's 1985 novel *Graal-Romance*. The events of this work occur ten years after Arthur's death, when a cleric, commissioned to write the king's story, comes to Brocéliande to interview Guinevere, Merlin and Viviane, and to consult the available documents. Although memories are shown to be unreliable and contradictory, a portrait of Arthur ultimately emerges, and it is not a happy one: he is remembered as a mad, drunken, self-pitying failure.

Jacques Roubaud and Florence Delay cannot easily be discussed with any of the preceding authors. The two of them have composed a cycle of dramas that stands as the most ambitious and most intriguing Arthurian effort in modern France, and Roubaud has authored several other books on Arthurian themes.

The drama cycle, entitled *Graal-Théâtre*, was planned as a group of ten plays, though only six have been completed. Several were published separately, and they were then gathered in two volumes issued in 1977 and 1981.[7] The plays are *Joseph d'Arimathie*, *Merlin l'enchanteur*, *Gauvain et le chevalier vert*, *Lancelot du Lac*, *Perceval le Gallois* and *L'Enlèvement de Guenièvre* (Delay and Roubaud have pointed out that these six plays are in fact numbers II–VII in the series, and that the last planned play, *Blaise de Northombrelande*, is designed to be numbered X, but to stand at the head of the cycle and lead into the rest). If the titles and much of the material are familiar, the juxtaposition of events is often surprising. For example, in the first play, Joseph of Arimathea encounters the Questing Beast in a dream, and *Gauvain et le chevalier vert*, after recounting the beheading test known to readers of the Middle English *Sir Gawain and the Green Knight*, then presents a visit by Perceval to the Grail Castle. The play ends with Gauvain himself at the Grail Castle.

The material offered in the other dramas is similarly traditional and familiar, but reconfigured and recombined in decidedly original fashion, with scenes sometimes repeated from one play to another, manipulation of temporal sequence and knowledgeable and effective use of the interlace technique that characterizes the medieval Arthurian prose cycles. The dramatic material is drawn from the authors' serious and mature knowledge of medieval sources, from Chrétien de Troyes to the Vulgate Cycle to *Sir Gawain and the Green Knight*, the *Baladro del sabio Merlín* and the *Mabinogion*.[8]

Roubaud is also the author of *Graal fiction* (a mixture of fictional recreation with textual commentary)[9] and of a novel *Le Roi Arthur au temps des chevaliers et des enchanteurs.* In 1997 he published a novel entitled *Le Chevalier Silence: une aventure des temps aventureux*, an extraordinarily original text drawn from, and playing off, the medieval *Roman de Silence,* but pairing the character Silence with Walllwein, who is Gauvain's illegitimate son.

A frequent practice among Arthurian authors writing in English is to update the legend and set events in the modern world. French authors have, for whatever reason, been less concerned with offering updated Arthurian works. Two who have done so are Pierre Benoit and Georges Perec, though it may be more accurate to describe their creations as 'pseudo-Arthurian', meaning that they offer narratives that reflect Arthurian themes or motifs, without dramatizing or retelling the Arthurian legend at all. Benoit's 1957 novel *Montsalvat* recasts the story of the Grail quest in a modern context: France under the Occupation (Baudry 1991). A professor and a student are seeking the Grail in the south of France, as are a group of Nazi soldiers. This, however, is a destructive Grail, not a healing vessel, and it provokes crises, deaths and despair. Benoit, whose previous novels had offered frequent reflections of Arthurian themes, is here inspired by Wagner, by Catharist themes and especially by the writings of Otto Rahn,[10] to produce one of the most curious of modern Arthurian creations in France, reasonably conventional in its narrative methods, strikingly eccentric in its vision and context.

Perec's 1978 *La Vie mode d'emploi* has in common with Benoit's work the notion of a quest and the use of a number of Arthurian motifs. The Arthurian connections are stronger, however, in Perec's novel, which may be considered a parody of Arthuriana. Not only is the protagonist named Percival (Percival Bartlebooth) but there is a clear, if exceedingly peculiar, quest, and also an Avalon (though it is the island off the California coast), a painting of Joseph of Arimathea and a counterfeit Grail sold by the 'Galahad Society'. Percival's quest here is an extraordinarily unconventional one: he travels the world for a considerable part of his life, painting seascapes that are then to be cut into puzzles that will eventually be reassembled over a period of years and then destroyed.

French films on Arthurian subjects are not numerous, in contrast to the situation in English-speaking countries in particular. Apart from the Tristan films discussed below, and a number of Arthurian documentaries, there remain a small number of cinematic treatments of Arthurian materials. The two major ones date from the 1970s: Robert Bresson's *Lancelot du Lac* and Eric Rohmer's *Perceval le Gallois*.[11] Both of these films systematically, though in radically different ways, establish a distance between viewer and representation. Bresson accomplishes this by using unnatural sound effects, camera angles and the exclusion of much of the action from the frame. His film, drawing from the tradition of the prose romances, and in particular from the *Mort Artu*, begins when Lancelot and other knights return from their unsuccessful Grail quest. Lancelot still loves the queen but, despite his temptation, vows to remain chaste. Eventually, Guinevere returns to Arthur, and in the climactic war against Mordred the king is joined by Lancelot, who is killed in the conflict.

Rohmer, to a considerable extent, simply films the text of the Perceval sections of Chrétien de Troyes's *Perceval*, though adding a new ending in the form of a Passion Play. He even retains linguistic archaisms and uses stylized and clearly artificial sets and actors who move much like automata. In both films the effect is to reinforce the temporal and cultural distance between the story and the viewer and to emphasize the unreality of the Arthurian world.

One of the fascinating and problematic phenomena within the modern French conception and presentation of the legend is the existence of marginally Arthurian texts in which the Arthurian elements are ephemeral and elusive (or merely *allusive*). The novels of Benoit and Perec, discussed above, may be considered marginal, insofar as they seize upon Arthurian images, symbols or allusions and construct non-Arthurian narratives around them. Far more striking and challenging, though, is a work such as Robert Pinget's *Graal Flibuste*, a surrealistic quest novel (Henkels 1979). The title implies a Grail quest, but there appears to be no Grail, or at least it is not the object with which we are familiar, or, for that matter, an object at all. It is, instead, a person; the title of the novel, linking the Grail to a reference to piracy, is the name of the monarch of the strange land in which the protagonist travels. Among discernible Arthurian themes we find only the notion of the quest – if indeed it is a quest – and a reflection of the motif of the Waste Land. And even the purpose of the quest or voyage is uncertain, for just as the quester, having passed through extraordinary and very strange lands, arrives at a large gate and prepares to enter, the text ends. Long before Pinget's work, André Gide had offered an even more marginal, pseudo-Arthurian text in his 1892 *Voyage d'Urien*, in which a number of characters are given Arthurian names: Urien (traditionally Yvain's father), Morgain, Agloval, etc. But apart from those names and the fact that there is a voyage (but not necessarily a quest), it is difficult to discern anything Arthurian in this text.

Farther removed still from the legend of Arthur is a composition such as Benoîte Groult's erotic novel *Les Vaisseux du cœur*, in which the first-person narrator gives her lover the pet name of Gauvain, presumably in recognition of his physical beauty and his prowess. Otherwise, there is nothing discernibly Arthurian about the novel. With this novel and a great many other works we find ourselves in a literary grey area, where all narrative traces of the legend disappear, though Arthurian names and images (most often the Grail) may remain and provide a source of allusion recognizable, to varying degrees, by all readers.

The legend of King Arthur in France has attracted far fewer modern authors (and readers) than has been the case in English-speaking countries. As in an anglophone context, however, Arthurian compositions run the gamut from scholarly presentations of the narratives (e.g. Paulin Paris) to recreations such as that of Barjavel, and from updated versions recounting, for example, a Nazi quest for the Grail to creations that offer little more than a set of names and images with Arthurian associations. But even though the types of Arthurian texts in modern French may mirror those in English, the character of the French works is far more diverse and elusive.

The explanation for this striking difference must be in part the diversity of the sources of Arthurian material available to French writers (Lacy 2000, 122–3, 130). In English, the author standing clearly behind most modern Arthurian works is either Malory or Tennyson; modern French writers, on the other hand, have drawn inspiration from German sources (especially Wagner, but occasionally Wolfram von Eschenbach), from English (Tennyson in particular, though not exclusively), and finally from 'native' medieval French sources, originally in truncated and summarized form, now finally available in authoritative editions and reliable translations. These multiple sources of inspiration foster highly individual and often 'hybridized' versions of the Arthurian legend, making it, as previously noted, virtually impossible to establish unambiguous categories within which we can offer a productive description, much less an analysis, of groups of texts.

The notable exceptions to these generalizations about the chaos of the Arthurian tradition in modern France, that is, about the near absence of unifying themes and approaches, are provided by Tristan texts, which in most cases descend from clearly discernible sources, even as they develop original contours and interpretations. It is therefore to the story of Tristan and Yseut that we now turn. [NJL]

The Tristan Legend in Modern French Literature and Film[12]

Of all the medieval French literary works that history has bequeathed to us none has enjoyed the popularity in modern France of the romance of Tristan and Yseut, now recognized universally as a founding myth of Western civilization. Moreover, the legend's evolution throughout the nineteenth and twentieth centuries has been closely linked to scholarship. The prose *Tristan* was a best-seller in the Middle Ages, and as stated in our introduction this monumental romance, along with its continuations, kept the legend alive, if only barely, from the sixteenth to the early nineteenth centuries. It is, however, the extant fragments of the Old French verse romances (i.e. those of Beroul and Thomas), and indirectly Gottfried von Straßburg's poem, that have captivated twentieth-century audiences to the virtual exclusion of the prose *Tristan*.

Two signal events occurred in the nineteenth century that were to determine dramatically the legend's evolution in modern times. Richard Wagner's opera

Tristan und Isolde, completed in 1859, premiered in 1865, provoked a stunning revival of the legend and had a prodigious impact on the French conception of it. Using Gottfried, Wagner transformed the early medieval verse tradition, based on a conflict between love and law, into a tale of love and death. He endowed the lovers with a death wish, from the first act on the boat bound for Cornwall, when they consumed the potion, believing it to be poison, to the soaring 'love duet' of the second act, to the final *Liebestod* 'transfiguration' sung by Isolde (Yseut) before joining Tristan in death. The idea of Eros and Thanatos intertwined was an elegant formula that was bound to captivate the French imagination, especially those with a romantic or decadent bent. So it is not surprising that Wagner's influence was felt not only in the various dramas of the late nineteenth and early twentieth centuries, but also in numerous novels and poems in which the protagonists (not necessarily explicit recreations of Tristan and Yseut) embarked on a quest for idealized love that inevitably ended in death. Baudelaire, Mallarmé, Verlaine and their Symbolist successors were all inspired by Wagner in their quest for a new language exemplifying the artist's aspiration to escape from the material world towards the spiritual realm.[13]

The second event of the nineteenth century that was crucial to the development of the legend was the discovery and publication by Francisque Michel (1835) of the Anglo-Norman Tristan poems, notably the long-lost fragments of Beroul and Thomas. This remarkable discovery of the earliest known Tristan poems invested the French with the paternity of a legend that had seemed to belong to the Germans, especially after Wagner, and it incited Joseph Bédier to attempt to reconstruct, on the basis of the various extant medieval versions, the disparate elements of the two traditions, which he called the 'Common Version' (Beroul and Eilhart) and the 'Courtly Version' (Thomas and Gottfried). His *Roman de Tristan par Thomas* appeared in 1902, followed in 1905 by a volume of notes, including fragments of the Beroul–Eilhart tradition, designed to reconstitute the non-extant 'archetype'.

Before Bédier had finished this monumental task of erudition, he published his *Roman de Tristan et Iseut* (1900), destined to become the best-selling *Tristan* of the twentieth century, not only in France but throughout the world.[14] Bédier wished to acquaint the general public with the Old French legends through a modern French adaptation of a romance that might reflect the elusive 'archetype' (which he dated to *c*.1120) that he believed had nurtured the more primitive of the two Tristan traditions. However, his nineteenth-century sensitivity caused him to tone down both the lovers' deceit and Mark's cruelty and to imbue all three characters with the noblest of feelings. Although he intended to draw mostly on Beroul and Eilhart, he used for the beginning of the romance the Thomas–Gottfried tradition, which ended up permeating the entire work. Not only was he aiming at a unified style but also the 'courtly' tradition appealed more to Bédier, who had been nourished on nineteenth-century novels (Corbellari 1997). Consequently, despite his intention to 'repatriate' the legend, to reclaim it for the French, he remained steadfastly under the sway of Wagner and unwittingly reinforced the German composer's influence.

In 1939 Denis de Rougemont published his influential study *L'Amour et l'Occident*, tracing the origin of western romantic love back to the Tristan legend.[15] He based his conception of the legend largely on Wagner, who, he believed, had distilled its essence, and he quoted liberally from Bédier's romance, which he mistakenly took for a French translation of Beroul. He opened his study by quoting the first line of Bédier's work: 'Seigneurs, vous plaît-il d'entendre un beau conte d'amour et de mort?' (*Lords, would you like to hear a beautiful tale of love and death?*). This unforgettable beginning was to reinforce significantly the tendency to equate the legend with the love/death complex in the French collective memory, and would perpetuate the influence of Wagner, Bédier and Rougemont.

In the two-score years between the appearance of the *Roman de Tristan et Iseut* and that of *L'Amour et l'Occident* few serious attempts were made to challenge the supremacy of Bédier's romance. He himself, with Louis Artus, wrote a play based on his romance; this was performed in 1929. In 1934 Nicolas Ségur set out to do for the chivalric Tristan of the prose romances what Bédier had done for the verse versions. But, rather than presenting Tristan primarily as a knight he strung together freely, making a fairly coherent whole, episodes from the prose *Tristan* that reinforced the hero's image as a tragic lover. Dedicating his work to Wagner, he intended his romance as an illustration of how fate conspires against love that is too perfect. Pierre Champion also worked with the prose tradition, but he attempted a faithful modern French translation of the 'parties anciennes' (*old parts*) of the fifteenth-century prose *Tristan* contained in BNF, fr. 103 (edited by Bédier 1902–5, II, 321–95).

The only version that remotely rivalled Bédier's romance during this period was André Mary's *Tristan* (1937), whose long subtitle spoke volumes about the author's intention.[16] Finding Bédier's version too sober, he decided to draw on the entire tradition, combining the varied tones of Beroul, Thomas and Gottfried into one harmonic whole and infusing his prose with the movement, colour and breadth of these accounts. A poet much enamoured of medieval literature, Mary wove freely into his version narrative devices and motifs drawn from other romances and epics as well. Subsequent printings of this *Tristan* featured a preface first by Jean Giono and then by Denis de Rougemont, who compared Mary's 'baroque' style with Bédier's more classical one.

The 1940s produced two musical adaptations, bearing inevitably the imprint of both Wagner and Bédier: *Le Vin herbé* by the Swiss composer Frank Martin,[17] a secular oratorio for twelve solo voices with string and piano accompaniment based on three chapters of Bédier, and an opera by Sylvain Arlanc (and Paul Gautier?). Bédier's prose also inspired Gabriel Mourey to plan an opera with Claude Debussy, but it was never completed.

Indisputably, the Tristan event of the decade was Jean Delannoy's film *L'Éternel Retour*, which launched Jean Marais's screen career and struck a chord with audiences craving escape from the depressing reality of the German Occupation.[18] Much credit for the film belongs to Jean Cocteau, who wrote the screenplay, basing it on Bédier's outline and incorporating significant Wagnerian elements (transcendent love, identification of the potion with poison), but infusing the whole with his idiosyncratic obsession relating to all-consuming love and transformative death.[19] The potion has the effect of a slow-acting poison, and the lovers' final demise seems a product of their will (Maddux 1995). The pair, Patrice and Natalie, both 'orphans of the sea', clearly do not belong in this world. As they lie on the overturned boat in the finale, they are transformed into marble *gisants* (statues), and the old boathouse becomes a chapel as the music swells to a crescendo. The otherworldly dimension of the film is offset by wonderful moments of poetic realism resulting from Cocteau's ingenious transposition of the legend into modern times (Grimbert and Smarz 2002). For the barons and Frocin he substitutes a dysfunctional family, with a malevolent dwarf as a son who conspires incessantly against both his handsome cousin and the incandescent beauty brought home to be Mark's wife. Patrice discovers Natalie in a bar, where he rescues her from the bully Morolt, her *'fiancé'*; finally, he spends his 'exile' working as a mechanic in a garage owned by an old friend and his lovely sister Natalie, whom Patrice nearly marries.

The authors of subsequent reworkings in the 1940s and 1950s, especially illustrated versions with appeal for the general public, no doubt hoped to cash in on the success of *L'Éternel Retour*.[20] The film's imprint is plain in *Tristan et Yseult, amants éternels* (1946), by Marcelle Vioux, which appeared in a collection called 'Les Destinées Romanesques' (*Romantic Destinies*). The protagonists' feelings are recounted at great length, and Bédier's influence is palpable in the sympathetic portrayal of Tristan, Yseut and Mark, as is that of Wagner and Cocteau in the depiction of a love that transcends time and space.

At the opposite end of the spectrum from Vioux's popular romance is situated Paul Claudel's *Partage de midi* (1949).[21] Because Claudel based the work on an incident from his own life, he injected the Romantic ethos with a Christian perspective, drawing on the dramatic structure of Wagner's opera and exploiting stark oppositions that are eventually resolved: noon/midnight, life/death, reality/dream, even male/female. In the first act, Mesa, whose vow to devote himself to God has been 'rejected', is bound for China on an ocean liner when he falls passionately in love with a married woman, Ysé, a *femme fatale* who claims to carry death within her. The two yield to their mutual forbidden desire in the second act, set at night in a Hong Kong cemetery, recalling the garden both of Tristan and Yseut's nocturnal rendezvous and of the Fall of Adam and Eve. The third act ends with the lovers' death. Mesa, like Wagner's Tristan, though not for the same reason, welcomes the embrace of Night, and when Ysé joins him the two share in a rapturous transfiguration in which they are finally at one with each other for all eternity, but in the presence of God. Ysé, who dies on the stroke of midnight, is transformed from a malevolent to a redemptive force as she witnesses the break of noon separating Time and Eternity, the flesh and the spirit.

Besides the popular retellings that appeared in the wake of *L'Éternel Retour* and had no scholarly pretensions, several versions composed in the next couple of decades were by scholars determined to present the legend in a more authentic light and thus to remove the Romantic veneer that Bédier had applied (Grimbert 1998). Although they were careful to pay elaborate homage to their illustrious predecessor, their criticism was less muted than Mary's. The first wave of retellings was designed to recapture the tone of the twelfth-century Anglo-Norman poems, but the following wave also sought to remove the feudal context provided by Beroul and Thomas, in order to return the legend to its Celtic roots. All these scholars justified their initiative on the basis of research by Celticists (e.g. Henri Hubert, Jean Marx and Jean Markale). Thus, the tradition of retelling the legend for a modern audience continued to be nurtured by the fruits of scholarly research, as is particularly clear from the prefaces penned by Marx and Markale.

The first of these retellings was by Robert Bossuat (1951), who praised Bédier's scholarly work on the legend (1902–5), but criticized his 1900 romance; he reproached him for including only the elements of the legend that had appealed to him personally and for infusing his characters with his own feelings and making them witness to his own dreams. In his *Tristan et Iseut: conte du XIIe siècle, reconstitué*, Bossuat set out to succeed where Bédier had failed: to present one of the earliest incarnations of the legend, and, by drawing mostly on Beroul, to replicate as closely as possible the supposed 'archetype' of the legend.

Five years later, Pierre d'Espezel dedicated his reworking to Bédier's memory but rejected his mentor's notion of an early, unified tradition. Espezel's desire to underscore the variegated aspect of the legend is clear from the full title.[22] He intended to show how the legend had sprung from a Celtic and pagan culture where love was a fatality superior to social bonds. Eschewing Bédier's 'homogenized' characters, he portrayed them as a glorious mixture of contradictory traits; he reproduced Beroul and Thomas faithfully, except for passages he thought were later accretions, and filled in the gaps from sources he deemed to be the oldest, based on the existence of Celtic and Irish analogues.[23]

The third in the series of scholarly reworkings designed to bring the legend out of Bédier's shadow was René Louis's *Tristan et Iseult*. Louis pays homage to

Bédier and acknowledges the efforts of Mary, Bossuat and Espezel, but asserts the necessity of removing another layer of veneer obscuring what he believes to be the legend's true spirit. He carefully preserves and highlights all the traces of primitive or barbaric customs and eliminates the chivalric/courtly backdrop, which he considered a betrayal of the original legend on the part of Beroul and Thomas. His version, steeped in material culled from his research into Celtic culture, is curiously didactic, which actually attenuates the primitive tonality he hoped to achieve. But one innovation – his most daring departure from the extant texts – was to resonate powerfully with modern audiences at a time when feminists were turning their attention to Yseut. Knowing that in Celtic culture and myth women had considerable power, Louis causes Brangien, who recognizes that her mistress is in love with Tristan, deliberately to substitute the potion for the wine and entrust it to Yseut. The latter, just as consciously, drinks it and passes it to the man of her desires, thus taking her destiny into her own hands.

Michel Cazenave's 1985 'novel' (*Tristan et Iseut: roman*) can also be seen as an attempt to revise Bédier. In accordance with the object of the collection in which it appears, 'Les Grands Mythes fondateurs de l'Occident' (*The Great Founding Myths of the West*), the author sought to revitalize the 'myth' by penetrating beyond the extant texts to discover its Celtic, and even pre-Celtic roots. Rejecting both Wagner's romantic vision of the lovers' transcendent end, and the tragic overtones imposed by a Christian feudal perspective in the twelfth-century poems, he wished to show how Yseut and Tristan, creatures of the sun and moon respectively, participate in a common network linking all creatures in a universe presided over by a pre-Christian God of love. While his adherence to the traditional plot seems to belie this optimistic vision, the addition of significant details underscores the lovers' privileged situation within the universe: Tristan spends seven years (the moon's cycle) under the protection of women; the love potion is consumed at high noon on the eve of the summer solstice; the potion's effects wear off exactly three years later; the lovers die at midnight on the eve of the winter solstice. Following the lovers' death, Brangien and Kaherdin put the lovers side by side in an open boat and push it out to sea, watching it head towards Ireland or those Blessed Isles 'où l'amour n'a des lois que la lumière du soleil, la douceur de la harpe et le cœur de l'amante' (*where love is bound by no laws other than those of the sun's light, the harp's sweet sound and the heart of a woman in love*, 279).

Whereas the fragmentary state of the early texts had been a source of frustration for the authors of earlier reworkings, many in the last decades of the twentieth century saw it as an invitation to embroider on the main themes of the legend, to let one's imagination take wing in the interstices of the texts. This impulse can be seen in two apparently contradictory currents that were to dominate from around the mid-1960s: the tendency to poeticize the legend further, and the determination to demystify it. In both cases, the resultant works departed significantly, often radically, from the extant medieval versions.

The 'poetic' versions were generally composed by poets, some of them tapping into their regional roots. Yves Viollier situated his *Un Tristan pour Iseut* (1972) in his own rural, modern Vendée, where the natural setting and belief in the aphrodisiac power of certain herbs makes the legend more credible. Tristan comes to town one evening for the celebration of the new wine, fights with and kills a local youth, Morhout, then falls in love with Yseut at the farm where he is taken for treatment of his thigh wound. In his 1971 reworking, *Tristan et Yseult*, Michel Manoll, recognizing in Tristan a kindred soul nourished by the Celtic earth and the sea's relentless flow, portrayed the lovers as personified natural phenomena, lying beyond the reach of the ethics and conventions governing human relations and abandoning themselves to the realm of dreams and poetry.

The natural elements, especially the sea, figure prominently in three other versions by modern poets. In 1971 Mas-Felipe Delavouët published a 500-line Provençal poem, entitled *Ço que Tristan se disiè sus la mar*, that recounts the musings on the sea of the ailing hero who, like his 'older brother' Ulysses, yearns to be reunited with both the woman he loves and his homeland. Recalling his childhood marked by the sea and the alliance of the sun and love, Tristan knows that he is now a different self, seeking refuge, dreaming of the sun in the dimmer light of the dying day. Pierre Dalle Nogare's *Tristan et Iseut* (1977) shows the lovers following their predestined path as if in a dream. Sights and sounds are so many impressions appearing on the margins of their consciousness, like the flickering light in the sky and on the sea, to which they are extremely sensitive. This haunting prose poem begins with Tristan languishing on the sea bound for Ireland and ends with Yseut arriving in Brittany where she lies down with her dead lover and loses herself in him, echoing thus the opening lines of the prologue:

> Il arrive que l'amour et la mort soient un seul mot pour deux personnages: ainsi de Tristan et Iseut venus en ce monde pour se reconnaître, se nommer et se perdre l'un dans l'autre, et disparaître ensemble (Dalle Nogare 1977, 61).

> (*It can happen that love and death are a single word for two people: thus it was for Tristan and Yseut who came into this world to recognize and name each other, lose themselves in each other, and perish together.*)

Finally, Pierre Garnier's 'spatial poem' (*Tristan et Iseut, poème spatial*, 1981), the most radical of the poetic versions, reduces the legend to key words and elements, mostly contraries, which are arranged on the page in geometric forms indicating a relationship of creative tension. In this poem, as in the other two, the lovers, rejected by society and rejecting it, take refuge in the unity of nature, and trust that their love will be accomplished in eternity.

The principal subgroup in the texts that demystify the legend emphasizes the woman's perspective. Per-Jakez Hélias's three-act tragedy, *An Isild a-heul* or

Yseult seconde (1964), published in Breton with facing translation in modern French, focuses on Tristan's divided loyalties recounted from the viewpoint of his wife, who feels unjustly relegated to the role of refuge. Although she reproaches Tristan for narcissistically preferring an impossible love, she eventually comes to believe in their love. She reports that the sail is black in order to discover if the lovers are worthy of each other and, if they are, to fulfil their greatest wish: to be united in death.[24] Agnès Verlet's *Yseult et Tristan: théâtre* (1978), as the inversion in the title indicates, is another play that highlights the feminine perspective, concentrating on Yseut the Blonde and restoring to her the power that Celtic heroines possessed to choose their lovers and their own destiny. Portrayed as the Great Sun Goddess of the ancient Celts, she is the opposite of the romance heroine who submits to the paternal or conjugal yoke, but Tristan, unable to accept her gift of passionate love, dies from his refusal to relinquish the traditional image of woman he cherishes.

Demystification is also at work in the two most recent film versions of the legend.[25] Yvan Lagrange calls his critically acclaimed *Tristan et Iseult* (1972) a 'visual opera', because the stark, visual contrasts (with scenes filmed in Iceland and Morocco) and music (by the French rock group Magna, using a non-existent phonetic language) evoke the universal themes of the myth: love, eternity, madness, fatality, impressions retained from having read several versions of the legend and forgotten them. As the myth is freed from all strictures of plot, time and place, cultural values are subverted and traditional eroticism is openly denounced as poetic mystification (Payen 1979, 54). Louis Grospierre's *Connemara* (1990) is situated in a primitive Ireland, but the legend, though imbued with political overtones, is more recognizable. The hero, Loup, becomes the locus of conflicted loyalties: his passion for the redheaded Sedrid, his loyalty to his uncle and his affection for Brangien, a mixed-breed slave who loves and betrays him.

Two entries in the demystification category might be termed postmodern. Grigori Sturdza's *Tristan sans Isolde, roman d'après les cahiers de Stanislas Tugomir* (*Tristan without Isolde, a novel from the notebooks of Stanislas Tugomir*) (1972) tells of a young nobleman who resists possessing a village girl because his love for her is actually nourished on a refusal. His journal is initially an attempt at a cure, but the novel that is to be the end result is postponed indefinitely so that he can continue living his frustrated desire. If Sturdza's 'novel' is the pretext for a meditation on the theme of impossible love, Michel Tournier's short story *Tristan Vox* (1978) explores the power of persona. A radio announcer calling himself 'Tristan' begins receiving letters from a woman who signs herself 'Isolde'. Although he is totally unlike the image his voice projects, even his secretary is drawn to it and begins writing to him. When another man's picture is published under the name 'Tristan Vox', that man takes over the show and begins receiving letters from the first announcer's wife.

Works that attempt to demystify a cultural artefact actually testify to its enduring power, and clearly the Tristan legend is alive and well in France today, especially in the form that Bédier gave it. Indeed, his romance was one of three works included in the examination theme 'La Passion amoureuse' that students had to prepare in 1991–3 to qualify for entry into the scientific *grandes écoles*; it was also one of three novels to be studied in preparation for the 2000–1 *baccalauréat*. More surprisingly, perhaps, in 1996 the well-known Arabist André Miquel, who has discussed analogies between the story of Majnun and Layla and the Tristan legend, transposed Bédier's romance into Alexandrine verse.

Indications of the legend's continuing popularity abound. It has become the object of a beautifully illustrated *bande dessinée* (comic) realized by X. Josset and F. Bihel in a collection devoted to famous legends. *La Quête de la fille aux cheveux d'or* (1991) recounts the story only up to the consumption of the *philtre* which Yseut deliberately drinks before handing it to Tristan. Given the venerable tradition of the French–Belgian *bande dessinée*, this version has more than juvenile appeal, unlike the one penned by Michel Manoll in 1959, and more recently by Florence Ferrier, whose *Tristan et Iseult* (1994) appears in a collection that targets young readers and includes numerous illustrations ranging from manuscript miniatures to movie stills. At the other end of the spectrum, the prolific novelist Catherine Hermary-Vieille has penned a torrid romance in her *Rivage des adieux* (1990) that draws on Bédier, Rougemont, Louis and Cazenave. She infuses her characters with a curiously, sometimes jarringly, modern sensibility, and while retaining the feudal context plants Yseut firmly in Celtic soil; a strong-willed but sensitive woman, she seizes every occasion to perform a Celtic *lai* or recount a legend (usually on the theme of love and death). Hermary-Vieille bases the lovers' deaths on Thomas, but prolongs them by allowing us to follow Yseut into the afterlife to witness her ecstatic reunion with Tristan.

The legend was performed in Paris in 2001 as a thoroughly modern musical. Although the plot would be incomprehensible to anyone who does not know the legend, the Pierre Cardin production, directed by Thierry Harcourt, boasts many brilliant features, including costumes by Cardin and breathtaking choreography: the Taiji Kung Fu troop assumes various secondary roles, from the evil barons to the lepers, and, on the fringes of the stage, two aerial trapeze artists (the Farfadais) underscore the erotic content of the songs performed onstage by the lovers. Considerably less successful was Thierry Schiel's disappointingly Disneyfied version of the legend, which appeared in 2002 as a feature-length animation.

Despite the legend's entry into pop culture, its evolution in modern times has generally been marked by decisive dates in the world of scholarship. Michel's publication of the Anglo-Norman poems, and Bédier's erudite work on the Beroul and Thomas traditions, enabled the French to claim the legend as their own, and students of Celtic culture explored the legend's ties with a vibrant civilization that was all but eradicated by the Roman conquest of Gaul. And now a cluster of modern editions has guaranteed the medieval poems a secure place in the French literary canon. In 1974 Payen published the twelfth- and thirteenth-century fragments in modern French translation with an edition in Old French at the bottom of the page. In 1989 the useful Lettres Gothiques collection offered a bilingual edition of the same poems on facing pages, along with the first modern French translation of Brother Robert's Old Norse *Saga*. But the crowning moment was the appearance of the prestigious Pléiade edition (1995) that marked both the 'canonization' of the legend and the recognition that it was an eminently European phenomenon. *Tristan et Yseut: les premières versions européennes* offers a bilingual edition of all the Old French poems and fragments, including the newly discovered Carlisle Fragment and the Tristan section of the *Roman de la poire*, followed by French translations of the German poems (Eilhart, Gottfried, Ulrich and Heinrich), the Old Norse *Saga*, the Middle English *Sir Tristrem*, six episodes of the Italian *Tavola ritonda*, several Scandinavian songs and four episodes from the Czech version. It is a delicious irony that the only important work (necessarily) missing from this comprehensive 'European' edition (besides the 'Book of Sir Tristram' from Malory's *Morte Darthur*) is the voluminous prose *Tristan*, the work that served as a pilot-light during the 'dark ages' of the legend linking the Middle Ages to modern times. **[JTG]**

Notes

[1] See Lacy ed. 1991* and Lacy and Ashe 1998. These two sources offer some information concerning the few original Arthurian texts produced in France between the Renaissance and the mid-nineteenth century – subjects noted only briefly in this chapter.

[2] On the composition and publication of Arthurian texts during the sixteenth century, see Frappier 1965–6. For the eclipse and later rediscovery of the Arthurian legend, as well as a brief survey of modern French Arthurian literature, see Lacy ed. 1991*, 162–6, and Lacy and Ashe 1998, 139–47.

[3] Quinet's is first in its importance, but it was preceded by Auguste Creuzé de Lesser's *Les Chevaliers de la Table Ronde* (Paris, 1812). This work was an unfortunate attempt to draw on Ariosto in order to present to a French public the full story of Arthur and the Round Table (see Glencross 1995, 158–63).

[4] To most readers this poem will be especially familiar because one of its lines, 'Et ô ces voix d'enfants, chantant dans la coupole!' ('*And oh, those children's voices, singing in the dome!*'), was used by T. S. Eliot in *The Waste Land*.

[5] Entirely different kinds of retellings are offered by scholars and writers such as Paulin Paris and Jacques Boulenger; these are modernizations that generally conform to the accounts offered by their medieval models. Paris was mentioned above; for Boulenger, see Boulenger 1922–3. A somewhat different approach was taken by Xavier de Langlais (1956–75), who identifies his five-volume

work as a 'renewal' of the legend; it is based on the Vulgate Cycle and on other French texts, but it also recasts material borrowed from Wolfram von Eschenbach, the *Mabinogion* and other sources.

⁶ A striking example, in addition to the poets mentioned above, is Joséphin Péladan. In 1888 he visited Bayreuth and was so moved by Wagnerian art and themes that he founded a Grail order, of which he was Grand Master, the purpose of which was to revive the Christian esoteric tradition and create a new chivalric tradition. In 1893 he wrote *Le Mystère du Graal*, an attempt to fuse eastern, Grail and Wagnerian traditions (Péladan 1893; Baudry 1991; Lacy 1996, 354).

⁷ The Merlin, Gauvain and Lancelot plays were presented in Marseille in 1979. On Delay and Roubaud, see Lacy 2000, 127–30, and Baudry 1998*, 168–9.

⁸ They also identify a number of modern sources, ranging from Calderón to the works of Jean Markale.

⁹ In *Graal fiction* Roubaud informs us playfully that this is but the first of twenty-six planned volumes.

¹⁰ Rahn, an admirer of René Guénon's *Le Roi du monde* and author of the 1933 *Kreuzzug gegen den Gral* (Crusade against the Grail), served also as a source of inspiration for Alfred Rosenberg, the principal theorist of Nazi racial policies. In addition to the role his book played in Benoit's novel, Rahn's theory of a Catharist Grail led Raymond Escholier and Maurice Gardelle to compose *Le Secret de Montségur* (Paris, 1952), in which the Grail quester is Richard Wagner himself.

¹¹ See Rider, Hull and Smith 1991; 2002; Grimbert 2000. A more recent Arthurian film, Denis Llorca's 1990 *Chevaliers de la Table Ronde*, is a four-hour reduction of his far lengthier 1984 theatrical presentation entitled *Le Cycle du roi Arthur*. This film, inspired by *La Queste del Saint Graal*, presents a panorama of events from Merlin's birth to Galahad's triumph in the Grail quest. It met with little critical or popular success.

¹² For this section I have drawn on material from Grimbert ed. 1995*, lxv–lxxix, and two entries in Lacy ed. 1996c, 162–6, 609–11. The form Yseut is used throughout except in titles of works and in quotations where a variant spelling occurs.

¹³ The *Revue wagnérienne* was founded in 1885. On Wagner's impact on world literature, see Furness 1982. On the legend's reception in France from the late eighteenth to the early twentieth century, see Linden 1988.

¹⁴ 'The book [*Le Roman de Tristan et Iseut*], in just twenty years after its appearance, was translated into German (twice), Dutch, Swedish, English, Greek, Czech, Norwegian, Italian and Catalan. The 576th edition appeared in 1946, and the *Figaro littéraire*, choosing in 1957 the twelve best French love novels of the half century, mentioned Bédier's book favourably (Corbellari 1996, 276). See Corbellari 2000; Gallagher 1995; Grimbert 1998; Schaefer 1991.

¹⁵ In 1940 Rougemont's *L'Amour et l'Occident* was published in Great Britain as *Passion and Society*, and in the United States as *Love in the Western World*.

¹⁶ The subtitle reads: *La merveilleuse histoire de Tristan et Iseut et de leurs folles amours et de leur fin tragique, avec toutes les aventures s'y rapportant, restituée en son ensemble et nouvellement écrite dans l'esprit des grands conteurs d'autrefois selon la droite poétrie et rhétorique gallicane.* This version is still available, reissued most recently in 2000 by Folio (the preface is by Rougemont).

¹⁷ Martin records his debt to Bédier's prose, which affected him 'by its extraordinary sense of rhythm, proportion, and exacting psychological movement' (Corbellari 1996, 276).

¹⁸ Two other film versions of the legend, both silent, preceded this one: Capellani (*Tristan et Yseult*, 1909), an attempt to bring opera to the screen, and Mariaud (*Tristan et Yseut*, 1920); see Harty 1999.

¹⁹ Cocteau also wrote the texts for the Moroccan film by Swoboda (*Noces de sable*, 1949), a retelling of an Islamic legend in which he recognized analogies with the Tristan legend.

²⁰ E.g. Vertut 1945, Nanteuil 1947, Reille 1951 and Gautier 1956.

²¹ An earlier draft dates from 1906. Other, less innovative plays include those by Silvestre

(*Tristan de Léonois*, 1897), Saint-Georges de Bouhélier (*Tragédie de Tristan et Iseult*, 1923), Moerman (*Tristan et Yseult*, 1936) and Fabre (*Tristan et Yseult*, 1945).

[22] The full title is: *Tristan et Iseut, renouvelé d'après les manuscrits de Thomas, des deux Béroul et de la 'Folie Tristan' de Berne conférés avec la 'Saga' du Frère Robert, avec Eilhart d'Oberg et Gottfried von Strasbourg*. The combination of homage and justification found in Espezel's introduction is echoed in the preface where Marx describes the 'scientific' reasons (based on recent research) validating the decision to propose a new version of the legend, one that Marx claimed would have met with Bédier's approval.

[23] Breton renderings of the legend also indicate an interest in its Celtic origins; see Langlais 1958 and Payen 1979.

[24] Another piece that highlights the second Yseult is Gastaud 1975 (*Yseult aux blanches mains: tapissererie d'un long hiver*); it consists of six chants subdivided into scenes set in Carhaix.

[25] Truffaut's *La Femme d'à côté* (*The Woman Next Door*, 1981), produced by La Carosse d'or, contains many elements associated with the Tristan legend, but there is no evidence that the director had this legend in mind; see Grimbert 1999.

Reference List

For items accompanied by an asterisk, see the General Bibliography.

Modern French Arthurian Literature and Film (exclusive of the Tristan material)

Editions of Medieval Texts

Le Roman de la charrette d'après Gautier Map et Chrestien de Troyes. Ed. by W. J. A. Jonckbloet (The Hague, 1850).
Le Roman du chevalier de la charrette par Chrétien de Troyes et Godefroy de Laigny. Ed. by P. Tarbé (Reims, 1849).
Robert de Boron, *Roman du Saint-Graal*. Ed. by F. Michel (Bordeaux, 1841).
Sala, Pierre. *Tristan, roman d'aventure du XVIᵉ siècle*. Ed. by Lynette Muir (Geneva, 1958).
Tressan, Comte de, L.-E. *Histoire de Tristan de Léonois et de la reine Yseut*, Bibliothèque Universelle des Romans (Paris, 1776), 53–239.
Tristan: recueil de ce qui reste des poëmes relatifs à ses aventures. Ed. by F. Michel, 3 vols (London and Paris, 1835–9).
Tristan de Léonois. Ed. by A. Delvau in vol. 4 of his *Collections des romans de chevalerie mis en prose française moderne*, Bibliothèque Bleue, 30 vols (Paris, 1869).

Primary Sources

Anon. 1498. *Prophecies de Merlin*, Paris.
Anon. 1516. *L'Hystoire du Sainct Greaal*, Paris.
Apollinaire, G. 1909. *L'Enchanteur pourrissant*, Paris.
Barjavel, R. 1984. *L'Enchanteur*, Paris.
Briant, T. 1975. *Le Testament de Merlin*, Nantes.
Cocteau, J. 1937. *Les Chevaliers de la Table Ronde*, Paris.
Creuzé de Lesser, A. 1812. *Les Chevaliers de la Table Ronde*, Paris.
Delay, F., and J. Roubaud. 1977. *Graal-Théâtre*, Paris.
Delay, F., and J. Roubaud. 1981. *Joseph d'Arimathie et Merlin l'Enchanteur: Graal-Théâtre*, Paris.

Escholier, R., and M. Gardelle. 1952. *Le Secret de Mont-Ségur*, Paris.

Gide, A. 1892. *Le Voyage d'Urien*, Paris.

Groult, B. 1988. *Les Vaisseux du cœur*, Paris.

Guénon, R. 1925. *Le Roi du monde*, Paris.

Laforgue, J. 1886. *Lohengrin, fils de Parsifal*, Paris.

Le Dantec, J.-P. 1985. *Graal-Romance*, Paris.

Le Guillou, P. 1991. *Immortels: Merlin et Viviane*, La Gacilly.

Maugin, J. 1554. *Le Premier Livre du nouveau Tristan prince de Leonnois, chevalier de la Table Ronde et d'Yseulte, Princesse d'Yrlande, Royne de Cornoüaille*, Paris.

Paris, P. 1868–77. *Les Romans de la Table ronde mis en nouveau langage et accompagnés de recherches sur l'origine et le caractère de ces grandes compositions*, 5 vols, Paris.

Péladan, J. 1893. *Le Mystère du Graal*, Paris.

Perec, G. 1978. *La Vie mode d'emploi, romans*, Paris.

Quinet, E. 1860. *Merlin l'enchanteur*, 2 vols, Paris.

Rio, M. 1989. *Merlin*, Paris.

Rio 1999. *Morgane*, Paris.

Rio 2001. *Arthur*, Paris.

Roubaud, J. 1978. *Graal fiction*, Paris.

Roubaud 1997. *Le Chevalier Silence: une aventure des temps aventureux*, Paris.

Sala, P. 1522. *Le Chevalier au lion*.

Verlaine, P. 1881. *Sagesse*, Paris.

Vian, B. 1974. *Le Chevalier de neige*, Paris.

Weingarten, R. 1983. *Le Roman de la Table Ronde, ou le livre de Blaise*, Paris.

Films

Bresson, R. 1974. *Lancelot du Lac*, Mara Films.

Rohmer, E. 1978. *Perceval le Gallois*. Produced by Margaret Menegoz, Gaumont-Films du Losange.

Llorca, D. 1990. *Chevaliers de la Table Ronde*, Les Films du Jeudi.

Studies

Baudry 1991. 'Échos arthuriens dans les romans de Pierre Benoit', in Van Hoecke, Tournoy and Verbeke eds. 1991*, 491–508.

Boulenger, J. 1922–3. *Les Romans de la Table Ronde, nouvellement rédigés*, 4 vols, Paris.

Bowden, M. 1930. *Tennyson in France*, Manchester.

Busby, K. 1998. 'Roman breton et chanson de geste au XVIIIe siècle', in D. P. and M. J. Schenck eds *Echoes of the Epic: Studies in Honor of Gerard J. Brault*, Birmingham, AL, 17–48.

Dakyns, J. R. 1996. 'French Symbolism', in Lacy ed. 1996c*, 168–9.

Forsyth, L. B. 1972. 'Apollinaire's Use of Arthurian Legend', *Esp*, 12:1, 26–36.

Frappier, J. 1965–6. 'Les Romans de la Table Ronde et les lettres en France au XVIe siècle', *RPh*, 19, 178–93; repr. in J. Frappier, *Amour courtois et Table Ronde*, Geneva, 1973, 265–81.

Glencross, M. 1995. *Reconstructing Camelot: French Romantic Medievalism and the Arthurian Tradition*, Cambridge, 58–88.

Grimbert, J. T. 2000. 'Distancing Techniques in Chrétien de Troyes's *Li Contes del Graal* and Eric Rohmer's *Perceval le Gallois*', *Arthuriana*, 10:4, 33–44.

Henkels, R. M. 1979. *Robert Pinget: The Novel as Quest*, University, AL.

Jones, C. M. 1999. 'S/X: Fictions of Embodiment in Cocteau's *Les Chevaliers de la Table Ronde*', *FR*, 72, 687–95.

Lacy, N. J. 1996. 'French Arthurian Literature (Modern)', in Lacy ed. 1996c*, 162–6.

Lacy 2000. 'From Medieval to Post-Modern: The Arthurian Quest in France', *SAR*, 65, 114–33.

Langlais, X. de. 1956–75. *Le Roman du roi Arthur*, 5 vols, Paris.

McLendon, W. 1968. 'Thèmes wagnériens dans les romans de Julien Gracq', *FR*, 41, 539–48.
Rider, J., R. Hull, and C. Smith. 1991. 'The Arthurian Legend in French Cinema: Robert Bresson's *Lancelot du Lac* and Eric Rohmer's *Perceval le Gallois*', in Harty ed. 1991*, 41–56; revised in Harty ed. 2002*, 149–62.

The Tristan Legend in Modern French Literature and Film

Editions of Medieval Texts

Le Roman de Tristan par Thomas: poème du XII. Ed. by J. Bédier, 2 vols, SATF (Paris, 1902–5).
Tristan et Iseut: les poèmes en français, la Saga norroise. Ed. and transl. by D. Lacroix and P. Walter (Paris, 1989).
Tristan et Yseut – les premières versions européennes. Ed. by C. Marchello-Nizia et al. (Paris, 1995).
Les Tristans en vers. Ed. and transl. by J.-C. Payen (Paris, 1974).

Primary Sources

Bédier, J. 1900. *Le Roman de Tristan et Iseut*, Paris.
Bédier, J., and L. Artus. 1929. *Tristan et Iseut: pièce en trois actes, un prologue et huit tableaux. La Petite Illustration*, no. 434 (15 July 1929); repr. Paris, 1944.
Bossuat, R. 1951. *Tristan et Iseut: conte du XII siècle, reconstitué*, Paris.
Cazenave, M. 1985. *Tristan et Iseut: roman*, Paris.
Champion, P. 1938. *Le Roman de Tristan et Yseut: traduction du roman en prose du quinzième siècle*, Paris; rev. edn 1958 by P. Galand-Pernet; 1979. *Tristan et Iseut*, preface by M. Tournier.
Claudel, P. 1949. *Partage de midi*, Paris.
Dalle Nogare, P. 1977. *Tristan et Iseut*, lithographs by Peverelli, Paris.
Dalle Nogare 1991. *Tristan et Iseut, le manuscrit de Vienne, codex 2537, commenté par Michel Cazenave et Edmond Pognon*, Paris.
Delavouët, M.-F. 1971. *Ço que Tristan se disiè sus la mar*, in his *Pouèmo: poèmes provençaux avec traduction française*, Paris, I, 173–217.
Espezel, P. d'. 1956. *Tristan et Iseut, renouvelé d'après les manuscrits de Thomas, des deux Béroul et de la Folie Tristan de Berne conférés avec la Saga du Frère Robert, avec Eilhart d'Oberg et Gottfried von Strasbourg*, preface by J. Marx, Paris.
Fabre, L. 1945. *Théâtre fabuleux: Tristan et Yseult, légende dramatique en 2 actes*, Paris.
Ferrier, F. 1994. *Tristan et Iseult*, Vanves.
Garnier, P. 1981. *Tristan et Iseut, poème spatial*, Paris.
Gastaud, E. 1975. *Yseult aux blanches mains: tapissererie d'un long hiver*, photo illustrations by the author, Paris; repr. 1989, Lyon.
Gautier, B. 1956. *Tristan et Iseut*, Paris.
Hélias, P.-J. 1964. *An Isild a-heul* or *Yseult seconde, tragédie en trois actes et un épilogue*, Brest.
Hermary-Vieille, C. 1990. *Le Rivage des adieux*, Paris.
Josset, X., and F. Bihel. 1991. *La Quête de la Fille aux cheveux d'or*, Brussels.
Langlais, X. de. 1958. *Tristan hag Izold*, Brest; French transl. 1994 by A. Roparz as *Tristan et Iseult*, Rennes.
Louis, R. 1972. *Tristan et Iseult . . . renouvelé en français moderne d'après les textes des XII et XIII siècles*, Paris.
Manoll, M. 1959. *Tristan et Yseult*, illustrated by G. Valdès, Paris.
Manoll 1971. *Tristan et Yseult*, illustrated by M. Gourlier, Paris.
Mary, A. 1937. *Tristan: la merveilleuse histoire de Tristan et Iseut et de leurs folles amours et de leur fin tragique, avec toutes les aventures s'y rapportant, restituée en son ensemble et nouvellement écrite dans l'esprit des grands conteurs d'autrefois selon la droite poétrie et rhétorique gallicane*, Paris.

Miquel, A. 1996. *Tristan et Iseut, d'après Joseph Bédier*, Paris.
Moerman, E. 1936. *Tristan et Yseult*, Brussels.
Nanteuil, G. 1947. *Tristan et Iseut, adaptation*, illustrated by J. Camus, Paris.
Reille, J.-F. 1951. *Un conte d'amour et de mort. Le roman de Tristan et Yseult renouvelé ... d'après le roman en prose français, les textes de Béroul, Thomas et Gottfried de Strasbourg*, Paris.
Saint-Georges de Bouhélier (G. Lepelletier de Bouhélier). 1923. *Tragédie de Tristan et Iseult, pièce en 4 actes et 18 tableaux*, Paris.
Ségur, N. 1934. *Nouvelles amours de Tristan et Iseult tirées des anciens romans*, Paris.
Silvestre, A. 1897. *Tristan de Léonois, drames en 3 actes et 7 tableaux dont 1 prologue en vers*, Paris.
Sturdza, G. 1972. *Tristan sans Isolde, roman à faire d'après les cahiers de Stanislas Tugomir*, Paris.
Tournier, M. 1978. *Tristan Vox*, in M. Tournier, *Coq de Bruyère*, Paris, 1980.
Verlet, A. 1978. *Yseult et Tristan: théâtre*, preface by J. Markale, Paris.
Vertut, G. 1945. *La Légende de Tristan et Iseut, poème renouvelé*, Paris.
Viollier, Y. 1972. *Un Tristan pour Iseut; Raymonde: récits*, Les Sables d'Olonne.
Vioux, M. 1946. *Tristan et Yseult, amants éternels*, Lyon.

Musical Adaptations

Arlanc, S. 1943. *Tristan et Yseut: version nouvelle d'après la légende des trouvères*, Rodez.
Demelemester, M., and J.-J. Genevard (music), J. Berthel (text). 2001. *Tristan & Yseult, 'légende musicale'*, produced by P. Cardin, Paris.
Martin, F. 1943. *Le Vin herbé*, Vienna.
Wagner, R. *Tristan und Isolde*. Opera Guide 6 (London, 1981).

Film Adaptations

Capellani, A. 1909. *Tristan et Yseult*, Pathé.
Delannoy, J. 1943. *L'Éternel Retour*, Discina International. Screenplay by J. Cocteau, music by G. Auric.
Grospierre, L. 1990. *Connemara*, Lapaca Productions.
Lagrange, Y. 1972. *Tristan et Iseult*, Film du Soir.
Mariaud, M. 1920. *Tristan et Yseut*, Nalpas.
Schiel, T. 2002. *Tristan et Iseut*, Onira Productions.
Swoboda, A. 1949. *Noces de sable*, Studio Maghreb. Texts by J. Cocteau.
[Truffaut, F. 1981. *La Femme d'à côté* (*The Woman Next Door*), La Carosse d'or.]

Studies

Corbellari, A. 1996. 'Joseph Bédier, Philologist and Writer', in R. H. Bloch and S. G. Nichols eds *Medievalism and the Modernist Temper*, Baltimore and London, 269–85.
Corbellari 1997. *Joseph Bédier: écrivain et philologue*, Geneva.
Corbellari 2000. 'Joseph Bédier: (d')écrire la passion: l'écriture et la fortune du *Roman de Tristan et Iseut*', in M. Gally ed. *La Trace médiévale et les écrivains d'aujourd'hui*, Paris, 107–20.
Furness, R. 1982. *Wagner and Literature*, Manchester.
Gallagher, E. J. 1995. '"This too you ought to read": Bédier's *Roman de Tristan et Iseut*', in Grimbert ed. 1995*, 425–50.
Grimbert, J. T. 1996. 'Tristan and Isolde in Modern French Versions', in Lacy ed. 1996c*, 609–11.
Grimbert 1998. 'In Bédier's Shadow: French Prose Retellings of the *Roman de Tristan et Iseut* (1937–85)', *Tris*,18, 77–91.
Grimbert 1999. 'Truffaut's *La Femme d'à côté* (1981): Attenuating a Romantic Archetype – Tristan and Iseult?', in Harty ed. 1999a, 183–201.

Grimbert, and R. Smarz 2002. '*Fable* and *Poésie* in Cocteau's *L'Éternel Retour*', in Harty ed. 2002*, 220–34.

Harty, K. J. ed. 1999a. *King Arthur on Film: New Essays on Arthurian Cinema*, Jefferson, NC, and London.

Harty 1999b. *The Reel Middle Ages: American, Western and Eastern European, Middle Eastern, and Asian Films about Medieval Europe*, Jefferson, NC, and London.

Lacy, N. J. 1996. 'French Arthurian Literature (Modern)', in Lacy ed. 1996c*, 162–6.

Linden, B. 1988. *Die Rezeption des Tristanstoffs in Frankreich vom Ende des 18. bis zum Beginn des 20. Jahrhunderts*, Frankfurt and New York.

Maddux, S. 1995. 'Cocteau's Tristan et Iseut: A Case of Overmuch Respect', in Grimbert ed. 1995*, 473–504.

Payen, J.-C. 1979. 'Le *Tristan et Iseult* de Lagrange comme un anti-Tristan', *Tris*, 4:2, 51–6.

Rougemont, D. de. 1939. *L'Amour et l'Occident*, Paris; rev. edn 1956.

Schaefer, J. T. 1991. 'The French Modern Prose *remaniements* of Tristan', in Van Hoeke, Tournoy and Verbeke eds. 1991*, II, 462–78.

Selcer, R. W. 1979. 'Yvan Lagrange: Impressions of a Filmmaker', *Tris*, 4:2, 44–50.

GENERAL BIBLIOGRAPHY

Glyn S. Burgess

This Bibliography, which complements the Reference Lists found at the end of each chapter, includes chiefly works published since 1980.

Bibliographies

The Arthurian Bibliography, I: Author Listing, C. E. Pickford and R. Last eds (Cambridge and Totowa, NJ, 1981); II: *Subject Index*, C. E. Pickford and R. Last eds (Cambridge and Totowa, NJ, 1983); III: *1978–1992, Author Listing and Subject Index*, C. L. Palmer ed. (Cambridge, 1998); IV: *1993–1998, Author Listing and Subject Index*, E. Barber ed. (Cambridge, 2002).

Arthurian Legend and Literature: An Annotated Bibliography, I: *The Middle Ages*, E. Reiss, L. H. Reiss and B. Taylor eds (New York, 1984).

Bibliographical Bulletin of the International Arthurian Society/Bulletin bibliographique de la Société Internationale Arthurienne (Paris 1949–66, Nottingham, 1967–75; Paris, 1976–84; Madison, WI, 1985–). [*BBIAS*]

Specialist Journals

Arthurian Literature. First published in 1981 (vols 1–6, Woodbridge, Suffolk and Totowa, NJ; vols 7–9, Cambridge and Wolfeboro, NH; vols 10– , Cambridge).

The Arthurian Yearbook. Three vols published (New York, 1991–3), K. Busby ed.; later incorporated into vol. 17 of *Arthurian Literature* (1999).

Arthuriana. First published in 1994 (Dallas, TX) and incorporating *Quondam et Futurus: A Journal of Arthurian Interpretations* (1990–3).

Studies

Arrathoon, L. A. ed. 1984. *The Craft of Fiction: Essays in Medieval Poetics*, Rochester, MI.

Atanassov, S. 2000. *L'Idole inconnue: le personnage de Gauvain dans quelques romans du XIIIe siècle*, Orleans.

Barber, R. W. 2004. *The Holy Grail: Imagination and Belief*, London.

Barron, W. R. J. ed. 1999. *The Arthur of the English: The Arthurian Legend in Medieval English Life and Literature*, Cardiff, 1999; rev. paperback edn 2002.

Baswell, C., and W. Sharpe. 1988. *The Passing of Arthur: New Essays in Arthurian Tradition*, New York and London.

Baudry, R. 1998. *Graal et littératures d'aujourd'hui, ou les échos de la légende du Graal dans la littérature française contemporaine*, Rennes.

Baumgartner, E. 1991. 'Retour des personnages et mise en prose de la fiction arthurienne au XIIIe siècle', *BBIAS*, 43, 297–314.

Besamusca, B., W. P. Gerritsen, C. Hogetoorn, and O. S. H. Lie eds 1994. *Cyclification: The Development of Narrative Cycles in the chanson de geste and the Arthurian Romances*, Amsterdam, Oxford, New York, etc.

Bloch, R. H. 1983. *Etymologies and Genealogies: A Literary Anthropology of the Middle Ages*, Chicago.

Bogdanow, F. 1984. 'The Changing Vision of Arthur's Death', in J. H. M. Taylor ed. *Dies illa: Death in the Middle Ages*, Liverpool, 107–23.

Bogdanow 1986. 'La Chute du royaume d'Arthur: évolution du thème', *Rom*, 107, 504–19.

Boutet, D. 1985. 'Carrefours idéologiques de la royauté arthurienne', *CCM*, 28, 3–17.

Boutet 1999. *Formes littéraires et conscience historique: aux origines de la littérature française (1100–1250)*, Paris.

Boutet 2000. 'Le Comique arthurien', *BBIAS*, 52, 323–51.

Bozóky, E. 1981. 'Les Éléments religieux dans la littérature arthurienne', *Cahiers du Cercle Ernest Renan*, 122, 125–37.

Bozóky 1984. 'En attendant le héros ... (pour une typologie de l'orientation de l'itinéraire du héros dans le roman arthurien)', in G. Mermier ed. *Courtly Romance: A Collection of Essays*, Detroit, 23–45.

Braswell, M. F., and J. Bugge eds 1988. *The Arthurian Tradition: Essays in Convergence*, Tuscaloosa, AL.

Bromwich, R., A. O. H. Jarman, and B. F. Roberts eds 1991. *The Arthur of the Welsh: The Arthurian Legend in Medieval Welsh Literature*, Cardiff; paperback edn 1999.

Brownlee, K., and M. S. Brownlee eds 1985. *Romance: Generic Transformation from Chrétien de Troyes to Cervantes*, Hanover, NH, and London.

Bruce, J. D. 1923/1928. *The Evolution of Arthurian Romance from the Beginnings down to the Year 1300*, 2 vols, Göttingen and Baltimore; 2nd edn 1928; repr. Gloucester, MA, 1958, Geneva 1974.

Bruckner, M. T. 1993. *Shaping Romance: Interpretation, Truth, and Closure in Twelfth-Century French Fictions*, Philadelphia.

Burns, E. J. 1993. *Bodytalk*: *When Women Speak in Old French Literature*, Philadelphia.

Burns 2002. *Courtly Love Undressed: Reading through Clothes in Medieval French Culture*, Philadelphia.

Busby, K. 1980. *Gauvain in Old French Literature*, Amsterdam and Atlanta, GA.

Busby 1988. 'Medieval French Arthurian Literature: Recent Progress and Critical Trends', in M. Pors ed. *The Vitality of the Arthurian Legend: A Symposium*, Odense, 45–70.

Busby ed. 1996. *Word and Image in Arthurian Literature*, New York and London.

Busby 2002. *Codex and Context: Reading Old French Verse Narrative in Manuscript*, 2 vols, Amsterdam.

Busby, and R. H. Thompson eds 2006. *Gawain: A Casebook*, New York.

Busby, and J. H. M. Taylor 2006. 'French Arthurian Literature', in N. J. Lacy ed. *A History of Arthurian Scholarship*, Cambridge, 95–121.

Chênerie, M.-L. 1986. *Le Chevalier errant dans les romans arthuriens en vers des XIIe et XIIIe siècles*, Geneva.

Dessaint, M. 2001. *La Femme médiatrice dans de grandes œuvres romanesques du XII*ᵉ *siècle*, Paris.

Dor, J. ed. 2000. *Conjointure arthurienne: actes de la Classe d'Excellence de la Chaire Francqui 1998, Liège, 20 février 1998*, Louvain-la-Neuve.

Dover, Carol. ed. 2003. *A Companion to the Lancelot–Grail Cycle*, Cambridge.

Dubost, F. 1991. *Aspects fantastiques de la littérature narrative médiévale, XIIème–XIIIème siècles: l'autre, l'ailleurs, l'autrefois*, 2 vols, Geneva.

Duggan, J. J. 1989. 'Oral Performance of Romance in Medieval France', in *Continuations: Essays on Medieval French Literature and Language in Honor of John L. Grigsby*, Birmingham, AL, 51–61.

Faral, E. 1929. *La Légende arthurienne: études et documents, première partie: les plus anciens textes;* vol. 1, *Des origines à Geoffroy de Monmouth;* vol. 2, *Geoffroy de Monmouth, la légende arthurienne à Glastonbury;* vol. 3, *Documents: Historia Britonum, Geoffroy de Monmouth: Historia Regum Britanniae, Vita Merlini*, Paris.

Faucon, J.-C. ed. 1999. *Temps et histoire dans le roman arthurien*, Toulouse.

Faure, M. ed. 1997. *Félonie, trahison, reniements au Moyen Âge: actes du troisième colloque international de Montpellier, Université Paul-Valéry (24–26 novembre 1995)*, Montpellier.

Fenster, T. S. ed. 1996. *Arthurian Women: A Casebook*, New York and London; paperback 2002.

Foulon, C. et al. eds 1985. *Actes du 14*ᵉ *congrès international arthurien, Rennes, 16–21 août 1984*, 2 vols, Rennes.

Gallais, P. 1992. *La Fée à la fontaine et à l'arbre: un archétype du conte merveilleux et du récit courtois*, Amsterdam and Atlanta, GA.

Goodrich, P. H., and R. H. Thompson eds 2003. *Merlin: A Casebook*, New York and London.

Gouttebroze, J.-G. 1999. 'De la dévolution du pouvoir en milieu celtique et arthurien: croyances, rituel, éthique', *MA*, 105, 681–702.

Gowans, L. 1988. *Cei and the Arthurian Legend*, Cambridge.

Grigsby, J. L. 1984. 'Truth and Method in Arthurian Criticism', *RPh*, 38, 53–64.

Grimbert, J. T. ed. 1995. *Tristan and Isolde: A Casebook*, New York and London; paperback 2002.

Grisward, J. 1983. 'Uter Pendragon, Artur et l'idéologie royale des Indo-Européens: structure trifonctionnelle et roman arthurien', *Europe*, 654, 111–20.

Groos, A., and N. J. Lacy eds 2002. *Perceval/Parzival: A Casebook*, New York and London.

Grundriß der romanischen Literaturen des Mittelalters, Heidelberg, 1972– . See especially vol. 1, *Généralités* (1972); vol. 4, *Le Roman jusqu'à la fin du XIII*ᵉ *siècle*, 1, Partie historique (1978); 2, Partie documentaire (1984) and vol. 8, *La Littérature française aux XIV*ᵉ *et XV*ᵉ *siècles*, 1, Partie historique (1988).

Guerreau-Jalabert, A. 1992. *Index des motifs narratifs dans les romans arthuriens français en vers (XII*ᵉ*–XIII*ᵉ *siècles)*, Geneva.

Halász, K. 1990. 'L'Ange, Josephes, Merlin, Robert, Gautiers et les autres: approche narratologique de quelques romans en prose', *Le forme e la storia*, new series 2, 303–14.

Hanning, R. W. 1985. 'Arthurian Evangelists: The Language of Truth in Thirteenth-Century French Prose Romances', *PQ*, 64, 347–65.

Harding, C. E.1988. *Merlin and Legendary Romance*, New York.

Harf-Lancner, L. 1984. *Les Fées au Moyen Âge: Morgane et Mélusine, la naissance des fées*, Paris.

Harty, K. J. ed. 1991. *Cinema Arthuriana: Essays on Arthurian Film*, New York and London.

Harty ed. 2002. *Cinema Arthuriana: Twenty Essays*, Jefferson, NC, and London.

Herman, H. J. 1989. 'Sir Kay, Seneschal of King Arthur's Court', *Arthurian Interpretations*, 4, 1–31.

Hindman, S. 1991. 'King Arthur, his Knights, and the French Aristocracy in Picardy', *YFS*, special issue, *Contexts: Style and Values in Medieval Art and Literature*, 114–33.

Holzermayr, K. 1984. 'Le Mythe d'Arthur: la royauté et l'idéologie', *Annales*, 39, 480–94.

Hüe, D., and C. Ferlampin-Acher eds 2002. *Le Monde et l'Autre Monde*, Orleans.

Jackson, W. H., and S. A. Ranawake eds 2000. *The Arthur of the Germans: The Arthurian Legend in Medieval German and Dutch Literature*, Cardiff; paperback 2002.

James-Raoul, D. 1997. *La Parole empêchée dans la littérature arthurienne*, Paris.

Kelly, D. 1992. *The Art of Medieval French Romance*, Madison, WI, and London.

Kelly, 1993. *Medieval French Romance*, New York and Toronto.

Kelly ed. 1996. *The Medieval Opus: Imitation, Rewriting, and Transmission in the French Tradition: Proceedings of the Symposium Held at the Institute for Research in Humanities, October 5–7 1995, The University of Wisconsin-Madison*, Amsterdam and Atlanta, GA.

Kennedy, A. 1981. 'The Portrayal of the Hermit-Saint in French Arthurian Romance: The Remoulding of a Stock-Character', in K. Varty ed. *An Arthurian Tapestry: Essays in Memory of Lewis Thorpe*, Glasgow, 69–82.

Kennedy, E. D. ed. 1996. *King Arthur: A Casebook*, New York and London; paperback 2002.

Kibler, W. W. ed. 1994. *The Lancelot-Grail Cycle: Text and Transformations*, Austin, TX.

Knight, S. 1983. *Arthurian Literature and Society*, London and New York.

Köhler, E. 1970. *Ideal und Wirklichkeit in der höfischen Epik: Studien zur Form der frühen Artus- und Graaldichtung*, Tübingen; translated by E. Kaufholz as *L'Aventure chevaleresque: idéal et réalité dans le roman courtois. Études sur la forme des plus anciens poèmes d'Arthur et du Graal* (Paris, 1974).

Korrel, P. 1984 *An Arthurian Triangle: A Study of the Origin, Development and Characterization of Arthur, Guinevere and Modred*, Leiden.

Krueger, R. L. 1993. *Women Readers and the Ideology of Gender in Old French Verse Romance*, Cambridge.

Krueger ed. 2000. *The Cambridge Companion to Medieval Romance*, Cambridge.

Lacy, N. J. ed. 1986. *The Arthurian Encyclopedia*, New York and London; paperback New York 1987 and Woodbridge 1988.

Lacy 1991. 'Medieval French Arthurian Literature in English', *Quondam et Futurus*, 1, 55–74.

Lacy ed. 1991. *The New Arthurian Encyclopedia*, New York and London. See Lacy ed.1996c.

Lacy ed. 1996a *Medieval Arthurian Literature: A Guide to Recent Research*, New York and London.

Lacy ed. 1996b. *Text and Intertext in Medieval Arthurian Literature*, New York and London.

Lacy ed. 1996c. *The New Arthurian Encyclopedia*, rev. edn, New York and London. See Lacy ed. 1991.

Lacy 1999. 'French Arthurian Literature', in D. Sinnreich-Levi and I. S. Laurie eds *Literature of the French and Occitan Middle Ages, Eleventh to Fifteenth Centuries*, vol. 208 of *Dictionary of Literary Biography*, Detroit and Washington, DC, 296–306.

Lacy, N. J., and G. Ashe. 1988. *The Arthurian Handbook*, New York and London; 2nd edn, 1997.

Lacy, N. J., D. Kelly, and K. Busby eds 1987–8. *The Legacy of Chrétien de Troyes*, 2 vols, Amsterdam.

Lagorio, V. M., and M. L. Day eds 1990. *King Arthur through the Ages*, 2 vols, New York.

Lathuillère, R. 1980. 'L'Évolution de la technique narrative dans le roman arthurien en prose au cours de la deuxième moitié du XIIIe siècle', in *Études de langues et de littérature françaises offertes à André Lanly*, 203–14.

Laurie, H. C. R. 1991. *The Making of Romance: Three Studies*, Geneva.

Le Nan, F. 2002. *Le Secret dans la littérature narrative arthurienne (1150–1250): du lexique au motif*, Paris.

Loomis, R. S. ed. 1959. *Arthurian Literature in the Middle Ages: A Collaborative History*, Oxford.

Loomis 1963. *The Development of Arthurian Romance*, London.

Luttrell, C. 1981. 'Folk Legend as Source for Arthurian Romance: The Wild Hunt', in K. Varty ed. *An Arthurian Tapestry: Essays in Memory of Lewis Thorpe*, Glasgow, 83–100.

McCracken, P. 1998. *The Romance of Adultery: Queenship and Sexual Transgression in Old French Literature*, Philadelphia.

MacDonald, A. A. 1990. *The Figure of Merlin in Thirteenth-Century French Romance*, Lewiston, Queenston and Lampeter.

Maddox, D. 2000. *Fictions of Identity in Medieval France*, Cambridge.

Maddox, D., and S. Sturm-Maddox eds 1996. *Transtextualities: Of Cycles and Cyclicity in Medieval French Literature*, Binghamton, NY.

Magie et illusion au Moyen Âge, Senefiance 42, Aix-en-Provence, 1999.

Mahoney, D. B. ed. 2000. *The Grail: A Casebook*, New York and London.

Markale, J. 1981. *Merlin l'enchanteur, ou l'éternelle quête magique*, Paris.

Martineau, A. 2003. *Le Nain et le chevalier: essai sur les nains français du Moyen Âge*, Paris.

Matthews, J. 1981. *The Grail: Quest for the Eternal*, London.

Méla, C. 1984. *La Reine et le Graal: la conjointure dans les romans du Graal de Chrétien de Troyes au Livre de Lancelot*, Paris.

Ménard, P. 1991. 'Problématique de l'aventure dans les romans de la Table Ronde', in Van Hoecke, Tournoy and Verbeke eds, II, 89–119.

Ménard 1997. 'La Réception des romans de chevalerie à la fin du Moyen Âge et au XVIe siècle', *BBIAS*, 49, 234–73.

Meneghetti, M. L. 1988. *Il romanzo*, Bologna.

Mertens, V., and F. Wolfzettel eds 1993. *Fiktionalität im Artusroman: dritte Tagung der deutschen Sektion der internationalen Artusgesellschaft*, Tübingen.

Morris, R. 1982. *The Character of King Arthur in Medieval Literature*, Cambridge.

Morris 1988. 'Aspects of Time and Place in the French Arthurian Verse Romances', *FS*, 42, 257–77.

Nicholson, H. J. 2001. *Love, War and the Grail*, Leiden and Boston.

Ollier, M.-L. 1984. 'Utopie et roman arthurien', *CCM*, 27, 223–32.

Ollier 2000. *La Forme du sens. Textes narratifs des XIIe et XIIIe siècles: études littéraires et linguistiques*, Orleans.

Payen, J.-C. ed. 1983. *La Légende arthurienne et la Normandie: hommage à René Bansard*, Condé-sur-Noireau.

Pearcy, R. J. 1991. 'Fabliau Intervention in some Mid-Thirteenth-Century Arthurian Verse Romances', *Arthurian Yearbook*, 1, 63–89.

Pickford, C. E. 1959/60. *L'Évolution du roman arthurien en prose vers la fin du Moyen Âge d'après le manuscrit 112 du fonds français de la Bibliothèque Nationale*, Paris.

Pickford 1982. 'The Maturity of the Arthurian Prose Romances', *BBIAS*, 34, 197–206.

Poirion, D. 1982. *Le Merveilleux dans la littérature française du Moyen Âge*, Paris.

Pors, M. ed. 1988. *The Vitality of the Arthurian Legend: A Symposium*, Odense.

Régnier-Bohler, D. ed. 1989. *La Légende arthurienne: le Graal et la Table Ronde*, Paris.

Rey-Flaud, H. 1983. *La Névrose courtoise*, Paris.

Rittey, J. 2002. *Amplification as Gloss in Two Twelfth-Century Texts: Robert de Boron's Joseph d'Arimathie and Renaut de Beaujeu's Li Biaus Descouneüs*, New York, etc.

Rockwell, P. V. 1990. 'Writing the Fountain: The Specificity of Resemblance in Arthurian Romance', *BBIAS*, 42, 267–82.

Ruck, E. H. 1991. *An Index of Themes and Motifs in Twelfth-Century French Arthurian Poetry*, Cambridge.

Ruh, K. 1982. *Lancelot: Wandlungen einer ritterlichen Idealgestalt*, Marburg.

Saly, A. 1994. *Image, structure et sens: études arthuriennes*, Senefiance 34, Aix-en-Provence.

Sargent-Baur, B. N. 1984. '*Dux bellorum/rex militum/*roi fainéant: la transformation d'Arthur au XIIe siècle', *MA*, 90, 357–73.

Schmolke-Hasselmann, B. 1980/1998. *Der arthurische Versroman von Chrestien bis Froissart: zur Geschichte einer Gattung* (Tübingen, 1980); translated by M. and R. Middleton as *The Evolution of Arthurian Romance: The Verse Tradition from Chrétien to Froissart* (Cambridge, 1998).

Schmolke-Hasselmann 1981. 'Untersuchungen zur Typik des arthurischen Romananfangs', *GRM*, 62 (new series 31), 1–13.

Schmolke-Hasselmann 1982. 'The Round Table: Ideal, Fiction, Reality', *AL*, 2, 41–75.

Schmolke-Hasselmann 1983. 'Der französische Artusroman in Versen nach Chrétien de Troyes', *DVj*, 57, 415–30.

Schultze-Busacker, E. 1981. 'Étude typologique de la complainte des morts dans le roman arthurien en vers du 12e au 14e siècle', in K. Varty ed. *An Arthurian Tapestry: Essays in Memory of Lewis Thorpe*, Glasgow, 54–68.

Schulze-Belli, P., and D. Dallapiazza eds 1990. *Liebe und Aventiure im Artusroman des Mittelalters: Beiträge der Triester Tagung 1988*, Göppingen.

Séguy, M. 2001. *Les Romans du Graal ou le signe imaginé*, Paris.

Shichtman, M. B., and J. P. Carley eds 1994. *Culture and the King: The Social Implications of the Arthurian Legend. Essays in Honor of Valerie M. Lagorio*, Albany, NJ.

Szkilnik, Michelle. 2003. 'Conquête et exploration dans le roman arthurien en prose', *BBIAS*, 55 (2003), 359–82.

Taylor, J. H. M. 1992. 'Arthurian Cyclicity: The Construction of History in the Late French Prose Romances', *AY*, 2, 209–23.

Tolhurst, F. 1998. 'The Once and Future Queen: The Development of Guenevere from Geoffrey of Monmouth to Malory', *BBIAS*, 50, 272–308.

Trachsler, R. 1996. *Clôtures du cycle arthurien: étude et textes*, Geneva.

Trachsler 1997. *Les Romans arthuriens en vers après Chrétien de Troyes*, Paris.

Tyson, D. B. 1981. 'King Arthur as a Literary Device in French Vernacular History Writing of the Fourteenth Century', *BBIAS*, 33, 237–57.

Vance, E. 1987. *From Topic to Tale: Logic and Narrativity in the Middle Ages*, Minneapolis.

Van Hoecke, W. G. Tournoy, and W. Verbeke eds 1991. *Arturus Rex 2: acta conventus lovaniensis*, Louvain.

Vermette, R. A. 1987. '*Terrae incantatae*: The Symbolic Geography of Twelfth-Century Arthurian Romance', in W. E. Mallory and P. Simpson-Housley eds *Geography and Literature: A Meeting of the Disciplines*, Syracuse, NY, 144–60.

Vinaver, E. 1971. *The Rise of Romance*, Oxford.

Vinaver 1980. 'The Questing Knight', in M. W. McCune, T. Orbison and P. M. Withim eds *The Binding of Porteus: Perspectives on Myth and the Literary Process*, Lewisburg, PA, and London, 126–40.

Vitz, E. B. 1986. 'Rethinking Old French Literature: The Orality of the Octosyllabic Couplet', *RR*, 77, 307–21.

Vitz 1999. *Orality and Performance in Early French Romance*, Cambridge.

Walters, L. J. ed. 1996. *Lancelot and Guinevere: A Casebook*, New York and London.

West, G. D. 1969. *An Index of Proper Names in French Arthurian Verse Romances, 1150–1300*, Toronto.

West 1978. *An Index of Proper Names in French Arthurian Prose Romances*, Toronto, Buffalo and London.

Wolfzettel, F. ed. 1984. *Artusrittertum im späten Mittelalter: Ethos und Ideologie / Vorträge des Symposiums der deutschen Sektion der Internationalen Artusgesellschaft vom 10.-13. 11. 1983 in Schloss Rauischholzhausen, Universität Giessen*, Giessen.

Wolfzettel ed. 1990. *Artusroman und Intertextualität (Beiträge der deutschen Sektionstagung der Internationalen Artusgesellschaft vom 16. bis 19. November 1989 an der Johann Wolfgang Goethe-Universität Frankfurt a. M.)*, Giessen.

Wolfzettel ed. 1995. *Arthurian Romance and Gender: Masculin/féminin dans le roman arthurien médiéval: Geschlechterrollen im mittelalterlichen Artusroman (Selected Proceedings of the XVIIth International Arthurian Congress/Actes choisis du XVIIᵉ congrès international arthurien/Ausgewählte Akten des XVII. Internationalen Artuskongresses)*, Amsterdam and Atlanta, GA.

Wolfzettel ed. 1999. *Erzählstrukturen der Artusliteratur: Forschungsgeschichte und neue Ansätze*, Tübingen.

Wolfzettel ed. 2003. *Das Wunderbare in der arthurischen Literatur: Probleme und Perspektiven*, Tübingen.

GENERAL INDEX

Epithets and status attached to individual characters, and their family relationships, can vary from text to text. The full or precise name-form shown may not, therefore, appear in all the works covered by the entries for a specific person. Further information on proper names is to be found in West 1969* and 1978*.

418; exchange of 114; from the anvil and stone 252, 284, 292; from floating stone (Galahad's) 306–7, 319–20, 356; knight with two, *see* Balain, Beaudous, Meriadeuc; marvellous 404, 416; *see also* David; Excalibur; John the Baptist
symbolism 306, 309–10, 327, 348, 377, 463, 465, 477, 480–1, 550
Symbolists, the 556
Symeu 302
Szkilnik, M. 421, 422, 511

table, brass 230
Tables, Three, *see* Three Tables
Taiji Kung Fu troop 563
tailleor (trencher, platter) 234, 238–9, 244–5, 254, 267
Taliesin 98
Tallac de Rougemont 425
Tallas, King of Denmark 435
Tanguy du Chastel 68
tapestry 35, 488
Taulat 536–7, 539–40
Tavola ritonda (Italian) 564
Taylor, J. H. M. 462–4, 495, 513
Templars, the 305
temptation 283, 279, 307–8, 468, 554, 549; *see also* Perceval, temptations of
Tennyson, Alfred Lord 548, 555
Tent Maiden, in *Perceval* 143, 169
'Terre Faee', *see* fairyland
Terre Foraine, la 279
test 144, 202, 206, 222, 230, 243, 252, 296, 307–8, 319, 404, 443, 516–7; by seduction 404; by sword 415, *see also* Arthur, Galahad; of faith 283; of knightly qualities 422; of love 408, 496; of loyalty 126; of prowess 141, 150–1, 435; of spiritual worth 301, 307; *see also* beheading; bridge; chastity; horn; mantle
Teutonic Knights 494
Thanatos 556
Thaningues 360
Thèbes, Histoire de 499; *Roman de* 191, 197; MS of 17
Thessala 139–40
Thibaut de Tintagel 169; his elder daughter 169
Thibaut V, Count of Blois 398–9
Thibaut V, Count of Champagne and Navarre 482
Thierry, Count of Forbach 415
Tholomer 279
Tholomer 353 (Merlin's scribe)

Thomas, Duke of Exeter 80
Thomas d'Angleterre, *Tristan* 2, 4, 10, 30, 36, 112, 117, 118–26, 326, 333, 402, 555–6, 559–60, 563, 557, 563, 566; dating of 85, 119; epilogue to 119, 121; MSS of 8, 14–15, 19–20, 22, 51, 118–19, 123, 130, 564; nineteenth-century edition of 547; pan-European adaptations of 10, 37
Thomas de Maubeuge 53
Thomas de Saluzzo, *Livre du chevalier errant* 450
Thomas de Useflete 36
Thomas of Woodstock, Duke of Gloucester 80
Thompson, A. W. 216–17, 219–21, 265
Thorpe, L. 443–4
Three Orders, the 164–6
Three Tables 311; *see also* Grail, Last Supper, Round Table
Tiergeville 53, 57
time: circular 464; in Other World 203
Tinpincarantin 231
Tintagel 119, 126, 169, 252, 292; Duke of, *see* Gorlois; tournament at 153, 169
Tintagoil, lay of 542
Titus, Emperor 249, 258; his son 358
Tobin, P. M. O'H. 19, 198, 203
tomb 160, 245, 296, 301, 307, 320, 438, 476; burning 279; knight in 228, 253; knight of 254; slab 302–3; tempest-provoking 511; *see also* Merlin, entombment of
Tor 349; his mother 349
Torec (Dutch) 34, 37
Torrez, 'chevalier au Cercle d'or', lost MS story of 33–4, 37
Tors, Le (in *Perceforest*) 508
Tory, Geoffroy, *Champ fleury* 28
Tournai 32, 437, 462, 482–3
tournament/s *passim*; and the Church 170, 312; death in 169, 220–1; historical 445–7, 488; injury at 169, 176, 398, 176; invention of 502, 506; narratives 445–7; regulation of 168, 447; three-day 416; violence of 169; women and 169
Tournier, Michel, *Tristan Vox* 562
Tournoi de Chauvency 332
Tournoiement Antechrist, Le, see Huon de Méry
Tournon family 43, 69; Blanche de Tournon 69; connections with Italy 69; Jacques de Tournon 69; Jehanne de Tournon 69; Just de Tournon 69; Justine de Tournon 69
Tours 27; bookseller's catalogue from 78–9
Tours des Chevaliers, knights of 375
tower, disappearing 308

INDEX OF MANUSCRIPTS